BOOKS BY

H.L.MENCKEN

THE AMERICAN LANGUAGE
THE AMERICAN LANGUAGE: Supplement One
THE AMERICAN LANGUAGE: Supplement Two
HAPPY DAYS ⎫
NEWSPAPER DAYS ⎬ which, taken together, constitute
HEATHEN DAYS ⎭ *The Days of H. L. Mencken*
A NEW DICTIONARY OF QUOTATIONS
TREATISE ON THE GODS
CHRISTMAS STORY
A MENCKEN CHRESTOMATHY (with selections from the *Prejudices* series, *A Book of Burlesques, In Defense of Women, Notes on Democracy, Making a President, A Book of Calumny, Treatise on Right and Wrong,* with pieces from the *American Mercury, Smart Set,* and *Baltimore Evening Sun* and some previously unpublished notes)
MINORITY REPORT: H. L. MENCKEN'S NOTEBOOKS
THE BATHTUB HOAX and Other Blasts and Bravos from the *Chicago Tribune*
LETTERS OF H. L. MENCKEN, Selected and Annotated by Guy J. Forgue
H. L. MENCKEN ON MUSIC, Edited by Louis Cheslock

These are BORZOI BOOKS *published by* ALFRED A. KNOPF *in New York*

THE AMERICAN LANGUAGE
SUPPLEMENT II

SUPPLEMENT II

THE

American Language

AN INQUIRY
INTO THE DEVELOPMENT OF ENGLISH
IN THE UNITED STATES

BY

H. L. Mencken

1962
ALFRED A. KNOPF
NEW YORK

THIS IS A BORZOI BOOK,
PUBLISHED BY ALFRED A. KNOPF, INC.

COPYRIGHT *1948 by Alfred A. Knopf, Inc. All rights reserved. No part of this book may be reproduced in any form without permission in writing from the publisher, except by a reviewer who may quote brief passages in a review to be printed in a magazine or newspaper. Manufactured in the United States of America and distributed by Random House, Inc. Published in Canada by Random House of Canada, Limited.*

Published April 5, 1948; second printing, March 1952; third printing, March 1956; fourth printing, May 1960; fifth printing, October 1961; sixth printing, August 1962.

W

PREFACE

This Supplement follows the plan of Supplement I. In the latter I tried to give some account of the new material relating to the subjects discussed in the first six chapters of " The American Language," fourth edition, 1936. In the present volume I deal with such material as relates to the five chapters following them. I had hoped also to give a little space to the subject of Chapter XII, to wit, the future of American English, and to present some new matter about the non-English languages dealt with in the Appendix. Yet more, I had hoped to take up in a second Appendix certain themes not discussed at all in the fourth edition — for example, the language of gesture, that of children, the names of political parties, cattle brands, animal calls, and so on. But my notes turn out to be so enormous that I have been forced to close the present volume with Chapter XI, lest it grow to an impossible bulk. It is highly improbable that I'll ever attempt a Supplement III, but meanwhile my notes are preserved and indeed still piling up, and I may be tempted from time to time to present some of them in articles for the periodicals devoted to or showing some interest in American speech. At my age a man encounters frequent reminders, some of them disconcerting, that his body is no more than a highly unstable congeries of the compounds of carbon. In order to avoid fretting about this unpleasant fact I have arranged that all my books, pamphlets, journals, newspaper clippings and letters on speech shall go, at my death, to a place where they will be open to other students. Meanwhile, I'll be glad as always to hear from such students, and ask them to address me at 1524 Hollins street, Baltimore-23.

I am not trained in linguistic science, and can thus claim no profundity for my book. It represents the gatherings, not of an expert in linguistics, but simply of a journalist interested in language, and if there appears in it any virtue at all it is the homely virtue of diligence. Someone had to bring together the widely scattered field material and try to get some order and coherence into it, and I fell into the job. My professional friends, I have no doubt, have often had their teeth set on edge by some of my observations and conclusions, but they have nevertheless shown a generous and accommodating spirit, and I owe a great deal to their friendly if somewhat pained interest. Many of them are given specific credit for their aid in my footnotes, and others have been thanked in previous prefaces. But I must recall once again some men and women who have helped me most, including laymen who have greatly augmented my materials. Mention the American language, and you have mentioned Dr. Louise Pound. Read this book, and you will find countless proofs of it. Others upon whom I have leaned heavily are Dr. Joseph M. Carrière, P. E. Cleator, Monsignor J. B. Dudek, Fred Hamann, Alexander Kadison, Charles J. Lovell, Dr. Raven I. McDavid, Jr., Lieut. Col. F. G. Potts and Dr. Harold Wentworth. But these are only a few: there have been many more. Most of all I am indebted to my secretary, Mrs. Rosalind C. Lohrfinck, whose heroic struggles with a maddening manuscript make her deserve a large part of the credit for the diligence that I have just claimed for myself.

As in my two previous volumes I have been very liberal with references. Experience has taught me that readers of such books as this one like to explore the byways of the subject, and thus do not object to frequent guideposts. Such explorations are greatly facilitated, as my own inquiries have been facilitated, by the incomparably efficient photostat service of the New York Public Library. Find your reference and send in your order, and you will have your photostat within a few days. The library very seldom reports that what is wanted is not on its shelves: its collections, especially in the more picturesque departments of Americana, appear to be unsurpassed on this or any other earth. Moreover, its staff is highly competent, and I have got frequent valuable help from one member in particular, Mr. G. E. Fielstra. I need hardly add my thanks to writers and publishers for permission to quote from their books and magazine articles, for my debt to them is visible on every page. Such a work as this, in fact, is essentially a collaboration, and in the present case it is a collaboration covering a large area. In the field of the speech of homicidal endeavor I have received contributions from generals and admirals, privates and seamen; in that of pedagogy from the presidents of universities and country schoolma'ams, and in that of language in general from high ecclesiastical dignitaries and lifers in prison.

The plan of this volume is exactly like that of Supplement I. It follows the order of " The American Language," fourth edition, and each section is hooked to that work by identical headings. But it is not necessary for the reader to have the fourth edition before him to make his way, nor even to have read it, for the new matter here presented is almost always self-contained, and I have included in brackets, wherever they seem useful, explanatory catch-lines or quotations. The figures at the beginnings of sections all refer to the fourth edition.

Baltimore, 1948   H. L. M.

Table of Contents

VII. THE PRONUNCIATION OF AMERICAN

1. Its General Characters	3
2. The Vowels	69
3. The Consonants	88
4. Dialects	101

VIII. AMERICAN SPELLING

1. The Influence of Noah Webster	271
2. The Advance of American Spelling	277
3. The Simplified Spelling Movement	287
4. The Treatment of Loan-Words	316
5. Punctuation, Capitalization, and Abbreviation	320

IX. THE COMMON SPEECH

1. Outlines of its Grammar	332
2. The Verb	353
3. The Pronoun	368
4. The Noun	383
5. The Adjective	387
6. The Adverb	388
7. The Double Negative	390
8. Other Syntactical Peculiarities	394

X. PROPER NAMES IN AMERICA

1. Surnames	396
2. Given Names	462
3. Place-Names	525
4. Other Proper Names	575

XI. AMERICAN SLANG

1. The Nature of Slang	643
2. Cant and Argot	652

LIST OF WORDS AND PHRASES

INDEX

ABBREVIATIONS

To save space some of the books referred to frequently in the text are cited by the following catch-words and abbreviations:

AL1   The American Language, by H. L. Mencken; first edition; New York, 1919.
AL2   The same; second edition; New York, 1921.
AL3   The same; third edition; New York, 1923.
AL4   The same; fourth edition; New York, 1936.
Bardsley   A Dictionary of English and Welsh Surnames With Special American Instances, by Charles Wareing Bardsley; London, 1901.
Barrère   Argot and Slang, by A. Barrère; London, 1887.
Bartlett   A Glossary of Words and Phrases Usually Regarded as Peculiar to the United States, by John Russell Bartlett; New York, 1848; second edition; Boston, 1859; third edition; Boston, 1860; fourth edition; Boston, 1877.
Bentley   A Dictionary of Spanish Terms in English, by Harold W. Bentley; New York, 1932.
Berrey and Van den Bark   The American Thesaurus of Slang, by Lester V. Berrey and Melvin Van den Bark; New York, 1942; fifth printing, 1947.
Black   The Surnames of Scotland, by George F. Black; New York, 1946.
Bristed   The English Language in America; in Cambridge Essays, Contributed by Members of the University; London, 1855.
Burke   The Literature of Slang, by W. J. Burke; New York, 1939.
Clapin   A New Dictionary of Americanisms, by Sylva Clapin; New York, n.d.
Concise Oxford   The Concise Oxford Dictionary of Current English, adapted by H. W. Fowler and F. G. Fowler; third edition, revised by H. W. Fowler and H. G. Le Mesurier; Oxford, 1934.
DAE   A Dictionary of American English on Historical Principles, edited by W. A. Craigie and James R. Hulbert; four vols.; Chicago, 1938–44.
Dunglison   Americanisms, in the *Virginia Literary Museum and Journal of Belles Lettres, Arts, Sciences, &c.*, signed Wy and supposed to be by Robley Dunglison; Charlottesville, Va., 1829–30.
Ewen   A History of Surnames of the British Isles, by C. L'Estrange Ewen; New York, 1931.
Farmer   Americanisms Old and New, by John S. Farmer; London, 1889.
Farmer and Henley   Slang and Its Analogues, by John S. Farmer and W. E. Henley; seven vols.; London, 1890–1904.
Grose   A Classical Dictionary of the Vulgar Tongue, by Francis Grose; London, 1785; new edition edited by Eric Partridge; London, 1931.

Heintze Die deutschen Familiennamen, by Albert Heintze; Halle a. S., 1903.
Holt American Place Names, by Alfred H. Holt; New York, 1938.
Horwill A Dictionary of Modern American Usage, by H. W. Horwill; Oxford, 1935.
Humphreys Glossary appended to The Yankey in England, by David Humphreys; n.p., 1815.
Jones An English Pronouncing Dictionary, by Daniel Jones; fourth edition, revised and enlarged; London, 1937.
Kennedy A Bibliography of Writings on the English Language From the Beginning of Printing to the End of 1922, by Arthur G. Kennedy; Cambridge & New Haven, 1927.
Kenyon and Knott A Pronouncing Dictionary of American English, by John Samuel Kenyon and Thomas Albert Knott; Springfield, Mass., 1944.
Krapp The English Language in America, by George Philip Krapp; two vols.; New York, 1925.
LA Linguistic Atlas of the United States; Linguistic Atlas of New England, by Hans Kurath, Miles L. Hanley, Bernard Bloch, Guy S. Lowman, Jr., and Marcus L. Hansen; Providence, R. I., 1939.
Maitland The American Slang Dictionary, by James Maitland; Chicago, 1891.
Mathews The Beginnings of American English, by M. M. Mathews; Chicago, 1931.
NED A New English Dictionary on Historical Principles, edited by James A. H. Murray, Henry Bradley, W. A. Craigie, and C. T. Onions; ten vols.; Oxford, 1888–1928.[1]
NED Supplement A New English Dictionary on Historical Principles; Introduction, Supplement and Bibliography; edited by James A. H. Murray, Henry Bradley, W. A. Craigie and C. T. Onions; Oxford, 1933.
Partridge A Dictionary of Slang and Unconventional English, by Eric Partridge; second edition; New York, 1938.
Pickering A Vocabulary or Collection of Words and Phrases Which Have Been Supposed to be Peculiar to the United States of America, by John Pickering; Boston, 1816.
Practical Standard Funk & Wagnalls New Practical Standard Dictionary of the English Language, edited by Charles Earl Funk; New York, 1946.
Schele de Vere Americanisms: The English of the New World, by M. Schele de Vere; New York, 1871; second edition, 1872.
Sherwood Gazetteer of the State of Georgia, by Adiel Sherwood; third edition; 1837.
Shorter Oxford The Shorter Oxford English Dictionary on Historical Principles, prepared by William Little, H. W. Fowler and J. Coulson, and revised and edited by C. T. Onions; two vols.; Oxford, 1933.
Stewart Names on the Land, by George R. Stewart; New York, 1945.
Supplement I Supplement I: The American Language, by H. L. Mencken; New York, 1945.
Thornton An American Glossary, by Richard H. Thornton; two vols.; Philadelphia, 1912. Vol. III published serially in *Dialect Notes*, 1931–39.
Tucker American English, by Gilbert M. Tucker; New York, 1921.
Ware Passing English of the Victorian Era, by J. Redding Ware; London, n.d.

[1] This work is often referred to as the OED or OD (Oxford Dictionary), but it seems to me to be preferable to use an abbreviation of its actual title.

Abbreviations

Warfel   Noah Webster, Schoolmaster to America, by Harry R. Warfel; New York, 1936.
Warrack   A Scots Dialect Dictionary, by Alexander Warrack; London, 1911.
Webster 1806   A Compendious Dictionary of the English Language, by Noah Webster; New Haven, 1806.
Webster 1828   An American Dictionary of the English Language, by Noah Webster; New York, 1828.
Webster 1852   An American Dictionary of the English Language, by Noah Webster; revised and enlarged by Chauncey A. Goodrich; Springfield, Mass., 1852.
Webster 1934   Webster's New International Dictionary of The English Language, edited by William Allan Neilson, Thomas A. Knott and Paul W. Carhart; Springfield, Mass., 1934.
Weekley   An Etymological Dictionary of Modern English, by Ernest Weekley; New York, 1921.
Wentworth   American Dialect Dictionary, by Harold Wentworth; New York, 1944.
Weseen   A Dictionary of American Slang, by Maurice H. Weseen; New York, 1934.
Woulfe   Irish Names and Surnames, by Patrick Woulfe; Dublin, 1923.
Wright   The English Dialect Grammar, by Joseph Wright; Oxford, 1905.
Wyld   A History of Modern Colloquial English, by Henry Cecil Wyld; London, 1920.

In some cases the authors whose principal works are listed above are also the authors of other works. All references to the latter are in full.

THE AMERICAN LANGUAGE
SUPPLEMENT II

VII

THE PRONUNCIATION OF AMERICAN

1. ITS GENERAL CHARACTERS

The fact that there are differences between the way the average literate American speaks and the way the average literate Englishman speaks has long been noted.[1] Many of these differences, as everyone is aware, have to do with vocabulary, and some are so striking that they inevitably attract attention. Thus the American, when he first hears an Englishman mention *corn*, is apt to assume that he means the Indian maize that goes under that name in this country, and is surprised to learn that he uses it as a generic term for all sorts of edible grain, including wheat, rye and barley. Contrariwise, the Englishman is puzzled and maybe a little upset when he discovers that *bowler*, which to him means what we call a *Derby* hat, means in the United States only a person engaged in bowling, and not any object at all. But these differences, though they still engage the scrutiny of persons who write about the two languages, are not as important as they used to be, for in recent years the English have picked up so many terms from the United States that they understand American more or less even when they do not undertake to speak it; and in any case the subject need not be pursued here, for it has been dealt with at length in Chapter VI of Supplement I and at various other places in the same book.

The differences in pronunciation, however, show a higher degree of resistance to change, despite the ever-growing influence of American talkies, and some of them promise to survive for a long while. They extend to many common words, *e.g.*, *can't*, *deficit*, and *secretary*. The Englishman, using the first of these, gives it a broad *a* that is rare in the United States save in those areas — for example,

[1] See AL4, pp. 3–12, and Supplement I, pp. 1–33.

the Boston region and the swankier suburbs of New York — where emulation of English usage is still potent in speechways; and most Americans, when they seek to imitate him or his imitators in speaking, are careful to throw in plenty of *cawnts*, and some even add a few *cawns*, though he actually pronounces *can* exactly as we do, to rhyme with *pan*. In words of the *deficit* class — other examples are *compensate*, *confiscate* and *demonstrate* — the difference is one of stress rather than of vowel-quality, for the Englishman puts the accent on the second syllable, whereas the American commonly stresses the first. In *secretary* what the Englishman does is to get rid of a syllable altogether, so that the word becomes, to American ears, *secretry;* the American himself almost always gives it its lawful four, and lays a slight but unmistakable second stress on the third, which he rhymes with *care*.

This last difference is typical of many others, for American speech, on the whole, follows the spelling more faithfully than English speech, and is thus clearer and more precise. A musician might describe the divergence by saying that the latter tends toward *glissando*, whereas the former is predominantly *staccato* and *marcato*. Why this should be so is not known with any assurance, though a great many persons have put forth confident theories, some of which have to do with alleged differences in the vocal apparatus of Americans and Englishmen, produced by differences in climate. But there is really no evidence that climate has any such effects. Even the adenoidal nasalization that Englishmen so often complain of in American speech, putting the blame for it on the comparative dryness of the American air, is really not peculiar to this country, for it is encountered also in the speech of the London cockneys, and is characteristic of the speech of all Frenchmen. Moreover, the mean annual rainfall in New York, Chicago and St. Louis is actually higher than it is in London, Liverpool or Edinburgh, and in the American South, where the American whine is seldom heard, it is higher still — in New Orleans, more than twice as high.[1]

My own guess, disregarding this nonsense about adenoids, is that Americans, taking one with another, speak more distinctly than Englishmen largely because their speechways were molded, for four generations, by Noah Webster's famous Spelling Book. From

[1] Encyclopedia Americana; New York, 1932, Vol. XXIII, p. 180.

1783, when it was first published, until the beginning of the Twentieth Century, when the wizards of Teachers College, Columbia, began supplanting it with spellers of their own, it was the most widely circulated book in the country,[1] and the most influential. Indeed, it was the only work on language that the average American ever saw, or even heard of. It had no traffic with slurring, but insisted that all words be pronounced as Jahveh had spelled them out to Adam and Eve in the Garden of Eden, or to the sons of Noah after the Flood.[2] Webster gave *secretary* four syllables, and noted that there was what he called "a half accent" on the third;[3] he insisted upon full *r*'s in such words as *far*, *fire* and *fore*, *hard*, *heart* and *cargo;* he frowned upon pronouncing *actual* as *actshual*, *aperture* as *apertshure* and *bounteous* as *bountcheous*, and he even insisted upon spelling pronunciations in such proper names as *Norfolk*, *Thames* and *Greenwich*.[4]

But though he was thus very influential in fixing the national standards of pronunciation in rather rigid molds, he was only giving voice and momentum to what was really a spontaneous natural tendency. The Americans, taking one with another, were a highly matter of fact people, and could see nothing save folly in the af-

[1] Down to 1814 it had sold more than 3,000,000 copies, and down to 1889 62,000,000. Mrs. Emily E. F. Skeel, the lexicographer's great-granddaughter, tells me that there were 304 editions before 1829. See AL4, p. 385.

[2] Webster's theory of the divine origin of language was set forth at length in his introduction to his American Dictionary of 1828, and it continued to appear in the successive editions thereof until twenty-one years after his death, when his heirs and assigns employed a German philologian named C. A. F. Mahn to revise it. In brief, old Noah accepted the statement of Genesis XI, 1 that after the Flood "the whole earth was of one language and of one speech" and concluded that this must have been what he called Chaldee. Also, he concluded that Chaldee remained the base of all the tongues inflicted upon the descendants of Noah when they built the Tower of Babel, and that it was thus the *Ur-Sprache* of the whole human race. See Etymology, Anglo-Saxon, and Noah Webster, by Charlton Laird, *American Speech*, Feb., 1946, pp. 3-15.

[3] He also gave four clear syllables to *territory*. This American pronunciation was noted by General Thomas P. Thompson in the *Westminster Review* for Oct., 1933. "There are [American] mispronunciations," he said primly, "which the English will never submit to; for example, a member of the Senate will never be excused for calling *territory Terry Tory*." The English pronunciation makes it something on the order of *territry*.

[4] *Worcester*, to be sure, stumped him, and though he rejected *Wooster* he was willing to compromise on *Worster*. Also, he allowed that it was best to pronounce *Mishilimackanac* as if it were spelled *Mackinaw*. He spelled and pronounced *Chicago Chickaugo*.

fected pronunciations that became fashionable in England during the latter half of the Eighteenth Century. Those pronunciations arose in the court circles of London, were adopted by the more pretentious sort of actors, and were propagated and given standing by the pronouncing dictionaries of Thomas Sheridan (1780) and John Walker (1791), both of whom had been actors and teachers of elocution before they put on the shroud of the lexicographer.[1] But in the United States such dubious authorities were combatted earnestly and even with some violence (despite a few concessions) by the peppery Webster, and in consequence they were impeded in making converts for their stretched vowels and macerated consonants. American speechways went back to an earlier and less self-conscious era,[2] and remained more logical and rational. If the peo-

[1] They were not, of course, the first English lexicographers to interest themselves in pronunciation, but they seem to have been the first to exert any important influence. The principal dictionary makers before them, e.g., Samuel Johnson, devoted themselves mainly to vocabulary, morphology and syntax. An elaborate and excellent study of the subject is in Standards of English Pronunciation According to the Grammarians and Orthoepists of the 16th, 17th and 18th Centuries, by Esther Keck Sheldon. This is a thesis submitted in 1938 to the Graduate School of the University of Wisconsin, where Mrs. Sheldon received the doctorate. It has not been published, but I have had access to it through the kindness of Dr. Robert C. Pooley, Dr. Miles L. Hanley and the author. It starts with Jean Palsgrave in the Sixteenth Century and ends with the attempts to reform and refine English pronunciation made by Sheridan, Walker and their contemporaries. "We think of the Eighteenth Century," says Mrs. Sheldon, "as the time when the desire to regulate and fix the language, above all to reform its speakers, predominated." See also Walker's Influence on the Pronunciation of English, likewise by Mrs. Sheldon, *Publications of the Modern Language Association*, March, 1947, pp. 130–46. I should note here, without detracting in the slightest from the value of her studies, that Henry Cecil Wyld calls attention in A History of Modern Colloquial English; London, 1920, p. 1, to the unsatisfactory nature of written records of speech. It is sometimes very hard to make out precisely what sounds an author undertakes to represent.

[2] James Boardman, who visited the United States in 1829, wrote in his America and the Americans; London, 1833: "The variations from the present usages of the mother-country in respect to many words and expressions really English can be accounted for by supposing the language now used in America to be the same imported by the Pilgrim Fathers and others to the period of the separation of the governments, since which the Americans have ceased to look to England as their model." "There can be no doubt," said Robert J. Menner, in The Pronunciation of English in America, *Atlantic Monthly*, March, 1915, p. 360, "that the number of native-born Americans at the time of the Revolution whose pronunciation was exactly the same as that of Englishmen was exceedingly small." The archaisms that survived are discussed in AL4, pp. 124–29 and in

ple of the young Republic were influenced at all by relatively recent English precept and example it was by the movement toward spelling-pronunciations which antedated by half a century the rage for actorial affectations. Their speech was thus marked by clarity,[1] and not only by clarity but also by a high degree of uniformity, so that nearly all the English travelers who ventured into the country after the Revolution were struck by the comparative absence of class and regional dialects. These Englishmen, accustomed to being beset by what they regarded as gross barbarisms the moment they got out of the ambits of the court, the theatres and the two universities at home, were astonished to discover that nearly all Americans talked alike, on the lower as well as the higher levels of society, and that their talk was generally clear and hence easily understood. There were, of course, some differences, and Webster himself often gave evidence that he was a New Englander and not a Southerner, but such differences were not numerous and none were important. Save, in fact, for a few oddities in vocabulary, it was perfectly possible to understand any man encountered along the road, even in the Far South or beyond the Alleghanies, and there was nothing anywhere that could be reasonably compared to the gnarled and difficult local dialects of Somerset, Lancastershire and Yorkshire, to say nothing of Scotland and Wales, or of proletarian London.[2]

Allen Walker Read has devoted two of his valuable studies in the history of American English to the observations of these travelers and of other Eighteenth Century Englishmen.[3] The first to discourse upon the subject was probably Hugh Jones, a clerical peda-

---

Supplement I, pp. 224-26. Their tendency to persist in an immigrant language is well exemplified by the case of Icelandic.

1 Edward Everett, writing on June 19, 1827, said: "The great difference between the American and English mode of speaking . . . has seemed to me that we are apt . . . to pronounce every syllable. Great pains are generally taken in our schools . . . to teach boys to pronounce *extra-ordinary*, *min-i-a-ture*, etc., which are the things that first strike an English ear." To say "the schools," in 1827, meant to say Noah Webster.

2 "It has often happened to me in our own island," said Sir Charles Lyell in his Travels in America in the Years 1841-2; New York, 1852, "without traveling into those parts of Wales, Scotland or Ireland where they talk a perfectly distinct language, to encounter provincial dialects which it is difficult to comprehend."

3 Amphi-Atlantic English, *English Studies*, Oct., 1935, pp. 161-78, and British Recognition of American Speech in the Eighteenth Century, *Dialect Notes*, Vol. VI, Part VI, 1933, pp. 313-34. I am indebted to both papers for much of the foregoing and for more of what follows.

gogue who spent the years from 1716 to 1721 at William and Mary College in Virginia, and while there wrote "An Accidence of the English Tongue" that was the first grammar-book ever begotten on American soil. In another work, "The Present State of Virginia," he testified that "the planters and even the native Negroes generally talk good English, without idiom or tone."[1] This was confirmed forty years later by a Scotsman of noble birth, Lord Adam Gordon, who made a progress through the colonies in 1764 and 1765. In Philadelphia, he said, "the propriety of language surprised me much, the English tongue being spoken by all ranks in a degree of purity and perfection surpassing any but the polite part of London." Five years afterward came William Eddis, who wrote home on June 8, 1770:

> In England almost every county is distinguished by a peculiar dialect, . . . but in Maryland and throughout the adjacent provinces . . . a striking similarity of speech universally prevails, and it is strictly true that the pronunciation of the generality of the people has an accuracy and elegance that cannot fail of gratifying the most judicious ear.
>
> The colonists are composed of adventurers not only from every district of Great Britain and Ireland, but from almost every other European government. Is it not, therefore, reasonable to suppose that the English language must be greatly corrupted by such a strange intermixture of various nations? The reverse is, however, true. The language of the immediate descendants of such a promiscuous ancestry is perfectly uniform and unadulterated, nor has it borrowed any provincial or national accent from its British or foreign parentage. . . .
>
> This uniformity . . . prevails not only on the coast, where Europeans form a considerable mass of the people, but likewise in the interior parts, where population has made but slow advances, and where opportunities seldom occur to derive any great advantages from an intercourse with intelligent strangers.

Such testimonies continued until near the end of the century, when the London reviews launched that ill-humored war upon American speechways which has gone on ever since, with prudent truces every time a pressing need for Yankee bayonets has made it impolitic to be too critical of Yankee talk.[2] Even the unhappy success of the Revolution, though it left some bitterness, did not provoke the attack, for the English, during the decade following Yorktown, seem to have entertained some hope that the wayward colo-

---

[1] Jones taught mathematics at William and Mary and was chaplain to the Virginia House of Burgesses. He published both of his books in London in 1724. Later he came back to America, remaining until his death in 1760.

[2] See AL4, pp. 12-23 and 28-48, and Supplement I, pp. 33-44 and 56-76.

nies might return, and, in any case, regarded them disdainfully in the rôle of political and commercial rivals. Indeed, there were Englishmen who spoke favorably of American speech while the struggle was actually going on, and one of them was the otherwise bitterly anti-American Jonathan Boucher,[1] who wrote on December 23, 1777 that " in North America there prevails not only, I believe, the purest pronunciation of the English tongue that is anywhere to be met with, but a perfect uniformity." On July 19 of the same year one Nicholas Cresswell, who came out in 1774 and remained three years, wrote that " though the inhabitants of this country are composed of different nations and different languages, yet it is very remarkable that they in general speak better English than the English do." " No country or colonial dialect is to be distinguished here," he went on, " except it be the New Englanders, who have a sort of whining cadence that I cannot describe." So late as 1791 the editor of an English reprint of Dr. David Ramsay's " History of the American Revolution " was moved to say in his preface:

> It is a curious fact that there is perhaps no one portion of the British empire in which two or three millions of persons are to be found who speak their mother tongue with greater purity or a truer pronunciation than the white inhabitants of the United States. This was attributed, by a penetrating observer, to the number of British subjects assembled in America from various quarters, who, in consequence of their intercourse and intermarriages, soon dropped the peculiarities of their several provincial idioms, retaining only what was fundamental and common to them all — a process which the frequency or rather the universality of school-learning in America must naturally have assisted.[2]

This Englishman's surmise as to the cause of the uniformity of speech visible in the United States is supported by the fact that immigration from one State or another has been active since the earliest days. The case of Ramsay, noted below, was not unusual even before the Revolution, and today it is a commonplace of observa-

---

[1] See AL4, p. 35n.
[2] Ramsay (1749–1815) was a Pennsylvanian who moved to South Carolina and there became a man of mark. He was a physician and served as a surgeon in the Continental Army. In 1776 he was elected to the South Carolina Legislature, and sat off and on until he was captured by the British in 1780. From 1782 to 1786 he was a member of the Continental Congress, and during the last two years its president. After the Revolution he returned to the South Carolina Legislature. He was murdered by a lunatic. Beside his History of the American Revolution, first published in 1789, he wrote a History of South Carolina, a History of the United States, and a biography of Washington. See AL4, p. 17.

tion that the population of the big cities is made up largely of native Americans born elsewhere, and to a considerable extent in distant States.[1] But the early levelling of dialects was more than a mere amalgamation, for the resultant general speech of the country was influenced much more by several of the British dialects than by all the rest. Which of these dialects had the greatest weight has been discussed at length without any unanimous agreement, but the preponderance of opinion seems to be that American English, at least in the North, got most of its characters from the speech of the southeastern counties of England. "While every one of the forty counties," said John Fiske in "The Beginnings of New England,"[2] "was represented in the great Puritan exodus, the East Anglican counties contributed to it far more than all the rest. Perhaps it would not be far out of the way to say that two-thirds of the American people who can trace their ancestry to New England might follow it back to the East Anglican shires of the mother-country; one-sixth might follow it to those southwestern counties — Devonshire, Dorset and Somerset — which so long were foremost in maritime enterprise; one-sixth to other parts of England." This is confirmed by Anders Orbeck, whose study of the Seventeenth Century town records of Massachusetts[3] leads him to conclude that if "Essex, Middlesex, and London, as well as Norfolk, Suffolk, Cambridgeshire, Northamptonshire, Bedfordshire and Hertfordshire" are included in the East Anglican counties, slightly over 71% of the pioneers of Plymouth, Watertown and Dedham who can be traced came from that area. Further confirmation is provided by Read, who has shown that the Americans of the early Eighteenth Century

---

[1] See State of Birth of the Native Population, 1940, prepared under the supervision of Dr. Leon E. Truesdell, chief of the population division of the Census Bureau; Washington, 1944. In California, in 1940, 48.7% of the native population had been born in other States; in Oregon, 49.4%; in Wyoming, 55.2%, and in the District of Columbia no less than 60.7%. Of the 5,316,338 white inhabitants of New York City, 76,399 came from Massachusetts, 113,987 from the Carolinas, 128,954 from New Jersey, and 145,869 from Pennsylvania. Alaska contributed 108, Nevada 229, Wyoming 477, Idaho 552, South Dakota 967 and Delaware 2994. Nor is this movement into metropolitan cities only. Chattanooga, Tenn., with 128,163 inhabitants, had 50,488 born in other States — 1030 in Ohio, 595 in Texas, 462 in New York, 204 in Oklahoma, 148 in Massachusetts, 45 in Vermont, 32 in Maine, and 15 in New Hampshire.

[2] Boston and New York, 1889, p. 63.
[3] Early New England Pronunciation; Ann Arbor, Mich., 1927, p. 129.

were quick to notice peculiarities in the speech of recent immigrants from the British Isles, but saw nothing to remark in that of those who came from east of Wiltshire or south of the Wash.[1]

Orbeck, in the monograph just mentioned, rehearses the contrary speculations of some of the earlier writers on the subject. In 1885 Senator George F. Hoar of Massachusetts, then president of the American Antiquarian Society, read at its annual meeting a paper in which he not only sought to show that the speech of New England was based upon that of Kent, but also argued that the same county, which he described as "the England of England," was the source of many other salient traits of the New England culture.[2] Hoar cited many familiar New England terms in support of his contention, *e.g.*, *slick* for *sleek*, *be* for *am*, *grub* (food), *to argufy*, *biddy* (a chicken), *to bolt* (food), and *brand-new*, but he ran these terms no further back than William Holloway's "General Dictionary of Provincialisms" of 1839, and his own evidence showed that many of them were also to be found in Sussex. A year later, before the same audience, his conclusions were challenged by Thomas Wentworth Higginson, who used the second edition of Francis Grose's "Provincial Glossary," 1790, and the supplement thereto, published as an appendix to the second edition of Samuel Pegge's "Anecdotes of the English Language," 1814.[3] Higginson rejected all of Hoar's evidence, and argued that American English showed very strong North Country influences. Of the terms that he investigated, he said, 109 came from that region, and only 18 from south-

---

[1] The Assimilation of the Speech of British Immigrants in Colonial America, *Journal of English and Germanic Philology*, Jan., 1938, pp. 70–79. The late Marcus L. Hansen in his chapter on The Settlement of New England in Handbook of the Linguistic Geography of New England; Providence (R.I.), 1939, p. 63, concluded that of the 4,000 families, embracing 20,000 individuals, who reached New England between 1628 and 1640, "the majority originated either in the eastern and southern counties of England, where Puritanism and agricultural change were in the air, or else in the western counties, where fishing and shipping were important occupations."

[2] Report of the Council, *Proceedings* of the society, April, 1885, pp. 342–71.

[3] Neither of the high contesting parties seems to have made any use of J. O. Halliwell-Phillipps's Dictionary of Archaic and Provincial Words; London, 1847; nor of Thomas Wright's Dictionary of Obsolete and Provincial English; London, 1857 (not to be confused with Joseph Wright's English Dialect Dictionary in six vols.; London, 1896–1905), nor of the publications of the English Dialect Society, which began to appear in 1873; nor of Edward Moor's Suffolk Words and Phrases; London, 1823.

eastern England. "The proportion of North Country words," he concluded, "is absolutely overwhelming," and many of them were also to be found in "the Lowland Scots of Scott and Burns."[1]

Years later a Scottish specialist in mythology, Lewis Spence, convinced himself that "the English spoken in the United States is to a great extent merely the popular Midland English of the Seventeenth Century brought more or less up to date by constant communication with the parent country, yet retaining more of the vocalization of the older form by reason of a certain degree of isolation." Spence admitted that he also found traces of influence from Norfolk and even from Cornwall, but insisted that the Midlands were the chief source, and professed to find evidences of Danish coloring, stretching back to the Ninth Century.[2] But the preponderance of opinion among writers on the subject has always inclined toward the East Anglican theory of American speech origins, which is supported more or less by many familiar New England place-names, *e.g.*, *Yarmouth, Ipswich, Haverhill* and the nearby (in England) *Cambridge* and *Boston*. A good example is offered by Schele de Vere. In his "Americanisms: the English of the New World," he declared flatly that the early New England immigrants brought from Norfolk and Suffolk "not only their words, which the Yankee still uses, but also a sound of the voice and a mode of utterance which have been faithfully preserved, and are now spoken of as the 'New England drawl' and 'the high, metallic ring of the New England voice.'"[3] In another place, in speaking of Southern American speech, he said that its disregard for the letter *r* should be laid upon "the shoulders of the guilty forefathers, many of whom came from Suffolk and the districts belonging to the East Anglians."[4]

[1] English Sources of American Dialect, *Proceedings of the American Antiquarian Society*, April, 1886, pp. 159–66. J. R. Bartlett, in the second edition of his Dictionary of Americanisms; Boston, 1859, pp. xxv and xxvi, also favored this North Country theory, though without offering any evidence.

[2] The American Accent and What it Really is, *Scottish Educational Journal*, Oct. 11, 1935, p. 1283, and The American Accent: What Was its Origin?, Edinburgh *Evening Dispatch*, Sept. 30, 1942.

[3] Americanisms: The English of the New World; New York, 1872, p. 427.

[4] p. 627. The old kingdom of East Anglia comprised the present counties of Norfolk and Suffolk, and part of Cambridgeshire. A list of books and articles on its speech in modern times is in Arthur G. Kennedy's Bibliography of Writings on the English Language From the Beginning of Printing to the End of 1922; Cambridge and New Haven, 1927, pp. 383 and 384, and another is in A Bibliographical List

Hans Kurath, editor of the Linguistic Atlas of the United States and Canada, agrees with this in so far as the coastal South is concerned. "Like the seaboard of New England," he says, "the Tidewater region of Virginia received most of its early population from Southeastern England."[1] But he holds that the speech of the areas back from the seacoast shows the influence of "Scotch-Irish who spoke ... the English of the Lowlands of Scotland or the North of England as modified by the Southern English standard." This, however, is not borne out by an investigation undertaken by Cleanth Brooks, Jr., who shows in "The Relation of the Alabama-Georgia Dialect to the Provincial Dialects of Great Britain"[2] that relatively few of the vowel and consonant forms now to be found in the area examined are also encountered in the Scottish and northern English dialects, but that 93% of the former and 95% of the latter are highly characteristic of southwestern (not southeastern) England. Though, says Brooks,

the agreement between the southwest dialects and the Alabama-Georgia dialect in a few particulars might be explained as accidental, their agreement in many — indeed, in nearly every instance in which the Alabama-Georgia dialect differs from standard English — makes any explanation on the basis of a merely accidental relationship untenable. ... This is not to say for a moment, of course, that the Alabama-Georgia dialect is the dialect of Somerset or Devon, but the fact that the former, wherever it deviates from standard English, *deviates with the latter*, indicates that it has been strongly colored by it.[3]

He goes on:

Whereas historical corroboration is lacking, there is nothing in the theory of southwest country influence which runs counter to the known facts. The southwest counties are coast counties and were from Elizabethan times active in exploration and colonization. Of the two companies founded in 1606 for the settlement of Virginia, one was composed of men from Bristol, Exeter and Plymouth.

The area studied by Brooks is a relatively small one, but I think it may be taken as typical of the whole lowland South,[4] saving only

---

of the Works That Have Been Published, or are Known to Exist in MS., Illustrative of the Various Dialects of English, edited by W. W. Skeat and published by the English Dialect Society; London, 1875. In the same works are bibliographies of the speech of the Midlands, the North Country and the West Country, and of most of the English individual counties.

[1] The Origin of Dialectal Differences in Spoken American English, *Modern Philology*, May, 1928, p. 391.
[2] *Louisiana State University Studies*, No. XX; Baton Rouge, 1935.
[3] pp. 72 and 73.
[4] His material came mainly from A Word-List From East Alabama, by L. W. Payne, Jr., *Dialect Notes*, Vol. II, Part IV, 1908, pp. 279-328,

Tidewater and the bayou region of Louisiana. He follows Krapp[1] in holding that in this area "the speech of the Negro and of the white is essentially the same" and that what are commonly regarded as "specifically Negro forms" are only "older English forms which the Negro must have taken originally from the white man, and which he has retained after the white man has begun to lose them."[2] To this another highly competent Southern observer, W. Cabell Greet, agrees. "As the Negro," he says, "has preserved the Methodist and Baptist camp-meeting hymns of a century ago in his spirituals, English dances in his clogs and jigs and reels, so he has kept old ways of speech."[3] Tidewater Southern differs in many ways from this bi-racial lingo but Greet shows that it is confined to a relatively limited area, radiating from the lowlands to such inland islands as Richmond, Charlottesville and the northern Shenandoah valley, but hardly extending beyond. The rest of the South, until one comes to the mountains, the French areas of Louisiana and the cattle country to the westward, follows the patterns described by Brooks. Tidewater Southern, like the dialect of the narrow Boston area and that of the lower Hudson valley, appears to have been considerably influenced by the fashionable London English of the Eighteenth Century. The reason is obvious. These regions, from the earliest days, maintained a closer contact with England than the other parts of the country, and their accumulation of wealth filled them with social aspiration and made them especially responsive to upper-class example. The Civil War shifted the money of the South from Tidewater to the Piedmont, but the conservative lowland gentry continued faithful to the speechways acquired in their days of glory, and the plain people followed them. But all the more recent intrusions of English ways of speech have entered in the Boston and New York areas and on the level of conscious Anglomania.[4]

---

and Vol. III, Part V, pp. 343–91. Payne reported on Lee, Macon, Russell and Tallapoosa counties, Alabama, and Troupe, Harris and Muscogee counties, Georgia. This is low country, with an average altitude, except for a narrow peninsula making down from the Appalachian chain, of less than 600 feet.

[1] The English Language in America; New York, 1925, Vol. I, pp. 248 ff. and Vol. II, p. 226.

[2] pp. 63 and 64.

[3] Southern Speech, in Culture in the South, edited by W. T. Couch; Chapel Hill (N.C.), 1934, p. 614.

[4] See Supplement I, pp. 511 ff. A writer in Town Topics, April 26, 1906, p. 13, reported that this emulation became marked in the 80s. Americans, he said, then began "landing in England with a twang and returning with that twang made more abominable by the ef-

There remains the speech of the overwhelming majority of Americans — according to some authorities, at least 95,000,000 of the 140,000,000 inhabitants of the continental United States. It is called Northern American by John S. Kenyon and Thomas A. Knott,[1] Western or General American by George Philip Krapp,[2] Middle Western by many lay writers,[3] and American Standard by George L. Trager,[4] and is described by the last named as "the pronunciation ... of the whole country except the old South, New England and the immediate vicinity of New York city." More, it is constantly spreading, and two of its salient traits, the flat *a* and the clearly sounded *r*, are making heavy inroads in the territories once faithful to the broad *a* and the silent *r*. "Only in the immediate neighborhood of Boston and in the greater part of New Hampshire and Maine," says Bernard Bloch,[5] "is the so-called Eastern pronunciation universal," and even in this region there are speech-islands in

---

fort to inflect and produce the English language as Londoners of fashion do. This curious importation has grown and developed until now the result is of an alarming ugliness. Compounded of bastard Briticisms and inescapable nasalities, it is delivered from a mouth apparently abrim with steaming porridge.... The syllables cannot really be said to issue at all. They mingle in one blend of inchoate vowel sound; the consonants die before they are decently born." The writer, with the lack of reticence characteristic of a society journalist, named some of the fashionables of the time who were most given to this lingual Anglomania: the Sloanes, Whitehouses, Havemeyers, Palmers, Stokeses, Brokaws, and Haggins. "Our spoken American," he said, "is threatened from the top down, and slang and all the perishing inventions of the vulgate do not menace it one tithe as sombrely as does this mannered mouthing by our millionaires." The increasing rage for English speechways had been lampooned by Mrs. Burton Harrison in The Anglomaniacs in 1887, and by Edgar Fawcett in A Gentleman of Leisure, *c*. 1880. See American English, by Gilbert M. Tucker, *Transactions of the Albany Institute*, Vol. X, 1883, p. 335.

1 A Pronouncing Dictionary of American English; Springfield (Mass.), 1944, p. xxxii, and American Pronunciation, by Kenyon alone, ninth ed., Ann Arbor (Mich.), 1945, p. vi. Kenyon is professor of English at Hiram College and rewrote the Guide to Pronunciation for Webster 1934. Knott was general editor of this Webster from 1926 to 1935, when he became professor of English at the University of Michigan and editor of the Middle English Dictionary. He died on Aug. 14, 1945.
2 The English Language in America; New York, 1925, Vol. I, p. 40.
3 For example, Lewis and Marguerite Shalett Herman in Talk American; Chicago, 1944, p. xi.
4 The Pronunciation of Short *a* in American Standard English, *American Speech*, June, 1930, p. 396.
5 Postvocalic *r* in New England Speech: A Study in American Dialect Geography, *Acts of the Fourth International Congress of Linguists*, Copenhagen, 1936, p. 198.

which it is challenged. New England west of the Connecticut river now belongs predominantly to the domain of General American, and so does all of New York State save the suburbs of New York, and all the rest of the country save the late Confederate States. Even the dialect of Appalachia, though it differs from General American, differs from it less than it differs from any regional variety.

What, then, was the origin of this widespread and now thoroughly typical form of speech, and why is it prevailing against all other forms? There are authorities who seek to answer, as in the case of New England, by pointing to population statistics. "The Piedmont of Virginia and the Carolinas, and the Great Valley," says Kurath in the paper lately quoted, "were largely settled, during the half-century preceding the Revolution, by the Scotch-Irish, who spoke . . . the English of the Lowlands of Scotland or the north of England as modified by the Southern English Standard. They neither dropped their *r*'s nor did they pronounce their long mid-vowels diphthongal fashion. The large German element from Pennsylvania ultimately acquired this type of English." Moreover, it also found lodgment in Western New England, which received a considerable admixture of Scotch-Irish during the same period, and the speechways of this region soon "became established in New York State and in the Western Reserve of Ohio," and thence moved into the whole of the opening West. Unquestionably this influence of Scotch-Irish example was powerful all along the frontier, and even nearer the coast it must have had some effect, for many of the early schoolmasters were Scotsmen or Irishmen. Though some eminent phonologists dissent, and I am mindful of Dr. Louise Pound's tart but just remark that "it is the amateur in phonetic matters who speaks with strongest conviction and feels surest of his message,"[1] I find it impossible to put away the suspicion that later tides of pedagogy considerably reinforced the movement away from the southeastern English speechways of the Atlantic seaboard and toward those of the Scotch lowlands and the English North. The original Scottish schoolmasters, to be sure, did not long outlast the Eighteenth Century, nor did the Irishmen who followed them. By the time the great movement into the West was well under way

[1] British and American Pronunciation: Retrospect and Prospect, *School Review*, June, 1915, p. 381.

both were beginning to be displaced by native young men,[1] and before the Civil War these native young men were giving way in their turn to females. Not many of the latter, in their primeval form, had any education beyond that of the common schools they taught in; the great majority, indeed, were simply milkmaids armed with hickory sticks. They could thus muster up no authority of their own, but had to depend perforce upon that of the books in their hands — and the book that was there invariably, before and above all others, was the aforesaid blue Speller of Noah Webster. When it got any support at all, it was usually from his unfolding series of dictionaries.

Webster was a New Englander, but he was not a Bostonian, and his central purpose, as he wrote to John Pickering, was "to deliver . . . my countrymen from the errors that fashion and ignorance" were seeking to introduce from England [2] — and succeeding more or less in the Boston and New York areas. He advocated, above all, clarity and consistency in utterance,[3] and was against all the vowel changes, sacrifice of consonants and other perversions that were imitated from contemporary England usage in the Anglomaniacal circles of the East. In particular, he was opposed to the artificial *Bühnenaussprache* that Sheridan had introduced, and that Walker was soon to reinforce, for his opinion of actors was almost as low as his opinion of political and theological rhetoricians.[4] He thus gave

1 It was almost the rule, between 1800 and 1835, for poor young men to earn their way through college by teaching school, and large numbers continued until they were ripe for politics or one of the professions. In the rural South and Middle West the custom survives more or less to this day.
2 Quoted by George H. McKnight in Modern English in the Making; New York, 1928, p. 484.
3 "If we examine the structure of any language," he said in his Dissertations on the English Language; Boston, 1789, pp. 27–29, "we shall find a certain principle of analogy running through the whole. We shall find in English that similar combinations of letters have usually the same pronunciation, and that words having the same terminating syllable generally have the accent at the same distance from that termination. . . . In disputed points, where people differ in opinion and practise, analogy should always decide the controversy."
4 Brander Matthews says in Essays on English; New York, 1921, p. 216, that the German *Bühnenaussprache* was revised in 1898 by a committee consisting of five professors of language and six actors and managers. American actors of the tonier sort still use some of the traditional pronunciations of the English stage, but Frank Vizetelly says in A Desk-Book of 25,000 Words Frequently Mispronounced; New York, 1917, p. ix. that these affectations are but little imitated outside the theatre, even in England. He gives some curious specimens — *aitches* for *aches, bird*

powerful, if not always conscious support to the Northern British influences — always in favor of relatively precise utterance — that were operating upon American speech west of the Hudson, and he was supported in turn by the natural tendency of hard-driven pioneers to say what they had to say in very plain language, without airs and fopperies.[1] The schoolma'am, without doubt, found it difficult to induce her pupils to speak with any elegance, just as her heirs (as we shall see anon) are finding it difficult today, but she at least taught them to articulate clearly and to pronounce words according to more or less logical patterns,[2] and in this benign endeavor her efforts were vastly facilitated by the popularity of the spelling-class and the spelling-bee, which broke up words into their component parts, and gave every part its full value.[3]

It is easy, of course, to over-estimate such influences, and every pedagogue is well aware that the speech actually acquired by the young is determined not only by what they are taught in school but also by what they hear outside. But I think it is unwise to argue, as some linguists have done, that the schoolma'am is a mere bystander in the process of speech change.[4] She needs a favorable environment to work her will upon her charges, but in the United States she has always had it, for Americans, from the days of their

---

for *beard*, *kwality* (with the *a* as in *at*) for *quality*, *rallery* for *raillery*, *Room* for *Rome*, *yur* for *your*, *moo-errn* for *mourn*, *ge-irl* for *girl*, and *England* with the *e* of *end*.

1 Said C. K. Thomas in the *Quarterly Journal of Speech Education*, Nov., 1927, p. 452: "The West, since it grew up with its attention on more urgent questions than niceties of speech, developed a more natural type, mainly free from the artificialities of polite speech."
2 In Sources of Pronunciation, *American Speech*, June, 1929, pp. 416-19, J. S. K[enyon?] discussed acutely the four dominant influences, to wit, tradition, analogy, borrowing and spelling. The last-named, he said, is always most powerful in the middle ground between the illiterate and the "educated and cosmopolitan." The overwhelming majority of Americans, as of other folk, have always stood in that middle ground.
3 I am reminded of this by Mrs. Delia H. Biddle Pugh, of New York, who writes: "In country schools in the old days spelling-classes stood up and spelled *extraordinary* as *E X ex*, *T R A tra*, *extra*, *O R*, *or*, *extraor*, and so on. This influenced the American tendency to give full value to every syllable." Certainly it worked powerfully against such English forms (borrowed in Boston and New York) as *extraw'n'ry*.
4 This is the conclusion, on the college level, of J. M. Steadman, Jr., in The Language Consciousness of College Students, *American Speech*, Dec., 1926, p. 131. "The imitation of the teacher as a superior linguistic authority," he says, "is by far the most important single cause of change."

beginning, have vastly esteemed so-called education and accepted precept and example so docilely that their culture has inclined more and more toward a nation-wide uniformity. As year chases year they tend in ever increasing multitudes to eat the same food, wear the same clothes, live in houses of the same sort, follow the same recreations, admire the same mountebanks, fear the same hobgoblins, cherish the same hallucinations and delusions, and speak the same language. That language is now being studied as it was never studied before, but in all probability a considerable time must yet pass before we attain to a really sound knowledge of its origins and growth.

The beginnings of this prevailing speech of the country, as opposed to the New England and Southern varieties, apparently date from the Revolution,[1] but until the closing years of the Eighteenth Century it seems to have attracted little notice, either from purists at home or from visiting Englishmen. Even the alert and far from amiable John Witherspoon, writing from his rectoral stool at Princeton in 1781,[2] had little to say about the pronunciation of Americans, but confined himself to their grammatical and semantic innovations. And what little he said was mainly favorable, perhaps because he was a Scotsman and hence no partisan of the currently fashionable form of Southern English. "The vulgar in America," he allowed, "speak much better than the vulgar in Great Britain, for a very obvious reason, *viz.*, that being much more unsettled and moving frequently from place to place, they are not so liable to local peculiarities either in accent or phraseology." His chief complaint was laid, not against this speech of "the vulgar" as he had encountered it in the Middle Colonies, but against the more pretentious discourse of the presumably educated classes. "I have heard in this country," he said, "in the senate, at the bar and from the pulpit, and see daily in dissertations from the press, errors in grammar, improprieties and vulgarisms which hardly any person of the same class in point of

---

[1] Says Eilert Ekwall in American and British Pronunciation; Upsala, 1946, pp. 29 and 32: "Educated American pronunciation on the whole remains at the stage which British pronunciation had reached about the time of the Revolution, while modern British pronunciation has left that stage far behind. . . . Educated American was under the influence of Standard British all through the colonial period, an influence probably stronger in the later than in the earlier part."

[2] His strictures are dealt with at length in Supplement I, pp. 4-14.

rank and literature would have fallen into in Great Britain."[1] But even here he was flogging what he presumed to be errors in usage, not errors in pronunciation. The same may be said for the English reviewers who loosed their torrent of objurgation toward the end of the century. They were dealing with written, not spoken American, and in consequence they lavished their scorn upon such American contributions to the vocabulary as *reliable, lengthy, bogus, to donate, to advocate, to progress, balance* (in the sense of remainder) and *to jeopardize*, and had nothing to say about the flat *a* or the resurrected *r*.

It remained for native Americans to set up the doctrine that the only right way to speak English was the ever-changing way of the English upper classes. Benjamin Franklin, despite his heterodoxy in other respects, seems to have inclined to this idea, perhaps because he had spent so much time in England,[2] and it was apparently supported more or less by the American Academy of Language and Belles Lettres organized in New York in 1820, with John Quincy Adams as its president.[3] Irving, always eager for English notice and favor, ran the same way, and so, after a somewhat timorous show of independence, did Cooper. Nor is there any evidence that any other American authors of the pre-Civil War era greatly resented the notion that spoken American, save for the differences in vocabulary, should conform to English standards, though Edward Everett and George Ticknor objected to the patronizing air of Englishmen who favored it, and Walt Whitman, characteristically substituting hopes for observation, predicted that Americans would eventually become "the most fluent and melodious voiced people in the world — and the most perfect users of words."[4] But all these writers scarcely more than played with the subject, and their acquiescence in the

---

[1] This judgment was confirmed forty-two years later by another Scotsman, John M. Duncan, whose Travels in America was published in Glasgow in 1823. In Vol. II thereof he said: "The inferior orders of society in America certainly speak more accurately than the inferior orders in Britain. . . . Here, however, my concessions stop. The educated classes do not speak by any means so accurately in America as in Britain; there are more deficiencies in grammar, in accent, in pronunciation." I am indebted here to Dr. J.-M. Carrière, of the University of Virginia.

[2] On Sept. 27, 1760, he wrote from London to David Hume: "I hope . . . that we shall always in America make the best English of this island our standard, and I believe it will be so." But this was before the Revolution.

[3] See Supplement I, pp. 18–20.

[4] Here I am indebted again to Allen Walker Read's Amphi-Atlantic English, before quoted.

theory that the speech standards of England should also prevail in America was mainly only tacit. The first Americans to give the language of the country what might be reasonably described as serious study were William C. Fowler and George P. Marsh, the former of whom published "The English Language in its Elements and Forms" in 1850, and the latter of whom followed with "Lectures on the English Language" in 1859. Fowler, who was a son-in-law to Noah Webster, was professor of rhetoric at Amherst and the first Northern pedagogue to undertake courses in Old English.[1] Marsh was a Vermonter who went in for politics and rose to high office, but had many outside interests and among other things tried to introduce the camel into the United States. Fowler distinguished between the language of New England, that of the South, and that of the rising West, but predicted that "the system of school education, and the use of the same textbooks in the institutions of learning, and of the same periodicals and reading books in families — in short, the mighty power of the press" would eventually iron out these differences and make "the people of America one in language as one in government."[2] He was willing to be polite to English example on the higher levels of speech — that of "the best authors and public speakers" — but he argued that "the great mass of the people of the United States speak and write their vernacular tongue with more correctness than the common people of England." Marsh took much the same position, but he noted that "a marked difference of accent" was already separating the speech of the two countries. This separation he deplored, saying,

If we cannot prevent so sad a calamity, let us not voluntarily accelerate it. Let us not, with malice prepense, go about to republicanize our orthography and our syntax, our grammars and our dictionaries, our nursery hymns [sic] and our Bibles, until, by the force of irresistible influences, our language shall have revolutionized itself. When our own metaphysical inquirers shall establish a wiser philosophy than that of Bacon; when a Columbian Shakespeare shall awake to create a new and transcendent genus of dramatic composition; and when the necessities of a loftier inspiration shall impel our home-born bards to the framing of a nobler diction than the poetic dialect of Albion, it will be soon enough to repudiate that community of speech which, in spite of the keenly conflicting interests of politics and of commerce, makes us still one with the people of England.[3]

[1] This was in 1841. It had been taught at Randolph-Macon College since 1839 and at the University of Virginia since 1825.

[2] p. 94.

[3] Lectures on the English Language; fourth edition, revised and enlarged; New York, 1870, p. 676.

But this, after all, was hardly more than a flourish of rhetoric, characteristic of the time and buried in the last pages of a long book, and it would be unjust to accuse Marsh of advocating an abject conformity to English standards. The first to do that in an all-out and undisguised manner was another amateur philologian, and one whose influence, for a good many years, was greater than that of Marsh or even of Fowler. He was Richard Grant White. In his "Words and Their Uses," undertaken immediately after the Civil War,[1] he apologized most humbly for his occasional criticisms of English usage, saying that "no insinuation of a superiority in the use of their mother tongue by men of English race in 'America' is intended, no right to set up an independent standard is implied."[2] And then he proceeded to formulate a criterion:

> The pronunciation of *a* in such words as *glass, last, father* and *pastor* is a test of high culture . . . next to that tone of voice which . . . is not to be acquired by any striving in adult years, and which indicates breeding rather than education. The full, free, unconscious utterance of the broad *ah* sound of *a* is the surest indication in speech of social culture which began at the cradle.[3]

To which he added in 1876, in a magazine article entitled "American Pronunciation of English":[4]

> It is only in a comparatively small, although actually numerous, circle of people of high social culture in New England and New York, and in the latter place among those of New England birth, or very direct descent, that the true standard of English speech is found in this country.

White republished this paper in a second volume, "Every-Day English," in 1881, but omitted the passage I have just quoted. He made up for it, however, with the following:

> The usage of polite society regulates pronunciation; and that there is very polite society in Texas and in California the dwellers in those places most vehemently declare, and I shall not deny. But with the utmost respect for its intelligence and politeness, we must all admit, I think, that it is not English society, or that it is so in a modified and limited sense of the term. Therefore, it is not to Texas, or to California, or to Maine, or indeed to any place in "America" that we should go to find out standard English, whether in word, in idiom, or in pronunciation. The language spoken in those places may be a

---

[1] The essays making up the book were first published in the *Galaxy* in 1867, 1868 and 1869, and appeared between covers in 1870.
[2] Preface dated New York, July 8, 1870. The passage is on p. 8 of the New Edition, Revised and Corrected; New York, 1876.
[3] p. 62.
[4] *Galaxy*, April, p. 523.

very polite one, very admirable in every respect, but it is not necessarily standard English; and just in so far as it deviates from the language of the most cultivated society in England it fails to be English.[1]

White was challenged by a number of other writers on speech, notably Fitzedward Hall and G. Washington Moon, but the most refined opinion of his time seems to have supported him, and his books remained authorities for many years. "Words and Their Uses," indeed, was the *Stammvater* of all the cocksure treatises on "correct" English which still appear in large numbers, and are accepted gravely by the innocent.[2] The schoolma'am followed it dutifully for more than a generation, either at first hand or at second, third or fourth, and the super-gogues who trained and indoctrinated her seldom showed any doubt of its fundamental postulates. It received a heavy reinforcement in 1905, when Henry James, the novelist, broke his voluntary exile in England long enough to harangue the year's graduating class at Bryn Mawr College on the evils of American speech.[3] James was no phonologist, and it was apparent that his notion of the speechways of his native land was

---

[1] Every-Day English; New York, 1881, p. 89. It will be noted that White put the word *America* into ironical quotation marks — a banal indication of his Anglomania. This animosity to the vernacular was denounced by Dante, so long ago as the first years of the Fourteenth Century, in Il Convivio. He found five causes for it, thus summarized by Gordon Hall Gerould in The Gawain Poet and Dante, *Publications of the Modern Language Association*, March, 1936, p. 33: "blindness in discernment, mischievous self-justification, desire of vainglory, the prompting of envy, and abjectness of mind, or cowardice." Of the last-named Dante said: "On account of this abjectness many disparage their own vernacular and praise that of others; and all such men as these are the abominable wretches in Italy who regard as low their precious vernacular, which, if it be low in anything, is only so in so far as it is heard in the bawdy mouth of these adulterers."

[2] White was a New Yorker, born in 1821, and after trying medicine and the law took to journalism. He soon attained to notice as a musical and dramatic critic, and in 1853 began a series of studies of Shakespeare which eventually produced the Riverside edition of the Bard, published in 1883. He had no training in philology, but was a very cocksure fellow, and did not hesitate to pit his opinions against those of such authorities as William D. Whitney. During the Civil War he served gallantly as a Federal jobholder in New York. His son Stanford, born in 1853, was the celebrated architect, put to death by Harry K. Thaw on June 25, 1906.

[3] His address was delivered on June 8, and got a great deal of attention in the newspapers. It was printed in The Question of Our Speech; Boston and New York, 1905.

picked up, not by direct observation,[1] but by a study of the barbarisms credited to Americans in the English comic papers, *e.g., popper, vanillar, vurry, Amurrica, tullegram* and even *Philadulphia.* He had, however, high prestige as a writer and imitated very effectively the lofty air of an Oxford don, so his ill-natured remarks made a considerable impression. He did not argue categorically that Americans should adopt English speechways — indeed, he made it plain that he believed that any such cultural ascent was beyond their poor powers —, but he at least indicated clearly that he thought their own were ignorant, uncouth and against God. If asked, he said, to define what he meant by speaking badly, "I might reply to you, very synthetically [*sic*], that I mean . . . speaking as millions and millions of supposedly educated, supposedly civilized persons — that is the point — of both sexes, in our great country, habitually, persistently, imperturbably, and I think for the most part all unwittingly, speak." He then proceded to rehearse his specimens of American speech from the English comic papers, and to denounce the American *r* as "a sort of morose grinding of the back teeth" and a "signal specimen of what becomes of a custom of utterance out of which the principle of taste has dropped," leaving in the air the conclusion that the only road to linguistic decency lay through its obliteration as in England, and the adoption of all the other refinements of Oxford English. This pronunciamento, despite its donkeyishness, was politely received in pedagogical circles, and so late as 1916, Fred Newton Scott was telling the schoolma'ams, male and female, of the National Council of Teachers of English, that "almost everyone who touches upon American speech assumes that it is inferior to British speech."[2]

Scott was wrong here, as he was wrong in other matters, for philologians of more weight than he had were already declaring for American autonomy in pronunciation. One of them was Dr. Louise Pound, who printed a paper in 1915 which noted the plain fact that English and American had already developed too many differences

---

[1] Born in New York in 1843, he spent the years 1855-59 in Europe, and in 1869 settled in England, where he remained until his death in 1916. He was perhaps the champion Anglomaniac of all time, not even excepting Walter Hines Page.

[2] Presidential address in New York, Dec. 1. This address was printed in the *English Journal*, Jan., 1917, and reprinted in The Standard of American Speech and Other Papers; Boston, 1926. A brief account of Scott is in Supplement I, pp. 134 and 135n.

to "be treated as orally identical." She expressed the pious hope that these differences would not lead, at least in the near future, to a complete separation of the two tongues, but she saw clearly that they were bound to "increase, not lessen." She went on:

> To the assumption of those who find at the present time very little departure from British standards, and who hold to the belief that cleavage may be held in check, may be opposed the fact that we have drifted so far apart that in each country the accent of the other serves for a comedy part on the stage.[1]

Other experts on the national speechways soon joined her, and in recent years nearly all the better texts on pronunciation accept American English as it is, and avoid any vain attempt to bring it into harmony with current English standards. This is true, for example, of the books of Krapp[2] and Kenyon,[3] the two most respected authorities. Even Larsen and Walker, the former an Oxford man and the latter of Harvard,[4] "do not advise any one who has not already acquired the speech characteristics of English Received Pronunciation in a natural way to attempt to acquire them artificially," on the ground that "an irritating affectation will surely result from any such attempt,"[5] though they advocate a broad *a* in such words as *path*, *grass* and *past*.[6] Krapp, in the book lately cited, p. x, had said: "It seems scarcely credible that one who knows the facts should think it possible to impose British standards upon American speech." To which may be added the verdict of a special committee

---

[1] British and American Pronunciation: Retrospect and Prospect, *School Review*, June, p. 392. Said William Schack in the *Millgate*, Oct., 1938, quoted in the Manchester *Evening News*, Sept. 28: "To an American vaudeville audience a broad *a* is as funny as a bit of slapstick comedy; and it would take a brave man to say *cahn't* in many an American gathering."

[2] The Pronunciation of Standard English in America, by George Philip Krapp; New York, 1919. See especially his discussion of the broad *a*, p. 64.

[3] American Pronunciation; Ann Arbor, Mich., 1924; ninth ed., 1945. Kenyon says, p. vi, that he has "based his observations on the cultivated pronunciation of his own locality — the Western Reserve of Ohio." He adds: "this is fairly representative of . . . the speech . . . which is virtually uniform in its most noticeable features from New York State west, in a region north of a line drawn west from Philadelphia."

[4] Pronunciation: a Practical Guide to American Standards, by Thorlief Larsen and Francis C. Walker; London and New York, 1930.

[5] p. 15.

[6] Some of their other recommendations are hardly in accord with the general American practise. See, for example, the pronunciations they recommend for *triolet, to annex, to convoy, abdomen, mamma, obscurantist, ordinarily* and *panegyrist*.

appointed by the Modern Language Association to draw up a report on "The English Language in American Education":

> Contemporary linguistic science views . . . American English not as a corruption but as the accepted English of the United States. . . . Realization that it is the American rather than the British forms of the English language which American students need to learn should not shock any teacher who knows what American English is. . . . The most practical pedagogical conclusion involved is that wherever the spelling, pronunciation, vocabulary or usage of the two great branches of the language differ, American students should be taught the American rather than the British form. . . . The English our American students should be helped to master is the standard English spoken and written in contemporary America.[1]

There remain, however, belated followers of White, especially in the New York region, who hope to achieve this impossibility, and occasionally they make some pother. This was the case, for example, during the years after 1918, when an Australian-born phonologist named William Tilly was appointed to foster speech elegance at Columbia, and proceeded at once to advocate a close approximation to the English standard.[2] He acquired a number of ardent disciples, mainly female, among teachers of what used to be called elocution but is now denominated speech correction, and some of them went to the length of arguing that all Americans hoping to be really refined should imitate the imitation of English speech prevailing among the tonier sort of American actors.[3] But this folly did not

---

[1] The report was published by the Commission on Trends in Education of the Modern Language Association; New York, 1945. The quotation is from pp. 5 and 6. The special committee consisted of Thomas Clark Pollock, of New York University; William Clyde DeVane, of Yale; and Robert E. Spiller, of Swarthmore. The report was approved by the Commission on Trends in Education on Sept. 17, 1944, and passed for publication by the Executive Council of the association on Dec. 27.

[2] Tilly was born in 1860 and died in 1935. He went to Germany in 1887, taught at the University of Marburg from 1892 to 1902, and then set up a phonetic institute in Berlin. On the outbreak of World War I he was interned by the Germans, but in 1916 they released him and he went to London. In 1918 he came to New York.

[3] Some of the extravagances to which this would have led were noticed a little while back. Very few American actors, in fact, have ever succeeded in acquiring an English accent that really fools the English. One of those who made the grade was Edwin Booth. On Nov. 24, 1880, he wrote from London, where he was presenting his répertoire: "The purity of my English is invariably praised, and even admitted by the carpers. Think of a blarsted Yankee speaking English!" But he seems to have fallen into his native American when he was off guard, for he added: "Wish I could speak as good English off as I do on the stage." See Memories

extend very far, and there is little sign that it will spread hereafter. In 1927 C. K. Thomas of Cornell printed a review of the subject [1] in which he attempted to summarize professional opinion under five headings, to wit:

1. Is there a world-standard of English pronunciation?
2. What claim has the speech of southern England to be considered a world-standard?
3. What claim has the speech of southern England to be considered the standard for America?
4. Is there a distinct American national standard?
5. What are the criteria of a good standard?

Dr. Thomas found that the answer to the first question was no. He could find no trace of a generally acknowledged world-standard. On the one hand a few phonologists of small authority favored " the worldwide acceptance of the southern English standard," but all the rest of the faculty seemed to favor national autonomy, and to regard it as inevitable. To the second question the answer was none.

---

and Letters of Edwin Booth, *Century Magazine*, Dec., 1893, p. 240. The old-time elocutionists all affected a pseudo-English pronunciation, chiefly marked by ludicrously broad *a*'s. The English themselves no longer imitate actors as they did in the Eighteenth Century. Said Henry Cecil Wyld, in The Historical Study of the Mother Tongue; London, 1906, p. 356: "The English of the stage . . . differs from the English of good society partly in being more archaic, partly also in being marred by certain artificialities and affectations of pronunciation." Said Thomas A. Knott, then general editor of the Webster Dictionaries, in an address to the Eastern Public Speaking Conference in New York City, April, 1933: "[If you are training] a college student who is a member of the debating team of the State University of Illinois . . . you don't want to teach him London stage speech. His audiences would laugh. Some of them wouldn't even understand what he was trying to talk about." This address was printed as How the Dictionary Determines What Pronunciations to Use, in the *Quarterly Journal of Speech*, Feb., 1935, pp. 1-10. A survey undertaken in 1941 by "a member of the faculty at Pennsylvania State College," reported in General American Speech, Dayton (O.) *Journal*, editorial page, Nov. 21, 1941, showed that 52% of the male film stars then reigning in Hollywood used the General American pronunciation. The rest varied between the Boston-New York City variety and efforts to imitate Oxford English. But among male stars of the legitimate stage only 24% used General American. The rest used the broad *a* and dropped their *r*'s. See Stage Versus Screen, by Marguerite E. DeWitt, *American Speech*, Jan., 1927, pp. 165-81.

[1] Recent Discussions of Standardization in American Pronunciation, *Quarterly Journal of Speech Education*, Nov., pp. 442-57. The title of this journal was abbreviated to the *Quarterly Journal of Speech* in 1928. It is the organ of the National Association of Teachers of Speech.

There were English authorities, to be sure, who defended Standard English as superior to any other form of the language, but there were other authorities, greater in number and fully equal in learning, who denounced it as one of the worst. The answer to the third question was likewise none. "The preponderance of authority," concluded Thomas, " is strongly against community of standard for British and American pronunciation." In answer to the fourth question he described the three major varieties of American, already discussed in this chapter — the Boston-New York, the Southern, and the Western or General —, and then found himself agreeing with Kenyon and Krapp that the last-named was already almost overwhelmingly dominant, and showed plain indications of increasing its area and authority in future. The answer to the last question resolved itself into a plea for letting nature take its course. " A good standard," said Thomas, " is a natural growth, not a manufactured article; and attempts to improve on this standard are like attempts to graft wings on human shoulders." In other words, the voice of the people, in the last analysis, must decide and determine the voice of the people. That the voting is now running heavily in favor of General American must be manifest. Kenyon, writing in 1927, rehearsed the evidence for it then visible;[1] the evidence available today is even more impressive, and it would undoubtedly be more impressive still if General American were studied as diligently as New England English has been studied. The Eastern colleges yearly outfit a ponderable number of Indianans, Iowans and Oregonians with the broad *a*, but most of them resume the flat *a* as soon as they return home, and meanwhile the Linguistic Atlas of New England finds two flat *a*'s in *half past* within the very shadow of the Boston Statehouse.[2]

[1] *Maître Phonétique*, Jan.-March, 1927, pp. 3 and 4.
[2] Vol. II, Part I, Map 80. Miss M. E. DeWitt hints in EuphonEnglish; New York, 1924, p. 49n, that something resembling the English standard is taught at Columbia, Hunter College, Smith and Vassar, but she does not enter into particulars. She even adds the State University of Iowa, but this is hard to credit. She notes that the New York Singing Teachers' Association " has adopted Daniel Jones's English Pronouncing Dictionary," which rests squarely upon the English standard, but that fact is of no significance, for singers, for obvious reasons, always use the Italian *a*. Incidentally, it may be noted that Jones himself, in his preface to his dictionary, p. x, says: " Several American teachers (mostly from New York and the Northeastern part of the United States) have informed me, somewhat to my surprise, that RP [*i.e.*, Received Pronunciation, his name for the English standard] or

The subject was revived in 1944 when the New York State Department of Education appointed a committee to draw up rules for the certification of teachers of "speech correction" in the public schools of the State. Thomas, who was one of its members,[1] found a sharp difference of opinion among his colleagues about the standard of pronunciation that should be recommended. Some were apparently in favor of General American, but others inclined toward the standard that had been advocated by Tilly. Thomas resolved to ask the advice of a number of outside phonologists of distinction, and accordingly prepared a questionnaire. Its first question was: "In a course of phonetics for prospective teachers of speech correction what standard or standards of pronunciation would you include?" This was sent to the following:

V. A. Anderson, Stanford University; author of "Training the Speaking Voice."

A. C. Baugh, University of Pennsylvania; author of "A History of the English Language."

W. Cabell Greet, Columbia University; editor of *American Speech* and speech consultant to the Columbia Broadcasting System.

Miles L. Hanley, University of Wisconsin; associate director of the Linguistic Atlas of the United States and Canada.

Hans Kurath, Brown University (now Michigan); director of the Linguistic Atlas and author of "American Pronunciation."

Mardel Ogilvie, State Teachers College, Fredonia, N. Y.; president of the New York State Speech Association.

J. M. O'Neill, Brooklyn College; former editor of the *Quarterly Journal of Speech*.

Louise Pound, University of Nebraska; former editor of *American Speech*; former president of the American Dialect Society and of the American Folk-Lore Society.

Loren Reid, University of Missouri; former president of the New York State Speech Association.

K. R. Wallace, University of Virginia, editor of the *Quarterly Journal of Speech*.

Harold Wentworth, Temple University; compiler of the "American Dialect Dictionary."

Robert West, University of Wisconsin; co-author of "Phonetics" and former president of the Speech Correction Association.

RP with slight modifications would be a suitable standard for teaching in American schools. Personally, I cannot think that any attempt to introduce this pronunciation into America is likely to meet with success."

[1] The others were H. J. Heltman, of Syracuse (chairman); Miss Agnes Rigney, of State Teachers College, Geneseo; Miss Mary Zerler, of the Yonkers public schools; and Mrs. Letitia Raubicheck, of the New York City public schools.

A. B. Williamson, New York University; former president of the Association of Teachers of Speech.

G. P. Wilson, Woman's College of the University of North Carolina; editor of the *Publications of the American Dialect Society*.

The replies were thus summarized by Thomas:

> Almost all the contributors recommend that General American be included in the content of the course. Several recommend that it be the principal content; not one rejects it. Since, however, many of the students in the course will speak some other type of American English provision must be made for their speech needs as well. If we follow the . . . threefold classification of American pronunciation into Eastern, Southern and General American, it will probably be salutary for the student to have some acquaintance with all three types. . . . It is noteworthy that not one of the contributors recommends the inclusion of the South British standard, and that several of them specifically reject it.[1]

One of the members of the Department of Education committee, Mrs. Raubicheck, objected to this referendum on the ground that the two New Yorkers consulted were not specialists in phonetics. She accordingly sent Thomas's questions to six others, all of them directly interested in teaching speechways. They were:

Almira M. Giles, Brooklyn College.
Edward W. Mammen, College of the City of New York.
Dorothy L. Mulgrave, New York University.
E. J. Spadino, Hunter College.
Margaret Prendergast McLean, author of "American Speech."
Jane Dorsey Zimmerman, Teachers College, Columbia, associate editor of *American Speech*.

This jury was somewhat more favorable to Tilly than the fourteen philologians polled by Thomas, but only Miss McLean rejected the claims of General American. "I should include," she said, "the pronunciation given as Eastern Standard by Kenyon and Knott[2] or that given by Daniel Jones in 'An English Pronouncing Dictionary.'"[3] Miss Giles preferred "acceptable varieties of Eastern speech," and explained that by acceptable she meant varieties showing all forms of the *a* in *half*, from that of *hat* to that of *father*, but added that she thought the course should also "touch briefly on General American and Southern standards." Mammen was of the opinion that "both Eastern and General American should be ac-

---

[1] A Symposium on Phonetics and Standards of Pronunciations, *Quarterly Journal of Speech*, Oct., 1945, pp. 318–327.

[2] *i.e.*, the Boston-New York City standard.

[3] *i.e.*, the Southern English or Oxford standard.

ceptable." Miss Mulgrave said: "If it were apparent that teachers were trained for New York State only I should be loath to recommend them as teachers of speech correction. . . . There seems to be no need to act as though New York has seceded." Spadino voted for " General American, with little importance given to geographical distinction," and described it as " a dialect embracing both Northern and Eastern regional pronunciations as defined and recorded in Kenyon and Knott," but did not say how these dialects were to be reconciled. Mrs. Zimmerman proposed to " make the standard of pronunciation a very flexible one " and to " include in it all commonly used variants which are consistent with good voice, clear articulation, accurate patterns of stress, phrasing and intonation, and which are acceptable to the professional or social group to which the student belongs or to which he wishes to belong." It will thus be seen that the Raubicheck jury, like that of Thomas, favored a thoroughly American standard, with special emphasis on the prevailing usage, and had but little to say for the effort to bring American speech into harmony with British.[1]

Lay opinion runs strongly in favor of General American, as was demonstrated by tests made by Walter H. Wilke and Joseph F. Snyder, of New York University, in 1940–42. They recorded by phonograph the speech of thirty-two persons from all parts of the country, and circulated the recordings among 2470 persons in forty localities, asking for preferences. The jury consisted mainly of " college students in elementary courses," but there were also some high-school students and miscellaneous adults. It was chosen to be representative of " that sector of the population likely to discriminate between the generally acceptable and sub-standard speech, yet typical enough of fairly well-educated persons to avoid any biases due to special study and emphasis on details of speech." The result of the poll was overwhelmingly favorable to General American. Of the thirty-two samples the five at the top of the list all belonged to it, and it also got more votes than any other form further on. The runner-up was Southern American. The Eastern speech of the Boston area came out very badly, and that of New York City even worse. " More widely used in the United States than any other dia-

[1] A Footnote on Phonetics and Standards of Pronunciation, Quarterly Journal of Speech, Feb., 1946, pp. 51–54.

lect," concluded the authors, "the General American type has the additional advantages that it is favorably regarded in all sections and that it is not identified with any single region. This experiment supports the view that General American is likely to dominate in the trend toward a more homogeneous national language."[1] Of considerable significance is the fact that Southern American got more votes than the speech of the Boston-New York region. To most Americans of other sections the latter shows what James M. Cain calls the "somewhat pansy cast" of Oxford English,[2] but Southern speech is everywhere regarded more tolerantly, partly, perhaps, because of what the Hartford *Courant* once described as the "honeyed languor" of the sub-Potomac voice, and partly because it is most familiar to the North and West in the talk of Negroes, and is thus associated with suggestions of the amiable and the amusing.[3] In the early days of the radio the primeval announcers sought to prove their elegance by affecting what W. Cabell Greet has described as speech of "an Eastern United States or pseudo-British type."[4] chiefly marked by long *a*'s, suppressed *r*'s, *eye-ther* for *ee-ther*, and the use of such multilated forms as *secretry* and *ordinry*, but it did not please the customers and before long there were many protests against it in the newspapers. In 1930 Josiah Combs, of Texas Christian University, for long an astute and diligent student of American speechways, flung himself upon it in *American Speech*,[5] and in 1931 he returned to the attack as follows: [6]

[1] American Speech Preferences, *Speech Monographs, Research Annual*, Vol. IX, 1942, pp. 91-110. I am indebted for this to Miss Elda O. Baumann, of Kalamazoo, Mich. See also the *World* Almanac, 1941, p. 676.

[2] Said Thomas A. Knott in the address lately quoted: "If you seize upon a student from . . . Red Wing, Minn., and return him to Red Wing talking like a native of Cambridge, Mass., . . . you probably have done him an irreparable injury." Knott explained that he had in mind an effort to make this student "regarded as an effective person in his community."

[3] This attitude, unhappily, has been changing since certain imprudent Negro leaders, like certain imprudent Jewish leaders, began objecting to the presentation of their people as humorous characters. Whatever has been gained for dignity by this reform has been more than lost in good will. Such saviors of the downtrodden always forget that people laugh *with* a comedian rather than *at* him, and that the general feeling he leaves behind him is one of friendliness. Potash and Perlmutter probably did far more to allay anti-Semitism in the United States than all the Zionists and Communists.

[4] A Standard American Language?, *New Republic*, May 25, 1938, p. 69.

[5] Broadcasting and Pronunciation, June, 1930, pp. 420-23.

[6] The Radio and Pronunciation, Dec., 1931, pp. 124-29.

Their attempts at imitating British pronunciation are, in most cases, foolish and stupid. . . . We wonder what would happen should they invade the stronghold of Oxford English as spoken by the tea- and cricket-hounds of that leisurely old university! . . . This Oxford pronunciation (the most offensive and illogical in the English-speaking world) is not practised by the majority of educated Englishmen. It is merely a link in the chain of icy exclusiveness long practised and fostered by loyal Oxfordians and their representatives in politics and among the landholding classes. It does not hesitate to assimilate, slur, chop, swallow and cut; in short, it stoops to anything in pronunciation that will make it as difficult as possible for average folks to imitate.

The early radio announcers, a generally uncultured and even barbaric class of men, recruited largely from the ranks of bad newspaper reporters, were not altogether to blame for their unhappy tendency to imitate English speech, for they were under pressure from various prophets of refinement, some of them of apparent authority. Part of this pressure came by way of the theatre and the movies, which still followed, more or less, the traditional stage pronunciations, already noticed. When the American Academy of Arts and Letters began offering gold medals to actors for chaste and genteel diction it soon became apparent that those following English models were favored, for among the early winners were George Arliss, Edith Wynne Matthison and Julia Marlowe. Meanwhile, the showmen's weekly, the *Billboard*, had employed a speech corrector named Windsor P. Daggett to police the pronunciation of public performers of all sorts, and he argued eloquently for the pseudo-English standard prevailing in the days of Augustin Daly.[1] But public opinion turned out to be strongly against any movement to extend this artificial polish to the speech of the current announcers, commentators and crooners, and as time wore on the radio companies were heavier and heavier beset by complaints against the la-de-da pronunciation of some of their hirelings. On February 4, 1931 the Columbia Broadcasting System sought to allay the uproar by setting up a school for announcers, and appointing the late Dr. Frank H. Vizetelly as its head. Vizetelly was born in London and lived there until he was well in his twenties, but he was no advocate of Oxford English and at once announced to his students that he was eager to " help in spreading the best traditions of American speech, which does not suppress its consonants nor squeeze the life out of its vowels."[2] In another lecture he said:

[1] The Spoken Word, *Billboard*, April 4, 1928.

[2] I am indebted here to Mr. Jesse S. Butcher, of the CBS. Vizetelly was

Those who have been there tell us that only an Oxford man can understand a man from Oxford and that neither would want to understand anyone else. . . . Thank God that we talk to be understood, and that in the aggregate the voices of our announcers are clear, clean-cut, pleasant, and carry with them the additional charm of personal magnetism, which cannot be said of the delivery of the Cockney-bred announcers of London.

The effects of Vizetelly's pedagogy were soon visible,[1] and in a little while the effort to talk like English actors was only a memory in the CBS studios, though not many members of the staff ever really attained to that "charm of personal magnetism" which he had so politely ascribed to them. On his death he was succeeded by Dr. W. Cabell Greet, editor of *American Speech*, whose views regarding American speech standards have been noted a while back. When World War II began Greet devoted himself to the preparation of manuals showing the correct pronunciation of the multitudinous foreign proper-names that swarmed in the news.[2] In the meantime he listened to broadcasts at the heroic rate of 600 a month, and kept his ears open for slipshod or affected pronunciations.[3] In 1939, after two years of this service, he thus summed up his observations:

---

born in 1864. He came to America in 1891 as associate editor of the Standard Dictionary, and became its chief editor in 1914, dying in that office in 1938. He wrote many books on speech, and edited many others. He was the editor for years of The Lexicographer's Easy Chair in the *Literary Digest*. He took to the radio in 1924.

[1] So late as April 26, 1931 the Chicago *Radio Weekly* was still denouncing both the CBS and the NBC for attempting to "oust the American language from the American home . . . and supplant it with English as she is spoken in England, or in the 'better' social centers of America, which is practically the same thing," but this was before Vizetelly really got under way.

[2] War Words: Recommended Pronunciations; New York, 1943; World Words: Recommended Pronunciations; New York, 1944. In his introduction to the latter he said: "The recurring question, 'Which is correct?' is best met by the doctrine of levels of usage. Ask not only which is correct, but correct for what purpose. To the style appropriate for the pulpit, the Supreme Court, after-dinner speaking, conversation, familiar speech, and so on we must add the style appropriate to radio. Radio is peculiar: though the subject matter may be serious and formal, the radio audience hears it in the familiar surroundings of home. The platform and pulpit styles become incongruous; the listeners wish the broadcaster to be natural and friendly, but well spoken and easily understood."

[3] The announcers of local stations, of course, were not bound to follow his recommendations, and though many of them did so others continued to fill the air with unearthly pronunciations, especially of foreign proper names. On June 25, 1944, a Cambridge reader of the Boston *Herald* reported in horror that he had heard *Cherbourg* pronounced *Chair-boor*.

The announcer is, of course, a kind of actor, and it is difficult for most actors to speak naturally. . . . They may play a part well, but without a part . . . their speech is likely to ring false and pretentious. . . . To appear in mufti is as difficult a task for an actor as for a uniformed official. And that is the announcer's job. . . .

Listeners are the arbiters of his success, and they have not hesitated to criticize. The criticisms are usually of two kinds: the announcer either does not pronounce a word correctly, or he speaks a highfalutin, unreal English with a so-called British accent. . . . Most listeners nowadays will sympathize with an announcer who is in revolt against the pseudo-correctness and the insincere voice of the typical announcers of the 20s, who were encouraged in their fake culture by the Academy's medal for good diction.[1]

The National Broadcasting Company, for a while, hesitated to appoint a speech expert to ride herd on its announcers,[2] but in the end it followed the CBS by recruiting Dr. James F. Bender, director of the speech and hearing clinic at Queens College, Flushing, L. I., and speech clinician at the Vanderbilt Clinic, New York, and the New York Post-Graduate Medical School and Hospital. Bender turned out to be an advocate, like Greet, of the General American pronunciation, and when he prepared a Handbook of Pronunciation for NBC broadcasters [3] he based it upon the speech of various eminent announcers who used that form of speech, and said in his introduction:

While there are those in America who are strongly in favor of imposing Received Standard Pronunciation [*i.e.*, Oxford English] upon American broadcasters — "to hasten the day when all English-speaking people will speak alike" — they are not numerous. Seemingly they are enchanted by speech that is radically different in some respects from varieties used by most educated Americans. . . . That pronunciation is best that is most readily understood, and that pronunciation is most readily understood that is used by most people. . . . If the station is a local one the broadcaster would do well to pronounce words as the educated people of his community pronounce them. . . . [But when he] speaks over a powerful or nation-wide hook-up he desires to use a pronunciation that is most readily understood by the majority of his listeners. In such an event the broadcaster would be well advised to use a pronunciation widely known among phoneticians as General American, the standard presented in this book.

1 The Announcers Have a Word For It, *Broadcasting*, Oct. 15, 1939, pp. 24 and 62.
2 Under date of May 26, 1931, its acting manager of press relations, Mr. Walter C. Stone, wrote to me: "We have never designated an individual or a group to censor our announcers. They are, however, constantly under the scrutiny of different members of our Program Department, and when one of them makes a bad slip he is quickly called on the carpet and shown his error."
3 New York, 1943.

Bender listed about 13,000 terms, some of them proper names, but mostly words in the ordinary American vocabulary. He ordained the flat *a* in *dance, grass, aunt*, etc., a clear terminal *r*, the retention of every syllable in such words as *secretary*, and the American pronunciations in *schedule, laboratory*, etc. He pursued the subject in various magazine and newspaper articles,[1] and became a frequently quoted authority. His labors, following those of Vizetelly and Greet, unquestionably influenced many American broadcasters,[2] but others, especially among the more vapid news commentators, still affect something they take to be the English standard. Said a popular writer on speech, Frank Colby, in 1946: "I have invented the term *microphonitis* to describe . . . this rash of *culchah* that is often induced by the radio germ. The disease manifests itself by the patient's aping of the British . . . : 'I have *bean aghast* at the *vahst disahster* at the *aircrahft plahnt*.'"[3]

In the early days of the British Broadcasting Corporation (BBC), a government monopoly, most of its announcers and commentators affected a somewhat extreme form of Oxford English. There were, in consequence, a great many protests from listeners in the North of England and in Scotland and Ireland, to whom this dialect was as strange, and indeed as offensive, as it would have been to Americans. In response to their protests the BBC appointed, in 1926, an Advisory Committee on Spoken English headed by the Poet Laureate, Dr. Robert Bridges, organizer in 1913 of the Society for Pure English[4] and a diligent student of speechways. The other members were Sir Johnston Forbes-Robertson, Logan Pearsall Smith, Daniel

---

[1] For example, This Problem of Pronunciation, *Printers Ink*, March 24, 1944, pp. 32–36; Ninety Millions Speak General American, New York *Times Magazine*, Aug. 27, 1944, pp. 17 and 29; If You Were a Radio Announcer, the same, Feb. 25, 1945, p. 23, and How Do You Pronounce It?, the same, July 15, 1945, p. 20.

[2] Under date of Nov. 16, 1937 Dr. H. K. Croessmann, of Du Quoin, Ill., wrote to me: "Graham McNamee's accent, twelve or fifteen years back, was very Eastern and broad. Today I listen as carefully as I can for this and don't hear it. He might be a native Illinoisan who never left the State." There is a discussion of the standards of Greet and Bender in Standards in American Speech, by Brobury Pearce Ellis, *Saturday Review of Literature*, June 1, 1946, pp. 5–42.

[3] Take My Word For It, Syracuse *Post-Standard* (and other papers), Jan. 16, 1946. Here Colby slipped on *disaster*. It would not be *disahster* but *disahsta*.

[4] The Society had to suspend operations on the outbreak of World War I, but resumed after the Armistice in 1918. In its Tract No. 1, issued in Oct., 1919, there is a statement of its objects and a list of its first members.

Jones, A. Lloyd James and George Bernard Shaw. On the death of Bridges, in 1930, Shaw succeeded him as chairman, and in 1933 the committee was considerably enlarged. It has since included representatives of the British Academy, the Royal Society of Literature, the English Association and the Royal Academy of Dramatic Art, and among its members have been H. C. K. Wyld,[1] S. K. Ratcliffe, Rose Macaulay, Lord David Cecil, Lady Cynthia Asquith, Lascelles Abercrombie and I. A. Richards. It now includes four so-called consultant members, all of them professional phonologists. When the BBC wants advice about the pronunciation of a given word or group of words it is submitted to these consultants, and they formulate their recommendation. This recommendation is then considered by the full committee, which, if it agrees, relays it to the BBC, which in turn announces what it is, thus giving all interested persons a chance to approve or protest before it is put into effect. The consultants have leaned, generally speaking, to the Southern form of English, but some of the members of the general committee, *e.g.*, Shaw and Bridges, have been tart critics of it, and in consequence modifications of it have been tolerated. Beginning in 1928 the BBC has printed a number of pamphlets listing the committee's recommendations.[2] Candidates for jobs as announcers are selected very carefully and put through rigid examinations. Each is asked to read, before a microphone, a short news bulletin, an S.O.S. in French, a programme of music in French, German and Italian, and a piece of literary prose. There is a professional phonetician in attendance, and he reports to a board of BBC officials as to whether

1. the candidate's voice is of good microphone quality;
2. it is free of speech defects, however small;
3. his pronunciation is likely to be intelligible to all listeners;
4. he reads the foreign languages tolerably; and
5. he reads intelligently.

One of the consultants, the late A. Lloyd James, professor of phonetics at the School of Oriental Studies, London, reported that "most candidates fail in this test." Many, he said, are rejected "be-

---

1 Dr. Wyld died in 1945.
2 They are entitled Broadcast English, and numbered. No. I, published under date of June, 1928, contained 322 words. In a second edition, published in 1932, this number was increased to 503, and in a third edition, in 1935, to 779. No. II (1930) was devoted to English place-names, No. III (1932) to Scottish place-names, and No. IV (1934) to Welsh place-names. These will be noticed in Chapter X, Section 3.

cause their English accent is . . . too much like what is sometimes called *haw-haw*," i.e., the extreme form of the Oxford accent. " The standard of performance in foreign languages," he added, " is usually exceedingly low, even in the case of university men with degrees in modern languages." The most expected of them, when it comes to German and Italian, is that they should know " more or less how intelligent people who talk about music and have a general knowledge of what is passing in the world pronounce the names of German and Italian composers, authors, politicians and scholars." But " during a period of three years, during which at least fifty candidates were heard, all but one were floored by *Gianni Schicchi*."[1] Those who pass this test are taken on as probationers and put to school to experts in English and the various foreign languages. If, after three months, they seem to be giving satisfactory service they get permanent jobs. About half of them have been through public schools (in the English sense) and either one or the other of the two older universities.

As I have said, the committee has included, from time to time, members who were by no means enamoured of Oxford English. So long ago as 1910, sixteen years before he was recruited, Dr. Bridges had described this dialect as " a degraded form of English."[2] What chiefly aroused his indignation was its slaughter of the final *r* in such words as *danger, pleasure, character* and *terror*. Not only, he pointed out, was the consonant obliterated, but the verbs preceding it were given the nondescript sound often described as neutral, such as appears, for example, in *thuh* for *the*. Thus *danger* became something on the order of *danguh* and *pleasure* became *pleasuh*. " Many of these corrupted vowels," he said, " are still carefully pronounced in the north of the island.[3] We have only to recognize the superiority of the northern pronunciation and encourage it against London vulgarity, instead of assisting London jargon to overwhelm the older tradition, *which is quite as living*.[4] If one of the two is to spread at the expense of the other, why not assist the better rather

1 The Broadcast Word; London, 1935, pp. 21 and 22.
2 His essay was first published in *Essays and Studies by Members of the English Association*, edited by A. C. Bradley. He revised and republished it as A Tract on the Present State of English Pronunciation; Oxford, 1913.
3 He might have added, " as also in all of the United States save the Northeastern seaboard and the South."
4 Bridges' italics.

than the worse? A Londoner will say that a Scotchman[1] talks strangely and ill: the truth is that he himself is in the typical attitude of vulgar ignorance in these matters." He seems to have been outvoted in many of the decisions of the BBC committee, and in 1929 he printed a somewhat elaborate criticism of its first list of pronunciations.[2] In support of this criticism he recruited an advisory committee of his own, including Lord Balfour, Lord Grey of Fallodon, Earl Russell, H. G. Granville-Barker and C. T. Onions. But the end result was not of much importance, for though one or another of these advisers objected to 99 of the 322 pronunciations listed, only 29 of them were opposed by two or more of the committeemen, and none was opposed by all five. Shaw seems to have had no part in this effort to police policemen. He occasionally broke into the newspapers with general assaults upon Oxford English,[3] but it was seldom possible to make out just what he objected to. Another Irish playwright, St. John Ervine, was a great deal more forthright. In a series of articles contributed to London newspapers from 1926 to 1938,[4] he argued that the Oxford pronunciation was, in large part, no more than glorified Cockney. " The English," he said in one of these diatribes,

are a lazy lot, and will not speak a word as it should be spoken when they can slide through it. Why be bothered to say *extraordinary* when you can get away with *strawdiny?* . . . Many of the Oxford Cockneys are weaklings too languid or emasculated to speak their noble language with any vigor, but the majority are following a foolish fashion which had better be abandoned. Its ugliness alone should make it unpopular, but it has the additional effect of causing confusion.

In another paper he quoted with approving gloats a piece of doggerel by an Ulster poetess named Miss Ruth Duffin, entitled " A Petition From the Letter *R* to the BBC," in part as follows:

[1] Bridges' use of this term, abhorrent to all Scotsmen, showed that he was not one himself. He was born in Kent, "the England of England," in 1844, was educated at Eton and Oxford, and spent most of his long life at Oxford.
[2] This was the list in Broadcast English No. I, already referred to. His criticism was published in *S.P.E. Tract No. XXXII.*
[3] For example, in the London *Times,* Jan. 25, 1934. The substance of his criticism is in AL4, pp. 329 and 330.
[4] For example, the Curse of *Refanement,* London *Daily Mail,* Aug. 30, 1926; English as Pronounced by the English and Americans, *Variety,* Oct. 9, 1929 (reprinted from the London *Evening Standard*); Ham Acting, London *Observer,* Feb. 9, 1936; the Oxford Cockneys, the same, Feb. 13, 1936, and Open Your Vowels, the same, March 13, 1938.

O culcha'd rulahs of the aia,
Listen to my humble praya!
There was a time when I knew my place,
But lately I have fallen from grace. . . .
I used to be alive in modern,
But now I find it rhymes with sodden. . . .
I cannot beah to heah of waw.
It irritates me maw and maw.
Anathemar on him who slays
His native tongue in suchlike ways!
Lawds of Culchah, lend an eah
And my sad petition heah.
Rescue me from this disgrace
And I shall be, aw neah aw fah,
Your slave the Letter *R* (or *Ah*).

Various other Britons, including not a few 100% Englishmen, have taken equally vicious hacks at the Oxford dialect. Some of them, *e.g.*, Wyndham Lewis, Sir John Foster Fraser, Richard Aldington, Dr. J. Y. T. Greig and H. W. Seaman, are quoted in AL4.[1] I add a few more at random:

Gomer Ll. Jones, of the National Council of Music, University of Wales: There is absolutely no comparison, in my opinion, between the virility of American and the emasculated insipidity of "standard English."[2]

James Howard Wellard: Genuine Oxonian simply cannot make accentual concessions. It keeps on with its impeccable bleating, whatever the company or whatever the circumstances. "But, my *deah* chap, *dewnt* you *ralize* . . ." It can be imitated quite well by placing a small round stone beneath the tongue, thrusting in the chin, and enunciating the words with a painful meticulousness.[3]

Campbell Dixon: Nine British films out of ten are unacceptable to America. . . . What maddens Americans is the thin, high-pitched bleat that a certain type of person associates with culture and a great many others with effeminacy. It would be a shock to a number of actors and actresses to know how many people in this country heartily agree with America.[4]

Nathaniel Gubbins: The American accent is . . . not nearly so funny as the dull buzzing that passes for conversation in rural England, the self-conscious "refinement" of Kensington Cockney, the strangled accents of English parsons, and the shrill screaming of the English upper class.[5]

---

[1] pp. 46, 48, 328, 329.

[2] Private communication, June 17, 1938. Mr. Jones spent two years in the United States. I should add that he finds "certain features of American pronunciation definitely displeasing, at least to a musician's ear, particularly the flat *a* and the broad *o*."

[3] Gentleman, Gent., Man, *Query* (London), No. 3.

[4] Voice That Lost Us the U.S. Market: Effeminate Accents Spoiling British Pictures, London *Daily Telegraph and Morning Post*, March 28, 1938.

[5] In the London *Sunday Express*, quoted in Many Mediums Strive to Tell British of U.S., by William W. White, Washington *Post*, July 15, 1942. I am indebted for this to Mr. Don Bloch.

George Bernard Shaw: Over large and densely populated districts of Great Britain [the Oxford accent] irritates some listeners to the point of switching off, and infuriates others so much that they smash their wireless sets because they cannot smash the Oxonian.[1]

I might extend considerably the quotation of such blasts, but it would probably serve no useful purpose, for they come from Boeotia. Nearly all the accepted speech experts of England stand up bravely for Oxford English, or for something closely resembling it. Dr. Daniel Jones, professor of phonetics at University College, London, describes it complacently as the Received Pronunciation, and says that it is the form " usually heard in everyday speech in the families of Southern English people who have been educated at the public schools,"[2] among " those who do not come from the South of England but who have been educated in these schools," and " to an extent which is considerable though difficult to specify from natives of the South of England who have not been educated at these schools."[3] He disclaims any intent to depict it " as intrinsically better or more beautiful than any other form of pronunciation," but all the same he is for it.[4] So is his pupil and disciple, Peter A. D. MacCarthy, lecturer in phonetics at the School of Oriental and African Studies, University of London.[5] So, too, though with certain prudent reservations, was his late colleague on the BBC board, A. Lloyd James, professor of phonetics at the same.[6] So, again, is T. Nicklin, warden of Hulme Hall, Manchester.[7] So, yet

---

1 Quoted in Oxford Accent Rated Low, by Frank Colby, Rochester (N.Y.) *Times-Union*, June 25, 1946.
2 He explains in a footnote that he means *"public school"* in the English sense, not in the American sense." The difference is explained in Supplement I, pp. 479n and 487n.
3 An English Pronouncing Dictionary; fourth edition, revised and enlarged; London, 1937, p. ix.
4 Jones's name indicates Welsh descent, but he does not give his birthplace in Who's Who. He was educated at Radley, University College School and Cambridge. He has written many other books on phonetics, including volumes on the pronunciation of Chinese, Russian, French, Sinhalese and Sechuana.
5 English Pronunciation: A Practical Handbook for the Foreign Learner; Cambridge (England), 1944, p. 1.
6 James was also a Welshman, educated at University College, Cardiff, and at Cambridge. In 1940 he lost his mind, and on January 14, 1941 he killed his wife, a violinist named Elsie Owen. Sent to an asylum, he soon afterward committed suicide. He was the author of many able books and papers on phonetics. His discussion of Southern English is in The Broadcast Word; London, 1935, pp. 153–72.
7 The Sounds of Standard English; Oxford, 1920, pp. 10 and 11.

again, is Dr. R. W. Chapman, secretary to the delegates of the Oxford University Press and an active member of the Society for Pure English.[1] So, to make an end, was the late Henry Cecil Wyld, professor of the English language and literature at Oxford, and author of many books on the history of English speech.[2] Wyld said that it might be called Good English, Well-bred English or Upperclass English, but preferred to call it simply Received Standard English.[3] He described it as "easy, unstudied and natural," with "sonorous" vowels, each of them clearly differentiated from all the others, diphthongs of high "carry-power and dignity," and consonants which need no bush. It is the speech, he said, of

speakers who do not need to take thought for their utterance; they have no theories as to how their native tongue should be pronounced, nor do they reflect upon the sounds they utter. They have perfect confidence in themselves, in their speech, as in their manners. For both bearing and utterance spring from a firm and gracious tradition. "Their fathers have told them" — that suffices. Nowhere does the best that is in English culture find a fairer expression than in R.S. speech.[4]

Wyld, so far as I know, never ventured into the American wilderness, but Jones made the trip in 1925 and James in 1936. Jones came over to give a course in phonetics at Smith College, and seems to have made a hit with the ladies of the faculty, for one of them testified afterward that he was very polite about American English and "never antagonized the most tender-minded of us."[5] James was imported by the Rockefeller Foundation, which was then consecrating "some of its dollars to the cause of improving English diction."[6] He conferred with the authorities of "both major broadcasting chains," listened to the pronunciation of Hollywood actors, and investigated the possibility that short-wave broadcasting, still a

[1] His defense of Oxford English is set forth in *S.P.E. Tract No. XXXVII*, published in 1932.
[2] Wyld was educated at Charterhouse, and at Heidelberg, Bonn and Oxford. He taught at Liverpool before being called to Oxford in 1920.
[3] *A History of Modern Colloquial English*; London, 1920, p. 2. This book traces the history of English pronunciation from the Middle English period to modern times, and is extraordinarily learned and valuable. Unhappily, consulting it is made very difficult by the lack of both index and word-list.
[4] *The Best English: A Claim for the Superiority of Received Standard English, S.P.E. Tract No. XXXIX*; Oxford, 1934, p. 614.
[5] Standards of Speech, by Elizabeth Avery, *American Speech*, April, 1926, p. 367.
[6] Predicts Radio Standardizing Spoken English, New York *Herald Tribune*, March 12, 1936.

novelty in 1936, might eventually iron out the differences between English and American pronunciation. "Everybody," he said, "seems to be terribly afraid of standardization of the spoken language. . . . But modern communications demand standardization. Our railway gauges are standardized, our voltages are standardized. The motor industry could not have achieved its energy or have brought us the benefits we have enjoyed from it without standardization." But by standardization he apparently meant a considerable degree of submission to the English standard, and there is no record that he got any encouragement for this, or that his visit had any other substantial effect. He said:

> In Britain our better class schools and our universities make it one of their cardinal principles to train people for the public service. It is from their graduates that we have long been accustomed to draw our parliamentarians and to staff our Civil Service, and it is from this reservoir of talent that the BBC has selected its announcers and commentators. Such an idea does not seem to hold quite so prominent a place among the American people as with us.[1]

What such trainees speak is obviously a class dialect, and the fact had been noted by nearly all the British phoneticians, including James himself. Writing a year before his American trip he had said:

> Here, as in every other aspect of social behavior, although much latitude is allowed, there are some things that simply are not done. You may show a fine independence by wearing Harris tweeds on occasions that are generally regarded as unsuitable, but you dare not wear brown shoes with a morning coat. So you may scatter your intrusive *r*'s as you please, but you had better not call the brown cow a *bre-oon ce-oo*, or ask for a cup of *cowcow*. It isn't done, and that is the end of the matter.[2]

Two years later he returned to the subject, as follows:

> It is easier for the camel to pass through the eye of a needle than for the child who speaks broad Cockney to pass into the Higher Civil Service or to become a shop assistant in a smart West End shop, despite the fact that he may become a man for a' that, and notwithstanding that she may become a very estimable woman for a' that.[3]

Wyld, in 1920, had described what he called Received Standard English as "the product of social conditions," and had shown how its origins went back to the Sixteenth Century, when, for the first

[1] The New York *Herald Tribune* report, just quoted.
[2] The Broadcast Word; London, 1935, p. 163.
[3] Our Spoken Language; London, 1938, p. 161.

time, "difference was recognized between upper-class English and the language of the humbler order of people."[1] It was, he said, by no means a regional dialect, despite the fact that it was often called Southern English. It was actually spoken by the upper social class, with inconsiderable local modifications, all over England. "Perhaps the main factor in this singular degree of uniformity," he went on, "is the custom of sending youths from certain social strata to the great public schools. If we were to say that Received English is Public School English we should not be far wrong."[2] Palmer, Martin and Blandford, in 1926, described it as "a special sort of dialect that is independent of locality,"[3] and H. C. Macnamara, in 1938, as "the language necessary for all English boys who aspire to be archbishops, field-marshals, Lords of Appeal, butlers and radio announcers."[4] Macnamara's mention of butlers was a true hit, for the fashionable English pronunciation falls very short of being learned. Indeed, some of its characteristics suggest the paddock far more forcibly than they suggest the grove of Athene. Nor does every Englishman of high position affect it. One of those who departs from it very noticeably is the Duke of Windsor, formerly King Edward VIII.[5] Even Winston Churchill, though he kept close

---

[1] Before this it was apparently unheard of. Helge Kökeritz says in Mather Flint on Early Eighteenth-Century English Pronunciation: Uppsala, 1944, p. xlv, that so late as 1685 "a gentleman could apparently speak Scottish or Northern English in London and still be a gentleman."

[2] A History of Colloquial English, before cited, pp. 2 and 3.

[3] A Dictionary of English Pronunciations With American Variants, by H. E. Palmer, J. Victor Martin and F. G. Blandford; Cambridge (England), 1926, p. xii.

[4] Is There an American Language?; Hong Kong, 1938. Many lay testimonies might be adduced. For example, Why Girls are Refæned, by Brevier, London News Chronicle, June 15, 1936: "Accent is the big barrier between classes in this country. Without the right accent, whether real or assumed, no girl will go far in the office world." American English, by H. B. Cohen, Boston Herald, June 19, 1934: "There is a certain coterie in England which makes pronunciation a test. If you pronounce words its way, you belong; if not, you don't. You must say *blackin'* and *puddin'*; you must pronounce the *t* in *valet* and the *s* in *Calais*. . . . It is little things like this that show a man up."

[5] The King's English, by W. Cabell Greet, Baltimore Evening Sun (editorial page), May 13, 1936. After describing it Greet was moved to demand: "If the King of England is strong enough to refuse the Oxford-BBC accents, now in positions of extraordinary prestige, cannot the free-born American teachers of speech be strong enough to resist the temptation of the unholy and really ridiculous American imitations of those accents?"

enough to it in his heyday to enrapture American Anglomaniacs, ameliorated its rigors sufficiently to avoid alarming the plain people.[1] Roosevelt II, whose native speech was a somewhat marked form of the Harvard-Hudson Valley dialect, toned it down with similar discretion when he spoke to his lieges, and his caressing rayon voice did the rest.[2]

The nature of the differences between Wyld's Received Standard English and the prevailing General American have been discussed at length by various authorities, but by none more comprehensively than by Palmer, Martin and Blandford in their before mentioned "Dictionary of English Pronunciation With American Variants."[3] They distinguish twelve major variants and fourteen minor ones, and for the 20,000-odd terms (including inflections and derivatives) that they list in their vocabulary they note differences in more than 5,000. Their twelve major variants may be reduced to six classes, as follows:

1. The English *o* in such words as *hot, box* and *stop* becomes, in General American "a vowel more or less approximating" the broad English *a* of *ask* and *path*.

2. This English *a* is replaced by a flat *a* in both of these words, and also in many others, *e.g., half, brass* and *last*.

3. The *r* following vowels, whether or not it is itself followed by consonants, is pronounced more clearly than in English.

4. There is a difference between the English *u* in such words as *hurry, worry* and *thorough* and the prevailing American *u*.[4]

5. The *-ary* at the end of a word has a clear *a* sound, whereas the English reduce it to the neutral vowel or omit it altogether.

6. So with *-ory*.

[1] His pronunciation was analyzed at some length in Churchill's Accent, by Frank Colby, Boston *Globe*, June 13, 1943.

[2] There is occasional newspaper discussion of the pronunciation of other American politicians. Examples: Mr. Hoover at the Microphone, Ottawa *Journal* (editorial), Aug. 13, 1932; How Do You Say It?, by James F. Bender, New York *Times Magazine*, Oct. 22, 1944, p. 47 (Roosevelt II and Thomas E. Dewey); Under My Hat, by Hannen Swaffer, London *Daily Herald*, March 3, 1938 (Glenn Frank).

[3] pp. xxxvii-xlvii.

[4] This vowel is discussed at length in Notes on the Pronunciation of Hurry, by C. K. Thomas, *American Speech*, April, 1946, pp. 112–15. Thomas shows that the American *u* prevails west of a line beginning in northern Vermont, running southward through Massachusetts to the Connecticut border, then westward through southern New York and northern Pennsylvania, then southward through Pennsylvania to the Ohio river then westward along the Ohio to the Mississippi, and then in a southwesterly direction through Missouri, Oklahoma and Texas.

46   *The American Language: Supplement II*

Palmer and his collaborators also note many minor variants, *e.g.*, the English pronunciation of *clerk* as *clark*, of *ate* as *et* (a vulgarism in the United States), of *lieutenant* as *leftenant*, and of *schedule* with its first syllable showing the *sh* of *she*. They also note the regional differences to be found in the Boston-New York area and in the South. Finally, they show that it is sometimes difficult to find any logical pattern or general tendency in a major variation between English and American speech. Thus, if we take the sentence, " Mr. Martin of Birmingham," and ask an Englishman and an American to speak it, the Englishman will reduce the *-ham* of *Birmingham* to a sort of *'m* but pronounce the second syllable of *Martin* distinctly, whereas the American will reduce *Martin* to *Mart'n* but give a clear pronunciation to the *-ham*. Here Englishman and American head both ways, and without apparent rhyme or reason.[1] It would not be difficult, indeed, to make up a short list of words in which the General American pronunciation is what one might expect to find in

---

[1] The curious will find other discussions of the differences between English and American pronunciation, with examples, in The English Language in America, by George Philip Krapp, Vol. II; New York, 1925; English English, by Claude de Crespigny, *American Speech*, Nov., 1926, pp. 71–74; British and American Pronunciation, by Anne Currie, *American Speech*, April, 1928, p. 347; British and American Pronunciation, by Louise Pound, *School Review*, June, 1915, pp. 381–83; English — According to American *Skedule*, by St. John Ervine, London *Evening Standard*, Sept. 23, 1929; Beware of Affected Speech: Ten Pronunciations of the Anglophile, by F. Sherman Baker, *Correct English*, Jan., 1938, pp. 5–28; A Comparison of Certain Features of British and American Pronunciation, by C. M. Wise, *Proceedings of the Second International Congress of Phonetic Sciences*, 1936, pp. 285–302; American Pronunciations, by H[ans] Kurath, *S.P.E. Tract No. XXX*; Oxford, 1928; A Desk-Book of 25,000 Words Frequently Mispronounced, by Frank H. Vizetelly; New York, 1917, pp. xiv–xvii; Trends in American Pronunciation, by Arthur J. Bronstein, *Quarterly Journal of Speech*, Dec., 1942, pp. 452–56; Some Observations on American Speech, by J. Howard Wellard, *Nineteenth Century and After*, March, 1935, pp. 374–84; Concerning Briticisms, by Charles Wendell Townsend, *American Speech*, Feb., 1932, pp. 219–22; The Pronunciation of Standard English in America, by George Philip Krapp; New York, 1919, Ch. III; American Pronunciation, by John Samuel Kenyon; 9th edition; Ann Arbor, Mich., 1945, pp. 82–86; Some Phases of American Pronunciation, by William A. Read, *Journal of English and Germanic Philology*, April, 1943, pp. 217–44; Colby Discusses Briticisms and Use of King's English, by Frank Colby, Providence (R.I.) *Journal* (and other papers), June 20, 1943; English Mispronouncing Section, *Word Study*, March, 1935, p. 3; From Evacuees Abroad, Liverpool *Echo*, April 18, 1941; The Story of Our Language, by Henry Alexander; Toronto, 1940, Ch. XIII.

Standard English, and vice versa. This is true even in the matter of stress, where there are plenty of exceptions to the stronger American tendency to throw the accent forward. But in general the prevailing tendencies in the two forms of the language are pretty well maintained, both in the values given to letters and in the placing of stress. Thus when an American hears *laboratory* or *doctrinal* with the accent on the second syllable and *artisan* or *intestinal* with the accent on the third,[1] he gathers at once that he is not listening to a compatriot. In this field even the most colonial-minded Bostonian commonly speaks American. He may sometimes go beyond the English themselves in his dealing with the *a*, as for example, in *drahmatize*, which has a flat *a* in English, though *drama* has a broad one, and *gas-mask*, in which *gas* is not *gahs* in England but plain *gas*, though *mask* is *mahsk;* but he seldom ventures to the length of putting the accent on the last syllable of *etiquette* or the third syllable of *fantasia*, or the second of *rotatory* and *miscellany*.[2]

The movement of stress toward the first syllable, of course, is by no means of American origin. It has been going on in English since Chaucer's day and there has been a considerable acceleration since the Eighteenth Century. Kökeritz has shown[3] that in 1723 *alcove*, *balcony*, *bombast*, *confiscate* and *expert* were all stressed on the second syllable, and that these pronunciations survived at least until 1791.[4] So late as *c*. 1825, in fact, Samuel Rogers the poet was saying: "*Cóntemplate* is bad enough but *bálcony* makes me sick."[5] Kökeritz also shows that *advertise*, *complaisance*, *fornicator* and *paramount* were accented on the third syllable down to 1791. But his study offers proof of a number of forward shifts between 1723 and

---

[1] I am indebted here to a list prepared in 1945 by Dr. James F. Bender.
[2] All four of these pronunciations are ordained in Broadcast English No. I; London, 1928.
[3] Mather Flint on Early Eighteenth Century English Pronunciation; before cited, pp. 159–60.
[4] His authorities are A Dictionary of All the Words Commonly Us'd in the English Tongue, by Thomas Dyche; London, 1723, and Walker's Dictionary.
[5] Stress on First Syllable Spreading in English Use, by Frederick W. Henrici, New York *Times*, July 21, 1940. "Through the centuries," says Henrici, "there seems to be a glacier-like movement of the accented syllables of English words, slow but irresistible, toward the front." In 1883 George R. Howells read a paper before the Albany Institute (published in its *Transactions*, Vol. X) in which he said: "There is a tendency to bring the accent as far forward in the word as possible. A few years ago not to say *balcóny* was regarded as evidence of want of culture, if not of illiteracy. Now we wonder that anybody ever pronounced it otherwise than *bálcony*."

1791, *e.g., arbitrator, expedite* and *reconcile*, in which the stress moved from the third syllable to the first, and *inbred, mischievous* and *theatre*, in which it moved from the second to the first. Rather curiously, he also turns up a few words in which the stress was on the first syllable in 1723, but has since moved back, *e.g., accessory, cement, construe, escheat* and *utensil*. But the prevailing movement is in the other direction, and is still in progress. "Twenty years ago," says Ernest Weekley, "*decádent* was permissible; now *décadent* is the rule. Such accentuations as *laméntable, interésting* are not uneducated, but archaic."[1] It is in the United States, however, that the movement seems to have most momentum. A great many examples, some from presumably educated levels, are in my collectanea, *e.g., dísplay, mágazine, dírect,*[2] *ínquiry,*[3] *állies, áddress, místache, ádvertising, détail, cément, cígarette, épitome,*[4] *múseum, lócate, détour, áddict, rébate, ánnex, rébound, rómance, décoy, máma, pápa,*[5] *príncess,*[6] *quándary, ábdomen,*[7] *quínine,*[8] *éntire, fínance, tríbunal,*[9] *récess, ídea, défect, bóuquet, pólice,*[10] *éxcess, dis-*

---

[1] The English Language; New York, 1929, p. 111. Broadcast English No. I ordains *décadence, lámentable* and *ínteresting*.
[2] Our Changing Language, by C. J. Gerling, St. Louis *Post-Dispatch*, Feb. 26, 1935.
[3] Palmer, Martin and Blandford give *inquíry* as the English form, and say that it is also used in America. But some water has gone under the bridges since they wrote in 1926.
[4] Our Agile American Accents, by John L. Haney, *American Speech*, April, 1926, p. 379.
[5] See AL4, p. 519.
[6] Larsen and Walker say that the second syllable is stressed in England, but not in such combinations as *Princess Mary*, in which the first is stressed.
[7] In Pronunciation of Medical Terms, *Journal of the American Medical Association*, Oct. 18, 1941, pp. 1377–78, Dr. A. Henry Clagett, Jr., recommended *abdómen*, but noted the prevalence of *ábdomen*, which is preferred, rather curiously, by Henry Cecil Wyld's Universal Dictionary of the English Language, though not, apparently, by any other English authority. A number of other medical terms are accented differently in England and America. The English, for example, use *capíllary, duódenum, esophágeal* and *éxhibit*, and make the first syllable of *fibrillation* rhyme with *bribe*. I am indebted here to Drs. Louis Hamman, Charles W. Wainwright and Benjamin M. Baker, Jr., of Baltimore. When penicillin was brought out the English used *pénicillin*, and it got the approval of the BBC, but Dr. Fleming, one of the discoverers of the new drug, preferred *penicíllin*, and it has prevailed in both countries. See the *Lancet* (London), Nov. 20, 1943, p. 648.
[8] There has been some effort among the elegant, in recent years, to convert *quinine* into *kin-éen*, but Webster 1934 prefers *qwéye-nine*, and so do most Americans.
[9] The last six are listed in Radioese Needs Correction, by Charlton Andrews, New York *Times*, Dec. 20, 1931.
[10] Pronunciation in the Schools, by Louise Pound, *English Journal*, Oct., 1922, p. 476.

charge[1] and *résearch*.[2] There is some exchange in fashions of pronunciation across the water. The English, after holding out a while for *armístice*, seem to have yielded to *ármistice*, but so far not many Americans have succumbed to the English *áristocrat*.[3] Running against the current, *barráge* and *garáge* survive in the United States against the English *bárrage* and *gárage*. But the American *réveille* balances the account by resisting the English *reveille*, pronounced *revélly*.[4]

In this matter of pronouncing loan-words there is much confusion in both countries, for it is just here, say Kenyon and Knott, p. xlvii, that "usage is most unsettled and uncertain." The English it seems to me, are rather more bold than we are in naturalizing foreign words, especially proper names, and the example of *Calais*, pro-

1 This is Army usage. See *American Speech*, Feb., 1946, p. 75.
2 There is an elaborate discussion of the shifting of accents in The Standard of Pronunciation in English, by Thomas R. Lounsbury; New York, 1904, pp. 121 ff. Its historical aspects in the Germanic tongues are dealt with in The Genesis and Growth of English, by J. S. Armour; New York, 1935, who summarizes his conclusions on p. 92. Its effects (or lack of them) on the early French loans in English are described in The Accentuation of Old French Loan Words in English, by Henry Dexter Learned, *Publications of the Modern Language Association*, Dec., 1922, pp. 707-21. The following is from The Laggard Art of Criticism, by Oscar Cargill, *College English*, Vol. VI, 1945, p. 245: "When atmospheric conditions altered the speech of Europeans settled in America, so that immigrants of all nationalities said *cóntents* when the dictionary then insisted on *conténts*, it was obvious that iambic verse, the great measure of the French and the English, did not provide a natural melodic line for the poets of this country.... Free verse, the emancipating invention of Walt Whitman, was the inevitable product of the long revolt against the heroic couplet; bu it is significant that the poet's most successful experiments all throw the accent forward, as the natural, incisive speech of his countrymen demanded." I am indebted here to Thomas Pyles: A New Meteorological Theory of Stress, *Modern Language Notes*, Nov., 1945, p. 497. Wentworth, in his American Dialect Dictionary, pp. 497-98, gives some curious examples of the forward shift on the level of folk speech, *e.g.*, *béhave, díspatch, cámpaign, pércent, résign, réquest, ádvice, défense, gúitar, ínsane, réprieve* and *súccess*. I have myself heard *dé luxe* in the name of an automobile.
3 *American Speech*, April, 1934, p. 155.
4 The varying stress in the same word when used as noun or verb, *e.g.*, *pérfect* and *to perféct*, *prótest* and *to protést*, *dígest* and *to digést*, remains fairly uniform in England and America, though of late there seems to be some tendency, in this country, to throw it forward in the verb also, as in *to rétail*. See Stress in Recent English as a Distinguishing Mark Between Disyllables Used as Noun or Verb, by A. A. Hill, *American Speech*, Aug., 1931, pp. 443-48, and The Sounds of Standard English, by T. Nicklin; Oxford. 1020, pp. 71 and 79

nounced *Calis*, rhyming with *pálace*, since Shakespeare's time, is in point. The consultors of the BBC do not hesitate to recommend essentially English pronunciations of such words as *carillon, chauffeur, conduit, cotillion, cul-de-sac, décor, liqueur, guillotin* and *harem*, and they appear to have a hearty contempt for the French *u* and the German *ö* (they convert *Röntgen*, for example, into *Runtgen*), but in many other cases they are at pains to preserve something resembling foreign pronunciations, e.g., in *compère* (the English equivalent of the American *master of ceremonies* or *m.c.*), *fête, enceinte, fiancée, hors-d'oeuvre, ennui, entourage, embonpoint* and *ski*. The late Lloyd James discussed the difficulties of the problem in "Broadcast English No. I." "In early days," he said, "such words were read as English words. French was read as though it were English, and the matter ended there. But since we have begun to learn French and to speak it with some attempt at giving our effort a French sound, it is thought desirable to give French words as near an approximation to their French pronunciation as possible." When James said *we* he meant, of course, the English upper class; the common people of England, like those of the United States, know no French, and show no desire to learn any. The result is inevitably a series of sorry compromises. "The only French sound in the average English pronunciation of the word *restaurant*," observed James sadly, "is the *s*, which is the same in English and French."[1] His colleagues, on the BBC board, I gather, have often been at odds over a given word, and sometimes they have changed their decisions. At their eighth meeting, for example, holden on January 17, 1930, they ordained that *ski* should be *skee*,[2] but by the time the third edition of "Broadcast English No. I" came out in 1935 it had become the correct Dano-Norwegian *shee*.

Most American authorities seem to be willing to let nature take its course. They have learned by bitter experience that their admonitions, at best, never reach below the penthouse of the educational structure, and that the plain people go ways of their own. Because of the presence of so many foreigners in the Republic, these Americans on the lower levels have picked up many more loanwords than Englishmen of the corresponding class, and not a few

[1] Broadcast English No. I, in which he had a principal hand, advises *réstarong*.
[2] On Naturalizing Words, by A. Lloyd James, *Radio Times* (London), Feb. 7, 1930, p. 309. See also Fixing English Pronunciation, Manchester *Guardian*, Feb. 7, 1930.

of those that have come in by word of mouth have retained more or less correct pronunciations, *e.g.*, the French *rouge*, the Spanish *cañon, adobe, siesta, corral, frijole, mesa, patio, sierra* and *tortilla*,[1] and the German *sauerkraut, pumpernickel, hausfrau, katzenjammer* and *delicatessen*. In other cases loan-words have been preserved only by changes in spelling, as in *ouch* (*autsch*) and *bower* (*bauer*). In yet other cases they have succumbed to folk-etymology, *e.g.*, the Dutch *koolsla*, pronounced *cole-slaw*, which has become *cold-slaw;* or suffered changes in their vowels, *e.g.*, the Spanish *peon* (whose derivative, *peonage*, rhymes the first syllable with *see*), *loafer* (from the German *laufer*), and *smearcase* (from *schmierkäse*). *Hofbräu* has become *huffbrow*, *rathskeller* has become *ratskiller*, *wanderlust* has acquired a last syllable rhyming with *rust*, the *sch* of *schweizer* has become a simple *s*, and the German *u* of *bummer* has become the English *u* in *rum*. The late Brander Matthews believed in the inevitability of such changes, and refused to denounce them. " The principle which ought to govern," he once said,

can be stated simply. English should be at liberty to help itself freely to every foreign word which seems to fill a want in our own language. It ought to take these words on probation, so to speak, keeping those which prove themselves useful, and casting out those which are idle or rebellious. And then those which are retained ought to become completely English, in pronunciation, in spelling, and in the formation of their plurals. No doubt this is today a counsel of perfection; but it indicates the goal which should be strived for. It is what English was capable of accomplishing prior to the middle of the Seventeenth Century.[2] It is what English may be able to accomplish . . . if we once awaken to the danger of contaminating our speech with unassimilated words, and to the disgrace which our stupidity or laziness must bring upon us, of addressing the world in a puddingstone and piebald language.[3]

Here, I suspect, Matthews's facile talk of a moral obligation was rather more pedagogical than wise: there is no actual offense to

---

[1] Rather curiously, Americans have preserved what seems to be the correct Spanish pronunciation of *rodéo*, though *ródeo* is used among the Mexican and American cattlemen of the Southwest. I am indebted here to Mr. William C. Stewart, of Southbridge, Mass.

[2] Says Logan Pearsall Smith in The English Language; New York, 1912, p. 36: " Speaking in general terms, we may say that down to about 1650 the French words that were borrowed were thoroughly naturalized in English, and were made sooner or later to conform to the rules of English pronunciation and accent; while in the later borrowings (unless they have become very popular) an attempt is made to pronounce them in the French fashion."

[3] The Englishing of French Words, *S.P.E. Tract No. V;* Oxford, 1921, p. 7.

God, I am advised by my chaplain, in trying to pronounce French words like a Frenchman. A more plausible objection to it was stated by Larsen and Walker in "Pronunciation: A Practical Guide to American Standards,"[1] to wit:

> Setting up a foreign standard of pronunciation for isolated words and phrases in an English context . . . would throw them out of harmony with the passage as a whole. Especially in the case of French the foreign language is so entirely different from English in intonation, in accent, and in tenseness of utterance that a perfect rendering of isolated French words . . . would involve an awkward shift of the whole vocal machinery. Borrowed words and phrases are adequately pronounced with a certain amount of compromise between the foreign sounds and the corresponding native sounds.[2]

They follow this with lists of French, German and Italian words in which an ingenious attempt is made to approximate the pronunciations of the original languages without setting the 100% American tasks beyond the power of his tongue, and on the whole they succeed admirably, though they encounter the usual difficulties with the German *ch*,[3] the French *l*, *u* and nasal *n*, and the Italian *c*. When a foreign word in wide use presents difficulties the plain people sometimes dispose of it by inventing a shortened form, as in *bra* (pronounced *brah*) for *brassière*.[4] Not infrequently a loan which has had polite treatment in the higher levels is dealt with barbarously when it becomes known lower down. This happened, for example, to *coupé*. It was commonly pronounced in an approximation of the French manner so long as it designated a four-wheeled, one-horse carriage,[5] in use only among the relatively rich, but when it was applied, *c.* 1923, to a new model of Ford car it quickly became *coop*.[6] In the same way *chauffeur* became *sho-f'r*, *liqueur* be-

---

1 London, 1930, p. 149.
2 Four years before this H. W. Fowler had said in Modern English Usage; Oxford, 1926, p. 194: "To say a French word in the middle of an English sentence exactly as it would be said by a Frenchman in a French sentence is a feat demanding an acrobatic mouth; the muscles have to be suddenly adjusted to a performance of a different nature, and after it as suddenly recalled to the normal state; it is a feat that should not be attempted. . . . All that is necessary is a polite acknowledgement of indebtedness to the French language indicated by some approach in some part of the word to the foreign sound."
3 The NBC Handbook of Pronunciation; New York, 1943, tackles *ch* with tongs and mallets. Thus it gives *ah-ler-herkst* for *allerhöchst*, *rike* for *reich*, *muhnch-ou-z'n* for *Münchhausen*, and *bahk* for *Bach*.
4 Miscellany, by Louise Pound, *American Speech*, Oct., 1941, p. 228.
5 The DAE says that it was first used in this country in the 1840s.
6 Some Established Mispronuncia-

came *lik-kewer*,[1] *chassis* became *shassis* or *tshassis*, and *chic* came close to *chick*. *Hors-d'oeuvre* has always been a stumbling block to Anglo-Saxons, and when, in Prohibition days, it began to be given to the embalmed fish, taxidermized eggs, salted nuts, salami, green and black olives, pretzels, pumpernickel and fragments of *Leberwurst* that were served with cocktails it was mauled very badly. In 1937 the sponsors of a Midwest Hotel Show at Chicago offered a prize for a likely substitute, and it was won by Roy L. Alciatore of New Orleans with *apiteaser*. One contestant proposed that the term be naturalized as *horse-doovers*. In 1938 the quest was resumed by a popular magazine,[2] and at about the same time the Hon. Maury Maverick of Texas, the foe of *gobbledegook*,[3] proposed *dingle-doos*.[4] Many Americans, in despair, have turned to the Italian *antipasto*, which is much less painful to the national larynx.

In 1935 Emily Post, then the unchallenged arbiter of elegance in the United States, was appealed to for advice about pronouncing the French words currently in vogue. She replied that those which had "already been Americanized" should be turned into "plain English," e.g., *menyou* for *menu* and *valet* with a clear *t;* and that those having sounds nearly equivalent to English sounds should be given the latter, e.g., *mass-her* for *masseur* ("emphasis is the same on both syllables"), *boo-kay* for *bouquet*,[5] *brass-yair* for *brassière*, *voad-veal* for *vaudeville*, and *showfur*, not *showfer* or *showf'r* ("accent both syllables equally or else slightly on the last"), for *chauffeur*. Such words as *garage*, *demi-tasse* and *fiancé* she described as "stumbling blocks," and advised her customers, in the last two cases, to substitute *black coffee* and either *betrothed* or *man I'm going to marry*.[6]

---

tions, by Annina Periam Danton, *Words*, Nov., 1937, p. 177.

[1] I am indebted here to Mr. K. L. Rankin.
[2] Name It and You Can Have It, *Esquire*, Jan., 1938, pp. 102-69.
[3] Supplement I, p. 414.
[4] Quaint Americanizations, by L. Sprague de Camp, *American Speech*, April, 1938, p. 154.
[5] Webster 1934 ordains *boor-bun* for *bourbon*, but the NBC Handbook makes it *boor-b'n*. In the bourbon country the prevailing and indeed almost universal pronunciation is *bur-b'n*. The Handbook recommends *boo-dwahr* for *boudoir*, *bool-yuh-base* for *bouillabaisse*, *boor-zhwah-zee* for *bourgeoisie*, and *boo-tuh-nyair* for *boutonnière*, with the accent on the final syllables of the three last-named.
[6] Mrs. Post added some advice about honorifics and proper names. Europeans, she said, always use their own titles in addressing Americans, so we should use *Mister*, *Misses* or *Miss* in addressing them, thus avoiding the snares of *Monsieur*, *Signora* and *Fräulein*. "Certainly it

54   *The American Language: Supplement II*

The bare sounds of spoken speech, of course, constitute only one of its characters, and that character, as the professors of phonemes [1] have taught us, is a variable quality, for a given phoneme may change its vowel, and yet remain the same phoneme, or, at all events, a pair of diaphones.[2] Even syllable stress changes more or less with the position of a word in a sentence and with the mood and intent of the speaker; hence it cannot be reduced to rigid rules. There are students of speech who hold that neither is as important, in distinguishing one dialect from another, as intonation, or, as some of them call it, pitch pattern.[3] When an American hears a strange Englishman speaking it is not the unfamiliar pronunciation that chiefly warns him to be on his guard, nor even the occasional use of unintelligible words; it is the exotic speech tune. Between the two forms of the language, says Hilaire Belloc,

there is not only a difference in rhythm and in tonal inflection — that is, in the musical notes of a sentence — but there is also a spiritual difference. . . . Different parts of the same phrase are emphasized. That means not only a difference in the sense of rhythm but some subtle difference in the mind of the speaker. So far as rhythm is concerned the main difference would seem to be . . . one

---

is in much better taste," she continued, " to call our American college *Noter Dayme* than to pronounce it as French, and yet we would (and should) say *Notrr Damme* when we mean the cathedral in Paris." There is a wise discussion of this problem in Broadcast English No. VI, by A. Lloyd James; London, 1937, pp. 7 and 8.

1 Supplement I, p. 102.
2 Phonemes and their proponents are dealt with somewhat boorishly in Supplement I, p. 102. There is a more seemly discussion of them in The Program of the Prague Phonologists, by R-M. S. Heffner, *American Speech*, April, 1936, pp. 107-15. Heffner says that these Prague phonologists defined the phoneme as " a phonological unit not susceptible of analysis into smaller units," but notes that when " one sound may be substituted for another without destroying or changing the meanings of the words, the two sounds represent phonic variants of the same phoneme." He quotes another definition of the phoneme by a Dutch phonetician, Eijkman, to wit: " The phoneme is the sum-total of single anthropophonical conceptions formed in the mind through the blending of the impressions acquired by the pronunciation of one and the same speech sound of one language." This definition he describes, with some plausibility, as " awe-inspiring." The phoneme was launched upon humanity in 1916 by Ferdinand de Saussure, a French phonetician.
3 Says John C. Diekhoff in Milton's Prosody in the Poems of the Trinity Manuscript, *Publications of the Modern Language Association*, March, 1939, p. 165: " There are so many degrees of stress possible in the normal reading of English, and the question of stress is so complicated by questions of pitch and quantity, that to use the simple, unqualified designations *stressed* and *unstressed* of given syllables must be in some measure unsatisfactory. At best it represents half-truth."

The Pronunciation of American 55

which I have discovered in many other departments of the national life beyond this medium of speech. The American rhythm is shorter. If you hear an Englishman pronounce a long sentence, such as, "I shall be very glad to see him again after such a long interval," and then compare it with the way in which the average American would pronounce identically the same printed words, you will discover . . . that the number of emphatic syllables in the English intonation is less than in the American. To take a metaphor from the movement of water, the waves are shorter and steeper. Further, the phrase lifts in tone at the end in English and falls in American.[1]

Unhappily, there is a good deal of conflict of opinion regarding the precise nature of the difference in intonation between typically English and typically American speech. Some observers report that, to their ears, Englishmen cover a wider range of tone in speaking, and carry it higher than Americans;[2] others, while agreeing that Americans pitch their voices within a very narrow range,[3] hold that their gamut lies further up the scale than that of the English.[4] Some think that Englishmen speak the faster, and some believe that Americans do.[5] In each case this may be only fresh evidence of the

---

[1] The Contrast; New York, 1924, p. 223-24.

[2] Speaking of English intonation in The Pronunciation of English; Cambridge (England), 1914, p. 60, Daniel Jones says that its range is "very extensive." "Most people in speaking," he goes on, "reach notes much higher and much lower than they can sing. . . . In declamatory style it is not unusual for a man with a voice of ordinary pitch to have a range of over two octaves, rising to F above the bass clef or even higher, and going down so low that the words degenerate into a kind of growl which can hardly be regarded as a musical sound at all." The voices of Englishwomen, he adds, show a much narrower range, often limited to the octave and a half between G in the bass clef and D in the treble.

[3] "The first complaint that I should make against our speech," said John Erskine in Do Americans Speak English?, *Nation*, April 15, 1925, p. 411, "is that it is horribly monotonous — it hasn't tune enough." "Perhaps the most apparent general characteristic of American speech, so far as cadence is concerned," said George Philip Krapp in The Pronunciation of Standard English in America; New York, 1919, p. 50, "is its levelness of tone. The voice rises and falls within a relatively narrow range, and with few abrupt transitions from high to low or low to high. To British ears American speech often sounds hesitating, monotonous and indecisive, and British speech, on the other hand, is likely to seem to Americans abrupt, explosive and manneristic."

[4] "Middle-class American speech seems to the English," says Oscar Browne in Normal English Pronunciation; London, 1937, p. 91, "to be spoken in a pitch unduly high. A high pitch does not carry well and requires extra volume, particularly when the tone is again raised for emphasized syllables or words." To which Krapp, just quoted, adds: "One reason for the relative levelness in pitch of American speech may be that the American voice in general starts on a higher plane, is normally pitched higher than the British voice."

[5] At the annual convention of the Association of Shorthand Report-

familiar fact that strange speech always sounds over-fast.[1] To these witnesses, all of them born to some form of English, I add the testimony of an alert and professionally trained foreigner who acquired it as a second language. She is Dr. Aasta Stene, a Norwegian philologian who went to England during World War II, spent the better part of four years there, and then came to the United States. On May 3, 1946, at a linguistic conference at the University of Wisconsin, she read a paper entitled "Unlearning My English," in which she discussed illuminatingly the differences noted by a foreigner trained in observing speechways between American English and the English of the English universities. She found that she needed to make only a few changes in her vocabulary in order to be understood by Americans, but that otherwise her acquired English had to be considerably modified in this country. She said:

My delivery is slower than in England, or in Norway for that matter. The average rate of speech in England seems to me to be appreciably faster than in the part of the United States I have got to know.[2] Retaining the faster English tempo results in the listener not understanding. . . . I find myself speaking considerably more loudly than in Britain. It is not acceptable here to speak as mutedly as is common in casual conversation in England. The threshold of accepted audibility is higher in America than in England. . . .

During the first few days I found that although, with English intonation patterns, I would occasionally rise to (or fall from) a higher level in my voice range than Americans do, the larger proportion of my speech-continuum was below my medium pitch level, and that this fact was socially unfortunate, as in much of American speech a more considerable proportion rises above medium pitch. In order not to create the impression of being bored, uninterested or supercilious I have had to increase the proportion of syllables pitched above the medium. But at the same time I have probably reduced the number rising to really high pitch. . . .

A wide pitch range is sometimes called for in English, but the fact that every intonation group has to come to roost at low pitch, and that a reduced pitch range is frequently used even for emphasis, keeps a considerable proportion of speech units at a low pitch level. In American a greater proportion of syllables reach into fairly high pitch levels. Such wide intonation ranges in

---

ers of New York, in 1929, someone reported that the tempo of American speech was increasing. The gain at that time was said to be averaging ten words a minute every twenty years. See A Measure of Speech, New York *Times* (editorial page), April 1, 1929, and Anent London, by Michael Foley, Bayonne (N.J.) *News*, April 2, 1929.

1 "It is doubtful," says Krapp, p. 51, "if on the whole American cultivated speech is any slower than British speech." He adds that the drawl Englishmen note in American speech is "partly produced by the levelness of intonation, partly by the retention of secondary stresses in polysyllables."

2 *i.e.*, the upper Middle West.

British would indicate emphasis, but they are used in American in statements that cannot be considered emphatic. Consequently, American speech sounds to an ear conditioned to English patterns as if it is uniformly emphatic.[1]

Finally, there is the question of timbre. To most Englishmen American speech is unpleasantly harsh and unmusical, whereas to most Americans that of Englishmen is throaty and gurgling.[2] These differences not only make it hard, on occasion, to take in the idea sought to be conveyed by a speaker from the wrong side of the Atlantic;[3] they also produce emotional responses that are nearly always hostile, for each dialect has its characteristic speech tunes, and hearing a strange one substituted for a familiar one is always disconcerting and sometimes extremely irritating. Said A. Lloyd James:[4] "It is the intonation that hurts. English spoken on Swedish intonation may sound petulant, on Russian intonation lugubrious, on German intonation offensive, on French intonation argumenta-

---

[1] I have had access to this instructive paper by the courtesy of Dr. Stene. An attempt to investigate the precise nature and significance of intonation is in The Intonation of American English, by Kenneth L. Pike; Ann Arbor (Mich.), 1946. It includes, pp. 3–19, a review of previous writings on the subject, beginning with the Orthograpie of John Hart, 1569. Unhappily, it is not susceptible to summarization for the lay reader.

[2] And not only to Americans. Compare the report of an anonymous New Zealander quoted by Frank H. Vizetelly in A Desk-Book of 25,000 Words Frequently Mispronounced; New York, 1917, p. vii: "I left England wondering what on earth the English voice was, and whereabouts in England people spoke English. . . . I heard the West End well-bred affectations produced, as it were, around a substantial marble wabbling in the region of the tonsils; I heard languid drawls, simpers, high-pitched silver-bell lisps; I heard terminal *aws* and clipped *g*'s and feeble *h*'s; but rarely did I hear what I should call just a fine, clear, interesting voice speaking good plain English."

[3] There is a large amount of evidence to this end. I choose a specimen testimony by an English dramatic critic, Harry W. Yoxall, in American Plays and English Reviewers, *Vanity Fair*, July, 1923, p. 68. The occasion was the London premier of Eugene O'Neill's Anna Christie with an American company. "Americans and Englishmen," said Yoxall, "seem to be under the delusion that because they speak more or less the same language they can automatically make themselves understood in each other's countries. In reality there is so much difference in intonation, rhythm and stress that the unpractised ear on either side of the Atlantic has much difficulty in interpreting the words that issue from the visitor's lips. It is quite certain that much of 'Anna Christie' . . . was clearly lost on the English house. . . . Englishmen speaking in the United States must abandon their national habit of swallowing the latter part of their sentences; Americans playing in London must . . . refine the nasal monotony of uneducated American speech and enunciate slowly and distinctly."

[4] The Broadcast Word; London, 1935, pp. 8 and 9.

tive, on many American intonations casual or cocksure. . . . What foreign languages sound like when spoken on British or American rhythms and intonations is best left to a lively imagination." James then quoted I. A. Richards: " Not the strict logical sense of what is said, but the tone of voice and the occasion are the primary factors by which we interpret."[1] To which an American testimony may be added: " Many as the differences of word and usage are, the vital difference which is dividing English and American speech far more rapidly than any change of vocabulary is the divergence in enunciation, pronunciation, and quality of voice. The same words sound quite different on English and American tongues."[2] There are Englishmen who, in their more reflective moments, admit that something is to be said for the superior clarity of American pronunciation, but they seldom hold to that line long. The general tune of American speech affects them as unpleasantly as the cockney whine of the Australians, and their discomfort relights in them the old passionate conviction of their nation that everything American is not only inferior, but also villainous and ignoble. Thus their typical attitude to the gabble of Americans, says Allen Walker Read, is " one of utter loathing."[3] It should be added at once that when they give voice to that loathing they fill the Americano with sentiments which match it precisely.[4]

The study of pronunciation, as I have hitherto noted, is of comparatively recent growth, and it was not until a time within the

---

[1] Science and Poetry; London, 1925.
[2] How Long Will Americans Speak English?, by Adelaide Stedman, *Christian Science Monitor*. I have no note of the date, but I think it was in 1937.
[3] Amphi-Atlantic English, *English Studies* (Amsterdam), Oct., 1935, p. 176. Richard Heathcote Heindel records in The American Impact on Great Britain, 1898–1914; Philadelphia, 1940, p. 277, the results of a poll of British school children in the 13–16 age group, made in 1936 and 1937. There was a strong agreement among them that " Americans speak very poor English."
[4] Inasmuch as I have been often accused of preaching, in my writings on speech a violent chauvinism, perhaps I may be permitted to note here that my general view of things American closely approximates that just described as the traditional English view. But the English dislike of American speech-ways I do not share. It seems to me that General American is better than any dialect now prevailing in the British Isles, and enormously better than Oxford English and its offshoots. It meets almost precisely the specifications for good English drawn up so long ago as 1531 by Sir Thomas Elyot in The Governour, to wit, that it must be " cleane, polite, perfectly and articulately pronounced, omitting no lettre or sillable."

memory of persons still relatively young that anything resembling scientific method was applied to it. Even so late as 1926 Dr. Kemp Malone could say in a professional paper, and with perfect truth, that "intonation, or pitch variation in speech," though "probably the most important constituent in the sum total of speech peculiarities that give one an accent," was "yet but little studied."[1] To be sure, the individual constituent sounds of English had been investigated with more or less diligence, and various attempts had been made to devise an alphabet that would represent them better than the conventional alphabet, but there was but little study of the traits of the spoken language as a whole. The pioneer in this field was Alexander Melville Bell (1819–1905), father of the inventor of the telephone, whose "Visible Speech" was published in 1867. But his ideas got much more attention in Europe than in the United States, and it was not until 1901, when Dr. E. W. Scripture, who was not a philologian but a medical man, brought out a volume called "Elements of Experimental Phonetics," that the new method of approach began to attract any considerable number of Americans.[2] It was given a vigorous impulse when Dr. C. E. Seashore, the Swedish-born professor of psychology at the State University of Iowa, began to apply its devices to the investigation of music, and since the time of Malone's lament it has flourished in a way that must delight him. Its practitioners have got together a really formidable armamentarium of instruments for detecting and recording precisely what goes on during the speaking of a sentence, and some of their discoveries, though rather beyond the comprehension of the layman, are of considerable importance.

Perhaps typical of their work is an investigation of accent undertaken by Dr. Wilbur L. Schramm, of the University of Iowa in 1935 and 1936.[3] He made use of "the microphone, high-quality amplification, the oscillograph, the high-speed output-level recorder and the recording phonograph,"[4] and came to the conclusion that

[1] Pitch Patterns in English, *Studies in Philology*, July, 1926, p. 372.

[2] Dr. Scripture, born in New Hampshire in 1864, had a Ph.D. degree from Leipzig and an M.D. from Munich. He became director of the psychological laboratory at Yale in 1892, and lectured at Columbia and the Johns Hopkins. Later he was professor of experimental phonetics at Vienna.

[3] The Acoustical Nature of Accent in American Speech, *American Speech*, Feb., 1937, pp. 49-56.

[4] Other phonologists have used the x-rays, the moving picture, the vibrograph, the resonator, the kymograph and, of course, the tuning-

accent is a far more complicated phenomenon than the old-time lexicographers ever suspected. "There may be," he said, "more than one kind of emphasis in speech; a dictionary accent is one thing, an accent which beats the drum for rhythm is another, and a logical emphasis which determines the meaning of the sentence is a third." One of his associates, Dr. Ruth Ortleb, found that stress itself is by no means an isolated phenomenon, measurable wholly in terms of intensity. It also drags out the duration of a syllable, raises its pitch, and augments its tonal range. And as with syllables, so with words. "In 98% of the cases the emphasized words were of longer duration, in 84% they moved through a wider pattern of inflection, in 75% they reached a higher pitch, and in 71% they reached a lower pitch." "It is apparent," concluded Dr. Schramm, "that our old explanations of accent are perhaps too simple," and that "a complete acoustical description would probably have to take into account at least seven elements: duration of phonation (plus pause, in some cases), magnitude of inflection, highest pitch level, lowest pitch level, average pitch level, average intensity level, and type of inflection."[1] Many other American phonologists now devote themselves to the precise measurements of speech sounds and speech tunes, and the literature of the subject is growing rapidly.[2]

For many years past philologians have been struggling with the difficulties of representing the gradations of speech in print. No alphabet of any actual language has enough letters to achieve the business, and no artificial alphabet so far contrived has done much more than complicate and obfuscate it. It is, in fact, full of downright impossibilities, as Robert Southey was saying more than a hundred years ago. "Sounds," he observed, "are to us infinite and variable, and we cannot transmit by one sense the ideas and objects of another. We shall be convinced of this when we recollect the innumerable qualities of tone in human voices, so as to enable us

---

fork and the laryngoscope. Their reports bristle with talk of decibels, centroids of energy and other such things. So far, nothing comparable to the electrocardiograph and electrocephalograph has been devised to study speech, but no doubt it will come. See A Brief History of Palatography, by Elbert R. Moses, Jr., *Quarterly Journal of Speech*, Dec., 1940, pp. 615-25.

[1] These categories were suggested by Dr. Joseph Tiffin.
[2] An annual bibliography is in the Supplement to the *Publications of the Modern Language Association*. From 1934 onward *American Speech* printed one quarterly, prepared by Dr. S. N. Treviño, of the University of Chicago, whose own contributions have been numerous and valuable.

to distinguish all our acquaintances, though the number should amount to many hundreds, or perhaps thousands. With attention we might discover a different quality of tone in every instrument; for all these there never can be a sufficient number of adequate terms in any written language; and when that variety comes to be compounded with a like variety of articulations it becomes infinite to us."[1] Nevertheless, hopeful if imprudent men began to grapple with the problem soon after Southey wrote, and during the 60s of the last century Prince Louis Lucien Bonaparte (1813–1891), a nephew of Napoleon and an amateur philologian of no mean attainments, proposed an alphabet which, at the hands of Alexander J. Ellis, an English phonetician (1814–90), eventually reached 390 characters — 77 for vowels and the rest for consonants and their combinations.[2] In 1877 Henry Sweet (1845–1912), another Englishman, reduced the number to 125, but this abbreviated alphabet was quickly found to be inadequate, and improvements upon it were undertaken during the 80s by Paul Passy, a French phonetician. The result was the International Phonetic Alphabet (IPA) of the Association Phonétique Internationale, the latter being Passy's artifact also.

This alphabet, which includes many new characters hitherto unknown on land or sea, has come into wide use, but its deficiencies are innumerable, and there have been constant changes in it. When, for example, the Practical Phonetics Group of the Modern Language Association adopted it in 1927, it was necessary to add a number of new symbols to indicate peculiarities of American speech,[3] and other additions have been since proposed by various other authorities. In 1926 it was given a drastic overhauling by a conference of philologians at Copenhagen, chiefly with the aim of making it more useful for the transcription of non-European languages.[4] In 1939 the editors of *American Speech* petitioned the council of the Association Phonétique Internationale for approval of

[1] The Doctor; London, 1834–47, Interchapter XXV.
[2] He called this alphabet Palaeotype. It is given in full in his Early English Pronunciation; London, 1869–74, Vol. I, pp. 3–12.
[3] The International Phonetic Alphabet, by John S. Kenyon, *American Speech*, April, 1929, pp. 324–27.
[4] Phonetic Transcription and Transliteration: Proposals of the Copenhagen Conference, April, 1925; Oxford, 1926. This report was prepared by Otto Jespersen and Holger Pedersen, both professors in the University of Copenhagen. There were twelve phoneticians in attendance, coming from Norway, Denmark, Sweden, Germany, Poland, Holland, England and France. The English representative was Daniel Jones.

two new symbols for American sounds devised by John S. Kenyon,[1] and at various other times, unless my eyes deceive me, they have slipped in other changes without waiting for a directive from GHQ. Very few practical phonologists have ever attempted to use the IPA without modification. It has become divided into a " broad " form and a " close " or " narrow " form, the former needing fewer symbols than the latter, but suffering a corresponding loss in precision. Daniel Jones used the " broad " form in " An English Pronouncing Dictionary," [2] but he had to borrow four extra vowel symbols from the " narrow " form in order to make his transcriptions intelligible.

In the pamphlets of the British Broadcasting Company he and his colleagues use both the IPA and what they call " modified spelling," e.g., ăkwáttic for *aquatic*, fayt for *fête*, plaak for *plaque*, and túrkwoyze for *turquoise*. No doubt this is a necessary concession to crooners to whom the Greek and Runic letters, the upside-down *e*'s, *c*'s and *v*'s, and the other strange symbols of the IPA would be impenetrable, and perhaps even maddening. Most of the other British phonologists have encountered the same difficulties. Peter A. D. MacCarthy, in his " English Pronunciation," [3] says that the symbols he uses are " in conformity with the phonetic alphabet of the International Phonetic Association," but proceeds at once to list changes that he has made in it, some of them borrowed from Sweet. In his bibliography,[4] listing fifteen works on phonetics by himself and other British authorities, he shows that two use one modification of the IPA, one uses another, six use a third, and five use a fourth. The late H. C. Wyld, in his monumental " History of Modern Colloquial English," already mentioned, rejected the IPA altogether, and used one of his own invention. " Books about the spoken word," said A. Lloyd James in " The Broadcast Word," " all suffer from a serious disadvantage: it is completely and absolutely impossible to represent on paper, by means of conventional print, the simplest facts of speech. . . . [Its] subtleties are such that no visual symbols can cope with them. The symbol *s* has to do duty for very many different noises that pass muster, up and down the world, for what is known as ' the sound of the letter *s*.' The ' sound of the let-

[1] A Petition, *American Speech*, Oct., 1939, pp. 206–08.
[2] Fourth edition, revised and enlarged; London, 1937. On pp. xxxvii and xxxviii he gives a list of other phonologists using it.
[3] Cambridge (England), 1944.
[4] p. 169.

The Pronunciation of American

ter *l*' has many variants in the English-speaking world, and the *l* sounds to be heard where English is spoken are legion."[1]

With this most American phonologists agree. The late George Philip Krapp made some effort to use the IPA in both "The Pronunciation of Standard English in America,"[2] and the second volume (on pronunciation) of "The English Language in America,"[3] but in the former volume he sounded a warning to the whole faculty (including himself) that no such artificial alphabet could ever solve the problem of representing all the shades of sound in print. He said:

> The professional student of phonetics seems to find it hard to resist the fascination which the game of inventing symbols exerts. The conventional alphabet is obviously inadequate for any scientific purposes, and scores of phonetic alphabets have been invented to take its place. If a phonetic alphabet is an evil, it is a necessary evil. But moderation should be practised in the exercise of this evil, for once started, there is obviously no limit to the number of symbols one may devise as records of his observations. It may be said, moreover, that in the end not even the most elaborate phonetic alphabet can record all the shadings and nuances of speech sounds current daily in good use. For one seeking absolute completeness and precision, some device richer in possibilities than an alphabet must be discovered.[4]

John S. Kenyon, in his "American Pronunciation," first published in 1924, used the IPA "in such ways as to adapt it to the peculiarities of American pronunciation," but apparently found it appreciably short of satisfying, for when he undertook his larger "Pronouncing Dictionary of American English" in collaboration with the late Thomas A. Knott in 1936[5] he issued a call for suggestions from other phoneticians.[6] Whether or not this call brought them anything of value I do not know, but they finally decided to retain the IPA in their dictionary, though with the addition of about twenty-five additional symbols for "less common English sounds and the sounds of foreign languages," *e.g.*, *y*, *w* and *h* upside-down, and *?* with the dot under the hook omitted. Their explanation of this vitaminized IPA occupied nearly a dozen pages of fine print in the introduction to their dictionary, and must have produced

---

1 pp. 11 and 14.
2 New York, 1919.
3 New York, 1925.
4 p. vi.
5 Knott died on Aug. 14, 1945.
6 Problems in Editing an American Phonetic Dictionary, by Kenyon and Knott, *American Speech*, Oct., 1936, pp. 227–31. Suggestions by Miles L. Hanley, L. Sprague de Camp, C. K. Thomas, Lee S. Hultzén and Cabell Greet were printed in *American Speech*, Dec., 1936, pp. 319–26. The Pronouncing Dictionary was finally published in 1944.

some symptoms of cephalalgia in untutored users of that otherwise able and valuable work. The common, or dirt dictionaries of both England and the United States avoid the IPA with great diligence. Webster 1934, of which Knott was the general editor, offers an explanation of it in the prefatory " Guide to Pronunciation," written by Kenyon, but in the body of the work it is abandoned for a system going back to Webster himself,[1] whereby such homely indicators as ā, ă and ä are interpreted by strings of everyday words running along the bottoms of the pages, e.g., āle, ădd and ärm.[2]

There was a time, not remote from today, when the pronunciations ordained by Webster, like his spellings, were accepted as gospel by all right-thinking Americans, and especially by the corps of schoolma'ams, but of late there has been a disposition to question dictionary authority, for the news has got about that language does not follow a rigid pattern but is extraordinarily flexible and changeable. In 1936 Dr. Edward W. Mammen, of the College of the City of New York, printed an analysis of Webster 1934, the Standard, the Century, and various other dictionaries, showing that some of the pronunciations they recommended were not in accord with those then prevailing " in educated colloquial American English." [3] In 1938 Dr. George P. Wilson, of the Woman's College of the University of North Carolina, followed with another and more devastating paper,[4] in 1939 Dr. C. K. Thomas, of Cornell, joined the attack (somewhat mildly) with a third,[5] and in 1940 Dr. Karl W.

[1] *American Speech* complained in a review, April, 1935, p. 140, that many of the pronunciations also go back to Noah. " Professor Kenyon's splendid piece of work," it said, " is in the preface; in the body of the dictionary are regularly the old, often provincial and unrepresentative pronunciations."

[2] Dr. Kenyon tells me that he is not convinced that this system is simpler than the IPA, as I ventured to say in AL4, p. 320. " Some five years of dealing with it," he says, " convinced me that it was more elaborate and complicated than that of the IPA with its one invariable symbol for every significant sound." Perhaps I should have said " more familiar " rather than " simpler." See Progress in Pronouncing Dictionaries, by Bert Emsley, *American Speech*, Feb., 1940, pp. 55-59; A Survey of English Dictionaries, by M. M. Mathews; London, 1933, pp. 90-92, and Pronouncing Systems in Eighteenth Century Dictionaries, by Esther K. Sheldon, *Language*, Jan.-March, 1946, pp. 27-41. The New Practical Standard Dictionary of 1946 uses a simplification of the Webster system, without any recourse to the IPA.

[3] Mispronunciations?, *American Speech*, April, 1936, pp. 137-41.

[4] American Dictionaries and Pronunciation, *American Speech*, Dec., 1938, pp. 243-54.

[5] American Dictionaries and Variant Pronunciations, *American Speech*, Oct., 1939, pp. 175-80.

Dykema, of Youngstown College, came on with a fourth, covering both dictionaries and handbooks of "correct" English.[1] Even before these attacks, the aforesaid Knott had entertained the savants assembled for an Eastern Public Speaking Conference in New York with a disillusioning account of the way in which dictionary pronunciations are determined, born of his hard experience with Webster 1934.[2] The dictionary editor, he said, has to disregard the sounds of words in sentences, and deal with them in isolation, paying no attention to the influence of a given one upon its neighbors and *vice versa*. Again, he has to frame a pronunciation that will be suitable for the most careful and precise utterance, *e.g.*, that of a public speaker, and pass over the looseness of "ordinary running colloquial." How, then, are these somewhat pedantic pronunciations arrived at? Knott answered:

> We habitually and periodically send around questionnaires containing a very carefully selected list of words with as many as sometimes six different known pronunciations, to just as many people as we dare, people of very widely different classes. . . . We include a limited number of college and university presidents, . . . a limited number of linguists and phoneticians, . . . as large a number as we dare of teachers, heads of departments of speech, [and] . . . a considerable number of heads of departments of English. . . . We select some lawyers. We select some of the principal public speakers down in Washington and from various parts of the country. We present them with just as many known pronunciations of these representative words that we have a decent record of, and ask them which one is the one that they prefer.

The answers, said Knott, usually show substantial votes for one or two of the pronunciations submitted. "We find about 125 out of 300 say that there is some one that they use prevailingly. Another hundred habitually use or hear type No. 2, and the other 75 are sprinkled out among the other candidates."[3] Knott said that Web-

---

[1] On Handbooks, *American Speech*, Feb., 1940, pp. 89-92.

[2] His speech was delivered in April, 1933. A stenographic report of it was printed in the *Quarterly Journal of Speech*, Feb., 1935, pp. 1-10.

[3] A table showing how seven standard dictionaries disagree as to the pronunciation of different words is in Webster 1934, pp. lix-lxxviii. The dictionaries covered are Webster itself; the New English Dictionary and its Supplement; Oxford, 1888-1933; Daniel Jones's English Pronouncing Dictionary, second edition, London, 1924; H. C. Wyld's Universal Dictionary of the English Language; London, 1932; the Century Dictionary; New York, 1911; Funk and Wagnalls's Standard Dictionary; New York, 1931, and the International French-English and English-French Dictionary, edited by Paul Passy, George Hempl and Robert Morris Pierce, 1904. The usage of 200 "educated, native-born citizens of the United States, not professional

ster 1934 did not use the IPA because " hardly anybody knows it yet." " Take it out," he went on, " to the first twenty-five teachers that you will meet in an ordinary city public-school system, and if there is one of them who has ever heard of it I should certainly be very, very greatly surprised." [1] And then, in closing:

> We probably get five letters every week from school teachers who tell us that such and such a word is not in the dictionary, and why isn't it? We write back and say: " It is on page 1041, column 2, eight lines from the bottom." *They don't know the alphabet.*

Krapp's longing for a device to record speech sounds that would be " richer in possibilities than an alphabet," lately noticed, was already in process of realization when he wrote in 1918. It was the phonograph, which the International Correspondence Schools had been using to teach foreign languages since 1901. But its use for embalming and studying spoken American had to wait until 1924, when Dr. Harry Morgan Ayres, of Columbia University, presented five records of the national speech at the annual meeting of the Modern Language Association. Three years later he and Dr. W. Cabell Greet began a diligent and systematic making of records at Columbia, and this accumulation went on until the beginning of World War II. The materials were obtained from various sources. In some cases radio speeches by eminent public characters, *e.g.*, Roosevelt II and his lady, the Hon. Frances Perkins, General Hugh S. Johnson, Nicholas Murray Butler and Dorothy Thompson, were recorded, and in other cases volunteers from various parts of the country were recruited to provide specimens of their talk. The latter were found mainly on the campus of Columbia, where 14,000 students are gathered annually for the sessions of the Summer School. The director of this Summer School assigns a tree on the campus as a rally-place for the students from each State, so they sort out very conveniently, and finding individuals who spoke the

---

radio speakers," is shown in Radio Pronunciations, by Jane Dorsey Zimmerman; New York, 1946.

[1] Dr. E. H. Sturtevant, of Yale, in explaining his failure to use any sort of phonetic alphabet in his Linguistic Change: An Introduction to the Historical Study of Language; Chicago, 1917, p. v, said: " Such a notation would have required a long explanation, which some readers would have skipped, and which would have caused others to lay the book aside." Dr. Leonard Bloomfield, also of Yale, agreed in The Stressed Vowels of American English, *Language*, June, 1935, p. 98: " Any transcription shocks and offends all but the few readers who have been inured to the free use of graphic symbols."

dialect, say, of Columbia, S. C. or Newburyport, Mass., was thus easy. Ayres and Greet were presently joined by Dr. Jane Dorsey Zimmerman, of Columbia, and advanced students were put to work, apparently as kitchen police duty, transcribing the phonograph records in a modified form of the IPA. These transcriptions were printed in *American Speech* under the editorship of Dr. Zimmerman, beginning in February, 1933, and continuing to the present day. In 1936 she brought out a collection of them running down to June of that year,[1] and in 1939 there was a revised edition coming to December, 1939. Most of the student guinea-pigs were set to reading a little fable called "Arthur the Rat," originally drawn up by the English phonologist, Henry Sweet, to exhibit all of the customary sounds of English, and later improved by Dr. Hans Kurath and Dr. Greet.[2] By 1935 records of the speech of no less than 3200 speakers were on file, most of them obtained either from the radio or at Columbia, but also including a number made on trips of exploration by Greet and others.[3]

Meanwhile, the Linguaphone Institute in New York undertook, on a large scale, the teaching of both foreign languages and English pronunciation by phonograph,[4] and in 1943 it added an American English conversation course in which the teachers were Ayres, Greet, Mrs. Zimmerman and various other phonologists.[5] It also

[1] Phonetic Transcriptions from *American Speech, American Speech Reprints and Monographs,* No. I; New York, 1936.
[2] The text is in On Teaching Speech, by Greet, Baltimore *Evening Sun* (editorial page), Dec. 26, 1934. Under the title of The Young Rat it first appeared in Sweet's Primer of Spoken English; Oxford, 1890, pp. 66–68. At Columbia the title was changed to Grip the Rat. Greet later changed it to Arthur the Rat, for *Arthur* allows for many more different pronunciations than *Grip*.
[3] A more detailed account of the beginning of this enterprise, with a description of the apparatus used, is in American Speech Records at Columbia University, by Ayres and Greet, *American Speech,* June, 1930, pp. 333–58. See also Diction of Roosevelt and New Deal Aides Recorded for Columbia Language Study, New York *Times,* July 12, 1934.
[4] In 1942 the Army and Navy, in association with the Linguistic Society of America and the Intensive Language Program of the American Council of Learned Societies, began teaching foreign languages to soldiers and sailors by the same method. Many (though apparently not all) of the recordings and manuals prepared for the purpose are now published by Henry Holt & Co. The linguistic theories embodied in the Intensive Language Program have been challenged by Ephraim Cross in Learning Foreign Languages: a Little Politics and Some Economics, *Modern Language Journal,* Feb., 1947, pp. 69–79.
[5] Linguaphone for Languages; New York, 1945, p. 3. The course ran

offered a course " in standard American pronunciation " prepared by Dr. Ray E. Skinner. Finally, it offered two courses in " The Sounds of English," one based on American pronunciation, prepared by Greet, and one based on British pronunciation, prepared by James. In 1941, cheered by these experiments and doubtful about the usefulness of the IPA, Dr. Bert Emsley, of Ohio State University, proposed boldly that the pronouncing dictionaries of the future be not printed, but recorded on phonograph plates.[1] He said:

> Pronouncing dictionaries have gone about as far as they can go, in print. Letters cannot duplicate a sound; they can only symbolize it. This situation resembles an older stage, when description of the sounds, which could not symbolize or represent them, had to be replaced, or at least supplemented, by respelling. Just as the Eighteenth Century advanced from description to respelling, it now appears that the Twentieth Century must go ahead from visible to audible devices. . . . Let us imagine an apparatus which will give (with or without general lexical information) an understandable and reputable pronunciation of any word on demand. Ultimately we should be able to hear the desired word alone, without going through *asphasia* to get to *asthma*. A list is not sufficient – there must be some way of sounding and repeating a wanted entry in isolation.

So far this clarion call has not been answered, but no doubt inventive men are busy with it.[2]

---

to sixteen ten-inch records of two sides each, and included " thirty conversational lessons and two lessons in phonetics."

[1] Talking Dictionaries, *Quarterly Journal of Speech*, April, 1941, pp. 274–81.

[2] The IPA, almost always with modifications, may be found in the standard words on phonology, e.g., A Pronouncing Dictionary of American English, by Kenyon and Knott, already cited. *American Speech*, with delicate humor, reprints it on the inside back cover of each issue – but without any explanation, understandable to a layman, of the significance of its symbols. They are used by all the philological journals, and are obtainable in various type faces. The Mergenthaler Linotype Company offers them in ten-point only but they come in both bold and Roman, and run to 202 characters. The Intertype Corporation offers but 38, but all of them come in both eight-point and ten-point, and some in other sizes up to fourteen. The Lanston Monotype Machine Company offers them in eleven faces, running variously from five-point to eleven. The American Type Founders, Inc., offers only a few of the characters, for it deals mainly in type faces that are not used in text composition. The Ralph C. Coxhead Corporation, which manufactures a typewriter called the Vari-Typer, offers three phonetic alphabets, one of more than 80 characters. Some sense of the inadequacy of the IPA must have been in the mind of Dr. Kenneth L. Pike when he wrote his revolutionary Phonetics: A Critical Analysis of the Phonetic Theory and a Technic for the Practical Description of Sounds; Ann Arbor (Mich.), 1943. Unhappily, his method of representing sounds, though it tells a lot to a phonologist, is apt to be baffling to the layman, for it represents the ordinary

2. THE VOWELS

"Every vowel sound without exception," said Hilaire Belloc in "The Contrast,"[1] "has taken on this side of the Atlantic [*i.e.*, the American side] some different value from what it has on ours [*i.e.*, the English side]. And in many cases the change is so great that the exact setting down of it in an accurate transliteration would involve a totally different spelling." Even "a totally different spelling," I am convinced, would not suffice to indicate these differences, for they are almost infinite in gradation and hence virtually innumerable. Consider, for example, the much debated *a*-sound, a favorite gauge of the disparity between English speech and American. At one end of the scale is the broad, solid *ah* that speakers of the Received English Standard put into such words as *fast*, *last*, *glass* and *dance*, and at the other end is the so-called flat *a*, as in *can* and *Daniel*, used by speakers of General American. Between the two stands the compromise of the Boston-Hudson Valley dialect, first given countenance, I believe, by Joseph E. Worcester in his "Comprehensive Pronouncing and Explanatory Dictionary" of 1830. But what, precisely, is this compromise *a?* There is actually no way to record it in print, even with the aid of the IPA and its extensions, for the sound sought to be recorded is not fixed, but variable, and in one form or another it runs all the way from virtual identity with the most extreme form of the English *a* to something that is very hard to distinguish from the *a* of General American. I have heard a group of six Bostonians, all talking at once, use six different variations of it, and in the New York region more are easily to be distinguished. In one community in Virginia, according to George P. Wilson, ten different ways of pronouncing *aunt* are in common use, and elsewhere in the State he has detected two more.[2] Most persons who attempt the compromise *a*, in fact, vary it considerably in their own speech, so that it is sometimes difficult to make out whether

---

[1] New York, 1924, p. 224.
[2] Some Unrecorded Southern Vowels, *American Speech*, Oct., 1934, p. 209. See also Some Phases of sound of the letter *f*, for example, by MaIlDeCVoeIpfocAPpdaldtlft-nransnfSrpFSs.
American Pronunciation, by William A. Read, *Journal of English and Germanic Philology*, 1923, pp. 237 and 238, and *Haf* and *Haef*, by C. H. Grandgent, *Dialect Notes*, Vol. I, Part VI, 1893, p. 271.

they use it or do not use it. So with the other vowels: they are all in a state of flux, and Arthur J. Bronstein has hinted that something analogous to the Great Vowel Shift of 1500, which separated Modern English from Middle English, may be in progress.[1]

The old-time grammar-books were content to inform the young that there were five vowels in English, but this was true, of course, only of the letters used to represent them, not of the sounds. In 1791 John Walker was constrained to distinguish ten vowels and diphthongs,[2] and in 1837 Isaac Pitman, the pioneer of modern English shorthand, went on to six long vowels,[3] six short ones, and four diphthongs. The number has been growing ever since, but no two phoneticians seem to be in agreement as to what it is precisely. Richard Paget, in 1925, was content with "thirteen separate vowels,"[4] but Daniel Jones, in the 1937 edition of his "English Pronouncing Dictionary," went to fifteen vowels and twelve consonants, and Leonard Bloomfield, in 1935, reported seventeen "syllabic phonemes" among "educated speakers in Chicago" alone.[5] In 1937 Oscar Browne reported in his "Normal English Pronunciation" that phoneticians distinguish seventy-two "variants of vowel sounds," but some of these, he added, are not heard in English. All such estimates, of course, are unreliable, for what they classify should be called, not vowels, but vowel-groups, and the differences within each group are too numerous and too minute to be described in words or symbols. "The vowel," says John W. Black, "is an ever-changing phenomenon during phonation. . . . Certain factors are constant and others are variable. . . . Each vowel is a succession of different structures. . . . Teachers . . . should not say that this

---

[1] Trends in American Pronunciation, *Quarterly Journal of Speech*, Dec., 1942, pp. 452–56.
[2] The Phonetic Concepts of John Walker and Daniel Jones, by Benjamin Newman, *Quarterly Journal of Speech*, Oct., 1941, p. 365.
[3] To wit, *ah, eh, ee, aw, oh* and *oo*.
[4] Paget's paper was first printed in French in the *Bulletin* of the Institut Général Psychologique in 1925. An English translation, made and revised by the author, is in *S.P.E. Tract No. XXII*; Oxford, 1925. See his p. 31. On p. 24 he apparently increases the number of vowels to fourteen. In The Sounds of Spoken English; Oxford, 1920, p. 31, T. Nicklin said that "there are in modern English nine simple vowels," but he actually listed eleven, and then added eight diphthongs.
[5] The Stressed Vowels of American English, *Language*, June, 1935, p. 97. In the same volume of *Language*, pp. 148–51, some of Bloomfield's conclusions are criticized by Morris Swadesh in The Vowels of Chicago English.

is the vowel in *top* without adding that this is one of the possible vowels in *top*."[1]

The sounds of vowels are produced by columns of air going through the two resonator-spaces above and below the tongue, with modifications effected by variations in the position of the tongue itself and the lips. Obviously, no two human mouths are precisely alike, and equally obviously the mechanism of speech thus differs from individual to individual, and in the same individual from time to time. "These positions of the vowels in the mouth," said Dr. Robert Bridges, "are like the places of the outfielders at cricket, whom the captain shifts about according to the idiosyncrasies of the bowler and batsman: their stations are named and relatively well established, but it cannot be foreseen on any occasion where any one of them will be standing; and in any case the accurate knowledge of the ideal vowel-position is of no more practical use to the speaker than the scientific millimetred analysis of the action of the complicated stops of a clarinet would be to the performer on it."[2] Nevertheless, Bridges believed that the five vowels of the old grammar-books sufficed "to represent the acme of the main distinctions of quality and timbre," and that getting any closer to their sounds would be possible only "if all speakers had exactly similar organs." As things stand, it is sometimes difficult to distinguish between *a* and *o* on the one hand and *a* and *e* on the other, or between *a* and the neutral vowel, but on most occasions they remain reasonably distinct, despite the wide range of sounds on both sides of the fence. "There can be considerable variation in the composition of the spoken vowel," says Leroy T. Laase, "and the character of the vowel still be clearly recognizable."[3] The quantity, *i.e.*, the length, of any vowel is conditioned mainly by the stress put upon it, and to a lesser extent by its position with relation to other sounds. Thus the exclamation *ah*, in isolation, shows a longer *a* than the one in *father* or *palm*, and the quantity thereof is further affected by the

---

[1] The Quality of a Spoken Vowel, *Archives of Speech*, July, 1937, pp. 15 and 25.
[2] Remarks on Paget's paper, lately cited, *S.P.E. Tract No. XXII*, p. 39.
[3] The Effect of Pitch and Intensity on the Quality of Vowels in Speech, *Archives of Speech*, July, 1937, p. 59. "Each vowel," say C. E. Parmenter and S. N. Treviño, *Quarterly Journal of Speech*, June, 1932, p. 366, "has a typical or characteristic position around which variations may take place."

surrounding consonants and the rapidity of speech.[1] "The pronunciation of a word in isolation," says R.-M. S. Heffner, "represents an unhampered shot at the goal of an ideal or normal pronunciation, while pronunciation in context represents a more or less disturbed or jostled shot at the same goal."[2] The most active factor, however, is stress, and Heffner concludes that "strong stress with falling intonation produces a slightly greater duration of the vowel than strong stress with rising intonation."[3] All such differences in quantity tend to become differences in quality, and in the long run they may produce entirely new vowels, or, at all events, variations so marked that they have to be represented by different symbols.[4]

That there is a movement in American English toward the shortening of vowels has been noted by various observers.[5] The English authorities ordain the long *e* in *evolution*,[6] and the long *i* in *isolation* and the words of the *fragile* class,[7] but in the United States the short *e* and *i* seem to be dominant in these words. There is also a tendency to substitute the short *a* of *radish* for the long *a* of *made* in *data, vagrant, aviator, Danish* and even *radio*;[8] the short *e* of *pen* for the long *e* of *scene* in *penalize, economics, detonator, scenic* and *electricity*; the short *i* of *sin* for the long *i* of *idea* in *sinecure*; the short *o* of *fog* for the long *o* of *bone* in *mobilize, soviet, choral* and

---

[1] The Effect of the Consonant on the Vowel, by John W. Black, *Journal of the Acoustical Society of America*, Jan., 1939, pp. 203-95. In The Stability of the Vowel, *Quarterly Journal of Speech*, Feb., 1939, Black shows that the vowels of a given speaker may change perceptibly within so short a time as two years, and that such changes, though not great, are "apparently consistent."

[2] Notes on the Length of Vowels, April, 1937, p. 128. Heffner continued the discussion of the subject in *American Speech* for Feb. and Dec., 1940; Oct., 1941, and Feb., 1942, and in *Language* for Jan.-March, 1940. See also Vowel-Length in General American Speech, by Harry A. Rositzke, *Language*, April-June, 1937, and Two Notes on Vowel and Consonant Quantity, by Norman E. Eliason, *American Speech*, Oct., 1942. In both papers there are references to previous studies of the subject.

[3] *American Speech*, Feb., 1942, p. 48.

[4] Outline of English Phonetics, by Daniel Jones; New York, 1932, par. 879, quoted by Heffner.

[5] For example, Henry A. Perkins, in Our Changing Vowels, Hartford *Courant*, April 27, 1938.

[6] Broadcast English No. I, p. 34; Jones, p. 151.

[7] Broadcast English No. I, p. 36; Jones, pp. 173 and 236.

[8] In 1937, after attending a meeting of the American Psychological Association, Dr. William J. Griffin, of the State Teachers' College, St. Cloud, Minn., wrote to me: "Among all the learned doctors there apparently is not one who speaks of *status, data, apparatus,* or *strata* with anything save the *a* of *hat*."

The Pronunciation of American

voltmeter, and the short *u* of *sum* for the long *u* of *cube* in *quintuplet*.[1] In both English and American usage there is a strong movement toward substituting the so-called neutral vowel for clearer vowels in unstressed syllables, especially in colloquial speech. Thus the *a* of *about*, the *e* of *the*, the *i* of *habit*, the *o* of *hillock* and the *u* of *upon* are all reduced to a grunt that has given considerable concern to the phonologists, for it varies somewhat in different situations, and differs in many of them in England and the United States.[2] In this country the schoolma'am, influenced by her veneration for spelling-pronunciations, makes war upon it, and I was myself taught in primary-school to enunciate the *e* of *the* clearly, making it identical with the *ee* of *thee*, but it is far too firmly lodged to be disposed of. The English, says C. H. Grandgent, prefer to omit the mauled vowel altogether, thus producing the collision forms that Americans always notice in their speech.[3]

There is no need to add much to the discussion of the individual vowels in AL4, pp. 334 *ff*. As we have already seen in the present book, the broad *a* did not begin to flourish in England until the Eighteenth Century, though it was, of course, used before then, especially in dialects. C. Cooper, whose "Grammatica Linguæ Anglicanæ" was published in 1685 and who has been described by Wyld as "by far the most reliable phonetician among the Seventeenth Century writers," recorded the flat *a* of what is now General American not only in *bath*, *gasp* and *path*, but also in *car*, *tar*, *quality*, *barge*, *carp*, *dart*, *larch* and *tart*. To this day, in fact, that *a* is retained by the English in a large number of words — perhaps in quite as many as show the broad *a* that Americans think of as so characteristic of England. Examples are *manse*, *fancy*, *pants*, *vassal*, *pantry*, *lass*, *crass*, *paraffin*, *pariah*, *can*, *mandate*, *mannequin*, *pamphlet*, *ant*, *ass* (the animal), *parasol*, *avoirdupois*, *bas-relief*, *candle*, *passenger*, *mammal*, *palate*, *parrot*, *saddle*, *latch*, *handsome*, *quagmire* and *passive*. "Some English Roman Catholics, mostly converts," says H. W. Seaman,[4] "insist on a long *a* in *mass*," but when the word is used to

---

1 I am indebted for these examples to Perkins, lately cited.
2 A Desk-Book of 25,000 Words Frequently Mispronounced, by Frank H. Vizetelly; New York, 1917, p. xxviii.
3 Old and New; Cambridge (Mass.), 1920, pp. 143 and 144. See also The English Language in America, by George Philip Krapp; New York, 1925, Vol. II, pp. 249 *ff*.
4 Private communication, June 27, 1944.

designate a quantity of matter the American *a* is used.[1] Wyld says[2] that the change from the old (and still American) flat *a* to the broad *a* of the English *past, bath* and *after* was still hanging fire in the early Eighteenth Century, and that it was " difficult for Englishmen at that time." James[3] ventures the opinion — " but that," he adds cautiously, " is only an opinion " — that " in the end the short vowel [*i.e.*, the American vowel] will prevail." " In the Sixteenth Century," he says, " [it] was universal." [4]

In the United States the long *a* survives before *r, l, k* and *m*, as in *charm, salt, walk* and *calm*, but it has pretty well disappeared before *s, th, n* and *f*, as in *pass, path, chance* and *laugh*. Writing in the early 70s, William D. Whitney said that " until quite recently it was admitted in the United States in *calf, halve, answer, chance, blanche, pant, can't, alas, pass, bask, clasp, blaspheme, last, path, lath, laugh, staff, raft, after* and in many other words like them," but that, save in " local usage (I cannot say how extensive) " [5] it was already being replaced by " the *a* of *fat* and *fan*," or by some " intermediate " *a*.[6] According to a writer in *American Speech*,[7] the broad Southern *a* is now losing ground even in Tidewater Virginia, but is holding out better among the women than among the men. " This," he says, " is probably because a man's friends are more likely to resent what they regard as a speech affectation. I have known several cases in which the mother used the broad *a* and the father didn't, and the children imitated the mother's pronunciation. However, when the children grow up there is a tendency for the boys to adopt the

1 For most of the foregoing examples I am indebted to Seaman, to Mr. R. Raven-Hart, to the Palmer-Martin-Blandford Dictionary of English Pronunciation, to Broadcast English No. I, and to The Phonetics of English, by Ida C. Ward; Cambridge (England), 1929, p. 78.
2 A History of Modern Colloquial English, before cited, p. 204.
3 The Broadcast Word, p. 99.
4 So long ago as 1874 A. J. Ellis noted, in Vol. IV of his Early English Pronunciation, p. 1148, the wide variation of usage in England, even among careful speakers. He said that at a performance of King John he had heard Mrs. Charles Kean give *calf* the flat *a*, whereas her *vis-à-vis*, Alfred Wigan, gave it the broad *a* of *palm*.
5 The context shows that he meant the usage of Boston and its colonies. The so-called compromise *a* of this region is not altogether unknown in England. In fact, it is reported by Robert Forby in The Vocabulary of East Anglia; London, 1830, Vol. I, p. 86. He says that " perhaps the nearest approach " to its sound " is the bleat of a very young lamb."
6 Oriental and Linguistic Studies: Second Series; New York, 1874, pp. 206–07.
7 Broad *A* in Virginia, by Chad Walsh, Feb., 1940, p. 38.

short *a*." When, at the Republican National Convention of 1944, Governor (later Senator) Leverett Saltonstall of Massachusetts made a speech in which he " pronounced *pass* as if it were spelled *pahss* " it brought forth what the Boston *Herald* described as a " mass snicker " from the assembled heirs of Lincoln.[1] So far as I know, the only words in which Americans use the broad *a* and Englishmen the flat one are *mall*, as in the *Mall*, at Washington, and the proper nouns, *Polack*, *Albany* and *Raleigh*.[2] In the case of *Polack* American usage has perhaps been influenced by German example.

The newspapers often engage in discussions of the " proper " pronunciation of *a* in this or that word, *e.g.*, *tomato*, *ate*, *again* and *to stamp*, for it remains an article of American faith that there is a right way and a wrong way in all the situations of speech. *Tomayto* is the common form, and James F. Bender ordains it for radio announcers in the " NBC Handbook of Pronunciation," but *tomahto*, which is English, is in use in the Boston *Sprachgebiet* and also in the Tidewater South, and seems to be making some progress among the elegant elsewhere. However, when Representative Allen T. Treadway, of Massachusetts, used it at a session of the House Committee on Ways and Means, in February, 1940, he was challenged by Representative Pat Cannon, of Florida, who demanded to know if he meant *tomayto*. " No," replied Treadway. " I mean *tomahto*." Cannon thereupon appealed to the Democratic majority in the committee, which decided in his favor. " We have a majority," he declared triumphantly. " You mean *tomayto*." Lieut. Col. F. G. Potts, of Mt. Pleasant, S. C., tells me that, south of Virginia, *tomahto* " sounds quite affected." Occasionally, he adds, *tomatto* is heard.[3] I have also encountered *termayter* and *termatter*, but only among *hoi barbaroi*.

Another debate that frequently engrosses the newspaper phonologists has to do with *again*. Should it be pronounced as it is spelled or made *agen?* Palmer, Martin and Blandford say that the former is good English usage and Bender advises American crooners to use

---

[1] An *A* for an *R* (editorial), July 3, 1944. On July 5, in the same paper, the Boston *a* was defended with eloquence by a correspondent in Middleton, R. I., signing himself E. O. Lux.

[2] I am indebted here to Mr. Hugh Morrison, of Mays Landing, N. J. The English give *Pall Mall* two flat *a*'s.

[3] Private communication, Jan. 20, 1945. There was a discussion of the word in the Boston *Traveler* in April, 1944.

agen, but there is contrary advice and custom on both sides of the water. The NED shows that the word as we have it is descended from two different early Germanic words, the one represented by the Old High German *gagen* and the other by the OHG *gegin*. The former, prevailing in the South of England, produced *again;* the latter, *agen*. Down to the Nineteenth Century the English poets freely rhymed *again* with *pen*, but this was not true invariably, for Shakespeare, as Frank H. Vizetelly pointed out,[1] also rhymed it on occasion with *twain, plain* and *slain*. The NED, whose *A* volume was published in 1888, ventured the opinion that *again* was then displacing *agen* in England, and this seems to be confirmed by the later English authorities, including Daniel Jones, but most American authorities, *e.g.*, Webster 1934 and Kenyon and Knott, hold out for *agen*. The English authorities sanction *et* for *ate*,[2] but in the United States it is generally regarded as a vulgarism, along with *eat* in the past tense.[3] *To stomp*, in the sense of to beat down forcibly, as with the foot, is only provincial in England, but in the United States it is in relatively good usage, though no American would ever speak of a *postage-stomp* or of *stomping* a letter.[4]

The pronunciation of *a* in this or that situation has changed often within the past two centuries, for, as Parmenter and Treviño say, it is " of all vowels the least stable in quality." [5] Boswell records in his Life how puzzled Samuel Johnson was when Lord Chesterfield advised him that " the word *great* should be pronounced so as to rhyme to *state*" and Sir William Yonge insisted that " it should be pronounced so as to rhyme to *seat*, and that none but an Irishman

---

1 In *Agane* or *Agen*, a letter to the New York *Herald Tribune* dated Feb. 1, 1938.
2 On Feb. 5, 1937 *John o'London's Weekly*, which specializes in language questions, printed an inquiry from a Scotswoman who wrote: "Can you explain the almost universal pronunciation, by English people, of the word *ate* as *ett?* The spelling of the word gives no justification for this pronunciation, and the sound *ett* is, to my mind, peculiarly ugly. For some obscure reason it suggests to me a wolfish, gobbling action, in contradistinction to the quiet dignity of *ate*." To this the editor replied: "My correspondent has my sympathy, but is she fastidious enough to complain of *red* and *delt* as the past tense forms of *read* and *deal?* In English ears today *ate* sounds rather falsely 'fastidious.'"
3 British *Eat* and American *Ate*, by Eston Everett Ericson, *American Speech*, Dec., 1937, pp. 322–23.
4 The Big *Stomp*, by J. H. M. C., Hartford *Courant*, Dec. 9, 1937.
5 Vowel Positions as Shown by X-Ray, by C. E. Parmenter and S. N. Treviño, *Quarterly Journal of Speech*, June, 1932, p. 354. There is an interesting discussion of the fermentation of *a* in the NED, Vol. I, p. 1.

would pronounce it *grait*." "Here," marvelled the lexicographer, "were two men of the highest rank, the one the best speaker in the House of Lords, the other the best speaker in the House of Commons, differing entirely."[1] In Webster's time, as he records in his "Dissertations on the English Language,"[2] *reesin* for *raisin* was in good usage in "two or three principal towns in America," and in our own time the Hon. Al Smith, LL.D. (Harvard), preferred *raddio* to *raydio*. The question whether *ration* should have the *a* of *passion* or that of *nation* is still being debated, and Kemp Malone has sought to resolve it by showing that the word is really two words, one derived from the Latin and the other from the French, and that both pronunciations are correct.[3] In 1943 a newspaper commentator[4] reported that among the eminentissimos of the time, Roosevelt II, Winston Churchill, Elmer Davis, Leon Henderson, James F. Byrnes and Eddie Rickenbacker used *rash-un*, but that Harold L. Ickes and Claude Wickard used *ray-shun*.[5]

When it comes to *e* the chief battle in the Republic continues to be between the advocates of *ee-ther* and those who prefer *eye-ther*.

[1] Boswell's Life, March, 1772.
[2] Boston, 1789, p. 116.
[3] Ration, American Speech, April, 1943, pp. 128-30.
[4] *Rash-un* or *Ray-shun*: Both are Correct for *Ration*, Jamestown (N.Y.), *Post Journal*, Jan. 13.
[5] There is a large literature on *a* in English and American, and anyone becoming heated up by the subject will find fuel for his flames in Fashion and the Broad *A*, by C. H. Grandgent, *Nation*, Jan. 7, 1915 (reprinted in Old and New; Cambridge (Mass.), 1920, pp. 25-30); Observations on the Broad *A*, by Miles L. Hanley, *Dialect Notes*, Vol. V, Part VIII, 1925, pp. 347-50; The Pronunciation of Short *A* in American Standard English, by George L. Trager, *American Speech*, June, 1930, pp. 396-400; One Phonemic Entity Becomes Two: The Case of Short *A*, by the same, *American Speech*, Oct., 1940, pp. 255-58; The Vowel in *Rather* in New England, by Herbert Penzl, *Publications of the Modern Language Association*, Dec., 1938, pp. 1186-92; Relics With Broad *A* in New England Speech, by the same, *American Speech*, Feb., 1938, pp. 45-49; The Compromise *A*, by the same, *Anglia*, Band LXIII, 1939, pp. 88-99; The Vowel Phonemes in *Father, Man, Dance* in Dictionaries and New England Speech, by the same, *Journal of English and Germanic Philology*, Jan., 1940, pp. 13-32; Flat *A* and Broad *A*, by J. S. K[enyon], *American Speech*, April, 1930, pp. 323-26; *Watch, Water, Wash*, by Sarah T. Barrows, *American Speech*, April, 1929, pp. 301-02; The *A* of *Father, Rather*, by Kemp Malone, *Modern Philology*, Vol. XVI, 1918, pp. 11-22; Umlaut in Middle English, by George Bond; Dallas (Tex.), 1937, pp. 86 *ff;* The English Language in America, by George Philip Krapp; New York, 1925, Vol. II, pp. 36 *ff; Vays, Vayz* or *Vahz*, by Janet R. Aiken, *North American Review*, Dec., 1929, pp. 716-21; and Mather Flint on Early Eighteenth Century Pronunciation, by Helge Kökeritz; Uppsala (Sweden), 1944, pp. 81-92.

In 1936 a lady phonologist named Miss Estelle B. Hunter, educational director of the Better Speech Institute of America, announced from Chicago that *ee-ther* and *nee-ther* were gaining on *eye-ther* and *nye-ther* as part of a movement in favor of General American and against "the sophisticated intonations of stage folk."[1] Noah Webster, in his "Dissertations,"[2] called *eye-ther* and *nye-ther* "errors," and classed them with *desate* for *deceit*, *consate* for *conceit* and *resate* for *receipt*, but he had to admit that the *ey*-sound was in general use "by the Eastern people," though not common in the South and West. At that time (1789), if we are to believe him, *ee-ther* and *nee-ther* were favored in England. The Rev. John Witherspoon, in 1781, denounced Americans for using *either* in reference to more than two objects, but had nothing to say about the pronunciation of the word. John Pickering, in 1816, was likewise silent on the subject. J. Fenimore Cooper, in "The American Democrat" (1838), came out strongly in favor of *eye-ther* and *nye-ther*, which he described as "polite." "This is a case," he said, "in which the better usage of the language has respected derivations, for *ei* in German is pronounced as in *height* and *sleight*, *ie* making the sound of *ee*." What German usage had to do with American standards he did not pause to explain. Nearly all the American authorities of the Nineteenth Century, including even the violently Anglomaniacal Richard Grant White, were in favor of *ee-ther*,[3] and most of those of the present century have followed them,[4] but it is my observation that *eye-ther* is holding out, and perhaps even making some progress. Certainly I have heard it of late in circles where, in my boyhood, it would have been derided.

One of the Briticisms that Americans appear to be most conscious

---

[1] *Eether* Now Heads *Eyether*, Associated Press dispatch from Chicago, *Christian Science Monitor*, March 13, 1936.
[2] p. 114.
[3] So was James Russell Lowell, who wrote in his famous essay On a Certain Condescension in Foreigners, 1869: "We said *eether* and not *eyther*, following therein the fashion of our ancestors, who unhappily could bring over no English better than Shakespeare's."
[4] For example, Kenyon and Knott, Louise Pound, Krapp and Bender. Krapp says (The Pronunciation of Standard English in America; New York, 1919, p. 77) that *eye-ther* "is popular and general nowhere in America," but admits that it is "heard often as a conscious refined pronunciation." Raven I. McDavid, Jr., in Dialect Geography and Social Science Problems, *Social Forces*, Dec., 1946, says that it is supported by "the snob-appeal of not using the same pronunciation as the uneducated or rustic people of one's own community." See AL4, pp. 341-43.

of is the change of *e* to a broad *a* in *clerk, Derby, Berkeley,* etc. Wyld in his "History of Modern Colloquial English,"[1] shows that this vowel shift began in the Thirteenth Century, and has left sediments in words that are now spelled with the *a* in both England and America, e.g., *to bark, barley, barn, carve, dark, farther, farm, harvest, heart, hearty, hearken, hearth, marvel, parson, smart, star, starling, start* and *starve*. There was a time when what Webster called "the yeoman of America,"[2] like the contemporary English, used this broad *a* in many other words now showing *e*, e.g., *mercy, servant, certain, clergy, (e)ternal, concern, learn, serpent, search, service, deserve, term* and *virtue*,[3] and it still survives in the dialect of Appalachia. Along with these words, though with the *a* of *lash* substituted for that of *palm*, are *thrash* and *rassle*. The latter, in fact, is often used by highly refined sports reporters in reporting wrestling-matches. In the general speech the only notable survivor seems to be *sergeant*.[4] But let us not forget the proper names *Hartford, Barclay* and *Barney*, the last-named a diminutive for *Bernard*, as in *Barney* Baruch. In England itself the *a* is not used invariably. H. W. Seaman tells me that though the Derby horse-race is the *Darby* "the inhabitants of Derby and Derbyshire pronounce the *er* in the moral or American way, and occasionally write to the papers protesting against the *ar*-sound." Seaman says [5] that *stern* (of a ship) is commonly pronounced *starn* in England, but in the adjective, according to Palmer, Martin and Blandford, the *e* of *persuade* is used. Wyld says that the change from *er* to *ar* started in the dialects of Southeastern England, and soon spread to East Anglia. It was rare in the London dialect before the Fifteenth Century, but became "increasingly fashionable until the last quarter of the Eighteenth," when it began to recede from all words save those which had come to be spelled with *a*, e.g., *dark*.[6]

Crick for *creek* is commonly regarded as an Americanism, and it has been traced by the DAE to 1608, when Captain John Smith used

---

[1] pp. 212–22.
[2] Dissertations, p. 105.
[3] There are many examples in The Beginnings of American English, by M. M. Mathews; Chicago, 1931.
[4] American *Sargeant* et al, by Robert Withington, *American Speech*, Oct., 1934, p. 234. See also Early American Pronunciation and Syntax, by Henry Alexander, *American Speech*, Dec., 1924, p. 145.
[5] Private communication, May 16, 1944.
[6] Wyld presents many examples. There are others in English Pronunciation from the Fifteenth to the Eighteenth Century, by Constance Davies; London, 1934.

it in his "Newes from Virginia," but the NED shows that, in the forms of *crike*, *krike* and *cryke*, it was in English use before the discovery of America. The late William Allen Pusey (1865–1940), sometime president of the American Medical Association, was greatly interested in the distribution of *crick*, and spent a lot of time gathering evidence about it. He found that it was almost unknown in the rural parts of his native State, Kentucky, and that it was rare in the South below North Carolina. He concluded that it was a Northernism.[1] Incidentally, *crick in the neck* is properly *crick* and not *creek*. The NED traces it to *c*. 1440 and says that it is "probably onomatopoeic, expressing the sudden check which the spasm causes."[2] Webster, in his "Dissertations," recommended many pronunciations that have since become vulgar, *e.g.*, *heerd* for *heard* and *deef* for *deaf*. For the former he had the support of Samuel Johnson,[3] and for the latter the "universal practise in the Eastern States" and general usage "in the Middle and Southern." He recorded that *def* was in use in England, but called it "a corruption," and cited the rhymes of Chaucer and of Sir William Temple in support of his position. Of *herd* for *heard* he said: "The Americans were strangers to it when they came from England, and the body of the people are so to this day. To most people in this country the English pronunciation appears like an affectation, and is adopted only in the capital towns, which are always the most ready to distinguish themselves by an implicit imitation of foreign customs." It was "almost unknown in America," he added, "till the commencement of the late war [of the Revolution], and how long it has been the practise in England I cannot determine." Webster, in those days, was a fiery linguistic patriot, and refused absolutely to follow English example. "If it is erroneous," he said, "let it remain so: we have no concern with it. By adhering to our own practise we preserve a superiority over the English in those instances in which ours is guided by rules, and so far ought we to be from conforming to their practise that they ought rather to conform to ours." But by the time he came to his "American Dictionary" of 1828 he was admitting *hurd*, though

---

[1] Private communications, Aug. 23 and 27, Sept. 8 and Nov. 14, 1937.
[2] The difference in meaning between *creek* in England and *creek* in America is discussed in Supplement I, p. 221.
[3] Boswell reported under date of Sept. 23, 1777: "[Johnson] said his reason was that if *heard* were pronounced *herd* there would be a single exception from the English pronunciation of the syllable *ear*, and he thought it better not to have any exception."

insisting that *deaf* was "more commonly *deef*" than *def* in America. While this dictionary was under way he was visited by Captain Basil Hall, R.N., and they fell into a discussion of the word. "Your way of pronouncing *deaf*," he said to Hall, "is *def* — ours, as if it were written *deef*; and as this is the correct mode, from which you have departed, I shall adhere to the American way."[1] Webster was apparently the first lexicographer to make note of the so-called neutral vowel. Of it he said in the introduction to his 1828 Dictionary:

> Let any man in genteel society or in public pronounce the distinct sound of *a* in the last syllable of *important,* or the distinct sound of *e* in the terminations *less* and *ness* in *hopeless, happiness,* and he would pass for a most inelegant speaker. Indeed, so different is the slight sound of a great part of the unaccented vowels in elegant pronunciation from that which is directed in books of orthoepy that no man can possibly acquire the nicer distinction of sounds by means of books — distinctions which no characters yet invented can express.

A hundred and seven years later A. Lloyd James returned to this melancholy vowel in "The Broadcast Word,"[2] as follows:

> The preacher or public speaker is perpetually in difficulties with it, and especially when it occurs in the final position, where the temptation to dwell on it is irresistible. It cannot be a lengthened version of itself, and so it must assume the quality of a stressed vowel that varies from speaker to speaker and from word to word. The favorite variety is the long *aa;* it makes *ever* sound like *evaa, scripture* becomes *scriptchaa,* and *idea* becomes *ideaa.*

Difficulties with *i* in the United States occur mainly in relatively recent words of scientific provenance, *e.g., appendicitis, iodine, quinine,* and so on. Bender, in his counsel to radio message-bringers,[3] follows what are probably the prevailing American pronunciations, which are far from consistent. Thus he gives the crucial *i* the diphthongal *ai-* sound in *iodine,* but the *ee-*sound in *chlorine* and *bromine,* and the sound it has in *in* in *ephedrine.* In *appendicitis, bronchitis, tonsillitis, neuritis, gastritis* and the like he ordains the *ai-*sound. Jones, in "An English Pronouncing Dictionary," gives precisely the same pronunciations for England, but notes that *iodine* is accorded the *ee-*sound by English chemists, and that the *ai-*sound "is rapidly given place to" it. The *ai-*sound, he says, "is an old-fashioned pronunciation used by people who are ignorant of chemistry, but are familiar with the substance as a household commodity." Kenyon and

[1] Travels in North America in the Years 1827 and 1828, by Hall; Philadelphia, 1829; Vol. I, p. 321.
[2] London, 1935, p. 180.
[3] NBC Handbook of Pronunciation; New York, 1943; third printing.

Knott note that the *ee*-sound is likewise preferred by chemists in America, and give *iodin*, with the last syllable rhyming with *pin*, as an alternative to *iodeyn*. Bender recommends *kwi'-nin*, with both *i*'s as in *nine*, for *quinine*, and so do Kenyon and Knott. Jones gives the *i* of *pin* to the first syllable and that of *nine* to the second. Vizetelly noted so long ago as 1917[1] that the highly artificial *kin-ne'en* was already going out. He appended an interesting note upon the orthoëpic adventures of the word in American dictionaries.[2] The synthetic rival of *quinine*, *atabrine*, has not yet acquired a settled pronunciation. I have heard both *atabreen* and *atabrine* (rhyming with *line*) from equally tony medical men.

"American English," says Louise Pound,[3] "is losing its short *o* and turning it into a long open *o*, or into *ah*. Should one say *dawg*, *fawg*, *bawg*, or *dahg*, *fahg*, *bahg*? There is a different usage for different parts of the United States; and there is no consistency observed even for words within the same group, *e.g.*, I say myself *dawg* but *fahg*. Some would-be purists go so far as to insist upon the vowel *a* of *artistic* in words like *Florence, orange, coffee, horrid*, although the real purist should strive for the preservation of the original short open *o*-sound, yet heard in British usage; not for the substitution of a sound which is not an *o*-sound at all." During the ten years before 1944 Charles K. Thomas, of Cornell, investigated the pronunciation of *horrid, orange, Florida, forest, borrow, foreign, horrible* and a number of other such words by speakers from nineteen States. He found that the territory they came from could be divided into an Eastern-Southern *ah*-section and a Western short-*o*-section, with the two divided by a line running southward from central Vermont, then westward across New York and Pennsylvania, then southward through Maryland and part of Virginia, then generally westward to southern Missouri, and then southward again through Texas. He learned that in some parts of the *ah*-region the preference for it is overwhelming, *e.g.*, Massachusetts, lower New York, New Jersey, Virginia, Tennessee, Arkansas and Louisiana. Unfortunately, his inquiry, as I have said, covered but nineteen of

1 A Desk-Book of 25,000 Words Frequently Mispronounced, p. 713.
2 The Linguistic Atlas of New England, Map 516, shows that *iodine* and *iodeen* are both in use throughout the territory covered, with what appears to be *iodæne* occasionally encountered in the western part. *Kwinine* seems to be almost universal (Map 517).
3 Pronunciation in the Schools, *American Speech*, Oct., 1922, p. 476.

the forty-eight States, and no one, so far as I know, has investigated the remainder.[1] Harold Whitehall has shown [2] that in colonial American *o* sometimes took a *u*-sound, or even an *oo*-sound. It still takes the former in *among, company*, and (at least in parts of the country) *constable*, but in nearly all other situations these aberrations have disappeared.

Hilaire Belloc says that to American ears the vowel used by the English in *hot, coffee, soft, cough, lost, off, gone, dog*, etc., sounds "ridiculous."[3] A. Lloyd James says [4] that it is a quite recent newcomer among English vowels, and that in Victorian days *dawg, crawss, cawf, gawn* and *frawst* were still "current in educated London speech." He adds that *awff* for *off* survives. The usual English *o* seems to most American ears to be nearly identical with the *u* of *hut*, so that that word and *hot* are hard to distinguish. Sometimes, in the United States, a neutral vowel resembling the one in unaccented *the* is substituted for *o*, as in *demuhcrat*. There is occasional discussion in the newspapers of the *o*-sound in the second syllable of *bureaucracy*, with one faction advocating the *o* of *rock* and another an *oh*-sound that is supposed to be the French *eau*-sound. All the principal authorities, English and American, seem to favor the former, though they ordain the *oh*-sound in *bureau* and *bureaucrat*. It is obviously stress that supports the *ock*-sound. H. W. Fowler, in "Modern English Usage,"[5] denounces *bureaucracy* itself, as "a formation so barbarous that all attempt at self-respect in pronunciation may perhaps as well be abandoned." "It is better," he goes on, "to give the whole thing up, and pretend that *-eau-* is the formative *-o-* that ordinarily precedes *-crat*, etc.; all is then plain sailing; it is only to be desired that the spelling could also be changed to *burocrat*, etc."[6]

The vicissitudes of the *u*-sound in early American speech have

1 The Dialectal Significance of the Non-Phonemic Low-Back Vowel Variants Before *R*, in Studies in Speech and Drama in Honor of Alexander M. Drummond; Ithaca (N.Y.), 1944, pp. 244–254. A bibliography is appended. See also Short *O* Vowels in American Speech; Massachusetts, by C. W. Dow, *Speech Monographs*, 1945, pp. 74–76.
2 An Elusive Development of Short *O* in Early American Speech, *American Speech*, Oct., 1941, pp. 192–203.
3 The Contrast; New York, 1924, p. 226.
4 The Broadcast Word; London, 1935, pp. 100 and 105.
5 Oxford, 1926, p. 59.
6 The *Rock* in *Bureaucracy*, by Alexander Kadison, New York *Times* (editorial page), Feb. 21, 1938.

been studied by Whitehall.[1] It became, on the one hand, *oo*, on the other hand a diphthong apparently identical with that of *how,* and on the third hand, so to speak, various other sounds. These variations, in the main, have vanished, and one no longer encounters *bull* spelled *bool,* or *blood* rhymed with *load,* or *dew* with *bough,* or *dust* with *host,* but *nooz* for *news* still remains the prevailing pronunciation in the United States, despite the English preference for *nyewz* and the effort of generations of schoolma'ams to import and propagate it. Webster was against it, and in his "Dissertations"[2] dismissed the intrusion of the palatal glide as a peculiarity of Virginia speech, and hence barbaric. In his Dictionary of 1828 he actually ordained *fig-ur, val-u, vol-um, moot* (for *mute*), *litera-tur,* etc., but he had to admit that it was already "the practise [in the North] to give *u* the sound of *yu* in such words as *nature, feature, rapture,* which are pronounced *nat-yur, feat-yur, rapt-yur,*" and after his death in 1843 his heirs and assigns quietly inserted the *y* in *figure, value* and *volume.* Krapp has shown[3] that old Noah, as on not infrequent other occasions, reported the educated speech of New England somewhat inaccurately, and Wyld has produced evidence that the *yu*-sound was already in wide use in England in the early Seventeenth Century.[4] The whole question is discussed by Krapp at length and with much learning. At the present time the English seem to employ *yu* more often than Americans, but it is nevertheless in constant use in this country. Kenyon and Knott give both *nyu* and *nu* for *new,* with the former first, but Bender prefers the latter. Most Americans use *doo* for *due, toob* for *tube, dooty* for *duty,* and *nood* for *nude,* but I have never encountered a native who used *moosic, booty* (for *beauty*), *poor* (for *pure*), or *aboose. Dew,* like *due,* is commonly *doo,* but *few* is seldom if ever *foo.*

H. W. Fowler ventures the opinion[5] that *yu* is yielding to *oo* in English usage. "It was formerly *de rigueur,*" he says, "to put in the *y*-sound; a *flute* had to be called a *flyoot,* or the speaker was damned

[1] Middle English *ū* and Related Sounds: Their Development in Early American Speech, *Supplement to Language,* Oct.–Dec., 1939. Some objections to his conclusion are stated in Development of Middle English *u,* by Eilert Ekwall, *American Speech,* Oct., 1940, pp. 306–10.
[2] p. 159.
[3] The English Language in America; New York, 1925, Vol. II, pp. 155–64.
[4] A History of Modern Colloquial English; London, 1920, pp. 242–44.
[5] Modern English Usage, lately cited, pp. 335–36. This discussion was first published in *S.P.E. Tract No XXII;* Oxford, 1925, pp. 47–48.

in polite circles. . . . But for most of us [Southern English] anything but *bloo* [*blue*] and *gloo* [*glue*] is surely now impossible, however refined we like to be where the trials of articulation are less severe." Fowler adds that *loodicrous, voloominous, loobricate, saloot* and *diloot* also prevail in England, and that *oo* is ousting *yu* from all accented syllables, *e.g.*, in *lunatic, lurid, aluminum, salute, lugubrious, lukewarm, fluent,* and from monosyllables. Krapp, in "The English Language in America," gives the history of the pronunciation of *lieutenant*.[1] It was originally *leftenant* in this country, as it is in England, but Webster, with his fondness for spelling pronunciations, declared for *lootenant*, and *lootenant* it now is.[2] An American police lieutenant is commonly *Loot* to his men, and the same abbreviation is not unknown in the Army and Navy. Sometimes the English use *liftenant* or *litenant* instead of *leftenant*.[3]

Jones says in "An English Pronouncing Dictionary"[4] that *route* is pronounced *rowt* by English soldiers, but *root* by the rest of the population. In the United States *root* seems to be prevailing, helped by the analogy of *routine*. Webster preferred *rowt*, but George R. Howells reported in 1883[5] that "ninety Americans out of a hundred," at that time, used *root*. Kenyon and Knott apparently prefer *root*, but also give *rowt*. Bender gives *root* without mentioning *rowt*. Larsen and Walker give *root*, and dismiss *rowt* as "*dial.*" Webster 1934 gives *root*, but adds that *rowt* "prevails in military use, among railroad men, and colloquially, of a delivery *route*." Krapp says that *rowt* occurs only "in very colloquial English, as in speaking of a milk-*route* or a mailcarrier's *route*."

The intrusion of *y* before the broad *a* as in *cyard* and *gyarden*, is still thought of by most Americans as a Southernism, but it actually goes back to Eighteenth Century England, when it was described by Walker (1791) as prevailing "in polite pronunciation." At the same time there was a fashion in London for inserting it before the diphthong of such words as *kind* and *cow*. Webster was against

---

1 Vol. II, pp. 163-64.
2 The NED shows that in the Fourteenth Century, when the word was just coming into English, both forms were in use in England. *Luftenand* and *leeftenaunt* are cited from 1375 and 1387 respectively. But *lutenand* also dates from *c.* 1375.

3 *Lif, Lef,* or *Loo,* Edinburgh *Evening News*, Sept. 27, 1943.
4 London, 1917; revised in 1924, 1926 and 1937.
5 *Transactions of the Albany Institute*, Vol. X.

this intrusion, and denounced it in his "Dissertations" in 1789. In the case of *ow* he called it characteristic of the "barbarous dialect . . . of the Eastern country people," and in the case of *ai* an affectation of "those polite speakers who are so fond of imitating the English stage pronunciation as to embrace every singularity, however disagreeable."[1] "It is presumed," he added prissily, "that the bare mention of such barbarisms will be sufficient to restrain their progress, both in New England and on [sic] the British theatre." But so late as 1853 *Punch* was still chiding the English actors for using *gyarden* and *kyind*."[2] After *k* and *g* the *y*-sound, says Krapp,[3] "can still frequently be heard, both in cultivated Virginian speech and in the Negro's naïve imitation of cultivated speech."[4] Greet, himself a Southerner, says[5] that there is much variation of usage among Southerners who affect the *y*-sound, and that they are seldom consistent. He tells, for example, of "two gentlewomen" who used *cigya* (for *cigar*), *cyahnly* and *cyahnt* (for *can't*), but nevertheless failed to insert the *y* in *car* and *garden*. It is not fashionable, he says, in words showing the vowels of *gift, get* and *carry*, but it occurs before the *u*-sound, as in *gyirls* for *girls*. To insert the *y*-sound before the *ow* of *cow*, he says, in "a real *fauxpas*." In this he agrees with Webster, who carried on, as we have seen, a war against *cyow, cyounty, tyown* and their like, which were common in the New England of his time, and still survive there among the remoter country people. Webster laid down specifications for schoolmasters eager to put down this *y*. "In order to pronounce *cow, power* or *gown* with propriety," he said, "the pupil should be taught, after placing the organs in the position required by the first consonant, to open his mouth wide before he begins the sound of *ow*. Otherwise, in passing from that position to the aperture necessary to pronounce *ow*, he will inevitably articulate *ee, keow*."[6]

---

1 p. 109.
2 Quoted in *Godey's Lady's Book*, Jan., 1854, p. 86, with the implication that American actors were doing likewise.
3 The English Language in America, Vol. II, p. 207. An excellent discussion of the history of the sound follows.
4 Dr. L. L. Barrett tells me that he once knew a professor at the University of Virginia who even introduced it into French, as in *regyarder* for *regarder*.
5 Southern English, in Culture in the South, edited by W. T. Couch; Chapel Hill (N.C.), 1934, p. 610. See AL4, p. 364.
6 All of us, of course, insert *y* before the *u* in *union* and the like, but *yarb* for *herb* and *yere* for *here* are definitely rustic and vulgar. Wyld shows that *yere* for *here* and *yearth* for *earth* were used by

In the dialect speech of the Republic the diphthongs have made heavy weather of it. Either they displace other sounds, as in the *thoid* of the Brooklyn dialect, or they are themselves displaced by other sounds, as in *hist* for *hoist*, *rile* for *roil*, *jice* for *joist*, *pisen* for *poison*, *snoot* for *snout*, and *thar* for *there*.[1] The use of the diphthong of *wine* in the words in *oi* was quite correct in England in the Seventeenth and Eighteenth Centuries. Samuel Butler's rhymes indicate that he heard it in *toil*, *purloin* and *enjoin*, Dryden's that it was then current in *toil* and *coin*, and Pope's that it was admitted in *enjoy* and *join*. But William Kenrick, whose "New Dictionary of the English Language" was published in 1773, indicated that the *oi*-sound was then ousting the *ai*-sound. He declared that it would still "appear affectation" to use the former in *boil* and *join*, but that the retention of *ai* in *oil* and *toil* had become "a vicious custom" tolerated only "in common conversation."[2] Some English observers detect a movement toward the diphthongization of vowels even in educated American speech. "To an Englishman," says Oscar Browne,[3] "an impression is given that many Americans have acquired habits of restricting the functions of the nasal sinuses, placing unorthodox values and pitches upon vowels, including a change of simple vowels into diphthongs."[4] On the vulgar level many other changes in vowels, *e.g.*, *jedge* for *judge*, *empire* for *umpire*,[5] *ingine*

Bishop Hugh Latimer in the sermons he published in 1549, and that *yearl* for *earl* was in use at the same period. It was probably a fear of such vulgarisms that knocked the *y* off *yeast*. It was pronounced *east* in Maryland in my boyhood, but the *y* has now been restored.

1 See AL4, pp. 345-46.
2 I take this from A Modern English Grammar, by Otto Jespersen; Heidelberg, 1922, Vol. I, pp. 329-30. Isaac Watts, in The Art of Reading and Writing English, 1721, listed *jice* as correct for *joist*, but Robert Nares in Elements of Orthoepy, 1784, denounced *hist* for *hoist* as a "low vulgarism."
3 Normal English Pronunciation; London, 1937, p. 91.
4 Mr. William R. Bradley, of New York City (private communication, Dec. 1, 1943), sends me a tearsheet from *Science* containing an article entitled Medical Orthoepy, by Dr. B. N. Craver, of the School of Medicine, Wayne University, Detroit, which says in part: "A very common error in the pronunciation of medical terms is to render as diphthongs vowels which should be sounded separately.... Thus, *protein*, correctly a three-syllable word, has been accorded but two; so also with *caffeine*, *rabies* and others. However, for such words as *oubain*, *sparteine*, *codeine*, *caries*, *facies* and others correct speech demands the pronunciation of all three syllables. *Syndrome*, analogous to *epitome*, should have all vowels sounded, but it has so long been mispronounced as a two-syllable word that lexicographers remark that pronunciation in medicine."
5 There was a contrary exchange in

for *engine*, *chaw* for *chew*,[1] and *shet* for *shut* still flourish more or less, but it is my impression that they are gradually succumbing to the schoolma'am. Whether the current plan to run every American moron through high-school will ever dispose of them altogether remains to be seen.

3. THE CONSONANTS

"In London and some parts of the South [of England]," said R. J. Lloyd in 1894, " the *r* following a vowel at the end of the word or syllable has disappeared, but there is no other part of the English-speaking world except Eastern New England where this is quite the case."[2] Lloyd might have excepted also the Tidewater South, but everywhere else in the United States, including even the Hudson Valley area, the *r* is usually sounded. The late C. H. Grandgent of Harvard (1862–1939) once estimated that, in the West, it appears before consonants, as in *card*, *north*, *part* and *farm*, 81 times out of 100, in the Middle States 64 times, in New England 36 times, and in the South 24 times.[3] Bernard Bloch, one of the collaborators in the Linguistic Atlas of New England, has since shown that it is now conquering even New England. In the Western third of the area he has found it prevailing in more than 75% of the cases, and even within the Boston territory there are speech-islands in which it is clearly sounded. The older speakers, he says, still omit it; the young ones insert it. Its eastward extension, he concludes, " reflects not merely the spread of a single feature from Southwestern New England, but a gradual victory of the chief

---

the Philippines after the promulgation of civil government on July 1, 1902. Thereafter the refined began speaking of the days before that event as those " of the *empire*," but the less tutored resident Americans preferred *umpire*. I am indebted here to Mr. Hartford Beaumont.

[1] *Chaw* must have been accepted in England during the Eighteenth Century, for Walker in 1791 described it as having " grown vulgar," apparently recently. It was permitted by Nares in 1784.

[2] Standard English, *Die neueren Sprache*, 1894, p. 53. I take this from Sidelights on the Pronunciation of English, by Giles Wilkeson Gray, *Quarterly Journal of Speech*, Nov., 1932, p. 556. Gray's paper gives a sympathetic and excellent account of Lloyd (1846–1906), who was a lifelong resident of Liverpool, and thus stood outside the Oxford influence that shows in nearly all other English phoneticians.

[3] Notes on American English, quoted by Gray, just cited.

type of American English over a specifically provincial dialect."[1] There are, to be sure, some neighborhoods in which a contrary tendency seems to be showing, but Bloch inclines to think that even there the *r* will finally conquer.

Archibald A. Hill has shown that the loss of *r* after vowels and before consonants is frequent in the English dialects,[2] and has produced examples from as long ago as the Fifteenth and Sixteenth Centuries, e.g., *hoss* for *horse* (1473–88), *assenycke* for *arsenic* (1530) and *cott* for *court* (1552).[3] Wyld says that it was lost earliest before *s* and *sh*.[4] It is sounded in England when it is followed by a vowel, as in *red, ride* and *rode*, but it is omitted when it stands at the end of a word, as in *car, fair* and *fur*. In the latter case, however, it is commonly restored when the word following begins with a vowel, as in " The *car* is at the door."[5] But this restoration is not invariable, and there are situations in which many speakers seem to find it difficult to decide whether they should sound the *r* or not. As a result, some of them, eager to be correct, insert it where it has no place, as in " the *idear* is " and " *vanillar* ice-cream." This confusion is promoted by the fact that many quite dissimilar words, e.g., *law* and *lore*, are pronounced precisely alike in Southern English. People so afflicted, says A. Lloyd James, " will not infrequently talk about the *lore of Moses* when they mean the *law of Moses*."[6]

The best discussion of the American *r* that I am aware of is in a paper by John S. Kenyon.[7] He describes at length the vocal mechanism whereby the various *r*-sounds, ranging downward from the

[1] Postvocalic *R* in New England Speech, *Acts of the Fourth International Congress of Linguists;* Copenhagen, 1936, pp. 195–99.
[2] Early Loss of *R* Before Dentals, *Publications of the Modern Language Association*, June, 1940, pp. 308–59.
[3] Just how *cott* was pronounced is not clear. It may have been the remote forerunner of the Southern *cote*, as in *co't-house*.
[4] A History of Modern Colloquial English; London, 1920, p. 298.
[5] I take this example from Broadcast English No. II, by A. Lloyd James; London, 1930, p. 14. James does not indicate how *door* is here pronounced, but other British authorities clip off the final *r* and make it nearly identical to the *doh* in the Southern cracker and Negro " Shet 'at *doh*."
[6] Our Spoken English; London, 1938, p. 99. James also discusses this blunder in The Broadcast Word; London, 1935, pp. 107, 108 and 183. Mr. George W. Thompson calls my attention to the fact that the Southern proletariat is lavish with redundant *r*'s, as in *holler* (noun and verb), *yeller* or *yaller, ager, marshmeller, Ednar, Emmar,* etc.
[7] Some Notes on American *R, American Speech*, March, 1926, pp. 329–39.

trilled *r* of German, French and Scots, are produced, and distinguishes between the mere muffling of the sound and its complete extinction. In many cases, in the middle ground, he says, *r* is reduced to a sort of vowel. He observes, like Ring Lardner before him,[1] that the literary custom of representing the vulgar pronunciation of *fellow, window* and their like by *feller, winder*, etc., is misleading, for the final syllable in most cases does not show *r* at all, but is simply the neutral vowel.[2] Why has *r* survived in General American? Kenyon rejects the theory that the schoolma'am, egged on by Webster, preserved it by insisting on spelling-pronunciations, and points out very wisely that there were more of her clan in Eastern New England, where it vanished, than to the westward, where it persisted. He rather inclines to believe that the character of the immigration into the West was mainly responsible. It was largely made up of Scotsmen, of Irishmen and of Englishmen coming from regions outside the influence of London speech, and " they brought their *r*'s with them." " There is much reason to think," he concludes, " that the Western treatment of *r* . . . is parallel to the Western pronunciation of words like *half*, which belongs to an ' older family ' than Eastern *hahf*." Even more than the use of the flat *a*, the sounding of *r* is the chief hallmark of General American speech; indeed, Leonard Bloomfield says that this General American, or, as he calls it, " Central-Western type of American Standard English," may be defined as " the type which preserves old *r* in final position and before consonants."[3] Its sound, one may admit without cavil, is very far from lovely,[4] but as the late Frank H. Vizetelly was fond of pointing out, it at least makes for intelligibility.[5]

---

[1] AL4, p. 425, n. 1.
[2] The nature of the sound in this position is discussed in New Light on the Origin of Eastern American Pronunciation of Unaccented Final *A*, by James L. Clifford, *American Speech*, Oct., 1935, pp. 173–75. Various correspondents assure me, *pace* Lardner, that they have frequently heard *feller*. It may be a spelling-pronunciation. See Notes, by Moyle Q. Rice, *American Speech*, Oct., 1937, p. 237.
[3] The Stressed Vowels of American English, *Language*, June, 1935, p. 97.
[4] Henry James described it, in The Question of Our Speech; Boston, 1905, p. 29, as resembling "a sort of morose grinding of the back teeth," and an editorial writer for the Hartford *Courant*, on July 6, 1938, accused the speakers of General American of hanging on to it " with the painful tenacity of a clumsy dentist drilling out a cavity." The Romans called *r* the *litera canina*, the dog's letter.
[5] Alas, even this is denied by a Southern correspondent, Lieut.-Col. F. G. Potts, U.S.A. (ret.), of Mt. Pleasant, S. C. Under date of Jan. 20, 1945 he writes: " American

— and the desire to convey ideas is the chief purpose of speaking at all.[1]

The dropping of the final g in words ending in -ing seems to be more widespread in England than in America, and is tolerated, if not exactly recommended, by most of the English authorities on speech. Kenyon says[2] that, in the United States, it "appears to be more common among the educated in the South than in the North and East." "The spelling-pronunciation," he goes on, "is now so general that it is in excellent usage, but it must not be hastily concluded that the pronunciation -in is necessarily a mark of ignorance or lack of cultivation. It is still commoner than most people suppose. It is a good illustration of the muddling through by which forms and usages regularly become established in standard use. Hundreds of people have religiously practised saying *coming* instead of *comin* without ever intelligently considering the facts, or whether the effort was worth while." Krapp shows[3] that -in is to be found plentifully in the early American records, and that it must have been general in the Seventeenth Century. He ascribes the prevalence of -ing to the rage for spelling-pronunciations, and notes that, among the innocent, "the analogy of words" has produced such forms as *kitching* and *garding*. Lardner noted that in the common speech the final g is commonly dropped in *nothing* and *something*, but retained in *anything* and *everything*.[4] Lieut.-Col. F. G. Potts[5] accounts for this on the plausible ground that "*anything* and *everything* have strong secondary accents on their last syllables, and are

---

r, carefully sounded, tends to make words indistinct, especially when two or more r's occur close together. Just have a Middle Westerner say *Yorkshire terrier* and see what you think of it. The rolled or trilled r's of Scotland, Ireland and the Continent ... are usually pleasant to listen to, and do not detract from clarity of utterance. But the American r is not only disagreeable in itself, but also the cause of modification in the pronunciation of nearby vowels, so that *Mary, marry, merry* and *Murray* are frequently pronounced alike, and *heart* becomes *hurt*."

1 Interesting speculations about r are in The English Language in America, by George Philip Krapp; New York, 1925, Vol. II, pp. 217-31; The Dog's Letter, by C. H. Grandgent, in Old and New, Cambridge (Mass.), 1920, pp. 31-56; Dropping of the R, by L. A., *American Notes & Queries*, Sept., 1945, p. 92, and Loss of R in English Through Dissimilation, by George Hempl, *Dialect Notes*, Vol. I, No. VI, 1893, pp. 279-81.
2 American Pronunciation; Ann Arbor (Mich.), 1945, p. 149.
3 The English Language in America, Vol. II, pp. 13-17.
4 AL4, p. 352, n. 2.
5 Private communication, Jan. 20, 1945.

pronounced as if those syllables were separate words." Americans, like Englishmen, seldom give a clear sound to the *g* in such words as *length* and *strength*. It becomes, at best, *k*, and this sound is recorded without comment by Jones in his "English Pronouncing Dictionary." Dr. Alfred D. Schoch argues that this substitution is quite rational. "The *g* in these words," he says, "is only an orthographic expedient; they really have no *g* in them — that is, no *g* sound. What they do have is a velar nasal consonant like the *n* in *ink*, which stands between two other sounds that are articulated forward in the mouth, and so stands to have its articulation shifted forward to the *n*-position. I don't remember, though, that I have ever heard these words with a plain *n*-sound. What is more likely to occur in ordinary talk is that the *ng* nasal consonant may disappear and leave the nasality of the *e* to take its place."[1]

It is as grievous to an Englishman of tone to be accused of dropping his *h*'s as it is to a white Southerner to be accused of using *you-all* in the singular. Nevertheless, both are guilty to some extent. Daniel Jones, in prescribing the usages of what he calls Received Pronunciation (RP), lists *hospital* with a clear *h* but allows both *hostler* and *ostler*, and when he comes to *hotel* says that "some use the form *otel* always; others use it occasionally, when the word is not initial."[2] All Americans believe that they sound the *h* invariably, but when they use *an* before *hotel*, which happens sometimes, they actually say *an 'otel*, for sounding *h* after consonants is phonologically unhandy, as the cases of *on his* and *to kiss* (or *neck*, or *shoot*) *her* sufficiently show. They are saved from cockneyism by the fact that, as a practical matter, they seldom use *an* before *hotel* and its allied words, despite the assumed influence on their speech habits of the King James Bible, which gives it before *haven*,[3] *hair*,[4] *host*,[5] *hedge*,[6] *helmet*,[7] *herb*,[8] *hidden*,[9] *high*,[10] *hand*,[11] *hole*,[12] *holy*,[13]

1 Private communication. *Strengths*, incidentally, must be a hard dose for foreigners learning English. It not only includes the difficult sound of *th*, but is a nine-letter word with only one vowel. But when it comes to clusters of consonants English is a relatively humane language. In his Notes on Duwamish Phonology and Morphology, *International Journal of American Linguistics*, Oct., 1945, p. 204, Jay Ellis Ransom says that Duwamish, one of the Indian languages of the northwest Pacific Coast, includes *sxw, gwlts, gwlgw, bdtcd, sqwqw, txw, djdtcd* and *bdtcdz*.
2 An English Pronouncing Dictionary, p. 211.
3 Genesis IL, 13; Acts XXVII, 12.
4 I Kings I, 52.
5 II Chronicles XIV, 9; do., XXVI, 11; Psalms XXVII, 3; do., XXIII, 16; Ezekiel I, 24; Daniel VIII, 12.
6 Job I, 10; Proverbs XV, 19. But in

horn,[1] horse,[2] house,[3] householder,[4] hundred,[5] hypocrite, etc.[6] In late years the more popular American prints of Holy Writ have quietly substituted *a* for *an* before all these words, though in a few aberrant cases *an* is retained. In the only instances in which *hen*, *hind*, *hot* and *huge* appear in the text with an indefinite article the King James Version itself uses *a*, which is also used before *horrible*. *Hunt* never appears as a noun and *hurt* never with an indefinite article.

It is hard to make out whether the use of *a* or *an* influences the pronunciation in more cases than the pronunciation influences the use of the articles. So far as I know the only study of English and American practise has been one reported by Louis N. Feipel in 1929. He investigated three hundred contemporary books by authors of decent standing on both sides of the water and found that the English used *an* much oftener than the Americans. In the case of *hallucination*, for example, the score ran three to one, in that of *horizon* four to one, and in that of *hysterical* five to one. *An historical* was found in six English writers and four Americans, but *a* was likewise used by six Englishmen and four Americans, which left a sort of stalemate. *An heroic* was used by eight Englishmen and four Americans — including Waldo Frank and Lewis Mumford —, but two Americans used *a heroic*, which all the English avoided. No author of either country used *a hour*, *a heir* or *a honest*, which seems to indicate that the *h* is dropped in all of them in both coun-

---

Ecclesiastes X, 8 and Mark XII, 1 *a* is used before *hedge*.

7 Isaiah LIX, 17; I Thessalonians V, 8. But in I Samuel XVII, 5 *a* is used.
8 Isaiah LXVI, 14.
9 Job III, 16; Proverbs XVIII, 11; do. XXI, 4; Isaiah XXX, 13; John XIX, 31; Acts XIII, 17.
10 Psalms CI, 5; Exodus XIV, 8; Numbers XXXIII, 3; do. XV, 30.
11 Ezekiel II, 9; do. VIII, 3; Daniel X, 10. But *a* is in Exodus XIX, 13.
12 Exodus XXVIII, 32; do. XXIX, 23. But *a* is in Jeremiah XIII, 4, Ezekiel VIII, 7; II Kings XII, 9.
13 II Kings IV, 9; Ezekiel XLV, 1; Acts X, 22; I Peter II, 5; Romans XVI, 16; I Corinthians XVI, 20; II Corinthians, XIII, 12; I Thessalonians V, 26; II Timothy I, 9. But *a* is used in Exodus XIX, 6; Isaiah XXX, 29; Romans XII, 1.

1 Luke I, 69.
2 Psalms XXXIII, 17. *An horseman* is in II Kings IX, 17. But *a horse* is in I Kings X, 29 and Isaiah LXIII, 13.
3 Exodus XII, 30; Judges XVII, 5; I Kings II, 24; do. XI, 18; do. XII, 31; Psalms LXXXIV, 3; Proverbs XVII, 1; do. XXIV, 3; Matthew X, 12. But *a* is in Job XX, 19 and Psalms XXXI, 2.
4 Matthew XII, 52.
5 *An hundred* occurs in the King James Bible more than seventy times.
6 Job XIII, 16; Proverbs XI, 9; Isaiah IX, 17.

tries. No American used *an hereditary*, *an hermaphrodite*, *an hermetically*, *an hydraulic*, *an hyena*, *an herculean*, *an hypnotic*, *an hypocrisy* or *an hilarious*, but a few Americans used *an heraldic*, *an habitual* and *an hiatus*. *Such an one* was used by twelve Englishmen and seven Americans, and *such a one* by six of the former and four of the latter.[1] Mark Twain was noting these differences in 1879, when he said to an Englishman encountered on a German train:

> Your educated classes say *humble* now, and *heroic*, and *historic*, etc., but I judge that they used to drop those *h*'s because your writers still keep up the fashion of putting an *an* before those words, instead of *a*. This is what Mr. Darwin might call a rudimentary sign that *an* was justifiable once, and useful — when your educated classes used to say *umble*, and *eroic*, and *istorical*.[2]

"In the American pronunciation," wrote Noah Webster in 1789, "*h* is silent in the following: *honest, honor, hour, humor, herb, heir*, with their derivatives. To these the English add *hospital, hostler, humble*. But an imitation of these, which some industriously affect, cannot be recommended, as every omission of the aspirate serves to mutilate and weaken the language."[3] Perhaps the best present-day American practise is set forth in the Style-Book of the *Atlantic Monthly*, as follows:

> Before words beginning with *h* use *a* with monosyllables and words accented on the first syllable: *a hat, a habit, a hurricane*. In such cases one bears heavily on the aspirate, so that it is equivalent to a consonant. Before polysyllables accented elsewhere than on the first syllable use *an*: *an habitual, an historical, an heretical*. In such words the *h* is naturally so slurred in pronunciation that its presence is scarcely apparent, and a distinct effort is required to pronounce it distinctly, as one must if *a* is used before it. With those words beginning with *hu* in which the combination is pronounced almost like *yu*, *a* should always be used, without regard to the accent: *a humane, a humility*.[4]

The leading English authority, F. Howard Collins's "Authors' and Printers' Dictionary,"[5] ordains *a* before *hope, horse, hospital* and

[1] *A* and *An* Before *H* and Certain Vowels, *American Speech*, Aug., 1929, pp. 442–54. See also Is It Pedantry?, by Clifford H. Bissell, *Saturday Review of Literature*, Aug. 13, 1927; *A* or *An?*, by J. T. Hillhouse, *Modern Language Notes*, Feb., 1928, pp. 98–101; *A* and *An* Before *H*, by Steven T. Byington, *American Speech*, Oct., 1929, pp. 82–85, and Initial Long *U*, by Edwin B. Davis, the same, April, 1944, pp. 152–53.

[2] Concerning the American Language," part of a chapter crowded out of A Tramp Abroad" (1880); in A Stolen White Elephant; New York, 1882, pp. 265–69.

[3] Dissertations, p. 122.

[4] Text, Type and Style: A Compendium of *Atlantic* Usage, by George B. Ives; Boston, 1921, p. 269.

[5] Seventh edition; London, 1933, p. 1.

humble, and also before *honorarium*, which last is somewhat puzzling, for Thomas R. Lounsbury, in 1904, listed *honor* as one of "four words beginning with *h* in which the initial letter is not pronounced by educated men anywhere," the others being *heir*, *honest* and *hour*. "This usage," he said, "extends of course to their derivatives."[1] "Whether," he went on,

> they will continue to hold out forever against the stream of tendency which is bringing about the resumption in speech of letters once silent must be left to the prophets to announce. In this instance their predictions can be uttered with perfect safety. None of those now living will survive to witness their fulfilment or non-fulfilment. So far no one has ever advocated the pronunciation in them of the initial letter save Walter Savage Landor. He may have been led to take this course by the irritation he felt at having his own usage criticized, for when he came to the employment of the *h* he is reported to have frequently exhibited distinct orthoepic frailty.[2]

When it appears in any save the initial position *h* is frequently dropped, even by speakers of General American. No one, for example, sounds it in *exhaust* and *exhort*, and many also omit it in *exhibit*.[3] The English long ago dropped it from *forehead*, which is *forrid* or *forred* in their speech. There was a time when they also dropped it in *blockhead, hothouse, hedgehog, greenhouse, abhor* and *adhere*.[4] The compensatory insertion of *h* in situations where it does not belong is purely dialectical in English and does not occur

---

1 The Standard of Pronunciation in English; New York, 1904, p. 195. Strictly speaking, *honorarium* is not a derivative of *honor*, for the former came into English direct from the Latin, whereas the latter came from the Anglo-French *onour*. But *onour* was itself of Latin origin, and *honorarium* is always associated with *honor* in the minds of those who use it.

2 In Talks With Ralph Waldo Emerson; New York, 1890, p. 51, Charles J. Woodberry reports that Emerson said to him of Landor: "He does not aspirate; drops his *h*'s like a cockney. I cannot understand it." Thomas Adolphus Trollope said of him in What I Remember; New York, 1888, p. 440: "He was, I think, the only man in his position in life whom I ever heard do so. That a man who was not only by birth a gentleman, but was by genius and culture — and such culture! — very much more, should do this seemed to me an incomprehensible thing. I do not think he ever introduced the aspirate where it was not needed, but he habitually spoke of '*and*, '*ead* and '*ouse*."

3 I do not pause over the not infrequent pedantic complaint that many Americans drop it in *which, where, when*, etc. As a matter of fact, sounding it there is almost beyond human power; to get it in it must be transferred to the first place in these words, so that *which* becomes *hwich*. That is where it was a thousand years ago. But it is not there today, and the effort to pronounce it is a mere affectation. See Phonetic Illusions, by Harold E. Palmer, *John o' London's Weekly*, Dec. 23, 1938.

4 The Sounds of Standard English, by T. Nicklin; Oxford, 1920, pp. 78 and 79.

in Standard Southern English. In American it is quite unknown, save only in such vulgar forms as *hit* for *it* and *overhalls*.[1] But Americans sometimes retain the *h* where English usage does not sound it, especially in proper names, *e.g., Northampton*.[2]

The elision of other sounds from vulgar American speech is discussed in AL4, pp. 352–54. Such forms as *bound'ry, comf'table*, and *prob'ly* are fit matches for the English *secret'ry* and *extr'odn'ry*. The sound most often dropped is that of medial *r*, and the late George Hempl (1859–1921), professor of Germanic philology at Stanford University, long ago published a formidable list of examples, *e.g., pa'tridge, su'prise, qua'ter, co'ner, the'mometer, pe'formance, lib'ary, yeste'dy*,[3] *sa'sparilla, pu'sy* (for *pursy*, usually encountered in *pussy-gut*), *pa'lor* and *Feb'uary*.[4] Some of these are to be found also in English usage. Other sounds that are likewise dropped on occasion are those of *k*, as in *e'cept*;[5] *n*, as in *kill* for *kiln*;[6] *th*, as in *scythe*;[7] *l*, as in *a'ready* and *cert'n'y*;[8] *v* as in *fi' cents*;[9] *d*, as in *We'nesday, kin'ness* and *tole; t*, as in *of'n*,[10] *apos'le* and *Chris'mas*,

[1] Wyld says that *hit* was in general use in England in the Sixteenth Century. I seize the chance to fill a small nook with a sentence from a London letter in the Penang Gazette, June 10, 1938: "*An* Hollywood seeress who is now in England has cast Mr. Chamberlain's horoscope." Obviously, this connotes the pronunciation of *Hollywood* as *Ollywood*.

[2] I am indebted here to Mr. Alexander Kadison. In Nov., 1946, the Rev. F. H. J. Newton, vicar of Blackheath, South England, advocated in his parish magazine that *h* be dropped from the alphabet. He argued that the Cockney version of "Has Herbert had his haircut?," to wit, "Azerbert addiz aircut?," "comes out almost as one word — and how beautiful it is, because it is effortless and not self-conscious."

[3] Perhaps oftener *yistidy*. *Yistidy* was approved in the late Eighteenth Century by Sheridan, Kenrick and Nares, but Walker was against it.

[4] Loss of *R* in English Through Dissimilation, Dialect Notes, Vol. I, No. VI, 1893, pp. 279–81.

[5] Two Observations on Current Colloquial Speech, by A. R. Dunlap, American Speech, Dec., 1939, p. 290.

[6] Kiln or Kill, by Joseph Jones, American Speech, Oct., 1931, pp. 73 and 74.

[7] Bender recommends *syth* in the NBC Handbook of Pronunciation, but Louise Pound reports (Some Folk-Locutions, American Speech, Dec., 1942, p. 247) that *sy* "is in rather common usage," and "seems to have fairly wide currency" from South Dakota to Maine. In Maryland, in the 80s, I never heard anything else.

[8] Wyld shows in A History of Modern Colloquial English, p. 175, that the English formerly omitted the *l* from *almost, almanac, falter* and various other words. It is still absent from *almond*.

[9] I am indebted here to Miss Jane D. Shenton, of Temple University.

[10] Bender recommends *awf'n*. So does Jones for England, but he lists *often* as an admissible variant. Miss Ward presents evidence, in The Phonetics of English, p. 27, that the *t* was omitted in England in

and *s* as in some of the almost innumerable deteriorated forms of *yes*.[1] Sometimes, in careless speech, one consonant is substituted for another, as in *grampa* and *robm* (*robin*), or two for two, as in *sebm* (*seven*);[2] sometimes a cluster of consonants is omitted, as in *gra'ma;* and sometimes there is elision of a combination of consonant and vowel, as in *pro'bition, guv'ment* and *o'n'ry*.[3]

Hilaire Belloc, in 1924, alleged that *th*, in American speech, was becoming *d*, " even in carefully pronounced words, traditional and in the mouth of a highly-educated man."[4] "*The*," he went on, " has not yet become *de*, but it is on the way." This change, so far as I know, has never been acknowledged by any American phonologist, but many of them have studied the parallel change of *t* to a kind of *d* that they call the voiced *t*, as in *water, butter, battle, twenty*, etc. An Englishman commonly pronounces the *t* in *pity* clearly, but in colloquial American speech the word often comes close to *piddy*. This voiced *t*, according to Kenyon,[5] " occurs most commonly between vowels, sometimes between a vowel and certain of the voiced consonants when it is at the end of an accented syllable before an unaccented one (*twenty*), or sometimes when it is at the beginning of an unaccented one where there is some doubt which syllable the *t* is pronounced with (*want to go*)." It also occurs between two unaccented syllables, as in *join us at eleven*. It does not occur at " the beginning of syllables initial in the phrase, whether accented or unaccented (*table, today*), nor at the end of syllables final in the

---

1701, but the frequent newspaper discussions of the pronunciation indicate that there is now a tendency to restore it. It long ago disappeared from *listen* and *castle*.

1 Popular Variants of *Yes*, by Louise Pound, *American Speech*, Dec., 1926, p. 132. This study was published before the great success of *oh yeah*. The vowel here, of course, is not that of *lay*, but a lengthened form of the *e* of *yes* itself. I am indebted for this to Mr. Edgar W. Smith, of Maplewood, N. J. See also *Yes* and Its Variants, by Albert H. Marckwardt, *Words*, Feb., 1936, pp. 7 and 18.

2 Some Recurrent Assimilations, by Louise Pound, *American Speech*, June, 1931, pp. 347-48. When *ph* appears for *f* it is often changed to *p*, as in *dip'theria, nap'tha, amp'itheater* and *dip'thong*. See AL4, pp. 352 and 407.

3 The DAE gives *onery* and *ornery*, tracing the former to 1860 and the latter to 1830. It derives both from *ordinary*. I can only say that in the Baltimore of my youth *o'n'ry* was the only form in general use, and that it was understood to signify, not ordinary, but vicious. Mr. L. Clark Keating tells me that *onery* is heard in Minnesota.

4 The Contrast; New York, 1924, p. 225.

5 American Pronunciation, ninth edition; Ann Arbor (Mich.), 1945, p. 232.

phrase, whether accented or unaccented (*repeat, rivet*), nor at the beginning of accented medial (*Miltonic*) or final syllables (*retain*)." In 1942 Dr. Victor A. Oswald, Jr., of Columbia, made an attempt to discover the extent to which this *d*-like sound was substituted for *t* in ordinary literate speech, using students of the Hazleton, Pa., Senior High School as laboratory animals. He found that in *bitter, betting, plotting,* and *sorted* the overwhelming majority of them sounded a clear *t*, but that in *bleating, waiting, hearty, hurting* and *writing* most of them used a consonant that sounded like *d*.[1] An ingenious correspondent [2] tells me that he hears this sound even in *street:* "most Americans say *sdreet*."[3] He also hears *g* for *k* in *score* and *b* for *p* in *sponge*. The use of *s* for *sh* before *r*, noted in many English dialects, seems to be common in the South. It was denounced by a Baltimore orthoepist, so long ago as 1856, as "the affected pronunciation of over-refined school-girls who cannot bring themselves to utter the homely English sound of *sh* when combined with an *r*, for fear apparently of distorting their faces,"[4] but it survives below the Potomac in speakers of all ages, though it is far from universal. Sir Richard Paget believes that both *s* and *sh*, along with *f* and the sound of *th* in *both*, should be "thrown out of our language" and replaced by their voiced equivalents, to wit, *z, zh* (as in *pleasure*), *v* and the *th* of *thy*. "These unvoiced or whispered sounds," he says, "are in every way inferior to the voiced sounds — as inferior, in fact, as whispered speech is to voiced speech. Their carrying power is one-tenth to one-twentieth of that of the voiced sounds; they are incapable of being sung or of carrying vocal inflection — they are the prime cause of all

---

[1] Voiced *T* — a Misnomer, *American Speech*, Feb., 1943, pp. 18-25. Oswald objected to calling this sound a voiced *t*. "From the point of view of phonemics," he said, "it is a combinatory variant of both *t* and *d*." See also Kenyon, before cited, pp. 232-33; Notes on Voiced *T* in American English, by Einar Haugen, *Dialect Notes*, Vol. VI, Parts XVI and XVII, 1938, pp. 627-34; Language, by Leonard Bloomfield; New York, 1933, pp. 81 and 100.

[2] Mr. Dooley Toepel, of Detroit; private communication, Sept. 2, 1940.

[3] The contrary substitution of *t* for *d*, as in *holt* for *hold*, has been long noted, but is not frequent.

[4] Punctuation and Improprieties of Speech; Baltimore, 1856, p. 68. I take this from Pronunciation of *Shrimp, Shrub* and Similar Words, by George H. Reese, *American Speech*, Dec., 1941, pp. 251-55, in which the occurrence of *s* in English dialects is reviewed. Reese says it became dominant in Standard English in the late Seventeenth or early Eighteenth Century, but was subsequently replaced by *sh*, "probably under the influence of spelling."

verbal misunderstanding. On the telephone they are practically inaudible."[1]

The displacement of consonants by metathesis, as in *prespiration, hunderd, modren, childern, calvary, neuraliga, govrenment, apurn* and *interduce*, is not pathognomonic of vulgar American but is ancient in English and has produced a number of everyday words, *e.g., third*, which started out in life in the Ninth Century as *thrid*. Equally widespread is the intercalation of redundant vowels, though many familiar examples are probably of American origin, *e.g., athaletic, reality (realty), fillum,*[2] *Cubéan, mountainious, golluf, cruality, mayorality*[3] and *municipial*. It was apparently commoner in the earlier days than it is today. Henry Alexander, in a study of the spellings in a pamphlet by an ill-educated New England farmer, written in 1798, finds *tremendious, conterary (contrary), constitutiants (constituents), docterin (doctrine), vagarant (vagrant)*, and *cuntery (country)*, all of them indicative of the author's customary speech.[4] This farmer also added a *g* to words ending with *n*, and in *brethering* he both intruded a vowel and added a *g*. The addition of *g* to the *n* of unstressed syllables has been traced by Wyld[5] to the Fifteenth Century. Some of his later examples are *chicking*, 1653; *lining (linen)*, 1657; *chapling*, 1662; *fashing*, 1664; *childering*, 1692; and *slouinglie (slovenly)*, 1549. In the American common speech

---

[1] The Nature and Origin of Human Speech, *S.P.E. Tract No. XXII;* Oxford, 1925, p. 32. Lieut. Col. F. G. Potts, of Mt. Pleasant, S. C., tells me that he believes that these sounds are more often voiced in the South than in the North. He cites *explosive, exclusive, Japanese* and *rinse* as examples. Bender ordains the unvoiced *s* in all of these save *Japanese*. Spellings, says Col. Potts, are sometimes misleading, and he reports hearing *Stee-fen* for *Stephen* instead of *Stee-ven*. Occasionally, he adds, one is taken aback by hearing a voiced consonant where it is not expected, as in *diagnoze* for *diagnose*. My mother (1858–1925), born and brought up in Baltimore, showed a liking for the voiced sounds, as in *zinc* for *sink* and *azzembly* for *assembly*, maybe due to Southern influence.

[2] Mrs. Pieter Juiliter, of Scotia, N. Y., says (private communication): "The correct modern Dutch pronunciation of *Delft, elf*, etc., has this same swarabhati vowel: *Deluft, eluf*, etc."

[3] Headline in the *Congressional Record*, May 2, 1939, first page of House section: "The Chicago Mayorality Election." The frequent use of the term in Ottawa was noted in That Fourth Syllable, Ottawa *Evening Journal*, Dec. 13, 1939.

[4] The farmer was William Manning and his pamphlet was The Key of Liberty. Alexander's investigation is reported in A Sidelight on Eighteenth Century American English, *Queen's Quarterly* (Kingston, Ont.), Nov., 1923, pp. 173 ff.

[5] p. 290.

such forms are still frequent, e.g., *kitching, capting, leming (lemon)*. Sometimes a *t* is added, as in *varmint (vermin)*, which is traced by Wyld to 1539 and is now reduced to dialect.[1] Often the *t* follows an *s*-sound, as in the familiar *wunst, twict, acrost* and *sinct*.[2] Wentworth traces *grievious* and *bretheren* to 1837, *hunderd* (I hear it as *hundert*) and *childern* to 1840,[3] and *modren* to 1905. The last is undoubtedly much older. *Bron-ix* seems to have arisen among the Jews of that borough, and *fil-lum* probably comes from Hollywood. There is a story about an author who, after a year or two in the movie Zion, quit in disgust. As his train pulled out of Los Angeles he apostrophized his place of exile thus: "What a people! They know only one word of more than one syllable, and that is *fil-lum*."[4] *Mountainious*, used quite seriously, is in *Harper's Magazine* for 1860,[5] and *Patapsico* is common in Maryland. I have heard *heightht* many times, and *lengtht, elevingtht* and *strengtht* more than once. According to a writer in *American Speech*[6] "intrusive *n* remains a recurrent phenomenon in oral and written speech,' e.g., *menance, prowness* and *grimance*. Other familiar forms are *chimbly*, traced by Wentworth to 1818; *conflab*;[7] *lozenger*, traced to 1850; *bronichal, asthema, blasphemious, mischievious, drownded, attackted, somewheres, portry* and *holler*.[8] Such changes as those which converted *licorice* into *likerish*,[9] *recipe* into *receipt*,[10] *jaundice* into *janders, picture* into *pitcher* and *larceny* into *larsensy* have been noted in AL4.[11] A lovely example of double metamorphosis is offered by *savage corpse* for *salvage corps*.[12]

[1] Wentworth offers examples from all parts of the country, ranging in date from 1837 to 1943.
[2] In Middle English *once* was *ones*, i.e., *one* in the genitive. It and the allied words were corrupted in the early Modern period by the influence of *against*, etc.
[3] *Hunderd* was listed as acceptable in John Jones's Practical Phonography, 1701.
[4] In a paper in *Dialect Notes*, Vol. V, Part V, 1922, pp. 133-38, Intentional Mispronunciations in the Central West, Louise Pound called attention to the fact that *fillum, ellum* and their congeners are often used by persons "wishing to contribute to the entertainment of others."
[5] Dec., p. 132.
[6] Dec., 1940, p. 360.
[7] The Reconteur, Montreal *Gazettte*, Jan. 19, 1924.
[8] The Hon. Sam C. Massingale of Oklahoma in the *Congressional Record*, Aug. 5, 1939: "Will Rogers came across the American scene with ... a hoot and a *holler*."
[9] *Dialect Notes*, Vol. I, Part II, 1890, p. 74.
[10] *Receipt-Recipe:* A Request for Information, by Wendell R. Fogg, *American Speech*, Feb., 1931, pp. 218-19.
[11] p. 353.
[12] There are many books on pronunciation, but most of them are of small value. Those of more dignity are listed in Kennedy; pp. 267-81,

4. DIALECTS

354. [All the early writers on the American language remarked its strange freedom from dialects.] This freedom, of course, was only relative, for differences between Northern speech and Southern speech were noted even before the Revolution, and when the movement into the west began the pioneers quickly developed dialects that were set off from all those prevailing along the seacoast. But the English travelers who toured the country in the intervals between the Revolution and the War of 1812 were right in reporting that the linguistic differences they found among Americans were vastly less than they had experienced at home.[1] In all its history, indeed, the United States has produced but one dialect that stumps a visitor from any other part of the country, and that is the so-called Gullah speech of the Negroes of the Southern sea-islands, to be dealt with hereafter. And even these Negroes, when they put their minds to it, can make themselves intelligible to fellow-Americans from thousands of miles away, and it is only a small minority of remote and sequestered individuals among them who find any difficulty in understanding a man from Maine, Texas, Iowa or California. The differences in pronunciation between American dialects seldom impede this free communication, for a man who converts *pass* into *pahs* or drops the final *r* in *father* is still usually able to palaver readily with one who gives *pass* the *a* of *Dan* and wrings the last gurgle out of his *r*'s. The differences in vocabulary are sometimes more puzzling, but they are not, after all, very numerous, and a stranger quickly picks them up. I have often noted that a newcomer to my Maryland Fatherland soon abandons *faucet*, or *tap*, or whatever it was that prevailed in his native wilds, and turns easily to the local *spigot*. In the same way an immigrant to the Deep South is rapidly fluent in the use of *you-all*, *yonder* and *to carry* in

---

429, 447 and 466; The Phonetics of English, by Ida C. Ward; Cambridge (England), 1929, pp. 169-70; An English Pronouncing Dictionary, by Daniel Jones, London, 1937, pp. xxvii and xxviii; and The Broadcast Word, by A. Lloyd James; London, 1935, pp. 201 and 202. Others are referred to in the text, hitherto and hereafter.

1 AL4, pp. 90, 354 ff and 416; Supplement I, pp. 4, 5 and 37. See also British Recognition of American Speech in the Eighteenth Century, by Allen Walker Read, *Dialect Notes*, Vol. VI, Part VI, 1933, pp. 313-34, and Two Early Comments on American Dialects, by Robert J. Menner, *American Speech*, Feb., 1938, pp. 8-12.

the sense of to convey. Differences in intonation present greater difficulties, but they are much less marked between any two parts of the United States than they are between any two parts of England, or than between England and this country as a whole.[1]

The origins in British speech of such American regional peculiarities as survive have been discussed in Section 1, and are summarized in various learned publications.[2] The differences implanted by successive waves of Eastern Englishmen, Western Englishmen, Scotsmen, Irishmen and other immigrants, each group with its own characteristic speechways, must have been considerable at the start, but they were soon being worn down and obliterated by the intermin-

---

[1] "The difference in speech between Boston and San Francisco," says the Encyclopaedia Britannica, fourteenth edition; London, 1929, Vol. XIII, p. 698, col. 2, "is less than what may be observed between two villages in Great Britain that are only a few miles apart." In other countries the same divergences are to be found, for nowhere else is there so much interstate migration as in the United States. The situation in Italy is thus set forth by Mr. Hugh Morrison (private communication, Feb. 8, 1946):
"Few Americans realize how fortunate they are in living in a country in which the differences in speech from place to place are slight. The following is a sentence, 'Inside there were written three words,' in the dialects of ten different places in Italy:
"Tuscany (standard Italian): Dentro c'erano scritte tre parole.
"Piedmont: Drenta a i era scrit tre parole.
"Lombardy: Denter gh'era scritt tre paroll.
"Venice: Drento ghe era scrite tre parole.
"Emilia: Deintr a i era scrett trai paroll.
"Rome: Drento c'erano scritte tre parole.
"Sicily: Dintra c'eranu scritti tri paroli.
"Sardinia: Intro ci vini inscrittas tres paraulas.
"Milan: Denter gh'erò scritti trè parol.
"Naples: Entro c'erano scritto tre paruolo.
"The study of the Tuscan dialect is required in all the schools in Italy, but it is a mistake to think that everyone learns it. When I was studying Italian in New York there were two young men fresh from Italy trying to learn their own language. They were not from backwoods communities but from cities — Milan and Bari. They had had the elementary schooling required of everybody, and all their textbooks were in standard Italian. They could read Italian all right, but in every other respect they were the poorest students in the class. They often resorted to English in talking to each other."

[2] For example, in The Origin of the Dialectal Differences in Spoken American English, by Hans Kurath, *Modern Philology*, May, 1928, pp. 385–95. Excellent expositions of the nature of the process whereby dialects rise and fall are in What is a Dialect?, by E. S. Sheldon, *Dialect Notes*, Vol. I, Part VI, 1893, pp. 286–97; Linguistic Change, by E. H. Sturtevant; Chicago, 1917, pp. 146–58; and English Words and Their Backgrounds, by George H. McKnight; New York, 1923, pp. 12–22.

gling of the population, and that leveling has been going on ever since, and at a constantly accelerated rate. Webster, in 1789, feared that "the body of the people, governed by habit," would "retain their [local] peculiarities of speaking, and for want of schools and proper books fall into . . . inaccuracies which . . . may imperceptibly corrupt the national language,"[1] but he noted at the same time that "the establishment of schools and some uniformity in the use of books" might very readily prevent this debasement, and he himself was destined to have more hand than any other in the operation of the second of the influences he named.[2] Bartlett, so late as 1859,[3] was still willing to predict that "in those parts of the country aside from the great thoroughfares," dialects would become so "firmly established" that "a thousand years might not suffice" to eradicate them, but there are no longer any regions that are really far from "the great thoroughfares," and hence no longer any dialects that stand entirely apart from the common speech. The railroad, the automobile, the moving-picture and, above all, the radio, have promoted uniformity in even the most remote backwaters, and there is every reason to believe that General American, which has been steadily widening its territory for two generations past, will eventually conquer the whole country.[4]

Because of its steady encroachment upon the other dialects the area it covers today is shifting and somewhat vague, but all authorities seem to agree that it begins in the East somewhere in the vicinity of the Connecticut river, runs southward to the line of the Potomac and Ohio, and covers the whole country, save for a few outcroppings of Southern or Appalachian-speech, west of the Mississippi. Kenyon and Knott call it Northern American[5] and Kurath calls it Western,[6] but in view of its immense spread it seems to me that

---

[1] Dissertations, p. 19.
[2] See Noah Webster, Schoolmaster to America, by Harry R. Warfel; New York, 1936, p. 3. Writing in Notions of the Americans; London, 1828, Vol. II, p. 165, J. Fenimore Cooper reported that the dialectal peculiarities of New England, New York and Pennsylvania "were far greater twenty years ago than they are now."
[3] A Glossary of Words and Phrases Usually Regarded as Peculiar to the United States, second edition; Boston, 1859, p. xviii.
[4] "Standardization of education and the migratory habits of the population," said the London Morning Post, Aug. 26, 1936, "have brought American citizens much nearer a common American than we are near a common English."
[5] A Pronouncing Dictionary of American English; Springfield (Mass.), 1944, p. xxxii.
[6] American Pronunciation, S.P.E.

General is preferable. It is, of course, not entirely uniform throughout its area, and Kurath distinguishes a Central or Midland speech from that of the Great Lakes Basin [1] and the Far West, but these differences are very slight, and a casual observer from some other *Sprachgebiet* notices no substantial variance between the speech of a Western New Yorker, that of a Michigander, that of a Nebraskan and that of an Oregonian. This General American, says Kurath, is spoken in "the Middle Atlantic States (New York, New Jersey and Pennsylvania), the Middle West (Ohio, Indiana, Illinois, Wisconsin, Minnesota, Iowa and Northern Missouri), and the Further West to the Pacific Coast." He might have added most of Delaware, Maryland and West Virginia, a part of Kentucky, and a not inconsiderable part of New England.[2]

Southern American marches with General American along the Potomac and Ohio, shows a few dips across the latter into Ohio, Indiana and Illinois, and leaps the Mississippi into Southern Missouri, Arkansas and Eastern Texas. Kurath shows that it is "more varied than either the Eastern or the Western, both geographically and as between the various classes of society." The educated Southerner tends to move toward General American, but the people of the lower classes, whether white or black, still cling to their ancient speechways,[3] and as a result "cultivated speech and dialects are more clearly separated than in the North."[4] Greet distinguishes three general sub-types of Southern speech — the coastal or Tidewater, the general lowland speech, and that of Appalachia — the Southern hill type. "The speech of the Virginia Tidewater," he says "has been transplanted successfully to the northern Shenandoah region and to Charlottesville, but outside of Virginia it has made no headway against the General Southern of the lowlands."[5] This General Southern is spoken in "the plantation up-country of Georgia

---

Tract No. XXX; Oxford, 1928, p. 268.
[1] *Language*, July–Sept., 1944, p. 151.
[2] See also A Standard American Language, by W. Cabell Greet, *New Republic*, May 25, 1938, pp. 68–70.
[3] "Local variants," says A. Lloyd James in Broadcast English No. I; London, 1935, p. 10, "become increasingly unlike one another as we descend the social scale."

[4] *S.P.E. Tract No. XXX*, before cited, p. 292.
[5] Southern Speech, in Culture in the South, edited by W. T. Couch; Chapel Hill (N.C.), 1934, p. 602. Greet returned to the subject in The South Today: The Direction of Southern Speech, an article released by the Southern Newspaper Syndicate, June 21, 1936.

and South Carolina, the cotton country of Alabama, Mississippi, Texas and Louisiana in so far as the speech is without French influence," and the Piedmont of Virginia. The speech of the hill people is quite different from both dialects of the Southern lowlands, and in some ways shows resemblances to that of rural New England. "There is no sharper speech boundary in the United States," says Kurath, "than that following the Blue Ridge from the Potomac to the James."[1] This mountain speech is also to be found in the Ozarks, which lie in the corner where Missouri, Arkansas and Oklahoma meet. It was taken there by immigrants from Appalachia and has filtered into the adjacent lowlands.

Dr. Louise Pound has called attention to the fact that the study of dialect, in both England and the United States, came in later than the study of folklore. The latter, she says, was "an offshoot of the Romantic Movement of the late Eighteenth and early Nineteenth Centuries," but the latter had to wait until 1870, when Aldis Wright and Alexander J. Ellis issued simultaneous calls for the organization of the English Dialect Society, which got under way in 1873, with W. W. Skeat (1835–1912) as its director and honorary secretary. There had been, of course, some investigations of dialectal differences before this, beginning with Francis Grose's "Provincial Glossary" in 1786, and including, for example, Robert Forby's "Vocabulary of East Anglia" in 1830,[2] but nearly all these had been undertaken by amateurs, and it was not until Skeat applied his extraordinary philological powers to the business that the study of the British dialects got upon a scientific basis.[3] After that the Society published a long series of excellent books upon them, covering nearly all the English counties, and Joseph Wright, deputy professor of comparative philology at Oxford, used the material thus amassed in his large "English Dialect Dictionary."[4] The American

---

[1] *Language*, July–Sept., 1944, p. 151.
[2] A full bibliography down to 1874 is in A Bibliographical List of the Works That Have Been Published or are Known to Exist in Manuscript, Illustrative of the Various Dialects of English, edited by Skeat and published by the Society in 1875. An extension to the end of 1922 is in Kennedy, pp. 380–404. Of the latter valuable work Kemp Malone said in *Modern Language Notes*, Dec., 1928, p. 500: "It is a model, and an ornament to American scholarship. It belongs to that limited number of books which, immediately upon their publication, become indispensable."
[3] He counted 30 of them in England and Wales, 7 in Scotland and 3 in Ireland.
[4] Six volumes; London, 1898–1905. It was reprinted in 1923. An English Dialect Grammar is in Vol. VI.

Dialect Society did not follow until 1889.[1] As I have suggested in Supplement I,[2] it probably owed its organization quite as much to the current discovery of and rage for dialect by American novelists as to the example of the English Society, but it had the advantage from the start of the interest of such competent philologians as E. S. Sheldon, C. H. Grandgent, F. J. Child and J. M. Manly, and until the appearance of *American Speech* in 1925 its organ, *Dialect Notes*, offered the only outlet for scholars investigating American speechways.

Its vicissitudes have been recounted in Supplement I, including the mysterious loss of its collection of 26,000 examples of American dialect words and phrases — a catastrophe which rocked the small world of 100% American *Sprachwissenschaftler* almost as dizzily as the larger world of American physical scientists had been rocked by the hanging of Professor John W. Webster of Harvard in 1850. This collection has not been recovered, but enough of it had been printed in *Dialect Notes* to launch Dr. Harold Wentworth[3] upon his " American Dialect Dictionary," published in June, 1944. Wentworth, however, was not content to depend upon *Dialect Notes;* he also mined *American Speech*, the newspapers and popular magazines, and the writings of such lay observers as Edward Eggleston, James Russell Lowell, James Lane Allen, Roark Bradford, William Faulkner, Joel Chandler Harris, Vance Randolph, James Whitcomb Riley and the early humorists.[4] As a result students of American speechways now have the use of a pioneer work of great value. It brings into one handy volume the accumulated observations of hundreds of men and women, extending over many years, and it is so arranged that consulting it is easy. It shares a defect of the Dictionary of American English, in that most of its materials come from printed sources, but Wentworth has studied them with a critical eye, and added first-hand examples whenever possible, some gathered in the field and the rest borrowed from other workers and the

---

1 The story of its organization is told in The First Year of the American Dialect Society, *Dialect Notes*, Vol. I, Part I, 1890, pp. 1-12.
2 p. 104.
3 Then of West Virginia University; later of Temple University. Wentworth was born at Cortland, N. Y., in 1904, and is a Ph.D. of Cornell. He was assistant editor of Webster 1934, and has been a frequent contributor to *American Speech* and other philological journals. See Supplement I, pp. 326n, 359, 367, 368, 369n, 372, 381 and 683n.
4 A list of his principal sources is in his dictionary; New York, 1944, pp. 737-47.

radio. Unhappily, he has omitted a good many interesting words and phrases without apparent reason, and as a result the student is not infrequently brought up by irritating gaps.

An inspection of the book makes clear the fact that, in the United States as elsewhere, dialect is mainly a function of the lower orders of the population. Persons of the educated class, though they show the influence of the circumambient patois, not only in vocabulary but also and more particularly in pronunciation and intonation, nevertheless approach the standard speech of the region whenever any care in speaking is indicated. Individuals of this class, living in the country, says Wyld,[1] will "gain inevitably a very fair knowledge of the local dialect in all its aspects. They can imitate the pronunciation, they know the characteristic grammatical 'mistakes,' and they know a considerable number of the typical words and idioms." Yet they do not use this dialect in conversation among themselves, and seldom if ever in speaking to "their humbler friends," for if they did so "it would be felt as an insult." Wyld is discussing Englishmen, but the same thing is true of Americans. No educated Southerner, save with teasing intent, ever uses what he understands to be Negro dialect in addressing Negroes, and no New Yorker, when forced to ask his way in the wilderness of Brooklyn, uses *thoid*. The plain people save on their very lowest levels, understand "good English" quite well, and many of them make not unsuccessful attempts, on occasion, to use it.

Wentworth's dictionary shows that any given dialect term is apt to be considerably more widespread than is commonly assumed. *To tote*, for example, seems to many persons to be a quite typical Southernism, but he finds examples of it from Maine, Pennsylvania, Illinois, Indiana and Oregon. *To carry*, in the sense of to transport or escort, is also associated in recent years with Southern speech, but he cites its use in Maine.[2] The same wide extension of terms is encountered among the names for common birds, most of which Wentworth does not list. The Florida gallinule (*Gallinula chloropus cachinnans*), for example, has at least a dozen different designations in various parts of the country, but it is a *mud-hen* in States as far apart as Alabama, California, Indiana, Iowa, Michigan, Missouri,

[1] A History of Modern Colloquial English; London, 1920, pp. 15 and 16.
[2] The NED traces it to 1513 in Scotch use, and shows that it was used by Pepys, Samuel Johnson and Benjamin Franklin.

New York and Texas, not to mention Quebec.[1] "Sometimes," says Bradford F. Swan, "a usage went West with the tide of settlers. On other occasions Western expressions have been spread across the whole nation and are now perfectly familiar to Easterners."[2] Not infrequently the evidence makes it clear how a given locution got from one place to another. There is, for example, the Pennsylvania use of *all* in such a phrase as "The bread is *all*." Its old home is in the German counties of its native State, and though it has got as far away as Nebraska and Kansas it is never encountered save in centers of German immigration. Many terms, sometimes thought of as dialectal, are really nearly universal, *e.g., to allow* in the sense of to think, guess or assert; *gallus*, suspenders; *h'ist*, hoist; *bub*, boy; *sass*, sauce; and *brung*, brought.[3] Some specimens of this class belong to ignorant English everywhere, but others seem to be American inventions. Appreciable progress has been made in late years in tracking down the history of the latter, chiefly in the colonial town-records,[4] but much remains to be done. What is needed is a coöperative dictionary on a comprehensive scale, following the method of the Dictionary of American English. Since the resurrection of the American Dialect Society in 1941 there have been some efforts, under the able leadership of Dr. George P. Wilson, of the Woman's College of the University of North Carolina, to interest a

---

[1] Local Names of Migratory Game Birds, by W. L. McAtee (U.S. Department of Agriculture, Miscellaneous Circular No. 13); Washington, 1937, p. 45. McAtee has published a bibliography of American bird nomenclature in Some Local Names of Birds, *Wilson Bulletin*, June, 1917, pp. 85–89. He is also the author of a series of valuable papers, Some Local Names of Plants, in *Torreya*, 1913–42.

[2] Review of Wentworth in the Providence *Journal*, Aug. 6, 1944.

[3] Southern Speech, by W. Cabell Greet, in Culture in the South, edited by W. T. Couch, Chapel Hill (N.C.), 1934, p. 595.

[4] The pioneer in this investigation seems to have been Albert Matthews (1860–1946). He was powerfully reinforced in 1925 by George Philip Krapp (1872–1934) in The English Language in America, Vol. II. Since then a large collection of materials has been made by Miles L. Hanley. These written records, of course, leave much to be desired, for even the most ignorant scribe, when he seized pen in hand, became self-conscious and literary. Said Erick Berry (Mrs. Herbert Best) in Collaborating on a Best-Seller, *Author & Journalist*, Dec., 1945, p. 8: "The recreation of a past mode of speech is particularly difficult, since in his diaries and letters the early American was much influenced by his reading of the Bible and the classics; he wrote with one eye on the elegancies of the language and never, oh never, indulged in local slang or swear words." But this is a difficulty that afflicts all compilers of dictionaries "on historical principles."

competent posse in such an enterprise,[1] but so far the response has been far from exhilarating. Meanwhile, Wentworth's volume is a monument to his extraordinary diligence and to the courage of his publisher.[2]

The Linguistic Atlas of the United States and Canada, launched in 1928, does not meet the need for the dialect dictionary just mentioned, for though it is on a large scale and is magnificently done it does not undertake to present the whole body of dialect terms, but confines itself to showing the distribution of a relatively small number — less than 800. Those chosen are adroitly selected, and the maps recording them tell the student a great deal, but the scheme inevitably overlooks many of the most interesting oddities of local speech. Not a few recorders of dialect object to it on that ground, and there rages an unhappy dispute between those who favor it and those who are against it. The former say that it offers the only feasible way to determine dialect boundaries with any precision — that the mere accumulation of terms is likely to lay too much stress upon those that are only aberrant and curious, and that the collector has no means of checking their distribution. The latter reply that the sample method, though much more accurate within its limits than their own, nevertheless fails to turn up many of the most interesting and significant specimens of local speech. Differences between philologists are apt to become waspish, and this one has already produced some flashes of sauciness. It is a pity that the brethren cannot get together on a joint or compromise scheme, and

---

[1] Wilson published Instructions to Collectors of Dialect as *Publication of the American Dialect Society No. 1* in April, 1944. This was preceded by Some Principles for American Dialect Study, by Raven I. McDavid, Jr., *Studies in Linguistics*, Dec., 1942. See also Organization of Source Material for the Study of American English and American Dialects, by Nathan van Patten, *American Speech*, Aug., 1939, pp. 425-29, and Regional Speech and Localisms, by Wilson, in Needed Research in American English, published by the American Dialect Society, May, 1943, pp. 2-4.

[2] Its defects are set forth in a sympathetic review by Wilson, *American Speech*, Dec., 1944, pp. 284-89. The publisher, the Thomas Y Crowell Company of New York, bore the whole cost and risk of publication. Wright's English Dialect Dictionary, according to its title page, was printed at his own expense, though he got some financial help from W. W. Skeat and others when he was gathering his materials. He had the assistance of hundreds of volunteer local informants and readers, but Wentworth was aided by an even smaller group than the one which coöperated in the DAE. See AL4, p. 106.

so pool their learning for the edification of all persons at interest and the glory of the Flag.[1]

The first part of the Linguistic Atlas, devoted to New England, was published in six elephant-folio volumes, 14 x 21 inches in size, between 1939 and 1943, along with a 240-page interpretative Handbook. The six volumes are made up of 734 double-page tinted maps showing, in phonetic symbols, the vocabulary and pronunciation encountered in 425 communities in New England and six in New Brunswick. The materials were all collected between September 1, 1931 and October 1, 1933, and less than a dozen field workers bore the heat and burden of gathering them. The arrangement is clear and admirable. Successive maps show how typical people of the communities investigated pronounce common words, *e.g., class, theatre* and *yesterday;* what names they use to designate common objects, *e.g., pail* or *bucket, garret* or *attic, purse* or *pocketbook;* how they conjugate common verbs, *e.g., swelled* or *swole, drove* or *driv, took* or *taken;* and what euphemisms they use for such words as *coffin, bull* and *ram.* The test-words were adroitly chosen, and though there was some variation in the use made of them by the field-agents, they undoubtedly produced a reasonably accurate and more or less comprehensive report on New England speech.

One of the strange facts unearthed has been noted already — that the broad *a* of the Boston area seems to be gradually succumbing to the flat *a* of General American, even within cannon-shot of the Harvard pump. Many other curiosities of American speech will reward the patience and stamina of any reader bold enough to struggle with the six hefty volumes and search the glosses accompanying the 734 maps. Map 372, for example, indicates that in 1933 the hideous *mummy*, borrowed from the English and now fashionable in all the big cities,[2] was just beginning to invade New England. It was supported by a somewhat similar form, apparently indigenous, to wit, *mumma*, but the overwhelming majority of natives, whether urban or bucolic, appear to prefer the more ancient *ma*,

---

[1] The opposing views are well stated in the program of the annual meeting of the American Dialect Society at Washington, Dec. 28, 1946, prepared by George P. Wilson, and in a review of Phyllis J. Nixon's Glossary of Virginia Words, by Raven I. McDavid, Jr., *Studies in Linguistics*, March, 1947. pp. 21–24.
[2] Supplement I, p. 519.

maw, mom, mahm, mum, mamma, mommy or *mother*. So with names for the other parent. Map 371 shows that *pa, paw, pap, pappy, papa, dad* and *daddy* are all in wide use, with marked differences on different age levels. One example of *pater* is reported from the Boston area and one of *governor* from the Maine coast, but both seem to be what the Handbook calls innovations. Such innovations, it says, are "derived from the literary language" or "through contact with the upper classes of society." Unhappily, the maps do not indicate social levels, and their statistical value is thus diminished.[1] But they show pretty clearly that the old Yankee dialect is fast losing many of what were once among its characteristic terms. *Pantry* is supplanting *buttery*, *clothes-press* is yielding to *clothes-closet*, *shopping* is driving out *trading*, and *to home* is succumbing to *at home*.

The Linguistic Atlas was originally suggested by Dr. E. H. Sturtevant of Yale, a linguistic scholar of eminence, now professor of linguistics emeritus at Yale.[2] Dr. Hans Kurath, then of Ohio State University, later of Brown and now of Michigan, was in charge of it from the start, and his extraordinary learning and energy vitalized the whole enterprise.[3] His principal collaborators were Miles L. Hanley,[4] Bernard Bloch,[5] the late Guy S. Lowman, Jr., the late

---

[1] This lack, of course, is inevitable. Says Joseph Wright in the preface to Vol. I of his English Dictionary, p. v: "It is not always easy to decide what is dialect and what is literary English; there is no sharp line of demarcation; the one overlaps the other."

[2] Sturtevant, a former president of the Linguistic Society of America, was born at Jacksonville, Ill., in 1875 and got his doctorate at the University of Chicago in 1901. He has specialized in late years in Hittite and is the author of standard works upon it. He has also written two excellent books for the general reader — Linguistic Change; Chicago, 1917, and An Introduction to Linguistic Science; New Haven, 1947. The early history of the Atlas is told in The Dialect Society and the Dialect Atlas, *Dialect Notes*, Vol. VI, Part II, 1931, pp. 65–78.

See also AL4, pp. 58–59; Supplement I, pp. 111–13, and How We Got Our Dialects, by Falk Johnson, *American Mercury*, Jan., 1947, pp. 68–70.

[3] Kurath was born in Vienna in 1891, but was brought to the United States as a boy and got his education in this country. He took his doctorate at the University of Chicago in 1920. He is also editor of the Middle English Dictionary.

[4] Hanley is an Ohioan, educated at Harvard. He was secretary-treasurer of the American Dialect Society, 1928–1940, and has done a great deal of valuable work in the field of American English. See Supplement I, pp. 105 and 109.

[5] Born in New York in 1907, Bloch took his Ph.D. at Brown in 1935, and has since been a member of the faculty there.

Marcus L. Hansen, Lee S. Hultzén and Herbert Penzl, and he was aided in organizing the field work by Jakob Jud, one of the editors of the Linguistic Atlas of Italy and Southern Switzerland,[1] and Paul Scheuermeier, a member of its staff. The gathering of materials in other parts of the country and Canada has been in progress for some years, with Albert H. Marckwardt in charge of the Great Lakes and Ohio valley regions, Henry Alexander in charge of Canada, Raven I. McDavid, Jr., in charge of South Carolina, and other competent linguists directing the work elsewhere. To this end funds have been provided by the American Council of Learned Societies[2] and Drs. Kurath, Bloch, Harold Whitehall and others have undertaken the training of field workers.[3] But it is hardly probable that any of the volumes to be brought out hereafter will be on the heroic scale of the New England folios, which cost about $250,000 to produce and were sold at $185 a set. Indeed, Sturtevant seems to be of the opinion[4] that a less formidable format, without maps, will be more useful.

It was the dialect of New England that first attracted the attention of writers upon speechways in the United States, and as a result the literature upon it is very large. That literature began with Noah Webster's amateurish effort, in his "Dissertations on the English Language," 1789, to account for the Yankee drawl,[5] and it has culminated in our time in such competent and valuable studies as the Linguistic Atlas and Anders Orbeck's "Early New England Pronunciation."[6] Two years before Webster, in 1787, the Yankee made his first appearance as a stage type in "The Contrast," by Royal Tyler, and thereafter he gradually took on popularity, was borrowed by the writers of humorous fiction,[7] and finally came to

---

[1] Sprach- und Sachatlas Italiens und der Südschweiz, edited by Karl Jaberg and Jakob Jud; 16 volumes; Zofingen (Switzerland), 1928-40.

[2] *Bulletin of the Linguistic Society*, 1946, p. 15.

[3] *Supplement to Language*, Oct.-Dec., 1946, p. 15; *Indiana University Bulletin*, Aug., 1946, p. 2.

[4] An Introduction to Linguistic Science, before mentioned, p. 37.

[5] p. 107. He believed that it was produced by the natural diffidence of a people unaccustomed to commanding slaves and servants and "not possessing that pride and consciousness of superiority which attend birth and fortune." This caused them "to give their opinions in an indecisive tone" and to drag out their words.

[6] Ann Arbor (Mich.), 1927.

[7] The first of them was apparently Seba Smith, whose Letters of Jack Downing was published in 1830, but the most successful was Thomas C. Haliburton, whose Sam Slick sketches began to appear in 1835. See Supplement I, pp. 128-30.

his apotheosis in "The Biglow Papers" of James Russell Lowell, the first series of which was published in the Boston *Courier* in 1846. When this series appeared in book form, two years later, Lowell added a preface on the Yankee dialect and a glossary thereof, and when a second series followed in 1867 (begun in 1862) he expanded these into a somewhat elaborate treatise. Unhappily, he was untutored in the ways of language, so he fell into two serious errors, all the more confusing because they were antagonistic. The first was the error of seeking to justify every Yankee locution he noticed by showing that it could be found in some English book, and the second was that of listing as Yankeeisms peculiarities of pronunciation and accidence which really belonged to the common stock of ignorant English, and were no more the monopolies of New England than boiled dinners and the Saturday night bath. Thus in his glossary of 1848 he listed *darsn't* as a Yankeeism, but in his dissertation of 1867 he showed that *darst* is to be found in Chaucer.[1] Again, he listed *shet* (*shut*), and then found it in Arthur Golding (*c.* 1556–*c.* 1605). Yet again, he listed *ben* (*been*), and found it in "Gammer Gurton's Needle." In the first series of "The Biglow Papers" Lowell lay down seven rules for distinguishing the Yankee dialect, but Krapp has shown that only two of them, both relating to the pronunciation of *a*, had any validity.[2] Krapp also showed that of forty words distinguished as dialect in six stanzas of Lowell's "The Courtin'," only six were really local to New England.[3] A later commentator, Miss Marie Killheffer,[4] has exposed the same deficiencies in one later and three earlier attempts to put the Yankee dialect into print. In "The Yankey in England," published in 1815, David Humphrey used a higher percentage of genuine Yankeeisms than Lowell or than any of the other three dramatists,[5] but in a glossary that he appended to the play, intended for the illumination of English audiences, he also included a great many terms that he himself described as "low words in general," *e.g.*, *agin* for *again*, *crittur* for

---

[1] It is actually traced by the DAE to *c.* 1175.
[2] The English Language in America; New York, 1925, Vol. I, pp. 232–33.
[3] p. 235.
[4] A Comparison of the Dialect of The Biglow Papers With the Dialect of Four Yankee Plays, *American Speech*, Feb., 1928, pp. 222–236.
[5] They were Tyler, whose The Contrast was first played in 1787; Joseph S. Jones, whose The People's Lawyer, or Solon Shingle appeared in 1839, and Denman Thompson, whose The Old Homestead was first presented in 1886 and continued to be the starring vehicle of the author until his death in 1911.

114   *The American Language: Supplement II*

creature, and *gal* for *girl*. In one soliloquy of 151 words Miss Killheffer finds 32 distinguished as dialectal, and of them only twelve are really peculiar to the Yankee.

Charles Astor Bristed, a dilettante grandson of the original John Jacob Astor, did an essay on "The English Language in America" for a volume of "Cambridge Essays, Contributed by Members of the University," published in London in 1855,[1] in which he warned the English that Haliburton's Yankee clock-maker in "Sam Slick" interspersed a good many Westernisms and much general slang with his Yankeeisms.[2] He said that the chief peculiarities of New England speech lay in pronunciation rather than in accidence or vocabulary, and went on: [3]

> Among its features of this sort may be mentioned a nasal intonation, particularly before the diphthong *ow*, so that *cow* and *now* are sounded *kyow* and *nyow*; a perverse misplacing of final *g* after *n*, almost equal to the Cockney's transposition of initial *h*, making *walkin* of *walking*, and *captin* of *captain*; a shortening of long *o* and *u* in final syllables; *e.g.*, *fortun* and *natur* for *fortune* and *nature*; on the other hand, a lengthening of various short syllables, as *naughtin* for *nothing*, and *genuíne* for *genuine*. Also, a general tendency to throw forward [4] the accent of polysyllables and sometimes even of dissyllables; *e.g.*, *territóry*, *legislátive*, *conquést*. This tendency, from which, by the way, the very best classes of New England society are not altogether free, has been noticed as a Scotticism, erroneously, we think, for though the Scotch sometimes misplace the accent, they throw it backward as often as forward, in *mágazine*, for instance. Some peculiar words, however, are found, as *doing chores*, for doing miscellaneous jobs of work, (a North Country word, *cf. char-woman*), and many peculiar uses of ordinary words.[5]

1 AL4, pp. 69–71.
2 Haliburton was a Nova Scotian, and it was the fashion at the time to denounce him for libelling the Yankee. But *Harper's Magazine* said of him in April, 1852, p. 705, col. 2: "It is a little singular, but it is true, that scarcely any native writer has succeeded better in giving what is termed the true Yankee dialect than a foreigner, an Englishman, Judge Haliburton, of Nova Scotia." This was six years after The Biglow Papers began to appear.
3 pp. 66 and 67.
4 It would be more natural today to say *backward* here, and to use *forward* where Bristed later uses *backward*.
5 All the more important discussions of New England speech down to 1922 are listed in Kennedy, pp. 413–16. Among those of interest that have appeared since are New England Dialect, by Windsor P. Daggett, *Billboard*, March 3, 1923; Yankee Twang — New England Dialect, by Gertrude McQuesten, *Emerson Quarterly*, March, 1925; The Real Dialect of Northern New England, by George A. England, *Writer's Monthly*, March, 1926; New England Provincialisms, 1818, by P. G. Perrin, *Dialect Notes*, Vol. X, Part IX, 1926, pp. 383–84; Die Volkssprache im Nordosten der Vereinigten Staaten von Amerika, by Johann Alfred Heil, *Giessner Beiträge zur Erforschung der Sprache und Kultur Englands und Nordamerikas*, Vol. III, 1927, pp. 205–311 (based on Lowell and other

Next to New England speech, the American dialect that has been most studied is that of the Southern mountains. According to Greet, it " comes down the Blue Ridge to southwestern Virginia, western North Carolina, eastern Kentucky. Thence it was carried to southern Indiana and southern Illinois, but there it has been overcome by the Middle Western variety.[1] It thrives in east Tennessee, west Tennessee and northern Alabama — in short, wherever the land is rocky, hilly and bad. Where the land is good, as in Middle Tennessee, in central and western Kentucky, in the neighborhood of Memphis, in the lowlands of Arkansas, Mississippi, Alabama, you find the plantation or general Southern type. The Southern Hill type was influenced and carried along by the Scotch Highlanders who came into the Shenandoah Valley from Pennsylvania and traveled on south and west." [2] Greet overlooks West Virginia, where it flourishes. It is encountered only sporadically in the mountains of Pennsylvania, but begins to appear in the western tip of Maryland, and then sweeps southward through the mountain coves

writers); The Language of the Salem Witchcraft Trials, by Henry Alexander, *American Speech*, June, 1928, pp. 390–400; Some New England Neologisms, by Julia W. Wolfe, *American Speech*, Dec., 1929, pp. 134–36; New England Words for the Seesaw, by Hans Kurath, *American Speech*, April, 1933, pp. 14–18; New England Words for Earthworm, by Rachel S. Harris, *American Speech*, Dec., 1933, pp. 12–17; New England Terms for Poached Eggs, by Herbert Penzl, *American Speech*, April, 1934, pp. 90–95 (the last three are based on the Linguistic Atlas of New England); Two New England Lists of 1848, by Allen Walker Read, *Dialect Notes*, Vol. VI, Part X, July, 1935, pp. 452–54; Dialect Mongers in New England, by Clarence M. Webster, *Yankee*, Sept., 1936, pp. 7–10; That Famous Harvard English is O.K., by Sebastian Smith, Boston *Post*, Dec. 27, 1936; Postvocalic *r* in New England Speech, by Bernard Bloch, *Acts of the Fourth International Congress of Linguists*, Copenhagen, 1936, pp. 195–99; Relics With Broad *a* in New England Speech, by Herbert Penzl, *American Speech*, Feb., 1938, pp. 45–49; The Yankee on the Stage, by R. M. Dorson, *New England Quarterly*, Sept., 1940, pp. 467–93; Early New England Words, by William Matthews, *American Speech*, Oct., 1940, pp. 225–31; The Stage Yankee, by Louis M. Eich, *Quarterly Journal of Speech*, Feb., 1941, pp. 16–25; New Englandisms of the Twenties, by George R. Potter, *American Notes & Queries*, April, 1943, p. 7; A New England Dialogue by B. J. Whiting, *American Speech*, Oct., 1944, pp. 227–28. Mr. Thomas S. Shaw, of Washington, calls my attention to a brief but interesting paper that Kennedy overlooked, to wit, Collection of Vulgarisms, or Yankeeisms, *American Magazine*, Sept., 1834, p. 416. Articles on the regional speech of the various New England States will be listed when we come to those States.

1 *i.e.*, by what I have called General American.
2 A Standard American Language?, *New Republic*, May 25, 1938, p. 68.

into Georgia and Alabama, with leaps into southern Illinois and the Ozarks of southwestern Missouri. The persons who speak it undiluted are often called, by Southern publicists, "the purest Anglo-Saxons in the United States," but this view of them seems to be disputed by less romantic ethnologists. Most of the latter describe them as predominantly Celtic in blood, though the fact is plain that there has been a large infiltration of English and even German strains. The dwellers in the more remote regions are thus dealt with by a distinguished English historian:

> The Appalachian has relapsed into illiteracy and into all the superstitions for which illiteracy opens the door. His agricultural calendar is governed by the phases of the moon; his personal life is darkened by fear, and by the practise of witchcraft. He lives in poverty and squalor and ill-health. In particular, he is a victim of hook-worm, a scourge which lowers the general level of vitality in Appalachia just as it does in India. . . . The Appalachian mountain people are the American counterparts of the latter-day white barbarians of the Old World: the Rifis and Kabyles and Tuareg, the Albanians and Caucasians, the Kurds and the Pathans and the Hairy Ainu . . . [They] are *ci-devant* heirs of the Western Civilization who have relapsed into barbarism under the depressing effects of a challenge which has been inordinately severe. . . . They may be traced back to a ruthless tradition of frontier warfare along the border between Western Civilization and "the Celtic Fringe" which . . . has been revived among these Scotch-Irish settlers in North America by the barbarizing severity of their Appalachian environment. . . . [Their] nearest social analogues . . . are certain "fossils" of extinct civilizations which have survived in fastnesses and have likewise relapsed into barbarism there: such "fossils" as the Jewish "wild highlanders" of Abyssinia and the Caucasus, or the Nestorian "wild highlanders" of Hakkiari.[1]

To this may be added the testimony of a Scots kinsman regarding those who have been lured into the mill-towns of the Piedmont and so converted from *hill-billies* into *lint-heads:*

> One cannot but sympathize with these poor relations of ours — Celts, most of them —, though their own bigoted ignorance and arrogant unprogressiveness have been the main causes of their misfortunes. They may realize by this time that it would have been better for them to educate themselves, co-operate in the improvement of their farms, and make common cause with the Negroes. Economic servitude and the dismal life of factory towns are the doom of a people who will not bring brain and purpose to bear upon their own rural polity.[2]

[1] A Study of History, by Arnold J. Toynbee; second edition; London, 1935, Vol. II, pp. 311–12. See also Vol. I, pp. 466–67.
[2] Poor Relations in America, by Looker-on, Glasgow *News*, Sept. 17, 1934. For the immigration of the Scotch-Irish see The Scotch-Irish in Colonial Pennsylvania, by Wayland F. Dunaway; Chapel Hill (N.C.), 1944.

It would be ridiculous to say that all the Appalachian mountaineers are on this low level, or to assume that their stock is wholly decayed. They produce, at somewhat longish intervals, individuals of marked ability — whether by chance adulteries or by some fortunate collocation and effervescence of Mendelian characters is not certain.[1] But such individuals usually escape from their native alps at the first chance, so that their genes do not improve the remaining population, which continues to go downhill, with excessive inbreeding to help it along. The speech of these poor folk, who have been called " our contemporary ancestors," is ignorant but very far from unpleasant, as I can testify who have heard it used to preach the Word in the mountains of eastern Tennessee.[2] It was first described with any approach to scientific precision by Calvin S. Brown, Jr., in two papers published in 1889 and 1891,[3] but during the years thereafter various other linguists began to study it at length, notably Josiah H. Combs. Combs's first report on it, published in *Dialect Notes* in 1916,[4] was so good a conspectus of the subject that there has been little for later inquirers to do save run down the leads he furnished. He not only described the dialect at length in its most typical form; he also noted its local variations,[5] and did not overlook the grotesque effects sometimes produced when a native rhetorician, say a Primitive Baptist preacher, attempts to " place it up on stilts." On two points subsequent research has questioned his first conclusions: it seems probable that the Celtic element in the mountain population, including Welsh as well as Scotch-Irish fractions,

---

1 See The Many-Sired Lincoln, by J. G. deRoulhac Hamilton, *American Mercury*, June, 1935, pp. 129-35. Lincoln was not a hillman, but the stock from which he issued was almost as deteriorated as that of the high Appalachians.

2 See The Hills of Zion in my Prejudices; Fifth Series; New York, 1926, pp. 75-86.

3 Dialectal Survivals in Tennessee, *Modern Language Notes*, 1889, pp. 409-16, and Other Dialectal Forms in Tennessee, *Publications of the Modern Language Association*, 1891, pp. 171-5.

4 Old, Early and Elizabethan English in the Southern Mountains, Vol. IV, Part IV, 1916, pp. 283-97.

5 "The dialect," says Horace Kephart in Our Southern Highlanders; New York, 1921, p. 279, " varies a good deal from place to place, and even in the same neighborhood we rarely hear all families speaking it alike. Outlanders who essay to write it are prone to err by making their characters talk it too consistently. It is only in the backwoods or among old people or the penned-at-home women that it is used with any integrity." See also Variation in the Southern Mountain Dialect, by Charles Carpenter, *American Speech*, Feb., 1928, pp. 22-25.

is larger than he was disposed to grant,[1] and there is a rising doubt that the linguistic fossils he discovered in large number are really inherited directly from Elizabethan England, as the title of his paper indicated. Many of them flourished along the Scotch-English border so late as the Eighteenth Century, and not a few survive there to this day, as a glance through Alexander Warrack's "Scots Dialect Dictionary"[2] is enough to show.[3] But this, after all, is an irrelevance, for Combs made it plain that the archaisms that appear in all American speech[4] are appreciably more numerous, whatever their immediate provenance, in the mountain dialect than in General American. He returned to the subject at various times after 1916,[5] and in 1931 summed up his observations in a paper contributed to *Publications of the Modern Language Association*.[6] In this paper he included an account of Appalachian place-names and given-names and a discussion of the mountain phonology. The latter was dealt with at greater length in 1942 by Joseph Sargent Hall,[7] who gathered his materials

---

[1] Combs, however, sticks to his guns, and may be right. He wrote to me under date of February 7, 1944: "In all the highlands except West Virginia I have not found a single ballad which savors of the Scotch dialect. I once collected at random about 200 family names and went over them with Dr. MacKenzie of Edinburgh University; we decided that less than 15% of them were of Scottish origin. Scotch Presbyterian missionaries come evangelizing into the South the past hundred years have given undue importance to the Scottish element in the highlands."

[2] London, 1911.

[3] Some examples cited by Combs: *afeared, steepy, tonguey, to argufy*.

[4] AL4, pp. 124–29; Supplement I, pp. 224–26.

[5] For example, in Dialect of the Folk Song, *Dialect Notes*, Vol. IV, Part V, 1916, pp. 311–18; Early English Slang Survivals in the Mountains of Kentucky, *Dialect Notes*, Vol. V, Part IV, 1921, pp. 115–17; Kentucky Items, *Dialect Notes*, Vol. V, Part IV, 1921, pp. 118–19; A Word-List From Georgia, *Dialect Notes*, Vol. V, Part V, 1922, pp. 183–84; Addenda From Kentucky, *Dialect Notes*, Vol. V, Part VI, 1923, pp. 242–43; A Word-List From the Southern Highlands, *Publication of the American Dialect Society No. 2*, Nov., 1944, pp. 17–23. At the annual meeting of the American Dialect Society in New York, Dec. 28, 1944, he entertained the members with a translation of Lincoln's Gettysburg Address into the vernacular of the Kentucky mountaineers. He has under way a book to be called The Language of Our Southern Highlanders. A commentary on his paper on Old, Early and Elizabethan English in the Southern Mountains, by H. M. Steadman, Jr., was published in *Dialect Notes*, Vol. IV, Part V, 1916, pp. 350–52.

[6] Language of the Southern Highlanders, Dec., 1931, pp. 1302–22.

[7] The Phonetics of the Great Smoky Mountain Speech, *American Speech Reprints and Monographs, No. 4*. Hall is also the author of Mountain Speech in the Great Smokies, No. 5 in a series of pamphlets entitled National Park Service Popular Study Series, issued by the National Park Service, Department of the Interior; Washington, 1941. In The Phonetics of the Great Smoky

in two counties of western North Carolina and three of eastern Tennessee. Unfortunately, his methodology has been sharply criticized by a competent authority.[1] Other investigators, not named above, who have contributed to our knowledge of this Appalachian speech are listed below.[2]

Vance Randolph, who has written so much and so well about the Ozarks since 1926 that he has converted them into his private preserve, says that the dialect of the region is " derived doubtless from the dialect of the Southern Appalachians,"[3] but that it has been reinforced in the remoter areas by words and phrases apparently of indigenous origin. Some of these, he says, are hardly more than gibberish, and he offers the theory that they are either engendered by the howling " in the tongues "[4] at mountain revivals or come from the jabber of imbeciles. " The people in these isolated hill-regions," he says, " intermarry excessively, and feeble-mindedness is very common; it is not unusual to find whole families and clans

---

Mountain Speech there is a bibliography, pp. 107-10.

[1] Raven I. McDavid, Jr., in *Language*, April-June, 1943, pp. 184-95.

[2] A Word List From Barbourville, Ky., by Abigail E. Weeks, *Dialect Notes*, Vol. III, Part VI, 1910, pp. 456-57; An Eastern Kentucky Word-List, by Hubert G. Shearin, *Dialect Notes*, Vol. III, Part VII, 1911, pp. 537-40; A Word-List From the Mountains of Western North Carolina, by Horace Kephart, *Dialect Notes*, Vol. IV, Part VI, 1917, pp. 407-19; Appalachian Mountain Words, by L. R. Dingus, *Dialect Notes*, Vol. V, Part X, 1927, pp. 468-71; American Speech as Practised in the Southern Highlands, by Maristan Chapman, *Century Magazine*, March, 1929, pp. 617-23; Elizabethan America, by Charles M. Wilson, *Atlantic Monthly*, Aug., 1929; Beefsteak When I'm Hungry, by C. M. Wilson, *Virginia Quarterly Review*, April, 1930, pp. 240-50; How the Wood Hick Speaks: Some Observations Made in Upshur County, W. Va., by Paul E. Pendleton, *Dialect Notes*, Vol. VI, Part II, 1930, pp. 86-89; Folk Speech in the Kentucky Mountain Cycle of Percy Mackaye, by B. A. Botkin, *American Speech*, April, 1931, pp. 264-76; Folk Speech of the Cumberlands, by Bess Alice Owens, *American Speech*, Dec., 1931, pp. 89-95; Variations in the Southern Mountain Dialect, by Charles Carpenter, *American Speech*, Feb., 1933, p. 22; Southern Mountain Accent, by C. G., *American Speech*, Dec., 1934, p. 251; Remnants of Archaic English in West Virginia, by Charles Carpenter, *West Virginia Review*, Dec., 1934, pp. 77-95; The Language of the Tennessee Mountain Regions, by T. J. Farr, *American Speech*, April, 1939, pp. 89-92; How to Say It In Smoky Speech, *Better English*, Jan., 1940, pp. 50-52; Southern Mountain Dialect, by Lester V. Berrey, *American Speech*, Feb., 1940, pp. 45-54 (includes a bibliography); More Tennessee Expressions, by T. J. Farr, *American Speech*, Dec., 1940, pp. 446-48; The Georgia Mountaineer's Vanishing Vocabulary, by Byron Herbert Reece, Atlanta *Journal Magazine*, March 3, 1946, pp. 8 and 9. (I am indebted for this last to Mr. John E. Ransom, of Atlanta.)

[3] Is There an Ozark Dialect?, *American Speech*, Feb., 1929, pp. 203-04.

[4] Mark XVI, 17.

of people who, while perfectly able to take care of themselves in their native hills, are easily recognized as definitely sub-normal if placed in a more complex environment. . . . It very frequently happens that such individuals . . . have a singular ability to coin impressive words at a moment's notice, or to pronounce words in some grotesque and ludicrous fashion." [1] " The chief differences between the Ozark dialect and the standard vulgate of the United States," he says in another place, " are matters of pronunciation and vocabulary rather than of grammar." [2] Most of his examples of pronunciation, however, show that of ordinary ignorant American English, e.g., *skeerce* for *scarce*, *bar'l* for *barrel*, *ketch* for *catch*, *extry* for *extra*, *yaller* for *yellow*, *laig* for *leg*, *deef* for *deaf*, *kittle* for *kettle*, *potater* for *potato*, *bresh* for *brush*, *sassy* for *saucy*, *neckid* for *naked*, *hist* for *hoist*, *onct* for *once*, *rench* for *rinse*, *dreen* for *drain*, and *brethern* for *brethren*, and nearly all the rest are encountered in Appalachia, e.g., *hit* for *it*, *malary* for *malaria*, *yander* for *yonder*, *goom* for *gum*, *vomick* for *vomit*, and *heathern* for *heathen*.[3] In the vocabulary he notes some curious changes in meaning:

> A *stew* is not a dish of meat and vegetables in the Ozarks, but a drink made of ginger, hot water and corn-whiskey. . . . *Ashamed*, when used with reference to a child or a young girl, does not mean ashamed at all, but merely timid or bashful. *Gum* means . . . a rabbit-trap — when the hillman wants chewing-gum he calls for *wax*. . . . When he says *several* he doesn't mean two or three or four, but a large number. . . . *Judge* or *jedge* is used to mean a fool or clown, and there is even an adjective, *jedgy*. *Enjoy* is used in the sense of entertain. *Lavish* is used as a noun, meaning a large quantity. . . . *Portly*, as applied to a man, means handsome. . . . *Out* is used as a verb meaning to defraud. . . . *Fine-haired* means aristocratic.[4]

Among the other more or less picturesque Ozark terms listed by Randolph are the following:

Arbuckle. A carbuncle.[5]
Arkansaw, v. To murder in what is regarded locally as an unfair way.

Boggy. Delirious.
Chaunk, v. To crush with the teeth.
Crimp, v. To writhe in pain.

[1] A Possible Source of Some Ozark Neologisms, *American Speech*, Dec., 1928, pp. 116-17.
[2] The Grammar of the Ozark Dialect, *American Speech*, Oct., 1927, pp. 1-11.
[3] Pronunciation in the Ozarks (with Anna A. Ingleman), *American Speech*, June, 1928, pp. 401-07.
[4] The Ozarks: an American Survival of Primitive Society; New York, 1931, pp. 70-71. Of these terms Wentworth finds *ashamed* in Pennsylvania, Louisiana and Kansas, *gum* in southeastern Virginia and *wax* in western Texas, but the rest seem to be either borrowed from Appalachia or peculiar to the Ozarks.
[5] Possibly by assimilation with the name of a popular brand of coffee.

Cripple, *v.* To limp.
Ducy. The penis.[1]
Fastly. Firmly, persistently.
Feather into, *v.* To shoot.[2]
Givey. Unsteady.
Hate, *v.* To be sorry.
Hoe. A stocking.[3]
Host, *v.* To entertain guests.[4]
Human rifle. A rifle of large calibre, suitable for homicide.
Love-hole. A ditch across a road.
Miller, *v.* To beat.
Nursement. Human milk.

Paw-pawer. A fugitive from justice.
Poot. An exclamation of disgust.
Saying. A speech.
Scoffle, *v.* To ridicule.
Shoot. An adolescent.
Snag. A tall tree-stump.
Squirrel-turner. A marksman.
Susy. Countrified.
Swoggle, *v.* To dip or stir.
Tutor, *v.* To pamper or indulge.
Wash-off. A bath.
Weather, *v.* To storm.[5]

Randolph's account of the extreme prudishness of the Ozarkers has been noticed in Supplement I, pp. 654–55. Many common words, *e.g., bull, buck, bitch, virgin, bed, leg, bag* and even *love*, are taboo among them,[6] but on the other hand they are free in the use of terms, *e.g., to snot* and *to give tittie*, that are frowned upon elsewhere.[7]

1 Mostly used, says Randolph, by old women.
2 Possibly a reminiscence of an old archery term.
3 A false singular for *hose*.
4 This appeared in the vocabulary of *Variety, c,* 1935.
5 A Word-List From the Ozarks, *Dialect Notes,* Vol. V, Part IX, 1926, pp. 397–405; More Words From the Ozarks, *Dialect Notes,* Vol. V, Part X, 1927, pp. 472–79.
6 Such terms are discussed at some length in AL4, pp. 300–11, and Supplement I, pp. 639–61. Beside those regarded as indecent many are frowned upon for other reasons, especially in the South. In Dialect Geography and Social Science Problems, *Social Forces,* Dec., 1946, p. 172, Raven I. McDavid, Jr., calls attention to the fact that Henry Wallace's *century of the common man* was regarded askance south of the Potomac because *common* is there "a term of contempt."
7 Verbal Modesty in the Ozarks, *Dialect Notes,* Vol. VI, Part I, 1928, pp. 57–64. This paper is reprinted in Randolph's The Ozarks; New York, 1931, pp. 78–96. His other writings include: The Ozark Dialect in Fiction, *American Speech,* March, 1927, pp. 283–89; Literary Words in the Ozarks, *American Speech,* Oct., 1928, pp. 56–57; A Third Ozark Word-List, *American Speech,* Oct., 1929, pp. 16–21; Dialectal Survivals in the Ozarks (with Patti Sankee), *American Speech,* Feb., 1930, pp. 198–208; April, pp. 264–69, and June, pp. 424–30; Recent Fiction and the Ozark Dialect, *American Speech,* Aug., 1931, pp. 425–28; Quilt Names in the Ozarks (with Isabel Spradley), *American Speech,* Feb., 1933, pp. 33–36; A Fourth Ozark Word-List, *American Speech,* Feb., 1933, pp. 47–53; A Fifth Ozark Word-List (with Nancy Clements), *American Speech,* Dec., 1936, pp. 314–18. Among the papers by other hands that contain useful information are: A List of Words From Northwest Arkansas, by Joseph W. Carr, *Dialect Notes,* Vol. II, Part VI, 1904, pp. 416–22; Vol. III, Part I, 1905, pp. 205–38; Vol. III, Part II, 1906, pp. 125–65; Vol. III, Part III, 1907, pp. 68–103, and Vol. III, Part V, 1909, pp. 392–406; Snake County Talk, by Jay L. B. Taylor, *Dialect Notes,* Vol. V. Part VI, 1923, pp. 197–225; On the Ozark Pronunciation of *It,* by Vernon C. Allison,

The division of Southern American into Appalachian, Tidewater and Lowland or General Southern has been noted earlier in this section. Tidewater, which is the most extreme form of the dialect, covers a relatively small area:[1] the majority of Southerners speak General Southern. But General Southern is a variable quantity, and more than one observer has noted the great range between the careful speech of an educated and self-conscious inhabitant of, say, Atlanta, Richmond or New Orleans and the casual talk of a Georgia cracker or Mississippi Negro. The former tends to approximate General American, though in dealing with *r* before consonants and at the ends of words it follows Boston speech in making the letter silent. Its vowels, according to a Louisiana authority, C. M. Wise,[2] are substantially those of General American, including the flat *a* in *pass, dance, can't,* etc. It inserts a *y*-glide before *u* after *t, n* and *d,* but not after *s, z* and *l,* e.g., *tyune, nyew* and *dyew,* but not *presyume* or *absolyutely*.[3] But this elegant Southern is a narrow class dialect, and is seldom encountered in its purest form. More commonly it is colored, even on the highest levels, by usages borrowed from below. These include the conversion of the flat *a* into something resembling *e,* as in *keint* for *can't;* the omission of the final *r* in *poor, floor* and *your,* and sometimes of the medial *r,* as in *throw* and *through;* the change of the diphthong in *cow* into a mixture of the flat *a* and *y* and of that in *I* into something resembling *ah;* the omission of the *l* from *twelve, self, help,* etc.; the voicing of the *s,*

American Speech, Feb., 1929, pp. 205–06; Ozark Words Again, by Napier Wilt, *American Speech,* Oct., 1937, pp. 234–35.

[1] Greet says in A Standard American Language?, *New Republic,* May 25, 1938, p. 68: "It runs up the coast from Savannah, flourishes at Charleston, weakens in North Carolina, blooms again in the Petersburg and Richmond (Williamsburg) district [of Virginia]. Families like the Byrds carried it to Winchester in the Shenandoah Valley. It crosses the Chesapeake to the Eastern Shore of Virginia and Maryland, and in certain old families has a hold on Delaware."

[2] Southern American Dialect, *American Speech,* April, 1933, pp. 37–43. Wise gathered his materials in Louisiana, Mississippi, Texas, Arkansas, Tennessee, Kentucky, Alabama, Florida, Georgia, Virginia and the Carolinas.

[3] This glide, of course, also appears before other vowels, e.g., *a,* as in *cyar* and *cyarry*. But only when *r* follows, silent or not: *Cyabell* is unknown. See an editorial, Ah Declah, Doctuh!, in the Richmond *Times-Dispatch,* Dec. 26, 1946, correcting some errors in a paper by Argus Tressider, a Northerner, published in the *Madison Quarterly*. I am indebted here to Mr. James M. Bowcock, of Richmond.

as in *greasy* and *blouse;* the use of *you-all;*[1] the dropping of *g* from the *-ing* words, and the omission of *t* from *next, best, soft,* etc., and of *d* from *land,* etc. Says Wise:

> Diphthongization, triphthongization and even what might be called double diphthongization are regular characteristics of what has been referred to as "typical" Southern speech. Collectively and popularly, these phenomena are called the Southern drawl. Tyros in the talking pictures and elsewhere who think this Southern drawl is nothing more than slow, attenuated speech produce most inaccurate and laughable results. Duration is probably the basis of the drawl, but it is by no means its end-result.[2]

Another Southern observer, this time of Texas,[3] agrees with Wise that the intrusion into cultivated speech of elements borrowed from the folk-speech is more frequent in the South than elsewhere: she might have added that these borrowings are not all phonological, but also include many examples of "bad" grammar, *e.g.,* the use of *don't* in the third person singular. She says:

> Family usage is an important factor in Southern speech. Children whose parents speak a rustic dialect are likely to preserve certain features of their rustic pronunciation even when they are well educated. It is only natural that an observer from another part of the country should feel justified in designating as cultivated Southern pronunciation certain features of the speech of educated Southerners whose speech habits have been acquired in rural communities or from more or less illiterate parents. . . . Nevertheless, the cultivated Southerner is quick to recognize and condemn the rustic features that appear even in the speech of the educated.[4]

But this, obviously, is a begging of the question. The Southerner from the great speech-belt which sweeps southward and westward from the Virginia Piedmont through all the late Confederate States, with branches projecting into Kentucky, Tennessee, Missouri and Oklahoma, and even into Southern Ohio, Indiana and Illinois, uses habitually a dialect that marks him off instantly, and is not concealed by education. Indeed, Miss Wheatley herself admits that a Southern university professor "may and often does" show speechways that he himself, as a cultivated man, "considers rural and vulgar." In the Tidewater region of Virginia and South Carolina, where the most elegant of all Southerners live and have their being, little effort

---

[1] *You-all* will be discussed in Chapter IX, Section 3.
[2] pp. 41–42.
[3] Southern Standards, by Katherine E. Wheatley, *American Speech,* Feb., 1934, pp. 36–45. Miss Wheatley gathered her materials in Louisiana and southeastern Texas.
[4] pp. 37–38.

seems to be made to conceal a way of speaking that sounds to many Northerners (as they say in their benighted fashion) somewhat niggerish. A Tidewater Virginian, when he escapes to the wilds of the damyankee, may throw off his native speechways more or less, but at home he clings to them, and Greet tells of a member of the distinguished Carter family who was forced to make its name *Cyahtuh* whenever he returned to visit an intransigent old aunt.[1]

Southern American has been neglected by Northern philologians, but some of the Southern brethren have made and published excellent studies of it, notably Cleanth Brooks, Jr.,[2] Raven I. McDavid, Jr.,[3] George P. Wilson,[4] H. P. Johnson,[5] James B. McMillan,[6] Atcheson L. Hench,[7] N. M. Caffee,[8] James T. Barrs,[9] the aforesaid Greet, Combs and Wise, and, above all, William A. Read.[10] Southern speech has suffered cruelly on the stage and in talkies, where kittenish

1 Southern Speech, before cited, p. 610. The late W. J. Cash, a very acute lay observer, noted in This is How We Talk: Babel in the South, Charlotte (N.C.), *News*, Dec. 12, 1937, a tendency among educated Southerners to drop, on informal and especially jovial occasions, into what he called *cornfield nigger*.

2 The Relation of the Alabama-Georgia Dialect to the Provincial Dialects of Great Britain, *Louisiana State University Studies, No. XX*; Baton Rouge, 1935; The English Language in the South, in A Vanderbilt Miscellany; Nashville, 1944, pp. 179–87.

3 The Unstressed Syllabic Phonemes of a Southern Dialect, *Studies in Linguistics*, Summer, 1944, pp. 51–55. The dialect investigated is that of the author himself, a native of Greenville, S. C., in the Piedmont. In 1941 McDavid read a paper on The Stressed Vowel Phonemes of a Southern Dialect before the annual meeting of the Linguistic Society of America at Durham, N. C.

4 Secretary-treasurer of the American Dialect Society and chairman of its committee on regional speech and localisms. In the society's *Publication No. 2*, Nov., 1944, he began a series of word-lists from the South to which he contributed one from Virginia and North Carolina. The other contributors were Leah A. Dennis, Josiah Combs, Hugh C. Laughlin, Cratis D. Williams, Francis C. Hayes, Constance Bey and L. R. Dingus. Wilson is the author of Some Unrecorded Southern Vowels, *American Speech*, Oct., 1945, pp. 209–13.

5 Who Lost the Southern R?, *American Speech*, June, 1928, pp. 377–83.

6 Vowel Nasality as a Sandhi-Form of the Morphemes *-nt* and *-ing* in Southern American, *American Speech*, April, 1939, pp. 120–23.

7 The Survival of *Start-naked* in the South, in Humanistic Studies in Honor of John Calvin Metcalf, *University of Virginia Studies No. I*, 1941, pp. 48–64. Hench is the author of other interesting studies of Southern speech, and I am indebted to him for friendly aid with the present book.

8 Southern *L* Plus a Consonant, *American Speech*, Oct., 1940, pp. 259–61.

9 Some Remarks on Southern Dialect, a paper read before the English Lunch Club at Harvard, Feb. 12, 1944. From March 19 to July 23, 1942, Barrs contributed weekly articles on South Georgia speech to the Douglas (Ga.) *Enterprise*.

10 The Vowel System of the Southern United States, *Englische Studien*, Vol. XLI, 1910; Some Variant Pro

actresses from the domain of General American think that they have imitated it sufficiently when they have thrown in a few *you-alls* and *honey-chiles* and converted every *I* into a long *ah*. Such outrages have brought forth some sharp protests from Southern philologians, and are frequently belabored in the Southern newspapers. In 1944 Walling Keith, editor of the Gadsden (Ala.) *Times*, was moved to organize a Society for the Prevention of Cruelty to Southern Accents, with the Hon. Cordell Hull as its president, and Governors Chauncey Sparks of Alabama and Ellis Arnall of Georgia among its trustees. Keith was especially incensed by the use of *you-all* in the singular by "goofy-eyed fake Southern belles," but he also laid about him on other counts, and got promises of help from many other Southern editors.[1] The exact phonetic nature of the Southern long *i* has been discussed by various sub-Potomac philologians, for example, Medford Evans, of the University of Chattanooga.[2] Evans points out that, in standard English, this phoneme is not a simple vowel, but a diphthong made up of the vowels *a* and *i* (*ah* and *ee*). In Southern speech, however, the latter half of the sound is dropped off, leaving a remnant that sounds to Northerners like *ah*. But it is not precisely *ah* to Southern ears: it is produced nearer the front of the mouth than the true Southern *ah*. Evans says that it appears only at the ends of syllables or before voiced consonants, and in this he is supported by other observers.[3] Thus the Southerner's first person *I* sounds *ah* to a Northerner, and the same vowel occurs in *my*, *ride*, *time*, *fine*, *alive*, *try* and *high*. But in *night*, *hike*, *ice*, *life* and *type* he uses the diphthong that is used by all the other speakers of English.

General American, though it is, technically speaking, as much a dialect as any other form of American speech, is less studied than the rest, no doubt because its immense and growing extension makes it seem obvious and commonplace. As I have noted, some materials

---

nunciations in the New South, *Dialect Notes*, Vol. III, Part VII, 1911, pp. 497–536.

1 For example, from his colleague of the Fort Smith (Ark.) *Times-Record* in a powerful editorial entitled That "Southern" Accent, Oct. 21, 1944.

2 Southern Long *i*, *American Speech*, Oct., 1935, pp. 188–90.

3 For example, by William B. Edgerton in Another Note on the Southern Pronunciation of Long *i*, *American Speech*, Oct., 1935, p. 190. But Edgerton denies that the Southern long *i* is a simple vowel. "There is," he says, "a scarcely perceptible glide toward *i*" [*ee*].

have been gathered looking to a Linguistic Atlas of it, but that atlas will probably not be completed for a good many years. In the early days its larval form, then called Western speech, attracted the attention of the contemporary philologians, for that form was the source of nearly all the current neologisms, many of them of an extraordinary pungency.[1] Webster and Pickering were too early to record more than a few of them, for the great movement into the West, with its vast proliferation of new words and phrases, did not begin in earnest until after the War of 1812, but by the time John Russell Bartlett put together his Glossary in 1848 many of them had come into notice in the East, and he listed a large number. The West was wild and woolly until the Civil War and for twenty years afterward, but in the middle 80s it began to succumb to the schoolma'am and the evangelist, and today it shares with the South the custody of what remains of Puritanism and is quite decorous in its speech. Nearly all the verbal novelties since 1900, in fact, have been generated in the East,[2] and the once-familiar term, *Westernism*, has ceased to have any significance.[3] Even in its palmy days the West introduced few novelties in pronunciation: its contributions were nearly all to the vocabulary. The two waves of pioneers, from the North and the South, met on its wide reaches and the reaction between their speechways produced what is now General American. The misfits lingered in Appalachia or took refuge in the Ozarks, and there hung on to the archaic patois that we have been lately examining. The Pike county dialect of the Mississippi Valley was only a transient phenomenon: it long ago disappeared from all save a few remote backwaters.

The speech of the Western cattlemen, once romantic nomads but now mere drovers,[4] is said by Greet to show a predominantly Southern sub-stratum.[5] "Its eastern boundary in the South," he says, "runs from Laredo to San Antonio, to Forth Worth, to Little Rock or close by. It extends west to the Pecos river and the Sacramento

---

1 See Supplement I, pp. 227-35. Also, see West, speech of, in the Index thereof.
2 See Supplement I, pp. 228 and 330.
3 The DAE traces it to the *Knickerbocker Magazine* for 1838, but it is probably older. The DAE's last example of its use is from *Harper's Magazine* for Oct., 1886. By that time the Old West was fast vanishing, and Chicago, in Eugene Field's phrase, was preparing "to make culture hum."
4 See Toynbee, before cited, Vol. III, p. 21, n. 1.
5 A Standard American Language?, *New Republic*, May 25, 1938, p. 68.

Mountains, jumping the Rio Grande Valley, where the influence is strong of New Mexican Spanish (fanning up into southern Colorado). It picks up again in Arizona, and extends north with the cattle industry, skipping the agricultural lands, into the Canadian provinces. The mining communities of the region share the cattlemen's speech." But this speech remains a good deal less regional than occupational, and in any case most of its terms have been made so familiar by the movies and by pulp fiction that it hardly strikes the average American as peculiar. In 1913, when Bartle T. Harvey, of the United States Bureau of Ethnology, undertook the first vocabulary of it,[1] he listed many words and phrases that are known to every schoolboy, *e.g., fall guy, bear* (a general term of approval: *It's a bear*), *to get in bad, to hit the hay, locoed, makings* (of a cigarette) and *to mooch*. A year later, adding to his list, he had little to offer save more of the same sort, *e.g., to buffalo, bull* (idle talk), *coffin-nail* (cigarette), *to goose, to be nuts over, to punch* (cattle) and *twister* (cyclone).[2] All the later contributors to the subject offered only more and more evidence that the speech of the old Wild West was being rapidly assimilated to General American.[3] The same may be said of the speech of the Southwest. It is, even today, much more heavily laden with Spanish loans than General American, but a great many such loans have been taken into the latter,[4] and meanwhile the Southwest seems to be gradually abandoning those that remain, so that New Mexican American promises, on some near tomorrow, to become indistinguishable from the American of the Middle West, as the American of New Orleans, once full of French loans, has become almost indistinguishable from

---

1 A Word-List From the Northwest, *Dialect Notes*, Vol. IV, Part I, pp. 26–28.
2 Addenda to the Word-List from the Northwest, *Dialect Notes*, Vol. IV, Part II, 1914, pp. 162–64.
3 For example, Benjamin H. Lehman, in A Word List From Northwestern United States, *Dialect Notes*, 1918, pp. 22–29. One of Lehman's entries was *blue-liz*, signifying a police patrol-wagon. I suggest that this may have suggested *tin-lizzie* for the Model T Ford, which appeared on Oct. 1, 1908, but did not reach a production of 1,000,000 until Dec. 10, 1915. See also A Word List From the Northwest, by R. M. Garrett, *Dialect Notes*, Vol. V, Part II, 1919, pp. 54–59, and Part III, 1920, pp. 80–84; Additional Words From the Northwest, by B. H. Lehman, *Dialect Notes*, Vol. V, Part V, 1922, p. 181; Westernisms, by Kate Mullen, *American Speech*, Dec., 1925, pp. 149–53; The Speech of the Frontier, by E. E. Dale, *Quarterly Journal of Speech*, Oct., 1941, pp. 353–63; and Westernisms, by Levette J. Davidson, *American Speech*, Feb., 1942, pp. 71–73.
4 Supplement I, pp. 312–13.

that of the rest of the lowland South.[1] "Perhaps the Middle West language, whatever it is," said an intelligent newspaper commentator in 1937,[2] "will prevail because it is a composite. While it has its own sectionalisms, it has rejected to a large degree the radical departures of the older areas of the South and East. Its Tarkingtons, Lardners, Sandburgs and others have created a literature as purely American as any yet produced."

The sectionalisms here mentioned, of course, are to be found all over the United States, for despite the general uniformity of speech in large areas there are still many local peculiarities, some of them purely regional and the rest determined by occupational and racial factors. In the small State of Maryland, for example,[3] there are five quite distinct speech areas, and several sub-areas. In the two far western counties the prevailing speech is that of Appalachia. To the eastward, under the Mason and Dixon line, the influence of the Pennsylvania German area of Pennsylvania is plainly apparent. On the Eastern Shore, south of the Choptank river, the dialect shows the influence of Tidewater Virginia, with occasional suggestions of Appalachia. On the Western Shore, below Annapolis, it is predominantly General Southern. In Baltimore and vicinity and around the periphery of Washington it is General American, with a few touches of Southern. Moreover, there are innumerable gradations where these areas meet, so that it is often difficult to say of a strange Eastern Shoreman, for example, whether he comes from below the Choptank or above. The same differentiations are to be found in many other States, even, as has been noted, in such apparently homogeneous areas as New England and the Deep South. It is thus

[1] But see The English Language in the Southwest, by Thomas Matthews Pearce, *New Mexico Historical Review*, July, 1932, pp. 210-32. In this paper, which was read before the Academy of Sciences, Arts and Letters of Albuquerque on May 23, 1932, Pearce takes a contrary view. A bibliography of other writings on the subject is in Supplement I, p. 313, notes 2 and 3. An early discussion, Southwestern Slang, by Socrates Hyacinth, *Overland Monthly*, Aug., 1869, pp. 125-31, is reprinted in The Beginnings of American English, edited by M. M. Mathews; Chicago, 1931, pp. 151-63. See also Trader Terms in Southwestern English, by the aforesaid Pearce, *American Speech*, Oct., 1941, pp. 179-86; and Spanish Words That Have Become Westernisms, by Florence A. Chapin, *Editor*, July 25, 1917, p. 121.
[2] Editorial, Grand Rapids (Mich.) *Press*, Oct. 27.
[3] It has but 12,210 square miles of area, and 2319 of them are under water. Counting only dry land, Texas could hold 21.76413+ Marylands.

very misleading to sort out American speechways by States. But that, unhappily, is just what has been done by most local writers on the subject, and as a result their reports are often very far from illuminating, for they put down as local variants locutions that are actually common to large areas. Wentworth's "American Dialect Dictionary" offers massive evidence of this: he shows that words and phrases credited to this or that State are often to be found in other States a thousand miles away, *e.g.*, the pronunciation *yarb* for *herb* occurs both along the Maine coast and in the Ozarks, *ground-hog* for *Arctomys monax* is common to central Pennsylvania and northwestern Arkansas, *bucket* (for the New England *pail*) ranges from the Philadelphia area to Alabama and Kansas, and *heap* from Connecticut through the South to the Far West.[1] But we must take the available material as it comes, and in the following notes I have tried to list and summarize, for the use of local inquirers, such papers on it as I have encountered.[2]

Alabama

The most comprehensive studies of Alabama lowland speech are those of Cleanth Brooks, Jr., already noted in the discussion of Southern speech in general,[3] and James B. McMillan [4] but there are

---

[1] Mark Twain defined it, in Roughing It, 1872, as "Injun-English for very much."

[2] The question where the best American is spoken is often discussed in the newspapers. Noah Webster, after his tour of the country in 1785–86, is said to have nominated Baltimore. In 1928 a group of 100 gradute students in English at Columbia, after hearing some of the phonograph records assembled by W. Cabell Greet, chose St. Louis. (It's in St. Louis That Americanese is Spoken, New York *World*, Nov. 9, 1928). Ann Royall, in her Sketches of History, Life and Manners in the United States, published in 1826, said: "The dialect of Washington, exclusive of the foreigners, is the most correct and pure of any part of the United States I have ever yet been in," and this was supported 117 years later by Francis X. Welch in the New York *Times*. (All Speech Pure to Speakers, Sept. 17, 1943). In 1936 a writer in *Business Week* voted for Benton Harbor, Mich. (Editorially Speaking —, June 6, p. 51). As for me, I wobble between Baltimore and Benton Harbor, inclining toward the former because it is my native place and fixed my own speech-habits, and toward the latter because it is in the same *Sprachgebiet* as Owosso, Mich., the birthplace of Thomas E. Dewey, whose General American is the clearest and best that I have ever heard from the lips of an American rhetorician.

[3] The relation of the Alabama-Georgia Dialect to the Provincial Dialect of Great Britain, *Louisiana State University Studies*, No. XX; Baton Rouge, 1935. There is a review by Kemp Malone in *Modern Language Notes*, Jan., 1938, p. 40.

[4] Phonology of the Standard English

others worth consulting by L. W. Payne, Jr.,[1] and Leah A. Dennis.[2] Payne's field of investigation was an area in eastern Alabama and western Georgia "centering around the town of Auburn, Ala., and extending south to include Macon and Russell counties, west to include Tallapoosa county, north to include the counties of Chambers and a small part of Randolph, and east to include the counties of Troupe, Harris and Muscogee in Georgia." His material was used in the study by Brooks just mentioned. He said of it: "I am convinced that the speech of the white people, the dialect I have spoken all my life and the one I have tried to record here, is more largely colored by the language of the Negroes than by any other single influence. In fact, the coalescing of the Negro dialect with that of the illiterate white people has so far progressed that for all practical purposes we may consider the two dialects as one."[3] "The dialect of white and Negro," said Brooks, writing twenty-six years later, "is substantially the same."

In 1941 McMillan and I. Willis Russell undertook a linguistic survey of the State with funds supplied by the University of Alabama. By 1946 they had accumulated phonographic records from 64 of the 67 counties. Their informants were mainly freshman students at the university, each a native of the county he or she represented, and usually also the child of natives. These informants read "Arthur the Rat" for one face of a record and a script prepared by McMillan and Russell for the other. Other material was gathered in the field. That used for McMillan's doctoral dissertation, lately mentioned, came mainly from Talladega county, to the eastward of Birmingham, but records were also made in Calhoun, Chambers, Clay, Cleburn, Coosa, Lee, Randolph and Tallapoosa counties. This region overlaps that studied by Payne and Brooks, but lies rather more to the northward. It covers, says McMillan,

most of the area ceded to the United States by the Creek Confederacy in 1832, and was opened as a unit to white settlement thirteen years after the State of Alabama was formed. . . . [It] is the southwestern tip of the great Piedmont crescent which extends northeastward, separating the Appalachian mountains

---

of East Central Alabama, a dissertation submitted for the doctorate at the University of Chicago, 1946. I am indebted to Dr. McMillan for access to this.

[1] A Word-List From East Alabama, *Dialect Notes*, Vol. III, Part IV, 1908, pp. 279-328; Part V, 1909, pp. 343-91.

[2] A Word-List From Alabama and Some Other Southern States, *Publication of the American Dialect Society No. 2*, Nov., 1944, pp. 6-16.

[3] p. 279.

and the coastal plain from Alabama to Virginia. It is a cotton-growing and textile-manufacturing region, like the Piedmont crescent through Georgia and the Carolinas. . . . The southern counties have a large Negro population, but in 1940 that of the whole region was only 30%. . . .

There are three loosely-defined classes: the dominant group (professional people, and planters), the white tenant-farmer and mill-worker group, and the Negroes, who are generally farmers or unskilled laborers. The dominant white group is not sharply divided from the poor-white group, but shades into it. Individuals and families rise frequently and rapidly into the upper class, changing some of their cultural traits as they rise, but retaining others unchanged. Thus a small-town business and civic leader may occupy a position of prestige and influence, yet, having risen from humble circumstances, he may have speech features generally considered characteristic of uneducated people.

McMillan's detailed description of this dialect shows that it is a mixture of Appalachian, Southern Lowland and General American. Post-vocalic and pre-consonantal *r* is sounded by many of the poor whites, as in General American, but is reduced to something resembling the neutral vowel by the gentry and the Negroes. *Sh* followed by *r* is commonly transformed into *s*, so that *shrink* and *shred* become *srink* and *sred*. Final *t* preceded by *p, k, f* and *s* is usually lost, so that *guest* becomes *gues* and *sects* and *sex* are homophones. *Mrs.* may be *miz, mis* or *miziz*, but is never *misiz*. The flat *a* is used normally in *aunt, dance, pass, half, bath*, etc., but transformed into what McMillan calls " a new diphthong, with an *i* off-glide, acoustically close to *ei*." Before *r* and *m*, as in *far, calm*, etc., the broad *a* is heard.

There is a chapter headed "Folklore and Folkways" in "Alabama: A Guide to the Deep South," in the American Guide Series,[1] but it offers only a few specimens of the local speech. The same book says that the early settlers were " small farmers from the Atlantic seaboard." It reports that there are French-speaking Cajans (Acadians) in the southwestern corner of the State, along the Louisiana border; a Russian colony at Brookside, near Birmingham, a colony of Swedes in Baldwin county, across Mobile Bay from Mobile, and one of Germans in the same county. These colonies have introduced some of their native folk customs, but they seem to have had no effect upon the local speech.

Arizona

Notes on Arizona speechways will be found in the discussions of Southwestern speech in general, already noted. In 1914 A. P. Man,

[1] New York, 1941, pp. 122-29.

Jr., printed in *Dialect Notes*[1] a brief vocabulary collected from the Western stories of Stewart Edward White.

Arkansas

In 1904 J. W. Carr, of the University of Arkansas, began the publication in *Dialect Notes* of a series of observations in the Ozark region of Northwestern Arkansas.[2] This part of the State, he said, "was settled largely by people from Kentucky, Tennessee and Missouri," and, like Randolph, he found their "peculiarities of speech" to be mainly Appalachian. His field-work was done in the vicinity of Fayetteville, in Washington county. During the same year an English Club was organized at the University of Arkansas, and one of its purposes was "to study the English spoken in Arkansas." Carr had the aid of its members, and especially of one of them, Rupert Taylor. He listed a number of locutions apparently peculiar to Northwestern Arkansas, *e.g.*, *to grabble*, to dig only the largest potatoes; *hickory-tea*, a whipping; *mush and molasses*, idle talk; *ciphering-match*, a contest in arithmetic; *cook-room*, a kitchen; *to jowl*, to quarrel, used only of dogs and children; *squat-drop* and *rousin' oil*, a purgative; *training-school*, a prep-school leading to the State university; *wire-road*, one along which a telegraph wire was strung; *Yankee*, a cheat; *blue*, mouse-colored; *calico*, a woman; *brought on*, imported, and some interesting names for children's games, *e.g.*, *Bill Brown's Big Black Hog*, *Black Man*, *Bring Home What You Borrowed*, *Chicago*, *Old Granny Hobble-Gobble*, *Crook Crab*, and *Frog in the Middle*. In this fourth paper he listed some Arkansas words and phrases also reported elsewhere, most of them from nearby States but some from as far away as Cape Cod. In 1937 James H. Warner undertook a complementary study of the speech of the Arkansas lowlands. This region is outside the Appalachian area, and shows both Southern and Western influences. Warner said of it:

> Into [it] have come settlers from Tennessee and Mississippi on the east, from Louisiana on the south, and from Texas on the west. . . . The most striking impression which I received came from the remarkable linguistic fecundity

[1] Vol. IV, Part II, pp. 164–65.
[2] A List of Words From Northwest Arkansas, Vol. II, Part VI, 1904, pp. 416–22; Vol. III, Part I, 1905, pp. 68–103; Vol. III, Part II, 1906, pp. 124–65; Vol. III, Part III, 1907, pp. 205–38, and Vol. III, Part V, 1909, pp. 392–406.

of the region. Colloquialisms referring to motion are especially frequent and interesting. [It's] speech abounds in distinctive and forceful similes which often spring directly from the occupations and conditions of the region. . . . Solecisms, improprieties and barbarisms [are numerous]. While these are confined largely to the more uneducated, . . . several, including *may can* and *might could*, are almost universal.

I add a few of Warner's examples, some of them common to the whole lowland South:

I *wouldn't be for knowing.*
You *might ought* to go.
If I'd *a-wanted* to *went* I couldn't *a-got* to *gone*.
I *taken* a liking to the boy.
That's the worst I ever heard of in all my *put-together*.
Battle-ax. A strong man.
Cousin. An easy victim.
Dog, v. To lie.
Fizz. A disturbed mental state.
Hard-down. Pure.
Pretty. Good; fine; excellent.
Stone pony. A hard worker.[1]

California

"California," wrote B. H. Lehman in *Dialect Notes* in 1921,[2] " offers a fine opportunity to the collector of words. Its size, its peculiar history, its natural diversity, the varied industry and varied idleness of its inhabitants, and a remarkable disposition to create words, all enrich the field." Lehman listed a number of terms, presumably of California origin, that have since come into general use, e.g., *jaywalker, hang-out, pearl-diver* (a dish-washer), *purp, patootie* (a sweetheart), and various words in *-eria, -ery* and *-atorium*.[3] Spanish terms, of course, are in more frequent use than in the East, and there is an appreciable infiltration of loans from the Chinook trade-language.[4] Percy Marks, who is a native of the State, tells me [5] that in its northern part English is spoken " closer to as it is spelled " than anywhere else in the country. The Californians there, he says, " are not nasal; they sound the *r*, and the *a* is usually flat; they slur less than any other people; they sound every syllable." But another

---

[1] A Word List From Southeast Arkansas, *American Speech*, Feb., 1938, pp. 3-7.
[2] A Word-List From California, Vol. V, Part IV, pp. 109-14.
[3] Supplement I, pp. 348 ff.
[4] Supplement I, pp. 310 and 311.
[5] Private communication, Oct. 18, 1939.

correspondent says that some curious dialectal peculiarities survive among the older inhabitants of San Francisco, including a diphthongization of *i* that suggests vaguely the *boid* and *goil* of Brooklyn. Of this I have no other evidence.

Colorado

So far as I know, the only published study of Colorado speech is in a paper by Louis Swinburne.[1] It is devoted mainly to the argot of cattlemen, but also lists some Indian and Spanish loans. In 1879, three years after the State entered the Union and a year after the beginning of the Leadville mine boom, a brief note on the subject was printed in the Denver *Tribune*,[2] but this note showed nothing beyond a few specimens of the general cow country speech of the time, e.g., *round-up* for a social party,[3] *to corral* in the general sense of to get,[4] *to go over the range* for to die, *to pass in one's chips*,[5] *to buck* (of a horse),[6] and *cow-puncher*.

Connecticut

Noah Webster was a native and almost lifelong resident of Hartford, Conn., and hence took a somewhat bilious view of the speech-habits of the Boston area. The fact may have had as much to do as the flow of immigration with the failure of the Boston dialect to make any progress west of central New England. The seam between it and the Connecticut speech-area, according to Hans Kurath,[7] "runs straight north from the mouth of the Connecticut river through Connecticut and Massachusetts to the southern boundary of Franklin county, where it swerves west and follows the southern boundary of Franklin county to the Berkshires. Here it turns north again and runs along the crest of the Green Mountains to the northern boundary of Vermont." The most distinctive feature in the pronunciation of the area west of this line, he adds, "is the rather general use of *r* in all positions, contrasting with the eastern habit of

1 The Bucolic Dialect of the Plains, *Scribner's Magazine*, Oct., 1887, pp. 505–12.
2 Reprinted in the St. Louis *Republican*, Oct. 22, 1879, p. 3, and in *American Speech*, Dec., 1941, p. 269.
3 Traced by the DAE to 1880.
4 Traced to 1860.
5 The DAE's earliest example is dated 1888.
6 Traced to 1864.
7 Handbook of the Linguistic Geography of New England; Providence (R.I.), 1939, p. 8.

pronouncing *r* only when followed by a vowel."[1] But there are also other differences in phonology, and in vocabulary there are a great many, as the maps in the Linguistic Atlas of New England show. The Connecticut dialect, moving up the Connecticut river valley, not only prevailed in most of western New England, but also barged into upper New York, and from there spread westward as the basis of General American. For that reason, says Kurath, " it impresses most Americans as less distinctive than that of the seaboard." This is not saying that it lacks local peculiarities — as a matter of fact, it still shows plenty of them —,[2] but at bottom it is less aberrant than the Boston dialect, and much less than those of Appalachia and the South.

E. H. Babbitt, one of the founders of the American Dialect Society in 1889, undertook soon afterward a study of the speech of his native region — the hilly district west of the Connecticut river, running along the Housatonic. He found that it was very close to the dialect of the Ithaca region in New York State — in other words, to General American.[3] In 1905 William E. Mead and George D. Chase followed with a report on the dialect of Middleton, on the west bank of the Connecticut river, with some additions from Windham county in the northeastern corner,[4] and in 1932 M. Cordelia Fuller made a brief one on that of Danbury, in the western end of the State, based upon the speech of her mother, then ninety-three years old.[5]

---

1 p. 19.
2 Says Odell Shepard in Connecticut Past and Present; New York, 1939, p. 255: " The thing about these peculiarities that most delights me is that most of them are not peculiar to the State at large, but to special districts, often to single towns. . . . Despite the levelling influence of highways, automobiles, radio and public education, the idioms and pronunciation of Connecticut people remain as testimony to that extreme localism, that strong independence and segregation of the towns, which has characterized us from the beginning." An example is *muggs*, a herb cellar, reported and discussed by Donald Barr Chidsey, of Lyme, in *American Speech*, April, 1947, pp. 154-55.
3 List of Words From Western Connecticut, *Dialect Notes*, Vol. I, Part VI, 1893, pp. 276-78; The Dialect of Western Connecticut, *Dialect Notes*, Vol. I, Part VII, 1894, pp. 338-43. Babbitt announced in the latter paper that he proposed to resume discussion of the subject in a book on American pronunciation, then in preparation, but apparently that book was never completed.
4 A Central Connecticut Word-List, *Dialect Notes*, Vol. III, Part I, pp. 1-24.
5 Word List From Danbury, Conn., *Dialect Notes*, Vol. VI, Part V, pp. 283-84.

Delaware

In 1933 Greet made a linguistic survey of the region that its inhabitants called Delmarva, *i.e.*, the Eastern Shore of Virginia, the lower Eastern Shore of Maryland, and most of Delaware. He found a variety of speechways, including Tidewater Southern, General Southern, and, rather curiously, even Appalachian. Indeed, he came to the surprising conclusion that the common dialect of Delmarva was closer to "the speech heard in the Blue Ridge Mountains in Madison county, Virginia," than to any lowland Southern dialect. Even the "more formal speech" of the region, he reported, was "similar to what you hear in the towns of southwestern Virginia and of Tennessee, in Fort Worth (Texas), and in the cattle country as far west as Roswell, New Mexico." He went on:

> There is an alternation of long and short syllables that is one kind of Southern drawl. Often the last syllable is raised in pitch (though not circumflexed, as in western Pennsylvania). The vowels are tense and fronted, and, in marked contrast to the Southern coast and middle-country dialect, there are many remarkable retroflex vowels. The consonant *r* is pronounced in all positions. . . . The broad *a* is very rare.

Greet did not offer any surmise as to how and why the Appalachian speech threw this anomalous outrider into a region so different geographically and so far away. In the lower reaches of Delmarva, of course, he found that the influence of Tidewater and General Southern was rather more marked, and on the islands in the lower Chesapeake and off the Atlantic coast he encountered people speaking a dialect "related to the speech of the Guinea region of Gloucester county, Virginia."[1]

Florida

The same influence of Appalachian is visible among the crackers of western Florida, "especially those living along the rivers which flow from the Georgia and Alabama uplands,"[2] but here it is ob-

---

[1] Delmarva Speech, *American Speech*, Dec., 1933, pp. 56–63. Some further observations on Delaware speech will be found under Maryland. Both States are included in the area to be studied for a proposed Middle Atlantic section of the Linguistic Atlas of the United States and Canada.

[2] Florida and Tennessee, by Joseph Leon Hicks, *American Speech*, April, 1940, p. 215.

viously due to immigration. So far as I know, no general investigation of Florida speechways has ever been made, and the literature of the subject is confined to a few brief notes. In 1916 the late F. Sturges Allen (1861–1920), then general editor of the Webster New International Dictionary, sent to *Dialect Notes*[1] twenty-five terms picked up mainly at St. Petersburg, but subsequent research by Wentworth and others has shown that only a few of them could be called peculiar to Florida, *e.g.*, *bomb*, a wad of paper soaked in kerosene, used to kindle a fire. The dialect of the Conchs, as they are called, who inhabit the Florida Keys, has been reported on by Thomas R. Reid, Jr.[2] He says that they lengthen the short *i* to a long *ee*-sound, confuse *w* and *v*, drop their *h*'s like Cockneys, use *ain't* for *won't* and *haven't*, and translate many Spanish idioms.

Georgia

The study of the speech of Georgia was begun during the 20s of the last century by the Rev. Adiel Sherwood (1791–1879), a New Yorker who had moved there for the benefit of his health. The State was then frontier territory, at least west of what is now Atlanta, and the last Indians were not dispossessed until 1838. When Sherwood printed a glossary of its speech in his "Gazetteer of the State of Georgia,"[3] most of the terms he listed were ignorant forms common to the whole frontier, *e.g.*, *mounting* for *mountain*, *Babtis* for *Baptist*, *bar* for *bear*, *cheer* for *chair*, *cotched* for *caught*, *oxens* for *oxen*, and *yaller* for *yellow*. The rest came from the Appalachian dialect or from General Southern. In a few cases he was the first to record words and phrases that have not been found elsewhere at earlier dates, *e.g.*, *crazy* for *sickly*, *power of* for *many*, *mushmillion* for *muskmelon*, and *done did it*, but that fact shows only that he was one of the first lexicographers in the field.[4] Cleanth Brooks's study of the dialect prevailing along the Georgia-Alabama border has been noticed under Alabama. Most of the later writings on the speech of the State are based, not on observation in the field, but on literary

---

[1] Vol. IV, Part IV, p. 302, and Vol. IV, Part V, pp. 344–45.
[2] A Philologist's Paradise, *Opportunity*, Jan., 1926, pp. 21–23.
[3] First published in 1827. A second edition omitted the glossary, but in a third, published in 1837, it was restored and extended.
[4] His vocabulary is reprinted in The Beginnings of American English, by M. M. Mathews; Chicago, 1931, pp. 118–21.

sources,[1] but there are a few exceptions.[2] The best early source is Augustus Baldwin Longstreet's "Georgia Scenes," first published in various newspapers and brought out as a book in 1840.[3]

Idaho

There is a glossary of Idaho terms in "Idaho Lore," one of the books published by the Federal Writers' Project of the Works Progress Administration,[4] but nearly all of them are common to the whole West, *e.g., bob-wire* for *barbed-wire; to high-tail,* to depart swiftly, and *sourdough,* an old-timer. The same volume lists some specimens of miners' argot from the Pierce City area, and of railroad men's terms. In 1931 Paul Jensen contributed a paper on the jargon of the *desert rats, i.e.,* harvest hands of Eastern Idaho, to *American Speech,*[5] and in 1944 Nancy Wilson Ross included a brief note on Idaho speech in her "Westward the Women."[6] Some of the terms listed by Jensen show Mormon origin, *e.g., down home,* meaning Utah. He says:

Sagebrush is known locally as *hickory. Dogwood* is a nick-name given because of the odor of the sagebrush when wet: it resembles that of a dog's wet coat of hair. . . . A forced overnight stay in the desert is *sage-henning it. Silk* is the euphemistic name for barbed-wire. . . . *Rib-stickers* are beans. . . . Bacon is *turkey.* . . . *Heinze,* the Shoshone word for friend, is a familiar form of address. . . . When some young man threatens to *clean your plow* he intends to defeat you in a fistic encounter. . . . A *wish-book* is the catalogue of Montgomery Ward or some other mail-order house. . . . The four-horse *spud-digger* is an implement for digging potatoes. The man who picks them from the *spud-row* is a *spud-glommer.*

Says Mrs. Ross:

A certain pictorial turn of phrase, peculiar to mining country, seems to be passing slowly from the language, though Idaho is still rich in the unique quality of its speech. Idahoans *fork* a horse when they mount it; they are

1 For example, A Word-List From Georgia, by J. H. Combs, *Dialect Notes,* Vol. V, Part V, 1922, pp. 183–84. This is also true to some extent of Brooks's paper.
2 For example, Tales of the Okefinokee, by Francis Harper, *American Speech,* May, 1926, pp. 407–20, and The Way We Say It, *North Georgia Review,* Winter, 1941, pp. 129–30.
3 Longstreet (1790–1870) was born at Augusta, Ga. He was, at various times, a lawyer, a judge, a journalist, a Methodist parson and a college president. Georgia Scenes had a great success in its day, but its author is said to have been ashamed of it in his old age.
4 Caldwell (Idaho), 1939, pp. 241–45. The State director was Vardis Fisher.
5 Desert Rats' Word-List From Eastern Idaho, Dec., 1931, pp. 119–23.
6 New York, 1944.

often *busier 'n Hattie's flea; clear grit* is to them the genuine article; and they sometimes find their fellow citizens *big as a skinned mule and twice as homely*. Every old town has its collection of tantalizing local personages. The wandering questioner still hears unlikely tales of *Jack the Dude, Johnny Behind the Rock, Diamond-Field Jack Davis, Senator Few Clothes*, and *Jimmy the Harp* — friends of the parlor house girls. [The girls themselves have names which] range from the imperious dignity of the *Irish Queen* and the *Cornish Queen* to the piquancy of *Spanish Rose, Molly b'Damn*, and the *Little Gold Dollar*, and finally to the more graphic appellations of *Em' Straight-Edge, Peg-Leg Annie, Velvet-Ass Rose*, and *Contrary Mary*.[1]

Illinois

The most interesting part of Illinois, linguistically speaking, is the lush region called Egypt, at the southern tip of the State — the northernmost extension of the coastal plain which follows the Mississippi up from the Gulf of Mexico. It was largely settled, at the time of the great movement into the West, by Carolinians who came by way of Kentucky and Tennessee, and its speech still shows Appalachian and General Southern influences. An account of this dialect was contributed to *Dialect Notes* in 1902 by William O. Rice, a native of Wisconsin who had lived in the region since Civil War times.[2] Some of the peculiarities that he noted were (*a*) the poverty of the vocabulary, so that one verb was used in a range of senses covered by many more in the general speech, *e.g., big* for all kinds and degrees of largeness; (*b*) the invariable use of *a* as the indefinite article, to the exclusion of *an, e.g., a* apple, *a* hour, *a* image; (*c*) the intrusion of *y* before *a* followed by *r* and *u* followed by *sh*, as in *gyarden* and *bryush*; (*d*) the use of a syllabic plural affix, clearly pronounced, as in *nestes* for *nests*;[3] and some items of vocabulary not recorded elsewhere, *e.g., explore* for *explosion, grab-gutter* for *greedy, foot-mop* for *door-mat, livers* to designate the whole viscera, and *packwater* for *drudge*.

The same dialect was investigated again, forty years later, by Grace Partridge Smith, also a resident of the region.[4] " When we

[1] Some Idaho terms, chiefly from the miners' argot of the Coeur d' Alenes region, are in A Word List From Northwestern United States, by Benjamin H. Lehman, *Dialect Notes*, Vol. V, Part I, 1918, pp. 22–29.
[2] The Pioneer Dialect of Southern Illinois, Vol. II, Part IV, pp. 225–49.
[3] Such plurals are common in the English dialects. Wright even records a triple form, *nestses*, in Essex.
[4] Speech Currents in Egypt, *American Speech*, Oct., 1942, pp. 169–73.

come to Egypt," she said, " we are on the edge of the South." Most of the words and phrases she listed were obviously of Southern or Appalachian origin, but she also added a few that Wentworth, in 1944, did not report elsewhere, *e.g.*, *frog-eye gravy*, the gravy left in the skillet after frying ham;[1] *to look the berries*, to stem them; and *shotgun-house*, a house whose rooms are all in one line. Jesse W. Harris, writing in 1946, reported that the predominant influence on Southern Illinois speech appeared to be Appalachian.[2] Geographically, he said, the region "belongs to the Ozarks, whose foothills extend across it from east to west. Most of the pioneer inhabitants came either directly from the Appalachian highlands or by way of Kentucky and inland Tennessee." Harris cited a number of characteristic Appalachian terms, still in wide use, *e.g.*, *feisty*, lively, frisky; *infare*, a reception given to or by a bridegroom; *fireboard*, a mantel; *budget*, a peddler's pack, and *ham-meat*, ham or bacon. He said that German colonies in St. Clair and Monroe counties and Italian settlements in the coal-mining regions have given the local speechways "their own individual peculiarities," but he offered no examples. The diaries and other records of the early settlers of the State are probably rich in specimens of frontier speech in the 1812–1840 era, but so far they have not been explored as Albert Matthews, M. M. Mathews, George Philip Krapp, Allen Walker Read and other philologians have explored the records of colonial and post-Revolutionary days in the East.

The study of the current speech of the State got a considerable impetus in 1937 when Albert H. Marckwardt, of the University of Michigan, launched plans to extend the Linguistic Atlas of the United States and Canada to the Great Lakes and Ohio valley regions, though on a scale less ambitious than that of the six volumes on New England. In a little while he had in hand field material from thirty-seven com-

---

[1] Miss Smith suggests that *frog-eye gravy* is analogous to *hush-puppy*. It is and it isn't. In most parts of the South *hush-puppy* means cornmeal cooked in the fat in which fish has been fried, with maybe onions added, and Mr. Davenport Edwards tells me that the term in this sense has got as far as California (private communication, Oct. 31, 1945). But Wentworth presents evidence that *hush-puppy* is also used to designate various other forms of fried mush, without fish. In the mountains of Tennessee, as in Egypt, it is applied to ham gravy.

[2] The Dialect of Appalachia in Southern Illinois, *American Speech*, April, pp. 96–99. See also his Pioneer Vocabulary Remains in Southern Illinois, *Journal of the Illinois State Historical Society*, Dec., 1945, pp. 476–80.

munities in Illinois, Ohio, Indiana and lower Michigan, of which ten were in Illinois.¹ The latter ranged from the Chicago region to Egypt. In each case the informant was a native of the community, of education that did not go beyond the grade school, and seventy years old or older. This, of course, was only a preliminary survey — undertaken, in Marckwardt's words, "to see if the result would justify going forward on a more intensive scale." The results were duly encouraging, and by 1943 there were records in hand from fifty communities, to which Dr. Frederick G. Cassidy, of the University of Wisconsin, presently added fifty more from that State. Unhappily, World War II and its aftermath and Marckwardt's absence on an educational mission in Mexico interrupted the work, and a great deal remains to be done. But Marckwardt has already published some illuminating discussions of the material already in hand,² and plans are under way to interest the State universities of the area in the project. Funds for the preliminary work were provided by the Horace H. Rackham Foundation of the University of Michigan.

In 1904 Carl D. Buck published a study of Chicago speech,³ but it had to do with the speech of immigrant groups only. In 1935 Leonard Bloomfield published a study of American vowels devoted chiefly to those heard in Chicago,⁴ and soon afterward the same subject was dealt with by Morris Swadesh.⁵ In 1908 George E. Hoffman sent me some interesting observations of the speech of Chicago children. Among the terms he listed were *Polish piano* for accordion; *Halstead street* for anything inferior; *back of the yards*, of the same general meaning; *to make off*, to pretend; *aft* for afternoon; and *to* as a substitute for *in* and *on*, as in "When we lived *to* Milwaukee" and "I live over *to* Wayne avenue."⁶ Hoffman also noted some curious pronunciations of proper names, *e.g.*, *Joán, Genóa* and *Devón*.

[1] Wisconsin has since been added, and it is proposed to add Kentucky and a part of Ontario later on.
[2] For example, Middle English ŏ in American English of the Great Lakes Area, *Papers of the Michigan Academy of Science, Arts, and Letters*, Vol. XXVI, 1941, pp. 56–71; Middle English *WA* in the Speech of the Great Lakes Region, *American Speech*, Dec., 1942, pp. 226–34, and The Survey of Folk Speech in the Great Lakes Area and Ohio River Valley, *Studies in Linguistics*, April, 1943, pp. 2–3.
[3] A Sketch of the Linguistic Conditions of Chicago, *Decennial Publications of the University of Chicago*, Series I, Vol. VI.
[4] The Stressed Vowels of American English, *Language*, June, p. 97.
[5] The Vowels of Chicago English, *Language*, 1935, pp. 148–51.
[6] Private communication, Aug. 2, 1938.

Indiana

Indiana seems to have set the fashions in Western speech in the period between the War of 1812 and the War with Mexico, for in those days *Hoosierism* was used almost as frequently as *Westernism* to designate one of the novel and usually uncouth locutions that flowed eastward across the mountains.[1] They were used freely by Edward Eggleston in "The Hoosier Schoolmaster," first published in 1871, and a subsequent generation of Indiana novelists labored them heavily. Eggleston (1837–1902) said in an edition of his book brought out in 1899 that he was encouraged to investigate and report upon the dialect by James Russell Lowell, and that "The Hoosier Schoolmaster" was the first American dialect novel dealing with a variety of speech other than that of New England. He was born at Vevay, a small Ohio river town in the southeastern corner of the State, and spent some of his earlier years traversing it as an itinerant Methodist preacher. He saw the influence of Irish immigration upon the Hoosier dialect of his youth, and also that of immigrants from the Pennsylvania German country, but he seems to have been unaware of the even greater influence of Appalachia. Two of the German loans he noted were *plunder*, household goods, and *smearcase*.[2] Seven years after "The Hoosier Schoolmaster" J. H. Beadle, also a native of Indiana, described the dialect in his "Western Wilds and the Men Who Redeem Them." His account of it was thus summarized by John S. Farmer in "Americanisms Old and New":[3]

> It abounds in negatives held to strengthen the sentence. "Don't know nothing" is common. "See here," says a native, looking for work, to the farmer, "you don't know o' nobody what don't want to hire nobody to do nothin' around here, don't you?" But it is in the verb *to do* that the Hoosier tongue is most effective. Here is the ordinary conjugation: *Present tense:* regular as in English. *Imperfect:* I, you, he done it; we, you, they uns gone done it. *Pluperfect:* I, you, he, etc. bin gone done it, etc. *First future:* I, you, he, etc., gwine to do it. *Second future:* I gwine to gone done it, etc. *Plural:* We, you, they uns gwine to gone done it, etc. Philologically, this language is the result of a union between the rude translations of Pennsylvania Dutch, the Negroisms of Kentucky and Virginia, and certain phrases native to the Ohio valley.

---

[1] The DAE traces *Hoosierism* to 1843. For *Hoosier* see Chapter X, Section 4.
[2] Eggleston's Notes on Hoosier Dialect, by Margaret Bloom, *American Speech*, Dec., 1934, pp. 319–20.
[3] London, 1889, p. 304.

In 1906 O. W. Hanley, a native of Vigo county on the Wabash (Terre Haute is its metropolis), contributed to *Dialect Notes* an extensive vocabulary of its speech.[1] He noted some of the characters reported from Illinois by Rice,[2] *e.g.*, the invariable use of *a* as the indefinite article, the intrusion of *y* before *a* followed by *r*, and the use of syllabic plurals, and added a number of forms that Rice had not found, *e.g.*, *crickled*, disabled; *eye-winker*, eyelash; *hen-down*, chicken dirt, and *muckle-dun*, mouse-colored, but at least nine-tenths of the terms he listed came from the common stock of the American vulgate, *e.g.*, *no-account, hist, to get religion, to fly the coop, bust, right smart* and *to pass the time of day*. In 1912 Rollo Walter Brown followed with another list from a region apparently a little to the northward, but with much the same result.[3] Here the investigation of Indiana speechways rested until 1937, when Marckwardt, mentioned under Illinois, undertook plans for his linguistic atlas of the Great Lakes area and the Ohio river valley. Marckwardt presented a report on his Indiana material to the Twenty-first Annual Indiana History Conference at Indianapolis on December 9, 1939.[4] In it he said:

> Indiana preserves a Southern type of pronunciation with a greater degree of unanimity than either of her neighboring States, Illinois and Ohio. Why? The answer is clear enough when we consider the census figures for 1860, and remember that this was when most of our informants, who average 80 years of age, were born. Indiana in 1860 had only 41,000 citizens who were born in New York and the six New England States, but it had 140,000 born in the four States of Virginia, Kentucky, Tennessee and North Carolina. On the other hand Illinois had 168,000 born in New York and New England and 144,000 born in the same four Southern States.

This finding was supported by a remarkable study of the dialect of a village in the north central part of the State, published by W. L. McAtee, already cited.[5] McAtee is a biologist, not a philologian, but he is greatly interested in speechways, and his account of the lan-

[1] Dialect Words From Southern Indiana, Vol. III, Part II, pp. 113–23.
[2] The Pioneer Dialect of Southern Illinois, lately cited.
[3] A Word List From Western Indiana, *Dialect Notes*, Vol. II, Part VIII, 1912, pp. 570–93.
[4] It was printed in the *Indiana History Bulletin*, Feb., 1940, pp. 120–40.
[5] Rural Dialect of Grant County, Indiana, in the Nineties; Chicago, 1942; followed by Additional Dialect of Grant County, Indiana; Chicago, 1943; Grant County, Indiana, Speech and Song; Chicago, 1946; two supplements to the last, 1946.

guage of his native village in his boyhood is one of the most searching and valuable reports on an American dialect ever made.[1] It gives not only an extensive vocabulary, but also a conspectus of the local pronunciation and some account of grammatical vagaries. The words listed, though they belong mainly to the common stock of vulgar American, include many that are characteristic of Appalachian and Lowland Southern, and McAtee says that he found high percentages of coincidence on comparing them with word-lists from Virginia and eastern Alabama. But he also reports some curious discrepancies, *e.g.*, the absence of *to carry* in the sense of to transport or escort, and of *to tote, you-all, fightingest, grits,* and *evening* (for *afternoon*). He lists twenty terms that are plainly of Scotch origin, thirteen loans from the French, twelve from the Dutch, eleven from Indian languages, ten from the German, and eight from the Spanish. He goes on:

> The rural folk of Grant county had a varied and graphic language. Americans are said to act as if the law of life were ceaseless hurry, yet the folk take time in talking to use many similes when single words would suffice, and employ numerous even more roundabout expressions apparently out of sheer love of the picturesque. The natural man (here reflected) was not content merely to say something was *big;* no, it was *as big as a whale* or *as big as all outdoors.* If you inquired, " How are you? " the answer would be no monosyllable but some such expression as, "Why, jest as fine as frog's hair," or "If I felt any better I'd have to see a doctor." This choice of language resulted from an underlying, imperishable sense of humor that probably was a vital factor in the people's endurance and overcoming of the hardships of pioneer life.[2]

McAtee later published a ten-page supplement, in a very small edition, of local words and phrases of an indecorous character, and prefaced it with a dignified plea for the scientific study of such terms, supporting the position taken by Allen Walker Read in 1934.[3] He said:

> There is such a thing as serious, scholarly study of these theoretically forbidden matters. There can be discussion of the supposedly worst words (choose what one may) that will not descend below the level of purposeful and

---

[1] The village was Jalapa, near Marion, and McAtee was born there in 1883. It lies on the Mississinewa river, a branch of the Wabash. McAtee was educated at the University of Indiana, and has occupied important posts with the United States Biological Survey, the National Museum, and the Fish and Wildlife Service, which last he now serves as technical adviser. He is the author of more than 700 professional papers, mainly on birds, insects and plants.

[2] *Cf.* Supplement I, p. 235.

[3] An Obscenity Symbol, *American Speech*, Dec., pp. 264-78.

dignified etymological and ethnological investigation. For such studies raw material in the form of recorded dialects is essential, and the words which some assure us that the public cannot tolerate should be included as an integral part of language. Those who speak of public distaste in this direction are mistaken, for the words involved are of the public. Even the ugliest of the so-called unprintable Anglo-Saxon monosyllables are known to every person in the land.[1]

The ethnologists have long ago got rid of the prudery here denounced, but among philologians it is still all too prevalent.

In 1926 Richmond P. Bond published in *American Speech* a long and interesting list of similes embodying comparisons with animal traits, in use in Indiana popular speech, *e.g.*, *as crooked as a dog's hind leg*, *as skittish as a colt* and *as tough as a mule*, and to it he added a great many other metaphors of the same origin, *e.g.*, *catnap, pussyfoot, pigheaded, goose egg* (zero), *to ferret out, road-hog, coon's age, bear-hug* and *snake-fence*.[2] Most of these, of course, are common American, but there are a number that I have not found elsewhere, *e.g.*, *as proud as a dog with two tails*, *as poor as a racehorse*, *as safe as a cow in the stockyards*, *as jealous as a cat*, *as sour as a billy-goat* (applied to milk), *as greasy as a muskrat*, *little buzzard* (a dirty child), *as tough as a biled owl*, and *as mean as a jaybird*. By some strange oversight Bond omitted *as durable as a hog's snout* and *to goose;* it is impossible to believe that they are unknown in Indiana, the native soil of James Whitcomb Riley and George Ade. He listed *as poor as Job's turkey*, but it is not peculiar to Indiana. The DAE traces it to 1824, when it appeared in the Troy (N. Y.) *Sentinel* in the form of *as patient as Job's turkey*. But by 1830 *poor* was substituted for *patient*, and has prevailed ever since. The simile, says the DAE, posits " an imaginary turkey having the qualities of patience and poverty, in allusion to the qualities of Job." But why a turkey? So far as I know, this question has never been answered. Bond listed *as hot as a mink*, an obvious echo of the widespread folk-belief that *Putorius vison* bursts with libido. McAtee notes this belief in the Supplement that I have lately noted, and says that it also prevails among the French-Canadians, whose name for the animal embodies a reference to it.

In 1939 Paul G. Brewster supplemented the Bond list in a paper in *American Speech* on Indiana folk-metaphors in general, and in 1941

[1] Supplement to the Rural Dialect of Grant County, Indiana, in the 'Nineties; Chicago, 1942, pp. 1 and 2.

[2] Animal Comparisons in Indiana, *American Speech*, Oct., 1926, pp. 42–58.

and 1942 he followed it with a second, and a third.[1] The materials for all three were gathered in ten counties in the southern part of the State, five of them fronting on the Ohio river. Some specimens:

A skinny person . . . *has the running-gears of a grasshopper*. People of stocky build are *built like a depot stove*. A red-head may be described by: "If you cut his hair he'd bleed to death." . . . A prominent and hooked nasal organ is a *cherry-picker's nose*, the possessor of which could hook it over a limb and thus support himself while he picked cherries with both hands. . . . An untrustworthy man is *so crooked he could hide behind a corkscrew*. . . . One who is not over-intelligent is *as dumb as a mine mule in low coal*, or *doesn't know sheep pearls*[2] *from cherry-seed*. . . . The person who is living beyond his means is said *to bore with too big an auger*. . . . Husband and wife who have separated are said to have *split the blanket*. . . . Ill health is indicated by *like a lead nickel with a hole in it* or *like I'd been shot at and missed*. . . . The busybody is advised to mind his own business by . . . "Go on with your rat-killin'." . . . Persons who are intimate are *as thick as three in a bed*.[3]

In addition to the Marckwardt survey for the Linguistic Atlas, Harold Whitehall and Edson Richmond, of Indiana University, are engaged upon an independent examination of the State speechways. says Whitehall: [4]

Its southern third belongs to what I call the transferred South, *viz.*, its fauna and flora have more in common with those of the States south of the Ohio than with those of the Indiana plain to the north. In dialect, too, it is the transferred South. From the Ohio to a point nearly two-thirds up the State the prevailing dialect is what some authorities like to call Hill Southern,[5] modified in centers such as Indianapolis with infiltrations from General American, but on the whole singularly typical of the matrix from which it originally

---

[1] Folk Sayings From Indiana, Dec., 1939, pp. 261–68; More Indiana Sayings, Feb. 1941, pp. 21–25; Still More Indiana Sayings, April, 1942, pp. 130–31.

[2] *i.e.*, droppings.

[3] In Provincial Sayings and Regional Distributions, *American Speech*, Feb., 1943, pp. 66–68. Raven I. McDavid, Jr., showed that many of the words and phrases collected by Brewster are also to be heard in the South. In Notes on Indiana Speech, *American Speech*, Oct., 1944, pp. 204–06, V. E. Giblens printed interesting glosses upon some of them. In *Dauncy, American Speech*, April, 1945, pp. 151–52, Allen B. Kellogg discussed the Indiana use of that word, which is not peculiar to the State, but is recorded by Wentworth for Maine, California, Pennsylvania, and nearly all the States of the South. In Jive Talkers Can't Sneeze at Old-Time Hoosier Chin Music, Indianapolis *Star*, Dec. 21, 1945, William L. Toms said: "In pretty nearly every second or third generation Hoosier is an outcrop of atavism, as evidenced by the occasional use of words and terms peculiar to his ancestors." I am indebted here to Miss Nelda A. Weathers, of Washington, D. C. For other aid I am obliged to Professor John B. Nykerk, of Hope College, Holland, Mich., and to Captain John Jamieson, of New York City.

[4] Private communication, Oct. 20, 1946.

[5] *i.e.*, Appalachian.

The Pronunciation of American 147

came. A high proportion of the population, particularly in the hill districts around Bloomington, is of Kentucky origin of a few generations back, and even in localities where it isn't the prevailing speech-type seems to have carried all before it. Along the Ohio, particularly in the river towns, there seems to be a compromise dialect that blends Kentucky Highland Southern with a form of Pennsylvania speech that must have come down the river from somewhere in the Pittsburgh region. This mixture is especially marked around New Albany.[1]

Iowa

"The impression is general," wrote Frank Luther Mott in 1922,[2] "that Iowa was settled from New England via New York and Ohio, and that in consequence its speech is generally Northern." This impression turned out, on investigation, to be erroneous. Mott found that, in the early days of the State at least, its people were predominantly of Southern origin, and that their speechways showed it. Indeed, in a vocabulary of the 1833-46 era, he detected 136 examples of clear Southernisms as against but 62 examples of clear Yankeeisms. This finding was supported by the local historian, Frank I. Herriott, who came to the conclusion that Iowa " was first settled by sons of the Old Dominion, interspersed with the vigor of New England,"[3] and by the Census returns of 1860, which showed two settlers born in the South to one born in the North. At a later period the State, which was admitted to the Union on December 28, 1846, received large accessions of population from the stream of European immigration, and today it shows many speech-islands in which the basic dialect has been considerably modified. One of these was described in 1929 by Miss Katherine Buxbaum,[4] of the Iowa State Teachers College at Cedar Falls, who said:

My parents, German born, came to Iowa in the 60s from New York State, where they had learned their English casually. . . . With the project of farming in the new location they combined storekeeping, which brought them into contact with other pioneers of widely different speech traditions. . . . Our

1 Raven I. McDavid, Jr., says in Dialect Geography and Social Science Problems, *Social Forces*, Dec., 1946, p. 170, that "the area settled predominantly from the South follows an irregular line a little south of the fortieth parallel in Ohio and Illinois, and a little north of it in Indiana." The fortieth parallel runs between Indianapolis and Muncie.
2 A Word-List From Pioneer Iowa and an Inquiry into Iowa Dialect Origins, *Philological Quarterly*, July, 1922, pp. 202-21; An Additional Word-List From Pioneer Iowa, the same, Oct., 1922, pp. 304-10.
3 Whence Came the Pioneers of Iowa?, *Annals of Iowa*, Series III, Vol. 7.
4 Some Iowa Locutions, *American Speech*, April, pp. 302-04.

Pennsylvania German neighbors, really Ohioans once removed from Pennsylvania, clung rather tenaciously to foreign idiom. *Still* was tacked illogically to sentences that seemed complete without it. *Was für (ein)* lost nothing in translation, for they always said "*What for* seeds are you going to plant?," or "He asked me *what for* books I wanted." My parents never used these expressions, but they did translate literally the German auxiliary, *sollen*, in its sense of "to be reported." It was not until I studied the modals from a German grammar and learned *er sollte sagen* that I understood why my mother, in reporting a bit of village gossip, had stated guardedly: "He should have said that Ernest was a thief."

Wentworth shows that the Pennsylvania German *all*, as in "The butter is *all*," has moved into Ohio, Indiana, Michigan, Kansas and Nebraska, and I am told by an Iowa informant [1] that the analogous use of the word as in "It's in a bad neighborhood, is *all*" is common among Iowans "of high and low degree." Another informant [2] says that the Pennsylvania German *waumus*, a jacket, was in general use in Monroe county, in southern Iowa, 1914–20.[3]

Kansas

The pioneer of dialect study in Kansas was Dr. W. H. Carruth (1859–1924), a native of Osawatomie who was graduated from the University of Kansas in 1880, took his Ph. D. at Harvard in 1893, and occupied various linguistic chairs at the former until 1913, when he became professor of comparative literature at Leland Stanford. His first contribution to the subject was a word-list published in the *Kansas University Quarterly* in 1892,[4] and he followed it with three

---

[1] Mr. C. F. Ransom, of the Des Moines *Register and Tribune:* private communication, July 8, 1939.

[2] Mr. William J. Griffin, of the State Teachers College at St. Cloud, Minn.; private communication, Sept. 26, 1937.

[3] The DAE derives *waumus* from the Dutch *wammes*, a jacket, but Kramer's Nieuw Engelsch Woordenboek shows that the more usual form of the word is *wambuis*. Wentworth says it is from the Pennsylvania Dutch, *i.e.*, German. Webster 1934 adopts the Dutch etymology, and relates the word to the Old French *wambais*. Marcus Bachman Lambert, in his Dictionary of the Non-English Words of the Pennsylvania-German Dialect; Lancaster, 1924, gives the form *wammes*, and so does J. William Frey in his Simple Grammar of Pennsylvania Dutch; Clinton (S.C.), 1942. Lambert marks it "dialectal German." In standard German *wamme* means paunch. *Warmus*, a form produced by folk-etymology, is recorded by Webster. Whatever the source of the term, it seems to have spread through the United States from Pennsylvania. Wentworth records it for Ohio, Indiana, Illinois, Iowa, West Virginia, Wisconsin and central New York.

[4] Dialect Word-List, Vol. I, No. 2, Oct., 1892, pp. 95–100.

others during the five years thereafter.[1] He listed nearly a thousand words and phrases altogether, but many of them were marked General or credited to other States, though encountered in Kansas. A number, however, have not been reported elsewhere in the United States, among them, *coddy*, odd, out of fashion; *boo*, dried mucous; *cod*, a piece of deceit; *girling*, a girlish boy; *huckleberry*, indifferent, as in " He's a *huckleberry* Christian "; *to jimmy with*, to meddle; *quill-wheel*, a rattletrap wagon; *skin-away*, a small boy; *skit*, a harmless lie; *sloomiky*, not neat; *snouge*, unfair; *Ely*, a success, as in " My name is *Ely* "; *to horsehead*, to cajole or wheedle; *rally-kaboo*, not up to standard; *tinker-tonker*, a small boy; *fizzle-dust*, anything very small; *Jumping Jesus*, a lame man; *skift*, a small quantity; *spool-pig*, a weakling; *bung-out*, empty; and to *crow-hop*, to back out.

Carruth turned up several words, later in widespread use, that seem to have been invented in Kansas, e.g., *calamity-howler*. He encountered others that were obviously loans, e.g., *lagniappe* from the French, *savey* from the Spanish, *wic-i-up* from some Indian language, and *smearcase, land-louper (landlaufer), waumus* and *all* (as in " The corn is *all* ") from the German. He also credited the local use of *hole*, as in " The wind is from the north *hole* today," to German example (Ger. *wetterloch*), and suggested that *blue-sky*, to indicate a bad investment, might be from the German *blauer dunst*. Becoming interested in these loans, he undertook an investigation of the islands of non-English speech in the State, and found them in 90 of its 105 counties. In 65 church services were still being held in foreign languages (1894), and in 41 there were schools so carried on. There were colonies of Swedes, Norwegians, Danes, Hollanders, Czechs, Hungarians, Irish, Russians, Frenchmen (chiefly from Canada, but some from Switzerland), Italians and Welsh, beside Germans speaking half a dozen different dialects. Carruth made two reports on these speech-islands, each with a map.[2] In the first of them he made an excellent plea for dialect study in the State. Kansas, he said:

[1] Dialect Word-List No. 2, *Kansas University Quarterly*, Vol. I, No. 3, Jan., 1893, pp. 137-42; Dialect Word-List No. 3, the same, Vol. VI, No. 1, Series B, Jan., 1897, pp. 51-58; Dialect Word-List No. 4, with Paul Wilkinson, the same, Vol. VI, No. 2, Series B, April, 1897, pp. 85-93.

[2] Foreign Settlements in Kansas: A Contribution to Dialect Study in the State, *Kansas University Quarterly*, Vol. I, No. 2, Oct., 1892, pp. 71-84, and Vol. III, No. 2, Oct., 1894, pp. 159-63.

is a peculiarly favorable field. We have here side by side representatives of nearly every State in the Union and from a dozen foreign countries. . . . The remark that there is no such thing as a Kansas dialect rests upon a misapprehension of what is meant by the term. In just the same way that we speak of the flora and fauna of Kansas we may speak of the dialect of Kansas. . . . Standard literary English is always a little behind the times. It is the stuffed and mounted specimen in the museum. Dialect is the living animal on its native heath.

Kansas has had another diligent student of its speech in Judge J. C. Ruppenthal, a native of Philadelphia who was taken to the State in childhood, and rose to be a district judge at Russell, a member of the State Judicial Council, and professor of law in the University of Kansas. His principal contributions to the subject were word-lists published in *Dialect Notes* between 1914 and 1923.[1] He said in the preface to his first list:

There are a large number of expressions that have come from the Germans, including the Pennsylvania Germans, and the Germanic elements or German-speaking peoples of central Kansas, who are natives not only of Germany, but of Russia, Austria, Switzerland, Luxemburg, etc. Although there is a large Slav element, and perhaps a larger Scandinavian element, neither of these appears to have contributed a single word or phrase to the language of central Kansas. In addition there are some English, Irish, Scotch, Welsh, French, Belgians, Greeks, and, recently, Mexicans. Negroes are few and much scattered. Excepting Mexicans and Negroes, all other elements seem to be rapidly absorbed into the general population.

The terms listed by Judge Ruppenthal came mainly from the central part of the State and many of them were picked up in his courtroom at Russell. They included a number not since unearthed by any of Wentworth's authorities in other States, *e.g.*, *beany*, mentally defective; *black dishes*, cooking utensils; *to bushwhack*, to borrow with intent to return; *one at a clatter*, one at a time; *dead in the shell*, worn out; *to do bandies*, to do stunts on a dare; *fast*, untrustworthy; *to gig back*, to back down; *to go south*, to be beaten; *go-back land*, cultivated land that has reverted to prairie; *goop*, a person of uncouth manners; *goose heaven*, the bourne of dead animal pets; *to hog*, to sow grain in unplowed land; *kolfactor*, a term of con-

---

[1] A Word-List From Kansas, Vol. IV, Part II, 1914, pp. 101–14; Vol. IV, Part V, 1916, pp. 319–331; Jottings From Kansas, Vol. V, Part VI, 1923, pp. 245–46. Prefaced to the last paper was a note saying that Judge Ruppenthal was "preparing another extended list of expressions found current in Kansas," but it never appeared in *Dialect Notes*, which was mainly given over, during the years following, to printing the third volume of R. H. Thornton's American Glossary.

The Pronunciation of American 151

tempt; *kump*, a deep dish, such as a soup-plate; *pass-word*, a greeting; *to penny-dog*, to fawn on; *like siz*, copiously, expressively; *spread-water*, the overflow of a stream; *dumb Isaac*, a simpleton; *elk-face*, in which the cheek furrows run nearly parallel with the nose; *to give one the flit-flaps*, to make one nervous; *to tit*, to milk a cow; and *weehaw*, askew, awry. He found some curious pronunciations, e.g., *alfathy* for *alfalfa*, *swullen* for *swollen*, *elder* for *udder*, *flavior* for *flavor*, *twell* or *twill* for *till*, *hearso* for *hearsay*, *side-draft* for *sight-draft*, *stalted* for *stalled*, *fochts*, with a German *ch*-sound, for *folks*; and *barrow*, *narrow*, etc., with a broad *a*. He encountered many German loans, e.g., *blutwurst*, blood sausage; *schwartenmagen*, souse or hog's head cheese; *to slurp*, to eat noisily (Ger. *schlürfen*); *heia*, an exclamation (Ger. *Herr Je* or *Herr Jesu*, Lord Jesus); *wassermucker*, a Prohibitionist (Ger. *wasser*, water, and *mucker*, a bigot); *schleckerig*, fastidious; *to take goodby; uhrgucker*, a clock-watcher; *mix-max*, a medley or confusion (Ger. *misch-masch*); *mush*, rotten (Ger. *morsch*); *sauerteig*, leaven; *half-brother*, the son of a father's brother (Ger. *halb-bruder*);[1] and several loans from the Yiddish, taken in through the German, e.g., *mazuma*, money, and *tookis*, the anus (Yid. *tochos*, the backside).[2] He also found some French and Spanish loans, e.g., *bayou* and *cabase*, the head (Sp. *cabeza*). In a paper upon the speech of the region of which Kansas City is the metropolis, contributed to *Dialect Notes* in 1926, Miss Josephine M. Burnham, of the University of

---

[1] In 1946 Dr. H. B. Reed, head of the psychology department at the Fort Hays Kansas State College, undertook a survey of the 2732 grade school pupils of Ellis county, which adjoins Judge Ruppenthal's Russell county to the westward. The Natoma *Independent* thus reported his findings on Aug. 8: "Test results showed 1616 had speech defects of one kind or another.... The most frequent was the German accent, found in 1226, or three out of five. Instead of saying '*We have pigs with big teeth*' they say '*Vee haf picks wit bik teet.*'" Other speech defects were in pitch, voice quality, and distinctness.

[2] In Russian Words in Kansas, *Dialect Notes*, Vol. IV, Part II, 1914, pp. 161–62, Ruppenthal listed some Russian terms in use among German immigrants who came to Kansas by way of the Volga region, where they had been settled since 1760, e.g., *ambar*, a granary; *arbus*, a watermelon; *brosch*, abandoned land; *gofta*, a short jacket for women (R. *kofta*); *klapot*, a lawsuit or other trouble; *knout*, a whip; *natschelnik*, a court official; *pachshu*, a garden plot; *plodnik*, a carpenter; *sotnik*, a constable, and *steppe*, a prairie. But these terms have not got into the common speech.

Kansas, listed a few other peculiarities,[1] e.g., the frequent use of *to get*, as in "He didn't *get to go*," and of *to do*, as in "*Do you have some ink?*". "The Kansans," said Miss Burnham, would never say, "We *have no* bananas," but always, "We *don't have any* bananas." The *a*, she added, was often omitted in *after a while*, and the *the* before *United States*, and *the* was inserted before *most*, as in "*The most* of the time."

In the great days of Bleeding Kansas the inmates of the State prided themselves upon the alleged fact that what they called the *Kansas language* was simpler, franker and more vivid than that of the decadent East. As one of their editors, Nelson Antrim Crawford, has recorded,[2] there was "no goddam grammar" in it. Its great professors were the politicians and world-savers who then howled from every stump, but it was also used by the State literati. Crawford reports that it is now vanishing. "Kansas," he says, "has become a conservative State, and most of its people consciously seek to become like the people of other conservative States. Something resembling the old-time Kansas language . . . is more likely to be heard today in Iowa or North Dakota than in Kansas."

Kentucky

What is now Kentucky was the first region beyond the mountains to be settled. Pioneers began to invade it before the Revolution, and by 1782 it had more than 30,000 population.[3] It was originally a part of Virginia, and the effort to organize it as an independent State took a great deal of politicking, but it was finally admitted to the Union on June 1, 1792, little more than a year after Vermont, the first new State to come in. During the period down to the War of 1812 many of the neologisms then called Westernisms were coined within its bounds, and some of its early heroes, notably Daniel Boone, made contributions to the store.[4] The present speech of the

---

[1] Some Observations Upon Middle Western Speech, Vol. V, Part X, pp. 391-96. Many of her examples were taken from the Kansas City *Star*, the principal newspaper of the region. "The collection," she said, "might almost — but not quite — be called 'Notes on Kansas.'"

[2] A Note on the Kansas Language, in We Liberals; New York, 1936, pp. 76-84.

[3] The first Federal census, in 1790, showed 32,211 males and 28,922 females.

[4] But Boone's so-called autobiography, published in 1834, was actually written by John Filson.

State, like that of Tennessee, ranges from Appalachian to General American, with the latter showing strong Southern influences. The first serious study of it was made by John P. Fruit, of Bethel College at Russelville, in the southwestern lowlands, in 1890.[1] Most of the terms he listed belonged to the common stock of vulgar American, especially in the West, e.g., *to crawfish; to saw gourds*, to snore; *gallus*, suspenders, and *ruckus*, a disturbance, but he also found some that have not been reported from other regions, e.g., *beastback*, horseback; *drats*, a game of marbles; *in a bad row of stumps*, in a tight place, and *whittlety-whit*, fifty-fifty. In 1910 Miss Abigail E. Weeks published in *Dialect Notes* a brief word-list from Barbourville in the southeastern corner of the State, but it consisted mainly of Appalachian terms.[2] A year later Hubert G. Shearin, of Transylvania University at Lexington, in the Bluegrass country, followed with a longer one from that region.[3] It offered some oddities in vocabulary, e.g., *red-nose*, discouragement; *dough-beater*, a housewife; and *slowcome*, a lazy fellow, but they were not numerous.

There was then a long wait until 1946, when Miss Virginia Park Matthias and Fred A. Dudley offered brief contributions to the subject. Both confined their inquiries to the Appalachian area. Miss Matthias[4] presented some interesting specimens of the local dialect, but most of them were common to the whole Appalachian range and not a few were old in the British dialects: *blinky*, soured (used of milk), *agin* (against) as a preposition, as in "He'll be home *agin* November," and *favor*, to resemble. Among her less familiar terms were *latch-pin*, a safety-pin; *natural-looking*, familiar, and *waste*, a hemorrhage. Dudley[5] added *caps*, popcorn; *carton-box*, carton;[6] *hoved out*, bulged or warped (used of woodwork) and *smothersome*, hot and humid.[7]

1 Kentucky Words and Phrases, *Dialect Notes*, Vol. I, Part II, 1890, pp. 63–69. Fruit followed this with Kentucky Words, *Dialect Notes*, Vol. I, Part V, 1893, pp. 229–34.
2 A Word-List From Barbourville, Ky., Vol. III, Part VI, pp. 456–57.
3 An Eastern Kentucky Dialect Word-List, *Dialect Notes*, Vol. III, Part VII, 1911, pp. 537–40.
4 Folk Speech of Pine Mountain, Kentucky, *American Speech*, Oct., 1946, pp. 188–92.
5 *Swarp* and Some Other Kentucky Words, *American Speech*, Dec., 1946, pp. 270–73.
6 Dudley did not mention the pronunciation. In most part of the United States the common form is *cartoon*.
7 Other Kentucky word-lists, chiefly from the Appalachian area, are in Early English Slang Survivals in the Mountains of Kentucky, by Josiah H. Combs, *Dialect Notes*, Vol. V, Part IV, 1921, pp. 115–17; Kentucky Items, the same, pp. 118–19; Kentucky Pioneers, by Atche-

Louisiana

"In the State of Louisiana, which was colonized by the French," said John Russell Bartlett, in the preface to the second edition of his "Glossary of Words and Phrases Usually Regarded as Peculiar to the United States,"[1] "there are many words of foreign origin, scarcely known in the Northern States. The geographical divisions, the names of rivers, mountains, bays; the peculiarities of soil and climate; all that relates to the cultivation of the earth, the names of fishes, birds, fruits, vegetables, coins, etc., retain to a great extent the names given them by the first possessors of the country." So far as I know, no effort was made to study this speech until 1890, when J. W. Pearce, of Tulane University at New Orleans, printed a brief word-list in *Dialect Notes*.[2] Pearce, however, paid no heed to the French sediment in it, but gave his attention mainly to pronunciations in the purely English vocabulary, *e.g.*, *axed* for *asked*, *riz* for *rise*, *jine* for *join*, *hender* for *hinder*, *maracle* or *meracle* for *miracle*, and *dreen* for *drain*, nearly all of them common to the vulgar speech of the whole country. He was followed twenty-six years later by a colleague at Tulane, E. Riedel, who had a sharper ear for French influence[3] and listed a number of characteristic loans, *e.g.*, *armoir*, a wardrobe; *brioche*, a kind of cake, *gris gris*, a magical formula to gain advantage in a game; *jambalaya*, a hash containing ham and rice; *picayune*, five cents, and *praline*, a candy made of brown sugar and nuts, but he somehow contrived to omit *lagniappe*.[4]

A little later James Routh, associate professor of English at Tulane and secretary of the American Dialect Society for the Gulf States, began supplying *Dialect Notes* with longer and better lists.[5]

---

son L. Hench, *American Speech*, Feb., 1937, pp. 75–76, and A Word-List From the Mountains of Kentucky and North Carolina, by Cratis D. Williams, *Publication of the American Dialect Society, No. 2*, Nov. 1944, pp. 28–31.
1 Boston, 1859, p. xx.
2 Notes From Louisiana, Vol. I, Part II, pp. 69–72.
3 New Orleans Word-List, *Dialect Notes*, Vol. IV, Part IV, 1916, pp. 268–70.
4 Supplement I, pp. 319–20. Wentworth finds that it has extended to Alabama, Mississippi and Texas.
5 Louisiana, Vol. IV, Part V, 1916, pp. 346–47; Terms From Louisiana, Vol. IV, Part VI, 1917, pp. 420–31; Louisiana Gleanings, Vol. V, Part VI, 1923, pp. 243–44. The editors of *Dialect Notes* seem to have had some difficulty with Routh's name. They made him *Rouse* on the cover of Vol. V, Part VI, and *Rontt* inside. Born in Virginia in 1879, he has held various professional posts in Georgia since 1918.

The Pronunciation of American

His first paper added *brulée*, an open place in a swamp; *flottant*, a soft prairie; *minnie*, a cat (Fr. *minet*); and *kruxingiol*, a cake eaten at Mardi Gras (Fr. *croquignole*); his second, *marronguin*, a large mosquito; *nanan*, a godmother; *pieu*, a fence built of boards; *rabais-shop*, a notion store; *briqué*, a red-haired mulatto; and *to coshtey*, to steal (Fr. *cocheter*); and his third, *bidon*, a man's hat; *boucan*, a smudge fire to keep off mosquitoes; *papiettes*, curl-papers; and *parin*, a godfather. He added some English forms apparently of local origin, *e.g., little small*, a small amount; *basin*, a channel; *down the street*, downtown; *onfinancial*, without money; *nick*, a pile of wood; *to skull-drag* and *to maul-drag*, to do servant's work, and *tin-a-fix*, a tinsmith, and recorded the diphthongization of *er* in *boid* (*bird*) and *desoive* (*deserve*), as in the Brooklyn, N. Y., dialect.[1] To his second list he added a large number of local bird-names, chiefly gathered from notes printed in the New Orleans *Picayune*, March–July, 1916, by Stanley Clisby Archer, *e.g., aigle noir*, the golden eagle; *becasse*, the woodcock; *biorque*, the bittern; *cou collier*, the kildee; *egret caille*, the blue crane; *goelan*, the gull; *moineau*, the English sparrow; *perdreaux*, the quail; and *zel rond*, the darter.

Pearce, in his pioneer study, had noted what appeared to him to be a German loan, to wit, *whatfer*, as in " *Whatfer* man is he?," from the German *was für*. He said that it was in common use in Red River parish. This is some distance above the so-called German Coast of Louisiana, which runs along both banks of the Mississippi for about forty miles, beginning twenty-five miles north of New Orleans, and was settled during the Eighteenth Century, but there was early penetration of the Red River valley by the German settlers.[2] In the same sense of *what sort of* the term is recorded by Wentworth in Lebanon county, Pennsylvania, and in West Virginia, western Maryland, central New York, and Iowa — all of them regions showing German influence. Two other possible German loans in the northern part of Louisiana were recorded in 1935, to wit,

---

He is a Ph.D. of the Johns Hopkins.

[1] Major William D. Workman, Jr., tells me that the compensatory *er* for *oi* is also heard, but that it is "softer and less nasal" than in Brooklyn. He says that *oyster* "is not so much *erster* as *uh-ister*." Private communication, Aug. 20, 1945. For the Brooklyn dialect see under New York.

[2] The Settlement of the German Coast of Louisiana, by J. Hanno Deiler, *German American Annals*, Jan.–Feb., 1909, pp. 34–63; March–April, pp. 67–102; May–June, pp. 123–63; July–Aug., 179–207.

to cook coffee and the use of *until* in place of *that*, as in "I was so hot *until* I nearly melted." The former is a common Pennsylvania Germanism, and the latter has analogues in Pennsylvania.[1] In this northern part of the State Gallicisms are relatively rare, and the speech in general is that of the Ozarks.[2] In the south, however, large numbers of French loans are in everyday use, *e.g., banquette*, a sidewalk; *gabrielle*, a loose wrapper; *îlet*, a city square; *jalousie*, a Venetian blind; and *to make ménage*, to clean house.[3]

With Dr. C. M. Wise of the Louisiana State University in charge, there is now in progress a survey of the State dialects upon a scientific basis, and in the course of a few years it should produce a valuable volume for the Linguistic Atlas of the United States and Canada. Wise was one of the scholars who took instruction in linguistic geography from Dr. Hans Kurath, editor of the Atlas, while Kurath was at Brown University. At the conclusion of this course the General Education Board, acting through the American Council of Learned Societies, established four scholarships in the South for scholars interested in studying its speech, and Wise was appointed for Louisiana. He decided to gather materials for a linguistic atlas of the State, and he and his graduate students have been engaged upon the project ever since. He read a paper describing their work before the Linguistic Society of America in July, 1942, and published a report upon it in *Studies in Linguistics* in 1945.[4] A provisional map that he has prepared shows that the area of French influence runs northward from the Gulf to the vicinity of Alexandria on the Red river. From there its boundary slopes southwestward to the mouth of the Sabine river, on the Texas-Louisiana border, and southeastward to Baton Rouge and then eastward along the north side of Lake Pontchartrain to the mouth of the Pearl river. In this area, says Wise, there are two phonological marks of the local speech. One is the change of *ar*, " final in a stressed syllable with or without a succeeding consonant or consonants, and not pre-

---

[1] Notes From Louisiana, by Pearl Hogrefe, *American Speech*, Feb., 1934, p. 79.

[2] Some specimens are given in Older English in Louisiana, by Herbert L. Hughes, *American Speech*, Dec., 1936, pp. 368–69.

[3] All of these are from the glossary in the New Orleans City Guide, in the American Guide Series; Boston, 1938, pp. 407–10. This glossary gives *minon* for *cat* instead of the *minnie* listed by Routh, and *papillote* for *curl-paper* instead of his *papiette*.

[4] The Dialect Atlas of Louisiana: a Report of Progress, Vol. III, No. 2, June, 1945, pp. 37–42.

ceded by the sound of *w*," into a vowel resembling the *a* of *chalk* and *although*, so that *yard* becomes something on the order of *yawd*. The other is the diphthongization of the vowel in *bird*, *heard*, etc., already noted. In the six parishes east of the Mississippi, but north of the French area, the speech is that of Mississippi and the rest of the lowland South. In the region lying along the Arkansas and Texas borders it is that of the Ozarks, which is to say, of Appalachia. A number of Wise's graduate students have completed intensive studies of the speech of communities in various parts of the State, and all the material amassed is being preserved in quadruplicate.

Maine

"Maine and New Hampshire," says Hans Kurath, "are the most conservative parts of New England. Both are rural and remote from the great population centers, with large areas that are sparsely settled and have been losing population for several decades. As a result, [they] preserve many dialectal features lost in the southern part of the Eastern area, and they still use currently other features now rare in eastern Massachusetts or losing ground in the Boston area."[1] All this applies, as Kurath explains further on, only to the southeastern coast and the western uplands, both of which were settled by immigrants from Massachusetts. "Northern Maine," he says, "belongs to the St. John river area of New Brunswick, which was settled by Loyalists from New York, New Jersey and western Connecticut," and therefore shows the influence of what has now come to be called General American. The dialects of the State have got a great deal of attention from linguists in recent years, and the literature dealing with them is extensive. It begins with a study of that of the Penobscot valley, contributed to *Dialect Notes* in 1907 by Joseph William Carr and George Davis Chase, of the University of Maine,[2] and it runs down to the detailed reports provided by the maps in the Linguistic Atlas of New England.[3] Carr and Chase,

---

[1] Handbook of the Linguistic Geography of New England; Providence (R.I.), 1939, p. 17.

[2] A Word-List From Eastern Maine, Vol. III, Part III, pp. 239-51. This was followed by the same authors with A Word-List From Aroostook, *Dialect Notes*, Vol. II, Part V, 1909, pp. 407-18. After Carr's early and lamented death in 1908 Chase continued alone with Lists From Maine, *Dialect Notes*, Vol. IV, Part I, 1913, pp. 1-6, and Maine, Vol. IV, Part II, pp. 151-53.

[3] These maps, however, stop short at the latitude of Bangor.

whose interest was chiefly in vocabulary, called attention to the influence of lumbering upon the speech of Maine, and also to the infiltration of terms from Canada. The investigators who followed [1] also devoted themselves mainly to vocabulary, and in their lists were many picturesque locutions that have never been reported, so far as I know, from any other region, e.g., *tie-up*, a cow-barn; *to cousin*, to visit relatives; *gorming*, clumsy, stupid; *pizen-neat*, over-neat; *spleeny*, vaguely ailing; *hog-wrestle*, a country dance; *burn*, burned-over woodland; *matterated*, infected; *drozzle tail*, a slovenly woman; *muster-bread*, a kind of ginger-bread; *claw-off*, an excuse; *pod*, a large belly; *all of a biver*, excited; *all of a high*, very eager; *booze-fuddle*, whiskey; *dingclicker*, a good-looking woman; *dite*, a small amount; *to gibbet*, to punish; *nimshy*, a young girl; *stool*, a sill or threshold; *potato thump*, mashed potatoes; *skulch*, swill; *rent*, any house or apartment for rent; *snug*, stingy; *yip*, noisy talk; *whee-up*, a fit of anger; and *smutter*, a cloud of dust. Some of the survivals of English dialect in the dialect were tracked down and listed by Dr. Anne E. Perkins in 1922,[2] and its phonology was discussed by Ezra Kempton Maxfield in 1926[3] and by W. Cabell Greet in 1931.[4] Maxfield thus described two of the Maine vowels:

> No alien has ever yet been able to master our so-called short *o*. It is extremely amusing to hear the actors in alleged "Down East mellerdrama" try to enunciate such words as *road, coat, boat, loan* and *stone*.... They say *rud, cot, bot, lud* and *stun*.... After puzzling over the phonetics of these words for some years I have discovered that the difficulty lies in thinking that we are dealing with a single vowel. There is no *o* that represents these words. Instead of a single sound it consists of two vowels so rapidly spoken that only one seems apparent.... Say very rapidly *ro-ud, co-ut, bo-ut, lo-und* and *sto-un*, and you will hit it almost in the eye.... Short *e* is often substituted for short

[1] Two Word-Lists From Roxbury, N. Y. and Maine, by Mrs. F. E. Shapleigh, *Dialect Notes*, Vol. IV, Part I, 1913, p. 55; Rural Locutions of Maine and Northern New Hampshire, by George Allan England, *Dialect Notes*, Vol. IV, Part II, 1914, pp. 67–83; Maine List, by E. K. Maxfield, *Dialect Notes*, Vol. V, Part IX, 1926, pp. 383–90; Notes From Maine, by S. E. Morison, *American Speech*, June, 1929, p. 356; Yankee Notes From Eliot, Maine, by Wendell F. Fogg, *Dialect Notes*, Vol. VI, Part II, 1930,

p. 90; More Notes on Maine Dialect, by Anne E. Perkins, *American Speech*, Feb., 1930, pp. 118–31.
[2] Boston *Transcript*, Dec. 2. This paper was republished in Colloquial Who's Who, by William Abbatt; Tarrytown (N.Y.), 1924, Vol. I, pp. 101–07, and again in *American Speech*, Dec., 1927, pp. 134–41.
[3] Maine Dialect, *American Speech*, Nov., pp. 76–83.
[4] A Record From Lubec, Maine, and Remarks on the Coastal Type, *American Speech*, Aug., pp. 397–403.

a. . . . A door *ketches* if it sticks, and . . . one consults the *kelender* to know the date. . . . *Accept* sounds identical with *except*. An officer *errests* a wrongdoer.

Maxfield said that the Maine *a*, as in *aunt*, is not *aw* or *ah*, but "something that sounds like *ar*, . . . [though] certainly not the gnarled sound that passes for *r* west of Albany and north of the Mason and Dixon line. . . . You would be laughed at if you asked the way to *Bath* (rhymed with *lath*). You must say *Barth*." Greet hears a flat *a* in *aunt*, *dance*, *can't*, *answer*, *grass* and *fast*, and says that it "is very flat." He agrees with Maxfield that *o* is often a diphthong, but says that it "is not marked." He goes on:

> The first vowel in *color* is almost *a*. *Was*, when stressed, is *wahz* . . . ; *do* and *due* are homonyms. . . . The final *r* is usually not pronounced, but the liaison *r*, as in *idear* is common. . . . This is the characteristic speech of the well-to-do citizen of the New England coast and the adjacent regions from Newburyport, Mass., to Lubec, Maine. I have examples from as far inland as Concord, N. H.[1]

Maryland

The first known study of an American dialect was Jonathan Boucher's of that of Maryland, written before 1775 though not published until 1832.[2] It took the form of a pastoral entitled "Absence" and was accompanied by explanatory footnotes and a glossary. It antedated John Witherspoon's treatise on American speech by six years.[3] Some of the words occurring in it are not traced further back, by the DAE, than Boucher's text, *e.g.*, *wring-jaw*, hard cider; *cushie*, a kind of pancake; *eggnog*, and *belly-bacon*. Not many of them, however, appear to have been peculiar to Maryland: they were simply specimens of the general speech of the colonies, *e.g.*, *mad* for angry, *Fall* for Autumn, *bug* for any kind of insect, *per*-

---

[1] See also One Man's Meat, by E. B. White, *Harper's Magazine*, Dec., 1940, pp. 107–08. I am indebted for useful suggestions to Mrs. Isaac Gerson Swope, of Wayne, Pa.; to Mr. Ray C. Faught, of Baltimore, a native of Maine; to Dr. George W. Blanchard, of New York City; and to Mr. John B. Wentworth, of Tenants Harbor, Maine.

[2] For Boucher see AL4, p. 35, n. 1. More about him is in Boucher's Linguistic Pastoral of Colonial Maryland, by Allen Walker Read, *Dialect Notes*, Vol. VI, Part VII, 1933, pp. 353–60, and in Additional Comment on Boucher, by M. M. Mathews, in the same issue of the same journal, pp. 360–63. See also Jonathan Boucher: Champion of the Minority, by Robert G. Walker, *William and Mary Quarterly*, Jan., 1945, pp. 3–14.

[3] For Witherspoon see AL4, pp. 4–7, and Supplement I, pp. 4–14.

simmon-beer, roasting-ear, possum, canoe, hominy, pow-wow, squaw and *yam*. But one of them, *johnnycake*, may have originated in Maryland,[1] and so may some of the tobacco-growers' terms listed but not defined, *e.g., twist-bud, thick-joint, bull-face* and *leather-coat*. Boucher defined *bandore*, which he noted was pronounced *banjor*, as " a rude musical instrument made of the shell of a large gourd or *pumpion*,[2] and strung somewhat in the manner of a violin." " It is much used," he added, " by Negroes."[3] He defined *pickaninny* as " a male infant," and said nothing of color. Some of his terms were borrowed, with credit, from books on the West Indies[4] but he indicated that they had come into Maryland use.[5]

Since Boucher's time there has been little study of the speech of the State, but an excellent investigation of that of at least one of the counties, Garrett, has been made by a native thereof, Miss Florence Warnick. This is reported in a pamphlet, " Dialect of Garrett County, Maryland," printed privately in 1942.[6] Garrett county is the westernmost county of the State and is surrounded by Pennsylvania and West Virginia. Geographically, it is part of Appalachia, but its speech has been influenced by immigration from the German areas of Pennsylvania. Some of the German loans noted by Miss Warnick are *hutchy*, a colt (Ger. dial. *hutsch, hutschel* or *hutschli*); *ponhoss*, scrapple (Ger. *pfannhase*, panned hare); *satz*, home-made yeast; *snits*, sliced and dried apples or other fruit (Ger. *schnitz*, a slice); *what-fer* (Ger. *was für*), and the Pennsylvania German use of *all*, as in " The butter is *all*," *i.e.*, exhausted. She suggests that another word, *blage*, gossip, may be from the French *blague*. Many of the terms she lists are obviously Appalachian, *e.g.*,

---

1 See AL4, p. 203.
2 *Pumpion* or *pompion* was the original English form of the word, traced by the NED to 1545. *Pumpkin* is traced by the DAE, in American use, to 1654.
3 The DAE's earliest example of *banjo* is dated 1774; it may not antedate Boucher. The word is derived from the Spanish and Portuguese *bandore*, first recorded in English use in 1591.
4 A True and Exact History of the Island of Barbados, by Richard Ligon; London, 1657, and The History, Civil and Commercial, of the British Colonies in the West Indies, by Bryan Edwards; London, 1793. I take these references from Read.
5 William Eddis praised the Maryland pronunciation in his Letters From America; London, 1792, p. 59. I am indebted here to Mrs. Lucy Leigh Bowie.
6 Miss Warnick, at that time, was secretary to W. L. McAtee, whose study of Indiana speech has been noted under Indiana. She was inspired to her work by his example. She was reared in a small village ten miles south of Grantsville, which lies just under the Pennsylvania line.

whistle-pig for what is called a *ground-hog* elsewhere in Maryland, but there are also a few that Wentworth does not find anywhere else, *e.g., cabbage-leaves,* large ears; *to chew,* to scold; *to cut up molly,* to act extravagantly; *to dance in the hog-trough,* used of an older brother or sister left unmarried after the marriage of a junior; *hanover,* a rutabaga;[1] *to make him scratch where he don't itch,* to put in a predicament; *pe-pippa,* a very little bit; *pooch-jawed,* fat-cheeked; *snoopy,* finicky about food; and *sollybuster,* any unusual thing. Miss Warnick notes that *ornery* is pronounced *onry* in Garrett county.

As I have noted in my introductory remarks on American dialects, there are at least five speech areas in Maryland. Some incidental mention of them is to be found in "Delmarva Speech," by W. Cabell Greet,[2] but there was no scientific attempt to delimit them until the late Guy S. Lowman, Jr., one of the editors of the Linguistic Atlas of New England, began accumulating material for a similar atlas of the South Atlantic States. At the time of his death he had in hand records of the speech of 400 informants in scattered communities in Maryland, Delaware, Virginia, North and South Carolina and Georgia. About a third of these informants were elderly persons who had lived in their birthplaces or nearby all their lives, a second third was made up of middle-aged persons of fair education, and the remainder were college graduates. This somewhat meagre material was worked up in 1940–41 by Miss Elizabeth Jeannette Dearden, a candidate for the doctorate at Brown University under Hans Kurath.[3] Miss Dearden found that the line dividing Appalachian speech from that of the Piedmont, represented by the use of [paper] *poke* in the former and *sack* in the latter, crosses Maryland from north to south in Washington county, rather less than 100 miles west of Baltimore, and that the *lightwood* line runs west to east through Washington and Annapolis, and then through Caroline county on the Eastern Shore into Delaware. She said:

> The linguistic situation in the region around Chesapeake Bay is very complicated. ... The area frequently has its own distinctive terms, which are not found at all in the adjoining territory. For instance, *head horse* is often used

[1] Possibly from *Hanover* county, Pennsylvania.
[2] *American Speech,* Dec., 1933, pp. 56–63.
[3] Her thesis has not been published, but I have had access to a copy of it by the courtesy of Mr. H. Glenn Brown, supervisor of readers' service in the Brown University Library.

for *lead horse* on the Eastern Shore and at the head of the Bay, and *bother horse* occurs in three communities. *Whetter* and *whet* instead of *whetstone* are used in a few places on the Eastern Shore. *Catch-all* for the Southern *lumber-room* is most frequent in Delaware, but also occurs in two communities on the Western Shore of Maryland. *Hind legs* or *hind feet* for *haunches* and *prim up* instead of *primp up* are found on both sides of the Bay, the former as far west as Carroll county, the latter frequently on the Eastern Shore. The Bay region also preserves some of the relic terms which have been found along the Virginia and North Carolina coast.

The great institutions of learning of Maryland appear to take but little interest in the curiously diverse and instructive speech of the State. Dr. Kemp Malone, of the Johns Hopkins, has concerned himself to good effect with American speech in general [1] but not with that of Maryland in particular, and J. Louis Kuethe, of the same university, has published several brief notes on the latter [2] but is mainly devoted to place-names and topographical terms. The Johns Hopkins participates officially in the field-work for the projected Linguistic Atlas of the Middle Atlantic States, supported by the American Council of Learned Societies, but apparently its participation is more formal than active.[3] I have long had it in mind to attempt a vocabulary of Baltimore speech in the 80s and 90s, for a number of terms that were in common use there and then do not seem to have been noted elsewhere, *e.g.*, *Araber*, a street huckster; *to arab*, to go huckstering;[4] *front steps*, the steps before a dwelling-house, usually in those days, of marble; and *Yankee jumper*, a sled for girls, with the platform raised 9 or 10 inches above the runners,

[1] See *American Speech*, 1925–1945: The Founders Look Back, *American Speech*, Dec., 1945, pp. 241–46.
[2] For example, Words From Maryland, *American Speech*, Dec., 1940, pp. 451–52.
[3] Its delegates are Malone and Dr. Isaiah Bowman, president of the university. Pennsylvania is represented by the American Philosophical Society; Virginia by Archibald A. Hill and Atcheson L. Hench, of the University of Virginia; and North Carolina by George R. Coffman and Howard W. Odum, of the University of North Carolina, and Paull F. Baum, of Duke University. The Rev. H. E. Zimmerman, of Myersville, a small town in the Pennsylvania German area, published a list of Maryland terms in *Dialect Notes*, Vol. IV, Part V, 1916, p. 343, but it ran to but 23 items. They included *Jersey wagon*, a wagon with a top; *limerick*, lingo; and *snatched up*, in a hurry. Some are already obsolete. There is a spoofing account of current Baltimore pronunciation in Baltimorese and Mountainese, Baltimore *Evening Sun* (editorial page), Oct. 16, 1946.
[4] I am reminded of these by Mr. Charles E. Fecher of Baltimore; private communication, Aug. 23, 1945.

and the runners curved upward in front. *Leapfrog* was always called *par*, and the word *garden* was almost unknown: it was always either the *backyard* or *frontyard*, or simply the *yard*. The outdoor privies that still survived in most backyards were called *postoffices*, and the men who cleaned them at intervals operated an O.E.A. (*i.e.*, odorless excavating apparatus). The grades in school were designated *first reader, second reader*, etc. The best public room of a house was always the *parlor*. The street before it, at least for purposes of play, was *out front*.

The sweetmeats bought by children from the little stores which then hugged every schoolhouse had names that are now forgotten, e.g., *nigger-baby, shoe-string*, and *cow-flop*. A *nigger-baby* was a small, hard, black licorice candy cast in the image of a colored baby. It sold at four or five for a cent. A *shoe-string* was a length of softer licorice candy, perhaps a foot or more long. It sold for a cent. A *cow-flop* was a round, flat cake made of flour and molasses, with some ginger added and ground cocoanut mixed in. No well-mannered child of the time would dare to refer to an actual *cow-flop*, but the term was tolerated when applied to the cake, and the resemblance between the cake and the droppings of a cow was acknowledged with winks. Another delicacy of the young was *Washington pie*, which was about two inches thick and was vended in blocks about two inches square. It was made of stale pies, gingercakes, etc., ground up and rebaked. The price was a cent a square. All the schoolhouse stores sold *spit-blowers*, which were thin cylinders of tin. A bad boy who owned one would buy a cent's worth of putty, and let fly with small pellets of it at schoolma'ams, blind men and the aged. Dried peas were also used for this purpose. In the schoolroom he concealed his *spit-blower* in one of the legs of his knee pants, with the lower end caught in his long stocking. When one was discovered by the teacher, the principal was called in, and the offender was rattaned. The same stores sold many other things now forgotten — for example, colored tissue for making kites and *passapool* (*i.e., Sebastopol*) flags.[1]

[1] Mrs. B. J. Cleaves, of Garrett Park, Md. (private communication, Feb. 19, 1946), calls my attention to the fact that the pronunciation of *donkey*, in Maryland, makes it rhyme with *monkey*. From Mr. John Wm. Siegle, of Baltimore (private communication, April 27, 1940), I have received some curious specimens from the vocabulary of his great-grand-

Massachusetts

How Massachusetts is divided between the Boston dialect and General American has been described in the section on American dialects in general. An enormous amount of material about both forms of Massachusetts speech is to be found in the six volumes of the Linguistic Atlas of New England, and there is more in the files of *Dialect Notes* and *American Speech* and in the phonological and lexicographical studies already mentioned in dealing with New England. Cape Cod alone has produced a considerable literature, and Nantucket and Martha's Vineyard have produced scarcely less. The first Cape Cod study of scientific pretensions was published by George Davis Chase, of Wesleyan University, in 1903;[1] it was followed by two others in 1904 and 1909.[2] Further reports have come from Herbert W. Smith,[3] Henry J. James,[4] and Mrs. Wendell B. Phillips.[5] Chase's first paper was based on the speech of his parents, both born and brought up at West Harwich, a small village on the south shore of the Cape, and it represented the dialect prevailing *c.* 1850. He said that this dialect was already changing when he wrote, chiefly under the admonitions of the schoolmaster, who frowned upon such pronunciations as *chimley* for *chimney* and *cramberry* for *cranberry*, and the use of *ar* instead of *er* in *serve, perfect, serpent, nervous*, etc. The *r* was usually dropped before consonants, *oi* became *ai*, the flat *a* was used before *l*, there was no *y*-glide before *ew*, and *w* itself often disappeared, as in *forrard* for *forward* and *ekal* for *equal*. The verb *to be* was inflected as follows:

---

mother, born in Baltimore in 1851, e.g., *bampoolap* (with the accent on the first syllable), an elderly dandy; *Dink Dare*, a saucy colored person of either sex; *flagary* (with the accent on the second syllable), a tantrum; *pechly poorly*, honestly ill and deserving sympathy; *aahaahoo*, a haunt. He also lists *pillgarlick*, a chronic groaner, reported by Wentworth from Cape Cod. For *Sebastopol* see my Happy Days; New York, 1940, pp. 15 and 136.

1 Cape Cod Dialect, *Dialect Notes*, Vol. II, Part V, pp. 289–303.
2 Cape Cod Dialect, *Dialect Notes*, Vol. II, Part VI, 1904, pp. 423–29, and Cape Cod Dialect: Addenda, *Dialect Notes*, Vol. III, Part V, 1909, pp. 419–22.
3 Addenda to the Cape Cod Lists From Provincetown and Brewster, Mass., *Dialect Notes*, Vol. IV, Part I, 1913, pp. 55–58; Cape Cod, *Dialect Notes*, Vol. IV, Part II, 1914, pp. 155–56, and Notes From Cape Cod, *Dialect Notes*, Vol. IV, Part IV, 1916, pp. 263–67.
4 Notes on Cape Cod Dialect, *Dialect Notes*, Vol. V, Part VII, 1924, pp. 286–88.
5 Cape Cod-erisms, *Atlantic Monthly*, Oct., 1927, p. 576.

Present Indicative	Emphatic	Negative	Interrogatory	Emphatic Interrogatory
I'm	I be	I (h)aint	em I?	be I?
you'm	you be	you (h)aint	em yi?	be yi?
he's	he is	he (h)aint	is he?	is he?
we'm	we be	we (h)aint	em wi?	be wi?
you'm	you be	you (h)aint	em yi?	be yi?
they'm	they be	they (h)aint	em they?	be they? [1]

There was a tendency to make strong verbs weak, *e.g.*, *growed*, *drawed*, *busted*, *clinged*, *drinked*, *freezed*, *teared* and *catched*,[2] and verbs remaining strong had the same forms for the past and perfect participle. Elderly people were called *Aunt* or *Uncle*, and a married woman was known by her own and her husband's given names, *e.g.*, *Hope Austin* (*Hope*, the wife of *Austin* Baker). Many of the terms in the local vocabulary came from the sea, *e.g.*, *aback*, at a standstill; *gangway*, any passage way; *to get to windward*, to gain an advantage; *to go by the board*, to be lost; *to keel up*, to be laid up by illness; *ship-shape*, in good order, and *stern foremost*, backward. Other localisms listed by Chase were *bitch-hopper*, a provoking woman; *blunderbuss*, a blunderer; *to buckle*, to run fast; *chicken-flutter*, excitement; *ginger-leap*, wintergreen; *lug-wagon*, a four-wheeled farm vehicle; *meet-up*, a crony; *quuf*, the letter G; *slobber-chops*, a child or animal that scatters its food; and *tuckout*, a fill of food. In his second and third lists he added *chowder-head*, a stupid person; *fiddle-a-ding*, a trifler; *gentleman passenger*, a well-behaved boy; *harness-cask*, a barrel for salt meat; *hog age*, a boy's awkward age; *Lady Haley*, a well-behaved little girl; *to limp-to-quaddle*, to hobble; *to talk underground*, to speak indistinctly; *yeppit*, a small boy; *boiled yarn*, a dish made of brown bread crusts boiled in sweetened milk and water; *grave-stones*, prominent front teeth, and *Jack White*, a shirttail. Smith dealt with more recent locutions, and listed, among others, *facultized*, versatile; *cow-storm*, rain without wind; *nail-sick*, applied to wood so rotten that it won't hold nails; *to fly-blow*, to depreciate; *narrow-gutted*, stingy; *fumble-heels*, a clumsy person; and *to rootle*, to root (as a hog). To these, in 1924, James added *cod-head*, a knee-length boot; *hog's back son-of-a-*

---

[1] In this paradigm, I assume, *i* is used to represent the *ee*-sound.
[2] In recent years there seems to be some movement in the other direction. Mr. Paul Grimley Kuntz, of Dennis, Mass. (private communication, Dec. 26, 1943), tells me that he has heard *wed* as the past tense of *to weed*.

bitch, boiled codfish with scraps of pork, and *fat cat,* leapfrog.

Nantucket and Martha's Vineyard, the two islands lying to the southward of Cape Cod, were both settled before 1650, and, like the Cape itself, show some survivals of archaic speech. The sea has played a salient part in their history, and its terms supply their dialect with frequent pungent metaphors, *e.g., poor craft,* a sorry figure of a man; *long-sparred,* having long limbs; *down by the head,* bowed by age or infirmity; *fair wind,* good fortune; *astern the lighter,* tardy; and *to square the yards,* to pay a debt. There is some animosity between the two islands, as is shown by the nicknames applied to the people of one by those of the other — *Scrap Islander* for a Nantucketer on Martha's Vineyard, and *Old Town Turkey* for a citizen of Martha's Vineyard on Nantucket.[1] In 1915 William F. Macy and Roland B. Hussey published a book on Nantucket which listed a large number of localisms.[2] Some of them were Cape Codisms, but others were words and phrases that have not been recorded elsewhere, *e.g., to clip in to,* to make a call at; *Coff,* a native of Cape Cod, and, by extension, any other off-islander; *cornstarch airs,* formal manners; *flink,* a good time; *gallied,* frightened; *gam,* a social visit; *huddle,* a dancing party; *polpisy,* awkward, countrified; *quint,* an old maid; *to shool,* to saunter; *to sit in the buttertub,* to marry well; *stingaree,* a persistent person; *to tivis,* to wander about; *wadgetty,* fidgety, and *to wilcox,* to lie awake at night.[3] In 1918 Byron J. Rees published a similar list of Martha's Vineyard terms, gathered at Chilmark the year before.[4] It included *current,* in good health; *flake,* any section or piece; *flared,* deranged mentally; *hickory,* rough, tempestuous; *pinkletink,* a young frog; *to studdle,* to stir up, and *turkler,* a man of great energy.[5]

The large literature upon the so-called Boston accent has been

1 Edgartown, the capital of the Vineyard, was formerly called *Old Town.*
2 The Nantucket Scrap Basket, printed by the *Inquirer and Mirror* Press in the town of Nantucket. Second edition, with additions; Boston, 1930. This word-list was reprinted in *Dialect Notes,* Vol. IV, Part V, 1916, pp. 332–37.
3 A word-list prepared by James Mitchell, a native of the island, in 1848, is printed in Nantucketisms of 1848, by Allen Walker Read, *American Speech,* Feb., 1935, pp. 38–42. In this paper Read quotes from other early accounts of the island speech.
4 Word-List — Chilmark, Martha's Vineyard, Mass., 1917, *Dialect Notes,* Vol. V, Part I, 1918, pp. 15–17.
5 Other Nantucket word-lists are in Nantucket, by W. P. Adams, *Dialect Notes,* Vol. IV, Part II, 1914, pp. 156–57; More Nantucket Sayings, by W. F. Macy, *Proceedings of the Nantucket Historical Asso-*

noticed in the preceding pages, and there is no need to return to the subject here.[1] In 1943 George L. Trager published a posthumous paper on its phonology by Benjamin L. Whorf, an amateur linguist of high attainments,[2] but that paper is too technical to be summarized for the lay reader. There has been some infiltration of loan-words in the sections of Massachusetts invaded by non-English-speaking immigrants, but if any study of them has ever been published I have not encountered it. Mr. Charles J. Lovell, an acute observer of speechways, tells me[3] that in the New Bedford and Fall River area two Portuguese loans, *cabaca*, head, and *lingreesa*, sausage (Port. *linguica*), are in common use. He also says that *bobo*, apparently from the Canadian French, is widely used for chamber-pot. The children of the immigrants reciprocate by speaking a magnificent vulgar American. Mr. Lovell offers the following specimens:[4]

> After supper my dad taken off his shoes and lain down on the couch.
> He gotten hell for what he done.
> You must have been brang up in a pigpen.
> His mother should of learned him not to pick the snots from his nose.
> I known her since she was a little girl.
> Mrs. Robinson given me those pants what Phil outgrown.
> She shouldn't of letten him touch her.
> I been down there myself.
> He helt on to Watkins and broughten him down.
> He use to work for me but I fire him.
> Teacher say I an' him should of went too.
> They all know he ain't no good.[5]

---

ciation, 1935, pp. 27–29; and Nantucket, the Far-Away Island, by W. O. Stevens; New York, 1936, Ch. VIII. For Martha's Vineyard see Country Editor, by H. B. Hough; New York, 1940. For the analogous dialect of New Bedford see There's Apt to be Katowse on Deck if Scuttle isn't Hitched When Sky Begins to Look Typestric, New Bedford *Standard-Times*, March 28, 1937.

1 The common speech of the city has been described as one-third Harvard, one-third hick, and one-third mick.

2 Phonemic Analysis of the English of Eastern Massachusetts, *Studies in Linguistics*, Dec., pp. 21–40. Trager followed it with a commentary, pp. 41–44.

3 Private communication, May 17, 1933.

4 Private communication, May 31, 1933.

5 Other papers on Massachusetts speech: Expressions, Chiefly of Whalers, Noted at New Bedford, Mass., by Edward Denham, *Dialect Notes*, Vol. IV, Part III, 1915, pp. 240–42; Pixilated, a Marblehead Word, by Fannie Hardy Eckstorm, *American Speech*, Feb., 1941, pp. 78–80; Boston Accent a Myth, Boston *Globe*, editorial section, April 25, 1937, p. 3; Boston Accent, by

Mrs. R. H. Hoppin, of Belmont, Mass.,[1] calls my attention to a number of locutions apparently peculiar to the Boston region, *e.g.*, *tonic* for *soda-water*, *drymop* for *dustmop*, *dry-cleansing* for *dry-cleaning*, *spa* for a sandwich and ice-cream shop, and *apparatus* for fire-engine, and Mr. Howard S. Russell reminds me[2] that the English *moor* survives on Nantucket and Martha's Vineyard, and that *common, green* and *brook* continue in use elsewhere in the State.

Michigan

Michigan is within the Great Lakes-Ohio river area being investigated by Albert H. Marckwardt and his associates, mentioned under Illinois and Indiana. They began by confining their inquiry, save for Sault Ste. Marie, to the lower peninsula of the State. I know of no other study of Michigan speech save a brief note on its phonology, published in 1934.[3]

Minnesota

All the writers upon the speech of Minnesota call attention to the influence of non-English dialects upon it, especially Swedish, Dano-Norwegian and German. In *American Speech* in 1946 there was an interesting account, by Mrs. W. L. S. Mackintosh, of Kampala, Uganda, East Africa, of the language of her native village of Hawley, in the northwestern part of the State, about thirty miles from the North Dakota border.[4] Mrs. Mackintosh's people, on her father's side, were Scots who came to the United States by way of Nova Scotia, and on her mother's side, half northern Irish, a quarter Scottish and a quarter Pennsylvania German. "I grew up," she said, "with Scandinavians for the most part, with a sprinkling of

---

J. H. Sweet, New York *Times Magazine*, Oct. 1, 1944, p. 24; Words Coined in Boston, by C. W. Ernst, *New England Magazine*, Nov., 1896, pp. 337-44 (also articles by the same author, of the same title, *Writer*, Vol. XII, 1899, pp. 145-47, and *Proceedings of the Bostonian Society*, 1900, pp. 39-47); Survivals in American Educated Speech. II. Bostonisms, by S. D. McCormick, *Bookman*, Nov., 1900, pp. 243-46; Slur on Boston "Dialect" Draws Broad-*a* Broadside, Boston *Evening Globe*, Sept. 28, 1945.

1 Private communications, July 8, 13 and 17, 1946.

2 Private communication, Aug. 5, 1946.

3 Notes on Michigan Speech, by John Seaman, *American Speech*, Dec., p. 295.

4 A Letter From East Africa to Mr. Mencken, Feb., pp. 51-60. The letter was dated Aug. 1, 1944.

English who were early settlers, a few later-arriving Scotch-Irish from Ontario, and a very few Irish and Germans who came later." She went on:

> All our Norwegian, Swedish and Danish friends and neighbors without exception said " Can I go *with?* " instead of " Can I go *with you?* " . . . They also said, in asking if a certain person was included in, or accompanied others at any gathering, " Was he *with?* " . . . Both of these expressions were exclusively Scandinavian, and others in town never used them except in quotation marks. . . . News to the Scandinavians in Hawley always *stood* in the *Herald*. . . . My mother often said when she lost or mislaid something, "I wonder what *went* of it." . . . I vaguely considered it Canadian, but none of the other Canadians used it. . . . We always said, as the town still does, " *Who-all* was there? " and " *What-all* did you do? " Many of the Irish also use *who-all* and *what-all*.[1] As children we asked, "May we have a *piece?*," which meant a between-meal snack of bread and butter, usually superimposed with brown sugar, jelly, peanut-butter or anything available. . . . We said in sleighing talk, " Let's *slug* around this next bend," whipped up the horses and skidded with as wide a sweep and swoosh as possible around the curve. . . . My younger sister caught me out in the use of *rense* for *rinse* in recent years, but . . . we never heard *rench*. . . . *A-going* sounded quite foreign to us, as did *that-a-way*, both of which were used by a Nebraska family which moved into our community. . . . We wore *tossle* caps, certainly never *tassel* caps, and there were *tossles* on the ends of bath-robe cords, but on articles of furniture or other garments they were *tassles*. . . . Children in Hawley studying for confirmation in the Lutheran church under the tuition of the minister always did, and still do, *read for the minister*. I have heard my Swedish sister-in-law say hundreds of times that she would now *cook* the coffee. . . . *To carry on* in Hawley and generally among Scandinavians in Minnesota means to make a fuss or a scene, as in " She *carried on* until we were ashamed of her." . . . *Chores* always carried with it a flavor of the barnyard. . . . The Scotch-Irish commonly said, " I don't *dast* " for " I don't dare." " I *dasn't* " was far more rarely heard.

Here we have linguistic legacies from all over. *Dast* is New England, but is also common in the South. *To stand* (in the newspaper) is used in Pennsylvania. Wentworth finds *piece* in Pennsylvania, Maryland, West Virginia and Ohio, and it appears in William Dean Howells's novel of early Ohio, " The Leatherwood God." [2] *That-a-way*, like *this-a-way*, is ancient in English, and was probably *that-there-way* originally. *Rense* is from New England, and appears in " The Biglow Papers." *Tossle* ranges from Maine to Louisiana. *To carry on* has been in almost universal American use for more than a century, and probably originated in the West: the DAE traces it to 1828, but it is not recorded in England until 1856. Nils Flaten called

---

1 But not, apparently, *you-all*.   2 New York, 1916.

attention to *to go with* so long ago as 1900:[1] he suggested that it was a translation of the Norwegian " Vil du *gaa med?*," but it may have come into Minnesota speech from the German, in which the analogous form is " Gehst du *mit?* "[2] Says William J. Griffin, of the State Teachers College at St. Cloud:[3]

> In central Minnesota we are well acquainted with the influences of Swedish, Norwegian, Finnish, German, and Irish. But the characteristic of the common speech that impressed me most is the pronunciation of *aunt*. The vowel (not at all diphthongized) is unbelievably broad. The closest analogy I can suggest is to *flaunt*. It is the only word which is given this broad value, so far as I have observed.

Sinclair Lewis, a native of Minnesota, says that the rustic speech of the State turns *creek* into *crick* and *muskrat* into *mushrat*. Wentworth presents evidence that the former is not common in Maine, in the South, or in Appalachia, but he finds *mushrat* in New England, in Appalachia, in up-State New York, and in Wisconsin. Several localisms of the Twin Cities have been reported by William Randel,[4] *e.g., resort* in the restricted sense of an individual establishment in a resort community, *boulevard* in the sense of the grassed area between curb and sidewalk on a city street, and *to go to the lake* in the sense of to go upon any holiday, whatever one's designation. Minnesota lies within the area of the Marckwardt survey of Great Lakes speech, and the study of its dialect has been undertaken by Harold B. Allen, of the State university. It will probably be some years, however, before the field-work for this investigation is completed.

Mississippi

In 1893 a young Mississippian named H. A. Shands, seeking his doctorate at the State university, chose the local speechways as the theme of his dissertation.[5] " No previous study of this special sub-

[1] Notes on American-Norwegian, With a Vocabulary, *Dialect Notes*, Vol. II, Part II, p. 118.
[2] A Word-List From Minnesota, by Fr. Klaeber, *Dialect Notes*, Vol. IV, Part I, 1913, p. 9.
[3] Private communication, Sept. 26, 1937.
[4] Minnesota Localisms, *American Speech*, April, 1945, pp. 153-54.
[5] Some Peculiarities of Speech in Mississippi; published by the author, 1893. I am indebted for the loan of a copy of this pamphlet, now very scarce, to Mrs. James D. Oliver, librarian of the University of Mississippi.

ject," he said in his introduction, " has, within the knowledge of the writer, been made," nor has there been any other, so far as I know, since. Shands did his work under the direction of the Rev. William Rice Sims, Ph.D., and had the aid of Dr. H. Schmidt-Wartenberg, professor of modern languages at the university. He gave attention to speech on three levels — that of the educated whites, that of the illiterate whites, and that of the Negroes. He omitted " the majority of the provincialisms that are noted as common by Bartlett or other lexicographers," and made an effort to disregard " those words and expressions that have been introduced into Mississippi by foreign immigrants." What he found was in substance what is now usually called Lowland Southern, though, as usual, it showed traces of Appalachian influence. Some of his observations follow:

1. The final *a* was converted into *i*, as in *Minnesoti* and *sofy*.
2. The palatal glide after *a* and before *r*, as in *gyarden*, *cyar* and *cyarpet*, appeared in the speech of all illiterates, and in that of educated immigrants from Virginia and South Carolina.
3. Among the illiterates *a* was flat almost invariably, as in *ask*, *answer*, *last*, *grass*, *calf*, *half*, and even *aunt*, *palm* and *calm*. *Papa* became *pappy*.
4. The flat *a* before *r* was broadened, so that *barrel* became *bahr'l* and *bare* became *bahr*. In *radish*, *carriage* and *carry* it became short *e*.
5. The long *e* in *teat*, *Negro*, *fear*, *here* and *steer* became short.
6. Negroes, but not whites, used *haid* for *head*, *aidg* for *edge*, *sont* for *sent*, and *sot* for *set*.
7. Both races used *tarrier* for *terrier*, *thrash* for *thresh*, *tarrible* for *terrible* and *trassel* for *trestle*.
8. The Negroes alone used *bres* for *bless*, *gwine* for *going*, *cyo* (with a long *o*) for *cure*, *heaben* for *heaven*, *gib* for *give*, *sabe* for *save*, *debl* for *devil* and *smoove* for *smooth*.
9. He found *r* " so seldom pronounced in the middle or at the end of words by any class that its pronunciation forms an exception." Such exceptions, he noted, were found only " in a class of very illiterate whites," and their occurrence constituted " the most distinguishing feature of the real po' white trash dialect as contrasted with the Negro dialect." [1]
10. In Negro speech *th* at the beginning of words often became *d* or *f*, and in other situations, *d*, *f*, *b* or *v*. Examples: *den*, *dat*, *dis*, *froo* (*through*), *nuffin* (*nothing*), *anudda* (*another*), *breaf* (*breath*), and the before-mentioned *smoove* for *smooth*. But they sounded *th* in *otha* (*other*), *thrash*, *thumb*, *thunder* and *thout* (*without*).
11. All persons of the verb *to be*, in the present tense, indicative, were " involved in inextricable confusion " by Negroes, who used *I is*, *I are*, *You is*, *We am*, etc.
12. As compensation for the use of *bile* for *boil*, *boil* was used for *bile*.

[1] Here, I suggest, the influence of Appalachian was visible.

13. There was a confusion between *ever* and *every*, as in "he hit *ever* man in the crowd."

14. *Very* was often used in a sense opposite to its usual meaning. "In spoken discourse its meaning depends entirely on the tone in which it is uttered. If it is pronounced quickly, without any special stress, it means small extent, to a very moderate degree. Thus, sometimes, when a thing is said to be *very good* it is meant that the thing is moderately good, or not so good after all; *e.g.*, if someone were asked whether a dog is a good one or not, and should reply, 'Well he is *very* good,' it would in all probability be meant that the dog was not entirely good, but that he had some good qualities. When the necessity arises for using *very* in its emphatic or intensifying sense Mississippians nearly always employ some other term, a few of which I shall give: *real, real down, mighty, quite, tarnation, awful, uncommon, monstrous, rattling*; all of which are used as adverbs when taking the place of *very*."

"The dialect of the illiterate whites of the extreme backwoods," said Shands, "possesses a characteristic that cannot be adequately represented by written characters — a kind of drawling, nasal twang." Most of the localisms he listed were loans from Appalachia, *e.g.*, *to hone for*, to pine for; *jewlarky*, a sweetheart; *to projick*, to trifle; *jodarter*, anything superior; and *we-uns*, but he also gave a few that have not been reported elsewhere, *e.g.*, *barbershela*, a friend (borrowed from the Choctaw and used only in the south central part of the State); *to bip into*, to attack; *jimmy-jawed*, with protruding lower jaw; *to give him scissors*, to lash with the tongue; *elected with*, provided with; *to be due one a compliment*, to owe an apology; *to chaw tobacco more than onc't*, to repeat; *brief*, dressed up, and *to fisticuff*, to fight. Rather curiously, he did not mention *you-all*.

Missouri

Missouri, said Allen Walker Read in 1932,[1] "presents a welter of speech-groups, with jumbled overlappings and complex origins. The early French occupation has left its mark (very distinctly in some speech-pockets), the Southern and Northern influences have jostled, immigrant races such as the German have contributed, the Negro has brought his characteristic speechways, and geographical factors have split the State even further: the distinctive river regions, the southeastern swamplands, the Ozarks, the plains near Kansas, the

[1] Folk-Speech in Missouri, *Arcadian Magazine*, June, p. 13. Read was then an instructor in English at the University of Missouri. See also his The Strategic Position of Missouri in Dialect Study, *Missouri Alumnus*, April, 1932, pp. 231–32.

corn country near Iowa. This variety makes, for dialect study, an unlimited wealth." Basically, Missouri speech is predominantly Southern, but most of the early schoolmasters were New Englanders, and they left many traces of their tutelage. The first formal study of the speech of the State, by R. L. Weeks, was published in 1893 [1] and dealt with the dialect of Jackson county, the county-seat of which is Independence, the home-port of the Hon. Harry S. Truman. Unhappily, the " peculiar words and usages " presented by Weeks were all common to various other parts of the country, and some of them were nearly universal. Nor was there much that was singular in his list of " pronunciations and grammatical points."

D. S. Crumb, who followed him in 1903 with a lengthy study of the speech of the southeastern part of the State,[2] unearthed a great deal more that was specially Missourian, *e.g., to run a blind calf over*, to impose on; *buckshot land*, poor clay soil; *to cheep*, to mention or hint at; *clay-bank*, cream colored, applied to a horse; *to cut the comb of*, to humiliate; *door-shutter*, a door; *enthralled*, in debt; *glut*, a large wooden wedge; *groundhog case*, an irremediable situation; *like a hog to war*, sideways; *meals*, a meal, used in the singular; *to pack guts to a bear*, to engage in a low occupation; *to rehaul*, to overhaul or repair; *slack-jaw*, impudent language; *snurl*, a gnarled place in a log, and *spouty* and *water-sobbed*, water-logged, none of them found elsewhere by Wentworth. Crumb found many Southernisms, *e.g.*, the *y*-glide before *ar*, *you-all*, *evening* for *afternoon*, and *hit* for *it* in emphatic situations. He also found a large number of Appalachianisms, apparently migrant from the Ozarks.[3] Perhaps the best report upon the dialect of eastern Missouri, along the Mississippi, is to be found in the works of Mark Twain. He knew it thoroughly and recorded it lovingly, especially in " Huckleberry Finn."[4]

---

[1] Notes From Missouri, *Dialect Notes*, Vol. I, Part V, pp. 235-42.
[2] The Dialect of Southeastern Missouri, *Dialect Notes*, Vol. II, Part V, pp. 304-37.
[3] Jay L. B. Taylor, in Snake County Talk, *Dialect Notes*, Vol. V, Part VI, 1923, pp. 197-225, included a long glossary from McDonald county, the most southwesterly of Missouri counties, in the heart of the Ozarks. It did not differ materially from those of Vance Randolph, already noticed.
[4] His vocabulary is discussed at length in Mark Twain's Vocabulary, by Frances Guthrie Emberson, *University of Missouri Studies*, July 1, 1935, and in A Mark Twain Lexicon, by Robert L. Ramsay and Dr. Emberson, the same, Jan. 1, 1938. A list of other contributions to the subject by students of Ramsay is in Attitudes Toward Missouri Speech,

Montana

In 1915 Marie Gladys Hayden published in *Dialect Notes* a list of words and phrases in use in the Judith basin of Montana.[1] It showed nothing that was not common to the speech of the West, and most of it came from the lingo of cattlemen or lumbermen, *e.g.*, *soogan*, a sheep-herder's blanket, and *flunkey*, a camp waiter. A later list was included in "Montana: A State Guide-Book,"[2] but it was likewise largely confined to cattlemen's terms, with some miners' terms added. Burke lists a "Glossary of Common Speech in Montana," published at Missoula in 1938, but I have been unable to find a copy of it.[3]

Nebraska

The fact that Dr. Louise Pound was born in Nebraska and has spent nearly all her life there[4] offers sufficient assurance that the speech of the State has not gone unstudied. She made her first report upon it, in fact, so long ago as 1905,[5] and thereafter she discussed it frequently, and used it as raw material for her numerous invaluable papers on American speechways in general. Her preliminary note upon the phonology of the dialect was an excellent treatise in miniature on the whole American vulgate, at least north of the Potomac-Ohio line and west of the Mississippi, for it described characters encountered everywhere, *e.g.*, *rassle* for *wrestle*, *ketch* for *catch*, *deef* for *deaf*, *kittle* for *kettle*, *deestrick* for *district*, *histry* for *history*, *fella* for *fellow*, *spose* for *suppose*, *pisen* for *poison*, *somewheres* for *somewhere*, *acrost* for *across*, *warsh* for *wash*, *chimbley* for *chim-*

---

by Allen Walker Read, *Missouri Historical Review*, July, 1935, p. 268, n. 39. See also A Word-List From Missouri, by Constance Bey and others, *Publication of the American Dialect Society No. 2*, Nov., 1944, pp. 53-62.

1 A Word List From Montana, Vol. IV, Part III, pp. 243-45.
2 New York, 1939, pp. 413-16. This volume was one of the American Guide Series prepared by the W.P.A. The list was first published in *Frontier and Midland*, Summer, 1938, pp. 246-48.
3 The vocabulary of Montana miners is discussed in The Folklore, Customs and Traditions of the Butte Miner, by Wayland D. Hand, *California Folklore Quarterly*, Jan., 1946, pp. 1-25, and April, 1946, pp. 153-78.
4 She was graduated from the State University in 1892, took her A.M. in 1895, became a fellow in English literature the same year, was made Ph.D. of Heidelberg under Johannes Hoops in 1900, returned to Nebraska as adjunct professor, became assistant professor in 1906, associate in 1908, and full professor in 1912.
5 Dialect Speech in Nebraska, *Dialect Notes*, Vol. III, Part I, pp. 55-67.

ney, shumac for *sumac, quanity* for *quantity, strenth* for *strength, prespiration* for *perspiration, hunderd* for *hundred, ellum* for *elm, Babtis* for *Baptist, bust* for *burst, cuss* for *curse, rine* for *rind, interduce* for *introduce, sassy* for *saucy, neked* for *naked, shet* for *shut, crick* for *creek, lozenger* for *lozenge, Gahd* for *God, Febuary* for *February,* and *probly* for *probably.* Not many of the forms she listed were peculiar to Nebaska: its speech on all levels, indeed, comes very close to the norm of General American, and she noted that loans from non-English languages were confined to the areas of relatively dense immigration. Nor was there any evidence in the vocabulary, as she presented it, of specifically Southern influence: it was fundamentally Northern, but the Northern of the West, not of New England.

Dr. Pound printed a second report on it in 1911 [1] and a third in 1916.[2] In both cases her material was gathered largely by the students who had begun to cluster about her at the University of Nebraska, and nearly every one of the locutions listed was turned in by at least six informants, " generally from different sections of the State." The lists included many additions to the store of common American, *e.g., dreen* for *drain, neuraliga* for *neuralgia, snoot* for *snout, atheletic* for *athletic, secetary* for *secretary* and *incidence* for *incident,* but also some pronunciations not general elsewhere, *e.g.,* the over-careful *frag-grant* and *extra-ordinary.* Some of the terms smelled of the college campus, but there were also a number of curious localisms of wider currency, *e.g., brashy,* having a tendency to fall sick; [3] *dabimit,* an exclamation of annoyance; *to horn,* to annoy; *hymaviffa-of-the-bivavva,* a person of great importance; [4] *jigger,* a cry of warning; *lick-dab,* gravy; *to puss,* to pout or sulk; *skite,* an unlikeable person; *kadoowy,* any substance of unknown nature; *skeehaw,* crooked or out of place; *squeechy,* a term of eulogy, and *wug,* a knot of hair. These later lists showed some German influence, *e.g.,* in the use of *longsome* for *long;* in the substitution of *by* for *to,* as in " I go *by* the house," and in the use of *all* for *finished* or *exhausted,* as in " The milk is *all."* The popularity in the

---

1 A Second Word-List From Nebraska, *Dialect Notes,* Vol. III, Part VII, pp. 541-49.
2 Word-List From Nebraska (III), *Dialect Notes,* Vol. IV, Part IV, pp 271-82.
3 In use in Maine to indicate easily broken.
4 Described as " current in eastern Nebraska."

1910–20 era of the pseudo-Russian suffix, *-ski*, was reflected by *darnfoolski, devilinski, dumbski* and *smartski*.[1]

Later studies of Nebraska speech have been made by E. P. Conkle, Melvin Van den Bark, M. A. Burwell, Mamie Meredith and Erma V. Grill, some of them students of Dr. Pound. Van den Bark, who afterward collaborated with Lester V. Berrey in preparing the best dictionary of American slang so far published,[2] gave his first attention to the contemporary speech of the Sandhill section of the State, a barren and forlorn area of 20,000-odd square miles in the north central part,[3] but he afterward turned to that of the pioneers of 1854–90.[4] There was, however, considerable overlapping, for he found that the Sandhillers, in their remote settlements, preserved many locutions of an earlier day. They were, indeed, simply the last wave of pioneers, and they had sought to tame a wilderness that their predecessors had rejected. Their talk, as Van den Bark reported it, indicated that most of them had come from north of the Ohio river, but in it there were not a few terms that seemed to be of their own invention. A few examples:

> Blow-out. A hole in the sandy soil, made by the wind.
> White-cap. A hill showing many blow-holes.
> Choppies, or chop-hills. Low hills bare of grass.
> Let-down. A place where the barbed-wire of a fence may be lowered to let cattle through.
> Jump-over. A crude bridge of planks.
> Corduroy bridge. One made of windmill piping set in cement.
> Dead-man. A weight fastened to a barbed-wire fence to hold it down.
> Jerker. A corn-husker.
> Jew peddler. One selling overalls, sewing-thread, cheap jewelry, etc.
> Prune peddler. One selling dried fruits, extracts, tea, coffee, spices, etc.
> Catalog woman. A wife acquired through a matrimonial agency.
> Music-box. A gayly painted house or shanty.
> Tailer. A cow so undernourished that it must be assisted to its feet by twisting its tail.
> Thunder-pump. The green heron, commonly known elsewhere as the *shite-poke*.[5]
> Juice, *v*. To milk a cow.

1 This suffix was discussed by Dr. Pound in Domestication of a Suffix, *Dialect Notes*, Vol. IV, Part IV, 1916, p. 304; Addenda to IV, 4, 304, the same, Vol. IV, Part V, 1916, p. 354, and Vogue Affixes in Present-Day Word-Coinage, the same, Vol. V, Part I, 1918, pp. 1–14.
2 The American Thesaurus of Slang; New York, 1942.
3 Nebraska Sandhill Talk, *American Speech*, Dec., 1928, pp. 125–33.
4 Nebraska Pioneer English, *American Speech*, April, 1931, pp. 237–52; Oct., 1931, pp. 1–17; Feb., 1932, pp 161–71, and Dec., 1933, pp. 48–52.
5 Supplement I, p. 251, n. 4.

Howl. A high wind.
On pump. On credit.
Hay-wire, *v.* To mend anything.

Van den Bark's studies of the speech of the Nebraska pioneers were based upon a diligent search of the literature describing the later stages of the great movement into the West, and his four papers make a valuable record of the speechways of the whole trans-Mississippi region. The foundations of those speechways were laid by the hunters and trappers who preceded the settlers, and they were enriched by the argots of the Army and the early cowmen. "The pioneers," says Van den Bark, "came from everywhere — from the East, the South, from England, Ireland, Germany, Bohemia, Holland, and the Scandinavias. The words and expressions they coined and the words to which they gave new meanings were generally simple, honest and direct. The talk of the cowboys . . . still lives vigorously on ranches, [and is] used as slang by townsmen who refuse, sometimes, to believe that there are still *soddies*[1] . . . in Nebraska." The other investigators mentioned have made lesser contributions to the speech-lore of the State. Conkle, in 1924, published a list of curious interjections from its southeastern part, *e.g.*, *edads*, *forevermore*, *ginger blue bird*, *oh girlie*, *heavenly day*, *oh poodle*, *whiff*, *woman alive* and the German *donner und blitzen*.[2] Burwell, in 1931, listed some locutions from the South Dakota border,[3] *e.g.*, *bummy*, spoiled, slightly ill; *misbobble*, a mistake, and *to nip*, to move with the shaky steps of old age. Miss Grill, in 1933, added *explosion*, a dance; *to partake of fresh air*, to take a drink, and *Sandhill pavement*, a sandy road covered with hay, to Van den Bark's list of Sandhill words and phrases. Vernon L. Hoyt, of the Columbus (Neb.) *Daily Telegram*, sends me three more curious phrases, not peculiar to the Sandhill country,[4] to wit, *to get a good scald on*, to do any job well;[5] *to make a lot of bag*, applied to any act or process which seems to portend an ominous event,[6] and *dinner's about*,

1 *Soddy*, a sod-house. The DAE's first example of *soddy* is recent, but it traces *sod-house* to 1872. In 1932 Van den Bark reported that there were still 22 *sod* schoolhouses in the State.
2 Interjections From Southeastern Nebraska, *Dialect Notes*, Vol. V, Part VII, p. 285.
3 Expressions From Boyd County, Nebraska, *American Speech*, Feb., pp. 230–31.
4 Private communication, May 29, 1944.
5 Obviously borrowed from the vocabulary of hog-killing.
6 Hoyt says that it was originally used, and is still used, of a cow about to calve, and hence showing a swelling of the udder.

dinner is about ready — the last apparently a loan from the German or Dano-Norwegian.

Nevada

Nevada has too small a population, scattered over too large an area, to have developed anything properly describable as local speechways. In part, its people speak the argot of miners and in part that of cattlemen; for the rest, they use General American. There are word-lists of both the argots mentioned in the guide to the State prepared by the Writers' Project of the WPA.[1]

New Hampshire

As we have seen under Connecticut, the line separating the speech of the Boston area from the Eastern sub-species of General American runs northward from the Berkshires along the crest of the Green Mountains. This leaves all of New Hampshire within the Boston area, but there are local differences sufficiently marked to give its dialect a considerable individuality. For one thing, the State is predominantly rural, not urban, and hence lacks some of the affectations that have colored the speech of Boston and vicinity. For another thing, its isolation has preserved archaisms that have disappeared elsewhere.[2] The Linguistic Atlas of New England reports on the speech of 46 informants scattered through 37 New Hampshire communities.

The first effort to compile a comprehensive word-list of the State was made in 1907 by Joseph William Carr,[3] whose valuable studies of the speech of Arkansas and Maine have been mentioned under those States. Carr, who was an eager and highly intelligent investigator of American speechways, was a native of Hampstead, N. H., a village in the southeastern corner of the State, and spent the first twenty-four years of his life in contact with its speech. Hampstead was settled by immigrants from Massachusetts, and was once in Norfolk county, Mass., which comprised all the towns of the Bay Colony north of the Merrimac river. Its speech is thus almost identi-

---

[1] Nevada: a Guide to the Silver State; Portland, Ore., n.d., pp. 58-63 and 75-78.
[2] Handbook of the Linguistic Geography of New England, p. 4.
[3] A Word-List From Hampshire, S. E. New Hampshire, *Dialect Notes*, Vol. III, Part III, pp. 179-204.

cal with that of northeastern Massachusetts, but there are still some peculiarities worthy of note. I take a few specimens from Carr's lengthy list, not recorded by Wentworth's authorities: *barge*, an omnibus; *Barrington beggars*, pedlers and basket-makers from Barrington, N. H.; *black snaps*, huckleberries; *checkermint*, wintergreen; *cowy*, use of contaminated milk; *grassee*, an artificial bank covered with grass; *guts-ache*, belly-ache; *pricker*, a brier; *straddle-bug* or *stromp*, a woman with a mannish gait, and *tough cud*, a hard character. Carr also unearthed some curious pronunciations, *e.g.*, *elk* for *yolk* and *geogaphry* for *geography*. He had a second word-list under way when he died in 1908.[1]

Other contributors to the study of the New Hampshire vocabulary have been C. N. Greenough,[2] George Allan England,[3] Leo Wiener,[4] and Jason Almus Russell.[5] Greenough's list was too short to be of any value. England's second one included *to stuboy*, to set a dog on a person, *tetnit*, a child born of elderly parents, and the pronunciation *skrivel* for *shrivel*. Wiener's was gathered in 1909 or thereabout from an informant who had lived at East Jaffrey, N. H., since 1858. He sent it to *Dialect Notes* but it was lost, and not until fifteen years later did he unearth his notes. He recorded *browcing*, a beating; *calamity*, old household goods; *to stay up*, to bandage, and the pronunciation *crotch* for *crutch* and *shivel* for *shovel*. England's material came from Hillsborough county, on the Massachusetts border, as did that of Russell, published six years later. Russell's additions were mainly survivals of "a dialect of former generations," *e.g.*, *meeting-house*, traced by the DAE to 1632; *burying-ground*, traced to 1759; *contribution-box*, to 1666; *to snoop*, 1832, and *cellar-way*, 1761.

Paul St. Gaudens, who was brought up in New Hampshire, tells me that the educated speech of the State has become assimilated to General American, and, though "not as harsh as the Middle West-

---

[1] There is an account of him in *Dialect Notes*, Vol. III, Part V, 1909, p. 406.
[2] Terms From S. E. New Hampshire, *Dialect Notes*, Vol. IV, Part I, 1913, p. 54.
[3] Rural Locutions of Maine and Northern New Hampshire, *Dialect Notes*, Vol. IV, Part II, 1914, pp. 67-83; Items From South Weare, New Hampshire, *Dialect Notes*, Vol. V, Part VII, 1924, p. 295, and The Real Dialect of Northern New England, *Writers' Monthly*, March, 1926.
[4] New Hampshire, *Dialect Notes*, Vol. IV, Part II, 1914, pp. 153-55.
[5] Colloquial Expressions From Hillsborough County, New Hampshire, *American Speech*, June, 1930, pp. 418-20.

ern" variety, is "untainted by Bostonese." But there is still, he says, "a surprisingly large number of folks back in the hills who somehow retain much of what must have been the manner of speech of the colonial settlers."[1] Some of the surviving terms he has noted are *prug*, pregnant; *screwbore*, a rifle; *down-street*, down-town; *to get a feel*, to feel the effects of alcohol; *to think for*, to think; *to put right into it*, to work hard, and *strong*, full measure. There used to be a speech-island on the Isles of Shoals, seven rocky islets off the New Hampshire coast, southeast of Portsmouth, but its dialect has been much modified by the talk of Summer visitors. The first to report upon it was Celia Thaxter (1836–94), daughter of the lighthouse keeper on White Island, who began to contribute articles on the island life to the *Atlantic Monthly* in 1867.[2] She said:

> The Shoals phraseology existing in past years was something not to be described; it is impossible by any process known to science to convey an idea of the intonations, quite different from Yankee drawl or sailor-talk. . . . Why they should have called a swallow a *swallick* and a sparrow a *sparrick* I never could understand, or what they mean by calling a great gale or tempest a *tantoaster*. . . . "I don't know whe'r or no it's best or no to go fishin' *whiles* mornin'," says some rough fellow. . . . Of his boat another says with pride: "She's a pretty *piece of wood*." . . . Two boys in bitter contention have been heard calling each other *nasty-faced chowder-heads*. . . . But it is impossible to give an idea of their common speech leaving out the profanity which makes it so startling.[3]

New Jersey

Francis B. Lee, of Trenton, began investigating the speech of New Jersey in 1892, and two years later he published the first of two reports upon it in *Dialect Notes*,[4] but since then the philologs of the State have neglected the subject, though there must be rich material in the dialect of the so-called *Pineys* or *Piners* in the central and southern counties and in that of the Jackson Whites in the Ramapo mountains along the boundary-line between New Jersey and New York — in full sight, on a clear day, of the topless towers of Manhattan. The noblesse of the Newark region and the Oranges

[1] Private communication, April 3, 1943.
[2] They appeared as a book under the title of Among the Isles of Shoals; Boston, 1878.
[3] pp. 69–72.
[4] Jerseyisms, Vol. I, Part VII, 1894, pp. 327–37. It was followed by Jerseyisms — Additions and Corrections, *Dialect Notes*, Vol. I, Part VIII, 1895, pp. 382–83. To the latter the Rev. W. J. Skillman, of Philadelphia, a native of New Jersey, made contributions.

speak something resembling the pseudo-English of the Hudson valley, and the proletarians of Hudson county show the influence of Brooklynese, but in the main Jerseymen use General American. Even along the Atlantic coast there is a gap in the broad *a* territory between Cape May and Sandy Hook.

The lists compiled by Lee showed, in the main, only such mispronunciations and other malfeasances as are common to all the varieties of vulgar American, *e.g.*, *ager* for *ague*, *afeared* for *afraid*, *chaw* for *chew*, *I be* for *I am*, *nary* for *never*, and *snew* as the preterite of *to snow*, but he also offered some locutions not recorded elsewhere, *bag o' guts*, a loafer; *beach*, a sand island; *belly-wax*, molasses candy; *garvey*, a small scow; *to go by water*, to follow the sea as a calling; *to goster*, to domineer; *hold-fast*, a sore; *to ground oak*, to inflict injury on the person, or to threaten to do so; *to lug*, to bark, as a dog; *shaklin*, shiftless; *to snag-gag*, to quarrel; *tickey*, coffee; *upheader*, a horse or man of proud bearing; *to bounder*, to scrub the person, and *do-ups*, preserves. He found a number of Dutch loans, also surviving in New York, *e.g.*, *blickey*, a small bucket (Du. *blikje*, from *blik*, tin); *pinxter*, Whitsuntide; *noodleje*, noodles, and *rooleje* (pro. *rollitsh*), chopped meat stuffed in sausage skins, to be sliced and cooked. He also found one that seemed to be German, to wit, *spack*, pork (Ger. *speck*, bacon, lard). He reported that *v* was often changed into *w* in South Jersey, *e.g.*, in *winegar* and *wittles*. He said that *applejack* was always called simply *jack* by its makers, and that *Jersey lightning* was "hardly used by natives."[1] He noted the archaic *housen*,[2] but did not mention the part or parts in which he found it. In 1938 George Weller reported it still in use among the Jackson Whites.[3] To Lee's first list William Marks and Charles Simmerman added a glossary of the argot of New Jersey glass-workers, and Lee himself one of the shingle-makers of South Jersey. Mr. L. Nixon Hadley, of Evanston, Ill., tells me that he has observed the substitution of a glottal stop for mid-*t* in Jersey speech, even on high levels, *e.g.*, *bo'le* for bottle. "I will always remember," he says, "the hilarity in a

---

[1] *Applejack* is traced by the DAE to 1816, and *Jersey lightning* to 1860.
[2] *Housen* is archaic, but not exactly ancient. The NED says that *houses* is actually older.
[3] A Reporter at Large: The Jackson Whites, *New Yorker*, Sept. 17, p. 30. See also A Pre-Phonograph Record, by Albert Payson Terhune, *North American Review*, May, 1931, p. 433.

phonetic class when a very charming girl said: 'I've tried and tried, but I simply can't make a *glo'al* stop.'"[1]

New Mexico

There is a larger admixture of Spanish in the English of New Mexico than in that of any other State. "Little boys, begging on the streets of Taos," says Spud Johnson, editor of the Taos *Valley News*,[2] "say '*Dame un dime*,' pronouncing the final *e* of *dime* like the final *e* of *dame*." In the vocabulary of the State's speech in the New Mexico volume of the American Guide Series[3] nearly all the 300 terms listed are Spanish loans. Spanish, indeed, is the house language of a great many New Mexicans, especially on the lower levels, and as a result the English they speak shows a marked accent and various other peculiarities. A dialect closely resembling it has been studied in Southern California by Douglas Turney, who reports that the familiar sentence, "Now is the time for all good men to come to the aid of the party" becomes "Na-hoo eess tay-ee tah-eemm fore old goohd mehnn to cahmm to tay-ee aidd ofe tay-ee par-tee." He says that its speakers have difficulty with the English long *i* and short *a* and the combinations *sh* and *ng*.[4] The local schoolma'am struggles against these aberrations diligently, but without much success. She is impeded by the fact that the so-called Spanish element of the population — it is actually largely Indian — has been made extremely race-conscious by the lofty scorn of the 100% Americans, and is thus not disposed to make any concession to Yankee ways. From time to time its politicoes launch plans to replace English with Spanish in the primary schools of the State. Though they have never reached that goal it is now the law that any local school-board may provide for the teaching of Spanish, beginning with the fifth grade. At last accounts about 8,000 children were being so taught.[5] The English spoken by what are called

[1] Private communication, Aug. 10, 1943.
[2] Private communication, June 15, 1935.
[3] New Mexico: a Guide to the Colorful State; second edition; Albuquerque, 1945, pp. 110-19.
[4] The Mexican Accent, *American Speech*, Aug., 1929, pp. 434-39.
[5] The political and cultural factors entering into this controversy are too complicated to be discussed here. They are dealt with sensibly in The Compulsory Teaching of Spanish in the Grade Schools of New Mexico, by Joaquín Ortega; Albuquerque, 1941. I am indebted to Dr. Ortega for friendly aid, and also to Dr. Antonio Rebolledo, Mr. Keen Rafferty and Mr. John D. McKee.

the Anglos of New Mexico is basically General American, but it is full of the aforesaid Spanish loans, along with many Indian loans, and also shows some influence of Appalachian speech, apparently exerted upon it by way of Texas.[1] The Spanish of the State has been studied at length by Dr. Aurelio M. Espinosa and his colleagues,[2] but its colorful English still awaits scientific investigation.

New York

When Oliver Farrar Emerson, a young Iowa schoolmaster, sought the degree of Ph.D. at Cornell in 1889, he chose for the subject of his thesis the phonology of the common speech of the Ithaca region. The result was the first really scientific study of an American dialect ever published.[3] Ithaca is in the central part of the State, at the lower end of Lake Cayuga, and has been the home of Cornell since 1868. It is in a region settled mainly by immigrants from New England, but with some infiltration from Pennsylvania, New Jersey, Maryland and Virginia. Its first settlers were veterans of the Revolution, and most of the New Englanders among them came from Connecticut. There were also some Massachusetts men, but they apparently came from the western end of the State, and in consequence the speech of the region, at the start, was free from the imitations of English fashions that had begun to creep into the Boston area. To this day it offers an excellent example of what has come to be called General American. That is to say, it prefers the short *a* before *f*, *th* and *s*, it usually sounds the *r*, and it runs to a generally clear and distinct style of pronunciation, though terminal *g* is sometimes dropped. "In comparison with standard English,"[4] said Emerson, "it represents a dialect of the Eighteenth Century, with certain peculiarities usually attributed to the Seventeenth Century. . . . It has remained practically uncontaminated by the speech of foreigners. . . . [Its] predecessor [was] probably the English of the eastern division of England." This surmise, as we have seen, has been amply confirmed by later investigations.[5]

1 The authorities on Spanish loans in the Southwest are listed in Supplement I, p. 313, n. 3.
2 See AL4, pp. 647-49.
3 The Ithaca Dialect: a Study of Present English, *Dialect Notes*, Vol. I, Part III, 1891, pp. 85-173; republished at Zwickau, Germany, 1931.
4 *i.e.*, with London or Oxford English.
5 Emerson was a charter member of the American Dialect Society, and at the start was its district secretary

Emerson's pioneer study directed the attention of philologians, both professional and lay, to the speech of upstate New York, and during the years following many other papers on the subject got into print. Among those who wrote them were B. S. Monroe,[1] B. L. Bowen,[2] Henry Adelbert White,[3] Mrs. F. E. Shapleigh,[4] Jason Almus Russell,[5] Gerald Crowningshield,[6] and, above all, C. K. Thomas, whose seven excellent studies of upstate pronunciation began to appear in *American Speech* in 1935,[7] and who followed them five years later with two of downstate pronunciation.[8] Monroe's investigation was confined to the speech of students at Cornell. He tested 141 of them, of whom 125 were natives of the State, distributed over all save seven of its counties, and the rest had been living in it since childhood. His report described an almost pure specimen of General American. In such words as *grass*, *path*, *pass* and *laugh* his subjects preferred the flat *a* by overwhelming majorities, never running to less than 127 to 14, and their preference for a clear terminal *r*, as in *door* and *tier*, was even more marked. The only students who elided the sound came from the Hudson valley, and even among these more retained it than dropped it. Monroe found a heavy predominance of the *ah*-sound in *fog*, *hog* and *frog*, but, rather curiously, a clear *o*-sound in *dog* and *log*. He reported, somewhat incredibly, that more than two-thirds of his subjects turned *kl* into *dl* in *clean*, *clock*, *Clark*, etc., and *gl* into *dl* in *gladness* and *inglorious*, and sought to account for it by the fact that

---

for western New York. He later served on its editing committee, and after that was secretary-treasurer until 1905, when he became president. He was professor of English at Western Reserve University, Cleveland, from 1896 until his death in 1927. His books include three histories of the English language and a Middle English reader.
1 The Pronunciation of English in the State of New York, *Dialect Notes*, Vol. I, Part IX, 1896, pp. 445–56.
2 A Word-List From Western New York, *Dialect Notes*, Vol. III, Part VI, 1910, pp. 435–51.
3 A Word-List From Central New York, *Dialect Notes*, Vol. III, Part VIII, 1912, pp. 565–69.
4 Two Word-Lists From (I) Roxbury, New York, and (II) Maine, *Dialect Notes*, Vol. IV, Part I, 1913, pp. 54–55.
5 Colloquial Expressions From Madison County, New York, *American Speech*, Dec., 1929, pp. 151–53. Howard F. Barker commented on this word-list in *American Speech*, Aug., 1930, pp. 493–95.
6 Dialect of Northeastern New York, *American Speech*, April, 1933, pp. 43–45.
7 Pronunciation in Upstate New York, April, pp. 107–12; Oct., 1935, pp. 208–12; Dec., 1935, pp. 292–97; Feb., 1936, pp. 68–77; April, 1936, pp. 142–44; Dec., 1936, pp. 307–13; April, 1937, pp. 122–27.
8 Pronunciation in Downstate New York, *American Speech*, Feb., 1942, pp. 30–41; Oct., 1942, pp. 149–57.

Noah Webster had advocated these prissy mispronunciations in his American Dictionary of 1828. But Webster quickly abandoned them, and it is hard to imagine them surviving on the Cornell campus of 1896.

Bowen's word-list of 1910 was gathered in Monroe county, ten miles west of Rochester. This is the Genesee country, which was settled largely by Massachusetts people, but there were also infiltrations from the South and by Irish and Germans. Bowen found a great many of the mispronunciations that are common to all vulgar American, e.g., *apurn* (apron), *attackted*, *bust*, *childern*, *crick*, *deef*, *dreen* (drain), *et* and *to rile*, and also not a few characteristic New Englandisms, e.g., *buttery*, *meeting-house*, *pail*, *I swan*, *spider* (frying-pan) and *tunnel* (funnel), but he could find no trace of Southern influence, and very few of the locutions he listed seemed to be of local invention. White's shorter word-list, published two years later, came from the region just east of Syracuse, which was settled largely by New Englanders, though there were also some Dutch among its pioneers, and later came Irish, Germans and Scandinavians. Like the Bowen list, it showed few if any local contributions to the vocabulary. Mrs. Shapleigh's list, based on the speech of Roxbury, a village on the east branch of the Delaware river, just west of the Catskills, was too short to be illuminating, but it contained one term not reported elsewhere, to wit, *skimmelton*, a noisy serenade to a newly-married couple, usually designated a *charivari*, *sherrivarrie*, *chivaree* or *callithump*. Russell reported on Hamilton, the seat of Colgate University, some miles southwest of Utica, and his list included a number of campus terms. Crowningshield investigated the dialect of the northeastern corner of the State, mainly settled by immigrants from western Massachusetts and Vermont. He found the flat *a* even in *aunt*, and reported that the broad *a* was never used elsewhere "except as an attempt at elegance and refinement." The *o* of *frog*, *hog* and *hot* and even *rob* and *doll*, he said, became *ah*, but not that of *log* and *dog*. The *e* was diphthongized to *ai* in *leg*, *edge* and *measure*. The *r* was never elided, except as an affectation, but the final *ng* was usually reduced to *n*.

Thomas, who is a first-rate phonologist, picked up the inquiry begun by Emerson in 1889, and carried it much further, partly because of the advances of phonetics since Emerson's time but mainly because of his own superior equipment. At the beginning of his inquiry he worked mainly with Cornell students who were natives of upstate New York, and in his first group were 223 individuals from 50 of the 53 upstate counties. Later he made field trips which increased his force of informants by about 50%, and in this new lot were many "persons without college education, in some cases with very little education." Still later he added more, some of them educated and some not, and in the end he had 666, representing all of the upstate counties, with the heaviest representation from the western part of the state and the lowest from the southern. His conclusions agreed pretty well with those of his predecessors. He found that some form of the short *a*, which he described as "one of the more variable American phonemes," was overwhelmingly prevalent, and that even in *aunt* the broad *a* occurred only in speakers who had picked it up from old-fashioned aunts — probably relatively recent immigrants from New England — who preferred it. The *r* was elided, he reported, "only in a few cases of dissimilation in which an unstressed *r* before a consonant drops out before a following *r* in the same word," e.g., *gove'nor, pa'ticular*, and it was seldom that he encountered the intrusive *r*, as in *idear, vanillar*. He made a particular inquiry into the nature of the *r*-sound, and found that, like the *a*-sound, it was very variable. He also found considerable variations in the *o*- and *u*-sounds. There were signs that *deef* was dying out, and *crick* with it. "A speaker," he noted, "may pronounce *creek* as *crick* when conversing, but as *creek* when reading." In the pronunciation of *either* and *neither* the *ee*-sound prevailed over the *eye*-sound. *Been* occurred as *bin* 228 times to 87 times as *ben*, and no time "in unaffected speech" as *bean*. *Ate* was pronounced as spelled 224 times to one time for *et*, and *eggs* 200 as spelled to 35 as *aigs*. In general, he found the upstaters speaking "in a rather close-mouthed fashion," but with relatively few losses of consonants: even the *h* of *forehead* was clearly articulated. His conclusion was:

> Upstate New York speech is more closely allied with General American than with either of the other main dialectal types, but it is less closely allied than is sometimes supposed. In the East, the traditional boundary line of the Hudson river is apparently of no present significance; the line between New York and New England is certainly no further west than the political boundary, and the line between upstate and metropolitan New York is almost at right angles to the Hudson.

Thomas is still pursuing his investigation of upstate New York speech,[1] but meanwhile he has turned aside for a look at that of New York City, and Nassau, Suffolk, Westchester and Rockland counties.[2] In this section he has found three different speech-areas — that of the city, including suburban Nassau county, that of the more rural parts of Long Island, and that of Rockland and Westchester, on the two banks of the Hudson above the city. "The historic roots of Suffolk speech," he says, "are in Connecticut"; that of Rockland and Westchester "shows some traces of upstate speech." Thomas's material came from 420 persons, about half of them Cornell undergraduates "who have always lived in the downstate counties," and whose ancestors, in not a few cases, "have lived there for some generations." This material excluded, on the one hand, the affectations of the Hudson valley Anglomaniacs, and on the other hand the perversions of the lower classes in New York City. Thomas found the flat *a* prevailing in all situations, least in *aunt, ask, dance, laugh* and *last*, but overwhelmingly in *after, basket, class, grass* and *path*. In *calm*, of course, the broad *a* had it, and the same sound occurred in *gong* and *pond* and *on*, though not in *laundry*, which showed an *o*-sound. *Been* was predominantly *bin*, not *bean*, and *either* was *ee-ther*, not *eye-ther*. On the educated level investigated there was but small evidence, of course, of *deef, crick* and the like. Curiously enough, Thomas concluded that, in its general characters, this downstate speech showed rather more resemblance to Southern American than to either General American or the New England type. "In population, if not in territorial extent," he said, it "seems worthy of recognition as a fourth main type, especially when we realize that it includes not only the nine counties of this article, but parts of southwestern Connecticut and northern New Jersey as well."

The vulgar speech of the New York City area, once known as

[1] In The Dialect of Up-State New York: a Study of the Folk-Speech in Two Works of Marietta Holley, *Studies in Philology*, July, 1945, pp. 690–707, E. E. Ericson undertook an investigation of the vocabulary of two once very popular books — Samantha at Saratoga; Chicago, 1887, and Samantha at the St. Louis Exposition; New York, 1904. Unhappily, it is not quite clear just what part of New York State housed Samantha Allen and her husband Josiah. Ericson's report indicates that their speech, as recorded by Miss Holley (1844–1926), differed very little from the general vulgar American.

[2] Pronunciation in Downstate New York, *American Speech*, Feb., 1942, pp. 30–41; Oct., 1942, pp. 149–57.

Boweryese but now generally called Brooklynese, seems to have attracted little attention until after the Civil War. Its chief characteristic today is generally assumed to be its conversion of the *er*-sound into *oi*, but that change apparently did not appear until a relatively late date. When William Cullen Bryant, visiting New York in 1818, made some notes upon the talk he heard, he put down *horl* for *hall, barl* for *barrel, boees* for *boys, sich* for *such* and *yesterday* with the accent on the last syllable, but he did not record *boid* and *thoidy-thoid*.[1] Nor did either of them or any of their analogues get mention in the introduction to John Russell Bartlett's "Glossary of Words and Phrases Usually Regarded as Peculiar to the United States," first published in 1848, though he noticed and remarked the loans from the Dutch still surviving in New York speech. When the *oi*-sound first appeared, and by whom it was first recorded I do not know, though there is evidence that the New York newspapers were aware of it by 1880, chiefly in the forms of *goil* and *loidy*. But even down to the 90s, when Edward W. Townsend began writing his "Chimmie Fadden" stories, the accepted hallmark of Boweryese was not *boid* or even *goil*, but the substitution of *t* or *d* for the two forms of *th*, as in *wit* or *wid* for *with*, and *dem* for *them*. When, however, E. B. Babbitt, then secretary of the American Dialect Society, published, in 1896, the first study of the New York City dialect from the standpoint of a competent phonologist, the *oi*-sound was duly noted and discussed.[2] Babbitt called it "the one distinctive peculiarity of the New York pronunciation," and said that it was "only sporadic, and very rare at that, outside the region under consideration," to wit, New York City, the adjacent parts of New Jersey, "the commutation district" along the Hudson, Long Island, and "the Sound cities of Connecticut, up to Hartford." It has since been found, as we have seen, in parts of the South,[3] and Babbitt himself noted its use by a Kentucky woman, but it still remains pathognomonic of New York

[1] His list appears in Dictionary of the New York Dialect of the English Tongue, *c.* 1820, by Cullen Bryant, *American Speech*, April, 1941, pp. 157–58.
[2] The English of the Lower Classes in New York City and Vicinity, *Dialect Notes*, Vol. I, Part IX, pp. 457–64.
[3] Raven I. McDavid, Jr., says in Dialect Geography and Social Science Problems, *Social Forces*, Dec., 1946, p. 170, that it occurs "in the plantation area from north of Charleston to South Georgia, along the Gulf coast to the mouth of the Mississippi, and up the Mississippi and its tributaries along the bottomlands as far inland as Decatur" [Ala.].

speech, and later observers have found that it rises therein to relatively high cultural levels.[1] Said Babbitt:

> In a schoolroom in Brooklyn, with 37 pupils, 35 had this pronunciation without doubt, and of the other two one proved to have been born in Scotland and the other in Bristol, Conn. Out of a hundred cases of guards on the elevated road at Eighty-first street, 81 announced *Eighty-foist,* and in seven of the other cases the guard was clearly an Irishman or a German. The sound is difficult to imitate consciously, and outsiders, unless they come to New York very young, rarely adopt it, but the genuine born-and-bred New Yorker rarely escapes it.

Brooklynese has since been studied by other philologians and discussed at great length by the newspapers, but a good deal of mystery still hangs about it,[2] and its history remains to be determined. The theory has been advanced that its substitution of *oi* for *er* is a legacy from Dutch times,[3] and may have been suggested by the pronunciation of the Dutch *ui,* as in *duivel,*[4] but, as Edwin B. Davis has argued, this notion is brought into doubt by the fact that the actual Dutch *ui* of colonial days has become, not *oi,* but the *i* of *bite,* as in *Spuyten Duyvil* and *Schuyler.*[5] Davis is rather inclined to account for *oi* by recalling that the "replacement of a consonant by a semivowel before another consonant in order to obviate some complexity of occlusion or constriction is a common phonetic phenomenon," but he neglects to explain why this one is not found in

---

[1] John Dyneley Prince, in Brooklyn and New York, *American Speech,* Dec., 1934, p. 295, noted that on these levels it is sometimes broken into its component parts, so that *thoid* becomes *tho-id.* In the same way *toilet* becomes *to-ilet.* "This pronunciation," he says, "is supposed to be refined."

[2] E. H. Sturtevant, in Linguistic Change; Chicago, 1917, p. 71, calls its *oi* a diphthong whose first element is "an abnormal vowel similar to German *ö* or French *eu* and whose second element is *i.*"

[3] A correspondent calls my attention to the fact that the following distich is in John Trumbull's M'Fingal, written between 1774 and 1782:
   As Socrates of old at *first did*
   To aid philosophy get *hoisted.*
But this leaves some questions unanswered. Did Trumbull give *hoisted* its correct pronunciation and so turn *first* into *foist?* Or did he think of it as *h'ist,* and so produce the impossible *f'ist?* In any case it is to be recalled that his rhymes were often very eccentric.

[4] For example, by Mr. Barrows Mussey: private communication, June 15, 1936. Mr. Mussey says that his mother had a New York Dutch great-aunt who used *oi* for *er* regularly. He also says that in a novel of the 90s the dialect forms of *girl* and *pearl* were spelled *geuil* and *peuil.* Mr. George Weiss, Jr., of Richmond Hills, N. Y., tells me that in the early 30s one of the New York newspapers suggested that *goil* and *thoity-thoid* be abandoned for *guyl* and *thuyty-thuyd,* as more accurate.

[5] Metropolitan *er, ir, ur, American Speech,* Feb., 1943, pp. 77-78.

other dialects. Greet, a very competent authority, says that it "may appear . . . throughout the South," but he finds that it is "tense and very marked" in the New York dialect, and that it is not reported in any of the dialects of England.[1] Kenyon and Knott say that it is unknown whether there is any connection between the occurrence of the sound in the South and in New York.[2] It has been suggested that its prevalence in New York may owe something to the influence of Yiddish,[3] but for that surmise there is no real evidence.[4] Indeed, there is evidence running the other way in the fact that *oi* seems to have come in before Yiddish began to be the second language of the area.

The compensatory change of *oi* into *er*, as in *erster* for *oyster* and *erl* for *oil*, is equally mysterious. In 1941 Dr. Lou Kennedy, chairman of the faculty committee on speech testing at Brooklyn College, devised a nonsense jingle to illustrate its occurrence, as follows:

> "O Father," cried the *Erster* Boy
>   To the *Erster* in the sea,
> "When I grow up to be an *Erster* Man
>   What will become of me?"
> The *Erster's verse* (voice) was choked with grief
>   And he shook till the water *rerled* (roiled)
> At the awful fate of *ersters*
>   For whom men fished and *terled* (toiled).
> "They *berl* (boil) us, Boy, or *brerl* (broil) us
>   And fry us deep in *erl* (oil),
> Or the ranks we'll *jern* (join)
>   If they lack the *kern* (coin)
> Of those who are caught to *sperl* (spoil)."

In 1926, as I have noted in AL4,[5] Henry Alexander, a Canadian phonologist trained in England, suggested that *oi* in *thoid* and *er* in *erster* are really the same sound — that the hearer, expecting *er* in the first place, hears it as *oi*, and expecting *oi* in the second place, hears it as *er*.[6] He said:

---

[1] Southern Speech, in Culture in the South, edited by W. T. Couch; Chapel Hill (N.C.), 1934, p. 608.
[2] A Pronouncing Dictionary of American English; Springfield (Mass.), 1944, p. xl.
[3] AL4, p. 368.
[4] The question is discussed in Jewish Dialect and New York Dialect, by C. K. Thomas, *American Speech*, June, 1932, pp. 321–26; In Re Jewish Dialect and New York Dialect, by Robert Sonkin, the same, Feb., 1933, pp. 78–79, and Curiosities of Yiddish Literature, by A. A. Roback; Cambridge (Mass.), 1933, p. 49.
[5] p. 367.
[6] *Soiving the Ersters*, *American Speech*, Feb., 1926, pp. 294–95.

> This phenomenon ... is found in several cases in the history of English. ... It probably lies behind the puzzling substitution of *w* for *v* recorded in Cockney English of the Victorian era, a peculiarity familiar to all readers of "Pickwick." The explanation is that Mr. Weller probably used a bilabial voiced fricative, *i.e.*, a *v* sound formed by the two lips instead of the lip and teeth, for both *v* and *w*. This sound is heard today in certain German dialects; it is the voiced form of the Japanese *f*-sound. Acoustically, it is a compromise between *v* and *w*. ... A similar explanation may account for the misuse of the aspirate ... [as in] *'am and heggs* (*ham and eggs*). If we assume that in all cases such speakers have a very weak *h*-sound, it is quite possible that this would impress itself on the ear as *h* when the hearer was expecting no *h* at all, and on the other hand would be insufficiently strong to sound like a real *h* when the hearer was prepared for a full *h*-sound.

But this ingenious theory has been attacked by various correspondents — for example, Dr. Roger A. Johnson, professor of mathematics at Brooklyn College.[1] "Contrary to Alexander," he writes, "there is nothing half-way about these sounds: they are definitely and clearly interchanged." He goes on:

> I am not an expert in these matters, but is it not possible to formulate a rule which might be called the Law of Reversal, to be stated somewhat as follows: When the replacement of one sound by another has for some reason become prevalent, there ensues a reversal whereby the second is replaced by the first? ... The lower-class English acquired the habit of eliding the *h* at the beginning of a word. In a misguided attempt to correct this error they succeeded in putting *h*'s in all the wrong places. ... Similarly, the attempt to correct *foist* leads to *erl* and *erster*. The result is not confusion between the two sounds, getting them sometimes right and sometimes wrong, but an out-and-out interchange.

A somewhat similar theory was launched by Howard K. Hollister in 1923,[2] and both got some support from Robert J. Menner, of Yale, in 1937.[3] "The New York pronunciation of *bird* with *oi*," said Menner, "is ridiculed as much as any pronunciation in the country, and in attempting to correct it New Yorkers sometimes lean over backward and pronounce *oil* with the *er*-sound." But other authorities reject this notion — for example, A. F. Hubbell, of Columbia.[4] The diphthong in *thoid*, he says, is actually variable, and sometimes it comes closer to *ui* than to *oi*. "These diphthongs," he goes on, "do not occur in all the words in which ... General

---

[1] Private communication, Oct. 26, 1945.
[2] The Origin of a Dialect, *Freeman*, June 2. There is a quotation from this paper in AL4, p. 368.
[3] Hypercorrect Forms in American English, *American Speech*, Oct., p. 169.
[4] *Curl* and *Coil* in New York City, *American Speech*, Dec., 1940, pp. 372–76.

American has *er*. They are heard only in syllables in which the written *r* is followed by one or more consonants which do not constitute an inflectional ending," e.g., *woik* and *woild*,[1] but not *stoid* (*stirred*). There is a like difference in the other direction. The change from *oi* to *er* is never made in words which end with the former, e.g., *toy, boy, enjoy*, or in their derivatives, or in those in which *oi* is followed by *al, z* or *t*, e.g., *loyal, noise*,[2] *loiter*, but it does occur in those in which it is followed by *l, n, nt, s, st* and *d*, e.g., *oil, join, joint, voice, oyster*[3] and *avoid*. Hubbell rejects the Menner-Hollister-Johnson theory on the ground that " speakers who use *r*-colored vowels in words like *coil* do so only in these words and not in words like *curl*," but he confesses that, for the present, he lacks " any satisfactory explanation " of the change.

Various other peculiarities of New York vulgar speech have been noted by other observers, e.g., a final *ng* is sometimes changed to *nk*, as in *singink*; an intrusive second *g* appears in a syllable ending with *g*, as in *Long Giland*; *s* and *sh* are voiced, so that *acid* becomes *azid* and *assure* becomes *azhure*; voiced consonants are unvoiced, so that *village* becomes *villitch* and *hills* becomes *hilce*; a glottal stop is substituted for medial *t*, as in *le'er* (letter);[4] the two sounds of *th* are confused, or converted into *t* or *d*, as in *t'row* and *wid*; final *r* often disappears, as in *cah* (car) and *fah* (far); an intrusive *r* is frequent, as in *I sawr*;[5] the long *i* and the short *u* are converted into *ah*, as in *tahm* (time) and *cahm* (come), and the flat *a* into *e*, as in *kesh* (cash). Even more curious changes have been reported. *Hit* becomes *hitth*, *dead* is indistinguishable from *debt*, and *trip* acquires an *f*-sound, making it something on the order of *tfip*. Many of these

---

1 Hugh Morrison, in New Yorkers Can't Speak English, *American Mercury*, Sept., 1938, pp. 42–46, says that the New York soap-boxers, in quoting the Communist Manifesto, say *Woikus of de woild, unite!*
2 But *poison* seems to offer an exception.
3 Here, of course, there is some competition from the common *ai*, as in *h'ist* (hoist).
4 The New York Lingo, New York Times Magazine, Oct. 10, 1943: "We write *lerrers*. We buy *buh-er*. We talk of the *innernational* crisis."
5 Says Dermot Cavanagh in The R in New Yorkese, *Word Study*, Oct., 1941, p. 7 (reprinted from the New York *Times*): " New Yorkers employ the *r*-sound for euphony only. They drop it out where it isn't needed, as in *fuh coat*, and leave it in where euphony commands, as in *furry animal*. When a consonant between words is needed, as in *raw egg*, the New Yorker slips in one of his surplus *r*'s and says *rawr egg*. Where there is already a consonant the New Yorker does not put in his *r*: he says *raw deal*."

forms are ascribed to "a common habit of holding the tongue nearly flat in the mouth during the articulation of *t, d, s, z, sh, zh, n* and *r*, instead of placing its tip somewhere upon the gum above the upper teeth."[1] It is a strange fact that a man born and bred to this dialect later became one of the most adept practitioners of Oxford English known to linguistic pathology. He was William Joyce, who alarmed the English during World War II in the character of Lord Haw Haw.[2] The Dutch loans in the New York vocabulary, some of them long since taken into the common speech of the country, are discussed in AL4[3] and Supplement I.[4]

North Carolina

One of the first Northerners to leave an account of his observations in the South was William Attmore, a Philadelphia merchant who visited North Carolina in 1787 to collect some lethargic accounts. In his diary for December 6 of that year he wrote:

It sounds strange to my ear to hear the people in Carolina, instead of the word *carry* or *carried*, commonly say *toat* or *toated*. I asked a boy what made

[1] The Speech of New York, New York *Times*, July 12, 1936. This is a report of an investigation in Brooklyn, by the aforesaid Dr. Kennedy in association with William Temple and David Driscoll. They found the worst speech errors in Williamsburg and East Flatbush, and the least in Flatbush and Midwood. Bensonhurst, Borough Park, Brownsville, East New York and Bushwick lay between. More difficulties with *th* were found in East New York than anywhere else. Glottal stops were most frequent in Williamsburg.

[2] Topics of the Times: Accents Across the Sea, New York *Times*, editorial page, Sept. 22, 1945. He was hanged Jan. 3, 1946.

[3] pp. 108-11.

[4] pp. 141-42 and 186-97. There is a section on The Local Vernacular in New York Panorama, the first volume of New York City: A Guide to the World's Greatest Metropolis, prepared by the Federal Writers' Project of the Works Progress Administration; New York, 1938, pp. 152-61, but in a review in the *New Republic*, Oct. 26, 1938, p. 340, Robert M. Coates denounced it for "devoting too much space to listing pseudo-Winchellisms and similar slang expressions and too little to the really absorbing peculiarities of New Yorkese and Brooklynese." In Some Words From Irvin S. Cobb, *American Speech*, Feb., 1945, p. 75, Steven T. Byington discussed some Long Island locutions in a story by Cobb, but not a few of them, *e.g., loblolly*, a muddy spot, and *swivit*, a hurry, are found in other places by Wentworth. See also New Yorkers Can't Speak English, by Hugh Morrison, *American Mercury*, Sept., 1938, pp. 42-46; Simple Language Guide to Brooklyn, New York *Times*, June 12, 1946, p. 29, and Brooklyn Primer, by J. F. Bender, New York *Times Magazine*, July 7, 1946, p. 14.

his head so flat; he replied "It was occasioned by *toating* water." This is the usual phrase. I am told the joiner charges in his bill for "*toating* the coffin home" after it is finished.[1]

To tote, of course, was not a North Carolinaism, nor was it new, for it had been recorded in Virginia in 1677, and there were many other records of it before 1787. Wentworth finds it in use from Maine to Oregon, but the DAE marks it "chiefly Southern," and Noah Webster called it "a word used in slave-holding countries, said to have been introduced by the blacks."[2] But it is highly characteristic of all the dialects spoken in North Carolina today — Appalachian, Tidewater and Lowland Southern.

The earliest study of the State's speech that I am aware of was contributed to *Dialect Notes* in 1918 by J. M. Steadman, Jr.[3] Nearly all the words and phrases on the list might have been found in a dozen other States, but there were nevertheless a few that have not, so far, been recorded elsewhere, *e.g., frensy* (or *frency*), the withered, dry leaves of tobacco or cotton; *high-bob* and *scoots*, a highchair; *to nullify* (or *nellify*), to balk; *shoe-round*, a dance; *to see monkeys*, to be overcome by the heat; *swamp-root*, moonshine whiskey, and *sore-back*, a Virginian.[4] Four later word-lists from North Carolina were published in 1944[5] and a fifth in 1946.[6] Like the Steadman list they consisted largely of locutions common to

[1] Journal of a Tour to North Carolina; edited by Lida Tunstall Rodman, *James Sprunt Historical Publications*, Vol. XVII, No. 2, pp. 1–45; Chapel Hill (N.C.), 1922. I am indebted for this to Miss Louise Hall, of Duke University.
[2] Supplement I, pp. 208–10.
[3] A North Carolina Word List, Vol. V, Part I, pp. 18–21. There was an earlier and briefer one, assembled by C. Alphonso Smith, in *Dialect Notes*, Vol. IV, Part V, 1916, pp. 343–44, but it was confined to student slang at the University of North Carolina.
[4] Steadman explained this as follows: "The North Carolinians say that they had to climb over the backs of the Virginians to get at the enemy during the Civil War and that the tar on their heels gave the Virginians sore backs." See the discussion of *tarheel* in Chapter X, Section 4.
[5] A Word-List From Buncombe County, North Carolina, by Hugh C. Laughlin, *Publication of the American Dialect Society*, No. 2; Greensboro (N.C.), Nov., 1944, pp. 24–27; A Word-List From the Mountains of Kentucky and North Carolina, by Cratis D. Williams, the same, pp. 28–31; A Word-List From North Carolina, by Francis C. Hayes, the same, pp. 32–37; and A Word-List From Virginia and North Carolina, by George P. Wilson, the same, pp. 38–52.
[6] A Word-List From Virginia and North Carolina, by C. M. Woodard, *Publication of the American Dialect Society*, No. 6, Nov., 1946, pp. 4–43. The North Carolina terms were heard in Pamlico county, 1900–10.

the whole South and a good part of the North, but again there were some exceptions, *e.g.*, *foot-pie*, an apple turnover; *goochy*, goosy; *lazy-gal* (or *lazy-wife*), a bucket running along a rope, used to bring water from a spring; *to softmouth*, to wheedle; *to talk short*, to speak angrily; *aboon*, above; *to belch back*, to rebound; *cha-cha*, the katydid; *dogwood Winter*, a spell of cold after dogwood is in blossom;[1] *lap-baby*, a child in arms; *sanky-poke*, a traveling-bag; *tourer*, a tourist; and *to unfeed*, to defecate. These came from all over the State — some from the mountains to the west, some from the low-lying and isolated coast country, and some from the Yadkin region, settled largely by Germans. The latter began to filter in in 1709, and their descendants continued to use German, *e.g.*, in church services, until *c.* 1850. The language is now forgotten, but it has probably left some sediment in the English of the area.

The dialect of the North Carolina coast differs considerably from the Tidewater speech of Virginia and South Carolina. It shows a number of archaic terms that seem to be survivors of the first settlements. An early report on it, published by Collier Cobb in 1910,[2] was chiefly devoted to these archaisms. A number of them have not been reported from other places in the United States, *e.g.*, *acre*, a furlong; *may*, a sweetheart; *kelpie*, a water-sprite; *to scoop*, to run away; *cracker*, a boaster; *to bloast*, to brag; *bloater*, a chubby child; *cant*, gossip; *to abrade*, to sicken; *birk*, a smart young fellow; and *fause*, a tidal creek; but nearly all of them are to be found in the English dialects. Cobb also listed some curious pronunciations, *e.g.*, *buer* for *butter*, *egal* for *equal*, *leuch* for *laugh*, *plead* for *pleased*, *fant* for *infant*, *fole* for *fool*, and *wharrel* for *quarrel*. He described the dialect as the language of "the better classes, or at least the middle classes, in England in the days of Elizabeth." He noted that, even in 1910, improving communications with the mainland — there called the country — were wearing it down.[3]

Elizabeth Jeannette Dearden, in her study of the materials accumulated by the late Guy S. Lowman, Jr., for a projected South Atlantic States section of the Linguistic Atlas, shows that the division be-

---

[1] Supplement I, p. 184.
[2] Early English Survivals on Hatteras Island, *University Magazine* (University of North Carolina, Chapel Hill), Feb., 1910, pp. 3-10.
[3] See also A Bit of Elizabethan England in America, by Blanch N. Epler, *National Geographic Magazine*, Dec., 1933, and Marooned for 300 Years, by George E. Basler, *Holiday*, preview issue, 1945.

tween Appalachian and General Southern speech lies more to the eastward in North Carolina than in Virginia. This she explains on the ground that "the Virginia Piedmont was settled by expansion from the coast," whereas that of North Carolina "was settled to a large extent by the Scotch-Irish and Germans who pushed out into the uplands from the mountains." "This area in North Carolina," she continues, "has acquired nowhere near the linguistic prominence and uniformity of the Virginia Piedmont. . . . There has been a spreading of mountain terms down the Cape Fear river." The isoglosses separating the mountain speech from that of the Piedmont enter North Carolina somewhere between Surrey and Warren counties. They are not very clearly marked, and a large area shows mixed speech. The extension of Piedmont speech eastward is blocked by the so-called pine barrens, where new terms "are stopped short because of the sparsity of the population and the high rate of illiteracy." There are many speech-pockets on isolated peninsulas along the coast: they show archaisms that have disappeared further inland, and no two of them are quite alike. Plans for a more comprehensive and scientific survey of North Carolina speech are now being furthered by George P. Wilson, secretary-treasurer of the American Dialect Society, and Hans Kurath. Wilson is accumulating word-lists, and Kurath is seeking to augment and analyze the material gathered by Lowman.[1]

North Dakota

I have been unable to find any report on the speech of North Dakota. Apparently it differs but little, if at all, from that of the adjoining States, especially Nebraska and Minnesota.

Ohio

Ohio, with an area of 41,222 square miles (nearly that of England) and a population of more than 7,000,000, shows a number of

[1] He read a paper on Dialect Areas in North Carolina at the meeting of the Linguistic Society of America in July, 1941, but it has not been published. Differences in time and pitch between the speech of a North Carolina girl and an Englishman using Oxford English were reported on by H. E. Atherton and Darrell L. Gregg in A Study of Dialect Differences, *American Speech*, Feb., 1929, pp. 216–23. They found that the girl spoke faster than the Englishman and showed less care in enunciation.

diverging speech areas, though most of its people speak General American. In the Western Reserve, comprising thirteen counties in the northeastern corner of the State, there is still some evidence that most of the early settlers came from New England, and in the extreme south, along the Ohio river, there are equally plain tracks of Southern influence. Also, there are areas in which foreign immigration has left its mark, notably that of Cincinnati, which was settled largely by Germans. Some surviving New England pronunciations in Hudson township, which straddles the Cuyahoga river just below Cleveland, were noted in the first issue of *Dialect Notes* (1890) by N. P. Seymour,[1] but he had to add that many that had been familiar in his youth were beginning to disappear, *e.g.*, *sneck* for *snake*, *bury* to rhyme with *fury*, *put* to rhyme with *hut*, *deestrict* for *district*, and *cheer* for *chair*. In 1917, John S. Kenyon, a highly competent phonologist born in 1874 in Medina county, also just south of Cleveland, contributed some valuable observations on the pronunciation of that country in his youth,[2] and in 1921 he followed with a few corrections.[3] Nearly all the terms he listed were of New England origin, and he himself traced the genealogy of most of them, but there were also a small number borrowed from non-Yankee immigrants, *e.g.*, *shillalah* from the Irish and *wampus* from the Pennsylvania Germans. In 1890 J. M. Hart and other members of the Philological Society of the University of Cincinnati contributed some local notes to *Dialect Notes*,[4] but only one of the words they offered showed German influence, to wit, *allerickstix*, which was described as a schoolboys' term meaning *all right* (Ger. *alles richtig*).

In 1916 W. H. Parry dealt with the dialect of six counties in the southeastern part of the State, three of them fronting on the Ohio river and facing West Virginia.[5] This area, he said, was settled by two streams of immigration, the first coming from New England by way of the river and the second from Maryland, Virginia and southern Pennsylvania over the mountains. The result was a mixed speech with some curious oddities, *e.g.*, the insertion of *r* between

[1] New England Pronunciations in Ohio, Vol. I, Part I, p. 17.
[2] Western Reserve, *Dialect Notes*, Vol. IV, Part VI, pp. 386–404.
[3] Western Reserve Terms, Vol. V, Part IV, pp. 122–23. In *Dialect Notes*, Vol. V, Part II, p. 76, there had been a commentary on his 1917 list by Arthur G. Brodeur.
[4] Notes From Cincinnati, Vol. I, Part II, pp. 60–63.
[5] Dialect Peculiarities in Southeastern Ohio, *Dialect Notes*, Vol. IV, Part V, 1916, pp. 339–42.

u or *e* and *sh*, as in *rursh* (rush) and *frersh* (fresh). "Occasionally," said Parry, "there is a sentence arrangement peculiar to German, such as the use of *once* as the German *einmal* and the use of the verb at the end of the sentence."[1] His list showed only a few terms not reported from other parts of the country, e.g., *tucks*, rheumatism; *bone-eater*, a dog, and *dry-hole*, a stupid person (from the oil field term).[2]

There has been a natural and considerable interchange of words and phrases between one part of Ohio and another, and the well-known Germanist, Dr. R-M. S. Heffner, who was born in 1892 at Bellefontaine, in the west central part of the State, testifies that New Englandisms were common there in his boyhood, though the area lies "well out of the sphere of influence of the Western Reserve.[3] He reports, indeed, that of the thousand-odd forms from the Maine coast listed by Dr. Anne E. Perkins in 1927 and 1929[4] no less than 630 are "entirely familiar to my ear from the usage of my father and his friends." The elder Heffner was born in Logan county, in which Bellefontaine is situated, and "his parents came over the mountains to Ohio from Pennsylvania." The speech of Athens, O., the seat of Ohio University,[5] has been reported by Lewis A. Ondis.[6] Athens is in the southeastern part of the State, adjoining the area discussed by Parry in 1916. Ondis says that the peculiarities he lists "are found on all social levels, including town officials, business people and even native school teachers," and that they "are quite general over an area of about thirty or forty miles about Athens, reaching the vicinity of Lancaster and Chillicothe." "The continual flow of students from all parts of the country and

---

1 To these Mrs. R. H. Hoppin, of Boston (private communication, July 8, 1946), adds the following from Alliance, which is but thirty miles from the Pennsylvania border: the omission of the auxiliary, as in "My hair *needs* combed"; *kidder* for *kid* (possibly under the influence of the Ger. *kinder*); *unelse* for *unless*, and the use of *anymore* as in "I do that all the time anymore."
2 Dr. William B. Bean, of Cincinnati (private communication, June 17, 1946), adds *jupe*, used to designate tuberculosis in southern Ohio and northern Kentucky. The patient is sometimes called a *juper*.
3 Maine Dialect in Ohio, *American Speech*, Feb., 1938, pp. 74-76.
4 Vanishing Expressions of the Maine Coast, *American Speech*, Dec., 1927, pp. 134-41, and More Notes on Maine Dialect, the same, Dec., 1929, pp. 118-31.
5 Not to be confused with Ohio State University, which is at Columbus.
6 Dialectal Peculiarities of Athens, Ohio, *American Speech*, Oct., 1945, pp. 232-33.

the permanent faculty of Ohio University," he continues, "have had hardly any influence on the natives." I quote from his paper:

-ish. This combination is invariably heard as *-eesh*. . . . A native will pronounce *fish, ignition, official, commission, vision, fissure* and *issue* as *feesh, igneetion, offeecial, commeesion, veesion, feessure* and *eesue*. Short *i* in any other position is normal.

-ush. Generally pronounced *-oosh*, especially in *bush, bushel, push*, which are invariably *boosh, booshel, poosh*. Long and short *u*, as in *fuse* and *tub*, are normal.

a. In this region and generally throughout Ohio the short *a* approaches the sound of short *e* as in *met, bet*, though somewhat prolonged. Such words as *calf, half, land, pass, past, salve* are usually pronounced *keff, heff, lend, pess, pest, sevv*.

au, aw. These digraphs approach the sound of *o* in *come, stop, done*, so that *caught, daughter, automobile, lawn* are pronounced *cut, dotter, ottomobile, lon*.

Ohio, of course, is in the area being investigated by Albert H. Marckwardt and his collaborators for the projected Linguistic Atlas of the Great Lakes and Ohio valley regions. They have already gathered material from the towns of Hiram, Medina, Ottawa, Mt. Vernon, Richmond, Bear's Hill, Worthington, Reynoldsburg, Marietta and West Union. In 1930 Hans Kurath, then of Ohio State University and later editor-in-chief of the Linguistic Atlas, made a detailed report upon the speech of a young woman junior at the university.[1] The subject was a native and lifelong resident of Columbus, born of a father of German ancestry (though he did not speak German), and a New England mother. Henry Sweet's "The Young Rat" was used to test her speech, which was recorded in a modification of the IPA alphabet. My impression is that this record shows a good specimen of General American, with a few Southern influences.[2]

Oklahoma

The educated Oklahomans speak General American, and in the speech of the lowly Okies there is little to distinguish it from that

[1] A Specimen of Ohio Speech, *Language Monographs*, No. VII, Dec., 1930, pp. 92–101. This was published in the Curme Volume of Linguistic Studies, brought out in honor of the seventieth birthday of Dr. George O. Curme, the distinguished grammarian.

[2] I should add that I am not too sure. It seems to me to be quite impossible, reading such a record aloud, to effect any save the most remote approximation of the speech of the subject. This is proved every month by the Phonetic Transcriptions in *American Speech*. Indeed, I long ago offered a confidential prize of a keg of beer to any phonetician who could identify the speech of President Truman by an IPA record.

of the adjacent wilds, especially the Ozark regions of Missouri and Arkansas. As far as I know, there has been no published study of the local vocabulary. A brief glossary appears in " Oklahoma: A Guide to the Sooner State," one of the WPA's series of State guidebooks,[1] but it is confined to oil-field terms. In 1938 Floy Perkinson Gates made a report on some of the words and phrases used in the Dust Bowl,[2] but offered no evidence that they were peculiar to Oklahoma. They included *black blizzard*, a very severe storm; *black roller*, of the same meaning, and *dust pneumonia*, apparently a variety of silicosis. Dean E. H. Criswell, of the University of Tulsa, has collected material from a dozen counties, and has interested some of his students in English in the work, but it will take a number of years to cover so large a State.[3]

Oregon

Save for a few terms borrowed from the Chinook jargon,[4] the speech of Oregon does not depart noticeably from the vocabulary of General American, and in phonology it sticks to the same normalcy. There are, of course, some pockets of different speech, mainly created by accidents of immigration. One such pocket is in the hills of Wallowa county, in the northeastern corner of the State. This inhospitable region was settled by fugitives from the Ozarks, and they brought with them the speech of Appalachia, with some traces of Lowland Southern. Says T. Josephine Hausen, the only observer to report upon it: [5]

> Such forms as *nestes* for *nests*, *postes* for *posts*, *holp* for *help* and *effen* for *if* may be heard in the ordinary speech. . . . The pupils in rural schools carry their lunch in a *poke* and sometimes *tote* their drinking water also. A pencil-sharpener is a *pencil-trimmer*, a library table is a *stand-table*. *You all* for *you*, *hit* for *it* are common expressions. . . . To feel *dauncy* is to feel dizzy, *to jeppo* means to cook for a crew of workmen.[6] In the Spring the *chillun* roam the hills in search of *wooly breeches* for greens, or scour the woods for *woodfish*, mushrooms. A *gap* is a gate, and *cowbrutes* are cattle. . . . A *ferrididdle* is a chipmunk, and a *varmint* may be any wild creature from a mouse to a cougar or bear.

1 Norman (Okla.), 1941, pp. 121-22.
2 Duststorm Words, *American Speech*, Feb., pp. 71-72.
3 Program of the annual meeting of the American Dialect Society, 1946, p. 2.
4 Supplement I, pp. 310-11.
5 Wallowa County, Oregon, Expressions, *American Speech*, Feb., 1931, pp. 229-30.
6 *To jeppo* is not recorded for the Ozarks.

Miss Hausen reports a number of borrowings from the argot of the cattlemen, *e.g.*, *pino*, a pony; *buckaroo*, a rider of wild horses; *to wrangle*, to round up cattle, and *bascal*, a Spanish cowhand.[1]

Pennsylvania

Pennsylvania, as a whole, belongs to the domain of General American, but its speech shows many peculiarities, not only in vocabulary and pronunciation but also in intonation, and in the Pennsylvania German area there is a dialect that has influenced not only the speech of the whole State, but also that of other States. The home territory of this dialect is coterminous with that of Pennsylvania German itself — a region described by Marcus Bachman Lambert as embracing 17,500 square miles, "or considerably more than twice the area of the State of Massachusetts."[2] Its base runs a little south of the Mason and Dixon line from the Delaware river to the longitude of Altoona and it extends northward to the vicinity of Williamsport on the west branch of the Susquehanna.[3] Its influence upon the local English has been heavy in vocabulary, but even heavier in intonation and syntax.[4] The early German settlers, when they began to acquire English, translated their native idioms, and in many cases those translations survive, and have been picked up by non-German natives, though not infrequently they do violence to accepted English usages, especially in the matter of prepositions. A familiar example is provided by the use of *all* in such phrases as "The soup is *all* (Ger.

[1] A few Oregon terms are in A Word List From Northwestern United States, *Dialect Notes*, Vol. V, Part I, 1918, pp. 22–29.
[2] A Dictionary of the Non-English Words of the Pennsylvania-German Dialect; Lancaster (Pa.), 1924, p. vi.
[3] Its boundaries are rather more sharply defined by Hans Kurath in German Relics in Pennsylvania English, *Monatshefte für deutsche Unterricht*, Vol. XXXVII, 1945, pp. 96–102. On the east, he says, they run from Stroudsburg through Easton to Doylestown and Norristown, where they turn westward to the dense German settlements of the Lancaster plain. The northeastern boundary runs from Stroudsburg to Lock Haven on the Susquehanna. To the west "we find no clear boundary": German loans simply become rarer and rarer until one lands in Ohio. But some of them, as Kurath's accompanying map shows, cover much wider areas, *e.g.*, *smearcase*, which is found all the way north to Erie, Pa., and in New Jersey, Delaware, Maryland, Virginia and West Virginia, to say nothing of speech-pockets in the Carolinas and the West.
[4] Says R. Whitney Tucker in Linguistic Substrata in Pennsylvania and Elsewhere, *Language*, March, 1934: "The psychological influence of the German substrata, reflected in syntax and idiom, is very great."

alle) — a form that, like *smearcase*, has been carried by Pennsylvania German immigrants, as we have seen, to many other States. Another is to be found in the substitution of *dare* for *may*, as in " Dare I go out?," which was obviously suggested by the German *darf*, of somewhat similar sound. A third lies in the redundant use of *once*, as in " Come here *once*," which parallels the German use of *einmal*. I take the following additional examples from Tucker and Kurath, from papers on the subject by William Prettyman,[1] W. H. Allen,[2] B. A. Heydrick,[3] L. Sprague de Camp,[4] E. K. Maxfield [5] and Claude M. Newlin,[6] and from reports by various correspondents:

Against, as in " These shoes look new *against* yours " (Ger. *gegen*).
Already, as in " I had algebra *already* in my freshman year " (Ger. *schon*).
Doppich. Awkward (Ger. *täppisch*).
Dress around, v. To change one's attire (Ger. *umkleiden*).
Dress out, v. To undress (Ger. *auskleiden*).
Get, v., as in " We are *getting* company " (Ger. *Wir bekommen besuch*) and *to get awake* (Ger. *wach werden*).
Grex, v. To complain (Ger. *krächzen*).
Have, v. Used in place of *to be*, as in " He *has* homesick " (Ger. *Er hat heimweh*).
It has, as in " *It has* fellows like me " (Ger. *es gibt*).
Leaven. Past tense of *to leave*, used in place of *to let*, as in " Why don't you *leaven* him go? " (Ger. *lassen*).
Let, v., as in " I *let* the book lying on the table " (Ger. *lassen*).[7]
Need, v., used without the infinitive, as in " The wine *needs* cooled " (Ger. " Der wein *gehört* gekühlt ").
On, used in place of *in* or *at*, as in " He sings *on* the choir " (Ger. *am*), and " Paw's *on* the table " (Ger. *am*).
Outen, v. To extinguish. Maybe influenced by the *-en* ending of German verbs.[8]
Should, used in place of *is said*, as in " He *should* have said that," i.e., " He *is said* to have said that " (Ger. Er *sollte* gesagt haben ").
Spritz, v. To sprinkle or squirt (Ger. *spritzen*).
Struwwely. Unkempt, used of the hair (Ger. *struwwel*).

[1] Dialectal Peculiarities in the Carlisle Vernacular, *German American Annals*, March and April, 1907, pp. 67–79.
[2] Pennsylvania, *Dialect Notes*, Vol. IV, Part II, 1914, pp. 157–58.
[3] Pennsylvania, *Dialect Notes*, Vol. IV, Part V, 1916, pp. 337–39.
[4] Scranton Pronunciation, *American Speech*, Dec., 1940, pp. 368–71.
[5] The Speech of South-Western Pennsylvania, *American Speech*, Oct., 1931, pp. 18–20.
[6] Dialects on the Western Pennsylvania Frontier, *American Speech*, Dec., 1928, pp. 104–10.
[7] Tucker says that *to leave* and *to let*, both *lassen* in German, are exchanged in meaning, e.g., " Leave me go," and " I *left* him do it."
[8] *Outen* occurred in Old and Middle English, but not as a verb. I am indebted here to Dr. F. W. Gingrich, of Albright College, Reading.

Till, used in place of *by, by the time that, before,* as in "I must get my shoes *till* Sunday" (Ger. *bis*).
Towards, used, like *against,* in place of *in contrast to, in comparison with* (Ger. *gegen*).
What for, as in "*What for* a man is he?" (Ger. *was für*).
Wonder, as in "*It wonders* me" (Ger. *mich wundert*).
Yet, used in place of *too,* as in "Do you want to be fanned *yet?*" (Ger. *noch*). Also used in place of *still,* as in "When we lived in the country *yet.*" Also as a general intensive, as in "And he's a preacher *yet*" (Ger. *doch*).

In the predominantly German areas, radiating out from Lancaster and York, this list might be considerably prolonged, and there are signs of German influence almost everywhere in the State. The speech of Philadelphia, investigated by Tucker, is essentially a variety of General American, but it shows both German and Scotch-Irish traces. In it, he says,[1] " final and preconsonantal *r* is rather generally pronounced, though not with so much emphasis as in upstate New York and the Middle West." He goes on:

In initial *wh* the aspirate is lost, so that *wheel* is pronounced like *weal, which* like *witch, where* like *wear,* etc. . . . All the diphthongs and long vowels . . . tend to be overlong, [which] gives an effect of slow speech, of drawling, a little unusual in urban dialects. . . . There is an unusually strong tendency to omit a following unaccented vowel, so that *mayor* is pronounced *mare.* . . . Short *o* [as in *God, dog*] remains fairly short and is pronounced *ah* in most positions, but before *f* and *ng,* and before *g, s* and *th* [as in *tooth*] when final or followed by another consonant, also in the word *on,* it is prolonged, tense and rounded. The same sound appears in such words as *awful, talk* and *thought.* In *oi, oy* the first element is long and close: *bo:i.* . . . Long vowels are usually pronounced as diphthongs. These diphthongs are greatly exaggerated in Philadelphia. It is [the sound of *o*] in *old, go,* more than any other, that makes Philadelphia speech seem affected or sissified to other Americans.

Tucker notes only a few peculiarities of vocabulary, *e.g., square* for *a city block, in the road* for *in the way, this after* for *this afternoon, spigot* for *faucet, to serve* for *to carry* or *deliver, well?* for *what?* in asking for the repetition of a remark or question, and *any more* in the sense of *now,* as in " Mary goes to high-school *any more.*"[2] He notes that some of the local terms are shared by New

---

[1] Notes on the Philadelphia Dialect, *American Speech,* Feb., 1944, pp. 37-42 — a paper read at the Indianapolis meeting of the Linguistic Society of America, Jan. 2, 1942.

[2] Kemp Malone pointed out in *Any More* in the Affirmative, *American Speech,* Aug., 1931, p. 460, that its use in the negative, as in " He doesn't do that *any more,*" is common English idiom. Wentworth adds that it is also used in questions, as in "Do you go there *any more?*" Most of the numerous examples that

York City; he might have added Baltimore for others, *e.g., square* and *spigot.* Rejecting the usual assumption that *any more* shows German influence, he suggests that it may have a Welsh source. Also, he points out importations from the Southern Piedmont. " Rather odd," he says, " is the intonation in short sentences beginning with *yes* and *no,* where there is a rising and falling pitch accent, in addition to special stress, on the last word: ' Yes it îs,' ' No we hâven't.' " This Philadelphia dialect extends into the three adjoining Pennsylvania counties, into northern Delaware (including Wilmington), and into New Jersey (including the shore resorts from Cape May to Atlantic City).

The speech of southwestern Pennsylvania, below the Allegheny river, has been studied by Maxfield.[1] This region was once a part of Virginia, and traces of Southern influence are still visible in its dialect. There is also a considerable sediment of German expressions. But the Scotch-Irish influence is predominant. The local speech-tune " is characterized by odd curves of pitch and tone, a question, for example, rising when one would expect it to fall, and descending at the most unexpected places." Maxfield lists a number of words and phrases that do not seem to be recorded elsewhere, *e.g., huthering,* a state of disorder; *all-day,* a sewing party lasting all day; *pine-tree,* any evergreen, and *to lend,* to borrow. *To neb,* to be inquisitive, and *to sleep in,* to sleep late, are also recorded for West Virginia, but whether they were taken there from Pennsylvania or *vice versa* is not known. *To want out* and *to want in* are in common use. The head of a family is the *mister.* The Appalachian *poke,* a small bag, is heard frequently. *Can* is used as an auxiliary, as in " I don't think I *will can.*" So is *get,* as in " I didn't *get to go.*" *On* is used in the dative, as in " His wife died *on* him " and " I wear white shoes *on* my baby," but is sometimes displaced by *for,* as in " The cow died *for* me," meaning " I lost my cow." The dialect of this region in

Wentworth cites come from either Pennsylvania or West Virginia, but he also has some from Iowa, Illinois, New York, Montana, Kentucky, South Carolina, Ohio, Maryland, Kansas, Indiana, and even Ontario. In all these regions there are other signs of German influence. In *Any More, American Speech,* Feb., 1932, pp. 233-34, D. W. Ferguson adds Michigan. There is a discussion of the phrase in West Virginia Peculiarities, by John T. Krumpelmann, *American Speech,* April, 1939, p. 156. In Affirmative *Any More* in England, *American Speech,* April, 1946, p. 151, Robert J. Menner calls attention to its use by D. H. Lawrence in Women in Love.

[1] The Speech of South-Western Pennsylvania, before cited.

pioneer days has been studied by Newlin,[1] using certain writings of the Whiskey Rebellion era, 1793–94, as material. His conclusion is that "at least four widely different types of English" were then spoken there — "Scottish English, Irish English, backwoods English and standard English."

De Camp, in reporting on the dialect of Scranton,[2] says that it should be "classed as a kind of General American," but that it has "distinctive features." He finds that the *r* following the *e* of *yet*, as in *very*, is clearly pronounced, that the vowel in such words as *ask*, *last* and *afternoon* "appears to be identical with that in *cat*," that the *u* in *new*, *tube*, *due*, *assume*, *blue*, etc., seldom shows a preceding *y*-sound, and that the two sounds of *th* are often changed to *t* and and *d*. Allen's material came from the Reading region and Heydricks's from Adams, York, Lancaster, Lebanon and Schuylkill counties, all within the Pennsylvania German *Sprachgebiet*. Allen reported the peculiar intonation before noticed: "the voice," he said, "is raised at the beginning of a question and lowered at the end."[3] He went on:

> Questions frequently contain an *ain't:* "It's a nice day, *ain't?*," "You'll do that, *ain't you will?*," "He's been a long time gone, *ain't he has?*." If one asks, "Have you any good apples?" the answer is "I *do*." "Don't you think?" with a falling inflection is often added to questions. . . . A sort of genitive of time is found in "She came *Saturdays* and left *Mondays*." In each instance this means one particular day. . . . Many words and constructions are obviously of German origin. *That* equals *so that*, as in "We like our mince-pie piping hot *that* it steams." . . . *To look* means to be fitting, as in "It doesn't *look* for two girls to go there alone." . . . You can *give* a person right and *give* him goodbye.

Allen listed a number of German loans in common use, *e.g.*, *tut*, a paper bag (Ger. *tüte*); *verdrübt*, sad; *freinschaft*, relationship (Ger. *freundschaft*); *glick*, to come out right (Ger. *glück*, luck); *hivvely*, rough (Ger. *hübelich*, knobby); *rutschi*, a sliding-place (Ger. *rutschen*, to rush); *siffer*, a drunkard (Ger. *säufer*), and *schussle*, a

---

[1] Dialects of the Western Pennsylvania Frontier, before cited.
[2] Scranton Pronunciation, before cited.
[3] Tucker, in Linguistic Substrata in Pennsylvania and Elsewhere, p. 4, describes it differently. "The voice," he says, "is raised in the middle of the sentence and lowered at the end, in contrast to the practise, usual in American English, of raising it at the end; thus, 'Is your *mother* home?,' 'Are you *going* down town?,' 'Are you going down *town* today?.' This phenomenon . . . seems to occur also in Pennsylvania German."

clumsy person (Ger. *schussel*). Heydrick added *butter-bread* (**Ger.** *butter-brot*), *saddy*, thank you (probably from Ger. *sag dank*), and *to stick*, as in " *Stick* the light out " (Ger. *ausstecken*). Prettyman in his study of the dialect of Carlisle, eighteen miles west of Harrisburg, found plenty of evidences of Scotch-Irish influence, along with many Germanisms. He argued that the frequent local use of *still*, as in " Don't yell: I heard you *still*," shows the former. He ascribed the use of *to flit*, to move, and *flitting*, household effects going from one house to another, to the same source, and likewise *strange* in the sense of bashful. But he concluded that *on the attic* was suggested by the German *auf dem boden*. The use of *that* in place of *it*, as in " *That's* a cold day today," puzzled him, for he found that the German *das* was not so used in Pennsylvania German. He ascribed " the frequent use of the present tense instead of the perfect to denote an action begun in the past but continued in the present, *e.g.*, ' I have had only one since I *am* here ' " to " the well-known German use of the present instead of the English perfect." He concluded:

> We have found a few survivals of obsolete or obsolescent English due to the influence of the Scotch-Irish, but it must be remembered that the persistence of some of these was traceable to the influence of similar German words. The vast majority of all the deviations from the English norm are directly traceable to the influence of the Germans, who, since the latter part of the Eighteenth Century, formed a considerable part of the population.

The most extensive vocabulary of Pennsylvania local terms is to be found in a pamphlet by Henry W. Shoemaker, first published in 1925.[1] It deals with the speech of the central mountain region, above the upper border of the Pennsylvania German area. The words and phrases listed, says the author, " are mostly of English origin: a few of them were familiar in Chaucer's day; more in Shakespeare's. Next in number are Gaelic roots, brought into Ireland by Highlanders who settled there after the Battle of the Boyne, or real Erse from the Irish Indian fighters of Revolutionary days. Other words are of German, Dutch, French or Shekener [2] beginnings, while a few hearken back to times of aboriginal associations and intermarriages

[1] Thirteen Hundred Old Time Words of British, Continental or Aboriginal Origins, Still or Recently in Use Among the Pennsylvania Mountain People; Altoona (Pa.), 1925; second ed., 1930. I am indebted for access to this work to Mr. A. Monroe Aurand, Jr., of Harrisburg.

[2] Penna. Ger. *Tschechener*, a gipsy.

with the whites." Shoemaker includes many terms from the days of the canal-boatmen and lumbermen and even from the Revolutionary era; most of them are now obsolete, and others still in use seem likely to follow them " as good roads, automobiles, picture shows and radios standardize the mountain people." His vocabulary seems to be predominantly Scotch-Irish, *e.g.*, *baachie*, nasty, filthy (Sc. *baach*, disagreeable to the taste); *boal*, a cupboard in a wall; *comb*, the crest of a mountain; *cot-betty*, a man fond of women's work; *bubbly-jock*, a turkey-gobbler; *cooser*, a stallion; *fey*, doomed to death or calamity, and *usquebaugh*, home-made whiskey, but there are many signs of German influence, *e.g.*, *bubeliks*, an endearing term for a baby (Penn. Ger. *bubli*, a small boy); *dudelsock*, a home-made bagpipe (Ger. *dudelsack*); *hex*, a witch; *geik*, a home-made fiddle (Ger. *geige*); *heaven's letter*, a written charm (Ger. *himmelsbrief*); *lusty*, cheerful, agreeable (Ger. *lustig*); *nochtogal*, whippoorwill (Ger. *nachtigall*), *rokenbrod*, coarse black bread (Ger. *roggenbrot*, rye-bread); *meyer*, an ant (Ger. *ameise*); *upstuck*, proud, aristocratic, and *wamus*, a jacket. There are also some loans from the Dutch, *e.g.*, *kloof*, a gap in the mountains and *vrow*, a wife; from the French, *e.g.*, *lupe*, a wolf, and from the language of the Pennsylvania German gipsies, *e.g.*, *mukkus*, a dull, stupid person (Gipsy *mukka*, a bear).

Many words seem to have been borrowed from the New Englanders who settled the northern tier of Pennsylvania counties, *e.g.*, *buttery*, pantry; *jag*, a load of hay or wood, and *vendue*, an auction sale, and others were either brought in from Appalachia or (perhaps more probably) exported to Appalachia, *e.g.*, *dulcimer*, *groundhog* and *poke*.[1] Shoemaker says that *Hog Dutch*, meaning speakers of High German as distinguished from Pennsylvania German, is from Ger. *Hochdeutsch*, but it may be pejorative. Pennsylvania German influence appears in a number of the terms having to do with witchcraft, *e.g.*, *bonnarings*, stars and circles painted on barns to ward off ill fortune, and *black book*, the reputed Seventh Book of

---

[1] Elizabeth Jeannette Dearden, in A Word Geography of the South Atlantic States, says: " *Paper bag* occurs everywhere in Pennsylvania and Delaware, as in Virginia and North Carolina. *Paper poke* is current in southwestern Pennsylvania and western Maryland. *Paper sack* is used around the fringes of the *poke* area. . . . The counties as far west as Sullivan, Luzerne, Carbon, Lehigh and Berks agree with the New England counties in using *want to get off* where the rest of the State says *want off*."

Moses. Two terms that may be indigenous are *Blackthorn Winter*, a late Spring snow after the thorn-trees are in bloom, and *Pigeon Snow*, a similar snow after the arrival of the wild pigeons: this last survives despite the fact that wild pigeons are now no more. Other words that do not seem to have been reported from other regions are *aethecite*, a mean, eccentric person (*atheist?*); *afterclap*, a child born long after its siblings; *to algerine*, to cut timber on another's land; *to arsle*, to sit unquietly; *blackie*, a small iron cooking-pot; *bull-driver*, a farmer from the back country; *botty*, a girl's backside; *cats'-heads*, women's breasts; *clipe*, a blow with a club; *cat's water*, gin; *codster*, a stallion; *cooster*, a worn-out libertine; *comb*, the crest of a mountain ridge; *castor-cat*, the beaver; *cooner*, a cute little boy; *to float*, to produce a miscarriage; *gow*, a gelding; *goose-cap*, a wayward girl; *goose-ground*, a common or market-place; *hog pig*, a castrated hog; *hawps*, a tall, awkward girl; *jit*, a bastard; *kadifter*, a blow on the head; *major-general*, a large, masculine woman; *pot-headed*, stupid; *to stamp*, to loaf on the boss's time; *sickener*, a tedious story; *spread*, a woman's shawl, *Summer-side*, the north side of a valley, and *tokens*, a girl's garters. Shoemaker reports that a noisy serenade to a bridal couple is called both a *callathumpian* and a *belling* — another indication of the mixed speech influences in the area. He also reports *dauncy*, unwell, which is mainly Appalachian, but has also been found in Maine, California and Oregon.

Kurath, in "German Relics in Pennsylvania," before cited, bases his study, which is mainly confined to the Pennsylvania German area, upon the materials collected by the late Guy S. Lowman, Jr., and upon investigations by Lester Seifert and Carroll Reed "for their doctoral dissertations at Brown University, 1942." He says that the most conspicuous German loans are "words for certain food stuffs and dishes, calls to domestic animals, terms for farm implements and parts of vehicles, names of insects and small animals, terms of endearment, . . . and [words for] parts of the house and the farm buildings." Among the cooking terms he lists *thick-milk*, curdled sour milk (Ger. *dickemilch*); *ponhaws* or *ponhoss*, scrapple (Ger. *pfannhase*); *fat-cake*, doughnut (Ger. *fettkuchen*), and *foss-nocks*, also doughnut (Ger. *fastnacht*). The calls to animals include *vootsie*, to pigs; *hommie*, to calves, and *bee*, to chickens. The farm terms include *over-den*, a loft (Ger. *obertenne*); *saddle-horse*, near-horse (Ger. *sattelgaul*); *saw-buck* and *wood-buck*, saw-horse (Ger.

sägebock and *holzbock*), and *shilshite*, swingle-tree (Ger. *silscheit*). Says Kurath:

> As one looks over the types of German or Germanized expressions that have survived in the English of Pennsylvania one is struck by the fact that they fall within the same range of meanings for which American English has widely retained local and regional terms. The conditions supporting the preservation of such terms, whether they are of English or foreign origin, are the same everywhere: everyday use in the home without countervailing influence of the school and the printed word.

During the Eighteenth Century German was more spoken in large parts of Pennsylvania than English, and in 1753 Benjamin Franklin voiced a fear that it might oust English altogether.[1] The white bond-servants of British origin had to learn it, and so did the Negro slaves.[2] Its lingering effects upon the English pronunciation of a century ago have been studied by Sara Gehman in the diary of an American-born Pennsylvania boy who began writing in German in 1826 and continued in English in 1832.[3] The fact that in Pennsylvania German *b* was a voiceless consonant very close to *p* gave him difficulty when he essayed to write English, and his book was full of such spellings as *pring* (*bring*), *petwene* (*between*) and *py* (*by*). In the other direction he wrote *broduck*, *biece* and *berson*. He also confused *d* and *t*, as in *pount* (*pound*), *remainter*, *hundret* and *United Staids*.[4] *Wh* and *th* baffled him sorely, and he wrote *wit*, *wealberow* and *mesot* (*method*). In 1871 his son continued the diary, but without showing a much better grasp of English phonology, for he wrote *grintstown* (*grindstone*), *kitel*, *blough* (*plow*) and *swinkeltree*, and imitated his father's *wealberow*. John Russell Bartlett, writing in 1859,[5] predicted that the German influence upon Pennsylvania English would last a long while. The German spoken in the State, he said, was "already much corrupted" and he believed that "in the course of time it must give way to English," but he thought it would "leave behind it an almost imperishable dialect as a me-

---

[1] Supplement I, p. 140.
[2] Bilingualism in the Middle Colonies, by Allen Walker Read, *American Speech*, April, 1937, pp. 93-99.
[3] Isaac Hunsicker's Copy-Books, *American Speech*, Feb., 1934, pp. 46-48.
[4] W. Matthews says in Two Notes Upon Seventeenth Century Pronunciation, *Journal of English and Germanic Philology*, July, 1933, p. 300, that such spellings as *Prodestant* were common in the Early Modern English period and "must represent genuine voicings."
[5] A Glossary of Words and Phrases Usually Regarded as Peculiar to the United States; second edition, p. xix.

mento of its existence." "It is a curious fact," said Kurath in 1943,[1] "that no one has recognized to this day the extensive contributions of Pennsylvania German to English. Our vague linguistic notions are obviously derived from our political history of the Nineteenth Century, which was dominated by the conflict between the North and the South."[2]

Rhode Island

Rhode Island belongs to what Hans Kurath[3] calls the Narragansett Bay speech-area, which also includes the adjoining counties of Connecticut and Bristol county, Massachusetts. "Here," he says, "expressions are current that have not been encountered elsewhere in southern New England. Some of these are confined to small districts, others are known on both sides of the bay, and some have spread to Buzzard's Bay, to Martha's Vineyard and Nantucket, to Cape Cod and to the New London area." He lists a number of terms that are common to the whole area, *e.g.*, *closet* or *kitchen-closet*, a pantry; *crib*, a corn-crib (*corn-house* and *corn-barn* are never used); *cade*, a pet lamb, and *apple-slump*, a deep-dish apple-pie, and others that are confined to parts of it, *e.g.*, *tippetybounce*, a seesaw; *fryer*, a frying-pan; *horning*, a serenade; *shacket*, a hornet; *squin*, the livers and lights of a pig, and *eaceworm*, an earthworm. Some of these have extended beyond the bounds of Rhode Island, but they seem to have been carried by immigrants from the State. The rural Rhode Islanders, in pronouncing *aunt*, wobble between the Boston *ahnt*

---

[1] Memorandum Concerning a Book of The English of the Eastern States.

[2] I am indebted for useful suggestions to the Rev. Benjamin Lotz, of Bethlehem (Pa.); Dr. F. W. Gingrich, of Reading; President David A. Robertson, of Goucher College; Mr. John Stanley Crandall, of Urbana (Ill.); Mr. Gerald G. McKelvey, of the Waynesboro Junior Chamber of Commerce; Mr. Donald M. Brown, of New York; Dr. George McCracken, of Otterbein College; Mr. Blaine A. Kelley, of Washington (D.C.); Mr. Conrad Richter, of Tucson (Ariz.); Lieut.-Col. F. G. Potts, of Mt. Pleasant (S.C.); Dr. Jacques Barzun, of Columbia University; Mr. Henry W. Edgell, of Cambridge (Mass.); and Miss Dawes Markwell, of New Albany (Pa.). See also Dutchisms in English, by Louis J. Livingood, Altoona (Pa.) *Morning Call*, Aug. 19, 1944; *Crazy Bait*, by Atcheson L. Hench, *American Speech*, April, 1942, pp. 133-34, and Provincialisms of the "Dutch" Districts of Pennsylvania, by Lee L. Grumbine, *Proceedings of the American Philological Association*, Vol. XVII, 1886, pp. xii-xiii.

[3] Handbook of the Linguistic Geography of New England: Providence (R.I.), 1939, p. 13.

and the General American *ant*. They sound a clear *f*, not a *v*, in *nephew*. They use *how ah yuh?* as a salutation, with an occasional descent to *how be yuh?* They say *judge*, not *jedge*. They sometimes omit the first *r* in *secretary*, but they sound the vowel in the penultimate syllable. When they do not use *Negro* or *colored man*, which seems to be usually, they call an Aframerican a *niggah*, a *dahkey* or a *coon*. *Calm* and its analogues have the broad *a*. *Deaf* is usually *def*, not *deef*. *Jaundice* is never *janders* and *drowned* is seldom *drownded*. *Depot* for *railroad station* is still in use, though it seems to be fading.[1]

The pronunciation of the Rhode Islanders in colonial days has been studied by Claude M. Simpson, Jr., who made use of the enormous collection of early spellings and rhymes assembled by Miles L. Hanley and his students at the University of Wisconsin,[2] and also of the town-records of Providence, Portsmouth and Warwick. In the latter he found a number of words used in senses not recorded in the NED, and others that antedated the NED's examples. Of the former he recorded *creasing-plane*, apparently a common tool in the Rhode Island of 1700; *to enlarge*, to compensate; *faultive*, a person at fault; *flag-collar*, a cheap horse-collar, possibly stuffed with dried flag plants; *in forwardness*, in advance of; *hobbing-iron*, an instrument of unknown character; *act of oblivion*, a cancellation of debts; *to offend*, to obstruct, as a road, and *wainscoat-plow*, a carpenter's tool. Simpson found old words in the town records that antedated "by over two centuries" the earliest examples given in the NED. His full dissertation has not been printed, but there is a copy of it in the custody of the American Documentation Institute at Washington, and microfilms and photostats are obtainable.

In 1936 Professor George Hibbitt, of Columbia, invading the town of Little Compton in search of local folk-lore, picked up phonograph records of the speech of the inhabitants, most of them descendants of immigrants who left the Plymouth colony at an early date. He reported on his return to New York that it was "clipped and sharply staccato, with no trace of the northern New England drawl." He found *stoop* and *piazza* in use to designate a porch, *help*-

[1] I take all these from the Linguistic Atlas of New England.
[2] Lexical Notes From Rhode Island Town Records, *Dialect Notes*, Vol. VI, Parts XII and XIII, 1936, pp. 517–27, and Early Rhode Island Pronunciation, 1636–1700, as Reflected in Published Town Records, *Dialect Notes*, Vol. VI, Part XIV, 1937, pp. 579–82.

keeper used for *housekeeper*, and such pronunciations as *lodge* for *large*, *hahly* for *hardly*, *krasligged* for *crosslegged* and *summus* for *summers*.[1] Another observer, reporting on the speech of Providence, lists *gangway*, a small street; *cleanser*, a cleaner of garments, and *rule*, a recipe. He says: "You hear broad *a*'s all up and down the street. One can't be kidded about them here, or be covertly suspected of affectation or undue attachment to things English. As a matter of fact, we're more consistent about our broad *a*'s than the English."[2]

South Carolina

South Carolina has produced an able phonologist in Dr. Raven I. McDavid, Jr., and as a result its speech promises to be studied more scientifically than that of any save a few other States.[3] Surveys for the Linguistic Atlas, begun by the late Guy S. Lowman, Jr., have been continued since his death in 1941 under McDavid's direction, and a great deal of first-hand material has been accumulated. The speech of the State, according to Greet, is partly Tidewater Southern and partly the General Southern of the country above the fall-line, excluding the mountains of Appalachia.[4] The division between the two areas, according to another Southern authority, is made "by a line drawn through Columbia parallel with the coast."[5] But McDavid has shown that the matter is rather more complicated than this, and that isoglosses mark off the different tides of early settlement.

---

[1] Shanghai Pierce, New Folk Hero, Had Voice One Could Hear 2 Miles, New York *Times*, Nov. 30, 1936. Shanghai was one of Hibbitt's discoveries — the Rhode Island equivalent of Paul Bunyan.

[2] In Perspective, by B. W. P., Providence *Journal*, March 6, 1944.

[3] McDavid was born at Greenville in 1911 and got his Ph.D. in English literature at Duke University in 1935. His interest in linguistics was aroused by attendance at the Linguistic Institute at the University of Michigan, where he pursued studies under Bernard Bloch in 1936, 1938, 1940 and 1941. His contributions include The Pronunciation of American English at Greenville, S. C., a paper read before the Linguistic Society of America in New York, Dec. 28, 1938; Low-Back Vowels in the South Carolina Piedmont, *American Speech*, April, 1940, pp. 144–48; The Unstressed Syllabic Phonemes of a Southern Dialect, *Studies in Linguistics*, 1943, pp. 51–55; Phonemic and Semantic Bifurcation, the same, 1944, pp. 88–90, and Dialect Areas of South Carolina, a paper read before the meetings of the South Atlantic and South Carolina Modern Language Associations in 1946.

[4] Southern Speech, in Culture in the South, edited by W. T. Couch; Chapel Hill (N.C.), 1934, pp. 594–615.

[5] Word List From Wedgefield, South Carolina, by Mary Celestia Parler, *Dialect Notes*, Vol. VI, Part II, 1930, pp. 79–85.

The first settlers along the coast were mainly southern English but there was also a considerable body of French Huguenots. They were followed by two groups that pushed into the interior — the first, south of the Santee river, made up principally of German-Swiss, and the second, above the river, of Baptists from Wales and Presbyterians from Scotland and Northern Ireland. Finally, a flood of Scotch-Irish and Pennsylvania Germans came down from the north along the eastern slopes of the Appalachian chain, " totalling perhaps as many as the white population of the coastal settlements and of the townships planted from the coast." The result was a formidable conflict of dialects, further complicated by later immigrations from the Northeast, but the commercial and cultural influence of Charleston was sufficient to make its speechways more or less dominant, and they are thus often encountered far in the interior.

The dialect of Charleston was first investigated so long ago as the 80s by Sylvester Primer, then a teacher at the College of Charleston.[1] Those were the cradle days of phonology in the United States, and Primer found it necessary to expound, even to a presumably professional audience, some of the elements of that dawning science. Like most of the other early investigators of American speechways he was struck by the number of archaisms he encountered. Charleston, he reported, was a speech-pocket in which many Briticisms of the Seventeenth Century still survived, though there were already signs that they would not last much longer. " A stranger in conversation with a Charlestonian," he said, " first observes a slight shade of difference in the pronunciation of certain vowels and words. Peculiarities of this kind are naturally more marked among the middle and lower classes, though the prevailing sound which a given letter may have acquired . . . pervades to a certain extent all classes of society." He went on:

[1] Charleston Provincialisms, *Transactions of the Modern Language Association*, Vol. III, 1887, pp. 84-99. A revision of this, under the same title, was printed in the *American Journal of Philology*, Vol. IX, 1888, pp. 198-213, and also in *Phonetische Studien*, Vol. I, 1888. Primer wrote other papers on the subject, including one on The Huguenot Element in Charleston's Provincialisms in *Phonetische Studien*, Vol. III. He was born in Wisconsin in 1842, but removed to New York as a child. He served in the Civil War as a cavalryman under Sheridan and Custer and was wounded at Antietam. After the war he took to language studies at Harvard, Leipzig, Göttingen and Strassburg, and in 1895 was given a Ph.D. by the last-named. From 1891 until his death in 1913 he was professor of Germanic languages at the University of Texas.

In the more common pronunciation of the words *ear* and *air*, *tear* (lacryma) and *tear* (to rend) are not distinguishable. *Hear*, *care*, *fair*, etc., also belong to this class.... The proper names *Pierce*, *Peirce*, *Pearce* always have the long *e*-sound and are never pronounced *pers*, as in New England. *Either* and *neither* fluctuate between *ee* and *eye*.... The pure *a*-sound, as in *father*, is rare in Charleston; the tendency is rather to the *ae*-sound, as in *man*, *cat*, *sad*.... We also have the same sound for *a* and *au* when they precede *f*, *ft*, *n*, *nd*, *th*, *s* and *sh*: *ask*, *demand*, *ant* and *aunt*, *glance*, *bath*, *laugh*, *example*, *launch*, *grant*, *command*, *dance*, *past*, *gaunt*, *jaunt*, etc., all of which have the sound *ae* and never *aa*.

Obviously, Primer was here describing a speech quite different from the Tidewater Southern of Virginia — one in which relics of various British provincial dialects had been preserved by the social intransigence of Charleston, and spread by the city's prestige to its dependencies. He continued:

The words *dog* and *God* always have the sound *aa*, as *daag*, *Gaad*.[1] ... That shade of the *u*-sound heard in *put*, *book*, *pull*, *pudding*, etc., has passed entirely over to its sound in *but*.... The *oi* in words like *boil*, *toil*, *oil*, often has among the lower classes the pronunciation of *bile*, etc. ... When *a* precedes *r*, *r* is almost inaudible, as in *hard*, *harsh*, *harp*. It disappears in words like *more*, *door*.... The introduction of an *i*-sound between *k*, *g* and a following *a*-sound has modified the character in words like *cart*, *garden* (*cyart*, *gyarden*). Here belong *kind*, *scarlet*, *sky*, *guard*, *guide*, *garrison*, *carriage*, *girl*, etc.

McDavid's studies began with the dialect of his native Greenville, a town of the Piedmont at the base of the Blue Ridge. His discussion of the phonology of that dialect is rather too technical to be summarized here, but it may be noted that, in the cases of two familiar words, to wit, *to hoist* and *to rear*, he shows how a divergence in meaning has flown from a divergence in pronunciation. He says:

In standard speech the noun *hoist* refers to a mechanical contrivance, the verb to the execution of a mechanical or formalized operation, like the *hoisting* of a flag. In the vernacular — the speech of rural, substandard urban or boys' groups — the noun *h'ist* refers to a lift or boost given with the arms or shoulders, the verb to the giving of such a lift. Such rural speakers hear of ammunition *hoists* and socially privileged boys hear others ask to be given a *h'ist* up the side of a fence; the two forms are borrowed back and forth until for practical purposes they exist side by side as independent words.

A more striking peculiarity is the existence of two forms, *rear* and *rare*, for *to rear*. The first of these is the general word; the second is a verb describing two types of action: (*a*) that of a horse rising on its hind legs, and (*b*) that of a man drawing himself back preparatory to throwing a missile or striking a blow, as in "I *rared* back and hit him" or "He *rared* back and threw the ball

[1] The context shows that he here had in mind the *a* of *all*, *war* and *law*.

as hard as he could." Whether decreasing familiarity with horses will make the metaphor less apparent and keep the doublet from spreading is a matter for speculation. The present existence of the doublet in at least one dialect is a fact.

Wedgefield, whose speech Miss Parler investigated in 1930, is a small village in Sumter county, about thirty miles east of Columbia. Among the terms she listed were *to put a bad mouth on*, to suggest an evil contingency; *big doin's, adj.*, conceited, haughty; *brass ankle*, a person who passes for white but is suspected of having Negro blood; *butt* or *butts meat*, fat salt pork; *to cap the stack*, to cap the climax; *carbox*, a box-car; *to cut up Jack and kill Jinny*, to raise a commotion; *embroidery*, ambrosia (a dessert of oranges and grated cocoanut); *lot*, a stable yard; *mutton corn*, green corn; *paratoed*, pigeon-toed; *sick'em*, said to anyone who sneezes; *sivvy beans*, Lima beans; *to specify*, to make good, and *yinnah*, a pronoun used for *you*, singular and plural. Miss Parler reported that coarsely ground corn is called *grits* before cooking and *hominy* afterward. Only the lowest class of poor whites (locally, *po' buckras*) call it *grits* after it is cooked. "This fact," she says, "has led some of the people who pride themselves on their breeding to ask for *hominy* in a store. A few others used carefully to ask for a quart of *grist*, partly because *grist* was considered more correct, but chiefly to avoid such a po' buckra word as *grits*." Miss Parler says that the addition of the redundant *own* to possessive pronouns, as in *his own, the doctor's own*, etc., is characteristic of upcountry South Carolina speech, and Dean J. C. Seegers, of Temple University, tells me that it is also to be found in Charleston, "usually among Charlestonians of German descent," who also used *all both*.[1] I am indebted to Dr. McDavid for the following additional observations:[2]

Psalm, calm, palm, etc., still rhyme with *jam* in rustic South Carolina speech, and also in the speech of the older generation in Charleston — not the so-called first families, but quite respectable people. The broad *a* of Boston or Oxford occurs only as an affectation in the *-s, -f* and *-n* words; the normal pronunciation is *tomayto* and *vayse*. *Lava* occurs only with the broad *a*; *gratis* with that of *hat* or *hate*; the second syllable of *asphalt* has the *aw*-vowel. The common pronunciation of *pretty* uses the vowel of *good*. In upcountry South Carolina there is no medial vowel between *ah* and *aw*. The first occurs in *swan, squalid* (varied, sometimes, by the *hate* vowel), and *wash*; the latter in *water. Swamp* and *God* may have either. The *oo* of *fool* occurs in *room* and *broom* and *coop* only rarely. The *uh*-vowel is heard occasionally in *constable*, especially in the vulgate, and almost always in *conjure*.

[1] Private communication, Feb. 5, 1937.
[2] Private communication, March 11, 1943.

216   *The American Language: Supplement II*

In "Low-Back Vowels in the South Carolina Piedmont," before cited, McDavid presents a statistical study of the speech of 75 students at Furman University, Greenville. He used 158 test words in which either the vowel of *father* or that of *law* may occur. He found that in the following, *inter alia*, the *ah*-sound was overwhelmingly prevalent, *horrid, orange, chocolate, wash, doll, swan, forest, God, quarrel, foreign, Chicago, John, moral, orator, Florence* and *borrow*, and that the *aw*-sound prevailed in *loss, cross, dog, gone, on* and *coffin*. In *log, daub, hog, frog, water, wasp, office, offer* and *swamp* there was divided usage.[1]

South Dakota

The glossary of South Dakota terms in the volume on the State in the American Guide Series [2] is headed "Language of the West," and in it there is evidence that the local speech differs but little from that of the adjoining States. There are separate lists of farmers', prospectors', cowmen's and sheepmen's words and phrases, and at the end a brief section of "General Terms." The latter includes nothing that has not been reported elsewhere save *honyock*, a homesteader, apparently a derivative of *hony*, an old American term for a poor white.

Tennessee

Most of the published studies of the speech of Tennessee deal with that of the Appalachian region, and need not be considered in detail here.[3] So far as I know, there are only three devoted to the

---

[1] McDavid's field-work in South Carolina and the other South Atlantic States was made possible by a fellowship from the Julius Rosenwald Fund in 1941, and later by an honorary fellowship from Duke University and a grant by the American Council of Learned Societies.

[2] A South Dakota Guide, Sponsored by the State of South Dakota, n.p., 1938, pp. 81-88.

[3] They include Tennessee Mountains, by H. A. Edson and others, *Dialect Notes*, Vol. I, Part VIII, 1894, pp. 370-77; Terms From the Tennessee Mountains, by Mary O. Pollard, *Dialect Notes*, Vol. IV, Part III, 1915, pp. 242-43; Dialect Survivals in Tennessee, by Calvin S. Brown, Jr., *Modern Language Notes*, Nov., 1889, pp. 410-17; Other Dialectal Forms in Tennessee, by the same, *Proceedings of the Modern Language Association*, 1891, pp. 171-75; Tennessee, by the same, *Dialect Notes*, Vol. IV, Part V, 1916, pp. 345-46, and Tennessee Expressions, by Stuart Neitzel, *American Speech*, Dec., 1936, p. 373.

speech of the lowlands, and all are short. The first, based on observations of J. Douglas Bruce and others, was published in *Dialect Notes* in 1913.[1] It included *change, dessert; to die out,* to die; *hunkle, haunch,* and *Lord's bread-wagon,* thunder. The second, published by T. J. Farr in 1936,[2] listed *bed-buddies,* bed-bugs; *black spot,* a shady place; *bug-dust,* cheap smoking-tobacco; *bush-house,* a brush arbor used for religious services; *cat's uncle,* a criminal; *cawked,* exhausted; *to chip out,* to have a misunderstanding; *cow-paste,* butter; *flinch,* coward; *goot,* a lunatic; *long-faced,* bald-headed; *mullock,* state of disorder; *to pad,* to seek work from house to house, and *triddler,* a woman gossip. The third, by Alfred Mynders,[3] added *on the drop edge of yonder,* at the point of death; *heart-burning,* consumed by love, and *miring-branch,* a stream with quicksand.[4] In 1934 Rebecca W. Smith undertook an examination of the diary of William Donaldson, a young Tennesseean who set out from Jefferson county for Springfield, Mo., in 1841. Its misspellings revealed pronunciations that still prevail in the mountains, *e.g., attackted, crep, tremendious, patridge* (partridge) and *famly.*

Texas

The speech of Texas as a whole still awaits scientific study, but that of the northeastern corner of the State has been admirably described by Oma Stanley.[5] Stanley's material was mainly gathered in Smith county, the chief town of which is Tyler,[6] but he also sought it in fourteen additional counties, and so covered an area larger than many States. It is a farming region lying to the east of Dallas, and its speech shows the influence of both Appalachian and Lowland Southern.[7] Most of its original settlers apparently came from either

---

1 Terms From Tennessee, Vol. IV, Part I, p. 58.

2 Folk Speech of Middle Tennessee, *American Speech,* Oct., pp. 275-76.

3 Originally published in the Chattanooga *Times.* Reprinted as The Way They Talk in Tennessee in the Richmond *Times-Dispatch,* Jan. 12, 1947. I am indebted here to Mr. James M. Bowcock, of Richmond.

4 Mynders's article is chiefly devoted, not to speechways, but to superstitions. They are also dealt with in Tennessee; a Guide to the Volunteer State, published by the WPA; New York, 1936.

5 The Speech of East Texas, *American Speech,* Feb., 1936, pp. 3-36; April, pp. 145-66; Oct., pp. 232-51; and Dec., pp. 327-55. These papers were reprinted with the addition of a chapter on The Sources of the Population of Texas, as *American Speech Reprints and Monographs No. 2;* New York, 1937.

6 Pop. 28,279 in 1940.

7 He calls the former the Hill Type and the latter the Plantation Type.

the Ozark region or the lowlands to the eastward, and there is little evidence in the dialect of the present inhabitants of any influence by General American or by such speech-pockets as that of the Germans of New Braunfels area, more than 250 miles to the southwest. "Education," says Stanley,

> has had virtually no influence on pronunciation among the vast majority of my subjects. Many people whose training, knowledge, profession, experience, and social position place them as distinguished members of the community use the same sounds as the dwellers on the farms or in the deep backwoods. Their grammar is more "correct," their vocabulary is larger, their competence in handling the language is greater, and their mental range is immeasurably wider than that of the illiterate white speakers. But phonetically they all belong to the same group.[1]

The Appalachian influence seems to be rather greater in the area studied than the Lowland Southern influence. The *r* is sounded before consonants, "with distinct quality, as generally in America," though not so emphatically as in the Middle West; the flat *a* is heard in *aunt, bath, dance, glass, laugh* and *path*, usually somewhat lengthened; and the mispronunciations and "bad grammar" that bristle in the dialect are mainly those of the highlands. The general American tendency to move the stress forward is exaggerated, and such forms as *pólice, ínsurance, víolin, éxpress* and *súpreme* are not uncommon. "*Governor*," says Stanley, "is always *guvner*, *perspiration* is *prespiration*, *adenoid* is universally *adnoid*, *turpentine* is *turpmtine*." The medial *t* is lost in *breastpin, costly, exactly, mostly, roast beef* and *strictly*, and the first *t* in *frostbite*. *Fifth* is usually *fith*, and *evening* is *e'nin'*. Final *d* after *n* is usually lost, "even when the following word begins with a vowel." Final *t* is lost after *k, p* and *s*, as in *correc', kep'* and *Methodis'*, and sometimes after *f*, as in *draf'* (draft). In careless or illiterate speech *v* changes to *b*, as in *lebm* (eleven). Sometimes *gl* changes to *dl* and *cl* to *tl*. The *th* of *these*, after *n*, becomes another *n*, as in "In *nese* days." Before vowels and diphthongs *g* and *k* are often followed by the glide *y*, as in *gyate* (gate) and *cyamel* (camel). *Texas* is *teksiz*. Stanley is chiefly interested in phonology, but he adds an appendix on East Texas grammar. In the main the conjugation of *to be* is in accord with the books, and *I be* is never used for *I am* or *I'm*. In the third person plural *are* is used with *they* but *is* with *them*. *Ain't* appears in all persons of the singu-

---

[1] I have hitherto called attention to the fact that this homogeneity is much more marked throughout the South than in the North.

lar. In the past tense *was* is often used in the second person singular and in all persons of the plural, though not invariably. The other verbs show the common peculiarities of vulgar American. Some of Stanley's examples:

> They oughta get somebody else to *brung* it.
> He oughtn to *done* it.
> I like to *froze* on that job.
> I told him he ought not to *et* it.
> I'd a *went* with him if he'd a-come by.
> I *done done* it.

The earliest report on the speech of Texas that I have been able to unearth was contributed to *Dialect Notes* in 1915 by Hyder E. Rollins, a native of Abilene, in the west central part, who had been instructor in English at the University of Texas in 1912–14.[1] His list was confined to such words and phrases as he had himself heard in use; it showed a great deal less Appalachian influence than the eastern dialect studied by Stanley. The argot of the cattlemen supplied a number of terms, *e.g.*, *maverick*, an unbranded calf; *locoed*, crazy; *son-of-a-bitch*, a meat and vegetable stew;[2] *chuck*, food; and *surface-coal*, cow dung. Rollins noted a curious pronunciation of *against*, as in "He fell *again* the door." He found that *back East* referred to any part of Texas east of the speaker, or any of the Southern States, but never to what is generally called the East. The Appalachian *poke*, a bag, was in use, and also *to grunt*, to complain, but the Appalachian *antigodlin*, out of plumb, askew, was transformed into *anti-goslin*. Some apparently indigenous forms were *Christmas*, whiskey; *Dutchman*, a contemptuous name applied to any foreigner or even to a disliked native; *spasm*, a stanza of a song, and *tank*, an artificial lake. Rollins listed *to goose* as meaning to tickle, with no reference to the special American meaning. He said that every lawyer in the area he surveyed was a brevet *judge* (pro. *jedge*), that syrup or molasses was *lick*, and that *molasses*, *mumps* and *measles* were always treated as plural nouns.

Other Texas word-lists were published during the years follow-

---

[1] A West Texas Word-List, Vol. IV, Part III, pp. 224–30. Rollins took his Ph.D. at Harvard in 1917. Since 1926 he has been professor of English there and since 1933 editor of the Harvard Studies in English. He edited the two volumes of poems in the Variorum Shakespeare, and is the author of many books.

[2] Other Texas lexicographers reduce this to *son-of-a-gun*.

ing by C. L. Crow,[1] Artemisia Baer Bryson,[2] Wilmer R. Park,[3] Charles H. Hogan,[4] and Carmelita Klipple,[5] and in 1944 John T. Krumpelmann contributed to *American Speech* a small group of early Texanisms unearthed from a German travel-book of 1848.[6] Crow's list was confined to terms picked up in Parker county, just west of Forth Worth, in 1896. It included *beyonst* for *beyond*; *hayseeder* for *hayseed*;[7] *library*, a bookcase; *to office with*, to share an office with, and *ransation*, spiritual libido at a revival. He added a few from other Texas counties, *e.g.*, *thunder-hole*, a storm-cellar; *to perdure*, to remain true to the faith, *e.g.*, Methodism; and *to cattle-mill*, to go round in a circle. Miss Bryson added *larrapin*, an adjective signifying superior;[8] *inland*, used of a town without a railroad, and *hissy*, a fit of anger, and also a few curious pronunciations, *e.g.*, *whelp* for *welt*, *poarched egg* for *poached*, and *pararie* for *prairie*. Park, writing from Lampasas, in the center of the State, not far from Austin and Waco, reported that he found "an appalling use of double auxiliaries, even among educated people," and cited *I might can, I might could, I used to could, it might would, he ought to could* and *she may can*. Hogan, a Northerner, noted *how that*, as in "It came to me *how that* we might get a new roof on the church"; *a-woofin*, lying or jesting; *flat-out*, bluntly, as in "*I flat-out* told him"; *come in this house*, an exclamation of greeting, and *bud*, a brother. Miss Klipple operated in a region a little to the south of that investigated by Park. She found a good many traces of Appalachian influence, with the flat *a* in *aunt*, *hit* for *it* in emphasized situations, and the loss of *d* in unstressed and intervocalic positions. "Although Spicewood people," she said, "say *krais* for *Christ*, when they come to form the possessive they know that *kraisiz* is wrong, so they say *kraistiz*. ... When they use *taken* in

---

[1] Texas, *Dialect Notes*, Vol. IV, Part V, 1916, pp. 347–48.
[2] Some Texas Dialect Words, *American Speech*, April, 1929, pp. 330–31; Homely Words in Texas, the same, Feb., 1934, pp. 70–71, and Texas Notes, the same, Oct., 1934, p. 213.
[3] A Letter From Texas, *American Speech*, April, 1940, pp. 214–15.
[4] A Yankee Comments on Texas Speech, *American Speech*, April, 1944, pp. 81–84.
[5] The Speech of Spicewood, Texas, *American Speech*, Oct., 1945, pp. 187–91.
[6] Some Americanisms From Texas in 1848, Feb., 1944, pp. 69–70.
[7] Also found in Maine.
[8] She suggested that it might be connected with the English *larrikin*, a street rowdy. Partridge says that *larrikin* is "originally and mainly Australian."

the preterite they often go on to pattern it after weak verbs and say *takened*. . . . For *Mrs.* neither General American *misiz* nor formal Southern *miziz* is heard: it is pronounced *miz* or more frequently *mizriz*. . . . In the sentence, 'I hear Martin,' both *r*'s are strongly articulated." [1]

Spanish is widely spoken along the Rio Grande, and is taught in the elementary schools there, beginning with the third grade and running to the eighth, but its use is by no means as prevalent as in New Mexico, nor has it left so heavy a deposit of loans.[2]

Utah

The speech of Utah is General American, but it has been influenced in vocabulary by the argot of the Mormons, and by those of miners and cattlemen. Miss Dorothy N. Lindsay [3] says that the Mormon terminology " has wide currency " in an area comprising all of the State, southern Idaho, northern Arizona, western Wyoming, and parts of Texas, New Mexico and California. Most of its words and phrases are ecclesiastical. A boy of twelve, aspiring to social security post-mortem, may sign for the *Aaronic priesthood* as a *deacon*, and thereafter win promotion to the ranks of *teacher* and *priest*. After that follows the *Melchisedek priesthood*, with the ranks of *elder*, *seventy* and *high priest*. Still higher are those of *bishop*, *patriarch* and *apostle*. The church is organized into *wards*, and several *wards* form a *stake*, whose head is a *bishop* or *stake president*. A non-Mormon is a *gentile* or *outsider*, and a Mormon who is expelled from the communion is said to be *cut off*. When a high church dignitary is seized with an idea and desires to propagate it he announces that he has had a *revelation*. Says Miss Lindsay:

[1] There is a glossary in Texas: A Guide to the Lone Star State, in the American Guide Series; Austin, 1940, pp. 669-70. It is chiefly made up of Spanish loans, with a few cattlemen's terms added. There is also a glossary in Sure Enough, How Come?, by Leslie Turner; San Antonio, 1943, pp. 107-09, and many localisms occur in Texas Brags, by John Randolph; Houston, 1944. See also Texas Speaks Texan, by John T. Flanagan, *Southwest Review*, Spring, 1946, pp. 191-92. I am indebted for various helps to Mrs. Elizabeth M. Stover, of Dallas; Judge Theodore Mack, of Fort Worth; Wilmer R. Park, of Lampasas; Miss Helen Sue Gaines, of Richland; Charles H. Hogan, of Kansas City (Mo.); William N. Stokes, Jr., of Houston, and Gordon Gunter, of Rockport.

[2] I am indebted here to Mrs. Pauline R. Kibbe and Miss Myrtle L. Tanner.

[3] The Language of the "Saints," *American Speech*, April, 1933, pp. 30-33.

A person may be *sealed* to another to whom he is not married, and may be married without being *sealed*. The two ceremonies are distinct, though they may occur simultaneously if both parties are Mormons, and they must occur if they *go through the Temple* for the marriage. Frequently a couple will defer the *sealing* for several years after marriage, possibly on the theory that since it endures for eternity it is not to be entered upon as lightly as a mere life contract. If husband and wife die without having been *sealed* their children often have the rite performed for them, so that the marriage may be perpetuated in the *spirit world*. Children may also be *sealed* to their parents, and . . . the living may be *sealed* to the dead.

Brother and *Sister* are used in place of *Mr.* and *Mrs.*, adds Miss Lindsay, "not occasionally or among the very pious, but constantly and among people of all types and ages. . . . The word *Mr.* does not enter the vocabulary of a child until he learns that there is a distinction between *saint* and *outsider*."

Vermont

Culturally and historically, Vermont has always been closer to New York than to eastern New England, and that fact is reflected in its speech.[1] The *r* in such words as *barn* and *four* is clearly sounded[2] in the western part of the State; the flat *a* is common, even in *aunt*,[3] and the vocabulary, save for some archaisms, seems to be mainly identical with that of General American. Rather curiously, the Vermont dialect has been very little studied. Indeed, the only report on it that I have encountered is but a fragment, and deals exclusively with the speech of the southernmost part of the State, bordering on western Massachusetts.[4] It shows no terms not to be found in other places. Even Calvin Coolidge's use of *to choose* in his famous "I do not *choose* to run"[5] has been reported from places as far distant as Alabama.[6]

[1] New York claimed it until after the Revolution, though the Green Mountain Boys had been fighting for independence since *c.* 1770. The State was admitted to the Union on March 4, 1791: it was the first to be admitted after the original thirteen.
[2] Handbook of the Linguistic Geography of New England, by Hans Kurath; Providence (R.I.), 1939, p. 19.
[3] Linguistic Atlas of New England, Map 384.
[4] Words From West Brattleboro, Vt., by Wiliam E. Mead, *Dialect Notes*, Vol. III, Part VI, 1910, pp. 452–55.
[5] Statement to the press at Rapid City, S. D., Aug. 2, 1927.
[6] A Word-List From East Alabama, by L. W. Payne, Jr., *Dialect Notes*, Vol. III, Part IV, 1908, p. 298. Schele de Vere, in Americanisms: The English of the New World; New York, 1872, p. 453, listed it as in universal use in the United States "by low-bred people." The DAE traces it to 1829, when it appeared in the *Virginia Literary Museum*.

Virginia

Some of the peculiarities of Virginia speech were noted before the Revolution — for example, by Philip Vickers Fithian, a young Princeton graduate who served as tutor to the children of Robert Carter on the great estate of Nomini Hall near Richmond in 1773 and 1774.[1] Others were recorded by Noah Webster in his "Dissertations on the English Language," published in Boston in 1789,[2] by John Pickering in his "Vocabulary" of 1816, by Robley Dunglison in the *Virginia Literary Museum* in 1829, by Mrs. Anne Royall in her "Letters From Alabama" in 1830,[3] and by uncounted lesser observers during the years before the Civil War.[4] In later times there has been a great deal of writing on the subject, beginning with a paper by Sylvester Primer, "The Pronunciation of Fredericksburg," published in 1890,[5] and including two whole books, B. W. Green's "Word-Book of Virginia Folk-Speech"[6] and Edwin Francis Shewmake's "English Pronunciation in Virginia,"[7] and a pam-

---

[1] Fithian's journal from 1767 to 1774 was published by the Princeton University Press in 1900. See its pp. 235-36. I am indebted here to Philip Vickers Fithian's Observations on the Language of Virginia (1774), by Claude M. Newlin, *American Speech*, Dec., 1928, p. 110.

[2] For example, on pp. 110 and 111.

[3] Mrs. Anne Royall as an Observer of Dialects, by M. M. Mathews, *American Speech*, Jan., 1927, pp. 204-07.

[4] For example, a sage signing himself Simeon Smallfry, who contributed a short article entitled Improprieties of Speech to the *Southern Literary Messenger*, 1857, pp. 222-23. This writer, after describing the elision of *r* in Virginia speech and the tendency to substitute the neutral vowel for *i* in such words as *possible*, cautioned his fellow Virginians against mocking Down East speech, then the chief butt of the national humorists. "As party names," he said, "are useful in giving a bodily form at which faction may hurl its missiles, thus facilitating the indulgence of men's natural tendency to hate and revile each other, so differences of language are hostile badges which guide, concentrate and inflame local animosity. . . . Difference of mere dialect is a greater cause of enmity than total difference of language, partly . . . because such near similarity implies relationship, and relations, when at variance, are always the bitterest enemies; partly, for the reason that slight differences commonly occasion the greatest animosities — that a heretic is deemed worse than an infidel, and a member of an opposite party in our own country is more hated than a foreign enemy."

[5] *Publications of the Modern Language Association*, pp. 185-99.

[6] Richmond, 1889; second ed., 1912.

[7] Privately published at Davidson (N.C.), 1927. This was "a dissertation submitted to the faculty of the University of Virginia in partial fulfillment of the requirements for the degree of doctor of philosophy" in 1920. In Dec., 1925 Shewmake published part of it in *Modern Language Notes*, pp. 489-92 as Laws of Pronunciation in Eastern Virginia. He has also published Distinctive Virginia Pronunciation,

phlet, Phyllis J. Nixon's "Glossary of Virginia Words."[1] Virginia speech is also dealt with in Elizabeth Jeannette Dearden's "Word Geography of the South Atlantic States," already noticed under Maryland and North Carolina, and there are studies of it in the philological literature by W. Cabell Greet,[2] Argus Tresidder,[3] G. G. Laubscher,[4] Guy S. Lowman, Jr.,[5] George P. Wilson,[6] A. P. Man, Jr.,[7] Chad Walsh,[8] Arthur Kyle Davis, Jr.,[9] J. Wilson McCutchan,[10] L. R. Dingus,[11] Richard H. Thornton,[12] C. Alphonso Smith,[13] Atcheson L. Hench,[14] and C. M. Woodward.[15]

Three main speech areas are commonly distinguished in Virginia — that of the Tidewater dialect, which runs up to the fall-line on the rivers; that of General Lowland Southern, which covers the Piedmont, and that of Appalachia. There are a number of small speech pockets, but they are not important. One is to be found in Gloucester county, in a small peninsula called Guinea Neck, be-

---

American Speech, Feb., 1943, pp. 33–38, and a note on the *ai* diphthong, *American Speech*, April, 1945, pp. 152–53.

1 *Publication of the American Dialect Society*, No. 5, May, 1946.

2 A Phonographic Expedition to Williamsburg, Va., *American Speech*, Feb., 1931, pp. 161–72; Two Notes on Virginia Speech (with William Brown Meloney), *American Speech*, Dec., 1930, pp. 94–96; Delmarva Speech, *American Speech*, Dec., 1933, pp. 56–63.

3 Some Virginia Provincialisms, *Quarterly Journal of Speech*, April, 1940, pp. 262–69; The Sounds of Virginia Speech, *American Speech*, Dec., 1943, pp. 261–72; The Speech of the Shenandoah Valley, *American Speech*, Dec., 1937, pp. 284–88; Notes on Virginia Speech, *American Speech*, April, 1941, pp. 112–20.

4 Terms From Lynchburg, Va., *Dialect Notes*, Vol. IV, Part IV, 1916, p. 302.

5 The Treatment of *au* in Virginia, *Proceedings of the Second International Congress of Phonetic Sciences*, 1936, pp. 122 ff.

6 A Word-List From Virginia and North Carolina, *Publication of the American Dialect Society*, No. 2, Nov., 1944, pp. 38–52.

7 Virginia, *Dialect Notes*, Vol. IV, Part II, 1914, pp. 158–60.

8 Broad *A* in Virginia, *American Speech*, Feb., 1940, p. 38.

9 Dialect Notes on Records of Folk Songs From Virginia (with Archibald A. Hill), *American Speech*, Dec., 1933, pp. 52–56.

10 Virginia Expressions, *American Speech*, Dec., 1936, pp. 372–73.

11 A Word-List From Virginia, *Dialect Notes*, Vol. IV, Part III, 1915, pp. 177–93.

12 Comment on A Word-List From Virginia, *Dialect Notes*, Vol. IV, Part V, 1916, pp. 349–50.

13 Dialect in Eastern Virginia and Western North Carolina, *Dialect Notes*, Vol. IV, Part II, 1914, p. 167.

14 Word-Hunting in Southern Maryland and Virginia, a paper read before the Present-day English section of the Modern Language Association at Boston, Dec. 28, 1940. Not printed, but reported in summary in the Richmond (Va.) *Times-Dispatch*, Dec. 29. I have had access to it by the courtesy of Dr. Hench.

15 A Word-List From Virginia and North Carolina, *Publication of the American Dialect Society* No. 6, Nov., 1946.

tween the York and Severn rivers at their mouths. This remote region is said to have been settled by Hessian prisoners disbanded at Yorktown, but no trace of German influence remains in its speech, which resembles, according to Greet,[1] that of Charleston, S. C. The inhabitants are fishermen, and there are no Negroes. One of the local peculiarities is the exaggerated use of singular nouns in the plural, as in *two doctor*. Another is the pronunciation of *here* as *hee*, with no trace of the *r* remaining and no substitution of *ah*. Another area of aberrant speech is the Shenandoah Valley, where terms and pronunciations borrowed from Pennsylvania, from Appalachia and from the Piedmont have been mingled with Tidewater. The speech of the Piedmont, according to Miss Deardon, "is more closely related to Tidewater than to mountain speech," mainly because the area was settled from the coast, and not by the movement of population down the eastern foothills of the Blue Ridge. The chief dialect boundary in the State, she says, " runs north and south parallel to the Blue Ridge." It enters the State between Frederick and Loudon counties, the first of which borders on West Virginia and the second on Maryland, and crosses the North Carolina line in the vicinity of Danville. It runs well to the east of the mountains in the southern part of the State.

Green's " Word-Book of Virginia Folk-Speech," a volume of 530 pages,[2] lists about 7200 terms and is thus the largest State glossary ever published. Green, who hailed from Warwick county on the James, not far from its mouth, in what is called the Lower Peninsula, dealt mainly with Tidewater speech, and found it heavy with archaisms. "It seems to resemble," he said, " the standard English of the time that the first immigrants came to the country, and there has been no foreign mixture, as the comers were English and few or none have come from other parts of the United States." Unhappily, his enormous word-list is by no means confined to Virginia localisms; on the contrary, it is burdened with many words and usages that are common to the vulgar speech of the whole country. In a number of cases, however, he records locutions that have not been noted elsewhere, *e.g.*, *akerel*, a man's given-name; *aquecope*,

---

[1] Two Notes on Virginia Speech, before cited.

[2] This is the second edition of 1912. The first edition of 1899 ran to 435. The second is augmented by the addition of a list of county names, with their derivations, and another of Indian place-names. The latter includes some names from Maryland and others that are not Indian.

an enlarged spleen following malaria; *berlue*, a noise or racket (from *hullabaloo?*); *by-blow*, a bastard; *drabbletail*, a slattern; *goer-by*, a passer-by; *hang-by*, a hanger-on; *minister's face*, the upper part of a hog's head, less the ears, nose and jowl; *smicket*, a small amount, and *to yuck*, to yank or jerk.

Man's word-list of 1914 was gathered between 1901 and 1907 in Louisa county, in the Piedmont region of the center of the State, northwest of Richmond. He noted that *air* and *hour* were both pronounced *aiah*, that *few* was used in the sense of any small amount, as in "a *few* mashed potatoes," that *on* was used before designations of time, as in *on yesterday* and *on last week*,[1] that hobgoblins were called *bineys* or *evils*, and that the local underprivileged were given to a number of curious outrages upon the normal conjugation of verbs, e.g., "*I'm is* the one." Dingus's list of 1915 came from the Clinch Valley in Scott county, in the far southwestern corner of the State, and thus showed mainly Appalachian terms, e.g., *fireboard*, a mantlepiece; *Good Man*, God; *holler-horn*, a disease among cattle, supposed to be cured by boring holes in their horns; *to lumber*, to make a loud noise; *new ground*, virgin land; *to norate*, to gossip; *piece*, a short distance; *rise of*, slightly more than, and *skift*, a light fall of snow. Dingus noted the usual Appalachian euphemisms, e.g., *male* for *bull* and *male-hog* for *boar*, and added one that seemed to be indigenous — *boar-cat* for *Tom-cat*. He added some notes on the phonology and syntax of the local speech. The *a* in closed syllables, he said, was invariably that of *man*, and at the end of a syllable it became the neutral vowel. The unaccented *o* at the end of words became *er*, with "the *r* always heard, even if it is indistinct." "Present participles used attributively are compared as other adjectives, e.g., *runnin'er* horse, *singingest* girl, *grown upest*, *worn outest*." Laubscher, in 1916, recorded *either* in the sense of *instead* at Lynchburg, as in "You can do that *either*," apparently a sign of Pennsylvania influence by way of the Shenandoah Valley. Thornton, commenting upon Dingus's word-list, found in it "survivals of pure Elizabethan English preserved among the mountains of southwestern Virginia for three centuries," and cited *agin* as a conjunction, *hope* as a variant of the old preterite *holp*, and *dremp* for *dreamed*.

[1] This is not peculiar to Virginia, but is the official style of the Congressional Record. See Supplement I, p. 122, n. 1.

Shewmake's "English Pronunciation in Virginia," unlike Green's "Word-Book of Virginia Folk-Speech," is confined to the speech of the State, and though it deals almost wholly with what is here called Tidewater, it attempts to differentiate between different speech levels, running from that of the educated gentry at the top to that of the most ignorant country Negroes at the bottom. "The city of Richmond," he says,

is regarded as the speech center of the territory in which the Virginia dialect prevails, though dwellers in other cities of eastern Virginia, as well as many rural folk of the same region, may speak this dialect in an equally representative way. . . . It would be inaccurate to say that the Virginia dialect is traceable in any marked way to Negro influence, for the details that make it up are, in the main, either different from typical Negro English or else are clearly derived from other sources. . . . Virginians are distinguished from other Americans less easily by their vocabulary than by their pronunciation. A speaker may talk for an hour without using many words or constructions that are not standard, but his peculiarities of pronunciation will reveal themselves in almost every sentence that he utters.[1]

Shewmake lists the more significant of these peculiarities as follows:

1. The insertion of the "glide or vanishing *y*-sound between *g* and *a* in words like *garden* and *garment*, between *c* or *k* and *a* in such words as *card* and *carpet*, and after *c* or *k* in words of the type of *sky* and *kind*. . . . It is heard chiefly in the speech of men and women of the older generation belonging to some of the old, highly cultured families." [2]

2. "The great majority of Virginians pronounce . . . words like *path* and *dance* . . . with the sound that *a* has in *man*, but the pronunciation with the so-called broad or Italian or Cavalier *a* and also that which includes what is known as intermediate *a*[3] are both heard at times."

3. "The so-called standard pronunciation of diphthongal *ou* is approximately that of *a* in *father* plus that of *oo* in *pool* or possibly that of *oo* in *foot*, but the pronunciation heard in Eastern Virginia is approximately that of *u* in *hut* plus the same sound used in standard pronunciation for the second part of the diphthong. . . . Typical eastern Virginia speech includes those who pronounce *about*, *house* and *out* with dialectal *ou*, and *crowd*, *how* and *loud* with standard *ou*." *Uh-oo* is used "when the diphthong is immediately followed in the same syllable by the sound of a voiceless consonant, but under all other conditions standard *ah-oo* is employed."

---

1 pp. 6, 7, 9 and 20.
2 In Survivals in American Educated Speech, *Bookman*, July, 1900, pp. 446–50, S. D. McCormick argued that this *y* was one of the hallmarks of F. F. V. (*i.e.*, first families of Virginia) speech, and "a recognized shibboleth of culture." He said that it appeared before *a* when followed by *n* as well as *r*, as in *cyandle* and *cyandor*. Some of his examples were *cyarcass*, *Cyarlyle*, *cyardinal*, *cyartoon*, *cyartridge*, *cyarpenter*, *disgyise*, *gyide* (*guide*), *cyarbon*, *gyarlic*, *gyarment*, *cyarbuncle* and *cyargo*.
3 *i.e.*, the Boston *a*.

4. "The standard sound of the diphthong . . . in such words as *bright, like* and *price* . . . is that of *a* in *father* plus that of *i* in *pin;* the dialectal sound is approximately that of *u* in *but* plus that of *i* in *pin*." This dialectal sound occurs when the diphthong is followed immediately by a voiceless consonant, e.g., *advice, bite* and *life,* and when it is followed in the next syllable by a voiceless consonant and an obscure vowel, e.g., *cipher, hyphen, rifle* and *viper.* In other cases the standard diphthong is heard, e.g., in *alibi, dialect, bridle, typhoid, advise.*

5. "The substitution of *n* for *ng* in unaccented syllables pervades almost all levels of speech in Virginia."

6. Following the *a* of *father,* the *e* of *her,* the *o* of *or* and the *u* of *fur, r* "is not sounded at all."[1] Initial or medial *r* preceded by any other vowel becomes a sort of neutral vowel. In other situations it has its full sound.

7. The following words have the sound of *oo* in *pool: aloof, boot, groom, proof, rooster, root, soon, spook* and *spoon.* The following have the sound of *u* in *pull: butcher, coop, Cooper, hoop, Hooper, nook* and *rook.* "The rest vary with different speakers: *broom, hoof, room.*"

8. "Virginians share the general lack of uniformity in pronouncing *God, log* and *fog.* Though the *aw-* or *au*-sound, or an approach to it, is often noticed, many, if not most Virginians use the short *o*-sound, as in *hot.*"[2]

Some of Shewmake's conclusions were challenged by Hans Kurath in *American Speech,* August, 1928, and by Argus Tresidder in the same journal, April, 1941, and Shewmake answered them in its columns in February, 1943. Tresidder resumed the discussion in December, 1943. He divided Virginia into four speech areas instead of the usual three — Tidewater, including the Eastern Shore; the Piedmont " extending from the fall-line to the slopes of the Blue Ridge, spreading out like an inverted funnel, two counties wide in the north and seven counties wide in the south, and embracing the largest part of the State "; the Valley and Ridge province, "made up of a very irregular series of linear ridges and valleys, including the Shenandoah," and the Appalachian plateau, " at the very southwestern corner of the State."[3] He continued:

About a third of the counties of Virginia are wholly or partly west of the Blue Ridge; these counties differ physically, socially, and almost spiritually

---

[1] This has been disputed. Said an anonymous Southerner, obviously a Virginian, writing in the Contributors' Club, *Atlantic Monthly,* July, 1909, pp. 135-38: "We do not drop the final *r* altogether, as many writers of Southern dialect falsely assert, but we do give it the sound of *ah.*"

[2] Shewmake's dissertation includes a review of previous studies of Virginia speech, a note on its use in dialect stories, and an attempt to indicate how it would sound in a reading of part of The Pickwick Papers.

[3] He had been content with three in Some Virginia Provincialisms, 1940, to wit, Tidewater, the Piedmont and the Shenandoah Valley.

from the rest of the State. ... Bean[1] estimates that 63% of Mecklenburg county[2] is of English stock, 57% of Augusta county[3] of Scotch, and 71% of Shenandoah county[4] of German descent. Several sections have been kept more or less separated from each other: the Eastern Shore counties are kept from the mainland by Chesapeake Bay; the long spine of the Blue Ridge and the various ridges west of the Alleghenies have tended to isolate many counties. Coastal influence is apparent in the speech of the Eastern Shore, which in some ways is more like the speech of coastal Maine or South Carolina than like that of the rest of Virginia. In the Shenandoah Valley Pennsylvania German phrases and whole communities of German speakers are to be found. In some parts of the Blue Ridge there are communities which, like those of the Tennessee, Kentucky and North Carolina highlanders, still keep some English idioms and pronunciations from the Eighteenth Century, such as *dauncy*, unwell; *sallet*, salad; and *poke*, sack.

Tresidder sought to get a cross section of Virginia speech by having 254 of the girl students of Madison College, at Harrisonburg in the Shenandoah Valley, read a test passage of 195 words. Of these girls, all of them " from average middle-class families," 74 were from Tidewater, 94 from the Piedmont, 76 from the Valley and Ridge province, and 10 from the Appalachian plateau. He concluded that " Virginia speech cannot be conveniently classified in geographical or ethnological divisions because in spite of physical and national differences the usages throughout the State, with some exceptions, are comparable." His girls, of course, hardly provided " an entirely satisfactory basis for speculation about Virginia speech, since they were all from the same social level, all were women, and all were college students." Perhaps these facts accounted in large part for the uniformities he noted: informants from the lower grades of society might have shown much greater differences. Even so he found a number of significant local usages, chiefly indicating that the maximum of elegance is in the Tidewater region, and that it declines steadily as one goes westward. Rather curiously, he found that the broad *a* was common only in *aunt*, *rather* and *can't*.

Primer's pioneer study of 1890 was devoted to the speech of the Northern Neck, between the Rappahannock and the Potomac. Of the palatal glide in *gyarden*, *gyirl*, *schyool* and their like he said: " the pronunciation is not general. Some consider it vulgar and avoid it,

[1] The Peopling of Virginia, by R. Bennett Bean; Boston, 1938.
[2] On the North Carolina line, due south of Charlottesville.
[3] In the Shenandoah Valley.
[4] Also in the Valley, about half way between Augusta county and the Potomac.

but it can be heard in the best families." He found both flat *a* and broad *a* in *pass, ask,* and *half,* and even in *calm* and *psalm,* but only broad *a* in *haunt*. He reported " the usual fluctuation " between *ee-ther* and *eye-ther* in Fredericksburg, and the absence of *r* from *door, more, war* and the like everywhere. Greet's phonograph expedition of 1930 was to Williamsburg, between the York river and the James, not far from the Warwick region investigated by Green. He encountered difficulties, for the indigenes objected to having their speech recorded, even by a man whose middle name was Cabell, but in the end he accumulated 170 records, some of them of the speech of visitors from Richmond, Norfolk and Petersburg, all of which are in the same *Sprachgebiet*. On his return to his Columbia University dissecting-room to anatomize his specimens he found that the speech of the Williamsburg region was " rather rapid " and that " drawl and laziness " were not characteristic of it. The *o* in such words as *log* and *long* often became *ah*, that in *go* and *know* a diphthong made up of *o* and *oo*, the diphthong in *out* became a combination of the first vowel of *further* and something resembling the *u* of *full*, the *a* in *car* and *far* was prolonged in compensation for the loss of the *r*, and the *i* in *I, mind, my, while* and *why* tended to approximate *ah*.

Davis and Hill, in their survey of Virginia folk-song crooners in 1933, found the same differences between the speech of the various Virginia regions before reported by others. They also recorded a " tendency to reduce the forms of the strong verbs to two instead of three," and even to one, but this is common to all forms of vulgar American. In Tresidder's paper on " The Speech of the Shenandoah Valley," published in 1937, he reported that it was " influenced by the Pennsylvania Germans and by the mountain people as well as by importations from eastern Virginia." He listed, as German loans, *to schnitz*, to peel, and the phrases " The salt is *all*," " *Give* me goodbye," " It's wettin' *down* out," " *Would* you go to ride?," " We're *fresh* out of pork " and " You can have the cart *either*." In a group of young women college students of the Valley he encountered such pronunciations as *melk* for *milk, cáydet* for *cadet, hangry* for *hungry, dahmitory* for *dormitory, bum* (with the *u* of *full*) for *bomb, wush* for *wish, roodge* for *rouge, arn* for *iron,* and *tard* for *tired.* Walsh, in 1940, reported that the so-called Cavalier accent was "becoming modified" in eastern Virginia, and "sometimes losing its most conspicuous feature, the broad *a*." [1]

Mrs. Nixon's "Glossary of Virginia Words," published in 1946 with a preface by Hans Kurath, is based upon 138 field records accumulated for the Linguistic Atlas of the United States and Canada. It is a list of about 275 terms, and all of them that have been reported in other parts of the country or in England are so marked. Unfortunately, the authorities consulted do not include Wentworth's "American Dialect Dictionary," published in 1944, and as a result a number of the terms appear as peculiar to Virginia though they are actually in use elsewhere, *e.g.*, *to change*, to castrate, which Wentworth reports from West Virginia and which is also common in Maryland. Among those that seem to be exclusively Virginian are *corn-stack*, used on the Eastern Shore in place of *corn-crib* or *corn-house; dry-land frog*, a toad; *green-beans*, used west of the Blue Ridge for *string-beans; home-made cheese*, a Shenandoah term for *cottage cheese* or *smearcase; johnny-house*, a privy, "fairly common in the James valley and the southern part of the Blue Ridge"; *milk-gap*, used in the southern Blue Ridge for cow-pen; *ox*, a bull, "used on the lower Rappahannock in the presence of women"; and *steer*, also a bull, used "on the Eastern Shore, on the lower Rappahannock and in the southern Piedmont in the presence of women." Wilson's word-list of 1944 was gathered along the North Carolina border and also includes many North Carolina terms. Mrs. Nixon does not list *you-all*. Wilson says of it: "So much can be said about this much discussed pronoun that nothing is being said here. In spite of many clarifying articles on the subject there is still much misunderstanding." But notwithstanding this despairing warning it will be tackled again in Chapter IX, Section 3.

Lowman, in his paper of 1936, reported that he had found no less than seven different variations of the diphthong in *house* in Virginia speech. His discussion was too technical to be summarized here, but the substance of it was that the substitution of a diphthong made up of either the *u* of *further* or the *a* of *sang* and the *u* of *full* — "the most widespread and generally considered the Virginia type" — was

---

[1] He has been quoted at length in Section 2 of the present chapter, in the discussion of American *a*.

"characteristic of the entire Piedmont north of the James," of "a narrow strip south through Buckingham to Halifax county," of "the Northern Neck peninsula between the Rappahannock and the Potomac," of "the section between the upper Rappahannock and the upper James, of the Norfolk-Newport News area, and of the Eastern Shore of the Chesapeake Bay." But with slight phonological differences he also found it in all other parts of the State — even among the Quakers of Loudoun county, the Scotch-Irish of the mountains, and the Germans of the Shenandoah Valley. Hench's paper, read before the Modern Language Association in 1940, was accompanied by a list of terms gathered mainly in the vicinity of Charlottesville, in central Virginia. It included *albatross*, a kind of sail-boat; *to backstand*, to stand up for; *cow-bug*, a large beetle with hook-like horns; *cunnyfingered*, butterfingered; *dick-in-a-minute*, immediately; *dirty-camp*, a brawl; *dog-trot house*, a house with an open passage between its two ends; *fairway*, a millrace; *flat-toned*, complete, absolute; *house-moss*, balls of dust; *inch*, a twelfth part of the daylight day ("I worked twelve *inches* today": "I worked from dawn to dark"); *to newspack*, to spread gossip; *rink*, a pile of firewood, and *sag*, a gap in a mountain ridge.

Woodward's word-list of 1946 was gathered at Salem, a town in the Shenandoah Valley, seven miles west of Roanoke. It consists mainly of terms in very wide American use, *e.g.*, *all the farther*, *backhouse*, *contrary* (disobedient), *gyp* and *hickey* (a pimple), but also includes some not reported from other areas by Wentworth, *e.g.*, *bird snow*, a late Spring snow; *breath-harp*, a harmonica; *clatterwhacking*, palaver; *gospel-fowl*, a chicken; *ice-pebble*, a hailstone; *misty-moisty*, threatening rain; *nibby*, inquisitive; *river-jack*, a stone from a stream, and *in a swither*, excited. He found Pennsylvania German influence in *pon hosh* (Ger. *pfannhase*). *Blue hen's chickens*, usually applied to natives of Delaware, is used to designate the local gentry.

Washington

The speech of Washington differs little from that of Oregon. Some of its terms were listed by Benjamin H. Lehman in 1918.[1]

[1] A Word-List From Northwestern United States, *Dialect Notes*, Vol. V, Part I, pp. 22–29. This list was not confined to Washington, but included terms from Oregon and Idaho.

They show many loans from the argots of the Western cattlemen and lumbermen, but a few are of local origin, e.g., *mothback*, an apple grower; *stopper*, a lodger for the night; *chix*, a chicken (singular), and *palouser*, a greenhorn, a home-made lantern, or a sunset. The last is from *Palouse*, " the fertile, rolling region lying north of the Snake river in eastern Washington," and *Palouse* in turn comes from the name of a tribe of Indians found by Lewis and Clark at the head of the Clearwater river.

West Virginia

In large part the speech of West Virginia is that of Appalachia, which has been dealt with a while back. But there are also signs of influence by the lowland speech of the South and even by Tidewater Southern, and traces of Pennsylvania infiltration are by no means lacking. In 1925 Carey Woofter, of West Virginia University, at Morgantown, enlisted his students in an effort to collect a vocabulary, and their gatherings were printed in *American Speech* two years later.[1] They worked mainly in the eight counties lying in the valley of the Little Kanawha river, and so covered a region that was partly in the mountains and partly on lower ground. They got altogether more than 800 words and phrases, and the speech thus revealed turned out to be very interesting. Some of the locutions found that have not been reported elsewhere were: *beaslings*, the first milk of a fresh cow; *boar's nest*, a camp of men without women; *bull's breakfast*, a straw hat; *to brouge*, to idle; *chestnut*, thin soil on northern slopes; *to be cold cocked*, to be knocked out; *consaity*, hard to please; *to crow-hop*, to take an unfair advantage; *to drive*, to take a female animal to be bred; *to pound hair*, to drive a team; *to help Andy*, to do nothing; *another hog off the corn*, one less person to feed; *to lap*, to whip; *sight of the eye*, the pupil; *sprag*, a dead branch on a tree, and *trink*, a minnow used for bait. Some curious pronunciations were encountered, e.g., *ahdn't*, hadn't; *keerpet*, carpet, and *severial*, several. The Pennsylvania loans included *snits*, dried apples, and the widespread *all*, as in " The potatoes are *all*."

[1] Dialect Words and Phrases From West-Central West Virginia, May, 1927, pp. 347–67. The first account of the speech of the State that I am aware of was in Dialectical Studies in West Virginia, by Sylvester Primer, *Publications of the Modern Language Association*, 1891, pp. 161–70. It was of small value.

The euphemisms in use were mainly Appalachian, *e.g.*, *outsider*, a bastard; *to jape*, to have sexual intercourse; *male-hog*, boar, and *male-cow*, bull. *You all* was found and also *whistle-pig* for *ground-hog*, the former common to the whole South and the latter characteristic of Appalachia. The dialect examined, though it was mainly rural, showed some influence from the argot of lumbermen, and also a good many smart words and phrases from the big cities, *e.g.*, *glad rags*, *to get one's goat*, and *hard-boiled*. A year after this excellent vocabulary was published Lowry Axley criticised it in *American Speech* on the ground that many of the terms listed were used also " in the mountains of the South, in other sections of the South and perhaps in other parts of the country," but this self-evident fact hardly needed laboring.[1]

In 1935 Hamill Kenny called attention to the prevalence of *to* in West Virginia folk-speech in places where Standard English uses other prepositions, as in " He spent a day *to* us," " I have a fear *to* water," " We stayed *to* home," " I had a course *to* (*i.e.*, *under*) Professor Blank," etc. He said that this last use was frequent in the colleges of the State. Wentworth calls it peculiar to West Virginia and southeastern Ohio, but lists examples of the use of *to* in place of *at*, *with*, *on*, *of*, *for* and *in* from Maine to Florida. In 1936 Dean B. Lyman, of the University of West Virginia, sent *American Speech* some idioms from southeastern West Virginia, in the Appalachian speech-area, *e.g.*, *any more* without a negative, as in " The store is closed *any more* "; *at all* used in the same way, as in " We had the best time *at all* "; the use of the long *e* in such words as *condition*, *position*, *wish*, making them *condeetion*, *poseetion*, *weesh*;[2] the use of *hope* for *wish*, as in " I *hope* you good luck "; and the inversion represented by " I *hope how soon* I'll see you," meaning " I hope I'll see you soon."[3] In 1939 John T. Krumpelmann followed with some locutions picked up at Huntington, on the Ohio river,[4] the metropolis of the State, *e.g.*, *to beal*, to suppurate; *budget*, a package, and *want* without the infinitive, as in " The dog *wants out*." The former two are common in other parts of the country, and the last is Pennsylvania German. Krumpelmann likewise noted the

1 West Virginia Dialect, *American Speech*, Aug., 1928, p. 456.
2 Woofter had called attention to *eetch* in 1927.
3 Idioms in West Virginia, *American Speech*, Feb., 1936, p. 63. Most of these seem to show Pennsylvania German influence.
4 West Virginia Peculiarities, *American Speech*, April, pp. 155-56.

change of the short *i* to a long one in *condeetion, feesh*, etc., and added the change of *u* to *oo* before *sh*, as in *poosh* (push) and *cooshion* (cushion).[1] I am told by Mr. C. E. Smith, of the Fairmont *Times*, that *feesh, deesh* and *poosh* are heard also in Fairmont, which is in the north central part of the State, not far from the Pennsylvania line.[2] In Nicholas county, in the center of the State, according to another correspondent,[3] *grist* is so pronounced that it rhymes with *Christ*.

The population of West Virginia is greatly mixed, with persons of Virginia origin probably predominating in the early strata, but with considerable elements of Pennsylvania, Maryland and Ohio stock mingled with them, and, in recent years, of immigrant Irish, Italians and Poles. In Taylor county, of which Grafton is the chief town, and in the adjoining Barbour county, there is an ancient settlement of mixed bloods known locally as the Guineas. Some of them claim to be of Dutch and Indian blood, but they show a Negro strain and a few of their surnames suggest German ancestry. There is an excellent study of them by William Harlen Gilbert, Jr.[4]

Wisconsin

On account of the eminence of the Milwaukee brewers Wisconsin is commonly thought of by Americans outside its bounds as a strongly German State, but as a matter of fact it was first settled by people from western New York, New England, Pennsylvania, Ohio and Michigan. The Germans, who began to filter in in 1839, did not come in large numbers until the middle 40s, and they were preceded by Norwegians and closely followed by Dutch, Czechs, Swedes and Poles. Dr. Frederic G. Cassidy, of the University of Wisconsin, who undertook a survey of the State for the Linguistic

---

[1] But *gush*, he said, never becomes *goosh*.
[2] Private communication, April 9, 1944.
[3] Mr. Ben D. Keller, of Fayetteville; private communication, April 23, 1937.
[4] Mixed Bloods of the Upper Monongahela Valley, West Virginia, *Journal of the Washington Academy of Sciences*, Jan. 15, 1946, pp.

[1-13] There are many similar groups of mixed bloods, always of low economic status, in the Eastern States, notably the Wesorts of southern Maryland, the Nanticokes of Delaware, and the Malungeons of southwestern Virginia, eastern Kentucky and Tennessee. The last named are supposed to be partly of Portuguese descent.

236 *The American Language: Supplement II*

Atlas, is of the opinion that these immigrants have had but little influence upon the local speechways, save in isolated communities. He says:

> The foreign-derived population has apparently adopted the current American lexical pattern, with insignificant variations. . . . Their own words have not generally entered the local American vocabulary. They have had a sort of negative influence by adopting the most current terms, and (lacking an English-speaking home environment) by promoting the decay of many less current, older, or domestic words by remaining unaware of them.[1]

Cassidy, whose doctorate comes from the University of Michigan, was trained in field work there under Marckwardt, and after experience in Michigan and Ohio gathered the Wisconsin material singlehanded. It comes from 25 communities, covering all parts of the State. It will not be published as a whole until the Great Lakes and Ohio valley section of the Linguistic Atlas is completed. In 1923 Howard J. Savage printed a brief word-list of Wisconsin speech,[2] but it showed only a small number of terms not in common use elsewhere, e.g., *elm-peeler*, a poor white; *fuskit*, an old army musket; *hi-open-hopens*, Fourth of July merrymakers; *mule-foot*, a hog with undivided hoofs; *penadie*, bread crumbs with butter, sugar and hot water; *smooth-bore*, a worthless fellow; *splint-shin*, a strain of the leg muscles, and *yelper*, a young turkey. Savage also listed some local metaphors, e.g., *to take his commission*, to castrate, and *to tip over*, to die. In 1940 Cassidy printed a few locutions in *American Speech*,[3] but they were mainly terms familiar, in some form or other, elsewhere.[4] In 1947 an immigrant from New Jersey contributed to the Milwaukee *Journal* the following observations on Wisconsin speech:

> Can it be that Wisconsin has a language all its own? Some of the people I have in mind are high-school graduates. Others have had further education, so apparently it isn't lack of training. A few examples:
> *That's for sure* in lieu of *definitely, absolutely* or *positively*. Panes of glass

---

1 Some New England Words in Wisconsin, *Language*, Oct.–Dec., 1941, pp. 324–39. In this paper Cassidy presents a map showing the main currents of immigration, and describes his method of collecting material.

2 Word-List From Southwestern Wisconsin, *Dialect Notes*, Vol. V, Part VI, pp. 233–40.

3 From Wisconsin Sources, Oct., pp. 326–27.

4 In 1942 he read a paper before the Indianapolis meeting of the Linguistic Society of America on Unstressed Final *o* in Wisconsin Speech, but so far as I know it has not been published.

are *window-lights*. The word *ever* appears constantly, as in "Is it *ever* cold" or "Was I *ever* glad," even in the newspapers and on the radio. Bedroom or house slippers are *morning slippers*. A gal's slip becomes an *underskirt*. Stockings are *socks*, regardless of the length. Pursued or chased is *took after*. A photographer's studio is a *picture gallery*. "I'll *borrow* you $5" is used instead of *loan* or *lend*. "Did you find *back* your pocketbook?" — why the *back?* I haven't heard anyone say *hello* or *how are you?* The accepted salutation is *hi*. At the movies, instead of requesting tickets for adults and children, they say *large* and *small*.[1]

One native, commenting upon this Jerseyman's strictures in the *Journal*, declared that the peculiarities noted were confined to Milwaukee, where "even teachers and radio announcers are not free from local errors."[2] Another, *pace* Cassidy, blamed the influence of various foreign groups. "We are," he said, "a melting pot and speak a mixed language with disregard for correct English."[3]

Wyoming

The first to report on the speech of what is now Wyoming[4] was P. W. Norris, superintendent of the Yellowstone National Park.[5] In 1884, in a book called "The Calumet of the Coteau,"[6] he included "A Glossary of Indian Names, Words and Western Provincialisms,"[7] and thought it necessary to define, for the benefit of Easterners, a number of terms that are now familiar to every American schoolboy, *e.g.*, *badlands*, *butte*, *cañon*, *geyser*, *mustang* and *pemmican*.[8] He also included some Indian words, from the Chinook and other dialects, that have since dropped out of use or become localisms, *e.g.*, *illahi*, my country; *ka*, no; *kamook*, a dog; *kokosh*, pork; *manonim*, wild rice; *odeona*, a village; *siwash*, a male Indian; *skookum*, brave, and *tillacume*, enemies. In 1911 Helen Bruner and Frances Francis contributed to *Dialect Notes* "A Short Word List

---

1 Wisconsin's Own Language, April 25, 1947. I am indebted for this and the following to Mr. J. A. Kapmarski.
2 Milwaukee's Odd English, Milwaukee *Journal*, May 9, 1947.
3 Other State Languages, Milwaukee *Journal*, May 5, 1947.
4 The Territory was organized in 1868, but the State was not admitted to the Union until July 10, 1890.
5 The Yellowstone became a national park in 1872.
6 The name of a tribe of local Indians. It was given to them by the early French (Fr. *coteau*, a knoll or hillock), apparently in reference to the country they inhabited.
7 Philadelphia, pp. 223–33.
8 *Badlands* is traced by the DAE, in Western use, to 1851, *butte* to 1805, *cañon* to 1834, *geyser* to 1854, *mustang* to 1808 and *pemmican* to 1804

From Wyoming"[1] made up chiefly of cattlemen's terms, *e.g.*, *biscuit-shooter*, a camp cook;[2] *dogie*, a motherless calf; *cavvies*, stray cattle, and *pail-feed*, a calf raised on skim milk. There is a much longer vocabulary of the cattlemen in the Wyoming volume of the American Guide Series.[3]

A curious speech-pocket has been reported on the Hilliard Flats in a valley in the Southwestern corner of the State, near the Utah line.[4] The inhabitants of this remote region are the descendants of English coal-miners who got converted to Mormonism in the early 80s, came to Utah in search of salvation, and were put to work in coal-mines not far from their present home. In 1895 there was an explosion in the mines which killed about a hundred of them, and the rest departed for Hilliard Flats, resolved to become farmers. Their speech still shows signs of their English origin. They drop their *h*'s, add a final *r* to such words as *law*, and preserve a number of Briticisms, especially of the Nottinghamshire dialect, *e.g.*, *dag*, a helping; *to dout*, to put out a fire; *hillins*, bed-clothing; *to marb*, to growl or grumble; *to piggle*, to pull or tug nervously; *to siden*, to put in order, and *to teem*, to pour from one vessel into another. They use *sempt* for *seemed*, *tret* for *treated* and *wed* for *weeded*.

Alaska

The Klondike gold rush of 1897 made all Americans familiar with a number of Alaskan terms, *e.g.*, *sourdough* and *to mush*, but few if any of them originated in Alaska. Some came from the Indian languages or from Eskimo or Aleut, others were heritages from the French-Canadian trappers of the Seventeenth and Eighteenth Centuries, and yet others were simply Western mining terms.[5] After Pearl Harbor there was another and vastly larger influx of Ameri-

[1] Vol. III, Part VII, pp. 550–51.
[2] The DAE does not list it in this sense, but traces it, in the transferred sense of a waitress, to 1898.
[3] Wyoming: a Guide to its History, Highways and People; New York, 1941, pp. 459–66.
[4] Note on Dialect in the Uinta Mountains of Wyoming, by Wilson O. Clough, *American Speech*, April, 1936, pp. 190–92.
[5] *Sourdough*, meaning a prospector who carries a lump of fermented dough to use as a leaven in making bread, was in use in California long before gold was discovered on the Yukon. It is not listed in the DAE, and neither is *to mush*. The latter, meaning to travel on foot, usually with a dog-team, is said by the NED Supplement to be "apparently from the French *marchez* or *marchons*, the command given to the dogs."

cans, made up of soldiers and construction workers, and the population of the Territory is now much greater than it was in 1940. Inasmuch as these newcomers hail from all parts of the United States, the local speech has become inordinately mixed and its earlier vocabulary has been enriched both by importations and by neologisms coined on the spot. One of the latter appears to be *no-see-um*, a biting insect too small to be seen.[1] Of the survivors from pre-Pearl Harbor days a good example is *mukluk*, defined in an advertisement of an Army supply house as boots made of tanned leather bottoms and canvas-duck tops, with a heavy felt lining and a laminated felt and leather sole.[2] Mr. Charles F. Dery, of Whitehorse, Y.T., who has been investigating speechways on both sides of the Alaska-Yukon border, reports that the newcomers have brought in terms from far-distant American dialects, *e.g.*, *link* as the singular of *lynx*, which is mistaken for a plural, and *mad-ax* for *mattock* from Appalachia; *till* for *to*, as in " a quarter *till* seven," from Pennsylvania, and *wait on* from the South.[3]

Hawaii

There is a somewhat full account of the American English of Hawaii in AL4, pp. 372–77, based on studies by William C. Smith[4] and John E. and Aiko Tokimasa Reinecke[5] and an article by a correspondent of the Christian Science *Monitor*.[6] English began to be taught in the schools of the islands so long ago as 1853, but the polyglot strata in the native speech of the population, to wit, Polynesian, Chinese, Japanese, Korean, Portuguese, Spanish and various kinds and levels of English, has made the work of the schoolma'am difficult. Some of the syntactical eccentricities encountered are listed in a series of test papers for pupils in the elementary grades, prepared by Madorah E. Smith and W. B. Coale and published by the

---

[1] *American Notes & Queries*, March, 1947, p. 183.
[2] I am indebted here to Mr. Nicola Cerri, Jr.
[3] I am indebted here to Mr. Dery, who has not yet published his observations.
[4] Pidgin English in Hawaii, *American Speech*, Feb., 1933, pp. 15–19.
[5] The English Dialect of Hawaii, *American Speech*, Feb. and April, 1934, pp. 48–58 and 122–31. See also Insular English, by T. T. Waterman, *Hawaii Educational Review*, Feb., 1930. Other authorities are cited in the Reinecke papers.
[6] Miss Elisabeth F. Smith, copyright supervisor of the *Monitor*, has been kind enough to make a diligent search for the author and date of this article, but without success.

University of Hawaii. Among them are difficulties with word order, e.g., "I feed *every day the rooster*" and "We *together went home*"; with number, e.g., "The boys *is* here," "Give *a* food to my pet" and "There were four *childs*"; with tense, e.g., "I *bring* it tomorrow," "I began to *fell* asleep" and "He did not *ran*"; with prepositions, e.g., "I must *to go to* Honolulu," "It's his turn *for do* that," "I attend *to* school every day" and "My sister *stays Japan*"; with the articles, e.g., "I must go to *the bed*," and with various common idioms, e.g., "*Lend* me look at the paper," "Give me *a* chalk," "I want to come *big*" and "We had *a* good *fun*." A number of Hawaiian locutions survive, e.g., "*Hemo* (take away) this desk" and "I go home *pau* (after) school,"[1] and there are English words and phrases that afflict the schoolma'am, e.g., "We laughed *like hell*." A curious habit of using geographical terms or their derivatives in place of the points of the compass, e.g., *waikiki, makai* and *ewa*, is noted in AL4, p. 377. Says Dr. Harold S. Palmer, professor of geology at the University of Hawaii:

Ewa lies to the west-northwest of Honolulu, so the direction *ewa* approximates west. *Waikiki* approximates east. But in the older Hawaiian usage *waikiki* would have approximated west to a person situated east of Waikiki beach. For analogy we may think of Albany, Buffalo, Cleveland, Toledo and Chicago, and say "Buffalo is *Cleveland* of Albany" and "Toledo is *Cleveland* of Chicago." The use of *mauka* (Hawaiian *ma*, toward and *uka*, mountain) and *makai* (Hawaiian *kai*, sea) is very practical in a region where the sun is close to overhead for some hours at midday for some months, so that shadows do not have pronounced directions."[2]

Lewis and Marguerite Shalett Herman, in their "Manual of Foreign Dialects,"[3] say that "the ordinary young Hawaiian speaks an American form of English with the exception of a few vowel and consonant variations and a smattering of grammatical changes," but add that "there is an infiltration of a slight Portuguese intonation, from which the Hawaiian dialect obtains its lilt and emphasis, as well as some Pidgin English and Beche le Mar." The first English spoken on the islands was undoubtedly Pidgin, but it began to give

[1] *Pau* is used in many other idioms, and has become, indeed, a counterword, e.g., "That's *pau* for now" and "She's *pau* on him." I am indebted here to Mr. John Springer.

[2] Private communication, March 13, 1938. I am also indebted here to Major William D. Workman, Jr.

[3] Chicago, 1943. The subtitle of this work indicates that its purpose is to instruct performers on "radio, stage and screen," but it is full of observations that are of interest to more methodical students of the language.

The Pronunciation of American 241

way to more orthodox English at least a century ago,[1] and, as I have noted, English has been taught in the schools since 1853. By an act of 1896, when Hawaii was still a more or less independent republic, English was declared to be " the medium and basis of instruction in all public and private schools," but in 1919 [2] this law was amended to provide that " the Hawaiian language shall be taught in all normal and high schools." In 1931, however, a further act reduced Hawaiian to the estate of an elective in junior and senior high-schools, and in 1935 a law providing that it should be taught in the grade-schools set up on land occupied by natives under a Homestead Act of 1921 was turned into absurdity by a provision that daily instruction in it should be for " at least ten minutes." [3]

The Hermans list the following as the most frequent vowel changes in Hawaiian English: the *a* of *take* and that of *bat* become the *e* of *get;* the *a* of *father*, that of *ball*, and the *aw* of *off* become the *u* of *but;* the *i* of *sit* becomes the *ee* of *seat;* the *oi* of *oil* becomes the *a* of *palm*. The sounds of long *ee*, as in *bee*, of *i* in *nice*, of *o* in *bone*, of *oo* in *food* and of *u* in *up* remain unchanged. Inasmuch as Hawaiian has but five vowels, *a, e, i, o* and *u*, and but seven consonants, *h, k, l, m, n, p* and *w*, with no diphthongs and no consonant clusters, for " no two consonants can be pronounced without at least one vowel between them," [4] the older natives have difficulty with many American words. But their Americanized juniors are learning to use *b, d, f, g, r, s* and *t*, though *d* and *t* are commonly dropped when preceded by another consonant, the *th* of *there* is changed to *d*, that of *thought* is changed to *t*, and *v* is changed to *w*. Also, diphthongs are creeping into such loans from the Hawaiian as *lai*, in which the vowels were clearly separated in the original.[5]

The Philippines

375. [Those Filipinos who have acquired American English in the public schools of the archipelago ... make changes in it. It is most unusual for one of them to speak it well.] This statement, with

[1] It still survives, however, as a *lingua franca*. See Pidgin English in Hawaii, by William C. Smith, *American Speech*, Feb., 1933, pp. 15-19.
[2] Hawaii was annexed to the United States Aug. 12, 1898.
[3] I am indebted here to Das Volksgruppenrecht in den Vereinigten Staaten von Amerika, by Heinz Kloss; Essen, 1940, Vol. I, pp. 589-95.
[4] The Hawaiian Language, by Henry P. Judd; Honolulu, 1940, p. 5.
[5] See also AL4, pp. 372-77.

the specifications following, was based upon an article by Emma Sarepta Yule, of the College of Agriculture, Los Baños, published in 1925.[1] A later report indicates that the Filipinos have made some progress, though not much, since the time of Miss Yule's paper. That report appeared in the Manila *Graphic* for September 22, 1938, in the form of an interview with Alice Mary Johnson, professor of English at Union College, Manila. She said:

> The mistakes which a native often commits are seldom if ever committed by an American. An American would not, for example, say "I *have gone* to the movies last night," but a native, unmindful of the definite past, would say just that. . . . Countless Filipinos still refer to a woman with the pronouns *he* or *him*, or to a man with *she* or *her*. Also, they use *him* for *he*, *she* for *her*, and the other way round. . . . A reputable story writer uses "work *in* the farm" for "*on* the farm." [2]

Of Filipino pronunciation her informant, Jose Luna Castro, said:

> The accent . . . is far superior to that of the natives of ten or twenty years ago. . . . They enunciate their vowels and consonants with admirable crispness. However (and nobody should be discouraged by this), the accent is none too correct or too pleasant to the American ear. . . . Twenty years ago Filipinos invariably spoke English with a nasal twang. It was considered smart. It was the result of listening to the early American soldiers, who spoke their own language nasally. Today only a few acquire the affectation, because wider contact with Americans has shown them that Americans themselves — that is to say, educated ones — avoid it. . . . The average Filipino who speaks and writes the language, and probably thinks in it, occasionally commits mistakes, but on the whole he knows it well enough to utilize it for ordinary use. After all, it is not every American or Englishman who speaks and writes English well enough to be a model.

Miss Johnson predicted that a distinctively Filipino form of English would evolve in the islands. "The great body of it," she said, will be "essentially American," and "the variations from the mother-tongue will be more evident in speech than in writing." At the end of 1945 it was estimated that no less than 5,000,000 of the 16,500,000 inhabitants spoke what is known locally as Bamboo English, as against but 500,000 speaking Spanish. Article XIII, Section 3 of the constitution approved by President Roosevelt on March 23, 1935 ordained:

---

[1] The English Language in the Philippines, *American Speech*, Nov., pp. 111–20.
[2] Other examples are in A Little Brown Language, by Jerome B. Barry, *American Speech*, Oct., 1927, pp. 14–20, and Bamboo English, by George G. Struble, the same, April, 1929, pp. 276–85.

The National Assembly shall take steps toward the development and adoption of a common national language based on one of the existing native languages. Until otherwise provided by law English and Spanish shall continue as official languages.

A great many proposals for carrying this mandate into effect were made in the Assembly during the years following, and in the end Tagalog was chosen to become official on July 4, 1945 alongside English and Spanish,[1] but it has made little more actual progress than Gaelic in Ireland, and the chances seem to be good that English will prevail in the long run. The Americans in the Philippines have taken a number of Spanish and Tagalog loans into their everyday speech, and some of them are in frequent use, *e.g.*, the Spanish *lavandera*, a laundress; *dulce*, sweet; *basura*, a garbage can; *sala*, a living-room; *aparador*, a clothes-press; *hombre*, man, and *komusta*, how are you? (Sp. *como esta?*), and the Tagalog *tao*, man, used of a native peasant. I am informed by a correspondent that there have been some miscegenations between Spanish and English, *e.g.*, *shoe-hombre*, a member of the native white-collar class — literally, one high enough in the world to wear shoes regularly.[2] A white man married to a native woman is a *squaw man* and half-breeds are *mestizos*. *Chit* (a check or note) and *tiffin* (lunch) have been borrowed from the vocabulary of the English in the Far East.[3]

Puerto Rico

"The Puerto Ricans," writes a correspondent, "are the only people in the world who have no language. They speak Spanish wretchedly and English twice as wretchedly." The first half of this was supported by Dr. Victor S. Clark, an economist who was the first president of the Insular Board of Education under the military government which followed the Spanish-American War, 1898–1902 "A majority of the people," he said, "do not speak pure Spanish. Their language is a patois almost unintelligible to the native of Barcelona and Madrid. It possesses no literature and little value as an intellectual medium. There is a bare possibility that it will be nearly as easy to educate these people out of their patois into English as

---

[1] *American Speech*, Dec., 1941, p. 303.
[2] Mr. Hartford Beaumont: private communication, March 11, 1938. I am also indebted here to Mr. James Ross, of Manila; Mr. James Halsema and Captain Henry L. Harris.
[3] See also AL4, pp. 375–77.

it will be to educate them into the elegant tongue of Castile." This "bare possibility" was the foundation of the educational scheme adopted for the island by its American saviors, and by 1912 98.4% of all the urban public schools were being taught in English exclusively. It worked very badly, and in 1930 Spanish was restored in the four lower grades, but English was retained through the higher grades and into the high-school and university. In that year a new commissioner of education, Dr. José Padín, made Spanish the sole medium of instruction in the first eight grades. But at some time before 1940 Roosevelt II ordered that English be given first place once more. A year later a native spokesman declared that "the system of education in Puerto Rico has been reduced to an absurdity, and our people are losing their own language without acquiring another."[1]

Thereafter the language question became an important part of the Puerto Rican movement for independence, and the discussion of it aroused bitter animosities. A minority of native Uncle Toms, derisively termed *pitiyanquis* (petite Yankees), declared themselves to be in favor of teaching even Spanish in English, but the overwhelming majority of Puerto Ricans demanded that all elemental teaching be in Spanish, with English taught only as a second language and in the higher grades. In May, 1946 the Puerto Rican Legislature passed an act adopting the latter programme, but it was vetoed by the Governor, Rexford G. Tugwell. The Legislature then repassed it over his veto, and under the Organic Act of March 2, 1917 it went for final decision to President Truman, who vetoed it on October 25. This second veto set off a fresh uproar, for under the same Organic Act the President was required to act upon such a repassed act within ninety days, failing which it became a law. Truman's defense was that it had not reached him until August 5, but the Puerto Rican Senate insisted that the ninety days should have been counted from the day the act was repassed, and accordingly appealed to the United States District Court of the island, which decided in its favor in March, 1947. The government thereupon appealed to the Su-

---

[1] The spokesman was a university student, Carlos Carrera Benitez, and his protest was part of a speech he delivered at an Inter-American Conference held at San Juan in April, 1941, under the management of Archibald MacLeish, the New Deal poet-statesman. See The Spanking of A. MacLeish, *New Masses*, May 20, 1941, pp. 21–24. Padín's ideas were set forth in English in Puerto Rico; San Juan, 1935 — a very effective piece of writing, far beyond the capacity of any but a microscopic minority of American pedagogues.

preme Court of Puerto Rico, and by the time these lines get into print the case may be before the Supreme Court of the United States.[1]

How many Puerto Ricans have acquired a working knowledge of American English is not known with certainty. In 1935 Padín estimated that 400,000 in a population of 1,600,000 had done so,[2] but in 1945 the Puerto Rican Teachers' Association (Asociación de Maestros de Puerto Rico) was still estimating the same number " ten years of age and over " in a population grown to 2,000,000.[3] Not many of these speak the language correctly, for most of them have been taught it by native teachers who are themselves far from at home in it. Spanish, indeed, is still the prevailing tongue of the island, save only in a narrow circle of Federal jobholders. Even the intellectuals educated in the United States speak it among themselves, and in the interior English is scarcely known at all. There was no English newspaper until March 7, 1940, when *El Imparcial* of San Juan began publishing a morning tabloid in the language of the liberators. The next day *El Mundo* followed with an afternoon *World Journal,* but it expired in 1946.[4] For the following notes upon the insular English I am indebted to Lewis C. Richardson, of the English Institute of the University of Puerto Rico:

> One of the effects of Spanish upon it is a tendency toward the simplification of the verb. The Spanish verb is actually much more complex than the English, but ordinary Puerto Rican speech tends to drop final consonants and this is carried over into English, so that the regular English verb has its four forms

---

1 *Weekly News Bulletin* of the American Civil Liberties Union, July 29, Sept. 30 and Nov. 4, 1946, and March 10 and 31, 1947. There is an admirable summary of the situation in The Teaching of English in Puerto Rico, by Mariano Villaronga, commissioner of education; San Juan, Feb., 1947. I am indebted for the chance to see it to Senator Guy Cordon, of Oregon. See also American Editors, Please Take Notice, *Puerto Rico Libre,* Oct. 30, 1946, and The Teaching of English in Puerto Rico, a Statement of Principles by the Puerto Rico Teachers' Association; San Juan, 1945. For help here and hereafter I owe thanks to Dr. Eugenio Vera, of Rio Piedras.

2 AL4, p. 596, n. 1.

3 The Teaching of English in Puerto Rico, before cited, p. 2. Since 1900 the population of the island has increased 120% as compared to 84% for the United States. It is now 618 per square mile, as compared to 47 for the United States. The island has consumed $1,000,000,000 of American money since 1898, but is still desperately poor. See the *Population Bulletin* of the Population Reference Bureau, Washington, May, 1946.

4 *Newsweek,* April 8, 1940; *Saturday Review of Literature,* July 20, 1946, p. 17.

reduced to two. Thus, of *flow, flows, flowed* and *flowing,* the forms *flow* and *flowing* are often the only ones remaining, and the past participle, the past tense, the third person singular of the present and the remainder of the present are consolidated in *flow.* This tendency is supported by the repugnance of Spanish to constellations of final consonants.

The same tendency sometimes operates to eliminate plurals formed without the addition of an extra syllable. Thus, as the Spanish *seiz pesos* may be reduced to *sei peso,* so the English *six dollars* becomes *sik dollar.*

No Spanish word begins with *s* plus another consonant. In consequence *stop* is likely to become *estop, skate* to become *eskate,* and *state* to be confused with *estate.*

Other peculiarities are the omission of initial *w* in such words as *woman,* the substitution of *t* and *d* or *s* for the two sounds of *th,* the rolling of *r*'s, a confusion between *b* and *v,* and a failure to distinguish between the short and long sounds of *i*.[1]

A Puerto Rican tends to put the stress on the pronoun rather than the preposition in such a sentence as "He was walking behind me," even when there is no contrast between *me* and some other person. Likewise, when a descriptive adjective is compounded with a noun, the accent is likely to fall upon the noun, as in *right ángle.*

"I want him to go" often becomes "I want that he go," following the pattern of the Spanish "Quiero que él vaya." The double negative similarly comes into Puerto Rican English through the Spanish, as in "I can't see nothing" from "No puedo ver nada." The auxiliary *to do,* which has no equivalent in Spanish, gives rise to such constructions as "Did he went?," "Where he went?" and "What means this word?"

Richardson says that Spanish also influences the Puerto Rican English vocabulary through deceptive cognates. Thus *actual* is used for *present* in "the *present* state of affairs," *sympathetic* is used for *agreeable, artist* for *actor,* and *compromised* for *engaged* (to marry). Synonyms of Romance origin are preferred to those of Germanic origin, *e.g., force* rather than *strength, implement* or *instrument* rather than *tool,* and *arm* rather than *weapon.* Most American newspapers spell the name of the island *Porto Rico,* but its people prefer the Spanish form *Puerto Rico,* and it is official in all government publications.[2] I know of no published study of the English spoken in Puerto Rico, but the Spanish has been the subject of a number of investigations.[3] It shows many loans from English.

---

1 As a result of this last *bedclothes* has become a euphemism for *sheet.*
2 United States Government Printing Office Style Manual; Washington, 1945, p. 41.
3 A Bibliographical Guide to Materials on American Spanish by Madaline W. Nicholas; Cambridge (Mass.), 1941, pp. 97–98. By the kindness of Dr. Vera, Mr. Richardson, Lcdo. J. M. Toro Nazario and Dr. del Rosario I have accumulated some interesting notes upon these loans, but they have been crowded out of the present volume along with all my other material relating to non-English languages. See AL4, p. 649.

The Virgin Islands

The English of the Virgin Islands, which is described briefly in AL4, p. 378, is basically archaic English, not American, and seems to be common, with local changes, to the whole British West Indies. The Danes held the group from 1668 to 1917, when the United States bought them for $25,000,000, but Danish never made any progress as the local language against English. The only report upon the speech of the native Negroes that I am aware of was made by Henry S. Whitehead in 1932;[1] it included a somewhat longish story told by a colored brother in St. Croix to the white pastor of his church. A specimen passage:

> A tek a liddle run, den A mek a jump, but A bin a foot too shart, so de two shoes drap in a' de water. Howsomeber, a'-wee go on till a'-wee mek Orange Grove bridge, when we cahl out foo res'. By de time a'wee was gwine tek de 'tart again, me foot get soak, an' ef yo' bin-a-go shoot me A couldn' move an inch. Me see one mahn da pass, so me beg 'im pull dem aff foo me, an' after he hab almos' drag-aff me foot an-'all A put dem shoes 'pon me unmrella-'tick, an' tell you what, it must-a bin a fine sight to see me in me old bell-topper, me frack-coat, an' me big crabat, da-mash de broad path wid me bare foot.

The use here of *a'wee* (*all-we*), a first person analogue of the Southern American second person *you-all*, will be noted. Whitehead reported a number of loans from West African languages, *e.g.*, *buckra*, a white man; *shandrámadan*, a rascally act, and *caffoon*, a fall or other mishap, and some survivals of French, Portuguese, French, Dutch and Spanish loans from Crucian (and St. Thomian) Creole, " a *lingua franca* invented [for the slaves] by early Moravian missionaries who combined the language of their European masters' families with their own African dialects, and who needed the common tongue to serve them when they passed by purchase or otherwise from one estate to another where a different European language was spoken." The basis of the dialect, he said, is " late Seventeenth and early Eighteenth Century English — traditionally the language of trade and of the buccaneers throughout most of the West India islands." This dialect, he added, is not only " the language of the normally English-speaking islands, such as St. Kitts and Antigua,

---

[1] Negro Dialect of the Virgin Islands, *American Speech*, Feb., pp. 175-79.

but also of Dutch Saba and Dutch and French St. Martin." It tends to throw the accent back whenever possible, so that *good-morning* becomes *gu-marnín;* it elides *s* before a consonant, so that *spoon* becomes *poon,* it changes *th* to *d,* and it includes many pronunciations recalling the American Negro, *e.g., sarmin, lebben, gwine, wuk* and *fotch.* There are also some traces of Irish influence, or perhaps they are only vestiges of Seventeenth Century English, *e.g., woife* and *toime.*[1]

Canada

Palmer, Martin and Blandford, in their "Dictionary of English Pronunciation With American Variants,"[2] group American and Canadian speech together as facets of the same gem. The earliest writer on the latter, the Rev. A. S. Geikie, noted so long ago as 1857 that a large number of Americanisms were already in use, *e.g., bug,* in the general sense of insect; *to fix,* in its numberless American senses; *to guess, to locate, first-class*[3] and *rooster,*[4] and his first successor, writing twenty-eight years later,[5] added *cars,* a railroad train; *dry-*

---

[1] Helen L. Munroe says in West Indian English, *American Speech,* Jan., 1927, p. 201, that "persons familiar with Montserrat claim that the blacks there have an Irish brogue." For the dialect of Barbadoes see American English as Spoken by the Barbadians, by Dorothy Bentz, *American Speech,* Dec., 1938, pp. 310-12, and The Well of English, by P. T. L., London *Morning Post,* Nov. 9, 1935; for that of Jamaica, The Runt Pig, by Ethel Rovere, *American Mercury,* June, 1945, pp. 713-19, and The English Ballad in Jamaica, by Martha W. Beckwith, *Publications of the Modern Language Association,* June, 1924, pp. 455-83; and for that of Trinidad, Getting Into Bassa-Bassa Over Trinidad's Lingo, Baltimore *Evening Sun* (editorial page), Feb. 2, 1938. The speech of Bermuda has been dealt with by Harry Morgan Ayres in Bermudian English, *American Speech,* Feb., 1933, pp. 3-10, and that of the Bush Negroes of Dutch Guiana, a very corrupt form of English, by A. G. Barnett, in Colonial Survivals in Bush-Negro Speech, *American Speech,* Aug. 1932, pp. 393-97; by Morton C. Kahn in Djuka: the Bush Negroes of Dutch Guiana; New York, 1931, pp. 161-74, and by an anonymous writer in Bush-Nigger English, Manchester *Guardian Weekly,* Oct. 21, 1931. See AL4, pp. 371-72 and 377-78.

[2] Cambridge (England), 1926, p. xxxvii.

[3] Whether or not *first-class,* in the general sense of excellent, is an Americanism remains to be determined. The English use it to designate the best compartments on a train and students taking the honors at university examinations, but their more usual term for excellence otherwise is *first-rate.*

[4] Canadian English, *Canadian Journal,* Vol. II, 1857, pp. 344-55.

[5] Canadian English, by W. D. Lightall, *Week* (Toronto), Aug. 16, 1889, pp. 581-83.

goods, sidewalk, store, and *dock,* a wharf.[1] In 1890 A. F. Chamberlain attempted a linguistic survey of the Dominion,[2] but had to confess that there was not enough material accumulated to make it comprehensive. He noted, however, that in Ontario, which was settled in Revolutionary days by fugitive Loyalists from New York and Pennsylvania, " much that characterized the English speech of those States " was " still traceable in their descendants," and that the speech of the Eastern Township of Quebec did not differ " to a very marked extent from that of the adjoining New England States." Says a more recent observer:

> There is practically no difference in the speech of Canada and the United States, for the intermingling of the people of the two countries is constant. Cross from Michigan into Ontario and the speech is identical. Toronto, Montreal, Winnipeg and Vancouver are as much American as Buffalo, Cleveland, Detroit and Seattle. The whole of the northwest of Canada is the same in speech as Minnesota, Montana and Washington, for a great number of the settlers there came from the States.[3]

This was rather too sweeping, for it disregarded the survival of regional dialects in the Maritime Provinces and Newfoundland, the prevalence of French loans in Quebec, and the effects of social aspiration in the larger cities. The last-named is powerful indeed, for it has sufficed to keep English spelling in countenance, so that *labour* and *centre* are still in use, though the American *tire, curb* and *jail* have conquered. The fashionable private schools, as in the United States, inculcate something vaguely approximating Oxford English, and many of their teachers are Englishmen. Among the super-loyal *noblesse* of Montreal *pram* is used for *baby-carriage, tin* for *can,*

---

[1] For *bug* see AL4, pp. 12, 86 and 310, and Supplement I, pp. 460, 462 and 660; for *to fix,* AL4, p. 26, and Supplement I, pp. 497–98, and for *to guess,* Supplement I, pp. 44, 52 and 78. *To locate* is traced by the DAE to 1652, *rooster* to 1772, *cars* (now obsolete) to 1826, *dry-goods* to 1701, *store,* in the sense of a retail establishment, to 1721, and *dock,* in the sense noted, to 1707. *Sidewalk* is old in England, but is rare there.

[2] Dialect Research in Canada, *Dialect Notes,* Vol. I, Part II, pp. 43–56. See Supplement I, p. 169, n. 1.

[3] Spoken English, by Thomas C. Trueblood, *Quarterly Journal of Speech,* Vol. XIX, 1933, pp. 513–21. Another phonologist, Martin Joos, agrees in A Phonological Dilemma in Canadian English, *Language,* Vol. XVIII, 1942, pp. 141–44. " Ontario English," he says, " differs from the neighboring General American speech (for instance, in rural New York or Wisconsin) in only two items of any phonological consequence." These are (*a*) *pod* and *pawed* are homophones, and (*b*) the diphthongs *ai* and *aw* (but not *oi* as in *boy*) each have two variants.

sweet for *dessert*, *level crossing* for *grade crossing*, *tram* for *street-car*, *braces* for *suspenders*, *long holidays* for *Summer vacation* and *shallot* for *scallion*. Also, *schedule* is pronounced with the *sch* soft, and the letter *z* is *zed*, not *zee*.[1] But this is a class dialect, not the common speech. Among the plain people *baby-carriage*, *street-car* and the like are in everyday use.[2] Moreover, the talkies, the radio and the constant travel across the border are bringing in the newest American inventions as they appear,[3] and nearly all the slang in current use is unmistakably American. " The Great Lakes and the St. Lawrence river," said an observer in 1939,[4] " are highways of communication rather than barriers. . . . Canadian is a variant of General American, but not so striking a variant as Southern American. . . . Canadian intonation is identical with General American, or nearly so." There are, of course, some differences, especially in pronunciation, and this observer thinks they are sufficient " to enable Canadians and Americans usually to place one another very quickly by speech alone." He lists some of them, *e.g.*, *cornet* is accented on the first syllable, not on the second, as in the United States;[5] *been* is *bean*, not *bin*; an intrusive *y* appears before *u* in *constitution*, *duke*, and the like; *economics* is *eek-*, not *ek-*; *lieu-*

---

[1] Montreal English, by Helen C. Munroe, *American Speech*, Oct., 1929, p. 21.

[2] A Note on Canadian English, by W. S. W. McLay, *American Speech*, April, 1930, pp. 328–29. " No Canadian, no matter how strongly his heart beats for the Empire," said a writer signing himself J. R. M. in the Winnipeg *Free Press*, June 20, 1936, " ever says *goods-train* or *lorry* or *petrol*." Under date of Dec. 3, 1945, Mr. Ralph O. Bates, of Melrose, Mass., writes: " The Canadian language lies between English and American, though much nearer to American. Canadians are likely to use the English *return ticket*, *nib* (pen point), *mudguard*, *braces* (suspenders) and *meat-pie* (pot-pie). In my boyhood in Canada both the American *hog-pen* and the English *pig-sty* were heard, but the most common term was *pig-pen*." The extent to which Americanisms are encountered in the debates of the Canadian Houses of Parliament was discussed in Parliament Goes Hollywood (editorial), Ottawa *Journal*, April 7, 1934.

[3] An unfamiliar Americanism, even an old one, is sometimes resisted stoutly by the Canadian equivalents of the English connoisseurs of American linguistic atrocities, but always in vain. In 1931, for example, there was an uproar from them when a Montreal coke company used *raise in pay* in an advertisement instead of the English *rise*. But nothing came of it. See *Raise or Rise*, by Helen C. Munroe, *American Speech*, Aug., 1931, pp. 407–10.

[4] A Note on Canadian Speech, by Morley Ayearst, *American Speech*, Oct., 1939, pp. 231–33.

[5] But I have often heard *córnet* in the United States, and destiny seems to be on its side, for the general tendency of American, as we have seen, is to move the accent forward.

tenant" is always *leftenant*"; *vacation* is *vuk-*, not *vaik-*, and "a few Canadians still say *clark* instead of *clerk.*"

But such differences are obviously small, and set against them are many popular preferences for American as opposed to English usage, *e.g.*, the *r* is always sounded, "if anything," says Ayearst, "more heavily than in the Middle West"; "*movies* are never the *cinema*"; "*street-car* and *sidewalk* are never *tram* and *pavement*"; and "*bloody* has no more shocking significance to a Canadian than to an American." In sum, "despite the best efforts of the pedagogue and the plaints of visiting Englishmen, . . . Canadian speech can only be regarded as a variant of Standard American, [and] it seems most probable that the tendency to assimilate American usage will continue." With all this another phonological observer agrees, at least for Ontario.[1] The dominant influence upon the local speech, she says, has been that of Scottish immigrants. The broad *a* is never heard, even in *aunt* and *rather*. The flat *a*, as in *care* and *carry*, often approaches the *e* of *yet*. In *not, log, watch, sorry, stop, on, rotten* and *foggy* the vowel is *aw*, not *ah*. "Most Canadians are inclined to regard American speech habits disparagingly, [but they] are no more fond of Southern British speech."

There is a considerable effort by social-minded persons of the tonier classes to put down the prevalent yielding to American example, but they are seldom clear as to what they want Canadian English to be. Sir Andrew Macphail, writing in 1935,[2] was content to argue that "the flat vowels in our Canadian speech" — especially, I assume, the flat *a* — were "unpleasant"; the only remedy he had to suggest was "to take thought, to listen acutely to beautiful [British?] speech, and to listen with equal acuteness to our own." "In England," he continued, "a man cannot pass from the lower to the higher social scale until he has mastered the letter *h*, and few succeed in the attempt. . . . But in England there is a standard of beauty and an established correctness of speech which the wise ones strive to achieve if it is not theirs by right, and they conform with that standard when they are to the manner born." Mr. Justice A.

[1] Ontario Speech, by Evelyn Ahrend, *American Speech*, April, 1934, pp. 136–39.
[2] Our Canadian Speech, Toronto *Saturday Night*, June 29. Macphail was born on Prince Edward Island in 1864, but spent his life on the mainland. He had some reputation as a pathologist, but, like Sir William Osler, had literary inclinations and wrote a number of non-medical books. He was knighted in 1918, apparently for his services in World War I.

Rives Hall, of the Canadian Court of Appeals, delivered many indignant pronunciamentoes on the subject during the 30s, but he was equally vague about what was to be done.[1]

The remoter parts of Canada, like the remoter parts of the United States, have developed local dialects that show some interesting oddities, but they are confined to small and thinly-populated areas, and give no sign of spreading. That of the Northwest is substantially identical with that of the American Northwest.[2] Those of New Brunswick, Nova Scotia and Newfoundland were the subjects of a report by W. M. Tweedie, of Sackville, N. B., in *Dialect Notes* in 1895.[3] Among the terms he listed were: *abito, bito* or *aboideau*, a sluice so arranged that water can flow through a dike at low tide; *admiral*, the oldest man in a settlement; *barber*, the vapor arising from water on a frosty day; *breastner, burn* or *turn*, a stick of firewood; *Colcannon Night* or *Snap-Apple Night*, Hallowe'en; *copying*, jumping from piece to piece of floating ice; *cracky* or *gaffer*, a small boy; *crunnocks*, kindling; *dirt*, bad weather; *drung*, a lane leading to a pasture; *dunch*, bread not properly baked; *dwy*, a sudden squall, with rain or snow; *all of a floption*, unawares; *hand-signment*, signature; *huggerum buff*, fish and potatoes fried in cakes; *to play jig* or *to slunk*, to play truant; *leaf*, the brim of a hat; *livier*, a merchant or trader; *nippent*, merry; *nunny-bag*, a bag for holding lunch; *prog*, food; *puck*, a blow; *rampole, rampike* or *ranpike*, the trunk of a dead tree; *to establish a raw*, to make a beginning; *silver thaw*, a sleet storm leaving trees covered with ice; *slob*, soft snow or ice; *to spell*, to gather; *starigan*, any small evergreen cut for firewood; *tilt*, a one-story house; *twinly*, delicate; *to yap*, to scold, and *yarry*, smart, quick. Most of these came from Newfoundland, and many of them were borrowings from various English and Scotch dialects.

---

1 Supplement I, p. 71. Other references to Canadian speechways are on pp. 90, 97, 178, 184, 320, 353, 477, 490, 545, 596, 599, 601 and 608. Not a few common Americanisms have come into the language from Canada, especially through Canadian French, *e.g.*, *chowder*, *toboggan* and *portage*.

2 The Polyglot Vernacular of the Canadian North West, by E. L. Chicanot, *Modern Language Review*, Vol. X, 1915, pp. 88–89; Western Canadian Dictionary and Phrase-Book, by John Sandilands; Winnipeg, 1912.

3 New Brunswick, Nova Scotia, and Newfoundland, Vol. I, Part VIII, pp. 377–81. To Tweedie's vocabulary the editors of *Dialect Notes* added some terms gathered by the Rev. William Pilot in Newfoundland.

In 1916 Lewis F. Mott added *handy*, nearby, and *just now*, shortly, from Newfoundland,[1] and in 1925 George Allen England [2] added the following, gathered in 1920 and 1922: *puckerin'* or *turned over*, sick in bed; *adurt*, across; *airsome*, cold, stormy; *andramarten*, a prank; *astray*, different; *bake* or *white-nose*, a newcomer; *batch*, a fall of snow; *baving*, thin kindling; *bedfly*, a bedbug or louse; *coaleys*, the court cards in a pack; *cockabaloo*, a bullying boss; *conkerbill*, an icicle; *corner boy*, a city man; *cowly*, hard, severe; *cozy*, energetic, fast; *cuffer*, an incredible story; *to douse*, to fool; *down the Labrador*, the North; *drop-ball*, an earring; *to fathom out*, to explain; *feller*, a son; *to fist*, to grasp; *flute*, the mouth; *front*, the region east of Newfoundland; *garagee*, a free-for-all-fight; *gazaroo*, a boy; *to glutch*, to swallow; *to go on the breeze*, to get drunk; *to go to oil*, to become valueless; *gobby*, crazy; *hang-ashore*, a loafer; *hardware*, intoxicants; *to heck it*, to walk quickly; *hocks*, boots; *humgumption*, common sense; *keecorn*, the Adam's apple; *lassie loaf*, bread and molasses; *to live hard against*, to have a grudge against; *liverish*, sick, nauseated; *look-after*, damages; *to make fire*, to make a row; *to make wonder*, to be surprized; *merry-me-got*, a bastard; *moor*, the root of a tree; *muckered* or *spun out*, exhausted; *omaloor*, an ungainly fellow; *oxter*, the armpit; *passionate*, patient in suffering; *on a pig's back*, in good condition; *proud*, glad; *rack*, a hair-comb; *raw*, a rough fellow; *to saddle*, to agree; *scheme*, mischief; *scudge*, a flurry; *shad*, a light fall of snow; *sharooshed*, taken aback, surprised, disappointed; *all of a slam*, in a hurry; *slinky*, thin; *slovey*, soft; *smack*, a short time; *smatchy*, tainted (as of meat); *snaz*, an old maid; *stage*, a wharf; *streel*, a slovenly woman; *to vamp it*, to walk, and *way*, home. England reported some curious pronunciations. Both sounds of *th*, he said, were commonly changed to *t*, the *h* was manhandled as in Cockney, *a* was often changed to *i*, and as often substituted for both short and long *e*, as in *age* for *edge* and *ape* for *heap*. *Oil* became *hile*; *easterly*, *easly*; *empty*, *empt*, and *pneumonia*, *eumonia*. *Flipper* was pronounced *fipper*. *Jersey* was *joisie*, as in New York City, and *to murder*, signifying to bother or pester, was *to moider*. The *f* often became *v*, as in *vin* for *fin* and *vur* for *fur*. As in the South, *evening* was used to designate the time

---

[1] Canada, *Dialect Notes*, Vol. IV, Part V, p. 332.
[2] Newfoundland Dialect Items, *Dialect Notes*, Vol. V, Part VIII, pp. 322–46.

from noon to 6 P.M. *Morning* was used for day in general, and any time after 6 o'clock was *night*. The preterite of *to save* was *sove*, and that of *to stow* was *stole*.[1]

The dialect of Labrador was discussed in papers by Mary S. Evans in 1903[2] and William Duncan Strong in 1931.[3] Miss Evans visited Fox Harbor on Lewis Bay, the southernmost large indentation on the Labrador peninsula, during the Summer of 1926. She found surviving many words and phrases that had been reported by an early explorer, George Cartwright, in 1792. She listed, among others, *to give a passage*, to give a lift in a boat, however short; *lop*, a wave; *puff-up*, the birth of a child, and *tickle*, a narrow neck of water. *He*, she said, was in common use for *it*, as in "I'll take *he*" (meaning any inanimate object). *Uncle* and *aunt* were applied to all elderly persons, every girl was a *maid*, and girls and boys used *my son* in addressing their younger brothers. Strong, who visited northern Labrador in 1927–28, added *lund*, quiet; *tidy*, swift; *scrammed*, almost frozen, and *chronic*, a gnarled tree, beside some curious names for the local fauna and flora. He said that in northern Labrador *she* was often used for *it* instead of *he*, as in "Put *she* in a bag," referring to a struggling fish.

The dialect of Lunenburg, Nova Scotia, which was settled by Germans in the Eighteenth Century, has been studied by a competent phonologist, M. B. Emeneau, of Yale.[4] German is no longer spoken there, but it is still understood by a few oldsters and its influence upon the local speech remains evident. Some of the examples cited by Emeneau are *what for* (Ger. *was für*); *to make* in the sense of to prepare, as a meal; *to get awake* (Ger. *wach werden*); *with* used as an adverb after *to go* and *to come* (Ger. *mitgehen*); *off* similarly used after verbs signifying cleaning (Ger. *abwaschen*); *all* used in place of *all gone*; *apple-snits* (Ger. *schnitte*); *lapish*, insipid

[1] See also Notes on the Dialect of the People of Newfoundland, by George Patterson, a paper read at a meeting of the Montreal branch of the American Folk-Lore Society, May 21, 1894, *Journal of American Folk-Lore*, Jan.–March, 1895, pp. 27–40. Patterson noted the Newfoundland use of *knowledgeable*, which became a counterword in England years later. See Supplement I, p. 423. Otherwise his word list did not differ materially from those I have abstracted. In the same journal, Jan.–March, 1896, pp. 19–37, he published some notes on Montreal speech, and in July–Sept., 1897, pp. 203–13 he followed with further notes on Canadian speech.

[2] Terms From the Labrador Coast, *American Speech*, Oct., pp. 56–58.

[3] More Labrador Survivals, *American Speech*, April, pp. 290–91.

[4] The Dialect of Lunenburg, Nova Scotia, *Language*, June, 1935, pp. 140–47.

(Ger. *läppisch*); *klotsy*, heavy or soggy (Ger. *klotzig*); *to fress*, to eat greedily (Ger. *fressen*); *hexed*, bewitched (Ger. *hexen*); *to grunt*, to complain (Ger. *grunzen*); *shimmel*, a very blond person (Ger. *schimmel*, a white mould), and *Fassnakday*, Shrove Tuesday (Ger. *Fastnacht*). Emeneau reports that all these loans show signs of dying out. The dialect has, in general, the characters of the general speech of Canada, and especially of Nova Scotia, *e.g.*, the tendency to change the diphthong of *how* into one made up of *o* and *u*, so that *couch* and *coach* become homonyms. But it drops the *r* in nearly all situations after verbs, whereas the letter is commonly sounded in the rest of Canada.[1]

The speech of the Dominion, and especially of the eastern part, is now being investigated in a scientific manner by Henry Alexander, professor of the English language and literature at Queen's University, Kingston, Ont., with a view to the preparation of a volume for the Linguistic Atlas of the United States and Canada. He is the author of an excellent short manual on the development of English, " The Story of Our Language," [2] and made a preliminary report on his field work at the Chicago meeting of the American Dialect Society in December, 1945. His researches on the coast of Nova Scotia, during World War II, provided proof that even philology has its dangers, and may some day have its martyrs. His questioning of local informants aroused the suspicion of the Army and Navy patrols guarding the coast against Hitler, and when he was arrested and a copy of the International Phonetic Alphabet was found upon him it was assumed to be some sort of code. Fortunately, he was finally brought before a naval officer who recognized this sinister-looking alphabet, and when he proved that he was an Englishman by birth and an Oxford man and that he had no police record in Kingston, he was liberated with nothing worse than a warning to sin no more.[3]

---

[1] Emeneau published A Further Note on the Dialect of Lunenburg, Nova Scotia, in *Language*, July–Sept., 1945.

[2] Toronto, 1940.

[3] The dialects of the other British possessions and of England, Scotland, Ireland and Wales lie outside the purview of this book, but I add a note on them for readers who may be interested. A bibliography running down to the end of 1922 is in Kennedy, pp. 380–405. For Cockney, since that time, see Cockney Past and Present, by William Matthews; London, 1938; Cockney H in Old and Middle English, by G. Ch. Van Langenhove, *Leuvensche Bijdragen*, Vol. XV, 1923, pp. 1–50; Bernard Shaw's Phonetics, by Joseph Saxe; London, 1936; Cockney, *John o'London's Weekly*, March

Other Dialects

In one of his invaluable historical papers Allen Walker Read has shown that the Americans of fifty years before the Revolution were already acutely aware of the existence among them of groups speaking English with tell-tale brogues and accents.[1] That aware-

---

25, 1938, p. 1017, and The Cockney Tongue, by W. M. Eager, *Contemporary Review*, Sept., 1922, pp. 363-72. The dialect of Australia is dealt with exhaustively in The Australian Language, by Sidney J. Baker; Sydney, 1945, an extremely valuable work, and Baker is also the author of A Popular Dictionary of Australian Slang; Melbourne, 1941, and New Zealand Slang; Christchurch, 1941. See also New Zealand English, by Arnold Wall; Christchurch, 1938; Meet New Zealand, a pamphlet issued for the guidance of American soldiers by the New Zealand Department of Internal Affairs; Wellington, 1942; Pocket Guide to Australia, issued by the American War and Navy Departments; Washington, 1942, especially pp. 46-48; Australian Slang, London *Morning Post*, June 15, 1936; Australian Slang, by Wilson Hicks, *Life*, May 18, 1942, pp. 15-17; Australian Slang, by E. S. Moore and others, London *Observer*, Oct. 23, Nov. 6 and 13, Dec. 11, 1938; *Fiddlers, Ropies* and *Skiddies*, *New Zealand Free Lance*, Aug. 18, 1943; How They Say it in Australia, by Philip Faxon, *This Week*, June 29, 1941; The Dinkum Oil, London *News-Review*, Aug. 2, 1945; Americans May Learn New Lingo in Australia, Baltimore *Evening Sun*, March 20, 1942; Timely Tips to New Australians, by Jice Doone (Vance Marshall); London, 1926; Australian Slang, in Slang Today and Yesterday, by Eric Partridge; second edition; London, 1935, pp. 414-21; Australia and the Mother Tongue, by B. T. Richardson, Baltimore *Sun*, Dec. 28, 1943; A Christmas Letter From Australia, by Robert B. Palmer, *Journal of the American Medical Association*, Dec. 11, 1943; I've Been in Australia, by Lucille Gordon, *Good Housekeeping*, Sept., 1942; Down Under, by John Oakes, *New Yorker*, Sept. 28, 1935; Pardon My Aussie Accent, by Harold Rosenthal, *Newspaperman*, Jan., 1945; *Cobber, Dinkum* and *Swag* Test Americans Down Under, *Christian Science Monitor*, Nov. 30, 1942; Slang Down Under, New York *Times Magazine*, Jan. 17, 1943; English as it is Spoken in New Zealand, by J. A. W. Bennett, *American Speech*, April, 1943, pp. 81-95, and The Pronunciation of English in Australia, by A. G. Mitchell; Sydney, 1946. See also Burke, pp. 146-48. For South African English the authority is South African English Pronunciation, by David Hopwood; Cape Town, 1928. For that of India it is A Glossary of Anglo-Indian Colloquial Words and Phrases, by Henry Yule and Arthur Coke Burnell; London, 1886. See also Some Notes on Indian English, by R. C. Goffin, *S. P. E. Tract No. XLI*, 1936, pp. 20-32. The English Dialect Society has brought out volumes on the speech of nearly all the English counties, and there are many more by private venturers. The British Museum is making phonograph records of all of them, for many are dying. For a general survey of English colonial speech see Spoken English, by Thomas C. Trueblood, *Quarterly Journal of Speech*, Vol. XIX, 1933, pp. 513-21.

1 Bilingualism in the Middle Colonies, 1725-1775, *American Speech*, April, 1937, pp. 93-99.

ness, indeed, must have gone back to at least a century before, for it is hard to imagine that the Indians who picked up the language of the Colonists at Plymouth and Jamestown learned to speak it correctly overnight, and before the middle of the Seventeenth Century the English were in frequent contact with Frenchmen and Dutchmen. Later came Swedes, Germans and Spaniards, and meanwhile the nascent Americans began to notice that the Scotch, Irish and Welsh immigrants who came in,[1] and even some of the English,[2] spoke in ways that were not their own. By 1775 the Southern Negro began to be differentiated in speech, by 1797 the rustic Yankee, and after the War of 1812 the Westerner.[3] After the great Irish immigration of the late 40s and the German immigration which followed it the Irishman[4] and the German became standard types in American comedy, alongside the Negro minstrel introduced by Thomas D. Rice (1808–60) in the 30s. They were followed, in the 50s, by the Chinaman, and in later years by the Scandinavian, the Italian and the Jew. So early as 1823 James Fenimore Cooper had attempted German, French, Irish, English and Negro dialects in " The Pioneers," though he made his Indians speak conventional English.[5] But there had been an attempt to render Indian English in a serious book published in 1675, to wit:

[1] The English at home had been aware of the curious dialect of the Welsh since Elizabethan times, as is shown by the speeches of Fluellen in Shakespeare's Henry V, c. 1599, e.g., " Got's plood! Up to the preaches, you rascals! Will you not up to the preaches? " (Act III, sc. II). The Englishman's French had been the butt of French humorists since the Middle Ages. See The Fabliau " Des Deux Anglois et de l'Anel," by Charles H. Livingston, *Publications of the Modern Language Association*, June, 1925.

[2] A Maryland court record of Sept. 11, 1762, printed in Documents Concerning Charles Willson Peale, *Maryland Historical Magazine*, Dec., 1938, p. 389, includes this: " She always understood and from his speech and pronunciation of his words believes he was an Englishman."

[3] Literary Dialects, in The English Language in America, by George Philip Krapp; New York, 1925, Vol. I, pp. 225–73. See also The American on the Stage, *Scribner's Monthly*, July, 1879, pp. 321–33, and Minority Caricatures on the American Stage, by Harold E. Adams, in Studies in the Science of Society, a *Festschrift* in honor of Albert Galloway Keller, edited by George Peter Murdock; New Haven, 1937, pp. 1–27.

[4] The best discussions of Irish-English that I know of are in English as We Speak It in Ireland, by P. W. Joyce; second edition; Dublin, 1910, and Irish Pronunciation of English, by Alexander J. Ellis, in his Early English Pronunciation; London, 1874, Vol. IV, pp. 1230–43.

[5] Cooper's Leatherstocking was given a dialect greatly resembling that of the contemporary Yankee. See The Dialect of Cooper's Leatherstocking, by Louise Pound, *American Speech*, Sept., 1927, pp. 479–88.

Umh, umh, me no stawmerre fight Engis mon. Engis mon got two hed, Engis mon got two hed. If me cut off un hed, he got noder, a put on beder as dis.[1]

German dialect apparently got its first literary recognition in 1856, when Charles Godfrey Leland wrote the earliest of his long series of "Hans Breitmann" ballads to fill an unexpected gap in *Graham's Magazine*. These ballads were very popular during the Civil War, and Leland continued to bring out volumes of them until 1895.[2] They were imitated by Charles Follen Adams, with almost equal success, in a "Leedle Yawcob Strauss" series which ran from 1877 to 1910. Here is a specimen of the dialect that both used:

> Der schiltren dhey vas poot in ped,
>   All tucked oup for der nighdt;
> I dakes mine pipe der mantel off,
>   Und py der fireside pright
> I dinks aboudt vhen I vas young —
>   Off moder, who vas tead,
> Und how at nighdt — like I do Hans —
>   She tucked me oup in ped.[3]

This stanza and the three that follow in the text well exhibit the earmarks of the German-American dialect as it was then understood, *e.g.*, the change of *ch* to *sh*, of *b* to *p*, of *p* to *b*, of *th* to *d*, of *t* to *dt*, of *d* to *t*, of *v* to *f* and of *w* to *v*, the diphthongization of *o*, and the tendency to put verbs and adverbs at the ends of sentences.[4] In the 70s the so-called Dutch comedian became a popular figure on the American stage, and during the 80s and 90s that was a

---

1 The Present State of New England, by a merchant of Boston; London, 1675, p. 12. I take this from Krapp, who speculates as to the meaning of *stawmerre* and concludes that it is either an Indian corruption of *understand* or an Indian term of the same meaning.

2 He was an amateur philologist of some skill, and published books on Pidgin English and the language of Gypsies. In 1889–90 he and Albert Barrère brought out A Dictionary of Slang, Jargon & Cant in two volumes; revised edition, 1897. He was born in 1824 and died in 1903. He was a native of Philadelphia, and after being graduated from Princeton, spent three years at Heidelberg and Munich. He wrote more than fifty books, including translations from Heine and other German authors. His most popular book, Hans Breitmann's Barty, was published in Philadelphia in 1868. In the preface to a subsequent English edition it is stated that the prototype of Breitmann was "one Jost, a German trooper of the Fifteenth Pennsylvania Volunteer Cavalry." I am indebted here to Judge Robert France.

3 Mine Schildhood, by Adams, *Harper's Magazine*, May, 1880, p. 952.

4 An earlier specimen of German dialect, in prose, is in the Editor's Drawer of *Harper's Magazine*, May, 1857, p. 859.

rare burlesque show or vaudeville which did not present at least one specimen of him.[1] He perished in World War I, though perhaps not altogether in consequence of it, for the Irish, Scandinavian and Negro comic characters perished with him, and the Jew moved from the stage to books. In 1913 or thereabout Kurt M. Stein, of Chicago, began contributing doggerels written in a different German dialect to Bert Leston Taylor's column in the Chicago *Tribune*. This dialect was not an English filled with Germanisms, but a German filled with Americanisms. A specimen:

> Den andern abend ging mein frau
> Und ich a walk zu nehme'.
> Of course, wir könnten a machine
> Affordern, but ich claime
> Wer forty waist hat, wie mein frau,
> Soll exzerseizah, anyhow.

These verses were well liked by the readers of the *Tribune*, and especially by the Germans among them, and they continued to appear until the entrance of the United States into World War I made everything German taboo. They were resumed after the war, and in 1925 a Chicago publisher brought out a volume under the title of "Die Schönste Lengevitch." It was an immediate success, and was followed by "Gemixte Pickles" in 1927 and "Limburger Lyrics" in 1932.

Since 1909, when the late Montague Glass's "Potash and Perlmutter" stories began to appear in the *Saturday Evening Post*, the speech of the immigrant Jews of New York, popular on the stage since the 90s, has been the dialect most cultivated by American comic writers, *e.g.*, Arthur Kober, Leo Calvin Rosten (Leonard Q. Ross) and Milt Gross.[2] It has been studied by Robert J. Menner,[3]

---

[1] Lewis Maurice (Lew) Fields and Joseph Weber, his most successful impersonators, first tackled him as juvenile comedians in 1877. They organized their own company in 1885, and opened their music-hall in New York in 1895. Fields was born in 1877 and died in 1941.

[2] Of these only Gross was born in the United States. Glass was of English birth, Kober is of Hungarian and Rosten is of Polish. Glass (1877–1934) published his first book of Potash and Perlmutter stories in 1910. Its characters were put into an enormously successful play in 1913. Kober and Rosten printed their stories in the *New Yorker*. Kober's first book, Thunder Over the Bronx, was published in 1935. Rosten's first, The Education of H*y*m*a*n K*a*p*l*a*n, appeared in 1937, and Gross's first, Nize Baby, in 1926.

[3] Popular Phonetics, *American Speech*, June, 1929, pp. 410–16.

Dolores Benardete,[1] C. K. Thomas,[2] Robert Sonkin[3] and Alter Brody.[4] Menner says that Gross's transcription is as accurate " as our poor alphabet will allow." One of the chief marks of the dialect is its change of the short *i*, as in *bit*, to the long *e*, as in *beet*, and *vice versa*. Says Menner:

> Gross makes his Mrs. Feitlebaum say *seex* for *six*, *dees* for *this*, *deesh* for *dish*, and *keetchen* for *kitchen* . . . but on the other hand he writes *quin* for *queen*, *itting* for *eating*, *stimhitt* for *steamheat*, *weesit* for *visit*, *spitch* for *speech*, and *keeds* for *kids*. . . . When the baby *sleeps* (slips) on the floor he is put " *queek* in de *bad* should go to *slip* (sleep)." Mrs. Feitelbaum's neighbor gives her child a *peel* (pill) when he eats up all the potato-*pills*. Now, if she uses long *e* incorrectly in *slip* and *peel* why can't she utter the sound where it properly belongs in *sleep* and *peel?* The real reason is that Mrs. Feitelbaum and her friends do not actually reverse these sounds. In both *slip* and *sleep* they use a sound which may be loosely ascribed as midway between short *i* and long *e*. For in their native Yiddish, presumably, they have not the exact equivalent of either. Our popular designations disguise the close relationship between short *i* and long *e*. To the phonetician, as to the Continental, both are varieties of an *i*-sound. In phonetic terms Mrs. Feitelbaum's *i* is probably a high-point tense *ee* shorter than the English *ee* in *sleep*, and yet not slack like the *i* in *slip*. . . . But if Gross's symbols are not phonetically exact, they nevertheless reproduce exactly the effect on the ordinary hearer of the Yiddish attempt to pronounce our vowels.

In the same way and for the same reason the speaker of this dialect confuses and interchanges the sound of *e* in *bed* and that of *a* in *bad*, so that *rang* becomes *reng* and *hat* becomes *het*. Again, the *o* of *don't* and the *u* of *run* are exchanged, so that *don't* becomes *dunt* and *punch* becomes *ponch*. Miss Benardete lists the following additional vowel changes: the *au*-sound in *mouth* becomes the *a*-sound of *mark* or the *o*-sound of *bow*, so that *down* becomes *dahn* and *now* becomes *no;* the *o*-sound of *not* is so shortened that it comes close to the *u*-sound of *cup*, so that *was* sounds like *vus;* the *au*-sound in *Maud* also turns into a kind of *u*, so that *yourself* is *yuself* and *because* is *bikus;* the *u*-sound of *cup* becomes an *a*-sound, so that *such* is *sahtsh* and *up* is *ahp*, and the vowel in *her* is changed to *oi*, so that *girl* is *goil* and *worth* is *woith*. Among the consonants *v* is changed to *f*, *w* to *v*, *v* to *w*, *d* and the *th* of *bath* to *t*, the *th* of *that* to *d*, and *g* to *k*.

[1] Immigrant Speech — Austrian-Jewish Style, *American Speech*, Oct., 1929, pp. 1–15.
[2] Jewish Dialect and New York Dialect, *American Speech*, June, 1932, pp. 321–26.
[3] In Re Jewish Dialect and New York Dialect, *American Speech*, Feb., 1933, pp. 78 and 79.
[4] Yiddish in American Fiction, *American Mercury*, Feb., 1926, pp. 206–07.

In their valuable handbook for character actors [1] Lew and Marguerite Shalett Herman describe all of the foregoing traits of the dialect, along with a number of others. In the initial position, they say, *d* is pronounced as in English, but in the medial position it changes to *t*, as in *rettesh* (radish), and at the end of a word, if preceded by another consonant, it is commonly dropped, as in *kain* (kind). The *k* that is substituted for *g* in the medial and terminal positions varies with the birthplace of the speaker: the German Jews make its sound that of *gk*, but the Eastern Jews use a plain *k*. In the initial position it remains *g*. *J* is often converted into *tch*, as in *tchahtch* for *judge*. In the combination *ng* the *g* is often sounded more clearly than by Americans, so that *singer* rhymes precisely with *finger*. At the beginning of a word *r* is usually pronounced correctly, but on occasion it may be preceded by the neutral vowel, so that *ribbon* becomes *uhreeb'n*. In the medial position, when followed by a vowel and another consonant, it is omitted, as in *pok* for *park*, but when followed by a vowel alone it is always sounded, as in *breenk* (bring). In the terminal position it is always dropped. The Lithuanian Jews, say the Hermans, have difficulty with *sh* and *tch*. The former is usually unvoiced, so that *fish* becomes *fees*, and the latter is reduced to *ts*, so that *bachelor* becomes *betseleh*. Most of the grammatical and syntactical peculiarities of Yiddish-American are common to the vulgar speech of the whole country, *e.g.*, the confusion of tenses, the use of *to lay* for *to lie*, the chronic misuse of *shall* and *will* and the substitution of *what* for *that*, as in " The girl *what* I seen." But it also has some aberrations of its own, *e.g.*, the substitution of *stood* for *stayed*, as in " He *stood* in bed "; the addition of an unnecessary auxiliary, as in " *Did* the work was did? "; the inversion of subject and predicate, as in " Was coming many peoples "; the omission of *of*, as in " Three kinds meat "; the use of *might* for *maybe*, as in " *Might* he will come "; the omission of *there*, as in " Is two men on the corner? " the substitution of *by* for *at*, as in " I was *by* his house "; the use of *as* following *better*, and the use of *mine* for *my*.[2]

[1] Manual of Foreign Dialects for Radio, Stage and Screen; Chicago, 1943, pp. 392-416.
[2] The Hermans' book also contains illuminating chapters on the Cockney, Oxford, Australian, Bermudan, East Indian, Irish, Scottish, German, French, Mexican, Filipino, Portuguese, Japanese, Chinese, Hawaiian, Swedish, Norwegian, Russian, Lithuanian, Jugoslav, Czech, Finnish, Hungarian, Polish and Greek dialects, and on Pidgin English.

Thomas's study is devoted to the speech of educated Jews in New York. He says that one of its chief characteristics is a slight change in tongue position in the pronunciation of *t, d, n, l, s* and *z*, producing the effect of a lisp. This lisp is even more noticeable in the speech of English Jews, and writers who attempt to transcribe that speech usually indicate it.[1] Brody, unlike Menner, is not content with the manner of rendering Yiddish-American followed by American writers. He does not mention Gross, but he is critical of Glass, and also of Anzia Yezierska, Myra Kelly and Bruno Lessing, whom he accuses of writing what he calls Yidgin English. His chief complaint is that, when a Yiddish preposition corresponds to two prepositions in English, they seek exotic color by translating it into the wrong one. An example is provided by *froon* (Ger. *von*), which may mean either *of* or *from*. Miss Yezierska makes it *from*, as in " God *from* the world," whereas *of* is correct. Brody thus translates II Samuel XVIII, 33:

> Oi weh! Mine son Absalom, Absalom mine son! God from the world! Better from far already I should have died, only if not he!

And thus Mark XIV, 36:

> Oi weh! So tired I am from the heart, till I could die! Mine Father from Heaven, everything it could be by You! So make it maybe I shouldn't have this bitter cup to drink!

Beginning August 26, 1933 J.X.J. (John J. Holzinger) published in the *New Yorker* a series of " Notes for an East Side Dictionary " which recorded amusingly some Yiddish-American pronunciations. A few examples:

> Dub. A large receptacle for water, as in *washdub*.
> Greens, *v.* Smiles broadly.
> Kettle. Steers and cows; livestock.
> Lift, *v.* Past tense of *to live*.
> Locker. Beer which has been stored some months before it is used.
> Mop. A gang, a crowd.
> Putter. A fatty substance obtained from milk and cream by churning; as in *pick putter-and-ache man*.
> Spit. Quickness in motion.[2]

---

[1] Jewish Speech in British Fiction, *American Notes & Queries*, Aug., 1941, p. 73; Dec., 1941, p. 135; Jan., 1942, pp. 158–59; April, 1942, p. 16.

[2] Says Albert Jay Nock in What Are Anthologies For?, *Encore*, Nov., 1944, p. 388: " This idiom has as distinct a place in American literary history as the French-English idiom of Louisiana as Mr. Cable presents it; the Negro-English idiom of the upper South as Mr. Harris presents it; and the German-English idiom of eastern Pennsylvania as you find it in ' Harbaugh's Harfe.' "

But of all the racial dialects on exhibition in the United States the one that has got the most attention, both from the literati and from students of linguistics, is that of the Southern Negroes. Tremaine McDowell says [1] that it made its first appearance in American fiction in Part I of Hugh Henry Brackenridge's satirical novel, " Modern Chivalry: Containing the Adventures of Captain Farrago and Teague O'Regan, His Servant," published in 1792,[2] but it had been attempted in plays so early as 1775 and there were traces of it in other writings even before.[3] One of the characters in " Modern Chivalry " is Cuff, an illiterate slave who discovers a petrified mocassin and is invited to Philadelphia to address the primeval scientificoes of the American Philosophical Society. A sample of his discourse:

> De first man was de black a-man, and de first woman was de black a-woman: and get two tree children; de rain vasha dese, and de snow pleach, and de coula come brown, yella, coppa coula, and at the last quite fite, and de hair long; and da fal out vid van anoda, and van cash by de nose, an pull, so de nose come lang, sharp nose.

Obviously, this could not have been good reporting, for *the* is sometimes *the* and sometimes *de*, *and* is sometimes *and* and sometimes *an*, *w* is sometimes *w* and sometimes *v*, and *r* is sometimes elided and sometimes not. But it at least gave some hint of one of the characters that must have shown itself in ignorant Negro speech in those days as it has shown itself ever since, to wit, a simplified grammatical structure. The origins of that structure was thus described by Krapp: [4]

> When the Negroes were first brought to America they could have known no English. Their usefulness as servants, however, required that some means of communication between master and slave should be developed. There is little likelihood that any masters exerted themselves to understand or to acquire the native language of the Negroes. . . . On the contrary, the white overlords addressed themselves in English to their black vassals. . . . This English . . . would be very much simplified — the kind some people employ when they talk to babies. It would probably have no tenses of the verb, no distinctions

[1] Notes on Negro Dialect in the American Novel to 1821, *American Speech*, April, 1930, pp. 291-96.
[2] The first two volumes of this Part I were published in Philadelphia. A third followed in Pittsburgh a year later and a fourth in Philadelphia in 1797. In 1804 and 1805 two volumes of Part II appeared in Philadelphia. Brackenridge (1748-1816) was a Scotsman who was brought to America as a child, and graduated from Princeton in 1771. He was a chaplain in the Revolution but afterward took to the law and became a judge in Pittsburgh.
[3] Some specimens are given by Krapp, Vol. I, pp. 255-65.
[4] The English of the Negro, *American Mercury*, June, 1924, pp. 190-95.

of case in nouns or pronouns, no marks of singular or plural. Difficult sounds would be eliminated, as they are in baby talk. Its vocabulary would be reduced to the lowest elements. . . . As the Negroes imported into America came from many unrelated tribes, speaking languages so different that one tribe could not understand the language of another, they themselves were driven to the use of this infantile English in speaking to one another.

The slaves, however, were not taught English by their white overlords but by the low-caste whites set over them as overseers and by the earlier comers of their own race. In Virginia, until the beginning of the Eighteenth Century, they worked side by side in the fields with white bond servants, and nearly everywhere else their management was entrusted to overseers who, in many cases, were former bond servants of non-English origin and in nearly all cases were either illiterate or next door to it. In another place [1] Krapp suggests that the result must have been the development of a dialect comparable to Pidgin English or Beach-la-Mar, and that this dialect survives more or less in the Gullah of the sea islands of Georgia and South Carolina, to be noticed presently. But its vestiges are also to be found in the speech of the most ignorant Negroes of the inland regions, which still shows grammatical peculiarities seldom encountered in white Southern speech, however lowly, *e.g.*, the confusion of persons, as in "I *is*," "*Do* she?," "*Does* you?," "*Am* you de man," and "He *am*"; [2] the frequent use of present forms in the past, as in "He *been die*," and "He *done show* me," and the tendency to omit all the forms of *to be*, as in "He *gone*" and "Where you *at?*." [3] The phonology of this mudsill Negro speech greatly resembles that of the lowest class of whites, so much so that many competent observers, among them Southerners, have declared that it is substantially identical,[4] but my own belief, after a lifetime spent in contact with Negroes of all classes, is that in intonation, at least, it shows

[1] The English Language in America, Vol. I, p. 253.
[2] In The Truth About *You-all*, American Mercury, May, 1933, p. 116, Bertram H. Brown, denied that *am* is ever so used. "Any Southern Negro I ever heard speak," he said, "would conjugate the present tense of the verb *to be* as follows: *I is; you is; he, she* or *it is; us is, you-all* (or *y'all*) *is, they is*." Krapp says in his *American Mercury* paper, before cited, that these are legacies from a northern English dialect. In Eloise, *American Speech*, June, 1932, pp. 349-64, Dolores Benardete gives the following conjugation of *to pray: ah prays, she pray, he pray, we prays, yuh prays, dey prays*.
[3] I am indebted here to Mr. George W. Thompson.
[4] *e.g.*, Krapp, p. 250; Cleanth Brooks and L. W. Payne, Jr., quoted under Alabama, and W. Cabell Greet in Southern Speech, in Culture in the South, edited by E. T. Couch; Chapel Hill (N.C.), 1934, p. 614.

special characters.[1] Even the educated Negro seldom loses this intonation, though in vocabulary and pronunciation his speech is identical with that of the corresponding class of whites.[2] Indeed, he tends to speak a shade "better," in the schoolma'am's sense, than whites on his own level, and it has been noted by more than one observer that in New York City, for example, the colored people seldom use *foist* and the other hallmarks of the so-called Brooklyn dialect. The representation of Negro speech in literature has always been imperfect, and often absurd. A familiar example is afforded by the *brer* of Joel Chandler Harris's stories. No Southern Negro ever actually uses *brer*. What he says, when he attempts *brother*, is something on the order of *bruh-uh* or *bruh,* maybe with a faint trace of *r* at the end.[3]

The Gullah or Geechee dialect of the Georgia and South Carolina coasts[4] is an anomaly among American Negro dialects, as it is indeed among American dialects in general, for it is the only one that is not easily intelligible in far parts of the country. Krapp was of the opinion that "very little of it, perhaps none, is derived from

[1] Said the late Grover C. Hall in a syndicated newspaper article, Feb. 2, 1936: "There are many similarities between the dialect of the unlettered Southerner and that of the unlettered Negro, but the differences are conspicuous to all sensitive ears."

[2] This approximation was noted by Nathaniel Beverly Tucker, a Virginia lawyer, so early as 1836. See McDowell, before cited, p. 295.

[3] See Krapp, Vol. I, p. 249; The Use of Negro Dialect by Harriet Beecher Stowe, by Tremaine McDowell, *American Speech,* June, 1931, pp. 322–26; The Vocabulary of the American Negro as Set Forth in Contemporary Literature, by Nathan van Patten, the same, Oct., 1931; The Negro in the Southern Novel Prior to 1850, by McDowell, *Journal of English and Germanic Philology,* Oct., 1926, pp. 455–73; The Negro Character in American Literature, by John H. Nelson, *University of Kansas Humanistic Studies,* Vol. IV, No. 1, 1926; Poe's Treatment of the Negro and of Negro Dialect, by Killis Campbell, *University of Texas Studies in English,* July, 1936, pp. 107–14, and The Philology of Negro Dialect, by Earl Conrad, *Journal of Negro Education,* Spring, 1944, pp. 150–54. But James Nathan Tidwell, in Mark Twain's Representation of Negro Speech, *American Speech,* Oct., 1942, pp. 174–76, argues that the speech of Jim in Huckleberry Finn is accurately reported. H. A. Shands says in Some Peculiarities of Speech in Mississippi, 1893, that *uh* is universally used by Mississippi Negroes in place of *er,* and that it is also the form of the indefinite article. "No sound of *r,*" he adds, "is ever apparent in the Negro pronunciation."

[4] It extends up the rivers for twenty miles or more. The origin of *Gullah* is disputed. It may come from *Gola,* the name of a tribe and language of the Liberian hinterland, or from *Ngola,* the name of a tribe in the Hamba basin of Angola. *Geechee* is probably from the name of another tribe and language of Liberia.

sources other than English," and not a few white linguists have supported him,[1] but this theory has now been considerably weakened by the studies of Dr. Lorenzo D. Turner, of Fisk University, a Negro linguist who prepared himself for his task by acquiring a working knowledge of the principal West Coast African languages. He began field work between Georgetown, S. C. and the Georgia-Florida border in 1930, and by 1944 had assembled no less than 6,000 loans from twenty-eight languages and dialects. Of these about a thousand came from Kongo, spoken in Angola and the Belgian Congo, and another thousand from Yoruba, spoken in Nigeria. About four-fifths of them appear today only as personal names, and others are used only in traditional African songs, mostly unintelligible to the singers, but the rest " are used daily in conversation."[2] Some of Turner's specimens from the surviving vocabulary follow, with the African terms from which they come:

Agali. Welcome. (Wolof *agali*).
Ban. It is done. (Vai and Bambara *ban*, to be finished).
Beng, or bing. A rabbit. (Fante *kping*).
Bong. A tooth. (Wolof *bong*).
Bubu. Any insect, but usually one whose sting is poisonous. (Fula *mbubu*, a fly; Hausa, *bubuwa*; Bambara, *buba*; Kongo *mbu*).
Bukra. A white man. (Efik and Ibibio *mbakara*, white man, from *mba*, he who, and *kara*, to govern).
Da, or dada. Mother. (Ewe *da* or *dada*).
Daf. Corn cooked in cakes. (Hausa *dafuwa*, boiled corn or rice).
Dajije. Sleep well. (Twi *dajije*).
Det. A hard rain. (Wolof *det*).
Dindi. A small child. (Vai *din din*).
Do. A child. (Mende *ndo*).
Dzadza, or dzagdza. A blackbird. (Mende *dzadzalo*).
Dzambi. A red sweet potato. (Vai *dzambi*).
Dziga. A sand flea. (Yoruba, Wolof, Mandinka and Hausa *dziga*).
Dzoga. A seesaw. (Wolof *dzogal*, to rise).
Enufole. Pregnant. (Ewe *fo le enu*, she is with child).
Fufu. A powder used to cast a spell. (Ewe *fufu*, dust).
Fukfuk. The viscera of an animal. (Mende *fukfuk*).
Fulafafa. A woodpecker. (Mende *fula*, to bore through; *fafa*, a small tree).
Gafa, or kafa. Rice. (Hausa *shinkafa*).
Guba. A peanut. (Kongo *nguba*, a kidney).

[1] For example, W. Cabell Greet in Southern Speech, in Culture in the South, edited by W. T. Couch; Chapel Hill (N.C.), 1934, p. 612; Reed Smith in Gullah, *Bulletin of the University of South Carolina*, Nov. 1, 1926, p. 32, and John Bennett in Gullah: a Negro Patois, Part I, *South Atlantic Quarterly*, Oct. 1908, p. 33.

[2] Notes on the Sounds and Vocabulary of Gullah, *Publication of the American Dialect Society No. 3*, May, 1945, p. 23.

Gumbo. Okra. (Tshiluba *tshinguhmbuh;* Umbundu *otshingumbo*).

Hudu, *v.* To bring bad luck to. (Hausa *hudu,* a form of gambling; Ewe *hododo,* lending or borrowing; *hodada,* a dice game).

Ibi, *v.* To vomit. (Yoruba *ibi*).

Kunu. A boat. (Bambara *kunu*).

Kuta. A tortoise. (Bambara and Malinke *kuta;* Dahomean *kulo;* Efik *ikut;* Buluba-Lulua *nkudu;* Djerma *ankura;* Hausa *kunkura*).

Landu, or dalandu. An alligator. (Kongo *ngandu,* a crocodile; Hausa *lando,* a lizard; Bobangi *landa,* to glide or move along).

Na. And. (Twi and Ibo *na*).

Nanse. A spider. (Twi and Fante *ananse*).

Nuna. A term of respect used in addressing an old woman. (Mandinka *nna;* Kongo and Bobangi *nuna;* Buluba-Lulua *nunu*).

Nyamnyam, or nyam, *v.* To eat. (Wolof *nyamnyam*).

Podzo, or odzo. A heron. (Mende *podzo*).

So so. A call to horses. (Vai, Mende and Jeji *so,* a horse).

Toko. Plenty. (Twi *toko,* plentifully; Dahomean *togogo,* overflowing).

Tot, *v.* To carry. (Umbundu *tuta,* to carry; Kikongo *tota,* to pick up; Mandingo *ta,* to carry on the head or in the hand).

Ula. A louse or bedbug. (Umbundu *ola* or *ona,* a louse; *ula,* a bed; Yoruba *ola,* a moth).

Vudu. Sorcery. (Dahomean *vodu,* a spirit or fetish; *vodudoho,* a curse; *vuduna,* a cult or religion; Ewe *vodu da,* a snake that is worshipped; *vodusi,* a priest).

Wanga. A charm. (Umbundu *owanga,* a charm or fetish).

Yan, *v.* To tell a lie (Wolof *yan*).

Some of these have got into the general American vocabulary, especially in the South, *e.g., buckra, gumbo, dzambi (yam), dziga (chigger), vudu (voodoo), hudu (hoodoo), guba (goober)* and *kuta (cooter).* It is possible also that *kunu* may have been the progenitor of *canoe* and *tot* of *to tote,* though it does not appear to be likely.[1] Other investigators, all working before Turner, sought to show that Gullah is simply an archaic form of English, strongly influenced by the British dialects, including Scots, and also by French. Bennett, before cited[2] compiled a list of Elizabethan and even earlier survivals in its vocabulary and phonology, and came to the conclusion that it comes closer to the dialect of Lancashire than to any other English dialect.[3] Arthur A. Norton, reporting on a trip to the South

---

[1] The difficulties that etymologists have had with *to tote* are described in Supplement I, pp. 208–10. Webster 1934 derives *buckra* from the Efik *mbakara* or *makara, yam* from the Senegal *inhame,* and *goober* from the Kongo *nguba.* It says that *canoe* is "of Arawakan or Cariban origin" and *chigger* "of Cariban origin." It derives *voodoo* from the Ewe *vodu* through Creole French, and calls *hoodoo* an apparent variant.

[2] Part I, p. 346.

[3] The same, Part II, Jan., 1909, p. 52.

Carolina coast in 1898, professed to find it "nearly similar to the broken English of the French-Canadians."[1] And Reed Smith, writing in 1926,[2] saw its genesis in "the English vocabulary as spoken on the coast by the white inhabitants from about 1700 on." What the Negroes did, he goes on, was to take "a sizeable part" of that vocabulary,

> wrap their tongues around it, and reproduce it changed in tonality, pronunciation, cadence and grammar to suit their native phonetic tendencies and their existing needs of expression and communication. The result has been called "the worst English in the world." It would certainly seem to have a fair claim to that distinction. To understand it requires a trained ear, and at first blush it is equally unintelligible to white people and colored people alike.[3]

Attempts upon the phonology and grammar of Gullah have been made by Smith,[4] Turner,[5] Albert H. Stoddard[6] and Guy B. Johnson,[7] and upon those of Negro American in general by James A. Harrison,[8] C. M. Wise,[9] Lupton A. Wilkinson[10] and Johnson.[11] Smith calls Gullah "a highly simplified form of English, both in phonology, grammar and vocabulary, with elision of difficult sounds, shortening of words, modification of every difficult enunciation, and a minimum of forms for person, number, case and tense." To which Stoddard adds: "[The Negroes'] ears could not take in nor their tongues encompass very much of our pronunciation. They lopped

---

[1] Linguistic Persistence, *American Speech*, Dec., 1930, p. 149.

[2] Gullah, before cited, p. 22. The substance of this paper seems to have been presented to the American Dialect Society at its 1923 meeting.

[3] Other testimonies to its difficulty are provided by Bennett, lately cited, Part I, pp. 336 and 340, and by Annie Weston Whitney in Negro American Dialects, *Independent*, Aug. 22, 1901, p. 1980. Both say that this difficulty once made it necessary to employ interpreters in the Charleston courts. Mrs. Whitney adds that, in the great days of the dialect, it threw off many subdialects. "Every large plantation," she says, "had its own. So distinct were these that a planter, by engaging a Negro in conversation, would tell at once who was his owner."

[4] Gullah, before cited.

[5] Notes on the Sounds and Vocabulary of Gullah, before cited.

[6] Origin, Dialects, Beliefs, and Characteristics of the Negroes of the South Carolina and Georgia Coasts, *Georgia Historical Review*, Vol. X, 1944, pp. 186–95.

[7] Gullah, in Folk Culture on St. Helena Island, South Carolina; Chapel Hill (N.C.), 1930, pp. 3–62.

[8] Negro English, *Anglia*, Vol. VII, 1884, pp. 232–79.

[9] Negro Dialect, *Quarterly Journal of Speech*, Nov., 1933, pp. 522–28.

[10] Gullah *versus* Grammar, *North American Review*, Dec., 1933, pp. 539–42.

[11] The Speech of the Negro, in Folk-Say: a Regional Miscellany; Norman (Okla.), 1930, pp. 346–58.

letters off words or added them on. They got the general idea of a word and used it in other senses." In Gullah the conjugations of verbs are disregarded, so that " the simple form *run* does duty for *run, runs, is* or *are running, has* or *have run, ran*, etc., singular and plural of all tenses ";[1] the possessive is indicated by juxtaposition, as in *Billy gun, we hat;*[2] adjectives and nouns are turned into verbs,[3] and verbs into nouns; " there is no distinction of pronouns with regard to sex: the feminine form is practically unused,"[4] and the singular of nouns commonly, though not invariably, also does duty as the plural.[5]

" Negro English," says Harrison, " is an ear language altogether." The result in Gullah is that many terms are changed by misunderstanding, *e.g., curly-flower* for *cauliflower, omelette* for *marmalade, sweet religion* for *sweet alyssum* and *Florida lime* for *chloride of lime*, and many others acquire liaison forms, *e.g., senkah* for *the same like, mona* for *more nor (more than), truwy* for *throw away*, and *shum* for *see them*. There is a marked economy of effort, so that the last means also *see it, him* or *her*, and *I see, do you see, can you see* and *don't you see it, him, her*, or *those. Sweet* is a sort of universal adjective, indicating any kind or degree of excellence. *To mash* means not only to crush, but also to beat, to dash, to strike upon, to throw weight upon. *One* and *only* become indistinguishable. *Too* is widened in meaning to include that of *very. To stand* is used for to exist, to be, and to live, and *to use* indicates any sort of indwelling or association. The broad *a* and the flat *a* exchange places, so that *psalm* becomes *psa'm* and *man* becomes *mahn*. The neutral vowel replaces the short *i* in *fish, mill, milk*, etc., and also the medial and final *r*, as in *bark, yard, part* and *tar*. Final *s, sh, ze* and *ns* become *ge* or *nge*, as in *sige* for *size, reinge* for *reins, chainge* for *chains* and *sneege* for *sneeze*. Initial *s* is commonly omitted, as in *kin* for *skin, pot* for *spot* and *tick* for *stick*. There are plenty of signs of African influence. *Ain't* becomes *yent, eye* becomes *yeye, young* becomes *nyoung, you* becomes *oonah* or *yoonah*,[6] and there are frequent African-like duplications, as in *one-one*, a swamp blackbird.[7]

1 Smith, before cited, p. 26.
2 Bennett, before cited, Part II, p. 50.
3 *e.g., to t'ief* for *to steal*.
4 Bennett, as before, p. 49.
5 Johnson: Folk Culture, before cited, p. 35.
6 Apparently from the *enu* or *yenu* of Umbundu or the *yeno* of Kisikongo.
7 Gullah was admirably reported in the stories and sketches of Ambrose E. Gonzalez (1857-26), author of The Black Border (with glossary), 1922; With Aesop Along the Black

Gunnar Myrdal, in "An American Dilemma,"[1] lists some of the terms prevailing among the urban Negroes of the country, *e.g.*, *Uncle Tom* or *handkerchief-head*, a Negro who defers to and flatters his white overlords, and *to play possum*, to beguile a white into doing what is wanted of him. Many others might be added, *e.g.*, *CPT* (colored people's time), meaning dilatory;[2] *ofay*, *pink*, *paleface* or *peckerwood*, a white person; *high yallah*, a light mulatto, and *bronze* and *sepia*, euphemisms for *colored*. The contributions of Negro wits to the vocabulary of jive will be noticed in Chapter XI, Section 2.[3]

Border, 1924; The Captain, 1924, and Laguerre, 1924. It was used in the character of Daddy Jake by Joel Chandler Harris, but not very effectively, for Harris knew best the Negro dialect of upland Georgia. See also Flaming Youth: a Story in Gullah Dialect, by John M. Rhame, *American Speech*, Oct., 1933, pp. 39–43. The first writer to attempt the dialect successfully was Charles Colcock Jones, Jr., whose Negro Myths of the Georgia Coast was published in Boston in 1888, but some notes on it by one subscribing himself Marcel were printed in the *Nation*, Dec. 14, 1865, pp. 744–45. A bibliography is in *American Speech*, July, 1926, pp. 559–61.

[1] New York, 1944, Vol. II, pp. 773–76.
[2] *American Speech*, April, 1940, p. 131.
[3] Some discussions of Negro speech other than those already mentioned: The Lingo of the Kentucky Negro, by John Uri Lloyd, *Dialect Notes*, Vol. II, Part III, 1901, pp. 179–84; The Negro Dialects Along the Savannah River, by Elisha K. Kane, the same, Vol. V, Part VIII, 1925, pp. 354–67; Aesop in Negro Dialect, by Addison Hibbard, *American Speech*, June, 1926, pp. 495–99; Negro Speech of East Texas, by Oma Stanley, the same, Feb., 1941, pp. 3–16; Survivals in Negro Vocabulary, by Morton Seidleman, the same, Oct., 1937, pp. 231–32; Some Negro Terms, by Norman E. Eliason, the same, April, 1938, pp. 151–52; Idioms of the Present-Day American Negro, by Ruth Banks, the same, Dec., 1938, pp. 313–14; Slang Among Nebraska Negroes, by Merle Herriford, the same, Dec., 1938, pp. 316–17; Negro-American Vocabulary, by A. D. Faber, *Writer*, July, 1937, p. 239; Story in Harlem Slang, by Zora Neale Hurston, *American Mercury*, July, 1942, pp. 84–96, with a glossary, and Negro Slang at Lincoln University, *American Speech*, Dec., 1934, pp. 287–90.

VIII

AMERICAN SPELLING

1. THE INFLUENCE OF NOAH WEBSTER

384. [The influence of Webster's Spelling Book was really stupendous. It took the place in the American schools of Dilworth's "Aby-sel-pha,"[1] the favorite of the Revolution generation, and maintained its authority for nearly a century.] Dilworth's book, the official title of which was "A New Guide to the English Tongue," was published in London in 1740. Seven years later Benjamin Franklin reprinted it in Philadelphia, and thereafter it was constantly on the press in America until the Webster Speller, first published in 1783, began to overhaul it.[2] Webster himself had been nourished upon it in youth, and was sufficiently convinced of its merits to imitate it, even to the extent of lifting whole passages. Dilworth's reading lessons, for example, began with a series of pious dithyrambs in monosyllables, more or less reminiscent of the Old Testament, and Webster's began with a palpable paraphrase of them. Thus:

Dilworth	Webster
No man may put off the law of God,	No man may put off the law of God.
The way of God is no ill way.	My joy is in his law all the day.
My joy is in God all the day.	O may I not go in the way of sin!
A bad man is a foe to God.	Let me not go in the way of ill men.

[1] A corruption of *abisselfa*, itself a corruption of *a-by-itself-a*. Allen Walker Read explains in The Spelling Bee: a Linguistic Institution, *Publications of the Modern Language Association*, June, 1941, that at the old-time spelling-bees a vowel which was also a syllable "was noted by a formula such as *a by itself, a*, which was contracted into *abisselfa*." The DAE's first example is from Augustus Baldwin Longstreet's Georgia Scenes, 1835, but Longstreet says that the term went back to "the good old days." Bartlett says that it was still in use in Suffolk (England) in 1848. Read finds a reference to the *a-by-it-self-a* system of spelling in The Petit Schole, by F. Clement; London, 1587.

[2] Charles Evans, in his American Bibliography; Chicago, 1903–14, lists 36 American editions between 1747 and 1792. I take this from Kennedy.

Dilworth	Webster
To God do I cry all the day. Who is God, but our God? All men go out of the way of thy law. In God do I put my joy, O let me not sin.	A bad man is a foe to the law. It is his joy to do ill. All men go out of the way. Who can say he has no sin?
Pay to God his due. Go not in the way of bad men. No man can see God. Our God is the God of all men.	The way of man is ill. My son, do as you are bid. But if you are bid, do no ill. See not my sin, and let me not go to the pit.
Who can say he has no sin? The way of man is ill, but not the way of God. My son, go not in the way of bad men. No man can do as God can do.	Rest in the Lord, and mind his word. My son, hold fast in the law that is good. You must not tell a lie, nor do hurt. We must let no man hurt us.

Dilworth shut down after six stanzas of this dismal doggerel, but Noah went on to ten, and then followed with five more printed frankly as prose. The latter began in the tone of the dithyrambs, but quickly proceeded to more worldly matters, thus:

> A good child will not lie, swear, nor steal. He will be good at home, and ask to read his book; when he gets up he will wash his hands and face clean; he will comb his hair, and make haste to school; he will not play by the way, as bad boys do.

Webster also borrowed the general arrangement of Dilworth, with lists of progressively more difficult words alternating with reading lessons, and not a few of his lists — e.g., *big, dig, fig, gig, jig, pig, wig* — he took over bodily.[1] He also levied upon Daniel Fenning's "Universal Spelling Book," first published in 1756, though he testified late in life that he had not studied from it in his boyhood. It was, he said, "in the country, but was not used in my neighborhood."[2] But we have his own testimony that he sweated through Dilworth in the Hartford primary-school, along with the New England Primer, a Psalter and the Bible. "No geography," he said in

[1] It is curious to note that both he and Dilworth put *cag* among the *-ag* words. This spelling and pronunciation of *keg* remained in favor until the end of the Eighteenth Century, though the NED traces *keg* (spelled *kegge*) to 1617. Webster stuck to *cag* to the end of his life. See AL4, p. 384.

[2] Warfel, p. 11. Fenning, in 1741, published a Royal English Dictionary which lasted for many years.

his old age, " was studied before the publication of Dr. Morse's small books on that subject, about the year 1786 or 1787.[1] No history was read, as far as my knowledge extends, for there was no abridged history of the United States."[2] The Catechism at the end of the Primer, as Warfel points out, greatly influenced American pedagogical method until the Revolutionary era, and Webster showed that influence by casting some of his hortations in the form of questions and answers, *e.g.*, " Henry, tell me the number of days in a year," " Charles, how is the year divided? " and " John, what are the seasons?." He was sufficiently homiletic, God knows, but now and then something almost akin to poetry crept into his lessons:

> Emily, look at the flowers in the garden. What a charming sight. How the tulips adorn the borders of the alleys, dressing them with gayety. Soon the sweet pinks will deck the bed, and the fragrant roses perfume the air. Take care of the sweet williams, the jonquils and the artemisia. See the honeysuckle, how it winds about the column, and climbs along the margin of the windows. Now it is in bloom: how fragrant the air is around it; how sweet the perfume after a gentle shower or amidst the soft dews of the evening. Such are the charms of youth when robed in innocence; such is the bloom of life when decked with modesty and a sweet temper.

Webster's Spelling-Book, even in its heyday, was by no means without rivals. It not only had to buck the entrenched Dilworth; it was also beset by innumerable imitations. There was no national copyright until 1790, and the States did not offer any protection to authors until 1782, when Webster himself began besieging their Legislatures. In his preface to his revised edition of 1803, he complained bitterly that his imitators " all constructed their works on a similar plan," borrowing his lists of words (as he had borrowed some of Dilworth's), or altering them " by additions, mutilations and subdivisions, numerous and perplexing."[3] But he had a stout heart and was a relentless salesman, and he could boast in the same preface that the sales of the Spelling-Book to date had reached 3,000,000. He went on:

---

[1] Dr. Jedidiah Morse's first geography was actually published in 1784.
[2] Letter to Henry Barnard, March 10, 1840, printed in the *American Journal of Education*, March, 1863, pp. 123-24. See also Warfel, p. 11.
[3] Webster always stipulated that authorized editions of his book should have blue covers, and his imitators usually adopted that color also. This was true, for example, of Thomas J. Lee's Spelling-Book Containing the Rudiments of the English Language; Boston, 1821, and Elihu F. Marshall's Spelling Book of the English Language; Bellows Falls (Vt.), 1819.

Its reputation has been gradually extended and established, until it has become the principal elementary book in the United States. In a great part of the northern States it is the only book of the kind used; it is much used in the middle and southern States, and its annual sales indicate a large and increasing demand.

How many copies were sold before it was at last displaced by more "scientific" texts is unknown, for it was republished, sometimes with the author's license and sometimes as piracy, by dozens of enterprising Barabbases in all parts of the country. Mrs. Roswell Skeel, Jr., Noah's great-granddaughter, tells me that she has heard estimates running to 400,000,000, but believes that 100,000,000 would be "very much nearer an accurate guess."[1] It seems to have made its way in the South more slowly than in the North, probably because schools were much fewer there, but once it was established it became almost immovable. During the Civil War discreetly revised editions were brought out at Macon, Raleigh and Atlanta, and Warfel reported in 1936 that it was still to be found in an occasional southern school. From 1930 to 1942 the American Book Company, the present publisher, averaged a sale of 4000 a year. Within recent years peddlers hawking the book from door to door have been in operation in Texas.[2]

Even more influential than the old blue-back speller was Webster's series of dictionaries, and especially the "American Dictionary" of 1828. He began work on them in 1800, and six years later brought out a preliminary draft under the title of "A Compendious Dictionary of the English Language." In 1807 he followed with "A Dictionary of the English Language Compiled for the Use of Common Schools in the United States." Both sold fairly well, but they were belabored with ferocity by Webster's numerous enemies,[3] and he spent a large part of his time during the next half dozen years in defending himself against their attack. Meanwhile, he continued to amass materials for the larger dictionary that he had in mind, and

---

[1] Mrs. Skeel has found records of six editions between 1783 and 1787 (while the Speller was still part of Webster's Grammatical Institute), of 105 after 1787 and before 1804, of 110 between 1804 and 1818, and of 83 between 1818 and 1828. (Private communications, Sept. 25, 1943 and Sept. 11 and 22, 1946.) On the cover of an edition published by D. Appleton & Co. in 1880 appeared: "More than 1,000,000 copies of this work are sold annually."

[2] I am indebted here to Mr. William W. Livengood, of the American Book Company.

[3] There is some account of these battles in AL4, pp. 9-12 and in Supplement I, pp. 21-33.

in 1824 went to Europe to consult the philologians and libraries of England and France. The former apparently paid him little attention, but he seems to have found what he wanted in the libraries, and in January, 1825, he finished his manuscript at Cambridge. He had a publisher in waiting, to wit, Sherman Converse of New York, but when the time came to make a contract with the printer, Hezekiah Howe of New Haven, it turned out that Converse was short of the needed money, so Webster himself had to borrow enough to cover Howe's bill. The first edition, in two volumes quarto, was of 2500 copies, selling at $20 a set. It went off quickly enough, but there was no profit in it, and in 1829 Webster employed Joseph E. Worcester (1784-1865) to prepare an abridgement in one volume. This abridgement sold very well, but Worcester followed it soon afterward with a dictionary of his own, and for years thereafter this dictionary and Webster's fought for favor.

Worcester's had one advantage: it was free from the attempts at reform in spelling and pronunciation that Webster had undertaken, and was thus preferred by the more conservative pedagogues of the time. But Webster's, though its etymologies were often fanciful and most of its innovations in spelling [1] had to be dropped after his death, gradually made its way with the plain people, and by 1840 it was generally accepted as the American authority *par excellence*. In 1840, when he was past eighty and close to death, old Noah mortgaged his home in Hartford to bring out a second edition. When he died in 1843 George and Charles Merriam, of Springfield, Mass., bought the rights to the dictionary from his quarreling heirs, and employed one of his sons-in-law, Chauncey A. Goodrich,[2] to prepare a new edition. This appeared in 1847, in one volume selling at $6. Warfel says that it "took immediate hold" and that "the presence of a Webster dictionary in almost every literate household dates from this year."

During the century since then Webster has had to meet some very stiff competition — from the Century Dictionary after 1891, from the Standard after 1895, and from the Concise Oxford after 1911 —, but it still holds its own, and four Americans out of five, when they think of a dictionary, think of it. The Merriams, who were smart business men, employed competent philologians to su-

---

[1] They are described at length in AL4, pp. 381-87.   [2] See Supplement I, p. 166n.

pervise the revisions which stretched from 1859 to 1934, and those revisions gradually made the position of the work unassailable. Today it is accepted as authority by all American courts, is in almost universal use in the schools and colleges, is the official spelling guide of the Government Printing Office,[1] and has the same standing in the overwhelming majority of American newspaper, magazine and book publishing offices.[2] How many copies of it have been printed and circulated to date cannot be ascertained, for as the copyrights on the successive editions expired many other publishers entered into competition with the Merriams, and scores of different editions are still in circulation. That the total sales of all these editions — some of them for the vest-pocket and selling for as little as ten cents — have equalled the sales of the Webster Speller is certainly possible, if not exactly probable. Thus Webster lives in American literary history as the author of the two champion best-sellers of all time. Nor has his singular success been confined to his native land. Said the *Literary Supplement* of the London *Times* on May 29, 1943:

> All the English-speaking nations can join this week in commemorating the centenary of the death on May 28, 1843, of that patriarchal dictionary-maker, Noah Webster. His actual dictionary, it is true, may now be out of date, just as Johnson's is; but it lives on eponymously — "a Webster" having become almost a synonym for a dictionary — and spiritually in the American language itself, which, though English, is no longer that of England or of colonial New England, but of a great and independent nation. Webster, in fact, was in his own sphere as much a founder of his nation as Washington, and consciously so; for he had the vision to perceive that his country, which ceased to be a colony when he was a young man, must henceforward grow its own culture, look no more to London and Europe for its sanctions, and speak and write no longer as a provincial. In his own way Webster was as the Pericles of his country, who presented it with an enduring temple in which to enshrine its words; or as its Augustus, who found its spelling to be of rough-cast and left it of polished marble.

[1] Says the Style Manual of the G. P. O.; Washington, 1945, p. 47: "To avoid the confusion and uncertainty of various authorities on spelling, the Government Printing Office must of necessity adopt a single guide for the spelling of words the preferred forms of which are not otherwise listed or provided for in this manual. The guide is Webster's New International Dictionary, which has been the accepted authority for Government printing for the past 80 years. Unless herein otherwise authorized, the Government Printing Office will continue to follow Webster's spelling."

[2] It is followed in all the style-books that I am aware of save those of the American Medical Association Press and the Princeton University Press, which prefer the Standard.

2. THE ADVANCE OF AMERICAN SPELLING

393. [American spelling is plainly better than English spelling, and in the long run it seems sure to prevail.] The first part of this is true enough in general, but it is easy to think of a few exceptions in particular. One is presented by *connexion*, which the English authorities still prefer to *connection*, though they usually add the latter as an alternative.[1] The word was borrowed from the French in the Fourteenth Century, and in the original it was spelled with *x*, not *ct*. But the NED shows that *connection* had appeared in good usage by 1680, and that not a few eminent writers of the century following preferred it, *e.g.*, Laurence Sterne and Lord Chesterfield. Its prevalence in the United States is due mainly to Webster, whose enthusiasm for analogy urged him to bring *connexion* into harmony with *affection, collection, direction,* etc. He also favored, and for the same reason, *reflection,* but when it came to *complexion* and *inflexion* he was content to endure the *x*. Of *reflection* the NED says: "The spelling with *x* is the earliest and is still common in scientific use, perhaps through its connexion with *reflex;* in the general senses the influence of the verb made the form with *ct* the prevailing one." In England the Wesleyan (or Methodist) *connexion* means what we would call the Methodist *denomination*. The word also appears in a familiar English law phrase, seldom encountered in the United States, to wit, *crim. con.*, meaning *criminal connexion*, meaning adultery. The NED shows that the same abbreviation sometimes represents *criminal conversation*, of exactly the same meaning; in this sense, in fact, *conversation* seems to be the older term. Not much is heard of *crim. con.* in the American courts. Our judges and lawyers, when it comes to infractions (never *infraxions!*) of Exodus XX, 14, prefer euphemisms based on *intimate*, not *criminal*.

Another English spelling that has something to recommend it is *whisky* for *whiskey*. Webster preferred *whisky* and the dictionaries bearing his name still do, but in this case his choice failed to prevail, and *whiskey* remains the common form in the United States. Rather curiously, the English reserve *whisky* for the Scotch variety;

[1] I am indebted here to Mr. Henry Elkin, of Atlantic City.

Irish or any other kind is *whiskey*. This differentiation is described by the NED as " modern trade usage." [1] There is also something to be said for the English distinction between *kerb* and *curb*, both of which come from a French verb, *courber*, meaning to bend. The English use *curb* the noun in the sense of a device to restrain a fractious horse, and as a verb in the sense of to hamper or restrain, but they prefer *kerb* for the border of a sidewalk. Unhappily, they also use *curb*, as we do, for the framework at the top of a well — and also for the rim of a brewer's kettle. Thus, though they call their *curb-brokers kerbstone-brokers*, if these *kerbstone-brokers* adjourned to a brewery they would become *curb-brokers*. The signs plentifully posted in New York reading " *Curb* Your Dog " are somewhat confusing to an English visitor. He can't make out whether they mean " Take him to the *kerb* when he shows certain signs " or " Prevent him yielding to his impulse altogether." I must confess that I am in the same doubt myself. The Authors & Printers Dictionary, the accepted English authority, ordains *curb* " for verb, and the *curb* of bridle," but calls *kerb* " more usual than *curb* " in *kerbstone*. Also, it warns printers not to spell *kerb* with an *i* instead of an *e* — an error impossible in the United States, even to a printer.

The English, in late years, have adopted a great many American spellings, e.g., *jail* for *gaol*,[2] *cider* for *cyder*, and *asphalt* for *asphalte*. They have even begun to succumb to *alright*, though I should add at once that it is often denounced by purists. The case against it was thus stated by a correspondent of a London weekly in 1936:

> It cannot be defended on the analogy of *almost, already, albeit*, etc. In these words the fusion of two ideas is complete, whereas *all* and *right* do not lend themselves to this welding process: the two ideas coöperate better than they unite. Even *already* does not express *all ready*, nor does *almost* mean the same as *all most*. In short, *alright* is *all wrong*.[3]

Two years later a controversy over the term raged in the London *Observer*, and one reader undertook to dispose of it as follows:

> I hope that your correspondents may succeed in giving this unhappy word its quietus, for it is as ugly as it is inaccurate. How such a stupidity came to be so widely distributed I cannot imagine, for it is by no means restricted, as one

---

[1] I am indebted here to Mr. Maurice Walshe, of London, formerly lecturer in English at the University of Vienna.

[2] Headline in the London *Daily Herald*, June 10, 1936: " There's No Place Like *Jail*."

[3] *Alright, John o'London's Weekly*, March 21.

of your contributors suggests, to illiterate servant girls. I would excuse them, but I find that it creeps into the documents of many so-called well educated persons. Here are some lines on the subject, which I clipped from a paper several years ago, and which may help to dispel the confusion:

Already, Almighty, Also,
Albeit, Almost and *Although,*
Altogether, Always and *Alone,*
But *Alright* is wrong, be it known.[1]

But this doggerel only brought a defense of *alright* from a Cambridge man signing himself Linguist, thus:

We recognize *almost* and *already* as compound words which are different in meaning from *all most* and *all ready*. That enables us in writing to distinguish between such pairs of sentences as "That is *all most* interesting" and "That is *almost* interesting," "They are *all ready* there" and "They are *already* there." Obviously, if *alright* represents a compound word which actually exists it has a certain justification. But is there such a compound? I believe there is.

The key to the problem of whether two words have fused in one is the accent with which they are spoken. When two words fuse they are pronounced with a different accent from the original pair. Let us take a sentence like "They are *all right*" and ask ourselves whether the accent of the last two words can be so varied that the sentence means two quite different things. We find that this can actually take place. If we pronounce the last two words so that they are equal in stress we find the sentence means "*All of them* are right"; if we pronounce them so that *right* is more strongly accented than *all* it means "They are not in danger; they are safe," or, more generally, "You needn't worry about them." It is easy to see that this second meaning of *all right* represents a fusion of the original elements.[2]

This learned correspondent, however, would not grant *alright* anything above colloquial status. It is, he said, "very convenient in everyday intercourse, but of no importance whatever in literary composition. I find that I use it regularly in ordinary conversation, but never have occasion to write it except in familiar correspondence. When I do write it, I spell it as two words." [3]

This English tendency to follow American example in spelling is not extended to two classes of words — those ending with *-or*, and those of the *defense* class. Here orthographical logic has little to do with the matter; it is, rather, one of national pride. "The American

---

[1] Ugly and Inaccurate, London *Observer*, Jan. 2, 1938.
[2] *Alright*, London *Observer*, Jan. 23, 1938.
[3] The NED Supplement calls *alright* "a frequent spelling of *all right*" and traces it in English use to 1893. It was used by the *Westminster Gazette* in 1897 and by Lord Curzon in 1925. Webster 1934 dismisses it as "a form commonly found but not recognized by authorities as in good use." The New Practical Standard refuses to mention it.

abolition of -*our* in such words," says H. W. Fowler in "A Dictionary of Modern English Usage,"[1] " has probably retarded rather than quickened English progress in the same direction. Our first notification that the book we are reading is not English but American is often the sight of an -*or*. ' Yankee,' we say, and congratulate ourselves on spelling like gentlemen; we wisely decline to regard it as a matter of argument; the English way cannot but be better than the American way; that is enough."[2] Unhappily, this English tenderness protects only relatively few words, *e.g.*, *honour*, *humour*, *odour*, *labour*, *favour*, *valour*, *vapour*, *vigour*, etc. Quite as many are already spelled with -*or*, *e.g.*, *governor*, *horror*, *pallor*, *tremor*, *author*, *censor*, *victor*, *tutor*, *donor*, *conqueror*, *juror*, *emperor*, *solicitor*, *visitor*, *tailor*, *warrior*, *error*, etc., and so are many of the derivatives of the -*our* words, *e.g.*, *honorary*, *odorous*, *laborious*, *valorous*, *vigorous*, *vaporous*, etc. There is, indeed, no order in the business, for *honorary* and *honorific* stand beside *honourable*, *laborious* stands beside *laboured*, *labourer*, *labouring* and *Labourite*, *odorous* beside *odourless*, *humorist* beside *humour*, *coloration* beside *colour*, *vigorous* beside *vigourless*, etc.[3]

In late years the English have moved from -*our* to -*or* in the agent-nouns, save in the single case of *Saviour*,[4] but the rule in other classes of words is so complicated and so full of exceptions that no lexicographer has been able to explain it.[5] In many cases the spelling has been changed, sometimes long ago and sometimes only recently. *Orator*, for example, was *oratour* to Chaucer but *orator* to Shakespeare. *Governor* was *governour* to Samuel Johnson in 1775, though Clarendon had written *governor* in 1647. Not infrequently -*our* has been dropped for -*or*, and later restored. John Wesley, writing in 1791, reported that the use of -*or* in *honor*, *vigor*, etc., was then a " fashionable impropriety " and denounced it as " mere childish affectation," but Coleridge was still spelling *honor* in 1809, though

---

[1] Oxford, 1926, p. 415.
[2] Said Basil de Sélincourt in Pomona, or, The Future of English; London, 1928, p. 40: "The Americans have dropped a *u* out of *humour* and other words; possibly we should have done so, *if they had not*." My italics.
[3] All these examples are from the Concise Oxford Dictionary of the Brothers Fowler; third edition; Oxford, 1934.
[4] In the United States even this solitary exception seems to be doomed. There is a Protestant Episcopal Church of Our *Savior* in Baltimore.
[5] For discussions of it see the before-mentioned Dictionary of Modern English Usage, p. 415, and the NED under -*or* and -*our*.

Wordsworth, in the same year, made it *honour*. Samuel Johnson spelled *errour* in his Dictionary of 1755,[1] and that spelling remained orthodox until the end of the Eighteenth Century, though Shakespeare, Ben Jonson and Sir Thomas Browne had used *error*. The use of *color* instead of *colour* was denounced by an English lady author so lately as 1937,[2] but the NED traces *colorific* to 1676, *coloration* to 1626, and *color* itself to 1663. H. W. Fowler seemed to be convinced that his fellow-Englishmen, soon or late, would adopt the *-or*-endings, despite their present distaste for them. He said:

> What is likely to happen is that either, when some general reform of spelling is consented to, reduction of *-our* to *-or* will be one of the least disputed items, or, failing general reform, we shall see word after word in *-our* go the way of *governour*. It is not worth while either to resist such a gradual change or to fly in the face of national sentiment by trying to hurry it; it would need a very open mind indeed in an Englishman to accept *armor* and *succor* with equanimity.[3]

The use of *c* instead of *s* in *defense* and *offense* is etymologically incorrect, but the English cling to it resolutely. Webster hazarded the guess that the change to *c* " was made or encouraged by printers, for the sake of avoiding the use of the old long *s*," but this was obvious nonsense, for Langland and Gower wrote *defence* in the Fourteenth Century, before there was any printing, and there is no evidence that printers ever objected to the long *s*. Gower also used *offence*, and so did Wyclif, but Lydgate preferred *offense*, and Chaucer used both spellings. The English use a *c* in *pretence*, but they have abandoned it for *s* in *expense* and *recompense*, so there is some hope that they may come over to the American way in other

---

1 "Nothing in language," said Webster somewhat patronizingly in his introduction to his American Dictionary of 1828, "is more mischievous than the mistakes of a great man. It is not easy to understand why a man whose professed object was to reduce the language to some regularity should write *author* without *u* and *errour* and *honour* with it."

2 Snob-Stuff From U.S.A., by Pamela Frankau, London *Daily Sketch*, Oct. 25: "The novelists have caught the snob epidemic so badly that we are now quite accustomed to find American spelling in English literature. *Color* may be a quicker way of spelling *colour*, but a calculation of the time saved in the process would shake Einstein. Me, I guess a twentieth of a second."

3 A Dictionary of Modern English Usage, p. 415. *Armor*, without the *u*, appeared in nearly all the English and colonial newspapers in 1938, in advertisements of Knight Without *Armor*, a film version of a novel by James Hilton. This movie was made in England, but its distribution was handled from Hollywood, and all the advertising electrotypes sent out spelled *armor* in the American manner.

words soon or late. In those beginning with *en-* or *in-*, *em-* or *im-*, they prefer the *e*, but there is a good deal of inconsistency in their practise. Thus they use both *to ensure* and *insurance, to endorse* and *indorsation*. The NED prefers *inquiry* to *enquiry*, but *enquiry* seems to maintain a considerable popularity in England.[1] Fowler recommends *en-* or *em-* in *to embed, to empanel, to enclose, to encrust, endorsement* and *to entrench*, but in the United States *in-* and *im-* are commoner. The English still use *æ* and *œ* in words in which, on this side of the ocean, simple *e* usually suffices, *e.g.*, *anæmia, anæsthetic, amœba, œcology, fœtus, œdema, œsophagus, œcumenical, hæmorrhage, mediæval, encyclopædia, gynæcology, diarrhœa* and *homœopathy*, but there seems to be a movement toward the American *e*.[2] The *Encyclopædia* Britannica retains the *æ* in its own name, and clings to *anæmia* and *anæsthetic*, but it now spells *hyena* as we do, not as *hyæna*. *Pediatrics, phenomenon, economy, pedagogy* and *penology* are now spelled by all English writers as they are in the United States: once they were *pædiatrics, phænomenon, œconomy, pædagogy*, and *pænology* or *pœnology*.

George Philip Krapp, in 1925,[3] described the spellings *honour, centre, defence, waggon* and *traveller* as rocks upon which the Englishman founds his pride, patriotism and faith. He might have added *storey* (of a house), *for ever* (two words), *nought, grey, cheque*, and *pyjamas*. Some of these rocks, alas, begin to show signs of faulting. When, in January, 1943, the British Foreign Office issued its first American White Paper, it made a graceful bow to Uncle Shylock by spelling *honor* and *labor* without the *u*.[4] All the English authorities that I am aware of (save, of course, the Simplified Spelling Society) still hold out for *centre, theatre, calibre, fibre*, etc., and also for *defence* and *offence*, but the Authors' & Printers' Dictionary has been recommending *wagon* with one *g* for years past, and the Concise Oxford confesses that there is something to be said for it by entering the word as *wag(g)on*.[5] The NED describes *forever*

---

[1] Even in the United States there is some wobbling, *e.g.*, in Philadelphia *Inquirer* and Cincinnati *Enquirer*.

[2] Urged on by Dr. George M. Gould (1848–1922), author of a standard medical dictionary and part-author of the incomparable Anomalies and Curiosities of Medicine, the American Medical Editors' Association declared for the simple *e* at Milwaukee, June, 1893.

[3] The English Language in America, Vol. I, p. 350.

[4] I am indebted here to Mr. H. W. Seaman.

[5] Nevertheless, the title of the movie, The Covered *Wagon*, became The

as "now chiefly U.S.," but its quotations show that making one word of the more usual *for ever* has been favored by eminent British authors of the past, including Carlyle.[1] So with *naught*. The NED calls it "now archaic" and prefers *nought*, but the Authors' & Printers' Dictionary ordains the American *naught*.

The amateur lexicographers who discuss and debate words in the English newspapers often go to the bat for *storey*, but the same high authority prefers *story* and is supported therein by Rules for Compositors and Readers at the University Press, Oxford.[2] The English, of course, have always used *story* to signify a tale, but they are loath to drop *storey* in the sense of a floor in a house. One of the arguments commonly heard in defense of it is that it serves to differentiate clearly the two meanings of the word, but how anyone could ever confuse a *story* in the *Saturday Evening Post* with one in the Al Smith Building is more than I can make out. All the classical British authors down to Dickens used *story* in the latter sense, but when Dickens wrote *storey* in "Barnaby Rudge" (1840) he was presently imitated by Harriet Beecher Stowe in "Uncle Tom's Cabin" (1852). Webster, however, preferred *story*, and at home he has had his way. It has also been argued that the English *nett* with two *t*'s, meaning free from deduction, serves to distinguish it from *net*, meaning a meshed fabric, but the Concise Oxford and the Authors' & Printers' Dictionary declare for one *t* in both cases, and it seems to be prevailing.[3]

When a London edition of the American soldiers' newspaper, the *Stars and Stripes*, was established during World War II, the English proofreader in the printing-office where it was printed corrected the American *defense* to the English *defence* every time he countered it in copy sent to the composing-room by the editors. "The proofreader," said the London *Times* in discussing this insular sabotage, "knew with one part of his mind that *defense*, considering the paper in which the word was to appear, was right, but another, and

---

Covered *Waggon* when it was presented in England. See the film column of the London *Daily Telegraph*, May 25, 1936.

[1] Charles Kingsley compromised by making it *for-ever*.
[2] *Story* and *Storey*, by Peter Duff, London *Observer*, Nov. 6, 1938.
[3] From a want-ad in the London *Morning Post*, Sept. 9, 1935: "Prompt Loans — 4¼ p. c. *net* yearly on reversions, life interest, incomes, legacies, freeholds, by will or deed." I should add that some of the advertisers in the same column used *nett*. I am indebted here to the collection of the late F. H. Tyson, of Hong Kong.

more influential, part was insisting that the unaccustomed looking *s* should give way to the decent and familiar *c*, and the unconscious gained yet one more victory over its eternal opponent."[1] There was a time when any such exercise of maternal authority would have been received humbly by decent-minded Americans, but no more. Even learned men now defend the national spelling without apology, and in the austere *American Journal of Philology*, so long ago as 1937, Dr. Kemp Malone, professor of English at the Johns Hopkins, gave Sir William Craigie and Professor James R. Hulbert a sharp rap over the knuckles for using the English *defence* and *offence* in the DAE.[2]

Thornton, in his "American Glossary,"[3] says that the reduction of two *l*'s to one in such words as *traveller*, *jewellery*, etc., began in the United States "about the year 1835," and that it was "a gradual process." There seems to be every reason for believing that Webster was responsible for it, though previous lexicographers, notably Walker and Lowth, had recommended it. In his "Compendious Dictionary" of 1806 he was content to record the spellings which then prevailed and still prevail in England, but in his "American Dictionary" of 1828 he not only gave the forms with one *l*, but defended them at length. The rule he set up was that when a final consonant appears in an accented syllable, it may be doubled in derivatives, but not when it appears in an unaccented syllable. Thus he arrived at *jeweler*, *traveler*, *counselor*, *duelist*, *marvelous*, etc., but permitted *distiller*, *forgetting*, *appalling*, *installment*, *beginning*, etc. Unhappily, he added some exceptions on dubious phonological or etymological grounds, *e.g.*, *metallurgy*, *chancellor* and *crystalline*, and most of these have survived. But even the English have now dropped the redundant *l* from *instalment*. Webster did not include *aluminum* in his dictionary of 1806, for the metal was not discovered by Sir Humphry Davy until 1808. Davy at first proposed to call it *alumium*, but in 1812 he changed its name to *aluminum*. To this the *Quarterly Review*[4] objected on the ground that *aluminum* lacked "a classical sound," *i.e.*, did not harmonize with the

---

[1] Defenders of *Defence*, London *Times*, Oct. 29, 1945. In this editorial, it will be noted, the *Times* used the American *proofreader* instead of *corrector of the press*, its orthodox English equivalent.
[2] July, 1937, p. 376.
[3] Vol. II, p. 905.
[4] Vol. I, 1812, p. 355.

names of *potassium, sodium, calcium*, etc., and proposed that *aluminium* be used instead. This was done in England, but Webster decided for *aluminum* in his dictionary of 1828, and it has remained *aluminum* in the United States ever since. The English, however, still stick to *aluminium*,[1] though the rule evoked by the *Quarterly* had been violated before 1812 by *aurum* (gold), *tantalum, platinum* and *molybdenum*, and has been violated since by *lanthanum*.[2] But this is only incidentally a matter of spelling. It is really the English and American names for the metal that are different.

The distinction between *practice* the noun and *to practise* the verb seems to be breaking down. Webster 1934 apparently prefers *practice* in both cases, and so do the Government Printing Office[3] and the American Medical Association Press,[4] but other authorities show a considerable uncertainty. Both noun and verb descend from an earlier *practic* or *practique*, and until Shakespeare's time both were spelled with an *s* and pronounced *practize*. The spelling with *c* apparently arose in imitation of *justice, service*, etc. Webster, in his 1828 dictionary, argued that "the distinction in spelling between the noun and the verb belongs properly only to words which are accented on the last syllable, as *device* and *devise*, where the verb has the sound of *-ize*." The use of *s* in the verb, he went on, encouraged the uneducated to pronounce it *practize*. My impression is that the use of *practise* for both noun and verb is increasing in the United States, despite the weight of authority against it. Perhaps the general use of *s* in *defense* and *offense* has had some influence here. But all the English authorities continue to distinguish between *practice* the noun and *to practise* the verb.

In AL4[5] I exposed Christopher Morley to the contumely of 100% Americans by showing that he had used the English spelling, *harbour*, in the name of an American town in his "Thunder on the Left."[6] He replied by putting the blame on his publishers. His manuscript, he said, showed *harbor* throughout, but his publishers

---

1 I am told by Mr. Percy A. Houseman, of Haddonfield, N. J., that the decennial index of *Chemical Abstracts*, an official publication of the American Chemical Society, used *aluminium* before 1916, but has since used *aluminum*.
2 I am indebted here to Mr. Ben Hamilton, Jr.
3 Style Manual, revised edition, Jan., 1945, p. 48.
4 *Practice* or *Practise*, Journal of the American Medical Association, April 26, 1930, p. 1342.
5 p. 391, n. 1.
6 New York, 1925.

insisted on English spelling "in any book of which they hoped to sell sheets in London."[1] This plea in confession and avoidance touched me on a tender spot, for my own publisher, Knopf, once followed the same practise, so I offered Morley my sympathy and apologies.[2] Knopf, indeed, went further: his first printing of his "Rules for the Guidance of Authors and Translators" actually set up the NED as his sole office authority, and ordained specifically such arrestingly English spellings as *anaemia, arbour, behaviour, defence, favour, for ever, jewellery, mediaeval, mould, neighbour, plough, sceptic, to-day* and *woollen*. To be sure, he permitted the American *ax* and *program*, but that, apparently, was only because the English had begun to tolerate them. Later on, however, he lowered the Union Jack and hoisted what English sailors call the Bedtick, and his current style-sheet sets up Webster 1934 as his office authority, with the NED to be followed only in books intended for English consumption. Most other American publishers do likewise, and English spelling is now rare in the United States, though it seems to hold its own in Canada, at least officially.[3] But the *-re* is still commonly used in *theatre* in the stage world, even though it occasionally produces such grotesqueries as *Center Theatre*,[4] and the *Racquet* and Tennis Club still survives in Park avenue, though the English themselves now prefer *racket*.[5] A Vogue *Tyre*, fortified with vitamins, was announced in 1945,[6] but *tire* continues to hold the American fort. Meanwhile, the following dispatch from the London correspondent of the *Christian Science Monitor*[7] shows how the wind is blowing in England:

[1] The Bowling Green, *Saturday Review of Literature*, April 24, 1937.
[2] Sulphur and Molasses, *Saturday Review of Literature*, May 15, 1937.
[3] In 1931 the Canadian Historical Association, the Canadian Geographical Society and the Royal Society of Canada declared for it. Canada Won't Even Import American Spelling, Baltimore *Sun*, editorial page, Aug. 5, 1931.
[4] There was one in New York in 1947.
[5] The word was borrowed from the French *raquette* in the early Sixteenth Century. It was spelled *racket* by Capt. John Smith in his General Historie of Virginia in 1624 and by John Locke in his Essay Concerning Humane Understanding in 1690. The spelling *racquet* seems to have arisen as a fashionable affectation during the Nineteenth Century. It did not last long in England. I am indebted here to Mr. H. W. Seaman.
[6] *Time*, Dec. 10, p. 52. I am indebted here to Mr. Charles J. Lovell.
[7] American Spelling Wins Recognition in London Schools, Sept. 21, 1938.

School children here who spell certain words the American way are not to be held guilty of mistakes that cost them marks in examinations conducted by the London County Council.

This decision was arrived at after close investigation of the problem as to whether or not children attending London County Council schools should be taught from textbooks in which American spelling and American idiom are used.

The special committee entrusted with the investigation agreed that there is something to be said for familiarizing English children with the variations in spelling and phraseology — " as distinct from slang " — which have been evolved by a great English-speaking people in another continent.

3. THE SIMPLIFIED SPELLING MOVEMENT

The Simplified Spelling Board, which walked high, wide and handsome during the lifetime of its angel, Andrew Carnegie, began to fade after his death in 1919, and since then not much has been heard from it.[1] But its English opposite number, the Simplified Spelling Society, is still affluent and active, and a large number of private spelling reformers whoop up various seductive but antagonistic schemes in both countries. One of the latter is Fred S. C. Wingfield, a Chicago printer who launched what he called Fwnetik Orthqgrafi in 1928, and has since supplemented it with a rather less alarming Systematized Spelling. Wingfield is a thoughtful student of the subject, and some of his publications are of decided value — for example, his study of the vowels in the present English alphabet,[2] and his discussion of the projects of other spelling reformers.[3] Among the latter he distinguishes five groups, as follows:

[1] Its history is told in some detail in Handbook of Simplified Spelling, by Henry Gallup Paine; New York, 1920, pp. 12–32. Among its original members were Richard Watson Gilder, editor of the *Century;* Justice David J. Brewer, of the Supreme Court of the United States; Isaac K. Funk, editor of the Standard Dictionary; Samuel L. Clemens (Mark Twain); William T. Harris, U. S. commissioner of education; Henry Holt, the publisher; Thomas R. Lounsbury, Thomas Wentworth Higginson, William James, Melvil Dewey and Brander Matthews. Mark Twain at first poked fun at the movement, but was later converted. See The Dizzy Rise (and Ensuing Bust) of Simplified Spelling, by H. L. Mencken, *New Yorker,* March 7, 1936. What remains of the Simplified Spelling Board is now denizened at Lake Placid, N. Y., with Godfrey Dewey, son of Melvil, in charge and its name changed to Simpler Spelling Association.
[2] Association Frequencies of the Vowel Sounds and Vowel Letters in the Conventional American-English Spelling; Chicago, 1941; second ed., Chicago, 1942.
[3] Among the Spelling Reformers, *American Speech,* Oct., 1931, pp. 54–57.

1. "Those wishing to improve the spelling of only certain words of the present orthography."
2. "Those wishing to spell phonetically by the addition of new letters to the present alphabet."
3. "Those wishing to spell phonetically by the inversion of some of the letters of the alphabet."
4. Those proposing an entirely new alphabet.
5. Those proposing to use the present alphabet, but with the addition of digraphs, e.g., *ah, au, aw, ay, ey, iw, iy, uh, uw*.

There is a specimen of Wingfield's Fwnetik Orthqgrafi, as it ran in 1931, in AL4, pp. 404–405. Since then he has changed it considerably, and by 1944 it had become Fonetik Crthografi.[1] In most of its forms it has used *dh* for *the* and the two sounds of *th*, *j* for *ee*, *q* for the *o* of *for* and the *a* of *father*, and *ei* for the *a* of *name*, but otherwise it has shown a great deal of variation from time to time, with a general trend toward simplification. In its latest incarnation it turns the first sentence of the Declaration of Independence into the following:

Hwen in dh kors v hiumn jvents, it bjkvmz nesiseri fcr wvn pipl ta dizqlv dh politikl baendz hwitsh haev k'nektd dhem widh anvdhr, and tu asu:m amvng dh Pqwrz v dh r:th, dh separeit and jkwal steishn tu hwitsh dh lcz v neitshr and v neitshrz Gqd entaitl dhm, a djsnt rjspekt tu dh opinynz v maenkaind rjkwairz dht dhei shwd diklaer dh kcz'z hwitsh impel dhem tu dh separeishn.

Here, says Wingfield, "nearly 11.9% of the words are unchanged; more than 28.4% are but slightly altered. Consequently 40.3% of the words can be immediately read without any prior study of the system." Even so, it seems to be too much for the customers, so its author has devised the aforesaid Systematized Spelling, which he calls "a reformed orthography for a new eera," as a sort of concession to their weakness. What it comes to is shown by the following rendering of the Gettysburg Address:

4 score and 7 years ago our fothers braut foerth on thiss continent a new nation, conceved in liburty, and dedicated tu the proposition that all men ar created eequal. Now we ar engaged in a graet civil waur, testing whether that nation or eny nation so conceved and so dedicated, can long endure. We ar met on a graet batlefeeld of that waur. We hav com tu dedicate a poertion of that feeld as a fienal resting-place for those hu here gave their lives that that nation miet liv. It is altugether fitting and propur that we shud du thiss. But

---

[1] Fonetik Crthografi: Krestqmathi, prejzentd widh komplimnts v dh Northwest Printery, 4617 w Grace str Chicago 41, Ills Nov 1944 – a pamphlet of twelve pages.

in a larger sence, we cannot dedicate, we cannot consecrate, we cannot hallo, thiss ground. The brave men, livving and ded, hu strugled here, hav consecrated it. . . .

Another diligent spelling reformer is Ralph Gustafson, of Moorestown, N. J. His system is based upon the Anglic of the late Professor R. E. Zachrisson, of Uppsala,[1] and an English scheme called Simpl Orderli Speling, but he has introduced modifications in order to get rid of "a strickli British stiel uv pronunsiaeshon tu wich moest Amerikanz ar not akustomed." In October, 1945, he sent out a circular warning his followers that his system "iz exsperimental and must not be regarded az definit or fienal."

After 1941 one of the most persistent American advocates of a wholesale reform in orthography was the Hon. Robert L. Owen, a former Senator from Oklahoma.[2] He had designed a new alphabet, adapted to all languages, at some time in the past, but it was the attack on Pearl Harbor, according to his own story, that determined him "to perfect this matter."[3] His alphabet, at the start, greatly resembled the series of strokes, curves and hooks used by the principal systems of shorthand, and the different characters in a word were usually joined by ligatures,[4] but he later simplified it, and in its final form it consisted of about 40 characters, to be printed separately as the letters of ordinary English are printed.[5] The hon. gentleman's years and past services got him friendly attention in Congress, and his pronunciamentos were frequently printed in the Appendix to the *Congressional Record* by amiable Senators and Representatives,[6] but when he had a hearing before the Senate com-

1 AL4, p. 405.
2 He served three terms in the Senate, from 1907 to 1925. Born in 1856, he was 85 years old when he set up as a spelling reformer. He died July 20, 1947.
3 Hearing Before the Committee on Foreign Relations, United States Senate, 78th Congress, Nov. 7, 1945; Washington, 1945, p. 6.
4 The Global Alphabet, by Hon. Robert L. Owen, Presented by Mr. Thomas of Oklahoma; Senate Document No. 49, 78th Congress, 1st Session; Washington, 1943, pp. 8 and 9.
5 The precise number is uncertain. In another pamphlet, also entitled The Global Alphabet, Senate Document No. 133, 78th Congress, 1st Session, Oct. 18, 1943, p. 1, the hon. gentleman mentioned "forms or letters representing 18 consonant sounds and 15 vowel sounds, each of which represents one and only one sound, approximately," but in a third pamphlet, also of the same title, Senate Document No. 250, 78th Congress, 2nd Session, Dec. 4, 1944, he spoke of "18 consonants, 18 vowel sounds and 6 compound consonants," and in the Hearing just mentioned, p. 5, he showed 44 characters.
6 See, for example, the *Record* for Dec. 15, 1942, p. A4647; Feb. 15,

mittee on foreign relations, in 1945, his claim that his alphabet was "a perfect key to all languages — a key which can be learned in one day " — suffered somewhat under the cross-examination of the learned Senator Theodore Francis Green, of Rhode Island. His chief adjutant in his crusade was Dr. Janet H. C. Meade, who also suffered at the same hands. She appeared as secretary of the World Language Foundation, Inc.

Wingfield occasionally reports on the schemes of rival reformers, with criticisms. Thus when a lady by the name of Miss Ruby Oliver Foulk announced " a refrmeishn v dh Ixglish laexgwidzh az wel az a nuli dyvaizd speling "[1] he dismissed it on the ground that, like the International Phonetic Alphabet, it made use of new characters — " an *aelfa*-laik keratr fcr dh vqwl in *father, army, not, aunt, guard,* and a simble rjsembling Grjk *thjta* fcr dh vqwl in *full, wolf, foot* " — and that these characters collided with the fact that " qur taipraitrz, lainotaips, mqnotaip mashjnz n dzhqb fqnts " were " nqt ikwipt widh " them. And when a Canadian brother, Ernest B. Roberts, of Toronto, launched a new system in a pamphlet entitled " Spel-Rid-Ryt " Wingfield reported that he could not " giv iz prapozd rifcrm a veri hai reiting, fcr it pru:vz ta by simpli anadhr nu letr skjm." Two of the new letters, he admitted, were " wel chosen: tailed *n* for *ng-singer* and the IPA sign for *sh*," but he had his doubts about " a *q*-like letter for *o-ode*," a reversed *c* for *ch*, an *e*-like character for *th-thin*, and a reversal of the *e*-like letter for *th-then*. So far as I know, Wingfield never examined the system projected by L. Julian McIntyre in 1925,[2] but it was noticed and dismissed loftily by an anonymous reviewer in *American Speech*.[3] Its author described it as " no panfuli rot out formula brot tu perfekshon bi yerz of pashent studi, but merli a common sens us of the karakturz olreadi provided and aksepted az substitutz for the spokn word " and estimated that it would save the American people more than $5,000,000 a year, but he apparently found that not many of them were interested. William Russell seems to have had no better luck with a far

---

1944, p. A795; Feb. 1, 1945, p. A4410; March 22, 1945, p. A1498; April 5, 1945, pp. A1790–91; April 17, 1945, pp. 3455–56; Oct. 10, 1945, p. A4578; June 21, 1946, pp. A3842–43; Aug. 1, 1946, p. A4989, and Jan. 23, 1947, pp. A264–66. His chief supporter is the Hon. A. S. Mike Monroney, of Oklahoma, for whom see *American Speech*, April, 1946, p. 85, n. 9.

1 Amxrikai Spek; Nu Yark, 1937.
2 An American Orthografi; Brooklyn, 1925.
3 April, 1926, p. 398.

more modest scheme that he proposed in 1946,[1] though he had kind words from a number of respected authorities on speech, including Arthur G. Kennedy and Josiah Combs. Russell mentioned Wingfield's Fonetik Crthqgrafi politely, but did not come out for it. His system consisted mainly of shortened forms that are already in more or less use, e.g., *apothem, brunet, burlesk, catalog, cigaret, fantom, foto, furlo, gild, nabor, nite, rime, sulfur, theater, tho, thoro, thru, vinyard, wilful* and *wo*. But " such forms as *BarBQ* and *R U going 2 the Cside*," he cautioned, " are not to be recommended."

A great many other private spelling reformers are in practise (or have been recently in practise) in the Republic, e.g., William J. Nixon, of Philadelphia; Iva Doty, of Bellflower, Calif.; Andrew C. Clark, of New Milford, Conn.; J. F. Hayden, of High Point, N. C.; William Simms Prosser, of San José, Calif.; John T. Gause, of New York; Carl A. Berg, of Minot, N. Dak.; William McDevitt, of San Francisco;[2] Edwin B. Davis, of Rutgers University; James Juvenal Hayes, of Oklahoma City; Arthur G. Smith, of Bryan, O.; Drew Allison, of San Antonio, Tex.; Robert E. Bullard, of Takoma Park, Md.; Elmer G. Still, of Livermore, Calif.; Frank C. Laubach and R. F. Chapin. Chapin's scheme was set forth in the *Rotarian* in 1939,[3] but I have heard no more of it. Bullard's, so far as I know, has never been printed, but he tells me[4] that its essential points are as follows: use *ä* for the *a*-sound in *hat*, *ae* for that in *ate*, and plain *a* for that in *halt*; drop *c, q, w* and *x* altogether, and *y* as a consonant; restrict *e* to the sound in *get*, *i* to that in *it*, *o* to that in *only*, *g* to that in *get*, *u* to that in *under* and *sunk*; use *y* for the *oo*-sound in *suit* and *boot*; use *ei* for the *i*-sound in *right* and *sign*, and *ie* for that in *beat* and *reek*; use *au* for the vowel in *cow*. Bullard estimates that his proposed changes would reduce the length of about 80% of all common words, leave 17% as now, and lengthen 3%.

Gause presents his project in the form of a game-book.[5] He proposes to use *y* with its tail turned to the right for the long *i*, and to indicate the other long vowels by putting dashes over them. He offers a capital *f* turned backward for the sound of *th* in *that* and a *v* upside down for the diphthong in *house*. Like most other spelling

---

[1] Better Spelling in a Post-War World; Athens (Ga.), April, 1946.
[2] AL4, p. 404.
[3] Phonetize English Spelling, April, pp. 60–61.
[4] Private communication, Dec. 9, 1938.
[5] Fun With Phoney Spelling; New York, 1941.

reformers he substitutes *k* for hard *c*, *s* for soft *c*, *kw* for *qu*, and *ks* for *x*. He puts *c* to use by giving it the sound of *oo* in *good*, and *q* by giving it that of *a* in *all*. He indicates the sound of *th* in *three* by putting an *h* before his reversed *f*, that of *ch* in *church* by using *tsh*, that of the middle consonant in *vision* by *j*, and that of the *j* of *jig* by *dj*. Nixon's system, which he calls E Z Speling,[1] is a sort of shorthand. He advocates using *&* for *and*, *u* for *you*, *2* for *to*, *too* and *two*, *c* for *see* and *sea*, *$* for *dollar*, *t* for *tee* and *tea*, *r* for *are*, *i* for *eye*, *8* for *ate*, *x* for *ex*, etc. He is a foe of all redundant letters and uses *iland*, *leag*, *lether*, *lo* (low), *mor*, *orfan*, *revu* (review), *si* (sigh), *tung*, *yern* and *hol* (whole). His system, of course, would vastly multiply homophones. He attempts to get rid of this difficulty by the use of spaces, so that *tal e* (tally), for example, is thus differentiated from *tale*. But there are plenty of other cases in which he seems unable to solve the problem, e.g., *borrow* and *borough*, both of which become *boro; soup*, which becomes *sup*, and *glean*, which becomes *glen*. He makes heavy use of figures and of the sounds of letters, so that *expose* becomes *x pose, eyebrow i bro,* and *energy n er g*. Sometimes he slips on pronunciations, as when he turns *nucleus* into *nuclus* and *opium* into *opum*.

One of the simplest of the American schemes of reformed spelling is that of Hayes, who is professor of English at Oklahoma City University.[2] He rejects *c*, *x* and *q* and adds no new characters, so that his alphabet is reduced to twenty-three letters. Like Gause, he proposes to indicate the long sound of vowels by putting dashes over them. The ordinary form of *a* is used for the sound in *father* and *alms*, *ā* for that in *claim* and *paint*, and *ae* for that in *bat* and *clam*. Ordinary *e* is used in *beg* and *crept*, and *ē* in *creep* and *degree*. Ordinary *o* suffices in *order*, but *ō* is substituted in *toad* and *enroll*. Ordinary *u* is used both in cases where it is pure, as in *up* and *shun*, and in cases where it is preceded by the palatal glide, as in *pure* and *refuse*. To indicate its sound in *urn* and *first*, *ur* is used — and Hayes disregards the possible confusion with *pure*. For the sound in *fair* and *error*, *er* is used, and for that in *wool* and *good*, *uu*. *Oi* is used in *boy, toil*, etc., *oo* in *food, do*, etc., and *ou* in *out, bough, crowd*, etc. *Kw* is generally substituted for *qu*, *tsh* for the *ch*-sound in *change*, *zh* for the first consonant in *azure*, *ks* for *x* in *vex*, and *gz*

---

[1] The Nixon System of E. Z. Speling; Philadelphia, n.d.

[2] Practical Phonetic English, *Words*, May, 1936, pp. 8–9.

for *x* in *exist*. The sound of *th* in *thin* is represented as now, but in *this* it is changed to *dh*. The result is as follows:

> Our Fadhr hoo art in hevn, haelōed bē dhī nām. Dhī kingdm kum. Dhī wil be dun in urth aez it iz in hevn. Giv us dhis dā our dālē bred. Aend forgiv us our dets aez we forgiv our detrz. Aend lēd us nat intoo temptāshn, but dē-livr us frum ēvl, for dhīn iz dhu kingdm, aend dhu pour, aend dhu glōrē, for evr. Amen.[1]

Davis's scheme greatly resembles that of Hayes, but it is less a formal and complete plan than a call for action. Not disheartened by the collapse of the Simplified Spelling Board, he argues that it is high time to make another attack upon "the pathetic unreasonableness, the archaic anarchy, the Gothic gargoyles of our present set-up," and he believes that the language pedagogues of the nation are bound in honor to make it. He advises them to begin by bedevilling the Legislatures of their respective States. "Get some solon," he says,

> to formulate a bill and some soft-hearted legislator to offer it this year, next year and sempiternally, with modified frills, until the people at the Capitol see they have some Pankhursts on their hands. Far be it for me to say what the bill should contain. I wouldn't know. But the school-book approach seems a good one. . . . Even bad publicity may be better than none. Better the dog-house than Nirvana.

Davis suggests that the short or unstressed vowels be left as they are, and that the long ones, when stressed, be indicated either by adding *e* to them or by putting lines above them. He proposes to omit silent vowels, to indicate the *a* of *father* by *ä*, *aa* or *ah*, to re-

---

[1] A large number of American books and articles proposing schemes of reformed spelling are listed in Kennedy, pp. 46–49, 293–97 and 430–32. Some items that Kennedy overlooked are in Krapp, Vol. I, p. 330. Many more might be added. So long ago as 1850 a *Wecli Fonetic Advocat* began to appear in "Sinsinati," and in 1852 the projectors thereof published a Fonetic Olmanac and Rejistur ov Speling and Ritin Reform. Not a few of the pre-Civil War reformers in other fields also toyed with simplified spelling. It was used, for example, in an anti-slavery monthly called *Leterz Political & Theological*, published at "Winooski Fallz," Vt., by Jon R. Forest from Jan., 1857 onward. Ten years earlier the *Anglo Sacsun* began to appear, and W. C. Bryant noticed it favorably in the New York *Evening Post*, June 29, 1848. Mr. Charles J. Lovell tells me that there is a partial file in the Boston Public Library. In 1852 some anonymous reformer brought out a Furst Fonetic Redur in Boston. In Aug., 1861 the Rev. B. M. Genung published a plea for a reform in spelling under the title of Orthography of Our Language in the *Ladies' Repository* (Cincinnati), pp. 486–87.

duce the variant spellings of *mood, do* and *prove* to one *oo*, to choose either the *ou* of *pout* or the *ow* of *cow* to represent the diphthong of both, and to settle on *ur, er* or *ir* to represent the sound in *turn, her* and *sir*. He is willing to let one letter serve for the *u* of *unit* and *duty*, but is uncertain what it should be. He asks for help with the *a* of *father*, and is stumped by the problem of distinguishing between the *u* of *tub* and that of *push*. When he comes to the consonants, he proposes to omit all that are silent, as in *thumb, yacht, psalm* and *wrong*.[1] He favors changing the hard *c* to *k* before *e* and *i*, but leaving it elsewhere; in his next paragraph he proposes to leave it before *e* and *i* when it has the *s*-sound, and to use *s* elsewhere. For the *th* in *breath* he suggests *th*, and for that in *breathe*, *dh*. To distinguish between the *ng* of *singer* and that of *finger* he apparently favors making the latter *ng̈*, but is willing to keep plain *ng* in both cases and endure the present confusion. Again, he proposes turning the *x* of *extra* into *ks* and that of *exist* into *gz*, but does not object seriously to keeping the present *x* in both.[2]

Beside such all-out reformers there are many who are willing to go a longer or shorter distance along the way, usually in the wake of the Simplified Spelling Board. The case of the Chicago *Tribune* up to the end of 1935 was reported in AL4.[3] Since then it has done some dizzy wobbling. Early in 1936 it reiterated its devotion to the new spellings it had introduced in 1934, *e.g., fantom, harken, aile, bailif, burocracy, herse, hefer, lether* and *yern*, but warned its readers that it would have to proceed slowly. Then, on March 26, 1939, it announced surprisingly that it was abandoning its programme and promised to sin no more. It went on:

> We're saying good-by to simplified spelling. We hope that no *hassocs* will be shied in our direction as we make our way down the *aile* to the mourners' bench. . . . There was *rime* and reason for every alteration. And yet we were deluged with protests. . . . We stood pat for five years, but now we cannot

---

[1] He also adds *houn!*

[2] See his English Spelling, *Modern Language Journal*, May, 1941, pp. 628–32. The scheme of Berg is expounded in Scientific Spelling Formula; Seattle, 1936; that of Hayden in Phonetic Spelling; High Point (N.C.), 1944; that of Clark in A Dicshunary of Reformed and Simplified Spelling; New Milford (Conn.), 1914, and that of Laubach in Wanted: a Global Alphabet, *National Education Association Journal*, Jan., 1947, pp. 28–29. I do not attempt a complete bibliography. Such works often appear as pamphlets in remote places, and others exist only in MS.

[3] p. 406.

overlook the obvious fact that everybody except us continues to write *heifer* and *leather* and that goes for those who applauded as well as those who cursed the innovation.[1]

But while this sad editorial was on the press there was another shift of mind in the *Tribune* office, and in later editions its title was changed from " Lacky, Pass the Hemloc " to " Not Yet the Hemloc," and a paragraph announcing that the eighty-odd words on its list of 1931 were being abandoned was omitted. A week later followed the announcement of a compromise with death. Some of the more alarming of the spellings on the 1934 list, *e.g.*, *aile, bailif, hammoc, jaz, hefer, lether, rifraf* and *yern*, were definitely doomed to the bone-yard, but forty-four were to be given a further trial. They included *agast, analog, bagatel, burocracy, cotilion, definitly, demagog, etiquet, genuinly, sherif, tarif, trafic* and *warant*. " Experience has shown," said the *Tribune*, " that spellings like *crum, lether, herse* and *quil* have made little or no progress in the last five years. Our own writers and compositors have not become fully accustomed to these forms. . . . Perhaps the dropping of one of the *f*'s in *sherif* and *tarif* is a little too sensible to be adopted generally, but we're going to give them a longer trial, and see what happens."[2] In 1946 it tried another nibble by adding *frate* to its list, and soon afterward it followed with *telegraf* and *geografy*. It also declared for *tho, thru* and *altho*. On August 7[3] it reported that it was " still too early to say how well or ill they have been received," but that it hoped that its readers, " including the editors of other publications, will come to accept the changes."[4] Alas, the only other paper to show any sign of emulation was the *Tribune's* daughter, the New York *Daily News*. But the *Daily News* has gone little beyond *nite, alright, foto, fotog* and *fotographer*, in all of which the influence of *Variety* seems to be quite as palpable as that of the *Tribune*. For some reason unknown, it boggles at *fotografer*.[5]

---

1 Lacky, Pass the Hemloc, editorial, March 26, 1939.
2 Simplified Spelling, editorial, April 9, 1939.
3 To Phyllis Who Might Spell It *Phreight,* editorial. I am indebted here to Mr. Arthur R. Atkinson.
4 Stanley Walker reported in the *New Yorker*, April 6, 1946, p. 87, that its readers were still showing signs of annoyance with *frate*. The *Tribune* comes by its weakness for phonetic spelling by inheritance. Its great editor, Joseph Medill (1823-1899), was a member of the council of the Spelling Reform Association.
5 *Foto*, Baltimore *Evening Sun*, May 16, 1936, p. 6. The *Evening Sun* argued for *foto*, but has never

Dr. Louise Pound long ago suggested that the spelling reform movement in the United States, if it had very little effect upon standard spelling, may have at least fanned the craze for whimsical spellings which still rages, especially among advertisement writers. An early stage of the craze was visible in the name of the *Ku Klux Klan*, organized in 1865, but the original Klan did not use all the strange nomenclature that marked its successor of 1920, *e.g., klavern, kleagle, klonvocation, kloran, klaliff* and *kludd*. Dr. Pound recalled that Walt Whitman was curiously attracted to *k*, and cited his *Kanada* and *Kanadian*.[1] In two previous papers[2] she had listed a large number of unorthodox spellings in American trade-names, *e.g., holsum* (bread), *nuklene* (shoe whitening), *porosknit* (underwear), *fits-u, keen-kutter* (cutlery), *kiddie-klothes, kum-a-part* (cuff buttons), *klearflax* (linen rugs), *klenzo* (tooth paste), *az-nu* (automobile enamel), *kutzit* (soap), *slipova* (children's garments), *kroflite* (golf balls), *da-nite* (bed), *evertite* (bags and purses), *sunbrite* (cleanser), *eatmor* (chocolates), *kantleek* (hot-water bottle), *veri-*

---

adopted it. See The Wayward Press, *New Yorker*, June 8, 1946, p. 90. *Fone* has got to England, and was denounced by a Captain Richard Pilkington in the London *Times*, June 7, 1943. On June 10 it was defended by George Bernard Shaw. *American Speech* reported *fotographer* on a Fifth avenue sign, April, 1936, p. 160. On Jan. 13, 1890, the Hon. Frank Lawler, of Illinois, introduced in the House of Representatives a resolution ordaining the use of *fotograf, alfabet, filosofy* and *paragraf* in public documents, but it died in committee. It was supported by Alexander Melville Bell (father of the inventor of the telephone); William T. Harris, then United States commissioner of education, and F. A. March, but opposed by A. R. Spofford, librarian of Congress. Allen Walker Read says in Amphi-Atlantic English, *English Studies*, Oct., 1935, p. 175, that when spelling reform was revived in Congress in 1906 "congressmen of both parties expressed subserviency to English models" and it died again.

[1] The Kraze for *K*, *American Speech*, Oct., 1925, pp. 43–44. In Nineteenth-Century Humor, *American Speech*, Aug., 1927, p. 460, Richmond P. Bond recalled that The Harp of a Thousand Strings, by S. P. Avery, published in New York in 1858, was described on its title page as "*konceived*, compiled and *komically koncocted* . . . and abetted by over 200 *kurious kutz*." *K* was the Greek *kappa*. The Romans changed it to *c*. Its subsequent history in the principal European languages is recounted in NED, Vol. V, p. 647. The *kraze* for *k* continues. In The Coming of the Big Freeze, *New Yorker*, Sept. 14, 1946, p. 72, E. J. Kahn, Jr., listed *Kol-Pak* and *Kold-Kist* among the new brand names of frozen foods, and on Sept. 28, 1946, pp. 19–20, the *New Yorker* added *Filto-Kleen* filters and *Kellogg Koiled Kords* ("Make ironing quicker, easier").

[2] Word-Coinage and Modern Trade-Names, *Dialect Notes*, Vol. IV, Part I, 1913, pp. 29–41, and Spelling Manipulation and Present-Day Advertising, *Dialect Notes*, Vol. V, Part VI, 1923, pp. 226–32.

best (canned goods), *quick-shyn* (shoe polish), *neu-tone* (paint) and *cof gums* (medicated gum-drops). One of the first of the long series was *uneeda*, introduced as the name of a cracker in 1898. Thirty-one years later, writing in *American Speech*,[1] Donald M. Alexander listed many more substitutions of *u* for *you*, e.g., *u-put-it-on* (weather strip), *wear-u-well* (clothing), *u-otto-buy* (used cars), *u-bet-u* (candy), *u-serve* (canned goods), *protectu* (a device for protecting checks), *while-u-wait, drive-ur-self* (cars for hire)[2] and *u-do-it* (graining compound), and argued that *U* in the second person is just as respectable as *I* in the first, which did not come in until after 1400. He reported that the roadside maps in Wayne county, Mich., indicated the passing automobilist's position by arrows bearing the legend *U Are Here*.

Meanwhile, *Variety* and its imitators continue to generate and disseminate a large number of simplified spellings of their own, e.g., *laff* (laugh);[3] *ayem* (A.M.); *nabe* as an abbreviation of *neighborhood*, extended to a neighborhood movie parlor; *whodunit* (who done it?), a mystery story or film; *burlesk* and *vodvil*.[4] Hollywood seems to have been responsible for the reduction of *and* to *'n*, as in *sit 'n eat, park 'n dine* and *dunk 'n dine*,[5] and perhaps also for *cash 'n carry, prun* (prune), *hiway, pare* (pear) and *traler* (trailer).[6] The substitution of *x* for *cks* is apparently of respectable age in the United States. *Sox* for *socks* has become almost universal, as in White *Sox*,[7] and Maury Maverick tells me that *sax* for *sacks* and *tax* for *tacks* are widely used among lumbermen. *Slax* for *slacks* was reported by one of the scouts of *American Speech* in 1936, when it was still a novelty,[8] but Louise Pound reported *trunx, chix* and *inx* in 1925.[9] *Variety* uses *crix* as an abbreviation of *critics*, and *drinx* is reported from England.[10] *Variety* always reduces *show* to *sho*, and is fond of *shobiz*.[11] *Shocard* is in common use. *Donut* is now so widely

1 Why Not *U* for *You*?, Oct., 1929, pp. 24-26.
2 *Drivurself* and *u-dryvit* had been reported from Cambridge, Mass., by Phillips Barry, *American Speech*, Sept., 1927, p. 514.
3 *American Speech*, Dec., 1941, p. 277.
4 See Supplement I, p. 327.
5 Showing Hollywood, by Cecilia Ager, *Variety*, July 23, 1930.
6 Notes of a Peninsula Commuter, by Joseph Burton Vasché, *American Speech*, Feb., 1940, p. 54.
7 See AL4, p. 407.
8 Dec., p. 374.
9 The Value of English Linguistics to the Teacher, *American Speech*, Nov., p. 100.
10 Saving a Letter, Liverpool *Daily Post*, July 27, 1944. I am indebted for this to Mr. P. E. Cleator.
11 Obituary of Lora Valedon, Sept. 18, 1946, p. 34.

accepted that there is a *Donut* Institute and in 1942 it proclaimed a National *Donut* Week beginning October 25, the twenty-fifth anniversary " of the making of the first *donut* by Salvation Army lassies in France in World War I."[1] The Jones Metabolism Equipment Company of Chicago uses *graf* in advertising the Jones Motor-Basal Metabolism Unit;[2] in Baltimore, in 1945, a drug-store was announcing *McNificent* food,[3] and at Essex, Md., there is (or was in 1946), a *Raynbo* Inn. Perhaps such whimsical forms as *izzatso*, *nuf sed*, *betcha*, *damfino* and *helluva* are too painfully familiar to need mention. To the same class probably belongs *Wanna Noit*, the name of " an extension culture club in a Western town."[4] *Ho-made* was first found in the Middle West in 1927[5] and has since made considerable progress. Now and then there is a nostalgic return to Bach. In 1946 the *New Yorker* reported[6] that the *Kwik* Products Company, of West Twenty-Eighth street, was also listed in the Manhattan Telephone Directory as the *Quick* Products Company.[7]

The collapse of the Simplified Spelling Board has put an end to organized and large scale agitation for spelling reform in the Republic, but at the same stroke it has helped to revive and restimulate the same great moral movement in England. This needs a little explaining. As I have hitherto noted, the angel of the Board, from its organization in 1906 until his death in 1919, was Andrew Carnegie. He started off by allowing it $15,000 a year but soon raised this subsidy to $25,000, and during his thirteen angelic years it saw, altogether, the color of $283,000 of his money. When it was found that he had forgotten it in his will the Board began to droop, but not long afterward it felt the kiss of fresh hope, for news seeped in that a rich British shipbuilder, Sir George Burton Hunter, had become violently interested in Simplified Spelling, and was resolved to promote it through the English speaking world.[8] Sir George began by

---

[1] *Nation*, Aug. 15, 1942, p. 133.
[2] *Journal of the American Medical Association*, Nov. 13, 1943, p. 54 (advertising section).
[3] Baltimore *Sun*, Aug. 1, p. 16, col. 2.
[4] *American Speech*, Oct., 1936, p. 274.
[5] *American Speech*, Oct., p. 70.
[6] Sept. 2, p. 19.
[7] *College English*, April, 1943, p. 438, in answer to a protest against *nu*, *glo*, *blu*, *sox*, *lite*, etc., remarked sagely that " their very unconventionality gives them a commercial value; that is to say, they call attention to themselves because they are not what the reader expects."
[8] Sir George was a Scotsman, and also laid out a lot of money on the National Temperance Federation. He was knighted in 1918. His firm built the *Lusitania*.

American Spelling

appointing "a personal secretary, Mr. T. R. Barber, to look after this side of his work,"[1] and presently the Simplified Spelling Society, the English opposite number to the American Simplified Spelling Board, was pleasantly in funds, and full of new zeal. On August 18, 1922, he set up a trust fund for its benefit, running for ten years, and when the ten years expired they were extended to sixteen. The terms of the trust provided that at the end of that time the trustees should divide the capital between the Society and "any other society or societies, association or associations" then "in existence or hereafter to come into existence" that had precisely the same objects. This trust finally expired in 1938, and meanwhile Sir George had died in 1937, at the age of ninety-two.

The trustees were then confronted with the question, Who should get the money? Should it all go to the Simplified Spelling Society, or should it be divided between the Society and some other organization or organizations, say, the Simplified Spelling Board? The trustees, unable to decide, appealed to the courts for guidance, and on March 1, 1939, the case came before Mr. Justice Bennett in the High Court of Justice, Chancery Division. The judge asked for expert evidence, and it was provided by Dr. Daniel Jones, professor of phonetics at the University of London, and Isaac James Pitman (later M.P.), grandson of Sir Isaac Pitman (1813–1897), inventor of the system of shorthand bearing his name.[2] Jones testified that "the Simplified Spelling Board of America" had "ceased to exist," and that the Simplified Spelling Society "was the only society of its kind in the world with which he was acquainted."

---

[1] New Spelling, by Walter Ripman and William Archer; London, 1940, p. 3.

[2] The *Ur*-Pitman was himself an ardent spelling reformer. In fact, the movement in England was launched by an article he printed in his stenographic magazine, the *Phonotypic Journal*, in Jan., 1843. See On Early English Pronunciation, by Alexander J. Ellis; London, 1874, Vol. IV, p. 1182. His phonetic alphabet included letters borrowed from the Greek and others of his own design. In 1849 he printed the Book of Psalms in it, and during the years following he brought out other books and pamphlets in it, but in his old age he abandoned it for the easier scheme of the Simplified Spelling Society. His publishing firm, Sir Isaac Pitman & Sons, Ltd., is still the Society's official publisher. He was knighted for his services to stenography in 1894. Like all other reformers, he was unsatisfied by one arcanum, and also embraced vegetarianism and teetotalism. There are lives of him by his younger brother, Benn (1822–1911), and by Alfred Baker, and a good short account of him is in The Man Who Wrote by Sound, London *Sunday Express*, Dec. 30, 1940.

Pitman swore that "he knew of no society with objects similar." Mr. Justice Bennett thereupon decided that the Simplified Spelling Society should get all the money, and the trustees turned over to it £18,200.[1] At once it began bringing out a long series of books and pamphlets in promotion of the cause, and it has been doing so ever since.

These publications show that the Society hopes to reform English spelling without bringing in any new characters, without putting accents on any of the existing letters (save the dieresis to separate successive vowels, as we use it now), and without departing from the more obvious phonetic values. It proposes to substitute *dh* for the *th* of *father*, but is willing to let *th* stand as it is in *thing*. It uses *zh* for the French *j*-sound, substitutes *k* for hard *c* in all cases, and uses *ur* wherever *er* or *ir* is now used in its place, *e.g.*, *urmin* (ermine) and *thurd* (third).[2] Hard *g* remains, but soft *g* is displaced by *j*. The consonants *b, d, f, h, k, l, m, n, p, r, s, t, v, w, y* and *z* are unchanged, and *ch* and *sh* are used as now. The present vowels retain their short sounds; their other sounds are indicated by simple devices. The long *a* of *father* becomes *aa*; the long *o* of *lower*, *oe*; the long *u* of *moon*, *uu*; the *a* of *made*, *ae*. The long *e* is always *ee*. The diphthongs are indicated substantially as now; the palatal glide by putting *e* after, not before, the *u*. The sound of *eye* becomes *ie*. S, whenever it is sounded as z, is written z. Silent letters are dropped. Useless doublings are reduced to single letters. What all this comes to is shown by the following:

> We instinktivly shrink from eny chaenj in whot iz familyar; and whot kan be mor familyar dhan dhe form ov wurdz dhat we hav seen and riten mor tiemz dhan we kan posibly estimaet? We taek up a book printed in Amerika, and *honor* and *center* jar upon us every tiem we kum akros dhem; nae, eeven to see *forever* in plaes ov *for ever* atrackts our atenshon in an unplezant wae. But dheez ar isolaeted kaesez; think ov dhe meny wurdz dhat wood hav to be chaenjd if eny real impruuvment wer to rezult. At dhe furst glaans a pasej in eny reformd speling looks "kweer" and "ugly." Dhis objekshon iz aulwaez dhe furst to be maed; it iz purfektly natueral; it iz dhe hardest to remuuv. Indeed, its efekt iz not weekend until dhe nue speling iz noe longger nue, until it has been seen ofen enuf to be familyar.[3]

Happily, the shock to Britons on encountering the American *honor* is evaded by going the whole hog to *onor*, *labor* is disguised

---

[1] London *Times*, March 2, 1939.
[2] But for some reason unknown it uses *erbaen* for *urbane*. Such inconsistencies are in all known simplified spelling systems.
[3] New Spelling, before cited, p. 90.

as *laebor*, and *color* becomes *kulor*, which seems somehow less obscene than *color*. In the same way *center* is toned down to *senter* and *meter* to *meeter*, but there is no way to get round the abhorrent *theater*. There are some logical but startling interchanges: *tyre* becomes *tier*, and *tier* becomes *teer*. The *tho* of the Simplified Spelling Board becomes *dhoe* and its *thru* becomes *thruu*. *To, too* and *two* are alike *tuu*. At first glance, the new system simply looks like "bad" spelling, but it must be said for it that even its most radical innovations, like those of "bad" spelling itself, are usually readily fathomed, *e.g.*, *hedkworterz, kwintesens, proelonggaeshon, forkloesher, miselaenyus* and *aproksimaet*.[1]

In England, as in the United States, there are many lone-wolf spelling reformers. The earliest recorded was a monk named Ormin, who lived and suffered at the beginning of the Thirteenth Century.[2] Many later English authors of the classical line made attempts to regulate and improve the spelling of their time, notably John Milton, who used *sovran* for *sovereign*,[3] *glimse* for *glimpse*, *hight* for *height*, and *thir* for *their*.[4] Swift seems to have been against simplified spelling, as Samuel Johnson was, and in 1712 denounced the "foolish opinion, advanced of late years, that we ought to spell ex-

---

[1] The Society published a Dictionary of New Spelling, compiled by Walter Ripman and including about 18,600 words, in 1941. After it received the Hunter trust money it greatly extended its list of publications, which now includes, *inter alia*, A Short Account of New Spelling; London, 1940; A Spesimen ov Nue Speling; Wallsend-upon-Tyne, 1940; Dhe Etimolojokal Arguement, by William Archer; London, 1941; Dhe Eesthetik Arguement, by the same; London, 1941; I Hav Lurnt to Spel, by the same; London, 1941; On the History of Spelling, by W. W. Skeat; London, 1941; The Best Method of Teaching Children to Read and Write; London, 1942; Dhe Proez and Konz ov Rashonal Speling; London, 1942; A Breef History of Inglish Speling; London, 1942; Braeking dhe Spel; London, 1942; Dhe Star, by H. G. Wells; London, 1942; How to Teach the New Spelling, by Walter Ripman; London, 1942; Dhe Fonetik Aspekt ov Speling Reform by Daniel Jones; London, 1942, and Views on Spelling Reform, by Ripman and others; London, 1944. Some of these are reprints of earlier publications. About half bear the imprint "Sur Isaac Pitman & Sunz, Ltd., London." I am indebted for information about the Society and its doings to Mr. Bernard C. Wrenick, of Walton-on-Thames, a member of its committee. Other members are Ripman and Dr. Jones. Its president, in 1946, was Gilbert Murray, formerly regius professor of Greek at Oxford.

[2] AL4, pp. 397–98.

[3] Comus, 1634, l. 41; Paradise Lost, 1667, I, l. 246. He was imitated by Coleridge, Lamb and Tennyson.

[4] Spare Hours: Second Series, by John Taylor Brown; Boston, 1867, p. 346.

actly as we speak," [1] but Southey somehow found authority in him for *tho'*, *thro'* and *altho'*.[2]

As everyone knows, George Bernard Shaw, in his heyday as a reformer, maintained a department of reformed spelling in his vast and bizarre Utopia. But save for a few somewhat banal innovations, *e.g.*, *havn't*, *program*, *novelet*, and *Renascence*, most of which were not really innovations at all,[3] he stuck closely to standard English spelling in his own writing, and even indulged himself in a few archaisms, *e.g.*, *to shew*.[4] In theory, however, he was always in favor of very radical changes, including the abolition of silent letters and the adoption of an entirely new alphabet. In a letter to the London *Times* in 1945 [5] he disported himself with the word *bomb*. The redundant *b*, he argued, " is entirely senseless and wastes the writer's time," and suggests " an absurd mispronunciation of the word exactly as if the word *gun* were to be spelt *gung*." He reported that he had made an experiment with *bom*, and found that he could write it twenty-four times in one minute, whereas he could write *bomb* but eighteen times. He proposed that the British government appoint a committee of economists and statisticians to deal with the matter, and closed by saying that " if the Phoenician alphabet were only turned upside down and enlarged by seventeen letters from the Greek alphabet it would soon pay for the war." Some months later, in an interview with Hayden Church, he explained that this new alphabet should have " at least forty-two letters, capable of indicating every sound in our speech without using more than one letter for each sound." [6] " The yearly cost of having to write my name with four letters instead of two," he went on, " is astronomical. The

---

1 A Proposal for Correcting, Improving and Ascertaining the English Tongue; a letter to the Earl of Oxford and Mortimer, London, Feb. 22, 1711/12. In this he proposed that an academy be set up for " ascertaining and fixing our language for ever." His position is discussed at length in Wyld, pp. 158-61.

2 This is on the testimony of Southey's son-in-law, in his notes to The Doctor. *Tho*, in fact, had been used by the before-mentioned Ormin, *c.* 1200. It is to be found in John Denham's Cooper's Hill, 1642; in Shaftesbury, 1711, and in a *Spectator* paper by Addison, No. 557, 1714, and Benjamin Franklin, though a purist, used it in a letter to Webster, 1789.

3 *Renascence*, for example, was used by Matthew Arnold in Culture and Anarchy, 1869.

4 The NED says that this spelling was " prevalent in the 18th c. and not uncommon in the first half of the 19th c." but is " now obs. exc. in legal documents."

5 Published Dec. 26.

6 *Saturday Review of Literature*, July 27, 1946, p. 10.

saving would repay the cost of the atomic bomb in a few months." But this argument was quickly demolished by Simeon Strunsky and Dr. Charles E. Funk in the New York *Times*. "Assume," said Strunsky, "that he saved himself 25 per cent. of time in writing. What percentage would it cost his readers whose eyes would pause constantly to puzzle out many strange spellings?"[1] Said Funk:

> Shaw wants to build a spelling reform upon pronunciation. That would be disastrous. Whose pronunciation would be the criterion? He naïvely suggests, broadly, "British pronunciation." As if all Britishers spoke any more alike than do all Americans! He cites *bomb* as his pet peeve. But, for the record, how does Shaw pronounce *bomb?* Many Britishers, especially the older generation, would phonetically spell it *bum,* according to the various British dictionaries on my shelves. That was the way the poet Southey pronounced it, but the poet Young called it *boom,* by analogy with *tomb,* while the earlier poet Matthew Prior called it *boam,* by analogy with *comb.*[2]

Another of England's fans for simplified spelling is William Barkley, one of Lord Beaverbrook's chief aides on the London *Daily Express*. His interest in the holy cause was first aroused by the late R. E. Zachrisson's Anglic scheme in the early 30s,[3] but he now seems to favor the rather simpler and more logical plan of the Simplified Spelling Society, though with some changes of his own. For one thing, he rejects the use of *dh* for the sound of *th* in *that*, and sticks to *th* in both words of the *that*-class and those of the *think*-class. Again, he rejects the Society's doubling of intervocalic *r*, as in *authorrity*. But in general he goes along, even when it comes to substituting *k* for *c* — for long a sign and symbol of extreme unenlight-

---

[1] Topics of the Times, editorial page, Dec. 29, 1945.
[2] Shaw's Scheme Scouted, New York *Times*, editorial page, Jan. 14, 1946. Funk is a nephew of Dr. Isaac K. Funk (1839–1912), the publisher of the Standard Dictionary and the *Literary Digest* and one of the most ardent of the early supporters of the Simplified Spelling Board. But the younger Funk has never followed his uncle into the wilderness.
[3] Bad Language, by William Barkley; London, 1945, p. 8. Anglic was launched by Zachrisson in the late 20s, and is described in detail in its inventor's Anglic: a New Agreed Simplified English Spelling; final revised edition; Uppsala (Sweden), 1931. Zachrisson was professor of English at Uppsala. His proposal was reviewed somewhat tartly by Janet Rankin Aiken in Or Shall We Go Anglic?, *Bookman*, Feb. 1931, pp. 618–20, and by A. G. K[ennedy?] in *American Speech*, June, 1931, pp. 378–80. For a while he promoted it in two periodicals, *Anglic, an Edukaeshonal Revue*, and *Anglic Illustrated*. He was not the only foreigner to undertake the reform of English spelling. The scheme of the Germanized H. Darcy Power is described in AL4, pp. 404–05. In 1932 a Japanese named Y. Okakura published The Simplification of English Spelling in Tokyo.

enment in English folklore, as in American. "There is," he admits, "a prejudice against *k*. Many people

think it is Teutonic. How much there is in habit can be seen at once in the spelling of the town of *Kanterbury*. How harsh and Teutonic! Yet this is the same word as *Kent*, and what is more purely and sweetly English than *Kent?* I fought against *k* for a time, thinking we could retain the *c* in many words. . . . [But] *k* is magnificently clean and clear in print. It takes three times as long to write it in longhand as *c*, more's the pity, but it will replace many conglomerations of *ch*, *cq* and *ck*. The addition of *k* to *c* in many words must have arisen because the printers felt *c* was not clear enough by itself. The dropping of *k* in such words as *publick* is one of the few spelling changes in the last two centuries, fought to the last ditch by Boswell.[1] We will restore his *k* but drop his *c*: *publik*.[2]

The spelling reform movement in both the United States and England, in its early days, had the support of many of the most eminent philologists then in practise in the two countries, and also of many distinguished literati, but it has never made any progress, and there is little evidence that it will do better in the foreseeable future. In this country it has been handicapped by the fact that, to Americans, phonetic spelling always suggests the grotesqueries of the comic writers stretching from Seba Smith[3] to Milt Gross, and by the further fact that popular interest in and respect for spelling prowess, fostered for more than a century by the peculiarly American institution of the spelling-bee, still survive more or less.[4] Also,

[1] And by Samuel Johnson. The word came in during the Fifteenth Century and was once spelled *publyke*, *publike*, *publique*, *publicte* and even *puplicke* and *puplik*. But *public* appeared in the statutes of Oxford University so early as 1645, and is to be found in Dryden, 1665. During the Eighteenth Century Jeremy Bentham, De Foe and Blackstone favored it. Noah Webster made it universal in the United States.

[2] Barkley's other publications on the subject include Ingglish, *Nineteenth Century and After*, May, 1938, pp. 602–15; The Two Englishes; London, 1941, and Article to End All Spelling Bees, London *Daily Express*, May 13, 1938. His colleagues of the *Daily Express* spoofed him gently by signing the last-named "by Wilyam Barkly."

"At least," they added, "that is how our Mr. William Barkley ought to spell his name if he had his way." The Two Englishes was noticed somewhat unfavorably in the London *Times Literary Supplement*, May 31, 1941, and Barkley replied on Aug. 30.

[3] Supplement I, pp. 128–31.

[4] The spelling-bee was promoted by Noah Webster's famous blue-back speller, for many years the only book, save the Bible, in general circulation in the country. But the name *spelling-bee*, though it had congeners running back to the Revolutionary era, is not recorded until the 1870s. Before that, beginning in the 30s, *spelling-class*, *-match* or *-school* was used. Introduced by the radio, the *spelling-bee* had a brief but furious vogue in England in the late 1930s.

there is reason for believing that the ardent and tactless advocacy of the Simplified Spelling Board scheme by Roosevelt I in 1906 produced vastly more opposition than support, for Americans, in those days, had not yet got used to government by administrative fiat, and resented it violently whenever it touched what they regarded as their private affairs. Finally, the fact is not to be forgotten that the patronage of Andrew Carnegie, which was not confined to his subsidy but also included active propaganda,[1] likewise irritated a tender nerve. He was then the richest man in the country, and memories of the Homestead strike of 1892 were still playing about him; it was not until some time later that he began to lose his diabolical character and to be admired by the underprivileged.

The advantages of spelling reform have always been greatly exaggerated by its exponents, many of whom have been notably over-earnest and under-humorous men. As I have noted, some of them and perhaps most of them have been advocates of other and even more dubious reforms. It is, indeed, rare to find a reformer who is content with but one sure-cure for the ills of humanity. Henry Holt, the publisher, one of the stout pillars of the Simplified Spelling Board, was also a spiritualist, and at no pains to conceal it. Sir George Hunter was a Scotch wowser who also whooped up Prohibition. George Bernard Shaw supported a dozen other arcana, ranging from parlor Socialism to vegetarianism. H. G. Wells toyed with Socialism, technocracy and Basic English. And so on down the line. As long ago as 1892 the old Spelling Reform Association was constrained to issue a warning that some of its members had "zeal without knowledge." "One of the favorite fallacies of the human mind," it said sadly, "is that whoever means well or engages in a good work is therefore entitled, no matter how incompetent, to the sympathy and aid of all good men."[2]

Some of the favorite arguments of the reformers are so feeble as to be silly — for example, the argument that the new spelling would greatly reduce the labor of writing and the cost of paper and printing. This was first put into speculative statistics in 1849 by Alexander J. Ellis, who figured that the fearsome phonetic alphabet he

[1] See his letter of Dec. 14, 1910, setting up the Carnegie Peace Fund, reprinted in the *Saturday Review of Literature*, June 1, 1946, pp. 20-21.

[2] Reformers and Cranks, *Spelling*, July, 1892, pp. 231-32.

was then advocating would result in a space saving of 17%. In 1878 J. H. Gladstone, then president of the English Spelling Reform Association, figured somewhat more modestly that "the mere removal of duplicated consonants would save 1.6% and of the mute *e*'s an additional 4%."[1] Such optimistic estimates always overlook the fact that many of the gains would be wiped out by compensatory losses. Thus the relatively mild scheme of the Simplified Spelling Society, though it reduces the seven letters of *thought* to the five of *thaut* and the six of the English *honour* to the four of *onor*, changes hundreds of other spellings without saving a single letter, *e.g.*, *hierling* for *hireling*, *pakt* for *pact*, *taterdemaelyon* for *tatterdemalion*, *survae* for *survey*, *inadekwasy* for *inadequacy*, and *furn* for *fern*, and in many other cases actually makes words longer, e.g., *furmentaeshon* for *fermentation*, *florrist* for *florist*, *insuelaeshon* for *insulation*, *asoeshyaeshon* for *association*, *kuupae* for *coupe*, *eksersiez* for *exercise*, and *mateeryaliez* for *materialize*.

The argument that phonetic spelling would be easier to learn than the present spelling is not supported by the known facts. In some cases it no doubt would be, but in plenty of other cases it would certainly not. Moreover, the number of "hard" words in English is always greatly overestimated.[2] It is undoubtedly surprising to a child to learn that *cough* rhymes with *off*, but it is probably a good deal less disconcerting than adults may fancy, for everything new is surprising to a child, and one marvel is taken in as facilely as another. Even adult foreigners find the standard spelling less baffling than is sometimes alleged, as more than one witness experienced in teaching them English has testified.[3] It is not infrequently argued that the inconsistencies of English are unknown to their native languages, but this is moonshine. No civilized language is really spelled

---

[1] Spelling Reform From an Educational Point of View, reprinted in *Spelling*, May, 1887, p. 27.

[2] Mr. Ed. C. Kruse, of Kansas City, tells me that in a Harmonized and Subject Reference New Testament, published at Delaware (N.J.) in 1904, the statement was made that "there are only thirty-three words in the English language pronounced as spelled." Nothing could be more ridiculous.

[3] For example, H. Johnstone Millar in the London *Times*, July 1, 1935. He said: "I still have correspondents from both Germany and France who hardly ever make spelling mistakes in the long letters with which they are kind enough to delight me." See also Spelling Reform, London *Times Literary Supplement*, May 27, 1944, p. 259.

phonetically, not even German, Spanish or Italian. German is actually full of sounds that are represented in its orthography by different characters, *e.g.*, *ch* and *g*, *f* and *ph*, *c* and *k*, and letters that have different sounds in different situations, *e.g.*, the *ch* of *loch* and *licht*, the *s* in *essen* and *hase*, the *r* in *rad* and *mutter*. So long ago as 1876 the Prussian minister of education, Adalbert Falk (1827–1900), one of the chief figures in the *Kulturkampf*, called a conference of philologists, pedagogues, publishers and printers to give the archaic German spelling of the time an overhauling, and in 1880 his successor, R. V. von Puttkamer (1828–1900), ordered the adoption of some of the changes this committee recommended, *e.g.*, the omission of the silent *h* after consonants. But the changes thus effected did not satisfy the more radical spelling reformers, who pointed out, *inter alia*, that there were still six signs for the sound of *k*, to wit, *k*, *c*, *ck*, *ch*, *qu* and *g*. These enthusiasts had formed a General Association for Simplified Spelling (Allgemeiner Verein für Vereinfachte Rechtschreibung) in 1876, and after 1877 it published a monthly journal, *Reform*. Unhappily, their scheme advocated the introduction of new characters for *ch*, *sch* and *ng*, and in consequence it met with so much opposition that it gradually faded out, despite the fact that the famous pathologist and politician, Rudolf Virchow (1821–1900), was in favor of it, and the further fact that the young Kaiser Wilhelm II, in 1890, ordered the ministry of education to " take the matter into consideration."[1]

Spanish and Italian come much closer to phonetic spelling than German, but their orthography is made difficult by the dialectal variations that are so plentiful in both. Says Hugh Morrison:

> In Latin-American Spanish *ll* and *y* are pronounced alike, and *z* and *c* before *i* and *e* are pronounced like *s*. *B* and *v* are universally pronounced alike, and *h* is always silent except in *ch*. . . . The Mexicans have the best pronunciation of all Spanish-speaking peoples, . . . [but] ask an average Mexican to write *vayas*, a form of the verb *to go*, and he will spell it in any one of eight different ways: *vayas*, *vallas*, *vayaz*, *vallaz*, *bayas*, *ballas*, *bayaz* and *ballaz*. . . .

[1] *Eclectic Magazine*, April, 1882, p. 571. *Spelling*, Sept., 1894, pp. 314–17. So recently as 1947 a conference of German teachers, publishers, writers and printers was held at Berlin to draw up a new scheme of spelling reform. Prof. Wolfgang Steinitz, a member of the preparatory committee, advocated the use of *ai* alone instead of both *ai* and *ei*, *eu* instead of *äu*, *ss* instead of *sz*, *f* in place of *v* and *ph*, *ks* in place of *x* and *chs*, *k* in place of *ch* when the sound is *k*, and the omission of *h* after *r*. See *Word*, Aug., 1946, p. 157.

Can you imagine anyone misspelling the pronoun *I*, or any word as common as that in any language in the world? . . . [In Spanish] the word is *yo*, and I have seen [Mexicans] write it *llo* hundreds of times.[1]

Of Italian Morrison says:

Italians in New York . . . assured me that Italian phonetics were foolproof, unlike Spanish, as *b* and *v* were pronounced as in English, there was no *y* at all, *z* was pronounced like *ts*, and *c* like *ch*, so neither one could possibly be confused with *s*. The *h*, they said, occurred only in the *ch* and *gh* combinations, which were phonetically watertight, and in four forms of the auxiliary verb *to have*, and these latter forms, *ho*, *hai*, *ha* and *hanno*, were all I really had to remember. . . . [But] I soon found out that standard Italian is a dialect of just one part of Italy, Tuscany, and that words are spelled as they are pronounced in that one province only. So, to a Neapolitan or a Sicilian, or, in fact, to nine-tenths of the people of Italy, the simplicity of the spelling system is a total loss. . . . Just as Mexicans misspell words as common as *I*, so Italians misspell words as common as *you*. . . . There are several second person pronouns, including *tu*, *ti*, *te*, *voi* and *vi*, and I have seen them spelled *du*, *di*, *de*, *foi* and *fi* many times.

Russian spelling, which had been static since it was fixed in the Eighteenth Century by M. V. Lomonosov (1711–65), the grammarian, was reformed by fiat by the Kremlin in 1924. The number of letters in the alphabet was reduced from thirty-seven to thirty-two, the crossing of the *t* and the dotting of the *i* were abolished, and various other simplifications were effected. But a proposal to abandon the Cyrillic alphabet for the Roman was rejected. In Bulgaria, in 1923, when the dictator, Alexander Stambolsky, undertook to anticipate the Kremlin's reforms, his Bulgarian lieges would have none of them, and the literate among them joined the Army in a revolt which led to his butchery on June 9.[2] In Turkey, a few years later, Kemal Pasha had better luck, for the Army was under his thumb and at least nine out of ten Turks were illiterate. He was therefore successful in substituting the Roman alphabet of Europe for the clumsy and difficult Arabic alphabet, and in bringing in what almost amounted to phonetic spelling.[3] In France the learned

---

[1] A Letter on Spelling Reform, *American Speech*, Oct., 1945, pp. 208–11. See also "Spanish is a Phonetic Language" — the quotation marks satirize the common delusion —, by Pierre Delattre, *Hispania*, Nov., 1945, pp. 511–16. Morrison's paper was questioned in Some Comments on Spelling Reform, by Mario A. Pei, *American Speech*, April, 1946, pp. 129–31.

[2] Literary Riots, Milwaukee *Sentinel*, editorial, July 6, 1923.

[3] The high illiteracy rate in Russia in 1924 also facilitated reform there. An article on that reform in *Science*, by John P. Harrington, was summarized in *American Speech*, Oct., 1925, pp. 60–61.

men of the Academy began considering spelling reform in 1893, and after six months of hard sweating decided to confine the silent *e*, as much as possible, to the feminine forms of nouns, and to substitute *f* for *ph*, also wherever possible. It turned out to be *im*possible in most cases, and by 1905 a savant named Paul Moyer was beating a tub for a new reform movement with teeth in it. Nothing came of it, and to this day French spelling is even less phonetic than English.[1]

In their effort to point up the inconsistencies and other absurdities of the latter, spelling reformers have frequently resorted to a kind of *reductio ad absurdum*. That is to say, they have undertaken to show how bad it would be if it were really as bad as, in their more soaring moments, they say it is now. Sometimes they concoct rhymes showing the unlikeness in current spelling of words that rhyme, and sometimes they carry the thing a step further by respelling words in what that spelling would come to if it were consistent in its worst inconsistencies. Everyone is familiar with such limericks as:

> There was a young girl in the *choir*
> Whose voice rose up *hoir* and *hoir*
>   Till it reached such a *height*
>   It was clear out of *seight*
> And they found it next day in the *spoir*.[2]

And such pedagogical rhymes as this:

> *Write* we know is written right,
> When we see it written *write;*
> But when we see it written *wright*,
> We know 'tis not then written right;
> For *write*, to have it written right,
> Must not be written *right* nor *wright*,
> Nor yet should it be written *rite*,
> But *write* — for so 'tis written right.[3]

The other device produces such monstrosities as *foolish* spelled *pphoughtluipsh* — the *f* as in *sapphire*, the *oo* as in *through*, the *l* as in *hustle*, the *i* as in *build* and the *sh* as in *pshaw;*[4] *fish* as *ghotti*

[1] Leonard Bloomfield says in Language; New York, 1933, p. 86 that Polish, Czech and Finnish are spelled phonetically, but inasmuch as he adds Spanish some doubts may linger.
[2] This appears on p. 8 of a 16-page pamphlet of such banal confectionery, Rimes Without Reason, issued by the Spelling Reform Association; Lake Placid (N.Y.), n.d.
[3] *Harper's Magazine*, Oct., 1852, p. 709.
[4] I take this from the just cited pamphlet of the Spelling Reform Association, inside back cover.

— the *f* as in *rough*, the *i* as in *women*, and the *sh* as in *nation*;[1] *potatoes* as *ghoughphtheightteeaux* — *gh* as in *hiccough*,[2] *ou* as in *dough*, *phth* as in *phthisic*,[3] *eigh* as in *neigh*, *tte* as in *gazette*, and *eaux* as in *beaux*;[4] *scissors* as *psozzyrrzz* — *ps* as in *psalm*, *o* as in *women*, *zz* as in *buzz*, *yrr* as in *myrrh*,[5] and *z* as in *whizz* —;[6] *root* as *lueed* — *l* as in *colonel*, *ue* as in *rue*, and *ed* as in *liked* —; *corn* as *kougholpn* — *k* as in *book*, *ough* as in *though*, *ol* as in *colonel* and *pn* as in *pneumonia* —; and *wish* as *juoti* — *ju* as in *Juanita*, *o* as in *women*, and *ti* as in *nation*.[7] The same words often appear in many of these somewhat feeble inventions, *e.g.*, *colonel*, *nation*, *pshaw*, *pneumonia*, *rough*, *dough*, *women* and *through*. Sometimes they deal with proper names, as when *Turner* becomes *Phtholognyrrh* — *phth* as in *phthisic*, *olo* as in *colonel*, *gn* as in *gnat* and *yrrh* as in *myrrh*.[8] One of the earliest is to be found in Alexander J. Ellis's century-old "Plea for Phonetic Spelling,"[9] where it is ascribed to William Gregory, professor of chemistry at Edinburgh. It takes the form of a letter to Isaac Pitman, then editor of the *Phonotypic Journal*, and runs in part as follows:

> Eye obzerve yew proepeaux two introwduice ay nue sissedem ov righting, bigh whitch ue eckspres oanly theigh sowneds anned knot thee orthoggerafey oph they wurds; butt Igh phthink ugh gow to fare inn cheighnjing owr thyme-onird alfahbeat, aned ading sew menny neau lebtors.[10]

All the American spelling reformers, beginning with Noah Webster, have made the capital mistake of trying to cover too much

---

[1] Would Spell *Fish Ghotti*, New York *Times*, March 5, 1944. This was a report of a lecture at University College, London, by Daniel Jones.

[2] Webster declared for *hickup* in his dictionary of 1806, and *hiccup* is now standard in both the United States and England.

[3] This was one of the marvels of my own schooldays, but every boy or girl of nine, not half-witted, could spell it. It has been supplanted in medical terminology by *tuberculosis*.

[4] *American Speech*, Jan., 1927, p. 217 says that *ghoughphtheightteeaux* appeared on the menu of the Lake Placid Club June 22, 1926.

[5] Why not *yrrh*?

[6] Sir Isaac Pitman's Life and Labors, by Benn Pitman; Cincinnati, 1902, p. 83. I am indebted here to Mr. Ed. C. Kruse, of Kansas City.

[7] The last three come from What a Language!, by J. Franklin Bradley, *English Journal* (College edition), April, 1938, pp. 349-50.

[8] I take this from an article in the *Youth's Companion*, reprinted in the *Writer's Monthly* in 1925.

[9] London, 1848, pp. 42-46.

[10] I leave the discovery of the spellings parodied here to readers serving leisured terms in the jug. In the rest of the letter Gregory made due use of *colonel*, *dough*, *psalm*, *phthisic*, *myrrh* and *sapphire*. Some of his horrible examples have since acquired more rational spellings, at least in the United States, *e.g.*, *accompt*, *drachm* and *gaol*.

ground at one operation. A very impressive number of Webster's innovations were accepted and are still the preferred American spellings, but many, many more were rejected.[1] The Simplified Spelling Board and its associated soothsayers suffered the same failure, and on a larger scale. When the National Education Association brought out its first list of proposed new spellings in 1898, to wit, *tho, altho, thru, thruout, thoro, thoroly, thorofare, program, prolog, catalog, pedagog* and *decalog*, they were met with considerable politeness, and some of them are in wide use today, but when the Simplified Spelling Board, intoxicated by Carnegie's money, began making the list longer and longer and wilder and wilder, until by 1919 it included such items as *eg, hed, bild, tipe, laf* and *leag*,[2] the national midriff began to tickle and tremble, and soon the whole movement was reduced to comedy. Of it Arthur G. Kennedy has said:

> Enthusiasm outran discretion, too many changes were urged in too short a time, and the movement soon lost momentum and lapsed into a state of indecision and discouragement. The discouragement was due, not so much to the opposition of "the ignorant and stubborn educated" against whom [Thomas R.] Lounsbury railed as to the great difficulties that would naturally be experienced by publishers, stenographers, teachers and all writers and users of the present well intrenched system of spelling. When the activities of the Simplified Spelling Board culminated in a Handbook of Simplified Spelling in 1920, the list of reformed spellings offered had become so formidable that one glance at the thousands of simplifications was sufficient to discourage most students of the English language.[3]

Sir William Craigie, one of the editors of the NED and chief editor of the DAE, made the same point in a wise paper printed in 1944:

> There would be better prospect of some success if the aim were less ambitious. Gradual changes in certain words or types of words, such as have been made in the past, might well be introduced by writers and printers, which in time would become so familiar that the older forms would take their place with those already discarded, as *horrour* and *terrour, musick* and *physick, deposite* and *fossile, chymical* and *chymist*. Such changes, however, could only be of a limited character, and would still leave the essentials of English

---

[1] AL4, pp. 381–87.
[2] The full list is in AL4, pp. 401–02.
[3] Recent Trends in English Linguistics, *Modern Language Quarterly*, June, 1940, p. 180. In the same paper, p. 181, Kennedy complains that "it is only quite recently that students of English have begun to make careful and detailed studies of important phases of the history of English spelling, and, to our shame, they have been foreign, chiefly German, students."

spelling intact. When all is said against it that can be said, it is well to bear in mind that it has now stood the test of three centuries, and in spite of all its alleged defects has not prevented English from attaining the world-wide position it now holds.[1]

In another paper Craigie called attention to an impediment that nearly all spelling reformers have passed over too casually:

> The question of the possibility or advantage of change becomes more difficult when the normalized spelling would reduce to a common form those homophones which at present are differentiated and on that account are immediately recognizable.[2] If the postal *mail* were respelled as *male*, the meaning of *male carriers* might well be in doubt in certain contexts, and if *sew* became *sow* it would not only eliminate a useful distinction but would add a third homograph to the noun *sow*.[3] This problem, of course, applies to all homophones with distinctive spellings, whether these have etymological justification or not. They form indeed one of the features of the English vocabulary which have to be taken seriously into account before it can be decided whether the present orthography can be usefully modified or replaced by one on a more phonetic basis.[4]

Craigie concludes that phonetic spelling is not necessarily possible to *all* languages. " Irish and Scottish Gaelic," he says, " are as far from being phonetically written as they could well be, but any one familiar with either form of the language knows how unintelligible they can become when any attempt is made to replace the conventional historic orthography by one which aims at representing the actual sounds." He also cites the case of Faeröese, an archaic Scandinavian dialect spoken on the desolate Faeroe Islands, 200 miles north of the Shetlands. When this language was first reduced to writing, toward the close of the Eighteenth Century, use was made of " an orthography which as far as possible represented the actual pronunciation," but it produced such uncouth effects that, after an experience of half a century, it was " replaced by a spelling closely based upon Icelandic." " That a phonetic spelling," says Craigie, " should in this way have been abandoned in favor of a historic after a fair trial is evidence that the value of the one or the other may depend upon the nature of the language to which they are applied." [5]

[1] Problems of Spelling Reform, S.P.E. Tract No. LXIII, 1944, p. 75.
[2] e.g., *to, too* and *two*.
[3] The English Simplified Spelling Society turns both *male* and *mail* into *mael* and both *to sew* and *to sow* into *soe*.
[4] Some Anomalies of Spelling, S.P.E. Tract No. LIX, 1942, p. 331.
[5] Some Anomalies of Spelling, just cited, p. 332.

Craigie hints that English is one of the languages which resist the phonetizing process, and for two reasons. The first is that it is made up of words coming from widely different sources — "the native, Romanic, classical and exotic" —, and each element has brought in its own traditions in spelling. If, in a proposed spelling reform scheme,

> the native standard is adopted, much of the Romanic and classical element becomes unrecognizable, e.g., if *seed* is taken as the natural representation of the sounds *s, ee, d*, then *cede* and *recede* must become *seed* and *reseed*. If *mesh* is normal, then both *cession* and *session* must become *seshon*, and *fissure* will fall together with *fisher*.[1] On the other hand if the Romanic and classical *fuse* or *muse* is taken as a model, then *news* will be *nuse*, and *huse* would represent both *hues* and the third person singular of the verb *hew*.[2]

The second obstacle lies in the fact that many of the commonest words in the language have traditional spellings that could not be changed without offending the eye and causing confusion. "No one will deny," says Craigie, "that . . . *ake, coff, enuff, enny, wimmen, tung, shure* and *berry* are better representation of the sounds of *ache, cough, enough, any, women, tongue, sure* and *bury* than the conventional spellings. The trouble is that to all who have a fair knowledge of orthography such forms, instead of being recognized as improvements, suggest only ignorance and illiteracy,[3] since they are such as would occur to anyone whose schooling had been decidedly imperfect."[4] A third difficulty lies in the fact that many words are pronounced differently in England and the United States, and even in different parts of the same country. There is, for example, *schedule*, which would have to be *shedyul* or something of the sort in England and *skedyul* in America. Again, there is *ci* in

---

[1] The Dictionary of New Spelling issued by the Simplified Spelling Society duly converts *cede* into *seed, recede* into *reseed* or *reesede*, both *cession* and *session* into *seshon*, and *fissure* into *fisher* or *fishuer*.

[2] Problems of Spelling Reform, before cited, p. 57. The Dictionary of New Spelling converts *news* into *nuez*, and both *hues* and *hews* into *huez*.

[3] This is true even when the writer is a learned man. I offer, for example, a few extracts from Albrecht von Haller and English Theology, by Lawrence Marsden Price, professor of German at the University of California, *Publications of the Modern Language Association*, Dec., 1926, pp. 942-54: "Shaftesbury . . . certainly *brot* the moral sense into prominence. . . . Haller used the same figure to express the same *thot*. . . . It is clear *enuf*. . . ."

[4] The Dictionary of New Spelling makes them *aek, kof, enuf, wimen, tung, shuur* and *bery*. The Simplified Spelling Board's Handbook of Simplified Spelling makes them *ak(e), cof, enuf, tung, sure* and *berri*. I can't find any substitute for *women* on its list.

such words as *association*, which would be *shy* in England and *si* in Scotland.[1] Said George Sampson, a retired inspector of school for the London County Council and formerly honorary secretary of the English Association:

> Radical reform in spelling means the exact phonetic representation of pronunciation. But whose pronunciation? There is Scottish English, Irish English, Welsh English, and American English of numerous kinds. There is even English English, of which I will offer some specimens.
>
> I was recently talking to some eminent persons about education. One spoke of "the *grät* (*ä* as in German) *vahyoo* of the *clahssics*," and mentioned "*Ahthuns*"; another spoke of "the *greet velyiew* of the *clessics*," and mentioned "*Ethins*"; a third thought it "a *gret shem* that the *univahsities* should *conten* so *mach infairior matairiel*." And the other day a lady told me she was "*afred bebby hed* a *pen* and *mäst hev gert* a *curled*."
>
> Well, there are a few specimens of "educated English." Again I ask, Whose pronunciation is to be represented in any *nu* spelling?[2]

The Dictionary of New Spelling conceals this difficulty by disregarding many of the pronunciations of standard English. Thus it renders *iron* as *iern*, *door* as *dor* and *carve* as *karv*, though the late Robert Bridges showed so long ago as 1919 that *iron* has become *ion* in England, *door* has become *daw*, and both *carve* and *calve* have become *caa'v*.[3] Bridges listed many other pronunciations that must strike an American not of the Southern Tidewater or the Boston area as strange, *e.g.*, *board*, *bored* and *bawd* as *bawd*; *hoar*, *whore* and *haw* as *haw*; *cork* and *caulk* as *cawk*, *lorn* and *lawn* as *lawn*, *source* and *sauce* as *sauce*, *stalk* and *stork* as *stawk*, *taut*, *tort* and *taught* as *taut*, and *saw*, *soar* and *sore* as *saw*. He also added *broach* and *brooch*, *desert* and *dessert*, *whoop* and *hoop*, *geyser* and *gazer*, *verdure* and *verger*, *reach* and *retch*, and *tray* and *trait* as homonyms, though they are certainly not so in General American. His search of the NED revealed 505 homonyms altogether, embracing 1075 words, but many of his pairs included words seldom encountered, *e.g.*, *acta-actor*, *wot-what*, *glose-glows*, *pyx-picks*, *cozen-*

---

[1] Simplified Spelling, London *Times Literary Supplement*, May 31, 1941.
[2] Reforms in Spelling, London *Times*, Feb. 26, 1936. I am indebted here to the late F. H. Tyson, of Hong Kong. Said Louise Pound in British and American Pronunciation, *School Review*, June, 1915, p. 393: "If one nation and not another simplified its spelling, or if different systems for reform were adopted by the two, or if both speeches were spelled phonetically, what severance already exists would be emphasized. They would differ to the eye as they already do to the ear. The process once started might be more rapid if the anchor of fixed spelling were torn loose."
[3] On English Homophones, *S.P.E. Tract No. II*, 1919, p. 14.

cousin, plaice-place, and *chase* (grove)-*chase* (printer's). He showed that phonetic spelling would greatly increase their number, but he professed, though without any show of surety, to be undaunted by that fact, for he argued that in the case of the average man, " as he learns new words, there will be a tendency, if not a necessity, for him to lose hold of a corresponding number of his old words, and the words that will first drop out will be those with which he had hitherto been uncomfortable, and among those words will be the words of ambiguous meaning." But all that this comes to is the doctrine that an increase in homonyms would lead to a corresponding impoverishment of the vocabulary.[1]

Though himself an advocate of a simplified spelling scheme, Bridges ended with this anticipation of Craigie:

> The complexity of [phonetic spelling] has driven off public sympathy and dashed the confidence of scholars, withdrawing thereby some of the wholesome checks that common sense might else have imposed on its practical exponents. The experts thus left to themselves, in despair of any satisfactory solution, are likely enough to adopt the simplifications most agreeable to their present ideas, and measure the utility of such simplifications by the accidental conveniences of their own science, independently of other considerations.[2]

Some years ago the London *Observer* sought to resolve the matter by advocating free trade in spelling. If a word is spelled so that it is instantly recognizable, what difference does it make, after all, *how* it is spelled? George Bernard Shaw, despite his puckish advocacy, in his hortatory moments, of an entirely new and impossible alphabet, was content to use the present alphabet in a free and easy manner in his ordinary writing, and I have myself, in my humbler way, found the same system to be comfortable and rewarding. It is, in fact, followed by the overwhelming majority of other Americanos, and by multitudes in the effete United Kingdom, and it works very well. Everyone can understand a policeman when he turns in a report of a *larsensy* or an applicant for a job when he

---

[1] Bridges listed a number of homonyms that have dropped out of English since Shakespeare's time, *e.g., neat* (an ox), *pill* (to plunder), *rede* (counsel), *ear* (to plow) and *speed* (aid), and also a few that he believed were in process of passing out in 1919, *e.g., cruse, clime, gambol, mien, rheum, wile, wrack* and *teem.*

[2] On English Homophones, before cited, p. 42. The most comprehensive study of homonyms is The Conflict of Homonyms in English, by Edna Rees Williams; New Haven, 1944. It is reviewed by Rudolph Willard in *American Speech,* Feb., 1945, pp. 61–62.

alleges that he is a licensed *chuffer, shoffer* or even *shofar*.[1] "Correct" spelling, indeed, is one of the arts that are far more esteemed by schoolma'ams than by practical men, neck-deep in the heat and agony of the world.

In Canada English spelling survives more or less, supported by the authority of the King's Printer,[2] but many American forms are in common use in the newspapers, *e.g., curb* and *tire*.[3] Indeed, the Printer himself sanctions *jail, aluminum, forever, net, program, story, wagon* and even *alright*, though he clings tightly to *draughtsman, mould, whisky,* and the *-our* and *-re* endings.

4. THE TREATMENT OF LOAN-WORDS

Sir William Craigie, in one of the papers I was lately quoting,[4] speaks of "the universal prejudice against accents in English," and says that "even if printers did not rebel against them they are yet distasteful and deterrent to readers out of all proportion to their complexity." This prejudice, I believe, is even more marked in the United States than it is in England, and as a result very few American newspapers make any effort to use the correct accents on foreign words. Said the editor of the *Editor & Publisher*, the chief journal of the newspaper trade, in 1939:

> Names like *führer, Göring, Brüning* become *fuehrer, Goering, Bruening* and so forth, while less famous names like *Dürer* usually become simply *Durer. Cañon* has been Americanized as *canyon*, but *mañana* becomes *manana*, not *manyana*, and *Azaña* gets into most American print as *Azana*, not *Azanya*. To Spaniards and Latin Americans, French and Germans and Scandinavians the diacritical marks are integral parts of the words, and their omission is as offensive as a gross misspelling is to an educated American. Not many newspaper offices, however, have these marks in their matrix fonts, and not many more have the time to spot them in from the pi channel, except in extraordinary circumstances.[5]

The *Editor & Publisher* apparently follows the procession, for on dipping into it at random I find *blaetter* in half a minute.[6] I turn to

---

1 Sojers Shad Lite on Simpul Spallin, by Raphael Avellar, New York *World-Telegram*, Jan. 9, 1946.
2 Preparation of Copy for the Printer, prepared and published under the authority of F. A. Acland, King's Printer; fifth edition; Ottawa, 1928.
3 A Note on Canadian Speech, by Morley Ayearst, *American Speech*, Oct., 1939, p. 232.
4 On English Homophones, p. 43.
5 Shop Talk at Thirty, April 22, 1939, p. 84. See also Foreign Words, by H. L. Mencken, San Francisco *Examiner*, Dec. 3, 1934.
6 German Papers Near 4 Million, Sept. 28, 1946, p. 54.

the *Saturday Review of Literature* and find *smorgasbord* for the Swedish *smörgåsbord*.[1] I turn to *Variety* and find it spelling the French original of its own name *variete*, not *variété*.[2] I turn to — but no more examples are needed, for they are flung at the American reader in endless number. At least one American newspaper, indeed, has declared categorically that accents, like italics, are unnecessary. There was a time, it says,

> when they were widely used. In the days when all type was set by hand, perhaps no great delay was occasioned by this practice, but when the type-setting machines came into general use, not to mention typewriters, both italics and accents were for the most part placed on the shelf. It would seem no possible benefit can be derived from reviving or expanding the use of accents. Few American readers will know the significance, whether it is attached to a place name or some common word in French, Spanish or whatever.[3]

I should add that this iconoclasm, while general, is by no means universal. The Baltimore *Sunpapers*, at least in theory, use the proper diacritical marks on all accented foreign words that have not been naturalized,[4] and the New York *Herald Tribune* uses them in " art, dramatic, editorial, literary and musical copy, and the Sunday fashion page." [5] Even the Chicago *Tribune*, despite its long-continued attempts to inflict simplified spelling on its readers, is orthodox when it comes to foreign words, and instructs its copy-readers (with what success I do not know) to put accents on *fête, façade, confrère, cortège, entrée, männerchor, portière, garçon, Maréchal Niel, Théâtre Français, Honoré* and *Götterdämmerung*.[6] The Government Printing Office favors naturalizing loans as soon as possible, and thus ordains *blase, boutonniere, brassiere, cafe, crepe, debut, de-*

1 S. J. P.'s Ilks, by Phil Stong, Sept. 21, 1946, p. 23.
2 Scully's Scrapbook, by Frank Scully, Jan. 17, 1945, p. 2. This article includes some interesting contributions to the history of *vaudeville*.
3 Rome (N.Y.) *Sentinel*, editorial, June 21, 1944.
4 The necessary linotype matrices were laid in by the *Evening Sun* in 1914 or thereabout. I was at that time a member of the editorial staff of the paper, and had been carrying on an intra-office campaign for their purchase since 1910. It took about five years to induce the copy-desk and proof-room to use them. The morning *Sun* followed ten or eleven years later. It was a long and bitter battle, and left me pretty well exhausted.
5 Style Book of the New York *Herald Tribune*, 1929, p. 2. On Dec. 25, 1938 it printed a Christmas editorial in which the following words all had accents: *marzipän, turrón, pfeffernüsse, gemüthlichkeit, crèche, Père Noël* and *Nürnberg*. This probably broke all American newspaper records. I am indebted here to Mr. Valdemar Viking, of Red Bank, N. J.
6 Chicago *Tribune* Rules of Composition, 1934, pp. 8-9.

collete, entree, facade, fete, melee, naive, nee, role and *roue,* but it still uses accents on *abbé, attaché, canapé, chargé d'affaires, communiqué, déjeuner, étude, fiancée, mañana, métier, pâté, précis, résumé, risqué, señor* and *vis-à-vis.*[1] The State Department, having a great deal of correspondence with foreigners, puts accents on all of these and also on *naïve.*[2] It uses *visa* instead of *visé,* which lingers on in England, but the French themselves have made the same change.[3] In England, as I have indicated, accents are used more frequently than in the United States, but even there a movement against them is visible. So long ago as November, 1923, the Society for Pure English prepared a list of foreign words that seemed ripe for complete naturalization, and it was adopted by the London *Times*, the London *Mercury* and other high-toned publications. It included *confrere, depot, levee, role* and *seance.*[4] Of these *levee* appeared without accents in Noah Webster's first dictionary in 1806, and *depot* and *seance* in his American Dictionary of 1828.

412. [Dr. Louise Pound notes that a number of Latin plurals tend to become singular nouns in colloquial American.] They are to be found plentifully, in fact, upon higher levels. I have encountered *data* in the singular in the *Congressional Record*,[5] in the *Saturday Review of Literature,*[6] and in a headline in the New York *Herald Tribune.*[7] In the *Editor & Publisher* I have found *media* used to designate one newspaper;[8] in the *Étude,* the Bible of all small-town music teachers, I have found *tympani* used for one drum;[9] and in *Life* I once found *Americana* used as a singular by the late William Allen White.[10] Dr. Pound long ago reported that *dicta, insignia, strata, criteria, curricula* and *phenomena* were coming into use as singulars

---

1 United States Government Printing Office Style Manual, revised edition, Jan., 1945, p. 49.
2 Style Manual of the Department of State, by Margaret M. Hanna and Alice M. Ball; Washington, 1937, p. 113.
3 Cassell's New French-English English-French Dictionary, edited by Ernest A. Barker; New York, 1930, p. 563.
4 S.P.E. Tract No. XXII, 1925, p. 65.
5 Extension of Remarks of Hon. Francis Case, of South Dakota, Nov. 23, 1945, p. A5440.
6 Two examples are on p. 9, Aug. 7, 1937, and a third is noted in Latin Plurals, by Mamie Meredith, *American Speech*, Oct., 1937, p. 178.
7 The headline was: Delay in Arms Merger Decision is Urged Until More Data is In. Someone must have squawked in the office, for in later editions this was changed to the equivocal Delay in Arms Merger Decision Urged Until There is More Data. I am indebted here to Mr. Alexander Kadison.
8 Censor's Office Discusses Rules of Advertising, March 7, 1942, p. 8.
9 Drum Hunt, Jan., 1944, p. 10.
10 The Hulls of Tennessee, April 8, 1940: "I have never seen a better *Americana.*"

American Spelling

among Americans of some education,[1] and since then she has added *emporia, memoranda, ganglia, stimuli, literati* and *alumni*,[2] and other pathologists of speech have added *propaganda*,[3] *agenda, arcana, nebulæ, meninges, bacilli, bacteria, automata, candelabra* and *sanitaria*. As for *data* it is so widespread that even Webster 1934 recognizes it, saying "although plural in form it is not infrequently used as a singular, as, This *data* has been furnished for study and decision." In compensation for these barbarities there is an occasional resort to a pseudo-Latin plural, as in *prospecti* and *octopi*.[4]

The tendency to replace all non-English plurals with indigenous forms is not recent, but goes back many years. When *halo* came in during the Sixteenth Century the Latin plural *halones* was used, but by 1603 it had become *haloes* and by 1646 *halos*. Many respectable authorities argue that most of the surviving Latin plurals had better be dropped. In 1925, for example, Robert Bridges declared for *nebulas* in place of *nebulæ*, *vortexes* for *vortices*, *gymnasiums* for *gymnasia* and *dillettantes* for *dilettanti*, though allowing that *automata* and *memoranda* had better be retained, and *forci, formulæ* and *indices* "in their scientific sense."[5] In 1938 Carleton R. Ball[6] proposed a sweep of all the surviving Latin plurals, both in scientific terminology and everyday speech, on the ground that

> Learning is unlimited. Time and talent are limited. Whatever uses time and ability unnecessarily is wasteful and should be avoided. Avoidable irregularity and diversity in the construction of a language make demands on time and talent that might be employed more profitably.

Some of the plurals he advocated were *abscissas, antennas, lacunas, nebulas, mammas* (for *mammæ*), *diplomas* (for the technical *diplomata*), *sarcomas, traumas, lumens* (for *lumina*), *analysises, axises*,

---

[1] The Pluralization of Latin Loan-Words in Present-Day American Speech, *Classical Journal*, Dec., 1919, pp. 163–68.
[2] Plural Singulars From Latin Neuters, *American Speech*, Oct., 1927, pp. 26–27.
[3] Latin Plurals, by Mamie Meredith, *American Speech*, Oct., 1937, p. 178.
[4] I take the former from Dozen Periodicals Fold, *Variety*, June 23, 1937; the latter is ascribed to John Steinbeck in *Minimum? Minimis? Minima?*, by Ernest Fuld, *Saturday Review of Literature*, Jan. 20, 1945, p. 23. The true Latin plural of *prospectus* is the singular unchanged, and the plural of *octopus*, according to Dr. Fuld, is *octopodes*.
[5] *S.P.E. Tract No. XXII*, pp. 66–67.
[6] Dr. Ball is a distinguished botanist. He was attached to the Bureau of Plant Industry of the Department of Agriculture in 1928. In 1931 he went to the University of California. He has been editor for agronomy of *Biological Abstracts* since 1926.

parenthesises, thesises, apexes, matrixes, testatrixes, vortexes, crisises, bacteriums, honorariums, criterions, agendums, erratums,[1] *stratums, bacilluses, funguses, polypuses, genuses, femurs, coccuses, focuses* and *colossuses*.[2] He was unable to find plausible English plurals for *caput, os, vas* and *corpus,* and some of his inventions, *e.g., synthesises* and *nymphæums,* were somewhat clumsy, but he was confident that he was on the right track. "Let us take these logical steps," he concluded, "in simplifying our English construction of plural nouns, and encourage others to take them. The gain will be great." The editors of the *Journal of the American Medical Association,* two years later, hinted that something of the sort was afoot in their art and mystery. "The most unpopular plural for a medical writer to accept at the hands of a manuscript editor," they said, "is the plural of *epididymis,* which is not *epididymes* but *epididymides.* Authors are so grudging, so reluctant, to accept this form that it betrays a bias in favor of the shorter spelling."[3] But the editors held out for *epididymides,* and in the same note declared that the true plural of *appendicitis* is *appendicitides,* and of *bronchitis bronchitides.* In their style book[4] they permit *appendixes, enemas, fibromas, gummas, spirochetes, serums* and *traumas,* but insist on *bronchi, criteria, foci, protozoa, sequelæ, stigmata* and *vertebræ.* Every now and then someone starts a crusade against loan-words that seem to be unnecessary, *e.g., questionnaire, per* instead of *a* in *per year,* etc.,[5] but it seldom comes to anything. The changes undergone in the process of naturalization are often curious. The case of *smearcase* (Ger. *schmierkäse*) is familiar. In a travel article published in 1876 the Japanese *jinricksha* appears as *djinrichia, geisha* is *guecha* and *samurai* is *samourai*.[6]

5. PUNCTUATION, CAPITALIZATION, AND ABBREVIATION

413. [In the first draft of the Declaration of Independence *nature* and *creator,* and even *god* are in lower case.] Sometimes, indeed,

1 Why not *errors?*
2 English or Latin Plurals for Anglicized Latin Nouns?, *American Speech,* April, 1928, pp. 291–325.
3 Plurals of Nouns Ending in *-itis,* July 26, 1930, p. 287.
4 Suggestions to Medical Authors; Chicago, 1919, p. 32.
5 In 1944 the Archbishop of Armagh wrote to the London *Times* denouncing *questionnaire* and proposed *questionary* in its place. Questionnaire, Liverpool *Daily Post,* July 1, 1944.
6 The Japanese Stage, *Galaxy,* Jan., 1876, pp. 76, 78 and 79 respectively.

American Spelling

small letters appear at the beginning of sentences and even paragraphs.[1] But Franklin, a conservative in this field as in so many others, stuck to capitals for all nouns, whether proper or common, to the end of his days, and wrote to Noah Webster from his deathbed, in 1789, protesting against the growing use of small letters. He said:

> In examining the English Books that were printed between the Restoration and the Accession of George the 2nd [2] we may observe that all Substantives were begun with a capital, in which we imitated our Mother Tongue, the German. This was more particularly useful to those who were not well acquainted with the English, there being such a prodigious Number of Words that are both Verbs and Substantives and spelt in the same manner, tho' often accented differently in Pronunciation. This Method has, by the Fancy of Printers, of late Years been laid aside, from an Idea that suppressing the Capitals shows the Character to greater Advantage, those Letters prominent above the Line disturbing its even regular Appearance.[3]

Charles J. Lovell, an assiduous delver into early American language records, tells me that the abandonment of capitals was apparently a function of the Revolution. "Beginning with Lexington and Concord," he says, "upper case letters were removed even from *Christianity* and the names of the various religious sects and political parties."[4] By 1791, a year after Franklin's death, the *American Museum* of Philadelphia was reducing all honorifics, including even *Mr.*, to lower case,[5] and using such forms as *six nations, bank of the United States, vice-president of the United States,* and *satan*. By the 1830s, as examples in the DAE show, *whig, tory* and *federalist* were usually l.c., though *Constitution* remained caps. Lovell sends me an extract from the Ohio Almanac (Cincinnati) for 1814 showing

---

1 The Declaration of Independence: the Evolution of the Text, by Julian P. Boyd; Princeton, 1945, pp. 19–21.
2 The English Restoration took place in 1660; George II ascended the throne in 1727.
3 Franklin's Vocabulary, by Lois Margaret MacLaurin; Garden City (N.Y.), 1929, p. 44. In this same letter Franklin denounced also the "fancy" that had lately "induced some Printers to use the short round *s* instead of the long one." The long *s* died hard. In Vol. I of the *Monthly Magazine and American Review* for 1800, Jan.–June, the longs and the shorts were still fighting it out.
4 Private communication, Oct. 28, 1945.
5 In its Sept. issue, p. 114, it put *dr.* before the name of Franklin himself, dead only a year! See AL4, pp. 413–14, for the use of *baron, colonel,* etc., before proper names by the Cambridge History of English Literature. Mr. Theodore E. Norton, librarian of Lafayette College, calls my attention to the fact that this is standard practise in preparing American library cards.

protestant episcopal church, methodist meeting house, quaker, jupiter, saturn and *venus*. He says that "just before the Civil War caps were coming back,[1] *State* was always capitalized, and personal names were written in small capitals."[2] At present there is considerable variation in the practise of American newspapers. The Chicago *Tribune* uses lower case for *company, union, university, board, hospital, bank, church, corporation*, etc., following proper names, but makes a curious exception in favor of *Line*, as in *Seaboard Air Line*, and *Foundation*, as in *Rockefeller Foundation*. The Baltimore *Sunpapers* capitalize all of these words. They use caps for the *Constitution* of the United States, but lower case for that of the States, including Maryland. They capitalize *Government, Administration* and *Cabinet*, as does the Providence *Journal-Bulletin*. Very few newspapers capitalize the names of the seasons, those of the points of the compass, or the numerical designations of centuries. All capitalize the names of *God* and His divine associates, and all pronouns referring to them save those beginning with *w*, but these pronouns are not capitalized in direct quotations from the King James Bible, where they are all l.c. Nearly all American publications now capitalize *Negro*.[3] The London *Times* still capitalizes *Street, Road, Crescent*, etc., and prints them as separate words; other English newspapers give them the form of *Park-lane, Bond-street*, etc.,[4] sometimes with the second element abbreviated to *-st., -rd.*, etc.[5] In the United States abbreviations are most commonly used, without capitals.

There is evidence of a Catholic campaign to induce American newspapers to capitalize *mass*. In the *Editor & Publisher*, in 1945, a letter appeared saying that capitalizing the word "would be regarded by Catholics as a gesture of understanding," and appealing to

---

[1] But Abraham Lincoln, in a letter written during the early part of the Winter of 1864-5, was still using small letters for the names of the days of the week, though he wrote *President*.

[2] That is, in caps and small caps. This custom survives on the editorial pages of the New York *Times*, the Philadelphia *Bulletin*, the Minneapolis *Journal* and various other old-fashioned newspapers. I am indebted here to Messrs. Carl B. Costello, of Duluth, Minn.; Douglas McPherson, of Philadelphia, and Theodore W. Bozarth, of Mount Holly, N. J.

[3] Supplement I, pp. 618-26.

[4] I am indebted here to Mr. R. E. Swartwout, of Cambridge.

[5] This leads to occasional uncouthness, *e.g., St. James's-street, Gray's Inn-rd.* and *Red Lion-square*. I am indebted here to Mr. Leslie Charteris, of Weybridge.

the editor thereof to "bring the matter to the newspaper field."[1] The writer thus stated the theological reason for his request:

> The Catholic Church teaches that Christ is present in the Mass as He was in the Last Supper, not in a representative way, but really, truly and substantially. This teaching is based on the words used by Christ, "This is My body" over the bread, and over the wine, "This is the chalice of My blood."[2] Thus, in the Mass, Christ is present as He was on Calvary, making the Mass and Calvary synonymous, and since Christ is a Divine Person and the Mass is Christ, in an unbloody manner, references indicating Christ are properly capitalized, *e.g., Son, Saviour, Mass* or *Lord*.

The Authors' and Printers' Dictionary, the standard British authority, ordains that in writing dates "the order shall be day, month, year as *5 June 1903*, not *June 5, 1903*,"[3] and this is usually followed by the English in letters. But in other situations they commonly make the order month, day, year.[4] The latter is the usual American practise, but during World War II the War Department came out for day, month, year,[5] and even before that the form had been in more or less use in both the Army and the Navy.[6] Not, however, in the other departments at Washington. The latest edition of the Style Manual of the Government Printing Office[7] ordains *July 30, 1914*, and even the State Department, which is otherwise excessively English, uses the same form.[8] There was a time when the English used a comma instead of a period (which they call a *full stop*) to divide the hours from the minutes in figures indicating times of the

---

[1] Capital *M*, by Robert C. Morrow, April 7, p. 68.
[2] Matthew XXVI, 26–28. The text quoted is that of the Douay Bible.
[3] In French, as the Dictionary notes (seventh edition, 1933, p. 84), the order is *5 Juin 1903* and in German *5 Juni 1903*. It will be noted that no comma appears after the name of the month.
[4] I turn, for example, to the London *Times*, Aug. 12, 1946, and find *August 12 1946* (no comma after *12*) in the flagstaff of the paper, *Aug. 12, 1944* in an In Memoriam notice, *September 14, 1946* in a legal notice, *Aug. 11* (no year) in the date-lines of many news dispatches, and *July 13, 1946* in a wedding announcement, though *31st August, 1946* appears in another legal notice.
[5] *New Yorker*, Sept. 16, 1944, p. 11;

American Notes & Queries, June, 1946, p. 40.
[6] I am told by a correspondent that when Rear Admiral Samuel McGowan, ret. (1870–1934), formerly paymaster-general of the Navy, became chief highway commissioner of his native South Carolina he ordered the use of *8 October, 1926* by his subordinates. But they went back to the usual American order after he left office.
[7] Revised edition, Jan., 1945, p. 139.
[8] Style Manual of the Department of State; Washington, 1937, p. 215. For discussions of the War Department order see *The Pleasures of Publishing* (a weekly press-sheet published by the Columbia University Press), July 15 and July 29, 1946.

day, *e.g.*, 7,25, but now they commonly use a period as we do, with the *a.m.* or *p.m.* following in small letters.[1]

In the use of the hyphen English practise and American practise seem to be substantially identical, though the English employ it in proper names rather more than we do, *e.g.*, *Stoke-on-Trent, Weston-under-Lizard, Weston-super-Mare, Ossett-cum-Gawthorpe, Hore-Belisha* and *Plunkett-Ernle-Erle-Drax*.[2] There is an elaborate and excellent discussion of hyphenization in "Compounding in the English Language," by Alice Morton Ball, one of the compilers of the Style Manual of the Department of State.[3] It includes a review of all the principal dictionaries, style books and grammars, with an attempt to set up rational rules. Like most other writers on the subject, Miss Ball makes a distinction between compounds used as nouns and the same used as adjectives. The former she prefers to leave separate, *e.g.*, *paper mill* and *holding company*, but the latter she hyphenates, *e.g.*, *paper-mill employee* and *holding-company bond*. This is the practise of most American newspapers. She prefers no hyphen in such compound titles as *vice president* and *under secretary*, but advises its use when prefixes or affixes are added, *e.g.*, *ex-vice-president* and *under-secretaryship*. She also recommends it when its absence might cause misunderstanding or mispronunciation, and when there is an inconvenient cluster of vowels or consonants, as in *bee-eater, egg-gatherer* and *brass-smith*. She prefers using a hyphen in *good-by* (Eng. *good-bye*), but it is my impression that *goodby* is supplanting *good-by* in the United States, as *today* and *tomorrow* have long supplanted *to-day* and *to-morrow*.[4] Of late there has been a tendency among American newspapers to amalgamate *-man* with a long series of nouns that were formerly separated, *e.g.*, *garbageman* and *newspaperman*. This, it seems to me, is irrational and confusing. In cases where the *-man* has been reduced to *-m'n* in pronunciation, *e.g.*, *workman, batsman* and even *longshoreman*, making one word of the compound is plainly allowable, but where the *-man* is still clearly enunciated, as in *garbage man, newspaper man, working man* and *end man* the most that can

---

[1] Authors' & Printers' Dictionary, seventh edition; London, 1933, p. 370.
[2] AL4, p. 502, n. 4.
[3] New York, 1939.
[4] Reginald Skelton, in Modern English Punctuation; London, 1933, p. 65, says that *tomorrow* is also "in regular use" in England. The Authors' & Printers' Dictionary, however, still ordains *to-morrow*, and likewise *to-day*.

be reasonably allowed is a hyphen.[1] Jacques Barzun has printed an eloquent protest against the excessive amalgamation of words that had better be kept separate,[2] listing some of the horrors that he has encountered, *e.g., picturegallery, hardshelled, fifteenyearold, ultraaustere, nonessential* and *midsummermadness*.[3] He adds a *reductio ad absurdum* in the form of a version of the Gettysburg Address beginning "*Fourscoreandseven years ago ourfathers broughtforth* . . ."[4]

Such a form as *St. James-place* would seem barbarous to an Englishman: he sticks to the possessive, and writes *St. James's-place* or *-pl*. In the United States the apostrophe seems to be doomed, for the Board on Geographical Names has swept it out of such old forms as *Prince George's* and *Queen Anne's* (counties in Maryland), and it has been dropped from the title of *Teacher's* College, Columbia, the Lhasa of American pedagogy.[5] In other respects American and English punctuation show few differences. The English are rather more careful than we are, and commonly put a comma after the next-to-the-last member of a series,[6] but otherwise are not too

[1] Some of the inevitable inconsistencies in Miss Ball's scheme are pointed out by Robert J. Menner in Compounding, *American Speech*, Dec., 1939, pp. 300–02.
[2] Unhyphenated American, *Nation*, Sept. 5, 1942, pp. 194–95.
[3] I add *sweetpotato* from the *Congressional Record*, April 2, 1946, p. 3050.
[4] The inconsistencies in Webster 1934 are reviewed by Miss Ball, pp. 9-11, and also in Note on Websterian Orthography, *Prairie Schooner*, Summer, 1946, p. 152. See also Hyphenation of Compound Words, by Arthur G. Kennedy, *Words*, March, 1938, pp. 36–38. H. W. Fowler's ideas on the subject, first set forth in *S.P.E. Tract No. VI*, 1921, pp. 3–13, are to be found in his Modern English Usage; Oxford, 1926, pp. 243–48. A discussion of the differences between English and American printers' practises in the division of words at the ends of lines is in Word Division, by Kenneth Sisam, *S.P.E. Tract No. XXXIII*, 1929, pp. 441–42.
[5] It survives, however, in the names of many colleges named after saints, *e.g., St. Mary's*, Winona, Minn., though it may be dropped when it would be inconvenient, *e.g., St. Francis*, Brooklyn, and *St. Mary-of-the-Woods*, Indiana. A correspondent of *American Speech* (April, 1937, p. 121) calls attention to the fact that when the sex of the students is indicated in a college name the singular *woman's* is commonly used for a college for females and the plural *men's* for one for males. This, of course, is because *man's* would sound incongruous. But why not *women's*?
[6] This practise is discussed by Steven T. Byington in Certain Fashions in Commas and Apostrophes, *American Speech*, Feb., 1945, pp. 22–27, and also the habit, common among newspaper headline writers, of printing a series of nouns without any *and* at all, *e.g.*, Committee Hears Protests of Millionaire, Educator, Philanthropist.

precise to offend a red-blooded American. There are frequent proposals that the semi-colon be abandoned, though its utility must be manifest.[1] The Style Manual of the Government Printing Office is content to say of it that it "is to be avoided where a comma will suffice,"[2] and this is repeated by that of the Department of State.[3] Next to the semi-colon, quotation marks seem to be the chief butts of reformatory ardor. The fact that quotes within quotes are often confusing, and unhinge the minds of thousands of poor copy-readers every year, has fanned these flames. Also, there is frequent complaint that the marks themselves, as they stand, are unsightly, with demands for something better. During the 1890s Theodore L. De-Vinne (1828–1914), then the premier typographer of the United States, designed a new type-face, including new quotes, for the *Century Magazine*. They consisted of pairs of nested carets or small parentheses laid on their sides, with those pointing west used to open a quotation and those pointing east to close it, and were imitations of characters adopted by the Didots, famous French printers, at the end of the Eighteenth Century. In explaining them[4] he said:

> When British printers decided to use quotation marks their type-founders had no characters for the purpose and did not make them. Whether this refusal was due to the unwillingness of the British printers to pay for a new character or to the prevalent dislike of everything French cannot be decided. All we know is that they decided to imitate them with the unfit characters in stock.

The DeVinne quotation marks were first used in the *Century* for November, 1895. No other publication adopted them, and after a few years they were abandoned for the more familiar *inverted commas*.[5] In 1941 another innovator proposed, with equal lack of success, a mark that he described as follows:

> It is a symmetrical elbow bracket, the size of a caret opened out to a right angle. It is placed at the top of the line like the strokes of the [present] quotation mark. Its nook is turned toward the quotation, like the angles of parenthetical brackets. I have called it the Text-quote.[6]

[1] Modern English Punctuation, by Reginald Skelton; London, 1933, pp. 41–47. Topics of the Times, New York *Times*, July 13, 1942.
[2] p. 121.
[3] p. 203.
[4] The *Century's* Printer on the Century Type, *Century*, Dec., 1895, pp. 794–96.
[5] Still the English term for what we call *quotation marks* or *quotes*.
[6] The Text-quote, by Ernest Boll, *American Notes & Queries*, June, 1941, p. 36.

Most American newspapers print the names of other newspapers, when they can't avoid mentioning them, in Roman, enclosed in quotation marks, but the Government Printing Office prints them without the quotation marks.[1] The relatively few that use italics [2] go on to caps and small caps when they mention themselves. The *Editor & Publisher* follows the irrational and unlovely system of using italics the first time a given newspaper is mentioned in an article, and then putting it in Roman every time it is repeated. The same newspapers which print unnaturalized loan-words without accents also print them in Roman, *e.g.*, *communique, tete-a-tete, hofbrauhaus, gemutlichkeit* and *a la carte.* "Most American newspapers," says the Style Book (printed *Stylebook*) of the Baltimore *Sunpapers*, not without a touch of ablonogastrigolumpiosity, "do not use italics; they are not even mentioned in the majority of style books. We should make our better practise stand out by using them correctly." [3]

The difficulties that 100% Americans have with the plurals of loan-words, mentioned in Section 4 of this chapter, are matched by their difficulties with the plurals of certain native words. Is *buses* correct, or *busses?* This problem first engaged the learned men of England when the first motor-bus appeared at Oxford, and one of the dons thereof made a pretty little poem upon it. It spread to the United States soon afterward and has been debated ever since, with no conclusion. Webster 1926 said " pl. *busses* or *buses*," but Webster 1934 evaded the question by giving no plural at all. H. W. Fowler, in his "Modern English Usage," accounts for *buses* by saying that it "is still regarded as an abbreviation of the regular *omnibuses*," but expresses the opinion that "when *omnibus* is for-

---

1 Style Manual, revised edition, Jan., 1945, pp. 21 and 145.
2 Many papers, and perhaps most, have no italic linotype matrices. Instead they use black-face.
3 The reader interested in the history of English punctuation will find nourishment to his taste in Historical Backgrounds of Elizabethan and Jacobean Punctuation Theory, by Walter J. Ong, S. J., *Publications of the Modern Language Association*, June, 1944, pp. 349–60; The Punctuation of Shakespeare's Printers, by Raymond Macdonald Alden, the same, Sept., 1924, pp. 557–80, and Shakespeare's Punctuation, by P. Alexander, *Proceedings of the British Academy*, Vol. XXXI, 1945. So far as I know, there is no history of American punctuation. Down to a century ago it was marked by a heavy overuse of commas, now happily abandoned. For the present practise in series see The Serial Comma Before *and* and *or*, by R. J. McCutcheon, *American Speech*, Oct., 1940, pp. 250–54.

gotten (and *bus* is now more usual than *'bus*) doubtless *buses* will become, as it should, *busses*."[1] And what of the plurals of *attorney-general* and its cognates? All the handbooks of "correct" English that I am aware of ordain adding the *s* to the first element, but *State Government*, the official organ of the Council of State Governments, puts it at the end.[2] Again, is the plural of *roof roofs* or *rooves? Proofs* pulls one way and *hooves* another. The NED finds *roofes* in 1600 and *roofs* in "Paradise Regained," 1671, but *roovis* in 1445. Yet again, is it *spoonsful* or *spoonfuls, brothers-in-law* or *brother-in-laws, Misses Smith* or *Miss Smiths?* Most authorities declare for the first of each of these pairs, but the others are undoubtedly in wide use. No less an authority than Sir William Craigie says that *sisteren* or *sistren*, now confined to the Christians, white and black, of the Get-Right-with-God Country, was common in Middle English and is just as respectable, etymologically speaking, as *brethren*. He also says that down to the Seventeenth Century *grieves* was the plural of *grief* and *strives* of *strife*.[3] Certain plurals of words ending in *-th*, though their spelling is established, present problems in pronunciation, e.g., *wreath*. Should the *th* of *wreaths* be that of *think* or that of *this?*[4] The plurals of the names of birds and animals have long engaged orthographers, and they still show a considerable difference of opinion. Webster's New International Dictionary, second ed., pp. 1896–7, says that there are four classes of them, as follows:

1. Those which use a plural differing from the singular, e.g., *bird* and its compounds, *dog, goat, mouse, owl* and *rat*. But when some of these words are preceded by *wild, native, sea, mountain*, etc., they may be unchanged in the plural, e.g., *wild pig, native horse* and *band of musk ox*.

2. Those which take plural forms in ordinary speech, but may be used in the singular "in the language of those who hunt or fish," e.g., *antelope, beaver, buffalo, duck, hare, muskrat, quail* and *fox*.

3. Those that are unchanged in form in the plural, e.g., *bison, deer, grouse, moose* and *sheep*.

4. Those that use a different plural form "only to signify diversity in kind or species," e.g., *trouts of the Rocky Mountains, fishes of the Atlantic*.[5]

[1] The varying practise of American magazine and newspaper was reviewed by Mamie Meredith in The Plural of *Bus, American Speech*, Aug., 1930, pp. 487–90. See also *Buses* or *Busses*, a powerful argument for the latter, by C. W. L. Johnson, New York *Herald Tribune*, editorial page, Dec. 6, 1940.
[2] *Attorney-Generals*, Jan., 1939.
[3] The Irregularities of English, *S.P.E. Tract No. XLVIII*, 1937, p. 287.
[4] The Plural of Nouns Ending in *-th*, by C. T. Onions, *S.P.E. Tract No. LXI*, 1943, pp. 19–28.
[5] Those Sporting Plurals; Washing-

American Spelling

Down to the advent of the New Deal the section on abbreviations, in the average American style book, filled only a few pages, and even the Style Manual of the Government Printing Office [1] exhausted the subject in six and a half. But now the number of them, chiefly emanating from Washington, is so enormous that the Manual refers its customers to a separate reference work, the United States Government Manual.[2] During the four years of American participation in World War II the Army and Navy spewed them out diligently, and so many new civil government agencies were set up, each with a long name and each name with an abbreviation, that no copy-reader in the country could keep up with them. Worse, more came pouring in from England and even more from Russia, and by 1945 George Erlie Shankle had assembled enough recognized abbreviations to fill a volume of 207 pages, set in small type in double columns.[3] The Russian contribution had found a recorder eight years before,[4] and that of the English helped fill a book of 104 pages by 1942.[5] All such volumes, alas, were incomplete, for new abbreviations came out faster than any press could run; moreover, the compilers, in sheer desperation, omitted many of the abbreviations used for the names of divisions, sub-divisions and ultradivisions in the new mobs of jobholders, *e.g.*, *EIDEBOEWABEW*,

---

ton, March, 1939. See also Predators Killing Off Game, by Ed Tyng, New York *Sun*, Jan. 25, 1946, in which both *fox* and *foxes* appear. Mr. Tyng, on inquiry, informed me (private communication, Jan. 30, 1946) that it is "increasingly common usage among anglers and hunters" to use the singular of *fox* and *skunk* in the plural, "as well as *deer*, *quail* and *grouse*." He said, however, that the singulars of *bear*, *rabbit*, *pheasant* and *squirrel* were not so used. He went on: "Fishermen use *trout*, *bass*, *perch*, *smelt*, *pickerel*, *pike*, *bluefish*, *shad*, etc., whether referring to one or many. *Muskellunge* (the name is spelled four or more ways) is used as both singular and plural, but the diminutive, *muskie* or *musky*, always becomes *muskies* in the plural. An angler never reports a catch of *eel* or *flounder*; it is always *eels* and *flounders*." In a report of George N. Dale, a high dignitary of the Newspaper Publishers Association, *Editor & Publisher*, Jan. 12, 1946, p. 8, I find "all mechanical *craft*" used twice. The use of *license*, *molasses*, etc., as plurals will be discussed in Chapter IX, Section 4.

1 Revised edition, March, 1933, pp. 55–61.
2 Style Manual, revised edition, Jan., 1945, p. 93.
3 Current Abbreviations; New York, 1945.
4 A List of Abbreviations Commonly Used in the U.S.S.R., compiled by George Z. Patrick; Berkeley (Calif.), 1937. This ran to 124 pp.
5 A Dictionary of Abbreviations, With Especial Attention to War-Time Abbreviations, by Eric Partridge, "with the able assistance of several other victims"; London, 1942.

which the *Editor & Publisher* reported in 1943 as the accepted abbreviation of *Economic Intelligence Division of the Enemy Branch of the Office of Economic Warfare Analysis of the Board of Economic Warfare*.[1]

How many such monstrosities were set afloat during the uproar no one will ever know, for many of them, like the pews at the public teat that they designated, had their names changed frequently. On April 7, 1943, the Hon. Earl C. Michener, a statistics-minded congressman from Michigan, filled nearly two columns of the *Congressional Record* with the names and their abbreviations of eighty-five high calibre lancets for bleeding taxpayers, ranging from the *Agricultural Adjustment Agency (AAA)* to the *War Shipping Administration (WSA)*.[2] Twelve days later the Hon. Walter E. Brehm, of Ohio, produced evidence [3] that the number had grown to ninety-two, and even while his list was being printed more were coming off the White House assembly line.[4] These, remember, were only major agencies, and the longest abbreviations recorded had only five letters, *e.g., OSFCW (Office of Solid Fuels Coördinator for War)*, and *PWRCB (President's War Relief Control Board)*. No wonder the newspapers and press associations began dropping the periods, and making all other possible condensations.[5] Thus the *W.A.A.C.* of 1942 became the *W.A.C.* of 1943 [6] and then the *WAC* or *Wac*. So early as 1939, in fact, the slaughter of periods had begun, and when J. S. Pope, managing editor of the Atlanta *Journal*, polled his fellow-editors on the subject in that year he found that the majority of them were in favor of it.[7] The New Deal saviors

---

1 *EIDEBOEWABEW*, Aug. 7, 1943.
2 pp. A1805–06.
3 *Congressional Record*, April 19, 1943.
4 When the United Nations organization was set up it began to add to the number, and by Oct. 21, 1946 its *Weekly Bulletin* was constrained to print a glossary. It included *ECITO (European Central Inland Transport Organization)*, *PICAO (Provisional International Civil Aviation Organization)*, *UNRRA (United Nations Relief and Rehabilitation Administration)* and *WHO (World Health Organization)*. The end, of course, is by no means yet.
5 William Hickey, the Walter Winchell of England, began reducing *U.S.A.* to *USA* in 1936, and his paper, the London *Daily Express*, on Aug. 29 of that year, announced that it would follow him. "We've dropped full-points in USA," it said, "because there's just no need for them; they're lumber in the way of a taut, streamlined style."
6 This change was made by the War Department when the WAAC became an actual part of the Army, the word *Auxiliary* being dropped.
7 Shop Talk at Thirty, by Arthur Robb, *Editor & Publisher*, April 22, 1939, p. 84. On March 29, 1947,

of humanity had barely got started by then, but there were plenty of other troublesome abbreviations, and the editors advocated taking the periods out of all of them, *e.g., CIO, TVA, CCC, GOP* and even *AFL.* "The *YMCA* informs us," wrote Lindsey Hoben of the Milwaukee *Journal,* "that it often drops the period nowadays and sees no possible objection to it. Neither *DAR* nor *WCTU* has protested our style."[1]

Meanwhile, the habit of making more or less pronounceable words of the new abbreviations, examples of which were provided by the Russian loan *Ogpu*[2] and the German *Nazi* and *Gestapo,* also began to spread. The English had already made a beginning in World War I with *Anzac* for *Australian and New Zealand Army Corps* and *Dora* for *Defense of the Realm Act;* in World War II they followed with *Mew* for *Ministry of Economic Warfare, Waaf* for a member of the *Women's Auxiliary Air Force Service; Wren* for a member of the *Women's Royal Naval Service,* and many another. The last-named, in fact, actually became official, and one of the ranks in the force, by the end of the war, was that of *Leading Wren.*[3]

---

in the same, p. 68, Robb reported that that majority had become almost unanimity.

[1] In its issue for May, 1933, p. 83, the *Delta Kappa Epsilon Quarterly* had been constrained to explain "for the benefit of recent initiates (and of some older dogs who have difficulty in learning new tricks)" that its name was made up of three Greek letters, and that when it was "written in English . . . there should be no periods after the letters."

[2] Defined as *Unified State Political Department* in a List of Abbreviations Commonly Used in the U.S.S.R., hitherto cited.

[3] Bits of Words, London *Times Literary Supplement,* Jan. 30, 1943.

IX

THE COMMON SPEECH

1. OUTLINES OF ITS GRAMMAR

My call for a comprehensive inductive grammar of the common speech of the United States, first made in a newspaper article in 1910 and repeated in piteous tones in AL1 in 1919, has never been answered by anyone learned in the tongues, though in the meantime philologists have given us searching studies of such esoteric Indian languages as Cuna, Chitamacha, Yuma and Klamath-Modoc, not to mention Eskimo.[1] There has even been an excellent grammar of Pennsylvania German, a decayed patois standing much further from standard High German than the American of an interstate truck-driver stands from the English of Walter Pater.[2] But while the wait has been going on for a savant willing to chart the vernacular in the grand manner there have at least been some approaches to the business by the writers on regional dialects — for example, Vance Randolph and Oma Stanley. Randolph, whose researches into the speech of the Ozark hillbillies have been noticed in Chapter VII, Section 4, points out that, in its grammatical structure, this speech is quite close to the underprivileged American norm,[3] and Stanley, whose examination of the dialect of East Texas has been dealt with in the same place, reports that "it is doubtful that anything will be found" there "that is not common to less well educated speakers everywhere in America."[4] Also, there has been an oblique attempt upon the common speech by I. E. Clark, who sought his materials,

[1] Most of these have appeared in the *International Journal of American Linguistics*, published by Indiana University under the auspices of the Linguistic Society of America, the American Anthropological Association, and a committee of the American Council of Learned Societies.
[2] A Simple Grammar of Pennsylvania Dutch, by J. William Frey; Clinton (S.C.), 1942.
[3] The Grammar of the Ozark Dialect, *American Speech*, Oct., 1927, p. 1.
[4] The Speech of East Texas, *American Speech Reprints and Monographs No. 2*; New York, 1937, p. 95.

not in the field but in the pages of that incomparable reporter, Ring Lardner.[1] Says Clark:

> The essence of Lardner's grammar is facility. His characters, like a great number of Americans, do not distinguish between the forms for the nominative and accusative case of pronouns, the preterite and past participle of the verb, and the comparative and superlative of the adjective. . . . The environment of the average [American] during his early years did not provide all the niceties of cultured English. School teachers tried desperately to improve his grammar, but they were unskilled in psychology, and their method was unconvincing. . . . He accepted the language spoken by his family, and by the friends he made before he started school. It was simple, it had lost useless forms, it permitted use of the handiest word. The language of the English teachers, enforced by the psychology of the Department of Education, only confused him.

That the grammar taught by these poor Holoferneses, male and female, is full of absurdities engendered by the medieval attempt to force English into the Procrustean bed of Latin was recognized by Noah Webster so long ago as 1789. "The most difficult task now to be performed by the advocates of pure English," he wrote in his "Dissertations on the English Language,"[2] "is to restrain the influence of men learned in Greek and Latin, but ignorant of their own tongue, who have labored to reject much good English because they have not understood the original construction of the language." And then: "They seem not to consider that grammar is formed on language, and not language on grammar. Instead of examining to find what the English language *is* they endeavor to show what it *ought to be* according to their rules."[3] Thomas Jefferson,

---

[1] An Analysis of Ring Lardner's American Language, or, Who Learnt You Grammar, Bud?; Austin (Texas), 1944. This is a thesis presented to the faculty of the graduate school of the University of Texas in partial fulfillment of the requirements for the degree of master of arts. It has not yet been printed, but I have had access to it by the courtesy of Mr. Clark. For Lardner see AL4, pp. 424–25. He founded a school that has included such sharp observers as Anita Loos and Damon Runyon, but its members would all agree, I am sure, that he was *facile princeps*.

[2] p. ix.

[3] p. 37. The extent to which the first English grammarians leaned upon Latin precedents is set forth in Early Application of Latin Grammar to English, by Sanford Brown Meech, *Publications of the Modern Language Association*, Dec., 1935, pp. 1012–32. All the technical terms that still survive were borrowed from the Latin, *e.g.*, *verb* (traced by the NED to 1388) from *verbum*, *noun* (1398) from *nomen*, *adjective* (1414) from *adjectivus*, *adverb* and *pronoun* (1530) from *adverbium* and *pronomen*, and to *parse* (1553) from *pars*. See also The Rules of Common School Grammars, by Charles C. Fries, *Publications of the*

with his invariable common sense, supported this on the plane of vocabulary in a letter to John Adams in 1820:

> Dictionaries are but the depositories of words already legitimated by usage. Society is the workshop in which new ones are elaborated. When an individual uses a new word, if ill-formed, it is rejected in society; if well formed, adopted, and after due time, laid up in the depository of dictionaries.

Unhappily, Webster's theory of the divine origin of language interfered with his excellent attempt to set up a truly inductive grammar, and when he passed from that theory to his doctrine of analogies he began to give considerable countenance to the pedants who sought to show what the language ought to be.[1] These pedants had the floor unchallenged throughout the first half of the Nineteenth Century, and their influence upon the American schoolma'am was enormous. Nothing was known at that time about the psychology of speech, and the discoveries in linguistics that were being made in Europe did not penetrate to the Republic until after 1850, when they were brought home from Tübingen and Berlin by William Dwight Whitney (1827–94). An Englishman, Robert Gordon Latham (1812–88), had raised some pother in the 40s by proclaiming that " in language whatever *is* is right," but he got no attention in this country, and so late as 1870 a favorite American authority, George P. Marsh,[2] was misunderstanding and denouncing him, though even Marsh was constrained to admit by that time that " the ignorance of grammarians " was " a frequent cause of the corruption of language."

The enormous proliferation of public-schools produced a heavy demand for text-books of grammar, and nearly all of them were written by incompetents who simply followed the worst English

---

Modern Language Association, 1927, pp. 221–37 and An Introduction to Linguistic Science, by Edgar H. Sturtevant; New Haven 1947, p. 54.

[1] Mrs. Charles Archibald (Mildred E. Hergenhan), in The Doctrine of Correctness in English Usage in the Nineteenth Century, says that the divine origin of language was held by John Locke and supported by Adam Smith, and that it survived into Goold Brown's Grammar of English Grammars, 1851, and even into Daniel Cruttendon's Philosophy of Language, 1870. She adds that the doctrine of analogies was part of the theory of language launched by George Campbell in his Philosophy of Rhetoric, 1776, a work long held in high esteem. I am indebted to Mrs. Archibald for access to her excellent study, which is not yet published.

[2] Lectures on the English Language: First Series, fourth edition; New York, 1870, pp. 645–46.

models. "The larger part of grammatical instruction," says Rollo LaVerne Lyman, "remained a slavish verbal repetition of rules and a desperate struggle with complicated parsing formulæ."[1] There were, of course, some grammarians, even so early as the 30s, who saw the futility of this method of instruction, and one of them, Warren Colburn, attempted a more rational grammar-book in 1831,[2] but the majority of the pedagogues of the time continued, as Lyman says, to favor "slavish memorizing, nothing more or less," and grammar remained a horror to schoolboys until the end of the Nineteenth Century. In 1870 the rambunctious Richard Grant White fluttered the pedagogical dovecotes by announcing the discovery that English really had no grammar at all,[3] but White was too pedantic a fellow to follow his own lead and during the rest of his life (he died in 1885) he devoted himself mainly to formulating canons of "correct" English which greatly aided the schoolma'am in afflicting her pupils.

The new philological learning brought to the United States by Whitney was a long while taking root. Even when, after fifteen years at Yale, he founded the American Philological Association, it was quickly engulfed by intransigent followers of Varro and Priscian, Posidonius and Apollonius Dyscolus, and the Sanskrit grammarians of the Fourth and Fifth Centuries B.C. When the Modern Language Association was launched at the new Johns Hopkins in 1883 it met a fate even more grisly, for the young college professors who flocked into it passed over the living language with a few sniffs and threw all their energies into flatulent studies of the influence of Lamb on Hazlitt, the dates of forgotten plays of the Seventeenth Century, the changes made by Donne, Skelton and Cowper in the texts of forgotten poems, and such-like pseudo-intellectual gym-

[1] English Grammar in American Schools Before 1850; Washington, 1922, p. 140. The subject was very little taught before the Revolution, but it became a favorite soon afterward, and by the end of the Eighteenth Century at least a dozen grammar-books were in circulation. Of these Lindley Murray's English Grammar, Adapted to the Different Classes of Learners, first published in 1795, was the most successful and by far. Lyman says that more than 1,000,000 copies of it and its successors were sold before 1850. Of the other grammars of the time about 4,000,000 copies were sold. A list in Seth T. Hurd's Grammatical Corrector; Philadelphia, 1848, pp. x and xi, shows that nearly 100 different ones had been published by 1847.

[2] Lyman, pp. 132–53. Colburn seems to have been influenced by the Swiss educational reformer, J. H. Pestalozzi (1746–1827).

[3] Words and Their Use; New York, 1870, Chapter X.

nastics.[1] Not until the Linguistic Society followed in 1924 was there any organized attack upon language as it is, not as it might be or ought to be, and even the Linguistic Society has given a great deal more attention to Hittite and other such fossil tongues than to the American spoken by 140,000,000-odd free, idealistic and more or less human Americans, including all the philologians themselves, at least when they are in their cups or otherwise off guard. On the level of the common, or dirt pedagogues [2] the notion that language should be studied objectively, like any other natural phenomenon, made even slower progress, and it was not until 1908 that any effort was made in that direction. That effort, at the start, took the form of trying to find out just what was in the common speech — in other words, to get together the makings of a purely descriptive and scientific grammar.[3] But in a little while the more intelligent inquirers — most of them *not* pedagogues, but philologians — began to ask themselves what validity there was, if any, in some of the rules inculcated by the schoolma'am, and to seek light in the speech habits of unquestionably cultured Americans. They found, as might have been expected, that few of the latter took the rules very seriously. Many used *it is me* habitually, and with no thought of sin. Others used *who* for *whom* in the so-called objective case. Yet others paid little if any heed to the delicate English distinctions between *shall* and *will*.

One of the first investigators to follow this line of inquiry was Sterling Andrus Leonard, professor of English at the University of Wisconsin, who had begun to flog the pedants in 1918, when he was still a young interne at Columbia.[4] In 1930 or thereabout he under-

[1] This frenzy to unearth the not-worth-knowing still goes on. *Publications of the Modern Language Association* occasionally prints a very useful paper, as readers of the footnotes to the present volume are aware, but in the main its contents are hardly worth embalming. See Supplement I, p. 101, n. 3.

[2] By a pedagogue I mean one trained in the so-called technic of teaching, but not in anything beyond the elements of the subject taught. This category embraces 99.9% of the teachers in the elementary schools, 95% of those in the high-schools and prep-schools, and probably 85% of those in all the colleges save a few dozen of the upper crust.

[3] This pioneer work is described in AL4, pp. 418-23.

[4] Old Purist Junk, *English Journal*, May, 1918, pp. 295-302. In this early paper he laid down the excellent principle: "A usage which one finds properly recorded as colloquial must certainly not be considered as thereby banned from the English classroom or from any but the most solemn and formal themes. Objection to real colloquialism is surely as wrong as that against genuine Americanisms,

took to find out what was really good usage by asking a committee of linguists, teachers of speech, authors, editors and business men, 229 in number, to pronounce their judgment upon 230 usages, ranging all the way from forms endorsed even by purists to forms seldom encountered outside the talk of baseball players and policemen. His report, published by the National Council of Teachers of English after his death,[1] made a sensation in pedagogical circles and was very influential in reorienting the traditional approach to English. It showed that at least 75% of the experts in linguistics approved *as regards, none-are, all dressed up, go slow, I don't know if, only* before the verb, *it is me, who are you looking for?, the reason was because, invite whoever you like, to loan, but what, I wish I was, everyone-they, providing* for *provided,* and *awfully* as a general intensive, and that between 25% and 75% of them favored *proven, four first, gotten, either of these three, I can't seem, older than me, neither-are, these kind, most anybody, it is liable to snow, in search for, ain't I?, don't* in the singular, *sure* as an adverb, *like* for *as if, off of, due to* for *on account of, some, little ways* and *different than.* All these forms had been banned by the school books for years, and likewise by the innumerable books of "correct" English for adults. Two years after Leonard's study appeared one of his students and successors at Wisconsin, Robert C. Pooley, supported its conclusions with examples from the historical dictionaries and the accepted *belles lettres* of the language, and concluded with a recommendation that the books be given a drastic overhauling.[2] Three of his specific proposals were:

> Whenever traditional grammatical classification ignores or misrepresents current usage, it must be changed.
> When custom has established two forms or usages on approximately equal standing, both must be presented.

---

which one finds even yet in the common attitude of purists toward such words as *depot* for *station.*" Leonard defended *none are, proven, try and see, to get sick, have got, quick* and *slow* as adverbs, *then* as an adjective, *through* for *finished,* and a number of other forms condemned by pedants.

1 Current English Usage: Chicago, 1932. The persons who gave him help in his investigation and completed his report after he was dead are listed on pp. xxi-xxii. He was born in California in 1888, and was drowned while canoeing on Lake Mendota, Wis., on May 15, 1931. There is an account of him in *American Speech,* June, 1931, p. 373.

2 Grammar and Usage in Textbooks on English, *Educational Research Bulletin No. 14* of the University of Wisconsin; Madison, Aug., 1933.

When current established usage conflicts with traditional rules, the rules must be modified or discarded.

A little while afterward Walter Barnes, of New York University, undertook to check the Leonard findings by a reëxamination of the locutions they covered, especially those set down as "illiterate" or "disputable." His referees and associates were students in his own seminar, but they also examined various printed authorities. In general they agreed with Leonard's jury, but in a number of cases they raised a given word or phrase a grade or more. Thus *complected*, which appeared as "illiterate" in the Leonard study, became "disputable" in that of Barnes, *good and cold* was lifted from "disputable" to "established," and *data* in the singular all the way from "illiterate" to "established." Barnes also submitted the locutions marked "disputable" on the Leonard list to a jury of 52 radio announcers, 29 writers and 40 business executives, and tabulated their votes. A majority of them approved *to fix* in the sense of *to repair*, the *one-he* combination, *in back of* (often denounced by English purists as an abhorrent Americanism), *right* in the sense of *direct, I can't seem, dove* for *dived, going some, good and cold*, and *to aggravate* in the sense of *to vex*.[1] Said the Barnes group in its summary:

> Certain self-appointed saviors of "English undefiled" have taken it upon themselves to put a stop to the evolution of the language, and to preserve it intact for future generations. They disregard the fact that it was far from a perfect tongue at the time from which their *status quo* begins.[2]

Between 1933 and 1937 Albert H. Marckwardt and Fred G. Walcott undertook a further study of the Leonard material[3] and found that a large percentage of the usages marked "disputable" were to be found in English and American authors of high rank, and that many of the rest were recognized as allowable in colloquial speech by generally accepted authorities. They unearthed *neither-are* from Johnson, Cowper, Southey and Ruskin, *like:* as in "Do it *like* he tells you" from Southey and William Morris, *try and* from Milton and Coleridge, *only* before the verb from Dryden and Tennyson, *slow* as an adverb from Byron and Thackeray, and *I wish I was* from

---

[1] Studies in Current Colloquial Usage; New York, 1933. There is a bibliography of language tests in Part IV, pp. 3 and 4.
[2] Part II, p. 2.
[3] Facts About Current English Usage; New York, 1938.

Defoe, Swift, Fielding, Jane Austen, Byron, Marryat, Thackeray, Dickens, Thomas Hardy, George Meredith and Oscar Wilde. Their conclusion was:

> Grammar is seen to be not something final and static but merely the organized description or codification of the actual speech habits of educated men. If these habits change, grammar itself changes, and textbooks must follow suit. To preserve in our textbooks requirements no longer followed by the best current speakers is not grammatical but ungrammatical. It makes of grammar not a science but a dogma.[1]

It is hard for grammarians, who have always been regarded as the archetypal pedagogues, to yield up this dogmatism, but in late years they have shown a considerable tendency to do so. That tendency, in truth, is not altogether new, for the once famous John Horne Tooke made an effort to clear away a lot of ancient grammatical rubbish in his " Diversions of Purley," the first volume of which was published in 1786, and some of his ideas were borrowed by Noah Webster in " A Philosophical and Practical Grammar of the English Language " in 1807,[2] and by William B. Fowle in " The True English Grammar " in 1827.[3] But it has not been until comparatively recently that these more or less amateurish reformers have got any substantial support from the professionals. The first break came when some of the latter began to turn their eyes from the written language to the spoken language, and to observe that what was true of the former, grammatically speaking, was not always true of the latter. The second came when others made a serious effort to find out just what rules, if any, governed the speech of the vulgar, and

---

[1] pp. 133–34. This was anticipated by a thoughtful layman of legal training and distinction, Walter Guest Kellogg. He wrote in Is Grammar Useless?, *North American Review*, July, 1920, p. 10: " Usage is standard and by usage English must be taught. No grammar or dictionary can lay down the law nor have the effect of a statute; they can only record what passes current among the people of the time and can only preserve the customs of today and the precedents of yesterday, as do the common-law reports."

[2] Warfel says, p. 84, that " Webster declared this work to be the one he was most satisfied with," but that it " never took hold, and only a few editions appeared." The established grammarians of the time were all against it.

[3] Published in Boston. The subtitle was " an Attempt to form a Grammar of English not modelled upon those of the Latin, and Greek, and other Foreign Languages." Fowle tried to reduce the parts of speech to nouns, verbs and adjectives. He argued that the articles were really adjectives, and that most proper names were the same. He recognized only two tenses, the present and the past, and tried to get rid of mood, number and person.

to consider whether those rules, at least in some cases, were not quite as " good " as those that had long adorned the grammar-books. The ensuing debate became a hot one and is still going on.

The pioneer study of errors in the speech of a typical group of American school children was made by G. M. Wilson, superintendent of schools at Connersville, Ind., in 1908.[1] It was followed by a similar study of the speech of school children in Boise, Idaho, by C. S. Meek, made during the years 1909–15,[2] and by a much more extensive investigation in the public schools of Kansas City, directed by W. W. Charters.[3] Many other local studies followed, and in 1930 one was begun on a national scale, directed by L. J. O'Rourke.[4] The result was the accumulation of a great deal of interesting (and often racy) information about the actual speech-ways of Americans,[5] but most of the grammarians were reluctant to grant the fair and indeed inevitable implications of their studies. This was especially true of O'Rourke, whose somewhat timorous conclusions were criticized sharply, immediately after they were published, by Janet

[1] Wilson's conclusions were first published in the form of a bulletin to his teachers, reprinted in the report of the Connersville School Board for 1908, and again as Errors in the Language of Grade Pupils, *Educator-Journal*, Dec., 1909, pp. 178–80. He found that ten errors constituted 58% of the total number unearthed, and urged the ma'ams of his flock to concentrate upon them. These ten, he said, " were reported again and again, and as persistently in the sixth, seventh and eighth grades as in the lower grades." They were the use of *ain't* or *hain't*, *I seen* and *I have saw*, the double negative, the coupling of plural pronouns with singular verbs, the addition of *got to* to *have*, *git* for *get*, *come* for *came*, *them* for *those*, *learned* for *taught*, and *me* and *him* in the nominative.

[2] Special Report of the Boise Public Schools, June, 1915, pp. 29–35, republished in Sixteenth Yearbook of the National Society for the Study of Education, Part I, pp. 89–91. I am indebted here to Mr. Frederick L. Whitney, of the Colorado State College of Education.

[3] A Course of Study in Grammar Based Upon the Grammatical Errors of School Children of Kansas City, Mo.; Columbia (Mo.), 1915. Its findings are summarized in AL4, pp. 418–21.

[4] Rebuilding the English-Usage Curriculum to Insure Greater Mastery of Essentials; Washington, 1934.

[5] A bibliography down to 1927 is in The Most Common Grammatical Errors, by Henry Harap, *English Journal*, June, 1930, pp. 444–46. It lists 33 titles. Since then there has been a heavy accumulation, mostly repetitive. But there is an original approach, along with a criticism of previous approaches, in Errors in the Oral Language of Mentally Defective Adolescents and Normal Elementary School Children, by Theodore Carlton and Lilyn E. Carlton, *Journal of Genetic Psychology*, Vol. LXVI, 1945, pp. 183–220. The Carltons, in this valuable study, report that four common errors accounted for between 40% and 55% of the total numbers they encountered, and that seven accounted for between 64% and 70%.

Rankin Aiken, of Columbia University, a woman grammarian of great originality and independence.[1] This was her conclusion:

> What the present writer wishes is that some competent scholar would take the O'Rourke tabulations and analyze them to show just where the English language stands today in respect to the wild flowers in its wood, the uncultivated usages which some of us find sweeter and more interesting than all the geraniums ever grown in pots. The competent scholar will then tell of his findings, not in the weary, flat reportese of the average survey, but in an English which is itself worth imitating as a model of freshness and flexibility.[2]

Later studies have come into greater accord with Dr. Aiken's demands, notably the one reported in "American English Grammar," by Charles Carpenter Fries.[3] The material used consisted of 2,000 letters from average Americans received by various departments of the Federal government at Washington. Fries recognized the difficulty lying in the fact that this material was all written, not spoken, but he used various ingenious devices to get rid of it as far as possible, and in his report he sought to separate his examples into three categories — Standard English, Common English, and Vulgar English. He found that what he called Common English was mainly a mixture of Standard and Vulgar, with few distinct characters of its own, so he gave it relatively little attention. His conclusions were conservative. He did not advocate any wholesale abandonment of the traditional grammar, but he called for a more intensive study of the language as it is, and advocated training pupils in that study. "Grammars with rules that were in part the rules of Latin grammar and in part the results of 'reason,'" he said, "did not and could not provide the tools of an effective language program. . . . To be really effective a program must prepare the pupil for independent growth, and the only possible means of accomplishing that end is to

---

1 O'Rourke and Leonard, *American Speech*, Dec., 1934, pp. 291-95.
2 Dr. Aiken, who died in 1944, published A New Plan of English Grammar; New York, 1933, in which she sought to reduce the traditional eight parts of speech to six functions, and to introduce other rationalizations. She followed this with Commonsense Grammar; New York, 1936, and Psychology of English (with Margaret M. Bryant); New York, 1940. Other efforts to the same end have been made by other teachers of grammar, *e.g.*, Patterson Wardlaw in Simpler English Grammar, *Bulletin of the University of South Carolina*, July, 1914, and James Hayford in American Grammar, *College English*, Oct., 1942, pp. 38-45.
3 New York, 1940. Fries's investigation was "financed by the National Council of Teachers of English and supported by the Modern Language Association and the Linguistic Society of America."

lead him to become an intelligent observer of language usage." This, of course, was somewhat vague, but it at least turned its back upon the cock-sure dogmatism of the old-time grammarians. It was not the long-awaited realistic grammar of the American common speech, but it brought that grammar a few inches nearer.

The movement to make the spoken language rather than the written language the objective of grammatical study seems to have been launched by E. H. Sturtevant, later eminent as a Hittite scholar, in 1917. "Whether we think of the history of human speech in general or of the linguistic experience of the individual speaker," he wrote, "spoken language is the primary phenomenon, and writing is only a more or less imperfect reflection of it."[1] This lead was followed by the English phonologist, Harold E. Palmer, in 1924,[2] and by various other writers on language during the years afterward, including the Dane, Otto Jespersen, probably the most profound student of English of the last half century.[3] Palmer explained in his introduction to his book that what he meant by spoken English was "that variety which is generally used by educated people in the course of ordinary conversation or when writing letters to intimate friends." He went on:

> One of the most widely diffused of the many linguistic illusions current in the world is the belief that each language possesses a "pure" or "grammatical" form, a form which is intrinsically "correct," which is independent of usage, which exists, which has always existed, but which is now in danger of losing its existence.... [The purist] is generally perfectly unconscious of the forms of speech which he uses himself. He warns the unsuspecting foreigner against what he calls "vulgarisms," and says to him, "Don't ever use such vulgar forms as *don't* or *won't:* you won't hear educated people using them," or "Never use a preposition to finish a sentence with," or he may say, "I don't know who you learn English from, but you are always using the word *who* instead of *whom*." Or we may hear him say, "Oh, I've got something else to tell you: don't say *I've got* instead of *I have*."[4]

[1] Linguistic Change; Chicago, 1917, p. 1.
[2] A Grammar of Spoken English on a Strictly Phonetic Basis; Cambridge (England), 1924.
[3] Essentials of English Grammar; New York, 1933.
[4] George O. Curme had published A Grammar of the German Language based on actual usage in 1905; revised edition, 1922. In his Grammar of the English Tongue, which began to appear in 1931, he gave studious attention to colloquial speech and even to vulgar speech. "Those who always think of popular speech as ungrammatical," he said in his preface to Vol. III, p. vi, "should recall that our present literary grammar was originally the grammar of the common people of England."

This movement against the traditional authoritarianism has not gone, of course, unchallenged. As I have recorded in AL4, p. 51, the National Council of Teachers of English established a Better-Speech Week in 1915, and it afflicted the schoolma'am and her pupils for nearly twenty years afterward. It finally blew up, but there remain respectable philologians who believe that the teaching of orthodox grammar is still useful, and ought not to be abandoned until the reformers perfect a coherent and effective substitute. One of these defenders of the old order is Dr. Reed Smith, dean of the graduate school of the University of North Carolina, who said in a paper published in 1938:

> The opponents of grammar have been outspoken against it, frankly and without apology. Let its advocates be equally outspoken in its favor. Unless future development and more convincing evidence prove that it is best to give up the teaching of grammar in whole or in large part, and until the opponents of grammar have a satisfactory substitute to offer, it is time for those who favor it to stop apologizing and begin fighting back.[1]

Tradition is also upheld by most of the authors of books on "correct" English, and by all save a few of the sages who answer language questions in the newspapers. The imbecilities of both groups have been exposed frequently, but to very little effect.[2] The schoolma'am clings to the same unhappy conservatism,[3] and so does the college tutor who wrestles, in Freshman English, with students who come up from the high-schools using *between you and I*.[4] Says

---

[1] Grammar: the Swing of the Pendulum, *English Journal* (College Edition), Oct., 1938, pp. 637-43. See also Smith's A College Man Looks at High School English, *English Journal*, May, 1942, pp. 375-84, and An Apology for Grammar, by W. Alan Grove, *Science and Society*, May 30, 1942, pp. 600-05.

[2] For the former see three papers by Reuben Steinbach, all in *American Speech* — On Usage in English, Feb., 1929, pp. 161-77; The Misrelated Constructions, Feb., 1930, pp. 181-97, and English as Some Teach It, Aug., 1930, pp. 456-62. For the latter, Grammar for the Populace, by Stuart Robertson, *English Journal* (College Edition), Jan., 1939, pp. 24-32.

[3] Schoolmarm English, by John J. De Boer, *American Scholar*, Winter, 1936, pp. 78-86, and American Youth and Their Language, by Walter Barnes, *English Journal* (College Edition), April, 1937, pp. 283-90.

[4] How English Teachers Correct Papers, by Sterling Andrus Leonard, *English Journal*, Oct., 1923, pp. 517-32; Are Our English Teachers Adequately Prepared for Their Work?, by George O. Curme, *Publications of the Modern Language Association*, 1931, pp. 1415-26, and The Failure of Freshman English, by Oscar James Campbell, *English Journal* (College Edition), March, 1939, pp. 177-85.

Curme, in one of the papers just cited: " Our school grammarians are not scholars. They do not inform themselves upon the subjects they teach. They are helpless if the little antiquated school grammars do not give them information. . . . I do not expect to see a much better condition in my lifetime." The hardest thing for these peewee pedants to understand is that language is never uniform — that different classes and even different ages speak it differently. What would be proper in a radio message-bringer " soaring in the high region of his fancies, with his garland and singing robes about him," would be only ridiculous in a schoolboy playing with his fellows; indeed it would be quite as ridiculous in the message-bringer himself, crooning to a manicure-girl or jawing his wife. The American of a Harvard professor speaking *ex cathedra* is seldom the same as the American of a Boston bartender or a Mississippi evangelist. Let the daughter of a hog-sticker in the Chicago stockyards go home talking like the book and her ma will fan her fanny. " Substandard students," said Thomas A. Knott, general editor of the Webster dictionaries, in 1934, " are not ' making mistakes.' They are simply talking or writing their own language." Knott suggested that, to some extent at least, the failure of pedagogy to teach them standard English might be lessened by thinking of standard English as a foreign language, and teaching it by the devices found effective in teaching French, German and Spanish.[1] But so far as I know, this proposal has never been put to trial.

In the General Explanations prefaced to the NED [2] Dr. James A. H. Murray, the chief editor thereof, undertook to show the interrelations of the various levels of English by means of a diagram. In the center he put what he called " the common words of the language " — the " nucleus or central mass of many thousand words whose Anglicity is unquestioned, the great majority at once literary and colloquial." Above this domain of the general and almost universal he put that of the literary language, with its greatly expanded vocabulary and tight grammar, and underneath he put colloquial speech, with its frequent counter-words and free use of outlaw idioms. Running out from this group he showed various branches or offshoots — that of the regional dialects, that of slang,

[1] Standard English and Incorrect English, *American Speech*, April, 1934, p. 88.

[2] Vol. I; Oxford, 1888, p. xvii.

that of technical language, and so on. In 1927 Sterling Andrus Leonard and H. Y. Moffett made this a little clearer by substituting two intersecting circles for Murray's somewhat crude diagram. One circle was labeled "formal or literary" and the other "informal or colloquial." Where they overlapped there was a common area, perhaps amounting to one-third of each, to indicate the usages appearing in both. Outside the circle were places for the smaller and less important categories — archaic forms of the language, slang and argot, technical vocabularies, dialects, and so on. They defined the four principal divisions as follows:

1. Formally correct English, appropriate chiefly for serious and important occasions, whether in speech or writing; usually called "literary English."
2. Fully acceptable English for informal conversation, correspondence, and all other writing of well-bred ease; not wholly appropriate for occasions of literary dignity; "standard, cultivated, colloquial English."
3. Commercial, foreign, scientific or other technical uses, limited in comprehensibility, not used outside their particular area by cultivated speakers; "trade or technical English."
4. Popular or illiterate speech, not used by persons who wish to pass as cultivated, save to represent uneducated speech, or to be jocose; here taken to include slang or argot, and dialect forms not admissible to the standard or cultivated area; usually called "vulgar English," but with no implication necessarily of the current meaning of vulgar; "naïf, popular, or uncultivated English."[1]

Two observations on this summary by its authors are worth recording. The first is that the levels of English are, to a large extent, social levels — that they indicate status by reflecting environment and education. The second is that "popular or illiterate speech is frequently just as clear and vigorous as more cultivated language." The former observation had been made long before by Ellis, Wyld and other English authorities, and is often repeated by lay writers on speechways.[2] The fact it exhibits is perhaps largely responsible for the persistence with which the outworn rules of "correct" English are rammed into the bewildered young by schoolma'ams and the lesser varieties of college pedagogues. The overwhelming majority of such poor quacks come from the lower cultural levels,

---

[1] Current Definition of Levels in English Usage, *English Journal*, May, 1927, p. 349.
[2] For example, William Feather, in the *William Feather Magazine*, May, 1945, p. 13: "For better or for worse, I move among those who insist on correct speech in business and social life. You can't do business and you can't drink cocktails with this bunch unless you speak the King's English."

and take a fierce and perhaps pardonable pride in the linguistic arcanum they have acquired, for it testifies to their improvement in status. If they issued from a more secure and tolerant social class they would be less doctrinaire, but with the ten-cent store and the filling-station barely escaped they are naturally eager to dig in. The easy way to improve their fitness would be to recruit them from better sources, but that would be as impossible, practically speaking, as trying to improve the race of washerwomen by recruiting them from café society. How the nervous vigilance of such fugitives from the folk produces frequent absurdities in speech has been amusingly described by Robert J. Menner, of Yale,[1] who shows that *I have saw* and its analogues were probably introduced into the American vulgate by schoolma'ams over-eager to eradicate *I seen*. Their excess of zeal convinced their alarmed customers that *saw* was elegant and *seen* incurably abominable, so a substitution was made across the whole board.[2]

The second observation of Leonard and Moffett supports their first. They say:

> It is not correct, as we have often done, to tell a boy who says "I didn't see no dog" that he has stated he did see a dog. His statement is clear and unequivocal. What we can tell him is that he has made a gross social *faux pas*, that he has said something which will definitely declass him, causing cultivated people to say "Who fetched that boy up?" as Mrs. Ruggles put it. Ungrammatical expressions are very rarely unclear. In fact they are often clearer and more forceful than their cultivated equivalents.[3]

To this Robert A. Hall, Jr., of Brown University, adds:

> In practical terms, if you say *it ain't me* instead of *it is not I*, or *I seen him* instead of *I saw him*, you will not be invited to tea again, or will not make a favorable impression on your department head and get the promotion you want. . . . [But] in itself, and apart from all considerations of social favor, one form of speech is just as good as another: *I seen him* has exactly the same meaning and is just as useful as *I saw him*, and there is of course no ethical "right" and "wrong" or "good" and "bad" involved. In many cases, however, certain forms are looked on with displeasure by certain people, often including those who are most influential. A complete description of the forms should, of course, include this fact; when we are telling others about the English language, for example, we need to describe the variation between *he did it* and *he done it*, and then to add: "If you say *he done it* some of your listeners

---

[1] Hypercorrect Forms in American English, *American Speech*, Oct., 1937, pp. 167–78. Allen Walker Read has used *hypersophic* to designate the same thing — a better word, and much needed.

[2] This explanation was anticipated by Leonard Bloomfield in Literate and Illiterate Speech, *American Speech*, July, 1927, p. 436.

[3] p. 348.

will consider you beneath them in social status, and will be less inclined to favor you than if you said *he did it*." ... It should be added that the choice of forms to be favored or disfavored varies from one social stratum to another. It is just as bad a break to say *it is not I* among workmen (who will accuse you of "talking like a school teacher") as it is to say *it ain't me* among school teachers (who will accuse you of "talking like a workman").[1]

The power of such social compulsions was analyzed by Carl G. F. Franzén, of Indiana University, as an incident to a study of speech levels made by him and his students between 1929 and 1933.[2] He concluded that "the only force which influences an individual to speak a better type of English than that to which he is accustomed is not the teacher in the schoolroom but the associates on the new level which he is trying to reach."[3] Robert C. Pooley, writing in 1937, stressed the fact, already noted, that a given individual frequently passes, under differing circumstances, from one level to another, and that sometimes his swing is very wide. The most illiterate speaker, he pointed out, is usually able, on occasion, to speak what passes for "good standard English," and even the most careful speaker occasionally descends to the lower levels. Of these levels Pooley distinguished six, to wit, the illiterate, the homely, the informal standard, the formal standard, the literary, and the technical.[4] The second he described as follows:

> It often has a slightly quaint or old-fashioned cast to it and displays, in many of its specific forms, the survival of words and idioms once widely used but now dropped from standard speech. It is heard in rural homes (excluding foreign influences), in the shops and homes of small towns, and among the older natives of large cities. In fact, it is so universal that few people in the United States escape its influence entirely, including all but a small portion of school teachers.

Franzén and his associates, in their search for material, examined current dialect stories and popular plays,[5] and recorded locutions heard in railroad and bus stations, on the radio,[6] in the courts, and

---

[1] Language and Superstition, *French Review*, May, 1944, p. 377.
[2] A Technique for Determining Levels in English Usage, *English Journal* (College Edition), Jan., 1934, pp. 57–69.
[3] This study was followed by A Study of Levels of English Usage, by Mayme Berns, one of Franzén's students. It is unpublished, but I have had access to it by his courtesy.
[4] The Levels of Language, *Educational Method*, March, 1937, pp. 289–98.
[5] Usage Errors in Oral English as Found in Representative Plays, by Alice E. McKeehan and Carl G. F. Franzén, *Journal of Educational Research*, Dec., 1945, pp. 300–04.
[6] The speechways of radio announcers have been discussed in Chapter VII, Section 1. In July, 1946, a press-agent disguised as an indig-

from "after-dinner speakers, preachers, lecturers and politicians." They might have found even better grist for their mill in popular songs and the comic strips.[1] Sigmund Spaeth, in a paper on the language of the former,[2] has shown that "bad grammar" has been their tradition for many years. Paul Dresser, author of the immortal "Banks of the Wabash" and brother to Theodore Dreiser the novelist, used the right pronoun in the title of his "Just Tell Them That You Saw Me," but in the text he indulged himself in "Remember I was once a girl like *she*." All old-timers will recall "He *Don't* Belong to the Regulars; He's Just a Volunteer," "Just Because She Made *Them* Goo-Goo Eyes," and the refrain of "Frankie and Johnnie": "He *done* her wrong."[3] "A song writer," says Spaeth, "would hardly dare to use *whom* in a sentence, even if he knew it was correct. Such things are just unsingable. . . . '*Who* do you love?' would lose all its enticing quality if it were made grammatically correct."[4]

426. [The vulgar American's vocabulary is much larger than his linguistic betters commonly assume. They labor under a tradition that the lowly manage to get through life with a few hundred or a few thousand words.] This nonsense seems to have been set afloat by the famous Anglo-German philologist, Max Müller (1823–1900).[5] It still survives in handbooks of "correct" English, but

---

nant schoolma'am got space in the newspapers by protesting against the Arkansas dialect forms used in sports broadcasts by Dizzy Dean, a former baseball player, *e.g.*, *slud* as the preterite of *to slide*, *respectable* for *respective*, and *confidentially* for *confidently*. See an Associated Press dispatch from St. Louis, printed in many morning papers the next day. Fans in large number supported Dizzy, and he was defended passionately by the *Saturday Review of Literature* (Aug. 3), the Baltimore *Sun* (Aug. 16), and *The Pleasures of Publishing*, press-sheet of the Columbia University Press (Aug. 12).

1 James D. Woolf, in The Difficult Art of Using Simple Words, *Printers Ink*, Sept. 29, 1944, p. 39, quoted *Life* as saying that "comic strips comprise the most significant body of literature in America to-day," read diligently by 51% of the nation's adults. The number of children following them is probably nearly 90%.

2 Stabilizing the Language Through Popular Songs, *New Yorker*, July 7, 1934, pp. 32–36.

3 A writer in *American Speech*, Oct., 1942, p. 181, says that in the Oxford Book of Light Verse this was changed to *did*. The first edition of Gray's famous elegy, published in 1751, had the title, An Elegy *Wrote* in a Country Church Yard.

4 See also Folk Song and Folk Speech, by Hans Kurath, *American Speech*, April, 1945, pp. 122–25.

5 The Science of Language; First Series; London, 1861, p. 277. Müller was challenged so early as Oct., 1865, by a writer in the *Eclectic Magazine*, p. 435. "A Derbyshire

there is no truth in it whatsoever. "The complete vocabulary of any full (not minimum or pidgin) language," says Robert A. Hall, Jr., "regardless of the cultural level of its speakers, is at least 20,000 to 25,000 words."[1] This is borne out by the anthropologist, A. L. Kroeber, who has been able to find 27,000 words in the vocabulary of the Aztec Nahuatl, and 20,000 in that of the Maya.[2]

It is not to be argued, of course, that any individual speaker of a language uses or even knows every word in it, but by the same token it must be borne in mind that no investigator, however competent and assiduous, can be expected to unearth all of them. Indeed, in the case of highly sophisticated languages, with machinery for inventing or taking in indefinite numbers of new words, it is impossible for even the most expert lexicographers to make complete reports. This is shown in English by the wide differences among them. Noah Webster's first dictionary of 1806 listed 28,000 words, the largest vocabulary assembled up to that time, but when he undertook his larger dictionary of 1828 he increased the number to 70,000. His successors kept on discovering more and more words, and the Webster's New International of today lists more than 550,000. Meanwhile, the Century Dictionary, in its final form, listed 530,000; the Standard, 455,000, and the NED, without its Supplement, 414,825.[3] These figures, of course, include combinations, and Robert L. Ramsay has argued plausibly[4] that many such combinations are really only variants, and should not be listed separately. Ramsay believes that the total number of different words in English is actually "something like 250,000" and that "over 50,000 of these are obsolete." He says that the best German dictionary lists 71,750 simple words and 112,954 compounds, or 184,704 in all, and that the figures reported for other languages are: French, 93,032; Spanish, 70,683; Italian, 69,642; Latin, 51,686; ancient Greek, 96,438 and Anglo-Saxon, 41,142. But it must be obvious that these vocabu-

---

peasant," said this writer, "uses eight different terms for a pigsty."

1 Language and Superstition, *French Review*, May, 1944, p. 378, n. 5.
2 Extent of Personal Vocabularies and Cultural Control, by J. M. Gillette, *Scientific Monthly*, Nov., 1929, p. 453. Hugh Morrison tells me of a French missionary in the Belgian Congo who is compiling a dictionary of the local language, and has already found 60,000 words. (Private communication, May 21, 1946.)
3 Millions of Words, by Frank H Vizetelly, New York *Herald Tribune*, March 5, 1933.
4 Taking the Census of English Words, *American Speech*, Feb., 1933, pp. 36–41.

laries are far from complete, and that nearly all dictionaries are based mainly on the written language alone. In the case of Latin and ancient Greek there is no other source. "English," says Ramsay, "should be roughly three times as wealthy in words as other languages, for its curious history has made its vocabulary to no small degree an amalgamation of three wealthy languages, Anglo-Saxon, French and Latin. But there is no occasion for exaggerating our advantages to the point of absurdity."

It is not easy to determine how many words a given man knows, and it is even harder to find out how many he uses. The method usually selected is to choose by some arbitrary method one word on each page of a dictionary, determine how many of the words thus gathered the subject can define, and then multiply the result by the number of pages in the dictionary. But this plan admits a large element of mere chance; moreover, it is limited by the limitations of the dictionary used. Gillette, in the paper already cited, criticized it severely and effectively. He found that his own vocabulary, when tested by a dictionary listing but 18,000 words, ran to but 16,833, but that when a large unabridged dictionary was used and due regard given to subsidiary words, it leaped to 127,800. This, to be sure, represented only words *known*, not words *used*. The former category is always larger than the latter, whether one considers speech or writing. But in any case the vocabulary of a given person, when adequately tested, turns out to be much more extensive than a layman would guess. E. A. Kirkpatrick has estimated that the average child in the second grade at school knows 4,480 words, the average sixth-grader 8,700, the ninth-grader 13,400, and the high-school senior 20,120.[1] Very young children, especially those of high IQ's, sometimes show astonishing vocabularies. Miss Margaret Morse Nice[2] records one who had 523 words at eighteen months, another who had 1212 at two years, and a third who had 1509 at thirty months. She shows that the average child of three years, living in a cultured family, has 910, and that this average goes up to 1516 at four, to 2204 at five and to 2963 at six. There is a report of a Ger-

[1] A Vocabulary Test, *Popular Science Monthly*, Feb., 1907. I take this and much of what follows from A Brief Outline of Vocabulary Measurement With a Summary of Some Methods Employed, *Word Study*, Feb., 1939, pp. 5–8.

[2] On the Size of Vocabularies, *American Speech*, Oct., 1926, pp. 1–7.

man boy who had 1142 at three.[1] E. H. Babbitt, writing in 1907, concluded that the vocabulary of the average American college sophomore, despite his superficial appearance of imbecility, runs to between 50,000 and 60,000 words, and that even non-college men and women, provided they read a few books, know between 25,000 and 35,000. F. M. Gerlach puts the average high-school student's vocabulary at 71,000 and the college student's at 85,000. Other inquirers offer more modest estimates, but I know of none who gives any countenance to the popular delusion that there are millions of people who get along with vocabularies of a few thousand or even a few hundred words.[2]

There is a plain fallacy in the frequent attempt to estimate an author's stock of words by counting those he uses in his writings. This has led to the notion that Shakespeare knew but 15,000 (some say 20,000), Milton but 8,000, and the translators of the Old Testament but 5642. In 1920 or thereabout some human adding-machine listed the different words in Woodrow Wilson's three books, " Congressional Government " (1885), " The State " (1889) and " A History of the American People " (1902), and found that there were but 6,221 altogether.[3] It was, however, manifest even to newspaper commentators that Wilson knew and used a great many more than that; indeed, the estimates of his vocabulary made by later pundits ranged from 62,210 to 100,000.[4] How far such nonsense can go was

1 References to many papers on the vocabularies of children are given in Miss Nice's study. Others worth consulting are listed in AL4, p. 426, n. 2. Yet others are Notes on Child Speech, by Urban T. Holmes, *American Speech*, June, 1929, pp. 390–94; The Speech of a Child Two Years of Age, by E. C. Hills, *Dialect Notes*, Vol. IV, Part II, 1914, pp. 84–100; Vocabularies of Children and Adults, by W. S. Gray, *Elementary School Journal*, May, 1945, and Speech Development of a Bilingual Child, *Northwestern University Studies in the Humanities No. 6*, 1939. Dr. Wilfred J. Funk, the lexicographer, once startled the readers of the New York *Times* (Topics of the Times, July 26, 1938) by declaring that the average intelligent dog could understand about 60 words of English, though unable to speak the language. He said that trick dogs could be taught more than 250 words, and in four or more languages.

2 The Story of a New Dictionary, issued by the publishers of the College Standard, says, p. 12, that "a parrot can learn 200–300 words, a bright child of six knows 2000–3000, a stupid adult knows 8000–10,000, the ordinary man knows 20,000–30,000, and the well-read man knows 35,000–70,000."

3 Says Average Man Uses 8000 Words, New York *Times*, July 15, 1923, p. 6.

4 Did Wilson Know 62,210 Words?, *Literary Digest*, April 3, 1926, p. 48.

illustrated years ago by a floating newspaper paragraph reporting that there were but 600 words in the vocabulary of Italian opera, and hinting that most singers knew no more. How hard it is to put down is shown by the following sentence in a 1944 issue of a putatively respectable literary review, written by a professional literatus of considerable pretensions: "The vocabulary of the average American business man, outside of profanity and pornography, is about a thousand words."[1] As a matter of fact, an investigation of the vocabularies of business executives, made in 1935,[2] indicated that they know more words, taking one with another, than so many college graduates. A good deal of this current balderdash about midget vocabularies is caused, I suppose, by confusion between words known and words in constant use. The very nature of language puts a heavy burden upon a relatively small number of common words, and so tends to conceal the number and importance of those used only seldom. So long ago as 1925 the late Leonard P. Ayres (1879–1946) made an investigation of the vocabulary[3] of everyday correspondence which showed that 542 words constitute seven-eighths of the average letter, that 43 constitute one-half, and that nine constitute one-fourth. The nine are *I, the, and, you, to, your, of, for* and *in*. Of these, the first three alone constitute an eighth.[4] But this really says nothing about vocabularies, for it must be manifest that all casual writing, like all casual talk, is made up very largely of a small group of common words.[5]

[1] For a Literary Lend-Lease, by Struthers Burt, *Saturday Review of Literature*, Nov. 4, 1944, p. 6. Unhappily, such delusions are shared even by philologians. In 1933 or thereabout a savant in practise at Harvard told his students that the average working vocabulary consists of but 2000 words. He was challenged by one of them, L. Clark Keating, later professor of Romance languages at George Washington University, who undertook to set down 2000 nouns alone without consulting a dictionary. He produced 1300 at a single sitting, and the next day added 1000 more.

[2] A Study of the English Vocabulary Scores of 75 Executives, published by the Human Engineering Laboratories of the Stevens Institute of Technology, Hoboken, N. J.

[3] The Spelling Vocabularies of Personal and Business Letters; New York, Feb. 13, 1925.

[4] In The Words and Sounds of Telephone Conversations, *Bell System Technical Journal*, April, 1930, pp. 290–324, N. R. French, C. W. Carter, Jr., and Walter Koenig, Jr., reported that the first nine recorded in telephone conversations are *I, you, the, a, on, to, that, it* and *is. And* is in tenth place, *of* in thirteenth, *in* in fourteenth, *for* in twentieth, and *your* in ninety-third.

[5] There is a large literature of vocabulary studies. Items down to the end of 1922 are listed in Kennedy, pp. 361–62. Various other papers

2. THE VERB

"The most surprising fact about the illiterate level of speech," says Pooley,[1] "is its widespread uniformity. It is not merely a haphazard series of lapses from standard English, but is rather a distinct and national mode of speech, with a fairly regular grammar of its own. It is characterized principally by inversions of the forms of irregular verbs, the confusion of regular and irregular verb tense forms, a bland disregard of number agreement in subjects and verbs and pronoun relations, the confusion of adjectives and adverbs, and the employment of certain syntactical combinations like the double negative, the redundant subject, and the widely split infinitive."

Most of these, of course, have long histories in the dialects of England, and crossed the ocean ready-made, but others seem to have originated in the Republic, or to have got a much firmer and more general lodgment here. Even *I seen*, though it is traced to *c.* 1440 by the NED, and had a prototype in *sehen* nearly two centuries earlier, has long had a formidable rival in England in *I seed*, and begins to take on a distinctively American color. It apparently did not gain its present wide vogue among the American underprivileged until the high tide of the Irish immigration in the 1840s. The Rev. John Witherspoon, writing in 1781,[2] denounced *I seed* and *I see* (in the past tense), but not *I seen*, and John Pickering, writing in 1815,[3] and Daniel Staniford, writing at about the same time[4] were content to echo Witherspoon. The glossary that David

---

are mentioned in AL4 or in the foregoing pages. Yet others worth consulting are Psychological Aspects of Language, by George C. Brandenburg, *Journal of Educational Psychology*, June, 1918; In Defense of Ezra, by L. E. Nelson, *English Journal* (College Edition), June, 1938; Size of Recognition and Recall Vocabularies, by P. M. Symonds, *School and Society*, Oct. 30, 1926; Vocabulary as a Symptom of Intellect, by Leta Stetter Hollingsworth, *American Speech*, Dec., 1925, pp. 154–58, and The Statistical Study of Literary Vocabulary, by G. Udny Yule; Cambridge (England), 1944. The last is devoted to devices for settling questions of disputed authorship, and its mathematics go beyond the equipment of the average layman, or even of the average philologist.

1 The Levels of Language, *Educational Method*, March, 1937, p. 291.
2 The Druid, VI, May 23.
3 A Vocabulary or Collection of Words Which Have Been Supposed to be Peculiar to the United States of America; Boston, 1816, p. 171.
4 A Short But Comprehensive Grammar; third edition; Boston, n.d., p. 84. Staniford's first edition appeared in 1807.

Humphreys appended to "The Yankey in England" during the same year, likewise listed *I seed* but not *I seen*, and so did the list of Southern provincialisms included in the Rev. Adiel Sherwood's "Gazetteer of the State of Georgia" in 1827. The NED offers no recent examples of *I seen* in England, but quotes *I see* from Thackeray and *I seed* from Scott and Kipling. Joseph Wright, in his "English Dialect Grammar,"[1] lists *I seed* and *I sawed*, but not *I seen*, and in his "English Dialect Dictionary" makes *I seen* chiefly Irish. Thornton's first American example is dated 1796, but after that he offers none until 1840. As I have noted in AL4, Robert J. Menner[2] believes that when *I seen* began to flourish in the American common speech it was "still in the perfect tense with the auxilary syncopated," *i.e.*, "I(ve) never seen it," but that it soon "came to be regarded as a real preterite and extended to all the functions of the past tense." Menner also believes that *I have saw* and *I have did* were probably launched and propagated by "the condemnation of *I seen* and *I done* by grammarians, teachers and family critics," as *between you and I* was prospered by the war on *it is me*.[3] His first example of *I have saw* is from Artemus Ward's "Scenes Outside the Fair-ground," *c.* 1862, and he says that "the grammarians of the early Nineteenth Century do not appear to include" it "in their 'exercises in false syntax,'" but I find it frowned upon as a Pennsylvania provincialism in the eleventh edition of Samuel Kirkman's "English Grammar in Familiar Lectures," 1829.[4]

There is great need for a study of the history of such forms in American English, but so far as I know only one attempt upon it has been made, to wit, by Henry Alexander in 1929.[5] Alexander found no inflections of the verb that had not been recorded in England, but his field of search was circumscribed and if it were extended to the whole body of colonial records it might produce something of great interest. The fact that most such forms are also to

1 Oxford, 1905, pp. 284 and 285. It is also included in Vol. VI of his English Dialect Dictionary; Oxford (reissue), 1923.
2 The Verbs of the Vulgate, *American Speech*, Jan., 1926.
3 Hypercorrect Forms in American English, *American Speech*, Oct., 1937, p. 173.
4 Boston, 1829, p. 207. Kirkman does not include it in his lists of New England, New York, Middle Atlantic, Southern and Irish solecisms. H. A. Shands, in Some Peculiarities of Speech in Mississippi, 1893, says: "The uneducated of Mississippi . . . use *seen* and *seed* for *saw*, *seed* for *seen*, *saw* for *seen*, and sometimes *see* for *saw*."
5 The Verbs of the Vulgate in Their Historical Relations, *American Speech*, April, 1929, pp. 307-15.

be found in English dialects is not of any significance, for American is itself an English dialect, and its vocabulary is largely made up of borrowings from its congeners. The important thing is that many forms have had histories in this country differing from their histories in England, and that some that are used only in narrow areas there have come into almost universal use in the American common speech. There are also archaisms to be considered, *e.g.*, *to loan* in the sense of *to lend*, and again there are forms that have undergone vocalic or consonantal changes, apparently in this country, *e.g.*, *to bust*.

The case of *to bust* would especially reward investigation, for it seems to have been evolved from *to burst* on these shores. The NED Supplement finds it in Dickens's "Nicholas Nickleby," published in 1839, just before his first visit to America, but he may have borrowed it as he borrowed more than one other Americanism, for the DAE shows that it was in use in this country in 1806, and that by 1830 it was widespread. Bartlett says that when, in 1832, Henry Clay, the Whig candidate, was defeated for the Presidency by Andrew Jackson, the following conundrum "went the rounds of the papers": " *Q.* Why is the Whig party like a sculptor? *A.* Because it takes Clay and makes a *bust*." The banks that blew up so copiously in 1837 did not *burst;* they *bust*. So with the boilers of the river-steamers. *To bust out laughing, to bust a blood-vessel* (or a *suspenders button*), *to go on a bust* (*i.e.*, a spree) [1] and the like became common phrases, and by 1845 *buster* was a popular designation for anything large or astounding and especially for a fat and hearty boy.[2] Not long afterward the last named became a nickname for such a boy, *e.g.*, Buster Brown, and survived in that capacity until our own time. *To bust a bronco* has been traced to 1888, but it is no doubt much older. *Trust-buster* appeared in 1877[3] and had a heavy run during the reign of Roosevelt I, and *gang-buster* was launched in 1935 to describe Thomas E. Dewey. *Bust-head*, meaning the cephalalgia following alcoholic indiscretion, is traced by the DAE to 1863, and *bustinest*, a synonym for *largest*, to 1851. "Pike's Peak or *bust*" was launched in 1858 and soon took on figurative meaning and almost proverbial

---

[1] John S. Farmer, in his Americanisms Old and New, London, 1889, p. 108, says of this: "Now common in England, but of California origin."

[2] Partridge says that it originated in the United States before 1850 and was naturalized in England *c.* 1858.

[3] Supplement I, p. 300.

dignity. Down to the 80s there was some effort by the hypersophic to preserve *burst*,[1] but they did not succeed. The Linguistic Atlas of New England [2] shows that *bust* and *busted* are widely prevalent in New England, and notes that *burst* or *bursted* " are felt as modern or refined." Berrey and Van den Bark, in the index to their " American Thesaurus of Slang," have nearly 200 entries for *to bust* and its derivatives, but only nine for *to burst*.

The paradigms of American vulgar verbs in AL4 [3] may stand with only minor changes. The majority of the forms listed are also to be found in one or more of the English dialects, and are given in Wright's " English Dialect Grammar." This is the case, for example, with the New England use of *be* for *am, is* and *are*, as in " I *be* going " and " *Be* he (or you) sick? " Pickering, in his Vocabulary of 1816, said that it was not then " so common as it was some years ago," and dismissed it as confined to " the interior towns or the vulgar," but the Linguistic Atlas of New England [4] shows that it was still flourishing in 1943. Some of the forms listed by the Atlas are: " I *be* what I *be*," " He says you *be* and I says I *ben't*," " I don't know as it *be*," " There you *be*," " They *be* good," " They *be* to Providence " and " You ain't going, *be* you? " [5] The NED says that both *be* and *ben't* survive in the Southern and Eastern dialects of England — the chief sources of the New England dialect —,[6] and cites both the singular form, " I *be* a-going," and the plural, " We *be* ready." In literary use *ic beo* (*i.e., I be*) is traced to *c.* 1000, and the NED adds that *be* remained a formidable rival to *are* until the time of Shakespeare. A long and very interesting discussion of the term in its various forms is appended.[7] It is described as " an irregular and defective verb, the full conjugation of which in modern English is effected by a union of the surviving inflexions of three originally distinct and independent verbs, *viz.* (1) the original Aryan

1 There are examples in *Harper's Magazine*, April, 1860, p. 710, and July of the same year, p. 277.
2 Vol. III, Part 2, Map 639.
3 pp. 427-36 and 444.
4 Vol. III, Part 2, Map 677.
5 Messrs. Leland O. Hunt and Roger A. Johnson, of New York, call my attention to the fact that *be* is rarely encountered in the United States in the third person singular.
6 In a translation of the First Epistle General of John into the Sussex dialect (*Click*, June, 1938, p. 13) Chapter I opens with: " It *be* about what has been from the beginning." Richard Paget says in The Nature of Human Speech, *S.P.E. Tract No. XXII*, 1925, p. 31, that the following paradigm also survives in the West Country: *I be, thou be, he be, we be, you be, they be.*
7 Vol. I, pp. 715-18.

substantive verb with stem *es-* ......, (2) the verb with stem *wes-* ......, and (3) the stem *beu.*" The DAE traces *I be* in American use (in the negative form of *I been't*) to Cotton Mather's "Magnalia," 1702. Wentworth reports examples from California, Ohio, Iowa, the Ozarks, central New York, Newfoundland, Florida and Appalachia, but the stronghold of *be* is and always has been New England.[1]

Attackted or *attacted* as the preterite and perfect participle of *to attack* is very widespread in the United States, but Wright indicates in his "English Dialect Dictionary"[2] that it is confined to relatively few regional dialects in England, *e.g.*, those of Essex, Somerset, Devonshire and the town of Newcastle. In Warwickshire, he says, it "is used by the uneducated above the lowest class, such as small tradespeople." The DAE traces it to 1689 in American use, and John Witherspoon denounced it in 1781 as "a vulgarism in America only."[3] The corresponding noun, *attackt*, has been traced to 1706, when it appeared in the Virginia state papers. John Pickering, in 1816, said that *attackted* was then confined, in the American seaports, to "the most illiterate people," but that in the interior it was "sometimes heard among persons of a somewhat higher class." He added that it was "used by the vulgar in London as well as in this country."[4] Oma Stanley notes it in "The Speech of East Texas,"[5] and Wentworth finds records of it in central New York, Tennessee, Nebraska, New Hampshire, Alabama, Georgia, Texas, Long Island, and the southern mountains. In October, 1937, the Hon. Alf M. Landon used it in a radio speech, and was held up to contumely therefor in *Newsweek*. A few weeks later he was defended by a fan who said that it had been used by "an Easterner," presumably of learning, "only a few hours before."[6] The analogous form *drownded* was used by Shaftesbury in his "Characteristics," 1711, and by Swift in his "Polite Conversation," 1738, but

[1] The negative forms, *ain't, amn't, an't* and *aren't* are discussed in AL4, pp. 51, 160, 202 and 445, and Supplement I, pp. 404–06. See also *Ain't I* and *Aren't I*, by Raven I McDavid, Jr., *Language*, Jan.–March, 1941, pp. 57–59.
[2] Reissue; Oxford, 1923, Vol. 1, p. 90.
[3] The Druid, No. VI, May 16.
[4] J. O. Halliwell, in his Dictionary of Archaic and Provincial Words; London, 1847, called it "a common participle, . . . but more extensively used in America." Thomas Wright (not to be confused with Joseph) in his Dictionary of Obsolete and Provincial English; London, 1862, did not mention it.
[5] New York, 1937, p. 62.
[6] Bobble, by G. M. Beerbower, Dec. 6, 1937.

the DAE says that it is "now vulgar." Witherspoon listed it as "a vulgarism in England and America" in 1781,[1] and Thomas G. Fessenden frowned upon it in "The Ladies' Monitor," 1818.[2] Wentworth finds it in use in all parts of the country, from Maine to Georgia and from New York to California. It is accompanied by *to drownd*, as in "He was scared of *drowndin'*."[3] Wentworth lists many other curious forms, *e.g.*, *foalded*, *swoonded*, *tossted*, *ailded*, *belongded*, *bornded*, *deceaseded* and *pawnded*, some of them confined to relatively narrow areas or classes, *e.g.*, Appalachia or the Southern Negroes, but others in use in all parts of the country.

To the same general class, more or less, belong such reinforced verbs as *to loaden, to quieten* and *to unloosen*. The NED shows that *to loose*, which is traced to *c.* 1225, had become *to loosen* in England by 1382, and *to unloosen* by *c.* 1450. The first has disappeared from the American common speech, and the third has pretty well displaced the second. In England *to unloosen* seems to be rare, but *to unloose* is preferred to *to loose* by respectable authorities.[4] *To loaden* is traced by the NED to a letter of Queen Elizabeth, 1568, and *to unloaden* to 1567. Wentworth finds the former in use in the hill country of Virginia, and a writer in *American Speech* offers evidence that it was in vogue during the high days of the Western expansion, 1830–60.[5] When *to quieten* first appeared in England, in 1828, it was denounced as "not English," but by 1852, the year of "Cranford," it was used by Mrs. Gaskell. The DAE does not list it, but Wentworth finds it in use in the Ozarks, Appalachia and Newfoundland, often with *down* following. Other such forms to be found in the records are *to shapen*,[6] *mistakened* for *mistaken*, *awe-*

---

1 The Druid, No. VI.
2 Published at Bellows Falls, Vt. See New England Provincialisms, 1818, by P. G. Perrin, *Dialect Notes*, Vol. V, Part IX, 1926, pp. 383-4.
3 The Leatherwood God, by W. D. Howells; New York, 1916.
4 For example, Jackdaw, a very popular writer on speech, in *John o'London's Weekly*, March 25, 1938. E. B. Osborn had written "when the full force of Liberal rancour was *unloosed* against him" in the *London Daily Telegraph and Morning Post*, and a correspondent at Torquay had asked for light upon it. Jackdaw replied:
"E. B. O. . . . might, had he wished, have written *loosed*, but he preferred *unloosed*, rightly I think. But why? Because here *unloosed* describes a slower and more reasoned act than *loosed*. It contemplates a rancour that has been chained up, not held ready on the leash: it had to be *unloosed* before it could be *loosed*, and by so much the more was deliberate."
5 Loadened, by J. D., Aug., 1930, p. 495.
6 Traced to 1535 by the NED but described as rare. In the adjectival form of *ill-shapened* it was found in Pills, Petticoats and Plows, by

strickened, ladened,[1] *to pinken,*[2] *soddened,*[3] *dampened, to safen,*[4] *to thinnen,*[5] *to rotten,*[6] *to smoothen,*[7] *stallded,*[8] *underminded,*[9] *confinded,* and even *misted* (*misseded*).[10] The impulse lying behind such inventions is plain enough. They are suggested by the countless accepted words that follow the same plan. Thus *to thicken* produces *to thinnen, to unbend* produces *to unloose,* which becomes *to unloosen,* and so on.[11]

The movement among verbs in English is apparently away from the so-called strong or irregular conjugation, *i.e., sing, sang, sung,* and toward the weak and regular, *i.e., wish, wished, wished; mean, meant, meant.* Charles C. Fries says in his "American English Grammar"[12] that there were 312 strong verbs, including those unchanged for tense, in Old English,[13] but that of the 195 which still survive at all 129, or 65%, have gone over to the weak category. In recent years the old strong verbs show a marked tendency to take refuge in the vulgar speech. Chaucer used *clombe* as the preterite of *to limb* without challenge, but by Shakespeare's time *climbed* had begun to supplant it, and today *clomb, clum* and the like must be

---

Thomas D. Clark, 1944, by a correspondent of *American Speech,* Oct., 1945, p. 186.

1 The last three, found in the Lawrence (Mass.) *Telegram,* Aug. 13, 1927, by Steven T. Byington, were discussed in *American Speech,* Dec., 1927, p. 163, by Louise Pound.
2 Headline in the Washington *Daily News,* Feb. 17, 1947, p. 9: "AYD's Aim is to *Pinken* U.S. College Students." AYD is a Communist-sponsored organization, American Youth for Democracy.
3 "He was found lying by the roadside *soddened* with drink." Reported in *American Speech,* April, 1928, p. 350.
4 "Let us *safen* your brakes." Reported in *American Speech,* April, 1931, p. 305. Also in The Changing Word, Minneapolis *Journal,* June 16, 1935.
5 "That diet ought to be *thinnening.*" Reported in *American Speech,* Sept., 1927, p. 515.
6 Reported from Maryland, Illinois, Alabama, Arkansas, Virginia, West Virginia, Indiana, Missouri, North Carolina and Tennessee by Wentworth.
7 Sherwin-Williams Home Painting Handbook and Catalogue, 1943, p. 10.
8 "My team *stalded* on the way to town." Recorded by Wentworth in Tennessee, Missouri, Arkansas, Alabama, Georgia, Kansas and Kentucky.
9 Found by Wentworth in Virginia, Missouri, Arkansas, Alabama and Georgia.
10 The last two are ascribed to the Middle West by Wentworth.
11 E. J. Harrison, in Verb Wanted, London *Observer,* June 30, 1935, called attention to the curious fact that English has produced no antonym to *to cheapen.* He suggested various possibilities, *e.g., to enhance,* but rejected them all as unsatisfactory. *To dear* was in use in the Fifteenth Century, but is long obsolete and forgotten.
12 New York, 1940, p. 60.
13 An interesting discussion of some of them is in Lost Preterites, *Every Saturday,* Oct. 16, 1869, pp. 481–92.

sought among the lowly. Similarly, *dove*, which once had plenty of authority behind it, is now vulgar, though of late it seems to be creeping back into more or less cultured use.[1] John Earle, in "The Philology of the English Tongue,"[2] gave a list of strong verbs that have become weak since Middle English days, e.g., *bow, beah, bowne; carve, carf, corfen; delve, dalfe, dolven; glide, glod, glode; gnaw, gnew, gnawn; help, holp, holpen; melt, malt, molten;*[3] *wash, wush, washen;*[4] and George P. Marsh, in his "Lectures on the English Language,"[5] predicted that the strong conjugations would disappear altogether. "Every new English dictionary," he said, "diminishes the number of irregular verbs." But he saw that the popular speech tended to preserve "many old preterites and participles which are no longer employed in written English."

This partiality for the old is opposed, however, by the plain fact that the weak conjugations are more logical than the strong, and hence easier to contrive and remember, and as a result there is a contrary movement toward them in the popular speech as well as on higher levels. Sometimes it goes to the length of providing regular inflections for verbs that are historically invariable in all situations, e.g., *to slit* and *to cast*;[6] sometimes it turns inflected verbs into invariable ones, e.g., *to sweat*;[7] and in many more cases it transfers a regular past participle to the place of an inflected preterite, e.g., *I taken*[8] and *I written*. In the latter event, as often happens, the admonitions of the schoolma'am sometimes have a greater effect

---

1 See AL4, p. 430, n. 5. In Hiawatha, VII, Longfellow wrote: "Straight into the water Kwasind *dove*." For the history of some of these forms in America see The Verbs of the Vulgate in Their Historical Relations, by Henry Alexander, *American Speech*, April, 1929, pp. 307-15.

2 Third edition; Oxford, 1879, pp. 261-64.

3 *Molten*, of course, is in use as an adjective.

4 Many of these survive in Wright's English Dialect Grammar, and some, e.g., *holp*, are listed by Wentworth.

5 Fourth edition; New York, 1870, p. 334.

6 From Public Service Responsibility of Broadcast Licensees; issued by the Federal Communications Commission in 1946: "The commercial program, paid for and in many instances also selected, written, *casted* and produced by advertisers and advertising agencies, is the staple fare of American listening." I take this from the *Editor & Publisher*, March 23, 1946, p. 8. See AL4, pp. 197 and 439.

7 Accountant Writer, by Giff Cheshire, *Author & Journalist*, Dec., 1945, p. 8: "I was not required to bleed for my country, but I *sweat*."

8 Joseph William Carr reported *he takened* in A List of Words From Northwest Arkansas, *Dialect Notes*, Vol. III, Part II, 1906, p. 160.

than she intends, and the discarded preterite is often used as the participle, *e.g.*, *I have took* and *I was broke*. This last change seems to be rare in the English dialects, but it has become very widespread in vulgar American, as readers of Ring Lardner, Will Rogers and other such reporters of it are well aware. Sometimes there are competing forms, *e.g.*, *I knowed* and *I known; I wish* and *I wisht*, both in the present tense; *I ate, I et* and *I eat*, all in the past;[1] *I sang* and *I sung;*[2] *he ran* and *he run*, in the past; *he did* and *he done*,[3] *he said* and *he sez; I win* and *I wan*, both in the past; *I give, I given* and *I guv*, again in the past; *I drag* and *I drug*, yet again;[4] *I got* and *I gotten; I brung,*[5] *I brang* and *I bring; they beat, they beaten* and *they bet;*[6] *they taken, they tuck, they takened* and *they tooken;*[7] *he shut*

1 I am indebted to Dr. Raven I. McDavid, Jr., for the addition of *I etten*, common in the South.
2 The New York *Times*, Aug. 29, 1936, p. 23, quoted Fries, lately cited, as saying that "in the past tense it should be agreed that the past tense of *ring* could be either *rang* or *rung;* of *sing*, either *sang* or *sung;* of *sink*, either *sank* or *sunk;* of *shrink*, either *shrank* or *shrunk;* of *spring*, either *sprang* or *sprung;* and for the participle of the verb *show*, either *showed* or *shown*."
3 In the negative there is no equivalent of *he done;* the form is always *he didn't*, usually pronounced *di'n't* or *di'n'*.
4 Caption under a picture in the Oklahoma City *Oklahoman*, July 25, 1924: "Turnbull captured it with his hands . . . and *drug* it out," *i.e.*, a 46-pound catfish out of a mudhole.
5 I am indebted to Mr. Alexander Kadison for the following from a poem entitled Old Homes, in Verses by the Way: Third Series;

New York, 1927, p. 47, by James Henry Darlington (1856-1930), Protestant Episcopal Bishop of Harrisburg, Pa.:
Sidesaddles, clocks, old portraits of
   fair women and strong men;
Tin candle-molds; sand-shakers, to
   dry the ink of goose-quill pen;
The pop corn; hams and strings of
   sage; herbs from the rafters hung;
A flintlock gun; three-cornered hat
   that from battle grandsire *brung*.
The Rev. Robert Forby says in The Vocabulary of East Anglia; London, 1830, that *I have brung* was used there, during the last twenty years of the Eighteenth Century, as often as *I have brought*. It was from that region, as we have seen in Chapter VII, Section 1, that many of the early American immigrants, especially to New England, came.
6 I am indebted here to Mr. Gilbert Chambers, of Newark, N. J.
7 Vance Randolph, in The Grammar of the Ozark Dialect, Oct., 1927, p. 2, says that the Ozark conjugation of *to take* runs as follows:

	Indicative	Subjunctive
Present	I take	Ef I take
Present perfect	I have tuck	
Past	I taken	Ef I taken
Past perfect	I had tuck	Ef I had of tuck
Future	I will take	

and *he shet;* lay, laid and *lain;*[1] bought and *boughten;*[2] *crep* and *crope; sat, set* and *sot;*[3] *wake, waked* and *woken;*[4] *pleaded* and *pled;*[5] *lent* and *lended;*[6] *drank* and *drunk;*[7] *drew* and *drawed;*[8] *leaped* and *lep;*[9] *braked* and *broke;*[10] *treaded* and *trod*,[11] and *heated, heat* and *het*.[12] It would be hard to disentangle the conflicting tend-

[1] Robert J. Menner, in Hypercorrect Forms in American English, before cited, p. 173, says that he has also heard *he lied,* apparently another unintended by-product of the schoolma'am's admonitions. In *American Speech*, June, 1927, p. 408, a correspondent reported finding *underlain* in a book by a professor at Teachers College, Columbia.

[2] Reported as prevailing in the Ozarks by Randolph, just cited.

[3] See Thornton, Vol. II, pp. 831–32.

[4] Usually followed by *up*. I find the following in the London *Observer*, June 21, 1936: "The epidemic of strikes . . . has threatened to include the concierges, among whose claims is one to the effect that they be no longer liable to be *woken up* at any hour of the night." I am indebted here to the late F. H. Tyson.

[5] *Pled*, which is ancient in English, has been creeping back into good usage of late. Pickering, in his Vocabulary of 1816, said that it was then "in the colloquial language of the Bar in New England." It was denounced as an Americanism in the *Port Folio*, Oct., 1809. But George Bernard Shaw used it in The Sanity of Art; London, 1907. I am indebted here to Mr. H. W. Seaman.

[6] Under date of March 2, 1940, Mr. W. C. Thurston, of Salisbury, Md., sent me a clipping from the local *Times* including "Group singing *lended* an atmosphere of good cheer." *To loan* is now widely used in place of *to lend* in all tenses. Miss Mary Lispenard Ward, of Asheville, N. C., tells me that in Baltimore children coming to borrow books at the Enoch Pratt Free Library branches often say that they want to *lend* them.

[7] Dr. Harold Wentworth sends me a clipping of an advertisement in the Morgantown (W.Va.) *Post*, Sept. 14, 1945, p. 7, sponsored by the local W.C.T.U. and containing the following: "Perhaps if one sits down and shuts his eyes and dreams he can make himself believe a glass of beer harmless when *drank* by the father in the home." Wentworth comments: "The W.C.T.U. won't use the word *drunk* even when it's right."

[8] In Pure English of the Soil, *S.P.E. Tract No. LXIV*, 1945, p. 103, Sir William Craigie shows that *drawed* was listed as the preterite of *to draw* in The Modern Husbandman, by William Ellis; London, 1745, along with *casted, growed, rended, rised* and *throwed*.

[9] Among American horse fanciers a jumping horse is called a *lepper*.

[10] Mr. Robert A. Johnson, of Brooklyn, tells me that in the palmy days of the trolley car the past tense of *to brake* was *broke* in both active and passive voices, *e.g.*, "That car *broke* all right yesterday," "I *broke* her a little coming into the curve."

[11] In The Past Tense of *to tread water, American Notes & Queries*, Feb., 1946, pp. 168–69, H. B. Woolf shows that *trod* is historically supported, but that *treaded* seems to be supplanting it. In 1939 the Baltimore *Evening Sun* made a low bow to history with "Buffaloes . . . bothered the railroads by *trodding* the tracks in great herds." On June 10 (editorial page) it poked fun at its own slip under the heading of New Words For Old.

[12] Mr. R. P. Whitmer, of the American Foundry & Furnace Co., Bloomington, Ill., tells me that *het* is almost invariably used for *heated* by workmen in the heating industry.

The Common Speech

encies visible here. Language, in fact, is very far from logical. Its development is determined, not by neat and obvious rules, but by a polyhedron of disparate and often sharply conflicting forces — the influence of the schoolma'am, imitation (often involving misunderstanding), the lazy desire for simplicity and ease, and sheer wantonness and imbecility.[1]

Mark Twain, in one of his philological moods, ventured the opinion that *got* is used as an auxiliary more frequently in England than in the United States, as in "I haven't *got* any money,"[2] but most other observers seem to believe that the reverse is really the case. When it comes, however, to *gotten* there is no difference of opinion, for all authorities agree that it is now one of the hallmarks of American speech. Says George O. Curme:

> The English colonists brought *gotten* along with them to their new American home. It wasn't after all an American blemish. It was good English.[3] But a great ocean lay between the English colonists and the mother country. English in England went on developing as in earlier times, and *gotten* became *got*, but in America *gotten* retained its original form. *Gotten* evidently belongs to the long list of American things.[4]

Today it is so firmly lodged that in some parts of the South, as Wentworth notes, *got* has come to be considered improper in the past tense. But in the present it flourishes lushly in the form of *gotta*, and in that form has completely obliterated *have*.[5] Other characteristics of vulgar American are the heavy use of *used to* as a general indicator of the past tense, and the use of *do* and *done* as

---

[1] The new verbs listed in Supplement I, pp. 382–406, belong mainly to rather pretentious levels of American speech, but there are always novelties on the popular level, *e.g.*, *to barbecue, to hitch-hike* and *laundried*. The NED gives *to launder* as the verb form of the noun, and *laundered* as its perfect participle, but *laundried* seems to be preferred. See The Value of English Linguistics to the Teacher, by Louise Pound, *American Speech*, Nov., 1925, p. 102.

[2] Concerning the American Language, in The Stolen White Elephant; Hartford, 1882, p. 269.

[3] The NED traces it to *c*. 1340, but marks it "now rare except in *ill-gotten*."

[4] *Gotten*, *American Speech*, Sept., 1927, pp. 495–96. See also *Get* and *Gotten*, by Wallace Rice, *American Speech*, April, 1932, pp. 280–96.

[5] In The Obsolescent Past Participle, *Saturday Review of Literature*, May 19, 1945, p. 15, Silas Bent quoted Bernard M. Allen, professor of Latin at Andover, as follows: "Some seventy-five or more years ago some American grammars began to talk against *have got* for possess or have. *Got* seemed superfluous. So grade teachers began to say, 'Don't say *have got*, say *have*. Don't use the *got*.' After a while it resulted in a subconscious avoidance of it in other uses, and going back to *gotten*."

auxiliaries. The former is always given the unvoiced *s* without a final *d*, and may be used also in the negative, as in "He *use to didn't* like it." For the following interesting observations upon it I am indebted to Mr. W. S. Hamilton, of Louisville: [1]

> I hyphenate the *to* because I believe it is felt to belong to *use* rather than to the following infinitive. In fact, the most striking thing about its employment throughout the South is that *use-to* is not always followed by the infinitive. For example:
> 1. He *use-to* wouldn't take a drink; now he drinks like a fish.
> 2. He *use-to* didn't care how he looked.
> 3. He *use-to* was always gambling, but he saves his money now.
>
> Now let's take a case in which the infinitive follows:
> 4. She *use-to* help me with my lessons.
>
> What can be made of all this? It seems that we are dealing with a handy past tense auxiliary which gives an habitual or continuing signification to the past action, somewhat as does the Latin imperfect as opposed to the perfect preterite. Greek, Latin, the Romance languages and German all possess, while English lacks, a tense form to express this shade of meaning. "She *helped me*," etc., would not have exactly the meaning of No. 4, and certainly the deletion of *use-to* would somewhat change the meaning of Nos. 1 and 2. No. 3 points to his reform better than it would if *use-to* were deleted.
>
> In the mouths of the vulgar it seems to distinguish itself from the old verb *to use* in four ways:
> 1. It is pronounced, not like the verb, but like the noun *use*.
> 2. It is uninflected.
> 3. It has acquired an inseparable suffix, *to*, which obviates the use of a preposition before a following infinitive. (In this power it is not unique. *Cf. dare-say* and *helped eat*.)
> 4. It is not limited to helping an infinitive. It may directly help to habituate (if the expression be admissible) the past tense of such modal auxiliaries as *could* and *would* and the negative intensive auxiliary *didn't*. It has been pointed out that the vulgar shy away from the subjunctive *be*. The very vulgar seem to shy away from even the infinitive *be* in the merely vulgar's *use-to-be*. And so, as in No. 3, they employ *use-to-was* as the habitual past tense of *to be*.[2]

Wentworth gives many examples of the employment of *used to* in his "American Dialect Dictionary" and says that the pronunciation discussed by Hamilton is "probably universal." He finds *used to could, would* and *was* in all parts of the country. The DAE ignores such forms, but *use-to could* was listed by the Rev. Adiel

---

[1] Private communication, Sept. 23, 1946.
[2] In A Letter From Texas, *American Speech*, April, 1940, pp. 214-15, Wilmer R. Park reports that *used to could* is often reinforced, in that great State, by *might could, might would, ought to could, may can* and *might can*. He says that these forms are encountered "even among educated people who should, and frequently do, know better."

Sherwood in the vocabulary accompanying his "Gazetteer of the State of Georgia," 1827, and in 1850 William C. Fowler put it among "ungrammatical expressions, disapproved by all," in his chapter on "American Dialects" in "The English Language."

Another peculiarity of vulgar American speech that has interested philologians is the use of *done* as an auxiliary, especially but by no means exclusively in the South. Oma Stanley[1] gives the following examples from East Texas: "He *done bought* a new hat," "He *done got* here," and "He *done done* it," and Wentworth adds the following from other parts of the country: "He's *done* in his grave," "I *done gone* went to town," "Bennie has *done married*," and "The chores *done been done*." *Done* is prefixed to a verb, says D. S. Crumb,[2] "only when action is completed. Most dialect writers stumble on this and use the word in a way it would never be heard in the South. 'The bread is *done burnt up*.' Never 'The bread is *done burning*.'" Robley Dunglison, who listed *done gone* and "What have you *done do?*" in the *Virginia Literary Museum* in 1829, called the use of the auxiliary "a prevalent vulgarism in the Southern States, . . . only heard amongst the lowest classes," and hazarded the guess that it was "probably obtained from Ireland." Adiel Sherwood cited *done said it* and *done did it* in his "Gazetteer of the State of Georgia," 1827, but without comment. The DAE offers no examples earlier than these of Sherwood.

The assimilation of *to* to the preceding verb, noted by Hamilton in the case of *use-to*, is a general process that in the opinion of William Randel may still have far to go.[3] "In the past," he says, "groups of words have coalesced, in either spelling or use. *Don* and *doff*, originally *do on* and *do off*, represent what verbs are capable of doing. Similar to this pair are various verbs that have absorbed prepositions as prefixes, *e.g.*, *overtake*, *undermine*, *inveigh*, *outplay*, *dismiss*. Such combinations . . . represent an important force in vocabulary growth." Combinations of the *use-to* form are numerous in the vulgar speech, *e.g.*, *gonna*, *gotta* and *hadda*, and there is reinforcement for them in the combinations with *have*, *e.g.*, *woulda* and *coulda*, and occasionally, among the nouns, with *of*,

---

[1] The Speech of East Texas, before cited, p. 98.
[2] The Dialect of Southeastern Missouri, *Dialect Notes*, Vol. II, Part V, 1903, p. 312.
[3] Verb Plus *to*, *American Speech*, Dec., 1939, pp. 319–20.

e.g., sorta. The final *a*, in fact, is often assumed to be *of* by the ignorant, and when Ring Lardner's baseball player takes pen in hand he writes *would of*, not *would have*. The DAE traces this form to 1844 and marks it an Americanism, but it is actually old in unstudied English and is to be found in the Verney Letters of the Fifteenth, Sixteenth and Seventeenth Centuries.[1] When, in 1938, a correspondent of the London *Observer* denounced it as an Americanism [2] he was answered by another who showed that it was common in England among persons "who have been denied more than the rudiments of education."[3] Vance Randolph, the authority on the Ozark dialect, says that in that speech "*could have* and *might have* are sometimes pronounced in three syllables, something like *could-a-of* and *might-a-of*, but *would have* is usually *would-a*."[4] Miss Brooke Jones reports hearing, in Oklahoma, the beautiful form, "Even if I *could of* knew I wouldn't *of* got to gone."[5] The NED describes this reduction of the OE *habben* (Ger. *haben*) to *a* as the *ne plus ultra* of the wearing-down tendency among English words.

To the discussion of the American use of *shall* and *will* in AL4,[6] and Supplement I [7] there is little to add. Their "so-called improper use," said Krapp,[8] "has been called the Irish difficulty, but it might as well be called the Scottish and the American and the British difficulty, for nowhere where the English language is spoken does there exist complete harmony between theory and practise in this mat-

---

[1] Wyld, p. 166. The DAE's first example is antedated, in the form of "I should *of* sent it before now," in a letter of Stutley Medbury, a Yankee pedlar, dated Paducah, Ky., Dec. 26, 1841. It is printed in New Light on the Yankee Peddler, by Priscilla Carrington Kline, *New England Quarterly*, March, 1939, p. 90. A modern example from Ringside View of Elliott Roosevelt, by Henry J. Taylor, New York *World-Telegram*, Feb. 8, 1947, p. 2: "Mr. Roosevelt, in Mr. Lewis' opinion, must not *of* known the meaning of the word *interloper*." I am indebted here to Mr. Alexander Kadison.
[2] *Might of*, by E. R. Wallace, June 5.
[3] *Of* and *Have*, by J. W. Sowan, June 12. Mr. W. G. Sullivan, of Indianapolis, calls my attention to the fact that "He *might of* been run over" and "people who gave theirselves airs which they had no business to *of* done" are in Compton Mackenzie's Youth's Encounter; New York, 1915, pp. 28 and 62. This book was published in England as Sinister Street.
[4] The Grammar of the Ozark Dialect, *American Speech*, Oct., 1927, p. 4.
[5] Piccalillie on the Vernacular, *Saturday Review of Literature*, March 3, 1945, p. 22. See also AL4, p. 444.
[6] pp. 199-201 and 445.
[7] p. 318.
[8] Vol. II, p. 264.

ter." Charles C. Fries has shown[1] that the first serious effort to differentiate between the two words was made by a grammarian named George Mason, whose "Grammaire Angloise," written in French, was published in 1622. In this forgotten work was the first adumbration of the rules still to be found in grammar-books, though it was not until 1765 that a successor named William Ward brought them up to their present state of muddled refinement. Ward was imitated by the grammarians who began to flourish after the Revolution, and especially by Lindley Murray, but Fries says that it was "only after the first quarter of the Nineteenth Century" that "the complete discussion of the rules for *shall* and *will* in independent-declarative statements, in interrogative sentences, and in subordinate clauses" became "a common feature of text-books of English grammar." These rules still survive, but the schoolma'am has failed to implant them in her pupils. The Americano, when it comes to the future tense, has abandoned *shall* altogether and even *will:* he has his say, as Sterling Andrus Leonard long ago noted,[2] by using "the much commoner contraction '*ll* and by the forms *is to go, about to go, is going to,* and the whole range of auxiliary verbs which mean both past and future." This was borne out by an investigation undertaken in 1933 by John Whyte, professor of German at Brooklyn College.[3] He submitted two German sentences, "Spielen Sie morgen?" and "Werden Sie morgen spielen?," to 139 colleagues and students, and asked them how they would ask the question in English. Most of them rejected "*Will* you play tomorrow" on the ground that they understood by it, not a simple inquiry, but an invitation, and only 2% admitted ever using "*Shall* you play?" "The first choice of the large majority of both teachers and students, with the students making it their unanimous choice," reported Whyte, was "*Are you going* to play tomorrow?"[4]

[1] American English Grammar, before cited, pp. 152-53.
[2] Shall and Will, American Speech, Aug., 1929, pp. 497-98.
[3] The Future Tense in English, College English, March, 1944, pp. 333-37.
[4] Says Eldon Emerson Smith, of Sterling, Colo. (private communication, Sept. 2, 1938): "The common speech future of all verbs in the indicative mode is 'I'm *gonna* bite,' or whatever verb. *Gonna* is pronounced with a long *o*. The future tense is frequently confused with the present progressive, as in 'I'm *going* to Europe next Summer.'" In the potential mode *may* has been almost completely displaced by *can*.

444. [The subjunctive . . . is virtually extinct in the vulgar tongue. One never hears "if I *were* you," but always "if I *was* you." In the third person the *-s* is not dropped from the verbs. One hears, not "if she *go*," but always "if she *goes*." "If he *be* the man" is never heard; it is always "if he *is*".] In a few counter-phrases, used now and then by the folk, the old form survives, *e.g.*, "*be* that as it may" and "far *be* it from me," but they carry an air of conscious sophistication. In ordinary talk the conjugation given in AL4, p. 444, prevails, to wit, *If I am, if I was* and *if I hadda been*. On higher levels, of course, the subjunctive shows more life, and there is ground for questioning the conclusion of Bradley, Krapp, Vizetelly, Fowler and other authorities that it is on its way out. Charles Allen Lloyd has shown [1] that it is still to be encountered plentifully in the newspapers [2] and even on the radio. But Thyra Jane Bevier has produced plenty of evidence [3] that it is by no means as often found in American writing as it was a few generations ago. "It was never actively alive in America," she concludes, "except about the period from 1855 to 1880."

3. THE PRONOUN

448. [The use of *n* in place of *s*, as in *ourn, hern, yourn*, and *theirn* is not an American innovation. It is found in many of the dialects of English, and is, in fact, historically quite as sound as the use of *s*.] Joseph Wright, in his "English Dialect Grammar," gives some curious double forms, analogous to *hisn*, *e.g.*, *hers'n* in Cheshire, *wes'n* in Gloucestershire, and *shes'n* in Warwickshire, Berkshire and other counties. David Humphreys, in his glossary of 1815, listed *hern* as an Americanism, and Adiel Sherwood, in 1827, put *hisn* into the same category, though noting that "many of our provincialisms are borrowed from England." Thomas G. Fessenden denounced both in "The Ladies' Monitor," 1818, as "provincial words . . . which ought to be avoided by all who aspire to speak or write the English language correctly." *Hern*, in the form

---

[1] Is the Subjunctive Dying?, *English Journal* (College Edition), May, 1937, pp. 369–73.
[2] Ernest Weekley, in On Learning English, London *Times Literary Supplement*, Aug. 12, 1944, p. 391.
says that the same is true for England.
[3] American Use of the Subjunctive, *American Speech*, Feb., 1931, pp. 207–15.

of *hiren*, is actually traced by the NED to 1340; *ourn*, in the form of *ouren*, to *c*. 1380; *yourn*, in the form of *youren*, to 1382, and *hisn*, in the form of *hysen*, to *c*. 1410. The grammarians of the Seventeenth Century declared war on all these possessives, and they have been denounced in the grammar-books ever since,[1] but they survive unscathed in the popular speech. Curme indicates that the somewhat analogous *thisn, thatn, thesen* and *thosen* are now mainly American, but shows that *whosen* occurs " in the south of England and in the Midlands."[2] I find some exhilarating specimens in my collecteana:

> Whatever is *ourn* ain't *theirn*.
> If it ain't *hisn*, then *whos'n* is it?
> I like *thisn* bettern *thatn*.
> Let him and her say what is *hisn* and *hern*.
> Everyone should have what is *theirn*.[3]

The last of these reveals a defect in English that often afflicts writers and speakers on much higher levels, to wit, the lack of singular pronouns of common gender.[4] When, on September 27, 1918, Woodrow Wilson delivered a speech at a Red Cross potlatch in New York, he permitted himself to say " No man or woman can hesitate to give what *they have*," but when the time came to edit it for his " Selected Literary and Political Papers and Addresses " he changed it to " what *he or she has*." Mrs. Eleanor Roosevelt fell into the same trap in 1941, when she wrote in " My Day ": " Someone told me last night that *they* . . ."[5] On lower levels there are specimens almost innumerable, *e.g.*, " When a person has a corn *they* go to a chiropodist."[6] Since 1858, when Charles Crozat Con-

---

[1] In the Art of Reading and Writing English; London, 1721, Isaac Watts the hymn-writer hazarded the guess that they were used " at first perhaps owing to a silly affectation, because it makes the words longer than really they are."

[2] A Grammar of the English Language. Vol. III. Syntax; Boston, 1931, p. 528.

[3] The origin of some of these *-n* endings is not settled, but it seems likely that the suffix may derive from *own*. Major William D. Workman, Jr., tells me that *his own*, as in " That is *his own*," is in use in Charleston, S. C.

[4] See AL4, p. 460.

[5] The DAE says, in discussing *everyone*, that "the pronoun is often plural: the absence of a singular plural of common gender rendering this violation of grammatical concord sometimes necessary," but under *everybody* it calls the sequence " incorrect." I am indebted here to An Author Replies, by C. A. Lloyd, *American Speech*, Oct., 1939, p. 210.

[6] A patient's letter in the *Journal of the American Medical Association*, March 25, 1939. Singular nouns are followed by plural pronouns in many other situations. Here is a

verse, the composer (1832–1918), tried to launch *thon* for *he or she* (and apparently also for *him or her*) and *thon's* for *his or her*, various ingenious persons have sought to fill this gap in English, but so far without success. In the days of her glory as the queen of American schoolma'ams, Ella Flagg Young (1845–1918), superintendent of the Chicago public schools, asked the National Education Association to endorse *hiser* (*his* plus *her*) and *himer* (*him* plus *her*), but the pedagogues gagged. Both terms, however, were listed in the College Standard Dictionary, 1922, and in 1927 the late Fred Newton Scott (1860–1930)[1] gave them a boost in a magazine article,[2] though with *hiser* changed to *hizzer*, *himer* to *himmer*, and *hesh* (*he* plus *she*) added. In 1934 James F. Morton, of the Paterson (N.J.) Museum, proposed to change *hesh* to *heesh* and to restore *hiser* and *himer*. But none of these terms has ever come into use, even among spelling reformers, nor has there been any enthusiasm for the suggestion that English adopt the French indefinite pronoun *on*, which is identical in singular and plural.[3]

This *on*, in the Fifteenth Century, seems to have begot the English pronoun *one*, but the latter continues to have so foreign and affected a smack that the plain people never use it, and even the high-toned seldom use it consistently, at least in this country. In England one occasionally encounters a sentence through which *ones* run like a string of pearls, but in the United States the second and succeeding ones are commonly changed to *he* or *his*.[4] In 1938 Gregory Hynes, an Australian lawyer, proposed *se* for *he* plus *she*, *sim* for *him* plus *her*, and *sis* for *his* plus *her*,[5] but there were no audible yells of ratification. Nor did any follow the suggestion of a reformer of Primghar, Iowa, Lincoln King by name, that *ha* be used in the nominative case, *hez* in the possessive and *hem* in the objec-

---

specimen from one of the late Will Rogers's newspaper pieces, 1931: "This is the heyday of the shyster lawyer and *they* defend each other for half rates." Also, singular pronouns are followed by plural verbs, as in the omnipresent *he don't*. One of the late Woodrow Wilson's daughters is authority for the statement that he used *he don't* in the family circle. See Current English Forum, by J. B. McMillan, *English Journal*, Nov., 1943, pp. 519–20.

[1] AL4, p. 134, n. 4.
[2] The New American Language, *Forum*, May, p. 754.
[3] French *on* — English *one*, by George L. Trager, *Romanic Review*, 1931, pp. 311–17.
[4] AL4, p. 203, and Supplement I, p. 425.
[5] See? *Liverpool Echo*, Sept. 21, 1938. I am indebted here to Mr. P. E. Cleator.

tive. Nor the suggestion of a correspondent of the Washington *Post*[1] that *hes, hir* and *hem* be adopted. Nor has *thon* ever got beyond the blueprint stage, though it made the Standard Dictionary and Webster 1934, along with *thon's*. In despair of getting rid of the clumsy *his or her* otherwise, the late Stephen Leacock (1869–1944) once proposed a bold return to "the rude days . . . when we used merely to use *his*."[2]

When, in 1926, the twenty-six linguists consulted by Sterling Andrus Leonard decided by a vote of 23 to 3 that *it is me* is sound English, and when, during the same year, the College Entrance Examination Board decided that nascent freshmen were free to use it, there was an uproar in academic circles but no noticeable jubilation among the plain people, for they had been using the form for centuries, and, what is more, they had been supported by many accepted authorities. Noah Webster allowed it in his "Grammatical Institute of the English Language," 1784, and the celebrated John P. Mahaffy, provost of Trinity College, Dublin (1839–1919), not only allowed it but did a lot of whooping for it. In defense of it he devised the following dialogue:

> A. We saw you and your wife on the beach this morning.
> B. Oh, but we didn't go out, so it can't have been *us*.

What rational person, demanded Mahaffy, would have said, "it can't have been *we?*"[3] Rather curiously, *American Speech*, then edited by Dr. Louise Pound, took an editorial slap at the College Entrance Examination Board for its action,[4] but this was atoned for in 1933 by the publication of a thundering defense of *it is me* by Wallace Rice.[5] Rice mustered an array of sages ranging from Joseph Priestley to W. D. Whitney, from A. H. Sayce to Havelock

---

[1] The Post Impressionist, Aug. 20, 1935.
[2] My Particular Aversions, *American Bookman*, Winter, 1944, p. 39. Many other holes in the English vocabulary have been noted by the ingenious. See Needed Words, by Logan Pearsall Smith, *S.P.E. Tract No. XXXI*, 1928, pp. 313–29; Words Wanted in Connection With Art, the same, pp. 330–32; The New American Language, *Forum*, May, 1927, pp. 752–56; Verbal Novelties, *American Speech*, Oct., 1938, p. 240 (*broster* is proposed for *brother and sister*) and Needed Words, by H. L. Mencken, Chicago *Herald-Examiner* (and other papers), Sept. 10, 1934. See also AL4, p. 175.
[3] I am indebted here to Mr. P. A. Browne, of the English Board of Education.
[4] Dec., 1926, p. 163.
[5] Who's There? — *Me*, Oct., 1933, pp. 58–63. The *Saturday Review of Literature*, then edited by Henry S. Canby, jumped aboard the C.E.E.B. band-wagon on Aug. 14, 1926, p. 33.

Ellis, and from Thomas R. Lounsbury to Alexander J. Ellis, all of whom upheld it as sound idiom. He might have gone much further, for George H. McKnight had assembled dozens of examples of *it is me* and even of *it is him* and *her* from sound authors in the first issue of *American Speech*,[1] and Otto Jespersen had brought together many others, and discussed the whole question with his accustomed good sense in 1894.[2] In Shakespeare's time the use of the objective pronoun had not yet established itself, and *it is I* was still the commoner form, though everyone will recall " Damned be *him* that first cries, ' Hold! Enough!,' "[3] but *c'est moi*, exactly analogous to *it is me*, had come into French in the Sixteenth Century, and it was soon influencing English.[4] Today most American philologians, though perhaps not most schoolma'ams, would probably agree with Rice:

> In the oral lessons given little children throughout the United States *it is I* is banged into their minds, and *it is me* is ranked with *ain't got none* and a long list of similar vulgarisms. . . . What a waste! What is accomplished? I can remember back sixty years to my share in a frenzied dance of the first form at school, a dozen of us yelling "*It is I, it is I!*" in derisive contempt for minutes together after we had just been told for the first time that this alone was correct. I believe this to be the normal attitude of the right-minded boy, and one that persists through life.[5]

J. M. Steadman found support for this when, in 1937, he polled the students of Emory University at Atlanta, Ga., to find out what words and phrases they considered affected. His tally-clerks reported that first place was taken by *limb*, but that *it is I* was a good second, and ran ahead of *expectorate*.[6] The Linguistic Atlas of New England[7] shows that *it is me* prevails overwhelmingly in that region, even within the Boston area. Most of the informants who reported *it is I* confessed that their use of it was the product of belaboring by the schoolma'am. " Whenever I used *me*," one of them said, " the teacher would say, ' Who is *me?*,' and then I'd change

1 Conservatism in American Speech, Oct., 1925, pp. 1–17.
2 Chapters on English; London, 1918, pp. 99–114. Reprinted from Progress in Language; London, 1894; second edition, 1909.
3 Macbeth, V.
4 Modern English in the Making, by George H. McKnight; New York, 1928, p. 195.
5 Who's There? — *Me*, above cited, p. 62. Any American politician who proposed to change the name of the Why-Not-*Me?* Club, the trades union of the fraternity, to the Why-Not-*I?* Club would go down to instant ignominy and oblivion.
6 Affected and Effeminate Words, *American Speech*, Feb., 1938, pp. 13–18.
7 Vol. III, Part 2, Map 603.

it quick." But not many of those consulted recalled the horrors of education so clearly. "If somebody knocked at my door and called 'It's *I*,'" a New York school teacher told a writer for the New York *Times* in 1946,[1] "I'd faint." In late years *it is me* has even got support from eminent statesmen. When, just before Roosevelt II's inauguration day in 1933, the first New Deal martyr, the Hon. Anton J. Cermak, was shot by a Nazi agent in Florida, he turned to Roosevelt and said, "I'm glad it was *me* instead of you," and when, in March, 1946, the Right Hon. Winston Churchill made a recorded speech at New Haven he introduced himself by saying, "This is *me*, Winston Churchill."[2] Just why *me* has thus displaced *I* is in dispute. A correspondent suggests that it may be because *I* "suggests the ego too strongly," but S. A. Nock thinks that it is because "the nominative *I* is colorless."[3]

Various authorities, including Sir William Craigie,[4] have suggested that the school grammarians' war upon *it is me* has prospered *between you and I*, just as their war upon *I seen* has prospered *I have saw*. Wyld shows that *you and I* was thus used by English writers of the Seventeenth Century,[5] and Henry Alexander produces examples from Pepys's Diary,[6] including *between him and I*. Robert J. Menner, dissenting from the Craigie theory, believes that the form came in because *you* and *I* were "often felt to be gramatically indivisible," and because *you* "had come to be used for both nominative and accusative."[7] He says:

Pronoun or noun plus *I* after preposition and verb ... is coming to be the natural usage at certain speech levels. Yet when the first personal pronoun *precedes* another pronoun or noun it is not normally in the objective

1 The Way You Say It, by Doris Greenberg, *Times Magazine*, April 7.
2 This is *Me*, *Time*, April 1, 1946. There is a legend at Princeton (*Princeton Alumni Weekly*, Feb. 4, 1927, p. 521) that when James McCosh was president there (1868–88) he one night knocked on a student's door, and on being greeted with "Who's there?," answered "It's *me*, Mr. McCosh." The student, unable to imagine the president of the college using "so ungrammatical an expression," bade him go to the devil. But that was a long while ago.
3 It is *Me*, *Saturday Review of Literature*. The date, unhappily not determined, was after Aug. 14, 1926.
4 The Irregularities of English, *S.P.E. Tract No. XLVIII*, 1937, pp. 286–91.
5 p. 332.
6 The Language of Pepys's Diary, *Queen's Quarterly*, Vol. LIII, No. 1, 1946. Other examples are in The Sullen Lovers, by Thomas Shadwell, I, 1668, and The Relapse, by John Vanbrugh, V, 1698.
7 Hypercorrect English, *American Speech*, Oct., 1937, pp. 176 and 177.

form in careless speech. I heard the following from one man calling to another from a porch:

A. They invited *me and Jim.*
B. (Not having heard) What?
A. (louder) They invited *Jim and I* to their party.

This is natural syntax among people who are neither at the lowest speech level, where *me* and *him* and *her* are common as nominatives, nor at the highest, where family tradition or academic training make the standard literary forms prevail.

Craigie says that "no one would venture to carry this confusion so far as to say *between you and we*," but I am not too sure, for I have encountered *he* in the objective following a preposition in the headline of a great moral newspaper.[1] Mark Twain, a very reliable (if sometimes unconscious) witness to American speechways, used *between you and I* regularly until W. D. Howells took him in hand.[2]

Whom need not detain us, for it does not exist in the American common speech. Even in England, says the NED, and on the highest levels, it is "no longer current in natural colloquial speech." When it is used on those levels in the United States it is frequently used incorrectly, as F. P. Adams used to demonstrate almost daily when he was conducting his newspaper column.[3] It was rejected as "effeminate" by Steadman's Emory University students,[4] and got as many adverse votes as *divine, dear* and *gracious* (exclamation). Indeed, only *sweet, lovely* and *darling* beat it. The Linguistic Atlas of New England shows that its use there is pretty well confined to the auras of Harvard and Yale, and that even so it is rare. George H. McKnight has supplied evidence that many English authors of the first chop, including Richard Steele, Jane Austen, George Meredith and Laurence Housman have used *who* freely in situations where *whom* is ordained by the grammar-books,[5] and I have no doubt that a similar inquiry among Americans would show many more. J. S. Kennedy, in 1930, printed a learned argument to the effect that the use of *who* in "*Who* did he marry?" need not be defended as a matter of mere tolerance, but may be ac-

1 Silva Says Killing Prompted by Insults at *He* and Buddy, Los Angeles *Examiner*, June 25, 1925, p. 2.
2 For example, in a letter from New York to the *Alta Californian* (San Francisco), May 18, 1867.
3 Horrible examples from *Liberty*, the *Red Book, Common Sense*, the *Commonweal* and an Associated Press dispatch are assembled by Dwight L. Bolinger in Whoming, *Words*, Sept., 1941, p. 70.
4 Affected and Effeminate Words, already cited.
5 Conservatism in American Speech, *American Speech*, Oct., 1925, p. 14.

counted for on the ground that *who,* in this situation, is actually in the objective case, and has been so almost as long as *you* has been in the nominative.[1] Just, he says, as "we have objective *you* and nominative *you* side by side, with *ye* preserved in the unstressed form in speech and also for very formal or archaic styles," so "we have nominative *who* and objective *who* side by side, with *whom* reserved for more formal style, chiefly written." In the common speech *that* is often substituted for both *who* and *whom,* as in "He's the man *that* I seen." Robert J. Menner has shown[2] that *that* has also largely displaced *whose,* as in "He's the fellow *that* I took his hat," and that often even *that* itself is suppressed by periphrasis, as in "He's the fellow I took his hat" and "She's the girl I've been trying to think of her name." The substitution of *them* for *these* or *those,* as in "*Them* are the kind I like," was denounced as a barbarism of the frontier South and West by Adiel Sherwood in 1827, but it has survived gloriously and Wentworth offers examples from all parts of the country. Says Horace Reynold:

> The use of *them* as a demonstrative is the mark of the manual worker. He finds *these* and *those* a little sissified and high-toned. He feels more comfortable in *them* shoes than in *these* shoes. *Them* is a word with a strong end; a man can get his teeth into it. Like the Irishman's *me* for *my, them* beats *these* hollow for force. The Irishman's "Give me some likker to temper *me* pain" has the same shirtsleeve, spit-on-me-hands wallop as the American's "Shut *them* winders!"[3]

The Southern *you-all* seems to be indigenous to the United States: there is no mention of it in Wright's "English Dialect Dictionary" nor in his "English Dialect Grammar." What is more, it seems to be relatively recent. Wentworth quotes "I b'lieve *you' all* savages in this country" from Anne Royall's "Letters From Alabama," 1830, but it is highly probable that this *you' all* was simply a contraction of *you are all. You-all* struck a Northerner visiting Texas as "something fresh" so late as 1869, though he had apparently been in the South during the Civil War and was familiar with *you uns.*[4] It was not listed by any of the early writers

---

[1] On *Who* and *Whom, American Speech,* Feb., 1930, pp. 25-55.
[2] Troublesome Relatives, *American Speech,* June, 1931, pp. 341-46.
[3] Piccalilli on the Vernacular, *Saturday Review of Literature,* Jan. 27, 1945, p. 14.
[4] South-western Slang, by Socrates Hyacinth, *Overland Monthly,* Aug., 1869, p. 131.

on Americanisms, and it is missing even from Bartlett's fourth and last edition of 1877. On the question of its origin there has never been any agreement. In 1907 Dr. C. Alphonso Smith, then head of the English department at the University of North Carolina,[1] published a learned paper on the subject in *Uncle Remus's Magazine* (Atlanta), then edited by Joel Chandler Harris,[2] in which he rehearsed some of the theories then prevailing. One, launched by a correspondent of the New York *Times* signing himself F. B.,[3] ascribed the pronoun to the influence of the Low German spoken by German settlers in Lunenburg, Mecklenburg, Brunswick and Charlotte counties, Virginia. This correspondent said:

A little imagination will help us see two old dignitaries meet and address each other with "Good'n morn, wohen wilt *ye all?*" (Whence will ye already?). And after the confab is over they will express their regret by saying "Wilt *ye all* gaan?" (Wilt ye already go?) and the answer, "Ya, *we* wilt *all* foort" (Yes, we will already forth).

Another theory, also advanced by a correspondent of the *Times*,[4] was thus set forth:

During the Cotton Exposition at New Orleans, 1885–86, I was in an official position which brought me into contact with hundreds of people from all parts of the Union, and as I was from Texas I seemed singled out for benevolent missionary work on the part of visitors from Northern States. With cheerful frankness they pointed out the many shortcomings of my people, and among them this idiom of *you-all*. I was boarding at the time with a Frenchwoman. I poured out to her my woes in English, and she expressed her sympathy in French. When I mentioned *you-all* as one of our sins she exclaimed: "Mais c'est naturelle, ça! On dit toujours nous tous, *vous tous!*"

Smith rejected both of these etymologies, and sought to show, by quotations from Shakespeare and the King James Bible, that *you-all* went back in England to Elizabethan times,[5] but his quota-

---

[1] Smith was a North Carolinian, born in 1864, and took his Ph.D. in English at the Johns Hopkins in 1893. After leaving the University of North Carolina in 1909 he became professor of English at the University of Virginia. In 1917 he moved to the Naval Academy as head of the English department, and there he remained until his death in 1924. He was the author of New Words Self-Defined, 1919, and many other books.

[2] *You All* as Used in the South, July. This paper was reprinted in the *Kit-Kat* (Cincinnati), Jan., 1920.

[3] Jan. 2, 1904.

[4] M. F. H., Jan. 16, 1904. Both communications were printed in the *Times Saturday Review of Books*.

[5] See also *You-all* in English and American Literature, by H. P. Johnson, *Alumni Bulletin* (University of Virginia), Jan., 1924, pp. 28–33; Shakespeare and Southern *You-all*, by Edwin F. Shewmake, *American*

tions offered him very dubious support, for those that were metrical showed the accent falling on *all*, not on *you*, and in another part of his article he had to admit that this shift of accent clearly distinguished the Southern *you-all* from *you all* in the ordinary sense of *all of you*. He sought to explain the difference as follows:

> In *you all*, *all* is an adjective modifying the pronoun *you*. But in *you-all* the parts of speech have changed places. *All* is the pronoun, standing for some other substantive, as *folks*, and *you* is the modifying adjective. This interchange is not without analogy in English. In such phrases as *genitive singular* and *indicative present* the first words were originally nouns, *singular* and *present* being adjectives. The plurals were *genitives singular* and *indicatives present*. But these phrases, borrowed from Latin, were exceptions to the usual position of words in English, which demands that adjectives precede nouns. The exception could not hold its own against the precedent established by the numberless phrases in which adjectives regularly preceded their nouns. After a while, such was the influence of mere position, the words *genitive* and *indicative*, standing in the normal position of adjectives, became adjectives, and the words *singular* and *present*, standing in the normal position of nouns, became nouns. Thus the plurals of these phrases are now *genitive singulars* and *indicative presents*. In similar fashion *you all* (pronoun plus adjective) passed into *you-all* (adjective plus pronoun).

Like any other patriotic Southerner, Smith devoted a part of his paper to arguing that *you-all* is never used in the singular, and to that end he summoned Joel Chandler Harris and Thomas Nelson Page as witnesses. This is a cardinal article of faith in the South, and questioning it is almost as serious a *faux pas* as hinting that General Lee was an octoroon.[1] Nevertheless, it has been questioned very often, and with a considerable showing of evidence. Ninety-nine times out of a hundred, to be sure, *you-all* indicates a plural, implicit if not explicit, and thus means, when addressed to a single person, *you and your folks* or the like, but the hundredth time it is impossible to discover any such extension of meaning. Eleven years before Smith wrote, in 1896, correspondents of *Dialect Notes* had reported hearing the pronoun in an unmistakable

---

Speech, Oct., 1938, pp. 163–68; The Southerners' *You-all*, by E. Hudson Long, *Southern Literary Messenger*, Oct., 1939. pp. 652–55, and *You-all* in the Bible, by Darwin F. Boock, *American Mercury*, Feb., 1933, p. 246.

[1] In Dixie is Different, *Printer's Ink*, Sept. 28, 1945, p. 23, D. C. Schnabel, of Shreveport, La., thus advised Northern advertisement writers: "And don't — don't — don't have your copy character in the South saying *you-all* to one person. (Hollywood please copy.) It sounds as incongruous in the South as to say *they is*."

singular in North Carolina, Delaware and Illinois,[1] and during the years following there had been a gradual accumulation of testimony to the same effect from other witnesses, including Southerners. In 1926 Miss Estelle Rees Morrison provoked an uproar by suggesting in *American Speech* that, when thus used in the singular, *you-all* was a plural pronoun of courtesy analogous to the German *sie*, the Spanish *usted*, and indeed the English *you* itself.[2] In May, 1927, Lowry Axley, of Savannah, declared in the same journal that in an experience covering " all the States of the South," he had " never heard any person of any degree of education or station in life use the expression in addressing another as an individual," and added somewhat tartly that the idea that it is ever so used " by any class of people . . . is a hydra-headed monster that sprouts more heads apparently than can ever be cut up." A correspondent signing himself G.B. and writing from New Orleans, offered Axley unqualified support three months later,[3] but after two more months had rolled round Vance Randolph popped up with direct and unequivocal testimony that *you-all* was " used as singular in the Ozarks " and that he had " heard it daily for weeks at a time."[4]

This encouraged Miss Morrison, and in 1928 she pledged her word that she had heard it so used at Lynchburg, Va., and also in Missouri.[5] The Southern brethren were baffled by this, for the Confederate code of honor forbade questioning the word of a lady, so Axley had to content himself with slapping down a German professor who had stated incautiously, on what he had taken to be sound sub-Potomac evidence, that *you-all* was often reduced to *you'll*.[6] The professor, of course, was in error: the true contraction, as Axley explained, was and always has been *y'all*.[7] At the same time Miss Elsie Lomax offered indirect testimony to the use of *you-all* in the singular by showing that a plural form, *you-alls*, prevailed in Kentucky and Tennessee. Early in 1929 a witness from Kansas testified that he was " addressed as *you-all* twice in the sin-

[1] Vol. I, Part X, 1896, p. 411.
[2] *You All* and *We All*, *American Speech*, Dec., 1926, p. 133.
[3] *You-all*, *American Speech*, Aug., 1927, p. 476.
[4] The Grammar of the Ozark Dialect, *American Speech*, Oct., 1927, p. 5.
[5] *You-all* Again, *American Speech*, Oct., 1928, pp. 54-55.
[6] The professor was Walther Fischer, of Giessen: *You-all*, *American Speech*, Sept., 1927, p. 496.
[7] *Y'all*, *American Speech*, Dec., 1928, p. 103.

gular, in one day, at Lawrence," the seat of the State university.[1] The Southerners thus seemed to be routed, but in June, 1929, Axley returned to the battle with a polished reply to Miss Morrison, in which he argued that, even if *you-all* was occasionally used in the singular in the South, it was not "widespread," and then retreated gracefully by referring unfavorably to Al Smith's use of *foist* for *first*, to George Philip Krapp's curious declaration that *a.w.o.l.* was pronounced as one word, *áwol*, in the Army, and to the imbecility of comic-strip bladder-writers who were trying to introduce *I-all*.[2]

In the years following various other depositions reporting *you-all* in the singular were printed in *American Speech*,[3] but the Southerners stuck to their guns, and in 1944 they got sturdy support from Guy R. Vowles, a Northerner who testified that, in nineteen years in the South, he had never heard *you-all* used in the singular.[4] Mr. Vowles added that he had often heard a second *all* added to *you-all*, as in "*Y'll all* well?," and cited support for it in the German ": Geht es euch *allen* gut?"[5] The *I-all* denounced by Axley is not recorded in any dictionary save Wentworth's, where it appears only as a jocosity by a radio crooner. But Webster 1934 lists *he-all*, though not *she-all*, *him-all* or *her-all*. It also lists *who-all*. Wentworth lists *he-all* from Webster and records *they-all*, *me-all* and both *we-all* and *we-alls*, but omits the others. Oma Stanley says in "The Speech of East Texas"[6] that the white freemen of that area use *you-all* "only as a plural," express or understood, but that the blackamoors "may use it with singular meaning as a polite form." Its declension in the Ozarks is thus given by Randolph:

[1] More Testimony, *American Speech*, April, 1929, p. 328.
[2] For more about *I-all* see Mr. Axley and *You-all*, by Herbert B. Bernstein, *American Speech*, Dec., 1929, p. 173.
[3] For example, in *You-all* Again, by T. W. Perkins, April, 1931, p. 304 (in Arkansas), and More *You-all* Testimony, by Thomas C. Blaisdell, June, 1931, pp. 390–91 (North Carolina).
[4] A Few Observations on Southern *You-all*, *American Speech*, April, 1944, pp. 146–47.
[5] Further discussions are in The Truth About *You-all*, by Bertram H. Brown, *American Mercury*, May, 1933, p. 116; *You-all* Again, New York *Times* (editorial), Jan. 15, 1945; As It is Spoken, *Journal of the American Medical Association* (Tonics and Sedatives), May 20, 1944, and *You-all*, by H. L. Mencken, New York *American* (and other papers), July 16, 1934. See also Bartlett's Familiar Quotations; eleventh edition; New York, 1937, p. 952.
[6] pp. 98–99.

	Singular	Plural
	First Person	
Nominative		we-all
Possessive		we-all's
Objective		
	Second Person	
Nominative	you-all	you-all, you-alls
Possessive	you-all's	you-all's
Objective	you-all	you-all
	Third Person	
Nominative		they-all
Possessive		they-all's [1]
Objective		

It will be noted that *us-all*, which Wentworth finds in Kentucky and North Carolina, is omitted, and also *he-all*, *she-all*, *her-all*, *him-all*, *his-all* and *them-all*. In the same paradigm from which I have just quoted Randolph gives the following declension of the analogous forms in *-un*:

	First Person
Nominative	we-uns
Possessive	we-uns
Objective	us-uns
	Second Person
Nominative	you-uns
Possessive	you-un's
Objective	you-uns

No singular forms and no third person forms are listed. Other observers, as Wentworth notes, have reported *he-un*, *she-un*, *them-uns*, *this-un* and *that-un*. Wentworth's examples show that the use of *-un* is especially characteristic of Appalachian speech, though it has extended more or less into the lowlands. Some one once observed that the eastern slope of the mountains marks roughly the boundary between *we-uns* and *you-all*, and that the Potomac river similarly marks off the territory of *you-all* from that of the Northern *yous*. But such boundaries are always very vague. In 1888 L. C. Catlett, of Gloucester Court-House, Va., protested in the *Century* [2] against the ascription of *we-uns* and *you-uns* to Tidewater Virginia speakers in some of the Civil War reminiscences then running in that magazine. He said: "I know all classes of people in Tidewater Virginia, the uneducated as well as the educated. I have never heard anyone say *we-uns* or *you-uns*. I have

[1] The Grammar of the Ozark Dialect, *American Speech*, Oct., 1927, p. 6.
[2] Aug., pp. 477-78.

asked many people about these expressions. I have never yet found anyone who ever heard a Virginian use them." But while this may have been true of Tidewater, it was certainly not true of the Virginia uplands, as a Pennsylvania soldier was soon testifying:

> At the surrender of General Lee's army, the Fifth Corps was designated by General Grant to receive the arms, flags, etc., and we were the last of the army to fall back to Petersburg, as our regiment (the 6th Pennsylvania Cavalry) was detailed to act as provost-guard in Appomattox Court-House. As we were passing one of the houses on the outskirts of the town, a woman who was standing at the gate made use of the following expression: "It is no wonder *you-uns* whipped *we-uns*. I have been yer three days, and *you-uns* ain't all gone yet."[1]

In the same issue of the *Century* Val. W. Starnes, of Augusta, Ga., reported hearing both *we-uns* and *you-uns* among "the po' whites and pineywood tackeys" of Georgia, and also in the Cumberland Valley and in South Carolina. Wentworth gives examples from every State of the South, both east and west of the Mississippi, and Miss Jane D. Shenton, of Temple University, tells me that *you-uns* and *you-unses* are also common at Carlisle, Pa.[2] Jespersen says that the pronouns in *-uns* are derived from a Scottish dialect.[3] The DAE omits *we-uns*, but traces *you-uns* to 1810, when it was reported in Ohio by a lady traveler.[4] It was new to her, and "what it means," she said, "I don't know." With this solitary exception, neither *you-uns* nor *we-uns* was recorded by any observer of American speech before 1860. Socrates Hyacinth said in 1869[5] that he had first heard the form in the South during the Civil War, and Bartlett said in his fourth edition of 1877 that it was "developed during the war."

"The pronoun of the second person singular" — to wit, *thou* —, says Wright in "The English Dialect Grammar,"[6] "is in use in almost all the dialects of England to express familiarity or con-

[1] Notes on *We-uns* and *You-uns*, by George S. Scypes, *Century*, Oct., 1888, p. 799. There is a similar story in Americanisms: The English of the New World, by M. Schele de Vere; New York, 1872, p. 569. A Confederate soldier captured by Sheridan in the charge through Rockfish Gap is credited with "We didn't know *you-uns* was around us all, and *we-uns* reckoned we was all safe, till *you-uns* came ridin' down like mad through the gap and scooped up *we-uns* jest like se many herrin'."
[2] Private communication, July 14, 1937.
[3] A Modern English Grammar; Heidelberg, 1922, Part II, Vol. I, p. 262.
[4] A Journey to Ohio in 1810, by Margaret V. (Dwight) Bell; not published until 1920.
[5] South-western Slang, *Overland Monthly*, Aug., p. 131.
[6] p. 272.

tempt, and also in times of strong emotion; it cannot be used to a superior without conveying the idea of impertinence. ... In southern Scotland it has entirely disappeared from the spoken language and is only very occasionally heard in other parts of Scotland." In the United States it dropped out of use at a very early date, and no writer on American speech so much as mentions it. The more old-fashioned American Quakers still use the objective *thee* for the nominative *thou*, and the singular verb with it, e.g., *thee is* and *is thee?* The question as to how, when and why this confusing and irrational use of *thee* originated has been debated at length, but there seems to be no agreement among the authorities.[1]

Margaret Schlauch suggests in " The Gift of Tongues "[2] that *this-here, these-here, those-there, them-there*, and *that-there* may reveal a pair of real inflections in the making. That is to say, *-here* and *-there* may become assimilated eventually to the pronouns.[3] Wright says in " The English Dialect Grammar "[4] that in some of the English dialects *-here* has begun to take on the significance of proximity, not only in space but also in time, and that *-there* similarly connotes the past as well as distance. Wentworth's examples show that *this-here* frequently occurs as *this-'ere, this-yere, this-yer, thish-yer*, and *this-hyar*, with like forms for *these-here*, and that the *-there* of *that-there, those-there* and *them-there* changes to *-ere, -ar, -thar, -air, -are* and *-ah*. Witherspoon, in 1781, listed *this-here* and *that-there* among vulgarisms prevailing in both England

---

[1] The Speech of Plain Friends, by Kate Watkins Tibbals, *American Speech*, Jan., 1926, pp. 193–209; Quaker *Thee* and Its History, by Ezra Kempton Maxfield, *American Speech*, Sept., 1926, pp. 638–44; Quaker *Thou* and *Thee*, by the same, *American Speech*, June, 1929, pp. 359–61; Nominative *Thou* and *Thee* in Quaker English, by Atcheson L. Hench, *American Speech*, June, 1929, pp. 361–63; Some Peculiarities of Quaker Speech, by Anne Wistar Comfort, *American Speech*, Feb., 1933, pp. 12–14; and *Thee* and *Thou*, by William Platt, and The Quakers, by Isabel Wyatt, both in the London *Observer*, March 6, 1938.

[2] New York, 1945, p. 147.
[3] *This* is itself the product of such an assimilation. The NED says that it was formed " by adding *se, si* (probably the Gothic *sai*, see, behold) to the simple demonstrative represented by *the* and *that*." It was, at the start, inflected for case and gender as well as for number, but " in Middle English these forms were gradually eliminated or reduced, until by 1200 in some dialects, and by the Fifteenth Century in all, *this* alone remained in the singular."
[4] p. 277.

and America, and noted that they were used "very freely ... by some merchants, whom I could name, in the English Parliament, whose wealth and not merit raised them to that dignity." This use, he added, exposed them "to abundance of ridicule." Mark Twain used *thish-yer* in his "Jumping Frog" story, 1865, and in "Tom Sawyer," 1876, and *this h-yere* in "Huckleberry Finn," 1884. The NED traces *this-here* to *c.* 1460, but offers no example of *these-here* before the Nineteenth Century. It traces *that-there* to 1742. All these forms are constantly and copiously in use in the American common speech.[1]

4. THE NOUN

461. [The only inflections of the noun remaining in English are those for number and for the genitive, so it is in these two regions that the few variations to be noted in vulgar American occur.] False singulars, made by back formation, are numerous, *e.g., Chinee, Portugee, Japanee, trapee, specie, tactic* and *measle,* nor are they confined to the untutored.[2] I have encountered *statistic* in a solemn pronunciamento by a Catholic dignitary,[3] in an uplifting editorial in a literary weekly,[4] in a paper in a leading scientific journal,[5] in a report of a committee of the American Society of Newspaper Editors,[6] and in the annual report of the Librarian of Congress.[7] The NED, which marks it "rare," presents only a few examples, the first of which, dated 1796, comes from an American book. Several correspondents report that they have heard *len* (from *lens*) and even encountered it in print.[8] *Pant* (from

---

1 See AL4, p. 452.
2 *Tactic* may really be called accepted. The NED has examples from Edmund Burke, Edward A. Freeman and Mark Pattison. Mr. Arthur D. Jacobs, of Manchester, tells me that it was used habitually by Sir Stafford Cripps in his Popular Front campaign of 1939. It has been used in this country by a writer as generally careful as Oswald Garrison Villard (Strategy of Good Manners, *Negro Digest*, Jan., 1946, p. 21) and appears frequently in the *Congressional Record*, *e.g.,* July 19, 1945, p. 7849, col. 2, and July 26, 1946, p. A4705, col. 2.
3 Catholics and Birth Control, by Monsignor John A. Ryan, *American Mercury*, April, 1944, p. 505.
4 The Library's Customers, by J. T. W(interich?), *Saturday Review of Literature*, Dec. 22, 1945, p. 16.
5 Heredity of the Agglutinogens M and N of Landsteiner and Levine, by Alexander S. Wiener, *Human Biology*, May, 1935, p. 231.
6 *Editor and Publisher*, Dec. 14, 1946, p. 78, col. 3.
7 For the year ended June 30, 1945, p. 37.
8 For example, Miss Jane D. Shenton, of Temple University, and Mr. Barrington S. Havens, of Schenectady, N. Y.

pants) was reported in the Middle West in *American Speech* in 1926,[1] and has since been found in Tennessee and South Carolina.[2] I have myself had the felicity to discover *homo sapien* in the Baltimore *Sun*.[3] When the English *innings* became *inning* in the United States is uncertain. The DAE shows that *innings* was used by Henry Chadwick in his pioneer treatise on baseball in 1868,[4] but that *Outing* was using the singular form in 1886. The NED says that in Great Britain the term is "always in the plural form *innings*, whether in singular or plural sense." It is traced as a cricket term to 1746. Partridge says that *to have a good innings*, meaning to be lucky, especially in money matters, has been in use in England since *c.* 1860, and in the sense of to live a long time since *c.* 1870, and that *to have a long innings*, in the latter sense, has been used since *c.* 1860.[5] A number of botanical terms ending in *-s*, e.g., *coleus* and *gladiolus*, are commonly assumed to be plurals in both England and the United States, and in consequence false singular forms are in use. The NED traces *gladiole* to *c.* 1420. Noah Webster noted in 1789[6] that the Americans of that time mistook *chaise* (borrowed from the French about 1700) for a plural, and so developed a singular form, *shay*, which the DAE traces to 1717. It did not appear in England until later.

Rather curiously, many obviously plural forms are used in the singular without change, e.g., *stockyards*, *grounds* and (golf) *links*. On the level of the common speech Dr. Louise Pound adds *ways*, as in "He walked a *ways* with her" and "The house is some *ways* off," and *suds*, as in a thick *suds*.[7] She adds that she has also heard *corp*, from *corpse*, and *appendic*, from *appendix*. She says:

> At first glance the plural-singulars first cited associate themselves vaguely with the adverbial *-s*, genitive in origin, which appears in *always*, *lengthways*,

[1] May, p. 460: "There is a Kalamazoo *Pant* Company at Kalamazoo, manufacturers of Kazoo trousers."
[2] I am indebted here to Mr. Hayden Siler, of Jellico, Tenn., and Lieut. Col. F. G. Potts, of Mt. Pleasant, S. C.
[3] Advertisement of the McKay Foundation, Dec. 27, 1945, p. 9: "Some say it's fifty or a hundred million years since the first *homo sapien* roamed the plains and hunted in the hills."
[4] The Game of Baseball: How to Learn It, How to Play It, and How to Teach It; New York, p. 41.
[5] *Paratroop*, by back formation from *paratroops*, has been reported from England (*American Speech*, Dec., 1944, p. 311), but so far as I know it has not come into use in the United States.
[6] Dissertations on the English Language, p. 118.
[7] Some Plural-Singular Forms, *Dialect Notes*, Vol. IV, Part I, 1913, pp. 48–50.

crossways, sideways, etc., as though *-s* were transferred from these adverbs to the singulars of the nouns. But though this association might help in the case of *a ways,* the commonest of the expressions – possible for this very reason – and often adverbial in function, it could hardly assist to account for *a thick woods* or for *a picnic grounds,* etc. Perhaps the speakers start with the singular in mind, as the presence of the indefinite article shows, then shift to the plural because the nouns involved are employed so frequently in the plural; note *roadways, crossways, pleasure grounds, playgrounds, woods* (as opposed to *wood,* the cut timber), *links, works, stockyards,* and the like. But, more probably, the plural forms are preceded by the indefinite article because treated as collective, as though to give the general impression of a singular, e.g., *a way(s)* made up of ways of different kinds or lengths, *a wood(s)* made up of separate trees or group of trees, *a ground(s)* made up of lawns, parks, and the like. In other words, the singular collective idea predominates over the grammatical form. Yet this tendency holds for certain expressions only. There is no such psychological confusion in the case of seemingly parallel words: for example, *a groves, a lawns, a parks* do not occur; this because the plurals of these words do not so promptly suggest, logically or through association, the idea of a singular.

I have never encountered any singulars, valid or false, for *scissors, spectacles, clothes, athletics, series* or *obsequies,* but *hoe* from *hose* is reported from the Ozarks [1] and *calv* from *calves* and *hoov* from *hooves* from Nebraska.[2] *Aborigine* from *aborigines,* though it is described by the NED as " etymologically as indefensible as *serie* or *indice,*" is traced in American use to 1858, though M. M. Mathews expresses doubt that it is an Americanism.[3] There is an interesting section on such forms in A. Smythe Palmer's " Folk-Etymology,"[4] a curious and useful work that has fallen into undeserved neglect. He points out, for example, that *Bible,* from the Latin *biblia,* is really a plural form, and it follows that such forms as the *Book,* the *Good Book* and the *Book of Books,* so often used by theologians, are incorrect. Palmer also reminds genealogists that the surname *Janeway* is from *Genoese* and used to be *Januweys* or *Januayes,* and that its present singular form is as questionable as *Chinee* or *Portugee.* Every high-school boy should be aware that *pea* is a false singular from *pease,* but Palmer is on less familiar ground when he points out that the original form of *potato,* from the Haitian *batatas,* was *potatus,* po-

[1] More Words From the Ozarks, by Vance Randolph, *Dialect Notes,* Vol. V, Part X, 1927, p. 475.
[2] Folk-Etymological Singulars, by Wilbur Gaffney, *American Speech,* Dec., 1927, p. 130.
[3] The New Element in American English, *American Speech,* April, 1945, p. 106.
[4] London, 1882, pp. 592–664.

tados or *potatoes* in both numbers, and that *sherry* is a false singular from *sherris* or *seres* (i.e., *Xeres* or *Jerez*, a town in Spain).

The use of *license, cheese, molasses* and *Baptist* as plurals is noted in AL4, p. 462. In the case of *cheese*, a false singular, *chee*, has developed, especially in the Southern mountains.[1] This confusion between singular and plural extends to many words ending in *-s, -ist, -ish, -ex,* and even *-age*. John Gerard, writing in the latter part of the Sixteenth Century,[2] said "*radish* are eaten raw," and Cotton Mather, in his Diary for 1711, wrote "a number of people of both *sex*." The surname of Tom *Collins*, inventor of the drink of the same name, was converted into a plural in a rum advertisement in a liquor trade paper in 1944.[3] *Baptist*, pronounced *baptizz*, is not only in almost universal use as a plural among the folk of the *Are-You-Saved?* country; it also makes frequent appearances in print.[4] In the same region *cabbage* is also a plural, as Wentworth shows by examples from North Carolina, Tennessee, Georgia, Florida and Arkansas. So is *sausage*. So, again, is *tourist*.[5] The late Will Rogers, a master of the common speech, even made one of *business*.[6] I find *enemy* as a plural in an official Army paper[7] and also in the London *Times:*[8] perhaps the Army borrowed it from the English.

Wentworth lists many double plurals in the common speech, especially in the South, e.g., *oxens, womens, dices, currantses, lices, folkses, sheeps, childrens, tomatoeses, nestes, postes, geeses, hogses, jeanses* and *(in)gredientses*. He also turns up two triple plurals, *feetses* and *menses (mens)*. Wright shows in his "English Dialect Grammar" that such forms are very common in the English dialects, and that some of them preserve the old *-en* plural ending, e.g., *geesen* and *micen*.

---

[1] Tennessee Mountains, by H. A. Edson and others, *Dialect Notes*, Vol. I, Part VIII, 1895, p. 376.

[2] The Herball, or General Historie of Plants; London, 1597. Quoted in *Encore*, Oct., 1943, p. 492.

[3] *Beverage Retailer Weekly*, Aug. 28, 1944, p. 9: "Thousands of Marimba *Collins* are being served and enjoyed every single day."

[4] Livermore (Ky.) *Times*, July 30, 1937, p. 1: "*Baptist* Hold Association." I am indebted here to Mr. Roger C. Hackett.

[5] *American Speech*, Jan., 1927, p. 217.

[6] Letters of a Self-Made Diplomat to His President; New York, 1926. Quoted in *Encore*, April, 1944, p. 395. I hope I need not add that Rogers was anything but illiterate himself. I saw him often in the 1925 era and we had many an hilarious palaver over the American vulgate.

[7] *Special Service Digest*, Oct. 30, 1944, p. 1.

[8] Gallantry on Northwest Frontier, Aug. 24, 1938.

5. THE ADJECTIVE

"In the dialects [of English]," says Wright, "the comparative suffix *-er* and the superlative *-est* are added to practically all adjectives, polysyllabic as well as monosyllabic. *More* and *most* are as a rule only used to supplement the regular comparisons, as *more beautifuller, more worst*."[1] He adds *betterer, betterest, bestest, worser, worsest, morer* and *mostest*. Wyld, in his "History of Modern Colloquial English,"[2] recalls Shakespeare's *most unkindest cut of all*, and traces *badder, more better, more surer, more gladder, more larger, more greater, more stronger, more fresher*,[3] *most best, most bitterest, most hardest* and *most nearest* to the Sixteenth and Seventeenth Centuries.[4] Jespersen notes that "the natural tendency in colloquial speech is to use the superlative in speaking of two," and that "this is found very frequently in good authors." Russell Thomas assembles examples from Mallory, Pope, Boswell, Coleridge, Emerson, Melville and many others.[5]

In the American common speech such forms are very numerous, and Wentworth lists *betterer* and *more betterer* from Georgia and Alabama, *more beautifuller* from Pennsylvania, *more better* from the Ozarks and South Carolina, *moreder* from Nebraska, *more hotter* from Virginia, *more resteder* from Appalachia, *more righter* from New England, *bestest* from Mississippi, *bestmost* from Arkansas, *mostest* from Indiana, and *leastest* from Massachusetts, Alabama, Georgia and Newfoundland. The ascription of the military maxim, "Git thar *fustest* with the *mostest* men," to the Confederate general, Nathan Bedford Forrest (1821–77), is probably apocryphal, but *mostest* is in everyday use today in his native wildwood. Adjectives not ordinarily subjected to the process are compared freely, *e.g., onliest, fightinest, dancinest, shootinest, loviner, growed-uppest* and *tore-downdest*. All these are reported from the Ozarks

---

[1] English Dialect Grammar, p. 267.
[2] p. 326.
[3] P. A. Browne sends me a magnificent modern English example: "John is *more taller* than Kate than she is than Jim."
[4] For the transition period immediately preceding see Dr. Louise Pound's dissertation, The Comparison of Adjectives in English in the XV and the XVI Century; Heidelberg, 1901.
[5] The Use of the Superlative Degree for the Comparative, *English Journal* (College Edition), Dec., 1935, pp. 821-29. See also The Grammar of English Grammars, by Goold Brown; New York, 1858, p. 294.

by Randolph,[1] and Wentworth adds examples from many other regions.[2] From New Jersey a correspondent sends in the following dialogue:

A. Ain't State street th' main street 'n 'is 'ere town?
B. Sure.
A. Well, if Ahm comin' down Warren an' your're comin' through State on my lef', then which is the *mainer?* [3]

The plain people pay no heed to the schoolma'am's distinction between *healthy* and *healthful,* and prefer *tasty* to *tasteful.*[4] In the phrase *healthy respect* the former is quite respectable. Of late there has been a strong tendency, especially in the field of victualling, to omit the *-ed* ending from adjectives, following the example of *ice-cream,* originally *iced-cream.*[5] Examples: *mash* potatoes, *hash-brown* potatoes, *whip cream.*[6] In Baltimore, in 1946, I saw a sign advertising Frostie, "an *old-fashion* root-beer." [7]

6. THE ADVERB

"In all the dialects [of English]," says Wright in his "English Dialect Grammar," [8] "it is common to use the adjectival form for the adverbial, as in 'you might *easy* fall.'" This is certainly true of the American vulgate. *Sure* as an adverb has become one of its chief hallmarks,[9] and *go slow,* often spelled *go slo,* has become official on

1 The Grammar of the Ozark Dialect, *American Speech,* Oct., 1927, p. 9.
2 Such forms are often used by the literati for humorous effect. In Notes on the Vernacular, *American Mercury,* Oct., 1924, pp. 235-36, Louise Pound offers *allrightest, nicerer, moderatest, far more superior, more outer, high-steppingest, goingest, orphanest, womanishest, outlandishest* and *pathetiker.* In Washington is Like That, by W. M. Kiplinger; New York, 1942, the Capital is described as "the *eatingest, drinkingest, gossipest* place in the world."
3 My debt here is to Mr. Harry Gwynn Morehouse, of Trenton.
4 The NED traces *healthy* in the sense of conducive to health to 1552, and shows that it was used by John Locke and John Wesley. It traces *tasty* to 1617 and provides examples from Goldsmith, Buckle, Hobhouse and Thackeray.
5 The NED traces *ice-cream* to 1769 and *iced-cream* to 1688.
6 I am indebted here to Mr. Douglas Leechman, of the National Museum of Canada, Ottawa.
7 The prevalence of incomplete comparatives in advertisements, e.g., "a *better* department-store" and "dresses for the *older* woman," is discussed in The Rise of the Incomplete Comparative, by Esther K. Sheldon, *American Speech,* Oct., 1945, pp. 161-67.
8 p. 299.
9 Milton wrote "God *sure* esteems the growth and completing of one virtuous person," in the Areopagitica, 1644, but the form has always been rare in England, save as a conscious loan from American.

road-signs throughout the country.¹ Both have been under fire by the schoolma'am, and the latter was denounced with some violence by a writer in *American Speech* in 1927,² but it was defended valiantly by Wallace Rice,³ who showed that many grammarians above the pedagogical level were in favor of it, and that it was listed as soundly colloquial in accepted dictionaries. Mrs. Charles Archibald, in her unpublished study, "The Doctrine of Correctness in English Usage in the Nineteenth Century,"⁴ shows that while adverbs shorn of the terminal *-ly* were countenanced by Noah Webster, it was not until the latter half of the century that the common run of grammarians made the discovery that many of them were etymologically sound.⁵ One of the first to see the light was the Rev. Henry Alford, dean of Canterbury, whose "Plea for the Queen's English," first published in 1863, is chiefly remembered today for its violent denunciation of Americans and the American language.⁶ Alford noted that most adjectives capable of use as adverbs "seem to be of one syllable," but so long as they qualified in that respect he had nothing against them, and in fact cited *soft, sweet, plain, bright* and *wrong* with approbation. Says S. A. Nock of *go slow:*

> An important element in the use of *slow* as an adverb is the necessity of emphasis. *Go slowly* means, when you see such a sign, "don't go too fast," but *go slow* means to go slow. The spondee and the rhyme are both effective.⁷

The use of *real* instead of *really* has been defended persuasively by Robert C. Pooley,⁸ who says that its position "is considerably higher than that of *sure*," and that "it is constantly heard in the professional and social conversation of cultured people." The same may be said of *bad*, as in "I feel *bad*." Wentworth offers examples of the former from North, East, South and West, and of the latter from places almost as far apart. He notes that *bad* sometimes precedes the adjective, as in "He was *bad* sick," cited from central

---

1 *Slow* was thus used by Shakespeare, Byron and Thackeray. The NED traces it to *c.* 1500.
2 Road Signs, by Ottilie Amend, Jan., pp. 191-92.
3 *Go Slow — Proceed Slowly, American Speech*, Sept., 1927, pp. 489-91.
4 A University of Wisconsin dissertation, quoted here by Mrs. Archibald's permission.
5 For the history of *-ly* see AL4, pp. 464-65.
6 It is quoted in AL4, p. 27.
7 Private communication, May 7, 1936.
8 *Real* and *Sure* as Adverbs, *American Speech*, Feb., 1933, pp. 60-62. See also *Real*, Adverb?, by Leah Dennis, *Words*, Sept., 1935, pp. 9-10.

New York, Kentucky, South Carolina, Florida, West Virginia, Kansas and Oklahoma. *Withouten*, which is both an adverb and a preposition, is found by him in the Appalachia area, but apparently nowhere else. The NED traces it as an adverb to *c.* 1000, but indicates that it is obsolete in England. As a preposition, traced to *c.* 1175, it was used by Gower, Byron and Kipling. *Outen*, without *with-*, prevails in the common speech all over the United States. Incidentally, it was used no less than eight times by H. W. Longfellow in his translation of Dante's " Divina Commedia." [1] Ramsay and Emberson say in their " Mark Twain Lexicon " [2] that Mark showed " a marked fondness for the old native suffixless or flat adverbs, which are sometimes unjustly stigmatized as ungrammatical uses of the adjective." They cite *awful, bad, cruel, fair, good, loud, near* (as in " I mighty *near* stepped on a snake "), *real, square, sure* and *tight*, but have to add the hypersophic *illy*, which occurs in " The Gilded Age " and may have been the contribution of Charles Dudley Warner. Wentworth finds it in West Virginia, and *muchly* in Alabama and Georgia, but does not list *thusly*. This last occurs mainly as conscious humor.[3] A correspondent tells me that Socialists and Communists frequently sign their letters *Yours comradely*, and that he has encountered *Yours friendly* at the end of a business letter. E. L. Thorndike, in a statistical study of adverbs in American use,[4] finds that there is an apparent taboo against those in *-lily*, *e.g.*, *oilily* and *lordlily*. He says: " *Holy, lonely, lordly* and other *-ly* adjectives in my records number over 3,000 occurrences without a single adverb in *-ly* formed from them."

7. THE DOUBLE NEGATIVE

" Not a single good reason except the tyranny of usage," says John S. Kenyon, " can be given for not using two or more negatives to strengthen negation. It is wholly in accord with linguistic

---

1 I am indebted here to Mr. Frederic R. Gunsky, of San Francisco. He reports that it appears in Cantos I, III and XXIV of the Inferno, VI, XI, XVIII and XXVIII of the Purgatorio, and XXIV of the Paradiso.
2 *University of Missouri Studies*, Vol. XIII, No. 1, Jan. 1, 1938.
3 But I find " The late Fremont Older penned it *thusly* " in the *Congressional Record*, Dec. 21, 1943, p. 11103, col. 3, apparently used seriously. However, it is often difficult to tell whether a congressman is serious or spoofing.
4 Derivation Ratios, *Language*, Jan.–March, 1943, pp. 27–37.

principle, being in the best of use in many other languages, as formerly in English, and is extremely effective, as in Chaucer's famous four-negative sentence.[1] It is still in full vigor in folk speech, where its great value keeps it alive; and it frequently occurs in disguise in cultivated use."[2] Noah Webster was of the same opinion, and said so in his " Philosophical and Practical Grammar " of 1807. Thus:

> The learned, with a view of philosophical correctness, have rejected the use of two negatives for one negation; but the . . . change has not reached the great mass of the people and probably never will reach them; it being nearly impossible, in my opinion, ever to change a usage which enters into the language of every cottage, every hour and almost every moment. . . . In this instance the people have the primitive idiom; and if the Greeks, that polished nation, thought fit to retain two negatives for a negation, in the most elegant language ever formed, surely our men of letters might have been less fastidious about retaining them in the English.

Examples of multiple negation swarm in the records of American folk-speech. Vance Randolph says[3] that in the Ozarks " the double negative, as in ' I *never* done *nothin'*,' is the rule rather than the exception. Often," he goes on, "*nohow* is added for greater emphasis, and we have a triple negative. Even the quadruple form, ' I *ain't never* done *nothin' nohow*,' is not at all uncommon. Occasionally one hears the quintuple, ' I *ain't never* done *no* dirt of *no* kind to *nobody*.' Such sentences as ' I *don't* want *but* one ' are used and defended even by educated Ozarkers." The free and irrational use of *but*, in fact, is almost universal in American English, especially in such forms as " I haven't any doubt *but that* "(or *but what*), and in AL4 I gave some examples from learned and eminent sources.[4] In the common speech *ain't* is often combined with *nobody* to give a multiple negative a final polish, as in " *Ain't nobody never* been there " (No one has ever been there) and " *Ain't nobody never* told me *nothing* about it." *Hardly* and *scarcely* are also used for this cosmetic effect, as in " I *don't* know *nothin' scarcely*," " We-all *can't* get her to eat *nothin' scarcely*," " It *didn't* take *hardly* ten

---

[1] This sentence is given in AL4, p. 470.
[2] Ignorance Builds a Language, *American Scholar*, Autumn, 1938, p. 477.
[3] The Grammar of the Ozark Dialect, *American Speech*, Oct., 1927, p. 8.
[4] p. 203. I add one from English English, found in the London *Times Literary Supplement*, Jan. 1, 1944, p. 8: " There can be no doubt *but that* it works."

minutes," " He *hardly hadn't never* saw her " and " It *don't hardly* amount to *nothin'*." Some miscellaneous specimens from my archives:

I *don't* believe it would do *but* little harm if he does.[1]
I *don't* kinda think it *ain't*.
Please *don't* buy *but* one.[2]
I will *not* be responsible for any debts *only* by myself after January 5, 1938.[3]
You *ain't* seen *nothing* yet.
They *didn't none* of them go.
I *haven't never* gotten able to work any yet.[4]
I *ain't* seen *nobody* roun' here at no time.
He *didn't* say *nothing* to *nobody neither*.[5]
Once a child gets burnt once, it *won't never* stick its hand in *no* fire *no* more.
There may *not* be *no nothing*.
Ain't you learned to *not never* argue with *no* woman *no* more? [6]
If it don't rain they *ain't no* use for 'em to come up *nohow*.
He *oughtn'* to *never* done it.[7]
I *ain't* got *nary none*.
That boy *ain't never* done *nothin' nohow*.
I *ain't never* seen *no* men-folks of *no* kind do *no* washin'.[8]
Hardly nobody don't chew *no* tobacco *no* more *nowheres*.
This government last year *could not* raise *but* $3,000,000,000.[9]
Ain't nobody hit *nothing*, has they?
Ain't nothing you *can't* do.
You can't get *nobody* out *nowhere* around *no* base without *no* ball.[10]
He *don't know from nothing*.[11]

1 From a letter signed Loyal Democrat in the Indianapolis *Times*, June 24, 1939.
2 Store advertisement in Baltimore, 1936.
3 Advertisement in the Toledo *Blade*, reprinted in the *New Yorker*, Sept. 24, 1938.
4 Tonics and Sedatives, *Journal of the American Medical Association*, May 18, 1940, p. 28.
5 The last two were reported from the Clinch Valley, Virginia, by L. R. Dingus in *Dialect Notes*, Vol. IV, Part III, 1915, p. 179.
6 Contributed to the *William Feather Magazine*, Feb., 1941, by Frank Richey. Mr. Richey amused himself by contriving a sentence containing ten negatives and a split infinitive; "I *ain't never* got *no* time for to *no* longer argue with *no* woman of *no* kind, *not never*, *no* more, *nohow*."
7 The last two are from The Speech of East Texas, by Oma Stanley, before cited, p. 103.
8 The last three are from Our Southern Highlanders, by Horace Kephart; New York, 1921, p. 287.
9 Letter of the Hon. Thomas L. Blanton, of Texas, *Congressional Record*, Jan. 25, 1935, p. 1037, col. 2.
10 Remark of a rustic baseball coach, contributed by Mr. E. W. Delcamp, of Lexington, Ky.
11 Julius G. Rothenberg, in Some American Idioms From the Yiddish, *American Speech*, Feb., 1943, p. 48, reports this from New York City. He says that it comes from the Yiddish *nisht zu wissen fin gornisht*.

You could *not* be *but* one person.[1]
There *didn't nobody* see him, did they?
Hardly *nobody don't*.
Don't everybody know how?[2]
Both good schemes, but *neither don't* put anybody to work.[3]
Don't nobody touch that.
Didn't I *never* tell, you *ain't* got *no* right to go out and chase after *no* ball when *nobody* ain't watching you? [4]
Nobody ain't never said *nothin'* about sendin' *no* flowers to *nobody*.[5]
I *never* set *no* hens, *nor nothing* of the kind.
Nobody's never wanted me.
You *can't* get *nowhere neither*.

The last three are from the Linguistic Atlas of New England,[6] which presents massive evidence of the prevalence of double and triple negatives in the area it covers. It distinguishes six main divisions, as follows:

1. The subject and the verb are negated, as in "*Nobody hadn't* ought to."
2. The verb and the predicate noun or adjective are negated, as in "That *ain't nothin'*."
3. The verb and the object are negated, as in "I *ain't* done *nothin'*."
4. The verb and the adverb are negated, as in "I *couldn't* get *nowheres* near him."
5. The object and the adverb are negated, as in "She *never* done *no* hard work."
6. Triple negation, as in "*Tain't no* place for *nobody*."

The *not-neither* combination, as in "I did *not* do it, *neither*," was in good usage until the end of the Eighteenth Century, and examples are to be found in Steele, Richardson, Burke and Cowper,[7] but for the past century it has been receding into the common speech, wherein it is still very much alive all over the United States. So with the *nor-not* combination, as in Shakespeare's "*Nor* do *not* saw the air." [8] The following note upon the double negative comes from an intelligent foreign observer:

It seems to me that the double negative is due, in great measure, to the ease with which *not* may be joined to the auxiliaries without increasing the number of syllables. Even *haven't, hasn't*, etc., are pronounced as monosylla-

---

[1] Letter in the *Baptist Record* of Jackson, Miss., Oct. 22, 1925.
[2] *i.e.*, "Everybody doesn't know how."
[3] Will Rogers, 1934.
[4] Reported from Germantown, Pa., by Jack Edelson, *Word Study*, Feb., 1946, p. 2.
[5] I am indebted for this to Mr. K. L. Rankin.
[6] Map 718.
[7] For the first three see the NED under *neither* A3. For Cowper see his letter to William Unwin, Feb. 24, 1782.
[8] Hamlet, III, *c.* 1601.

bles. If, in place of *no* and *not*, there were longer, or less simple, negating adverbs the double negative would not be possible because of the extra speech-effort required. The construction of the Scandinavian languages simply will not permit it; and so with German. I doubt that you have ever heard a German say anything comparable to: "Ich habe ihm *nicht nichts* abgenommen" or "Er gebraucht *niemals nicht keine* Seife." It can't be done.[1]

8. OTHER SYNTACTICAL PECULIARITIES

The long-awaited grammarian of vulgar American, when he spits on his hands at last, will have a gaudy time anatomizing such forms as "He is the girl I go *with's* brother,"[2] "I'd *like* to froze to death," "Where are we *at?*," "Who are you taking music lessons *offen* (or *offa*)?" "I *sorta, kinda* like it," "He *done* like I done," "Try *and* stop me," "He *gone and done* it," "I hit him good *and* hard," "Us *he's* would like to know," "What do you think of *this here, now,* Henry Wallace?," "*How old of a* mule have you ever *saw?*," "I ain't sure, the way things happen," "I used *to could do* it," "I'll call you up, *without* I can't," "I'd like *for* to go there," "It ain't hot *to what* we had yesterday," "You *want* to take this medicine every hour,"[3] "It ain't so *worse*," "I seen the *bothen* of 'm," "Them dogs are *us'n's*," "If I *hadda* been there," "A girl *which* I know," "They must *not* be *no* mistake," "Some men *lets their wife* run *them*," "He hadn't *only* one hat," "We *boughten* some *furniture*," "Both *her* and *you is* welcome," "*She's* a fine car," "It's O.K. *by me*," "Once you try it *once* it goes easy," "*Iffen* I had the money," "I *wisht* I was there," "It must be *somewheres*," "It was some place *else*," "I *been* there," "*Who* are you laughing at?," "So *what?*," and "He had *the* malaria."

Some of these forms, e.g., *good and* as an adverb and such verb compounds as *try and* and *come and*, have gradually worked their way into polite usage;[4] others, e.g., *like for*, are accepted in limited

---

[1] Mr. Valdemar Viking, of Red Bank, N. J.; private communication, Sept. 1, 1938.

[2] See Group Genitives, by Josephine Burnham, *American Speech*, Nov., 1926, pp. 84–85. A swell example is in Idea Man, by Claude Binyon, *Variety*, Jan. 8, 1947, p. 7: "You mean that fellow who took over when Hays left's office?"

[3] For *should*. See *You Want To*, by Louise Pound, *American Speech*, Aug., 1932, pp. 450–51.

[4] *Good and*, by Steven T. Byington, *American Speech*, Oct., 1944, p. 229.

regions, but not generally;[1] yet others, *e.g.*, *boughten*, are still definitely and apparently hopelessly vulgar. But there is no telling what will happen in language, and it is perfectly possible that most of the last class will one day gain acceptance, just as " It is *me*," *like* as a conjunction, *to loan* for *to lend*, the use of the plural pronoun with *anyone*, *everyone*, etc., *somebody else's*, *gotten* as a past participle, the *one-he* combination, the split infinitive, the terminal preposition, and a hundred other forms, all of them once damned from hell to high water by the grammarians, have gained acceptance. In such matters there is simply no telling, for language is a great deal more an art than a science. Once, exploring the upper Middle West, I mislaid my shaving-brush in a hotel-room, and called in a chambermaid of unknown nationality to help me hunt for it. When I found it hidden behind the Gideon Bible and let go with a cry of triumph she asked politely, " *Did* you *got* it? " This, by prevailing rules, was " bad " English. But why? And how long will it continue " bad "? I'd not like to answer too positively, for *did* is undoubtedly a sound preterite and *got* is equally a sound perfect participle.

[1] *Like for*, by A. R. Dunlap, *American Speech*, Feb., 1945, pp. 18–19.

X

PROPER NAMES IN AMERICA

1. SURNAMES

477. [*Smith* remains the predominant surname in the United States, followed by *Johnson, Brown, Williams, Jones, Miller, Davis, Anderson, Wilson* and *Moore* in order.] On May 2, 1939 the Social Security Board issued an analysis of the 43,900,000 names then on its roll, showing that ten per cent of the persons listed shared but fifty names, beginning with 471,190 Smiths, 350,530 Johnsons, 254,750 Browns, 250,312 Williamses, 240,180 Millers and 235,540 Joneses. The rest ran as follows:

Standing	Name	Approximate Number
26	Adams	70,000
19	Allen	81,000
8	Anderson	144,000
34	Bailey	45,000
23	Baker	71,000
33	Bell	47,000
36	Bennett	43,000
49	Black	27,000
46	Brooks	30,000
45	Burke	30,000
37	Butler	40,000
41	Cohen	33,000
7	Davis	177,000
32	Edwards	52,000
47	Elliott	26,000
43	Ellis	31,000
29	Evans	60,000
35	Fisher	43,000
38	Foster	39,000
21	Green	78,000
20	Hall	80,000
17	Harris	96,000
16	Jackson	105,000
40	James	33,000
42	Jenkins	33,000

Proper Names in America

Standing	Name	Approximate Number
47	Johnston	28,000
44	Jordan	30,000
24	King	70,000
18	Lewis	85,000
14	Martin	112,000
12	Moore	117,000
25	Nelson	70,000
50	Nichols	26,000
51	Owens	26,000
28	Phillips	61,000
27	Roberts	66,000
22	Robinson	77,000
31	Rogers	52,000
10	Taylor	118,000
11	Thomas	118,000
15	Thompson	108,000
30	Turner	56,000
39	Walker	38,000
13	White	113,000
9	Wilson	133,000 [1]

It will be noted that all these first fifty names save *Cohen* are of British origin, but it should not be forgotten that many of them, notably *Smith*, *Johnson* and *Miller*, conceal large numbers of non-British names that have been changed.[2] The German name of *Müller*, for example, has almost vanished from American directories: the umlaut has either been dropped, making it *Muller*, or is represented by *ue*, making it *Mueller*, or there has been a bold leap to *Miller*. Most of the dominating British names are English, but there are several that suggest Scottish origins, *e.g.*, *Johnston*,[3] or Welsh, *e.g.*, *Jones*, *Lewis* and *Owens*, and at least one, *Burke*, is Irish. All other efforts that have been made to analyze the national onomatology have led to closely similar results. Of 2,474,502 officers and men of the Navy in World War II, 21,476, or one in every 115, were named *Smith*, and following came 15,045 *Johnsons* and 11,035

---

[1] I am indebted here to Mr. Max Stern, director of the Informational Service of the Social Security Board.
[2] AL4, p. 477.
[3] *Johnston* was originally territorial — *John's ton*. *Ton*, *tun*, *toun*, *toune* and *tone* meant a farm, manor, parish or other well-defined piece of land. The founder of the John- ston(e) clan gave his name to lands in Annandale, Dumfriesshire, *c.* 1174. In the early days the name was frequently confused with *Jonson* or *Johnson*. Black gives a list of 16 variant spellings, including *Jhonestowne*, *Johanstoun*, *Johngston*, *Johnnesone*, *Joneston*, *Johnstoun* and *Joniston*.

Joneses.[1] In the Army there were 54,180 *Smiths*, 41,580 *Johnsons*, 29,960 *Browns*, 28,140 *Williamses*, 25,720 *Joneses* and 25,620 *Millers*.[2] On the roll of the Veterans Administration, in 1946, there were 13,000 *John Smiths*, and 8,000 of them had no middle initial.[3] On June 1, 1929 the American Council of Learned Societies' Committee on Linguistic and National Stocks in the Population of the United States issued a report showing the estimated numbers of persons in each 100,000 of population bearing the 200 most prevalent surnames. Its figures follow:

Adams	172	Clark	252	Graham	92
Alexander	87	Cohen	57	Grant	60
Allen	220	Cole	75	Gray	112
Anderson	444	Coleman	84	Green	200
Andrews	62	Collins	140	Griffin	85
Armstrong	68	Cook	135	Hall	210
Arnold	70	Cooper	110	Hamilton	93
Austin	67	Cox	108	Hansen	90
Bailey	112	Crawford	74	Hanson	64
Baker	186	Cunningham	71	Harper	52
Barnes	91	Davis	472	Harris	252
Beck	50	Dixon	53	Harrison	77
Bell	127	Duncan	51	Hart	72
Bennett	110	Dunn	69	Hawkins	58
Berry	68	Edwards	127	Hayes	84
Black	72	Elliott	65	Henderson	90
Boyd	69	Ellis	84	Henry	67
Bradley	64	Erickson	55	Hicks	56
Brooks	108	Evans	150	Hill	170
Brown	630	Ferguson	64	Hoffman	67
Bryant	62	Fisher	94	Holmes	72
Burke	78	Fitzgerald	51	Hopkins	53
Burns	102	Ford	81	Howard	112
Butler	103	Foster	103	Hudson	52
Campbell	166	Fox	70	Hughes	116
Carlson	88	Freeman	68	Hunt	64
Carpenter	52	Fuller	51	Jackson	270
Carr	55	Gardner	68	James	88
Carroll	71	Gibson	70	Jenkins	86
Carter	138	Gilbert	49	Jensen	64
Chapman	54	Gordon	72	Johnson	873

1 Washington dispatch in the Baltimore *Evening Sun*, March 8, 1944.
2 The Linguist Anthology; New York, 1945, p. 51.
3 Associated Press dispatch from Washington, Feb. 23, 1946. The resultant confusion gave a headache of high amperage to General Omar N. Bradley, the administrator, and he smote his bloomin' lyre on the subject in a speech to the American Veterans of World War II, meeting in Washington.

Proper Names in America 399

Johnston	66	Palmer	68	Stephens	53
Jones	566	Parker	131	Stevens	76
Jordan	70	Patterson	89	Stewart	131
Kelley	70	Payne	57	Stone	64
Kelly	164	Perkins	58	Sullivan	150
Kennedy	94	Perry	88	Taylor	310
King	196	Peters	55	Thomas	269
Knight	51	Peterson	172	Thompson	293
Lane	53	Phillips	140	Tucker	64
Larson	76	Porter	69	Turner	142
Lee	156	Powell	72	Wagner	76
Lewis	212	Price	96	Walker	216
Long	102	Reed	122	Wallace	83
Lynch	67	Reynolds	92	Walsh	74
Marshall	73	Rice	74	Ward	122
Martin	276	Richards	57	Warren	58
Mason	64	Richardson	103	Washington	61
McCarthy	56	Riley	66	Watkins	53
McDonald	94	Roberts	158	Watson	104
Meyer	64	Robertson	66	Weaver	58
Miller	526	Robinson	204	Webb	67
Mills	56	Rogers	122	Weber	52
Mitchell	154	Rose	59	Welch	55
Moore	302	Ross	106	Wells	77
Morgan	115	Russell	104	West	78
Morris	134	Ryan	104	Wheeler	52
Morrison	53	Sanders	88	White	292
Murphy	188	Schmidt	71	Williams	600
Murray	96	Schultz	61	Williamson	50
Myers	102	Scott	180	Willis	50
Nelson	230	Shaw	70	Wilson	371
Newman	80	Simmons	77	Wood	132
O'Brien	100	Simpson	72	Woods	66
O'Connor	52	Smith	1132	Wright	188
Olson	104	Snyder	84	Young	210 [1]
Owens	65	Spencer	55		

It will be noted that this list shows a number of plainly non-British names, *e.g.*, *Meyer, Schultz, Cohen* and some of the forms in *-son* and *-sen*. A great many German and Jewish *Schmidts* must be concealed among the *Smiths*, but there is still room for 71 *Schmidts* per 100,000, or more than the number of *Armstrongs, Bradleys, Dixons, Elliotts* or *Fergusons*. As for *Cohen*, it outranks *Carpenter, Chapman, Dixon, Duncan, Fuller, Harper, Hopkins, Knight* and *Spencer*, and crowds *Grant, Hawkins, Perkins, Warren*

[1] I am indebted for this table and for much else to Mr. Howard F. Barker, one of the committee's research associates and the foremost authority on American surnames.

and *Weaver*. *Smith*, of course, is an occupational name, but in modern times the number of smiths in the population is certainly not enough to account for its dominance among surnames. The explanation lies in the fact that in the days when it was first used the term signified any craftsman employing a hammer, and hence included wood- and stone- as well as metal-workers.[1] There is some reason for believing that *Smith* was once an even more common surname than it is today. In 1876, for example, a writer in the *Galaxy*[2] said that one out of every 70 New Yorkers then bore it, and that the ratio had been one in 83 in 1825, but today the Manhattan telephone directory shows not much beyond one in 300. This decline, of course, is partly to be accounted for by the extraordinarily heavy non-British immigration into the New York area. The Army and Social Security figures and the telephone directories of other cities and towns show that elsewhere about one American in every hundred is still a *Smith*. Thus it remains the leading surname in the United States, as it is in England, Scotland and Wales.[3] It is surpassed by *Cohen* in Manhattan[4] and by *Johnson* in Chicago, but in both cases it is a close runner-up, and nearly everywhere else it is first.[5]

[1] This is on the authority of the NED, Vol. X, Part I, p. 278. In Icelandic *smithur* is still used in the sense of "blacksmith, carpenter, builder." See Icelandic: Grammar, Texts, Glossary, by Stefan Einarsson; Baltimore, 1945, p. 450. Samuel Grant Oliphant, in his otherwise instructive The Clan of Fire and Forge, or, The Ancient and Honorable *Smiths*; Olivet, Mich., 1910, p. 6, falls into the error of restricting the original meaning of *smith* to "the worker in metals."

[2] The Inconvenience of Being Named *Smith*, April, pp. 498–504. This article was signed John Smith, but the *Galaxy's* index credited it to Col. Nicholas Smith.

[3] For the British ranking of names see the *World* Almanac for 1914, p. 668. The report of the Registrar-General for Scotland for 1937; Edinburgh, 1938, pp. lvi and lvii, shows that the ten leading names in Scotland in 1860 were *Smith*, *MacDonald*, *Brown*, *Wilson*, *Thomson*, *Robertson*, *Campbell*, *Stewart*, *Anderson* and *Johnston*, and that in 1935 *Smith*, *MacDonald* and *Brown* still held the first three places.

[4] Six More Listed Surnames, New York *Sun*, Oct. 6, 1943.

[5] Said Leigh Hunt in The Seer, XXXVII, 1840: "An Italian poet says he hates his name of *John* (*Giovanni*) because if anybody calls him by it in the street twenty people look out of the window. Now let anybody call 'John Smith' and half Holborn will cry out 'Well?'" Said the once famous Fanny Fern (Sara Payson Willis Parton): "When Adam got tired of naming his numerous descendants he said, 'Let all the rest be called *Smith*.'" (Fanny Fern: a Memorial Volume, edited by James Parton; New York, 1873, p. 208.) Said the *New Yorker*, March 2, 1940: "Moving into one of those apartment buildings that are supplied with electricity by a contract-

Among the names that follow it there are differing arrangements in different places. For the United States as a whole the order is *Smith, Johnson, Brown, Williams, Miller, Jones, Davis, Anderson, Wilson, Taylor, Thomas, Moore, White, Martin, Thompson, Jackson, Harris* and *Lewis*, with *Cohen* in forty-first place and *Burke* in forty-fifth, but in New York City *Cohen* is in first place and *Murphy, Kelly, Meyer* and *Schwartz* are among the first ten.[1] In Chicago, with *Johnson* in first place, those that follow in order are *Smith, Anderson, Miller, Brown, Peterson, Jones, Williams, Wilson* and *Thompson*. In Philadelphia the order is *Smith, Miller, Brown, Jones, Johnson, Wilson, Kelly, Williams, Taylor* and *Davis*. In Boston the first five are *Smith, Sullivan, Brown, Johnson* and *Murphy*, in New Orleans they are *Smith, Levy, Miller, Williams* and *Brown*, in San Francisco they are *Smith, Johnson, Brown, Miller* and *Williams*, and in northern New Jersey they are the same, but arranged *Smith, Miller, Brown, Johnson* and *Williams*.[2] The Social Security returns show that other common surnames tend to clump in distinct regions. Thus *Adams, Bailey, Jenkins* and *Nelson* are most numerous in Ohio, Kentucky and Michigan, and *Moore* in Pennsylvania, Delaware and New Jersey. In Grand Rapids, Mich., in a region of heavy Dutch settlement, the first five names are *Smith, Johnson, Miller, Brown* and *Anderson*, but the sixth is the Dutch *DeVries*, the ninth is *DeYoung (DeJong)* and the eleventh is *Van Dyke*.[3] Throughout Minnesota *Johnson* is so widespread that bearing it is

ing company which buys juice from Edison and meters it out to individuals, a Mr. Levy was surprised and hurt, since he always pays his bills before the tenth of the month, to get a request for a ten-dollar deposit. He made a fuss about it, and finally a representative of the company called upon him to explain. 'Whenever we get a new customer named *Smith, Brown, Cohen, Jones, Levy*, or *Johnson*, we always ask for a deposit,' he said. 'It's too much bother to look up their credit ratings.'" Said Anthony L. Ellis in Prisoner at the Bar; London, 1934, p. 25: "In all the wide vocabulary of the English language are there two words which, conjointly, suggest a finer guarantee of simple faith than the name *John Smith?* The words are the embodiment of honesty, of purpose, the epitome of rugged sincerity and truth." But enough of this Smithiana.

1 An investigation undertaken in 1933 by clients of the Emergency Unemployment Relief Committee showed that the lead of *Cohen* in Brooklyn, at least among telephone subscribers, was then tremendous. There were 11,314 *Cohens* listed, to 6,817 *Smiths*, 5,614 *Millers*, 4,384 *Browns* and 2,005 *Joneses*. See 11,314 Brooklyn *Cohens*, New York *Sun*, Feb. 28, 1933.

2 Our Leading Surnames, by Howard F. Barker, *American Speech*, June, 1926, pp. 470-77.

3 I am indebted here to Mr. Daniel Litscher of Grand Rapids.

a political asset, and some years ago a member of the clan became a formidable candidate for office by simply announcing his name: though he offered no platform and made no campaign he polled 44,049 votes out of 151,686 cast.[1]

Howard F. Barker estimates that only about a third of present-day Americans have English surnames by virtue of English blood in the male line, but to them, of course, must be added the large numbers whose ancestors acquired such names in Scotland, Wales or Ireland, the perhaps even larger numbers who have adopted English surnames in place of non-British names, and the Negroes. Counting in variants, about 35,000 native surnames are in use in England, but the number is less in the United States, for there has been a tendency here since the earliest days, save only in New England, to abandon unusual forms and spellings for commoner and more familiar ones. Thus *Leigh* and *Lea* have been largely absorbed by *Lee*, *Davies* by *Davis*,[2] *Cowper* by *Cooper*, *Baillie* by *Bailey*, *Forster* by *Foster*, *Colquhoun* by *Calhoun*, and *Smyth* and *Smythe* by *Smith*. *Baker*, *Carter* and *Moore*, no doubt because they are short and easy to remember, are relatively more frequent in this country than in England, and have probably engulfed various similar names, e.g., *More*, *Mohr* and *Muir*. *Parker* and *Hall* hold their own among us, maybe for much the same reasons.[3] Barker notes several general tendencies that seem to be peculiar to the United States. One wars upon final *e*, so that *Browne* and *Greene* become *Brown* and *Green*. Another lops off the *-son* ending, so that *Harris* runs far ahead of *Harrison*. A third adds a final *s* to various short names, so that *Hay* becomes *Hayes*, *Brook* becomes *Brooks* and *Stephen* becomes *Stevens*.[4] A fourth converts such difficult endings as *-borough*, *-holme* and *-thwaite* into simple forms, e.g., *-bury*, *-om* (as in *Newsom* from *Newsholme*) and *-white*. Many Americans of Scottish

---

[1] Believe It or Not, by R. L. Ripley, Buffalo *Evening News*, Aug. 25, 1936.
[2] In the English Who's Who, in 1937, there were 98 *Davieses* and but 31 *Davises*; in the American Who's Who there were 163 *Davises* and but 14 *Davieses*. I am indebted here to Mr. Roger Howson, of New York.
[3] *Hall, Parker*, and Company, Surnames, by Howard F. Barker, *American Speech*, Aug., 1926, pp. 596–607.
[4] "Surnames [in *-son*]," says Louise Pound, *American Speech*, April, 1936, p. 187, " occur often with a simple *s* and those who come to know such forms first remain eternally oblivious of divergences. The added *s* need not be thought of as a plural sign. Usually it is an old possessive patronymic ending."

ancestry have dropped the *Mac* from their names, and many Irish families that came in as *Mc's* or *O's* have similarly abandoned the prefixes. Barker says that *Mack* and *Gill*, which are much more common in the United States than in Great Britain, " serve as substitutes or contractions for a host of ' hard ' Irish names," such as *McGillicuddy*, *McIlhatton*, and *McGeoghegan*. The Welsh form seen in *ap Lloyd, i.e., son of Lloyd*, is almost unknown here, though it survives in Wales. But in such vestigial forms as *Floyd, Bowen, Powell, Price, Pumphrey, Pugh, Prichard* and *Upjohn*, from *ap Lloyd, ap Owen, ap Howell, ap Rhys, ap Humphrey, ap Hugh, ap Richard* and *ap John*, it flourishes.[1]

The earliest known list of English surnames comes from the Pipe Roll of 1159–60. Ewen says that no less than 94% of the persons listed had them in some form or other. Of these names, 5% indicated racial extraction, 35% were geographical, 19% were occupational, 21% showed descent, and 14% remained unidentifiable. The first Irish names are recorded in documents nearly three centuries older than the Pipe Rolls, and many of them are still common, e.g., *O'Connor, O'Donnell, O'Neill, O'Loughlin, O'Donovan* and *O'Brien*.[2] Since the setting up of the Irish Free State (Saorstat Eireann) on January 15, 1922,[3] and indeed since the dawn of the Irish Literary Renaissance, *c*. 1890, there has been a fashion among Irish politicians and literati for reviving the ancient Gaelic forms of both surnames and given-names, and as a result such forbidding examples as *MacEochain (Geoghegan), O Tuathail (O'Toole), MacSuibhne (McSweeney), OSuileabhain (O'Sullivan), Omarchadha (Murphy)* and *O Muircheartaigh (Moriarty)* now spot the Irish newspapers, but in America this romantic but somewhat ab-

---

1 It is dealt with in A History of Surnames of the British Isles, by C. L'Estrange Ewen; New York, 1931, pp. 206–08 and 255. "In Wales," adds Ewen, "there is little variety among native surnames, since they are nearly all of the genealogical class, and in order to add distinction a custom has grown of bestowing the mother's maiden name as a Christian name, and for the subsequent generation to couple the two by hyphen." David *Lloyd George*, the politician, got his surname by this route. His father was a *George* and his mother a *Lloyd*. He never used a hyphen, but always insisted that his surname was *Lloyd George*, not simply *George*.

2 Irish Names and Surnames, by Patrick Woulfe; Dublin, 1923, pp. xvi-xx. Ireland, says Woulfe, "was the first country after the fall of the Western Empire to adopt hereditary surnames."

3 The name was changed to Eire on Dec. 29, 1937.

surd affectation has found very few imitators.[1] The public records of Scotland, with few exceptions, do not go back in time beyond the beginning of the Fourteenth Century, and as a result the study of Scottish surnames, many of them common in America, is full of difficulties. But George F. Black, a Scottish-American scholar, has tackled those difficulties ingeniously and pertinaciously in a book that is one of the best works on surnames ever published.[2]

It shows that many familiar Scottish names are not Gaelic in origin, but Norman, English, Flemish, Danish or Irish. *Carlisle*, for example, comes from the name of the town in England, *Bruce* is a French territorial name, and *Macaulay* is from the Norse. There is little assurance, when an indubitable Scot sports an ancient and famous surname, that his arteries run blood of the clan to which he apparently belongs. The plain people of the early days simply took the names of the bloodletters whose banners they followed, and not infrequently they changed their names as they switched clans. During the early Seventeenth Century, a time of great turmoil in Scotland, so many ruffians thus enrolled themselves as *MacGregors* that an act was passed on April 3, 1603, abolishing that surname altogether, and making its use a capital offense. Many of the bogus *MacGregors* thereupon took other names — those of Perth, for example, announced that " in all tyme heirefter " they would " tak to thame and call thameselffis the name of *Johnnestoun* " —,[3] but the overwhelming majority resisted the law, and in 1661 it was suspended by King Charles II. A generation later the MacGregors took to the bush again, and in 1693 the law was reënacted, but the bearers of the name continued to cling to it and during the Eighteenth Century not a few of them came to America, bringing it along.[4] But most of their descendants are probably no more related

[1] Many examples are in Woulfe's Irish Names and Surnames, lately cited, pp. 55–161. The *O* is never separated from the name by an apostrophe. Either it stands alone or it joins the next capital without a space. The *Mac* is always separated. The feminine form is *Ni*.

[2] The Surnames of Scotland; Their Origin, Meaning, and History; New York, 1946. Black was born at Stirling, Scotland, in 1865, and after taking his degree at Edinburgh entered the service of the Scottish National Museum of Antiquities. In 1896 he joined the staff of the New York Public Library, where he remained for thirty-five years.

[3] Others joined the clans of *Stewart*, *Grant*, *Dougall*, *Ramsay* and *Cunninghame*.

[4] The act was finally repealed in 1784. By 1863, according to the Annual Report of the Registrar-General of Scotland, by James Stark, quoted in the Report of the

to the King Giric who is said to have founded the clan, *c.* 900, nor even to that later chief who boasted that wherever he sat was the head of the table, than Booker T. *Washington* was related to George. Other famous Scottish names attracted recruits in the same wholesale manner, notably *Stewart, Campbell* and *MacDonald*. Thousands of the proscribed *MacGregors* became *MacDonalds*, and to this day *MacDonald* is the most common of all surnames in Scotland, next to *Smith*. Even in the United States it ranks above such familiar English names as *Barnes, Ellis, Ford, Graham* and *James*. As for *Campbell*, it outranks *Mitchell, Turner, Cook* and *Lee*. As for *Stewart* in its various forms, it is ahead of *Ward, Rogers* and *Edwards* and on a par with *Parker* and *Morris*.

The first non-British immigrants to appear along the Atlantic seaboard in considerable numbers were the Dutch, who settled on Manhattan island in 1613 and held most of what is now New York until 1664. They occupied a large part of Long Island and nearly the whole valley of the Hudson, and also spilled into New Jersey, but even in the earliest days their hegemony was challenged by Frenchmen and Englishmen, to say nothing of Swedes and Germans. Marcus L. Hansen estimates[1] that by 1790 there were but 55,000 persons of Dutch descent in New York in a total population of 314,366. Many of these Dutch had retained their native names, *e.g.*, *Schuyler, Schermerhorn, Stuyvesant* and *Ten Eyck*, and some had even enforced the true Dutch pronunciation thereof, but many others had been compelled to yield to the pressure of English speechways. An example is offered by the *Van Kouwenhoven* family, whose progenitor, Wolphert Gerretse of that ilk, arrived in America in 1625. Some of his descendants retain the family name to this day, but others first changed *Kouwenhoven* to *Couwenhoven*, and then proceeded from *Couwenhoven* to *Cowenhoven, Cowan, Konover* and *Conover*.[2] In the same way, no doubt, many

---

Committee on Linguistic and National Stocks of the American Council of Learned Societies, before cited, p. 211, there were 10,000 of them again at large on the old soil.

[1] The Minor Stocks in the American Population, in the Report of the Committee on Linguistic and National Stocks in the Population of the United States, before cited, p. 370.

[2] 300 *Van Kouwenhoven* Descendants Visit Fair, New York *Herald Tribune*, Sept. 2, 1939. See also The Descendants of Wolphert Gerretse van *Kouwenhoven* Through His Son, Jacob Wolfertsen van *Couwenhoven*, by Lincoln C. Cocheu; New York, 1943.

a *Gerretse* became a *Garrett*, many a *Vosmaer* became a *Foster*, and perhaps even some of the *Stuyvesants* became *Stevensons*. The carnage of names closely resembling English forms, *e.g.*, *Smid*, *Visscher*, *Jong*, *Prins* and *Kuiper*, must have been great indeed: it is still great among the later Dutch of Michigan.[1] Says a correspondent who is a descendant of Hudson Valley pioneers:

> In 1680 the present name of *Blauvelt*[2] was *Blaeuwveldt*; it became *Blawveldt*, *Blawfelt* and *Blawvelt* before, a century later, it settled down to its surviving form. Many *Coopers* are descended from Klass Van Purvaments. His son, a cooper, subscribed himself Cornelius Klassen *Cuyper*, and *Cuyper* finally became *Cooper*. Harmanus *Dauws(e)*, an interpreter, took the occupational surname of *Taelman* (in present-day Dutch, *taalsman*), and his descendants are now *Tallmans*. *Bomgaert* became *Boogaert*, *Bogardus*, *Bogert* and *Bogart*. *Boetcher* became *Butcher*; *Haringh*, *Haring* or *Herring*; *Ten Eyre* and *Tenure*, *Turner*; *Lammaerts*, *Lambert*; *DeKlerke*, *Clark*; *Concklijn*, *Conkling*; *DeKype*, *Kipp* or *Kip*; *DeHarte*, *Hart*. Surnames, in the early days, were often patronymics fashioned from the given-names of fathers. Thus came *Gerrittsen*, which is now *Garrison*; *Theunissen*, which is *Tennyson*; *Dircksen* and *Derricksen*, which are *Dickson*, *Dickinson* and *Dickens*; *Harmansen*, which is *Harrison*, and *Karlsen*, which is *Carlson*.[3]

Sometimes, of course, the thing ran the other way, and it is highly probable that some of the early English settlers assumed Dutch names. Indeed, there is record of one named *Marston*, whose descendants became distinguished under the Dutch-sounding name of *Masten*.[4] I have also heard of an *O'Dell* family descended from a Hollander named *Odle* or something of the sort. French names were not uncommon among the early Dutch, and they were reinforced by the names of settlers who were really Frenchmen, *e.g.*, *Demarest* (*Des Marest*), *Deronde* (*DuRonde*) and *Harcourt*. Despite the grandiose social pretensions of some of their descendants, not many of the Dutch settlers of New Amsterdam were of gentle blood: the great majority of them, like the great majority of all other groups of immigrants, were farmers, traders and mechanics. The *Van* in

---

[1] AL4, p. 485.
[2] Represented by twelve entries in the Manhattan telephone directory, Summer–Fall, 1946.
[3] Mr. Everett DeBaun, private communication, Jan. 23, 1945. For *Longstreet* and *Pennypacker* see AL4, p. 480. For other Dutch names see The Origin and Meaning of English and Dutch Surnames of New York State Families, by George Rogers Howell, a paper read before the Albany Institute, May 15, 1894, and later printed as a pamphlet. This pamphlet is in the New York Public Library.
[4] *Marston* is an English territorial name, meaning the town on the marsh, and is traced to 1273 by Charles Wareing Bardsley in A Dictionary of English and Welsh Surnames; London, 1901, p. 517.

the names of so many of them is not to be confused with the German *von*, which connotes the *Adelstand*.[1] Readers of Alexander W. Thayer's monumental life of Beethoven will recall that poor Ludwig, during one of his litigations in Vienna, had to confess on the stand that the *Van* before his name did not indicate noble blood, and that he was thus not entitled to trial in the courts reserved for the nobility. In the United States some of the persons of Dutch descent have sought to enhance their status by writing the *Van* of their names as *van*, but the rest take it lightly, and many of them amalgamate it with other particles or with the stem or with both, e.g., *Vanderbilt*, *Vandenberg*, *Vander Veer* or *Vanderveer* (sometimes reduced to *Vandeveer* or *Vandiver*), *Vandergrift* and *Vandervelde*. *Van de Venter* also appears as *Van Deventer* and *Vandeventer* and *Van Nuys* as *Vannuys* or *Vannice*. Many other families have dropped the *Van* altogether, notably the *Roosevelts*, who were originally *Van Roosevelts*.[2] The sonorous names borne by latter-day Hollanders of aristocratic pretensions, e.g., A. F. H. *Troostenburg de Bruyn*, George *van Tets van Goudriaan* and A. W. L. *Tjarda van Starenburgh Stockouwer*,[3] are quite unknown among Dutch-Americans. *Jansen*, a common Dutch surname, probably made heavy contributions to the multitude of American *Johnsons*.[4]

The Germans were the first immigrants to undergo this name-changing process on a really large scale. They were represented in the colonies of John Smith in Virginia, of the Dutch in New York and of the Swedes on the Delaware, but the first whole shipload of them to arrive landed in 1683. After that they came in increasing numbers, chiefly to Pennsylvania, and by the middle of the Eighteenth Century they or their children made up a third of the population of the province. But the Quakers and so-called Scotch Irish had been ahead of them, and when their names were enrolled as the laws of the time required the enrolling officials made a dreadful mess of the business. Nearly all the newcomers spoke rustic dia-

---

[1] This is true, of course, only when it is written with a small *v*. The capitalized *Von* is no more significant than the Dutch *Van*.

[2] AL4, p. 480, n. 2.

[3] The first was once secretary of the Netherlands legation at Washington, the second was private secretary to Queen Wilhelmina, and the third was governor-general of the Netherlands East Indies.

[4] AL4, p. 477. See also pp. 479, 481 and 485.

lects of German and many of them were illiterate, so the difficulty of recording their true surnames, in numerous cases, amounted to impossibility. There were, for example, the frequent names in *bach*, including *Bach* alone. The German *ch*-sound did not daunt the Celtic jobholders, for, as Barker has suggested, it existed in their own speech, but in that speech it was often spelled *gh*, as in *MacLaughlin*, *Dougherty* and *McCullough*, so it was turned into *gh* on the records, and there thus arose the innumerable *Baughs*, *Baughmans*, *Harbaughs*, *Ebaughs* (*Ebach* or *Ibach*) and the like.

At the start, in all probability, these names were pronounced more or less correctly, but before long they acquired spelling pronunciations, and at present the *baugh* in them is usually *baw*, though in some instances it stops at the half-way point of *bock*, rhyming with *clock*. In other names the *ch* was changed to *k* forthwith, so that *Bloch* became *Block*, *Hoch* became *Hoke*, and *Koch* became *Cook* or *Coke*. In yet others it was changed to an *i*-sound, so that *Albrecht* became *Albright*, or to *x*, so that *Trechsler* became *Trexler*. And in still others the guttural *g* was changed to *y*, so that *Hollweg* became *Holloway*. To these Barker, in the Report of the Committee on Linguistic and National Stocks,[1] adds *Rock* and *Rugh*, both from *Rauch*; the membership rolls of a German parish in Maryland add *Upperco* from *Opferkuchen*;[2] a list from the Valley of Virginia adds *Churchman* from *Kirchman* and *Newkirk* from *Neukirch*,[3] and one from Wisconsin adds *Slaght* for *Schlacht*.[4]

The other common changes in German names are discussed in AL4[5] – the dropping of the umlaut, *e.g.*, *Sanger* from *Sänger*, *Furst* from *Fürst*, *Lowe* from *Löwe*, *Warfel* from *Würfel*, *Burger* or *Berger* from *Bürger*, *Custer* from *Köster*,[6] *Ohler* or *Oler* from *Oehler*, *Muller* from *Müller*;[7] the change of *sch* to simple *s*, *e.g.*,

[1] Before cited, p. 288.
[2] Saint Paul's Lutheran Church of Arcadia, Baltimore County, in the report of the Society for the History of Germans in Maryland; Baltimore, 1929, p. 27.
[3] Anglicized and Corrupted German Names in Virginia, by Herman Schuricht, *Pennsylvania-German*, Vol. XII, 1911, pp. 305 and 306.
[4] Orthographic and Phonological Changes in the German Surnames of Potosi, Wisconsin, by Elda O. Baumann. This paper, which was read before the Modern Language Association, is unpublished, but I have had access to it by the courtesy of the author.
[5] pp. 482–85.
[6] AL4, p. 480.
[7] The cases of the composers *Glück* and *Händel* are familiar. For *Händel* see *Handel*, by Herbert Weinstock; New York, 1946, p. xiii.

Snyder from *Schneider*[1] and *Small* from *Schmal;* the dropping of the terminal *e, e.g., Keen* from *Kühne, Lang* from *Lange;* the frequent changes of vowel, *e.g., Hayes* from *Heisse, Harman* from *Hermann, Lantz* from *Lentz, Spilman* from *Spielmann, Warner* from *Werner,* or of consonant, *e.g., Smith* from *Schmidt, Hite* from *Heid, Hood* from *Huth, Lowther* from *Lauter, Mitchell* from *Michel, Shriver* from *Schreiber;* the transliterations, sometimes involving other changes, *e.g., Cline* from *Klein, Bloom* from *Blum, Price* from *Preus, Eisenhower* from *Eisenhauer, Gates* from *Goetz, Hines* from *Heinz, Cole* from *Kohl, Kramer* from *Kraemer, Coon* from *Kuhn, Shane* from *Schön, Russell* from *Rössel, Saylor* from *Seiler, Frietchie* from *Fritsche, Lawrence* from *Lorenz, Early* from *Oehrle, Crouse* from *Kraus, Royce* from *Reuss, Coler* from *Kohler, Snead* from *Sniedt, Deeds* from *Dietz, Stine* from *Stein, Ewell* from *Uhl, Bower* from *Bauer,* and the almost innumerable translations, *e.g., Wise* from *Weiss, Baker* from *Becker, Carpenter* from *Zimmerman, Friend* from *Freund, Green* from *Grün, Goodman* from *Gutmann, Young* from *Jung, Hunter* from *Jaeger, Booker* from *Bucher, Bishop* from *Bischof, Brewer* from *Brauer, Fox* from *Fuchs, Brown* from *Braun, Weaver* from *Weber, Stone* from *Stein, Slaughter* from *Schlachter, Wanamaker* from *Wannemacher, Miller* from *Müller, Long* from *Lang, Short* from *Kurtz, Newman* from *Neumann, Lewis* from *Ludwig, Sharp* from *Scharf, Taylor* from *Schneider, Shoemaker* from *Schumacher, Black* from *Schwarz* and *Steel* from *Stahl.*[2]

The American tendency to add *s* to short British names, already noted in the cases of *Hayes, Brooks* and *Johns,* extended to names originally German, and there are examples in *Ames* from *Oehm, Richards* from *Reichardt, Bowers* from *Bauer* and *Sowers* from *Sauer.* In the somewhat decadent village of Potosi, Wis., Miss Baumann[3] has found a curious habit of preserving the original German

---

[1] In 1914 *Snyder* was forty-sixth in frequency among Philadelphia names, outranking *Wood, Hall* and *Burns,* and standing close to *Jackson, Harris* and *Collins.*

[2] I take most of these from Pennsylvania German Family Names, by L. Oscar Kuhns; New York, 1902. The original form of a name often survives alongside a translation, transliteration or respelling. In 1947 General Dwight D. *Eisenhower,* G. C. B., flourished in Washington and Miss Thelma von *Eisenhauer,* a talented soprano, in Detroit, and there were *Isenhours* in Minnesota.

[3] Orthographical and Phonological Changes in the German Surnames of Potosi, Wisconsin, lately cited.

spellings, even when the pronunciation of names has changed greatly. Thus a man always called *Smith* still writes his name *Schmidt*, and one called *Bryan* writes it *Broihahn*.

Donald Herbert Yoder has offered the plausible theory that many of the changes in Pennsylvania German names, making them different from the standard German forms, were not produced by pressure from the English-speaking population but by phonetic peculiarities of the dialects spoken by the immigrants, and especially by the Palatinate dialect that gradually engulfed all the others. Yoder calls this a Dutchifying of names, and says that "the immigrants and their descendants simply learned to spell their surnames as they themselves pronounced them." "Our family names," he goes on,

> bear the same relation to the High German forms as do many of our dialect words. That is to say, they show the same vowel and consonant shifts.... On a visit through Berks, Schuylkill, Dauphin and Northumberland counties, visiting some of our older cemeteries, I took particular notice of the name changes. Often in the same cemetery tombstones stood side by side bearing the High German and the Dutchified forms of the name, as for example *Hertlein* and *Hartlein* in the Oley Reformed Cemetery at Spangsville, Berks county.[1]

Yoder lists twelve common vowel changes and seven consonant changes, as follows:

a to *o*, as in *Spahn* to *Spohn*, *Graff* to *Grove*, *Rahn* to *Rhone*, and *Fahrni* to *Forney*.
au to *aw*, as in *Lauffer* to *Lawfer* and *Kaufmann* to *Coffman*.
au to *o*, as in *Stauffer* to *Stover*.
e to *a*, as in *Berger* to *Barger*, *Bernhardt* to *Barnhart*, and *Spengler* to *Spangler*.
ei to *oi*, as in *Meyer* to *Moyer*,[2] *Beyer* to *Boyer*, and *High* (originally *Hoch*) to *Hoy*.
eu to *ei*, as in *Kreuzer* to *Kreitzer*, *Kraeutler* to *Kreidler*, and *Baeumler* to *Bimeler*.
i to *a*, as in *Hirschberger* to *Harshbarger* and *Hirtzell* to *Hartzell*.
i to *e*, as in *Pfirsching* to *Pershing*.
oe to *e*, as in *Hoeppler* to *Hepler* and *Goetz* to *Getz*.
ue to *e*, as in *Zuericher* to *Zercher*.
ue to *ie*, as in *Kuefer* to *Kieffer*.
ue to *i*, as in *Guengerich* to *Gingerich*, *Buechsler* to *Bixler*, and *Nuessli* to *Nissley*.

1 Dutchified Surnames, Allentown (Pa.) *Morning Call*, Sept. 21, 1946.
2 Mr. Clyde V. *Moyers*, of Birmingham, Ala. (private communication, Aug. 16, 1946), tells me that his surname is pronounced *Meyers*.

b to *v*, as in *Gruber* to *Gruver*, *Eberhart* to *Everhart*, and *Gerber* to *Garver*.

g to *k* or *k* to *g*, as in *Gintner* to *Kantner* and *Kreider* to *Greider*.

k or *g* to *ng*, as in *Daenliker* to *Denlinger* and *Nafziger* to *Naftzinger*.[1]

ig to *ich*, as in *Neidig* to *Neidich*.

p to *b* and *b* to *p*, as in *Pressler* to *Bressler* and *Bitsche* to *Peachy*.

pf to *p*, as in *Stumpf* to *Stump*, *Pfeffer* to *Pepper*, *Pfaelzer* to *Pelzer* and *Pfaffenberger* to *Poffenberger*.

t to *d*, as in *Tressler* to *Dressler*, *Jotter* to *Yoder*, and *Rautenbusch* to *Roudebush*.

In addition, Yoder notes the frequent change of names by interpolation, as in *Minnich* from *Muench* and *Yearick* from *Goerg*.[2] All these forces, sometimes working together and sometimes in opposition, have produced a great variety of forms. For example, the *Huber* family from which President Herbert Hoover descended has left progeny named not only *Hoover*, but also *Hoeber*, *Hover*, and *Hoofer*, and many preserve the original name of *Huber*. Whenever one of the Pennsylvania German families holds a reunion this diversity is as apparent as it is when the Knickerbocker *Van Kouwenhoven-Conovers* have a party. Many of the *Schwarzes* are now *Swartzes* and others are *Blacks*.[3] In Maryland there are *Kaelbers* who have become *Calvert*[4] but others remain *Kaelber*. The name *Leipersberger* became *Leibelsperger*, *Leibensperger* and *Livelsberger* in Pennsylvania, and *Livelsberger*, *Livelsparger* and *Livenspire* in Ohio.[5] *Pfoersching* became *Pfirsching* in western Pennsylvania, and then *Pershin*, and finally *Pershing*. Some of the *Knoches* became *Knoxes* and others became *Bones* or *Boones*. Some of the *Günthers* became *Gunthers* and others became *Ginters*. Among the descendants of the primeval *Kleins* are *Klines*, *Clines* and *Kleins*. Some of the latter-day *Schnaebelis* are *Snabelys*, others are *Snavelys*, and yet others are *Snabels*. "Whenever William Penn could translate a German name into a corresponding English one," says an early chronicler,[6] "he did so in issuing patents for land in

---

[1] Yoder notes that "later Amish immigrants in Ohio and elsewhere spell this name *Noffsker*."

[2] Recorded by Heintze as a variant of *Georg*.

[3] Hanover (Pa.) *Sun*, Aug. 16, 1942: "One hundred and four were present ... when the annual *Swartz-Black* reunion was held."

[4] Death notice in the Baltimore *Sun*, Oct. 23, 1942.

[5] History and Genealogy of the Leibensperger Family, by Elmer I. Leibensperger; Reading (Pa.), 1943.

[6] Milledulcia: A Thousand Pleasant Things From *Notes & Queries*; New York, 1857, p. 34. I am indebted here to Mr. Huntington Cairns.

Pennsylvania; thus the respectable *Carpenter* family in Lancaster are the descendants of a *Zimmerman.*" But *Zimmerman* is still a more common name in Pennsylvania than *Carpenter.* The *Allgeiger* family which settled in Maryland in the Eighteenth Century has left descendants named *Allgeier, Algeier, Allgier, Allgeyer, Allgire* and *Algire.* The *Bortz* offspring are *Borz, Portz* and *Ports.* Those of *Eltzroth* are *Elserote, Elseroad, Elserode, Elsrode* and *Elsroad.* Those of *Lautenschläger* are *Laudenslager, Lautenslager* and *Lautenschleger.*[1]

It would be possible to compile an enormous catalogue of Americans of mark who have borne names originally German. *Pershing, Custer* and *Hoover* have been mentioned. George *Westinghouse,* the inventor of the air-brake, was the descendant of a Westphalian named *Wistinghausen.*[2] George W. *Crile,* the surgeon, descended from a German *Kreil.* Owen *Wister's Ur-Grossvater* was a *Wüster.* The forefathers of the Hon. John W. *Bricker* lie in a Frederick, Md., churchyard under the names of *Brücker* or *Brücher.*[3] The evangelist Billy *Sunday* was the son of a Union soldier named *Sonntag.*[4] Buffalo Bill Cody's actual surname was *Kothe* or *Köthe.*[5] Wendell L. *Willkie's* father was a German named *Willcke.*[6] Dr. Frederick A. *Cook,* the arctic explorer, was the son of a German *Koch.* Lew *Dockstader,* the old-time minstrel, was born *Clapp,* and got his stage name from an earlier minstrel whose original name was *Dachstädter.* General W. S. *Rosecrans,* who lost the battle of Chickamauga, was a *Rosenkrantz.* William *Wirt,* candidate for the Presidency in 1832, was a *Wörth.* The *Rockefellers* were originally *Roggenfelders.* General Nicholas *Herkimer,* killed in the Revolution, was the son of a *Herchheimer* born near Heidelberg in 1700.[7] The name of Peter Stenger *Grosscup,* once a celebrated Federal judge, was originally *Grosskopf.*[8] Daniel *Boone* may have been the

[1] I take these Maryland examples from Saint Paul's Lutheran Church, before cited.
[2] George *Westinghouse,* by Albert B. Faust, *American-German Review,* Aug., 1945, p. 6.
[3] *Bricker* of Ohio, by Karl B. Pauly; New York, 1944, p. 15.
[4] Billy *Sunday:* His Tabernacles and Sawdust Trails, by Theodore Thomas Frankenberg; Columbus (O.), 1917, p. 22.
[5] Cousin of Buffalo Bill Dies Here at Age of 94, Baltimore *Sun,* March 23, 1936.
[6] Public Men In and Out of Office, by J. L. Salter; Chapel Hill (N.C.), 1946, p. 54.
[7] Deutsche Namen in Amerika, by Stephan Kekule von Stradonitz, *B.Z. am Mittag,* Sept. 22, 1927.
[8] His mother's surname was *Bowermaster,* possibly from *Bauermeister.*

grandson of a *Böhn*.[1] The William *Rittenhouse* who was the first American paper-maker and grandfather of the first American astronomer arrived in Pennsylvania by way of Holland as William *Rittinghuysen*, originally the German Wilhelm *Rittershausen*.[2] Pal *Moore*, the lightweight pugilist, who died in 1943, started out in life as Paul Walter *von Frandke*.[3]

Where the early Germans encountered forerunners who were not British they often changed their names to accommodate non-English speechways, *e.g.*, French. On the so-called German Coast of Louisiana, settled in the Eighteenth Century, many of their surnames were thus Gallicized almost beyond recognition. *Buchwalter* became *Bouchevaldre*, *Wichner* became *Vigner*, *Wagensbach* became *Vacquensbac*, *Zehringer* became *Zerinque*, and *Huber* became *Houbre*, *Houver* and *Ubre*.[4] The same process has been recorded in France itself, and also in Spain, Italy and the Slavic lands.[5] The Germans have made the balance even by Germanizing many non-German names at home and also in their settlements in this country. To balance a German *Lesch* family which became *Lech*, *Laiche*, *Lesc*, *Leichert* and *Lecheux* in Louisiana [6] there was a French *Lecher* family in Pennsylvania which became *Lesher*, and a French *Lessecq* family which became *Lessig*.[7] An old tale tells of a Scotsman named *Ferguson* who, on settling among Germans in western New York, suffered the change of his name to *Feuerstein*, and then, on moving to an English-speaking settlement, had to submit to its translation into *Flint*. One of his grandsons, on immigrating to Louisiana, became *Pierre à Fusil*, and a son of this grandson, on returning to civilization, became Peter *Gun*.[8] To this may be added

---

1 Dr. T. G. Pullen, Jr., State Superintendent of Education of Maryland, tells me that he has been so informed by a member of the Boone family.
2 The First 100 Years, published by the Perkins-Goodwin Company, New York, 1946, p. 11.
3 Pal *Moore*, Ex-Boxer, Dies at Age of 52, Baltimore *Sun*, Dec. 23, 1943. For many others see The German Element in the United States, by A. B. Faust; New York, 1909.
4 The Settlement of the German Coast of Louisiana and the Creoles of German Descent, by J. Hanno Deiler, *German American Annals*, July and August, 1909, pp. 194–97.
5 Deutsche Familiennamen unter fremden Völkern, by Stephen Kekule von Stradonitz, *Mitteilungen der Akademie zur Wissenschaftlichen Erforshung*, April–May, 1928, pp. 901–15.
6 Deiler, lately cited, p. 195.
7 Pennsylvania English, by George W. Hibbitt, *American Speech*, Feb., 1939, p. 43.
8 *Ladies' Repository* (Cincinnati), Nov., 1861, p. 691. The story is there credited to "Mr. Livingston in his admirable answer to Mr. Jef-

the fact that when William *Wordsworth*, the English poet, settled at Goslar in the Hartz in 1798 the local Dogberrys recorded him on their scrolls as *Waetsford*.[1]

Americans of German descent who have clung to the original spelling of their names must submit to their mauling in pronunciation. Frederick Henry *Koch* (1877–1944), professor of dramatic literature at the University of North Carolina and founder of the folk-play movement, was always called *Kosh*, i.e., *coach* without the *t*-sound. As we have seen, the *sch*-cluster, as in *Schlens*, *Schleicher* and *Schneider*, is usually reduced to simple *s*, but not before *r*, as in *Schreiner*. The difficult *ch*-sound is seldom attempted; when it does not become *sh* it becomes *k*. The long German *u* is shortened, so that the first syllable of *Gutman* rhymes with *but*. The umlaut disappears, as in the name of Whittier's Maud *Muller*, that of the banking firm, *Kuhn*, Loeb & Company, and that of the New York restaurant, *Luchow's*.[2] Any unusual German name is bound to be mispronounced and misspelled. Mr. F. C. *Fiechter*, Jr., a lawyer of Philadelphia, has amused himself by collecting such distortions of his surname, e.g., as *Fletcher, Flechter, Feichter, Feighter, Frechter, Fichter, Fietcher* and *Fiescher*,[3] and Dr. Alfred D. *Schoch*, of Chicago, has matched them with fifty or more misspellings of his name, e.g., *Shock, Schooh, Schloch, Schack, Schoock,*

---

ferson concerning the *batture* case at New Orleans." Another version, recorded by Olaf Sölmund in Namen Wandern, New York *Staats-Zeiting*, in 1940, makes the original name of the Scotsman *Freyerstone*.

[1] William Wordsworth: His Life, Works and Influence, by G. McL. Harper; New York, 1916; Vol. I, p. 366.

[2] There was a wholesale change of German names in England during World War I. King George V led by changing his surname from *Wettin* to *Windsor* by proclamation on July 17, 1917. At the same time the *Tecks*, Queen Mary's family, changed their name to *Cambridge*, and the *Battenbergs* became *Mountbattens*. Simultaneously the head of the former family, Adolphus Charles Alexander Albert Edward George Philip Louis Ladislaus, Duke of *Teck*, became Marquess of *Cambridge*, Earl of *Eltham* and Viscount *Northallerton*, and his brother Alexander Augustus Frederick William Alfred George became Earl of *Athlone* and Viscount *Trematon*. The *Battenbergs*, whose German titles went back only to 1858, simply translated their surname. The head of the clan became Marquess of *Milford Haven*, Earl of *Medina* and Viscount *Alderney*, and his brother became Marquess of *Carisbrooke*, Earl of *Berkhampsted* and Viscount *Launceton*. Many well-known English families have surnames originally German, e.g., the *Barings* (Earl of *Cromer*, Earl of *Northbrook*, Lord *Revelstoke*), *Goschens* (Viscount *Goschen*), *von Donops*, and *Gleichens*.

[3] Private communication, Nov. 20, 1941.

Scooch, Sikoch, Sochs, Schmoch, Schoach, Sikoch and *Scochoch*.[1] Even German names that have become well known, *e.g.*, *Schurz*, *Mayer* and *Steinmetz*, are seldom pronounced correctly.[2]

497. [Of all the immigrant peoples in the United States, the Jews seem to be the most willing to change their names.] This willingness did not originate in the Republic; they brought it with them. In the Russian Pale from which so many of them came the eldest son of a family was exempt from military service, and in consequence the custom arose of younger sons bribing the 100% Russian officials to change their surnames, thus enabling them to pass as the eldest sons of mythical families.[3] It was also common for Jews who got on in the world to exchange their distinctively Jewish and usually commonplace names for new ones sounding more Russian and more elegant. In one of the stories of Sholom Aleichem there is a character named *Peshach Pessi* who adopts the sonorous *Platon Pantolonovich Lokshentopov*. His wife becomes *Pantomina*, and one of his cousins takes the style and appellation of *Fanfaron Faaronovich Yomtovson*. In another Aleichem story *Yenkel Voroner* — that is, *Yenkel of Vorone*, a town in Lithuania — becomes *Yakov Vladimirovich Voronin*.[4] Many of the principal recent figures in Russian history, bearing Russian names, came into the world with Jewish ones. The martyred *Lev Davidovich Trotsky*, for example, was born *Bronstein*, and the diplomat, *Maxim Maximovich Litvinoff* or *Litvinov*, was born *Finkelstein*.[5] In all other countries where name-

[1] Private communication, Jan. 1, 1940.
[2] But Abraham Lincoln knew how to pronounce *Schurz*, and liked to show off the fact. See Sumner's "Right Grand Division," by Darius N. Couch, Century Magazine, Aug., 1888, p. 636. The Baltimore Evening Sun once observed (Jan. 1, 1941) that while most American music-lovers manage to pronounce *Richard Wagner's* surname with some approximation to the German fashion, few of them so pronounce his given-name.
[3] I am indebted here to Mr. David Otis, of Brooklyn.
[4] The World of Sholom Aleichem, by Maurice Samuel; New York, 1943, pp. 275 ff.
[5] This name-changing among the comrades was not due wholly, of course, to a desire to get rid of Jewish names; another, and stronger, purpose was to confuse and throw off the police. Jews and non-Jews alike adopted aliases. *Nikolai Lenin*, for example, was that of a man originally *Vladimir Ilyitch Ulianov*, and *Joseph Vissarionavitch Stalin* is that of *Iosiph Djagashvilli, Djugashvilli* or *Dzhugashville*. When Earl Browder, then the putative head of the American Communists, was charged with getting a passport under a false name, part of his defense was that "party" names were commonly assumed by members of the party. Many of the Jews among them use English-sounding names.

changing is, legally speaking, relatively facile, Jews assume names borrowed from the local onomasticon. In England there are thousands of *Mosses* who were originally *Moseses*, *Brahams* who were *Abrahamses*, and *Montagues*, *Mortons*, *Taylors*, *Gordons*, *Leftwiches*, *Harrises*, *Davises*, *Morrises*, *Phillipses*, *Lewises* and *Lees* who have no blood kinship to those ancient tribes.[1] In France there has been a similar assumption of protective coloration in names, but it has been limited by statutes forbidding changes without legal permission by persons holding professional licences from the state — for example, for the practise of medicine. These statutes are sometimes violated, but probably not often, for violations are prosecuted. Said the Paris correspondent of the *Journal of the American Medical Association* in 1933:[2]

> Many foreign physicians seek to change their names on the pretext of making them easier to pronounce, but the main object is to conceal their nationality. These changed forms of names consist sometimes of simple translations, which deceive the public. *Klein* becomes *Petit*, *Delbrück* becomes *Dupont*, for example. A Rumanian physician by the name of *Fliesmann*, having acquired his diploma in the proper manner at the Faculté de Paris, opened an office in Paris, after assuming the French name *Florian*. He has been sentenced to pay a fine of $5 and an indemnity of $50, payable to the syndicate of the physicians of the Seine region, who brought suit against him.

The willingness of Jews to change their surnames is no doubt also helped along by the fact that those surnames, in many cases, are relatively recent, and hence do not radiate old associations and family pride. It was not until 1782 that the Jews of Austria were compelled to assume surnames, and not until 1812 and 1813 that those of Prussia and Bavaria, respectively, had to follow.[3] This

---

[1] Howard F. Barker notes in Surnames in *-is*, American Speech, April, 1927, p. 317, that *Davis*, *Harris*, *Lewis* and *Morris* are also very popular among American Jews, and that the fact may help to account for the high place held by these surnames on American namelists. The English Jews, on being made peers, always take names that offer no suggestion of their origin, *e.g.*, *Beaconsfield*, *Burnham*, *Melchett* and *Reading*.

[2] July 29.

[3] See AL4, p. 501. The authority quoted here in Dr. H. Flesch: Place-Names and First Names as Jewish Family Names, *Jewish Forum*, April, 1925. He adds that certain Jews took surnames as early as the Sixteenth Century, but that they tended to be variable. "The son," he says, "did not always retain the father's surname; with the change of market place or place of residence the surname changed. Thus Akiba *Nausch* from *Neuzze* near Frankfort, had a grandson called Akiba *Lehrer*, from *Lehrensteinfeld*; Tebi *Aschkenasi* had a son called Jacob *Emden*, and Samuel *Kelin* (from *Kolin*) had a son, Wolf *Boskowitz*."

compulsion was resisted by large numbers, and the harassed officials punished them by giving them names of a grandiose or otherwise ridiculous character, *e.g.*, *Edel* (noble), *Lilienthal* (valley of lilies), *Wohlgeruch* (perfume), *Armenfreund* (friend of the poor), *Ochsenschwanz* (ox tail), *Wanzenknicker* (louse cracker), *Drachenblut* (dragon's blood) and *Schöndufter* (sweet smeller).[1] Not infrequently a Jew was blackmailed by being threatened with a name that was obscene or otherwise ruinous,[2] but those who paid handsomely were permitted to choose names grateful to their sometimes florid fancy. This last fact, I suppose, accounts for the large number of surnames in *Gold-*, *Fein-* (fine) and *-blum* (flower) among the German Jews.

Flesch, in the article lately cited, shows that many very familiar Jewish names are translations of Hebrew given-names into German, Polish, Russian or some other language of the *Diaspora*. Thus *Naftah* (defined in Genesis XLIX, 21 as "a hind let loose") became *Hirsch* (deer) in German, and from *Hirsch* flowed a number of other names, *e.g.*, *Herz*, *Herzl* and *Herzler*. Similarly, *Jehuda* or *Judah* (defined in Genesis XLIX, 9 as "a lion's whelp") became *Löwe* (lion), and produced *Loew*, *Loeb*, *Leon* and even *Levin* and *Levinsohn*; *Schalom* (peace) was turned into *Frieden* (German: peace), and produced *Fried* and *Friedman*; and *Simcha* (joy) became *Freude* (German: joy), and produced *Freud*, *Freudman* and various other derivatives. Sometimes one Hebrew name sufficed to engender two or more in German, according to the way it was translated. Thus *Asher* (defined in Genesis XLIX, 20 as one whose "bread shall be fat"), gave rise to *Lamm* (lamb) because fatness suggested the sacrificial mutton, and also to *Selig* (blessed), apparently on the theory that good eating was a form of blessedness. Out of *Lamm* has come *Lämmle* (a diminutive), and out of *Selig* two common Jewish names, *Seliger* and *Seligman*. The formation of surnames by the addition of some form of *-son* to a father's given-name was as common among the Jews as among Christians. In German *-sohn* was used and in the Slavic languages *-ice*, *-ovice* or *-ovitch*. Many surnames were also made by the additions of diminutives to given-

---

[1] I take these examples from Die deutschen Familiennamen, by Albert Heintze; second edition; Halle a. S., 1903, pp. 66–68. For more see AL4, p. 501.

[2] An example is given in AL4, p. 501, n. 2.

names, e.g., -ig, -ich, -el, -la, -lein, -ing and -ung. Not infrequently phonetic change showed itself, as when the guttural *ch* of *Chayim* became *k* in *Keim* and *h* in *Hein, Heineman, Heyman* and *Hyman*. Many Russian, Polish and Rumanian Jews assumed such Germanized Jewish names at the time of the first big immigration to America from Eastern Europe. The German Jews were here before them, and had won to a respected position, and it seemed good policy to seek the shelter of that position. Says Jane Doe in a paper entitled " Concerning Hebrew Names ": [1]

> By that time . . . *Goldstein, Weinberg, Schoenberg*, etc., were considered by the Jews themselves to be Jewish names. Where the newly arrived immigrants from Slavic countries had borne Slavic names there they took German names here. At any given period of Jewish history some branch of Jewry plays the aristocrat. At that time the aristocrat was the German Jew.

The assumption by Jews of well-known non-Jewish names is sometimes protested by the bearers of the latter; indeed, even Jews of the older stock have been known to object, as happened, for example, when a Philadelphia dentist named *Isaac Solomon Cohen* began subscribing himself *I. Solis Cohen*, the patronymic of an ancient and honored Jewish medical family of that city. Again, there was an uproar from the *Cabots* of Boston when, in 1923, a Russian Jew named *Kabotchnick* [2] denized there, gave notice that he had shortened his name to *Cabot*,[3] and another in Baltimore in 1941, when a Dr. Henry Lyon *Sinskey* proposed to adopt the name of *Sherwood*, to the disquiet of a rich oil man of that name. But such objections, when they are taken into court, seldom profit the plaintiff, for under American law a man has a right to change his name at will, though it is common for a would-be changeling of any means to ask the countenance of a court of record, that there may be no trouble thereafter about voting rights and the conveyance of property.[4] The *Solis Cohens*, in fact, were advised that restrain-

[1] *Reflex*, Nov., 1928, pp. 27–31.
[2] United Press dispatch from Boston, Aug. 16, 1923.
[3] *Cabot* itself does not appear to be a British name, and Ewen does not list it in his History of Surnames of the British Isles. The first American *Cabot* to make a mark on history was George (1751–1823), a politician whose life was written by Henry *Cabot* Lodge the elder; Boston, 1877. The mariner, John *Cabot*, was an Italian whose real name was Giovanni *Caboto*.
[4] In England the law is substantially the same as in the United States but it is customary for a man seeking to change his name to do so by applying for a royal license, which may be obtained as a matter of course by paying a large fee, or by advertising his intention in the

ing Dr. Cohen was impossible under Pennsylvania law, and they did not go to court. The *Cabots* went and lost.[1] In Baltimore the complaining *Sherwood* seems to have scored a sort of dog-fall, for on November 19, 1941, Judge J. Abner Sayler, sitting in the local Circuit Court, approved the adoption of *Sherwood* by one of the *Sinskey* children, a young lawyer, but refused to approve its use by the father, who was still *Sinskey* in 1947.

Once a new name has been recognized, whether by judicial approval or by common consent, it becomes as much the bearer's possession as his original name, and may be used and defended in all situations in which the latter may be used and defended. This was decided in 1923 by Judge Learned Hand, then a Federal district judge in New York, in the case of the Goldwyn Pictures Corporation *vs.* Samuel Goldwyn. Goldwyn, who was born *Gelbfisch* and later called himself *Goldfish*, changed his name to *Goldwyn* in 1918, and as *Goldwyn* rose to fame and wealth as a movie magnate. But he lost control of the Goldwyn Pictures Corporation to others, and when, in 1923, he resumed making pictures and launched a screen version of "Potash and Perlmutter" on

---

newspapers and filing a deed-poll with the clerk of the Supreme Court. The aim in each case is to make it possible for him to continue under his new name whatever property or other rights he had under his old one. It is also possible to have a name changed by act of Parliament, but this is seldom resorted to. A. C. Fox-Davies and P. W. P. Carlton-Britton argued in A Treatise on the Law Concerning Names and Changes of Name; London, 1907, that "from the earliest times the Crown has made the assertion that change of name and the sanction thereof are within its prerogative," but this was disputed, and indeed disproved, by a writer in the London *Academy*, May 4, 1907. This writer was probably C. L'Estrange Ewen, for the same arguments appear in his History of Surnames of the British Isles, pp. 408–13. Since 1919 the Aliens' Restriction Act has forbidden any alien to assume a name by which he was not known before Aug. 4, 1914. But exemptions may be granted by royal license or by any Secretary of State. A British subject is still free to change his name as he pleases. For the law in New York see The How and Why of Name-Changing, by Helen P. Wulbern, *American Mercury*, June, 1947, p. 719.

[1] The issue of this case inspired a Boston wit to the following parody of a well-known quatrain:
I come from good old Boston,
  The home of the bean and the cod,
Where the Lowells speak only to
  Cabots,
And the *Cabots* speak Yiddish,
  by God.

A variorum version, ascribed (no doubt apocryphally) to Woodrow Wilson, made the last two lines read:
Where the Lodges can't speak to
  the *Cabots*,
'Cause the *Cabots* speak Yiddish, by God.

Broadway, the corporation got a temporary injunction against him, and he was ordered to credit the production on his billing to *S. G. Inc.* On the hearing of an application to make the injunction permanent Judge Hand vacated it, with the provision, accepted by Goldwyn, that he should add "not connected with Goldwyn Pictures Corporation" to all his public announcements. The learned judge's decision said:

> A new name, when honestly assumed and worn, may well be of as much or nearly as much consequence to its bearer as though it were familial. Our names are useful or dangerous to us according to the associations they carry among those who hear them. If we have by our past conduct established a good name, that is an interest, pecuniary or honorific, of which we may well object to being deprived, and which may exceed in value that which we inherited. A self-made man may prefer a self-made name.
>
> Under circumstances like that at bar it appears to me that *Goldwyn*, who has familiarized the public — with the acquiescence of the plaintiff — with that name, has as much right to complain of its loss as though he had not inherited the less euphonious *Gelbfisch*, or its equivalent, *Goldfish*. . . .
>
> The plaintiff's business was built up, in part at any rate, by *Goldwyn's* activity, and I may take it, I think, by his capacity and imagination. . . . The defendant accepts the necessity of some limitation upon his rights; he only objects to complete obscurity.[1]

The marriage, death and other personal notices in the newspapers frequently record changes in Jewish surnames. I reach into my collectanea and bring forth *Burstein* changed to *Burr*,[2] *Abrahams* to *Allen*,[3] *Loewenthal* to *Lowell*,[4] *Butensky* to *Burton*,[5] *Fleischer* to *Fleming*,[6] *Bogitzky* to *Bogart*,[7] *Abrams* to *Adams*,[8] *Ginsborg* to *Gilbert*,[9] *Bernstein* to *Brett*,[10] *Markowitz* to *Marlowe*, *Cohen* to *Coliver*,[11] *Lewisohn* to *MacLevy*,[12] *Feinstein* to *Fenton*,[13] *Katzenstein* to *Kaye*,[14] *Leven-*

---

[1] The case is reported in *Variety*, Oct. 25, 1923, p. 19.
[2] Death notice, New York *Times*, April 12, 1946.
[3] Announcement of engagement, New York *Herald Tribune*, Feb. 27, 1946.
[4] Wedding notice, New York *Times*, March 3, 1946.
[5] Death notice, the same, Feb. 24, 1946.
[6] Same, same, Feb. 26, 1946.
[7] Same, same, Sept. 7, 1946.
[8] Joey *Adams*, author of From Gags to Riches; New York, 1946, says in his book that *Abrams* is his family name.
[9] Wedding notice, New York *Times*, Feb. 25, 1946.
[10] Death notice, same, April 21, 1946.
[11] Baltimore *Sun*, Sept. 8, 1944: "As a rule Army captains do not greet Navy lieutenants with a kiss, but that is what happened in Brisbane recently when two Baltimore brothers, Lieut. Jonas H. *Cohen* and Capt. Norman *Coliver*, met for the first time in 27 months."
[12] Noted in New York by a correspondent who chooses to remain anonymous.
[13] Death notice, New York *Times*, April 22, 1946.
[14] Same, Baltimore *Sun*, July 11, 1945.

thal to *Lawrence*,[1] *Finkelstein* to *Flint* and to *Fenton*,[2] *Schlesinger* to *Walter*,[3] *Schneittacher* to *Snedeker*,[4] *Isaac* to *Ives*,[5] *Wohlgemuth* to *Wall*,[6] *Weinstein* to *Winston*, *Leberstein* to *Livingston*, *Rosenberg* to *Robinson* and to *Ruskin*,[7] *Edelstein* to *Addleston*, *Wasserzweig* to *Vassar-Smith*,[8] *Reizenstein* to *Rice*,[9] *Schmetterling* to *Smith*,[10] *Leibowitz* to *Leidy*,[11] *Finkelstein* to *Finn*,[12] *Pulitzer* to *Stevens*,[13] *Rothstein* to *Ross*, and *Goldberg* to *Gould* and *Coburn*.[14]

Changes are frequently made in Jewish names that are not abandoned altogether. *Cohen*, which is the commonest of such surnames in the United States,[15] is to be encountered as *Cohn, Cone, Cowan, Conn, Cahan, Cohon, Coyne, Cohan, Coen*,[16] *Kohn, Kohan, Kohon, Kahn, Kann* and *Kohen*.[17] Some of these forms are not arbitrary,

---

[1] Announcement of engagement, New York *Times*, Jan. 24, 1946.
[2] Wedding notice, Brooklyn *Eagle*, April 18, 1946; notice of engagement, New York *Herald Tribune*, June 28, 1946.
[3] The case of the orchestra conductor, Bruno *Walter*, recorded in his autobiography, Theme and Variations; New York, 1946, p. 89. The change was made before he immigrated to America.
[4] Death notice, New York *Times*, Jan. 26, 1946. *Snedeker* or *Snediker* is a Dutch name.
[5] Wedding notice, same, Feb. 1, 1946.
[6] Death notice, same, Feb. 1, 1946.
[7] Both found in the Harvard quinquennial catalogue by Miles L. Hanley and reported in *American Speech*, Oct., 1933, p. 78.
[8] Court Circular, London *Times*, Sept. 20, 1945.
[9] The author of The Adding Machine, Street Scene and other popular plays. See Current Biography: Who's News and Why; New York, 1943, p. 617.
[10] I am indebted for many of these specimens to Mr. Alexander Kadison, of New York, a diligent collector of onomastic Americana. "It is claimed," says Dr. A. A. Roback in *Sarah* to *Sylvia* to *Shirley*, Commentary, Sept., 1946, p. 274, "that a characteristically Jewish name is a drawback in the matter of a career. What is meant, of course, is that it is a drawback to be known unmistakably and immediately for a Jew. . . . [But] the fact probably is that when a Jew appropriates a fancy Anglo-Saxon or Scotch name like *Gainsborough* or *Stewart* the Anglo-Saxons and Scotch dislike him all the more for it."
[11] Seeks to Change Surname, Baltimore *Sun*, Nov. 3, 1927.
[12] Obituary in New York *Herald Tribune*, April 17, 1947.
[13] Discards *Pulitzer* Name, New York *Times*, Feb. 27, 1947.
[14] The last two are from The How and Why of Name-Changing, by Helen P. Wulbern, before cited.
[15] Samuel H. Abramson shows in Abramson Blames the Goldbergs, *Canadian Jewish Chronicle*, March 20, 1942, that it also leads in Canada, where it is followed by *Greenberg, Freedman*, or *Friedman, Katz, Levy, Goldberg, Rosenberg, Bernstein* and *Abramson* in order.
[16] *Cohan(e)* and *Coen* are Irish names. Woulfe, in his Irish Names and Surnames, says that the former was originally *O Cathain* or *O Ceochain* and the latter *O Comhdain, O Comhghain* or *Mac Eoghain*.
[17] Many other *Cohens* have changed their surnames to unrelated forms, e.g., *Crane* and *Quinn*.

but have history and foreign custom behind them. *Cohen* is a Hebrew word, *kohen*, signifying, originally, a prince or priest, but later a priest only. By Jewish tradition the name and the office are restricted to descendants of Aaron, but that tradition, like many others, has long since lost force. The Sephardic Jews pronounce the word *ko-hén;* the German Jews make it *koh'n*, in one syllable; the Polish Jews make the first syllable rhyme with *now*, and the Russian Jews prefer *káy-hun*.[1]

Levy is another Jewish patronymic that has many permutations. It is derived from the name of the Levites, who were priests of an inferior order. The original Hebrew designation of them was *Lewi*, and from it have sprung *Levi, Levy, Lewy, Levie, Leavy, Leevy, Levey, Levvy, Levay, Leve, Levee, Levin, Levine, Levene, Levien, Leveen, Leven, Levins, Levita, Levitan, Levitas, Levitz, Levitski, Levninsky, Levinson, Levinsohn, Levenson, Levison, Lewison, Lewisohn, Lewis, Lewin, Levanne, Lever* and a host of other forms, including *Halevy* (Hebrew *ha*, the).[2] *Lév-vy*, with the accent on the first syllable, is sometimes heard; it probably comes closer to the original Hebrew pronunciation than either *lée-vee* or *lée-vy*, the latter with the *vy* rhyming with high. The Sephardic Jews use *lay-vee*, with the accent on the first syllable, and convert the *v* into our *f*. A number of American *Levys* have changed their name to *Lee*,[3] and one family has chosen *Leeds*. I have also encountered

---

[1] Here I am indebted to Dr. Solomon Solis Cohen, of Philadelphia; private communication, May 7, 1937. William B. Ziff says in The Rape of Palestine; New York, 1938, p. 189, that many of the Jews now resettled in Palestine have gone back to Hebrew names. Mr. Gershon Aronsky, editor of the *Palestine Post* (Jerusalem) supplies me with some examples taken from public notices of name changes in the *Palestine Gazette*, 1946. They include *Steinberg* to *Harsela, Perlmutter* to *Dar, Moscovitz* to *Doron, Wasserman* to *Tavor, Braun* to *Bar-On, Gutman* to *Bar-Tov, Hoffman* to *Ben Yaaqov, Lederman* to *Yeredor, Loewenstein* to *Zur-Ayre, Fischer* to *Ben-Nun, Aronsheim* to *Beit Aharon, Rosenfelder* to *Vared, Miller* to *Sinay, Niedermann* to *Nasi, Bernstein* to *Ben-Horin, Bergenbaum* to *Oren, Weinstein* to *Hagiti,* and *Dudelzak* to *Halili*.

[2] Mr. B. G. Kayfetz, of Toronto, tells me that many of these are not American inventions, but are encountered among Jews all over Europe. The forms with German or Slavic suffixes, e.g., -*thal*, -*sky*, -*sohn* and -*stein*, were all imported.

[3] *Lee* is also a favorite with other immigrant groups, and that fact may account in part for its high frequency among American surnames — 156 in every 100,000 of population, which is much higher than its frequency in England. It is adopted in place of difficult German names, e.g., *Liebknecht* and *Lietsche;* common Jewish names other than *Levy,* e.g., *Leon,* and the

Proper Names in America

Levis,[1] *LeVie*, *LaVey*, *Delavie*, *Dellevie*, *Leylan* and *Lewynne*,[2] some of them borne by French or French-Canadian Jews. Another name with many variations, especially in spelling, is *Ginsberg*, e.g., *Ginzberg*, *Ginsburg*, *Ginsburgh*, *Ginsbury*, *Guinesberg*, *Gainsburg*, *Guynzburg*[3] and *Ginsborough*. Many other familiar Jewish names are similarly transmogrified. *Goldstein* becomes *Goldstone*, *Golston*, and finally *Golson* or *Golsan*; *Goldberg* becomes *Goldhill*, *Goldboro*, *Golboro*, or *Goldsborough*; *Schapiro* or *Shapiro* becomes *Schapira*, *Schapierer*, *Shapero*, *Shapera*, *Shapereau*,[4] *Chapereau*,[5] *Chapiro* or the terminal *Rowe*.[6] I have encountered *Guggenheim* spelled *Goughenheim*[7] and *Labovitz* turned into *LaBovith*. Many of the German-Jewish names in *-berg*, *-thal*, *-feld*, *-mann*, and so on have both elements translated, so that *Rosenberg*, for example, becomes *Rosehill*,[8] *Blumenthal* becomes *Bloomingdale*, *Wassermann* becomes *Waterman*, and *Schwarzmann* becomes *Blackman*.[9]

Not a few Jewish names of German origin present phonological difficulties to the average American, and thus suffer changes in pronunciation like those undergone by the names of German and other non-Jewish immigrants. All the *Strauses* and *Strausses* who mention the pronunciation of their names in "Who's Who in America" give the *au* the sound of *ou* in *out*, but there seems to be a growing tendency to make the name *Straws*, especially in the South. More-

---

Chinese *Li* and Scandinavian *Lie*. In New York the German-Jewish name *Lehman(n)* is fast acquiring the pronunciation of *Lee-man* (AL4, p. 500, n. 1); in time it may become simple *Lee*. Already it is common to find *Lees* with Jewish given-names.

1 Abrahamson Blames the Goldbergs, by Samuel H. Abramson, before cited.
2 Dr. Pepys' Diary, *Journal of the American Medical Association*, Oct. 7, 1944.
3 This appeared in a news story in the Baltimore *Sun*, last page, April 20, 1937.
4 Tonics and Sedatives, *Journal of the American Medical Association*, Dec. 16, 1939.
5 This was the form used by the defendant in a smuggling case in New York in 1938.
6 Engagement notice, New York *Times*, Aug. 30, 1946. Johannes Hoops, in Shakespeare's Name and Origin, Studies for William A. Read; University (La.), 1940, p. 70, lists *Chacsper* as one of the early variants of *Shakespeare*.
7 *Billboard*, Dec. 29, 1934, p. 99. The French form is *Gougenheim*.
8 A death notice in the New York *Times*, Feb. 23, 1946, recorded the change of *Rosebush* to *DesRosiers*, but *Rosebush* may not have been a Jewish name.
9 The Sephardic Jews, who are relatively few in number, usually stick to their original names, e.g., the Spanish *Acosta*, the Portuguese *de Silva* and the French *de Casseres*. I am indebted here to Dr. L. L. Barrett, of the University of North Carolina.

over, even when it is not *Straws* it has the American *s*-sound at the start, not the German *sh*-sound. Several *Goldsteins* in "Who's Who" ordain that the *-stein* of their name be pronounced *steen*, but Dr. Albert *Einstein*, the physicist, sticks to *stine*.[1] This appearance of *ei* as *ee* is a curious phenomenon, not yet explained. If it represents an effort at elegance it is quite silly, for *-steen* is surely no more lovely than *-stine*. Happily, it seems to prevail only when *-stein* is terminal. In such names as *Einstein*, *Feinstein* and *Weinstein* one often hears *-een* in the last syllable, but never in the first. Nor does it appear in *Weinburg*, *Klein*, *Fein*, *Steinbeck*, *Brandeis*, *Eichelberger*, *Eisenhower*, *Eisner*, *Dreiser* and the like, some of them Jewish and some not, nor in simple *Stein*, nor in numerous Jewish names in *-heim* and *-heimer*. In names in *Braun-* and *Blau-* the German *au* is often pronounced *aw*, so that *Braunstein* becomes *Brawnsteen* and *Blaustein* becomes *Blawsteen*. In the same way *Morgenthau* becomes *Morgenthaw*, with the *au* pronounced *aw* and the German *th* changed to the English *th* in *think*. Something of the sort also happens in the case of the terminal *-baum*, which becomes *bawm*, as in *Barenbawm* for *Barenbaum*. *Kühn* at first dropped its umlaut and became *Kuhn*, pronounced to rhyme with moon; now it shows signs of going on to *Kyun*, but without any further change in spelling. Many of the early Jewish immigrants from the German lands, like the Germin *Goyim*, changed the spelling of their names in order to preserve the pronunciation. Thus *Gorfein* became *Gorfine*, *Schön* became *Shane* or *Shain*, and *Klein* became *Kline*.[2] In innumerable cases, however, this was inconvenient or impossible, so the Jews, like other immigrants, had to submit to the mispronunciation of their names. Thus *Sachs* became *Sax* and has remained so, and *Katz*[3] came to be identical in sound with *cats*, and *Adler* acquired a flat American *a*. In the common

---

[1] In the NBC Handbook of Pronunciation, compiled by James F. Bender; New York, 1944, p. 119, both *Ine-stine* and the German form *Ine-shtine* are given.

[2] But I have heard even *Gorfine* turned into *Gorfeen*, and likewise *Durstine* into *Dursteen*.

[3] Rabbi Jacob Tarlau, of Flushing, L. I. (private communication, April 30, 1937), tells me that *Katz* has nothing to do, as it is sometimes assumed, with the identical German word, signifying a cat. It is a characteristic Hebrew abbreviation of two words, *kohen tzedek*, and indicates that the man bearing it is a descendant of Aaron, and hence a priest. The name of a late chief rabbi of France, *Zadoc Kahn*, was simply *Katz* reversed.

speech of New York the element *-berger* or *-burger* changes to *-boiger*, and I have heard it with a soft *g*.

Louis Adamic says in "What's Your Name?"[1] that "Poles and Polish Americans seem impelled to more name-changing than any other group" — that is, with the exception of the Jews —, but his own evidence shows that many of them resist stoutly the changes forced upon them by the fact that Polish accents are unintelligible to most Americans and many Polish sounds are unpronounceable. Thus the names of *Krzyzanowski*,[2] *Kosciuszko*, *Andrzejski*, *Szymkiewicz*, *Szybczyński*, *Korzybski* and *Mikolajezyk* still survive in American reference books and even in newspaper dispatches, though it is highly unlikely that more than one non-Polish-American in ten thousand can pronounce them.[3] But many more Polish names have been simplified, *e.g.*, *Winiarecki* to *Winar*, *Czyzcwicz* to *Chasey*, *Zmudzinski* to *Zmuday*, *Gwzcarczyszyn* to *Guscas*, and *Modrzejewski* to *Modjeski*,[4] or translated into English, *e.g.*, *Smith* for *Kowalczyk*, *Wheeler* for *Kolodziejcak*, *Gardner* for *Ogrodowski*, and *Cook* for *Kucharz*, or abandoned altogether for common British names, *e.g.*, *Izydorczyk* for *Sherwood*, *Wawrzynski* for *Stone*, *Szczepanski* for *Sheperd*, *Chrzanowski* for *Dunlap*, *Matykiewicz* for *Rodgers*,[5] *Valuzki* for *Wallace*,[6] and *Kedjerski* for *Kent*.[7]

---

[1] New York, 1942, p. 50.

[2] A general officer in the Civil War and the first Governor of Alaska. His descendants retain the name unchanged.

[3] The thing, of course, runs the other way, and Polish-American writers encounter difficulties when they try to represent American loan-words in Polish print. I offer a few examples from *Oredownik Jezykowy*, a Polish monthly published at St. Francis, Wis., by the Rev. B. E. Goral: *ajskrimsoda* (ice-cream-soda), *akjurejt* (accurate), *autsajd* (outside), *baj gasz* (by gosh), *Dzio* (Joe), *bendedz* (bandage), *berykejda* (barricade), *blosz* (blush) and *blesfana* (blast furnace).

[4] The name of a distinguished engineer (1861-1940) whose mother, Helena *Modjeska* (1844-1909) was a distinguished actress. The difference between the feminine and masculine suffixes will be noted. The Poles, like the Russians, also inflect proper names for case, etc.

[5] I am indebted for these examples to Mr. Charles C. Arensberg, of the Pittsburgh Bar. They come from the records of the Allegheny County Court of Common Pleas. Most Poles applying for registration of new names explain why they want to get rid of their old ones. Some of these reasons are that the old name is "hard to spell and pronounce," or is "embarrassing socially and in business," or that the new one is the name of some American relative-in-law or a cherished friend, or is "of better euphony."

[6] Death notice, New York *Times*, Oct. 6, 1940.

[7] Same, same, March 20, 1946. I am indebted for the last two to Mr. Alexander Kadison.

Sometimes the old name is retained as a middle name, as when Anthony *Mierzejewski* became *Anthony Mierzejewski Mackey*. And not infrequently, the new name chosen is not English but Irish or German, e.g., *Micsza* to *McShea*, *Koscielniak* to *Moran*, *Golebiewski* to *Kress*, *Pruchniewski* to *Prosser* and *Smialkowski* to *Schultz*.[1]

The Czechs, Slovaks, Serbs, Russians, Ukrainians and other Slavs all go the same route. Louis Adamic, in the book I was lately citing, describes the changes of name among his countrymen, the Slovenes. His own name, originally *Adamič*, i.e., *Adamson* or *Little Adam*, presented an accented consonant that Americans could not fathom, and a stress, *Ah-dáh-mitch*, that they could not be expected to follow, so in his youth in America he cast about for something less burdensome. He considered *Adamich*, *Adamitch* and *Adamage*, but finally decided on *Adamic* without the accent. "Each time," he says, "a book of mine appears inquiries come from librarians, booksellers and lecturing book reviewers as to its 'correct' pronunciation. Going about the country, I hear myself called *Adámic* almost as often as *Ádamic*. To inquiries I reply that I prefer *Adamic* but am willing to let the pronunciation establish itself."[2] The troubles of the Slovaks, who have surnames not unlike those of the Slovenes, have been described by Ivan J. Kramoris.[3] He says:

> Slovak names, invariably accented on the first syllable, undergo various shifts when pronounced by the American tongue. *Krámoris* becomes *Kramóris*; *Lédnicky*, *Lednícky*; *Bístricky*, *Bistrícky*; *Zémanovič*, *Zemánovic* or *Zemanóvic*, and *Péterka*, *Petérka*. *Jelačič*, shorn of diacritical markings, is no longer pronounced with the *j* as *y* in *yet* but as *j* in *jello*, and with the shift in accent the name changes from *Yélahchich* (the *ch* as in *church*) to *Jelássick*. . . . *Budiač*, written *Budiac*, might be pronounced *Búhdeeack*, and the attempt to phonetize it in the spelling *Budeach* results in the loss of the middle syllable and evokes the pronunciation *Buhdeach*, in effect a new name. . . . *Andic* prompts the pronunciation *Andik*, yet the owner would have it *Anditch*. The addition of the *h* to make it *Andich* would confuse the Slovak reader, for then, instead of pronouncing the name *Andeech* (as when written *Andič*) or *Andeetz* (if written *Andic*), he would make of *ich* the guttural *ch* as in German *ich* or *ach*.

1 Baltimore *Sun*, Jan. 28, 1936. Dr. Alfred Senn says in Lithuanian Surnames, *American Slavic and East European Review*, Aug., 1945, p. 134, that *-ski* in Poland designated nobility and that many parents had their children registered under names so terminating in order to smooth their way in life.
2 What's Your Name?, pp. 11–13.
3 The Americanization of Slovak Surnames, *Slovak Review*, Autumn, 1946, pp. 67–73.

Kramoris says that the Slovaks in America rejoice when they happen to bear surnames which fall in with American speechways, e.g., *Kuban*, *Toman*, *Urban*, and *Polak* or *Polack*. Those with more difficult names sometimes find it so hard to teach Americans how to pronounce them that they are abandoned altogether. For example:

> Dropping the diacritical mark in *Vlčansky* without adding an *h* to make it *Vlchansky* elicits the American pronunciation *Vulkánskee*. Adding the *h*, however, would change the Slovak pronunciation. Since the possessor of the name is an aspirant for a political office, to Americanize it is highly important. The insertion of the *h* will not do this for him, . . . so he resolves on a new name, a good vote-getting name, a name familiar to and respected by all Americans: *Rockne*. . . . Business men also think it advisable to make changes. *Brlety* may or may not know of the principle of metathesis in linguistics, but *Brilty* is more euphonious, and *Brilty* his name becomes. *Greguška* opens a fur store and changes his name to *Greeg*. . . . The *Kuvulič* family retains the name, but Doctor *Kavulič* changes his right in it to *Kaval*. The novelist of Slovak descent, Thomas *Belejčak*, becomes Thomas *Bell*. The *Hudak* sisters, a quartette singing for a commercial radio programme, change their name to *Harding*. In Hollywood Lillian *Micuda* becomes Lillian *Cornell*. . . . Your name may be *Burovsky* and you change it to *Bury*, or it may be *Gorčiansky* and you apocopate it to *Gor*, or it may be *Molitoris* and you ellipsize it to *Moris*.[1]

The discussion of Czech surnames in American in AL4,[2] based on the studies of the Right Rev. J. B. Dudek,[3] needs no amplification here. Russian and Ukrainian names, save those borrowed by Jews, are relatively rare in this country, and I know of no adequate investigation of them.[4] The American Lithuanians, who are Balto-Slavs, and thus bridge the gap between the Slavs and the Teutonic peoples, are fortunate in that their surnames, taking one with another, are considerably more amenable to American speech habits than those of the Poles, and that they are thus under less

---

[1] Kramoris has kindly given me access to a much more extensive paper, Notes on the Americanized Slovak Surname, but it is not yet published.

[2] pp. 486–88.

[3] Czech Surnames in America, *American Mercury*, May, 1925; The Americanization of Czech Surnames, *American Speech*, Dec., 1925; Czech-American Names, *Czechoslovak Student Life* (Lisle, Ill.), April, 1928.

[4] *Life* reported in 1946 that one of its photographers, *Jerry Cooke*, "was born *Jury Kuchuk*, of Russian parents." *The New Yorker*, March 9, 1946, p. 20, mentioned a New York orchestra leader named *Coolidge*, originally the Russian *Kudisch*. *Variety*, Nov. 17, 1943, recorded the death of a Victor *Hyde* who immigrated to America as a Russian dancer named *Haidbura*. Many female dancers bearing Russian names are actually Englishwomen. *Boris Karloff*, the movie actor, says in Who's Who in America that his real name is *William Henry Pratt*.

pressure to change them. Such names as *Klypa, Surgailis, Grigonis, Varnas, Asmantas* and *Zadeikis* may seem a bit strange to a 100% American who encounters them for the first time, but they do not really alarm him. There are, however, other Lithuanian names that do, especially in their written form, and their bearers are thus constrained to change them. One of the commonest changes is made by substituting English consonants for the Lithuanian consonants, so that *Sŭekevičius*, for example, becomes *Sukevicius* and *Valančiūnas* becomes *Valanciunas*. This, of course, involves a change in pronunciation, but it is sometimes only slight. Other names are changed by omitting the original endings, e.g., *-aitis, -onis* and *-unas*, which are authentically Lithuanian, and *-evicius, -avicius, -auska* and *-inskas*, which are Polish. Thus *Norkaitis* becomes *Norkat, Keturakaitis* becomes *Keturakat*, *Šalinskas* becomes *Shalins*, *Jakubauskas* becomes *Jakubs*, and *Bertašius* becomes *Bertash* or *Bartash*. Sometimes the same name is changed differently by different members of the same family, e.g., *Aukštikalnis*, meaning a high hill, which is converted into *Colney* by one Lithuanian and into *Hill* by his cousin. Finally, there are the usual bold leaps to English names, sometimes related and sometimes not, e.g., *Alksninis* to *Andrews, Tamošitis* to *Thomas, Bogdžiūnas* to *Borden*, and *Pilipavičius* and *Pilipauskas* to *Philipps*.[1] As in Russian, surnames are inflected for gender, so the wife of a man named *Vabalas* is Mrs. *Vabalienė*. Moreover, there is a special inflection to distinguish unmarried women, so that the daughter of this couple is Miss *Vabalaitė*. At home in Lithuania "it would be unthinkable and utterly ridiculous" to speak of *Mrs.* or *Miss Vabalas*, but in America these old inflections have broken down, and the masculine form is used "regardless of the sex of the person referred to."[2] Says the paper just quoted:

The Lithuanians are fully aware of the strong foreign imprint on their stock of surnames and they feel embarrassed about the situation. The Slavic elements are especially painful to their national pride. During the short period of Lithuanian independence[3] serious efforts were made to eliminate or at

[1] I am indebted here to the kindness of Dr. Alfred Senn, of the University of Pennsylvania, the foremost American authority on Lithuanian.
[2] Lithuanian Surnames, by Alfred Senn, before cited, pp. 127-37 — a paper read at a meeting of the Modern Language Association in New York, Dec. 28, 1944. In an earlier form it was read at a meeting of the Linguistic Society of America at Chapel Hill (N.C.), July 11, 1942.
[3] The Lithuanian republic was

least reduce foreign suffixes and replace them with Lithuanian formations in order to give the surnames a more Lithuanian appearance. A special Committee for the Restoration of Lithuanian Surnames was charged with the task of advising people with foreign-looking surnames "how to return them to their former Lithuanian purity." This movement spread across the Atlantic and reached the Lithuanians in the United States. A very frequent procedure would be simply to cut off the Slavic suffix, *e.g.*, to make *Končius* out of *Koncevičius*. Just as frequently the objectional suffix was replaced by a Lithuanian suffix, *e.g.*, *Antanavičius* was changed to *Antanaitis*. In other cases the change went deeper, *e.g.*, when *Dzimidavičius* was transformed into *Daumantas*, with the explanation that this had actually been the original form. Not only surnames of living persons were changed, but also those of historical personages.

The other Baltic peoples have varying fortunes when they bring their names to America. The Finns, who are neither Slav nor Teutons, but Finno-Ugrians and hence allied to the Hungarians, have plenty of surnames that are quite easy for Americans and call for no change, *e.g.*, *Ikola*, *Hakala*, *Talvio*, *Holsti*, *Irkonen*, *Kallar*, *Kesti*, *Zilliacas* and *Kosola*, but there are also others that pop the Yankee eye even when they do not strain the Yankee larynx, *e.g.*, *Koskenniemi*, *Sillanpää*, *Voionmaa*, *Tuomikoski*, *Päivärinta*, *Wuorijäri*, *Vuolijoki*, *Wäänänen* and *Määrälä*, and these must be changed. Some of the old forms that are commonly abandoned, along with new forms adopted in their places, are listed in AL4.[1] Many more are to be found in a paper by John Ilmari Kolehmainen, published in *American Speech*.[2] Kolehmainen says that these changes are most frequent in the large cities, "where the pressure for phonological adjustment has been stronger," and least in the rural regions. Names are simplified by dropping their prefixes, *e.g.*, *Niemi* from *Parhaniemi*, *Syrjäniemi* and *Kangasniemi*, *Saari* from *Pyöriasaari*, *Koski* from *Kalliokoski*, and *Maki* (often spelled *Mackey* or reduced to *Mack*) from *Kaunismäki*, *Myllymäki*, *Kortesmäki*, *Lamminmäki*, *Niinimäki* and many other names in *-mäki* (Finn. hill); by dropping their suffixes, *e.g.*, *Niemi* from *Nieminen*, *Kallio* from *Kalliokowski*, *Lamp* from *Lamppinen*, *Wain* from *Wäinömöinen*, and *Maki* from *Mäkelä*, *Mäkitalo*, *Mäkivuori* and their cognates; by dropping both prefix and suffix, *e.g.*, *Kane* from *Nykänen*; by more or less crude transliteration, *e.g.*, *Harris* from *Harrus*, *Marlowe* from *Määrälä*, *Jervey* from *Järvi*, *Perry* from *Piira*, *and William(s)*

---

launched Aug. 1, 1922, and sunk without trace by the Russian liberators July 21, 1940.

[1] pp. 492–93.
[2] Finnish Surnames in America, Feb., 1939, pp. 33–38.

from *Wiljamaa;* by translation, either of the whole name or of a part, *e.g., Sandhill* from *Hietemäki* (Finn. *hiekka,* sand; *mäki,* hill), *Lake* from *Järvinen* (Finn. *järvi,* lake), *Rose* from *Ruusu, Stone* from *Kiviniemi* (Finn. *kivi,* stone), *Churchill* from *Kirkkomäki,* and *Smith* from *Seppänen* (Finn. *seppä,* blacksmith); and by the bold assumption of unrelated but popular British names, *e.g., Harrison* for *Pirilä, Stephens* for *Nousiainen, Daniels* for *Puhakka,* and *Kelley* for *Karikanta.* Kolehmainen says that "the name *Wilson* has had the greatest fascination." The long cultural dependence of Finland upon Sweden introduced many Swedish and other Scandinavian surnames, and large numbers of Finns arrived in the United States bearing them — in different groups, according to Kolehmainen, from 20 to nearly 50%. Among these names "the most common were *Anderson, Abrahamson, Erickson, Gustafson, Hendrickson, Jacobson, Johnson, Larson, Michelson* and *Peterson,*" with *Johnson* the commonest by far. Most of them have been retained in the United States.[1]

The Finnish language is as unlike the Scandinavian languages, fundamentally, as English is unlike Arabic, but it has borrowed a large number of terms from them, and its way of representing vowel and consonant sounds in writing closely resembles that of Swedish. What happens to certain of those sounds in America, when they are imported in Swedish surnames, is discussed at some length in AL4,[2] mainly on the authority of Roy W. Swanson.[3] Some observations in a subsequent study by E. Gustav Johnson may be added here, though it deals mainly with Swedish placenames.[4] Johnson says that the custom of using surnames, in our sense of the word, did not become general among the Swedish peasantry until "the early part of the Nineteenth Century." Before that patronymics were used, as among the medieval Jews, so that the son of *Johann Gustafsson,* on being baptized with his grand-

---

[1] John Morton, one of the signers of the Declaration of Independence, was the descendant of a Finn named *Marttinen.* Albert Payson Terhune, the writer about dogs (1872–1942), was descended from a Finnish *Terhunen.* The Finnish republic was established June 17, 1919; its liquidation by the Russian liberators began Nov. 30, 1939.

[2] pp. 490–92.

[3] The Swedish Surname in America, *American Speech,* Aug., 1928, pp. 468–77.

[4] The Study of American Place-Names of Swedish Origin, *Covenant Quarterly,* Nov., 1946, pp. 1–16.

father's given-name, became *Gustaf Johansson*, and *his* son in turn, named *Johann* after his grandfather, became *Johann Gustafsson*. "Thus some Christian names would be continued in a family from generation to generation, but no definite *family* name would be associated with them." When these patronymics began to be made permanent a difficulty arose, for a daughter who, in the past, would have been *Anna Gustafsdotter*,[1] became *Anna Gustafsson*, which set the yokels to tittering. In time they got used to it, and many an *Anna Gustafsson* is to be found in both Sweden and America to-day, but the incongruity set them to hunting for other surnames, and they soon had a stock comprising all the familiar categories. The Swedish government helped the process along by circulating the suggestion that various common nouns be combined in euphonious forms, and the result was a great proliferation of names in *alm* (elm), *kvist* (twig), *lund* (grove), *strand* (shore), *sten* (stone), *dal* (valley), *berg* (mountain), *ek* (oak) and *gren* (branch). Says Johnson:

> The alteration of [Swedish] surnames [in America] takes place in two distinct ways.... A man named *Kilgren*, for instance, may ... change the spelling to *Chilgren*, since the *k* is soft in Swedish before front vowels and that sound is best represented in English by the consonant digraph *ch*, or he may choose to adopt the English hard sound of *k* and keep the Swedish spelling. The name *Örnberg* may be altered either into *Earnberg*, in which case the English pronunciation would approximate the Swedish, or into *Ornberg*, since diacritical marks are too troublesome to retain, in which case the English pronunciation of *o* would be adopted. An additional difficulty results here from the fact that in Swedish the *g* in *berg* is pronounced like the English consonant *y*: the Swede with a name ending in *-berg* therefore usually accepts the normal English pronunciation of the word, that is, with the *g* pronounced as a voiced guttural stop.

Johnson says that very few Swedish-Americans have the courage and patience to insist upon the retention of Swedish diacritical marks in their names. The umlaut vowels are *å*, pronounced like the English *o* in *more; ä*, which has the sound of *a* in *sad*, and *ö*, which is identical to the German *ö* in *böse*. Transliteration produces

---

[1] This practise still survives in Iceland, and it survived in the Shetland Islands, which were settled by Scandinavians, until the middle of the Eighteenth Century, *e.g., Margaret Nicholsdaughter* was the sister of *John Nicolson*. See A Shetland Merchant's Day-Book in 1762, by William Sandson; Lerwick, 1934. Lerwick is the most northerly town in the British Isles.

Monson from *Månson*,[1] *Backman* from *Bäckman* and *Turnwall* from *Törnwall* — all of them approximations. Says Johnson:

> The *bj* in such names as *Björk* and *Bjurman* is a combination difficult for Americans; therefore Swedish immigrants with these names usually change them to *Burk* and *Burman*. In names like *Hjelm* and *Hjort* the *h* is silent and the *j* is pronounced like the continental *y*, but ordinarily immigrants retain the *h* and eliminate the *j*; thus *Hjelm* becomes *Helm* and *Hjort, Hort*. In a name like *Ljungkvist* the initial *l* is also silent; the Swedish-American, however, nearly always transmutes this name into *Youngquist*. In Swedish *sj* represents a sound somewhat similar to *sh* in England. *Sjöholm* will therefore either write his name *Shoholm* or translate the first part and make it *Seaholm*.[2] . . . One of the *s*'s in names like *Gustafsson* and *Pettersson*, the first of which is really the possessive *s*, is usually dropped. The *i* in *Nilson* is changed to *e*, and *Karlson* is spelled with *c* instead of *k*. Silent letters are sometimes inserted merely for ornamental purposes: *Dalgren* becomes *Dahlgren*;[3] *Olson, Ohlson;* and *Berg, Bergh*, but in *Dahlgren* the *h* serves also to lengthen the vowel. The *v* and *w* are used interchangeably, since in Swedish there is no distinction in sound between them. In fact, the *w* is not called *double u;* it is called *double v*, and is used only in names.

The Norwegian immigrants who began to swarm into the Middle West toward the middle of the Nineteenth Century brought with them a system of nomenclature that was even more vague and unstable than that of the Swedes. They came chiefly from the remoter farming areas of their country, and most of them had no surnames at all, but only patronymics. *Ole* the son of *Lars* was *Ole Larssen*, but *Johannes* the son of *Ole* was not *Ole Larssen;* he was *Johannes Olessen* or *Olesen*. If any further identification was needed it was supplied by appending the name of the family farm, for all farms in Norway had names. But this farm-name was hardly a surname in our sense, for if a given *Lars* or *Ole* moved from the paternal farm to another, whether as its new owner or tenant, or as the husband of its heiress, or simply as a hired hand, he sometimes took the name of the latter. Usually, however, he did not use this farm-name save for official purposes; in everyday life he was simply *Ole Olesen*. This simple system sufficed in the isolated communities of rural Nor-

---

[1] Mr. Charles F. Dery tells me of a Rhode Islander born in Quebec whose Swedish great-grandfather became *Munson* there, and who is himself now *Mongeon*.

[2] It was thus that Professor C. H. Seashore, of the University of Iowa, translated *Sjöstrand*.

[3] John Adolf *Dahlgren* (1809–70), a Federal admiral in the Civil War and the inventor of the cannon bearing his name, was of Swedish ancestry. When he occupied Charleston in Feb., 1865, the commander of the collaborating land force was General *Schimmelpfennig*.

way, but when immigrants from all parts of the country were thrown together in America it caused hopeless confusion.

Many of these immigrants then recalled the names of their home-farms and began to use them as surnames, but others simply froze their patronymics as surnames for their children, so that the son of *Lars Olesen* was not *Nils Larsen*, as at home, but *Nils Olesen*. But this did not disperse the confusion, for the number of Norwegian given-names was limited, and it was not uncommon for *Olesens* or *Larsens* of a dozen different parts of Norway to be gathered in one American village. To this day the Norwegian-Americans have a great many more names in *-sen* and *-son* than any other group, but the number is much less than it used to be. The census of 1850 showed that it then ran to 93% of all the Norwegian names in Wisconsin, but by 1860 the percentage had dropped to 89 and by 1870 to 77. What it is today, I don't know, but it is probably less than 33. Gradually the suffix *-sen* was changed to *-son* to bring it into accord with American speechways, and for the same reason the redundant *s* was deleted. Thus *Johannessen* became *Johnson*, *Anderssen* became *Anderson*, *Peterssen* became *Peterson*, and so on. Not infrequently yet other changes were made, *e.g.*, from *Karlssen* to *Carlson*, from *Swenssen* to *Swanson*, and from *Knutsen* to *Newton*.[1]

The Norwegian-Americans, when they began to adopt settled surnames, did not confine themselves to those suggested by logical associations. If their traditional farm-names were those of remote and meagre farms, connoting poverty to their fellow Norsemen, they collared better ones, connoting opulence. Certain names became fashionable, and others went below the salt. A name in *-hof* stood at the head of the list, and was followed, in the order of pres-

---

[1] I am indebted here and for most of what follows to the work of Dr. Marjorie M. Kimmerle. Her doctoral dissertation at the University of Wisconsin, written under the direction of Dr. Einar Haugen, professor of Scandinavian languages, was devoted to a study of the names in the church records of two Norwegian Lutheran congregations in Dane county, Wisconsin. This dissertation was summarized in Norwegian-American Surnames, *Norwegian-American Studies and Records* (Northfield, Minn.), Vol. XII, 1941, pp. 1–32. Dr. Kimmerle has since published Norwegian-American Surnames in Transition, *American Speech*, Oct., 1942, pp. 158–65, and A Study in Connotation, in Elizabethan Studies and Other Essays in Honor of George F. Reynolds, *University of Colorado Studies*, Oct., 1945, pp. 337–43.

tige, by names in -*boer*, -*vin*, -*heimr*, -*saetr*, -*land*, -*stadir* and -*rud*. Of names other than those of farms, -*skiold* (shield) and -*hjelm* (helmet) hinted at nobility, and a Latin suffix at learning. "Very few trade names were used," says Dr. Kimmerle,[1] "because every Norwegian looked upon himself as being principally a farmer."[2] Often two or more sons of the same father chose different names, and the result was a disorder that still afflicts Norwegian-American genealogists. Some of the American immigrants who chose farm names used those brought from Norway; others used those of their American farms, or of farms owned by their wives, or their mothers, or their wives' first husbands, or of some rich *kulak* whom they worked for and admired. Others elevated nicknames to the estate of surnames, *e.g.*, *Aslak*, little, or *Vesle*, the younger. Yet others shortened their patronymics, so that *Clemetsen* became *Clemet*. A few even took trade names.

Unhappily, many of these names were written in official Norwegian, which was basically Danish, but pronounced in the fashion of one or another of the Norwegian dialects, so that a given man had a name in two forms, and not infrequently Americans could not master either. In consequence there was the usual wholesale change to American equivalents, real or fancied, so that *Praestegaard* became *Prescott*; *Asbjørnsen*, *Aspenwall*; *Laurentsen*, *Lawrence*; *Eigildsen*, *Eggleson*; *Kjaerret*, *Cherrie* or *Cherry*, and *Fjeld*, *Field*. Long names were ruthlessly shortened, *e.g.*, *Halsteinsgaardbakken* to *Bakken* and *Magnusholmen* to *Magnus*. Some of the Norwegian vowel-sounds were changed considerably.[3] The *a* in *Hagen*, *Hanson*, *Fladen* and the like, corresponding to the English *a* in *art*, was commonly shortened to the *a* in *band* or *cat*, but remained unchanged where it was supported by *h*, as in *Dahl*. The *u* in *Gunderson* and *Munson* became the short American *u* of *grunt*. The *ø*

---

[1] Norwegian-American Surnames, before cited, p. 17.

[2] The reference here, of course, is to rural Norway. In the larger towns the merchants began to take surnames in the Fifteenth Century, chiefly influenced by German example. The names of the nobles and of the learned were also imitations of German usage. The clergy did not use family names until the Seventeenth Century.

[3] Dr. Harold S. Palmer, of the University of Hawaii, writes: "My mother was born in Norway and her maiden name was *Schjøth*, which I cannot pronounce properly, though it is my middle name and also my older brother's. I usually use only the middle initial, and when I have to give my name in full I avoid the *ø*. I try for an umlaut over the *o* if I think it will stick. If not, I use *oe*."

suffered various mutations, mainly into the *u* of *curt* or the *o* of *cod*. The *d*, often silent in Norwegian names (though not in the elegant form of the language), was usually sounded, as in *Gunderson* and the names in *-stad* and *-rud*. The Norwegian *th*, pronounced *t*, became the American *th*, as in *Thorstad* — a change hitherto noted in such German Jewish names as *Morgenthau*. Very often the pronunciation of a name was changed without any change in its spelling, *e.g.*, *Brager* (*Brahkah* in Norwegian), which became *Bragger*. But more often the spelling was changed also, so that *Bjørnson* became *Benson*, *Gaarden* became *Gordon*, *Terjesen* became *Toycen* and then *Tyson*,[1] and *Viig* became *Week*. This process began at home in Norway, especially in the towns. There such British names as *Scott*, *Hall* and *Frost* became established long ago,[2] along with a number of German spellings, *e.g.*, *Baer*, *Schroeder* and *Wahl*. In Bergen Scotch names are common, *e.g.*, *Campbell*, *Christie* and *Ross*. The composer Edvard Hagerup *Grieg* (1843–1907) was the grandson of a Scotsman named Alexander *Greig*, born in Aberdeen in 1739.[3]

Of the names of Latin immigrants, those of the Spanish have fared the best in this country. Most Americans are familiar with such Spanish surnames as *Gomez*, *Sanchez*, *Gonzalez*, *Alvarez*, *Lopez*, *Rodriguez* and *Garcia* and pronounce them at least as accurately as the plain people of Latin-America, who commonly follow Andalusian speechways and so neglect the *th*-sound of the Castilian terminal *z*. Very few of the Cubans and Mexicans who have come to the United States have changed their names — probably because they usually settle in regions where Spanish is the second language.

---

1 I am indebted here to Mr. Wallace Lomoe, of Milwaukee. His own name, originally *Lömoe*, is now pronounced *LaMoe*, with the accent on the second syllable.
2 Norwegian Surnames, by George T. Flom, *Scandinavian Studies and Notes*, Vol. V, No. 4, 1918, pp. 139–54.
3 Edvard *Grieg*, by David M. Johansen; New York, 1938, p. 11. I am indebted here to Dr. Einar Haugen. *Greig* or *Gregg* is a common Scottish surname, traced by Black to *c*. 1214. Danes and Norwegians who settled in isolated American communities, out of contact with their countrymen, sometimes had their surnames changed without their let or leave. In Among the Isles of Shoals; Boston, 1878, Celia Thaxter tells of one named *Ingebertsen* who invaded that remote region. "To expect any Shoaler," she says, "to trouble himself to utter such a name as that was beyond reason. At once they called him *Carpenter* apropos of nothing at all, for he never had been a carpenter. The name was the first that occurred to them."

The Portuguese are less fortunate, perhaps because they are always surrounded by a population which can't fathom their language, which is considerably more difficult to Americans than Spanish. In Southeastern Massachusetts and also in Hawaii many common Portuguese surnames undergo radical changes in spelling and pronunciation, e.g., *Roach* for *Rocha*, *Marks* for *Marques*, *Perry* for *Perreira* or *Pereida*, *Tachera* for *Teixeira*, *Martin* for *Martines*, *Morey* or *Morris* for *Moreira*, *Cole* for *Coelho*, *Sylvia* for *Silva*, *Jordan* for *Jordão* and *Rogers* for *Rodrigues*.[1] Sometimes a name is translated, as when *Silva* becomes *Wood* or *Forest*, and *Reis*, *King*.[2] Many Spanish names in *-ez* have corresponding Portuguese forms in *-es*: the bearer of one of the latter tells me that most Americans insist on regarding it as Spanish, and pronouncing it as they think Spanish should be pronounced.[3] Neither the Spaniards nor the Portuguese in the United States maintain the system of surnames prevailing in their homelands, especially among the upper classes. In Spain a son's full name consists of his given-name, the surname of his father and the surname of his mother, the last two connected by *y* (and), thus: *Juan Espinosa y Pelayo*, which may be abbreviated on occasion to *Juan Espinosa y P.*, or *Juan Espinosa P.*, or even plain *Juan Espinosa*. A daughter's name follows the same plan, but when she marries she drops her mother's surname and substitutes that of her husband, preceded by *de*.[4] The Portuguese combine the paternal and maternal surnames in the same way, but with *de* in place of *y*, e.g., *Manuel Silva de Dias*. But in America they commonly use their mothers' surnames as middle names, as many Americans do, e.g., *Manuel Dias Silva*.[5]

The slaughter of French surnames that went on in colonial days is described briefly in AL4.[6] It continues among the descendants of the early settlers along the Mississippi, and the later French-Canadian immigrants to New England and the Lakes region. J.-M. Car-

---

[1] I borrow most of these from Personal Names in Hawaii, by John E. Reinecke, *American Speech*, Dec., 1940, p. 350.
[2] I am indebted here to Mrs. G. A. Meek, of Oakland, Calif. Mr. Charles J. Lovell tells me that it is also common for *Smith* to be substituted for *Silva*. In New Bedford, Mass., *Sylvia* is the commonest surname, followed by *Smith*, which conceals many *Silvas*. Third place is held by *Perry*.
[3] Albert R. *Lopes*, of Loyola University, New Orleans.
[4] *Amigos* (Chicago), Oct., 1941.
[5] I take this from Personal Names in Hawaii, lately cited, p. 350.
[6] pp. 481-82 and 495.

rière reported in 1939[1] that the following spellings had come in during the "last generation or two" in a settlement of French origin in the foothills of the Missouri Ozarks: *Rulo* for *Rouleau*, *Courteway* for *Courtois*, *Pashia* for *Pagé*, *Partney* for *Parthenais*, *Degonia* for *Degagné*, and *Osia* and *O'Shea* for *Augier*. The early French system of surnames was strange enough to make for confusion,[2] and that confusion was increased as the years passed, both along the Mississippi and along the northern border, by the frequent modification of spellings and pronunciations. McDermott, just cited, gives nineteen forms, for example, of the name *Kiercereau*, including *Kiergerau, Kergzo, Quiercero* and *Tiercero*, some suggesting German or Spanish influences. These changes in spelling, in the course of time, as Carrière says, tended "to conform to primitive phonetic patterns based upon English orthography," so that *Archambault* eventually became *Shambo*[3] or *Shampoo*;[4] *La Riviere, Larraby*; *L'Archeveque, Larch*; *Tetreault, Tatro*; *Guertau, Tetaw*;[5] *Bon Coeur, Bunker*;[6] *Chequelin, Jucklin*; *Thiebaud, Kabo*;[7] *Gauthier, Goochey*; *Gagne, Gonyer*; *Lavoie, Lovewear*; *Choquette, Shackway*; *Le Houx, Lou*;[8] *Renaud, Reno*;[9] *Guizot*,

---

[1] Creole Dialect of Missouri, *American Speech*, April, p. 119 n. 29.
[2] It is described by John Francis McDermott in French Surnames in the Mississippi Valley, *American Speech*, Feb., 1934, pp. 28-30. There were patronymics, *dit* names referring to some personal characteristic or item of personal history, and names borrowed from estates. The latter did not always descend to sons, who not infrequently acquired estates and names of their own. Thus Charles *Le Moyne* (1656-1729) a famous figure in early Canadian history, had the territorial surname of *Longueuil*, but five of his sons came to fame in Louisiana as *Iberville, Bienville, Sauvolle, Chateaugué* and *Serigny*.
[3] Reported from Bristol, Conn., by Mr. Epaphroditus Peck; private communication, July 2, 1936.
[4] Name Tragedies, by C. P. Mason, *American Speech*, April, 1929, p. 329.
[5] The last three are reported from northern Vermont by Mrs. Albert T. Stearns; private communication, July 3, 1937.
[6] The eponym of *Bunker Hill* was not a *Bon Coeur*, but the descendant of an English *Bunker* who immigrated before 1635. See AL4, p. 481, n. 2. But I am informed by Mr. Barrington S. Havens, of Schenectady, N. Y. (private communication, March 3, 1938), that his own paternal grandmother was a *Bunker* descended from a French Huguenot *Bon Coeur* who came to America by way of England and founded a family long settled on Nantucket.
[7] Mr. Alexander Johnson, of Fort Wayne, Ind., tells me (private communication, Jan. 28, 1924) that he once encountered a man in Switzerland county, Indiana, who spelled his name *Thibaud* and pronounced it *Kabo*. In Missouri *Thibaud* or *Thibeau* has become *Teebo*.
[8] The last five are from Notes on French-Canadian Proper Names in New England, by Robert E. Pike, *American Speech*, April, 1935, p.

Gossett or *Cossett* or *Cozart* or *Cozatt*;[1] *Beaumont, Bement* or *Bament*;[2] *Aubert, Obear; Bourgeois, Bushway; Blancpied, Blumpy; La Joie, Lashaway; Benoit, Benway;*[3] *Lareau, Laro; Poitevin, Potwin; Rossignol, Russel; Gervaise, Jarvis.*[4]

The statement of Schele de Vere[5] quoted in AL4,[6] that *Peabody* is an Americanized form of *Pibaudière* appears to have been no more than a rash surmise picked up from Captain Frederick Marryat.[7] I am informed by various members of the *Peabody* family of New England that their *Stammvater* was actually an English immigrant named *Paybody*, who landed about 1636. The name later changed to *Pabody, Pabodie* and *Peabody*.[8] Many Americans who have retained the French spelling of their names have been forced to suffer changes in the pronunciation. Among those of the Charleston, S. C., region *Huger* is pronounced *Hewgée; Legare, Legrée; Gaillard, Guilyard*, with a hard *g* and the accent on the first syllable; *Gourdin, Guddine*, rhyming with *divine; de Saussure, Déssosore; Girardeau, Jírrardo;*[9] and *Des Portes, Déssports*.[10] The tendency of the accent to go forward will be noted. Many familiar British names, of course, are of French origin, though their present forms often conceal the fact. According to Bardsley, *Sidney* was originally *St.*

---

118. Pike also records some translations, *e.g., Lapierre* to *Stone* and *Boisvert* to *Greenwood*.

9 Jesse Lee *Reno*, a Union major-general in the Civil War, was killed leading a charge at South Mountain, Sept. 14, 1862. One of his sons, Jesse Wilford, invented the escalator, and another, Conrad, made inventions in the field of radio. *Reno*, Nev., the divorce metropolis, was named after the general. Mr. Victor T. *Reno*, of Los Angeles (private communication, May 30, 1946), tells me that the founder of the American family was a Huguenot who came to America about 1700.

1 A Tragedy of Surnames, by Fayette Dunlap, *Dialect Notes*, Vol. IV, Part I, 1913, pp. 7–8.

2 I am indebted here to Mr. Hartford *Beaumont*, of New York; private communication, March 11, 1938.

3 The last five are from Corruptions, by Francis Dale, a letter to the New York *Times* dated April 16, 1929.

4 The last four are reported from Vermont by Mr. Paul St. Gaudens; private communication, Nov. 1, 1943. He tells me that his own name is frequently changed to *Gordons* or *Gordon*.

5 p. 112.

6 p. 482.

7 A Diary of America; New York, 1839, p. 153.

8 It is not listed by Ewen, but Charles Wareing Bardsley, in his Dictionary of English and Welsh Surnames; London, 1901, reports that there was a Thomas *Paybodie* at Oxford in 1615. What the name means, he goes on, "I cannot say."

9 But the name of the Missouri river town is pronounced *Jirrárdo*.

10 I am indebted here to Lieut. Col. F. G. Potts, U.S.A., ret., of Mt. Pleasant, S. C.; private communication, Jan. 20, 1945.

Denis, Sinclair was *St. Clair, Seymour* was *St. Maur*, and *Garnett* was *Guarinot*. Black lists many Irish names as of Norman-French origin, and Woulfe adds some Irish names.

The changes in Italian surnames in the United States have been studied by Joseph G. Fucilla.[1] He finds all the familiar processes at work. Those Italian names that present no difficulties to the native American are commonly retained intact, though usually with some change in pronunciation, *e.g., La Guardia, Di Georgio, Marcantonio, D'Alesandro, Martini, Russo, Pizzi, Papini, Moneta, Valentino, Moretti, Zucca* and *Serra*, but those that baffle him have to yield. Sometimes the change effected amounts to no more than the dropping of vowels, so that *Olivieri* becomes *Oliver*, and *Bonifazio* becomes *Boniface;* sometimes the final vowel is changed to an American equivalent, as when *Spellaci* becomes *Spellacy* and *Conte* becomes *Contey;* sometimes Italian consonant-sounds are saved by changes in spelling, as when *Amici* becomes *Ameche, Cecco* becomes *Checko, Paglia* becomes *Palia, Mazzola* becomes *Matzola*, and *Sciortino* becomes *Shortino*. Translations are by no means infrequent, *e.g., Bianco* to *White, Vinciguerra* to *Winwar*,[2] *Barbieri* to *Barber, Molinari* to *Miller, Chiesa* to *Church*, and *Casalegni* to *Woodhouse*. And it is not uncommon for Italian names to acquire the favorite American *s* as a suffix, as when *Alberti* becomes *Alberts; Giacobbe, Jacobs; De Clemente, Clements; Riccardi, Richards; De Pietro, Peters* and *Landi, Landis*.[3] Finally, there are the bold changes to purely British forms, as when *Cestaro* becomes *Chester; Canadeo, Kennedy; Melone, Malone; Zicaro, Seegar; Marino, Manning; Baratta, Barry; Rosellini* or *Rubba, Russell;*[4] *Scaccia, Scott; Marsala, Marshall*, and *Francescone, Frank*.[5] Sometimes, says Fucilla, the effort to Americanize Italian names leads to grotesque

---

1 The Anglicization of Italian Surnames in the United States, *American Speech*, Feb., 1943, pp. 26–32.

2 Frances *Winwar* is a well known woman writer who was brought from her native Italy at the age of seven as *Francesca Vinciguerra*.

3 Says Dr. Vincenzo Campora in Hammonton Notes, *Columbus* (New York), Sept., 1945, p. 7: "Hammonton was ... founded by Charles K. *Landis*, a Philadelphia gentleman whose original name in the Seventeenth Century was *Landi*, changed to *Landis* when the family immigrated to America from Italy."

4 Says Campora, just quoted, p. 36: "Lino *Rubba* is an executive of high calibre and has a very amiable personality. So is his worthy partner, Frank *Rubba*. Another brother of theirs is Capt. *Russell*, M.D., serving overseas."

5 Here I am indebted to Mr. Charles C. Arensberg, of Pittsburgh.

results, as when *Arteri* is turned into *Artery* and *Speziale* or *Speciale* into *Special*. Some Italians discard the frequent prefixes to their names, *e.g., di, de, della, la, li* or *lo*, when they kiss the flag, but not many, though it is not uncommon for the particle to be incorporated, as when *La Rocca* becomes *Larocca* and *Di Matteo, Dimatteo*.[1]

Now and then an Italian-American, having worn an American-sounding name for years, reverts to his original Italian name — usually as a matter of reviving national pride but sometimes only because Americans seem to be gradually getting used to Italian surnames and finding many of them less difficult than aforetime. The same phenomenon has begun to show itself among Greek-Americans, though the latter reason is seldom operative in their case. In 1941 a Chicago Greek who had been known as *Harris* petitioned one of the local courts to let him go back to *Haralampopoulas*. He kept a store, he explained, in a Greek neighborhood, and *Haralampopoulas* was easier to most of his customers than *Harris*.[2] But it is far more common for a Greek to try to get rid of his long name and substitute something shorter and easier, *e.g., Kar* for *Karamouzis*,[3] *Caloyer* for *Calogeropoulus*,[4] *Pappas* for *Pappadimitracoupoulos, Poulos* for *Gerasimopoulos* and *Chronos* for *Pappapolychronopoulos*.[5] The same route is followed by other immigrants from Eastern Europe. When a Hungarian's name is *Feleky, Bertok, Bartus, Simko, Balassa, Kormos* or *Yartin* his new neighbors are able to pronounce it more or less correctly, but if it is *Mészöly, Hrivnyák, Skalička, Csokonai, Szécskay, Eötvös, Karácsonyi, Erdijhelyi, Gyongyosy, Csongradi, Csüry, Ujváry, Nyitray, Szigligeti, Czatkai* or *Görg* he has to change either the pronunciation or the spelling, and sometimes he changes both.[6] At home the surname goes first, *e.g., Hunyadi Janos* (John), but in this country he adopts the usual order. So with the Armenians, Syrians, Bulgarians and Rumanians.[7]

1 See AL4, pp. 493–94.
2 United Press dispatch from Chicago, July 8, 1941. On April 29, 1947, a Baltimorean named Henry Wise Wood *Distler* petitioned the local Circuit Court for permission to resume the ancient surname of his family, to wit, *Distler und Derecsenyi zu Dercsen*, and it was granted by Judge Edwin T. Dickerson.
3 *Congressional Record*, July 2, 1946, p. 8295.
4 This is from the Pittsburgh court records, and I am indebted for it to Mr. Charles C. Arensberg.
5 See AL4, pp. 485–86.
6 I take most of these from The Magyar in America, by D. A. Souders; New York, 1922. See also AL4, p. 496.
7 For Rumanian names see AL4, p. 494.

The Arabic-speaking Syrians in the United States occasionally bear surnames that fit into the American pattern easily enough, e.g., *Kassab, Totah, Barsa, Azar, Saliba* and *Katibah*, but more often they have to make changes. Sometimes it is sufficient to substitute new spellings, e.g., *Arbeely* for *'Arbīlī*, *Beetar* for *Bītār*, *Mallouk* for *Mallūk*, *Boutross* for *Butrūs*, *Lian* for *Liyān*, *Mouakad* for *Mu'aqqad*, *David* for *Dāwūd* or *Da'ud*, *Diab* for *Diyāb*, *Jemail* for *Jumayyil*, *Gibran* for *Jubrān*,[1] *Namora* for *Nammūrah*, and *Arout* for *'Ayrūt*, but more frequently there are more substantial changes, e.g., *Sleyman* for *Sulaymān*, *Moran* for *Mārūn*, *Corey* for *al-Khūri*, *Malooly* for *Ma'lūli*, *Bonahom* for *Bū-Na'ūm*, *Jacobs* for *Yaqūb*, *Kadane* for *Qa'zān*, *Bourjaily* for *Abu-Rujayli*, *Boujalad* for *Abu-Jalad*, *Beters* for *Butrūs*, *Abbott* for *'Abbūd*, *De Bakey* for *Dabaghi*, and *McKaba* for *Muqabba'ah*.[2] The most distinguished of Armenian-Americans, William *Saroyan*, born in Fresno, California, has been able to keep his family name, but only at the expense of consenting to putting the accent on *roy*, where it does not belong in Armenian.[3] Many of his *Landsleute* have been less fortunate, for such names as *Megerditchian, Khatchadouryan, Soonkookian* and *Hovsepian* seem to be difficult to Americans.[4] As a result, the usual translations and transliterations are not infrequent. *Jermakian*, for example, becomes *White* (Arm. *jermak*, white), *Novsepian* becomes *Joseph*, and *Boghossian* becomes *Paul*. Fresno once had a citizen named *Paul Paul* whose original name was *Boghos Boghossian*. A Nazicide who made some stir during World War II under the name of John Roy *Carlson* came into the world as *Derounian*.[5] Many Armenians arrived in the United States bearing names imposed upon them by their Turkish overlords. These, in some cases, have been turned into true Armenian names, as when *Chilingirian* became *Darbinian*, both meaning *Smith*.[6]

---

1 The Syrian author and painter, Kahlil *Gibran* (d. 1931) was the author of a mystical book, The Prophet (written in English) that has had large sales for years.

2 I take these examples from Arabic-Speaking Americans, by H. I. Katibah and Farhat Ziadeh; New York, 1946.

3 Mr. Saroyan tells me that family tradition makes the original form of the name *Sarou Khan*, meaning blond lord, but the present form has been in use for generations.

4 Not all Armenian surnames end in *-ian* or *-yan*. In proof hereto Mr. Saroyan offers *Ardzeooni, Chituni, Rushdooni, Totoventz* and *Charentz*.

5 Westbrook Pegler's column, Nov. 13, 1946.

6 I am indebted here to Mr. Richard Badlian, of Boston; private communication, Sept. 28, 1936. Relatively

The Gypsies, who originated in Northern India but came to the United States by way of Europe, sometimes bear Slavic names, but these are usually converted in this country into what they call *nav gajikanes*, or Gentile names. Thus *Ivan Stefanovitch* becomes *John Stevenson* and all the *MiXails* become *Mitchells*. Gypsy names are often patronymics. *Giori*, the son of *Tsino*, becomes *O Giorgi de Tisasko*, and *Mary*, the daughter of *John*, becomes *Mary John*. Such grotesque forms as *Millie Mike* and *Rosie Pete* are not uncommon among the women.[1] In England most of the Gypsies have taken British surnames, *e.g.*, *Burton*, *Hughes*, *Jenkins*, *Taylor*, *Gray*, *Lewis*, *Lee*, *Lovel* and *Smith*. Many of these are translations or transliterations. Thus *Taylor* comes from *Chokamengro*, a tailor; *Gray* from *Gry*, a horse; *Lee* from *Purum*, a leek; *Lovel* from *Kamlo* or *Kamescro*, a lover; *Marshall* from *Makkado-tan-engree*, a dweller in a marsh; and *Smith* from *Petulengro*, a blacksmith. Some of these names are also common among the Gypsies in the United States, notably *Lee*.[2]

The Chinese in the United States have only about sixty different family names, of which *Chan*, *Wong* and *Lee* (*Li*) are the most often encountered.[3] The number to be found in all China has been variously estimated at from 150 to 400. The Chinese seldom change their surnames, which are really clan-names, but the business of representing them in English presents serious phonetic difficulties, and as a result there are many variants. Thus the same name is encountered as *Lok*, *Look* and *Luke*, and another common one appears as *Hiu*, *Heu* and *Hew*.[4] Even worse difficulty is caused by the fact that the same ideograph is pronounced differently in different parts of China, so that a Northern man named *Tsur* may be called *Chow*

few actual Turks have immigrated to America: the persons of Turkish birth shown by the census returns are mainly Armenians, Greeks or Jews. It was not until 1924 that Mustafa Kemal decreed that all Turks should have surnames, and not until 1934 that the Ankara National Assembly implemented this decree with legislation imposing a fine of $45 for non-compliance after one year. At that time, according to a United Press dispatch from Istanbul, July 21, no more than two or three hundred Turkish families already had surnames; the rest were content with given names alone. Kemal himself adopted the name of *Atatürk*.

1 Gypsy Fires in America, by Irving Brown; New York, 1924, p. 20.
2 The Gypsies, by Charles G. Leland; fourth edition; Boston, 1886, pp. 304–07.
3 Chinatown Inside Out, by Leong Gor Lum; New York, 1936, p. 55.
4 Personal Names in Hawaii, by John E. Reinecke, *American Speech*, Dec., 1940, p. 347.

in the South and *Jo* elsewhere.[1] But though surnames, which are proud possessions, are almost always retained, the Chinese frequently and in fact even usually adopt American given-names when they come to this country, as we shall see in the next section of the present chapter. Also, they often change the order of their names, for at home the surname goes first, as with the Hungarians, and this causes misunderstanding and confusion among Western strangers. Thus *Lee Loy*, in order to avoid being called Mr. *Loy*, becomes *Loy Lee*.[2] In the early days of Chinese immigration Americans mistook the honorific *Ah* for a given name, and many Chinese became *Ah Fu, Ah Sing*, and so on. This preserved their surnames, but some of their descendants have since adopted such combined forms as *Asing* and *Afong*.[3] In Hawaii a few of the younger Chinese have taken Hawaiian names, *e.g.*, *Akana* and *Ahuna*, for they carry a certain amount of social prestige in the islands. But very few have taken American names.[4]

Japanese personal names follow the order of American names, with the surnames last, and most of the latter are easily pronounceable, so there is no motive for changing them. Says Reinecke of Japanese nomenclature in Hawaii:

> In contrast to the diversity of spellings of Chinese names is the uniformity of the Japanese. The Hepburn system [5] is followed pretty consistently, with some minor variations such as *Shimizu, Shimidzu; Inouye, Inoue; Okazaki, Okasaki; Hirata, Hilata.* The phonemic difference between short *o* and long *o*

---

1 Inside Asia, by John Gunther; New York, 1939, p. 158. Other examples are *Oong, Wong* and *Wen, Chang* and *Jong, Feng* and *Fung*.

2 *Dong Kingman*, the San Francisco water-colorist, is commonly called *Kingman*, but his surname is actually *Dong*. The *Kingman*, which is his given-name, represents two Chinese words — *king*, meaning scenery, and *man*, meaning literature or grammar. He was born in California in 1911 but was taken to China at the age of five, and remained there until 1929. I am indebted here to Mr. *Dong* himself; private communication, Oct. 16, 1942. According to Gunther, just cited, *Chiang Kai-shek* is called Mr. *Chiang* by his party followers, with *Lao* (old) *Chiang* as an affectionate diminutive. His wife calls him *Kai*.

3 Reinecke, lately cited, p. 348.

4 According to Arthur H. Smith, in Village Life in China; New York, 1899, p. 253, Chinese at home who are adopted into a family bearing a different surname often take that surname. But adoption is rare among Chinese immigrants. See also Reinecke's Additional Notes on Personal Names in Hawaii, *American Speech*, Feb., 1943, pp. 69-70.

5 A scheme of transliteration devised by James C. Hepburn (1815-1911), an American medical missionary who made the first translation of the Bible into Japanese. His Japanese-English and English-Japanese Dictionary; Tokyo, 1867, remained a standard work for many years.

is ignored in Anglicization except in the name of *Ohta* and sometimes in a few other surnames; *Ono* and *Onoh* are found side by side. The syllable *ji* is often wrongly transliterated *gi*, so that the given-name *Mitsuji* and *Mitsugi* are confused. While Chinese and Koreans can sometimes deliberately Anglicize the spelling of their names, e.g., *Young* instead of *Yong*, *Park* instead of *Pahk*, the Japanese cannot. The very numerous Japanese surnames represent for the most part highly distinctive combinations of a limited number of ideographs, mostly denoting geographical features, which cannot well be Anglicized, translated, or shortened. Virtually no Japanese have tried to alter their names.[1]

The surnames of the American Indians are in a state of apparently hopeless confusion, as the Indians themselves are in confusion. Some of them have adopted names wholly American, e.g., *Philip Marshall*, *George Williams* and *Alfred B. Richards*;[2] others have hitched their native surnames to American given-names, e.g., *Moses Bull Bear*, *Charles Little Dog* and *Fred Cut Grass*; yet others have retained their native names unchanged. This last category, alas, is small and seems to be vanishing. I can find no example among the signatures to the petition just cited, nor among those to a similar petition from Choctaws,[3] nor in a list of graduates of the United States Indian Industrial and Training School at Carlisle, Pa., running from 1889 to 1913.[4] The original Redskins bore nothing properly describable as fixed surnames, and even their given-names were frequently changed. Said a contributor to the *Atlantic Monthly* in 1881:[5]

Ordinarily, the appellation an Indian receives is obtained at random, and is likely to be changed any time, either by the wearer or his friends. In fact, it is quite the thing for a warrior to change his name after each exploit, always adopting some descriptive and complimentary title; or perhaps, — unfortu-

---

[1] Lafcadio Hearn's children by his Japanese wife adopted Japanese names. His second son, known as *Iwao Inagaki*, became a teacher of English. The Japanese *John Smith*, according to the Associated Press correspondent in Tokyo, writing on Oct. 2, 1938, is *Taro Sazuki*, but according to Ray Cromley, correspondent of the *Wall Street Journal*, Dec. 20, 1946, p. 1, he is *Taro Tanaka*.

[2] I take these from a petition submitted to Congress in 1946 (*Congressional Record*, July 19, p. A4506) by the Oglala Sioux of the Pine Ridge Reservation. Not a few of the surnames appended to this petition were non-English, e.g., Cassidy, Shangreau, Condelario, Dubray, Lamont, Bissonette, Colhoff and Romero.

[3] *Congressional Record*, April 2, 1946, pp. A1953–54.

[4] Carlisle (Pa.), 1914. The school was housed in buildings belonging to the War Department. They were repossessed in 1918 for use as a hospital and rehabilitation center, and the school shut down. Founded in 1879, it never realized its objectives, and has not been revived. Its male students made something of a splash in athletics, especially football and running, but none of its graduates ever attained to any genuine distinction.

[5] Nov., p. 716.

nately for him, — in case of failure in an expedition, cowardice, or some evidence of weakness, he has it changed for him by his friends. All Indians seem to possess a very remarkable fondness for nicknaming; and while the leading man in the tribe may insist on being called by his own choice title, nothing prevents his being known and designated by a very different, and perhaps uncomplimentary, name. As deformities, peculiarities and character, or accidents to limb or feature often suggest fit names, it is sometimes impossible to know by the appellation whether the warrior is in contempt or honor amongst his associates. Daughters' names are never altered, and as married women do not take their husbands' names there is nothing to indicate whether an Indian woman is married or single.

When Indians began to come in from the warpath and settle on reservations this chaos gave great difficulty to the Indian agents, and eventually the Indian Bureau issued orders that every individual must have a surname and stick to it. The need for the regulation became even more pressing in 1887, when the passage of the Allotment Act made it necessary to identify precisely every Indian who received a parcel of the tribal land. In 1903 the Indian Bureau employed Dr. Charles A. Eastman to overhaul the surnames of the Sioux [1] and various others were put to work at the same task among other tribes. Whenever a child entering school or an adult entering a government hospital lacked a name in the American fashion one was supplied. If there was already a native name it was commonly translated, which explains the origin of such surnames as *Little Cloud*, *Fast Horse* and *Lone Wolf*. Unhappily, many a poor buck, at the time of the registration, was bearing a derisive name, and in consequence it still afflicts his progeny, *e.g.*, *Fool Head*, *Long Visitor* and *Broken Nose*.[2] Even more unhappily, the average Indian agent had only a meagre grasp of the native languages, and thus made some bad mistakes in translation, as when a name meaning *Young Man Whose Very Horses are Feared* became *Young Man Afraid of His Horse*. In the early days there were many names of like length, but the Indian Bureau discouraged them, and now it is rare to find an Indian bearing one. The surnames that survive mainly relate to personal characteristics, *e.g.*, *Black Eye* and *Yellow*

---

[1] Eastman, himself the son of a full-blooded Santee-Sioux and a half-bred Sioux woman, was born in 1858. He became a homeopathic doctor and held various posts in the Indian Service. The later years of his life were spent in delivering lectures and writing books.

[2] I am indebted here and for part of what follows to Indian Personal Names From the Nebraska and Dakota Regions, by Margaret Cannell, *American Speech*, Oct., 1935, pp. 184–87.

Boy,[1] or were suggested by a fancied likeness to some bird or animal, e.g., *Red Owl, Flying Hawk, Fast Horse* and *Crazy Horse,* or some feature of the landscape, e.g., *Howling Water, High Pine* or *Red Cedar*.[2] It is not surprising that many of these surnames should be opprobrious: the same is true of many Indian tribal names.[3] In the Indian tongues they tend to be jaw-breakers, and the early white colonists found them difficult. William Nelson lists the following monstrosities from the early days: *Abozaweramud* (1681), *Mokownquando* (1708), *Wallammassekaman* (1687), *Kekroppamont* (1677) and *Rawautoaqwaywoaky* (1709).[4] Sometimes these names embodied syllables which passed on from father to son, to become primeval equivalents of surnames, e.g., *baq* (bone), *ik* (pepper), *kok* (tortoise), *may* (tobacco), *pek* (stone), *seb* (clay), *yat* (fly), *gwuq* (seven) and *sam* (snot).[5]

The surnames of American Negroes have been studied by Howard F. Barker,[6] Newbell Niles Puckett,[7] and Lorenzo D. Turner.[8]

---

[1] Mr. Willard W. Beatty, director of education of the Office of Indian Affairs, tells me that sometimes an Indian word that was merely descriptive was mistaken for a surname and applied to an Indian without change. Thus many Navahos came to be called *Yazzi,* which means little, or *Begay,* which means son. Very often the same designation was translated differently by different government agents. Thus the name which appears as *Stand-for-them* on the Rosebud Reservation in South Dakota is rendered *Defender* on the Standing Rock Reservation in North Dakota.

[2] On July 17, 1937, the United Press correspondent at Watonga (Okla.) reported the marriage of Emma *Standing Elk,* described as "a pretty 18-year-old Montana Cheyenne princess," to Horace *Howling Water.* Among the spectators at the ringside were Jane *Walking Coyote,* Louise *Long Bear,* Mollie *White Bird,* Eva *Old Crow,* Hugh *Yellow Man,* Rose *Shoulder Blade* and James *Night Walker.* I am indebted here to Dr. Claude M. Simpson, Jr., of the University of Wisconsin. Mr. Bruce Nelson, of Bismarck, N. D., reports finding a Montgomery Ward *Two Bellies* in Montana; private communication, Jan. 4, 1946.

[3] American Indian Tribal Names, by Maurice G. Smith, *American Speech,* Feb., 1930, pp. 114–17.

[4] Indian Words, Personal Names and Place-Names in New Jersey, *American Anthropologist,* Jan.–March, 1902, pp. 183 ff.

[5] Notes on the Kekchi Language, by Robert Burkitt, *American Anthropologist,* July–Sept., 1902, pp. 441 ff.

[6] The Family Names of American Negroes, *American Speech,* Oct., 1939, pp. 163–74, and How We Got Our Surnames, the same, Oct., 1938, pp. 48–53.

[7] Names of American Negro Slaves, in Studies in the Science of Society Presented to Albert Galloway Keller; New Haven, 1937, pp. 471–94.

[8] Dr. Turner's studies are still unfinished, but I have had access to them through his courtesy. They are summarized in The Myth of the Negro Past, by Melville J. Herskovits; New York, 1941.

Barker estimates that of the 10,000,000-odd Negroes living on the American mainland in 1924, 7,500,000 bore English or Welsh surnames, 1,300,000 Irish names, and 1,200,000 Scottish names, with a very small minority bearing Dutch, German, Spanish, French or Jewish names.[1] It is commonly assumed that the surnames of Afro-Americans are those of the masters of their ancestors in slavery times, but Barker shows that this is by no means always the case. The name of Samuel *Hairston*, the largest slave-owner in the South at the outbreak of the Civil War, is very rare among colored folk, and those of other large slave-owners, *e.g.*, *Hampton*, *Haynes*, *Pinckney* and *Rutledge*, are anything but common.[2] The favorite is *Johnson*, which accounts for no less than 190 Negroes in every 10,000. Next in order come *Brown*, *Smith*, *Jones*, *Williams*, *Jackson*, *Davis*, *Harris*, *Robinson* and *Thomas*. It may be that the popularity of John *Brown* of Ossawatomie put his surname into second place, and the fame of George *Washington* apparently accounts for the fact that *Washington* is far commoner among Negroes than among whites,[3] but how are we to account for *Johnson*? It can hardly be a patronymic, for relatively few slaves had the given-name of *John*, and Andrew *Johnson* was certainly not its eponym, for Dr. Carter G. Woodson has shown that it stood in first place, and among free Negroes, so early as 1830.[4]

The fact is that freed slaves probably adopted the names of overseers as often as they took those of masters, and in even more cases chose names that were simply common where they lived and thus

---

1 The *Amsterdam News* reported on Feb. 1, 1944, p. 2-A, that a Negro Coast Guardsman named George Jack *Goldstein* was visiting in Harlem. He was born in New York City.

2 In a letter from Francis Scott Key to Benjamin Tappan, dated Washington, Oct., 1838, and published in Notes on the United States of America During a Phrenological Visit in 1838-39-40, by George Combs; Philadelphia, 1841, Vol. II, p. 361, there is mention of "a gentleman in Maryland, upwards of thirty years ago, who emancipated by his will between two and three hundred Negroes," and the statement is made that "they all took (as they were required to do) his name." There was no such requirement in the Maryland law, but the testator may have imposed it upon his beneficiaries.

3 Booker T. *Washington* says in Up From Slavery; New York, 1900, pp. 34-35, that his slave mother called him *Booker Taliaferro*, but that he grew up knowing only that he was *Booker*. When he went to school and discovered that surnames were necessary he added *Washington*. Later, informed of the *Taliaferro*, he made it his middle name and reduced it to its initial. He was born *c.* 1858-59. Of his father he says: "I have heard reports that he was a white man on a nearby plantation."

4 Barker, lately cited, p. 168.

seemed regular and proper and suitable to their station in life. Very few of them named themselves after Abraham *Lincoln*, and even fewer after *Garrison, Grant* and *Sherman*. Their favorite among all their liberators was General O. O. *Howard*, head of the Freedmen's Bureau from 1865 to 1874. Barker says that more than one-third of all the *Howards* in the United States are now colored. Unusual surnames are rare among Negroes, though Barker calls attention to the fact that, as is the case with whites, they are relatively frequent among persons of distinction, *e.g.*, *Du Bois, Chesnutt, De Priest, Vann, Douglass, Hastie, Schuyler, Robeson, Garvey, Bethune* and *Carver*. The female students in the Southern Negro colleges and normal schools, when they marry before graduation, often hook their surnames to those of their husbands, but this is not done to enhance their social prestige, but simply to identify their credits on the registrars' books.[1] Otherwise, hyphenated names are very rare among colored folk.[2]

The popular literature of onomatology is largely given over to discussions of strange and unearthly surnames. Their collection was begun by William Camden, who listed some interesting specimens in his "Remains Concerning Britain," first published in 1605,[3] *e.g.*,

[1] I am indebted here to Dr. J. D. Bowles, acting dean of the Houston College for Negroes, Houston, Texas; private communication, May 10, 1940.

[2] The Rev. Ben Hamilton, formerly in the Liberian consular service and now a missionary in French Equatorial Africa, tells me that many of the civilized natives of Liberia adopt Christian given-names but preserve their tribal surnames, *e.g.*, Isaac *Twe* and Robert *Okai*. Others preserve their full tribal names, *e.g.*, *Abayomi Karnge* (justice of the Liberian Supreme Court) and *Momulu Massaquoi* (formerly consul-general at Hamburg). Sometimes, when American surnames are adopted, native names are retained as middle names, *e.g.*, Nathaniel H. *Sie* Brownell (professor of mathematics at Liberia College), or the new names are joined to the old ones by hyphens, *e.g.*, T. E. *Kla*-Williams (editor of the *Liberian Patriot*).

Descendants in the male line of American Negro settlers retain, of course, their family names. J. S. Smith reported in the *Pylon*, April, 1939, that the natives of other parts of West Africa sometimes translate their original names into English, *e.g.*, *Fineboy, Alligator, Strongface* and *Cookey*. The followers of Father Divine in New York, both blacks and whites, abandon their lawful names on conversion, and adopt new names which indicate their semi-celestial status, *e.g.*, *Glorious Illumination, Crystal Star, Flying Angel, Quiet Love* and *Daniel Conqueror*. I am indebted here to The Psychology of Social Movements, by Hadley Cantril; New York, 1941, p. 128, and to Roman Influence, *Converted Catholic*, Nov., 1941, p. 240.

[3] This book was made up in part of selections from his Britannia, published in Latin in 1586 but not translated into English until 1610.

Bigot, Devil, Pentacost, Calf, Hoof, Loophole and *Gallows*. The bibliography in the United States apparently began with N. I. Bowditch's "Suffolk Surnames," published privately in Boston in 1857 and brought out in enlarged form the year following. The Suffolk of the title was the Massachusetts county, but Bowditch also included names from other parts of the country. Some of his prize specimens were *Ague, Cheer, Darkies, Dudgeon, Gotobed, Lighthead, Oxx, Rain, Strachatinstry, Ugly* and *Wedlock*. Edward Duffield Ingraham, a Philadelphia lawyer, followed in 1873 with "Singular Surnames," the materials for which came chiefly from the Philadelphia newspapers of the 20s, 30s, 40s and 50s. He listed, among others, *Allchin, Bitsh, Christmas, Forthfifth, Glue, Oyster, Toad, Whisker* and *Yeast*. The collection of such monstrosities still goes on, and the newspapers frequently report the discovery of one hitherto unwept, unhonored and unsung. I offer a few from my own archives:

Acid	By	Glymph	Ix
Acorn	Cabbage	Goforth	Jelly
Anger	Camphor	Gotoff	Junk
Argue	Cashdollar	Guitar	Kick
Army	Casebeer	Gubernator	Kidney
Baby	Cheesewright	Hailstone	Killbride
Barefoot	Clock	Hair	Laughinghouse
Beanblossom	Cobbledick	Hark	Laughter
Bible	Crysick	Hash	Lillywhite
Bilious	Death	Hatchet [3]	Liver
Boop [1]	Dialogue	Hogshead	Louis XVI [5]
Breeding	Dingbat	Holy	Loveall
Brightfellow	Dippy	Human	Lung
Buffaloe	Dose	Hush	Matches
Buggerman	Dumbell	Ice	Mayhem [6]
Bulpitt	Fatter	Ill [4]	Midwinter
Burp	Flowerdew	Inch	Minx
Buttermilk	Girl [2]	Itt	Mossaback

[1] I am indebted for this one to Dr. C. C. Branson, of Brown University.

[2] Christian *Girl*, who began as a mail carrier and ended as a millionaire manufacturer of automobile springs, died at Cleveland, O., June 10, 1946. I am indebted here to Mr. Alexander Kadison.

[3] Truly *Hatchett* is a real estate broker in Baltimore.

[4] Reported from Newark, N. J., by Mr. Pierre A. Banker, of New York.

[5] The surname of a French-Canadian family living in Rockland, Ont. Contributed by Dr. Douglas Leechman, who says that it is pronounced *Louis Seize*.

[6] Boulder (Colo.) *Daily Camera*, July 12, 1946. I am indebted here to Mr. W. M. Spackman, of Boulder.

450   *The American Language: Supplement II*

Necessary	Pinwheel	Sinus [3]	Tank [7]
Nicht	Plaintiff	Six	Tart
Oatmeal	Purple	Snowball	Teats
Only	Ram	Sodawasser [4]	Tickle
Organ	Ratskin	Sofa	Ut
Outhouse [1]	Roast	Spinach	Veal
Oxx	Secundo	St. Clergy	Walkingstick
Pancake	Sewer	Stolen	Wash
Parsonage	Sex	Such	Whale
Permission	Shortsleeve	Sugarwater [5]	Wham [8]
Piano	Shovel [2]	Sunshine	Yopp [9]
Pickle	Sickman	Swill [6]	
Pimple	Sinner	Sycamore	

Miss Mary C. Oursler, formerly administrative assistant in the Census Bureau, is authority for the statement that 30% of the heads of families in three of the thirteen original States in 1790, when the first census was taken, bore " names appearing as parts of speech in everyday conversation," *e.g., Dumb, Looney, Gushing, Soup, Vinegar, Waffle, Grog, Grapevine, Petticoat, Hornbuckle* and *Turnipseed*.[10] Many of these have succumbed to the ribald humors of the populace, but the foregoing list shows that a liberal sufficiency remains. When such names are combined with the weird given-names that will be considered in the next section the effect is often startling, *e.g., Uffie Grunt, Sunny Piazzi, Ima Hogg, Byzantine Botts, Joline Joy* and *Sudis Fat*.[11] A learned man in Canada tells me of a

[1] Oklahoma City *Oklahoman*, Jan. 8, 1940.
[2] Sir Cloudsley *Shovel* (1650–1707) was a British naval hero.
[3] Reported from Brooklyn by Mr. Robert H. Quinn, of that great city.
[4] Probably an Americanized form of Ger. *Spritzwasser*.
[5] *Berkshire Evening Eagle* (Pittsfield, Mass.), July 6, 1937.
[6] Found in Brooklyn by Mr. James Cowden Meyers, of New York.
[7] New London (Conn.) *Day*, Oct. 21, 1941.
[8] Fountain Inn (N.C.) *Tribune* of unknown date.
[9] Many of these names come from the collectanea of the late John W. Thomson, of Pittsfield, Mass., kindly put at my disposal by Mr. Robert G. Newman, librarian of the Pittsfield Public Library. For others I am indebted to Miss D. Lorraine Yerkes, of Chicago; Mr. E .P. Rochester, of San Antonio, Tex.; Mr. Paul St. Gaudens, of Barnard, Vt.; and Queer Names, by Howard F. Barker, *American Speech*, Dec., 1930, pp. 101–09.
[10] She Could Answer, How Old is Ann?, by Katherine Scarborough, Baltimore *Sun*, April 18, 1943.
[11] I take the last from Surnames in the Blue Ridge of Virginia, by Miriam Sizer, *American Speech*, Dec., 1937, p. 269. Miss Sizer says that *Fat* is all that remains of *Lafayette*, popular as a given-name a century ago and eventually adopted as a surname. It was pronounced *Lay-fat*. " The not understood and hence unimportant *Lay*," she explains, " was naturally thrown to the discard, but the good old name of *Fat* was retained, not

pretty immigrant girl who came to school in Manitoba bearing the name of *Helen Zahss*, and was much upset when the first roll-call produced titters. All surnames in the foregoing list were gathered in the United States, but England can match them hands down. Charles Wareing Bardsley, in his "Dictionary of English and Welsh Surnames," lists *Barefoot, Brass, Caitiff, Coiner,*[1] *Dam, Evilchild, Foulfish, Godspenny, Ham, Ironfoot, Jericho, Killer, Lent, Makehate, Obey* and scores like them, and other English professors of morbid onomatology have reported *Smallbones, Gotobed, Hogflesh,*[2] *Allways, Body, Burnup, Calf, Catchpoll, Cheese, Cuss, Doll, Egg, Eye, Galilee, Gent, Goodbeer, Hustler, Kisser, Maggot, Pink, Poorgrass, Shoppee, Smelt, Tout, Venus,*[3] *Candy, Shakelady, Ughtynton,*[4] *Trampleasure,*[5] *Hiccup,*[6] *Bugg,*[7] *Sucksmith, Smy, Ghost, Maw, Pitchfork,*[8] *Eighteen, Whist, Gumboil, Handsomebody, Cutmutton, Sleep,*[9] *Yallow, Gathergood, Gee* and *Rump.*[10]

The American nomenclature shows nothing like the fearsome batteries of hyphenated surnames that are common in England,[11] but it has a compensatory oddity of its own in the intrusion of second

---

for convenience alone, but because it embodies a mountain ideal of physical beauty."

1 English for *counterfeiter*.
2 Uncommon Names, by G. H. Brierley, London *Morning Post*, Jan. 20, 1936.
3 The last twenty-one come from The Romance of Names, by Ernest Weekley; London, 1914.
4 The last three are from The Personal Names of the Isle of Man, by J. J. Kneen; Oxford, 1937.
5 The *Trampleasures* by Jane Gillette *Trampleasure, Time and Tide*, June 20, 1935. Miss *Trampleasure* says that her name is pronounced *trample-sure*.
6 The following want-ad appeared under Personal in the London *Morning Post*, May 15, 1936, p. 1: "Advertiser, whose name is *Hiccup*, with broadcasting ambitions, wishes to adopt another name without publicity of change by deed poll. Suggestions welcome."
7 Mr. *Original Bugg*, Liverpool *Echo*, July 14, 1938. See also AL4, p. 310 and Supplement I, pp. 462 and 660.

8 The last five come from Surnames, by Ernest Weekley; New York, 1916.
9 The last six are from English Surnames, by Mark Antony Lower; London, 1875.
10 I am indebted for the last four to Mr. Sinclair Lewis.
11 AL4, p. 502. It is the custom there, when a hyphenated name runs to three syllables or less altogether, to use it in full in addressing the bearer, but when it is longer only the last member is commonly used. Winston *Churchill's* true family name is *Spencer-Churchill*, and he is always so designated in the Court Circulars issued from Buckingham Palace. When the Eightieth Congress assembled in January, 1947, two hyphenated surnames appeared on the roll of the House – the first recorded there for years. They were borne by the Hon. Horace *Seely-Brown* of Connecticut and the Hon. A. *Fernós-Isern*, resident commissioner for Puerto Rico.

capitals into names, e.g., *GaNun*,[1] *VirDen*,[2] *KenMore*,[3] *KlenDshoj*,[4] *KleinSmid*,[5] *RossKam*,[6] *RiDant*,[7] and *ViSKocil*.[8] Names that are really two names, separated by a space and not hyphenated, are occasionally encountered, e.g., *Be Bee*,[9] *Bel Geddes* [10] and *Ben Ami*,[11] but the early American custom of hitching territorial or occupational appendices to surnames, e.g., *Charles Carroll of Carrollton, John Randolph of Roanoke, John Ridgely of Hampton* and *Charles Carroll the Barrister*, seems to have passed out, and so, save in a few areas, has the custom of affixing father's initials to distinguish between two cousins of like given-name and surname, e.g., *Joseph Brown of A* (the son of *Albert*) and *Joseph Brown of D* (the son of *David*).[12]

1 *GaNun* & Parsons are opticians in New York City.
2 Originally *Virden*, the name of a settler on the Delaware in 1745. The *d* was raised by a clerical descendant "under the impression that the name was French." I am indebted here to Mr. Ray *VirDen*, of New York.
3 The *KenMore Kollector*, house organ of the *KenMore* Stamp Company, was quoted on the New York *Sun's* philately page, Aug. 15, 1941.
4 The name of a medical man recorded in the *Journal of the American Medical Association*, Aug. 16, 1941, p. 535.
5 Rufus Bernhard von *KleinSmid* became president of the University of Southern California in 1921. He was born in Illinois in 1875.
6 Charles K. *RossKam* "took out the Chicago Stock Company, one of the last of the larger rep companies to quit the road." See T. Dwight Pepple Recalls More Popular Old-Time Rep Troupes, *Billboard*, Aug. 2, 1941.
7 Hugh *RiDant* appeared as accompanist at a concert of the Germania Orchestra and Maennerchor at Saginaw, Mich., Oct. 21, 1946.
8 Miss Helen *ViSKocil* is a partner in the Purnell Art Galleries in Baltimore. Her name, she tells me, is of Czech origin and was originally *Vyskocil*. How and when its spelling was changed she has been unable to determine. According to the *New Yorker*, Feb. 15, 1947, p. 44, quoting the Scranton *Times*, John and Justina *Sawkulich* of Scranton had lately petitioned a local court for permission to change their name to *SaCoolidge*.
9 A gentleman named Hiram *Be Bee*, convicted of killing a city marshal, was sentenced to death at Manti, Utah, in 1946.
10 The name of Norman *Bel Geddes*, the stage designer, was so entered in the Manhattan telephone book for Winter-Spring, 1946, though he gives his father's name as *Geddes* in Who's Who in America, 1946-47.
11 Among curious forms of other sorts are *T'Serclaes, H'Doubler, Mis-Kelly* and *U'ren*. The first was reported by the Berkshire *Evening Eagle* (Pittsfield, Mass.), July 6, 1937. The second is the name of a distinguished surgeon of Springfield (Mo.), born in Kansas. A writer signing himself M.M.D. says in Irish Prefix, New York *Sun* (editorial page), Dec. 3, 1943, that *Mis-Kelly* is to be found in South Carolina, along with *Mis-Campbell*. Woulfe, in his Irish Names and Surnames, says that the *Mis* represents *Mac. U'ren* was the name of a well-known political reformer of the Bryan era.
12 A famous San Francisco editor of the early days, killed in a street duel, was *James King of William*.

"Almost every discarded fashion of spelling," says John Earle in "The Philology of the English Tongue,"[1] "lives on somewhere in proper names." The early scribes and notaries played hob with them, as Anders Orbeck shows for colonial America in his "Early New England Pronunciation,"[2] and many of the variants they propagated survive to this day, *e.g.*, *Millar-Millard*, *Farrar-Farrow*, *Buckminster-Buckmaster*, and *Haywood-Hayward*. Miss Oursler, before quoted, reports that in the census returns for 1790 *Kennedy* and *McLaughlin* were spelled in thirty-two different ways, and *Campbell* in twenty-seven. *Shakespeare's* name, in his day, was spelled in eighty-three.[3] George *Washington's* forefather, Laurence, was registered at Oxford as *Wasshington* in 1567; *Jefferson* was once *Jeffreson* and *Giffersonne*; *Adams* is interchangeable with *Addams*, *Adamson* and *Addamson*; *Jackson*, in its day, has been *Jakson*, *Jacson*, *Jackeson*, *Jakeson* and *Jaxon*; and *Lincoln* has gone through the forms of *Linccolne*, *Lyncoln*, *Lincon* and *Linkhorn*.[4] On Cape Cod *Mayo* and *Mayhew* are forms of the same name,[5] and so are *Harding* and *Hardin*; *Hamblen*, *Hamlin* and *Hamline*; *Merrick* and *Myrick*; *Shelley* and *Sherley*; *Crow* and *Crowell*; *Burge*, *Birge* and *Burgass*. Any American with an uncommon name is bound to find it grossly misspelled in his correspondence. The Hon. Thad *Eure*, formerly Secretary of State of North Carolina, was addressed by his constituents as *Ure*, *Euri*, *Ewar*, *Uue*, *Euria*, *Aure*, *Yuer*, *Erra*, *Eura* and *Eyre*,[6] and Wilberforce *Eames*, the bibliographer, cherished a collection of envelopes directed to *Anies*, *Bames*, *Earres*, *Gaines*, *Rames*, *Trames*, *Wames*, etc.[7]

1 Third edition; Oxford, 1879, p. 158.
2 Ann Arbor (Mich.), 1927, pp. 11–13. See also Krapp, Vol. I, pp. 201–05.
3 Orthography of *Shakespeare's* Name, by Richard Grant White, *Putnam's Monthly*, March, 1854, p. 295; *Shakespeare's* Name and Origin, by Johannes Hoops, in Studies for William A. Read; University (La.), 1940, pp. 67–87. The latter contains references to other discussions.
4 I take most of these variants from Bardsley's Dictionary of English and Welsh Surnames; London, 1901. Nicolay and Hay say in Abraham *Lincoln*: A History (*Century Magazine*, Nov., 1886, p. 6) that "there are *Lincolns* in Kentucky and Tennessee belonging to the same stock with the President whose names are spelled *Linkhorn* and *Linkhern*."
5 I am indebted here, and for what follows, to Mr. Gustavus Swift Paine, of Southbury, Conn. In England *Mayhew*, in the past, has been written *Maheu*, *Mayeu*, *Mayowe*, *Mayhoe* and even *Matthew*.
6 *New Yorker*, Jan. 6, 1940.
7 What's In a Name?, *Bulletin of the New York Public Library*, Nov., 1942, pp. 957–58. See also a letter

454 *The American Language: Supplement II*

But it is in pronunciation rather than in spelling that surnames suffer their greatest mutations. As we have seen in Chapter VII, Section 1, the general tendency in American pronunciation is to throw the accents forward, so that *addréss* becomes *áddress*, but in surnames it is often reversed. Thus *Moran, Bernard, Costello, Waddell, Savile, Mahony, Maurice, Jacoby, Sinclair* and *Purcell*, all of which are accented on the first syllable in Britain, are usually accented on the second here.[1] Another tendency is toward spelling-pronunciations, so that *Crowninshield*, which is *Crunchell* in England, is given the full value of all its syllables here, and *Harwood* is no longer *Harrod*, and *Heyward* is seldom *Howard*, and *Powell* is never *Po-ell*, and *St. John* is only rarely *Sin-jun*, and *Carew* is not *Carey*. But this tendency is not universal, and in the older parts of the country it meets with many checks. B. W. Green, in his "Word-Book of Virginia Folk Speech,"[2] lists a number of curious pronunciations in Tidewater Virginia, *e.g., Umsted* for *Armistead*,[3] *Beard* for *Baird, Belfur* for *Balfour, Barnet* for *Bernard, Blunt* for *Blount*,[4] *Bowthe* for *Boothe, Boler* for *Boulware, Brookenburro* for *Brockenbrough, Carroll* for *Callowhill, Kemp* for *Camp, Granger* for *Crenshaw, Druit* for *Drewry, Gouge* for *Gooch, Horton* for *Haughton* and *Hawthorne, Hickerson* for *Higginson, Munger* for *Ironmonger, Langon* for *Langhorne, Murray* for *Maury, Nazary* for *Norsworthy, Partrick* for *Patrick, Turnton* for *Turlington, Wait* for *Wyatt, Tolliver* for *Taliaferro* and *Darby* for *Enroughty*.

The last two have attracted much attention from students of names. The *Stammvater* of the American *Taliaferros* was Robert of that ilk, who was born in England about 1625 and came to Virginia some time before 1650, where he married, about 1653, Sarah Grymes, the daughter of the Rev. Charles Grymes of Brandon, a large landowner, and left a progeny that married into nearly all the prominent Virginia families of the time. Whether the surname was originally French or Italian is disputed. The French theory con-

---

about the troubles of the *Postlethwaites* in the *New Yorker*, July 9, 1938.

1 There are, of course, exceptions. Thus *Carnegie* and *Carmichael*, which have the stress on the second syllable in Britain, are commonly stressed on the first here.

2 Richmond (Va.), 1899, pp. 13–16.

3 *Armistead* is a rare surname in England, though Bardsley traces it in Yorkshire to 1379. In Virginia it is usually derived from the German *Armstädt*. See AL4, p. 479.

4 This is the accepted pronunciation in England also.

nects it with a Norman knight named *Taillefer,* who came to England with William the Conqueror. The Italian theory, which was supported by Thomas Jefferson and Chancellor George Wythe, connects it with a Venetian musician named Bartolomeo *Taliaferro,* who immigrated to England in Elizabethan times. Whatever the fact, there are still plenty of *Tallifers, Telefers* and *Tollivers* in England, and the American family has produced many men of distinction, *e.g.,* Major General William Booth *T.* (1822–98), of the Confederate Army; Benjamin and John *T.* (1750–1821 and 1768–1853), Virginia congressmen; James Piper *T.* (b. 1847), a Senator from Florida, and Dr. William H. *T.* (b. 1895), professor of parasitology at the University of Chicago and editor of the *Journal of Infectious Diseases.* Others have been successful lawyers, educators, bankers and business men, and no less than four are in " Who's Who in America" for 1946–47. Two of the latter note that they pronounce the name *Tól-i-ver.* This change seems to go back to an early date in England, but the actress Mabel *Taliaferro,* born in New York in 1887, used *Tal-ya-fér-ro.* Whether *Taliaferro* was her family name or only a stage name I do not know.[1]

There are *Enroughtys* in Virginia who pronounce their name *En-ruff-ty* and others who pronounce it *Darby.* How this confusion arose has been thus described by F. W. Sydnor:

> The records [of Henrico county] show one *Darby Enroughty* to have been living near Four-Mile creek[2] in 1690. He had a son named *John* and one named *Darby.* Later there were two *John Enroughtys* living in the same locality, cousins, whose names are frequently found in the records. Double Christian names were rarely used in those days, and it became necessary to distinguish between the two *Johns. John Enroughty,* the son of *John,* was known by his Christian name, but *John,* the son of *Darby Enroughty,* was designated *John Enroughty the son of Darby, John Enroughty of Darby,* and at least once as *John Darby.* The *Enroughtys* of Henrico and those known as *Darby* (real name *Enroughty*) are all descendants of *Darby Enroughty.* Those bearing the name *Enroughty* are the descendants of his son

---

[1] There is a considerable literature on the name and genealogy of the family, *e.g.,* The *Taliaferro* Family, by John Bailey Calvert Nicklin, *Tyler's Quarterly Historical and Genealogical Magazine,* Vol. VII, pp. 12–28; The *Taliaferro* Family, by William Buckner McGroarty, the same, pp. 179–82; The *Taliaferro* Family, by the same, *William and Mary College Quarterly Historical Magazine,* Vol. IV, pp. 191–99, and The Name and Family of *Taliaferro;* Washington, n.d. I am indebted here to Dr. Taliaferro and to Messrs. Sidney F. and H. M. Taliaferro.

[2] The county-seat of Henrico county is Richmond. Four-Mile creek was apparently a branch of the James river.

John, and those bearing the name of *Darby* are the descendants of his son *Darby*.[1]

This disposes of the legend, current in Virginia, that the original *Darby* took the name of *Enroughty* on marrying into the family or on inheriting property from one of its members, but insisted on retaining his own name in society. Also, it reveals the falsity of the theory that the *Darby-Enroughtys* are really *Enroughtys* who pronounce the name *Darby*. They actually bear two names — *Enroughty* in writing and *Darby* in speech.[2]

Lists of English surnames with strange pronunciations often appear in the newspapers, *e.g.*, *Chumly* for *Cholmondelay*, *Looson-Gore* for *Levesson-Gower*, and *Marshbanks* for *Majoribanks*. Some other curious examples follow:[3]

Abergavenny	Abergenny	Beauchamp	Beecham [6]
Alcester	Awlster	Beauclerc	Bóclare
Alnwick	Annick	Beaulieu	Bewly
Anstruther	Anster [4]	Beaworthy	Bowry
Arundel	Árrundel [5]	Bellingham	Bellinjam
Ayerst	I-erst	Belvoir	Beaver
Ayscough	Askew or Asko	Bentinck	Bentick
Bagehot and		Bertie	Barty
Bagshot	Baggot	Bicester	Bister
Barfreeston	Barson	Blyth	Bly [7]
Bartelot	Bartlett	Bolitho	Bolytho [8]
Barugh	Barf	Bottomley	Bumly [9]

[1] Richmond *News-Leader*, May 16, 1930. I am indebted here to Howard F. Barker, whose information comes from Lemuel N. Enroughty, of Richmond.
[2] See Note on Prof. Wilson's Article, by Ted Robinson, *American Speech*, April, 1939, p. 155.
[3] Many of these names come from Ewen's History of Surnames of the British Isles, pp. 344–45; Titles and Forms of Address; London, 1929, pp. 15–27; Broadcast English, Vol. VII, by A. Lloyd James; London, 1939; and These Names are Difficult, London *News Chronicle*, Nov. 28, 1936. For others see AL4, p. 503.
[4] But *Anstruther*, with the *u* as in *but*, and the *th* as in *there*, is also heard.
[5] In the United States the accent is commonly put on the second syllable. The Maryland county, *Anne Arundel*, is *Ann-rán'l* to many of its citizens.
[6] The given-name of *Champ* Clark (1850–1921), Speaker of the House of Representatives, 1911–19, was originally *Beauchamp*. The last syllable must have been pronounced *Champ* to get the abbreviation.
[7] But sometimes it is pronounced as spelled, with the *th* as in *there*.
[8] Letter from Hector *Bolitho* in Wild Names I Have Met, by Alfred H. Holt; Williamstown (Mass.), n.d., p. 7: "My name is Cornish, and it is pronounced: *bo* as in *low*, *li* as in *pie*, *tho* as in *low*. The accent is on the middle syllable." Ewen says it is from the Gaelic *bol ithing,* the great belly, *i.e.*, hill.
[9] Mr. P. R. Coleman-Norton writes

Proper Names in America

Bourchier	Bowcher	Crichton	Cryton [7]
Bowie	Boh-ie or Bow-ie [1]	Croghan	Crowan
Brahan	Brawn	D'Aguilar	Dágwiller
Broke	Brook	Dalzell or Dalziel	Dee-áll [8]
Brougham	Broo-am	Daventry	Daintree
Buccleuch	Buklóo	Decies	Déeshees
Burghley	Berly	De la Mare	Déllamair [9]
Campbell	Cámbel [2]	De La Pasture	Deláppature
Cassilis	Cassels	Dillwyn	Dillon
Cecil	Sissil [3]	Drogheda	Dráweda
Chalmers	Chahmers	Dumaresq	Dumérrick
Chandos	Shandos	Dymoke	Dimmuck
Charteris	Charters [4]	Falconer	Fawkner
Claverhouse	Clavers	Featherstonhaugh	Fétherstonhaw [10]
Clough	Cluff	Fenwick	Fennick
Cockburn	Coburn	Findlay	Finly
Coghlan	Colan or Coglan [5]	Foljambe	Fooljum
Colclough	Cokely	Foulis	Fowls
Colquhoun	Cóhoon	Froude	Frood
Combe	Coom	Gallagher	Gállaher
Compton	Cumpton	Galsworthy	Gawlsworthy
Conisborough	Cunsbra	Geikie	Geeky
Corcoran	Corkran	Geoghegan	Gaygun
Cottenham	Cottnam	Gilkes	Jilks
Coutts	Coots	Glamis	Glahms
Cowper	Cooper [6]		

---

under date of Sept. 20, 1937: "This was current during Horatio Bottomley's palmy days, some fifteen years ago." He was sent to prison for wholesale frauds in 1922. It is possible that *Bumly* was suggested by the disrepute of *bum* in England. See AL4, p. 156.

1 With the *ow* as in *how*. In America it is commonly *Boo-ie*.
2 *Camel* is apparently not in use.
3 This is used by the Marquess of Salisbury, whose family name it is. But the Marquess of Exeter, another *Cecil*, uses *Sessel*.
4 But the Earl of Wemyss, a *Charteris*, pronounces it as spelled.
5 The usual spelling in America is *Coughlin*, with *Coughlan* as a variant. There are eight times as many names in *Cough-* in the Manhattan telephone directory as names in *Cogh-*. In origin all are identical. *Coughlin* is sometimes pronounced *Coglan*, sometimes *Coklan*, sometimes *Cooglin*, and sometimes *Coflin*. I am indebted here to Dr. George McCracken, of Otterbein College.
6 But the name of the poet, William C., is often pronounced as spelled.
7 This is also the pronunciation of *Creighton*.
8 Black says that, in Scotland, "some of the name call themselves *Dalyell*, some *Dalzell*, and some *Dal-zeel*." He gives *Dalyell, Dalyiel, Diyell, Deill, Daliel, De Yell, Deyell, Dalyhel, Dalyelle, Dyell, Dalzel, Dalzelle, Dyayell* and *Deell* as variant spellings. The name is traced to 1259.
9 The first part as in *Delaware*.
10 Titles and Forms of Address, p. 18, gives no variants, but Broadcast English offers *Fanshaw, Feesonhay* and *Feerstonhaw*. Writing in the *New Yorker*, June 25, 1938, Duane Featherstonhaugh, of Schenectady, said *Fan-shaw* is favored in Canada and *Featherstonhaw* in the United States. In England, he added, the

Greaves	Graves	Leiston	Layson
Greig	Gregg	Leominster	Lemster
Halkett	Hackett	Lea and Ley	Lee
Heathcote	Hethcot	Leishman	Leeshman
Hertford	Hartford	Le Queux	Le Kew
Hoey	Hoy	Leven	Leeven
Home	Hume	Livesey	Livzy
Hotham	Huthum [1]	Loughborough	Lufburra
Houghton	Hawton, Howton or Hoton [2]	Lygon	Liggon
		Lympne	Lim
Houston	Hooston [3]	M'Eachern	Mackékrun
Inge	Ing	M'Gillycuddy	Maclíkuddy
Jekyll	Jeekel	Mahon	Mahn [5]
Jervis	Jarvis	Mainwaring	Mannering
Jamieson	Jimmisson [4]	Marlborough	Mawlbra
Keighley	Keethly or Keely	Maugham	Mawm
Keightley	Keetly	Meagher	Mayer
Kerr	Carr	Menzies	Mengiz [6]
Keynes	Kayns	Meynell	Mennel
Kirkby	Kirby	Meyrick	Merrick
Kirkcudbright	Kirkóobry	Millais	Míllay
Knollys	Noles	Molyneaux	Mullinewks
Lascelles	Lássels	Montgomery	Muntgummery [7]
Layard	Laird	Moray	Murry
Leicester	Lester	Moule	Mole

lower classes sometimes make it *Freeze-ting-haze* and sportive persons of higher elegance *Feston-hog*.

[1] With *th* as in *there*.

[2] The pronunciation of this name seems to be unsettled in England, as it is in America. When Alanson B. Houghton (1863–1941) was appointed ambassador to Germany, in 1922, he announced that he preferred *Howtun*. One of the *Houghtons* in Who's Who in America, 1946–47, prefers *Hotun* and another *Hot'n*. Holt says in Wild Names I Have Met that even within the board of *Houghton* Mifflin, the Boston publishers, two pronunciations are used — *Hoton* and *Howton*. Elsewhere in New England it is often *Hooton*. The people of *Houghton*, Mich., call it *Hoton*. Says Holt: " Anything will do — except *Huffton*."

[3] This is also the New York pronunciation. In the Texas city it is *Hyooston*.

[4] Broadcast English, Vol. VII, gives *Jaymisson* and *Jammisson* as variants.

[5] Also used for *Mahan*.

[6] Broadcast English, Vol. VII, prefers *Mingiss*, but also gives *Mengiz*. It says that *Menziz* is used in Australia. The name is Scottish. Black says that it was originally *de Meyners*, which has become *Manners* in England. It is traced to 1214. There have been many variants in spelling, including *Megnies, Mainzeis, Mengues, Menyas, Menzheis, Mennes* and *Menzas*. Said a writer in the Sydney (Australia) *Bulletin*, Jan. 1, 1936: " *Mingies* in England merely represent the attempts of Southerners to imitate the Scottish pronunciation, for no Scot ever called it that. The modern spelling is the result of a confusion by the early Scottish printers of the letters *y* and *z*, their tails making them look alike. The correct spelling is *Menyies*, which is nearer the correct pronunciation, though the Scotch say it with a twang it is impossible to reproduce in writing."

Proper Names in America

Moynihan	Moynian [1]	Selous	Selóo
Murtagh	Murta	Sewell	Syooel
Myerscough	Maskew	Seymour	Seemer
Newnes	Newnz	Shrewsbury	Shrohsb'ry
Norreys	Norris	Slaithwaite	Slo-it
Outram	Ootram	Sotheby	Sutheby [4]
Pauncefote	Pownsfoot	Southey	Suthy
Pepys	Peeps [2]	Stanhope	Stannup
Petrie	Peetry	St. Clair	Sinclair
Ponsonby	Punsunby	St. Maur	Seymour
Pontefract	Pumfret	Stourton	Sturton
Portishead	Pozzet	Strabolgi	Strabogie
Powys	Pó-is	Strachan	Strawn [5]
Pretyman	Prittyman	Straton	Stratton
Pulteney	Poltny	Swaffer	Swoffer
Raleigh	Rawly or Rally	Symons	Simmons
Rathbone	Rathbon	Synge	Sing
Rhondda	Rontha	Teignmouth	Tinmuth
Rhys	Reese	Theobold	Tibbald
Rolleston	Rolston	Touche	Toosh
Romney	Rumny	Trevelyan	Trevilian
Rothwell	Rowell	Tyrwhitt	Tirrit
Ruthven	Rivven or Ruffen	Urquhart	Erkert
Sacheverell	Sasheverel	Vaux	Vox or Vokes
Sandys	Sands	Villiers	Villers
Sawbridgeworth	Sapsed [3]	Waldegrave	Wawlgrave
Scone	Scoon	Warwick	Worrick
Scrope	Scroop	Wauchope	Waukop [6]
Sedburgh	Sedber	Wemyss	Weems

---

7 A touchy English *Montgomery* is said to send the following letter to persons who make the first syllable of his name *Mont:* "During our conversation today I noticed with regret that you were finding some difficulty in correctly pronouncing my name. As *Montgomery* is one of the many words in which the letter *o* is pronounced as a *u*, I think perhaps it might help you if I were to remind you of some of the other words in this large category: 'London company's governor's accomplished comedy mother coming to Tonbridge Monday. One son working constable, other brother recovering.' You will agree that if these words were pronounced as spelt they would sound horrible. That is precisely what happens when I hear people mispronouncing *Montgomery*."

1 This is the pronunciation given by Broadcast English, but William Hickey says in the London *Daily Express*, Sept. 7, 1945, that *Munian* is often heard.
2 Titles and Forms of Address says that *Peeps* is used by living members of the clan, but that *Peppiz* was used formerly. Broadcast English says that the Earl of Cottenham, whose family name it is, sticks to *Peppiss*.
3 The *Reader's Digest*, Nov., 1935, said that this pronunciation has now been given up, and the name is pronounced as it is spelled.
4 The *th* as in *there*.
5 But sometimes it is pronounced as spelled and sometimes it is *Strahn*. *Strachey* is always *Straytchy*.
6 *i.e.*, almost *walk up*.

Wescott	Westcot	Wolseley	Woolzly
Whalley	Whawly	Wortley	Wertly
Whitefield	Whitfield	Wriothesley	Roxly
Whytham	Whitam	Wrotham	Rootham
Wightwick	Wittick	Wrottesley	Rotsly
Wilbraham	Wilbram	Yeats	Yayts
Winder	Win-der [1]	Youghal	Yawl

Regarding the pronunciation of many other British surnames usage differs in different places, and as a result the authorities do not agree. Very often, indeed, the same authority gives two or more forms. Thus "Titles and Forms of Address" says that *Devereux*, which is an Irish name derived from France, is pronounced both *Déveroo* and *Déveroox* (*de* as in *devil*), and A. Lloyd James adds *Dévveruh* (with the neutral vowel at the end) and *Dévverecks*. Again, *Ffoulkes* is both *Fokes* and *Fooks*,[2] *Gell* takes both the hard and the soft *g*, *Heygate* is both *Haygait* and *Haygit*, *Lisle* is both *Lile* and *Leel*, *Onions* is both *Unnionz* and *Oníghons*, and *Coughtrey* is variously pronounced *Cowtry*, *Cawtry*, *Cootry*, *Cotry* and *Coftry*, with the initial syllables of the first four forms rhyming with *how*, *saw*, *stew* and *low*. In parts of Scotland *Cunningham* is pronounced *Kinnicum*,[3] and in Lord *Byron's* day he was usually called *Birron* by his intimates.[4] Similar aberrations, of course, are

---

[1] The *Maryland Historical Magazine*, Sept., 1944, p. 177, n. 1, says that this name is pronounced *Win-der* in England and *Wine-der* in the United States. Brig.-Gen. William Henry *Winder* (1775–1824) was in command of the American troops at Bladensburg, Aug. 24, 1814, and got a famous licking.

[2] *Ffoulkes*, like *Ffrench*, *Ffarington*, *Fford*, *Ffennell*, *Ffinch*, etc., is Welsh, but the form has been imitated in England and Ireland. The initial *Ff* is sometimes written *ff*, but this is an error. Says Trevor Davenport-*Ffoulkes* in Two Little *f*'s, London Sunday *Times*, April 22, 1934: "Actually there exists no such thing as two little *f*'s. The Welsh alphabet provides by its ninth letter the double *f* in the same way as the English alphabet provides the double *u* (*w*). The pronunciation of the Welsh single *f* is *v*, as in *ever*, *Eva*, etc.; the double *f* provides for the sound of the English *f*. . . . If families holding such names were to use the Welsh single *f* the pronunciation would be *Vookes*, *Vrench*, *Varington*, *Vinch*, and in my own case, *Voulkes*." This indicates that Mr. Davenport-*Ffoulkes* sounds the *l* in his second name. I am indebted here to Mrs. Delia H. Biddle Pugh, of New York.

[3] See W. E. Henley's note in The Letters of Robert Louis Stevenson; New York, 1923, Vol. II, p. 305. Black gives *Cunygam*, *Cuninggame*, *Conighame* and *Cwnynghame* as early spellings.

[4] Memoirs of My Times, Including Personal Reminiscences of Eminent Men, by George Hodder; London, 1870, reprinted in Personal Reminiscences of Barham, Harness and Hodder, by Richard Henry Stoddard; New York, 1875, p. 321.

also frequently encountered in the United States. Some of those prevailing in Virginia have been listed; in New Hampshire *Pierce* is pronounced *Purse*, and *Franklin* of that ilk (1804–69), fourteenth President of the United States, was so called by his friends, one of whom, Nathaniel *Hathorne*, changed the spelling of his own name to *Hawthorne* in order to bring it into accord with his notion of its euphonious pronunciation.[1] Not a few Americans of eminence have borne changed names. John *Fiske* the historian (1842–1901) was Edmund Fiske *Green* until 1855, and Henry *Wilson*, Vice-President under Grant (1812–75), was Jeremiah Jones *Colbath* until 1833.[2]

Howard F. Barker says[3] that the surnames of the American people have been greatly stabilized by the wholesale regimentation introduced by World War I. Many of the conscripts rounded up for that war had only the vaguest idea of the spelling of their names, and not a few were uncertain as to what their names were, but by the time they were discharged every man had a name that was imbedded firmly in the official records, and he had to stick to it in order to enjoy any of the benefits and usufructs of a veteran. Barker continues:

> On the heels of this came the general spread of life insurance, a powerful stabilizing force. Men who had carried $10,000 in insurance during the war were prone to take out at least a few thousand in civil life. Thereby they again wrote themselves down as being specifically *Houlihan, Holohan* or *Holoughan*, and stayed that way. Then came the automobile registration. Automobiles not only changed the face of the American landscape; they also went a long way toward stopping changes of family names. Automobile titles soon constituted a formidable body of property records, and annual licenses reinforced them. Every million cars meant another million families named for good. After some years came Social Security, and it was soon followed by other like devices, each involving the registration of millions of names. By 1940 American family nomenclature was vastly more stable than it had been in 1910, or even in 1920.[4]

[1] For *Pierce* see A Word-List From Hampstead, S. E. New Hampshire, by Joseph William Carr, *Dialect Notes*, Vol. III, Part III, 1907, p. 196, and Colloquial Expressions From Hillsborough County, New Hampshire, by Jason Almus Russell, *American Speech*, June, 1930, p. 420. Carr says that *Ordway* is commonly pronounced *Orderway* in New Hampshire. For *Hawthorne* see Salem With a Guide, by George Arvedson; Salem (Mass.), 1926, p. 38, n. 4. I am indebted here to Mr. Alexander Kadison.

[2] The Life and Public Services of Hon. Henry Wilson, by Thomas Russell and Elias Nason; Boston, 1872, pp. 19–20.

[3] Private communication.

[4] The literature of surnames is very large. There are lists of books, pamphlets and articles on the subject down to the end of 1922 in Kennedy's Bibliography, pp. 57–58, 149–50, 187 and 328–37, and others

2. GIVEN NAMES[1]

When, in 1920, Simon Newton undertook a survey of the given-names of American males [2] he found that *John* led all the rest, with *William, James, Charles, George, Thomas, Henry, Robert, Joseph* and *Edward* following in order. In 1938 Daniel Francis Clancy unearthed evidence which led him to believe that *William* had displaced *John*, with *John, Charles, George, James, Frank, Henry, Robert, Arthur* and *Edward* following,[3] but his sample was by no

---

are noted in AL4, Chapter X, Section 1, and in the preceding pages. In The Theory of Proper Names; Oxford, 1940, Alan H. Gardiner says, p. 43: "A proper name is a word or group of words recognized as indicating or tending to indicate the object or objects to which it refers by virtue of its distinctive sound alone, without regard to any meaning possessed by that sound from the start, or acquired by it through association with the said object or objects.... The purest of proper names are those of which the sounds strike us as wholly arbitrary, yet perfectly distinctive, and about which we should feel, if ignorant of their bearers, no trace of meaning or significance." The following may be useful to the inquirer desirous of pursuing the subject: The Story of Surnames, by William Dodgson Bowman; New York, 1931; The Ancestry of Family Names, by Howard F. Barker, *Atlantic Monthly*, Aug., 1935; Family Names, by Jerome C. Hixson, *Words*, Feb. and March, 1937; These Names of Ours: A Book of Surnames, by Augustus Wilfrid Dellquest; New York, 1938; What's Your Name?, by Lewis H. Chrisman, *Journal of Education*, May, 1944; Surnames and the Chronology of the English Vocabulary, by Ernest Weekley, in Adjectives — and Other Words; London, 1930; Personal Names, by George H. McKnight, in English Words and Their Backgrounds; New York, 1923; Irish Gaelic Clan Names and Family Names Abundant in America, by J. N. Enos, *Americana*, July, 1927; Middle English Surnames of Occupation, 1100–1350, With an Excursus on Toponymical Surnames, by G. Fransson; Lund (Sweden), 1935; Scottish Clans and Families Represented in America, by J. N. Enos, *Americana*, July, 1923; Early Anglo-Norman, English, Welsh and Scottish Families in Ireland Now Represented in the United States, *Americana*, July, 1926; What's the Name, Please? A Guide to the Correct Pronunciation of Current Prominent Names, by Charles Earle Funk; New York, 1936; revised edition, 1938; and The Founders of New England, by Howard F. Barker, *American Historical Review*, July, 1933.

1 In this section a few passages are lifted from Notes on American Given-Names, a paper I contributed to Bookman's Holiday, a *Festschrift* in honor of Harry Miller Lydenberg; New York, 1943. I am indebted for permission to use them to Mr. Deoch Fulton, head of the New York Public Library Press.

2 *World* Almanac, 1921, p. 150. His studies were based upon "100,000 names in biographical dictionaries, Army and Navy registers, Masonic rosters, etc., and the Detroit City Directory."

3 More *Williams* Than *Johns*, Chicago *Tribune*, March 9, 1938.

means as large as Newton's and other investigations tend to show that *John* is still in the lead.¹ If so, it has held its place in the English-speaking lands for a long, long while, for the roster of the first Common Council of London, held in 1347, showed 34 *Johns*, 17 *Williams*, 15 *Thomases*, 10 *Richards* and 8 *Roberts* in a total enrolment of 133.² In the interval there have been passing fashions for other given-names, but not one of them has forced its way into the top bracket.³ That, of course, is not saying that *John*'s frequency continues to be absolute as well as relative. On the contrary, there is reason to believe that it is slowly losing ground in the United States, along with all the other ancient saints' names.⁴ They continue, however, to be almost unchallenged on the Continent of Europe, and have been so for a thousand years, for in the Catholic areas Canon 761 of the Canon Law ordains that such a name must be given to every child at baptism, and even in the Protestant areas

1 Frank J. Fay, register of births, deaths and marriages in Boston, reported in 1942 that *John* led among the male children whose births were reported in the city during the first six months of the year. *Mary* and *John*, Boston *Herald* (editorial), July 14, 1942.
2 N or M, London *Times Literary Supplement*, March 30, 1946, p. 151. But in the Domesday Book of *c.* 1086 there had been 68 *Williams*, 48 *Roberts* and 28 *Walters* to but 10 *Johns*, and at the end of the Twelfth Century, according to E. G. Withycombe in The Oxford Dictionary of English Christian Names; New York, 1947, p. xxiii, *William* accounted for 15% of the recorded given-names, with *John* accounting for but 2%. A century later, however, *John* had jumped to first place with 25%, followed by *William* with 15%, *Robert* with 11%, *Ralph* with 10% and *Richard* with 8%.
3 An example is *Michael*, which arose to popularity among the English upper classes *c.* 1900 and was imitated by American Anglophiles. *Peter* had a similar vogue a bit later — launched, according to Eric Partridge in Name This Child; London, 1936, by the popularity of J. M. Barrie's *Peter* Pan, 1904. The curious spread of *Carl* in the United States is noted in AL4, p. 506, n. 1. In the House of Representatives of the Eightieth Congress no less than seven out of the 435 members bore it. It stands in forty-second place in the Newton list of 1920. The rise and fall of various women's names has been frequently noted. The cases of *Barbara*, *Ella*, *Emma*, *Joan*, *Muriel*, *Phyllis* and many others are discussed by Miss Withycombe in The Oxford Dictionary of English Christian Names, just cited. For *Joan* see also *Joan*, by B. H. P. Fisher, London *Times Literary Supplement*, Feb. 16, 1946, p. 79, and the *William Feather Magazine*, Nov., 1944, p. 24. For *Maud* see Life With Salt on the Side, by E. V. Durling, New York *Journal-American*, June 5, 1946.
4 It seems to be resented by some of its bearers on the ground that it is too common. "If you should have a boy," wrote John Keats to G. A. Keats, Jan. 13, 1820, " do not christen him *John;* 'tis a bad name and goes against a man." Perhaps he was envious of the mellifluous name of his rival, *Percy Bysshe Shelley*.

they are still dominant. Canon 761, which is a reaffirmation of ancient legislation, was promulgated by Pope Benedict XV on May 22, 1917, and reads as follows:

> Curent parochi ut ei qui baptizatur christianum imponatur nomen, **quod** si id consequi non poterunt, nomini a parentibus imposito addant nomen alicuius Sancti et in libro baptizatorum utrumque nomen perscribant.[1]

This may be Englished thus:

> Let pastors take care that a Christian name be given to the one baptized; and, if they cannot accomplish this, let them add to the name given by the parents the name of some saint, and inscribe both names in the book of baptisms.

Even in such strongholds of Protestantism as Prussia, Denmark and Sweden, where the Canon Law has no authority, Canon 761 is generally followed.[2] It is also followed, of course, by Catholics in the United States, if not by parents then at least by priests. In case a child is presented for baptism by a mother or father who insists upon giving it some non-canonical name the priest is required to add a saint's name. He may do it *sotto voce*, but do it he must, and the saint's name goes on the records of the parish.[3] Sometimes

---

[1] Codex Iuris Canonici; Rome, 1917. The commission which edited the code was appointed by Pope Pius X on March 19, 1904. It consisted of cardinals only, with the Pope himself as president, but it took the advice of many consultors, some of them resident in Rome and some not. The code was made binding upon all "patriarchs, primates, archbishops, bishops and other ordinaries and . . . the professors and students of Catholic universities and seminaries," and hence upon all lay Catholics. It was promulgated by the bull *Providentissima Mater Ecclesia*. On Sept. 15, 1917 Pope Benedict XV set up a commission of cardinals to interpret it, and that commission has since handed down many decisions. On Dec. 19, 1917 it decided that all *dubia* (questions) must be submitted by or through bishops or the "major superiors of orders and religious congregations."

[2] In France, during the Revolution, an effort was made to abolish, or, at all events, to limit the use of saints' names, but it came to nothing, and nearly all Frenchmen of today bear them. See Encyclopedia of Religion and Ethics, edited by James Hastings; New York, 1928, Vol. IX, p. 150. In England a constitution of John Peckham, Archbishop of Canterbury (d. 1292) still seems to have some force. It provides that "ministers shall take care not to permit wanton names, which, being pronounced, do sound to lasciviousness, to be given to children baptized, especially of the female sex; and if otherwise it be done, the name shall be changed by the bishop at confirmation." Ernest Weekley says in Jack and Jill; London, 1939, p. 2, that "this change has often been effected." He also says that candidates for holy orders sometimes change their given-names at ordination.

[3] This is done also, of course, in the case of adult converts, who may

this causes difficulties later on, as when a boy named, say, *Woodrow* applies for a birth certificate, and discovers to his astonishment that he is really *Joseph Woodrow* or *Woodrow Joseph*. There has been some murmuring against Canon 761 among American Catholics in recent years, especially in the Middle West, for it works against the fanciful names that are in vogue there, and many priests have seen fit to lean as far backward as possible in their interpretation of it. In one of the current treatises on moral theology it is watered down to the following:

> Parents should choose suitable names for their children, avoiding such as are obscene, ridiculous, or impious. It is advisable that the name of a saint or of some other person distinguished for holiness be chosen, for this will be of a spiritual advantage to the child and an edification to others.[1]

Not a few of the common saints' names, of course, are of heathen origin — for example, the Greek *George*, the Latin *Paul* and the Germanic *Charles* — but that fact has been long forgotten; all that the Canon Law now demands is that saints on the Calendar or prophets of an earlier day once bore them. Thus, in an official list of permissible baptismal names published in 1935 by authority of Patrick Cardinal Hayes, then Archbishop of New York,[2] both *Adolf* and *Benito* appear, though the former is an ancient Teutonic name signifying "like a wolf" and the latter is a pet-name derived from *Benedetto*. They qualify because *Adolf* was the name of an Osnabrück saint of the Thirteenth Century, remembered for his devotion to the poor, and because *Benito*, like *Benedetto* itself, is an accepted form, in Italy, of the name of *Benedictus* (signifying blessed), the great founder of Western monasticism who passes in England and the United States as *Benedict*, in France and Belgium as *Bénédict* or *Benoît*, in the German lands as *Benedikt*, and in Spain and Portugal as *Benedicto*.

---

bear such abhorrent given-names as *Darwin*, *Wesley* or *Luther*, and desire to keep them. In 1942 a young priest named *Ellsworth* S. Fortman celebrated his first mass at Holy Cross Church, Baltimore. In the account of the event in the Baltimore *Catholic Review* there was no hint as to what the *S.* stood for, but no doubt it was a saint's name. The case of Bishop *Duane* G. Hunt, of the Salt Lake City diocese, is not so easily accounted for, for his middle name is *Garrison*.

[1] Moral Theology: A Complete Course, by John A. McHugh and Charles J. Callan; New York, 1930, Vol. II, p. 650.

[2] Baptismal and Confirmation Names, by Edward F. Smith; New York, 1935.

The official list just mentioned sanctions some far from dignified distortions of prophets' and saints' names, *e.g., Abe, Abie, Aggie, Al, Aleck, Alex, Alf, Alick, Allie, Andy, Annabelle, Archy* and *Atty* (from *Attracta,* the name of an Irish saint of the Fifth Century), to go no further than the *A*'s. It also permits *Dolores,* which is not a given-name at all, but comes from one of the titles of the Virgin Mary — *Mater Dolorosa* (Sorrowful Mother). *Virginia,* which is likewise permitted, gets in by much the same route. Such American favorites as *Homer, Horace* and *Ulysses* are banned, for they are the names of invincible heathen, but *Caesar* is admitted on the ground that there was a saintly Archbishop of Arles of that name in the Sixth Century, and *Virgil* because it was borne by an Irish missionary saint of the Eighth Century who helped to convert the heathen Germans and became Bishop of Salzburg. Even in Italy, I gather, there is some encroachment of non-canonical names. Consider, for example, the case of Monsignor *Amleto* Giovanni Cicognani, Archbishop of Laodicea in *partibus infidelium,* who became Apostolic Delegate to the United States in 1933. His Excellency was not only a high Roman dignitary; he was also a former professor of Canon Law and the author of a standard treatise on the subject;[1] yet the first of his two given names was the Italian form of the old Danish *Amleth* or *Hamleth,* the appellation of a probably fabulous heathen prince of the Second Century who has been immortalized by Shakespeare as *Hamlet.*[2]

It was the English Puritans who, toward the end of the Sixteenth Century, staged the first revolt against saints' names in Europe. They were opposed to honoring any of those on the Roman calendar who had lived since apostolic times,[3] and so turned to the Old Testament for names for their children.[4] It was then that

---

[1] Canon Law, tr. by Joseph M. O'Hara and Francis Brennan; Philadelphia, 1934.

[2] There are two *Amleth* sagas in Icelandic, in which he appears as *Ambales.* His story was first told by the Dane, Saxo Grammaticus, *c.* 1200.

[3] They were encouraged in this attitude by John Knox's Calvinist Book of Discipline, 1560, their favorite guide to conduct. It said: "Let persuasions be used that such names that do not savor of either paganism or popery be given to children at their baptism, but principally those whereof there are examples in the Scriptures."

[4] The translation they use was the Genevan of 1560 — called the Breeches Bible because of its rendering of Genesis III, 7: "They sewed fig leaves together and made themselves breeches." It was the first English Bible printed in small format. Charles W. Bardsley says

Abraham, Moses, Daniel, Samuel, Joshua and their like began to have a vogue,[1] though they had been permissible names to Catholics all the while. Unhappily, that vogue extended to the unsaved,[2] and, as Bardsley says,[3]

> the sterner Puritan found a list of Bible names that he would gladly have monopolized, shared in by half the English population.[4] That a father should style his child *Nehemiah*, or *Abacuck*, or *Tabitha*, or *Dorcas*, he discovered with dismay, did not prove that that particular parent was under any deep conviction of sin. This began to trouble the minds and consciences of the elect. Fresh limits must be created. As *Richard* and *Roger* had given way to *Nathaniel* and *Zerrubabel*, so *Nathaniel* and *Zerrubabel* must now give way to *Learn-wisdom* and *Hate-evil*.[5]

The more extreme Puritans made names of various other pious hopes and admonitions, *e.g.*, *Fear-not, Faint-not, Stand-fast, Increase, More-trial, Joy-again, From-above, Free-gifts, Be-faithful, More-fruit, Hope-still, Sin-deny, Dust, The-Lord-is-near, Fly-fornication*, and *Praise-God*,[6] and many of these, along with the Old Testament names, were brought to America by immigrants to New England. Most such inventions were so clumsy that they had to be abandoned,[7] but a number survived into the Eighteenth Cen-

---

in Curiosities of Puritan Nomenclature; London, 1880, p. 38, that it "ran through unnumbered editions, and for sixty years, if not for seventy, was the household Bible" of England. Among the American Puritans it survived even longer. In the favorite American edition a list of approved Biblical given-names was printed in an appendix.

1 The more earnest Puritans unearthed some really formidable specimens, *e.g.*, *Zerubbabel, Zaphenathpaneah* and *Mahershalalhashbaz*. See In the Driftway, *Nation*, Feb. 7, 1923, p. 150.

2 In Puritan Christian Names, London *Times Literary Supplement*, July 25, 1935, W. Fraser Mitchell suggested that their popularity was often "a sign of education rather than of piety." He cited the fact that Foston Watson, in The English Grammar School to 1660, offered evidence "of the teaching of Hebrew in leading grammar schools" in the Puritan period, and went on: "A parent familiar with the meaning of a Hebrew name was as likely to bestow it on his son as parents familiar with classical names were to draw upon these — a practise very prevalent in the same period and for a century longer."

3 Curiosities of Puritan Nomenclature, just cited, p. 118.

4 Mr. James Whittaker tells me (1944) that such names are still common in the North of England — the present Bible Belt of the country.

5 Such names, of course, were opposed by the orthodox clergy of the Church of England. In A Priest to the Temple, 1632, George Herbert thus described the duty of a parson baptizing children: "He admits no vain or idle names, but such as are usual and accustomed."

6 Ecclesiastical History of Great Britain, by Jeremy Collier; London, 1708–14.

7 The Editor's Drawer, *Harper's Magazine*, April, 1855, p. 709: "A good old lady died, within our

tury, *e.g., Increase* and *Preserved*, and a few are occasionally encountered even today. The Old Testament names that preceded and accompanied them are now apparently more popular in the South than in New England, though even in the South they are going out. There must have been a revolt against them at the time New England Puritanism began to fade into Unitarianism, for it is recorded that *Noah* Webster, the lexicographer, disliked his given-name[1] and refused to let it be given to any of his male descendants. The Puritan names for girls, *e.g., Grace, Charity, Hope, Constance, Mercy* and *Faith*, were nearly all permissible for Catholics, for they had been borne by female martyrs in the early days of Christianity, but the Puritans gave them a new lease of life, and most of them are still much more frequent in the United States than anywhere else.

The chief competition that saints' names encounter in the Republic today does not come, however, from Puritan names; it comes from the use of surnames as given-names and the wholesale invention of entirely new and unprecedented names in the Bible country of the South and Southwest. Many names of the former sort, *e.g., Howard, Dudley, Douglas, Stanley, Sidney, Clifford, Spencer* and *Russell*, are now in wide esteem in both England and the United States, but they did not appear in England until the latter part of the Sixteenth Century and were not imitated here until a little later. The first mention of them that I have been able to find is in William Camden's "Remains Concerning Britain," first published in 1605.[2] Camden noted that their use was then a novelty of "late years" and sneered at an unnamed "wayward old man" for alleging that it went back to the reign of Edward VI (1547–53). He also noted that it was purely English and was to be encountered "nowhere else in Christendom." He gave twelve current examples, to wit, *Pickering, Worton,*[3] *Grevil,*[4] *Varney,*[5] *Bas-*

---

circle, not many years ago who was familiarly known as *Aunt Tribby*, but who was baptized with the more extended title of *Through-Much-Tribulation-We-Enter-Into-the-Kingdom-of-Heaven Crabb.*" See also The Historical Aspect of the American Churches, *Eclectic Magazine*, Aug., 1879, p. 201.

[1] Warfel, p. 329.
[2] My quotations are from the reprint of the seventh edition of 1674, in the Library of Old Authors; London, 1870, pp. 56–57.
[3] Not to be confused with *Wharton*. Bardsley, in his Dictionary of English and Welsh Surnames; London, 1901 says that *Worton* comes from the name of "several vil-

singburne, *Gawdy, Calthorp, Parker, Pecsal,*[1] *Brocas,*[2] *Fitz-Raulf* and *Chamberlain.* Of these only *Parker* appears to have ever attained any marked popularity, and it has been swamped in recent years by *Cecil, Spencer, Seymour, Howard, Douglas, Dudley, Desmond, Stanley* and *Clifford,* to mention only a few shining examples. At the start, according to Camden, the use of given-names as surnames was confined to "worshipful ancient families," and proceeded "from hearty good will, and affection of the godfathers to shew their love," but it soon spread to lower and lower strata, and by the middle of the Seventeenth Century *Percy, Howard, Sidney* and *Cecil* had become common given-names in England, though not, apparently, in Scotland and Ireland.

In the English colonies in America the favorite English names were soon reinforced by American additions, *e.g., Chauncey* (originally *Chauncy*), *Clinton, Eliot, Dwight, Schuyler, Cotton, Bradford, Endicott, Leverett* and *Winthrop,* and by the time of the Revolution the custom of naming children after conspicuous persons, not relatives, was already sufficiently noticeable to be remarked in the newspapers. Says Dr. Arthur M. Schlesinger:

> The meeting of the first Continental Congress in the Fall of 1774 ... crystallized the growing sense of nationality, helped to dissolve intercolonial prejudices, and highlighted leaders hitherto of only local renown. Thenceforth the giving of patriotic names to infants became a newsworthy event, reported by the press along with the latest political developments. ... From the outset John *Hancock* proved a prime favorite on baptismal occasions. ... Though his bold chirography was yet to appear on the Declaration of Independence he was president of the First Continental Congress (and later of the Second), and therefore personified the united colonial effort. Before 1774 drew to an end his namesakes were recorded in Providence, R. I., and Marblehead, Mass.[3]

But the outbreak of actual war, as Dr. Schlesinger records, offered stiff competition to Hancock's popularity, and thereafter the favorite name for male babies was *Washington.* The first upon whom it was bestowed seems to have been the infant son of Col.

---

lages so called in County Oxford" and traces it to 1273.
4 A Norman name. The usual modern spelling is *Greville.*
5 A variant of *Verney* — cf. *clerk-clark* —, traced by Bardsley to 1273.
6 Possibly a variant of *Pechel,* a name of French origin.

2 A name of French origin, traced by Bardsley to 1315. It is nearly extinct in England.
3 Patriotism Names the Baby, *New England Quarterly,* Dec., 1941, pp. 611-18.

John Robinson of Dorchester, Mass., who was christened toward the end of July, 1775. After that infants named for the commander of the American forces began to be reported in all directions, and in April Alexander Anderson of New York, on being presented with twins of opposite sexes, named one *George Washington* and the other *Martha Dandridge*. The first real hero of the Revolution was Joseph Warren, who was killed at Bunker Hill, June 17, 1775. He was scarcely in his grave before babies were being named after him, and by the next year the custom was so firmly established that thousands were being baptized *Franklin, Jefferson, Otis* and *Adams*,[1] to be followed in due course by *Hamilton, Marshall, Jackson, Harrison, Lincoln, Grant, Lafayette*,[2] *Madison, Tyler, Scott, Lee, Sherman, Sheridan* and so on, not to mention *Irving*, leading down to the *Grover Cleveland, George Dewey, Theodore Roosevelt* and *Franklin Delano* of our own era.[3] Among the thirty-two Presidents of the United States up to 1947, three had surnames as given-names, and seven had them as middle-names. Of the latter, three dropped their given-names and used their middle-names. The long survival of names taken over during the Revolutionary period

---

[1] Dr. Schlesinger notes that certain Loyalist families retorted by naming their sons after English governors and generals. In March, 1776, a Stanford, Conn., couple named Edwards thus had a boy baby christened *Thomas Gage*, then still Governor of Massachusetts. Three days after the christening an army of 170 neighboring women marched on the Edwards house and undertook to tar and feather the mother. She was saved only by the valor and military skill of her husband.

[2] For the permutations of *Lafayette* see *American Speech*, Dec., 1941, p. 312; Dec., 1942, p. 225, and April, 1946, p. 155. Says Mr. Edgar W. Smith of Maplewood, N. Y. (private communication, July 27, 1936): "It is quite natural that the flat *a* should have got into *Lafayette*, for it is in strict correspondence with Parisian usage — at least as the *a* in *la* is pronounced there today. I know some over-precise Americans who call the *LaSalle* automobile the *Lah Sahl* under the impression that they are using the correct French pronunciation. But the Parisian French, and practically all other Frenchmen save those from the deepest Midi, call it a *LaSalle* with both *a*'s short, the closest American sound being the *a* in *ant*."

[3] See What's In a Name?, by Joyce G. Agnew, New York *Times Magazine*, Nov. 5, 1944, p. 38. After the Civil War many admirers of *Stonewall Jackson* named their sons, not *Jackson*, but *Stonewall*. Such names usually date their bearers. The distinguished Southern editor, *Grover Cleveland* Hall, was born in 1888. On March 15, 1941 the Oklahoma City papers reported the inducting of twins named *Woodrow* and *Wilson* Calloway, born in 1918. On Oct. 31, 1944 the Associated Press reported the death of a Seattle pioneer whose given-names were the surnames of seventeen officers of his father's Civil War regiment. But for everyday purposes he passed as *William Cary*.

was shown by the cases of *Franklin* Pierce, *Warren* Harding and *Franklin* Roosevelt. Rather curiously, the most popular nomenclature relic of that time in vogue today, not excepting *Washington*, is *Elmer*, which is said to be derived from the name of two heroes so far forgotten otherwise that it does not appear in any of the ordinary reference books. Of it the New York *Herald-Tribune* said in 1935:

> The name does not occur in Burke's or any other peerage, knightage or companionage. Nor is it found in any easily available English or American histories; but if the curious inquirer will delve into old collections of biography or into American histories written in the middle of the last century, he will soon encounter the brothers Ebenezer and Jonathan *Elmer*, of Cumberland county, New Jersey. They were Revolutionary pamphleteers, organizers of Revolutionary militia, surgeons and officers in command of troops throughout the Revolution, members of Congress and fierce debaters of a hundred stirring issues of their times, enjoying a fame and popularity that is easier to understand than their present oblivion. The name *Elmer* therefore has such an honorable genealogy that it is time for America's countless *Elmers* to know it and stand up for it.[1]

Elmer is encountered from end to end of the United States, but it seems to be most popular in the Middle West. In 1940, traveling through Central Indiana by automobile, I found that it was in common use there as a greeting-name for strangers.[2] *Waldo*, though it is not unknown elsewhere, is a specialty of New England: it seems to have come in as a surname, but its early history is obscure.[3] In the same way *Truman* is mainly found in the Pennsylvania German country and its colonies, *Clay* in Kentucky, *Randolph* in Virginia,

---

[1] In Defense of *Elmer* (editorial), Jan. 18, 1935. If *Elmer* was actually derived from the surname of these brothers it was probably made popular by the fact that it was borne by Col. Ephraim *Elmer* Ellsworth, the first hero of the Civil War, killed at Alexandria, Va., May 24, 1861. As a contraction of the Saxon *Ethelmer*, meaning noble and renowned, it was listed by Camden in 1674. Weekley, in Jack and Jill; London, 1939, p. 34, relates it to *Aylmer*, a not uncommon German given-name, though not a saint's name. Both *Aylmer* and *Elmer* are extremely rare in England, but the latter is in sixty-first place on the Newton frequency list of American given-names, and thus stands above *Franklin*, *Chester*, *Harvey* and *Lloyd*. Some day there may be an American saint named *Elmer*.

[2] In the early editions of his American Spelling-Book Noah Webster listed "the most usual names of men." His list did not include *Elmer* nor was there any mention of *Washington*, *Jefferson* or *Franklin*, but *Bennet*, *Bradford*, *Clark* and *Luther* were included.

[3] It is of German origin, and Reclams Namenbuch; Leipzig, 1938, says that it is a shortened form of *Walderich*, the root of which is *walten*, meaning sway or rule. See also Jack and Jill, by Ernest Weekley; London, 1939, p. 45.

Harlan in Iowa [1] and *Pinckney* in South Carolina.[2] On the origin of *Chester* as a given-name (it has been borne by one President of the United States) I can throw no light. The names of the Protestant heroes, *Luther, Calvin* and *Wesley*, have become so common in the United States that they are often borrowed by immigrants of non-British stock, usually in an attempt to Americanize names they have brought with them, *e.g., Wesley* for the Czech *Václav*.[3] All three sometimes appear in Catholics, though Canon 761 forbids them, just as it forbids *Jupiter, Mohammed* and *Satan*.[4]

Though the English invented the use of surnames as given-names, and have acquired a large répertoire of them, they make less frequent and less bold additions to it than we do. Nevertheless, such additions are not unknown among them, as the cases of *Rudyard* Kipling, *Nassau* W. Senior, *Hartley* Coleridge, *Hallam* Tennyson, *Aldous* Huxley, *Almroth* Wright and *Garnet* Wolsley bear witness.[5] Where they run ahead of us is in the multiplication of given-names, sometimes all of them saints' names but usually a mixture of saints' names and family names. Those of the Duke of Windsor are *Edward Albert Christian George Andrew Patrick David*, and those of the Earl of Carrick are *Theobald Walter Somerset Henry*. The American custom of giving a boy his mother's surname as a middle-name originated in England, but is now far more widespread in this country. Many girls are similarly named, and in the South, at least, some are given surnames as their first-names, *e.g., Sidney* and *Beverly*. The English eschew the American custom whereby

---

[1] Iowa Personal Names, by Jerome C. Hixson, *Words*, Jan., 1937, p. 22. James *Harlan* (1820–99) was an Iowan who became Secretary of the Interior in Lincoln's Cabinet. His daughter married Lincoln's son Robert. There is an account of him in my Prejudices: First Series; New York, 1919, pp. 249–50.

[2] Dr. Raven I. McDavid, Jr., tells me that *Pinckney* is oftenest encountered in the Charleston area, along with *Heyward, Rutledge, Ashmead, Huger* and *Pringle. Hampton* and *Moultrie* are common throughout the State. The Carolina Baptists commemorate two of their heroes in *Broadus* and *Boyce*. The Irish, in the South as elsewhere, often use *Emmet* in honor of the patriot, Robert *Emmet*, hanged Sept. 20, 1803. *Emmet* is not a saint's name, but the Catholic priests apparently pass it as a variant of *Emeric*, which is.

[3] See AL4, p. 511 and 513.

[4] *Luther* stands in one hundred-and-fourth place on the Newton list. It is thus above *Mark, Vincent,* and *Christian*, and far above *Washington*, which has been dropping out of late.

[5] The use of surnames as middle names is relatively common, *e.g.*, J. *Ramsay* MacDonald, Andrew *Bonar* Law and William *Ewart* Gladstone.

a woman, at marriage, drops her baptismal middle-name and substitutes her maiden surname. This custom was launched, though perhaps not established, before the Civil War.[1] After Harriet Elizabeth Beecher, the sister of Henry Ward Beecher, married the Rev. Calvin E. Stowe in 1836 she thus dropped the *Elizabeth* in her name and substituted *Beecher*. Said an English commentator in 1867, apparently forgetting (or unaware) that Mrs. Stowe no longer used *Elizabeth*:

> It is not a bad plan for girls to have only one name, so that they may retain their maiden surname after their marriage, as that honored lady, Mrs. Harriet *Beecher* Stowe, has done.[2]

But this English commendation of Mrs. Stowe's example has not been followed by imitation.[3] Nor does an English grass-widow, on getting rid of her husband, *John*, cease, in the American fashion, to be Mrs. *John* Smith and become Mrs. *Jones* Smith, the *Jones* being her maiden surname. The American custom of representing a middle name by its simple initial, though it is not altogether unknown in Britain, is not common, and such a form as *George B.* Shaw would strike most Englishmen as odd. Said Simeon Strunsky in one of his "Topics of the Times" columns in the New York *Times:*[4]

> This middle initial in American personal names continues to puzzle the British mildly and amuses them enormously. The late G. K. Chesterton was always writing about American multi-millionaires called *Philoxenus K. Hunks*, in which most of the fun was in the middle *K*. The serious Englishman simply drops the middle letter and speaks of Mr. *Myron* Taylor or Mr. *William* Tilden, Jr. When an American spells out his middle name, as in William *Allen* White or James *Branch* Cabell the English drop the first name and say *Allen* White or *Branch* Cabell. The gentleman from Emporia still calls himself *William*, but Mr. Cabell has actually gone over to the British practice and dropped his *James*.[5] The practice is becoming common over here.
>
> We must not call it British obtuseness. Perhaps the people over there are misled by the habit of our Presidents, *Grover* Cleveland, *Woodrow* Wilson

---

1 The anonymous author of Our Given Names, *Putnam's Monthly*, Jan., 1855, p. 59, said that it originated among the Quakers.

2 *Happy Hours*, reprinted in *Every Saturday* (Boston), June 8, 1867, p. 716.

3 An American who married a Bermudian lady tells me that when she adopted her maiden surname as a middle-name and returned to Bermuda her bank there refused to cash her checks and that when she applied for a renewal of her passport she had to resume her maiden given-names.

4 Aug. 3, 1938.

5 Cabell later restored the *James* White died in 1944.

and *Calvin* Coolidge; so the British fail to see why not *Myron* Taylor or *William* Bullitt.[1]

Camden says that second given-names were "rare in England" in his time, *c.* 1605, though common in the Catholic countries. James I had been christened *Charles James* and his son was *Henry Frederick*, but it was not until his other son, later Charles I, married *Henrietta Maria* of France in 1625 that they came into any popularity. Even so, they were confined for a long while to the gentry. In America they were adopted only slowly. The first graduate of Harvard to have one is said to have been *Anmi Ruhamah* Corlet, who set up as a schoolmaster at Plymouth, Mass., in 1672. Mr. Gustavus Swift Paine, of Southbury, Conn., who has made an extensive study of nomenclature on Cape Cod, tells me that middle names were not in general use there until late in the Eighteenth Century. Before then, he says,

the naming of children was something like this: Frequently, but not always, the first son was named after the father's father or the mother's father; the first daughter was named after the father's mother or the mother's mother; the second son and daughter were named after the grandparents previously neglected; then the next children were named after the father and mother. If a child died in infancy its name was often repeated for the next child of that sex, and sometimes three or four were thus given the same name successively. Some children were named after brothers and sisters, uncles and aunts, of the parents. When middle names came in, the mother's family name was often thus preserved in the naming of offspring. Sometimes, however, a child was named after an admired friend or distant relative.

Of all the remembered worthies of the early days only *John Quincy* Adams,[2] *Robert Treat* Paine and the two Virginia Lees, *Richard Henry* and *Francis Lightfoot*, had middle names,[3] and of the first seventeen Presidents only *John Quincy* Adams, *William Henry* Harrison and *James Knox* Polk. They were more numerous among the literati, *e.g.*, *James Fenimore* Cooper, *Nathaniel Parker* Willis, *Francis Scott* Key, *Charles Brockden* Brown and *William Ellery* Channing, but so late as 1859 they were still rare enough in the general population, even on the educated level, for a writer in

---

[1] Usually *Myron C.* and *William C.* in the United States. *Cf.* John D. Rockefeller.

[2] He was named after Josiah *Quincy,* who had been associated with his father, John Adams, in the defense of the British soldiers implicated in the Boston massacre of March 5, 1770.

[3] *John Paul* Jones was originally *John Paul;* he added the *Jones* for reasons still undetermined.

Harper's Magazine to be arguing that they should be bestowed more frequently. He said:

> We might very easily, and perhaps wisely, revive the Roman usage, and give children, besides their own proper name and that of the family, a middle name, taken from the most important ancestor or the most characteristic branch that has been grafted into the family tree. No harm would be done if several, or even all the children had the same middle name. The mother's own family name may furnish the needed cognomen; and if variety is needed, it may be, according to a frequent classic usage, found in the name of the father's mother or the mother's mother, so as to perpetuate in the children the ancestral surnames of the paternal and maternal side. Such a custom does good by cherishing a proper family feeling, and suggesting the important truth that a man's blood is a fact significant enough to be looked after, whether to correct failings or to encourage virtues that run in its arteries.[1]

In late years there have been three curious tendencies in the naming of American children: (*a*) the growing popularity of nicknames as given-names, (*b*) the bestowal of mere initials on boys instead of names, and (*c*) the fashion for inventing new and unprecedented names for girls, often of an unearthly and supercolossal character. All three tendencies are most marked among the evangelical tribesmen of the South and Southwest. Until the political explosion of 1946 the Texan who served as Speaker of the House of Representatives, officially the third in rank among all American statesmen, described himself in the Congressional Directory as *Sam* — not as *Samuel* but as plain *Sam* —, and under his eye, when an appropriation bill was on its passage and all hands crowded up to vote, were two other *Sams*, five *Freds*, four *Joes*, two *Eds*, two *Wills*, a *Pat*, a *Pete*, a *Ben*, a *Mike*, a *Sol*, a *Thad*, a *Fritz*, a *Dan*, a *Jack*, a *Nat*, a *Jed*, a *Jere*, a *Jerry*, a *Cliff*, a *Newt* and a *Harve*. Many of these homespun Hampdens succumbed to the explosion aforesaid, but even in the Eightieth Congress, with its Republican majority,[2] there were five *Freds*, three *Joes*, two *Sams*, two *Mikes*, and a *Jack*, a *Wat*, an *Abe*, a *Walt*, a *Si*, a *Cliff*, a *Jere*, a *Ben*, an *Ed*, a *Chet*, a *Hal*, a *Pete*, a *Jay*, a *Ray*, a *Toby*, a *Tom*, a *Harry*, a *Sid*, a *Harve*, a *Jamie* and a *Runt*,[3] though *Sam* the Speaker had returned to the floor and was displaced by a sedate *Joseph* from Massachusetts.

---

[1] Editor's Table, Dec., 1859, p. 122.

[2] Republican politicians are usually much more decorous than Democrats, not only in their names but also in their dress, rhetoric, and eating and boozing habits. See my Making a President; New York, 1932, pp. 8–9.

[3] For this gentleman see *American Speech*, April, 1946, p. 84, n. 7.

Nor were all of these bob-tailed brethren Southerners: some came from the outposts of Biblical science in the upper Middle West and on the Pacific coast and several actually emanated from Pennsylvania, New Jersey and New York.

It is in the South, however, that such stable-names are most frequently conferred upon he-babies at the sacrament of baptism. I turn to the Register of the Texas Christian University for 1942-43 and find two *Joes*, two *Dons*, a *Jack*, a *Fred*, a *Herb*, a *Sam*, a *Harry* and a *Bob* among the students listed upon a single page.[1] I linger a bit in the same instructive work and find an *Ed*, a *Dan* and a *Harry* among the trustees and a *Lew*, a *Mack*, a *Fred* and a *Will* on the faculty. I reach into my collectanea and bring forth a *Lum*,[2] an *Artie*, an *Andy*, a *Dick*, a *Dolph*, a *Cal*, a *Bennie*, a *Bernie*, a *Charley*,[3] a *Zach*,[4] a *Gene*,[5] a *Billie*, an *Alex*, a *Louie*, an *Eddie*, a *Jimmie*, an *Archie*, a *Terry*,[6] a *Phil*, a *Link*, a *Jeffie*,[7] a *Josh*,[8] a *Larry*, a *Sammy*,[9] a *Hy*, a *Jess*,[10] a *Nels*,[11] a *Jed*,[12] a *Nat*,[13] a *Bert*, a *Fritz*, a *Johnnye*,[14] a *Wash*,[15] an *Edd*,[16] a *Ned*,[17] an *Ollie*[18] and a *Gus*.[19] Nearly all these names

---

[1] p. 149.
[2] Oklahoma City *Oklahoman*, Sept. 16, 1945. The name of a Baptist pastor, so appearing in a wedding notice. Apparently an abbreviation of *Columbus*.
[3] A captain in the Regular Army, promoted from first lieutenant June 12, 1940.
[4] On the faculty of the Georgia Teachers College, May, 1946.
[5] Appointed a second lieutenant in the Marines, June 5, 1946.
[6] The last seven were made ensigns in the Navy, June 5, 1946.
[7] The last three are contributed by Mr. E. P. Rochester, of San Antonio, Tex. *Link* is apparently a shortened form of *Lincoln*. An eminent Arkansas statesman was the Hon. *Jeff* Davis (1862-1913). He was Governor of the State from 1900 until 1907 and one of its United States Senators from the latter year until his death.
[8] The Hon. *Josh* Lee was a Senator from Oklahoma, 1937-43. While he was in the Senate he so described himself in the Congressional Directory, but in Who's Who in America he appeared as *Joshua* Bryan. It is thus probably unfair to count him.
[9] Public Records and Vital Statistics, Oklahoma City *Oklahoman*, March 7, 1946.
[10] The last two are from a list of residents of Elwood, Ind., printed in *Life*, Aug. 26, 1940, p. 2.
[11] From *Nelson*, possibly influenced by *Nils*.
[12] The Hon. *Jed* Johnson, of Oklahoma, was a member of the Seventy-eighth Congress.
[13] The Hon. *Nat* Patton is a statesman of Texas.
[14] The last three belong to members of the Linguistic Society of America.
[15] For *Washington*. I am indebted here to Mr. James F. Rennicks, of Camden, Ark.
[16] *Edd* Kiespert was charged with reckless driving in Oklahoma City, June 19, 1941.
[17] The Hon. *Ned* R. Healy, of California, was a member of Congress in 1946.
[18] The Hon. *Ollie* M. James (1871-1919) was a member of Congress from Kentucky, 1903-13, and a Senator from 1913 until his death.

come from official records, in which both given-names and surnames are recorded with care.[1]

The custom of giving boys simple initials instead of given-names [2] is not quite new, but it seems to have been growing rapidly of late, especially in the South. The President of the United States at the time I write is the Hon. Harry S. Truman of Missouri, whose middle initial, according to the Associated Press,

is just an initial — it has no name significance. It represents a compromise by his parents. One of his grandfathers had the first-name of *Solomon;* the other, *Shippe.* Not wanting to play favorites the President's parents decided on the *S*.[3]

Mr. Truman was born in 1884, when the custom under discussion was in its cradle days, but he had forerunners. One of them may have been U. S. Grant, for Captain Charles King says in "The True Ulysses S. Grant," published in 1915: "Grant was never formally baptized until late in life, and then, by his own choice, as *Ulysses S.* He would not take the full [middle] name of *Simpson* [the surname of his mother], but elected to be baptized as he had been so long and well known to the nation."[4] In the generation

---

19 An ensign in the Navy. *Congressional Record*, May 13, 1946, p. 5017.

1 Other examples: *Joe Ben* Jackson, a regent of the University of Georgia in Talmadge days; *Will* Rogers and his politician son of the same name; *Tom* Peete Cross, professor of English and comparative literature at the University of Chicago, to whom the Aug., 1945 issue of *Modern Philology* was dedicated. One from England: the Right Rev. *Tom* Longworth, bishop suffragan of Pontefract. The Hon. *Tom* Clark, of Texas, Attorney-General of the United States as I write, seems to have been baptized *Thomas Campbell*, but he switched to *Tom* as he rose in public responsibilities.

2 Given-name is an Americanism, traced by the DAE to 1827 and apparently in use in New England some time before. The NED Supplement's first example of its use in Great Britain is from a Scottish novel by S. R. Crockett (1860–1914), published in 1895. In England *Christian-name* is still in general use, though it has been omitted from many official forms since World War I as a result of protests by Jews. See Strange Names, London *Observer*, Sept. 6, 1936.

3 Dispatch from Washington, April 12, 1945. I am informed by Mr. Truman's secretary, Charles G. Ross, that the full name of his paternal grandfather was Anderson *Shippe* Truman and that of his maternal grandfather Solomon Young.

4 There is some conflict in testimony regarding Grant's given-names. His father, Jesse Grant, said in The Early Life of General Grant, New York *Ledger*, March 14, 1868, that he "was christened *Hiram Ulysses*, but was always called by the latter name." When he was appointed to West Point, the congressman who named him, one Hamer, mistakenly entered him as *Ulysses Simpson*, misled by the fact that *Simpson* was his mother's maiden name and that there was another son named *Simpson* in the family. "My son,"

478   The American Language: Supplement II

between Grant's and Truman's there were a number of conspicuous Americans bearing initials as given names, *e.g.*, *W J* (no periods) McGee, the anthropologist (1853-1912), and *D-Cady* Herrick, candidate for the governorship of New York in 1904 (1846-1926). Also, there have been others among Mr. Truman's contemporaries, *e.g.*, Ferris *J* Stephens, curator of the Babylonian collection at Yale;[1] Dr. *J* Milton Cowan, secretary of the Linguistic Society of America, who signs himself *J M.*;[2] *J* Spencer Weed, former president of the National Horse Show; *DR* Scott, of the University of Missouri;[3] Mrs. *Bj* Kidd, secretary of the Advertising Federation of America and a well-known writer of and on advertising,[4] and the late *Ed L* Keen, vice-president of the United Press.[5] But the fashion

---

said the father, "tried in vain afterward to get it set right by the authorities." Hamlin Garland says in his Ulysses S. Grant: His Life and Character; New York, 1898, pp. 30-31, that when Grant set off for West Point and noted that his trunk bore the initials H.U.G., he feared that the other cadets would nickname him *Hug*, and so registered as *Ulysses Hiram*. This seemed to pass official scrutiny, but when he proposed to change further to *Ulysses Simpson* permission was refused. But he told the other cadets that *Ulysses Simpson* was his true name, and they nicknamed him *Uncle Sam* and *Sam*. I am indebted here to Mr. Lloyd Lewis, who refuses on the advice of counsel to choose between these discordant stories.

1 Mr. Stephens, like Mr. Truman, got his middle initial by compromise. His mother desired that he have no given-name save her own surname, but family pressure induced her to consent to *J*, derived from *James* and *Jefferson*, the given-names of his two grandfathers.

2 Dr. Cowan tells me that his father, whose given-name was *James* and who was the son of another *James*, favored bestowing the name on *his* son, but that the son's mother objected. They compromised on the initial, with the understanding that its bearer could fill it out later if he so desired. He says: "I never considered the matter of sufficient importance to do anything about it."

3 He writes: "My father's name was *David Roland* Scott. I was given his two initials as a given-name. The problem of translating it into written language was left to me. The form I use was not a matter of positive choice but rather the result of unwillingness to use any other form."

4 *Editor & Publisher*, Feb. 1, 1947, p. 17: "Christened *Elizabeth Jane*, she grew up as *Betty Jane*. In the business world she signed interoffice correspondence *BJK*, and from that achieved the pen-name of *Bj*."

5 He was christened *Edward Legget*, but always used *Ed L*. To the list might be added *Will-A* Clader, of Philadelphia (AL4, p. 517), and *Will-B* Hadley, of the same city. Men without any given-names at all are by no means unknown. One was Dr. Gatewood, a Chicago surgeon. See Dr. Gatewood Dies; Never Had a First Name, New York *Herald Tribune*, May 24, 1939. Another was Tifft, who carried on business in New York under the style of *Tifft Bros.* for many years. He wrote to me in 1939: "I have never had a first name, nor considered one." A third

for giving boys initials instead of given-names did not make any progress among the plain people until the interval between the two World Wars. By the time World War II was on us it had developed so vastly that the Army and Navy had to devise means of dealing with it, to avoid uncertainty and confusion. The Navy's plan was to distinguish between simple initials and those representing actual names by enclosing the former in quotation marks, without periods, *e.g.*, "*C*" "*L*" Keedy, Frank "*A*" Downs, Harold "*B*" "*J*" Barnes, Herbert J. "*A*" Hillson and John "*C*" S. Coffin.[1] The Army, in the early days of World War II, marked off the bearers of initials by inserting (*IO*), *i.e.*, initials only, between the initials and the surnames, and used (*NMI*), *i.e.*, no middle initial, after the given-names of those who had but one. But by Army Regulation No. 345-1, March 11, 1944, these marks were abandoned, and *John James Jones* and *J J Jones* both became *Jones, J. J.*[2]

The craze for afflicting girl babies with bizarre and unheard of given-names is a phenomenon of relatively recent years and is principally manifest, as I have noted, in the South and the rural Middle West, but it appeared sporadically in the North before the Civil War, and the swarming of the underprivileged before and during World War II carried it to the Pacific Coast. In a list of "the most usual names" of American women, published in an 1814 edition of Webster's Spelling Book the 69 names given included such old favorites as *Ann, Dorothy, Elizabeth, Helen, Jane, Katharine, Margaret* and *Mary*, along with such Puritan survivals as *Abigail, Deborah, Faith, Priscilla, Prudence* and *Temperance*, but the utmost advance of fancy forms was represented by *Clarissa, Huldah* and *Susannah*, none of them novel. In 1834, however, Longworth's Directory listed *Aletta, Blandina, Coritha, Dovinda, Elima, Hilah, Keturah, Parnethia* and *Zina*.[3] This was a beginning, and in a little while there were contemporary Connecticut records of *Minuleta, Typhosa, Irista, Zeriah* and *Wealthena* — all of them worthy of the best efforts of an Oklahoma mother today.[4] Other name-lists of the

who uses no given-name is Arki-Yavensonne, manager of the Hotel Fensgate in Boston.

1 I take these examples from the *Congressional Record*, June 10, 1946, pp. 6707-11. I am indebted here to Mr. H. Bartlett Wells.
2 I am indebted for a copy of this regulation to Major-General Edward F. Witzell, the Adjutant General.
3 I am indebted for this to Dr. Joseph M. Carrière, of the University of Virginia.
4 For these I am indebted to Mr. Lockwood Barr, of New York.

1840–60 period show *Rodintha, Finette, Sula, Delvina, Luzertta, Auria, Calina, Milma,*[1] *Isaphene, Algeline, Levantia* and *Philena.*[2] After the Civil War there was a great access of romanticism in all departments of American life, and the naming of infants marched shoulder to shoulder with the crocheting of tidies and the jig-saw adornment of suburban villas. Says Van Wyck Brooks:

> The new age was Hellenistic and it was also Tennysonian. . . . Steeped as it was in all the poets, Greek, German, French and English, it was losing the Hebraic flavor, although it preserved the Hebrew names when these were euphonious also. . . . One observed a similar change in the country districts, where the Hebraistic imagery was dying also. The country-people had vaguer standards, but they too longed for something pretty and were not concerned to scrutinize its source and value. They sometimes invented names that struck them as having associations with the classical world or the world of the poets and romancers. In these less critical regions, one encountered such names as *Liverius, Lurella, Lucina, Levina, Zepheretta, Loretta* and *Zerrilla.*[3]

The same madness showed itself in England, and in 1882 a writer in the *Cornhill Magazine*[4] was denouncing such "inventions of ignorance" as *Almetana, Annarenia, Berdilia, Elderline, Fortituda, Henerilta, Margelina, Perenna* and *Ulelia.* In this country the new fashion was short-lived in the Northeast, but it went into the Southwest and West with the immigration of the post-Civil War period, and there it began to flourish after 1900. Before then it was apparently only a feeble growth, for lists of frontier women born before 1890 show only a few of the more grotesque names, though such diminutives as *Lovie, Dolly, Hattie* and *Nellie* are numerous.[5] Just where and when the current epidemic got its start I do not know, but it must have been south of the Potomac and west of the Alle-

---

author of a history of clock-making in Bristol, Conn.

[1] These were unearthed from New Hampshire records by Mr. Paul St. Gaudens.

[2] The last four were found at the Ontario Female Seminary, Canandaigua, N. Y., in 1841 by an English traveler, J. S. Buckingham. I am indebted here to Mr. Charles J. Lovell.

[3] New England: Indian Summer — 1865–1915; New York, 1940, p. 149.

[4] Oddities of Personal Nomenclature, reprinted in the *Eclectic Magazine,* April, 1882, p. 533.

[5] Many examples are to be found in Belles and Beaux of 40 Years Ago, by J. Marvin Hunter, *Frontier Times* (Bandera, Texas), March, 1944, pp. 269–73. In the *Century Magazine,* March, 1888, pp. 809–10, E. W. Denison complained bitterly against "the strange fatuity which makes grown-up women, and business women at that, announce themselves to the world as *Jennie, Mattie, Maggie,* etc., *ad nauseam.*" "How can they help seeing," he demanded, "the increased dignity of *Jane* and *Martha* and *Margaret?*" This fashion did not last long.

Proper Names in America

ghanies. With its center in Oklahoma, it now has fastnesses in Texas and the Deep South, and there are outposts stretching all the way from up-State New York to the Los Angeles region of California. It has gained little local headway in any of the large cities east of the Mississippi, but some of them, *e.g.*, Chicago, Detroit and Baltimore, acquired large colonies of Okie and Linthead females bearing its stigmata during World War II. Perhaps it will be most profitable, before undertaking a discussion of the anatomy and physiology of such names, to give a somewhat extensive list of them. The following, though some of them may seem almost impossible, are all typical. They were mainly gathered in the Southwest, and all of them are supported by printed sources, though I have omitted references in most cases.[1]

Adenesia	Ahmelda	Alfa [5]	Aloha
Adula	Alapluma [2]	Alga	Aloyd
Adyhon	Alcarla [3]	Aliene [6]	Alsenatha
Aerielle	Alease [4]	Alla Jo	Altamease [7]
Agnella	Alexanderene	AlMeda	Alto

[1] I am heavily indebted here to Miss D. Lorraine Yerkes, of Chicago, a diligent collector of American onomastica. She has got together a collection on cards, mainly gathered from newspapers and telephone directories, that runs to many thousands of examples, and has generously put it at my disposal. I have also had access to an unpublished Prolegomena in Arte Onomastica, by the Right Rev. J. B. Dudek, whose previous studies in American English contributed so much to the various editions of AL4 and to Supplement I. Various other readers who have helped me are mentioned in the footnotes to the following list. Others who should be added are Mrs. Ethel Austin, of Granby, Conn.; J. C. Bibb, Jr., of New Orleans; Miss Alice S. Emery, of Taunton, Mass.; Frank Field, of Johnson City, Tenn.; Mrs. J. P. Gardner, of Lexington, Ky.; Miss Marjorie Gardner, of Baltimore; Lester Hargrett, of Washington; William S. Hoffman, of State College, Pa.; Miss Charlotte Matson, of Minneapolis; James Cowden Meyers, of Ridgewood, N. J.; Mrs. Charles I. Mosier, of Gainsville, Fla.; Mrs. Douglas Rigby, of New York City; Miss Elizabeth Rigby, of Putney, Vt.; Mrs. John W. Robertson, of Livermore, Calif.; E. P. Rochester, of San Antonio, Texas; Hyder R. Rollins, of Cambridge, Mass.; Mrs. Fred. Schmitt, of Oak Park, Ill.; Mrs. F. W. Schnirring, of New York City; Miss Esther Smith, of Lonaconing, Md.; Mrs. Wellman Topham, of Belmont, Calif.; Mrs. Mary M. Webb, of Fort Lauderdale, Fla.; and Howard M. Wilson, of New York City.

[2] Reported from Cortez, Colo., by Mr. Don Bloch, 1945.

[3] Oklahoma City *Times*, July 24, 1945.

[4] From *Alice* or *Elise*. Other forms: *Aleese, Allece, Aliece, Alyce, Alys, Aylisse*.

[5] Probably from *Alfred*. Also — *Alfredia, Alfretta*.

[6] One of the many forms of *Aileen*. Others are *Aleyne, Alieen, Alleen, Allene, Alleyne, Aleene, Aeileen, Erleen, Erlene* and *Ilene*.

[7] Found in Jacksonville, Fla.

Al Verne	Argeree	Arvigne	Avola
Amasca [1]	Argigene	Arzonia	Aytla [22]
Amerette	Arind	Arylne	Azadia
Aminnia	Arjesta	Asenath	Azuba [23]
Andina [2]	Arlenzor [8]	Atha	Azuna [24]
Ana [3]	Arloine	Attelia [15]	Bardiene
Anajean [4]	Armadilla	Aubrigene	Bashie [25]
Angelle	Armemaryvetta [9]	Auburn	Be Ann
Anniece [5]	Armilda	Au Dell	Beatfred [26]
Anthonette	Armista [10]	Audery [16]	Begonia
Aola	Armderdeen [11]	Aulana	Belziazona [27]
Apalonia	Armyl	Aura	Benenia [28]
Apple	Arnez [12]	Austaphine	Bennie Mae
Ara	Arsula [13]	Australia [17]	Berdella
Arazona [6]	Artesia	Authalene [18]	Berna Dean [29]
Arcelia	Arthurene [14]	Autice [19]	Beronest
Ardeal	Artonsia	Avayd [20]	Berry Jayne
Arene [7]	Arvesta	Ava Marie [21]	Berthie [30]

1 Reported from California by Mrs. G. A. Meek.
2 Probably from *Andy*. An analogue is *Andrice*.
3 *Anah, Aner* and *Anner* are also reported.
4 This is one of many analogues, e.g., *Anajean, Analon, Anajoe, Anamarie, Aniceta, Anliza, Anneene,* etc.
5 Divorced in Oklahoma City, Oct. 11, 1945. Other forms are *Anneice, Annice* and *Annyce*.
6 Found in Jacksonville, Fla., 1945.
7 A new spelling of *Irene?*
8 Found in Jacksonville, Fla., 1944.
9 Found on Cape Cod by Mr. Gustavus Franklin Paine.
10 *Armistice* is also encountered.
11 Divorced at Oklahoma City, March 6, 1946.
12 From *Inez?*
13 From *Ursula?*
14 Enrolled at the State Teachers College, Florence, Ala., 1938–39. On the same roll were an *Adrene*, a *Waltherene*, an *Olene*, an *Olgalene* and a *Willene*. At the same time an *Ethelene* was enrolled at the similar college at Troy, Ala. Simultaneously the Sam Houston State Teachers College at Huntsville, Texas, had an *Earlene* and a *Haleene*. *Arthuree* and *Arthuritus* are also recorded.
15 From *Ottilie?*
16 Apparently an attempt at *Audrey*. Other forms encountered are *Audie, Audra, Autra* and *Audrae*.
17 Described by the San Francisco *News*, April 20, 1938, as "an old-time client" of the local social workers.
18 From the Ozarks.
19 From Alabama.
20 Oklahoma City *Times*, Dec. 7, 1945.
21 Reported by Mr. Kenneth Rockwell, of Arlington, Texas.
22 Reported from the Sacramento Valley, Calif.
23 Reported from California by Mrs. G. A. Meek.
24 Found in Florida by Dr. Mary Parmenter.
25 From Iowa. Mr. Charles B. Anderson of New York tells me that this is short for *Bathsheba*.
26 A daughter of *Frederick* H. and *Beatrice* Haas. Her father died at Deer Park, L. I., Jan. 18, 1945.
27 Reported from Jacksonville, Fla.
28 Reported from Baltimore by Mr. Francis R. St. John.
29 From *Bernardine?*
30 Reported from Western New York in *Dialect Notes*, Vol. III, Part VI, 1910, p. 437. A pet-name form of *Bertha*. I have also encountered *Birtha, Burtha, Beartha, Byrtha* and *Berthella*.

Proper Names in America 483

Besma [1]	Bozana	Canaliza	Charla [18]
Besshunter [2]	Brazell [11]	Candelaria	Cherubim [19]
Betress	Breza	Capitola	Chestannie
Bette [3]	Brightie	Carbena	Chineeah
Bewsie	Brooxie	Carlee [14]	Chizella
Bezzie [4]	Brunetta	Carnell	Chlorine [20]
Bibianna	Brytha [12]	Carrine	Christoria
Billye [5]	Buena Vista [13]	Casindania	Chyna
Birdeen [6]	Byioba	Catharan [15]	Cirrelda
Blanka	Bythella	Catrisa	Civilla
Bleba [7]	Calara	Cecyle	Clalie
Bobby [8]	Calista	Celethal	ClarEtta [21]
Bocalvia [9]	Cama	Cementa [16]	Clata
Boncilla	Camolia	Cerilla [17]	Clazene [22]
Bonnie [10]	Camyada	Chairynne	Cleatus [23]

1 Providence (R.I.) *Journal*, May 29, 1935.
2 Found in Chicago.
3 A common spelling of *Betty*, along with *Bettye*, *Betti*, *Betta* and *Bettha*. All of them appear in many double names, e.g., *Bette Lou*, *Betty Fae*, *Bettye Joe* and *Bettijune*.
4 Apparently a recherché form of *Bessie*, a shade higher in tone than *Bessye*.
5 Also *Byllye*.
6 The fancy forms of the primitive *Birdie* are innumerable, e.g., *Birdell*, *Birdelle*, *Birdella*, *Birdellis*, *Birdine*, *Byrdice*, *Byrdyce*, *Byrdell*, *Byrdella*, *Byrdalice*, *Byrdalyce*, *Birda*, *Birdena*, and *Birtie*.
7 Reported from the Cumberland Mountains, *American Speech*, April, 1930, p. 306.
8 A very common girl's name, often used in combination, e.g., *Bobby Jean*. Variants are *Bobba*, *Bobbye*, *Bobbie* and *Boby*.
9 From Georgia. Father: *Calvin*; mother: *Roberta*. Called *Bo*.
10 Often used in combination, e.g., *Bonnie Mae*.
11 Also *Brazelle*, *Braziel* and *Brazielle*.
12 Oklahoma City *Times*, May 24, 1940.
13 Both *Buena* and *Vista* are also used singly.
14 Oklahoma City *Times*, May 24, 1940. The popularity of *Carl* as a boy's name, noted in AL4, p. 506, n. 1, has produced a large crop of feminine variants, e.g., *Carlyne*, *Carla* and *Carlina*. The cognate *Carroll* has produced *Carol*, *Caral*, *Carell*, *Carul*, *Caryl*, *Carriell*, *Carrall*, *Carolie*, etc. See *Karleen*.
15 From Oklahoma. Other common spellings are *Cathern* and *Kathern*.
16 On a headstone at Westminster, Vt. The two sisters of the deceased were *Amenta* and *Belenta*.
17 Reported from Crown Point, Ind.
18 Simple *Charles* is in some use as a girl's name in the South, but apparently nowhere else. Among the feminine derivatives in my collection are *Charlsie*, *Charlcie*, *Charlyne*, *Charlena*, *Charlene*, *Charlis*, *Charlyne*, *Charleye*, *Charelle*, *Charleere*, *Charlaine*, *Charline*, *Charlatta*, *Charlyse*, *Charlye*, *Charlie* and *Chas*.
19 The mother of *Cherubim* E. Lee died at Mt. Vernon, N. Y., Jan. 19, 1945.
20 Headline in the Oklahoma City *Oklahoman*, March 17, 1941: "Mrs. *Chlorine* Craighead Honors Son at Party." Also reported from Alabama.
21 In this and all similar forms the second element is carefully capitalized. This puts a heavy burden on the reporters, copy-readers, compositors and proof-readers of the Oklahoma papers, but they have got used to it.
22 From Leaksville, N. C.
23 An Edmond, Okla., bride, 1945.

484   *The American Language: Supplement II*

Cleopatria [1]	Cozella	De'An [14]	Dixie Lou [22]
Clesta	Crenna	Dee-Dee [15]	Dodis
Clevanel	Cudell	DeKina	Dondeline
Climena [2]	Cylistine	Delavendra	Don Elda
Cloa	Cylvia	Delette	Donna Bee
Clome	Cyra	De Lores [16]	Doozie
CloVera	Dabney [7]	DelRose	Dorabelle
Cly	Dacel	Delymaine	Dorethe [23]
Coita [3]	Daffodil	Demis	Doris Jean [24]
Colita	Daisybee	DeNell [17]	Dorlye
Commoleen	Danny Lou [8]	Deoda	Dorraine
Congetta	Dardanella	Dereen [18]	Doyel
Connace	Darel-Gene [9]	Detta	Druesylla [25]
Cordula	Darlene [10]	Deucie	Drulla
Corean [4]	Darthilda [11]	Dewdrop [19]	Dullere
Cosy	DaRue	Dialtha [20]	Duphemia [26]
Covadonga [5]	Dasy [12]	Dicey Mae [21]	Dura
Coweene [6]	Dawnette [13]	Disa	Dustia

[1] Here, as in many other cases, the spelling follows the local pronunciation.
[2] Providence (R.I.) *Journal*, May 29, 1935.
[3] In a list of students at Oklahoma College for Women, Oklahoma City *Oklahoman*, Sept. 19, 1945.
[4] Other popular spellings of *Corinne* are *Coreen, Coreine, Corienne, Corrine, Corene, Corinn* and *Correne*, not to mention *Korene*. It has also produced *Corilla* and *Corise*.
[5] Reported from Florida.
[6] Also *Coweta*.
[7] A not uncommon girl's name in Virginia.
[8] Oklahoma City *Oklahoman*, Nov. 17, 1946. Names derived from *Daniel* are common, e.g., *Danelle, Dannine, Danna, Danial, Danele, Dannie* and *Dana*.
[9] From *Geraldine*; also *Darel-Jean, Darrell-Gene*, etc.
[10] A common girl's name from Florida to Oregon. Variants: *D'Arline, D'Arlene* and *Darlean*.
[11] From Nebraska.
[12] Also *Dayse*.
[13] Oklahoma City *Oklahoman*, Dec. 2, 1945.
[14] Also *DeAnn* and *DeeAnne*.
[15] Oklahoma City *Oklahoman*, March 27, 1941.
[16] Other forms of *Dolores: De Lauris, Delares, Deloris, Dolorous, Dolaris, Dolorosa* and *Dolorez*.
[17] Reported from Nowata, Okla., by the Oklahoma City *Oklahoman*, May 31, 1940.
[18] Oklahoma City *Times*, May 2, 1941: a graduate of one of the local high-schools.
[19] Married at Oklahoma City, Sept. 14, 1940.
[20] A junior high-school miss in Oklahoma City.
[21] Found in an Alabama orphans' home by Mrs. Ethel Austin, of Granby, Conn.
[22] Oklahoma City *Times*, May 24, 1940. *Dixie* is common both singly and in combination.
[23] From the students' directory of Fresno (Calif.) State College, 1940–41. Many other variants of *Dorothy* are to be found, e.g., *Dorotha, Dorthea, Dortha, Dorathy, Dorethe, Dorothe, Dortho, Dorathe, Dorothye* and *Dorthy*.
[24] Sometimes *Doris* is spelled *Dorris* or *Dorriss*.
[25] A variant of *Drusilla*, from Florida. Others found there are *Druecellar* and *Drewsiller*.
[26] Reported from South Carolina by Mr. Paul St. Gaudens, April 17, 1943.

Proper Names in America 485

Duta	Elpha	Eulice	Fayrene [21]
DuWayne	Elura	Euphia	Faythe
Dynama	Elvaree	Eurah	Feby [22]
Ealeta	Elvis	Eutanna	Felesta
Earthel [1]	Elzada	Eutha [15]	Fema [23]
Easlyn	Ema Jane [7]	Eutris	Fermetta
Echo	Enolia [8]	Euzelle [16]	Ferra
Edgarta	Empo	Evannah	Filleul
Edgealea	Enclyn	Evarista	Fledarea
Edina [2]	Endamile	Evassa	Floay
Edneau	Enrechetto	Evelyene [17]	Flodeen
Eduta	Eola [9]	Everdiena	Floradawn
Eidel	Ermyl	Ever Mae	Florestine
Elah [3]	Ernadine [10]	E-Vetta	Floscella
Elcie [4]	Ernestyne [11]	Evon [18]	Flosye
Electamae [5]	Erneze	Exaverm [19]	Flowanna
Eledice	Esterine [12]	Exolda [20]	Foleeta [24]
Elgretta	Etalea [13]	Ezza	Fomby
Elicious	Ethna	Fae	Foncilla
Elleuvinia [6]	Ethol [14]	Fairy	Fondanell
El Louise	Etna	Fan El	Forsha
Elmonia	Etoyle	Farl	Foy
Elodee	Etrulia	Faucette	Fra
Elore	Euarda	Faynola	Fragoletta [25]

[1] Reported from Franklin, Ind., by Mr. John Jamieson, of New York.
[2] The medieval Latin name of *Edinburgh*, so used by Burns. But here it probably comes from *Edward* or *Edwin*. Other attempts at feminization: *Eddene, Eddis, Edice, Edwarda, Edenia, Edolia, Edonna,* and *Edrin*.
[3] Probably a fancy form of *Ella*.
[4] From *Elsie?*
[5] A dancer figuring in a San Francisco dispatch to *Variety*, dated Sept. 17, 1940.
[6] Found in Colusa county, Calif.
[7] *Emma* seldom appears with two *m*'s. Sometimes it is *Emi, Eme, Emo* or even *Emer*. Common compounds are *Ema Jane* and *Emalou*. More nobby are *Emelda, Emaelera* and *Emelle*. *Emily* produces *Emalee*.
[8] Found in Baltimore by Miss Marjorie Gardner.
[9] Found in Peoria, Ill., by Mr. Fred Hamann.
[10] From western Nebraska.
[11] This and *Ernestein* indicate the prevailing pronunciation of *Ernestine*.
[12] Applied for a divorce in Oklahoma City, Aug. 30, 1945.
[13] Oklahoma City *Times*, May 24, 1940.
[14] Probably an attempt at *Ethel*. *Ethyl, Ethylyn, Ethalene* and *Eythel* also occur.
[15] Charlotte (N.C.) *Observer*, March 24, 1940.
[16] Reported from Colusa county, Calif.
[17] Oklahoma City *Oklahoman*, Oct. 30, 1945. Also *Evelynne, Eveline* and *Evylan*.
[18] *Yvonne?*
[19] Marriage Licenses, Oklahoma City *Oklahoman*, Jan. 11, 1944.
[20] The same, Oct. 7, 1945.
[21] A lady murdered in Arkansas: *Master Detective*, Nov., 1945, p. 34.
[22] *Phoebe?*
[23] Reported from Texas in *Townsfolk*, Chicago, Dec., 1940.
[24] From rural Indiana.
[25] Found in the Ozarks.

Francelia	Ghaska	Gueresy	Idress
Frankie Bell	Ghyneth	Gyilil	Iduma
Franklinina	Gilleen	Hallijean	Ietta
Fray	Girtha [5]	Halloween [12]	Ifla
Freddie Mae	Gladis [6]	Hannora	Ilo
Freelin	Glamora [7]	Harolyne	Imilda
Frema	Glanda	Harrietta	Imojean [21]
Froeda	Glary Ann	Harvesta	Ineda
Gae	Glassie	Hathyel	Iness [22]
Galeen	Glea	Hele	Inolia
Galween	Glenoulia	Henriola [13]	Iovia
Gamelle	Glineva	Heroina [14]	Irealia
Gara	Glinner	Hertasene [15]	Iril
Garguerite [1]	Gloe	Hesba [16]	Isalona
Garnada	Gloriola	Hexie	Isma
Gatha	Glovetta	Hiramette	Isota
Gaylene [2]	Glowrene	Holly Jo	Itealia
Gaynelle	Glucinda	Horlene	Ithama
Gazelle	G'Ola [8]	Horres	Itrice
Geann	Goletha	Hygiene	Iturna
Gearldina [3]	Gommerray	Hosa	Ivan Dell
Gelda	Gondra	Hughzetta	Iverna
Gemmalee	Gradena	Hywana	Iville
Geneal	Grava-Nell [9]	Ibada	Ivynnelle
Genia	Groveline [10]	Icel [17]	Izola
Georgeilein [4]	Guandoln	Iceyphenolia [18]	Jacel
Geronia	Guarito	Iddela	Jackaline [23]
Gesnia	Guela	Idoline [19]	Jackie Jane
Getalea	Guen [11]	Idoree [20]	Jacoba

1 Found in California by Mrs. G. A. Meek, of Oakland.
2 From New Mexico. Her sister is *Joyrene*.
3 With a hard *G*.
4 Oklahoma City *Oklahoman*, Aug. 15, 1945.
5 Reported from Fort Worth, Texas.
6 Other variant spellings of *Gladys* (originally the Welsh *Gwladys*) are *Gladyes*, *Gladdis*, *Gladous* and *Gladyce*.
7 Accent on the second syllable.
8 The death of Mrs. *G'Ola* Nagle, a school-teacher, was reported in the Oklahoma City *Oklahoman*, May 12, 1944.
9 Reported from Lawton, Okla., 1940.
10 *Southwest Courier*, Oklahoma City, May 18, 1940.
11 An attempt at *June?*
12 An applicant for a divorce at Oklahoma City, Sept. 28, 1940.
13 From Los Angeles.
14 A member of the faculty, Georgia Teachers College at Collegeboro, 1946.
15 Participant in a beauty contest in Mississippi, 1945.
16 Reported from New Orleans, 1945.
17 Reported from Iowa, *American Speech*, Oct., 1933, p. 73.
18 Strange Carolina Names, by Burke Davis, Baltimore *Evening Sun*, editorial page, Feb. 26, 1947.
19 Found in Baltimore in 1908.
20 Accented on the last syllable.
21 Apparently from *Imogene*. I have also encountered *Imajane*.
22 *Inez?* Other forms are *Inos* and *Inice*.
23 One of several forms of *Jacqueline*. Others are *Jacklynn*, *Jacquelyn* and *Jacquelynne*.

Proper Names in America 487

Jahala [1]	Jo [6]	Karleen [12]	Lalan
Ja Jaye	Joanita	Kashatta [13]	La Morte
Jamie Lou	JoAnn [7]	Keldora	Lanivine
Janann	Jocelia	Kerry [14]	LaOba
Jarmie	Jodine	Keturah	La Phalene
Jaunelda	Joeeda	Kewpie	Lapriel
Jaunice [2]	Johnah [8]	Kimona	Larada [16]
Jayne	Johnny-v [9]	Kiwanis	Larceny [17]
Jayrene	Joi	Kizize	Lasarian
Jeanita	Joma	Kona	La Terulia
Jearl	Jonnie Lee	Koral	Latrina [18]
Jeeta	Joreath	LaBelle	Lauginia
Jeffanna	Joveta	Lacene	L'Aurelia
Jelessia	JoyRene	Ladelle [15]	Lausia
JeNanne	Jozelpa	LaDellys	Lava [19]
Jennyberry	Juanzell	La Duska	Lavalette [20]
Jeoneta	Julaine	Ladye	LaVassar [21]
Jeoraldean [3]	Juneesia	LaFern	LaVaughne
Jerryline [4]	Juva [10]	Lahoma	La Vieve [22]
Jessoise	Jymme	Lala	Lavisa
Jimmie [5]	Kaloola [11]	La Lahoma	Laweese [23]
J'Nette	Kanzadah	Lalabelle	Lazella [24]

1 Reported from Bartlesville, Okla., by the *Southwest Courier*, June 1, 1940.
2 Oklahoma City *Oklahoman*, Dec. 4, 1943.
3 An Oklahoma City schoolma'am, listed by the Oklahoma City *Times*, May 24, 1940.
4 Reported by Mr. Kenneth Rockwell from Arlington, Texas.
5 In 1944 Miss *Jimmie* Bugg Middleton was treasurer of the National Association of College Women.
6 A favorite name, seldom written *Joe*. It appears either alone or in head-or-tail combinations, e.g., *Billy Jo* and *Jo Verleen*.
7 Oklahoma City *Times*, May 2, 1941.
8 Possibly from *Jonah* but more likely from *John*. Derivatives of *John* are numerous, e.g., *Johnaline, Johnaphene, Johnena, Johnella* and *Johnetta*. Sometimes the masculine form is used without change, though usually with a feminine indicator following, e.g., *John Marie*.
9 Found in California by Mrs. G. A. Meek, of Oakland.
10 *American Speech*, Oct., 1942, p. 173.

11 Found in California by Mrs. G. A. Meek.
12 Variants: *Karla, Karlene, Karldene,* and *Karlette*. See *Carlee*.
13 Found in Arkansas by Mrs. James F. Rennicks.
14 An apparent attempt to gild *Carrie*.
15 An Ardmore, Okla., bride, 1945.
16 Reported from Iowa by Miss Harriet Perley. *Larada's* sisters are *Valora* and *Fama*.
17 Brought out to civilization from the mountains of Tennessee by a traveling bishop. Pronounced *Larcée-ny*.
18 Christian Names in the Cumberlands, by James A. Still, *American Speech*, April, 1930, p. 306.
19 An Oklahoma City schoolma'am.
20 Oklahoma City *Times*, May 24, 1940.
21 Oklahoma City *Oklahoman*, July 1, 1941.
22 On the staff of the Kirksville College of Osteopathy and Surgery, Kirksville, Mo.
23 *Louise?*
24 Reported from Peoria, Ill., by Mr. Fred Hamann.

Lazette
L'Dean [1]
LeAda
Leafy Ella
Leannette
Learlene
Lebita
Ledell
Lee Ona [2]
Legna [3]
Lejitta
Leletia
Lemma
Lendol
Lenva
Leonodine
Leota Glee
Lepha [4]
Lepoline
Leroyal
Letha
Letress
L'Etta
Lettucia
LeTulle

Leumiza
Levala
Levonna [5]
Lexine
Leyetta
Liddane
Ligretta
Lillious
Lincolna [6]
Liora
Livera [7]
Lloa
Lloydine [8]
Loaine
Lo Bella
Loberta
Locust
Loe Mae
Lonzetta
Lorama
LoRayne
Loree
Lorna Jo
Lo-ruhmah
Lotolia

Louah
LouCille
Louiezon
Lounoma
Lousetta [9]
Louwillie
Loventine
Lovelady
LoVina
Lovorn
Loxi
Loy
L'Rue
LuAlice
Luanda
LuCiel [10]
Luda [11]
Luena [12]
Lugarda
Lush
Lutellia
Luttie
Luvna
Luweoda
Luzelle

Lyligh
Lyndyll
Lynovecta
Lyska
Mebele [13]
Macena
Madalyne [14]
Madame [15]
Madora
Mae [16]
Maela
Ma'ene
Maeola
Mafalda
Magalone [17]
Magnease
Mahleen
Maimai
Majel
Malaoa [18]
Malixia
Malma
Malta Jean
Mamel
M'Amis

1 Oklahoma City *Times*, May 2, 1941.
2 *Leona? Lee* is very popular as a second name, as in *Una Lee, Dora Lee*, etc.
3 *Angel* spelled backward. From Virginia.
4 From Elwood, Ind.; *Life*, Aug. 26, 1940.
5 Reported from Marlette, Mich., in *Comfort* (Augusta, Maine), July, 1940.
6 *Lincolna* Summers, aged five, was the subject of a kidnaping scare in Denver, Colo., in 1946.
7 From Sullivan county, New York.
8 Reported from Florida by Mr. Paul St. Gaudens.
9 The first syllable rhymes with *few*. Other forms: *Louza, Louzon, Louzella*, and *Lousella*.
10 Described by the *Covered Wagon*, University of Oklahoma (reprinted in the *New Yorker*, Nov. 26, 1938) as "blond Alpha Chi Omega dream dancer divine."
11 Reported by Mr. Tom C. Mead, of Boulder City, Nev. He says that it is a contraction of *Lucinda*, vice an earlier *Sin*.
12 Murdered at Hampton, Tenn., Jan. 6, 1938 (*True Detective Mysteries*, Sept., 1938, p. 13), along with her sisters *Sonia* and *Roma Jean*.
13 The common variants are *Mable, Mayble, Maybelle* and *Mayble*.
14 Other forms: *Madelline, Madeliene, Madelyn, Madline, Madolene, Madalyne* and *Madlyne*.
15 This comes from Maine, and Mrs. Frederick G. Fassett, Jr., of Cambridge, Mass., tells me that it is pronounced *May-dá-me*.
16 I am informed that this spelling was rare before 1900. The name occurs very frequently in combination, usually as the second element, e.g., *Allie Mae, Fannie Mae*, etc. It is often uttered in address. Often it is assimilated, e.g., *Olamae*.
17 Reported from Alabama.
18 From Minnesota.

Proper Names in America 489

Manaloa [1]	Matina	Meroah	Murva
Manassas [2]	MauDee	Merry Lou	Muzelta
Mandalina	Maudella	Metarie	Myda
Manifee	Maudleigh	Mia	Myricille
Manila	Mauva	Mickey [15]	Mystia
Maomi [3]	Mauzell	Milada	Nadda
Marcalee	Mava	Milca	NaDine
Marcellette	Mavance	Mildren	Nadinola [20]
Mardella	Mavontiene	Millinee	Naevene
Margaline [4]	Maymire	Milta	Naio
Margell	Mayola	Minian	Najala
Margileth	Mayozie	Minnewa	Naparia
Mariedythe	Mazelle	Mirta	Narylyn
Mariel	Mazura [10]	Mocolee	Nasrine [21]
Marijo	McNora	Modaine [16]	Nauvelene [22]
Marine [5]	Mecca [11]	Mohelia	Navelle [23]
Marmette	Media	Molvene	Needa
Marschula	Medrith	Moma	Neketia
Marseille	Mega	Monima	Neldagae
Marsylvia [6]	Melbourine [12]	Monteze	Nelma
Marthamarcella	Melcena	Morveen	Nerva
Martyl	Meniola	Mosetta [17]	Neval
Marvee	Mercidean	Mosiellee [18]	Newana
Marye [7]	Merdelle [13]	Moslyn	Nicoma
Ma'Su	Merdine [14]	Motare	Nieca
Mateel [8]	Merhize	Moyett	Nissie
Matha [9]	Merma	Murdena [19]	Nix

1 From Minnesota.
2 Reported from Leaksville, N. C., by Mr. Durward King.
3 Probably suggested by *Naomi.*
4 From a list of high-school graduates in the Oklahoma City *Times,* May 9, 1941.
5 For *Maureen?*
6 Found on Cape Cod by Mr. Gustavus Franklin Paine.
7 For *Mary* see *Words,* March, 1937, p. 55, and my Treatise on the Gods; New York (revised edition), 1946, pp. 149-50. *Maryea* and *Mayry* are reported from Oklahoma. Many combinations are to be found, *e.g., Marynell, Marylynn.*
8 For *Mathilde.*
9 Oklahoma City *Times,* May 24, 1940.
10 From Missouri. Probably a fancy form of the name of the State.
11 Found in Oakland, Calif.
12 *American Speech,* Oct., 1942, p. 173.
13 *American Speech,* April, 1933, p. 55.
14 A young lady of Altus, Okla. Her sister is *Verdine.* Oklahoma City *Oklahoman,* Sept. 19, 1945.
15 Found in Oklahoma. Variants: *Micki* and *Miki.*
16 Reported from Oakland, Calif.
17 Providence (R.I.) *Journal,* May 29, 1935.
18 From Arkansas. Pronounced *Mossy Lee.*
19 Found in the Providence (R.I.) city directory. The Sideshow, Providence *Journal,* May 29, 1935. See *Merdine.*
20 Reported from New Orleans, 1945.
21 *Nazarene?*
22 Her engagement was announced by the Oklahoma City *Oklahoman,* Feb. 27, 1945.
23 Applied for a divorce in Oklahoma City, Oct. 9, 1945.

490   *The American Language: Supplement II*

Noba	Opaloma	Permelia	Ravola
Nolia [1]	Orabelle	Persotia	Raychel [21]
Nookie	Ordis [6]	Petula	Reasta
Nordamyrth [2]	Orene	Phadalee	ReDonda [22]
Norissa	O'Rhaitia [7]	Phalla	Refolla
Normarie	Orilla	Phaye	Reinette
Norvain	Orr-Lyda	Pheotine	Revola
Nylotis	Orsavilla [8]	Philelle	Rheufina
Nynn	Ortice	Phra [11]	Rhumelle [23]
Oaxim	Oscaretta	Phygenia	Rhygene
Obanon	Ostella	Phylistice [12]	Rocille
Oberzine	Ostenia	Pleasantina	Romalice [24]
O'Dwaine	Othema	Polo [13]	Roseola [25]
Odyle	Otta	Pomalee	Roumaine [26]
Ogalallah	Ova	Prucia [14]	Roxaner
Ogeal	Owaelah	Prunice	Royalene
Okemah	Oyonna	Pyola [15]	Rozetta
Okla	Ozell [9]	Qay	Ruburdia
Olgalene	Paradine	Quaintillia [16]	Rumba Jo
Olinzea	Parzola	Quejette [17]	Ruy
Omadell	Patriola	Queena	Rylda
Omelia	Patti Jo	Quida	Sabra
Onema	Paulala	Rae [18]	Sadelle
Onza [3]	Pava	Ragine [19]	Safronia
Oolooah [4]	Pearline	Ramarion	Saidee [27]
Oota [5]	Pencilla [10]	Raola [20]	Salathia

1 From Mississippi.
2 Reported from the Middle West by Mr. James M. Bowcock, of Richmond, Va.
3 *American Speech*, April, 1930, p. 306.
4 Found in North Carolina by Mrs. Robert L. Morehouse.
5 From the Chicago region.
6 Oklahoma City *Oklahoman*, May 5, 1946.
7 The name of a girl born on a train. Perhaps it was suggested by *all right*.
8 Found in Michigan.
9 Oklahoma City *Times*, May 2, 1941.
10 Found in California by Mrs. G. A. Meek.
11 Found in California.
12 Oklahoma City *Oklahoman*, Dec. 2, 1945.
13 Oklahoma City *Oklahoman*, July 29, 1945.
14 Found in Alabama.
15 Reported from Thomasville, Ga., by Miss Kathryn Tucker.
16 Reported from Alabama by Miss Kathryn Tucker.
17 A student at Mississippi State College for Women in 1920.
18 Apparently from *Ray*. In wide use in combination, *e.g., Edna Rae, Lois Rae*, etc. Sometimes *Rhey*.
19 From Oklahoma. *Ray* plus *gene*, and so pronounced.
20 Reported from Florida by Mr. Paul St. Gaudens.
21 Also *Racheal* and *Rachelle*.
22 Married in Oklahoma City, Dec. 22, 1946.
23 Reported from North Carolina.
24 A contribution from Texas.
25 Many other home-made derivatives of *Rose* are in use, *e.g., Rosia, Rosiena* and *Rosile*.
26 From a list of public school-teachers, Oklahoma City *Times*, May 24, 1940, p. 22.
27 Also *Saidhe* and *Saydhe*.

Proper Names in America

Saline [1]	Swan [9]	Tomi [12]	Uva
Sally Ben	Syreath	Tonkajo [13]	Vadna
Saphrona	Syveta	Toovone [14]	Vae
Satyra [2]	Tahwahnah	Tosa [15]	Valeita
Scharlott	Talicia	Totus	Valerica
Seena	Taloah [10]	Townzella [16]	VaLeta [22]
Serene	Tamora	Traina	Valfred
Sewlliea	Tasceil	Travette	Valla
Sharmeen	TeAta	Trevania	Valoise
Shelby Lee	Teletha	Tryphena [17]	Vandetta
Shelta	Tenya	Twitty	Vangele
Shelvia	Teretha	Twylah [18]	Varbel
Shir Lee [3]	Tesa	Tydfyl	Vardrene
Sibeth	Teyna	Tyi	Varice
Sina [4]	Texana [11]	Uarda	VaRue
Sing [5]	Thallis	Ukdene	Vasoline [23]
Sireen	Tharyn	Ulala	Vaughncille
Sivola [6]	Thava	Ullainee [19]	Vavelle
Sonora	Thella	Ulyssia [20]	Vaye
Srilda	Theral	Uneveigh	Vella [24]
St. Clair [7]	Therica	Urath	Velondia
Stenola [8]	Theyva	Urcell	Velva Jo [25]
Susunah	Thuda	Ureatha [21]	Vema
Suvada	Thurolene	Urlda	Venazulia
Sva	Tolee	Utahna	Veneriece [26]

1 Reported from Leaksville, N. C., by Mr. Durward King.
2 Providence (R.I.) *Journal*, May 29, 1935.
3 Baltimore *Evening Sun*, June 30, 1945.
4 Participant in a beauty contest in Mississippi, 1945.
5 Reported from Houston, Texas, joined to *LeTulle* as a middle-name.
6 Enrolled at the State Teachers College, Jacksonville, Ala., 1938-39.
7 Reported from South Carolina by Dr. Raven I. McDavid, Jr.
8 Oklahoma City *Oklahoman*, Aug. 15, 1945.
9 A teacher in Gainesville, Fla., 1940.
10 Pledged by Em Hil sorority at Chickasha, Okla., Sept. 18, 1945.
11 One of the long series based on *Texas*, e.g., *Texarilla*, *Texola*.
12 Also *Tomme* and *Tommye*. There are many other forms, e.g., *Tomaline*, and *Tommie* is popular in combinations, e.g., *Tommie Ann*.
13 Reported from Kansas by Miss Rachel Ann Nixon. A compound of *Tonk*, the nickname of the bearer's grandfather, and the popular *Jo*.
14 Oklahoma City *Oklahoman*, May 27, 1945.
15 From western Nebraska.
16 Reported from Kentucky in the *Princeton Alumni News*, Nov., 1940.
17 From California.
18 From Minnesota.
19 Found by Mr. Winslow Ames in Illinois.
20 Reported from Baltimore by Mr. Francis R. St. John.
21 Reported from western Maryland.
22 One of three sisters in Bethany, Okla. The others are named *Vela* and *Zoya*.
23 From Alabama.
24 From Iowa. *American Speech*, Oct., 1933, p. 73.
25 Yukon (Okla.) *Sun*, Aug. 8, 1940.
26 *Propeller* (Galesburg, Ill.), Sept. 1, 1943.

Venie [1]	Vonda	Weltha	Yabel [21]
Ver	Vondilee [7]	Willie Mae [16]	Yetza
Verdavelle	Vonnez	Wilsonia	Yondah
Ve Ree	Voy	Wilvarine	Zadean [22]
Verma [2]	Vura	Wimmie [17]	Zadonna [23]
Vermilla	Vyrillia	Windi	Zala
Vernola	Wacile	Winnaretta	Zannis [24]
Veroqua [3]	Wah-Leah	Winnell	Zanola
Vesnelle	Wahlelu [8]	Winola	ZaZelle [25]
Vetelia [4]	Wahneta [9]	Wona	Zdenka [26]
V-Etta	Waive [10]	Wreatha [18]	Zeema
Viadell	Walsena	Wroberta	Zefferine
Vilentia	Wanahda [11]	Wyena	Zelvateen
Vinnierenn	Wanda Verline [12]	Wylvia Jayne [19]	Zemma
Violintta	Wanoka	Wymola	Zenana [27]
Viora	Wanza [13]	Wyneese	Zenoda
Virjama	Warrenetta	Wynelle [20]	Zerietha
Vitoline [5]	Wathena [14]	Wyvine	Zessie
Viviaette [6]	Wauhilla	Xie Mae	Ziba [28]
Vlene	Weeda [15]	Xina	Ziona
Vomera	Welo	Xmay	Zippa [29]

1 Sterling (Kansas) *Bulletin*, Dec. 5, 1946.
2 Found in California by Mrs. G. A. Meek.
3 Married in Chicago, Aug. 18, 1945.
4 *American Speech*, Oct., 1942, p. 173.
5 From Sullivan county, New York.
6 Enrolled at the State Teachers College, Jacksonville, Ala., 1938–39.
7 *American Speech*, Oct., 1942, p. 173.
8 A high-school teacher at El Reno, Okla.
9 Obviously an attempt at *Juanita*. Others are *Waneta, Wanita, Wanneta, Wanetta, Wanerta* and *Waunita*. The last appeared in a list of notables of Elwood, Ind., in *Life*, Aug. 26, 1940, p. 2. See *Joanita*.
10 Reported from Iowa in Front Row, by Elizabeth Clarkson Zwart, Des Moines *Tribune*, May 8, 1940.
11 Reported from Lawton, Okla.
12 Oklahoma City *Oklahoman*, Sept. 14, 1945.
13 The name of the winner of six beauty contests in Louisiana.
14 Reported from Watonga, Okla.
15 Ouida? *American Speech*, April, 1933, p. 35. I have also encountered *Weta*.
16 This combination is a favorite throughout the Fancy Names Belt. It is accompanied by many derivatives of *William*, e.g., *Willia, Willetta, Williamina, Willieva, Willith, Willena, Wilda, Willedra, Willola* and *Willow*. On June 6, 1945 the New Orleans *Picayune* announced the discovery of a two-year-old girl at Ellabelle, Ga., bearing the name of *Williweze*.
17 Found in Alexander, La.
18 From Indiana.
19 A bride in Oklahoma City, 1946.
20 A member of the faculty at the Georgia Teachers College, Collegeboro, 1946.
21 Reported from the Sacramento Valley, Calif.
22 Married in 1939 at Lexington, Okla.
23 Reported from Elkader, Iowa, by Mr. J. J. Hyde.
24 From the Blue Ridge of Virginia, *American Speech*, April, 1933, p. 35.
25 An Oklahoma City schoolma'am.
26 Found in Colusa county, Calif.
27 From the Sacramento Valley, Calif.
28 Found in Pekin, Ill., by Mr. Fred Hamann.
29 From the Oakland, Calif. region.

Zle [1]	Zonza	Zula Bell	Zymole
Zoan [2]	Zoualda	Zuma	Zzelle
Zoda	Zoya [4]	Zwilla	
Zola [3]	Zudeen	Zylphia	

Despite the seeming chaos here the judicious reader will at once observe certain patterns and tendencies. Many of these names, he will note, are more or less plausible and euphonious modifications of common male names, usually by the addition of suffixes generally thought of as feminine, e.g., *Philelle, Ulyssia, Lloydine, Alexanderene, Oscaretta, Alburtis.* Others are diminutives of male names, often given a feminine flavor by combining them with accepted women's names, e.g., *Bennie Mae, Jimmie Lou, Mary Jo.* Yet others are surnames converted into given-names, e.g., *Beverly, Sidney, Shirley, Dabney, Powell, Shelby.* And still other are geographical names — sometimes used unchanged, e.g., *Manila, Sonora, Elba,* and sometimes modified to please a whimsical fancy, e.g., *Texana, Utahna, Arzonia, Denva, Melbourine, Okla, Venazualia, Hiburnia.* All these processes, though they have been carried further in the Fancy Names Belt than anywhere else, have roots in the past. The ancient German man's name of *Albert* produced *Alberta* at a very early date, and there was a saint thus called in the Third Century. So with *Julia*, which comes down from Roman times and was borne by a saint of the same era. So, again, with *Philippa, Theodora, Henrietta, Caroline* and many another. So, even, with *Sophia*, which was originally one of the Names of Jesus, and hence masculine, though it was transferred to women in Apostolic times and has been accepted by Holy Church ever since.[5] *Mary Jo* and their like may be traced to the day before surnames, when it was common to distinguish between two women of the same name by appending their fathers' given-names. Nor is there anything precisely new about giving girls surnames as given-names: it apparently came in simultaneously with the custom of using such names for boys. Camden says, in fact, that *Douglas* was thus adopted in England shortly before his time, and Henry Howard, Earl of

---

[1] A girl who suffered a broken neck in an automobile accident at Dallas, Texas, April 13, 1940.
[2] From Arlington, Texas.
[3] An Oklahoma City schoolma'am.
[4] Oklahoma City *Oklahoman*, Feb. 1, 1941.
[5] Camden, in his Remains Concerning Britain, says that it was frowned upon by "some godly men" of his time, c. 1600, as too pretentious and hence "irreligious."

Northampton (1540–1614), had a daughter of that name who became the wife of Sir Arthur Gorges, the cousin and companion of Sir Walter Raleigh, and was herself the subject of a poem by Spenser.[1] This use of surnames as given-names for girls has always been commonest in the South, where it marks the gentry rather than the plain people. But in recent years it has flourished lushly among the lowly of Oklahoma.

Another large class of non-canonical girls' names is produced by adorning old names with new and mellifluous terminations, *e.g.*, *Carrine, Marcellette, Olgalene*, or by making collision forms of two or more, *e.g.*, *Gracella, Alouise, Hannora, Mariedythe, Harrietta, Agnella, Abbieann*. With it goes a long series of novel abbreviations, *e.g.*, *Affie, Berthie, Oshie*, and another and longer of rococo spellings, *e.g.*, *Cylvia, De Lores, Wroberta, Jayne, Mable, Dasy, Scharlott, Jaann*,[2] *Phaye*. Such spellings were once fashionable in the great Babylons of the East, with *Edythe, Kathryn* and *Sadye* as familiar examples, but in late years they have passed out there. In the Dust Bowl and its colonies, however, they continue to flourish, and some of them are of a great boldness, *e.g.*, *Feby (Phoebe), Gladdis, Rhey* and *Qay*. In some cases their forms suggest that mere illiteracy may lie at the bottom of them, as for example in *Anner, Cloteel, Drewceller, Milderd, Kathern* and *Roxaner*,[3] but it is much more common for a highly self-conscious artfulness to be manifest, and the same is also visible in the lavish misuse of particles, capitals, apostrophes and other such alarms and delights to the eye and psyche, *e.g.*, *ClarEtta, Da Rue, M'Amis, De'An, Du Wayne, G'Ola, Je Nanne, Ja Jayne, La Doris, DeDonda, AlMeda, E-Vetha, Lo Venia, McNara, Del Rose, El Louise, Le Olive* and *La Lahoma*.[4] The last example presents a case of doubling of *la*, not at all infrequent in my material, and the two cases immediately preceding show masculine articles used before feminine names. How one is to account for such forms as *Garguerite, Maomi, Orene* and *Omelia*, in which old names are turned into new ones by the simple device of chang-

---

[1] *Publications of the Modern Language Association*, Sept., 1928, p. 645.
[2] The name of a young lady of Denver, Colo. Whether it represents *John* or *Jan* I do not know.
[3] There are other examples in Feminine Names, *American Speech*, Nov., 1925, p. 130.
[4] The incomparable *Shir Lee* falls under three headings. It is a surname, it is a doublet of the *Betty Jo* class, and it involves an orthographical novelty.

ing the initial letters, I do not know. It may be ingenuity that operates here, and it may be only ignorance.

There remains the large group that defies analysis and even classification. All that one may say of its masterpieces is that they show a resolute determination to achieve something hitherto unmatched and unimagined, at whatever cost to tradition and decorum. It is as if the ambitious mother of a newly-hatched darling wrote all the elements of all the ancient girls' names upon slips of paper, added slips bearing syllables filched from the terminology of all the arts and sciences, heaved the whole into an electric salad-tosser, and then arranged the seethed contents two by two or three by three. On what other theory is one to arrive at the genesis of such prodigies as *Flouzelle, Glitha, Lephair, Ulestine, Delector, Luvader, Wheirmelda, Gentervee, Margileth* and *Moonean?* They bear no apparent relation to the ordinary nomenclature of the language, but seem to be altogether synthetic. It is easy to imagine the exultation of a poor woman who achieves so shining a novelty. She not only marks off her little darling from all other little darlings within ear- or rumor-shot; she also establishes herself in her community as a salient social reformer and forward-looker and is quickly rewarded with the envy and imitation of other mothers. In the heat of this creative urge, alas, she sometimes contrives something that may wring snickers from city slickers, *e.g., Faucette, Vomera, Uretha, Melassia, Fondanell, Onema, Leyette, Glanda, Morene, Phalla, Ova, Merdine, Eutris, Gelda, Tryphena* or *Coita,* but her friends and admirers are unaware of any cryptic meaning or suggestion, and so is she herself.[1] These are names wholly new to the human record, and she thinks that they are pretty ones, and even gorgeous. The woman next door who, in revolt against the stereotyped, can fetch up nothing better than *Echo, Fairy, Dreamy, Kewpie, Kiwanis, Dewdrop* or *Apple* is plainly of an inferior order of advanced thinker.

Most such inventions, I gather from the documents, come from mothers in the lower income brackets, but by no means all. Some of the most extraordinary specimens on my list are taken, not from the police news in the Bible Belt newspapers, but from rosters of

[1] All borne by actual girls, mainly in Oklahoma. An affidavit to that effect, witnessed by my pastor, is deposited in a time capsule buried on my estate at Hohenzollern, Md. Names in *Merd-* are numerous, *e.g., Merdena, Merdelle* and *Merdis*.

college students and the elegant gossip of the society columns. Indeed, the impulse to make strange names for their daughters sometimes seizes upon women on the highest cultural levels, and as a result not a few female Americans of considerable dignity bear them. In AL4 [1] I made note of a lady professor in California named *Eschscholtzia* — whether in honor of the California poppy or of the Russian naturalist who was its eponym I do not know. *Irita*, the charming given-name of the charming woman who is editor of the New York *Herald Tribune's Books*, was concocted, according to her own account, "with no excuse except that it pleased my parents' fancy." [2] *Tallulah*, the name of a very successful actress, is geographical and has been borne by ladies of her family, the Bankheads of Alabama, for several generations. The four daughters of the late Owen Cattell, one of the editors of *Science*, are *Coryl, Roma, Quinta* and *Jayjay*.[3] Miss M. *Burneice* Larson, director of the Medical Bureau in Chicago, finds her name so spelled because her mother objected to the way that *Bernice* was pronounced by the Cornish miners of the Michigan copper country where she was born, to wit, *Búrniss*, and determined to do something about it.[4]

I have noted the frequency of strange given-names among lady professors, especially in the South; the same frequency seems to prevail among librarians. One named *Ullainee* is reported from Illinois, and others named *Vannelda, Zola Mae, Azaleen* and *Mirth* have been found below the Potomac. Still another lady of the craft, *Tommie* by name, is said to have once suffered the embarrassment of being booked to share a room with a he-colleague at a professional convention. In Canada there is a female public official, now retired, whose given names are the simple initials, *O P*. In Oklahoma there is a female pianist named *James*.[5] In 1940, writing in the *Reader's Digest* upon the strange names borne by some of the wives of Southern congressmen, *e.g., Clarine, Ivo,*[6] *Nobie, Merle* and *Lady*

---

1 p. 522, n. 5.
2 Wild Names I Have Met, by Alfred H. Holt; n.p., n.d., p. 17.
3 Owen Cattell, 42, Magazine Official, New York *Times*, March 28, 1940.
4 I am indebted here to the courtesy of Miss Larson herself. Miss D. Lorraine Yerkes reports finding the following other variants in the Chicago area: *Burneace, Burnus, Bernece, Burnis* and *Burnuce*.
5 At all events, the Oklahoma City *Oklahoman* so reported on Oct. 20, 1941.
6 This is a male name, countenanced by Holy Church. I am informed by the Rev. *Ivo* O'Sullivan, O.F.M., of Hupeh, China, that it is a Latinized form of *Ives*, the name of a

Bird, I fell into the error of including *Ocllo*, and was politely called to book by its bearer, Mrs. *Ocllo* Gunn Boykin, wife of a representative from Alabama. It is not, in fact, a given-name of native manufacture, though it is unusual: it is that of the sister and consort of Cachi, one of the legendary founders of the Inca dynasty of Peru, and was bestowed upon Mrs. Boykin because of her grandfather's admiration for that dynasty.

When the invention and adoption of such names began I do not know, but it must have been long ago. Sydney Smith gave the name of *Saba* to his eldest daughter, born *c.* 1800, in an effort to find something striking enough to divert attention from *Smith*.[1] *Belva* Lockwood, born in 1830, was the first woman admitted to practise before the Supreme Court of the United States, and ran for the Presidency on the Equal Rights ticket in 1884 and 1888; she is one of the saints of the feminist calendar, and many admirers of her generation named their girl babies after her. General George E. Pickett's second wife was baptized *LaSalle*, and General Richard S. Ewell's had the name of *Lizinka*.[2] Cornelius Vanderbilt II, in 1869, married as his second wife, a lady of Mobile, Ala., named *Frank* Crawford. *Lamiza* has come to its fifth generation in the Breckenridge family, and has been borrowed outside.[3] It appeared in the New York Social Register for 1933–34 along with the following:

Ambolena	Dinette	Fononda	Mosolete
Anzonetta	Edelweiss	Helentzia	Symphorosa
Attaresta	Engracia	Isophene	Thusnelda
Berinthia	Etelka	Lotawana	Velvalee [4]
Credilla	Exum	Mellona	

The process of forming such names, on a level far above that of the unlettered, was described by the Oklahoma City *Times* some

---

holy lawyer-priest of Brittany who died in 1303. *Yvette* and *Yvonne* are feminine forms. In Ireland, where *Ivo* is not uncommon, it may also be related to the name of St. *Ibar* of Begerin island, in Wexford harbor, who flourished in St. Patrick's day and died in 500. There was also a St. *Ivo*, Bishop of Chartres, who died in 1116.

1 A Memoir of the Rev. Sydney Smith by His Daughter, Lady Holland; London, 1855, II.

2 This was a Russian loan: she was born in St. Petersburg while her father was American minister there. Her first husband was one Brown, and Ewell always introduced her as "my wife, Mrs. Brown." See Lee's Lieutenants, by Douglas S. Freeman; New York, 1943, Vol. II, p. 606.

3 Mrs. Breckenridge Lambert, of St. Louis, tells me that family legend makes it of Indian origin.

4 I am indebted here to Mrs. Delia H. Biddle Pugh, of New York City.

years ago in an article dealing with the five beautiful daughters of a Mrs. Arthur Wilbur White of that city, to wit, *Wilbarine, Yerdith, Norvetta, Marlynne* and *Arthetta*. A group photograph of them was included, and under it one of the bright young men of the *Times* wrote "not a trite name in the bunch." I quote:

> Mrs. White . . . started early, with the first daughter, *Wilbarine*, 20-year-old junior at Oklahoma City University. That's a name you won't find in most folks' family trees. Mrs. White thinks you won't find it anywhere. She made it up. Got part of her idea from her husband's middle name, and then added a few letters for the sake of euphony.
>
> When the next daughter came along, Mrs. White couldn't let her down. So she set about manufacturing a name. This time it was *Norvetta*, who is a junior at Classen high-school. Mrs. White smiled as she recalled the time she had getting that name together. She liked the name *LaVeta*, but she had to have something different. So she used part of her maiden name, *North*.
>
> It was too late to turn back when the third daughter arrived, and besides Mrs. White likes to manufacture names. *Yerdith*, 11-year-old pupil at Harding junior high-school, is proud of hers. *Yerdith*, Mrs. White explained, is a composite of *Yvonne* and *Edith*, with a little letter twisting to make it sound pretty.
>
> When the fourth daughter showed up, Mrs. White wanted to show her favoritism for the name *Marilyn*, but Lindbergh was pretty much in the public eye. So — she shook her name basket. And up came *Marlynne*, who's 10 years old and in the 5B grade at Wilson school.[1]
>
> Six years ago another daughter arrived by stork express, and Mrs. White thought it was time father was remembered again. So, the baby of the family, a first grader at Wilson, is *Arthetta*.[2]

That the fashion for artificial names may be spreading is indicated by the fact that they have begun to be listed in the handbooks for puzzled parents got out by enterprising publishers. In one of these books, for example, I find *Adabel, Arvia, Cerelia, Rosel, Sidra, Thadine* and *Xylia*,[3] and in another *Airlia, Darlene, Gelda, Marette, Xanthe* and *Zella*.[4] But even in the heart of the Swell Names Zone the older girls' names have not yet gone wholly underground, and elsewhere they hold out stoutly. I turn, for example, to a list of 346 recent graduates of the Capitol City High-school of Oklahoma City, about equally divided between girls and boys. Among the former, despite the throng of *Frenas, Phillie Joes, Narasonas* and *Twylas*, I yet find two *Katherines* and *Helens*, three *Margarets* and *Dorothys*,

[1] Why *Marlynne* should be thought closer to *Lindbergh* than *Marilyn* is not explained.
[2] Oklahoma City *Times*, Sept. 17, 1941, p. 12.
[3] What Shall We Name the Baby?, edited by Winthrop Ames; New York, 1935.
[4] Naming Your Baby, by Elsdon C. Smith; New York, 1943.

four *Ruths*, nine *Marys* and no less than seventeen *Bettys*. These old names have been facing the competition of successive waves of newer ones for centuries, but they still hold out. Ernest Weekly once undertook an examination of the names of women dead before *c.* 1750, embalmed in the Dictionary of National Biography: he found that *Agnes, Alice, Cicely, Joan, Matilda* (or *Maud*), *Margaret, Elizabeth* and the related *Isabel* " recur almost monotonously " — and all of them continue to flourish to this day.[1] There are recurrent crazes for naming girls after the heroines of novels and movies and the stars of stage and screen, but they do not last. The old names go into disuse for a while, and then come back triumphantly. " The only thing that has kept girls' names from collapsing into sheer frivolity or worse," wrote a Canadian observer in 1935, " has been the astonishing recrudescence of *Ann* and *Jane*." [2] Both have flourished with occasional short eclipses, since the Fourteenth Century. So have *Amy, Beatrice, Blanche, Mary, Philippa, Helen, Emma, Katherine* and *Sibyl*. Dr. Morris Fishbein reported in 1944[3] that one-twenty-fourth of all American women were then named *Mary*, with *Elizabeth, Margaret* and *Helen* following in order. He added, however that *Mary* was apparently receding somewhat, with *Elizabeth* threatening to run ahead of it, and *Helen, Dorothy, Margaret, Marie, Katherine, Louise, Ruth* and *Eleanor* following.

" The names of women," says the Manu-smriti, the ancient Brahman code of laws, " should be easy to pronounce, not implying anything dreadful, possess a plain meaning, be pleasing and auspicious, end in long vowels, and contain a word of benediction." [4] " Let no man," it continues in another place, " marry a woman named after a constellation, a tree or a river, nor one bearing the name of a low caste, or of a mountain, nor one named after a bird, a snake or a slave, nor one whose name inspires terror." Later sages have offered more specific advice. Coleridge declared that every woman's name should be a trochee — that is, of two syllables, with the accent on the first, *e.g., Mary, Alice, Agnes, Ellen*. But Gelett Burgess has

[1] Jack and Jill; London, 1939, p. 17.
[2] Improper Nouns, by J. H. Simpson, Toronto *Saturday Night*, March 16, 1935.
[3] What's In a Name?, *Hygeia*, March, p. 173.
[4] The Laws of Manu, translated by G. Bühler; Oxford, 1886, p. 35. This code is supposed to come down from Manu, the creator of the world, just as the Hebrew Pentateuch is supposed to come from Moses. The existing version of the text was probably prepared in the second century of the Christian era.

complained that the trochee suggests "a persistent, hammering force," and that the iambus, in which the accent is on the second syllable, *e.g., Elaine, Jeannette, Louise,* suggests "a decisive vigor." His choice seems to be the dactyl — an accented syllable followed by two without accents, *e.g., Emily, Adelaide, Abigail, Isabel* —, though he also has a kind word for the anapest — three syllables, with the accent on the last, *e.g., Antoinette, Marianne.* The former, he says, shows "limp, ragdoll ease" and the latter "is just the thing for sparkle and pep."[1] Another recent professor of the subject, Elsdon C. Smith, contents himself with advocating names embodying "the more sonorous consonants, *r, l, m* and *n,* and next to these *t, p* and *d.*" He warns against *q* and the hard *g,* but says that "the soft *e* is pretty, as in *Evelyn.*" A good girls' name, he concludes, should be easily spelled and pronounced, it should not give ready birth to a disagreeable diminutive, it should be free from unpleasant connotations or associations, and it should not be "so odd or unusual as to evoke constant comment."[2] But I greatly fear that the principal and often only excuse for some of the grotesque names I have listed is precisely that they "evoke constant comment."

Two fashions in boys' names have been mentioned — that for diminutives[3] and that for mere initials. A third of almost equal oddity converts *Junior* from an indicator following the surname into a middle-name, *e.g.,* John *Junior* Jones. In a list of 88 students, male and female, graduated from the Marshall, Mo., High-School in the class of 1946 I find no less than three boys thus named, and in a roster of Army recruits from the same town I find two more. One of the Marshall *Juniors* applied to the local Circuit Court in 1946 for permission to drop his middle name on the ground that it had "caused him difficulty and confusion."[4] Even when the adjective is in its proper place it is common for an American boy to be called *Junior* by his family and friends, to distinguish him from his father. In writing, *Jr.* is in most frequent use in the United States, but in England *Jun.* seems to be preferred.

[1] Make a Name For Yourself, *Saturday Review of Literature,* Jan. 25, 1947, pp. 9-41.
[2] Naming Your Baby; Evanston (Ill.), 1943, pp. 5-11.
[3] Said Joseph William Carr in A List of Words From Northwest Arkansas, II, *Dialect Notes,* Vol. II, Part I, 1905, p. 102: "They are liked evidently because they lack dignity and formality and suggest popularity. Such names are useful in politics."
[4] Marshall *Democrat-News,* June 19. I am indebted here to Dr. W. L. Carter.

The use of *2nd*, *3rd*, etc. is marked an Americanism by the DAE and traced to 1803. At the start *2nd* seemed to have been only a substitute for *Jr.*, but now it often indicates, not the son, but the grandson or nephew of the first bearer of the name. A writer in *Putnam's Monthly* in 1855 described it as "common in New England."[1] The use of the Roman numerals, *II*, *III*, etc., came much later. It is frowned upon in England as an invasion of royal prerogative, and also by the American Army and Navy, which use only *2d*, *3d*, etc., in their lists.[2] A somewhat unusual form is favored by Edward H. Butler, editor and publisher of the Buffalo *Evening News*, who describes himself on the masthead of his paper as Edward H. Butler *(Son)*. This recalls the German use of *Vater* and *Sohn*, as in Johann Strauss *Vater* and Johann Strauss *Sohn*. But the Germans also use *d.J.* (*der Jungere*) and *d. Ä.* (*der Ältere*). There was a time when *Sr.* was encountered almost as frequently as *Jr.*, but it seems to be passing out: the old man now evades admitting his age by using his name unadorned.

The invention of new and unearthly boys' names has not, so far, enlisted all the feverish fancy that has enriched and glorified the American répertoire of girls' names; nevertheless, it has made notable advances since the turn of the century, and has developed some talented virtuosi. Its lag is probably explicable on the ground that fathers ordinarily have more to say about the naming of their sons than about the naming of their daughters, and oppose masculine Toryism to feminine advanced thinking. My list of revolutionary boys' names is thus shorter than the foregoing list of girls' names, and shows fewer genuine prodigies:[3]

Ace	Alsex	Apollo	Arla
Adjoil	Amburs	Aorum	Arlando
Airoy	Amel	Arben	Armon
Allieu[4]	Amer	Arch	Arrow
Almouth	Anvil[5]	Ardis	Arson[6]

1 Our Given Names, Jan., 1855, p. 59.
2 But Commodore Allen George Quynn, U.S.N., reports in Who's Who in America that his son is *Allen George VIII*. I am indebted here to Mr. Alexander Kadison.
3 My specimens come mainly from newspapers, and my heaviest borrowings are from lists of war heroes. I have been aided by the kindness of the persons mentioned at the head of the roll of girls' names, with the addition of Paul Flowers, of Memphis, Tenn., and John P. Shepard, of Detroit.
4 Reported from Peoria, Ill., by Mr. Fred Hamann.
5 Christian Names in the Cumberlands, by James A. Still, *American Speech*, April, 1930, p. 307.
6 Reported from the South in Christian Names, by Katherine Bux-

Arville	Cad	Colonel [11]	Dolphus
Ather [1]	Caldeen	Comma	Donaco
Aud	Camma	Commodore	Dorcine
Audif	Cara	Corne	Dorotha
Ausby	Carolle	Coy [12]	Dove
Austell	Cash	Creed [13]	Doyal [18]
Author	Ceal	Crellon	Duane [19]
Baysul	Cellow	Cullus	Dub
Bearl [2]	Centurlius	Curilee	Dude
Belvin	Ceola	Cyclone [14]	Earven
Benjiman	Champ	Dalvin	Ecton
Berlin [3]	Chan	Daymono	Edgard
Bernis	Chastain	Dee [15]	Edysol
Beryl	Chick	DeLaine	Eldo
Billy Dee	Cho-Wella [8]	Delores	Eleck
Birvin [4]	Christo	DeLoyce [16]	Elesten
Bishop	Clarise	Del Ray	Elgne
Blois	Clarmond	Dencred	Eligh
Blue [5]	Claudere	Denver	Elmer Dee
Bo	Clauzell	Deo	Elvan
Bok [6]	Cleodus	Derald	Elvcyd
Brownelle [7]	Clere	DeRoin	Elvis
Brunis	Cletis [9]	Dewight [17]	Elzie [20]
Bud	Clevern	Dial	Emitt
Bulas	Clint	Dink	Enel
Bun	Clodean	Dixie	Era
Buster	Clois [10]	Doc	Errett
Byard	Cluke	Doke	Erron

baum, *American Speech*, Oct., 1933, p. 73.
[1] Christian Names in the Blue Ridge of Virginia, by Miriam M. Sizer, *American Speech*, April, 1933, p. 36.
[2] Also *Bearle*.
[3] Also *Berlyn* and *Burlin*.
[4] Also *Burvine*.
[5] Oklahoma City *Oklahoman*, March 15, 1942.
[6] *Buck?*
[7] Oklahoma City *Times*, March 13, 1942.
[8] Oklahoma City *Times*, April 4, 1942.
[9] Reported from the Tennessee mountains by Mr. Hayden Siler, of Jellico, Tenn. Common in Oklahoma in the form of *Cletus*.
[10] From Long Grove, Okla. Also *Cloys*.
[11] *Colonel* Fred Docstader, of Fonda, N. Y., was inducted into the Army as a private at Albany, May 22, 1941.
[12] A very popular name in Oklahoma. Also *Coe*.
[13] Christian Names in the Cumberlands, before cited.
[14] From Galveston, Texas.
[15] Often used as a second name.
[16] Oklahoma City *Oklahoman*, March 4, 1942. *DeLos* is reported from Los Angeles.
[17] Perhaps from or for *DeWitt*.
[18] Probably from *Doyle*, assimilated with *Royal*.
[19] A very popular name, sometimes spelled *Dwain, Dwane, Dwaine, Dewane, Duayne, DuWayne*, or *Dee Wayne*.
[20] This name is common all over the Bible country. Sometimes it becomes *Elza* or *Elzia*.

Proper Names in America 503

Ersie	Foy	Hulon	Komal
Erville	Frederique	Human [13]	Koran [21]
Esco [1]	Gareld [7]	Idris	Laddie
Eson	Garl	Iloath [14]	LaFerry
Esther Mae [2]	Gayfree	Irby [15]	Laron
Estra	Gladson [8]	Irl	Lathal
Etci [3]	Glenace	Ivy [16]	Laurel
Eubert	Glenneth [9]	Izell	Leandrew
Euclid	Glore	Jamanuel [17]	Lector
Evern	Gora	Jat	Leeanard
Evitmus	Gotha	Jaydee	Legnial
Ewul	Gov [10]	Jewehe	Lelis [22]
Exton	Guyenn	Jimmie Lee	Lemial [23]
Fain	Gwendel	Joela	LeMon
Fareign	Gyle	Johnathon	Lesley [24]
Faye [4]	Habert	Jonie	LeVon
Felmet	Harce [11]	Jorene	Lig
Fern	Harlinza	June [18]	Lillard
Finace	Headlee	Junian	Lilon
Finis [5]	Hilry	Kark	Limon [25]
Flake	Hollene	Kazan	Loarn
Flavel	Hope	Keleel	Lodell
Florns	Hoyd	Kennis	Loenial
Foil [6]	Hozen	Kleo Murl [19]	Loeties
Fonzo	Huckleberry [12]	Koith [20]	Lonnie [26]

1 Christian Names in the Cumberlands, before cited.
2 Associated Press dispatch from Columbia, S. C., April 19, 1941: "*Esther Mae* may join the Army, but boys, don't get excited if you hear the name at call some morning. He — and the gender is right — is awaiting classification with Richland county draft board."
3 Oklahoma City *Oklahoman*, March 6, 1946.
4 A gallant soldier of Council Hill, Okla.
5 The name of a Tennessee statesman. It appears also as *Phynis* and *Finice*.
6 From LeFlore, Okla.
7 Also *Gerold, Jerrold, Jerell,* and *Jirl*.
8 Perhaps from *Gladstone*.
9 From Midwest City, Okla.
10 Death notice in the Oklahoma City *Oklahoman,* May 4, 1942.
11 The usual pronunciation of *Horace* in Alpine Tennessee.
12 From Stilwell, Okla.
13 Reported from Arnaudville, La.
14 Reported from Iowa by Miss Katherine Buxbaum.
15 Christian Names in the Cumberlands, before cited. Common in Oklahoma.
16 *Ivy* Lee (1877-1934), born in Georgia, was the press-agent of John D. Rockefeller I.
17 Oklahoma City *Oklahoman,* March 31, 1942.
18 Christian Names in the Blue Ridge of Virginia, before cited.
19 Oklahoma City *Oklahoman,* April 5, 1942.
20 Reported from Iowa by Miss Katherine Buxbaum.
21 Also *Koren*.
22 From Sapulpa, Okla.
23 *Lemuel?* There is also *Lemul*.
24 Also *Lessly*.
25 Reported from Tennessee. *Lyman?* His middle name was *Beecher*.
26 Originally, this seems to have been a diminutive for *Alonzo*, but it now flourishes on its own. *Lonzo* is also common.

Loran	Monzell	Odas	Oris
Lotus	Moose	Ode	Orlen [20]
Lououn	Mord [7]	Oder [14]	Ormal
Lovis	Mosco	Odis [15]	Orman
Loy	Muriel [8]	Odix	Orpha
Loyd [1]	Murt	O'Henry	Orray
Lum [2]	Naith	Ohmart	Orsamus
Lural	Nello	Oid	Orv
LuReign [3]	Nenzil	Okey [16]	Osie [21]
Luvan [4]	Nerton	Ol	Osman
Luvardia	Nevada	Olander	Othal [22]
Lynel	Nias [9]	Oleah	Ottis
Lysle [5]	Novert	Ollus	Otwa [23]
Mac	Noyce	Olva	Oval
Malene	Nuel	Omae	Overy [24]
Manvin	Nylan	Onus [17]	Ovid
Mariana	Oadeous	Ophni	Ozmay
Marion	Oarly [10]	Oral [18]	Ozro
Mavo	Oby [11]	Oran	Pallis [25]
Melirn	Oceail	Oras	Para
Merl [6]	Occum [12]	Oravell	Pasco
Modrel	Oceaphus	Orban	Phin
Monar	Ocie	Orbra	Pink
Monk	Od [13]	Oriel [19]	Pleas [26]

1 Also *Loid*.
2 Christian Names in the Cumberlands, before cited. An abbreviation of *Columbus*. The bearer's twin brother is named *Lem*.
3 Made an ensign in the Navy June 5, 1948. *Congressional Record*, June 10, p. 6710.
4 Found in Peoria, Ill., by Mr. Fred Hamann.
5 Also *Lyle, Lyall* and *Lyal*.
6 Reported from Iowa by Miss Katherine Buxbaum, *American Speech*, Oct., 1933, p. 72. His brother was *Verl*. Other forms: *Murrel, Mirl, Muirl, Merl, Myrl* and *Murl*.
7 Christian Names in the Cumberlands, before cited.
8 Also *Murel*.
9 Christian Names in the Blue Ridge of Virginia, before cited. Maybe from Ananias.
10 Christian Names in the Cumberlands, before cited.
11 Also *Obie* and *Oba*.
12 Reported from New Hampshire by Mr. Paul St. Gaudens.
13 From Tulsa, Okla.
14 Christian Names in the Cumberlands, before cited.
15 Also *Odys*.
16 Found in Peoria, Ill., by Mr. Fred Hamann.
17 From Konawa, Okla. Also *Onis*.
18 Christian Names in the Cumberlands, before cited. This name is very common in Oklahoma, along with *Orel*.
19 From Iowa. *American Speech*, Oct., 1933, p. 72.
20 Also *Orlin*.
21 Christian Names in the Cumberlands, before cited. Reported from Iowa in the form of *Osey*, *American Speech*, Oct., 1933, p. 72. Also used as a name for girls.
22 Also *Othul*.
23 A major in the Army from Oklahoma.
24 Marriage Licenses, Oklahoma City *Oklahoman*, March 11, 1942.
25 Reported from the Tennessee mountains by Mr. Hayden Siler, of Jellico, Tenn.
26 Pronounced *Plez*. An abbreviation of *Pleasant*, a favorite given-name. Sometimes spelled *Ples*.

Proper Names in America

Poke	Solomao [7]	Tye	Virtus
Pulis [1]	Son	Uel	Vital
Rada	Speaker	Uhlan	V-J [16]
Reo	Sturgeon	Uliey	Von
Quannah	Sugar [8]	Une	Voyd
Rephord	Synn	Ura	Vulon
Retel	Tal	Urxula	Wave
Rofey	Tandy	U S [13]	Wazell
Rolla [2]	Tee	Usona [14]	Whestone [17]
Rolen [3]	Tera [9]	Utis	Wras
Roman	Terbert	Valourd	Yale
Ronal [4]	Thaddies	Vanis	Yick [18]
Rowdy [5]	Thaine	Vasso	Yuvon
Royal	Thelbert	Vaudie	Zale
Rue	Themious	Veon	Zay
Sank	Theoplies [10]	Verbilee	Zedore
Satis	Theorda [11]	Verle [15]	Zee
Sceva	Thoas	Vernace	Zelmer
Semion	Thrantham	Vernal	Zephro
Senus	Throniall	Vernet	Zeylus
Sestee	Torl	Veskel	Zine
Sion	Toxie [12]	Veston	Zoheth
Siro	Travois	Vin	Zota
Solen [6]	True	Virgle	Zurr

It will be noted at once that nearly all the categories of girls' names that we have examined are represented here, though the specimens as a whole are a good deal less rich. In not a few cases, indeed, girls' names also reappear as boys' names — a phenomenon certainly not new in the world, as the bisexual use of *Evelyn* in England, *Florence* in Ireland and *Maria* in Latin Europe testifies. It is not uncommon in Oklahoma for a male *Dixie* or *Marion* or

---

1 Buried at Oklahoma City, Aug. 9, 1940.
2 Not a feminine form of *Rollo*. Borne by a member of the 80th Congress.
3 *Roland?* Sometimes spelled *Rolin* or *Rollin*.
4 From *Ronald?* Also *Ronell*.
5 Oklahoma City *Oklahoman*, Jan. 8, 1941.
6 *Solon?*
7 From *Solomon?* Or *O sole mio? Salomica* is also reported.
8 Tulsa dispatch, May 4, 1942.
9 Christian Names in the Blue Ridge of Virginia, before cited.
10 Apparently from *Theophilus*, a saint's name. Also *Theople*.
11 Encountered in the Army by Mr. Hugh Morrison.
12 From Ellisville, Miss.
13 Reported from Lake Village, Ark., by Mrs. Helen F. Gaines, 1940. His brother is 2 S.
14 From *United States of America*. Reported from New Jersey by Mr. Henry Burnell Shafer, of Haddon Heights.
15 Very common in Oklahoma. Also *Verl* and *Vurl*.
16 Reported from Detroit by the New York *Times*, Aug. 17, 1945.
17 Christian Names in the Cumberlands, before cited.
18 From Greenville, Miss.

LaVerne or even *Beryl*[1] to espouse a lady of the same given-name, and in 1941 R. L. Ripley unearthed an *Ora* Jones married to an *Ora* Jones. Manuel Prenner has published a study of the names most frequently found in both sexes, *e.g.*, *Beverly, Carmen, Carol, Cecil, Cleo, Darryl, Fay, Gail, Hope, Jean, Lee, Leslie, Lynn, Merle, Ray, Sidney, Vaughn* and *Vivian*.[2] To this list, from my Oklahoma material, may be added *Delores, Dorotha, Laurel* and *Osie*.[3]

Odd spellings seem to be almost as numerous among boys' names as among those of girls, but whether they are produced by a deficiency in orthographic science or by a sophisticated artfulness is hard to determine. The former may account for *Amel* (*Emil*), *Byard, Gareld, Hilry, Malcum, Markus* and *Virgle*, but I suspect that the latter is responsible for *Benjiman, Eligh, Frederique, Johnathon, Lesley* and *Seymore*. Such bizarre spellings as *DeLaine, Del Ray, LaFerry, LeMon* and *LuReign*, so common among girls' names, seem to be relatively rare. So are the combinations and collision forms, *e.g.*, *Jamanuel, Landrew, Edgard, Jimmie Lee* and *Joela*. But the making of new names by changing letters in old ones, *e.g.*, *Arlando, Garl, Terbert, Bearl* and *Urxula*, is more frequent. As we have already seen, diminutives are often bestowed at baptism and some of them show novelty, *e.g.*, *Chan, Clint, Dolphus, Od, Orv* and *Ulys*, and equally popular are the pet-names, *Bo, Bud, Buster, Chick, Dink, Dub, Doc, Laddie, Monk* and *Rowdy*. Names of literal significance, *e.g.*, *Cash, Comma, Cyclone, Dude, Human, Moose, Onus, Orange, True* and *Vital*, are often encountered, but those suggesting medical matters, *e.g.*, *Cardia, Toxie* and *Voyd*, are not as numerous as among girls. Nor are common given-names with fancy suffixes, *e.g.*, *Carolle* and *Claudere*, nor geographical names, *e.g.*, *Denver, California* and *Nevada*.[4] But the deficit is made up for

1 Apparently pronounced as one syllable, for it is often spelled *Burl* or *Byrl*.
2 *Ora* Jones Married *Ora* Jones, by Manuel Prenner, *American Speech*, April, 1942, pp. 84-88, and Dec., 1942, p. 282.
3 One of the attorneys for Jahveh, at the trial of Scopes at Dayton, Tenn., in 1925, bore the name of *Sue*, though his he-ness was manifest. In 1941, according to Prenner, *Case and Comment*, the lawyers' magazine, unearthed male barristers named *Slare, Velma, Shirley, Ormie* and *Gail*. In the Seventy-ninth Congress there were two members of the House named *Clare*, one male and one female. See Bulletin on Hon., by H. L. Mencken, *American Speech*, April, 1946, p. 81. For a he-*Ruby* of eminence see Supplement I, p. 532.
4 Captain *California* C. McMillan, of the Coast Guard, retired in 1938 after 36 years service, and died in San Francisco, Dec. 4, 1946.

by titles, *e.g., Colonel, Commodore, Count, Earl, Gov, Speaker;* by the popularity of well-worn surnames, especially *Clay, Floyd, Wayne, Dwight, Dallas, Lyman, Preston, Harlan* and *Taylor;*[1] and by the surviving if gradually diminishing vogue, throughout rural America, for names borrowed from the heroes of Hellenic history and legend. In Oklahoma I have encountered *Ovid, Solon, Euclid, Virgil, Apollo* and even *Deo.* As for *Homer,* it flourishes from Bangor to San Diego.

Nothing here is really new. Paul St. Gaudens has unearthed *Sterling* and *Urian* from the Killingly, Conn., records of 1725–40; *Irastus, Delor* and *Ozno* from New Hampshire records of 1850–70; *Aldace, Milon, Erdix, Royal, Volney, Alvah, Nonnus* and *Sardis* from the rolls of Kimball Union Academy at Meriden, N. H., 1834–48; and *Noble, Leroy, King, Earl, Lysander, Delbert, Euclid, Romaine, Osro, Hector,* and *Dolph* from various New England account-books of 1850–60. The fame of Ralph *Waldo* Emerson (1803–82) after his Phi Beta Kappa oration at Harvard in 1837 started a vogue for his middle-name. William *Tecumseh* Sherman, born in 1813, was not the first American to bear an Indian name,[2] nor was *Kenesaw Mountain* Landis, born in 1866, the first to be named for a battle.[3] Geographical names began to be used as givennames in the period of expansion into the West. *Wisconsin Illinois* and *Arizona Dakota* were two North Carolina brothers,[4] and *Lewes Delaware* was a Washington physician. In Connecticut, a generation or two ago, there was a politico surnamed *Bill* whose given-names were *Kansas Nebraska.* He had brothers named *Lecompton Constitution* and *Emancipation Proclamation,*[5] and sisters

---

[1] On June 29, 1940, the United Press reported from Springville, Utah, that a filling-station there had both a *Taylor Burt* and a *Burt Taylor* on its faculty. Mrs. James Nye Ryman, of Houston, Texas, tells me that the number of surnames in use as given-names in that great State is augmented by the custom of naming boy babies after the doctors who deliver them.

[2] Lloyd Lewis says in Sherman, Fighting Prophet; New York, 1932, p. 517, that Sherman was christened simply *Tecumseh,* but that *William* was later prefixed at the sugges-tion of his foster-father, Thomas Ewing.

[3] Sherman was defeated by Joseph E. Johnston at Kenesaw Mountain, near Marietta, Ga., June 27, 1864. Dr. *Malvern Hill* Price, a Washington physician, maybe preceded Landis, for Malvern Hill was fought on July 1, 1862. I am indebted here to Dr. John B. Nicols, of Washington.

[4] I am indebted here to Mr. Thomas E. Street, of Enfield, N. C.

[5] I am indebted here to Mrs. L. B. Bailey, of South Freeport, Maine.

named *Louisiana Purchase* and *Missouri Compromise*. Long before their time Governor William H. Gist, of South Carolina, named a son *States Rights*. This *States Rights* was graduated from the Harvard Law School in 1852, joined the Confederate Army in 1861, rose to be a brigadier-general, and was killed at the battle of Franklin, Tenn., November 30, 1864.[1]

The austere pages of "Who's Who in America" are adorned with many strange names, *e.g.*, *Champion, Dallas Dayton, Erdis*,[2] *Zeno, Balpha, Doel, Amor, Ival, Tubal, Zellmer* and *Cola*, though they are naturally less numerous than among the sturdy yeomen of Oklahoma and Texas. There are congressmen (1948) named *Omar, Rolla, Prince, Oren, Wint, Fadjo* and *Thor*, and bishops named *Angie, Noble* and *Vedder*. The newspapers are constantly turning up given-names of a fantastic improbability. In 1944 *E. Pluribus Unum* Husted was found in Oklahoma City, though he was a native of Quincy, Ill.[3] In 1936 *Willie ⅜* Smith was unearthed in rural Georgia.[4] In 1901 *Loyal Lodge No. 296 Knights of Pythias Ponca City Oklahoma* Smith was baptized at Ponca City.[5] The late Cap Anson, manager of the Chicago baseball club, was baptized *Adrian*

---

1 I am indebted here to Lieut. Col. Frederick Bernays Wiener of the Judge Advocate General's department of the Air Force. The general's niece, Elizabeth Lewis Gist, married David Edward Finley and became the mother of *States Rights* Gist Finley, general superintendent of the Chattanooga Electric Power Board. Roger Butterfield says in The Millionaires' Best Friend, *Saturday Evening Post*, March 8, 1947, p. 80, that he is known in the family as *States*. I am indebted here to Messrs. Alexander Kadison and Simon Hochberger.

2 Borne by *Erdis* Robinson, a distinguished citizen of Columbus, O. He thus explains its origin: " My father was a pioneer in engineering education and an inventor. When I, his only son, was born, he felt that no ordinary name would do for me, so he invented one. He proceeded thus: He opened at random a book on mechanical engineering and with eyes closed touched the page with his pencil point and recorded the letter struck. Another page, another letter, and so until he had a long line of letters. Of this series he chose the first five letters in sequence that formed a pronounceable word. The result was *Erdis*." Private communication, March 28, 1940. The late Dr. *Lewellys* F. Barker (1867–1943), the Johns Hopkins consultant, explained in his autobiography that he was christened *Lewellys* because *Llewellyn*, which was traditional in his family, had become trite in his native Ontario.

3 Oklahoma City *Oklahoman*, Aug. 8, 1944.

4 I am indebted here to Mr. Leonard G. Pardue, of Jacksonville, Fla.

5 I get news of him from Dr. Raven I. McDavid, Jr., of Greenville, S. C., whose information comes from the officiating clergyman.

Constantine because his mother was born at *Adrian*, Mich., and his father at *Constantine* in the same State.[1]

Every Southern town boasts a Negro denizen who is exhibited to strangers as *Seaboard Airline Railway* Jackson, *Way Down Upon the Swanee River* Johnson, *Are You Ready For the Judgment Day* Brown or *Sunday Night Supper* Jones, but most such grotesque names, I am convinced, are invented by sportive whites and accepted only to gain their attention and favor. They may be bestowed now and then at baptism in the village creek, but that is only because the majority of Southern blackamoors regard pedobaptism as unscriptural, and hence do not go into the water until they have passed their nonage — long after their names have been determined, whether by Caucasian fiat, by their own choice, or by public acclamation. All the students who have investigated Aframerican onomastics in a scientific spirit have found such monstrosities to be few and far between, and when a particularly amazing specimen is reported the news of it usually comes at second or third hand. Dr. Urban T. Holmes, of the University of North Carolina, who undertook, in 1930, a survey of the names of 722 Negro schoolchildren in a typical mill-town of that State, found that 544 bore ancient and commonplace names on the order of *Mary* and *Margaret*, *James* and *William*, that 136 boasted such fancier but none the less familiar names as *Clarissa* and *Eugenia*, *Elbert* and *Gordon*, and that only 44 were adorned with such inventions as *Orcellia* and *Margorilla*, *Sandas* and *Venton*.[2]

In a study of the names of 22,105 colored college students — 12,220 females and 9,885 males —, reported in 1938, Dr. Newbell N. Puckett, of Western Reserve University, found a considerably higher incidence of what he called "unusualness," to wit, 15.3% among the females and 8.4% among the males, but he neglected, unhappily, to define "unusualness" or to give any examples of it, so his figures must be accepted with caution. On examining the Negro given-names in "Who's Who in Negro America," includ-

[1] On the Side, by E. V. Durling, Baltimore *News-Post*, July 13, 1945. Anson, says Durling, "thanked the Lord his mother had not been born in Ypsilanti and his father in Kalamazoo."

[2] A Study in Negro Onomastics, *American Speech*, Aug., 1930, pp. 463-67.

ing those of parents, spouses and children, he found a "rate of unusualness," for the two sexes together, of 7.6% among individuals born before 1870, one of 9.8% among those born between 1870 and 1900, and one of 15.6% among those born since the latter year. Here, again, he failed to define "unusualness," but inasmuch as his criterion, whatever it was, was apparently applied alike in all three periods, it is safe to accept his conclusion that "the rate of unusualness with the females seems to be on the increase." The same applies to his examination of lists of students in two colored colleges — one in South Carolina and the other in Arkansas. At the former he found 10.3% of "unusualness" before 1901, and 17.5% in 1935. At the latter the rate was 14.6% from 1900 to 1919, 22.4% from 1920 to 1929, and 35.6% in 1935.[1]

Here the effect of the circumambient white *Kultur* is well displayed. The fact that fancy names were more than twice as numerous among the Negroes of Arkansas as among those of South Carolina was precisely what one might have expected. My own examination of lists of Southern colored students indicates that their density, as among the white population, runs in inverse proportion to the degree of local civilization. In a roster of undergraduates at the North Carolina College for Negroes at Durham, a high-toned seminary, I find less than a dozen fancy names among nearly 600, and in the catalogue of Tuskegee Institute for 1946–47, listing students of a decidedly ambitious and superior class, with relatively cultured home backgrounds, the ordinary given-names run to at least 90%. I encounter, to be sure, some eyebrow-lifting *Arrenwinthas*, *Berneths* and *LaFauns*, but they would be outnumbered at least six to one by the *Fledareas*, *Jessoises*, *Merhizes* and *Oyonnas* in any comparable white list from Oklahoma, Arkansas or the Baptist areas of Louisiana and Texas.

On the lowest social level the study of Negro given-names is impeded by a fact already mentioned — that the sacrament of baptism is delayed among the majority of blacks until they are sturdy

---

[1] Negro Names, *Journal of Negro History*, Jan., 1938, pp. 35–48. In Names of American Negro Slaves, to be noticed presently, Puckett found that the order of frequency in names among Negro college students of today runs *James, William, John, Robert, Charles, George, Edward, Joseph, Thomas, Henry, Samuel* and *Walter* for the men, and *Mary, Annie, Ruth, Helen, Dorothy, Thelma, Louise, Alice, Katherine, Elizabeth, Lillian* and *Ethel* for the women.

Proper Names in America

enough to stand a violent ducking, by which time they have often become known to their friends by pet-names or nicknames, and are disinclined to change them. Many of them are illegitimate, with less family ties than a wild thing in the woods. Thus it is not surprising to find occasional names like the following, all of which are supported by plausible evidence:

Alligator [1]	Cupid	Gee-Whiz	Magazine [20]
Ape	Cutie [8]	Goat	Mama's Baby [21]
Big Boss [2]	Damfino [9]	Goose [13]	Me
Blasphemy [3]	Deck [10]	Handbag [14]	Mister [22]
Bootjack [4]	Doodle Bug	Himself [15]	Monkeydo [23]
Bo-peep [5]	Dove-Eye [11]	Ivory [16]	Nerve
Buckshot [6]	Extra [12]	Jingo [17]	Pill [24]
Bugger [7]	Fraidy	Loven Kisses [18]	Ping [25]
Bus	Frog	Luck [19]	Possum

[1] Dark Town, by J. Andrew Gaulden, *Negro Digest*, June, 1945, p. 11.
[2] From Louisiana. Chicago *Tribune*, Feb. 10, 1939, p. 8.
[3] Reported by Mrs. R. C. Coffy, of Muskogee, Okla. Reduced familiarly to *Feemy*.
[4] *American Mercury*, March, 1927, p. 305.
[5] Reported from Texas by Mr. Stanley Walker.
[6] From Louisiana. Chicago *Tribune*, Feb. 10, 1939, p. 8.
[7] Found in Georgia by Mr. Thomas Caldecot Chubb, of New York City.
[8] Some Curious Negro Names, by Arthur Palmer Hudson, *Southern Folklore Quarterly*, Dec., 1938, p. 188.
[9] Reported from Georgia by Mr. S. B. Tolar, Jr., of Waycross.
[10] Oklahoma City *Oklahoman*, July 1, 1940.
[11] The last two are from Some Curious Negro Names, before cited, p. 188.
[12] *Georgia's Health*, Sept., 1942, p. 3.
[13] The last two are from a list compiled by the Atlanta police and discussed in Names, Raleigh (N. C.) *News-Observer*, Aug. 19, 1940. It is probable that they are not given-names at all, but merely criminal monikers.
[14] *American Mercury*, March, 1927, p. 305.
[15] Reported by Mr. Donald Moffatt, of Brookline, Mass.
[16] Reported from Pine Bluff, Ark., by Miss Helen Cockrum, of Little Rock.
[17] Reported by Mrs. Louise B. Ellison, of Charleston, S. C.
[18] A steward's mate in the Navy, reported by Rear Admiral T. H. Robbins, Jr.
[19] Reported from Florida by Dr. Herman H. Horne, of New York University.
[20] Found in North Carolina by Miss Beverly Entsler, of Goldsboro.
[21] Found in Florida by Dr. Thomas B. Shoup, of the University of Florida. Its bearer registered for the draft as *M. B.*
[22] Found at Plymouth, N. C. As we have seen, titles are often used as given-names by whites also. But they cover a somewhat wider range among the blacks, *e.g.*, *Judge, Sergeant, Preacher, Deputy* and *Rabbi*. The last is reported from Texas by Mrs. D. J. Condit, of Tulsa, Okla.
[23] Some Curious Negro Names, before cited, p. 188.
[24] Some Curious Negro Names, before cited, p. 185.
[25] From Tulsa, Okla.

Pudding [1]	Satchel	Sugar [2]	Trouble [4]
Radio	Sausage	Sunbeam [3]	Two-Bits [5]
Rascal	Sooner	Trigger	Victrola
Rat			

Many of the double names in vogue among the dark blanket Christians of the South are the product of piety, for the Negro, on all save his highest levels, is almost as religious as the white cracker. Examples are *King Solomon, Queen Esther, Holy Moses* and *Virgin Mary*.[6] Once in a while these combinations run to formidable length, recalling the worst imbecilities of the Puritans, *e.g.*, *I Will Arise and Go Unto My Father*,[7] *Jesus Christ and Him Crucified*, *Matthew Mark Luke John Acts of the Apostles*. There are also cognate prodigies in the secular field, *e.g.*, *Pictorial Review*,[8] *Quo Vadis, Lake Erie*, and, when a romantic colored mother decides to shoot the works, *Christine Nancy Luanna Jane Rio Miranda Mary Jane, George Washington Thomas Jefferson Andrew Jackson*,[9] *Georgia May Virginia Dare Martha Annie Louise*,[10] *Mary Beatrice Love Divine Ceeno Tatrice Belle Caroline*[11] or (a mixed example) *Daisy Bell Rise Up and Tell the Glory of Emanuel*.[12] Some of the pious names show a considerable shakiness in Bible scholarship, *e.g.*, *Deuteronomy, Ecclesiastes, Judas Iscariot, Ananias, Verily*,[13] *Balaam, Cain, Herod, Archangel* and *Onan*. I have even heard of a colored boy baptized *Jehovah*.[14]

Among the secular names showing the same talent for absurdity I find *Delirious, Anonymous, Neuralgia*,[15] *Iodine, Sterilize, Sal Hepat-*

---

[1] Dark Town, before cited.
[2] The last three are from Some Curious Negro Names, before cited.
[3] Dark Town, before cited.
[4] The last two are from Some Curious Negro Names, before cited.
[5] From Louisiana. Chicago *Tribune*, Feb. 10, 1939, p. 8.
[6] Some Curious Negro Names, by Arthur Palmer Hudson, *Southern Folklore Quarterly*, Dec., 1938, pp. 179–93.
[7] *Willie* for short.
[8] Called *Torial* for short. Reported from Greensburg, Pa., by Miss Lenora Lund.
[9] On Aug. 16, 1936, R. L. Ripley reported a Negro in Pilot Grove, Tex., named *Daniel's Wisdom May I Know Stephen's Faith and Spirit Choose John's Divine Communion Seal Moses Meekness Joshua's Zeal Win the Day and Conquer All Murphy, Jr.* When he went to war, according to *This Week*, Sept. 12, 1943, he was entered upon his company books as *D. C. Murphy, Jr.*, and answered to *Dan*.
[10] Reported by Mr. Durward King, of Leaksville, N. C.
[11] Reported from Bladen county, N. C., by Mr. Worth B. Baldwin, of Laurinburg.
[12] I am indebted for this to Mr. A. Wilson Dods, of Fredonia, N. Y.
[13] Mistaken for a name. *Cf.* Matthew VI, 18.
[14] Found by Mrs. Louise B. Ellison, of Charleston, S. C.
[15] Reported from Virginia by Mrs.

ica, Morphine, Castor Oil, Ether, Constipation,[1] *Castile, Jingo, Vaseline* and *LaUrine*.[2] Public events and wonders often suggest names to Negro mothers, *e.g., Submarine,*[3] *Radio, High Water, Prohibition,*[4] *Blitzkrieg,*[5] *Pearl Harbor,*[6] *Hardtimes* and *NRA*.[7] It is not uncommon for a boy given the name of some great hero, clerical or lay, to take the hero's title as well, *e.g., Sir Walter Raleigh*[8] and *Saint Patrick*.[9] But all such oddities remain relatively rare and are seldom if ever encountered among Negroes above the total immersion level.

The names of black slaves have been investigated by Puckett.[10] His material ranges in date from 1619 to 1865, and embraces 12,000 names. He finds that the earliest slaves usually had commonplace English or Spanish given-names, with *John* and *Mary* in the lead. His first example of what later came to be regarded as a characteristically Negro name, to wit, *Sambo,* is found in Maryland in 1692. During the Eighteenth Century *Cuffy, Cudjo, Mungo* and *Quashie* appeared, and the prevailing classical influence showed itself in such names as *Caesar, Cato, Hannibal* and *Ulysses.* But the old names held their own, as they did among the whites, with *John* in the lead for men, followed by *Henry, George, Sam, Jim, Jack, Tom, Charles, Peter, Joe, Bob* and *William,* and *Mary* in the lead for women, followed by *Maria, Nancy, Lucy, Sarah, Harriet, Hannah, Eliza, Martha, Jane, Amy* and *Ann.* By the beginning of the Nineteenth Century Negro nomenclature began to take on the patterns it shows today. After Emancipation it was assimilated by the given-

---

John Allen Leathers, of Louisville, Ky.

[1] The last five are from Some Curious Negro Names, by Arthur Palmer Hudson, before cited. He says that *Constipation's* stable-name is *Consto.*

[2] Reported from Oklahoma. A Negro maid. Pronounced *You-reen,* with the accent on the second syllable.

[3] Associated Press dispatch from Crowley, La., Aug. 12, 1940.

[4] From Smithfield, N. C., reported by Mr. Don Wharton, of New York City.

[5] On July 4, 1940 the Associated Press reported that Negro twins born at Franklin, Texas, had been christened *Blitz* and *Krieg.*

[6] Reported from Pike county, Miss., by the Jackson *Daily News,* Dec., 1941. I am indebted here to Miss Anabel Power, of Jackson.

[7] Pronounced *Nira.* Reported by Mr. Harris Booge Peavey, of Maplewood, N. J.

[8] Found in a law report by Mr. Manuel Prenner.

[9] Negro's Liquor Sentence is 18 Days a Gallon, Oklahoma City *Oklahoman,* Sept. 23, 1941.

[10] Names of American Negro Slaves, in Studies in the Science of Society Presented to Albert Galloway Keller; New Haven, 1937, pp. 471–94. A previous study by Miss Blanche Britt Armfield, of Concord, N. C., is noted in AL4, p. 523, n. 3.

name patterns and fashions of the whites, though perhaps with a larger admixture of downright ridiculous names and a lesser admixture of mere fancy names. Says Puckett:

> With freedom, . . . *Romeo* Jones signed his name *Romey O.* Jones, and *Pericles* Smith became *Perry Clees* Smith. A boy who had always been known as *Polly's Jim*, having learned to read the New Testament,[1] became Mr. *Apollos James*. Slave *Sam* of Mississippi became *Sam Buck* when his master acquired another *Sam*, but under the exhilaration of freedom he expanded into *Sam Buck Jeemes Ribber Higboo* and indulged in other vagaries, such as feeding his dog gunpowder to make him brave. *Corinthia Marigold Wilkinson Ball Wemyss Alexander Jones Mitchell* owed her collection of names to the fact that she had been owned successively by half a dozen families and after Emancipation took the names of them all.[2]

The American Negroes, save in one small and isolated area, have dropped the names they brought with them from Africa, and also the Indian names that they picked up in the New World. That single area is the Gullah country along the South Carolina and Georgia coasts, including the offshore islands. Its speech, as we have seen in Chapter VII, Section 4, has been studied by Dr. Lorenzo D. Turner, of Fisk University. Most of the 6,000 African words that survive in Gullah are personal names. " In some families on the Sea Islands," writes Dr. Turner,[3] " the names of all the children are African. Many have no English names, though in most cases the African words in use are mere nicknames. Very few of the Gullahs of today know the meaning of these names; they use them because their parents and grandparents did so." Some of Turner's examples, with their languages of origin and original meanings, are:

Abeshe (Yoruba): worthless.
Aditi (Yoruba): deaf.
Agali (Wolof): welcome.
Alamisa (Bambara): born on Thursday.
Alovizo (Jeji): inflamed fingers or toes.
Anika (Vai): very beautiful.
Arupe (Yoruba): short.
Asigbe (Ewe): market day.
Bafata (Mende): high tide.
Bambula (Kongo): to transfer by witchcraft.
Boi (Mende): a first-born girl.
Dodo (Ewe): a forest.
Dutala (Mandinka): midnight.

[1] Acts XVIII, 24.
[2] Puckett gives authorities for all these names.
[3] Private communication, June 5, 1944.

Foma (Mende): a whip.
Hama (Mende): the rainy season.
Hawa (Mende): lazy.
Holima (Mende): patience.
Ishi (Kimbundu): the ground.
Kowai (Mende): war.
Kuta (with the *u* like *oo* in *foot*): a salt-water turtle, the totem of some of the clans of Gambia.
Lainde (Fula): a forest.
Mandze (Mende): a girl born at night.
Maungau (Kongo): a hill.
Momo (Bambara): to pry into.
Mumu (Mende): dumb.
Randa (Wolof): a thicket.
Sanko (Mende): one of triplets.
Simung (Mandinka): time to eat.
Sina (Mende): a female twin.
Suango (Mende): proud.
Suni (Bambara): fasting.
Sukuta (Mandinka): night is arriving.
Tiwauni (Yoruba): it is yours.
Winiwini (Jeji): delicate.

It will be noted that many of these relate to personal characteristics or to the place or circumstances of birth. Turner reports that the Gullahs carry this habit of name-making into English. " In addition to the names of the months and day," he says, " the following are typical: *Blossom* (born when the flowers were in bloom), *Wind, Hail, Storm, Freeze, Morning, Cotton* (born in cotton-picking time), *Easter* and *Harvest*." He does not include the once familiar *Cuffy* in the list of names he sends me, but I am told by Mr. Marcus Neville, of London,[1] that it is in common use on the Gold Coast, and is there thought to be derived from a Fanti word, *cofi*. The DAE traces it to 1713 and calls it " of African origin." It died out after the Civil War.[2] In my boyhood in Maryland the name commonly applied to a colored girl whose actual name was unknown was *Liza*, and a strange colored boy was similarly called *Sam* or *Rastus*, but both are now extinct.

The Mormons, in their early days, extracted a roster of names for their male offspring from the Book of Mormon, and to this day some of them are still called *Nephi, Mahonri, Lehi, Laman* and *Moroni;* also, the custom survives among them of naming the sev-

[1] Private communication, Feb. 1, 1943.
[2] Big as *Cuffy*, by George Stimpson, *Negro Digest*, Jan., 1947, p. 194.

enth son of a seventh son *Doctor*.[1] Other curious names, chiefly loans from afar, *e.g., Luana* and *Aloha*, testify to the fact that every pious Mormon must go on a missionary journey in his youth. But all these names are falling into disuse and the young of today bear the same fancy appellations that prevail among other Bible searchers, *e.g., Filna, Geneal, WaNeta, LeJeune, Janell* and *Myldredth* for girls; *Legene, Rondell, La Mar, Herald* (*Harold?*) and *Wildis* for boys, and *LaVon* and *LaVerne* for both sexes.[2] Indeed, it is possible that this murrain of made-up names was launched upon the country by the Saints, for as long ago as the 1836–44 era their prophet and martyr, Joseph Smith, had wives named *Presindia, Zina, Delcena* and *Almera*.[3]

The willingness of Jews to change their surnames, noted in Section 1 of the present chapter, is more than matched by their willingness to adopt non-Jewish given-names. This process is anything but new, for the Jewish exiles brought back many names from the Babylonian Captivity, and Moses himself apparently bore an Egyptian name.[4] Other names were borrowed from the other great nations of antiquity, *e.g., Feivl* and *Kalman*, from the Greek *Phoebus* and *Kelonymos*.[5] From medieval times onward borrowing and adaptation have gone on in all countries. Thus *Abraham* has been transformed in Russia into *Abrasha*, in France into *Armand*, in Germany into *Armin*, in Austria into *Adolf*, in England into *Bram*, and in the United States into *Albert, Arthur* and *Alvin*.[6] In the same way *Isaac*, an ancient Hebrew name meaning to laugh, has become *Ignatz* in Galicia, *Isidor* in France and Germany, and *Irving, Irwin, Edward* and even *Edmund* in the United States,[7] and *Samuel* has been supplanted by *Sidney, Stanley, Sylvan, Seymour, Sanford* and

---

[1] I am indebted here to Mr. J. F. Hill, of Salinas, Calif.
[2] I am indebted here to Mrs. George Lucas, of Ogden, Utah.
[3] No Man Knows My History, by Fawn M. Brodie; New York, 1945, pp. 335–36.
[4] Exodus II, 10 seeks to relate it to the Hebrew root *mashah*, to draw out, but most scholars reject this etymology as fanciful. Its actual source seems to lie in the Egyptian *mes* or *messu*, a son or child. Indeed, the late Sigmund Freud wrote a book seeking to prove that Moses was not a Jew at all, but an Egyptian.
[5] *Sarah* to *Sylvia* to *Shirley*, by A. A. Roback, *Commentary*, Sept., 1946, p. 272.
[6] Roback, just cited, predicts that "the next phase will be *Aldrich*."
[7] "Next in line," says Roback, "are *Eugene, Evan* and heaven knows what." He adds: "*Irving* came into vogue some sixty years ago. Lately, it has fallen from grace – for the obvious reason that too many Jews bear it."

Salwyn or *Selwyn*, some of which also do duty as substitutes for *Solomon*. Even the sacred name of *Moses* has given way in Russia to *Misha*, in France and Italy to *Moïse*[1] or *Maurice*, in Germany to *Moritz*, and in the United States to *Morris, Morton, Mortimer, Marcus, Marvin, Melvin, Martin, Milton, Murray* and even *Malcolm*.

It will be noted that in nearly all these cases the initial letter is preserved.[2] Roback, lately cited, says that often the original Jewish name survives " underneath and complementary to the protective Gentile name " and " it is this original name that is pronounced over them, following a whispered conference between rabbi and relatives, just before the last remains are gathered to their fathers." In many cases the widespread adoption of Gentile names by Jews has led to their abandonment by Gentiles. This is true, for example, of *Moritz* and *Harry* in Germany,[3] and it probably had something to do with the gradual disappearance of certain Old Testament names, *e.g., Abraham, Isaac* and *Moses*, in mid-Nineteenth Century America.[4] In not a few cases the Jews have adopted names of distinctively Christian character, *e.g.*, the Yiddish *Nitul*, which is related to *Natalie*, meaning a child born at Christmas. *Dolores*, taken from *Mater Dolorosa*, one of the names of the Virgin Mary, offers another example. In the same way *Alexander* and *Julius* were borrowed from the heathen centuries ago.

Of late the Jews have taken to naming their sons *John, Thomas, Mark, James* and *Paul*, not to mention *Kenneth, Chester, Clifton, Bennett, Leslie, Lionel, Tracy* and *Vernon*.[5] Roback reports that of the four presidents of the leading Jewish theological seminaries

---

1 I am indebted here to Mr. *Moïse* K. Cohen, of New York. *Moïse* is common among the Jews of Louisiana, and in South Carolina it is a surname.

2 " Usually," says Jane Doe in Concerning Hebrew Names, *Reflex*, Nov., 1928, p. 29, " a Jewish child is named after some ancestor. It has become a recognized custom of loyalty to take the first letter of the ancestor's given-name and give the newly born an Anglo-Saxon name beginning with the same letter."

3 *Harry*, there, is a diminutive of *Hershel*, a derivative of *Hersh* or *Hirsh*, which is not Jewish at all, but German. Roback says that in the United States it has generated *Henry, Herbert, Harold, Howard* and *Harvey*.

4 In later years *Max* seems to have fallen under the same blight. I once knew a politician named *Max* in Baltimore who lost an election because his opponents spread the report that he was a Jew.

5 Earl and Samuel G. Wiener, in On Naming the Baby, *Zeta Beta Tau Quarterly*, Dec., 1926, call such names as the last eight baronial. See AL4, pp. 507-08.

of the United States in 1946 three were named *Stephen*, *Louis* and *Julian*. Another distinguished rabbi has the name of *Beryl*,[1] a late president of the Central Conference of American Rabbis was *Edward*, and a rabbi who got into the *Congressional Record* with an Armistice Day address in 1945 was *Norman*.[2] The changes that have gone on during the past century and a half are well shown by the family-tree of the American Guggenheim family.[3] The founder was *Simon*, born in 1792, and his wife was *Rachel*. Their son was *Meyer* and their oldest grandson was *Isaac*. Among their other grandsons were *Daniel*, *Solomon* and *Benjamin*, but interspersed among them were *Murry*, *Robert* and *William*. In the fourth generation the *Stammhalter* was *Robert*. After that the male line began to languish, but meanwhile there were many daughters, and among them were *Lucille*, *Natalie*, *Diana*, *Margaret*, *Joan*, *Beulah*, *Edyth*, *Helen*, *Marguerite*, *Eleanor* and *Gertrude*. Some of these daughters (not counting those who married *Goyim*) had children or grandchildren named *Jean*, *Jack*, *Roger*, *Norman*, *Betty*, *Gene*, *Janet*, *Terrence*, *Gwendolyn*, *Harold*, *Willard*, *Timothy* and *Mary Ann*. Thus Jewish given-names are being rapidly assimilated to the general American stock, including the stock of fancy names. *Shirley* is now probably more common among Jewish girls than among Christians, and *Tommie Mae*, *Luciel* and *V-Etta* may be only around the corner. The Sephardic or Spanish Jews seem to cling to their traditional given-names much more firmly than the Ashkenazim [4] e.g., *Benjamin*, *Elias*, *Abraham*, *David*, *Emmanuel*, *Nathaniel*, *Solomon*, *Nathan*, *Isaac*, *Miriam*, *Rachel* and *Rebecca*,[5] but even the Sephardim have begun to weaken, and there are individuals of their proud clan in New York named *Ernest*, *William*, *Robert*, *Harold*, *Edgar* and *John*.[6]

The impact of Hitler made the American Jews acutely race-conscious, and from 1933 onward there was some tendency to go back to Jewish names.[7] But it did not proceed very far. Among

---

1 *Bloch's Book Bulletin*, Jan.-Feb., 1945, p. 18.
2 Nov. 16, p. A5291.
3 The Guggenheims: The Making of an American Dynasty, by Harvey O'Connor; New York, 1937.
4 Originally applied to the Jews of Germany, but later extended to those of Eastern Europe. The Sephardim hail from the Latin countries, Holland and the Levant.
5 I am indebted here to the late Benjamin De Casseres.
6 De Casseres himself admitted to having two female cousins named *Lulu*.
7 Mr. Marcus Rosenblum, of New York, tells me of a Jewish woman

the refugees in Palestine, however, it went to great lengths and is still in progress.[1] The *Palestine Gazette* is full of notices of changes of name registered with the Commissioner for Migration and Statistics, *e.g.*, *Leopold* to *Bezalel, Adolf* to *Abraham* or *Zeev, Stefan* to *Yaaqov, Bernhard* to *Dov, Eugen* and *Leo* to *Yehuda, Dora* to *Devora, Kurt* to *Yoel* or *Amnon, Felicia* to *Ilana, Gottfried* to *Yedidya, Franz* to *Yehiel, Wilhelm* and *Felix* to *Uri, Nina* to *Suad, Mendel* to *Menahem, Veronica* to *Adina, Edith* to *Dina, Zelda* to *Yardena, Frida* to *Tsipora, Irma* to *Miriam* or *Naomi, Clara* and *Rose* to *Shoshana* and *Sylvia* to *Shifrah*.[2] Moses Levene, in a pamphlet designed to interest English Jews in their ancient given-names,[3] says that the following, among others, have been revived in Palestine:

Male		Female	
Abindav	Itamar	Adina	Daliah
Achimelech	Itiel	Ahuda	Hassidah
Amikam	Joab	Aviva	Orah
Asaph	Jonadav	Beruria	Tikvah
Elnathan	Mevasher-Tov	Carmelit	Yonah
Hanina	Yigoel	Chemdah	Ziona [4]

Among the first German immigrants to America such characteristic given-names as *Johann, Hans, Franz, Conrad, Caspar, Gottfried, Andreas, Otto, Herman, August, Anton* and *Dietrich* were

---

who had changed her own name of *Sarah* to *Karen* at the age of sixteen, but named her daughters *Drazia* and *Avram*, both ancient Jewish names.

[1] Says William B. Ziff in The Rape of Palestine; New York, 1938, p. 189: "In Palestine, when a Jew changes his name, which is frequent, he selects the most Jewish one he can find."

[2] I am indebted here to Mr. G. Agronsky, editor of the *Palestine Post*, Jerusalem. But apparently this movement has its limits. On June 11, 1947, a Major *Wesley* Aron, of Palestine, appeared in Baltimore to advocate the unrestricted immigration of Jews.

[3] Hebrew Names: Their Meaning and Historical Connections; London, 1944.

[4] Levene calls attention to the curious fact that *Shem*, from whom the Jews are supposed to be descended, has had very few namesakes among them. Some traditional Jewish given-names, he says, are not Biblical, but originated in the Middle Ages, *e.g., Chaim, Hamina, Meyer, Nachman, Pesach. Chaim*, which means life, may have had forerunners in the period of the Babylonian Exile. An analogue was the Latin *Vitalis. Haym* is a modern form. Levene says that it is added to the names of sick people to stave off death. This change of name at a time of crisis is common among orthodox Jews. I am indebted here to Mr. R. G. Wasson, of New York, and Miss Dorothy C. Walter, of Providence, R. I.

very common,[1] but with the flight of the years most of them have been transformed into their British equivalents or abandoned altogether. The former process was facilitated, of course, by the fact that not a few were already identical with British names in spelling, though usually not in pronunciation, *e.g., Robert* and *Arnold*. The one brilliant exception to this obliteration has been mentioned before, to wit, *Carl*, which is now quite as common in the United States as it ever was in Germany.[2] I suspect that German influence may have helped to popularize certain girls' names, *e.g., Anna, Elsa, Emma, Ernestine, Gertrude, Ida, Irma, Meta, Regina* and *Selma*, but it certainly did not suffice to naturalize *Kunigunde, Waldburgia, Irmingard* and *Sieglinde*.[3] The Scandinavians in the Northwest have added *Helma, Karen*[4] and *Ingeborg* to the American répertoire, especially in that region, but for every name they have thus managed to preserve they have lost dozens. So with their boys' names, *e.g., Olaf, Gunnar, Axel, Nils, Anders, Holger, Knut, Jens*: of the whole lot only *Erik*, spelled *Eric*, seems to have been adopted by Americans.

Dr. Nils Flaten, of St. Olaf College, Northfield, Minn., in a study of the given-names of the students enrolled there in 1937–38, found that though nearly all of them were of Norwegian ancestry, wholly or in part, only 42 of their 702 different names were genuinely Norwegian.[5] *Anders, Fritjof, Halvor, Leif, Nils* and *Thorvald* each appeared but once, even among males whose parents were both Norwegian; among those with but one Norwegian parent they were lacking altogether. Among the girls *Astri, Ragna, Sigrid* and *Solveig* likewise appeared but once, and again only in children of pure

---

1 A Collection of Upwards of 30,000 Names of German, Swiss, Dutch, French and Other Immigrants in Pennsylvania From 1727 to 1776, by I. Daniel Rupp; second edition; Philadelphia, 1927.

2 Dr. Alfred Senn says in Unsere Namen, *Schweizer Journal* (San Francisco), Nov. 8, 1944, p. 1, that *Carl* or *Karl* was unknown in Germany until relatively recent times. In a list of 100,000 names from Breslau, *c.* 1400, it does not occur once. It first appeared in German Switzerland, in the form of *Carli*, in 1688.

3 An excellent list of German given-names, with their meanings, is in Reclams Namenbuch, a pamphlet in the Reclam series; Leipzig, 1938.

4 In 1947 Dr. Clifford R. Adams, of Pennsylvania State College, reported that *Karen* was the favorite of the co-eds there assembled, followed by *Dianne, Catherine, Linda, Ellen, Barbara, Gail, Carol, Margot* and *Kathleen* in order.

5 Dr. Flaten's report has not been published, but I have had access to it by his courtesy.

Norwegian stock. The favorite boys' names were *Arthur, Clifford, Clarence, Donald, Gordon, Harold* (from *Harald*), *Kenneth, Lloyd, Norman, Orville, Paul, Robert, Thomas* and *William:* these, taken together, were found no less than 124 times. The favorite girls' names, with the number of their occurrences, were *Helen,* 17; *Margaret,* 15; *Ruth,* 14; *Dorothy* and *Marion,* 12 each; *Lois* and *Mary,* 9 each; *Mildred,* 8; *Elaine* and *Esther,* 7 each; *Charlotte, Eunice, Irene* and *June,* 6 each. Fancy names of the sort we have been admiring in the Dust Bowl were numerous, *e.g., Brunell, Daryl, Durwood, Erliss, Glendor, Judean, Kermon, Murley, Selmer* and *Theos* among the males, and *Alette, Ardis, Edellyn, Erdine, Ferne, Juella, La Vaughn, La Verne, Marolyn, Monne Fay, Ninnie, Norena* and *Selpha* among the females.[1] Dr. Flaten says that when the early Norwegian immigrants sent their American-born children to the public-schools it was not uncommon for the schoolma'ams to give them " American " names. Thus *Knut* Larson became *Kenneth* and *Nils* Olson became *Nelson*. Some of these children kept both names through life, one for family and *Landsleute* and the other " to serve when dealing with Yankee neighbors."

As I have noted in AL4,[2] the Latin immigrants to the United States have had relatively little difficulty in retaining their often beautiful given-names, though occasionally a Mexican named *Jesús* is constrained to change to *José* or *Joe* in order to allay the horror and check the ribaldry of 100% Americans, or one named *Angel* adds an *o* for the same reason, and thus becomes an Italianate *Angelo*.[3] In the Southwest many American girls have been given Spanish names, *e.g., Dolores, Juanita, Anita* and *Constancia*, and some of these have got into wide circulation, but in compensation the Mexican girls have taken to American names, *e.g., Margaret, Annie, Edna, Lulu* and *Lucile*.[4] In theory, at least, every Mexican girl of pious parents is christened *María*, with the addition of one of the titles of the Virgin Mary, *e.g., María de los Dolores, María del Rosario, María del Pilar* —, but in practise the *María* is com-

---

[1] Miss Magda Houkon, of New York, the daughter of a Norwegian pastor in Minnesota, tells me that her father once baptized two sisters, one named *Lutine Clipporine Blanchine Annie-Ann* and the other *Purl*.

[2] p. 508.

[3] I am indebted here to Mr. Hugh Morrison, who says that this addition of *o* occurs in other cases.

[4] I am indebted here to Mr. J. Marvin Hunter, editor of the *Frontier Times* (Bandera, Texas).

monly dropped, and *Dolores, Rosario* or *Pilar* is used alone.[1] The Portuguese in Massachusetts and Hawaii have a few given-names for boys that are very hard worked, *e.g., José, João, Manoel, António* and *Francisco*, usually Americanized to *Joseph, John, Manuel, Antone* (or *Tony*) and *Frank*,[2] but in recent years they have begun to bestow purely British names upon both boys and girls, and in a little while, no doubt, there will be Portuguese *Elmers* and *Douglases, Doryses* and *LaVaughns*.[3]

The Slavs and Greeks in America find it difficult to retain their native given-names and large numbers of them seem to have abandoned the effort. An account of the situation among the Czechs, based upon the researches of Monsignor J. B. Dudek, is given in AL4.[4] The Slavic *Jan*, like the Scandinavian *Karen*, has gained some popularity among Americans, male and female, in the Fancy Names Belt,[5] but the Slavs themselves show a strong tendency to adopt American names. Ivan J. Kramoris[6] says that the Slovak *Jaroslav* is frequently changed to *Jerry* and *Miloslav* to *Milo*, and that *Kenneth, Lee, Wayne, Deane, Anita* and *Gail* are growing in popularity. Some of the Slovak girls have even adopted *Karen*. Once I received a letter from a Pole in Detroit who asked me to devise a plausible American substitute for his given name of *Zdzislaw*, which had been reduced to the unlovely *Zelo* in school. Unhappily, the best I could think of was *Elmer*. In 1940 another Detroit Pole, this time bearing the quite easy given-name of *Antoni*, applied to the local probate judge for permission to change it to *Clinton*. The reason he gave was that some of his American friends called him *Tony*, some *Anton* and some *Anthony*, to his confusion and embarrassment. But he did not propose to change his surname, so *Antoni Przybysz* became *Clinton Przybysz!*[7] Greek given-names

1 I am indebted here to Mr. L. Clark Keating, of Minneapolis.
2 Personal Names in Hawaii, by John E. Reinecke, *American Speech*, Dec., 1940, p. 350.
3 An interesting note upon given-names in Brazil, where anti-clericalism has warred upon the ancient saints' names, and brought in *Milton, Jefferson, Newton, Gladstone* and even *Calvin* and *Luther*, is in Brazil: an Interpretation, by Gilberto Freyre, New York, 1945, pp. 130–31. In Names on Puerto Rico, by Lawrence S. Thompson, *American Notes & Queries*, Sept., 1945, pp. 83–86, there is a discussion of the nomenclature that has displaced the old formal Spanish name system among the lower classes of the island.
4 pp. 511–12.
5 The pronunciation is changed to make it rhyme with *fan*.
6 The Americanization of Slovak Surnames, *Slovak Review*, Autumn, 1946, p. 70.
7 *Newsweek*, Jan. 15, 1940.

are so often changed in America that in 1943 the Greek War Relief Association found it necessary to issue a list of twenty-six of the more frequent ones, showing their original forms, the usual American equivalents, and the true English translations or transliterations.[1] *Konstantinos*, it revealed, is commonly turned into *Gus* or *Frank*, *Vasilos* into *William* or *Bill*, *Athanasios* into *Thomas* or *Tom*, *Panayiotis* into *Peter* or *Pete*, *Stavros* into *Steve* or *Sam*, *Dimitrios* into *James* or *Jim*, *Harilaos* into *Charlie*, *Ilias* into *Louie*, and *Anestis* into *Ernest*. Among the Greek waiters in New York, according to the *New Yorker*,[2] " *Demosthenes* becomes *Dick*, *Francopolous* turns out to be *Frank* or *Franklin*, and there was a Greek named *Demetrios Garfakis* who, on going to work in a hotel, became, not without stateliness, *James Garfield*."

Among the Armenians there has been a wholesale change of native given-names into more or less equivalent American forms, e.g., *Hovsep* into *Joseph*, *Garabed* into *Charles*, *Levon* into *Leon*, *Dikran* into *Dick* or *Richard*, *Misak* into *Mike*, *Mehron* into *Henry*, *Manoog* into *Mano*, *Sumpad* into *Sam*, *Davite* into *David*, *Vart* into *Rose*, *Aghavni* into *Dove* or *Dovey*, *Asthike* into *Stella*, *Nishan* into *James*, *Kevrok* into *George*, and *Hrant*, *Harutyoun* and *Hriar* into *Harry*.[3] In a directory of the State College at Fresno, Calif., I find girls with Armenian surnames named *Bernice*, *Isabel*, *Margaret*, *Betty*, *Dorothe*, *Dorthea*, *Roxie*, *Grace*, *Blanche*, *Doris*, *Aurora* and *Mary Jane*, and boys named *Milton*, *Luther*, *Karl*, *Martin*, *Jacques*, *Harold*, *Albert*, *Ralph*, *Ray* and *Vaughn*. The Arabic-speaking immigrants, mainly Syrians, frequently change the spelling of their names to make them less difficult to Americans, and sometimes drop them altogether. *Mahmūd* is changed to *Mike*, *Dāwūd* to *David*, *Najīb* to *Jimmie*, *Monsūr* to *Monte*, *Wādi'* to *Wade*, and *Abu* to *George*. A painter of Lebanese descent, originally *Fu'ād Sāba*, is now *Clifford Saber*, and various Arabic artistes have the names of *Julia*, *Selma*, *Elvira* and *Lucile*. But there are plenty of Arabic names that fit into English speechways without serious change, and these tend to be preserved, e.g., *Aziz*, *Habib*, *Salīm*, *Gibran*, *Salom*, *Fadwa*, *Khalil* and *Farhat*.[4] The Finns and Hungarians, who bridge

[1] I am indebted here to Mr. J. H. Young, of the Association headquarters in New York.
[2] June 1, 1935, p. 21.
[3] I am indebted here to Mr. William Saroyan, the Armenian-American dramatist and story-writer, and to Mr. Richard Badlian, of Boston.
[4] All these Arabic names are from Arabic-Speaking Americans, by

the gap, philologically speaking, between Europe and Asia, make many changes in their given-names, e.g., *Jussi* and *Juhana* to *John*, *Taavetti* to *David* and *Imari* to *Elmer* among the Finns.[1] The Hungarians change *Ferenz* to *Frank* or *Frederick*, *Istvan* to *Stephen*, *Mihály* to *Michael*, *János* to *John*, *Mór* to *Maurus* or *Maurice*, *József* to *Joseph*, *Géza* to *George* and *Elémer* to *Elmer*, but some of their other names, e.g., *Arpád*, *Béla*, *Lajos* and *Imre*, seem to be surviving.

The Chinese in America commonly keep their surnames but abandon their clan and given-names for American given-names, and at the same time shift their surnames from first position to last, so that *Lu Chi-hsin*, for example, becomes *David Lu*.[2] Some of the names adopted have a curious smack. Among the Chinese laundrymen of Baltimore *Tom*, *Bennie*, *Harry*, *Willie* and *Charlie* are common, and there is at least one *Wesley* and one *Lear*.[3] And in lists of Chinese intellectuals I have encountered *Daniel*, *Pearl*, *Jane*, *Rose*, *Jimmy*, *Eric* and *William*.[4] The Japanese in this country, like the Chinese, seldom change their surnames, and until the rise of the first American-born generation were similarly tenacious of their given-names, but of late many of them have begun to adopt American given-names. In the same Fresno State College Directory already quoted for Armenian names I find boys with Japanese surnames named *George*, *James*, *Hugh*, *Ben* and *Don* and girls named *Ruth*, *Olive*, *Ethel* and *Enid*. Reinecke, before cited, says that of 400 *Matsus* listed in the Hawaii Directory for 1934–35 only 1.2% had American given-names alone, and only 12.2% American names plus the initials that almost always stand for Japanese names, but these percentages have probably been increased since Pearl Har-

---

H. I. Katibah and Farhat Ziadeh: New York, 1946. In The Arab Village Community of the Middle East, in the Annual Report of the Board of Regents of the Smithsonian Institution for 1943; Washington, 1944, p. 537, Afif I. Tannous says that "when the first boy is born to a married couple people cease to call them by their name. Instead they are called after the name of their son — for example, *Abu-Ahmed* and *Um-Ahmed*, i.e., the father and mother of *Ahmed*." This practise, of course, is abandoned in America.

1 More examples are in AL4, p. 510.
2 *Parade*, April 14, 1946, p. 18.
3 13 Fines Assessed on Trash Counts, Baltimore *Evening Sun*, Jan. 4, 1946, p. 29.
4 Chinese in the United States Today, by Rose Hum Lee, *Survey Graphic*, Oct., 1942, p. 419. For more, see AL4, p. 513. On Feb. 18, 1946 *Donaldine Lew*, a Chinese soprano, sang at the Hotel Ambassador in New York.

bor. Even in 1934–35 the Japanese teachers in the public-schools, a highly Americanized class, showed 56% of American given-names. The Japanese do not run to nicknames and are chary of using given-names save in the family. Said a Japanese Rotarian in 1937:

> We Rotarians of Japan are told that calling a man by his first name or a nickname is a Western custom based upon a desire to be friendly, yet it does seem a bit extraordinary to us. We lay great stress on courtesy and ceremony. Most Japanese would consider addressing a man by his nickname as somewhat coarse and of questionable taste.[1]

Reinecke reports that many native Hawaiian given-names, *e.g.*, *Leilani*, *Iwalani*, *Maunaloa* and *Leimoni*, continue to flourish in the islands, and even carry a certain prestige, especially among mixed bloods. A child of such mixed bloods, even if it bears an American first-name, is usually also outfitted with an Hawaiian middle-name, and such middle-names are sometimes of formidable length, *e.g.*, *Kekoalauliionapalihauliuliokekoolau*, meaning " the fine leaved kaotree on the beautiful green ridges of the Koolau mountains." So long a name, of course, has to be abbreviated for everyday use. Some of the mixed bloods show strange and wonderful combinations of genes, ranging from Hawaiian to German, and from Japanese to French, Italian and Portuguese. These mongrels, especially those having Filipino blood, which is itself badly mixed, have a liking for curious double names, *e.g.*, *Dorothy Dot* and *Moses Moke*.[2] Others, says Reinecke, have " tasteless names reminiscent of those found in Southern directories," *e.g.*, *Luckie*, *Buddy*, *Sonny*, *Sweetheart* and *Loving*.

3. PLACE-NAMES

The need of a comprehensive treatise on American place-names, sufficiently well-informed to content specialists in the subject and yet written with enough sense of the picturesque to please the general reader, was met in 1945 by the appearance of Dr. George R. Stewart's " Names on the Land." It begins with a discussion of the lovely but somewhat repetitive names that the early Spaniards be-

[1] A Japanese View of Rotary, by S. Sheba, *Rotarian*, March 1937, p. 5.
[2] Additional Notes on Personal Names in Hawaii, by John E. Reinecke, *American Speech*, Feb., 1943, pp. 69–70. See also English Hawaiian Words, by O. Shaw; Milwaukee, 1938, pp. 71–80.

stowed upon the coasts and rivers of their discovery, and proceeds to the banal and unimaginative town names of the New England Puritans, to those borrowed from the French, Dutch, and later immigrants, to those carried westward by the first flights of pioneers, and to those issuing from the exuberant fancy of the same.[1] It does not linger long over Indian names, though they are always the first to attract the attention of a forcigner glancing at a map of the United States, but this perhaps is not illogical, for Indian place-names were in a state of chaos among the Indians themselves, and to this day the meaning of large numbers of them is in dispute or quite unintelligible.

Consider, for example, one of the most familiar: *Allegheny.* "The name," says a leading authority on Pennsylvania names, "has been a battleground for the Indian etymologists; no less than six different explanations are current."[2] More, there is no general agreement as to the spelling. The United States Geographic Board, in its heyday, made an effort to win universal acceptance for *Allegheny,* but in vain, and the two variants, *Allegany* and *Alleghany,* still survive and flourish.[3] Two other examples are *Penobscot* and *Milwaukee.* The meaning of the former has been debated for years, but with no result save the agreement that it somehow relates to water falling over rocks.[4] The latter is said by some authorities to be derived from an Indian word, *milioke* or *miloaki,* meaning good earth, and by others from *mahnah-wauk-seepe,* meaning a council ground near a river; yet others favor *man-a-waukee,* meaning a place where the Indians harvested a medicinal root called *man-wau.* A French map of 1648 made it *Meleke;* Father Louis Hennepin, the Franciscan missionary and explorer, spelled it *Melleoke* in 1679, and John Baisson de St. Cosme used *Milwarick* in 1699. The first postoffice established on the site of the present city was called *Melwakee,* but that was soon changed to *Milwaukie,* which continues to this day to be the name of a town in Oregon. Other forms in the past have been *Millicki, Melwarik, Milwacky* and *Milwackey.*[5]

Great confusion prevails especially among the Indian names of

---

[1] See AL4, pp. 234–36.
[2] Pennsylvania Place Names, by A. Howry Espenshade; State College (Pa.), 1925, p. 120.
[3] See AL4, p. 539.
[4] There is a good discussion of it in Indian Place-Names of the Penobscot Valley and the Maine Coast, by Fannie Hardy Eckstorm; Orono (Maine), 1941, pp. 1 and 2.
[5] The etymology of the name is discussed at length in A History of

the Eastern seaboard, for at the time they were adopted but little was known about the Indian languages, and since the study thereof has been tackled by competent linguists, the number of persons speaking them has greatly diminished, and in many cases fallen to zero. Moreover, those that survive have apparently changed considerably since the early days, and knowledge of most of them is still too scanty to give a sure footing to so difficult a discipline as etymology.[1] Says the preface to the Sixth Report of the Geographic Board, 1890 to 1932:[2]

> Many of the sounds occurring in the vocables of the Indian languages were strange to the early colonists. Some of them were quite unknown to the European languages. Hence the utterance and proper apprehension of these sounds were naturally subject to the influence of two effective causes of phonetic change and corruption, namely, (1) orosis, or the mishearing and misapprehension of the sounds uttered by the Indians, and (2) the tendency to compression and abbreviation of words in order to achieve ease of utterance. Conversely, the effect of these two causes was also influenced by the phonetics peculiar to the vernacular language of the recorder — whether it was Swedish, Dutch, French, English, Spanish or Russian. Such a recorder has a strong tendency to imagine that he heard sounds peculiar to his own mother tongue, and the availing records bear clear testimony to this fact. Some sounds common to the Indian languages were not apprehended at all, which often became the source of false identification of terms with other quite unrelated words.

The Indians themselves often forgot the meaning of their names for hills, meadows and streams: they became simply arbitrary words, like so many of our own proper nouns. Moreover, one tribe frequently borrowed a name from another using a different language or dialect, and had no more idea of its significance than we have today. Thus the Hurons got the name *Susquehanna*, meaning a muddy river, from the Delawares, and presently transformed it into a meaningless word which went into French as *Andastoei* and then into English as *Conestoga*, and in English became the name of a branch of the Susquehanna, of a town on that branch, and of a heavy wagon first built in the vicinity.[3] A crude folk-etymology

---

the Origin of the Place Names in Nine Northwestern States; Chicago, 1908, pp. 102–03.

[1] "The main problem of American place-name study," said the distinguished German philologian, Max Förster of Munich, in *American Speech*, Oct., 1939, p. 213, "seems to me the investigation of American names of Indian origin. . . . There is only one drawback: that the scientific study of Indian languages and dialects is hardly advanced enough to form a safe basis."

[2] Washington, 1933, p. 12.

[3] Sixth Report of the United States Geographic Board, just cited, pp.

often transformed Indian names into forms that seemed (and still seem) to be of English origin. There is, for example, *Crow Wing*, the name of a village in Minnesota, which was originally *Kakakiwing*, a Chippewa term meaning " at the place of the raven." The first two syllables were more or less correctly translated as *crow*, but *wing* was mistaken for the English word, though there was no reference to wings in the Indian name. *Port Tobacco* in Maryland, originally *Pentapang* or *Pootuppag*, was transmuted into its present form when the early colonists began loading tobacco in an adjacent arm of the Potomac. The *Rockaways* on Long Island were originally *Reckawackes* and seem to have got into English by way of Dutch; *Loyalhanna* and *Loyalsock*, two Pennsylvania townships, were originally *Laweelhanna* and *Lawisaquik*,[1] and *Tia Juana* (California), which seems to be Spanish for *Aunt Jane*, is actually an Indian term, *tiwana*, meaning " by the sea." [2]

Many other non-English place-names have been subjected to the same barbarization. The *Low Freight*, a stream in Arkansas, was originally the French *L'Eau Froid;* the *Ambrosia* in Indiana was the French *Embarras; Gramercy Park* in New York City was the Dutch *Kromme Zee* (crooked lake); *Baraboo* in Wisconsin was the French *Baribault; Waco* in Texas was the Spanish *Hueco* and so on.[3] Numerous bastard names have been formed by outfitting non-English stems with English indicators, *e.g., Romeroville, Glenrico, Point Loma, Ninaview*[4] and *Pass aux Huitres*[5] and this process is still in full blast, especially in the naming of new resorts and suburbs, *e.g., Buena Park* and *Mount Alta*. Non-English names are naturally

---

13-14. The DAE shows that there was an inn called the *Conestoga Waggon* in Philadelphia in 1750.

[1] American Place-Names, by Louis N. Feipel, *American Speech*, Nov., 1925, p. 83.

[2] Spanish and Indian Place Names of California, by Nellie Van de Grift Sanchez; San Francisco, 1914, p. 47. The Geographical Board long ago declared for *Tia Juana*, but most American newspapers use *Tijuana*.

[3] The process was witnessed on a large scale in France during the two World Wars. *Ypres* became *Wipers, Isigny* became *Easy Knee,* and *Bricquebec* became *Bricabrac*.

The French themselves began it in Napoleonic times by giving a village in Spain the name of the English *Horse Guards* — and then turning it into *Hossegar*. See Some Folk Etymologies for Place Names, by J. W. Aston, *Journal of American Folklore*, April–June, 1944, pp. 139-40.

[4] A Dictionary of Spanish Terms in English, by Harold W. Bentley; New York, 1932, p. 17.

[5] Language Mixture in American Place Names, by Mamie Meredith, *American Speech*, Feb., 1930, p. 224.

most prevalent in the areas in which the languages from which they come have been most spoken, *e.g.*, Spanish in the Southwest,[1] German in Pennsylvania,[2] Dutch in New York, French in Louisiana[3] and along the Canadian border, and Scandinavian in Minnesota.[4] But some of them have wandered far, so that there are substantial numbers of Spanish names in Pennsylvania, and of German names in California.[5] In most cases they were carried by immigrants, but returned soldiers also had something to do with it — for example, after the Mexican War.

When an Indian name is borne by a place of any importance its spelling and pronunciation tend to become more or less fixed, as we have seen in the case of *Milwaukee*, but there is seldom any agreement about the names of smaller places. The Geographic Board and its successor, the Board on Geographical Names, have spent a great deal of time and energy settling such differences. The former, taking up the problem of determining the true name of a small lake in New Hampshire, was confronted by no less than 132 different forms. It finally decided upon *Winnepesaukee*, but soon afterward found reason to change to *Winnipesaukee*. The familiar *Mohawk*, the name of a river, a valley, a lake, a town and various villages in New York State, appears in the literature of the early frontier in 142 spellings, all coming down, apparently, from an Iroquois word *maqua* or *mahaqua*, meaning a bear. Even *Seneca* has been spelled in 110 ways, and *Oneida* in 103. Some of the Indian names that survive in remote places are very formidable, *e.g.*, *Souadabscook, Quenshukeny,*[6] *Kiskiminetas, Quohquinapassakessa-*

---

[1] Bentley just cited, says that there are more than 400 in California and more than 250 in New Mexico.

[2] Der deutschamerikanische Farmer, by J. T. Och; Cincinnati, 1913, pp. 228-35.

[3] French Names in Our Geography, by Henry G. Bayer, *Romanic Review*, July-Sept., 1930, pp. 195-203.

[4] Roy W. Swanson, in Scandinavian Place-Names in the American Danelaw, *Swedish-American Historical Bulletin*, Aug., 1929, p. 8, says that he has counted more than 400 in that State. In The Viking and the Red Man; two volumes; New York, 1940-42, Reider T. Sherwin argues that many place-names presumed to be of Indian origin were actually borrowed by the Indians from Norse settlers of a thousand years ago. These settlers, he says, were absorbed by the Indians, and gave many Norse loans to their languages.

[5] In the *Hamburger Tageblatt*, July 8, 1934, briefed in the *American-German Review*, Dr. Norbert Zimmer called attention to the curious fact that most of the German place-names of the United States are of Low German origin, though the early German immigration was predominantly from Western, Central and Southern Germany.

[6] A run feeding the north branch of

managnog[1] and *Chargoggagaugmanchaugagoggchaubunagungamaugg.*[2]

Worse, not a few of them, when their original meanings are dredged up, turn out to be opprobrious or obscene. The Indians often had several or even many names for the same place, and some of them were far from flattering. In other instances they had no names at all, for what was huge, obvious and inescapable seemed to them to be hardly worth naming. When a white colonist, in the former case, pressed them for the name of some river, valley or hill they sometimes gave him the worst one current, and in the latter case they replied with the aboriginal equivalent of " That is a river " or " Go to hell! "[3] The most reliable opinion today is to the effect that *Chicago*, as the sportive Indians imparted it to the first whites, meant " the place of strong smells " or *Skunktown*.[4] At different times in the past it has been spelled *Cheggago, Cheegago, Tzstchago, Stktschagko, Chirgago, Shecago, Shikkago, Shercaggo, Schenkakko, Zheekako, Ztschaggo, Chiccago, Checago, Chicawgo, Chikkago, Chiggago, Shakakko, Schuerkaigo, Psceschaggo, Stkachango* and *Tschakko*.[5]

The early English settlers were dull dogs, and, as Stewart has

---

the Susquehanna. The Geographic Board warns that it is not to be written *Quenshhague, Quineshakony* or *Quinneshockeny*.

[1] The name of a brook in New Hampshire. I should add that the Geographic Board abolished it in 1916 and ordered that the brook be called *Beaver*. Many other Indian names have been similarly displaced. J. H. Trumbull, in his Indian Names and Places, Etc., In and On the Borders of Connecticut; Hartford, 1881, recorded that the *Anchamaunnackkaunack*, a pond near Stonington, had become *Lake Amos*, and that an eminence originally *Puckhunkonnuck* was *Pendleton Hill*. In her Letters From the United States, Cuba and Canada; New York, 1856, p. 324, the Hon. Amelia M. Murray was deploring the disappearance of *Natchovtashmuck* and *Nassamasschaick* from the map of the Massachusetts Berkshires, and as far back as Sept.

23, 1837, a writer in the New York *Mirror* was calling *Coosawda, Catawba, Tuscaloosa, Talapoosa*, etc., " softer, more appropriate and more descriptive " than *Johnstown, Jamestown, Millerstown* and the like. I am indebted for the last two references to Dr. Joseph M. Carrière.

[2] This monster is reported in Connecticut Past and Present, by Odell Shepard; New York, 1939, p. 100. It is the name of a lake commonly called *Webster*.

[3] The process is well described in The Aleut Language, by Richard Henry Geoghegan; Washington, 1944, p. 87.

[4] Stewart adds " or something worse." See Great Skunk Theory Stands Up, Chicago *Tribune*, Sept. 12, 1939, p. 14.

[5] A History of the Origin of the Place Names in Nine Northwestern States, before cited, pp. 55–56.

noted, very few of the names they bestowed upon the land showed any imagination. The Pilgrim Fathers could think of nothing better than *Plymouth Rock* to call the place of their landing, and their opposite numbers in Virginia, though they succumbed to a few lovely Indian names, displaced many others with such banalities as *James, York, Charles, Henry, Williamsburg* and *Richmond*.[1] So many of the place-names of New England are mere repetitions of the names of English towns that there is a Namesake Town Association there,[2] with a long membership and a longer list of eligibles. "The determination of the colonists," said the *Knickerbocker Magazine* in 1837,[3] "was to eradicate everything that perpetuated the native tribes, and the ancient names of *Naumkeag, Shawmut* and *Mooseasuck* gave place to . . . *Salem, Boston* and *Providence.*" The same loan was used over and over again, and to this day there are sixteen towns with names based on *Newton* within a few miles of Boston.[4] Nor was there much improvement when the ties with the Motherland began to loosen. The first patriot to think of calling some frontier village *Washington* had immediate and numerous imitators and by 1839, according to Captain Frederick Marryat,[5] there were already 43 *Washingtons* on the American map, with 41 *Jacksons*, 32 *Jeffersons*, 31 *Franklins*, 26 *Madisons*, 25 *Monroes*, 22 *Perrys*, 14 *Lafayettes* and 13 *Hamiltons* following.[6] Hundreds of names were made by prefixing *New* to some existing name,[7] or

---

1 "The Americans," said Robert Southey in The Doctor, CV, 1834-47, "have given all sorts of names, excepting fitting ones, to the places which they have settled or discovered." "Our country," said Washington Irving in the *Knickerbocker Magazine*, Aug., 1839, "is deluged with names taken from places in the Old World, and applied to places having no possible affinity or resemblance to their namesakes. This betokens a forlorn poverty of invention, and a second-hand spirit, content to cover its nakedness with the borrowed or cast-off clothes of Europe." I am indebted here to Dr. Joseph M. Carrière.
2 Place Names, by Jerome C. Hixson, *Words*, Sept., 1936, p. 13.
3 Jan., p. 19.
4 I am indebted here to Mr. L. Clark Keating.
5 A Diary in America, p. 151.
6 In an editorial entitled What's In a Name? the Boston *Herald* reported on Sept. 3, 1944 that 27 *Washingtons* remained. The writer in the *Knickerbocker Magazine* for 1839, just quoted, said that there was then "a county or town of *Washington* in every State and Territory of the Union, except Delaware," and that in the majority there was both a town and a county. Delaware still lacks a *Washington*, though it has a *Lincoln*. *Washington* Territory was organized March 2, 1853 and became a State on Nov. 11, 1889.
7 The writer in the *Knickerbocker Magazine*, just quoted, said that

by borrowing the name of some local animal or tree. Both processes were followed by the pioneers who penetrated to the eastern end of Lake Erie toward the close of the Eighteenth Century. First, with gorgeous lack of humor, they called their village of sticks and mud *New Amsterdam* and then they switched to *Buffalo*, which was instantly borrowed for scores of other hamlets in what was then the Far West.

The classical place-names which engaud the map of central New York, *e.g.*, *Troy*, *Utica*, *Ithaca* and *Syracuse*, have often been credited to Simeon DeWitt, surveyor-general of the State from 1784 to 1834, who laid out the bounty lands for Revolutionary soldiers on which they occur. But he denied in his old age that he had anything to do with the matter[1] and hinted that they were actually chosen by the Commissioners of the Land Office, to wit, Governor George Clinton, Lewis A. Scott, Gerard Bancker and Peter T. Curtenius. This was at a meeting held in New York City on July 3, 1790,[2] at which DeWitt was not present. There remains, however, some mystery about the business, for the names bestowed at that meeting, though they included many personal names, *e.g.*, *Brutus*, *Cicero*, *Romulus* and *Pompey*, did *not* include such place-names as *Troy*, *Utica* and *Syracuse*. Whatever the actual provenance of the latter and in spite of the ridicule which the wits of the time heaped upon them,[3] they appealed to the American imagination, and were presently imitated upon a large scale in the new West. So late as 1929 Evan T. Sage reported[4] that there were still 2200 on the American map, including 31 *Troys*, 22 *Athenses*, 20 *Spartas*, 19 *Carthages* and 13 *Uticas*, and that they were to be found in every one of the 48 States.[5]

---

there were 257 town-names embodying *New* in the United States in 1839. Today there must be many more. There are also four State names out of forty-eight.
1 Krapp, Vol. I, p. 194.
2 The Classic Nomenclature of Western New York, by Victor H. Paltsits, *Magazine of History*, May, 1911, pp. 246-49.
3 For example, Fitz-Greene Halleck and Joseph Rodman Drake in one of their Croaker Papers in the New York *Evening Post*, June 17, 1819. They assumed that DeWitt was to blame and declared that he had "reared for himself an everlasting monument of pedantry and folly."
4 Classical Place-Names in America, *American Speech*, April, pp. 261-71.
5 See also Classical Names in New York State, by Edward E. Hale, *American Speech*, Feb., 1928, p. 256; Origin of Classical Place-Names of Central New York, by Charles Marr, *Quarterly Journal of the New York State Historical Association*, July, 1926, pp. 155-67; New York Classical Names Due to Governor Clinton, New York *Times*, Feb. 26,

There were similar wholesale bestowals of place-names in later years, especially after the railroads began to run everywhere. When the Southern Pacific was opened from Mojave, Calif., to the Colorado river " an alphabetical order was used — *Bristol, Cadiz, Daggett*, etc."[1] It was not uncommon, indeed, for the guests of the first train over a new line to be given the privilege of naming the stations along the way — most of them, of course, mere knots in the telegraph wire at that stage, but some of them substantial towns in the days following.[2] The Postoffice was also active in naming new communities, sometimes by deciding between rival contenders and at other times by inventing names of its own, and the Geological Survey and later the Forest Service commonly determined the names of newly-surveyed lakes, streams, mountains and valleys.[3] Washington Irving, in 1839,[4] charged that " the persons employed by government to survey and lay out townships " in his day were largely responsible for the embalming of politicians' cognomens as place-names. " Well for us is it," he said, " when these official great men happen to have names of fair acceptation, but woe unto us should a *Tubbs* or *Potts* be in power, for we are sure, in a little while, to find *Tubbsvilles* and *Pottsylvanias* springing up in every direction." But most such names, of course, were invented and bestowed by Tubbses or Pottses who happened to have land in the vicinity, or by their local admirers or parasites. In 1837 a writer in the New York *Mirror* suggested that eponymous names might be made measurably more bearable by varying their suffixes. He said:

1928, p. 5, and Classical Place Names in Tennessee, by A. W. McWhorter, *Word-Study*, Nov., 1933, pp. 7 and 8.

[1] American Place-Names, by Louis N. Feipel, *American Speech*, Nov., 1925, p. 89. " On a certain railroad in western Iowa," says Allen Walker Read in Observations on Iowa Place Names, *American Speech*, Oct., 1929, " are three towns at intervals of five miles named *Plover, Mallard* and *Curlew*. The explanation seems to be that the first president of the railroad, Charles E. Whitehead, was a great hunter and had often hunted through the region before the railroad was built."

[2] Observations on Iowa Place Names, just cited, pp. 28–29. The *New Yorker* reported, Feb. 15, 1947, p. 21, that a composer named Ernst Krenek had lately used the names of the stops on the Santa Fe between Albuquerque and Los Angeles as the text for a chorus *a cappella*.

[3] How one officer of the Forest Service bestowed scores of names upon natural features of the Wenatchee National Forest in Washington is described at length in Place-Names in the Northwest, by A. H. Sylvester, *American Speech*, Dec., 1943, pp. 241–52.

[4] In the *Knickerbocker Magazine*.

Take the favorite name of *Pitt*, for instance,[1] and see in how many shapes it may be complimented without copying the familiar ones of *Pittstown, Pittsfield* and *Pittsburg*. In addition to the other common terminations of *-ville, -ford, -haven, -port* and *-borough*, we have, first, *Pittstade* (being the name of a place situated upon a sea or river); second, *Pittstead* (when the place is inland); third, *Pittsteppe* (when on a hill); fourth, *Pittstein;* fifth, *Pittsdorf;* sixth, *Pittsdale;* seventh, *Pittshithe;* eighth, *Pittsthorpe;* ninth, *Pittsheim;* tenth, *Pittside;* eleventh, *Pittshame;* twelfth, *Pittsmore;* thirteenth, *Pittscliffe;* fourteenth, *Pittsbourne;* fifteenth, *Pittsleigh*. The meaning of these last terminations the reader will find in Johnson's and other dictionaries, and by altering the prefix he may coin as many names as he pleases. The word *Ravenswood*, for instance, thus altered, will make a dozen as fine-sounding names as the original of Scott. The master of *Ravenscliffe, Ravenstein* and *Ravensleigh* would boast as sound a title as the hero of "Lammermoor." [2]

This proposal, which was apparently made quite seriously, seems to have had no immediate effect, but in the long run it may have launched the spate of *Ferndales, Stoneleighs, Woodmeres, Briarcliffes, Elmhursts* and the like which began to afflict the country after the Civil War.[3] The craze for such fancy names has survived into our own time, but of late it has shown some signs of abating. During the high tide of the great movement into the West, between the end of the War of 1812 and the first battle of Bull Run, it raged only among a small minority of aesthetes, chiefly clotted along the Atlantic Coast. The hearty Philistines who swarmed over the Alleghenies and then over the Rockies were quite innocent of it. In the main they were content to give their new settlements names brought from the East or fashioned of familiar materials and in time-worn patterns; for the rest, they preferred humor to poetry. This was the period which saw the founding of such surrealist communities as *Hot Coffee*, Miss.;[4] *Hog Eye, Gourd Neck, Black Ankle, Lick Skillet* and *Nip and Tuck*, Texas;[5] *Social Circle*, Ga.; *Sleepy Eye*, Minn.; *Gizzard*, Tenn.; *Noodle*, Texas; *Wham* and *Waterproof*, La.; *Oblong*, Ill.;[6] *Peculiar*, Mo.;[7] *Santa Claus*, Ind.;[8]

[1] William Pitt, first Earl of Chatham (1708–78), remained popular in America because of his opposition to Lord North's harsh treatment of the colonies and his vigorous defense of them in the French and Indian War. This popularity, in 1758, caused the unlovely *Pittsburgh* to be substituted for the charming *Fort Duquesne*.
[2] Names of Places, New York *Mirror*, April 15, 1837, p. 335. I am indebted here to Dr. Joseph M. Carrière.
[3] See Stewart, pp. 330–32.
[4] Strangers in Mississippi Find *Hot Coffee* is Place, Baltimore *Evening Sun*, Oct. 21, 1932.
[5] These Texas specimens are from South-western Slang, by Socrates Hyacinth, *Overland Monthly*, Aug., 1869.
[6] The last seven come from Newark Library: Books' Baedeker, Newark

Wages, Colo.; *Drain*, Ore.; *Goodnight*, Texas; *Ox*, Ohio; *Okay*, Okla.; *Grit*, Ky.; *Loco*, Okla.; *Plush*, Ore.;[1] *Rabbit Hash*, Ky.; *Bug*, Ky.; *Bumble Bee*, Ariz.; *Blue Eye*, Mo.; *Fireworks*, Ill.; *Huzzah*, Mo.; *Ice*, Ky.; *Jitney*, Mont.; *Only*, Tenn.; *Rat*, Mo.; *Razor*, Texas; *What Cheer*, Iowa; *Wink*, Texas; *Zigzag*, Ore.;[2] *Bowlegs*, Okla.; *Bugtussle*, Texas;[3] *Braggadocia*, Mo.; *Big Arm*, Mont., and *Defeated*, Tenn.

The popularity of such grotesque names in the new West seems to have been first noted by James Hall (1793–1868), a Philadelphian who went down the Ohio by keelboat in 1820, settled on what was then the frontier, became a judge in Illinois, and finally engaged in banking at Cincinnati. In 1828 he published a book in which he described the new country, and in it he printed a jingle recording some of its curious nomenclature, *e.g.*, *Horsetail, Dead Man, Custard, Brindle* and *Raccoon*.[4] But it was after the plains and Rockies were crossed that the pioneers really spit on their hands and showed what they could do. Many of their inventions have become part of the romantic tradition of the Pacific Coast and have thus taken on a kind of improbability, but *Humbug Flat, Jackass Gulch, Gouge Eye, Red Dog, Lousy Level, Gomorrah*,[5] *Shirt Tail* and *Hangtown* were very real[6] and so late as 1876

News, May 23, 1938. Who's Who in America gives *Waterproof* as the birthplace of Franklin O. Adams, a distinguished architect. Neal O'Hara reported in the Boston *Traveler*, Aug. 12, 1946, that a Louisiana newspaper once made a sensation by printing the headline: Seven *Waterproof* Negroes Drown. I am indebted here to Mr. Alexander Kadison.

7 American Towns Bear Odd Names, New York *Times*, Feb. 7, 1932.

8 A village in Spencer county, not far from the Ohio river. At Christmas time many thousands of American children write to Santa Claus there. When the Postoffice proposed to change its name the Indiana delegation in Congress made loud and effective objection.

1 The last eight are from Titular Tour, *Atlantic Monthly*, Nov., 1934, pp. 639–40.

2 The last thirteen are from U.S. is Full of Odd and Wonderful Names, *Life*, Jan. 31, 1944, p. 57.

3 For the last two I am indebted to Capt. Morris U. Lively, of Norman, Okla.

4 Letters From the West, Containing Sketches of Scenery, Manners and Customs, and Anecdotes Connected With the First Settlements of the Western Sections of the United States; London, 1828. For this I am indebted to An Early Discussion of Place Names, by John T. Flanagan, *American Speech*, April, 1939, pp. 157–59.

5 Long before this there was a *Sodom* in New York State, and it still exists. It is in Warren county.

6 California Gold-Rush English, by Marian Hamilton, *American Speech*, Aug., 1932, p. 425.

Henry T. Williams was printing a long list which included *Ragtown, Dead Mule, Chucklehead, One Eye, Puke, Rat-Trap, Port Wine, Ground Hog's Glory, Nigger Hill, Blue Belly, Swellhead, Centipede, Seven-by-Nine, Gospel Swamp, Nary Red, Gas Hill, Paint Pot, Pancake, Chicken Thief, Hog's Diggings, Shinbone, Poodletown, Puppytown, Git-Up-and-Git* and *Poverty Hill*.[1] In the years since then many of these names have been changed to more elegant ones,[2] and others have vanished with the ghost towns they adorned, but not a few still hang on. Indeed, there are plenty of lovely specimens to match them in the East, in regions that were also frontier in their days, *e.g.*, the famous cluster in Lancaster county, Pennsylvania: *Bird in Hand, Bareville, Blue Ball, Mt. Joy, Intercourse* and *Paradise*.[3] Pennsylvania also has towns named *Cyclone, Cypher, High Dry, Holiday, Local* and *Obelisk*, and I have heard of one named *Poison*, though it is not on the maps. *Hog Island*, Pa., which got into the newspapers often during World War I, had namesakes in Virginia, Texas, Maine, New York, Vermont and Massachusetts. Maryland has a *Blue Ball* to match Pennsylvania's, and also a *Basket*, a *Bald Friar*, a *Fiery Siding*, an *Issue*, a *Number Nine*, a *Gott* and a *T.B.* New Jersey has a *Dolphin*, a *Seaboard*, a *Straws* and a *Wall*.

The new State of Michigan, admitted to the Union on January 26, 1837, sought to stem the tides of nomenclatomania then running by enacting a law forbidding calling a town " after any other place or after any man without first obtaining the consent of the Legislature." " The consequence is," said a writer in the Providence *Journal* later in 1837,[4]

---

[1] The Pacific Tourist; New York, 1876.

[2] *Gouge Eye*, for example, is now *Pleasant Grove*, and *Hell's Neck*, Mo., has become *Neck City*. I am indebted for the last to Mrs. Vernon A. Rea, of Waygata, Minn.

[3] Some of these got their names from old inn signs, as did *Red Lion* in York county, *Broad Axe* and *King of Prussia* in Montgomery, *Rising Sun* in Lehigh, and *Compass* and *White Horse* in Chester. But the origin of *Intercourse* is mysterious, and A. Howry Espenshade does not discuss it in his Pennsylvania Place-Names; State College (Pa.), 1925. The village, which is near Lancaster, does a roaring trade in postcards with passing motorists. Some Western geographical names of an indelicate nature are listed in Nomina Abitera, by W. L. McAtee; Washington, 1945, pp. 3 and 4.

[4] The precise date I do not know. The article was reprinted in the New York *Mirror*, Oct. 21. I am indebted here to Dr. Joseph M. Carrière.

that Michigan is destitute of *London, Paris* and *Amsterdam*. Unlike her sister States she boasts neither *Thebes, Palmyra, Carthage* or *Troy*. No collection of huts with half a dozen grocery-stores has been honored with the appellation of *Liverpool*, nor has any embryo city, with a college or an academy *in contemplation*, received the name of *Athens*. She is the only State but has a *Moscow* and a *Morocco* in the same latitude, and an *Edinburgh* and an *Alexandria* within thirty miles of each other. *Babylon, Sparta* and *Corinth*, though they have been transplanted to every other part of the Union, are destined never to flourish on the soil of Michigan. No *Franklin* or *Greene* or *Jefferson*, which would make the five hundredth, no *Washington*, which would make the ten thousandth of the same name, is to be found in her borders.

This writer, alas, was too optimistic, for the law turned out to be as unenforceable as the Volstead Act, and at the present moment Michigan has a *London*, a *Paris*, a *Palmyra*, a *Troy*, an *Athens*, a *Sparta*, a *Moscow*, a *Franklin* and a *Washington*, to say nothing of a *Rome*, a *Dublin*, an *Oxford*, a *Turin*, a *Sans Souci*, a *Topaz*, a *Payment*, an *Eden*, a *Zion* and a *Dice*. It was not, in fact, until more than half a century afterward, on February 15, 1890, that any effective effort was undertaken to bring place-names under official regulation. On that day Captain H. F. Picking, the hydrographer of the Navy, set up a board in his office to consult with the hydrographers of foreign nations about the forms and spellings of names appearing on mariners' charts. The British Admiralty had published rules of its own in 1885, and Captain Picking's board was soon in communication with the Admiralty authorities, and with those of France, Germany, Spain, Canada, Chile, the Netherlands, Italy, Austria-Hungary, Mexico, Japan and China. The result was a report published by the Navy Department in 1891.[1] It dealt wholly with foreign place-names, but its preparation naturally suggested the need of a similar study and control of American names, and on September 4, 1890 President Benjamin Harrison appointed a United States Board on Geographic Names consisting of representatives of the Postoffice, the Smithsonian, the Hydrographic Office of the Navy, the Engineer Corps of the Army, the Lighthouse Board, the State Department, the Geological Survey, and the Coast and Geodetic Survey. The authority of this board, at the start, was confined to settling disputes regarding place-names which arose in the depart-

[1] Report on Uniform System for Spelling Foreign Geographic Names. See Foreign Geographic Names on the Mariner's Chart, by James B. Hutt, *United States Naval Institute Proceedings*, Jan., 1946, pp. 39–47. I am indebted here to Rear Admiral G. S. Bryan, U.S.N., ret.

ments, but on January 23, 1906 President Theodore Roosevelt widened its scope by charging it with "the duty of determining, changing and fixing" all such names "within the United States and insular possessions," and a little later its name was shortened to United States Geographic Board. Representatives of the General Land Office, the Government Printing Office, the Census Bureau, the Biological Survey and other agencies were added to it from time to time, and it continued to flourish until 1934. It issued frequent announcements of its decisions, and in 1933 published an 834-page report in which all of those reached down to 1932 were assembled.

Unfortunately, it was treated parsimoniously by an otherwise lavish government. Down to 1917 it had no appropriation of its own, but fed its members out of the salaries they got from the various departments, and down to 1929 it had no paid secretary.[1] On April 17, 1934, as an incident of the departmental reorganization then in progress, it was abolished, its functions were transferred to the Interior Department, and it there reappeared as the United States Board on Geographical Names. For some time it seems to have escaped the notice of the idealists then fashioning a new world, and so late as 1935 its staff was confined to an executive secretary, an assistant and a clerk. But then its potentialities were grasped by the forward-looking Secretary of the Interior, the Hon. Harold L. Ickes, and after Pearl Harbor it began to move into high gear. On February 25, 1943, it was reorganized with a director at $8,000 a year, an assistant at $5,000, two grand divisions of five sections each, a staff of geographers and philologians, and a working force of 110 altogether.[2] During the war years it naturally gave most of its attention to foreign place-names, for the Army and Navy were then penetrating to many far places, and where even the Army and Navy could not go airships were carrying agents soliciting clients for Lend Lease. Thus the board, in July, 1945, brought out a brochure on Tibet by which it appeared that the proper spelling of the name of the Tibetan village lying at the intersection of Lat. 27° 30′ N and Long. 85° 14′ E was *Mendong Gomba*, not *Mendong Gompa*, and that to call it *Men-tung-Ssu*

[1] Its first report, issued Dec. 31, 1890, was published at the cost of the Smithsonian; its second, May 25, 1891, at that of the Coast and Geodetic Survey; and its third, Aug. 1, 1891, at that of the Lighthouse Board.

[2] Say Now, Shibboleth, *Nation's Business*, Aug., 1943, pp. 76–78.

was altogether incorrect. Other brochures dealt with the place-names of Mongolia, Portuguese Timor and the Lesser Sunda islands, but those of the United States were rather neglected, and nearly all of the few dealt with were the names of mountains, rivers, etc., not of inhabited places.

With the end of the war, however, the board returned to its home grounds, and since then it has been carrying on the work of getting something approaching order into the American map. Like its predecessor, it seems to be determined to knock all apostrophes out of the national place-names, even at the cost of logic. Thus the county in Maryland which was *St. Mary's* for centuries is now *St. Marys* and the county which used to be *Prince George's* is *Prince Georges*.[1] Why the *s* was not deleted with the apostrophe I do not know. In various foreign names, *e.g.*, that of *St. John's*, the capital of Newfoundland, the board has been constrained to retain the apostrophe, but not within the continental limits of the United States.[2] Accents appear to be similarly doomed. What was once *Santa Fé*, N. Mex., is now plain *Santa Fe*, though *Santa Fé* in Argentina remains unshorn. So with *Wilkes-Barre*, Pa., once *-Barré*. So with *San José*, Calif. So with *Coeur d'Alêne*, Idaho. The board also advocates simplified spelling and has changed *centre* to *center* in many town-names, and lopped the final *h* from *-burgh*,[3] and dropped many a redundant *City*, *-town* and *-ville*.

But in one respect, at least, it is conservative: it gives no countenance to such clumsy collision forms as *Jonespoint*,[4] *Annarbor*, *Limesprings*, *Burroak*, *Wallawalla* and *Coscob*.[5] Also, it frowns upon the false delicacy that wars upon picturesque old names. Its

---

1 In the earliest records, *c*. 1634, *St. Mary's* appeared as *St. Maries;* by the end of the Seventeenth Century it had become *St. Mary's*. *Prince George's* was so denominated by an act of the Assembly, 1695, and *Queene Anne's* by an act of 1706.
2 One of the few exceptions is *Martha's Vineyard*. Here the apostrophe was saved by vigorous local protests.
3 But not in *Pittsburgh*, where local indignation stayed it.
4 A landing on the Hudson river. Local usage seems to have made it *Jone's Point* originally, with the apostrophe ahead of the *s* instead of after it. Then it became *Jonespoint*. The board prefers *Jones Point*.
5 In the Revolutionary era even worse amalgamations were common. The *Village Record* of Amherst, N. H., used *Newhampshire*, and other papers used *Newbedford*, *Rhodeisland* and *Newengland*. This madness was followed by the wide use of hyphens, *e.g.*, *New-York*, which was the practise of all the New York papers in the 30s and 40s. I am indebted here to Mr. Charles J. Lovell.

predecessor consented to changing the name of *Dishwater Pond* in New Hampshire to *Mirror Lake*, but it resisted the visionaries who sought to change *Cow Creek* on the Chesapeake into *Big Creek*, *Ironjaw Lake*, Mich., into *Crescent Lake*, and *Cat Island*, Mass., into *Lowell Island*. In general, however, it tries to follow local desires, and when a village or natural object has a name which arouses mirth it usually gives its imprimatur to a change. Thus it consented to turning *Muskrattown*, Md., into *Little Georgetown*, *Bug Lake*, Minn., into *Herriman Lake*, and *Great Gut*, Va., into *Houseboat Creek*. In most such cases it finds support for its decisions in local history or legend. In the matter of foreign names it has favored using native forms of the names of towns, *e.g.*, *Firenze*, *'s Gravenhage* and *München*, on outgoing mail in order to facilitate ultimate delivery, but the usual English forms for the names of countries, *e.g.*, *Germany*, *Greece* and *Switzerland*, to facilitate sorting in the American Postoffice. It apparently looks forward to the day when the American names for foreign cities, *e.g.*, *Florence*, *The Hague*, *Naples*, *Vienna* and *Munich*, will disappear altogether, but that day is not yet.[1]

The synthetic place-name seems to be indigenous to the United States: it may be encountered, now and then, elsewhere, but it must surely be rarely. Characteristic examples are *Texarkana* (*Texas* + *Arkansas* + *Louisiana*),[2] *Penn Yan* (*Pennsylvanian* + *Yankee*), *Reklaw* (*Walker* spelled backward), *Wascott* (*W. A. Scott*), *Paragould* (*W. J. Paramore* and *Jay Gould*), *Carasaljo* (*Carrie* + *Sally* + *Josephine*), and *Asco* (*Atlantic Smokeless Coal Company*). Of the first class there are many examples along the borders of the States, *e.g.*, *Kenova* (*Kentucky* + *Ohio* + *West Virginia*),[3] *Texhoma* (*Texas* + *Oklahoma*), *Calexico* (*California* + *Mexico*), *Kanorado* (*Kansas* + *Colorado*), *Dakoming* (*Dakota* + *Wyoming*), *Nosodak* (*North Dakota* + *South Dakota*), *Mardela* and *Delmar* (*Maryland* + *Delaware*), *Delmarva* or *Delmarvia* (*Delaware* + *Maryland* +

---

[1] The question is discussed at length in First Report on Foreign Geographic Names; Washington, 1932. The American press associations, on April 8, 1944, decided to use native forms in their foreign correspondence in all save 78 cases. These exceptions include *Moscow* instead of *Moskva*, *Athens* instead of *Athenai*, and *Limerick* instead of *Luimneach*. A full list is in the *Editor and Publisher*, April 15, 1944.

[2] The Name Texarkana, by M. E. Melton, *American Speech*, Nov., 1926, p. 113.

[3] *American Speech*, Dec., 1933, p. 80.

Virginia),[1] *Arkana* (*Arkansas* + *Louisiana*), *Tennga* (*Tennessee* + *Georgia*,[2] *Viropa* (*Virginia* + *Ohio* + *Pennsylvania*), *Pen-Mar* (*Pennsylvania* + *Maryland*), *Vershire* (*Vermont* + *New Hampshire*), *Moark* (*Missouri* + *Arkansas*), and *Nypenn* (*New York* + *Pennsylvania*).[3]

All the other varieties of blend-names show numerous examples. Hamill Kenny reports *Ameagle* (*American Eagle Colliery*), *Anjean* (*Ann* + *Jean*), *Champwood* (*Champ Clark* + *Woodrow Wilson*), *Cumbo* (*Cumberland Valley Railroad* + *Baltimore & Ohio Railroad*), *Itmann* (*I. T. Mann*), *Mabscott* (*Mabel* + *Scott*), and *Gamoca* (*Gauley* + *Moley* + *Campbell*) from West Virginia;[4] Fred I. Massengill reports *Maryneal* (*Mary* + *Neal*), *Alanreed* (*Allen* + *Reed*), *Fastrill* (*Farrington* + *Strauss* + *Hill*), *Gladstell* (*Gladys* + *Estell*), *Normangee* (*Norman G. Kittrell*), *Saspamco* (*San Antonio Sewer Pipe Company*) and *Tesnus* (*sunset* spelled backward) from Texas,[5] and Dorothy J. Hughes reports *Alkabo* (*alkali* + *gumbo*), *Cando* (from *We can do*), *Golva* (*Golden Valley*), and *Seroco* (a memorial of the fact that the first piece of mail reaching the village postoffice was a *Sears Roebuck* catalogue) from North Dakota.[6] Some curious specimens are to be found in other States, e.g., *Benld* in Illinois, a blend of *Benjamin L. Dorsey*; *Westkan* in Kansas, from *West Kansas*; *Miloma* in Minnesota, a blend of *Milwaukee* and *Omaha*, not formed directly from the names of the

---

1 This is the name, not of a town, but of a whole region — the lower peninsula between the Chesapeake Bay and the Atlantic. There is a *Delmarva News* at Selbysville, Del., and at Wilmington, Del., there is a *Delmarvia Review*. There are *Delmars* in various States far from those here named, but their names seem to be derived from the Spanish term for "by the sea." I am indebted here to Mr. Donald L. Cherry, of Watsonville, Calif.

2 I take the last two from Two State Towns and Cities, by Miriam Allen deFord, *American Notes & Queries*, Oct., 1945, p. 112.

3 The last two are from *American Notes & Queries*, Sept., 1946, p. 91. Henry J. Heck printed fifty specimens in State Border Place-Names, *American Speech*, Feb., 1928, pp. 186-90. Stewart says, p. 364, that such names "never became popular in the East and Middle West," but that there are "about sixty" examples in the South and Far West. "The three chief railroads," he continues, "cross the California line at *Calneva*, *Calzona* and *Calexico*. Many boundary names also record a location on the line between two counties or near the junction of three."

4 The Synthetic Place Name in West Virginia, *American Speech*, Feb., 1940, pp. 39-44. See also his West Virginia Place Names; Piedmont (W.Va.), 1945, pp. 57-58.

5 Texas Towns; Terrell (Texas), 1936.

6 Coined Town-Names of North Dakota, *American Speech*, D 1939, p. 315.

two cities, but from those of the *Milwaukee Chicago & St. Paul* and the *Chicago, Minneapolis and Omaha Railroads; Marenisco* in Michigan, from *Mary Relief Niles Scott; Centrahoma*, from *central* + *Oklahoma; Ladora* in Iowa, from *la, do* and *re* of the musical scale; *Ardenwald* in Oregon, from *Arden Rockwood*, with the last syllable translated into German; *Ti* in Oklahoma, made up of the initials of *Indian Territory* reversed; *Pawn* in Oregon, the initials of *Poole, Aberley, Worthington* and *Nolen;*[1] *Marhattianna* in Oklahoma, from *Mary, Hattie* and *Anna; E. T. City* in Utah, named for *E. T. Benson*, " an early miller and Mormon official," and *Veyo* in the same State, " coined from the words *verdure* and *youth* by a group of Mormon Beehive Girls."[2] Another American invention is the addition of *Courthouse* or *Court House* to the name of a county-town. Such forms are more prevalent in Virginia, but they are also to be found in New Jersey and North Carolina.[3] The low amperage of patriotic passion during World War II saved twelve of the thirteen *Berlins* in the United States from rechristening. The one casualty was *Berlin*, Ala., which became *Sardis*.[4] An effort by Easterners to induce the people of *Berlin*, Ore., to change its name to *Distomo* was rejected at a mass-meeting on October 10, 1944.[5] But the name of *Kobe*, Alaska, was apparently changed to *Rex* in 1944.[6]

The Board on Geographical Names, save in very rare cases, does not concern itself with the pronunciation of place-names, and when other governmental agencies venture to do so it is seldom to much edification. The Legislature of Arkansas decided solemnly in 1881

---

[1] I borrow the last four from Stewart, p. 363.
[2] The last two come from Origins of Utah Place Names, third edition; Salt Lake City, 1940.
[3] They are discussed in Some American Place-Name Problems, by George R. Stewart, *American Speech*, Dec., 1944, pp. 289–92. In the same paper he also discusses the common American practise of referring to a county by its proper name only, omitting *county*.
[4] *American Notes & Queries*, Jan., 1946, p. 155.
[5] *American Notes & Queries*, Jan., 1946, p. 157. The original name of the village was *Burrell Inn*, but *Berlin* had been adopted for convenience. *Distomo* was a town in Greece, destroyed in the war.
[6] U.S. Board on Geographical Names, Decision List No. 4408, Aug., 1944, p. 169. The democratic flavor of the new name will be noted. Stewart says, p. 372, that World War I " left less effect upon the map than the average presidential election of a hundred years earlier." *Berlin*, Ga., became *Lens*, but reverted to *Berlin* after the war. *Potsdam*, Mo., became *Pershing; Brandenburg*, Texas, became *Old Glory*, and *Kiel*, Calif., became *Loyal*, but *Bismarck*, the capital of North Dakota, kept its name. In Canada *Berlin*, Ont., became *Kitchener* and has so remained.

that the name of the State "should be pronounced in three syllables, with the final *s* silent, the *a* in each syllable with the Italian sound, and the accent on the first and last syllables,"[1] but it will be noted that the *a*'s in the second and third syllables, as one now hears them in *Árkansáw*, are actually anything but Italianate. Moreover, the name of the *Arkansas* river is the *Arkánsas* along its course through Kansas and so is the name of *Arkansas City*, which is in Kansas just over the Oklahoma line. "The *Arkansaw* Traveler," the national hymn of the State, is always, however, *Árkansáw*, and evidence assembled by the DAE shows that the Indians who infested the region in the early days were called *Arkansaws* so early as 1772, and that Congress thus spelled the name in 1819. Indeed, there are Arkansawyers who argue spitefully that *Kansas* itself should be *Kansaw*.[2] Meanwhile, *Arkansaw* for the State has been accepted by the British Broadcasting Corporation, though it makes the Kansas town *Arkánsas City*.[3] The same authority now ordains *O-hígh-o* for *Ohio* and *Massachóosets* for *Massachusetts*, though the English schoolboys of past generations were taught to say *Ó-he-ó* and *Massátchusetts*.[4] The *Arkánsas* pronunciation, so abhorrent to all patriotic citizens of the State, may have arisen by assimilation with that of *Kansas*, and perhaps it was helped on by the Eastern schoolma'ams who once tried to substitute *Gloucéster* for *Gloster* and *Worcéster* for *Wooster*.[5] Similarly, the presence of an *a* in-

---

[1] This joint resolution was approved March 15, 1881. It is given in full in The Basis of Correctness in the Pronunciation of Place-Names, by Allen Walker Read, *American Speech*, Feb., 1933, pp. 42-43. It was during the debate on this resolution that one of the legislators loosed a speech that has come down in stag-party humor as "What! Change the name of *Arkansaw?* Never!" A much bowdlerized version of it is in Native American Humor, edited by James R. Aswell; New York, 1947, pp. 359-60.

[2] Mr. Charles J. Lovell tells me that The Ohio and Mississippi Pilot; Pittsburgh, 1820, p. 132, says: "The name *Kanzaw* is applied to the country watered by the river *Kanzas*, which should be pronounced *Kanzaw*." It is spelled *Konza* in the report of Major Stephen H. Long's journey from the Mississippi to the Rocky Mountains, made in 1819-21. See The Pronunciation of *Arkansas*, by Robert T. Hill, *Science*, Aug. 26, 1887, pp. 107-08.

[3] Broadcast English, VI, by A. Lloyd James; London, 1937, p. 22.

[4] Dr. James T. Barrs, in a speech before the English Lunch Club at Harvard, Feb. 12, 1944, said: "South Georgians, along with other Southerners, have trouble in pronouncing *Ohio*. They treat the *hi* as if it were *how*, and say *Ohowo*."

[5] This, at all events, was the theory of John Murdoch (1852-1925), librarian of the Smithsonian, and he set it forth tartly in *Science*, Sept. 2, 1887, p. 120.

stead of an *i* at the end of *Missouri, Cincinnati, Miami*,[1] etc., is probably the end product of a schoolma'amish war upon an early tendency to turn every terminal *a* into *y*, e.g., *Indiany, Ithacy, Floridy, Uticy, Alabamy, Caroliny, Susquehanny, Philadelphy, Nebrasky, sody, opery, asthmy, balony*.[2]

The pronunciation of *Missouri* has been under debate for many years and has produced a large literature, some of it marked by anything but scholarly calm.[3] Allen Walker Read has published a characteristically comprehensive review of the whole matter.[4] In that review he rejects the theory just mentioned, first launched by E. S. Sturtevant,[5] that the *-a-*ending represents a fastidious effort to get rid of the apparent vulgarism of the *-y-*ending, though Sturtevant has since been supported by such accepted authorities as George Philip Krapp[6] and John Samuel Kenyon.[7] Instead he seeks an explanation in the disinclination of the carnivora of a proud and once bloodthirsty State to let it pass under a name which suggests a diminutive.[8] But he overlooks the unchallenged presence of the same diminutive in *Mississippi*,[9] one of the least infantile names on the American map, and in the names or pet-names of such testosteronic towns as *Boise*, Idaho; *Tulsy*, Okla.;[10] *Hickory*, N. C., and *Corpus Christi*, Texas. The early authorities show that *Missouri*,

[1] The Ohio town, county and river, not the Florida hellmouth.
[2] Harold Wentworth, in his American Dialect Dictionary; New York, 1944, pp. 722–23, prints about 200 examples.
[3] Franz Boas says in Geographical Names of the Kwakiutl Indians; New York, 1934, p. 20, that *Missouri* is derived from an Indian term, *m'nisose*, meaning roily water.
[4] Pronunciation of the Word *Missouri*, American Speech, Dec., 1933, pp. 22–36. See also The Word *Missouri*, Missouri Historical Review, Oct., 1939, pp. 87–93.
[5] Linguistic Change; Chicago, 1917, pp. 79–80.
[6] The Pronunciation of Standard English in America; New York, 1919, pp. 80–81.
[7] American Pronunciation; ninth edition; Ann Arbor (Mich.), 1945, pp. 168–69.
[8] To this effect he quotes the St. Louis *Post-Dispatch* as follows: "*Mizzoura* rolls from the tongue with mellifinous [sic] grandeur. It must be spoken with open mouth and erect head. It suggests beauty and greatness. *Mizzoury* . . . ends in a piping squeak. A lion's roar to a peewee's pipe! . . . *Mizzoury* is a pretty name for a nice little school girl, but it will never do for the Queen of the Union."
[9] H. A. Shands says in Some Peculiarities of Speech in Mississippi, 1893, that in that State *Massasip* is "sometimes used by Negroes and illiterate whites for *Mississippi*," but is apparently unused on higher levels.
[10] The use of the diminutive in this case is justified historically, for *Tulsa* was named after an Osage chief named *Tulsey*. I am indebted here to Capt. Morris U. Lively, of Norman, Okla.

not *Mizzoura*, was first in the field, and that it apparently remained in favor until the Civil War era. At that time a craze for elegance seized the nascent *intelligentsia* of the State, and the *-a*-ending was urged upon the plain people with such fervor that the overwhelming majority of them adopted it and have continued to use it to this day.[1] But in the early 90s or thereabout a new wave of pedagogues, chiefly, it would appear, from the East, launched a counter-attack in behalf of the *-i*-ending, and a bitter battle was soon joined. The gogues might have had some chance of success if they had been content to argue only for the *-i*-ending; unhappily, they also tried to unvoice the two *z*'s in the middle of the name, and so convert the manly Roman sound of *buzz* and *whizz* into the puny Phoenician cheep of *kiss* and *bliss*. This was a fatal blunder, for even those Missouri sophisticates who were willing to accept *-i* revolted against *-ss-* in disgust and indignation. Today even the dictionaries and encyclopedias, which are usually at least a generation behind-hand, prefer the *-zz-* to the *-ss-*, and most of them have also surrendered to the *-a*-ending.[2]

Three other conspicuous American place-names whose pronunciation has kicked up controversy are *Iowa*, *Los Angeles* and *San Antonio*. *Iowa* is borrowed from the name of an Indian tribe, and the history of that name was thus told by the late Dr. Frank H. Vizetelly:

> The *Iowas* were a branch of the main group of a southwestern Sioux tribe which received the name of *Pahoja*, or *Gray Snow*,[3] which they retained, but they were known to the white people by the name of *Ioways* or *Aiaouez*. This name was spelled phonetically in both cases — one for the guidance of the English-speaking people, and the other for the guidance of the French-speaking people.
>
> In 1689 the spelling *Aiaoua* was that used in American literature, and is to be found in Perrot's Memoirs, p. 196. The form varied at that time, and the plural was given as *Aiaouais* and *Aiaouez*. In 1702 Iberville used *Ayooués* (the

---

1 Read says "perhaps two-thirds." I incline to think that his estimate is too low.

2 The local preference extends to regions outside Missouri, especially to the southward. When, in 1911, Dr. William A. Read, of Louisiana State University, polled college students in Alabama, Arkansas, Florida, Georgia, Kentucky, Louisiana, Mississippi, North Carolina, Tennessee, Texas and Virginia on their pronunciation, he found that 162 out of 238 preferred the *-a*-ending and all save one preferred *-zz-* to *-ss-*. See *Dialect Notes*, Vol. II, Part VII, 1911, p. 500.

3 The New International Encyclopedia gives *Pahotcha* or *Pahucha* as the form and says that it meant dusty noses. The Encyclopedia Americana makes it *Palinchas*, of the same meaning.

acute accent gives the word the sound of *e* in *they*). By 1731 *Ayoouais* was used by Beauharnois and Hocquet, but varied in 1761 to *Aiauway*, a form to be found in the Journal of Lewis A. Clark. In the following century (1804) *Aieways* was used, and *Aiowais* was used by Pike in his travels (1811), but in 1810 we had *Ioway* as a variant. In 1824 *Iawas* and *Iaways* were used, and in 1825 *Ihoway*, which latter form is to be found in Senate Document No. 21 of the Eighteenth Congress, Second Session. The forms current in 1848 were *Ayavais* for the plural and minus the *s* for the singular. And *Ioway*. By 1858 the name took the form *Ayeovai* in the singular, with an *s* in the plural, and in 1905 *Iaways*.[1]

Ioway seems to be preferred by the plain people of the State, and the name so appears in the State song, but the Geographical Board long ago declared for *Í-o-wa*, and it is supported not only by the majority of outsiders but also by a formidable faction within the State. There is even a body of opinion in favor of putting the accent on the second syllable, but it is apparently feeble. Nearly all the accepted authorities ordain *I-o-wa*, but the Thorndike Century Senior Dictionary[2] gives *I-o-way* as an alternative, and the Funk and Wagnalls New Practical Standard Dictionary[3] notes it as used locally. The controversy over the pronunciation of *Los Angeles* has been going on for years, and will probably never end. As I noted in AL4, p. 542, the Los Angeles *Times*, the chief guardian and glory of the local culture, advocates what it renders in type (somewhat darkly) as *Loce Ahng-hayl-ais*, but a dozen other forms are to be encountered in the town. The gabbers of the British Broadcasting Corporation are instructed to use *Loss Anjileez*[4] and those of the National Broadcasting Company are encouraged to attempt *Laws-an-j'l-uhs*,[5] but most other authorities wobble. Even Frank H. Vizetelly, usually so sure of himself, could not decide between *Los Anggeles*, with the *o* as in *go*, and *Los Anjuhliz*, with the *o* as in *not*,[6] and one local expert has actually recommended different pronuncia-

---

1 *Atlantic Monthly*, April, 1931, p. 62 of Advertising Section. The DAE records *Ioway* for 1836, 1839 and 1841, but *Iowa* for 1810, 1840 and 1853. The Encyclopedia Americana adds *Ayanways* and *Ajowes* to the early forms of the name. The *Iowa* tribe came into what is now *Iowa* from Minnesota. In 1861 it was concentrated on reservations in Kansas and the present Oklahoma.
2 Chicago, 1941.
3 New York, 1946. References to other discussions are in The Basis of Correctness in the Pronunciation of Place-Names, by Allen Walker Read, *American Speech*, Feb., 1933, p. 43.
4 Broadcast English VI, by A. Lloyd James; London, 1937, p. 45.
5 NBC Handbook of Pronunciation; New York, 1943, p. 189.
6 A Desk Book of 25,000 Words Frequently Mispronounced; New York, 1917; p. 561.

tions in successive editions of the same book.[1] Webster 1934 gives both *Los Anggeles* and *Los Anjeles*, the New Practical Standard gives *Los Anjilus*, *Los Anjileez* and *Los Ang-guh-lus*, Robert Shafer gives four forms in a phonetic alphabet that I refuse to try to interpret,[2] and Kenyon and Knott give half a dozen pronunciations without deciding between them, and record despairingly that "a resident phonetician says: 'The only one I've never heard is *Los Angheles.*'"[3] Many of the inhabitants abbreviate the name to *L.A.*, and others use *Los*.[4] The controversy over *San Antonio* has to do with the question whether the people there ever call the town *Santóne*. The Hon. Maury Maverick, its best-known citizen, assures me that they do not. "The average person," he reports, "says *Santónyo*, although the well-informed generally say *San An-tón-i-o*. The Mexicans, of whom there are some 90,000 in San Antonio, pronounce the word with a broad *a* and sound every syllable."[5] But other observers insist that *Santóne* is in common use, and Charles H. Hogan says that the first syllable is frequently stressed.[6] Dr. E. G. Reuter, a resident, tells me that he has also heard *San Antone*.[7]

As I have recorded, the Geographical Board follows local usage, whenever possible, in the spelling of place-names. The same policy with respect to pronunciation was advocated by Noah Webster so long ago as 1803.[8] "The true pronunciation of the name of a place," he said, "is that which prevails in and near the place." But he defended and indeed advocated changes in Indian names to bring them

[1] Harry L. Wells, author of California Names; Los Angeles. His first edition of 1934 gives *Los Ahng-hay-lays*, but in his edition of 1940 he makes it *Ahn-hay-lays*.
[2] The Pronunciation of Spanish Place Names in California, *American Speech*, Dec., 1942, p. 241.
[3] A Pronouncing Dictionary of American English; Springfield (Mass.), 1944, p. 260. This phonetician seems to have overlooked the fact that Nellie Van de Grift Sanchez, in her Spanish and Indian Place Names of California; San Francisco, 1914, p. 339, had recommended *Loce Ahng-hell-ess*.
[4] The full name of *Los Angeles*, in Spanish times, was *El Pueblo de Nuestra Señora la Reina de Los Angeles de Porciuncúla*. Harry L. Wells, in California Names, before cited, says that *Los Angeles de Porciuncúla* was the name of a shrine of St. Francis Assisi in Italy, and that it was given to the Los Angeles river by Padre Crespi in 1769. *Porciúncula* is Spanish for a small portion or allowance.
[5] Private communication, March 21, 1935.
[6] A Yankee Comments on Texas Speech, *American Speech*, April, 1945, p. 82. I am also indebted here to Mr. William C. Stewart, of Southbridge, Mass., and to Dr. Josiah Combs, of Fort Worth.
[7] Private communication, Dec. 28, 1946.
[8] The American Spelling Book; revised impression; Brattleborough (Vt.), 1814, p. v.

in accord with "the genius of our language, which is accommodated to a civilized people." This is the line taken by Allen Walker Read in his excellent review of the subject.[1] He rehearses and answers the argument that the pronunciation of place-names should follow the spelling or be decided by self-constituted authorities on language or by legislative action, and concludes that it should be determined "simply by impartial observation of selected speakers in the locality of the places named." Even this rule, of course, cannot be followed slavishly, for sometimes there is a sharp difference of opinion, even among natives, as to the true pronunciation of a given name, and more often an accepted local form is challenged by another prevailing somewhere else, or even generally. We have just seen examples in the cases of *Arkansas, Los Angeles* and *Iowa*. Another is provided by *Chicago*, which is *Chicawgo* in the city itself but *Chicahgo* in the rest of the country.

Read raises the question as to what is to be done about a name which, while designating the same place or object, differs in pronunciation in two regions, *e.g.*, that of the *Arkansas* river. Is it, he asks, "to change its name for different parts of its course?" Well, why not? If the people of Kansas prefer *Arkánsas* for that part of the river within their boundaries, then it *is* the *Arkánsas* there, and if those of Arkansas prefer *Árkansaw* for their own share of it, then it becomes the *Árkansaw* as the border is crossed. The name of *Beaufort* is pronounced differently in the two Carolinas — and both forms are "correct."[2] The best pronouncing dictionary of American place-names, that of Alfred H. Holt, first published in 1938,[3] avoids all vain speculations as to how names *ought* to be pronounced, and is content to record accurately how they *are* pronounced. Holt's authority is always local, and he is careful to find out if there are variations on different cultural levels. His method of indicating pronunciations is so simple and effective that it puts to shame the phonetic alphabets invented by learned men, and he relieves the tedium of what might otherwise be a depressing subject by cracklings of pawky humor.

The study of place-names is comparatively recent in the United

[1] The Basis of Correctness in the Pronunciation of Place-Names, *American Speech*, Feb., 1933, pp. 42–46.
[2] There is an interesting discussion of this question in Broadcast English, II, by A. Lloyd James; London, 1930, pp. 6-10.
[3] American Place Names; New York.

States. Washington Irving printed some observations upon them in the *Knickerbocker Magazine* in 1839 and Henry R. Schoolcraft discussed the Indian names of New York before the New York Historical Society in 1844,[1] but it was not until 1861 that a separate work upon the subject appeared. This was a pamphlet of thirty-two pages by a surgeon named Usher Parsons, entitled "Indian Names of Place in Rhode-Island."[2] Parsons' interest was mainly in the Indian names in use in the State "when civilization commenced" and his stated purpose was to provide a supply "for the convenience of those who may hereafter wish to apply them to their country villas, factories or institutions," but within those limits he made a good job of it, and it was more than thirty years before a better study of Rhode Island place-names appeared. In 1870 James Hammond Trumbull followed with a work which remains one of the classics of the subject,[3] and by the 80s Henry Gannett had begun an investigation which was to result in gazetteers and "geographical dictionaries" of Connecticut, Massachusetts, New Jersey, Rhode Island, Kansas, Utah, Texas, Delaware, Maryland, Virginia, West Virginia, Colorado and the Indian Territory, and an omnibus volume entitled "The Origin of Certain Place Names in the United States."[4] It was this book which set the study of American place-names on its feet.

1 There is a good account of Schoolcraft in Lost Men of America, by Stewart H. Holbrook; New York, 1946, p. 208. He was an eccentric fellow, and some of the Indian names he listed were actually inventions of his own.
2 Providence, 1861. Parsons (1728–1868) was a Maine man who studied medicine in Boston under the celebrated John Warren and served as a naval surgeon in the War of 1812. At the battle of Lake Erie he was in sole charge of the American wounded. He became professor of anatomy at Brown University in 1823.
3 The Composition of Indian Geographical Names, Illustrated From the Algonkin Languages; Hartford, 1870. Trumbull (1821–97) was a native of Connecticut and a graduate of Yale. He held several public offices, but gave most of his time to the study of the Indian languages. From 1863 until his death he was librarian of the Watkinson Library at Hartford and president of the Connecticut Historical Society. In 1874 he was president of the American Philological Association. He supplied the polyglot quotations used as chapter headings in The Gilded Age, by S. L. Clemens (Mark Twain) and Charles Dudley Warner, 1873.
4 Washington, 1902; second edition, 1905. A volume of 334 pages, listing nearly 9,000 names. Gannett (1846-1914) was a native of Maine and a graduate of Harvard. He became chief geographer of the Geological Survey in 1882 and was one of the original members of the United States Geographic Board. He also published gazetteers of Cuba and Puerto Rico.

Unhappily, that study is yet to be organized on a national scale, and in consequence the work done so far is spotty and incoördinate.[1] In some States, *e.g.*, Oregon, Arizona, South Dakota, California and Missouri, the record is substantially complete, and in others, *e.g.*, Pennsylvania, Nebraska, Minnesota, Wyoming and West Virginia, admirable progress has been made, but in yet others, *e.g.*, Maryland and New Jersey, there is hardly a beginning. The excellent discussion of place-names in George Philip Krapp's " The English Language in America," published in 1925,[2] awakened new interest in the subject, and in 1927 Dr. Robert L. Ramsay, professor of English at the University of Missouri, undertook a systematic effort to investigate the nomenclature of that State. He had the invaluable assistance of Allen Walker Read, then an instructor on his staff, and Read presently launched the enterprise with a paper in the *Missouri Historical Review*.[3] Thereafter, Ramsay's graduate students began a study of Missouri place-names that went on until 1945, by which time eighteen reports, covering all the 114 counties of the State, had been completed. The material thus accumulated, running to 32,324 names, was entered upon three sets of cards, one of which was deposited with the Board of Geographical Names in Washington. At the beginning of this huge enterprise Ramsay published an " Introduction to a Survey of Missouri Place-Names " which amounted to a treatise upon the whole technic of place-name research, and remains the best American handbook on the subject.[4]

Meanwhile, Lewis A. McArthur, a Portland business man, had been carrying on an inquiry into the place-names of Oregon, and in 1928 there appeared the first edition of his " Oregon Geographic Names," a truly admirable work.[5] It is not based upon local tradi-

---

[1] At its annual meeting in Dec., 1938, the Present-Day English section of the Modern Language Association appointed a committee on place-names and passed a resolution expressing "a strong interest" in the subject, but nothing has been done about it since. See The Place Name Committee, *American Speech*, April, 1939, pp. 136-38.
[2] Vol. I, pp. 169-200.
[3] Plans For the Study of Missouri Place-Names, Jan., 1928, pp. 237-41.
[4] *University of Missouri Studies*, Jan. 1, 1934. Ramsay is at work upon an analytical dictionary of his whole material, to be brought if possible into one volume, but when this will be finished is undetermined.
[5] The second edition, published by the Oregon Historical Society in 1944, is a volume of 581 pages and lists about 4,000 names. McArthur is secretary of the Oregon Geographical Board and a fellow of the American Geographical Society. He was aided in his long inquiry by Miss Nellie B. Pipes, librarian of the Oregon Historical Society, who

tion alone, but represents a diligent and thorough examination of all the available records, and shows an extraordinary resourcefulness. How much time and labor went into it is beyond estimate, but certainly very few works of American scholarship have ever enlisted more.[1] The only compilations that rival it and Ramsay's in scientific value are "West Virginia Place Names," by Hamill Kenny;[2] "Arizona Place Names," by Will C. Barnes;[3] "South Dakota Place Names," sponsored by the department of English of the State university,[4] and "California Place Names," by Erwin G. Gudde.[5]

The literature of the subject is extensive, but a large part of it is concealed in pamphlets and papers published locally, and hence difficult of access. A bibliography listing 195 titles was presented to the Modern Language Association in December, 1938, by Harold W. Bentley and M. Robert Snyder, and since then Richard B. Sealock, librarian of the Gary, Ind., Public Library, and Pauline A. Seely, of the Los Angeles County Public Library, have completed a much more extensive one covering the United States, Alaska, Canada and Newfoundland. It is in press as I write.[6]

There is room here for no more than brief notices of the more important contributions to the subject. To take them alphabetically by States, the place-names of Alabama have been reported on by Peter A. Brannon, Frank H. Elmore and others in various issues of *Arrow Points*, the monthly bulletin of the Alabama Anthropological Society, and the Indian names among them have been studied at length by William A. Read[7] and H. S. Halbert.[8] The place-names

---

is now Mrs. McArthur. The publication of additions to the edition of 1944 was begun in the *Oregon Historical Quarterly*, Dec., 1946.

[1] In 1944 the *Oregon Journal* of Portland brought out an abbreviated edition with illustrations by Marilyn Campbell.

[2] Piedmont (W.Va.), 1945. This is a volume of 768 pages, listing more than 3,500 names.

[3] *University of Arizona Bulletin*, Jan. 1, 1935. A volume of 503 pages, listing about 4,000 names. It includes a bibliography.

[4] Vermillion (S.Dak.), 1941. A volume of 689 pages, listing about 7,000 names. There are maps and a bibliography.

[5] Berkeley, 1947. This work is still in press as I write, but I have seen some specimens of it by the courtesy of Dr. Gudde. It will run to about 750 pages and will list about 7,500 names.

[6] It is being published by the American Library Association. I have seen the MS. by the courtesy of Mr. Sealock, and can testify to the thoroughness of the work. It lists more than 2,000 items.

[7] Indian Place-Names in Alabama, *Louisiana State University Studies* No. 29; Baton Rouge, 1937. This learned work is reviewed in *American Speech*, Oct., 1937, by John R. Swinton, of the Bureau of American Ethnology, with some minor

of Alaska were first investigated by Marcus Baker, whose report was published by the Geological Survey in 1900.[1] In 1940 John Drury Clark and L. Sprague de Camp printed a brief but illuminating note upon them, listing about seventy,[2] and three years later the WPA brought out a report on the geographical nomenclature of the coastal areas.[3] The map of Alaska is sprinkled with names borrowed from the Eskimos, the Russians and various Indian tribes, and includes such strange forms as *Aniahwagamut, Metlakatla, Ouzinkie, Egegik, Chickaloon, Iditarod* and *Bogoslof*. Clark and de Camp show that there is a tendency among the American settlers to give English values to vowels encountered in print and to place accents according to English patterns. "A feature of Alaskan idiom," they say, " is the use of the names of rivers, without the word *river*, to indicate general regions, or, more accurately, watersheds. Sometimes the word *country* is added; sometimes not. . . . A man will say 'I've been up in the Chandalar,' meaning the Chandalar river watershed."

Will C. Barnes's "Arizona Place Names," before mentioned, is a painstaking and excellent compilation; indeed, it comes close to exhausting its subject. Barnes complains of a tendency common all over the country, to wit, to ascribe to " Indian origin " every place-name for which no other etymology is available. There are, he says, more than twenty tribes in the State, and running down such vague ascriptions is seldom rewarding. He finds some mellifluous names of Spanish origin, e.g., *Huerfano* (orphan), *Nogales* (walnut), *Tortolia* (little dove) and *Tinja* (an earthen water-jug), and others authentically Indian, e.g., *Huachuca* (Chirchua-Apache: thunder), *Vekol* (Papago: grandmother), *Topock* (Mohave: bridge), *Parish-hawampitts* (Piute: boiling water), *Cochibo* (Papago: *kochi*, pig,

---

corrections and additions. In it there is a bibliography of other writings on Alabama names, pp. 80–84. It disposes of the old theory that *Alabama* comes from an Indian term meaning "Here we rest." The real meaning, says Read, is "those who clear the land." In John Palmer's Journal of Travels in the United States; London, 1819, p. 131, there is the interesting observation that the Alabamians of that era pronounced the State name *Ol-aw-baw-ma*.

8 Choctaw Indian Names in Alabama and Mississippi, *Transactions of the Alabama Historical Society*, Vol. III, 1898–99, pp. 64–77.

1 Twenty-first Annual Report, Part II, pp. 489–509. There was a second edition in 1906.

2 Some Alaskan Place Names, *American Speech*, Feb., pp. 60–61.

3 Geographic Names in the Coastal Areas of Alaska; Washington, 1943.

and *bo*, pond), and *Shato* (Navajo: sunny side), but most of the pioneers were matter-of-fact men and were content with such banal names as *Milltown, Maryville, New London, Shultz, Sunset City* and *Smithville*, with an occasional ascent to *Grasshopper, Frog Tanks, Tombstone* and *Total Wreck*.[1] In Arkansas the place-names of French origin have been studied by Branner and Renault,[2] and there is a discussion of the State names in general by Fred. W. Alsopp.[3]

Those of California, now dealt with at length in Gudde's study, before mentioned, have been listed by many other fanciers, beginning with C. M. Drake.[4] As everyone knows, the map of the State is adorned with a large number of charming Spanish names, many of them worn down considerably by American speech habits, *e.g.*, *Los Angeles*, but the rest fairly well preserved. Walt Whitman, in "An American Primer," objected to the saints' names among them on the ground that they had "a tinge of melancholy and of a curious freedom from roughness and money-making" and hence knew nothing "of democracy — of the hunt for gold leads and the nugget or of the religion that is scorn and negation." "Chase them away," he exclaimed, "and substitute aboriginal names." Fortunately, his fatuous counsel went unheard for years and when it was heard at last it was not heeded.[5] The sonorous Spanish names were described romantically in 1914 by Nellie Van de Grift Sanchez[6] and more soberly by various other writers afterward, *e.g.*, Joseph B. Vasché,[7] Gertrude Mott,[8] Martha A. Marshall,[9] Archibald A. Hill,[10]

[1] Barnes prints a bibliography, but overlooks Arizonology, by Elwood Lloyd; Flagstaff, 1933, which lists about 2,000 names.

[2] Some Old French Place-Names in the State of Arkansas, by John C. Branner and Raoul Renault, *Modern Language Notes*, Feb., 1899, pp. 33-40, and March, 1899, p. 96.

[3] Arkansas Place-Names, in Folklore of Romantic Arkansas; New York, 1931, Vol. I, pp. 59-64 and 65-107.

[4] California Names in Their Literal Meanings; Los Angeles, 1893.

[5] An American Primer was published posthumously in the *Atlantic Monthly*, April, 1904. But most of it had been written in the 50s, before the appearance of Leaves of Grass.

[6] Spanish and Indian Place Names of California; San Francisco, 1914.

[7] Trends in the Pronunciation of Spanish Place-Names of California. *American Speech*, Aug., 1931, pp. 461-63.

[8] A Handbook For Californiacs: A Key to the Meaning and Pronunciation of Spanish and Indian Place Names; San Francisco, 1926.

[9] A Pronouncing Dictionary of California Names in English and Spanish; San Francisco, 1925.

[10] California Place-Names From the Spanish, *American Speech*, April, 1932, pp. 317-18, and April, 1933, p. 75.

Laura K. McNary[1] and Robert Shafer.[2] Most of these authors make some effort to expound the true pronunciations, but usually without much effect, for there is a difference of usage and opinion in and about many names beside *Los Angeles*. The commonest error, says Vasché, is the substitution of the *a* in *cat* for the Spanish *a* in *father*, but almost as bad are the substitutions of the *a* in *father* or the *u* in *up* for the Spanish *o* and of the *i* in *it* for the Spanish long *i*, as in *machine*. The California place-names of Indian origin have been studied by the anthropologist, A. F. Kroeber.[3] One of them, *Pasadena*, is commonly assumed to be Spanish, but it actually comes from a Chippewa term said to mean " crown of the valley " and was suggested to the first settlers by a missionary to Missouri who was a relative of one of them.[4]

Henry Gannett's gazetteer to Colorado, brought out in 1906, held the field alone until 1932, when Levette J. Davidson and Olga Hazel Koehler published a paper on " The Naming of Colorado's Towns and Cities " in *American Speech*.[5] They recalled that in the days following the Mexican War what is now the State narrowly escaped being named *Idaho* and that soon afterward it was actually called *Jefferson Territory*. The name finally chosen was taken from that of the river *Colorado*, a Spanish term meaning florid or ruddy. *Denver*, the capital and metropolis, was first called *Montana City*. It presently had an adjacent rival named *St. Charles City* and then a second, *Auraria*. In the end *St. Charles City* engulfed the other two and was renamed *Denver* in honor of James W. Denver, Governor of Kansas Territory. Davidson and Koehler listed some of the

[1] California Spanish and Indian Place Names; Los Angeles, 1931.
[2] The Pronunciation of Spanish Place Names in California, *American Speech*, Dec., 1942, pp. 239–46. There is an anonymous article in the California Historical Nugget, Vol. I, 1924, pp. 59–66.
[3] California Place Names of Indian Origin, *University of California Publications in Anthropology and Ethnology*, Vol. XII, No. 2, June 15, 1916, pp. 31–69.
[4] Francis P. Farquhar published Place Names of the High Sierra, *Sierra Club Bulletin*, Vol. II, 1923, pp. 380–407. Other contributions to the subject are in California Names; Their History and Meaning, by Thomas P. Pollok; San Francisco, 1934; Origin of *California*, by Nellie Van de Grift Sanchez, *Motor Land*, Sept., 1933, pp. 9–13; Dictionary of Spanish-Named California Cities and Towns, by Henry M. Moreno; San Luis Obispo, 1916, and The Dictionary of California Land Names, by Phil Townsend Hanna; Los Angeles, 1946. The last-named gives the Spanish pronunciation of all the Spanish names listed. There is a bibliography and nearly 4,000 names are discussed.
[5] Feb., pp. 180–87.

more picturesque place-names of the State, many of them now only memories of ghost-towns, *e.g.*, *Tin Cup*, *Buckskin Joe* and *Tarryall*. In 1935 Eleanor L. Richie and George L. Trager, followed with reports on its Spanish place-names.[1] There were only a few Mexican settlements within its bounds before the American occupation, but some Spanish names had got in along the southern border and others later penetrated northward. Miss Richie says that most of them have become Americanized in pronunciation, including *Colorado* itself, which is frequently *Colo-ray-do*. *Raton Pass* is *Rah-tone* in New Mexico, but *Ra-toon* in Colorado. *Garcia* is *Garsha*, *San Luis* is *San Loo-ie* or *San Loo-is*, *Alamosa* is *Ala-moosa*, and *Rio Grande* may be *Ree-o Grand* or *Rye-o Grand*. In 1939 the Colorado Writers' Project undertook an examination of all the town names of the State, of whatever provenance, and its reports were printed in the *Colorado Magazine*, beginning in January, 1940, and running to May, 1943. The field-workers made a diligent search of all the State records, examined early newspaper files and consulted many old settlers, but in the end they had to confess that the origin and meaning of large numbers of names, especially those of ghost-towns, were lost to human memory.[2]

J. H. Trumbull's early work on Indian place-names, beginning in 1870, had chiefly to do with those of Connecticut. He was followed in 1885 by F. B. Dexter with a paper on Connecticut town names in general,[3] and in 1894 Gannett contributed one of his gazetteers. Trumbull devoted himself largely to interpreting various Indian prefixes and suffixes, and to this subject Stanley Martin returned in 1939.[4] During the same year H. A. Wright published a paper on the corruption of Indian place-names in Connecticut and the adjacent States.[5] That corruption, he found, had been produced in the early days by the fact that the Algonquin Indians of the region spoke many different dialects, some of them so unlike as to be mutually unintelligible. In one dialect *l*, *n* and *r* were interchanged; in an-

1 *American Speech*, April, pp. 88-92, and Oct., pp. 203-07.
2 I am indebted here to Mr. Harry Simonson, supervisor of the project.
3 The History of Connecticut as Illustrated by the Names of Her Towns, *Proceedings of the American Antiquarian Society*, New Series, Vol. III, 1885, pp. 421-48.
4 Indian Derivatives in Connecticut Place-Names, *New England Quarterly*, June, pp. 364-69.
5 Some Vagaries in Connecticut Valley Indian Place-Names, *New England Quarterly*, Sept., 535-44.

other *l* was not used; in yet another, *r*; in a fourth, neither *r* nor *l*. Thus the Indian name of the Northampton, Mass., area appeared variously as *Norwotock, Nonotuck, Nolwotogg, Nanotuck* and *Nalwottoge*. The elements here were two roots meaning a far away place, common to all the dialects, but they varied so much from one to another that the name became greatly distorted, and the English settlers changed it further to *Nauwot, Nawwatick* and *Nawwatuck*. In 1941 it was announced in *American Speech* that Odell Shepard and Arthur H. Hughes, of Trinity College, Hartford, were engaged upon "a list of Connecticut place-names and notes of their origin and development," but Shepard withdrew from the enterprise in 1946 and Hughes has not yet published his accumulations. So far as I know, nothing has been done about the place-names of Delaware save what is to be found in Gannett's 15-page gazetteer of 1904, and his "Origin of Certain Place Names in the United States" of two years before. As I have hitherto noted, the State is the only one in the Union without a *Washington*, but it can boast of a *Rehoboth*, a *Lebanon* and a *Bethany Beach*, beside an *Angola*, a *Smyrna*, a *Glasgow*, a *Leipsic*, an *Odessa*, a *Mount Cuba*, a *Viola*, a *Brickyard*, a *Canal*, a *Sandtown* and a *Slaughter*, so its nomenclature should be well worth investigating.

Mrs. Annie McRae, of St. Petersburg, Fla., undertook a work on Florida place-names, eventually running to about 1300 items, in 1940, but it is still unpublished. The Indian names on the State map have been studied at length, and with great learning, by William A. Read.[1] Most of them come from the Seminole-Creek language, *e.g.*, *Tampa, Tallahassee, Hialeah* and *Palatka*, but there are others from the Choctaw, *e.g.*, *Pensacola*, and Hitchiti, *e.g.*, *Apalachicola*. The numerous names ending in *-hatchee* are derived from a Seminole-Creek word meaning river. Some names from the Indian languages of the North, *e.g.*, *Muscogee* and *Ocoee*, were brought in by white settlers. The origin of a few very familiar ones, *e.g.*, *Kissimee, Ocala* and *Suwanee*, remains undetermined. An effort has been made to interpret *Suwanee* as a corruption of the Spanish *San Juanito*, but Read says that it lacks ground. Gannett sought to derive it

---

[1] Florida Place-Names of Indian Origin and Seminole Personal Names; Baton Rouge, 1934. See also Some Florida Names of Indian Origin, by Frank Drew, *Florida Historical Society Quarterly*, April, 1926, pp. 181–82, and April, 1928, pp. 197–205.

from an Indian term, *sawani*, meaning echo,[1] but Read dismisses this also, calling it " no doubt purely fanciful." [2] The name of *Key West* reveals a curious corruption. The Spanish called it *Cayo Hueso*, meaning bone key, but the Americans turned *hueso* into *west*.[3] Some notes on early Georgia place-names are in Adiel Sherwood's gazetteer,[4] but in recent years the subject has been neglected. There is an M.A. thesis, Georgia County Place-Names, by Margaret W. Godley, 1935, in the library of Emory University, but it has not been published. Nor has a paper, Our Names and How We Got Them, by Dr. Guy H. Wells, president of the Georgia State College for Women, read to a group of graduate students in 1940.[5] Many Georgia names, like many Florida names, end in *-hatchee* and show the same Indian origin.[6]

The name of *Idaho* is generally supposed, though on dubious grounds, to be derived from two Indian words, *edah hoe*, meaning light on the mountains, but this etymology was challenged by Dr. Edward P. Roche, of Bath, Maine, writing in the Boston *Journal* in 1889.[7] Dr. Roche said that, in the Autumn of 1865, he met in New York one C. C. Cole, later a Congressman from Idaho, and that Cole told him the following story: At a time shortly before the organization of the Territory,[8] Cole and another man were riding through one of its ranges of barren mountains, and fell into a discussion of the various names that had been suggested for it. While so engaged they emerged upon a small plateau, and saw before them an Indian cabin. Just before they reached it an Indian woman came out of it and yelled. The word she uttered sounded to Cole like *Ee-dah-hoo-oo-oo*, with " a drop from the first *e* to the second, a

1 The Origin of Certain Place Names in the United States, before cited.
2 In a review of Read in *American Speech*, Oct., 1934, pp. 218-20, John R. Swanton, of the Bureau of American Ethnology, offered some valuable additions. A note by Read on *Caxambas*, the name of a pass making in from the Gulf of Mexico, is in *Language*, July-Sept., 1945.
3 I am indebted here to Dr. Alfred D. Schoch. A note on the name *Jupiter* is in *American Speech*, Oct., 1938, pp. 233-34.
4 Charleston (S.C.), 1827; second edition, Washington, 1837; third edition, Washington, 1837; fourth edition, Macon and Atlanta (Ga.), 1860.
5 Dr. Wells tells me that "most of the work on the names of Georgia towns" was done by Dr. Edward Dawson, of the college English faculty.
6 *Ee* Places in Georgia, New York *Sun*, March 30, 1938.
7 I have been unable to locate his article. What follows is from a reprint in the *Idaho Statesman* (Boise), of July 3, 1939, p. 10.
8 It was organized on March 3, 1863.

long *a*, almost as in *ah-ah*, and a musical, long drawn *hoo*, using the full force of the lungs in espuration [1] and crescendo." The caller's tone "was a combination of those of the Swiss yodler, the Spanish Indian and the Louisiana Negress." The travelers assumed that she was calling her husband, but it turned out that she was really calling her daughter, "an Indian girl about nine years of age, clean and better looking than many of her race." The idea occurred to Cole that the name of this damsel would make a good name for the new Territory, and he and his companion advocated it on their return to the settlements, and with success. How it became changed from *Eedahoo* to *Idaho* does not appear, nor why *Idaho* had been proposed as a name for the present *Colorado* several years before, as recorded in the discussion of Colorado place-names.[2]

There is little in print about the place-names of Illinois save a paper by William D. Barge and N. W. Caldwell.[3] Indiana has been better served, and a bibliography of the subject prepared by Richard B. Sealock and Pauline A. Seely in 1945 shows thirty-five items, but many of these are no more than *obiter dicta* in historical works of a more general character, and others are still in manuscript.[4] Iowa is more fortunate than either Indiana or Illinois, for Allen Walker Read, during his novitiate at the University of Missouri, made an extensive investigation of its place-names,[5] and T. J. Fitzpatrick has

---

[1] This word appears in no English dictionary and is unknown to music. It may be a mistake for *aspiration*.

[2] In the same issue of the *Idaho Statesman* from which I have quoted, p. 62, is an article giving the origins of the names of the Idaho counties, by Clyde A. Bridger. It is reprinted in the *Northwest Quarterly*, April, 1940, pp. 187–206. See also Some Non-English Place Names in Idaho, by E. W. Talbert, *American Speech*, Oct., 1938, pp. 175–78.

[3] *Journal of the Illinois State Historical Society*, Oct., 1936, pp. 181–311. Minor notes are in The Naming of Bloomington, by V. A. Syfert, the same, July, 1936, pp. 161–67, and Speech Currents in Egypt, by Grace Partridge Smith, *American Speech*, Oct., 1942, p. 173.

[4] I am indebted to Mr. Sealock for a copy of this bibliography. In the *Saturday Review of Literature*, Nov. 21, 1942, p. 24, Virginia Scott Miner, a resident of Kansas City but apparently Hoosier-born, printed some dithyrambs on the charm of Indiana place-names "from the *Wabash* banks to *Tippecanoe*, from *Vincennes* to *Buzzards' Glory*." There are some minor notes by Jacob Piatt Dunn, the State historian, in the *Indiana Magazine of History*, and a card-index of Indiana place-names is kept by the State Historical Society.

[5] Observations on Iowa Place Names, *American Speech*, Oct., 1929, pp. 27–44. This was followed by *Liberty* in Iowa, the same, June, 1931, pp. 360–67.

printed excellent studies of those of various counties, *e.g.*, Appanoose, Des Moines, Lee and Van Buren.[1] Read says that some of them "have grown up by common consent," but that the majority have been "given upon authority." When the State was opened to settlement immigrants poured in in large numbers, and there was a great deal of wholesale naming, "practically parallel to the naming of Pullman cars." The results were a proliferation of banality and many confusing repetitions; for example, there are still twenty townships called *Liberty*, and dozens of towns and villages have been so called at different times, past and present.

Read notes that the Iowans have always been hostile to long and clumsy names, *e.g.*, *Portlandville* and *Rocksylvania*, and have diligently avoided prefixes indicating relative situation. "The subsidiary position of being *West* Something," he says, "seems derogatory to the reputation of the town." Since they abandoned their frontier ways and took to golf, psychoanalysis and Kiwanis, they have purged their map of many old names of a ribald or otherwise embarrassing character. Thus the *Skunk Grove* of the early days is now *Rose Grove*, and *Barkersville*, named after a pioneer who later got into woman trouble, is now *Attica*. Many of the early settlements had the grandiloquent *City* attached to their names, and Fitzpatrick shows that Appanoose county has a *Pearl City* and a *Walnut City*, both of them small villages, to this day, but as hopes faded most such boastful appendages were dropped. Fitzpatrick's lists contain very few names of any originality or even of any appositeness. To every *Beetrace* (commemorating a route used by the Indians in hunting honey), *Jaybird* and *Snort Creek* there are a dozen commonplace *Centervilles* and *Pleasant Hills* and a score of such steals as *Cincinnati, Memphis* and *Philadelphia*.

The literature of place-names in Kansas seems to be confined to some local pamphlets and newspaper articles and a brief series of papers by W. H. Carruth, published in 1901–02. There is a card-index in the headquarters of the State Historical Society, but it is far from complete. Kentucky has even less to offer. Louisiana, like Florida, owes the investigation of its Indian names to William A. Read.[2] Nearly all come from the Longtown dialect of the Choctaw

[1] The names of Appanoose are dealt with in *American Speech*, Oct., 1927, pp. 39–66; the others, in *Annals of Iowa*, 1929–39.

[2] Louisiana Place-Names of Indian Origin; Baton Rouge (La.), 1927.

language and some have a considerable mellifluousness, *e.g.*, *Okaloosa*, *Panola*, *Shongaloo* and *Tchoupitoulas*. Many, as they stand today, show early efforts at folk-etymology, either by the French or the succeeding Americans, *e.g.*, *Funny Louis*, which comes from the Choctaw *fani*, a squirrel, and *lusa*, black. A few names are borrowed from northern Indian languages, *e.g.*, *Chautauqua* and *Chenango*, and at least one, *Plaquemine*, comes from the old Mobile trade language through Creole French.[1]

Maine is richer in picturesque Indian names than any other State, and they have been competently studied by Fannie Hardy Eckstorm,[2] a native and life-long resident of Brewer, near Bangor. Some of them are of appalling length, *e.g.*, *Chemquasabamticook* and *Moosetocmaguntic*, and in the early days there were many others, now abandoned, *e.g.*, *Kassanumganumkeag* and *Matchihundupemabtunk*.[3] They have been borrowed mainly from the Abnaki and Maliseet languages, both of which are still spoken by Indians in the State, but others seem to come from the Micmac, the original speakers of which lived over what is now the Canadian border but no doubt made forays into Maine. Mrs. Eckstorm's study includes a valuable treatise upon the Indian languages, especially Abnaki, which she mastered in the field. She warns against the facile assumption, so productive of absurd folk-etymologies, that the Indians formed words as we do, and that their grammatical categories were identical with our own. She gives all due credit to her predecessors, but does not spare a certain asperity in dealing with those who indulged themselves in speculations more donkeyish than perspicacious.

A study of the place-names of Maryland was undertaken during the 1930s by J. Louis Kuethe, of the Johns Hopkins, but he was soon diverted to other matters, and there remains nothing of his inquiry

---

[1] Read published More Indian Place-Names in Louisiana, *Louisiana Historical Quarterly*, July, 1928, pp. 445–62, mainly made up of addenda and corrigenda. There is a note on Place Names in New Orleans Parish (chiefly French), in the New Orleans City Guide compiled by the Federal Writers' Project; Boston, 1934, pp. 403–06.

[2] Indian Place-Names of the Penobscot Valley and the Maine Coast; University of Maine Studies, Second Series, No. 55; Orono (Maine), Nov., 1941.

[3] In AL4, p. 531 I quoted one stanza of a satirical poem on these names by R. H. Newell (Orpheus C. Kerr). Another such poem, by Francis B. Keene, was printed in the *Saturday Review of Literatur* July 13, 1946, p. 32.

save a few preliminary papers [1] and a file of notes. The place-names of Massachusetts got some attention from the scholars of an earlier day,[2] but the banality of so many of them apparently discouraged the inquiry, and in late years the only contribution to it has been a pamphlet published by the Federal Writers' Project as a by-product of a " general research upon historical subjects."[3] The vain effort of the first Legislature of Michigan to get rid of eponymic and imitative place-names has been mentioned; since that primeval day both the statesmen and the scholars of the State have held aloof from its nomenclature, which includes some far from commonplace names, e.g., *Ann Arbor, Sault Sainte Marie, Kalamazoo,*[4] *Ypsilanti, Au Train, Baie de Wasal, Hamtramck, Grosse Pointe, Lulu, Defiance, Bravo, Bovine, Male, Dice* and *Zilwaukee*.[5] Minnesota also has many picturesque place-names, e.g., *Mille Lacs, Good Thunder, Yellow Medicine, Sleepy Eye, Pigs Eye,*[6] *Blue Earth, Fond du Lac, Ah-quah-ching,*

1 Maryland Place Names Have Strange Oddities, Baltimore *Sun*, May 23, 1937, Sect. II, p. 2; Maryland Place Names Have Varied Origins, the same, March 24, 1940; Maryland Place Names, the same, Sept. 8, 1940. Dr. Hermann Collitz printed a note on the meaning of *Baltimore* in the *Johns Hopkins Alumni Magazine*, Jan., 1934, pp. 133–34. See also The Place-Names of Baltimore and Harford Counties, by William B. Marye, *Maryland Historical Magazine*, Dec., 1930, pp. 321–65.
2 An Essay Relating to the Names of Towns in Massachusetts, by W. H. Whitmore; Boston, 1873; The Indian Names of Boston and Their Meaning, by Eben N. Horsford; Cambridge, 1886; Massachusetts Names, by A. E. Winship, *Journal of Education*, Aug. and Sept., 1898, pp. 109–10 and 142–43; Indian Names of Places in Worcester County, by Lincoln N. Kinnicutt; Worcester, 1905, and Dictionary of American Indian Place and Proper Names in New England, by R. A. Douglas-Lithgow; Salem, 1909.
3 The Origin of Massachusetts Place Names of the State, Counties, Cities and Towns; New York, 1941.
4 Father Chrysostom Verwyst, O.S.F., says in Geographical Names in Wisconsin, Minnesota and Michigan Having a Chippewa Origin, *Collections of the State Historical Society of Wisconsin*, Vol. XII, 1892, pp. 390–98, that *Kalamazoo* is a corruption of the Chippewa *kikanamoso*, it smokes, or he is troubled with smoke, *i.e.*, in his wigwam. He derives *Michigan* from *michagami*, a large body of water; *Saginaw* from *osaginang*, the place of the Sacs; *Mackinac* from *mikinak*, a turtle, and *Petoskey* from *pitoskig*, between two swamps.
5 William L. Jenks has written upon the county names of Michigan, and there are many short articles on local names in the *Michigan Historical Magazine*.
6 I am told by Mr. E. P. Brown, of Minneapolis, that *Pigs Eye Landing* was the original name of St. Paul, but no citizen of St. Paul has corroborated this. *Pigs Eye*, its eponym, was a half-breed trader whose legal name was Pierre Parrant. Mr. Brown says that *Sleepy Eye* was named after a Sioux chief named *Ishtaba*, meaning sleepy eye.

Albert Lea, Lac qui Parle, Wang, Triumph, Plato and *Moe*. There is a comprehensive study of the State's geographical nomenclature in " Minnesota Geographic Names," by Warren Upham.[1] Those of Indian origin have been studied by A. W. Williamson[2] and Joseph A. Gilfillan[3] and those of Scandinavian origin by Roy W. Swanson.[4]

The indefatigable Henry Gannett tackled the place-names of Mississippi in 1902,[5] but his inquiry did not go very far and I know of no other discussion of the subject save some brief mention in a paper devoted mainly to those of Alabama[6] and a note on the etymology of *Natchez*.[7] The map of the State shows some striking Indian names, *e.g., Chulahoma, Issaquena, Oktibbeha* and *Pascagoula*, and also some recalling the days when it was French soil, *e.g., Bay St. Louis, Picayune* and *Bonhomie*, and frontier, *e.g., Logtown, Increase, Kiln, Sunflower, Lost Gap, Turkey* and *Bells*, but the majority of its present names belong to the depressing category of *Batesville, Franklin, Oxford, Rosedale* and *West Point*. The magnificent work of Robert L. Ramsay and his associates in Missouri I have already described.

Thanks to the initiative of Dr. Louise Pound, the place-names of Nebraska were investigated in the 1920s by one of her students, Lillian Linder Fitzpatrick, and the result was a report so comprehensive that it has not been surpassed since.[8] Miss Fitzpatrick showed that more than half the names on the State map are bor-

---

[1] A volume of 735 pp., published by the Minnesota Historical Society in 1920.
[2] Minnesota Names Derived From the Dakota Languages; St. Paul, 1884.
[3] Minnesota Geographical Names Derived From the Chippewa Language, in annual report of the Minnesota Geological and Natural History Survey, 1886, pp. 451-77.
[4] Scandinavian Place-Names in the American Danelaw, *Swedish-American Historical Bulletin*, Aug., 1929, pp. 5-17. See also North Shore Place Names, by William E. Culkin; St. Paul, 1931. A State Geographic Board was set up in 1937.
[5] The Origin of Certain Place Names in the State of Mississippi, *Publications of the Mississippi Historical Society*, 1902, pp. 339-49.
[6] Choctaw Indian Names in Alabama and Mississippi, by H. S. Halbert, before cited, pp. 64-67.
[7] Note on the Origin of *Natchez*, by Henry P. Dart, *Louisiana Historical Quarterly*, Oct., 1931, p. 515. He suggested its derivation from a Caddo Indian term meaning timber-land.
[8] Nebraska Place-Names, *University of Nebraska Studies in Language, Literature, and Criticism*, No. 6; Lincoln, 1925. Miss Fitzpatrick took her M.A. under Dr. Pound in 1924, and then proceeded to Cornell for her Ph.D. Unhappily, she died soon afterward.

rowed personal names, chiefly those of early settlers and railway builders. The next largest division embraces descriptive names, often combined with such trite suffixes as *-town, -view, -dale, -field, -port, -side, -ford* and *-grove*. Indian names are relatively rare, though they include the name of the State and that of its largest city, *Omaha*. *Nebraska* is derived from an Omaha Indian term, *Nibthaska*, meaning flat water and referring to the Platte river. This combination of sounds was baffling to the pioneers, so they inserted an *r*, which was not found in the Indian speech, for the sake of euphony. *Omaha* was taken from the name of the circumambient tribe. In the original it was *O-mán-ha*, signifying upstream and with the accent on the second syllable. Most Nebraska names are commonplace, but there are a few exceptions. *Horsefoot* and *Keystone* were named from cattle-brands, and *Enola* is *Malone* spelled backward, with the *m* omitted. *Sarben* is a backward spelling of the first two syllables of *Nebraska*. *Whynot* is said to have been suggested by an early settler who asked, "Why not name the town *Why Not?*"[1]

I know of no published work on Nevada place-names save some brief papers in the annual reports of the State Historical Society, but it is noted frequently in the newspapers that the local pronunciation makes the first *a* in the State's name that of *cat*.[2] Mr. Gustavus Swift Paine calls my attention to the fact that a number of its town- and geographical-names include the syllable *pah*, e.g., *Tonopah, Illipah, Pahranagat, Pahroc, Weepah, Pahrump* and *Timpahute:* he suggests that it may be an Indian term meaning water, which also appears in the name of the *Piute, Paiute* or *Pah Ute* Indians. He says that *Chinatown* was first used in 1857 to designate a settlement in which is now Nevada near what is now Dayton. The DAE's earliest example is dated 1877. The place-names of New Hampshire and New Jersey have got but scant attention from recent students of geographical nomenclature. On the former there is little save a brief but excellent paper on the naming of *Mount Washington*, by Lawrence Martin,[3] two others on the nomenclature of the White Moun-

---

[1] There is a good bibliography in Miss Fitzpatrick's monograph. A section on Nebraska place-names is in the Nebraska volume of the American Guide Series, prepared by the Federal Writers' Project.

[2] Holt says that in the Iowa town of the same name the *a* is that of *blade*. I am indebted here to Mr. Daniel L. Reardon, of Reno.

[3] *Geographical Review*, April, 1938, pp. 303–05. He says that it was

tains by Frank H. Burt,[1] and one on the county names of the State by Otis G. Hammond.[2] On New Jersey I can find nothing since Henry Gannett's " Geographic Dictionary " of 1894 save a far from comprehensive Federal Writers' Project pamphlet,[3] two short papers in the *Proceedings of the New Jersey Historical Society* in 1925–26,[4] and three even shorter newspaper articles published in 1937.[5] The material in the last-named seems to have been mainly derived from Gannett. Some of the place-names of northern New Jersey are of Dutch origin, *e.g.*, *Barnegat*,[6] *Sandy Hook* and *Kill van Kull*. In the Pine Barrens to the southward there are many abandoned villages with picturesque names, *e.g.*, *Chicken Bone*, *Hogwallow*, *La-Ha Way*, *Ong's Hat*, *Loveladies* and *Batsto*.[7] There is, so far as I know, no formal treatise upon the colorful place-names of New Mexico, but Dr. Thomas M. Pearce, of the State university, has published a paper upon some of those that have acquired folk-etymologies, *e.g.*, *Mora*, *Cimarron*, *Socorro*, *Lemitar*, *Pie Town* and *Picketwire*.[8] Not a few are the linguistic stumps of what were once long and sonorous Spanish names, *e.g.*, *Santa Fe*, which was originally *La Villa Real de Santa Fe de San Francisco de Assisi*,[9] and *Picketwire*, which is traditionally a folk-Americanization of *El Rio de las Animas Perdidas en Purgatorio* (The River of Souls Lost in Purgatory). Some charming early names survive, *e.g.*, *Alamogordo*, *Berna-*

---

called *White Mountain* or the *Sugar Loaf* down to 1786 and that its renaming may have followed George Washington's visit to New England in 1789. The first known map showing *Mount Washington* is one by a German named Sotzmann, published in Hamburg in 1796.

[1] *Appalachia*, Dec., 1915, pp. 359–90, and June, 1918, pp. 261–68.
[2] *Magazine of History*, Jan., 1909, pp. 48–50.
[3] The Origin of New Jersey Place Names, 1939; reissued by the New Jersey Public Library Commission, 1945. It lists less than 900 names.
[4] New Jersey: Some Early Place Names, by C. C. Vermeule; New Series, Vol. X, pp. 241–52, and Vol. XI, pp. 151–60.
[5] Origin of New Jersey Names, by John Venable. The first two appeared in the Perth Amboy *Evening News*, but I have been unable to determine the exact dates. I am indebted here to Miss Katharine L. McCormick, of Perth Amboy.
[6] Originally, *Barende-gat*, meaning an inlet with a heavy surf. See *Barnegat*, by A. R. Dunlap, *American Speech*, Oct., 1938, pp. 232–33. According to *Poughkeepsie*: the Origin and Meaning of the Word, by Helen Wilkinson Reynolds; Poughkeepsie, 1924, p. 69, the term also designated a lime-kiln.
[7] Ghost Towns, by Alfred S. Campbell, *Holiday* (preview issue), p. 83.
[8] New Mexico Folk Etymologies, *El Palacio*, Oct., 1943, pp. 229–34.
[9] I am indebted here to Mr. J. Nixon Hadley, of Evanston, Ill.

lillo, Carrizozo, Hilario, Los Vigiles, Tierra Amarilla, Tres Piedras, Ojo Caliente and *San Ildefonso*, but *La Junta* has been degraded to *Hondo*.

As I have hitherto recorded, the Indian place-names of New York early attracted the attention of the learned Schoolcraft, and since his day they have been studied by William H. Beauchamp,[1] William W. Tooker[2] and others.[3] Also, there have been monographs on various individual names, *e.g., Manhattan,*[4] *Poughkeepsie*[5] and *Krom Elbow*.[6] In the 1840s there was a movement to substitute Indian names for some of the more banal place-names of the States, *e.g., Horicon* for *Lake George* and even *Ontario* for *New York*, but it got nowhere.[7] In 1944 L. Sprague de Camp published a long and interesting list of upstate names, showing their local pronunciation.[8]

The study of the place-names of North Carolina goes back to 1888, when Kemp P. Battle printed a pamphlet on those of the counties,[9] but the field has been neglected since.[10] The same thing

1 Indian Names in New York; Fayetteville (N.Y.), 1893. In 1907 this was reissued, greatly expanded, by the New York State Museum under the title of Aboriginal Place-Names of New York. I am indebted here to Mr. Alvin G. Whitney.
2 Some Indian Names of Places on Long Island, N. Y., and Their Correspondences in Virginia, *Magazine of New England History*, July, 1891, pp. 154–58; Indian Place Names on Long Island and Islands Adjacent; New York, 1911.
3 For example, J. Dyneley Prince in Fragments From Babel; New York, 1939, pp. 165–71. Only a year after Schoolcraft B. F. Thompson printed a paper on the Indian names of Long Island in the *Proceedings of the New York Historical Society*, 1845, pp. 125–31.
4 *Mannahatta*, by John Howard Birss, *American Speech*, April, 1934, pp. 154–55. See also *American Speech*, April, 1930, p. 444.
5 *Poughkeepsie:* the Origin and Meaning of the Word, by Helen Wilkinson Reynolds, before cited. In The Ithaca Dialect, *Dialect Notes*, Vol. I, Part III, 1891, Oliver Farrar Emerson recorded some local pronunciations of Indian names, *e.g., Chenang* for *Chenango, Tiog* for *Tioga, Cayugy* for *Cayuga* and *Weego* for *Owego*.
6 *Kromme Ellebog:* A Seventeenth Century Place-Name in the Hudson Valley, by Helen Wilkinson Reynolds, Yearbook of the Dutchess County Historical Society; Poughkeepsie, 1933, pp. 58–68. I am indebted here to Mrs. Amy Ver Nooy.
7 It was approved in an editorial in the *Democratic Reflector* of Hamilton, March 26, 1845. I am indebted here to Mr. Charles J. Lovell.
8 Pronunciation of Upstate New York Place-Names, *American Speech*, Dec., pp. 250–65. A State Board of Geographic Names was set up by Chapter 187 of the Acts of 1913, but it has been inactive.
9 The Names of the Counties of North Carolina and the History Involved in Them; Winston, 1888.
10 Some curious specimens from the mountain section are recorded by Josiah Combs in Language of the Southern Highlanders, *Publications*

may be said of North Dakota and Ohio, the place-name bibliographies of which are limited to a few superficial items. For Ohio the most interesting is "Origin of Ohio Place Names," by Maria Ewing Martin, though it deals with the history of the settlement of the State rather than with its nomenclature, and is now sadly dated.[1] The Indian place-names of the State come from the languages of a dozen or more different tribes, and in pre-settlement days the same place often bore as many successive names. *Scioto* is Wyandot, *Chillicothe* is Shawnee, *Coshocton* is Delaware, and *Miami* is from the Ottawa word for mother. The early whites abandoned most of the Indian names and substituted trite inventions of their own, mainly brought from the East, e.g., *Farmington, New Philadelphia, Newark, Dover* and *North Amherst*.[2] For North Dakota the most interesting paper is a brief one on coined town names by Dorothy J. Hughes,[3] e.g., *Alkabo*, from *alkali* and *gumbo; Grenora*, from *Great Northern Railway*, and *Sandoun*, from *sand-dune*.

The place-names of Oklahoma have been dealt with at length by Dr. Charles N. Gould, director of the Oklahoma Geological Survey and professor of geology in the State University[4] and its French names have had separate treatment.[5] Gould says that less than one percent of them are of French origin and less than a quarter of one percent Spanish. He calls attention to "the rather unusual abundance of feminine names of postoffices," and lists more than a hundred, ranging from *Abbie* and *Addielle* to *Violet* and *Zula*. The

---

of the *Modern Language Association*, Dec., 1931, p. 1312, e.g., *Pinch Gut, Lick Log, Broken Leg, Naked Place, Burnt Pone, Four-Killer, Chunky Gal, How Come You, Jerkem Tight, Big Bugaboo* and *Barren She*. The Federal Writers' Project brought out How They Began — the Story of North Carolina County, Town and Other Place Names in 1941, but it need not detain us.

[1] It was read before the State D.A.R. at Toledo, Oct. 29, 1903, and published in *Publications of the Ohio Archeological & Historical Society*, June, 1905, pp. 272-90.

[2] But Wooster is not a respelling of the Eastern (and English) *Worcester*. Lowell W. Coolidge shows in *Words*, March, 1937, p. 60, that it was actually named after a Major-General David *Wooster*, of the Revolutionary Army. For *Cincinnati* see *American Speech*, Jan., 1926, p. 226.

[3] *American Speech*, Dec., 1939, p. 315. There is a State Geographic Board, and a report on its work was published in the *North Dakota Historical Quarterly*, Oct., 1927, pp. 53-56, but that work does not seem to have been productive.

[4] Oklahoma Place Names; Norman (Okla.), 1933.

[5] Some Geographic Names of French Origin in Oklahoma, by Muriel H. Wright, *Chronicles of Oklahoma*, June, 1929, pp. 188-93.

place-names of Oregon are discussed at length in the excellent monograph of Lewis A. McArthur, already mentioned — in many ways the best study of its sort yet done in America. The origin of the State name has been long debated. Stewart produces impressive evidence in "Names on the Land" that it may be derived from *Ouaricon*, which in turn was derived from *Ouriconsint*, an early French name for a vague "River of the West," apparently borrowed from the Indians.[1] If this theory is sound, then *Oregon* and *Wisconsin* both came from the same source.[2]

A. Howry Espenshade's "Pennsylvania Place Names"[3] is a volume of 375 pages and lists more than 1200 names. It is not to be mentioned in the same breath with McArthur's "Oregon Geographic Names," but there is nevertheless a lot of useful information in it, and it will form a springboard for some later, more comprehensive and better arranged work. It was preceded by small studies by Henry W. Shoemaker[4] and Stephen G. Boyd[5] and followed by others by George P. Donehoo[6] and William Pierce Randel.[7] Rhode Island, as I have recorded, produced one of the earliest studies of American place-names, that of Usher Parsons in 1861, but since then little has been done in the field.

1 The Source of the Name *Oregon*, American Speech, April, 1944, pp. 115–17.
2 Stewart is supported in *Ouaricon* and *Oregon*, by Frederick Bracher, American Speech, Oct., 1946, pp. 185–87. In Features of the New North-West, Century Magazine, Feb., 1883, p. 553, E. V. Smalley noted some of the curious place-names of the State, e.g., *Glad Tidings, Needy, Sublimity, Hardscrabble, Humbug, Whiskeytown, Louse* creek, *Jump-off Joe* creek and *Eltopia* (from *hell to pay*). *Sublimity, Humbug* creek, and two *Whiskey* creeks and one *Whiskey* run still survive.
3 State College (Pa.), 1925.
4 Place Names and Altitudes of Pennsylvania Mountains; Altoona, 1923.
5 Indian Local Names With Their Interpretation; York, 1888. In 1822 the Rev. John G. E. Heckewelder (AL4, p. 110) published a work on the Lenni-Lennape or Delaware Indian place-names of Pennsylvania, New Jersey, Maryland and Virginia.
6 A History of the Indian Villages and Place Names in Pennsylvania; Harrisburg, 1928. Donehoo also collaborated with Shoemaker in Changing Historic Place Names in Pennsylvania; Altoona, 1921.
7 The Place Names of Tioga County, Pennsylvania, American Speech, Oct., 1939, pp. 181–90. This is an excellent paper and lists more than 150 names. A Pennsylvania Geographic Board was set up in 1923, and three years later it published a list of decisions (American Speech, Dec., 1926, pp. 163–64). An amendment of 1929 made it consist of the Secretary of Forests and Water, the Secretary of Highways, the chairman of the State Historical and Museum Commission, and an officer of the Department of Internal Affairs. Its chairman in 1947 was Admiral Milo S. Draemel. U.S.N., ret.

There is a State Geographic Board and in 1932 it brought out an "Official Gazetteer of Rhode Island" in collaboration with the United States Geographic Board, but the remaining literature is mainly only local in interest. In 1941 the Federal Writers' Project for South Carolina published at Columbia a volume entitled "Palmetto Place Names," but it was far from complete and is now out of print.[1]

The fact that South Dakota has a volume on its place-names comparable to McArthur's on those of Oregon is due to the enterprise of Dr. Edward C. Ehrensperger, professor of the English language and literature in its State University at Vermillion.[2] At the suggestion of Robert L. Ramsay of Missouri, before mentioned, he put some of his candidates for the M.A. degree to work investigating the place-names of the State, and presently he had in hand a series of valuable theses. When the Federal Writers' Project undertook to deal with the same names, he lent his materials and his skill to the business, and the result was a really first-rate report. It is laid out upon a somewhat unhandy plan, with separate alphabets for towns, counties, rivers, mountains, etc., but the extraordinary richness of the data assembled makes the user forget this defect, and soon or late it will probably be remedied in a revision based upon a single alphabet. There is no comprehensive treatise on Tennessee names, but there have been brief discussions of them by Horace Kephart,[3] P. M. Fink,[4] A. W. McWhorter[5] and James A. Still.[6] Kephart lists such curiosities as *No Time*, *Big Soak* and *Go*

---

[1] Dr. Raven I. McDavid, Jr., in the course of his studies for the projected Linguistic Atlas of the South Atlantic States, has picked up some picturesque names in South Carolina, *e.g.*, *Hell Hole Swamp*, *Gobbler's Knob*, *Pumpkinville*, *Tigertown* and *Fingerville*. A suburb of Greenville is *Apeyard*, and a section of Greenville county is *'Possum Kingdom*.

[2] Ehrensperger was born in Indiana and educated at Harvard, where he became Ph.D. in 1921. He later studied at Bonn and at Lund (Sweden) with Eilert Ekwall, editor of the Concise Oxford Dictionary of English Place-Names, and the greatest living authority upon the subject. After seven years at Wellesley Ehrensperger went to South Dakota in 1932.

[3] Our Southern Highlanders; New York, 1921, pp. 299-304.

[4] Smoky Mountains History as Told in Place-Names, *Publications of the East Tennessee Historical Society*, Vol. VI, 1934, pp. 3-11, and (with Myron H. Avery) The Nomenclature of the Great Smoky Mountains, the same, Vol. IX, 1937, pp. 53-64.

[5] Classical Place Names in Tennessee, *Word Study*, Nov., 1933, pp. 7-8.

[6] Place Names in the Cumberland Mountains, *American Speech*, Dec., 1929, p. 113.

Forth from the Tennessee Pamirs and Fink unearths *Venus, Bacchus* and *Lesbia* from the effete lowlands.[1]

Texas has a good guide to the names of its 2,148 postoffices in "Texas Towns," by Fred I. Massengill.[2] J. Frank Dobie, the authority on the folklore of the Southwest, has published some papers on other place-names of the State,[3] and there is a book on the 254 county names by Z. T. Fulmore,[4] but the rest of the writing on the subject is journalistic and thin.[5] Utah has a mimeographed volume in the Federal Writers' Project series,[6] but "origin of name unknown" follows many of its 400-odd entries. It shows that the Mormons have had relatively little influence upon the geographical nomenclature of their Zion. They failed at the outset in their effort to call it *Deseret*, a term appearing in the Book of Mormon,[7] and had to submit to *Utah*, the name of a tribe of Shoshone Indians, chiefly notable for their thieving and neglect of personal hygiene.[8] No Utah county bears a name taken from the Book of Mormon, though several have the names of early Mormon worthies. There is a small village called *Deseret*, and others bearing the Mormon names of *Lehi, Manti, Nephi* and *Moroni*, but such borrowings are not numerous. Most of the settlements of the State have flabby names, *e.g., Centerville, Riverdale, Coal City, Clearfield* and *Lakeside*. *Upalco* is derived from Uintah Power and Light Company, and *Veyo* was begotten by butchering *verdure* and *youth* and then grafting their fragments. Most of the picturesque early names have been obliterated by the growth of delicacy. What was once the

---

1 *Muscle* Shoals, not *Mussel* Shoals, is correct for the rapids and dam on the Tennessee river. The reasons therefor were set forth at length in Why *Muscle* Shoals?, by Gerard H. Matthes, New York *Times* (editorial page), May 9, 1926.

2 Terrell (Texas), 1936.

3 Stories in Texas Names, *Southwest Review*, Jan., 1936, pp. 125–36; April, 1936, pp. 278–94, and July, 1936, pp. 411–17.

4 The History and Geography of Texas as Told in County Names; Austin, 1915; new edition, 1926.

5 For example, Beauty and Humor in Texas Place Names, by Tennessee Farris, Dallas *Morning News*, Nov. 2, 1930; Around the Plaza, by Jeff Davis, San Antonio *Light*, June 9, 1936; Firearms and Texas Towns, by W. E. Dancy, *American Rifleman*, Feb., 1938. A brief note by Artemisia Baer Bryson is in *American Speech*, June, 1928, p. 436.

6 Origins of Utah Place Names; Salt Lake City, June, 1938; third edition, March, 1940.

7 It is defined therein (Ether II, 3) as meaning a honey bee. A beehive is still the State emblem and appears on the State seal.

8 Whether or not *Utah* is identical with *Eutaw* seems to be in doubt. The latter is a frequent place-name in the South, where it commemorates the battle of *Eutaw Springs*, S. C., fought Sept. 8, 1781.

village of *Carcass Creek* is now *Grover, Poverty Flat* is *Torrey, Sahara* is *Zane* (from *Zane* Gray), and *Sodom* is *Goshen.*

I come to Vermont, and have nothing to say, for its place-names seem to have been given no attention by its native savants.[1] Those of Virginia have done but little better. Forty years ago Charles M. Long published a book on the names of the State's counties,[2] and in 1940 George Davis McJimsey produced an exhaustive and excellent study of its topographical terms (not place-names),[3] but aside from these there is not much to report.[4] The State of Washington has books on its place-names by Edmond S. Meany[5] and Henry Landes,[6] but both belong to an earlier generation, and there has been but little activity in the matter in recent years. In West Virginia, as I have noted, there is the book of Hamill Kenny, published in 1945 — a large and extremely valuable work, worthy to be ranked with those of McArthur on Oregon and Ehrensperger on South Dakota. Indeed, there are details in which it is superior to everything else of its sort — for example, in the richness of its notes on history and legend. It is preceded by an admirable introduction dealing with the methodology of place-name study, and there is a good bibliography.[7] The study of the place-

[1] The Rev. Samuel A. Peters (1735-1826), whose General History of Connecticut; London, 1781, is still considered scandalous in that State, claimed to be the sponsor of *Vermont.* This was in 1768 and he called it *Verdmont.* His claim appears in his History of the Rev. Hugh Peters; New York, 1807. There is an account of him in Supplement I, pp. 211–12.

[2] Virginia County Names: Two Hundred Years of Virginia History; New York, 1908. It was followed by Virginia County Names, by M. P. Robinson, *Bulletin of the Virginia State Library,* Vol. IX, 1916, pp. 1–283.

[3] Topographic Terms in Virginia, *American Speech,* Feb., pp. 3–38; April, pp. 149–79; Oct., pp. 262–300; Dec., 381–419. These papers were reissued in one volume as *American Speech Reprints and Monographs,* No. 3; New York, 1940. They will be noticed presently.

[4] A master's thesis on French Place-Names in Virginia, by J. W. Goi-don, of the University of Virginia, was noted in *American Speech,* Feb., 1937, p. 73. The manuscript is in the Virginia room at the university. A brief discussion of the Virginia custom of speaking of counties without adding *county* to their names, by Atcheson L. Hench, is in *American Speech,* April, 1944, p. 153.

[5] Origin of Washington Geographic Names; Seattle, 1923. The contents of this work were published serially in the *Washington Historical Quarterly,* 1917–23. Meany also published Indian Geographic Names of Washington; Seattle, 1908.

[6] A Geographical Dictionary of Washington, *Bulletin of the Washington Geological Survey,* No. 17, 1917.

[7] Some of the founders of West Virginia wanted to call it *Kanawha,* but in the constitutional convention of 1862 *West Virginia* won by

names of Wisconsin was begun in 1854 with a report to the State Historical Society by Alfred Brunson. It was resumed by the Rev. Chrysostom Verwyst in 1892 with a monograph upon those of Chippewa origin,[1] and continued a decade later by Henry E. Legler,[2] but after that there was nothing more until Dr. Frederic G. Cassidy, of the State university, undertook a study of the place-names of Dane county, surrounding Madison.[3] This brings us to Wyoming, the literature of which appears to be confined to a pamphlet on its stream-names, brought out by the State Game and Fish Department [4] and a brief but excellent paper by Dr. Wilson O. Clough, of the State university.[5]

The French names of Canada resemble the Spanish names of the Southwest in that they are frequently very long, *e.g.*, *Saint-Jean-Baptiste de l'Ile Verte*, *Notre-Dame de Lourdes de Montjoli* and *Coeur-Très-Pur de la Bienheureuse Vierge Marie de Plaisance*, but usually though not always, it is the last element that is used for everyday purposes, not the first or a middle one, as in the case of *Los Angeles*. Some of the combinations of French and English are not without humor, *e.g.*, *Notre-Dame de l'Assomption de Mac-Nider* and *Saint-Henri des Tanneries*. Canada has had a Geographic Board like our own since 1897,[6] and there is another for Quebec alone, where the great majority of place-names are French, and a Nomenclature Board for Newfoundland. The first has endeavored to preserve locally accepted name-forms whenever possible, but is required by law to follow forms " found in the statutes, proclamations, orders in council or other official acts of a Province "

---

30 votes to 9. *Western Virginia*, *Allegheny* and *Augusta* received two each. *Columbia* and *New Virginia* were also proposed, but they got no votes.

1 Geographical Names in Wisconsin, Minnesota and Michigan, before cited.
2 Origin and Meaning of Wisconsin Place-Names, With Special Reference to Indian Nomenclature, *Transactions of the Wisconsin Academy of Sciences, Arts and Letters;* Vol. XIV, No. 1, 1903, pp. 16–39.
3 Not yet published at the time of the present writing. It will run to 1500 entries. The Federal Writers' Project produced a 50-page mimeographed pamphlet, Wisconsin Place Name Legends, but the edition was exhausted before I could collar a copy.
4 Wyoming Stream Names, by Dee Linford; Cheyenne, 1944.
5 Some Wyoming Place Names; Laramie, 1942. An enlargement of a paper read before the Western Folklore Conference at Denver, July 9, 1942.
6 It has issued no reports since its nineteenth in 1930. I am indebted here to Mr. P. E. Palmer, its secretary.

establishing districts or communities, and it has frequently been troubled by the fact that, in the French districts, many towns have two names, one French and the other English, *e.g.*, *Trois-Rivières* and *Three Rivers*. Also it has been considerably harassed by demands from Quebec that all the *c*'s in place-names be changed to *k*'s, on the ground that, in French, *c* is used only in foreign loans.[1] The board has got rid of the offending *k* in many Indian names by approving the substitution of French names, *e.g.*, *Dufresnoy* for *Kajakanikamak*, but it survives defiantly in many others, *e.g.*, *Kakekekwaki*.[2]

Canada, like the United States, is afflicted by the heavy duplication of names. There are thirty-seven *Blanche* rivers in Quebec alone, and hundreds of names, in the Dominion as a whole, embodying *Moose*, *Trout*, *Bear*, *Deer*, etc. The picturesque names translated from the Indian languages by the pioneers, or invented by their own fancy, are under fire and many have been changed. *Moose Factory*, on James Bay, is now *Moosonoe*, *Rat Portage* is *Kenora* and *Pile O' Bones* creek is *Regina*. But *Medicine Hat* and *Moosejaw* happily survive.

The Geographic Board has published a number of valuable monographs on the place-names of various parts of Canada, *e.g.*, Manitoba, Prince Edward Island and the Thousand Islands. There is also a considerable literature on the subject by private inquirers, among them Pierre-Georges Roy,[3] W. F. Ganong,[4] H. L. Keenleyside,[5] George H. Armstrong,[6] John T. Walbran,[7] W. F. Moore,[8] Frank

1 *Le Petit Journal*, Montreal, Nov. 22, 1931.
2 The Quebec Geographic Board has changed *Makamik* to *Macamic* but the Geographic Board of Canada sticks to *Makamik*.
3 Les Noms Géographiques de la Province de Québec; Lévis (Quebec), 1906.
4 His monographs appeared in the *Transactions of the Royal Society of Canada* from 1895 onward.
5 Place-Names of Newfoundland, *Canadian Geographical Journal*, Dec., 1944, pp. 255–63. Keenleyside notes the refreshing absence of *Centervilles*, *Fairviews* and *New Londons* from the Newfoundland map, and praises the bold picturesqueness of many of its geographical names, *e.g.*, *Empty Basket*, *Breakheart Point*, *Milliner's Arm*, *Dog Pen*, *Hog's Nose*, *Lord and Lady*, *Burnt Arm*, *Iron Skull*, *Blowme-Down*, *Ha Ha*, *Stepaside*, *Cuckold's Cove*, *Pick Eyes*, *Horse Chops*, *St. Jones*, *Femme*, and *Our Lady's Bubbies* (two islets in the Strait of Belle Isle). He protests against the Philistinism which has induced the Nomenclature Board to change *Maggotty Cove* to *Hoylestown* and *Mother Hicks* to *Regina*.
6 The Origin and Meaning of Place Names in Canada; Toronto, 1930. This work contains a bibliography.
7 British Columbia Coast Names, 1592–1906; Ottawa, 1909. Some of

Eames,[1] Charles N. Bell[2] and Thomas J. Brown.[3] The origin of *Canada* has long engaged geographers and many fantastic etymologies have been offered, but the predominance of opinion today seems to favor its derivation from an Indian word, *kanata*, which is defined by Roy as meaning *ville, village, amas de cabànes, bourgade, bourg, groupe de tentes, campement de plusieurs*. The Indian guides of the early explorers called out *kanata* every time they passed a village on the St. Lawrence, and the explorers mistook the word for the name of the country.[4]

In AL4, p. 115, I have listed some of the novelties in geographical nomenclature which appeared with the settlement of America. Such ancient English terms as *moor, heath, dell, fell, fen, weald* and *combe*[5] disappeared from the vocabulary, and in place of them there arose a large stock of novelties, *e.g.*, *branch, run, fork, bluff, hollow, bottom, lick, neck, gap, notch, divide, knob* and *flat*. A few of these, to be sure, were known in England, but they were not common there, whereas in the new land they became words of everyday. As the settlements extended terms were borrowed from the French, *e.g.*, *rapids, prairie* and *butte*; from the Dutch, *e.g.*, *hook* and *kill*,[6] and from the Spanish, *e.g.*, *canyon, mesa* and *sierra*.[7] Rather curiously, no Indian term seems to have been taken in[8] save

the Indian names of the British Columbia coast are formidable, *e.g.*, *Ahwhichaolto, Coqueisenejigh, Nequiltpaalis* and *Incomappbeaux*.

[8] Indian Place Names in Ontario; Toronto, 1930.

[1] *Gananoque*: the Name and Its Origin; Aouan Island, 1942. *Gananoque* is the name of a river, a lake and a town in southern Ontario. Eames traces it to an Iroquois term meaning "the door to the flint at the mountain." He records 42 different spellings, including *Gaunuhnauqueeng* and *Guansignougua*, and in a mimeographed appendix he adds 13 more.

[2] Some Historical Names and Places of the Canadian Northwest; Winnipeg, 1885.

[3] Nova Scotia Place Names; North Sydney, 1922.

[4] I am indebted here to Dr. David Robertson, president of Goucher College, who kindly gave me access to a letter from Lawrence Burpee, of the International Joint Commission, Ottawa.

[5] *Moor* and *fen* are in Beowulf, and the NED traces *combe* to 770, *heath* to c. 1000, *weald* to 1018, *dell* to c. 1220 and *fell* to c. 1300.

[6] Other examples are in Dutch Place-Names in Eastern New York, by A. E. H. Swaen, *American Speech*, June, 1930, p. 400, and Dialectal Evidence in the Place-Names of Eastern New York, by Edward E. Hale, *American Speech*, Feb., 1930, pp. 154–67.

[7] Others are in Geographical Terms From the Spanish, by Mary Austin, *American Speech*, Oct., 1933, pp. 7–10.

[8] Says J. D. Whitney in Names and Places; Cambridge, 1888, p. 77: "A considerable number of Indian words form all or part of various proper names, and have thus become quite familiar to us, as, for

only *bayou*, which came from the Choctaw *bayuk* through the French. Many of these terms are confined to relatively small areas. Those from the Dutch are scarcely to be found outside southeastern New York and northern New Jersey, and many from the Spanish are understood only in the Southwest, *e.g., arroyo* and *vega. Butte* and *coulee*, which are from the French, are pretty well limited to the West, and I am assured by a Southern correspondent that *run* is rare south of Virginia,[1] just as *pond* for a natural body of water is rare outside New England. *Gulch*, which is of uncertain origin, is commonly thought of as Western today, but the DAE's first example, dated 1835, is from Newfoundland. *Notch* is used in New England for what is commonly called a *gap* south of New York. *Creek*, which is mainly applied to an arm of the sea in England, has the same sense along the Chesapeake, but elsewhere it usually means a small country stream. *Swamp*, as I have noted in Supplement I, pp. 496–97, is unknown in England save as an exoticism, and so are *barrens, bad lands* and *bluff*.[2]

How many place-names are there in the United States? Allen Walker Read, in a paper read before the American Dialect Society at Indianapolis, December 30, 1941, ventured to guess "well over a million," and in view of the fact that Ramsay and his associates have unearthed 32,324 in Missouri alone this estimate seems quite reasonable. In addition, there are many thousands of obsolete names,

---

instance, *sipi, minne, squam, kitchi* and many others, but no one of all these words has been generalized so as to have become applicable to any class or form of scenic feature."

[1] Lieut.-Col. F. G. Potts, of Mt. Pleasant, S. C.; private communication, Jan. 20, 1945.

[2] The most exhaustive study of American topographical names is in Topographic Terms in Virginia, by George Davis McJimsey, before cited. McJimsey traces many terms beyond the first dates given in the DAE, and adds a full bibliography. See also Geographical Terms in the Far West, by Edward E. Hale, *Dialect Notes*, Vol. VI, Part IV, 1932, pp. 217–34, likewise with a bibliography; Nomenclature of Stream-Forks on the West Slope of the Sierra Nevada, by George R. Stewart, *American Speech*, Oct., 1939, pp. 191–97; and What is Named? — Towns, Islands, Mountains, Rivers, Capes, by the same, *University of California Publications in English*, No. 14; Berkeley, 1943, pp. 223–32. *American Speech* prints frequent papers on place-names, but there is no journal specially devoted to the subject, and nothing equivalent to the English Place Name Society, founded in 1922 and skillfully guided until his death by Sir Allen Mawer (1879–1942). In Germany, Holland and Scandinavia the study of place-names has been long pursued. Germany has a journal called the *Zeitschrift für Ortsnamenforschung*, first issued in 1925, and Sweden has *Namn och Bygd*, founded in 1913.

recoverable from old maps and records, and George R. Stewart once told me that he thought they might amount to another million. Thus the field of place-name study is immense, with room in it for an army corps of investigators.

4. OTHER PROPER NAMES

The literature dealing with other American proper names is somewhat extensive, and deals, *inter alia*, with the names given to apartment-houses, bungalows, cemeteries, churches, colleges, theatres, warships, merchant ships, newspapers, magazines, express trains, eating-houses, bars, night clubs, station-wagons, political factions, athletic teams, telephone exchanges, quilts and domestic animals. In most instances it may seem to the casual observer that names are chosen arbitrarily and even irrationally, but investigation shows that in some cases well defined systems are followed, planned carefully to avoid or get rid of difficulties.

That used by the New York Telephone Company in naming the telephone exchanges of Manhattan Island was described at length in 1941 by Pitt F. Carl, Jr., one of the assistant vice-presidents of the company.[1] The first New York telephone directory, issued in 1878, did not show any exchanges at all, but only the names of subscribers, then 241 in number. A subscriber who wanted to talk to another simply asked for him by name and address. But as the number of subscribers increased this method broke down, and it was necessary to give each subscriber a number, and a little while later the numbers had to be apportioned to exchanges, each of which had to have a name. The first chosen were familiar neighborhood names, *e.g.*, *Gramercy*, *Chelsea*, *Murray Hill* and *Madison Square*, but soon these ran out, and the telephone engineers had to discover or invent new ones. This was not the easy business that it may have seemed to the layman, for every new name had to differ clearly from every name already in use, and in addition had to be " easy to read, easy to say, easy to hear, and easy to remember."

It sooned turned out that the number of such names, whether borrowed or invented, was anything but unlimited. In fact, long experiment showed that there were only about 240 of them. When

[1] *Word Study*, Oct., 1941, pp. 6 and 7.

200 had been put to use it became necessary to devise a new plan, and this was effected in December, 1930, by adding numbers to the exchange names, so that *Plaza*, for example, was divided into *Plaza-1*, *Plaza-2*, and so on. Inasmuch as the usual four-digit number had to follow, this had the disadvantage of giving every subscriber a number of five digits, but telephone users soon got used to them, and after a little while they caused no trouble. They showed the merit of greatly facilitating the introduction of dial telephones. The subscriber using such a telephone dials the first two letters of the name of the exchange. This would have presented an almost insuperable difficulty under the old system, for not a few of the 240 eligible exchange names began with the same two letters, but the addition of numbers multiplied every existing exchange by ten, and so disposed of that difficulty. Mr. Carl thus concluded:

> To sum up, the selection of central-office names for use in a large city is a major engineering problem. The names in use include as large a supply of neighborhood and historic names as fall within the technical requirements for calling either by dial or by voice. They are survivors from among thousands of names which, for one reason or another, fail to meet all the complex requirements of service for a great city.[1]

Apartment-house names show a rich efflorescence in the United States, and many gaudy and almost incredible examples are to be found. Those of New York City have been studied at length by Arthur Minton.[2] He finds that of the 5500 apartment-houses listed in the Polk directories of the five boroughs about a fourth have names. This proportion was probably much higher at an earlier time, for there has been a movement against names of late, chiefly on the ground of their frequent absurdity, and it is now fashionable to live in a house, however huge, that shows only a street address. In the 1947 Manhattan telephone directory more than 1000 such nameless apartments were listed. Mr. Minton finds that in the remainder (including those of Brooklyn, the Bronx, Queens and Richmond) the names in favor follow a few banal patterns. Some-

[1] Unhappily, the introduction of the dial telephone brought the telephone engineers a fresh headache. Thus Louis Azrael in the Baltimore *News-Post*, Feb. 22, 1946, p. 25: "When the *Towson* area gets dial phones something will have to be done about the name of the *Towson* exchange or the *University* exchange. Why? Because when you dial *TO* you are also dialing *UN*." This was because not only two but three letters were grouped in each compartment, *e.g.*, *TUV* and *MNO*.

[2] Apartment-House Names, *American Speech*, Oct., 1945, pp. 165-77.

thing between a quarter and a third include the words *Arms* or *Court*, and a great many of the rest include *Hall, Manor, Towers, Gardens, Terrace, House, Chambers, Plaza* or *Gables.* Sometimes two designations are combined, as in *Chelsea Court Tower.* "For the most part," says Minton, "these generic elements are obviously derived from English usage — *Arms*, for example, from English inn names, and *Court, Hall* and *Manor* from names of English dwellings and estates. In them, as even more markedly in other elements, Americans are seen turning to British life for connotations of prestige and security." The non-generic parts of the names, he continues, come mainly from five sources — the names of adjacent streets and localities, personal names, those carrying historical or romantic associations, those of "natural features of the landscape," and those coming out of a sheer exuberance of fancy. Of the first class, *Kingsbridge Vanity Court* (in the Kingsbridge section of Brooklyn) and *Parkside Arms* (on *Parkside* avenue) offer examples; of the second, *Florence Towers, Mary Arms* and the *Bertha;* of the third, *Caledonia, Ivanhoe, Jeffersonian, Cinderella Hall* and *Mona Lisa;* of the fourth, *Ocean Towers, Hillcrest* and *Superview;* and of the fifth *Shergold, El-Mora, Dalmac* and *Empec Court.* The names based on personal names show some lush incongruities, *e.g., Kaplan Court, Rossoff Terrace, Leibman Manor* and *Hochroth Arms.*[1] But the strongest visible tendency is toward British-sounding names, and there are many examples in *-leigh* and *-moor*, the former of which was once put to heavy use in the naming of second-rate suburbs. Says Minton:

> To judge by ... the large and ever-growing number of British and British-sounding names, ... New Yorkers are rabidly Anglophile. A recently built apartment-house or "development" (that is, group of apartment-houses) — if it is named — is likely to be blessed with a name that pretends to some aura of Albion. Among the tony examples are: *Oxford Knolls, Dorchester Gardens, Balfour Arms, Tilbury Court, Chiselhurst, Rossmore, Sherwood Hall, Windsor Castle.* ... The names *Windsor* and *Georgian* occur eleven times in Polk's lists, and *Tudor* sixteen times. Brooklyn has an *English Village.* The residents of *Tudor Manor*, a large Manhattan apartment group, live without stifling in units called the *Cloisters, Essex, Haddon Hall, Hardwick Hall,* the *Hermitage* and the *Manor.* Another Manhattan nest bears the promising name of *Dartmoor.*

[1] In Venice, Calif., there is (or was) a *Finklestein Arms* and a *Burkeshire Arms.* The *New Yorker* (March 9, 1946, p. 18) reports a *Venus Arms*, and *American Speech* (Feb., 1946, p. 75) a *Magdalene Arms*, both in Brooklyn.

578   *The American Language: Supplement II*

The names of American hotels show measurably less yielding to Anglomania, though in New York there are still some evidences of it, *e.g., Berkshire, Broadmoor, Clarendon, Cornish Arms, Cumberland, Devon, Gladstone, Oxford, Piccadilly, Prince George, St. Albans, Stratford House* and *Arms, Surrey* and *Sussex*. There was a time when American hotels commonly were named after the owners or managers, *e.g., Astor, Gilsey, Vanderbilt* (all in New York), *Parker* (Boston), *Willard* (Washington), *Rennert, Barnum's* (both Baltimore), *Hollenden* (Cleveland), *Palmer* (Chicago), *Galt* (Louisville), *Delevan* (Albany) and *Burnett* (Cincinnati), but that fashion has passed, and most of those of more recent construction take their names from history or mere fancy. Of late a number, imitating the apartment-houses, have abandoned names altogether, and are known by their street numbers. When a new hotel in some large city makes a conspicuous success, it is common for its name to be borrowed in smaller places: there are *Plazas, Astors* and *Ritzes* all over the hinterland. Up to 1900 or thereabout many an American hotel used *House* after its name, but that fashion has gone out, and when *House* now appears in the United States it is usually applied to an apartment-house or an office-building, in imitation of English usage.[1]

The English fashion for giving names to individual dwelling-houses has never got lodgment in this country, save in the case of country residences with more or less extensive grounds,[2] but the bungalows in Summer colonies are often given names, sometimes puns or satirical misspellings. Ida M. Mellen, in 1927, listed a number of specimens encountered " on a sand bar off the New York coast,"[3] *e.g., Wendoweeat, Jusamere Home, Camp Rest-a-bit, Hatetoleaveit, U Kan Kum Inn, Unous, Kumhavarest, Villa-de-*

[1] When the custom of attaching *House* to the name of a hotel arose in the United States I do not know: the DAE does not mention it. Neither does the NED or its Supplement mention the use of *House* in the name of an office-building in England.
[2] The discomforts it produces in England were once set forth as follows by William Carr in the London *Telegraph:* " On a dark night one may walk up one side of a long street in a new district looking for *Rosynook* with an electric torch, only to find it on the other side. Alternatively, darting from one side of the road to the other with danger to life and limb, one may walk up a garden path, newly planted with privet cuttings, to find ' The Elms ' painted over the front door when it would have been more easily seen on the front gate. Numbers should be made compulsory."
[3] Naming the Bungalow, *American Speech,* March, 1927, p. 269.

Proper Names in America

Luxe, Fallen Arches, Kamp Takiteze, You Know Me Al, and *Cat's Meow.* To these, in 1944, Mrs. Edith Morgan King added many more, dividing them into classes as follows: [1]

1. Names of the owners in reverse, *e.g., Nitsua* (Austin), *Elyod* (Doyle) and *Notluf Farm* (Fulton).[2]
2. Conjugal combinations, *e.g., Virma* (Virginia-Martin), *Ludor* (Louis-Dorothy) and *Wiso* (William-Sophia).
3. Whimsies and puns, *e.g., Suitsme, Welcomyn, Biltover, Dunrenten, Rope's End, Sutzanna, Upson Downs, Headacres* and *Holme Run.*
4. Bogus Indian names, *e.g., Wa-a-wa, Waywayanda* and *Caplunk.*

Other explorers have added *Hop Inn, Dew Drop Inn, Moneysunk, Dunhuntin,*[3] *Uncle Tom's, Kum-on-Up, Nodaway, G-E-M, Laff-a-Lot, Weona Place, Linger Longer, Lotta Joy, O-So-Kozy, Bide-a-Wee, Look See, Here-I-Is, Ken-Tuck-You-Inn, Gid Inn, We-Blu-Inn, Klimb Inn, Curl Inn* and *Snussle Inn.*[4] The revival of *inn* as a punning substitute for *in* in some of these names restores a word that threatened to be lost to the American language. Before the Revolution inns were relatively rare in the colonies save in the larger towns, but with the movement into the wilderness that began after the Treaty of Paris they multiplied enormously. Lewis H. Chrisman says[5] that after the completion of the turnpike from Philadelphia to Lancaster, in 1794, " almost every mile had an inn of some kind." During the same year Congress passed an act for their regulation. They all bore names and their signs commonly showed images of the persons, animals or objects after whom or which they were named. As towns grew up about the more prosperous of them their names were commonly transferred thereto, and that was the origin of some curious town names noted in Section 3 of this chapter, *e.g., Bird-in-Hand, King of Prussia,*[6] *Red*

---

[1] No Namee, *New Yorker,* Aug. 26, 1944, pp. 55–57.
[2] This device is frequently used for other purposes. Mr. B. P. Brodinsky, of Washington, tells me that the dramatic club at the University of Delaware used to be called the *Citamard* (dramatic), that a city-wide celebration in Omaha is called the *Aksarben* (Nebraska), that a patent medicine is called *Serutan* (nature's), and that a Jewish club in Cincinnati is the *Learsi* (Israel). General Felix Agnus, for many years publisher of the Baltimore *American,* called his home in the Green Spring Valley near Baltimore *Nacirema.*
[3] I am indebted here to Mr. W. R. Smith, of Rockledge, Fla.
[4] I take all these save the first four from Cabin Names From Colorado, by Joseph Jones, *American Speech,* Oct., 1936, pp. 276–78.
[5] Early Inns in the Philadelphia Region, *American Speech,* Dec., 1937, p. 318.
[6] Rendezvous im *König von Preussen,* by Karl T. Marx, *American-German Review,* Feb., 1946, p. 28:

Lion and *Blue Ball* in Pennsylvania, and *Bishop's Head, Rising Sun* and *Cross Keys* in Maryland.[1]

The florid fancy which shows itself in bungalow names is also visible in those of eating-houses catering to the migratory trade. In 1939 Marguerite Cooke Goodner undertook a study of more than 4000 such establishments in fifteen Texas towns, ranging from Amarillo to Waco, and presented her findings as a thesis at the Southern Methodist University, Dallas.[2] She found that the banal attempts at humor visible in Summer camp names showed in many of their names, *e.g., Do Drive Inn, Snak-Shak, Chat-N-Nibble, Dime-a-Mite, Chat and Chew, Eatwell, Kool Kave, Elbow Room, Suits Us, Just-a-Bite, Goodie Goodie, Taste Rite* and *Tastee.* About "thirty-four per cent. carried the names of the owners in some form," *e.g., Berry's Thrifty Corner, Carroll's Eat Shop, Jimmie's Tamale House, Jerry's Kitchen, Pete's Hamburger Place, Pinkie's Tin Shack* and *Irene's Bar and Café*.[3] Miss Goodner reported that first names were most popular, as promoting "a bond of friendship and understanding." "Men who are forced to eat day after day in commercial eating-houses," she said, "are apt to seek the friendly establishment where they can call their host by his first name." A feminine name, she added, was even more attractive, but in 1940 the Texas *mores* still frowned on the coupling of such a name with the word *bar*, though large numbers of the eateries employed young girls to serve both food and drink. The reappearance of *place*, an old American euphemism for *barroom*, was significant, but Miss Goodner did not record *shoppe* in *eat shop, sandwich shop*, etc. Mr. Don Bloch tells me[4] that similar fanciful names are given to grocery-stores in Denver, *e.g., Pay and Save, Sellrite, Save-a-Nickle, Rite Spot, Save-U-More, Best Yet* and *King Klean*.

In the early days of the railroad it was common to give names to locomotives, and in recent years some of the roads have revived this custom, but it is no longer general. Whether or not the mellifluous names of Pullman cars will survive, now that the Pullman

---

"Das Gasthaus heisst *King of Prussia*, ja selbst die Ortschaft heisst noch so."

1 *Cross Keys* was a village near Baltimore, now absorbed by the city. From time immemorial it has been mainly inhabited by colored folk.

2 It was summarized in The Names of Texas Eateries, Baltimore *Evening Sun*, editorial page, Feb. 8, 1940.

3 Probably pronounced *kaif*. See AL4, p. 347.

4 Private communication, Dec. 14, 1944.

Company has been sawed in two by court order and the operating half turned over to a syndicate of the larger railroads, remains to be seen. But names for fast trains seem likely to go on; indeed, the introduction of stream-liners has promoted their invention. Some of them are merely gaudy, but others have no little charm, *e.g.*, the *Lark*, which is given to a night train between Los Angeles and San Francisco, arriving in the morning, and the *Flamingo*, on the Atlantic Coast Line. So far as I know, the only discussion of such train names in print is in an article by Charles Angoff, published in the *American Mercury* in 1928.[1] He lists, among others, the *Chief* of the Atchison, Topeka & Santa Fe (now reinforced by a streamlined *Super-Chief*), the *Panorama Special* of the Denver & Rio Grande, the *Pine Tree Limited* of the Boston & Maine, the *Red Bird* of the Chicago Great Western, the *Sooner*, of the Missouri, Kansas & Texas, and the *Golden State Limited* of the Southern Pacific. To these may be added the *Hiawatha* of the Chicago & Milwaukee, the *South Wind* of the Atlantic Coast Line, the *Black Diamond* of the Lehigh, the *Rocky Mountain Rocket* of the Rock Island, the *Zephyr* of the Burlington, the *F.F.V.* (first families of Virginia) of the Chesapeake & Ohio, the *Royal Blue* of the Baltimore & Ohio, the *Argonaut* of the Southern Pacific, the *Twentieth Century Limited* and *Empire State Express* of the New York Central, the *Silver Meteor* and *Sun Queen* of the Seaboard Air Line, the *Royal Palm* and *Ponce de Leon* of the Southern, and the decorously named Washington-New York expresses of the Pennsylvania — the *Congressional*, the *Constitution*, the *Senator*, the *Speaker*, the *Judiciary*, the *Legislator*, the *Representative*, the *Executive*, the *Embassy* and the *President*, with the *Patriot* and the *Legion* thrown in to stir the heart. The Pennsylvania has a *Mount Vernon* and an *Arlington*, the Chesapeake & Ohio a *George Washington*, the Seaboard a *Robert E. Lee*, the Norfolk & Western a *Pocahontas*, the New York Central a *Commodore Vanderbilt* and a *Paul Revere*, and the Lehigh a *John Wilkes* and an *Asa Packer*. During the tire shortage of World War II the Florida East Coast put on a *Tiresaver*. *Express train* is not an Americanism, for the English were using it in 1841, whereas it is not traced beyond 1849 in this country. But *limited*, which is traced by the DAE to 1879, probably is, and *cannonball*, traced to 1888, undoubtedly is.

[1] The Railroads at Bay, Jan., p. 89.

582   The American Language: Supplement II

The first Pullman cars bore numbers, and then letters, but the letters soon ran out, and the numbers conflicted with those of other railroad cars. The first to have a name was the *Pioneer*, which started out as *Car A*. It was hastily completed in 1865 for use in the train which bore Abraham Lincoln's body on its long and eventful trip from Washington to Springfield, Ill. It cost $20,000 and was the first car built from top to bottom by George M. Pullman: its predecessors had all been converted day-coaches. When the Pullman Company took over the remains of the Wagner Company, in 1899, it was found that about 300 of the Wagner cars bore names duplicated by Pullmans. Richmond Dean, then a Pullman vice-president, was told off to get rid of this difficulty, and he did so by visiting the Chicago Public Library with a corps of clerks, and searching ancient history. The result was a rash of classical names for the Wagner cars, and for a number of years thereafter they astonished and enchanted the country. It was once widely reported that Mrs. Frank O. Lowden, the daughter of George M. Pullman, was in charge of naming the cars, at a fee variously estimated at from $1 to $100 apiece. There was no truth in this: they were actually named by the officials of the company, often following suggestions made by the railroads using them.

In 1943 the Pullman Company issued a revised list of its cars,[1] and in 1944 a supplement followed.[2] These documents showed cars named *Ann McGinty, Arthur Brisbane, Babette, Beethoven, B'nai B'rith, Central Park, Chief Iron Tail, Chinatown, Civic Center, Diogenes, Eiffel Tower, Evening Star, Frugality, Game Cock, Gwladys, Huey* (without the *Long*), *Ibsen, Kentucky Home, La Boheme, Marco Polo, Milton H. Smith, Molasse* (no final *s*), *Night Glow, Okoboji, Roentgen, Skokie Club, Sunburst, Tsankawi, Umatilla, Vassar College, Wall Street, Wood Violet, Yvonne* and *Zeno*. But in general, the list revealed only a feeble fancy. Whenever the company's onomasticians hit upon a name that suggests a whole series they throw away their aspirin, give thanks to God, and work it for all it is worth. Thus, when one of them thought of calling a car after a Scotch *glen* there ensued a long row of names in *Glen*, now running to more than 130 numbers, and including such pain-

[1] List of Standard, Private and Tourist Cars; No. 34; Chicago, Oct. 1, 1943.

[2] Supplement No. 1 to List of Cars No. 34; Chicago, Dec. 15, 1944.

fully un-Scotch forms as *Glen Beach, City, Hollow, Rapids* and *Rio*. *Cascade* produced almost as many, *e.g., Cascade Bluff, Den, Elf, Gully, Moon, Whirl* and *Whisper*, and so did *Clover, e.g., Clover Bed, Colony, Gem, Nest, Plot* and *Veldt*. The names in *Mc* are almost innumerable, and range from *McGonigle* and *McGillicuddy* to such curious forms as *McCreadyville* and *McZena*. The advantage of such serial names is that they serve to identify types of cars. Thus, nearly all the *Mc* cars are old-fashioned sleepers with twelve sections and one drawing-room, and all the *Cascades* are new models with ten roomettes and five double bedrooms.[1] In 1937 the late Arthur Guiterman, a poet in large practise, was inspired by the Pullman nomenclature to a set of dithyrambs beginning as follows:

> In peace unvexed by jolts and jars
> I rise, with sundry aims,
> On those palatial Pullman cars
> That bear such lovely names
> As:

Mark Twain	*Castor*	*Zanzibar*
Lake Pontchartrain	*John Jacob Astor*	*L. Q. C. Lamar*
Chief Gall	*Helicon*	*Fort Dodge*
Independence Hall	*Lake Pelican*	*Senator Henry Cabot Lodge*
Samuel Morse	*McTwiggan*	*Vancouver*
Chief American Horse	*Kate Douglas Wiggin*	And *Hoover*[2]

In the heyday of canals all the boats had names and some of them were alarming, *e.g., Bluddy Pirate, Wild Irishman, Bridge-smasher* and *Larger Bier* (lager beer).[3] The boats have now deteriorated into barges, and most of them have only numbers, but the naming of larger craft goes on apace, and during World War II it put considerable strain upon the onomastic engineers and poets of the Maritime Commission. This was the plan finally adopted:[4]

Liberty ships

Liberty ships proper (EC-2s) were named "for deceased persons who made notable contributions to the history and culture of America, and for merchant seamen who lost their lives in the service."

---

1 I am indebted for the foregoing to Mr. George A. Kelly, vice-president of the Pullman Company.
2 Pullman Ode, *New Yorker*, March 27, 1937, p. 69.
3 These were names of boats on the Morris Canal. I take them from Among the Nail-Makers, *Harper's Magazine*, July, 1860, p. 149.
4 I am indebted here to Mr. Robert W. Horton, director of the commission's division of information.

Liberty type hulls converted into colliers were named for major American coal seams.

Victory ships

The first 34 were named for the United Nations, with the word *Victory* appended. The next 218 were named for American towns and small cities, e.g., *Canton*, O., *Luray*, Va., and *Rushville*, Ill., also with *Victory* added.[1] The remainder were named after American colleges and universities, e.g., *Calvin Victory*, *C. C. N. Y. Victory*, *Notre Dame Victory*, *Loyola Victory*, *Tuskegee Victory* and *Wesleyan Victory*.

Standard type cargo vessels

C-1s were named for capes. C-2s for famous clipper ships, C-3s for birds, fishes and animals prefixed by *Sea*, and C-4s for the same prefixed by *Marine*.

Tankers

Coastal tankers (T-1s) were named for American oil-fields. T-2s were named variously — for American battles, for historic forts, settlements and trails, and for California missions. One series was named for California oil-fields with *Hill* in their names.

Miscellaneous cargo vessels

C1-S-D1s, made of concrete, were named for "deceased individuals who have made important contribution to the development of concrete and concrete engineering."

N-3s, for coastal use, were named for captains of the clipper ship era.

C1-M-AV1s were given the names of various sailors' knots.

Minor types

Concrete barges were named for minerals or chemical elements.
Wooden barges were named for trees.
V-2 tugs were named for American ports.
V-3 tugs were given names, both nouns and adjectives, "denoting strength."
V-4 tugs were named for American lighthouses.[2]

The Maritime Commission built many vessels for the Army, the Navy, foreign governments and private owners, but had nothing to do with their naming. The Navy followed a system of naming its ships that goes back, in its essentials, to March 3, 1819, when Congress passed an act providing that "all ships of the first class ... shall be called after the States of the Union, those of the second after the rivers, and those of the third after the principal cities and towns." This act was amended on June 12, 1858, leaving the

---

[1] There was an *El Reno Victory*, named, not after the Nevada divorce mill, but after *El Reno*, Okla.

[2] The private lines, before and after the war, have usually given their ships synthetic serial names, often unlovely, e.g., *Deloreans*, *Delargentino* and *Delbrazil*. Cf. the names of the old Cunarders, ending in *-ania*, and those of the White Star ships, ending in *-ic*.

first two classes untouched,[1] but giving the President the right to name third-class ships " as he may direct." There were further amendments in 1908, one of them providing that no first-class battleship should be named " for any city, place or person until the names of the States shall have been exhausted," and another allowing the President discretion in naming monitors. These rules are still followed by the Navy, but as new types of ships have come in it has had to seek new kinds of names for them. The schedule followed during World War II was as follows: [2]

Battleships

All are named for States.

Cruisers

For American cities, the capitals of American territories and possessions, and those territories and possessions themselves.

Destroyers

For " deceased persons in the following categories: Naval, Marine Corps and Coast Guard personnel who rendered distinguished service to their country; Secretaries and Assistant Secretaries of the Navy; members of Congress who were closely identified with naval affairs; inventors."

Destroyer Escorts

For " personnel of the Navy, Marine Corps and Coast Guard killed by enemy action in World War II."

Submarines

After " fish and denizens of the deep." [3]

Mine layers

After monitors formerly on the Navy list.

Mine sweepers

After birds.[4]

Patrol vessels

After American cities and towns, and American territories and possessions.

Yachts

After ships formerly on the Navy list, gems, and with " logical and euphonious words."

---

[1] The first was defined to include ships carrying 40 guns or more, and the second to include those carrying from 20 to 39.

[2] I am indebted here to Lieut. Leonard C. Hall, USNR, of the aviation and ship section of the Navy's office of information.

[3] Most of them are more commonly known by their numbers.

[4] In the last two cases it is provided that " logical and euphonious words " may be substituted.

Colliers, repair ships and tenders

After characters in mythology. Aircraft repair ships were also named after "personnel associated with naval aviation" and destroyer tenders after "localities and areas of the United States."

Ammunition ships

After volcanoes and with terms "suggestive of fire and explosives."

Provision storeships

After astronomical bodies.

Cargo ships

After astronomical bodies or "counties in the United States."

Aircraft ferries

After "historical places pertaining to aviation."

Miscellaneous auxiliaries

After islands in the United States or in American territories and possessions.

Surveying ships

After astronomers and mathematicans.

Amphibious force flagships

After mountains in the United States or in its territories and possessions.

Hospital ships

With "synonyms for kindness" or "other logical and euphonious words."

Net-laying ships

After monitors formerly on the Navy list.

Tankers

After the Indian names of rivers.

Transports

After the names of American counties, "places of historical interest, deceased commandants of the Marine Corps and deceased Marine Corps officers, signers of the Declaration of Independence, famous women of history, famous men of foreign birth who aided our country in her struggle for independence."

Barrack-ships

After the names of American counties.

Transports fitted for evacuating wounded

After deceased surgeon-generals of the Navy.

Repair ships

After the names of island possessions.

Salvage ships

"Names descriptive of their functions."

Submarine tenders

"Names of pioneers in submarine development; characters in mythology."

Submarine rescue ships

Names of birds.

Ocean tugs

Names of Indian tribes.

Seaplane tenders

Names of straits, bays and inlets in the United States and its possessions.

Landing ships

Names of places of historical interest.

Miscellaneous vessels

Names of vessels formerly on the Navy list, and of animals.

Fuel oil barges

Oil-field terms.

Net tenders

Names of trees, or of Indian chiefs "and other noted Indians."

Harbor tugs

"Names of Indian chiefs, other noted Indians, and words of the Indian language."

In 1897 Prince Louis of Battenberg, then a captain in the British Navy,[1] published a little book in which he discussed the names of British warships and of those of fifteen other countries, but not including Japan.[2] In his preface he said that nearly all the names on the current British list had "a long record of past services, covering three centuries in some cases." One ship, the *Vesuvius*, was the eleventh since 1693, and another, the *Lion*, was the fourteenth since 1546. The *Dreadnaught* of the time, a second-class battleship, launched in 1875, was the seventh since 1573. The revolutionary *Dreadnaught* of 1904, with its turbine engines, its speed of 21 knots, its ten 12-inch guns and its displacement of 17,900 tons, was the eighth. The English seem to follow no set system for the naming of their warships, but a glance at their Navy List is enough to show that they have a liking for saucy names, calculated to scare the foe, *e.g., Furious, Terrible, Invincible, Powerful, Victory, Inflexible, Wildfire, Bulldog, Conqueror, Daring, Devastation, Haughty, Hercules, Hotspur, Intrepid, Aggressor, Thunder, Infernal, Shark,*

---

[1] Born in 1854, he died in 1921. He rose to the rank of admiral. In 1917 he and all the other members of his family living in England changed their surname to *Mountbatten*, and he was created *Marquess of Milford Haven*.

[2] Men-of-War Names: Their Meaning and Origin; London, 1897; second ed., 1908.

Wolf, Tiger, even *Hyena*.[1] The Japanese, in their heyday, apparently preferred more romantic ones, *e.g., Siranui* (Phosphorescent Foam), *Yakaze* (Wind of an Arrow's Flight), *Natusio* (Summer Tide), *Urakeze* (Wind in the Bay), *Kasumi* (Mist of Flowers), and *Asagumo* (White Cloud of the Morning).[2]

All naval ships are given nicknames by their crews, and some of those in use in the American Navy are picturesque and amusing. The cruiser *Salt Lake City* is the *Swayback Maru,* the battleship *California* is the *Prune Barge,* the battleship *Tennessee* is the *Ridge Runner,* the *Idaho* is the *Spud Peeler,* the *Milwaukee* is the *Milk Wagon,* the *Mississippi* is *Old Miss,* the *Missouri* is *Misery* or *Old Mo,* the *Nevada* is the *Cheer Up Ship,* the *Brooklyn* is the *Teakettle,* the *Dayton* is the *Blue Beetle,* the *Boise* is the *Reluctant Dragon,* the *Marblehead* is *Old Ironsides,* the *Brooklyn* is the *Busy B,* the *Cincinnati* is the *Can Do Ship,* the *South Dakota* is *Battleship X,* the *New York* is the *Old Nick,* the *Franklin* is *Big Ben,* the *Pope* is *Honest John,* the *Langley* is the *Covered Wagon,* and the *Guam* is the *Mighty G*.[3] One of the curious byways of homicidal nomenclature takes us into the names of battles, and history shows that the contesting peoples often call the same one by different names. *Waterloo* is *Belle Alliance* to the French and even to the

[1] These names were noted during the Eighteenth Century by Francis Grose, author of A Classical Dictionary of the Vulgar Tongue. In a posthumous collection of essays called The Olio; London, 1792 (second ed., 1796), he called them "boastful" and warned that the hazards of war might make them ridiculous. "An unfortunate day," he said, "may engage the *Gazette* writers in an awkward combination of words, by being obliged to inform the public that the *Victory* was beaten off, the *Invincible* overpowered, the *Inflexible* forced to yield, and that the *Dreadnaught* escaped by crowding all the sail she could carry." Grose favored naming warships after admirals, "who may without much impropriety be spoken of as an old woman" — *i.e.,* as *she* —, or, anticipating American usage, after the counties of England. "When we hear a sailor say," he went on, "that the *Prince of Wales* has been on board *Poll Infamous* or that the *Princess Royal* has much injured her bottom, should we not tremble for the health of the royal offspring?" I am indebted here to Mr. Hugh Morrison.

[2] I take these from First Snow of the Season, New Yorker, Jan. 17, 1942.

[3] I am indebted for all these save the last to Sailor Nicknames for Fighting Ships, U. S. Naval Institute Proceedings, Jan., 1946, p. 83. Grose, in the paper I have lately quoted, gave some examples from the British Navy of his time. The *Eolus,* he said, was the *Alehouse* to its crew, the *Belliqueux* was the *Belly Cook,* the *Agamemnon* was the *Eggs and Bacon,* the *Bienfaisant* was the *Bonny Pheasant,* the *Boreas* was the *Bare Arse,* and the *Castor and Pollux* had "a misnomer too gross to repeat."

Germans who fought with the English, and the battle which Grant called *Pittsburg Landing* became *Shiloh* to the Confederates and is now *Shiloh* to most other Americans. These differences were thus discussed by the Confederate General D. H. Hill in one of *Century Magazine's* " Battles and Leaders of the Civil War " series: [1]

> The conflict of September 14, 1862, is called the battle of *South Mountain* at the North and the battle of *Boonsboro'* at the South. So many battlefields of the Civil War bear double names that we cannot believe that duplication has been accidental. It is the unusual which impresses. The troops of the North came mainly from cities, towns, and villages, and were, therefore, impressed by some natural object near the scene of the conflict and named the battle from it. The soldiers from the South were chiefly from the country, and were, therefore, impressed by some artificial object near the field of action. In one section the naming has been after the handiwork of God; in the other section it has been after the handiwork of man. Thus, the first passage of arms is called the battle of *Bull Run* at the North — the name of a little stream. At the South it takes the name of *Manassas*, from a railroad station. The second battle on the same ground is called the *Second Bull Run* by the North, and the *Second Manassas* by the South. Stone's defeat is the battle of *Ball's Bluff* with the Federals, and the battle of *Leesburg* with the Confederates. The battle called by General Grant *Pittsburg Landing*, a natural object, was named *Shiloh*, after a church, by his antagonist. Rosecrans called his first great fight with Bragg the battle of *Stone River*, while Bragg named it after *Murfreesboro'*, a village. So McClellan's battle of the *Chickahominy*, a little river, was with Lee the battle of *Cold Harbor*, a tavern. The Federals speak of the battle of *Pea Ridge*, of the Ozark range of mountains, and the Confederates call it after *Elk Horn*, a country inn. The Union soldiers called the bloody battle three days after *South Mountain* from the little stream, *Antietam*, and the Southern troops named it after the village of *Sharpsburg*. Many instances might be given of this double naming by the opposing forces.[2]

The first study of church names ever undertaken in the United States was published in 1891 by two anonymous laymen of Rhode

---

[1] The Battle of *South Mountain*, or *Boonsboro'*, Century, May, 1886, p. 137.

[2] Hill was a philosophical fellow, and his reflections on his murderous trade are well worth reading. In the same paper he thus discussed the moral propaganda that makes wars: "The war songs of a people have always been written by non-combatants. The bards who followed the banners of the feudal lords, sang of their exploits, and stimulated them and their retainers to deeds of high emprise wore no armor and carried no swords. So, too, the impassioned orators who roused our ancestors in 1776 with the thrilling cry, 'Liberty or Death,' never once put themselves in the way of a death by lead or steel, by musket-ball or bayonet stab. The noisy speakers of 1861, who fired the Northern heart and who fired the Southern heart, never did any other kind of *firing*. One of the most noted of them frankly admitted that he preferred a horizontal to a vertical death." After Appomattox, Hill took to the birch. He died in 1889 as president of the Middle Georgia Military and Agricultural College.

Island.[1] They were pious Episcopalians, and confined their inquiry to churches of their own communion. They found that there were then 3918 in operation in the United States, and that all save 54 of this number bore the names of saints, of higher personages in the heavenly hierarchy, or of salient events, objects or doctrines, *e.g., Ascension, Atonement, Mount Calvary, Incarnation* and *Advent*. Not less than 385 were dedicated to *St. Paul* — 18 more than were dedicated to *Christ*. The latter, however, were reinforced by 67 churches called *Good Shepherd*, 38 called *Redeemer*, 26 called *Our Saviour*, 21 called *Messiah*, and perhaps a score more of similar names. *St. John* followed *St. Paul* with 366 churches, and then came *Trinity* with 354, *Grace* with 279, *St. James* with 178, *St. Luke* with 142, *St. Mark* with 136 and *St. Peter* with 122. The Episcopalians fight shy of Mariolatry, so there were only 97 dedicated to *St. Mary* and three to *St. Mary the Virgin*. But 87 were dedicated to the First Person of the Trinity, 85 under the name of *Emmanuel*, one under that of *Emmanuelo* and one under that of *Our Father*. The dedications to the Third Person numbered 8, all of them called *Holy Spirit*. The anonymous ecclesiologists found but 54 Episcopal churches in the whole country which lacked pious names, nearly all of them in Virginia and Maryland. In both States it was the custom, in colonial days, to name churches, not after saints, but after the communities in which they were built, and those old names have survived. Some of the curious church names unearthed by this inquiry were *House of Prayer, Gloria Dei, Reconciliation, Bread of Life, Holy Fellowship, Regeneration, St. Ansgarius, Saint Esprit* (French for *Holy Ghost*) and *St. Mary Magdalene*. To it was appended a survey of British churches, which turned up, in England, *Charles King the Martyr, Saint Cross, SS. Cyricus and Julieta, St. Gaffo, SS. Gluvias and Budoke, Holy Paraclete, St. John in the Wilderness, St. Peter Port, St. Ursula and the Eleven Thousand Virgins*, and *St. Delta*, and, in Wales, *St. Cwfig, St. Cyffelach, SS. Dyunog, Iddog and Menw, St. Llanwddog, St. Tyclecho, St. Wrthwl* and *St. Ynghednoddle*. The English are much less shy of Mariolatry than American Episcopalians, so they have 2453 churches

[1] On the Dedications of American Churches: An Enquiry Into the Naming of Churches in the United States, Some Account of English Dedications, and Suggestions for Future Dedications in the American Church; Cambridge (Mass.), 1891.

named *St. Mary the Blessed Virgin*, and perhaps a hundred more showing *Mary* in other combinations.[1]

The authors of this study reported, with ejaculations of satisfaction, that they could find very few Episcopal churches named after the persons who built them, but they had to add that this was a common custom in the early days, when the founder was usually promoted to sainthood later on if his church turned out well.[2] The Methodists, Baptists, Presbyterians and other such non-conformists still honor founders in this way, and sometimes a process not unlike canonization follows. They use actual saints' names sparingly, but name many churches after streets or neighborhoods, or numerically. All the Christian Science dispensaries are numbered, and in such citadels of the faith as Los Angeles they have gone into high figures. The colored brethren have some favorite church names that seem to be peculiar to them, *e.g., Shiloh* (not the battle, but the village in Palestine where the sons of Benjamin got themselves wives by making off with the female dancers at a vintage festival),[3] *Ebenezer* (a monument set up to mark the site of Samuel's victory over the Philistines), *Canaan, Sharon, Bethel, Berea, Macedonia, Abyssinia* and *Zion*. Some of the Negro store-churches in the South[4] have extremely curious names. I once found one in Baltimore whose sign showed that it was the *Watch-Your-Step Church of God*.[5] Catholic Churches usually have saints' names, though such forms as *Corpus Christi, Immaculate Conception* and *Sacred Heart of Jesus* are common. They are never called after streets, neighborhoods or founders. Of late the cult of the *Little Flower* has multiplied places of worship dedicated to her, but they are called *shrines*, not churches.[6]

---

[1] See also Names of Churches, *Current Religious Thought*, Nov., 1945, p. 6, and Church Dedications of the Oxford Diocese, by K. E. Kirk; Oxford, 1946.

[2] "It was not until 1170 that the Roman Church reserved to herself the right to canonize; and only about 250 years ago that the regulations were laid down for substantially the present Roman procedure." (pp. 30 and 31.)

[3] Judges XXI, 16–23.

[4] A *store-church* is one set up in a vacant store or in the front room of a dwelling house. All it needs to get under way is a brother fired to preach, and a sufficiency of sisters to applaud him and feed him.

[5] For the sake of the record, I add that this was in Gilmor street above Lexington, little over three blocks from my house in Hollins street.

[6] The use of the names of Catholic churches by athletic teams made up of their younger members produces some startling incongruities in sports-page headlines, *e.g., All Saints vs. Corpus Christi* and *Holy Cross Beats Holy Rosary*. Combats

The tendency to seek mellifluous euphemisms for such terms as *cemetery*, *churchyard*, *burial-ground* and *graveyard*, noted in Supplement I, p. 570,[1] long ago influenced the naming of cemeteries, and there are many *Heavenly Rests*, *Memory Groves* and *Sweet Homes* throughout the country. Among the colored people of the South some bizarre names are in use, *e.g.*, *Furnace Hill*, in Lowndes county, Mississippi. Miss Lila M. Herring, of the State Bureau of Vital Statistics at Jackson, has collected many others from the State, *e.g.*, *Saint's Rest*, *Last Hope*, *Evening Star*, *Twilight*, *Mount Comfort*, *Wonder Home*, *Love Joy*, *Harmonia*, *Pleasant Dreams*, *Tribulation*, *Peter Rock*, *Sunflower*, *Little Hope* and *Traveler's Rest*.[2] In the South, as elsewhere, many cemeteries bear the names of the local communities. The aforesaid *Furnace Hill* is probably an example, and others from Mississippi are *Corn Cob*, *Red Bone*, *Freewill*, *Toe Nail*, *Stockfarm*, *Jumpertown*, *Society Hill*, *White Cloud*, *Yellow Leaf*, *Pickle*, *Remus*, *Turtleskin* and *Cistern Hill*. To the bucolic regions of the country also belong the traditional names of quilts, though here the original inventors were probably all Caucasians. A large number from the Ozarks were listed by Vance Randolph and Isabel Spradley in 1933,[3] and more from other regions by Carrie A. Hall and Rose G. Kretsinger in 1935,[4] *e.g.*, *Turkey Tracks*, *Star in a Mist*, *Joseph's Coat*, *Ham Shank*, *Widower's Choice*, *Leap Frog*, *Rose of Sharon*, *Spider Web*, *Spider's Den*,

---

between the colleges of the older British universities provide other examples, *e.g.*, *Jesus Still Head of River*, a headline in the London *Daily Telegraph*, June 15, 1936. I am indebted here to the late F. H. Tyson. At a village called *Sacred Heart* in Oklahoma there is a cotton-gin known simply as the *Sacred Heart Gin*. It is listed in Oklahoma Manufactures, 1940, Publication No. 49 of the Engineering Experiment Station of the Oklahoma Agricultural and Mechanical College, fifth ed., April, 1941, p. 98. I am indebted here to Mr. Winslow Ames.

1 *Churchyard* is traced by the NED to 1154. In the early days the gentry were buried under the floor of the church itself, and the common people in the consecrated ground surrounding it. *Cemetery*, which was first used to designate the subterranean Christian graves in the Roman catacombs, came into general use in the Fifteenth Century. *Graveyard*, an American invention, is traced to 1773, and *burial-ground* to 1803.

2 Cemetery Names Give State Distinction, Jackson *News*, March 5, 1939, p. 24. I am indebted here to Miss Anabel Power, of the State Department of Public Welfare, Jackson, and for other help to Mr. Carl Kastrup, of Rockford, Ill.

3 Quilt Names in the Ozarks, *American Speech*, Feb., pp. 33–36.

4 The Romance of the Patchwork Quilt in America; Caldwell, Idaho, 1935.

High Wind, Grandmother's Fan, Rattlesnake Shake, So Mote it Be, Mill Wheel, Rob Peter and Pay Paul, Hearts and Gizzards, and *Steps to the Altar.*[1]

"Names, Reader," said Robert Southey in "The Doctor,"[2] "are serious things." He then proceeded to devote a long chapter to them, beginning with the names of lodges of Odd Fellows in England, *e.g., Rose of Sharon, Poor Man's Protection* and *Apollo and St. Peter,* and going on to those of gooseberries, apples, pears, roses, bulls, horses, pigeons, and the devils of Hell. With the decay of theology most of the last-named have passed out, but there are some that certainly deserve revival, if only for use as objurgations, *e.g., Cocabelto, Kellicocam, Motubizanto, Ju, Arraba, Lacahabarratu, Oguerracatam, Buzache, Baa, Kelvoryvybegg, Keileranny, Cnocknatratin, Drung* and *Knockadawe.* Southey listed no name for a bull save *Comet,* but C. A. Bond, extension editor of the State College of Washington, at Pullman, Wash., has published an instructive report on the names given to cows in that great State.[3] Some were apparently suggested by "outstanding anatomical or physiological peculiarities," *e.g., Hatrack, Washtub, Leaky* and *Shimmy;* others by sentiment, *e.g., Grandma, Purity, Fairyland* and *Desire;* yet others by "humor and perhaps downright disgust," *e.g., Twerp, TNT, Little Rat* and *Bot Fly,* and still others by "literature, history and the drama," *e.g., Sheba, Portia* and *Imogene.* Mr. Bond found a cow named *Napoleon* and another named *George.*[4]

"There remains one stronghold," said Willis Thornton, writing in 1926,[5] "where the romance of names is undimmed: it is the turf." In support thereof he offered some mellifluous specimens from the roll of American thoroughbreds, *e.g., Summer Sigh, Carmencita, Altar Fire, Dream of Allah, Midnight Bell, Simoon, Satana,*

---

[1] "What is known as the *crazy-quilt,*" say Randolph and Miss Spradley, "is simply a wild jumble of small patches, apparently put together without any particular design." The DAE traces the term to 1886 and marks it an Americanism. It is probably much older.

[2] Ch. CXXXIX. The Doctor was written between 1834 and 1847.

[3] What's in a Name?, *Country Gentleman,* Feb., 1937, p. 97.

[4] The Borden Company's *Elsie* was the first cow to be a radio crooner and the first to travel by air. She was not, in fact, one cow, but "a troupe of well-bred Jerseys," with headquarters at East Shodack, N. Y. Her story was told in the Borden Company's annual report for 1946, pp. 26–27.

[5] O Tempora, O Nomina!, *American Speech,* July, pp. 529–60.

Ponjola, Monday Morning and *Ethereal Blue*, and also a few on the sportive side, *Doughnut, Brainstorm, Whiff, Spot Cash, In Memoriam, Nose Dive* and *Jealous Woman*. But he forgot to add that the naming of colts headed for the big tracks is rigidly regulated by the Jockey Club, and that the fancy of breeders and owners is thus seriously hobbled. The rules in force in 1947 were as follows:

1. Names are limited to fourteen letters, and are to consist of not more than three words; space, punctuation marks, etc., to count as letters.
2. Names of living persons are not eligible unless their written permission to use their names is filed with the Jockey Club.
3. Names of stallions whose daughters are in the stud are not eligible.
4. Names of famous horses are not eligible.
5. Names whose spelling or pronunciation is similar to names in use are not eligible.
6. Names of famous or notorious people are not eligible.
7. Trade names, etc., or names claimed for advertising purposes are not eligible.[1]

Race-horses commonly have stable-names to go with their registered names, so that one appearing on the register as a *Whirlwind* or *Cleopatra* may be *Jack* or *Molly* to his or her intimates. The same is true of blooded dogs. In the stud-books of their breeds they often bear names that approximate genealogies, but at home even the proudest champion is usually only *Butch* or *Lassie*. Captain William Lewis (Will) Judy, a leading American authority, reports that of 116,000 dogs entered in a radio contest in 1939, 1400 were named *Prince*, 1200 *Queenie*, 1000 *Spot*, 500 *Rover*, and 30 each *Rags, Towser, Muggsie* and *Fido*.[2] It will be noted that *Fido*, once a favorite, is now slinking into the shadows. So are *Ponto* and *Bruno*, and in 1946 the New York *Daily News* reported that *Rover* was yielding to *Butch*,[3] which was apparently introduced by a popular comic-strip, along with *Sandy*. Other color names are also in vogue, *e.g.*, *Whitie, Red, Buff* and *Blackie*, and the two World Wars gave a lift to *Colonel, Major, Captain* and *General*.[4] Dogs of German origin are often called *Fritz* or *Heinie*, and many Irish terriers are *Tim, Terry* or *Mickey*. Other names now favored are

---

[1] I am indebted here to Mr. Marshall Cassidy, executive secretary of the Jockey Club.
[2] Care of the Dog; Chicago, 1940; second ed., 1943, p. 19. Captain Judy is also editor of the *Dog World*.
[3] *Rover* Gives Way to *Butch* as Dog's Tag, Sept. 18.
[4] I am indebted here to Mr. Frank E. Bechman, of Battle Creek, Mich.

Mitzie, Rex, Dixie and *Danny*.[1] Dorothy Parker once had a dachshund named *Robinson*, and I have heard of several hounds, all of them vicious, named *Mencken*.

"Editors of early newspapers in America," said Cedric Larson in 1937,[2] " delighted to give their organs pretentious names. Patriotism was exuberant . . . and the tyrannies of Europe were real." The result was a great spate of such titles as *Vox Populi, Herald of Freedom, Flag of Our Union, Freeman, Spirit of Democracy* and *Genius of Liberty*. That fashion abated when the movement into the West began, and was succeeded by one for homelier and more picturesque names, often humorous, *e.g., Hustler, Avalanche, Breeze, Clarion, Tomahawk, Searchlight, Meteor, Headlight, Eagle, Scout, Plain Dealer* and *Bazoo*, most of them indicating a hot concern with the community interest. Walt Whitman, in " Slang in America," recalled some curious Western examples: the Tombstone *Epitaph* in Arizona, the Fairplay *Flume* in Colorado (it still exists), the Ouray *Solid Muldoon* in the same State, and the *Jimplecute* in Texas; and Farmer, in his " Americanisms Old and New " added a *Rustler*, a *Cyclone*, a *Prairie Dog*, a *Cowboy*, a *Knuckle* and a *Lucifer*. Nearly all of these yielded to the ideas of elegance which came in after the Civil War, and Larson shows that most American newspapers, in the smaller towns as in the big cities, now have extremely decorous names. The favorite is *News*, which was borne by 375 of the 3,000-odd dailies of 1936, and it was followed in order by *Times, Journal, Herald, Tribune, Press* (including *Free Press*), *Star, Record* (or *Recorder*), *Democrat, Gazette, Post, Courier, Sun, Leader* and *Republican* (or *Republic*). The amalgamation of newspapers that has gone on since World War I has produced a large number of hyphenated names, and many a town of only a few thousand population has a *Times-Herald*, a *Star-Gazette* or a *Journal-Standard*. Many village weeklies seek to gain additional dignity by substituting in their names the name of the county they serve for that of the town, and some take in even larger areas, say a valley, *e.g.*, the *Aroostook Republican* of Caribou, Maine, the *Everglades News*, of Canal Point, Fla., the *Sierra Valley News*, of Loyalton, Calif., and the *Eastern Shore Republican*, of Princess Anne, Md.

[1] I am indebted here to Miss Alice Rosenthal, editor of the *Dog News*.

[2] American Newspaper Titles, *American Speech*, Feb., 1937, pp. 10-18.

As I have said, not many of the old racy names survive, but here and there one is to be found, *e.g.*, the *Rustler-Herald* of King City, Calif., the *Headlight* of Terry, Miss., the *Searchlight and Republic* of Culbertson, Mont., and the *Flashlight* of Eureka Springs, Mo. Among the college papers a more picturesque nomenclature remains more or less in fashion: there are specimens in the *Diamondback* at the University of Maryland, the *Polygraph* at the Billings (Mont.) Polytechnic Institute, the *Stilletto* at the Kirksville (Mo.) College of Osteopathy, and the *Sour Owl* at the University of Kansas. The little magazines which flourished in the 1890s usually had uncommon names, and in 1942 John Valentine listed some of them [1] — *Angel's Food, Gray Goose, Kit-Kat, Lucky Dog, White Elephant, Owl, Kiote* and *Black Cat*.[2] The papers published by soldiers during World War II — not the official papers edited by Army press-agents, but those produced by soldiers on their own — often had amusing names, but so far there has been no attempt to make a full list of them. In 1942 Thomas R. Henry[3] recorded a *White Falcon* in Iceland, a *Kodiak Bear* on Kodiak Island, a *Fever Sheet* at the Carlisle (Pa.) Army Hospital, a *Jungle Cat* in Panama, a *Horned Toad* at Las Vegas, Nev., and a *Midnight Sun* in Alaska.[4]

522. [All the States have nicknames, and some have more than one.] The eldest seems to be *Old Dominion*, applied to Virginia. In its present form the DAE does not trace the term beyond 1778, but in an earlier form, *Ancient Dominion*, it goes back to the end of the Seventeenth Century. *Ancient Dominion*, however, was not, strictly speaking, a nickname, but simply a formal legal designation, born of the fact that Charles II, on ascending the English throne in 1660, quartered the arms of the Virginia colony upon his royal shield, along with those of his four other dominions, England, Scotland, Ireland and (in theory) France. Three years

---

1 *Saturday Review of Literature*, Aug. 8, 1942, p. 16.
2 Mr. Valentine said that there was an almost complete bibliography in Ephemeral Bibelots, by Winthrop Faxon; Boston, 1903.
3 In a dispatch from Washington printed by newspapers of the North American Newspapers Alliance, Aug. 19.
4 For the names of American colleges see American College Names, by Harold B. Allen, *Words*, March, 1937, pp. 70–72; April, pp. 86–88, and May, pp. 110–112. For the nicknames of football elevens see *American Speech*, April, 1937, pp. 158–59.

later Charles granted Virginia a new seal, with the motto *En dat Virginia quintam*, and it continued in use until October, 1779, when it was supplanted by the present seal, with the new motto, *Sic semper tyrannis*, quoted with approbation by John Wilkes Booth on the evening of April 14, 1865. Both quartering and motto were graceful acknowledgments of the fact that Virginia was the first British possession to recognize the restored monarch. Two other once-familiar nicknames for the State, the *Cavalier State* and the *Mother of Presidents*, have lost vogue in recent years, the first because the researches of iconoclastic historians, both damyankee and native, have demonstrated that many of the early settlers were not cavaliers at all, but proletarians and even malefactors, and the second because though Virginia supplied the Republic with seven of its first dozen Presidents, it has hatched but one since the death of Zachary Taylor in 1850, to wit, Woodrow Wilson. The State has also been called the *Mother of States*, an allusion to the fact that a number of the new States west of the Blue Ridge were carved out of its soil and settled by its people. But this name, if the DAE searchers are to be trusted, was not applied to Virginia until 1855, whereas it had been given to Connecticut seventeen years earlier. Another old name for the State was *Mother of Statesmen*, but it fell into disuse when the Civil War broke up its old political hegemony. Since that time Virginia has produced very few statesmen of any size.

The DAE presents evidence that so long ago as December 2, 1784 George Washington referred to New York as "the seat of Empire," but the term *Empire State* did not come into general use until the census of 1820 showed that the State had gone ahead of Virginia in population. After the opening of the Erie Canal in 1825 New York City acquired a commercial and financial preeminence that it has not lost since. At this time, and for that reason the State was dubbed the *Gateway to the West*, but the sobriquet is now forgotten. Another obsolete name, *Excelsior State*, was suggested by the fact that *Excelsior* is the motto on the seal of the State, adopted by the State Senate on March 18, 1778. It was assumed by the political Latinists at Albany that *excelsior* was an adverb meaning upward, and it was used in this sense by Henry Wadsworth Longfellow in 1841 as the title of one of his most popular poems, but long years afterward the Oxford dons of the NED announced that the word was really an adjective meaning simply higher. During the Civil War era of highfalutin *excelsior* became a common term indicating excellence, and was applied to regiments, restaurants, new strains of grain, and various manufactured products. It still survives as the name of the thin wood shavings used for stuffing upholstery and packing fragile objects, introduced in 1860. But *Empire State* goes on in full glory, and is in frequent use. The New York City telephone directory bristles with the names of companies embodying it, or its back-form, *Empire*. The *Empire State Express*, a celebrated train of the New York Central System, has been running since October 26, 1891, and for many years was the fastest long-run train in the United States.[1] The *Empire State Building* at Fifth avenue and Thirty-fourth street, the highest structure on earth — 1287 feet, including its 102 stories and spire — was opened on May 1, 1931, and made the first pages of the world on July 28, 1945 by being rammed though not sunk by an Army airplane lost in a fog. Its captain, for many years, was the Hon. Al Smith, but he escaped this unprecedented experience by dying on October 14, 1944.

Another of the older State nicknames is that of Pennsylvania, the *Keystone State*. The DAE's first example is dated January 23, 1818, when *Niles' Register* said that "the powerful population and ample resources" of the State made it stand "as the *keystone* of the Federal arch." This seems enough to account for the nickname, but there have been a number of more fanciful etymologies, two of which are given in George Earle Shankle's "American Nicknames,"[2] and may be sought there by the curious. Pennsylvania, at one time or another, has also been called the *Coal State*, the *Oil State* and the *Steel State*, in each case for obvious reasons, but these names are seldom heard today. The designation *Quaker State* is sometimes used, but not nearly so often as *Quaker City* for Philadelphia. The DAE traces the latter to 1841, but it must be older.

[1] I am indebted here to Mr. C. W. Y. Currie, of the New York Central. He tells me that it made a record of 112.5 miles an hour, west of Batavia, N. Y., so long ago as May 10, 1893, drawn by the famous locomotive, 999. Its first trip in streamlined, stainless-steel equipment was made on Dec. 7, 1941.

[2] New York, 1937, p. 410. Dr. Shankle's work is one of the best reference books ever published, and deserves to be in every library. It is heavily documented, and shows few omissions. I am indebted to it for much of what follows. For permission to quote it I owe thanks both to him and to his publisher, the H. W. Wilson Company.

Bay State, for Massachusetts, is traced to 1801, and *Old Bay State* to 1838. Both refer to the colony of Massachusetts Bay, founded in 1628. *Old Colony*, traced by the DAE to 1798, refers to the settlement within the arms of Cape Cod, founded eight years earlier. Shankle records that Massachusetts, at different times, has also been called the *Puritan State*, the *Rock-ribbed State* and the *Baked-beans State*, but these designations are now seldom heard. Vermont, so far as I know, has never been described as anything save the *Green Mountain State*, which the DAE traces only to 1838, though *Green Mountain Boy*, to designate an inhabitant, goes back to 1772, a year after the militia so called was organized to protect the present territory of the State against forays from New York. The adjoining New Hampshire is usually called the *Granite State*, which the DAE traces to 1830. It has also been called the *White Mountain State*, the *Mother of Rivers*, and the *Switzerland of America*. These nicknames, however, have not had much vogue, for *White Mountain State* collides with the more popular *Green Mountain State*, the five rivers that arise in New Hampshire are all second-rate, and *Switzerland of America* is disputed by West Virginia, Colorado, Maine and New Jersey, not to mention the Ozark region and the Canadian Rockies country.

Connecticut, as everyone knows, is commonly called the *Wooden Nutmeg State* or *Nutmeg State* in facetious remembrance of the fact that in the early days the pedlars it sent into the back country were sharp traders and devised a thousand ways to rook the settlers, most of whom were of low mental visibility. One of these schemes, according to legend, was to sell them nutmegs made of wood. It has been suggested by various historians of the language that Judge Thomas C. Haliburton, author of "Sam Slick," was the originator of this fable,[1] but the evidence seems to be against them, for Haliburton did not begin to publish his Yankee sketches until 1835, and the DAE finds a reference to wooden nutmegs so early as 1824.[2] At the start *Land of Wooden Nutmegs* seems to have been

---

[1] *e.g.*, M. Schele de Vere, p. 620, and Shankle, p. 129.

[2] Albany *Microscope*, March 27. The same article also referred to gunflints made of horn, and buttons made of basswood. In 1826 Timothy Flint, in his Recollections of Ten Years Passed in the Valley of the Mississippi, added straw baskets and "pit-coal indigo," apparently an anticipation of the synthetic indigo suggested by Adolf Baeyer in 1880. In 1833 S. A. Hammett, in A Stray Yankee in Texas, added wooden hams, and in 1838 a Western paper quoted by the Baltimore

applied to the whole of New England, but it soon became confined to Connecticut, which took an early lead in manufacturing. At other times the State has been called the *Constitution State,* the *Blue Law State,* the *Brownstone State,* the *Freestone State,* and the *Land of Steady Habits. Constitution State* refers to the fact that the Fundamental Orders drawn up by Thomas Hooker at Hartford in 1639[1] were the first formal constitution written on American soil. *Blue Law State,* which is traced by the DAE to 1839 but is no doubt older, refers to the Blue Laws alleged to have been in force in Connecticut in colonial days. Whether or not they were ever actually passed and executed has been much debated by historians. They were first made known to the world in a before-mentioned " General History of Connecticut " published in London in 1781 by Samuel A. Peters, a Tory clergyman who had been forced to leave the colony on the outbreak of the Revolution.[2] His bias was only too manifest, and for more than a century the existence of the laws he quoted was doubted by the learned, though it was believed in by Americans in general. But of late there has been a tendency to admit that he did not imagine them altogether, though he unquestionably embellished them. The DAE's earliest example of *blue law* is from Peters's history. The term quickly came into common use. *Brownstone State,* which is not listed by the DAE and is long obsolete, referred, according to Shankle, to the brownstone quarries at Portland on the Connecticut river, which flourished mightily in the Brownstone Era of the 60s and 70s. *Freestone State,* also obsolete, referred to similar quarries. It is listed as the only nickname of Connecticut in an article headed " Names and Nick-names of the Several States " published in *Brother Jonathan* on August 12, 1843,[3] and is there credited to an Albany newspaper. It is also given, along with *Nutmeg State* and *Blue Law State,* by

---

Commercial added cast-iron axes. I am indebted here to Thornton.

[1] Hooker (*c.* 1586–1647) was an English Puritan clergyman who was driven to Holland by Laud, then Bishop of London, and in 1633 proceeded to New England. He became pastor of a flourishing congregation at Cambridge, and a man of mark in the colony. In 1636 he and his people migrated to the Connecticut Valley. In 1643 he had a hand in organizing the United Colonies of New England, the remote progenitor of the United States.

[2] See Supplement I, p. 211.

[3] p. 441. I am indebted here to Dr. Joseph M. Carrière.

Schele de Vere.[1] The DAE does not trace it beyond Schele. *Land of Steady Habits* appeared in John Neal's "Brother Jonathan" in 1825,[2] and seems to have been in intermittent use for a long while afterward, but it is now heard only seldom. Schele de Vere, in his manuscript notes to his "Americanisms: The English of the New World,"[3] applied it to the whole of New England.

Rhode Island, the smallest of the States in area, is now usually called *Little Rhody*, but the DAE's earliest example is dated no further back than 1851. In the *Brother Jonathan* list, just quoted, the nickname given to it is the *Plantation State*, an obvious reference to its official name — the *State of Rhode Island and Providence Plantations* — though there are few plantations within its bounds today. It has also been called the *Lively Experiment*, in commemoration of a phrase in its original charter of 1663: ". . . to hold forth a *lively experiment*, that a most flourishing civil state may stand and best be maintained . . . with a full liberty in religious concernment."[4] A list of State nicknames that used to be published annually in the *World* Almanac gave New Jersey four of them, to wit, *Mosquito State, Garden State, Jersey Blue State* and *New Spain*, but in the course of time *New Spain* was omitted, and then *Jersey Blue State*, and the *Mosquito State*, and now *Garden State* is the only one that remains. It seems to be relatively recent, for Schele de Vere, in 1872, said that Kansas was then the *Garden State*, and J. H. Beadle, in "Western Wilds and the Men Who Redeem Them," 1833,[5] gave the name to Minnesota. *Jersey Blues State* (with *Blues* plural) appears in the *Brother Jonathan* list of 1843. It was derived from the nickname of the Jersey militia in colonial times: the men wore blue uniforms. The DAE traces it in this sense to 1758. It was transferred to the patriot troops during the Revolution, but by 1850 had degenerated to the lowly estate of a name for a breed of fowl.

In the 80s and 90s New Jersey was known almost universally as the *Mosquito State*, mainly because of the swarms of the insects

---

1 p. 658.
2 This book is not to be confused with the magazine *Brother Jonathan*.
3 Written in 1873 or thereabout. These notes are now in the possession of Dr. Atcheson L. Hench, of the University of Virginia.
4 I am indebted here to Mr. Bradford F. Swan, of the Providence *Journal*.
5 I take this from the DAE.

that beset New York City from the Jersey marshes, but after the Spanish-American War they began to abate, and on March 24, 1930 the State librarian, Charles R. Bacon, was writing to Shankle that "a considerable number of other States have fully as many, if not more." These Jersey mosquitoes were frequent themes of the comic artists of the years before 1900, and were represented as having snouts resembling bulldozers or flame-throwers. Shankle says that *New Spain* arose in 1817, when Joseph Bonaparte, ex-King of Spain, settled in Bordentown, remaining there until 1832 and returning for two years more in 1837. Bordentown's possession of the splendors of his court aroused the envy of socially ambitious Philadelphians, and they gave vent to it by dubbing New Jersey *New Spain*, the *State of Spain* and the *Foreigner State*. All these nicknames, of course, are now forgotten. Shankle also lists *Camden and Amboy State* (or *State of Camden and Amboy*), *Clam State* and *Switzerland of America*. The first harks back to the time when the promoters of the Camden and Amboy Railroad ran the politics of the State, and is now obsolete. *Clam State* refers to the clam fisheries of the Delaware Bay and the Atlantic seacoast, and is still occasionally heard. As I have noted in connection with New Hampshire, *Switzerland of America* is shared with four other States. It must seem grotesque to travelers across the melancholy flats which lead to the Jersey coast resorts, but it is justified by some fine scenery along the western border.

Maryland has had half a dozen or more nicknames since colonial times, but only *Old Line State* and *Terrapin State* have any remaining vitality today. Both are under formidable competition from *Maryland Free State*, which was invented in 1923 by Hamilton Owens, then editor of the Baltimore *Evening Sun*. The story is thus told in "The *Sunpapers* of Baltimore": [1]

> Some time in 1923, at the height of the debate over Prohibition, Congressman William D. Upshaw, of Georgia, a fierce dry, denounced Maryland as a traitor to the Union because it had refused (largely through the urgings of the *Evening Sun*) to pass a State enforcement act. Mr. Owens thereupon wrote a mock-serious editorial headed "*The Maryland Free State*," arguing that Maryland should really secede from the Union and go it alone. The irony in this editorial was somewhat finely spun, and on second thought Mr. Owens decided not to print it, but the idea embodied in the title stuck in his

[1] By Gerald W. Johnson, Frank R. Kent, H. L. Mencken and Hamilton Owens: New York, 1937, p. 389.

mind, and in a little while he began to use it in other editorials. It caught on quickly, and the *Maryland Free State* is now heard of almost as often as Maryland.

It was first used in the *Evening Sun* on April 4, 1923, in the headline over a brief extract from a "Geographical Compilation for the Use of Schools," published in Baltimore in 1806. The late Albert C. Ritchie, then Governor of Maryland, adopted it with delight, and it spread over the country during his campaign for the Democratic presidential nomination in 1924. It appealed greatly to Marylanders, for it was a convenient crystallization of a body of ideas that had been traditional in their State since colonial days, and had been revived and revivified by the *Evening Sun* after its establishment in 1910. These ideas were all favorable to personal liberty, and had been exemplified in a radical and even somewhat scandalous manner in Articles 6 and 44 of the State Declaration of Rights, adopted September 18, 1867, as follows:

> That . . . whenever the ends of government are perverted, and public liberty manifestly endangered, and all other means of redress are ineffectual, the people may, and of right ought reform the old or establish a new government; the doctrine of non-resistance against arbitrary power and oppression is absurd, slavish and destructive of the good and happiness of mankind.
> That the provision of the Constitution of the United States and of this State apply as well in time of war as in time of peace, and any departure therefrom, or violation thereof, under the plea of necessity, or any other plea, is subversive of good government, and tends to anarchy and despotism.

Once he had launched the *Maryland Free State* Mr. Owens used it assiduously and it was taken up by other editors throughout the nation, and soon spread the idea that Maryland was a sanctuary from the oppressive legislation and official usurpation that beset the country in general and most of the other States in particular. This idea was given powerful reinforcement in 1938, when President Franklin D. Roosevelt came into the State in an effort to purge the United States Senate of one of the Maryland Senators, Millard E. Tydings, then an active opponent of the New Deal. In a speech made at Denton, Md., on September 5 Roosevelt sought to disarm the Marylanders by describing "the *Free State of Maryland*" as "proud of itself and conscious of itself," but then proceeded to argue for submission to "the flag, the Constitution and the President." The result was that Tydings was reëlected by an overwhelming majority.

Maryland Free State, of course, was suggested by *Irish Free State (Saorstat Eireann)*,[1] which was apparently suggested in turn by *Orange Free State*.[2] Some of the staff contributors to the *Evening Sun* occasionally referred to the *Free State* as the *Saorstat Maryland*, but this form did not prosper, and *Maryland Free State* is now used exclusively.[3] It has overshadowed all the old nicknames of the State, including *Old Line State* and *Terrapin State*. The former is generally assumed to recall the Maryland Line in the Continental Army, described by a historian as "among the finest bodies of troops in the Army," but the DAE says that it really refers to the Mason and Dixon Line.[4] The DAE's earliest example is dated 1871, but the designation is much older. *Terrapin State* is a melancholy memorial to the State's former glory, *Malacolemmys palustris*, now on tap in only a few of the more backward-looking clubs of Baltimore and a fast diminishing array of private houses. Shankle says that Maryland was once also called the *Cockade State*, and quotes King's "Handbook of the United States" to the effect that the Maryland Line was made up largely of "patrician young men" who wore "brilliant cockades." The DAE does not list the nickname, and the explanation of it seems somewhat incredible, for the Maryland Line was by no means predominantly aristocratic and cockades were worn by many other Continental troops. Other names that have been applied to Maryland are *Monumental State*, *Queen State* and *Oyster State*. The first was an extension of *Monumental City*, still often used of Baltimore; it was listed by *Brother Jonathan* in 1843. The second I have never heard in Maryland, though I was born there the better part of a century ago. The

---

[1] Proclaimed on Dec. 6, 1922, after a struggle with England that had gone on off and on since 1171. Under the new constitution of Dec. 29, 1937 the name was changed to *Eire*.

[2] The *Orange Free State* declared its independence on Feb. 23, 1854. It was annexed by England on May 24, 1900, and became the *Orange River Colony*.

[3] There is a *Free State* Brewery in Baltimore, and also a *Free State* Roofing Co., a *Free State* Oil Corporation, a *Free State* Press, and a chain of *Free State* grocery-stores.

[4] The boundary between Maryland and Pennsylvania, run in 1763–67 by two English surveyors, Charles Mason and Jeremiah Dixon. It was, until the Civil War, the dividing line between the free States and the slave States, and is still generally regarded as marking off the North from the South. The actual division between the two sections, culturally and politically, runs an irregular course through Maryland, crossing below Baltimore. The Northern counties of the State belong either to the Appalachian or to the Pennsylvania cultural spheres.

third, like *Terrapin State*, recalls a faded and now half forgotten pride, for the Chesapeake oyster has been deteriorating steadily for fifty years, and is now seldom encountered in its former state of perfection.

Delaware, which lies cheek by jowl with Maryland, is usually called the *Blue Hen State*. Shankle quotes the following account of the origin of the name from W. A. Powell's " History of Delaware ":[1]

> Captain Caldwell of Colonel Haslet's regiment from Kent county, Delaware, took into the Revolutionary War with his company two game cocks of the breed of a certain blue hen, well known in Kent county for her fighting qualities. When put in the ring these cocks flew at each other with such fury and fought so gamely that a soldier cried: " We're sons of the Old Blue Hen, and we're game to the end! "

A related but rather more plausible etymology was printed in the *Niles' Register* in 1840, as follows:

> Captain Caldwell had a company recruited from Kent and Sussex, called by the rest " Caldwell's game cocks," and the regiment, after a time in Carolina, was nicknamed from this " the Blue Hen's Chickens " and " the Blue Chickens." . . . After they had been distinguished in the South the name of the *Blue Hen* was applied to the State.

How much truth is in this story I do not know, but in one form or another it is believed and cherished in Delaware. The DAE traces *blue hen's chicken* for " a fiery, quick-tempered person " to 1830, and *Blue Hen State* to 1840, but the latter was not listed by *Brother Jonathan* in 1843. Delaware has also been called the *Diamond State*,[2] *New Sweden* and *Uncle Sam's Pocket Handkerchief*. The DAE says that the first was probably suggested by the small size of the State, as the third unquestionably was. *Diamond State* is traced to 1869 by the DAE, but *Uncle Sam's Pocket Handkerchief* is not listed, and Shankle says he has been unable to discover anything about its history. *New Sweden* is simply a translation of *Nye Sverige*, the name of the original settlement of Swedes on Christiana creek, founded in 1638. *Brother Jonathan* listed *Little Delaware* in 1843, but this was hardly a nickname.

The two Carolinas have been called variously, but *Tarheel State* for North Carolina and *Palmetto State* for South Carolina seem

---

[1] Boston, 1928, p. 155.
[2] One of the races run at the Wilmington track is the *Diamond State Stakes*.

likely to prevail. Of the origin of the former the *Overland Monthly* gave the following account in 1869:

> A brigade of North Carolinians . . . failed to hold a certain hill, and were laughed at by the Mississippians for having forgotten to tar their heels that morning. Hence originated the cant name.

This story, of course, did not please the North Carolinians, and in 1901 Walter Clark offered a more flattering version in his " History of the Several Regiments and Battalions From North Carolina in the Great War, 1861–65 ":

> The following, familiar to all the army of Northern Virginia, illustrates the complacent pride with which the North Carolina soldiers adopted the distinctive sobriquet of *Tar Heels*, first banteringly given them. . . . Thus, after one of the fiercest battles, in which their supporting column was driven from the field and they successfully fought it out alone, in the exchange of compliments of the occasion the North Carolinians were greeted with the question from the passing derelict regiment: " Any more tar down in the Old North State, boys? " Quick as thought came the answer: " No; not a bit. Old Jeff's bought it all up." " Is that so? What is he going to do with it? " was asked. " He is going to put it on you'uns heels to make you stick better in the next fight." [1]

In a speech in 1915 Major William A. Graham, a North Carolina veteran of the Confederate Army, repeated this story substantially as it is told here, but followed it with a quite inconsistent variorum version, as follows:

> The Fourth Texas had lost its flag at Sharpsburg.[2] Passing the Sixth North Carolina a few days afterward, they called out " Tar Heel! " and the reply was, " If you fellows had some tar on your heels you would have brought back your flag from Sharpsburg."

Obviously, the point here is lost unless it is assumed that North Carolinians were known as *Tarheels* before the date of the incident, or, at all events, that some notion of tar was associated with them. That this was the case is shown by the DAE, which offers evidence that they were called *Tar-boilers* so early as 1845, and that their State was the *Turpentine State* by 1850. No one, so far, has unearthed an example of *Tarheel* older than the Civil War, but I suspect that a more diligent investigation than the searchers for the DAE undertook might produce many. At the start, it appears, the term was regarded as opprobrious by the North Carolinians, but

---

[1] I owe this to Shankle.
[2] The Southern name for the battle known to Northerners as *Antietam*. It was fought at Sharpsburg, Md., on Sept. 16 and 17, 1862.

that is certainly not true today. How their view of it was changed was represented by Major Graham in his speech to be as follows:

> It was recognized as a term of affront until 1864. Governor Vance,[1] when he visited the Army of Northern Virginia, in opening his speech, said:
> "I do not know what to call you fellows. I cannot say 'fellow soldiers' because I am not a soldier, nor 'fellow citizens' because we do not live in this State, so I have concluded to call you 'fellow *Tar Heels*.'"
> There was a slight pause before the applause came, and from that time *Tar Heels* has been honored as an epithet worthy to be offered to a gallant North Carolina soldier.[2]

Whatever the truth of all this, the fact remains that *Tarheel* has now lost all derogatory significance in North Carolina. The newspaper of the students at the University of North Carolina has been so called since 1892, and when, in 1922, the State bankers launched a monthly organ at Raleigh it was given the name of *Tarheel Banker*. Other nicknames recorded for North Carolina by Shankle and other authorities are *Old North State, Land of the Sky* and *Rip Van Winkle State*. The first arose naturally out of the geography and history of the State, and the DAE traces it, on the authority of Bartlett, to the campaign which made William A. Graham, apparently the father of the aforesaid Major Graham, Governor from 1845 to 1849. *Land of the Sky* is logically applicable only to the beautiful mountain country in the far western part of the State; Eastern North Carolina is far closer to the bottom of the Atlantic than to the sky. *Rip Van Winkle State* remains unexplained. It appears on the *Brother Jonathan* list of 1843, but is not recorded by the DAE. Washington Irving's "Rip Van Winkle" was first published in his "Sketch Book" in 1819.

---

[1] Zebulon B. Vance (1830–94) was an opponent of Secession, but when his State left the Union raised a company which became part of the Fourteenth North Carolina Infantry, C.S.A. He was later elected colonel of the Twenty-sixth North Carolina, and commanded it in the Seven Days' Battles of the Peninsula campaign, June 25–July 1, 1862. While still in the field he was elected Governor of his State. On May 20, 1864, he was imprisoned, but was released on July 5. In 1870 he was elected to the United States Senate. He was refused admission, but was reëlected in 1879, and served in the Senate thereafter until his death.

[2] The Graham speech, the theme of which was Agricultural Achievements in North Carolina, was delivered before the Southern Commercial Congress at Muskogee, Okla., April 25, 1915. Graham was then commissioner of agriculture in North Carolina. The speech was reprinted in the Miami (Fla.) *Daily News*, Nov. 19, 1925, and in *American Speech*, March, 1926, p. 355. It is from the latter that I take it.

The palmetto, a variety of fan palm, has been associated with South Carolina since colonial days, though it also grows in other States. The DAE traces its use as a common noun to 1739. *Palmetto State* appeared in both the *Knickerbocker Magazine* and *Brother Jonathan* lists in 1843. During the turmoils preceding the Civil War *palmetto* was used in various terms associated with the Nullification and Secession movements — e.g., *palmetto speech*, 1840, *palmetto cockade*, 1846, and *palmetto banner*, 1860 — and at the outbreak of the war the *palmetto flag* was the shining symbol of the Confederacy. The prevailing American belief in those days was that the South Carolinians were an especially bellicose folk, so the State was sometimes called the *Gamecock State* or the *Harry Percy of the Union*. The DAE traces the former to 1862, but it was probably not new at that time. Both it and *Harry Percy of the Union* have vanished as the fires of the South Carolinians have cooled. Their State has also been called the *Rice State*, the *Iodine State*, the *Swamp State* and the *Sand-lapper State*. Between the Revolution and the Civil War those living on the low-lying coastal plain were often called *Ricebirds* by the people of higher regions. *Rice State*, however, is not recorded by the DAE, nor are *Swamp State* and *Iodine State*. During the years before the Civil War the inhabitants of sandy regions throughout the South were often called *Sand-lappers*. In "The Scout," 1841 (also published as "The Kinsman"), W. G. Simms described one of them as "a little, dried up, withered atomy — a jaundiced *sand-lapper* or *clay-eater* from the Wassamasaw country." *Sand-hiller* was a variant. *Clay-hiller* belonged to both Carolinas. Thornton defines the term on the authority of a mysterious Ida May, as follows:

> A miserable set of people inhabiting some of the Southern States, who subsist chiefly on turpentine whiskey [1] and appease their craving for more substantial food by filling their stomachs with a kind of aluminous earth which abounds everywhere. This gives them a yellowish-drab-colored complexion, with dull eyes and faces whose idiotic expression is only varied by a dull despair or a devilish malignity. They are looked down upon by the Negroes with a contempt that they return with a hearty hatred.[2]

[1] The DAE says that this was "moonshine whiskey of a low grade."

[2] Clay-eating is an aberration known to pathologists as chthonophagia or geophagism. It is encountered only in persons of low mentality, and is usually accompanied by theological delusions of an extravagant character.

They were finally dissuaded from this diet by the Public Health Service doctors and nurses who began purging them of hookworms in the early days of the present century.

Georgia was listed as the *Pine State* by *Brother Jonathan* in 1843, but by 1872 Schele de Vere was calling it the *Cracker State*, though he added with some haste that it "little deserved" the nickname. *Cracker* as a designation for a low-down Southern white man is traced by the DAE to 1767, and from the start it seems to have been felt that such persons were especially numerous in Georgia. The origin of the term is obscure. It was used in the sense of a boaster by Alexander Barclay in "The Shyp of Folys" in 1509, and by Shakespeare in "King John" in 1595, and in this sense it seems to have been suggested by a verb common to all the Germanic languages, signifying to make a short, sharp sound, as of something breaking.[1] But it is hard to connect the verb with the Southern *cracker*, so amateur etymologists have looked elsewhere. One school holds that many of the early *crackers* were teamsters, and got their name by their loud and incessant cracking of their whips. Another believes that it came from their eating of cracked corn. Yet another teaches that it derives from their manner of speaking, which sounded like a mere crackling to strangers. *Crackers*, of course, were (and are) by no means confined to Georgia; they are to be found in all the States south of the Potomac and Ohio. In 1819 a correspondent of the Lancaster (Pa.) *Gazette* reported them in Florida, and in 1856 a traveling English lady said that Kentucky was then called the *Corncracker State*.[2] There was a time when Georgians bitterly resented *Cracker State*, but of late they seem to have become more philosophical, and for some time past the Atlanta *Journal*, which "covers Dixie like the dew," has been maintaining in Washington a correspondent named Ralph Smith who contributes to it a daily column of "Southern angle, home-State stuff" headed "*Crackerland* in Washington."[3]

At various times in the past Georgia has suffered even more

---

[1] Cf. the German *krachen* and the American *wise-crack* and *wise-cracker*.
[2] Letters From the United States, Cuba and Canada, by the Hon. Amelia M. Murray; New York, 1856, p. 324. I am indebted for this to Dr. Joseph M. Carrière.
[3] Advertisement of the *Journal* in the *Editor and Publisher*, July 15, 1944, p. 25.

opprobrious nicknames, *e.g.*, *Buzzard State*, and also basked in some very flattering ones, *e.g.*, *Empire State of the South*. The DAE traces *Buzzard* for Georgian to 1845, and during the same year it appeared in a list of such names in the *Broadway Journal*, one of whose editors was Edgar Allan Poe. Walt Whitman, as we have seen, copied this *Broadway Journal* list into his paper, "Slang in America," included in "November Boughs" in 1888. He changed or omitted some of the items, but he let *Buzzard* for Georgian stand.[1] *Empire State of the South* is traced by the DAE to 1857. It has been disputed by Texas, but is well deserved by Georgia, which is the largest State east of the Mississippi. *Yankee Land of the South* was launched by Frederick Law Olmsted in his once famous book, "A Journey in the Seaboard Slave States," published in 1856, where he credited it to a native Alabamian. It still has a plausible sound, for many Yankee enterprisers flocked to Georgia after the Civil War, and the Atlanta of today has been described as a half-Northern city. But it is highly improbable that any native, or dirt Georgian relishes being called a Yankee, even in compliment. *Goober State*, yet another nickname for Georgia, is traced to 1877 by the DAE. It comes from a common Southern name for the peanut, traced to 1848 but apparently older, and supposedly derived from *nguba*, an African name for the same plant. Georgia is a heavy producer of peanuts, and the hams of its peanut-fed hogs are highly esteemed by connoisseurs. Before the Civil War era *Goober-grabber* was a common nickname for a backwoods Georgian, but it was also applied to Alabamians, and the simple *Goober* was a nickname for North Carolinians.

We have now reviewed the Thirteen Original States, and perhaps it will be more convenient to proceed alphabetically hereafter, beginning with Alabama. It is credited by the *World Almanac*, 1947, with the nickname of *Cotton State*, and Shankle says that this refers to its central position in the cotton-growing area east of the Mississippi, now in sad decay. *Cotton States* is a generic name for the whole group, traced by the DAE to 1844, with *Cottondom* (1861), *Cotton Belt* (1871), *Cotton Country* (1671) and *Cottonia* as variants. Shankle also notes *Cotton Plantation State*, *Lizard State* and *Yellow-hammer State* as nicknames for

[1] See Nicknames of the States: a Note on Walt Whitman, by John Howard Birss, *American Speech*, June, 1932, p. 389.

Alabama. *Lizard State* derives from an early nickname for the Alabamians, first recorded in 1845. The origin of this nickname is obscure, but it seems to be clear that it was intended to be opprobrious, for the lizard has always been offensive to *Homo sapiens*. Another nickname, *Yellow-hammer State*, is more flattering, for the yellow-hammer (*Colaptes auratus*) is a beautiful variety of woodpecker. But Shankle cites Mrs. Marie B. Owen, director of the Department of State Archives and History at Montgomery, as authority for the explanation that the nickname was suggested during the Civil War by the fact that the home-dyed uniforms of the Alabama troops had a yellowish tinge.[1]

Arizona is called the *Baby State* by the *World* Almanac: it was the last of the forty-eight to be admitted to the Union — on February 14, 1912, more than a month after its sister-State, New Mexico. There is, however, nothing infantile about its *Kultur*, for it was settled by the Spaniards so long ago as 1580, and its Indian civilization goes back to a remote antiquity. Shankle shows that it has also been known as the *Apache State*, the *Aztec State*, the *Sand Hill State*, the *Italy of America*, the *Sunset State* and the *Valentine State* — the last because it was admitted on St. Valentine's Day, and the others for obvious reasons.

In 1923 the Legislature of Arkansas, prodded by the visionaries of the Arkansas Advancement Association, passed an act designating *Wonder State* as its nickname,[2] but in the past it was the *Bear State*, the *Hot Water State*, the *Bowie State* and the *Toothpick State*. Bartlett recorded *Bear State* so early as 1848, and in 1872 Schele de Vere reported that the local pronunciation was *Bar State*. California and Missouri, in those days, pretended to the same nickname, and there are bears on their State seals to this day. *Hot Water State*, of course, refers to the springs at Hot Springs and elsewhere. Both *Bowie State* and *Toothpick State* recall the *Bowie-knife*, the favorite weapon of the hardy blood-letters who wrested the Southwest from the Mexican, the Indian, the bear, the catamount and all lesser fauna. It was commonly made by grinding a flat, broad file, nine or ten inches long, to a fine point, sharpening both edges to razor

---

[1] Another and far less probable etymology is given in Alabama: a Guide to the Deep South, in the American Guide Series; New York, 1941, p. 128.

[2] There is a weekly *Wonder State Herald* in Kensett, Ark., population 889.

keenness, and fitting a hilt or guard between blade and handle. The DAE says that it was named after Col. James Bowie, who was killed at the Alamo on March 6, 1836, but the available evidence indicates that it was really invented by his brother, Rezin Pleasant Bowie (1793-1841), at some indefinite time before 1827. Its popularity, however, seems to have been due to James, who used it with great effect during the latter year in a famous mass duel at Natchez, Miss. In this gory affair Bowie was brought to his knees by a pistol shot, and an heroic opponent named Major Wright ran upon him with a sword, seeking to dispatch him. But Bowie's right arm was still working, and with it he plunged his *Bowie-knife* into Wright's heart, twisting it " to cut the heart string." [1] How the *Bowie-knife* came to be associated with Arkansas is not known, for the Bowies operated in Louisiana and Texas. But the DAE shows that it was being described as an *Arkansas toothpick* in an act of the Alabama Legislature so early as 1837. The legend was that the Arkansans of the time used it not only for murder, but also for fighting wild animals, butchering cattle, cutting up their victuals, and picking their teeth.

California was called the *Gold State* by the Hon. Amelia M.

[1] The history of the *Bowie-knife* has been heavily labored by historians, with no general agreement. The most plausible account of it is in The Bowie Brothers and Their Famous Knife, by Matilda Elanor Bowie Moore, a daughter of Rezin P. Bowie, *Frontier Times* (Bandera, Texas), Feb., 1942, pp. 199-205. Mrs. Moore was long dead in 1942, but she had prepared a history of the Bowies during her lifetime, and this was sent to the *Frontier Times* by her granddaughter, Mrs. Bessie Bird Moore Bryant. It showed that the *Bowie-knife* was invented by Rezin after he had been seriously wounded by a hunting knife with which he had attempted to cut the throat of a wild heifer. The thought occurred to him that this "could have been prevented had there been a guard between the blade and handle of the knife." He accordingly had the blacksmith of his plantation on Bayou Boeuf, La., make a new one of a broad file, with such a guard affixed. His daughter testified that he intended it to be used as a hunting knife only. But its usefulness for homicide soon attracted public attention, and in a little while it was the weapon of choice of the whole Southwest. The Bowies were descendants of a Scotsman who immigrated to America during the Eighteenth Century, along with two of his brothers. He settled in Natchez, Miss., but his brothers chose Maryland, and there they became the progenitors of a number of distinguished men, including Oden Bowie, Governor of the State from 1868 to 1872. Oden Bowie was a Democrat, and his election marked the final rescue of the State from the abhorred damyankee. I am indebted to Judge Robert T. Neill, of San Angelo, Texas, for the *Frontier Times*. See also *Bowie Knife*, by Eston Everett Ericson, *American Speech*, Feb., 1937, pp. 77-79.

Murray in her "Letters From the United States, Cuba and Canada" in 1855,[1] but the DAE shows that by 1867 this had become the *Golden State*. The State did not appear at all on the *Brother Jonathan* list of 1843, for that was five years before the discovery of gold on Sutter's ranch. It has, in late years, got much more glory and money out of its oil wells, orchards, vineyards, truck farms and movie lots than it has got out of its gold-mines, but the glamour of 1849 survives, probably helped by the suggestion in that most romantic of geographical names, *Golden Gate*. In 1849 *El Dorado* came into use as a nickname for California,[2] but it was by no means new, and had been applied previously to various other regions promising fabulous riches. Shankle also records *Grape State* and *Eureka State*, the latter borrowed from the motto on the state seal,[3] but neither seems to have ever had much vogue. Schele de Vere adds *Bear State*, also claimed by Arkansas, and explains that the California bear is a grizzly.

Colorado is usually called the *Centennial State*, for it was admitted to the Union in 1876. The DAE's first example of the use of the term is dated 1878. There was a time when it was often called the *Silver State*, but this designation was disputed by Nevada so long ago as 1871. It has also been called the *Switzerland of America*, which is challenged, as I have already noted, by Maine, New Hampshire, New Jersey and West Virginia, and the *Treasure State*, which is disputed by Montana. Shankle lists, in addition, *Lead State* and *Buffalo Plains State*, neither of which is recorded by the DAE.

The most common designations for Florida are *Everglade State* and *Peninsula State*, though it has had a number of others. The latter is favored by the *World* Almanac, 1947, which apparently reflects a local preference. The DAE offers no example of *Everglade State* dated earlier than 1893, but it must be considerably older. It gives no example at all of *Peninsula State*, nor of *Alligator State*,

---

[1] I am indebted for this to Dr. Joseph M. Carrière.
[2] *Dorado* is Spanish for golden, or gilt.
[3] *Eureka* is Greek for "I have found it." The NED says that it should be spelled *heureka*. It is the legendary exclamation of Archimedes (c. 287–212 B.C.) on his discovery of a way to determine, by specific gravity, the amount of base metal in a golden crown of King Hiero II of Syracuse (c. 308–216 B.C.). He made the discovery in a public bathhouse, and was so excited by it that he ran home naked. *Eureka State* is traced by Charles J. Lovell to 1857; the DAE overlooks it.

nor of *Flower State*, nor of *Orange State*, nor of *Land of Flowers*, all of them noted by Shankle as in occasional use. He also adds *Gulf State*, but this would hardly be a recognizable designation of Florida, for it is applied in the plural to all the States bordering on the Gulf of Mexico, to wit, Florida, Alabama, Mississippi, Louisiana and Texas. The boosters who swarm in Florida have made diligent efforts to devise a nickname connecting it with the Fountain of Eternal Youth which Juan Ponce de León sought there in 1513, but so far without success. Ponce de León returned for a second search in 1521, and was killed by the Indians. Florida entered the Union in 1845, soon after the second Seminole War of 1835-42, but it seems to have escaped, somehow, being called the *Seminole State*. It was listed as the *Shell State* by the Hon. Amelia M. Murray in 1856, but this designation apparently never had any vogue.

Idaho prefers to be called the *Gem of the Mountains*, or the *Gem State*, but *Little Ida* has also been recorded.[1] The DAE overlooks all of them, but the *World* Almanac gives *Gem State*. Illinois has had many nicknames in the past, *e.g.*, *Garden of the West*, *Corn State* and *Prairie State*, but *Sucker State* seems to be the only one surviving. The DAE traces *Sucker* for an Illinoisan to 1835, and the *World* Almanac still lists *Sucker State*.[2] The origin of *Sucker* is not established, though all the earlier authorities seem to have derived it from the name of a fresh-water fish of the *Catostomus* genus, related to the catfish and plentiful in the Western rivers. This fish swam up the rivers in the Spring and returned in the Autumn. When the lead mines at Galena, in the far northern part of the State, were opened in the 1820s, they were manned largely by itinerants from the southward, who came up the river with the fish and returned with them. Thornton gives this as the origin of the name on the authority of Charles Fenno Hoffman, who visited the region in 1833-34.[3] But Schele de Vere quotes the Providence *Journal* of some unnamed date before 1872 to the effect that the nickname originated in the fact that the pioneers, in dry seasons, would suck up water from crawfish holes through reeds. By the

---

[1] A Book of Nicknames, by John Goff; Louisville, 1892, p. 13, quoted by Shankle.
[2] There is a weekly called the *Sucker State* at Mahomet, Ill., population 729.
[3] A Winter in the Far West; London, 1835, I, p. 207n. This book was also published in New York during the same year as A Winter in the West.

1830s *sucker* had become a common term in the Western country for a gull or easy mark, and it has since got into almost universal American use. In the form of *gone sucker* the DAE traces it to 1832. The name of *sucker* for the fish is recorded in 1753 in the British Isles and in 1772 in this country. The DAE traces *Prairie State* for Illinois to 1857. It had been in use before that, in the plural, as a general designation for all the States in the plains area, from Indiana in the east to Kansas and Texas in the west. A writer in the *Atlantic Monthly* for March, 1867 quoted by the DAE, even included Missouri, Wisconsin and Minnesota.

Egypt has long been the common designation for the region of deep black soil in the southern part of Illinois, surrounding Cairo, where the Ohio river enters the Mississippi. Thornton says maliciously that the name was applied to it "with reference to the supposed intellectual darkness of the inhabitants" and quotes the Oregon *Argus* for September 8, 1860, as alleging that the majority of its people were then "exceedingly illiterate," but a contributor to the Editor's Drawer of *Harper's Magazine* in 1858 [1] offered the following far more flattering etymology:

> The Southern part of Illinois has long been called *Egypt,* and some have supposed it was so called as being a "land of darkness" — one of the benighted parts of the earth. A very intelligent correspondent of ours who lives there writes that the name had a very different origin; and he is desirous that it should be given in the Drawer, and then everybody will know it. He says: "This portion of the State was first settled, and afterward the Northern counties. The new settlements of the North had to depend on the South for their corn until they could raise it for themselves, and hence they were in the habit of saying, 'they must go down into *Egypt* to buy corn.' [2] This is the *real* source of the name; and as to the darkness, that is all in your eye." [3]

Indiana is listed in all the reference books as the *Hoosier State,* and seems to have no other nickname. The DAE's first example of *Hoosier* is dated 1832 and comes from a pioneer paper called the *Indiana Democrat.* The month and day are not given,

---

[1] June, p. 133.
[2] A reference to Genesis XLII, 2: "And he said, Behold, I have heard that there is corn in *Egypt;* get you down thither, and buy for us from thence; that we may live, and not die."
[3] The following is from The Field, the Dungeon and the Escape, by Albert D. Richardson; Hartford, Conn., 1865, p. 186: "'*Egypt* to the rescue!' is the motto upon the banner of a new Illinois regiment. Southwestern Illinois, known as *Egypt,* is turning out men for the Mississippi campaign with surprising liberality."

but the Indiana historian, Jacob Piatt Dunn, has shown that the precise date was January 3, 1832, when the term appeared in a set of verse supposed to be addressed to the readers of the paper by its carrier-boys — in the hope, apparently, of inducing them to give liberal New Year's presents. Here it was spelled *Hoosier*, as now, and on April 4, 1832 it so appeared again in a news item in the *Northwestern Pioneer and St. Joseph's Intelligencer* of South Bend.[1] When, in 1866, an aged Indiana poetaster named John Finley printed in Cincinnati a volume called "The *Hoosier's* Nest" he made the claim in a footnote that his title poem was written in 1830. Whether or not this was true cannot be ascertained today, but Dunn[2] has demonstrated that no record of the publication of the verses can be found before January 1, 1833, when they appeared in the Indianapolis *Journal* as a similar New Year's greeting from carrier-boys to readers. When Finley assembled and copyrighted his book in 1865, says Dunn, he "used his privilege of revising his work, and while he may have improved his poetry he seriously marred its historical value."[3] In both versions he described the *Hoosier nest* of his title as "a buckeye cabin," possibly meaning a log-cabin made of logs from the Ohio buckeye (*Aesculus glabra*), said by Eva W. Brodhead to rot at one end and sprout at the other.[4] In the Indianapolis *Journal* version *Hoosier* was used in the title, but thereafter *Hoosher* occurred seven times, and *Hoosheroon*, signifying an Indian child, once.[5] In his book Finley used *Hoosier* only. It appeared four times in his somewhat short-

---

[1] The Word *Hoosier*, *Indiana Magazine of History*, Vol. VII, 1911, p. 62.

[2] Dunn was born in 1855 and died in 1924. He was secretary of the Indiana Historical Society from 1886 until his death. He was on the staff of the State library from 1889 to 1893, on that of the Indianapolis *Sentinel* from 1893 to 1904, and city comptroller of Indianapolis from 1904 to 1906 and again from 1914 to 1916. He was the author of the volume on Indiana in the American Commonwealth Series, of a History of Indianapolis published in 1910, and of a book called Indiana and Indianans, published in 1910.

[3] The Word *Hoosier*, *Indiana Historical Society Publications*, Vol. IV, No. 2; Indianapolis, 1907, p. 4.

[4] Bound in Shallows; New York, 1897, p. 142. I take this reference from the DAE.

[5] No printed copy of the *Journal* of Jan. 1, 1833 is known to exist, but Dunn had access to a copy of the poem in the possession of the poet's daughter, Mrs. Sarah Wrigley, and on it the date was noted. It is probable that Finley made the copy after the poem was published, and changed the spelling of his title. The DAE traces *Hoosheroon* to 1834, by which time it had come to signify an adult as well as a child.

ened version of "The *Hoosier's* Nest" of 1833, and also in several other poems in the collection.

Its etymology has been much disputed and remains in doubt. Thornton, in his "American Glossary," called attention to the fact that *whoosher* was listed in a dictionary of 1659 and defined there as "a rocker, a stiller, a luller, a dandler of children asleep," but there was obviously no connection between this *whoosher* and *Hoosier*. The earlier American etymologists all sought to connect the term with some idea of ruffianism, and evidence was adduced that it was first applied to backwoodsmen in general, not only to Indianans. Said the Hon. Jere Smith, an aged resident of Winchester, Ind., in a speech reported by the Indianapolis *Journal* on January 20, 1860:

> My recollection is that the word began to be used in this country [1] in the Fall of 1824, but it might have been as late as 1826 or 1827, when the Louisville & Portland canal was being made. I first heard it at a corn-husking. It was used in the sense of *rip-roaring*,[2] *half horse and half alligator*,[3] and such like backwoods coinages. It was then, and for some years afterwards, spoken as if spelled *husher*, the *u* having the sound it has in *bush*, *push*, etc. In 1829, 1830 and 1831 its sound glided into *hoosier*, till finally Mr. Finley's "*Hoosier's* Nest" made the present orthography and pronunciation classical, and it has remained so since.[4]

In 1838, in the first edition of his "Dictionary of Americanisms," John Russell Bartlett gave the following account of the term by "a correspondent of the Providence *Journal*":

> Throughout all the early Western settlements were men who rejoiced in their physical strength, and on numerous occasions, at log-rollings and house-raisings, demonstrated this to their entire satisfaction. They were styled by their fellow citizens *hushers*, from their primary capacity to still their opponents. It was a common term for a bully throughout the West.[5] The boatmen

---

[1] *i.e.*, on the frontier.

[2] Traced by the DAE to 1834, but probably older.

[3] Defined by the DAE as "an appellation used by or about boasting frontiersmen and boatmen in the West." James K. Paulding, in his Westward Ho!; New York, 1832, Vol. I, p. 83, hinted that it embodied the idea that the boatmen were amphibious, and could proceed overland as well as afloat. The DAE's earliest example is dated June 12, 1812, but Thornton shows that the term had occurred in Washington Irving's Knickerbocker's History of New York, 1809. Thornton presents many examples from the 20s and 30s. The term was often reinforced with additions, *e.g., and a little of the snapping turtle, part earthquake and a little steamboat*, etc. It was an important constituent of the Tall Talk of the frontier, for which see AL4, pp. 136 and 137.

[4] I take this from Dunn's 1907 paper, p. 11.

[5] The term is not noted by either the DAE or Thornton.

of Indiana were formerly as rude and as primitive a set as could well belong to a civilized community, and they were often in the habit of displaying their pugilistic accomplishments upon the levee at New Orleans. Upon a certain occasion there one of these rustic professors of the noble art very adroitly and successfully practised the "fancy" upon several individuals at one time. Being himself not a native of this Western world, in the exuberance of his exultation he sprang up, exclaiming, in foreign accent, "I'm a *hoosier*, I'm a *hoosier*." Some of the New Orleans papers reported the case, and afterward transferred the corruption of the epithet *husher* (hoosier) to all boatmen from Indiana, and from thence to all her citizens. The Kentuckians, on the contrary, maintain that the nickname expresses the gruff exclamation of their neighbors, when one knocks at a door, etc., "Who's yere?"

To the second of these etymologies Schele de Vere added the following variorium version in 1872, quoting "America by River and by Rail, or, Notes by the Way in the New World," by William Ferguson:[1]

> The ... *Hoosiers* ... are proverbially inquisitive. They are said to have got their nickname because they could not pass a house without pulling the latchstring and crying out, "Who's here?."

Dunn rejects both etymologies. "Nobody," he says,[2] "has ever produced any evidence of the use of the word *husher* as here indicated, ... and there is no greater evidence of the use of the expression 'Who's yere?' when approaching a house. As a matter of fact, the common custom when coming to a house and desiring communication with the residents was to call 'Hallo the house!'" Dunn then rehearses an equally improbable etymology that was circulated on the authority of "the Rev. Aaron Wood, the pioneer preacher," as follows:

> When the young men of the Indiana side of the Ohio river went to Louisville, the Kentucky men boasted over them, calling them *New Purchase greenies*, claiming to be a superior race, composed of half horse, half alligator and tipped off with snapping turtle. These taunts produced fights in the market house and streets of Louisville. On one occasion a stout bully from Indiana was victor in a fist fight, and having heard Colonel Lehmanowsky[3] lecture on "The Wars of Europe," who always gave martial prowess to the German *hussars*, pronouncing *hussars hoosiers*, the Indianan, when the Kentuckian cried "Enough!," jumped up and said: "I am a *Hoosier*," and hence the Indianans were called by that name. This was its true origin. I was in the State when it occurred.

[1] London, 1856, p. 338.
[2] In his 1907 paper, p. 12.
[3] John Jacob Lehmanowsky, who had served as an officer under Napoleon, and came to Indiana after Waterloo. His descendants survive in Indiana to this day.

But this is folk-etymology at its worst, and Dunn disposes of it without difficulty. Only one of his points needs noting — that it is impossible to imagine a Polish officer mispronouncing the word *hussar*. Dunn ascribes another incredible derivation of the term to James Whitcomb Riley, the poet, as follows:

> The early settlers . . . were very vicious fighters, and not only gouged and scratched, but frequently bit off noses and ears. This was so ordinary an affair that a settler coming into a barroom on a morning after a fight and seeing an ear on the floor would merely push it aside with his foot and carelessly ask, "Who's year?"

Dunn shows that all these etymologies save Riley's were discussed, though with differences in detail, in an article in the Cincinnati *Republican,* republished in the *Indiana Democrat* so early as October 26, 1833. Mordecai M. Noah, then editor of the New York *Evening Star,* was therein credited with the story that the man who pronounced *hussar* as if it were *hoosier* (or *hooshier*) was not Lehmanowsky, but "a recruiting officer who was engaged during the last war in enlisting a company of hussars." Another etymology cited by Dunn is to the effect that *Hoosier* comes from the patronymic of one of the contractors for the Louisville & Portland canal, under construction from 1826 to 1831. This contractor recruited his laborers from the Indiana side of the Ohio river, and "the neighbors got to calling them *Hoosier's* men, from which the name *Hoosier* came to be applied to Indiana men generally."[1] Yet another seeks to derive *Hoosier* from *hoosa,* an Indian name for maize — but no such term has been unearthed by philologians. In 1851, when the Hon. Amelia M. Murray, the English tourist, visited Indianapolis, she picked up the story that the term "originated in a settler's exclaiming 'Huzza!' upon gaining victory over a marauding party from a neighboring State,"[2] but Dunn, in 1907, dismissed this as moonshine.

---

[1] A rather more probable eponym was the Rev. Harry *Hoosier,* a Negro Methodist evangelist who ravaged the frontier in the 1800 era. Born a slave in North Carolina, he died in Philadelphia in 1810. He was a famous alarmer of sinners and was much esteemed by his white contemporaries, Francis Asbury (1745-1816), Thomas Coke (1747-1814) and Richard Whatcoat (1736-1806). Says A. B. Hyde, in The Story of Methodism, 1894, p. 409: "If these eminent men were sick the congregations were glad if only Harry were there, and Asbury owned that they preferred Harry to him." I am indebted here to Mr. J. A. Rogers.

[2] Letters From the United States, Cuba, and Canada; London, 1856, p. 324.

His own inclination was to find the origin of the term in some old word brought from England, and he suggested three possibilities — *hoose,* indicating a cattle disease marked by "staring eyes, rough coat with hair turned backward, and hoarse wheezing"; *hoo,* an archaic English word signifying high, and surviving in a few geographical names; and *hoozer,* a Cumberland dialect term applied to "anything unusually large." He showed that *hoosier* was used in the latter sense by the Vincennes *Sun* on November 29, 1834, in describing a load of giant pumpkins, and by the *Northwestern Pioneer and St. Joseph's Intelligencer* on April 4, 1832, in recording the spearing of a huge sturgeon in the St. Joseph river. He also noted a Hindustani word taken into English, to wit, *huzur,* "a respectful form of address to persons of rank or superiority." But this last etymology collided with the plain fact that the early Indianans were not notable for "rank or superiority," and Dunn returned to his theory of an English origin, though without settling upon a definite one. *Hoosier,* he concluded, "carries Anglo-Saxon credentials. It is Anglo-Saxon in form and Anglo-Saxon in ring. If it came from any foreign language, it has been thoroughly anglicized."[1]

The discussion of the nickname still goes on, but without plausible etymological result. It was revived in 1944 when Queen Elizabeth of England said to an Indiana flyer: "You come from Indiana. That's the *Hoosier State.* What does *Hoosier* mean?" The flyer, it appeared, could not answer.[2] But on one point, at least, all authorities seem to be agreed: that *Hoosier,* at the start, did not signify an Indianan particularly, but any rough fellow of what was then the wild West. Dunn, in his 1907 paper, presented a great deal of evidence to this effect. The term, in fact, is still in more or less common use in Tennessee and the Carolinas and even in parts of Virginia to indicate a mountaineer or any other uncouth rustic. In 1857, as the DAE notes, E. L. Godkin was using it in the sense of a Southern *cracker,* and in 1900 J. F. Willard (Josiah Flynt) was

---

[1] This is from his 1907 paper, p. 25. Why he regarded *-ier* as a characteristically Anglo-Saxon ending he did not pause to explain. It is actually rare in English, and appears mainly in words showing French influence, *e.g., brigadier, cashier, financier, cavalier, grenadier, brazier, soldier* and *farrier.*

[2] *Hoosier* Inquiry Started by Queen, Bridgeport (Conn.) *Post,* July 30, 1944.

recording in "Tramping With Tramps" that in the argot of the road it was used for farmer.

In Indiana, however, the term apparently became restricted to a resident of the State at an early date. As far back as January 8, 1833, an orator named John W. Davis [1] proposed a toast to "The *Hooshier* State of Indiana" at a Jackson dinner at Indianapolis, and on August 3 of the same year J. B. Ray [2] and W. M. Tannehill issued a prospectus at Greencastle for a weekly to be called the *Hoosier*.[3] When, in 1833, Charles Fenno Hoffman was making the explorations reported in "A Winter in the Far West,"[4] he encountered "a long-haired *Hooshier* from Indiana" and later entered "the land of the *Hooshiers*," to find "that long-haired race more civilized than some of their Western neighbors are willing to represent them." The term *Hoosier*, he went on, "like that of *Yankee* or *Buckeye*, [was] first applied contemptuously, but has now become a sobriquet that bears nothing invidious, to the ear even of an Indianan."[5] Dunn says that the Finley poem of 1833 was "unquestionably the chief cause of the widespread adoption of [the term] in its application to Indiana." This poem "attracted much attention at the time,"[6] and exactly a week after it was printed the word was used by the aforesaid speaker at a public dinner in Indianapolis. It threw off derivatives at an early date. Thornton shows that *Hoosierland* and *Hoosierdom* were heard in the debates of Congress in 1848, and the DAE traces *Hoosier State* to January 4, 1834. *Hoosierism* goes back to 1843 and *to hoosierize* to 1852. James Whitcomb Riley (1853–1916) was known universally as the *Hoosier* poet.

Iowa is listed as the *Hawkeye State* in the *World* Almanac and by all other authorities that I know of, and is so called in the subtitle

---

1 Not, of course, to be confused with the Hon. John W. Davis of Wall Street, W. Va., Democratic candidate for the presidency in 1924.
2 Ray had been Governor of Indiana from 1825 to 1831.
3 By May 10, 1834 the Indianapolis *Journal* was reporting that the *Hoosier* (it spelled the word *Hooshier*, though Ray and Tannehill had used *Hoosier*) had "sunk into repose." Greencastle is now the seat of De Pauw University, founded in 1837. There is a weekly called the *Hoosier Democrat* at Flora, another called the *Hoosier State* at Newport, a *Hoosier Business Woman* at Monticello, and a *Hoosier Banker, Farmer, Legionnaire, Motorist* and *Sentinel* at Indianapolis.
4 London, 1835.
5 Vol. I, p. 223.
6 Dunn, 1907, p. 4.

of the volume on it brought out by the Federal Writers' Project.[1] The DAE traces the nickname to 1859, and *Hawkeye* as a designation for an Iowan to 1845, but both dates are probably too late. The origin of the name still engages etymologists, both professional and amateur. The Encyclopedia Americana derives it from that of "a great Indian chief, the terror of the early settlers," and the New International calls it "apparently an allusion to J[ames] G[ardiner] Edwards, familiarly known as *Old Hawkeye*, editor of the Burlington *Patriot*, now the *Hawkeye and Patriot*." Webster 1935 lists it as "of obscure origin," but indicates (without directing attention to) its probable source in "one of the sobriquets of Natty Bumppo," the hero of J. Fenimore Cooper's "Leatherstocking Tales." Natty, who figures under this name in "The Last of the Mohicans," published in 1826, was everything that the pioneer of those days fancied himself to be — brave, resourceful and honorable. In "The Prairie," which appeared in 1827, he died nobly. According to a "Commercial and Statistical Review of the City of Burlington," published by local boosters in 1882, p. 63, the name was added to the title of Edwards's paper at the suggestion of his wife, and began to be used on September 5, 1839. Mrs. Edwards, like her husband, was a romantic person,[2] and it is highly likely that she was a diligent reader of Cooper. Whether or not someone else had applied *Hawk-*

[1] Iowa: a Guide to the Hawkeye State; New York, 1938.
[2] Her maiden name was Eleanor T. Dunlap and she was born at Portsmouth, N. H., in the early years of the century. She suffered the pangs of conversion in her youth, and was preparing to go to Palestine to save the Jews when she met Edwards. He was born in Boston on Jan. 23, 1802, and for some years worked there as a printer. In 1826 he and Eleanor met and loved, and she quickly fanned his sense of sin. They were married on Sept. 14 of the same year, and in 1829 went to Jacksonville, Ill., then a sink of frontier carnality, as missionaries. They failed in this capacity, but when, in 1830, Edwards set up a pious paper called the *Western Observer* he seems to have spread a passion for printer's ink among the boys of the vicinity, for during the years since then they and their sons and grandsons have made many notable successes as editors and publishers. In December, 1831, giving up the salvation of the Jacksonvillains as hopeless, he changed the name of the *Western Observer* to the *Illinois Patriot*, and on March 24, 1838 he moved it to Fort Madison, Ill. It died soon, and on September 1 of that year he set out for Burlington, then a booming frontier trading-post. There he set up the Burlington *Patriot*, which gave way on June 6, 1839 to the *Iowa Patriot*, the progenitor of the *Hawkeye and Patriot* of today. As I have noted, *Hawkeye* was added to the title in 1839. The paper suffered various changes of name afterward, and in 1843 was suspended for a few weeks, but *Hawkeye* survived in its title. I am indebted here to two papers in the *Palimp-*

eye to the Iowans before she added it to the name of her husband's paper is not known at this writing,[1] but a search of the files of the early Iowa *Käseblätter* might furnish an answer. Edwards, though a printer by trade, was a very religious fellow, and indeed something of a fanatic. In all his papers he denounced the Catholics and the Mormons as agents of Antichrist. He died in 1851, but his widow seems to have survived for some time. It was not he who made the *Hawkeye* famous, but Robert J. Burdette, who joined its staff in 1873.[2] Shankle says that Iowa was once called *Land of the Rolling Prairies*, but this must have been no more than an invention of boosters that failed to please the customers, for it seems to have disappeared. In the town of Centerville there is an evening daily called the *Iowegian and Citizen*, but I have not found *Iowegian* elsewhere: perhaps it is only a compliment to local Norwegians. In Mt. Vernon (population, 1441) there is a weekly *Hawkeye-Record*.

Shankle lists no less than ten nicknames for Kansas — the *Battleground of Freedom*, the *Central State*, the *Cyclone State*, the *Garden State*, the *Garden of the West*, the *Grasshopper State*, the *Jayhawker State*, the *Navel of the Nation*, the *Squatter State*, and the *Sunflower State*. *Battleground of Freedom* seems to have been passed out with the Civil War; it referred, of course, to the sanguinary combats between Abolitionists and slavery men which reddened the soil of the State in the heyday of John Brown of Ossawatomie. *Garden State* is challenged by New Jersey and *Garden of the West* by Illinois, and neither has ever had much vogue, though the former was listed in preferred position by Schele de Vere in 1872. *Squatter State*, also listed by Schele de Vere, is long

---

sest (Iowa City) for March, 1938, one by Philip D. Jordan and the other by John Ely Briggs.

[1] A Guide to Burlington, Iowa; Burlington, n.d., produced by the Federal Writers' Project, says that "Edwards was the man who originated the appellation of *Hawkeyes* for the people of the Iowa country," but no evidence for this is offered.

[2] Burdette (1844-1914) was born in Greensboro, Pa., and educated in Illinois. He served in the Civil War as a private. He began his newspaper career in Peoria, Ill. His writings in the *Hawkeye* attracted nation-wide attention. In 1876 he took to the lecture platform, and in 1887 he was converted to Christianity and became a Baptist preacher. From 1887 onward he was pastor of the Temple Baptist Church in Los Angeles, and helped to lay the foundations of that great city as the theological capital of the United States. He belonged to the flight of American newspaper humorists headed by Eugene Field and Bill Nye.

obsolete, for no one remembers any more, nearly three generations after the Civil War, the once explosive issue of *squatter sovereignty*.[1] *Cyclone State* and *Grasshopper State*, of course, refer to two of the many calamitous acts of God from which Bleeding Kansas has suffered, and to them *Dust Bowl State* might be added. The DAE traces *Grasshopper State* to 1890, but does not list *Cyclone State*.[2] *Sunflower State* seems to be favored in Kansas itself, for the sunflower is the State flower, and was used on his guidons and gonfalons by the Hon. Alf M. Landon, its Republican candidate for the presidency in 1936.[3] It has, however, a formidable rival in *Jayhawk* or *Jayhawker State*. The latter is traced by the DAE no further than 1885, but *Jayhawker* for a Kansan goes back to 1875,[4] and in the wider sense of a fighting Abolitionist to 1858. In the still wider sense of a hardy pioneer it is said to have been used in California so early as 1849.[5] " The name," says Kirke Mechem, secretary of the Kansas

---

[1] *Squatter* is marked an Americanism by the DAE and traced to 1788, when it was used by James Madison. It was listed by John Pickering in his pioneer Vocabulary of 1816 and defined as " a cant name in New England for those people who enter upon new lands and cultivate them without permission of the owners." *Squatter sovereignty* meant the right of settlers in the Western lands to make their own laws. It is traced to 1854, and *squatter law* to 1857.

[2] *Cyclone* is apparently not an Americanism. The DAE traces it in this country to 1856, but it was proposed in 1848 by an English nautical writer named Piddington. *Cyclone-cellar*, however, is an American invention, traced by the DAE to 1887.

[3] When *Sunflower State* came in is uncertain. A writer in *Harper's Magazine* for June, 1888, quoted by the DAE, reported that it was already used " affectionately " at that time.

[4] Mr. Charles B. Driscoll, a native, tells me that it is never *Jayhawk*, but always *Jayhawker*.

[5] *Jayhawkers*, by Rockwell D. Hunt, *Nation*, April 30, 1903, p. 374. Hunt gave as his authority Death Valley in '49, by William Lewis Manly, pp. 321-22. In describing the trip of a party of young emigrants from Illinois through Death Valley during the Winter of 1849-50 Manly said: " These Illinois boys were young and full of mirth and fun, which was continually overflowing. . . . One of the boys was Ed Doty, who was a sort of model traveller in this line. . . . One day when Doty was engaged in the duty of cooking flap-jacks, another frolicsome fellow came up and took off the cook's hat and commenced going through the motions of a barber, giving his customer a vigorous shampoo, saying: '*I am going to make a Jayhawker out of you, old boy.*' Now it happened at the election for captain in this division that Ed Doty was chosen captain, and no sooner was the choice declared than the boys took the newly elected captain on their shoulders and carried him around the camp, introducing him as *the King Bird of the Jayhawkers*. So their division was afterwards known as the *Jayhawkers*, but whether the word originated with them or was some old frontier word used in sport on the occasion, is more than I will undertake to

State Historical Society, "became common during the territorial troubles and was at first applied to both sides. Jennison's regiment of Free-State men, as well as Quantrill's raiders, were at one time called *Jayhawkers*.[1] The name finally stuck to the anti-slavery side and eventually to all the people of Kansas."[2]

The common belief in Kansas is that *Jayhawk* was borrowed from the name of a predatory bird which lives by plundering the nests and food supplies of other birds, but there is no mention of it in any of the standard works on American ornithology. In 1932 Dr. Raymond C. Moore, professor of geology in the University of Kansas, suggested sportively that it might be a descendant of *Hesperornis regalis*, an extinct avian monster, six feet in height, whose remains have been found in the cretaceous rocks of Western Kansas. Dr. Moore proposed the name of *Jayhawkornis Kansasensis* for the *jayhawk* itself, but did not pause to describe it particularly or to tell where living specimens could be found.[3] The rest of the State *scientificos* held aloof, and no more was heard of the matter until early in 1944, when the supergogues of the State Board of Education discovered that one of the textbooks used in the State schools listed the *jayhawk* as a real bird and gave Kansas as its habitat. They set up a pother over this, and ordered all mention of the creature to be expunged, but this order was resisted energetically by various patriotic Kansas editors. One of them was Miss Marion Ellet, of the Concordia *Blade-Empire*, who let go as follows on January 20, 1944:

> I'm pretty sore at the pedagogues who want to take all the color and romance out of Kansas history. They've told the boys and girls of Kansas that there isn't any *Jayhawk* and they've set out to bar the pot-bellied little bird from the textbooks. It's facts they want. Or so they say. Well, I'll tell you a few facts.
> Sure, Virginia, there's a *Jayhawk*. And don't let your skeptical school

---

say." Manly added that when they returned to Illinois they formed an organization called the *Jayhawkers' Union*.

[1] Cf. Nebraska Pioneer English, by Melvin Van den Bark, *American Speech*, Dec., 1933, p. 50.

[2] The Mythical *Jayhawk*; Topeka, 1944, p. 2. Albert Matthews in the *Nation*, April 9, 1903, p. 291: "The noun *Jayhawk* . . . and the verb [to] *Jayhawk* . . . were used in Kansas as early as November or December, 1858, at which time they were applied to James Montgomery and his men, who, in retaliation for the atrocities committed on Free-State settlers by the Border Ruffians, raided the pro-slavery settlers and their abettors from Missouri."

[3] Discovered: Ancestor of *Jayhawkornis Kansasensis*. *Graduate Magazine of the University of Kansas*, Lawrence, April, 1932, p. 10.

teachers tell you there isn't. There were *Jayhawks* in the early history of Kansas, and there are *Jayhawks* yet. The first *Jayhawks* came from down around Trading Post in Linn county. They were there before the Trading Post massacre. They were Free Staters and they were raising their kids to be good Free Staters. They were raising them up proper in the little red district school house.

But the school district happened to be half in Missouri and half in Kansas. The school house was built on the Kansas side very near to the State line. Of course, some Missouri kids attended the school. Their parents were known as something worse than *Jayhawks*. They were called *Pukers*. Yes, Virginia, there were *Pukers* in Missouri in those days. There are *Pukers* in Missouri yet. And don't let any fastidious school teacher tell you it's an improper word.

These early day *Pukers* decided that the school house which their kids attended should be on sacred soil — in Missouri. So they up and stole the school house, moved it over the border. The Kansans set up a terrible hullabaloo, as Kansans will. And they moved the school house back. The *Pukers* moved it again. And the Kansans, raising their habitual hullabaloo, moved it back.

Because they raised such an unconscionable racket and because they lifted the little red school house so many times, the *Pukers* called the Kansans after the two Kansas birds which raise the biggest racket and do the most plundering. The scrapping Kansans were christened *Jayhawks*. And they have borne the title proudly ever since.

Sure, Virginia, there's a *Jayhawk*. Wherever there is habitual scrapping "for the principle of the thing," wherever there is argumentation and high temper and political plundering there is a *Jayhawk*. And don't let any blue-nosed pedagogue tell you different.[1]

This adroit parody of the New York *Sun*'s famous editorial on Santa Claus [2] had a powerful effect, and Mechem reports that when the smoke cleared away and the roars of indignation ceased to reverberate " it was hard to tell from appearances whether the educators were the hunters or the hunted." Having learned from the combat that there was no description of the *jayhawk* in the official literature of Kansas, he at once unearthed one from the pages of " a famous Spanish ornithologist " of Coronado's day, " now unfortunately apocryphal," and it was printed in his brochure, lately mentioned. It ran as follows:

[The *Jayhawk*] has a narrow short face, except for the beak, which is long and grotesque, being yellow in color and curved to a sharp point. The brow of those of the commonest size is two palms across from eye to eye, the eyes sticking out at the sides so that when they are flying they can see in all directions at once. They are blue and red, the feathers shining like the steel of a Toledo sword, iridescent, wherefore it is not possible to say where

[1] I am indebted to Miss Ellet for a copy of this editorial.
[2] Is There a Santa Claus?, Sept. 21, 1897. It is reprinted in Casual Essays of the *Sun;* New York, 1905, pp. 1-3.

one color leaves off and another begins. They have long talons, shaped like an eagle's. These claws are so powerful that many of our men, among which even the priest was one, aver that these birds have been seen to fly off with one of those hump-backed cattle in each claw.[1]

Mechem explained in a gloss that the learned Spaniard here referred to the buffaloes which then roamed the Kansas steppes. He adorned his brochure with beautiful drawings of the *jayhawk*, one of them by Frank Miller of the Kansas City *Star*. His labors lifted the bird at one stroke to the level of the guyascutus, the lunkus, the cutercuss, the lufferlang, the flitterbick, the billdad, the club-tailed glytodont, the wiffle-poofle and other such fauna of the Great Plains,[2] and greatly increased the pride taken in it by loyal Kansans.[3]

Kentucky has been the *Blue Grass State* since the Civil War era, and is the heir to a much larger *Blue Grass region* that once included Tennessee and even extended into Ohio, Indiana, Virginia and Pennsylvania. Bartlett, in the second edition of his "Dictionary of Americanisms," 1859, described this area as "the rich limestone land of Kentucky and Tennessee," and Schele de Vere, in 1872,[4] added Pennsylvania. The DAE's first example of *Blue Grass State* as applied specifically to Kentucky comes from John S. Farmer's "Americanisms Old and New," 1889, but it is probably considerably older, though Schele de Vere omitted it from his list of accepted designations for the State. In place of it he gave *Bear State*, which has been disputed by Arkansas, and *Corncracker State*, the *cracker* part of which has been collared by Georgia. In the years immediately following the Revolution Kentucky was often called the *Dark and Bloody Ground*, which was supposed to be a translation of the Indian phrase from which its name was derived. That name, at the start, was variously spelled *Kentuck, Kentucke, Kaintuck* and even *Caintuck*, and after the War of 1812 *Old* was often prefixed to it. *Dark and Bloody Ground* alluded, not to battles between Indians and the first white settlers, but to contests between Northern and Southern tribes of Indians, but by 1839, as the DAE shows, it had come to be accepted as a reference to "the

---

[1] The Mystical *Jayhawk*, p. 6.
[2] See Supplement I, pp. 245–252.
[3] For many years the battle-cry of the University of Kansas students at football games was *Rock Chalk! Jayhawk! K.U.!* I am indebted here to Mr. L. V. Graham of San Francisco, a former Kansan.
[4] Americanisms, p. 407.

slaughter of white pioneers." Kentucky has also been called the *Hemp State*, the *Rock-ribbed State* and the *Tobacco State*, but without much frequency. The first of these was applied to it, not because of the activity of its busy and accomplished hangmen, but because it produced large crops of hemp. It is rather surprising that the State has acquired no appellation calling up the speed of its race-horses, the traditional beauty of its women, or its Bourbon whiskey. The DAE's first example of *Bourbon* whiskey is dated 1850, but the example given shows that the name was already preceded by *good old*.

Pelican State for Louisiana goes back to 1859, and seems destined to outlive all rivals, for the *World* Almanac now lists it without an alternate. The pelican has appeared on the seal of the State since before the Civil War, and a committee of the State Convention of 1861, appointed to prepare a new State flag and seal, resolved to keep it there on the ground that it had "long been the cherished emblem of Louisiana." The pelican was chosen originally because it is plentiful along the Gulf coast of the State. Schele de Vere, in 1872, listed *Creole State* as an alternative nickname for Louisiana, and explained that it had arisen "on account of the large number of its inhabitants who are descendants of the original French and Spanish settlers." This designation was borne proudly so long as it was generally understood that a *Creole* was a Caucasian,[1] but when ignorant Northerners began assuming that the term connoted African blood it passed out of favor. The DAE traces it to 1792, and shows that it began to be applied especially to the people of New Orleans by 1807. Shankle says that Louisiana was once called the *Sugar State*, and Charles J. Lovell traces the nickname to 1855, but the DAE does not list it. It appeared as the *French State* in the Hon. Amelia M. Murray's "Letters From the United States, Cuba, and Canada" in 1856, but that designation has also vanished.

Maine is the *Pine Tree State*, and a pine tree appears upon its seal. The DAE's first example of the use of the term is from *Harper's Magazine* for March, 1860, but it appears in Bartlett's second edition of 1859, and must be older. On the *Brother Jonathan* list of 1843 Maine is called the *Lumber State*, which is not listed at

[1] See Supplement I, pp. 597 and 631n. See also *Creole* and *Cajan*, by William A. Read, *American Speech*, June, 1926, p. 483, and *Creole* and *West Indies*, by E. C. Hills, *American Speech*, March, 1927, pp. 293-94.

all by the DAE. Shankle also lists *Border State, Polar Star State, Old Dirigo* and *Switzerland of America*. The first seems to have gone out when the States bordering on slave territory began to be called *Border States* (traced by the DAE to 1849), and the last is disputed, as we have seen, by Colorado, New Hampshire, New Jersey and West Virginia. *Dirigo* is taken from the motto on the State seal, a Latin word signifying "I direct, or guide." This motto long antedated the saying, "As Maine goes, so goes the country," which was first heard in the national campaign of 1888 and is now obsolete. Otherwise, Maine has led the country on but one occasion — when, in 1858, it passed a Prohibition law which paved the way for the Eighteenth Amendment of 1919. There is a single star on the State seal, but that it is Polaris, the pole star, is not in evidence.

Michigan is the *Wolverine State* in the *World* Almanac, but it has also been called the *Lady of the Lakes*, the *Lake State* and, in recent years, the *Auto State*. *Wolverine State* is traced by the DAE to 1846, when it appeared in the *Knickerbocker Magazine*. Schele de Vere said in 1872 that it was suggested by "the number of *wolverines* (literally, little wolves) which used to abound in the peninsula, and gave the inhabitants their name of *Wolverines*, by which they are still generally known." The DAE's first example of *Wolverine* is dated 1835. It appears also in the *Brother Jonathan* list of 1843. A writer in the Detroit *Free Press*,[1] quoted by Shankle, calls it the impromptu invention of a young girl of 1800, based on the jocosity of a tavern-keeper named Conrad Tan Eyck. Tan Eyck was in the habit of telling his guests that any meat they had eaten in his house was a wolf steak, and when he launched his waggery on the girl she replied: "Then I suppose I am a *wolverine*." But *wolverine* was not actually new in 1800, for it had been in use since the early Eighteenth Century to describe a small mammal of the marten family, plentiful in all the Northern woods. John Gyles, in his "Memoirs of Odd Adventures, Strange Deliverances, &c," published in 1736, described it as "a very fierce and mischievous creature, about the bigness of a middling dog," and Dr. Robert W. Hegner, in his "College Zoölogy,"[2] says that it is so greedy and so enterprising that it steals bait from traps, and even makes off with the traps themselves.[3] Why the name of this voracious creature

[1] Nov. 30, 1918.
[2] New York, 1912, p. 656.
[3] Its European counterpart is the glutton (*Gulo luscus* or *articus*).

should have been given to the people of Michigan is still a matter of speculation. In *American Notes & Queries* for March, 1944,[1] a Michigander named M. M. Quaife pointed out that the early fur-trade inventories offer no evidence that " the *wolverine* ever lived or was trapped in our Michigan southern peninsula," and that during the 30s of the last century, when the people of the State became *Wolverines*, the State still had no northern peninsula. Nevertheless, the nickname was already current at that time, for in " A Winter in the West," published in 1835, Charles Fenno Hoffman told of meeting a typical *Wolverine* at " Prairie Ronde, Kalamazoo Co., M.T." This specimen he described as " a sturdy yeoman-like fellow whose white capot, Indian mocassins and red sash proclaimed, while he boasted a three years' residence, the genuine *Wolverine*, or naturalized Michiganian." [2] *Lake State* for Michigan early collided with *Lake States*, which began to be applied generally to all the States bordering upon the Great Lakes so early as 1845.

Minnesota chooses to be called the *North Star State*, and has the motto, *L'Étoile du Nord*, on its seal. Schele de Vere, in 1872, listed it as the *New England of the West*, and before that it had been the *Gopher State* and the *Beaver State*. But *Gopher State* was also claimed, *c.* 1845, by Arkansas, and *Beaver State* was claimed, at various times, by other States, *e.g.*, Oregon. Shankle quotes Charles E. Flandrau, author of " The History of Minnesota and Tales of the Frontier," [3] to the effect that the advocates of *Gopher State* and those of *Beaver State* fought it out bitterly in the 50s, and that the latter won. But *Gopher State* survived and the people of Minnesota are still called *Gophers*. Shankle also lists *Bread Basket of the Nation*, the *Bread and Butter State*, the *Cream Pitcher of the Nation*, the *Playground of the Nation* and the *Wheat State*, but all of these reflect the passion of boosters rather than *vox populi*.

Schele de Vere, in 1872, reported that Mississippi was the *Mudcat State*, after " a large catfish abounding in the swamps and the mud of the rivers," and this designation was listed by the Encyclopedia Americana so late as 1932, but it seems to be obsolescent. The nickname of choice is now *Magnolia State*. It has rivals, ac-

---

Both belong to the *Mustelidae*, and are related to the otters, minks and badgers.
[1] pp. 181–82.

[2] I am indebted for this to Dr. Joseph M. Carrière, of the University of Virginia.
[3] St. Paul, 1900, pp. 242–44.

cording to Shankle, in *Bayou State, Eagle State, Border-eagle State, Ground-hog State* and *Mud-waddler State*. *Bayou State* is listed by the New International Encyclopedia, and was included in the *World* Almanac list in 1922, along with *Eagle State*, but both seem to be passing out. The DAE traces *Bayou State* to 1867, but overlooks *Eagle State*. The latter is said to have been suggested, like *Border-eagle State* (traced by Lovell to 1846), by the fact that there is an eagle on the State seal. But there are also eagles on the seals of Alabama, Florida, Illinois, Iowa, Maryland, Michigan, New York, Oregon and Pennsylvania.

Missouri, which in former days was the *Iron Mountain State*, the *Bullion State*, the *Lead State*, the *Ozark State*, the *Puke State* and the *Pennsylvania of the West*,[1] but now it is known universally as the *Show Me State*. The origin of this designation is not yet established, but it seems to have been given nation-wide currency by a speech made by Willard D. Vandiver, then a congressman from Missouri, in Philadelphia in 1899 or thereabout.[2] The occasion was a dinner of the Five O'Clock Club. Vandiver, who, as a member of the Naval Affairs Committee of the House of Representatives, was in Philadelphia on public business, had not expected to be invited, and had thus brought no dress clothes. Neither had another impromptu guest, Congressman John A. T. Hull, of Iowa. They decided to go in their ordinary clothes, but at the last minute Hull somewhere found a dress-suit, and thereby greatly embarrassed Vandiver, who was the only diner without one. When the time came for speeches Hull delivered an eloquent eulogy of Philadelphia, and the toastmaster then called upon Vandiver. Let him now tell his own story:

> I started with no serious thought, . . . but determined to get even with Hull in a good-natured way. I made a rough-and-tumble speech, saying the meanest things I could think of about the old Quaker town . . . in the worst style I could command; and then, turning to Hull, followed up with a roast something like this:
> "His talk about your hospitality is all bunk; he wants another feed. He tells you that the tailors, finding he was here without a dress suit, made one

[1] In her Letters From the United States, Cuba, and Canada; New York, 1856, p. 324, the Hon. Amelia M. Murray called it the *Wolverine State*, but this was an obvious slip. I am indebted here to Dr. Joseph M. Carrière.

[2] Vandiver (1854–1932) was a pedagogue turned politician. He served in Congress from 1897 to 1905. His later years were mainly devoted to the insurance business, though he was assistant United States treasurer at St. Louis from 1913 to 1920.

for him in fifteen minutes. I have a different explanation: you heard him say he came here without one, and you see him now with one that doesn't fit him. The explanation is that he stole mine, and that's why you see him with one on and me without any. This story from Iowa doesn't go with me. I'm from Missouri, and you'll have to show me.

It will be noted that Vandiver did not claim the invention of the phrase; all he apparently intended to suggest was that his apt use of it before an Eastern audience served to spread it. It was further spread by its frequent use during the presidential campaign of 1912, when Champ Clark of Missouri was one of the candidates for the Democratic nomination. But its origin plainly goes beyond Clark and Vandiver; indeed, there are Missouri antiquarians who seek to run it back to pioneer days. A number of the etymologies that have been suggested were recorded in 1941 in an article by Paul I. Wellman, published in the Kansas City *Times*.[1] The first was given as follows:

> Claim was once made by General Emmett Newton, of Missouri, to having originated the phrase at Denver in 1892, when he was attending a convention of Knights Templars with his father. Newton, then a boy, was collecting badges, and a man smiled at him and said: "I have a better collection than you, I'll bet." Newton instantly replied: "I'm from Missouri. You'll have to show me."

Another:

> Dr. Walter B. Stevens, author of "A Centennial History of Missouri,"[2] cites an incident in the Civil War when an officer of a Northern army fell upon a body of Confederate troops commanded by a Missourian. The Northerner demanded a surrender, saying he had so many thousand men in his command. The Confederate commander, game to the core, said he didn't believe the Northerner's boast of numerical superiority, and appended the now famous expression, "I'm from Missouri; you'll have to show me," to his note refusing to surrender.

Yet another:

> W. M. Ledbetter, a former reporter of the Kansas City *Times*, said he heard the phrase first in Denver, during the mining excitement. At that time he was in a hotel where there was a green bell-hop. The clerk called to one

---

[1] Reprinted as Why Is Missouri the Show-Me State?, St. Louis *Post-Dispatch*, July 11, 1941.

[2] Published in two volumes in 1921. Stevens (1848–1939) was a native of Connecticut, but went to work for St. Louis newspapers as a young man. He was secretary of the St. Louis Exposition of 1904, and in that office picked up a glittering battery of foreign decorations. His first book, Through Texas, was published in 1892. After that he wrote more than twenty others, including a history of St. Louis, lives of various local worthies, and two volumes on Robert Burns.

of the more experienced boys, and said: "He's from Missouri; you'll have to show him."

Mr. Ledbetter said he frequently heard the phrase used in the mining towns, particularly Leadville. There were many Joplin miners there, and they, experienced in lead mining, did not know the methods used in silver mining. The pit bosses were constantly saying: "That man is from Missouri; you'll have to show him."

The last etymology was confirmed by Joseph P. Gazzam, an old mining man, in a letter to the St. Louis *Post-Dispatch* on July 14, 1941. He said:

> I was superintendent of the Small Hopes Consolidated Mining Co., at Leadville, Colo., in 1896. "Big Bill" Haywood, Moyer and Pettibone of Butte came to Leadville with a number of gunmen and shut down the mines in the early Summer.
>
> We had a sufficient number of native-born Americans, whom the Butte gunmen let severely alone, to keep the mines dry and in condition. We tried to arbitrate, but without success. In September, the owners decided they must either "pull the pumps" and let the mines drown or import labor from the outside.
>
> S. W. Mudd, general manager of the Small Hopes, told me their plans. I suggested that, if they decided to import labor, they bring in miners from the Joplin, Mo., district, as they were native-born Americans and would not be intimidated. My suggestion was accepted and plans were made to bring in the miners. Operations were started on the Coronado, a downtown mine, and the Emmet and R.A.M. shafts of the Small Hopes.
>
> "Big Bill," however, decided to block this plan by destroying the mines before the Missourians came in.
>
> About 2 A.M., September 21, the Coronado was attacked and the mine set on fire. The defenders put up a stiff fight, but their position was untenable. They then came out to the Emmet, but we had a tenable position and the attackers were defeated.
>
> The Missourians arrived in a few days and as the Coronado had been destroyed, they were all sent out to the Emmet and the R.A.M.
>
> I distributed them among the old miners, who were told that the Missourians did not understand our system of mining and would have to be shown our methods of operation. So it became a common saying in Leadville: "He is a Missourian and will have to be shown."[1]

Wellman says, on the authority of Vandiver, that Herbert S. Hadley, while Governor of Missouri (1909-13) "tried to have the expression supplanted, believing it uncomplimentary" and "even offered $500 for the best substitute," but if this is true he seems to have stood alone, for Missourians in general have always been proud

---

[1] I am indebted to Mr. Gazzam for this letter, and also for the Wellman article above quoted. He tells me that he found the phrase current among the miners of South Africa in 1903.

of it. Said Norman J. Colman, a farm-paper editor who became the first Secretary of Agriculture in 1889:[1]

> These fewer than half-score of simple Anglo-Saxon words contain a correct estimate of Missouri character. It is true that we are not a people who will accept as truth statements of moment which the maker should be able to demonstrate as fact.

Show me, adds Wellman complacently, " is the watchword of a canny people." Perhaps one reason why Missourians are fond of *Show-Me State* is that it has mercifully obliterated *Puke State*, which seems to have prevailed for many years. The origin of *Puke* to designate a Missourian is not known. It appears in the *Brother Jonathan* list of 1843, and is traced by the DAE to 1835. A humane theory, apparently favored in the State, is that it is simply a misprint for *Pike*, the name of a Missouri county bordering on the Mississippi, the county-seat of which is Bowling Green, the home of Champ Clark. In nearby Marion county is Hannibal, where Mark Twain spent his boyhood and which he later immortalized in " Huckleberry Finn." There is another Pike county across the river in Illinois, and in the early days the two were grouped together as the habitat of a singularly backward type of yokel. In 1849 a good many such yokels flocked to California, and there they were known as *Pike countyans*, a term which gradually came to embrace any newcomer of rustic aspect, whatever his origin.[2] But Missourians were called *Pukes* some time before this, and it is not easy to believe that the term began as a corruption of *Pike*.[3] Bullion

---

[1] Before that the office was only a commissionership. Colman was the last commissioner and first secretary. He served under Grover Cleveland. He was born in 1827 and died in 1911.

[2] In a prefatory note to Huckleberry Finn; New York, 1884, Mark Twain said: " In this book a number of dialects are used, to wit: the Missouri Negro dialect; the ordinary *Pike-County* dialect; and four modified varieties of this last. The shadings have not been done in a haphazard fashion, or by guesswork, but painstakingly and with the trustworthy guidance and support of personal familiarity with these several forms of speech."

[3] Letters from two Missourians, protesting against *Puke*, were in *Life*, Nov. 2, 1942, pp. 8 and 10. The editors replied that " like it or not, Missourians have been called *Pukes* for years," though " nobody knows just why." They added that certain unnamed " scholars " traced " the inelegant term to the Galena, Ill., lead-mine boom of 1827," when " so many Missourians rushed to the mines that the blunt miners said Missouri ' had taken a *puke*,' meaning it had vomited up all its people." The first occurrence of *to puke* in English is in Jaques' famous " All the world's a stage " speech in As You Like It, 1600: " At first the infant, mewling and

State is traced by the DAE to 1848, and is thought to have been suggested by *Old Bullion*, the sobriquet of Thomas Hart Benton (1782–1858), Senator from Missouri from 1821 to 1855 and a conspicuous advocate of a metallic currency.

Montana, in its earlier days, was the *Bonanza State* and the *Stubtoe State*, the first referring to its mineral riches and the second to its precipitous slopes, but it is now, because of its mining and smelting industry, the *Treasure State*.[1] Nebraska was listed by the *World* Almanac, in 1922, as the *Antelope State* and the *Black Water State*, but is, by formal act of its Legislature, the *Tree Planters State*. This designation was adopted by a resolution approved by the Governor on April 4, 1895. The resolution explained that the nicknames before prevailing were "not in harmony" with the State's "history, industry, or ambition."[2] The New International Encyclopedia made it the *Blackwater State* in 1916, "from the dark color of its rivers," with *Tree Planter State* (in the singular) as an alternative. Shankle adds *Bug-eating State* and *Corn Huskers' State*. The DAE lists none of these save *Tree Planters State*, but notes that *Bugeater*, as a nickname for a Nebraskan, goes back to 1872, and quotes *American Notes & Queries*, 1888, to the effect that it was used derisively "by travelers on account of the poverty-stricken appearance of many parts of the State." Nebraska, like Kansas, has suffered frequently from the more murderous and fantastic acts of God, and has produced a long line of statesmen pledged to prevent them by legislation, headed by William Jennings Bryan. *Bug-eating State*, according to Shankle, does not imply any hint that the human inhabitants ever ate bugs, but simply that they were the favored diet of a local bat, *Caprimulgus europeus*. *Cornhuskers* was at first applied to the University of Nebraska football eleven, and was only later extended to the State and its general population.

---

puking in the nurse's arms." It is possible that Shakespeare invented it, but it is much more likely that it was borrowed from some branch of German, and is related to the modern German verb, *spucken*, to spit.

1 *Congressional Record*, 1945, p. A1264: "The Anaconda Copper Corporation, which owns and operates the great copper mines of Butte, Mont., has for years endeavored to keep a tight rein on Montana politics. Owning or controlling, also, most of the State's vast industries — lumber, coal, silver, zinc, public utilities, hydroelectric plants, etc. — it has also added to its assets nearly all the daily newspapers in the *Treasure State*."

2 The full text is given by Shankle.

Nevada, according to the *World* Almanac for 1947, prefers to be called the *Battle-born State*, to recall the fact that it was admitted to the Union on October 31, 1864, while the Civil War was raging, but it is usually called the *Sage-brush State* or the *Silver State*,[1] with many votes, since the rise of Reno, for the *Divorce State*. *Sage-brush State* has been challenged by Wyoming and *Silver State* by Colorado. *Sage State* and *Sage-hen State* have also been heard, the first, like *Sage-brush State*, in compliment to *Artemisia tridentata*, which is the State flower, and the second in compliment to *Centrocercus urophasianus*, in the early days the chief victual of the pioneers. *Centrocercus* still feeds on *Artemisia* and acquires thereby a flavor seldom to the taste of a tenderfoot.

New Mexico glories in the plausible appellation of the *Sunshine State*, but has also been called the *Spanish State*, the *Cactus State*, the *Land of the Cactus*, the *Land of the Montezumas*, the *Land of the Delight Makers*, the *Land of Heart's Desire*, the *Land of Opportunity*, and the *Land of Enchantment*, the last five being the inventions of boosters. Which brings us to North Dakota, the *Sioux State*, with *Flickertail State*, *Great Central State* and *Land of the Dakotas* lurking in the background. The Sioux Indians roved the wilds that are now North Dakota for many years, and were hostile when the first white settlers appeared. In 1851 they were induced to cede some of their land to the invaders, but it was a long while before they became reconciled to the boons of civilization. *Flickertail State* comes from the popular name of *Citellus richardsonii*, a ground squirrel which, according to a local authority cited by Shankle, is found in North Dakota only.

Ohio, the first of the Middle Western States to be admitted to the Union (1803), is the *Buckeye State*, and has been recorded as such since 1835. It appears under that appellation on the *Brother Jonathan* list of 1843, and on all other lists that I am aware of. During the first years of the Nineteenth Century it was often called the *Yankee State*, apparently in allusion to the fact that many of its settlers came from New England, but that designation was abandoned long ago. There was a time when some of its boosters, having Grant, Hayes, Garfield, Benjamin Harrison, McKinley, Taft and

---

[1] This is used in the subtitle of the State Guide brought out by the Federal Writers Project. Lovell traces the name to 1851. In The Background to Mark Twain's Vocabulary, *American Speech*, April, 1947, p. 96, he traces *Silverland* to 1863.

Harding in mind, claimed for it the nickname of *Mother of Presidents*, once borne by Virginia, but that project blew up after the débâcle of the Hon. James M. Cox in 1920. *Buckeye* is derived from the name of a native horse-chestnut (*Aesculus glabra*), so called, according to Schele de Vere, because of "the resemblance its fruit bears to a deer's eye." The term was first used for the tree in 1784 or thereabout, but when and why it came to be applied to the people of Ohio is not known. According to William M. Farrar, a local historian quoted by Shankle,[1] it was because of the following incident:

> The first court conducted by the settlers of Ohio was located at Marietta in a large wooden fortress known as the Campus Martius. On September 2, 1788, while the judges were marching in a body to this fortification a Colonel Sprout, who led the procession with glittering sword and was a very tall, erect man, six feet, four inches in height, so impressed a group of onlooking Indians that they shouted "Hetuck! Hetuck!," meaning Big Buckeye. It was that incident, coupled with the abundance of the buckeye tree, which caused *Buckeye State* to be applied to Ohio.

This tale is far from persuasive, but all the authorities seem to agree that *Buckeye* for an Ohioan was somehow borrowed from the name of the tree. It goes back to 1823. There is a weekly called the *Buckeye* at Archibald (population, 1185), another called the *Buckeye State* at Lisbon, a third called the *Buckeye News* at Lithopolis, a fourth called *Buckeye Lake Topics* at New Concord, and a *Buckeye Grocer* at Springfield.

Oklahoma is the *Sooner State*, which is borrowed from the term used to designate the early settlers who sneaked across the border before the land of the State was thrown open to white settlement. The proclamation of President Benjamin Harrison opened it as of noon of April 22, 1889. At that time, about 20,000 progenitors and predecessors of the later *Okies* were gathered along the border, ready to rush in, hoping to find Utopia. Unhappily, many of them discovered, when they came to likely looking tracts, that there were claimants there ahead of them. How these claimants got in was not determined officially, but many of them succeeded in holding their claims. They were called *sooners*, and in a little while the term began to be applied to all the citizens of the State. The DAE notes that by 1892 it had been extended to any one of "that

---

[1] Why is Ohio Called the *Buckeye State*?, Historical Collections of Ohio (Columbus), 1890, Vol. I, p. 202.

numerous class of . . . people who insist upon crossing bridges before they come to them." The *sooner dog*, not listed by the DAE, had no relation to the human *sooner:* he was one who would sooner fight than eat. In England, according to Eric Partridge,[1] he was one who " would sooner feed than fight." With this latter sense in mind, *sooner* became British naval slang for a shirker. Shankle lists two other nicknames for Oklahoma — the *Boomer's Paradise* and the *Land of the Red People*. The latter is based on the theory that the name of the State is derived from a Choctaw word meaning red men or red people.

Oregon is the *Beaver State* officially, but has been known as the *Sunset State*, the *Web-foot State* and the *Hard-case State*. *Sunset State* was once disputed by Arizona, but now seems to be in the public domain. *Hard-case State*, which is traced by the DAE to 1845, had reference to the large number of evil characters who flocked into the Oregon country in the early days: their descendants are now austere Rotarians and Shriners. *Hard case*, to designate such a character, is marked an Americanism by the DAE and run back to 1842. Schele de Vere, in his manuscript notes to his " Americanisms," noted both *Old Webfoot* and the *Land of Red Apples* as designations for Oregon *c.* 1873. *Webfoot*, for a citizen of the State, is traced by Charles J. Lovell to 1853. The early examples of its use show clearly that it was suggested by the copious rainfalls between the Cascade Range and the Pacific Ocean. At Astoria, the first settlement in the valley of the Columbia, it is 77.2 inches a year, as compared to 42.87 inches at New York City and 33.5 inches at Chicago. Mr. Leo C. Dean of the Salem *Capital Press* tells me that the State newspapers always make *Webfoots*, not *Webfeet*, the plural of *Webfoot*. To use *Webfeet* would be as gross a gaucherie as to make *meese* the plural of *moose*.

South Dakota, which was joined to North Dakota until 1889, is the *Coyote State*. In its first days it was known variously as the *Blizzard State*, the *Artesian State*, the *Sunshine State* and the *Land of Plenty*, but *Sunshine State* has been taken over by New Mexico, and the others have passed out. In 1898 the *Monthly South Dakotan* of Mitchell was predicting that *Coyote* as a designation for a citi-

---

[1] A Dictionary of Slang and Unconventional English; New York, 1937, p. 801.

zen for the State would "probably last," and this prophecy has been fulfilled. The name comes, of course, from that of the prairie wolf (*Canis latrans*), borrowed by the Spaniards from a Nahuatl Indian word, *coyotl*. It has been sound American since the 30s of the last century, though for a long while there seems to have been some uncertainty about its spelling, and such odd forms as *cayote, collote, cayeute, chiota, koyott, ciote, cayotah, kiote* and *kiota* are listed by Thornton and the DAE.

Tennessee prefers to be the *Volunteer State*,[1] but since the Scopes trial at Dayton in 1925 it has been called the *Monkey State* with painful frequency, and will probably be a long time living down that derisive designation. The effort to repeal natural selection by law made the State ridiculous throughout the world, and its civilized minority has suffered severely from its ensuing ill fame. The DAE traces *Volunteer State* to 1853, but it really goes back to 1847, when Governor Aaron V. Brown issued a call for three regiments to serve in the Mexican War — and 30,000 men responded. At various times Tennessee has also been known as the *Big Bend State*, the *Hog and Hominy State* and the *Lion's Den*. The last-named was listed by *Brother Jonathan* in 1843, but its origin is mysterious. Perhaps it arose from the fact that the border ruffians of the early days were sometimes called *lions of the West*, or simply *lions*. *Hog and Hominy State*, of course, refers to the favorite diet of the Tennessee yeomanry — a diet popular throughout the Bible and Bilbo country. *Hog and hominy* means, colloquially, fatback and any preparation of corn-meal: the term is traced by the DAE to 1792. This combination is deficient in vitamins, and those who feed upon it often suffer from pellagra. There was a time when certain patriotic Tennesseans began calling the State the *Mother of Southwestern Statesmen*, but the nickname did not last, for the Southwest was soon moving beyond the Mississippi, and the researches of historians revealed that all three of the Presidents claimed by the State — Andrew Jackson, James K. Polk and Andrew Johnson — were born outside its boundaries. Another of its nicknames is *Big Bend State*, which refers to the various big bends in the Tennessee river, especially the one at Chattanooga.

[1] It appears in the subtitle of the guide to the State brought out by the Federal Writers' Project under the sponsorship of the State Department of Conservation.

Texas, as everyone knows, is the *Lone Star State*. This was the device on the flag of the Texas Republic (1836-45), and it remains the device on the State flag and seal today. Attempts have been made at various times to substitute *Banner State, Jumbo State, Blizzard State* and *Beef State*, but in vain. An important part of Texas is the *Panhandle*, which runs up between Oklahoma and New Mexico in the northwest. West Virginia has another such panhandle, projecting in a thin strip between Pennsylvania and Ohio, and has been called the *Panhandle State* because of it. Idaho has yet another. The term, which was apparently suggested by the handle of a frying-pan, is traced by the DAE to 1861, and was applied to the Texas *Panhandle* so long ago as 1873. At the time of the Texas Centennial Exposition of 1936, the Hon. William C. McCraw, then attorney-general of Texas and soon afterward an unsuccessful candidate for the Democratic gubernatorial nomination, launched a campaign to put down " the insidious use of the terms *panhandle* and *panhandling* for beggars and the act of begging." For a while this holy war got some attention in the newspapers, but it then subsided, and *panhandler* is still in wide use. Its origin was thus described by the Chicago *Tribune* at the time:

> The expression grew up among hoboes, or casual laborers, to describe their plight after they had spent all their wages and found themselves jobless and broke in a city. They call street begging *panhandling* because it is descriptive of the mendicant who sits on the sidewalk holding out his hand or a cup.[1]

Utah calls itself the *Beehive State*, and sports on its seal " a conical beehive with a swarm of bees round it, emblematical of the industry of the people," [2] but the designation *Mormon State* is far more popular, and seems likely to stick. The State, which did not enter the Union until 1896, delayed by the long battle over the polygamy issue, has also been called the *Deseret State*, the *Salt Lake State*, the *Land of the Mormons* and the *Land of the Saints*. *Deseret* is borrowed from a word in the Book of Mormon [3] signifying a honeybee and appearing in a passage describing the wanderings of the

[1] Texas Protests: You Shouldn't Say *Panhandler*, May 7, 1936. In Southwestern Slang, by Socrates Hyacinth, *Overland Monthly*, Aug., 1869, Texas is called the *Rawhide State*, but this was probably only a nonce use.

[2] Political Americanisms, by Charles Ledyard Norton; New York, 1890, p. 64.

[3] Ether II, 3.

prophet Jared and his brother and their families in search of the Promised Land. Reaching the valley of Nimrod, they pastured their flocks, turned loose edible fowl, stocked the streams with fish, liberated swarms of bees, and planted "seeds of every kind." The cantonment in which Brigham Young quartered his nineteen wives and fifty-seven children was commonly called the *Beehive* by infidels. In 1922 the *World* Almanac listed *Desert State* as a nickname for Utah, but this was probably only a typographical error. Washington is both the *Evergreen State* and the *Chinook State*, with the latter apparently the more in use. *Chinook* is the name of a local tribe of Indians, once numerous at the mouth of the Columbia river. They gave their name to a trade language that was in common use along the coast for more than a century, and is still spoken by a few old-timers.[1] It provided a number of words for American English, e.g., *skookum*, *siwash*, *potlatch*, and maybe also *cayuse* and *hooch*. The DAE traces *Evergreen State* to 1909. It refers, of course, to the State's immense stretches of conifer forest.

West Virginia, as I have noted, is one of the five contending *Switzerlands of America*, but it is now more generally known as the *Mountain State* or the *Panhandle State*, the former because a large part of its area is in the Allegheny chain, and the second because of the panhandle which juts up between Pennsylvania and Ohio and is in places less than ten miles wide, though it includes the metropolitan area of Wheeling, the largest in the State, and Moundsville, the seat of the State Penitentiary. The people of the State often speak of it proudly as *West by God Virginia*. Wisconsin is the *Badger State*, and its people are *Badgers*. The latter appellation seems to have arisen, like *Sucker* for Illinoisan and *Puke* for Missourian, at the Galena, Ill., lead mines in the 20s of the last century. These mines were near the place where Illinois, Iowa and Wisconsin meet, and many Wisconsin pioneers were occasionally employed in them. There were no houses for them, and they commonly lived in caves in the hillsides, resembling badger burrows. Hence they were called *Badgers*, and the nickname stuck when they returned home. Charles Fenno Hoffman, traveling in Michigan Territory in 1834, recorded that he there encountered " a keen-eyed, leather-belted *Badger* from the mines of Ouisconsin." But Schele

---

[1] See Supplement I, p. 309-11.

de Vere, in 1872, said that *Badger State* arose from the prevalence of the *Badger* (*Taxidea taxus*) in the wilds of the State. *Badger* is not an Americanism, but was brought from England, and is first recorded in America in 1654. Finally, there is Wyoming, the *Equality* or *Suffrage State*, so called because its Territorial Legislature made the first grant of the suffrage to women voters. This was in 1869.

XI

AMERICAN SLANG

1. THE NATURE OF SLANG

The boundaries separating true slang from cant and argot are wavering and not easily defined. The latter two are differentiated from slang by the fact that they belong to the speech of relatively small and cohesive groups, and cant is separated from both argot and slang by the fact that one of its purposes is to deceive or mystify the outsider, but there is a constant movement of words and phrases from one category to another. When, in 1785, Captain Francis Grose published the first edition of his "Classical Dictionary of the Vulgar Tongue," the word *slang* itself seems to have been confined mainly to the argot of criminals and vagabonds, but by the beginning of the Nineteenth Century it had begun to be used generally as a new and piquant synonym for *jargon*, and today it appears unchallenged in all dictionaries, though no one, as yet, has worked out its etymology.[1] The movement of novelties is in both directions: sometimes from above to below, *e.g.*, *bones* for *dice*, which Chaucer used quite seriously, *c.* 1386, and sometimes from below to above, *e.g.*, *to stump* in the political sense, which was a Western slang phrase when it came in more than a century ago,[2] but is now almost as respectable as *to caucus*. As everyone knows, most slang terms have relatively short lives, and nothing seems more stale than one that has passed out, *e.g.*, *skiddoo, snake's hips, nerts, attaboy* and *I don't think*, but now and then one survives for years and even for centuries, without either going into eclipse on the one hand or being elevated to standard speech on the other. *To bamboozle* is still below the salt and would hardly be used by a bishop in warning against Satan, but it is more than

---

[1] See AL4, p. 555.
[2] The DAE traces *to stump* to Peter Pilgrim; Philadelphia, 1838. The author of this tale of Western adventure was Robert Montgomery Bird, famous in his day for Nick of the Woods.

two hundred years old and was listed as slang by Richard Steele in the *Tatler* in 1710. *Gas* (talk) has been traced to 1847, *kibosh* to 1836, *lip* (impudence) to 1821, *sap* to 1815, *cheese it* to 1811, *to chisel* to 1808, *racket* to 1785, *hush-money* to 1709, *to knock off* (to quit) to 1662, *tick* (credit) to 1661, *grub* to 1659, *to cotton to* to 1605, *bat* (a loose woman) to 1612, *to plant* (to hide) to 1610, *brass* (impudence) to 1594, *duds* (clothes) to 1567 and *to blow* (to boast) to *c.* 1400: all remain in use today and all continue to be slang.[1]

It would be hard to figure out precisely what makes one slang term survive for years and another perish quickly and miserably, but some of the elements which may shape the process are discernible. One of them is the degree to which a neologism fills a genuine need. It may do so by providing a pungent name, nearly always metaphorical, for an object or concept that is new to the generality of people, *e.g., ghost-writer* and *caterpillar* (running gear), or it may do so by supplying a more succinct or more picturesque designation for something already familiar in terms more commonplace, *e.g., bellhop, sorehead, rubberneck* and *killjoy*. Many of the best slang-terms are simple compounds, as the examples I have just given show; others are bold tropes, *e.g., bull* (a policeman), *to squeal, masher, cold feet, yellow* (cowardly), *baloney, apple-sauce, cat's pajamas* (something very rare) and *hitched* (married); yet others are the products of a delirious delight in language-making which throws phonemes together helter-skelter, *e.g., fantods, heebie-jeebies, nifty, whoopee, hubba-hubba, to burp* and *oomph*. When a novelty is obvious it seldom lasts very long, *e.g., shellacked* for drunk, *skirt* for a woman, *peach* for a beautiful girl, *trigger-man* and *to put on the spot*, and when its humor is strained it dies as quickly, *e.g., movie-cathedral, lounge-lizard, third-termite*, and the frequent inventions of the Broadway school. Moreover, its longevity seems to run in obverse proportion to its first success, so that over-night crazes like *skiddoo* and *goo-goo eyes*[2] are

[1] I take these from Modern Slang, by J. Louis Kuethe, *American Speech*, Dec., 1936, pp. 293-97.
[2] This was broadcast in 1900 by Just Because She Made Dem *Goo-goo Eyes*, a coon-song by Hughie Cannon (words) and Johnny Queen (music). It deserved to live and in fact seems to be still alive in some parts of the country, for on March 25, 1944 the *New Yorker* reported, p. 22, that a man had been lately arrested in Houston, Texas, for violating a city ordnance prohibiting "making goo-goo eyes" on the street.

soon done for, whereas novelties of slower growth, *e.g.*, *booze*, *to goose* and *gimcrack* last a long, long while. The same autointoxication seems to cut short the silly phrases of negation that come and go, *e.g.*, *aber nit, sez you, oh yeah, I don't think* and *over the left*, and the numerous catch-phrases that have little if any precise meaning but simply delight the moron by letting him show that he knows the latest, *e.g.*, "How'd you like to be the ice-man?," "Wouldn't that jar you?," "O you kid," "Tell it to Sweeney," "Yes, we have no bananas," "Ish kabibble" (and its twin, "I should worry"), and "Shoo fly, don't bother me."[1]

Slang tends to multiply terms for the same concept: its chief aim seems to be to say something new, not necessarily something good. Thus there is a constant succession of novel synonyms for *girl, head, money, drunk, yes, good, bad* and other such words of everyday. Between 1860 and 1900 the American vocabulary swarmed with picturesque terms for *beard* in general and for the various varieties, but in this age of almost universal shaving they retain only a historical interest, *e.g.*, *galways, burnsides,* and *chinners*. Slang terms relating to the head always have a derogatory significance, and many of them hint at idiocy. In 1928 Mamie Meredith listed some of those then current, *e.g.*, *bean, coco* and *nut*, along with the fashionable derivatives, *e.g.*, *bonehead, pinhead* and *mutt* (from *muttonhead*), but all of these are now obsolete. The vast vogue of *sheik* (pronounced *sheek*, not *shike*) for a predatory male will be recalled by the middle-aged: it is now as extinct as *masher*.[2] The late George Ade, in 1935, attempted a list of sub-

[1] It might be worth while to attempt a history of such banalities, with dates. In 1869 the Boston music publishers, White, Smith & Perry, published a song called Shew, Fly, Don't Bother Me, with music by Frank Campbell. It was sung by Cool Burgess and Rollin Howard. Many other catch-phrases have been popularized by songs, *e.g., Yes, we have no bananas*. In American Notes & Queries, Aug., 1946, p. 74, Peter Tamony traced *Nay, Nay, Pauline* to Yale Yarns, by J. S. Wood; New York, 1895, p. 232. In The Kilroy Story, *Esquire*, April, 1946, David Scheyer attempted to account for *Kilroy was here*. Another etymology is in *American Notes & Queries*, Feb., 1947, pp. 173–74, and yet another in Air Words, by Fred Hamann; Seattle, 1946, p. 33. *Open the door, Richard,* came in on its heels and was as quickly defunct. The English are very fond of such phrases, *e.g., How's your poor feet?, Does your mother know you're out?, Cut yourself a piece of cake* and *Keep your hair on*. See It Makes You Think, London *Star*, May 10, 1940, and Let Me Tell Yo-o-ou, Dundee *Telegraph and Post*, Oct. 9, 1941.

[2] Sinclair Lewis, in Cass Timberlane; New York, 1945, pp. 323–24, listed some of the terms then in use for

stitutes for such words as *girl, married, idiot, begone* and *drunk*, arranging them in categories of "old," "later" and "latest."[1] Most of the terms he entered under the last heading are now almost forgotten, *e.g., cutie, babe, eyeful, pip* and *wow* for a pretty girl, *loud noise* and *main stem* for a "chief executive or person of importance," and *dumbbell, goof* and *total loss* for "an unsophisticated person." William Feather, searching "The American Thesaurus of Slang," by Lester V. Berrey and Melvin Van den Bark,[2] found that it listed 52 synonyms for *wife*, and that there was "not an affectionate reference in the lot."[3] I have mentioned the fact that the same thing is true of neologisms for *head*. Indeed, it is characteristic of all slang, which commonly represents no more than the effort of some smartie to voice his derision, not infrequently for some person, object or idea obviously above his own lowly thought and station. The folk, as such, invent nothing, but their spokesmen share their inferiority complex, and many of the most successful contrivances of those spokesmen are but little removed from pejorative. The wit of Broadway, now the chief source of American slang, is thus essentially opprobrious, and many of its brighter words and sayings may be readily reduced to "Oh, you son-of-a-bitch."

Nevertheless, it is from this quarter that most American slang comes, a large part of it invented by gag-writers, newspaper columnists and press-agents, and the rest borrowed from the vocabularies of criminals, prostitutes and the lower orders of showfolk. There was a time when it was chiefly propagated by vaudeville performers, but now that vaudeville is in eclipse the torch has been taken over by the harlequins of movie and radio. A good deal of this slang comes close to being obscene, *e.g.*, the *hot mamma* of a few years ago, the *jerk* of yesterday, and the Yiddish loans that come and go,[4] but their literal meanings are soon lost, and they are presently on the tongues of multitudes of college students and even

---

"the sort of male once described with relish as an *agreeable scoundrel*," *e.g., lug, jerk, louse, stinker, twirp, rat, crumb, goon* and *wolf*. Most of them soon passed out.

[1] A Check-Up on Slang in America, Baltimore *Sun* (and other papers), Sept. 8, 1935.

[2] New York, 1942.

[3] *William Feather Magazine*, Oct., 1943, p. 19.

[4] Some American Idioms From the Yiddish, by Julius G. Rothenberg, *American Speech*, Feb., 1943, pp. 43–48. The slang words for to cheat, to swindle are often identical with those for to have sexual intercourse.

school-children.[1] It would certainly be absurd, however, to argue that slang is wholly, or even predominantly vulgar and debased, or to dismiss its inventions, like the English prig, Allen Monkhouse,[2] as no more than "the ghosts of old facetiousness." It is, in fact, the most powerful of all the stimulants that keep language alive and growing, and some of the most pungent and valuable words and phrases in English, and especially in American English, have arisen out of its bilge. J. Y. P. Greig, the Scots professor just quoted, was quite right when he described *rubberneck* as "one of the best words ever coined."[3] It may be homely, but it is nevertheless superb, and whoever invented it, if he could be discovered, would be worthy not only of a Harvard LL.D., but also of the thanks of both Rotary and Congress, half a bushel of medals, and thirty days as the husband of Miss America. *Blah* is another masterpiece, and, like *rubberneck*, seems destined to live much longer than the normal term.[4] *Stooge* is yet another,[5] though it has many competitors, and *yesman* is a fourth. Others are *fan, piker,*[6] *stag-party,*[7] *stunt,*[8] *to*

[1] "The commonest stimuli of slang," said Professor J. Y. P. Greig, an esteemed Scots authority, in a university address in 1938 (Edinburgh *Evening Dispatch*, Aug. 24), "are sex, money and intoxicating liquor."
[2] A Bookman's Notes, Manchester *Guardian*, March 8, 1935.
[3] Breaking Priscian's Head; New York, 1929, p. 83. Said Benjamin R. Bulkeley in Something Literary: Slang and Colloquialisms, Boston *Herald*, May 5, 1928: "While it should today be ruled out of a sermon or a sonnet we do not know what the next century may allow."
[4] Eric Partridge says in A Dictionary of Slang and Unconventional English; second edition; London, 1938, p. 61, that it arose in the United States at some time before 1925, and was adopted by the English in 1927. He seeks to derive it from the German *blech*, a slang term for nonsense, and explains that there are "millions of Germans in the United States," but this sounds suspiciously like *blah* itself. Dr. Louise Pound lists many synonyms for it in *American Speech*, April, 1929, pp. 329-30, but not one of them comes within miles of it.
[5] *New Yorker*, Oct. 2, 1943: "On Sunday, September 12, the [New York] *Times* used *stooge* in the headline of a story. . . . It was not set off by quotation marks."
[6] The DAE's first example is dated 1869, when *piker* meant a yokel from Pike county, Missouri, then the common symbol of everything poverty-stricken and uncouth. It began to take on its present significance in the 1890s, when it appeared in the New York stock market to designate a petty operator.
[7] Traced by the DAE to 1856 and marked an Americanism. Partridge says that the English adopted it *c.* 1870.
[8] The DAE's first example comes from a word-list in *Dialect Notes*, Vol. I, Part VIII, 1895, p. 400, but I recall hearing it before that. Partridge suggests that it may be derived from the German *stunde*, an hour, but I am aware of no evidence for this.

debunk, to hike,[1] O.K.,[2] racketeer,[3] nut,[4] boom,[5] boost,[6] phony,[7] highbrow,[8] tight-wad, strong-arm, loan-shark, hard-boiled, he-man, soap-boxer, get-away, square-shooter, fifty-fifty, double-cross, kicker and the almost innumerable verb-phrases, e.g., to get together, to stop over, to eat crow, to saw wood, to bawl out and to play possum.[9]

Americans seem to be vastly more adept at making new slang than Englishmen, just as they are more adept at making more seemly neologisms.[10] There was a time when this was not true, and most of the slang that American purists frowned upon was of English origin,[11] but after the War of 1812 and the beginning of the

[1] In the sense of to run away to hike is old in the English dialects and was listed by Francis Grose in the second edition of his Classical Dictionary of the Vulgar Tongue; London, 1788. Partridge says that it sank into disuse in England, and was revived at some uncertain date in the United States and readopted in England c. 1926.

[2] The history of this most successful of all American slang terms is given in Supplement I, pp. 269-79.

[3] Racket is old, but racketeer was a product of Prohibition.

[4] In the sense of a half-wit. On May 8, 1946, in a speech to a Highway Safety Conference at Washington, President Harry S. Truman said: "It is perfectly absurd that a man ... can go to a place and buy an automobile and get behind the wheel — whether he has ever been there before makes no difference, or if he is insane or a nut or a moron." In reporting this speech the New York Times used nuts in its headline, enclosed in quotation marks. See "Nuts" and Morons, Boston Herald (editorial), May 20, 1946. As a noun meaning the head the word has been traced to 1858 in England, and in the sense of something agreeable, as in "It was nuts to him" it goes back to Shakespeare's time.

[5] The noun, in the sense of a barrier in a river to retain floating logs, is traced by the DAE to 1676 and marked an Americanism. The earliest example of the verb in the sense of to whoop up is dated 1873. Partridge says that it reached England c. 1885.

[6] Boost the noun has not been found before 1825 but the verb is in the glossary attached to David Humphreys' The Yankey in England, 1815. It is defined therein as to raise up, lift up or exalt. Partridge says that it reached England c. 1860 and the noun c. 1865. The etymology is undetermined.

[7] Robert Lynd predicted in Horrible New Words, London News Chronicle, March 18, 1939, that it would be as dead, "a few years hence," as "the tony and top-hole of previous generations," but within a year the English papers were calling the early, inactive stage of World War II the Phony War; on April 3, 1940, the term was used by Paul Reynaud, then premier of France, and on Aug. 24, 1945, the staid Edinburgh Scotsman was printing an editorial, Apt Phrases, which described it as a "typical outsider from across the Atlantic that has strengthened its position as a result of the war" and added that it "may have come to stay."

[8] See Supplement I, p. 325, n. 3.

[9] Many more are listed in AL4, pp. 197-98.

[10] See Supplement I, pp. 440-53.

[11] Such was the case, for example, with the locutions denounced by John Witherspoon in No. VII of The Druid, May 30, 1781, and it

great movement into the West Americans began to roll their own, and for years past the flow has been in the other direction.[1] Not only the movies and talkies but also American comic strips have flooded England with the latest confections of the Broadway and Hollywood neologists, and the fecund American key-hole columnists have been widely imitated. Now and then, to be sure, some hunkerous patriot, in D. W. Brogan's phrase, "sounds the clarion and fills the fife" against the invasion,[2] but meanwhile the wholesale adoption of American slang words and phrases goes on, and, as the London correspondent of the Baltimore *Sun* reported in 1937, "Britons are gradually growing reconciled to the Americanization of their language."[3] Many of them, indeed, go further: they declare that they like it. "American slang," wrote Horace Annesley Vachell, in 1935 or thereabout, "is not a tyranny, but a beneficent autocracy," and then he proceeded to argue for the superiority of the American *lounge-lizard* and *to be tickled pink* to the English *top-hole* and *putrid*. "English slang at its best," he went on, "has to curtsey to American slang, and at its worst it is *toppingly* the worst in the world." Even the Manchester *Guardian* and the London *Times* have praised the neologisms that the invasion brings in. The *Guardian*, in 1932, spoke editorially of "its Elizabethan

seems to have been the case with "the empty sarcastical slang so common to all the coxcombical gang" that Washington Irving derided in *Salmagundi*, June 27, 1807. To this day, in fact, many slang terms of English origin continue in everyday American use, e.g., *horse-laugh*, *soft-soap*, *cold-shoulder* and *lady-killer*. An acute observer, Thomas Adolphus Trollope (1810–92), notes in his What I Remember; New York, 1888, pp. 34–36, that the vocabulary of slang in the early part of the century was limited, and that most of it was better described as class argot.

1 The Canadian humorist, Stephen Leacock, said in Our Living Language: a Defense, New York *Times Magazine*, Feb. 26, 1939, p. 9: "American slang contains a much greater percentage of cleverness than English. To call a professional at cricket a *pro*, or breakfast *brek*-*ker*, or political economy *pol. econ.* saves time, but that is all. To call a pair of trousers *bags* is a step up: there is a distinct intellectual glow of comparison. But it is only twilight as compared with such American effects as *lounge-lizard*, *rubber-neck*, *sugar-daddy*, *tangle-foot* and *piece of calico*."

2 The Conquering Tongue, London *Spectator*, Feb. 5, 1943, p. 120. James Agate summed up in the London *Express*, June 4, 1936, by headlining an article with the sombre and final judgment: "I Loathe This American Slang." In the Carlisle *Journal*, April 5, 1946, a local Rotarian declared that it "has its roots in Negroid patter" and that "the whole influence of these clipt, shoddy and ugly terms is vulgarizing and lowering to the intelligence."

3 English Potpourri, by **Paul W.** Ward, Aug. 1.

vigor and its sometimes more than Elizabethan capacity for uncouth inventiveness "[1] and in 1937 of its "rich wit and expressive metaphor,"[2] and the *Times*, so long ago as 1931, granted "the variety of the sources, the ingenuity of the adaptation, and the lively vigor of these hard-hitting words."[3]

When, in 1937, an English schoolma'am named Miss Gwatkin set off a bomb at a convention of the Association of Head Mistresses at Brighton by employing *to debunk* in a speech and by boldly arguing that English school children were tiring of lessons in "correct" English and that "slick Americanisms meet their need and are far more effective," she was supported heartily by the press, including the ultra-conservative *Morning Post* and the *Daily Telegraph*. "To complain," said the *Telegraph*, "that girls and boys use these phrases before they are naturalized is to beg the question; it is they who give them their naturalization papers."[4] The *Morning Post* went further. "Not only the English language," it said, "but we ourselves have grown richer by the importation of such words [as *O.K., to debunk* and *highbrow*]. What substitute can we offer for *highbrow*? *Intellectual snob* is our best, and that is both longer and inexact."[5] A contributor to *Answers*, signing himself Philemon, thus summed up in 1941: "Let the purists be shocked! Let the precisions be offended! Let us drop a bomb among schoolmarmy talkers!"[6]

Maurice H. Weseen's "Dictionary of American Slang,"[7] which I was constrained to describe in AL4, p. 570, as "extremely slipshod and even ridiculous," has been supplanted since by "The American Thesaurus of Slang," by Lester V. Berrey and Melvin Van den Bark,[8] and there has appeared an excellent bibliography of slang, cant and argot by W. J. Burke.[9] In England the indefatigable Eric Partridge has followed his "Slang Today and Yesterday"[10]

[1] Still More American Language, Aug. 19.
[2] American Slang, June 28.
[3] American Slang, May 11.
[4] Debunking the Taboo on Slang, June 14, 1937.
[5] English and Slang, June 14, 1937. See also Conquest of England (editorial), New York *Times*, July 4, 1937.
[6] What Slanguage!, Sept. 13.
[7] New York, 1934. Weseen, who was associate professor of business English at the University of Nebraska, died April 14, 1941.
[8] New York, 1942. A second edition, including a supplement on the teen-age and jive jargon and the Army, Navy and Air Corps argot of World War II, was published in 1947.
[9] The Literature of Slang; New York, 1939.
[10] London, second edition; 1935.

and his annotated edition of Francis Grose's "Classical Dictionary of the Vulgar Tongue"[1] with a large "Dictionary of Slang and Unconventional English"[2] and William Matthews has published "Cockney Past and Present,"[3] and in Australia Sidney J. Baker has brought out "A Popular Dictionary of Australian Slang"[4] (which has many resemblances to American) and a large and valuable work on Australian English in general.[5] The Berrey-Van den Bark thesaurus, in its revised form, is a huge volume of 1231 pages. Its chief virtue is its comprehensiveness: it includes virtually every word of slang, cant or argot that had got into print at the time its forms closed. Moreover, its contents are arranged in such a way that looking up the vocabulary of any given trade, profession or graft is made easy. Its principal defect is that the inquirer who starts from a word instead of a category finds himself confronted with a 341-page, four-column index that is based on a complicated and sometimes maddening scheme of reference. Unhappily, no effort is made to date its entries, nor are there any etymologies — two valuable features of Partridge's "Dictionary of Slang and Unconventional English." Various other dictionaries of American slang seem to be under way as I write; in fact, I hear of a new one every few months. But it is not likely that the work of Berrey and Van den Bark will be supplanted in the near future, for scholars of their extraordinary diligence are very rare. Meanwhile, *American Speech* occasionally publishes useful papers on this or that aspect of American slang, and there is frequent (if seldom illuminating) discussion of the theme in the newspapers.[6]

1 London, 1931.
2 New York, 1937; second edition, revised and enlarged, 1938. It includes the numerous Americanisms that have become naturalized in England.
3 London, 1938.
4 Melbourne, 1941; second edition, 1943.
5 The Australian Language; Sydney, 1945. Baker has also published Australian Pronunciation; Sydney, 1947, and New Zealand Slang; Christchurch, 1940, and Arnold Wall has done New Zealand English; Christchurch, 1938.
6 Burke's The Literature of Slang, which ran serially in the *Bulletin of the New York Public Library* in 1936–38, is close to complete down to the latter year. Most of the later works of any value are mentioned in the footnotes to the present chapter.

2. CANT AND ARGOT

The common slang of the United States, as I have noted, is a catch-all for the inventions of various quite different classes of wits, though most of them have the common quality of being more or less disreputable. A neologism coined by a smart Harlem wise-cracker today may be raging in all the fashionable finishing-schools tomorrow, and there is a constant infiltration from the argots of innumerable lawful occupations and the cants of innumerable rackets. We owe many common words and phrases, for example, to the circus folks, *e.g.*, *guy*, *ballyhoo*, *three-ring* and *to shoot the chutes*; many more to the hobos, *e.g.*, *jungle*, *hand-out*, *panhandler* and probably *hobo* itself; and yet more to downright criminals, *e.g.*, *bull* (for policeman), *third-degree*, *to gyp*, *to bump off*, *to take for a ride*, *to shake down*, *to hi-jack* and *once-over*. We have borrowed *by a head*, *to scratch* and *to tout* from the race-tracks; *nineteenth-hole*, *to stymie* and *birdie* from the golf-links; *dope*, *coke*, *hop* and *to needle* from the drug-addicts, and *understudy*, *barnstormer*, *star*, *angel*, *box-office*, *to ring down the curtain on* and *full house* from the stage. In addition, large numbers of terms that belong to argot or cant are understood and occasionally used by Americans, though they have not yet entered (and perhaps never will enter) the common slang of the country.

The cant of modern criminals began to be formulated in western Europe in the early Fifteenth Century, when roving bands of a strange, dark race of petty thieves appeared from the mysterious East and were presently intermingled with the native tramps, beggars and other fly-by-night rogues. These newcomers, at the start, were assumed to be Egyptians, which explains our English name of *Gipsies* for them, but later studies of their history and language have demonstrated that they actually came from northwestern India. They were in Germany by 1414, in Italy by 1422, in France by 1427 and in England by the early 1500s. Two of the largest classes of indigenous vagabonds that they encountered were those of the begging friars and the displaced Jews. Both of these borrowed words and phrases from them and in turn reinforced their language with home-made inventions, and by the end of the Fifteenth Century there had developed in Germany a rogues' jargon that was based on German, but included many Hebrew and Gipsy terms. Some of these survive to the present day, even in the United States, *e.g.*, *pal* from the Gipsy [1] and *ganov* from the Hebrew.

The first writings in and on this jargon were done in Germany, and the earliest of them that have been preserved seem to have been based upon reports of a series of criminal trials at Basel in Switzerland, prepared by John Knebel, one of the clergy of the cathedral there.[2] This was in 1475, but it was not until 1512 or thereabout that Knebel's material got into print. It then appeared at Augsburg in the once-famous "Liber Vagatorum," which ran through many editions during the ensuing half century, including one edited at Wittenberg in 1528 by Martin Luther. All the Englishmen who wrote about thieves' cant during the Sixteenth Century seem to have made use of it, but there was no English translation until 1860, when John Camden Hotten brought out one in London under the title of "The Book of Vagabonds and Beggars, With a Vocabulary of Their Language."[3] Hotten, in his introduction, put the chief blame for the growth of vagabondage in the later Middle Ages, not on the coming of the Gipsies, but on "the begging system of the friars." He said:

[1] Mr. Everett DeBaun, of Philadelphia, calls my attention to other apparent loans from Romany speech, *e.g.*, *benny*, an overcoat (Rom. *bengree*, a waistcoat); *can*, a jail or privy (Rom. *caen*, to stink): *to cop*, to steal, and maybe also *cop* or *copper*, a policeman (Rom. *cappi*, booty, gain); *cush*, money (Rom. *cushti*, good); *shiv*, a knife (Rom. *chiv*, a blade), and *stir*, prison (Rom. *staripen*, a prison).

[2] Knebel's MS. is still preserved in the university library at Basel. It was printed for the first time in *Taschenbuch für Geschichte und Alterthum in Süd-Deutschland*, by Heinrich Schreiber; Freiburg (Switzerland), 1839. Records of the trials were also made by Hieronymus Wilhelm Ebner, and his MS. is also preserved at Basel. It was printed in Exercitationes Iuris Universi, by Johann Heumann; Altdorf, 1749.

[3] The text of Liber Vagatorum, with Luther's prefaces, is in the *Weimarisches Jahrbuch für deutsche Sprache, Litteratur und Kunst* for 1856, Vol. IV, pp. 65-101. This *Jahrbuch*, which lasted only a few years, was edited by Hoffmann von Fallersleben, the author of Deutschland über Alles. Hotten (1832-73) was an English bookseller and bibliographer who was in America from 1848 to 1856. In the latter year he set up as a publisher in London, and in 1859 issued his Dictionary of Modern Slang, Cant and Vulgar Words, several times reprinted, with additions, during the years following. In 1866, when Moxon suppressed Swinburne's Poems and Ballads in response to an uproar from Puritans, Hotten took it over. He was the first English publisher to publish Lowell, Artemus Ward, Charles Godfrey Leland, Bret Harte and Ambrose Bierce. He wrote biographies of Dickens and Thackeray, and also a History of Signboards, 1867.

These religious mendicants, who had long been increasing in numbers and dissoluteness, gave to beggars sundry lessons in hypocrisy, and taught them, in their tales of fictitious distress, how to blend the troubles of the soul with the infirmities of the body. Numerous systems of religious imposture were soon contrived, and mendicants of a hundred orders swarmed the land. Things were at their worst, or rather, both friars and vagabonds were in their palmiest days, towards the latter part of the Fifteenth Century, just before the suppression of the religious houses.[1]

But the German authority, Schreiber,[2] laid more stress upon the influence of the Gipsies, thus:

The beggars of Germany rejoiced in a Golden Age which extended through nearly two centuries, from the invasions of the Turks until after the conclusion of the Swedish war (1450 to 1650). During this long period it was frequently the case that begging was practised less from necessity than for pleasure — indeed, it was pursued like a regular calling. . . . Mendicancy became a distinct institution, was divided into various branches, and was provided with a language of its own. Besides the frequent wars, it was the Gipsies — appearing in Germany at the beginning of the Fifteenth Century — who contributed most of this state of things.

"Liber Vagatorum" lists the twenty-nine principal varieties of German rogues of the time, and provides a glossary of their *Rotwelsch*, or cant. I transcribe some specimens, with explanations:

Acheln, v. To eat (Heb. *akal*).
Barlen, v. To speak (Fr. *parler*).
Betzam. An egg (Heb. *beytzah*).
Bosshart. Meat (Heb. *basar*).
Bergen, v. To beg.[3]
Dallinger. A hangman (Ger. *galgener?*).
Fetzen, v. To work (Ger. *fetzen*, tatters).
Floss. Soup (Ger. *floss*, flowing water).
Galch. A priest.
Gatzam. A child (Heb. *gatam*).
Gfar. A village (Heb. *chafar*).
Gugelfranz. A monk.
Gugelfrenzin. A nun.
Hans Walter. A louse.
Himmelsteig. The Lord's Prayer (Ger. *Himmel*, heaven, and *steig*, a path).
Hornbock. A cow.
Iltis. A policeman (Ger. *iltis*, a polecat).
Joham. Wine (Heb. *yahyin*).
Kabas. The head (Lat. *caput*).
Platschen, v. To preach (Ger. *plätschern*, to murmur, to ripple, to splash).

[1] In England the monasteries were dissolved in 1539.
[2] *Taschenbuch für Geschichte und Alterthum*, before mentioned.
[3] Hotten suggests that this may be a corruption of Ger. *predigen*, to preach.

Quien. A dog (Fr. *chien*, dog).
Regenwurm. A sausage (Ger. *regenwurm*, an earthworm).
Schreiling. A child (Ger. *schrei*, a cry).
Versenken, *v.* To pawn (Ger. *versenken*, to sink).
Wunnenberg. A pretty girl.
Zickus. A blind man (Lat. *caecus*).
Zwicker. A hangman (Ger. *zwicken*, to pinch).

575. [The earliest English reference to the subject are in Robert Copland's "The Hye Way to the Spittell Hous," 1517, a dialogue in verse between the author and the porter at the door of St. Bartholomew's Hospital, London.] Burke says in "The Literature of Slang," that this book was probably not actually published until *c.* 1535. Copland was a printer who once worked for Wynken de Worde and maybe also for William Caxton. "The porter in 'The Hye Way to the Spittell Hous,'" says Burke, "talks the language of rogues, and there are passages entirely in cant." But Copland's source does not appear to have been "Liber Vagatorum"; he borrowed, rather, from a French translation of Sebastien Brant's "Das Narrenschiff," a somewhat earlier work which also included some thieves' jargon but was not a formal treatise on the subject. Brant (1457–1521) wrote a great deal of Latin poetry and also a number of legal and theological works, but he is chiefly remembered for "Das Narrenschiff," which appeared at Basel in 1494. "It was," says George Madison Priest, in his "Brief History of German Literature,"[1] "the first German work that achieved fame abroad. After the manner of the humanists it ridicules the weaknesses and crimes of the age as unreasoning, absurd follies; the 'fools' are adulterers, unbelievers, usurers, and the like." Brant, continues Priest, "studied the classics, and thus received a humanist's education," but he "did not accept the humanist ideal of pure humanity, and remained true to the medieval doctrines of the church. Indeed, German humanism in general, in contradistinction from that of Italy, never became wholly detached from religion. It was for the most part limited to scholars who despised the common people." Brant's book was given over chiefly to the follies of the upper and middle classes; what he added about rogues and vagabonds seems to have been derived from the same Basel records that have been mentioned as the probable sources of "Liber Vagatorum." Alexander Barclay's "The Ship of Fools," first printed in 1509, was a very free render-

[1] New York, 1909, p. 60.

ing of "Das Narrenschiff," with most of Brant's classical pedantry omitted and many additions of purely English material. Like its original, it had an enormous success, and is still pored over by the learned.[1]

Copland's "Hye Way to the Spittell Hous" was followed by many other books embodying specimens of English criminal cant, and among their authors were such remembered writers as Thomas Dekker and Robert Greene, but the first formal glossary did not appear until nearly two centuries later. This was "A New Dictionary of the Terms Ancient and Modern of the Canting Crew, in its Several Tribes of Gipsies, Beggars, Thieves, Cheats, Etc., With an Addition of Some Proverbs, Phrases, Figurative Speeches, Etc.," published in London in 1698. Its author concealed himself behind the initials B. E., and has never been identified. "From his dictionary," says Burke, "one gathers that he was an antiquary. Some of his words and definitions bear no relation to slang and cant, but merely gratify his whim for curiosa. . . . [His] is perhaps the most important dictionary of slang ever printed, since it had such an influence upon later compilations." It was reprinted in John S. Farmer's "Choice Reprints of Scarce Books and Unique MSS.,"[2] and there is a later facsimile reprint, undated, which often bobs up in the second-hand bookshops. The vocabulary runs to 176 double-column pages, and prefixed to it is a preface of six pages. In that preface the author confines himself mainly to discussing the origin of Gipsies and beggars. Beggars appeared in the world, he says, when slavery was put down. He goes on:

> The Jews, who allow'd of slaves, had no beggars. What shall we say, but that if it be true that the emancipation or freeing of slaves is indeed the making of beggars, it follows that Christianity, which is daily employed in redeeming slaves from the Turks, ransom'd no less than all at once from pagan slavery at first, at no dearer a rate, than the rent-charge of maintaining the beggars, as the price and purchase of our freedom?

The English here is somewhat thick, but the meaning is plain enough. In England, continues B. E.,

> it may be observed that the first statute which makes provision for the parish poor is no older than Queen Elizabeth, from which it may be fairly collected

---

[1] The best edition is that of T. H. Jamieson in two vols.; Edinburgh, 1874. It contains a good account of Barclay, pp. xxv ff.

[2] London, 1899; Vol. III.

that they entered with us upon the dissolution of the abbeys, as with them abroad upon the delivery of the slaves.[1]

B. E.'s glossary shows a number of terms that are still more or less in vogue. In the following list of specimens those that appear in the Berrey-Van den Bark "American Thesaurus of Slang" are marked with asterisks, and in all cases the spelling, punctuation and capitalization are modernized:

*Anglers. Cheats, petty thieves, who have a stick with a hook at the end, with which they pluck things out of windows, grates, etc.; also those that draw in people to be cheated.[2]

*Antidote. A very homely woman.[3]

*Aunt. A bawd.

*Bad job. An ill bout, bargain, or business.

*Balderdash. Ill, unpleasant, unwholesome mixture of wine, ale, etc.[4]

Beetle-head. A heavy, dull blockhead.

Belsh. All malt drinks.

Budge. One that slips into a house in the dark, and takes cloaks, coats, or what comes next to hand.

Buffer. A rogue that kills good sound horses, only for their skins, by running a long wire into them.

*Case. A house, shop or warehouse. *To tout the case:* to view, mark or eye the house or shop.

*Cat. A common whore.

*Chink. Money, because it chinks in the pocket.

*Clap. A venereal taint.

Cleymes. Sores without pain raised on beggars' bodies by their own artifice and cunning (to move charity), by bruising crowsfoot, spearwort and salt together and clapping them on the place, which frets the skin; then, with a linen rag, which sticks close to it, they tear off the skin and strew on it a little powdered arnica, which makes it look angrily or ill-favoredly, as if it were a real sore.

Clunch. A clumsy clown; an awkward or unhandy fellow.

Cob. A dollar (in Ireland).[5]

---

1 The first English poor law was passed in 1601.
2 Now used in the sense of a confidence man.
3 Here is a use of *homely* in the American sense, to indicate lacking in beauty. In current English usage the word means simple, unpretending, and is not applied opprobriously. But it was good English in the American sense down to the Eighteenth Century, and was so used by Shakespeare in The Comedy of Errors, II, 1590.
4 It seems to be likely that this was the original meaning of the word. In that sense the NED traces it to 1611, whereas in the sense of nonsensical words its goes only to 1674. Its origin is unknown. Ernest Weekley suggests in his Etymological Dictionary of Modern English; London, 1921, that it may have some connection with the Dutch *pladder*, meaning both a weak tipple and foolish talk, but this is only a guess.
5 *Dollar* was used in England to designate the German *thaler* from the middle of the Sixteenth Century. Toward the end of that century it came also to designate the Spanish

Cockale. A pleasant drink, said to be provocative.[1]
*Coltish. Said when an old fellow is frolicsome or wanton.
Cony. A silly fellow.[2]
*Cotton. *They don't cotton:* they don't agree well.
Crap. Money.[3]
*Crony. A comrade or intimate friend.
Cully. A fool or silly creature that is easily drawn in and cheated by whores or rogues.
Curmudgeon. An old covetous fellow, a miser.[4]
Damme-boy. A roaring, mad, blustering fellow, a scourer of the streets.
Dells. Young buxom wenches, ripe and prone to venery, but have not lost their virginity.
Doctor. A false die.
Dromedary. A thief or rogue.
*Elbow-grease. A derisory term for sweat.
Ewe. A top woman among the canting crew, very beautiful.
*Fence. A receiver and securer of stolen goods.
*File. A pickpocket.
Fireship. A pocky whore.
Flibustiers. West Indian pirates or buccaneers; freebooters.[5]
Fork. A pickpocket.
Fortune-tellers. Judges.
Fubbs. A loving, fond word used to pretty little children and women.
*Gag. To put iron pins into the mouths of the robbed, to hinder them crying out.
*Gang. An ill knot or crew of thieves, pickpockets or miscreants.
*Gelt. Money.
*Gimcrack. A bauble or toy.
*Glim. A dark lantern used in robbing houses.
Goat. A very lascivious person.
*Green-bag. A lawyer.

---

peso or *piece-of-eight*. It was adopted as the name of the unit of American currency by an act of the Continental Congress on July 6, 1785.

1 This, conceivably, may have been the original form of *cocktail*. See Supplement I, pp. 256–60.

2 Originally, a young rabbit. It began to be applied to dupes toward the end of the Sixteenth Century, and for many years thereafter swindling was called *cony-catching*.

3 It is possible that the origin of *crap*, the American dice game, may be found here. *Crap* is always listed in dictionaries as *craps* – a curious pedantry, for it is called *crap* by the players, and appears in the singular in *crap-shooter* and *to shoot* *crap*. It is traced by the DAE to 1843. *Crap* in the sense of excrement, and often used in the United States as a derogatory term for foolish talk, is also always singular.

4 *Curmudgeon* retained this narrow meaning until the Nineteenth Century. It now connotes churlishness rather than miserliness. *Cf.* Autobiography of a *Curmudgeon*, by Harold L. Ickes; New York, 1943.

5 *Filibuster*, in the American sense of one fomenting insurrection, came in in 1850. It was given wide currency by William Walker's expedition to Nicaragua in 1855. The offspring verb, signifying an attempt to delay the action of a legislative body, is traced by the DAE to 1853.

American Slang

*Grinders. Teeth.
Gropers. Blind men.
*Gugaws. Toys; trifles.[1]
Gunpowder. An old woman.
*Half seas over. Almost drunk.
*Pump. To wheedle secrets out of anyone.
*Rhino. Ready money.
Romer. A drinking-glass.[2]
Salamander. A stone (lately) found in Pennsylvania, full of cotton, which will not (as a modern author affirms) consume in the fire.[3]
Scandal-proof. One hardened or past shame.
*Screw. To exact upon one, or squeeze one in a bargain or reckoning.
*Shark. A sharper.
*Shop-lift. One that steals under pretense of cheapening.
*Skin-flint. A griping, sharping, close-fisted fellow.
Smart-money. Given by the king when a man in land or sea service has a leg shot or cut off, or is disabled.
*Smutty. Bawdy.
Snudge. One that lurks under a bed, to watch an opportunity to rob.
*Sock. To beat.
Soul-driver. A parson.
Split-fig. A grocer.
Stamps. Legs.
*Stretching. Hanging.
*Tom-thumb. A dwarf or diminutive fellow.[4]
*Trimming. Cheating people of their money.
Turk. Any cruel, hard-hearted man.
Whiddle, *v.* To tell, or discover. He *whiddles:* he peaches.
Woodpecker. A bystander that bets.

After the publication of this dictionary by B. E. there was an interval of nearly a century before England saw another work of importance in the same field. Then, in 1785, came the first edition of Captain Francis Grose's "Classical Dictionary of the Vulgar Tongue," the foundation of every treatise on thieves' cant and likewise on ordinary slang that has been done since. There was a second edition in 1788, and a third in 1796, five years after the author's death. In 1811 there was a fourth, brought out under the title of " Lexicon Balatronicum " by Hewson Clarke, a literary hack of the time,[5] and in 1823 there was a fifth, with the original title restored

---

1 Now *gewgaws*.
2 Probably from the German *römer*, meaning the same. It had degenerated into *rummer* even before B. E.'s time.
3 Asbestos. *Salamander-stone*, at a somewhat earlier period, was applied to a stone that, " once set on fire, can never be quenched." (NED, 1583).
4 P. T. Barnum's *Tom Thumb* was Charles Sherwood Stratton, born at Bridgeport, Conn., in 1838. He died in 1883.
5 " The merit of Captain Grose's Dictionary," said the preface, " has

and Pierce Egan serving as editor.[1] Finally, there is the reprint issued in 1931, edited by Eric Partridge and limited to 550 copies. This reprint is based on the third edition of 1796, which seems to have embodied corrections and additions prepared by Grose himself. Partridge adds a brief biography of the author, and enriches the dictionary itself with a large number of glosses, some of them very valuable.

Grose was the son of a Swiss jeweler who came to England early in the Eighteenth Century, set up business in London, and acquired a moderate fortune. The son was born in 1731 or thereabout and received a good education, though he did not proceed to a university. His early interests were divided between drawing and military affairs. He was for many years adjutant and paymaster of the Hampshire militia, and meanwhile he became so well regarded as a draftsman and water-colorist that in 1766 he was elected a member of the Incorporated Society of Artists. On his father's death in 1769 he came into enough money to put him at ease, and thereafter he devoted himself largely to antiquarian studies. Between 1773 and 1787 he published six volumes of "The Antiquities of England and Wales," and at the time of his death in 1791 he had done two more on "The Antiquities of Scotland" (1789–91), and had nearly finished two on "The Antiquities of Ireland." He was married and had seven children, one of whom rose to be deputy governor of New South Wales, but he was a gay dog and put in a large part of

---

been long and universally acknowledged. But its circulation was confined almost exclusively to the lower orders of society: he was not aware, at the time of its compilation, that our young men of fashion would at no very distant period be as distinguished for the vulgarity of their jargon as the inhabitants of Newgate; and he therefore conceived it superfluous to incorporate with his work the few examples of fashionable slang that might occur to his observation." The additions, as a matter of fact, were not numerous, but some of them have survived, e.g., *bang-up.*

[1] Egan (1772–1849) is chiefly remembered (and collected) today because George and Robert Cruikshank illustrated his Life in London, 1821. In 1824 he began publication of a weekly, *Pierce Egan's Life in London and Sporting Guide,* which later became *Bell's Life in London,* and was merged, in 1859, in *Sporting Life.* Life in London was a great success in its day, and so was a series of pamphlets called Boxiana, or Sketches of Antient and Modern Pugilism, which he began in 1818 and continued until 1829. There are interesting notes on him in the London *Times Literary Supplement,* Aug. 7 and 21, 1943.

his leisure investigating the night life of London. He also made a number of exploratory tours of the British Isles, and on one of them had a meeting with Robert Burns in Scotland which developed into a close friendship. Burns wrote two poems about him, in one of which, " On Captain Grose's Peregrinations Through Scotland," occur the famous lines:

> A chiel's amang ye, taking notes,
> And, faith, he'll prent it.

This couplet has been taken over by journalists as referring to their mystery, but it actually alludes to Grose's antiquarian researches. Egan says that his nocturnal tours of the London underworld were made in company with a retainer named Batch, and goes on:

> Batch and his master used frequently to start at midnight from the King's Arms in Holborn in search of adventures. The back slums of St. Giles's were explored again and again, and the captain and Batch made themselves as affable and jolly as the rest of the motley crew among the beggars, cadgers, thieves, etc., who at that time infested the Holy Land [*i.e.*, St. Giles's]. It was from these nocturnal sallies and the slang expressions which continually assailed his ears, that Grose was first induced to compile " A Classical Dictionary of the Vulgar Tongue."

This last may be true, but it is somewhat misleading. The fact is that Grose's dictionary leaned heavily upon the before-mentioned " New Dictionary " of B. E., though neither Egan nor Partridge calls attention to it.[1] A number of his definitions are taken over from B. E. unchanged,[2] and many others are changed but little.[3] Grose even preserved B. E.'s plurals where the singular form would have been more rational. But it is not to be gainsaid that he added a great deal of new matter of his own and got rid of many of B. E.'s nonce-words and literary affectations, so that his dictionary came much closer to the actual vulgar speech than its predecessor. And if he mined B. E., then all his successors have mined Grose; indeed,

---

[1] In all probability this influence may have been exerted through A Collection of the Canting Words and Terms Both Ancient and Modern Used by Beggars, Gypsies, Cheats, House-Breakers, Shop-Lifters, Footpads, Highwaymen, &c. appended to Nathan Bailey's Universal Etymological Dictionary; third edition; London, 1737, for Bailey also borrowed from B. E.

[2] For example, those of *Abram cove, acteon, Adam's ale, altitudes, artistippus, armor* and *autem,* to go no further than the *a*'s.

[3] For example, those of *Adam-tiler, ambidexter* and *anglers.*

his dictionary remained the best thing of its sort until Partridge began to investigate English slang during World War I. With Partridge's glosses his book still makes excellent reading. It came out at just the right time. That large facility for concocting new and picturesque words which characterized the English of the Seventeenth Century had begun to yield, by the last half of the century following, to the policing of the purists, and thereafter its prodigies were transferred to America, but there was still enough good slang in currency to be worth recording, and Grose recorded it with eager diligence and appreciation. In his first edition of 1785 there were about 3,000 entries, and in his third of 1796 the number had grown to nearly 4,000. It is thus impossible to give more than a random sampling here. But certainly the following, none of them to be found in B. E. and all now obsolete, deserve to be remembered:

Babes in the wood. Criminals in the stocks or pillory.
Baptized. Spirits that have been lowered with water.
Barrel fever. He died of the barrel fever: he killed himself by drinking.
Beau trap. A loose stone in a pavement, under which water lodges, and, on being trod upon, squirts up.[1]
Betwattled. Surprised, confounded.
Blowse, or blowsabella. A woman whose hair is dishevelled and hanging about her face; a slattern.
Blubber cheeks. Large, flaccid cheeks.
Bookkeeper. One who never returns borrowed books.
Bran-faced. Freckled.
Cleaver. One that will cleave; used of a forward or wanton woman.
Collar day. Execution day.
Fish. A seaman.
Gummy. Clumsy.
Hen-house. A house where the woman rules.
Jacob. A ladder.
Oven. A great mouth.
Peery. Inquisitive, suspicious.
Pound. A prison.
Scapegallows. One who deserves and has narrowly escaped the gallows.
Sea crab. A sailor.
Slush bucket. A foul feeder.
Smear. A plasterer.
Sneaksby. A mean-spirited fellow, a sneaking cur.
Snip. A tailor.
Strangle-goose. A poulterer.
Suds. *In the suds:* in a disagreeable situation.
Traps. Constables and thief-takers.

[1] In the Baltimore of my boyhood, c. 1890, a loose brick was called a *she-brick*. *She-bricks* have disappeared as the old brick sidewalks of the town have yielded to cement.

American Slang

Many of the other terms listed by Grose have survived to our day. Some still belong to slang or the lower levels of colloquial speech, *e.g.*, *cow-juice, to crook the elbow, duds, grub, hush-money, leery, to lush, pig-headed, sky-parlor, spliced* (married), *to touch* (borrow) and *uncle* (pawnbroker), but others have climbed to more respectable standing, *e.g.*, *crocodile tears, of easy virtue, elbow room, fogy, foul-mouthed, to fuss, gingerbread* (decoration), *greenhorn*,[1] *humbug, lopsided, mum, pin-money, pug-nose, sandwich*,[2] *tidy* and *white lie*.

Grose, in his preface to his first edition of 1785, differentiated clearly between the cant of rogues and ordinary slang. "The vulgar tongue," he said, "consists of two parts: the first is the cant language, called sometimes pedlar's French or St. Giles's Greek; the second, those burlesque phrases, quaint allusions and nicknames for persons, things and places which, from long uninterrupted usage, are made classical by prescription." In this last, of course, he was in error: slang may be quite evanescent and still be true slang. When, as and if it becomes "classical" it usually enters into the ordinary vocabulary, though it may never take on much dignity there. Grose borrowed his account of the origin of cant from William Harrison's "Description of England" prefaced to Raphael Holinshed's famous "Chronicles of England, Scotland and Ireland," published in two volumes in 1577–78.[3] Said Harrison:

> It is not yet fifty years sith this trade [of beggars] began, but how it hath prospered sithens that time it is easy to judge, for they are now supposed, of one sex and another, to amount unto above ten thousand persons, as I have heard reported; moreover, in counterfeiting the Egyptian rogues they have devised a language among themselves, which they name canting, . . . a speech compact thirty years since of English and a great number of words of their own devising, without all order or reason, and yet such it is as none but themselves are able to understand. The first deviser thereof was hanged by the neck, as a just reward no doubt for his deserts and a common end to all of that profession. A gentleman, Mr. Thomas Harman, of late hath taken great pains to search out the secret practices of this ungracious rabble, and among other things he setteth down and prescribed twenty-two sorts of them.

---

1 B. E., 1698, lists *greenhead*, "a very raw novice, or unexperienc'd fellow."
2 The NED traces *sandwich* to 1762, but it was still rather slangy in 1785.
3 Harrison (1534–1593) was a Londoner and an ardent antiquary. He was a clergyman and became canon of Windsor in 1586. His Description of England is an amusing, informing and altogether excellent piece of work. Shakespeare borrowed heavily from Holinshed.

The book by Harman, here mentioned by Harrison, was entitled "A Caveat or Warening For Commen Cursetors [1] Vulgarely Called Vagabondes." It was published in London in 1567, and not a few of the terms it listed survived in B. E.'s "New Dictionary" of 1698 and even into Grose. Not much is known about Harman save that he was a country gentleman and apparently interested in police matters. He indicated that the region in which he lived was hard beset, in his time, by troops of wandering rogues, and he describes their depredations at length. At the end of his book there is a brief vocabulary of "the leud, lousey language of these lewtering luskes and lasy lorrels," [2] including the following: [3]

Belly chete. An apron.
Bousing ken. An alehouse.
Bowse, *v.* To drink.[4]
Cante, *v.* To speak.
Chattes. The gallows.
Cly the gerke, *v.* To be whipped.
Couch a hogshead, *v.* To lie down and sleep.
Crashing chetes. Teeth.
Cutte, *v.* To say.
Darkemans. Night.
Drawers. Hosen.
Gan. A mouth.
Gentry morte. A noble or gentle woman.
Glasyers. Eyes.
Glymmar. Fire.
Hearing chetes. Ears.
Ken. A house.
Lage. Water.
Lap. Buttermilk or whey.
Lightmans. Day.
Margery prater. A hen.
Myll a ken, *v.* To rob a house.
Mynt. Gold.
Nab. A head.
Nosegent. A nun.
Nygle, *v.* To have to do with a woman.
Pannam. Bread.
Patrico. A priest.
Prat. A buttock.

[1] *Cursetor* or *cursitor* was a polite synonym for *vagabond* in the Sixteenth and Seventeenth Centuries. The NED's first example is taken from Harman's title-page.
[2] *i.e.*, loitering loafers and lazy blackguards.
[3] I have modernized the spelling of the definitions.
[4] *Bouse* and *bowse* were early forms of *booze*.

Prygge, *v.* To ride.
Quyerkyn. A prison.
Roger, or tyb of the buttery. A goose.
Rome bouse.[1] Wine.
Salomon. An altar or mass.
Slate or slates. A sheet or sheets.
Smelling chete. A nose.
Stamps. Legs.
Stow you, *v.* Hold your peace.
Strommell. Straw.
The ruffian cly thee. The devil take thee. (Ger. *klauen,* to claw, to clutch).
Togeman. A cloak.
Towre, *v.* To see.
Tryninge. Hanging.
Yaram. Milk.[2]

Harman apparently picked up some of these from the fugitive literature of the time,[3] but the rest seem to have come out of his own observation. As I have noted, many works dealing with rogues and vagabonds and recording more or less of their cant appeared in England during the Seventeenth Century and more followed in the Eighteenth. There is a bibliography of them in Burke and they are discussed in " The Development of Cant Lexicography in England, 1566–1765," by Gertrude E. Noyes.[4] Dr. Noyes shows that most of the lexicographers of roguery followed B. E. in pilfering from Harman. This was especially true of Dekker, who brought out " The Gull's Hornbook " in 1609 and followed it with other things of the same sort, and of the anonymous author of " The Groundwork of Coney-Catching," 1592. In turn these thieves supplied material to later ones, for example, Richard Head, whose " The English Rogue " appeared in 1665, followed by " The Canting Academy " in 1673.

The literature of criminals' cant since Grose has been voluminous, but on the whole it was of small value until recent years. Godfrey Irwin's " American Tramp and Underworld Slang," brought out in 1931, was mainly devoted to the argot of tramps, but within its limits it was well done, and I know of no later book that is better.[5]

[1] This suggests Gipsy influence. *Romany* is the Gipsies' name for themselves.
[2] Harman's list was reprinted in full in The Oldest Rogues' Dictionary, *Encore,* Sept., 1942, pp. 343-45.
[3] In W. J. Burke's Literature of Slang there is listed but one such work antedating Harman's Caveat, to wit, The Hye Way to the Spittell Hous, but it is certain that many such things have been lost.
[4] *Studies in Philology* (Chapel Hill, N.C.), Vol. XXXVIII, 1941, pp. 462-72.
[5] It is significant that Irwin had to go to England to find a publisher. There he got aid from Eric Par-

At about the same time Dr. David W. Maurer, of the University of Louisville, began to interest himself in the subject, and has since become the chief American authority upon it. He has two important qualifications for his task: he is a man trained in scholarly and especially philological method, and he has an extraordinary capacity for gaining the confidence of criminals. He has published a book upon the techniques and speech of the confidence men who constitute the gentry of the underworld [1] and papers in the learned journals and elsewhere upon the argots of various lesser groups, ranging from forgers and safecrackers to drug-peddlers and prostitutes, and he has been at work for some years past upon a comprehensive "Dictionary of American Criminal Argots." [2] A century ago the cant of American criminals was still largely dependent upon that of their English colleagues, stretching back for centuries, but though it still shows marks of that influence [3] it is now predominantly on its own. Its chief characters, says Maurer, are " its machine-gun staccato, its hard timbre, its rather grim humor, its remarkable compactness." [4] It differs considerably, of course, from specialty to specialty, but within a given specialty " it appears to be well standardized from coast to coast and from the Gulf into Canada." It shows the cosmopolitan quality of all American speech, and includes loans from Yiddish, Spanish, German, French, Chinese and even Hindustani. Like slang in general, it is the product, not of the common run of criminals, but of individual smarties, so it tends to increase in picturesqueness as one goes up the scale of professional rank and dignity. Says Maurer:

> Why do criminals speak a lingo? There are several reasons, perhaps the most widely accepted of which is that they must have a secret language in order to conceal their plans from their victims or from the police. In some instances it is undoubtedly used for this purpose — for instance, *flat-jointers*,[5]

---

tridge. His material was accumulated during "more than twenty years' experience as a tramp on the railroads and roads of the United States, Canada, Mexico and Central America, and on tramp steamers in Central American waters."

[1] The Big Con; Indianapolis, 1940.
[2] His plans for it are set forth in *Studies in Linguistics*, April, 1943.
[3] For example, in the survival of rhyming slang. An account of the argot of American criminals of the 1900 era is in The Lingo of the Good People, by David W. Maurer, *American Speech*, Feb., 1935, pp. 10–23. A great deal of it is now obsolete.
[4] The Argot of the Underworld, *American Speech*, Dec., 1931, pp. 99–118.
[5] Petty swindlers who follow carnivals, fairs, etc.

three-card monte men, and other *short-con workers* [1] sometimes use it to confuse or deceive their victims. But most professional criminals speak argot only among themselves, . . . for using it in public would mark them as underworld characters whether or not they were understood. . . . There is a very strong sense of camaraderie among them, a highly developed group-solidarity. . . . A common language helps to bind these groups together and gives expression to the strong fraternal spirit. . . . Professional crime is nothing more than a great variety of highly specialized trades; hence it is only natural that many of the same factors which operate among legitimate craftsmen should affect criminal speech.[2]

The vast upsurge of crime brought in by Prohibition made all Americans familiar with a large number of criminal words and phrases, and many of these, as I have noted, have entered into the everyday speech of the country. How much of the argot of the Volsteadian racketeers was the product of their own fancy and how much was thrust upon them by outside admirers, *e.g.,* newspaper reporters and movie writers, is not easily determined, but Maurer is convinced that a substantial amount of it came from the latter, including even such apparently characteristic terms as *big shot.* He says [3] that actual members of the *mob* called the brass hats of the profession *wheels* (in the plural). But *trigger-man, torpedo, gorilla, pineapple* (bomb), *whiskers* (a Federal agent: a reference to Uncle Sam), *hot* (a stolen object or a criminal pursued by the law), *on the lam, to snatch* (to kidnap), *moll* and *racket,* whatever their provenance, were really in use. The gentlemen of the *big con, i.e.,* swindlers who specialize in rooking persons of means, constitute the aristocracy of the underworld, and hold aloof from all lesser criminals. They are, taking one with another, of superior intelligence, and not many of them ever land in prison. Their lingo thus shows a considerable elegance and also some humor, *e.g., apple, savage* or *Mr. Bates* for a victim; *big store,* the bogus poolroom or brokerage office to which *apples* are lured; *coarse ones,* large bills; *ear-wigger,* one who tries to eavesdrop; *excess baggage,* a member of a mob who fails to pull his weight in the boat; *to fit the mitt,*

[1] *Short-con workers* operate on a modest scale, and are usually content with whatever money the victim has on him at the time he is rooked. They seldom employ the *send* — that is, they seldom send him home for more.
[2] The Big Con, before cited, pp. 270-71.
[3] Private communication, April 7, 1940. The anonymous author of The Capone I Knew, *True Detective,* June, 1947, p. 80, says that *syndicate,* used by Al to describe his mob, was "picked up from the newspaper stories about him."

668   *The American Language: Supplement II*

to bribe an official; *Joe Hep,* a victim who tumbles to what is happening; *larceny,* the itch for illicit money that lures a victim on: " He has *larceny* in his heart "; *to light a rag,* to run away; *to play the C,* to operate a confidence game; *to sting,* to swindle; *suckerword,* a term not used by professionals,[1] and *yellow,* a telegram. The craft is called the *grift,* not the *graft.*[2]

At the opposite pole from practitioners of the *big con* are the crude and brutal fellows who follow the *heavy rackets, i.e.,* those involving violence. They include burglars, safe-blowers (yeggs), hijackers, kidnapers, automobile thieves, window-smashers, mail robbers, pay-roll grabbers, purse-snatchers, and so on. They had their heyday during the thirteen delirious years of Prohibition, and there was a revival of their art, made much of by the newspapers, following World War II, but on the whole they seem to be declining in prosperity, and the new methods of thief-taking organized by the Federal Bureau of Investigation have landed large numbers of them in prison. They range in professional dignity from the *jug-heavies* or *bank burglars,* who stand at the top, to the mere hoodlums, many of them young neophytes, at the bottom. Among the cant terms of the *jug-heavies* are *bug,* a burglar alarm; *to case,* to spy out; *cutter,* a prosecuting attorney; *dinah* or *noise,* dynamite; *double,* a false key; *forty,* O. K.; *gopher,* an iron safe; *hack,* a watchman; *soup* or *pete,* nitroglycerine; *stiffs,* negotiable securities; *swamped,* surprised and surrounded, and *V,* a safe. Maurer says [3] that there are some regional differences in *jug-heavy* speech, *e.g.,* a bank is a *jug* everywhere but sometimes a *jay* in the Middle West or a *tomb* in the East, and a policeman is an *elbow* on the Pacific Coast, the *law* or the *works* in the Middle West, and a *shamus, fuzz* or *goms* in the East. The automobile thieves who once raged in large and well-organized gangs also had an argot of their own, *e.g., doghouse,* a small garage; *bent one* or *kinky,* a stolen car, and *consent job,* a car stolen with the connivance of an owner eager for the insurance,[4] and so did the hijackers who arose during Prohibition

1 I take all these from Maurer.
2 The glossary in The Big Con is also in The Argot of Confidence Men, *American Speech,* April, 1940, pp. 113–23, and Confidence Games, by Carlton Brown, *Life,* Aug. 12, 1946, pp. 45–52.
3 The Lingo of the *Jug-Heavy,*

Writer's Digest, Oct., 1931, pp. 27–29.
4 I Wonder Who's Driving Her Now, by William G. Shepherd, *Journal of American Insurance,* Feb., 1929, pp. 5–8 (reprinted in *American Speech,* Feb., 1930, pp. 236–37); Hot Shorts, by T. J.

and flourished in the aftermath of World War II, *e.g.*, *baloney*, an automobile tire; *box*, a truck trailer; *to carry the mail*, to drive fast; *crate*, a truck; *dark horse*, a watchman; *girl scout* or *hairpin*, a female associate; *in creeper*, in low gear; *on the I. C.*, on the lookout; *powder-wagon* or *blast-furnace*, a sawed-off shotgun; *red eye*, a stop signal; *stick*, a crowbar; *toby*, a highway; *traveler*, a hijacker, and *whistler*, a police-car.[1] The stick-up men who specialize in robbing pedestrians often operate in pairs. One clasps the victim around the neck from behind and chokes him while the other goes through his pockets. This is often done very violently and sometimes the victim is badly hurt. It is called *mugging* in New York, but *yoking* in most other places.[2]

Forgers, counterfeiters (*penmen*) and other such intellectuals have a certain standing in the underworld and even pickpockets are respected more or less as the masters of a difficult art, but they do not rank with the princes of the *big con* nor even with the more daring heroes of the *heavy rackets*. Among forgers, says Maurer,[3] there is a "sharp division of labor." The men who produce forged checks (*makers*, *designers*, *scratchers* or *connections*) are usually wholesalers who supply the actual *passers*, but do not tackle the public. The former, like their allies, the counterfeiters, often operate in safety for years on end, but the latter are frequently taken. The *passer* is also called a *paperhanger*, but the colleague who works off counterfeit money is a *paper-pusher*, *pusher* or *shover*. A forged check is *paper*, *scrip* or a *stiff*, and when it is a cashier's check it is a *jug-stiff* or *cert*. *Bouncer* and *rubber-check*, both in common use among laymen, do not seem to be in the professional vocabulary. The *paperhanger* does most of his *spread* on Saturday, after the banks close; in consequence he is usually broke by Friday, and he thus calls a dismal countenance a *Friday face*. To him a store-detective is a *shamus*, *Mr. Fakus* or *Oscar*, a warrant for his arrest is a *sticker*, a credit manager is a *credie* or a *Joe Goss*, a check-book is a *damper-pad*, and the confidence talk which precedes his passing of a bad check is the *business*. Among pickpockets the act of pick-

---

Courtney, *Saturday Evening Post*, Nov. 30, 1935, pp. 12-13, 72-74.
1 Hijacker's Argot, Chicago *Tribune*, Jan. 22, 1939.
2 *Yoking* Means Just That, Baltimore *Evening Sun*, July 16, 1946, p. 32.

Ordinarily, *to mugg* means to photograph, especially for the Rogues' Gallery.
3 The Argot of Forgery, *American Speech*, Dec., 1941, pp. 243-50.

ing a pocket is called the *beat*, the *sting* or a *come-off*, a watch is a *toy, thimble, turnip, kettle* or *super*,[1] a policeman is a *buttons, fuzz* or *shamus*, a victim is a *chump, mark, yap*, or *hoosier*, the member of a mob who does the actual stealing is a *claw, wire* or *tool*, his assistants are *stalls*, a wallet is a *poke, leather, hide* or *okus*,[2] an empty wallet is a *cold poke, dead skin* or *bloomer*, a ring is a *hoop*, paper money is *rag* or *soft*, and an overcoat is a *tog*. All pickpockets are *guns, cannons* or *boosters*, and a lady of the profession is a *gunmoll*.[3] *Dip* for a practitioner is now obsolete in America, though it is still used by lay writers upon crime waves and seems to survive in England.[4] Shoplifters, or *boosters*, have some resemblance to pickpockets, but they are much less daring. Many of them are women, and most of the women are amateurs. The professionals often carry a *booster-box*, which is a box resembling an ordinary shopper's parcel, but with a trap-door for receiving the loot.[5]

A large part of the vocabulary of the rum-running mobs of Prohibition days passed into the general speech, e.g., *the real McCoy*,[6]

1 Says Maurer in *American Speech*, April, 1941, p. 154: "Modern thieves call a stolen watch a *super* (or *super and slang* if the chain accompanies it), . . . not realizing that the word is really *souper*, a pun on the older form, *kettle*."
2 In Along the Main Stem, *True Detective*, March, 1942, p. 73, a writer signing himself The Fly Kid suggested that *okus* (or *hokus*) may have issued from *poke* by way of *hocus-pocus*. *Hocus-pocus* itself has long been a headache to etymologists. The NED inclines to the theory that it came from the pseudo-Latin patter and assumed name of a juggler during the reign of King James I, but Weekley believes that it may have arisen as a blasphemous perversion of the sacramental blessing, *hoc est corpus (filii)*. It has analogues in Norwegian, Swedish and German.
3 I am indebted here to Mr. Everett DeBaun, of Philadelphia. He tells me that *gun* and *cannon* have nothing to do with artillery. The former is derived from the Yiddish *ganov*, a thief, and *cannon* is simply a more elegant form. During the Golden Age of the Dillingers the newspapers took to calling a racketeer's girl a *gun-moll*, but this was an error. A pickpocket who specializes in robbing women is a *moll-buzzer*, whether male or female. Inasmuch as most women operators confine their work to their own sex, they are usually *moll-buzzers*. See The Language of the Underworld, by Ernest Booth, *American Mercury*, May, 1928, p. 78.
4 In The Argot of the Underworld, by James P. Burke, *American Mercury*, Dec., 1930, pp. 454–58, *catholic* is given as another name for a pickpocket, but without any attempt at an etymology.
5 I am indebted here to Mr. Victor T. Reno, of Los Angeles. See Slick Fingers, by Ralph L. Woods, *Forum*, Dec., 1939, pp. 273–77.
6 The origin of this term has been much debated and is still unsettled. Etymologies relating it to Kid McCoy, the pugilist, and to Bill McCoy, an eminent rum-runner, are given in AL4, p. 580, n. 1. Both are improbable. The late Alfred E. Smith, appealed to for light, once derived it from the name of a Bow-

American Slang

to take for a ride,[1] torpedo, trigger-man, bath-tub gin,[2] alky, to muscle in, to cut (to dilute), hide-out, jake (all right), to needle (to add alcohol), piece (a share), tommy-gun and hijacker,[3] and some of them seem likely to stick, along with the Yiddish loans that these public servants also made familiar, e.g., kosher (reliable), meshuga (crazy) and to yentz (to cheat).[4] The assorted ruffians who adorned the same glorious era made every American schoolboy aware of the meaning of to rub out, mob, to scram,[5] G-man,[6]

---

[1] Herbert Asbury says in Gem of the Prairie; New York, 1940, p. 327, that this lovely euphemism was coined by Hymie Weiss, one of the four ranking dignitaries of Chicago gangdom, the others being Johnny Torrio, Al Capone and Dion O'Banion.

ery oracle named McCoy, whose word on any subject was accepted as the low-down (Smith Gives the Origin of Phrase the Real McCoy, New York Times, Nov. 27, 1936), but Al actually knew no more about the matter than any other Harvard LL.D. DeBaun says that the phrase first got into circulation in 1915, just after the passage of the Harrison Anti-Narcotic Act, and he believes that it was derived from the name of a British firm which sold superior drugs, but Maurer tells me that it has been in use among safecrackers since c. 1900 at the latest to designate commercial nitroglycerine in contrast to homemade soup or stew cooked out of dynamite. He says that the older safecrackers believe that it comes from the name of an old wildcatter in the Pennsylvania oilfields who diverted nitroglycerine to them. Others derive the term from an Irish ballad, c. 1870, telling of a woman named McCoy who gave her husband a beating, thus proving to him that she was the real McCoy. Yet others say that it comes from the real McKaye, a Scottish phrase of similar meaning. Mr. G. Dundas Craig, of Berkeley, Calif., tells me that he heard the rale McKay "long before 1898." Another correspondent says that the real MacKay goes back to the Jacobite troubles of 1715-45, when doubt arose as to who was the true chief of the clan. But Partridge says that it comes from the American the real McCoy and did not reach England until c. 1929.

[2] Like big shot, this one was probably invented by some smart newspaper reporter and imposed upon the racket. Mr. Fred Hamann tells me that on the revival of bootlegging during World War II it became blitz-water, bang-water or ceiling-buster.

[3] Said H. K. Croessman in the American Mercury, June, 1926, pp. 241-42: "The first time I heard hijacker was from the lips of an Oklahoman. He explained it as coming from the command customary in hold-ups: 'Stick 'em up high, Jack,' or, more simply, 'Up high, Jack,' Jack being the common generic name for any male person of unknown or uncertain identity. Thus, the Oklahoman explained, both stick-up and hijack originate from the same command. The change from high to hi is a corruption typical of a tendency in America."

[4] Terms prevailing during Prohibition among boozers, though not among bootleggers, e.g., homebrew, are listed in Wet Words in Kansas, by Vance Randolph, American Speech, June, 1929, pp. 385-89 See also Volstead English, by Achsah Hardin, the same, Dec., 1931, pp. 81-88.

[5] The first appearance of to scram in print seems to have been in Walter Winchell's column, Your

672   *The American Language: Supplement II*

canary,[1] *to put the heat on, gat,*[2] *on the lam,*[3] — *or else,*[4] *gangster,*[5] *racketeer* [6] and *public enemy*.[7]

"One might expect prison slang," says Maurer, "to be a composite of the various specialized argots, but while some bonafide argot crops out in it, it is, on the whole, a separate institutional lingo which differs somewhat from prison to prison." He goes on:

Broadway and Mine, Oct. 4, 1928. See *Scram* — a Swell Five-Letter Word, by V. Royce West, *American Speech*, Oct., 1937, pp. 195–202. Partridge says that it reached England in the movies by 1930. Its etymology remains mysterious. For speculations on the subject see Partridge's Dictionary of Slang and Unconventional English, the West paper just mentioned, and notes by G. Kirchner in *American Speech*, April, 1938, pp. 152–53 and April, 1940, p. 219.

6 In A Couple of Cops, *Commonweal*, Jan. 31, 1936, p. 373, Roger Shaw says that the celebrated Machine-Gun Kelly complained of the deadly efficiency of the *G-men* when he was captured at Memphis, Tenn., Sept. 26, 1933, and that "newspapers, fictioneers and the movies took it up." It is from *government-man*.

1 One who *sings, i.e.,* confesses to the police.

2 Apparently from *Gatling-gun*. But Booth, before cited, derives it from *catting up*, meaning to rob itinerant workers at pistol point. Those so engaged, he says, "were known as *cat-up men*. Soon *cat* was corrupted to *gat*." This is confirmed by Godfrey Irwin in American Tramp and Underworld Slang, but it seems improbable.

3 Says Peter Tamony in Origin of Words: *Lam*, San Francisco *News Letter & Wasp*, April 9, 1939, p. 5: "Its origin should be apparent to anyone who runs over several colloquial phrases for leave-taking, such as *to beat it, to hit the trail*. ... The allusion in *lam* is to *beat*. *Beat it* is old English, meaning to leave. During the period of George Ade's Fables in Slang cabaret society delighted in talking slang, and *lam* was current. Like many other terms, it went under in the flood of new usages of those days, but was preserved in criminal slang. A quarter of a century later it reappeared." An article in the New York *Herald Tribune* in 1938 said that "one of the oldest police officers in New York" reported that he had heard *on the lam* "about thirty years ago." *To lam* in the sense of *to beat* is traced by the NED to 1595.

4 This phrase, so often used by virtuosi of *muscling in*, is neither new nor American. In A History of Our Own Times; London, 1879, Vol. II, p. 275, Justin McCarthy told of a threat sent by one Irish chieftain to another: "Pay me my tribute — *or else*." I am indebted here to Mr. Alexander Kadison.

5 In *American Speech*, Oct., 1936, p. 278, V. Royce West recorded the appearance of *gangster* in England, France, Germany and Holland. The DAE traces it in American use only to the same year, but it must be considerably older.

6 *Racket*, in the current sense of an anti-social enterprise, appeared in A New and Comprehensive Vocabulary of the Flash Language; London, 1812. But *racketeer* is American.

7 *Public enemy*, usually followed by a numeral, is said to have been coined by the Hon. Homer S. Cummings, LL.D., Attorney-General of the United States, 1933–39. The original *Public Enemy No. 1* was John Dillinger, killed by F.B.I. men in Chicago, July 22, 1934.

Relatively few successful professionals ever *do time*, and when they do they tend to hold themselves somewhat apart from the general run of prisoners. They count upon their strong political connections to secure preferment and often associate with the prison administration on intimate terms. The great bulk of prison populations is composed of amateurs or failures; hence the fallacious belief among some psychologists and criminologists that criminals are subnormal in intelligence. Thorough-going and successful professionals are usually superior in intelligence and have nothing about them to suggest the popular conception of a criminal. If you mixed a hundred of them with an equal number of business and professional men all the statistics of a Hooton or a Lombroso would never set them apart.[1]

But the residuum actually behind the bars is of generally low mentality [2] and in consequence the lingo of the average prison, save in so far as it is reinforced by the inventions of the aloof minority or by contributions from outside, shows little imagination. Its basis, says James Hargan, is "a variety of Anglo-Saxon terms dealing mainly with the sexual and simpler life processes, which have survived the centuries in defiance of the dictionary's refusal to receive them."[3] A large part of it, adds Hargan, shows a "euphemistic, often humorous understatement" by which the prisoner "softens an otherwise too unpleasant reality into something bearable," *e.g.*, *kimona*, a coffin; *dance-hall*, the death house; *sleeping time*, a short sentence; *mouse*, a spy or informer; and *bird-cage*, a cell. The animal appetites naturally take a major place in his thinking, and much of his humor, such as it is, is devoted to flings at his always monotonous and usually tasteless fare. I quote from a convict lexicographer:

On our first morning at breakfast a waiter came along calling "*Strawberries*" and we gullibly pushed our plate out — to have it filled with red beans. . . . Stew is *slum*, coffee is *jamoca* and water is *sky juice*. When someone yells for the *sand* one passes him the salt. Hamburger balls are entitled *jute-balls*. . . . Gravy and pork sausages go under the pseudonym of *hog and mud*, while pork, gravy and boiled potatoes are *hog, mud and rocks*. Bread parades under the alias of *sawdust*.[4]

1 Private communication, April 7, 1940.
2 A survey of all the male inmates of the State prisons of New York showed that 80.2% of them were of less than normal intelligence. My authority here is Dr. H. Curtis Wood, Jr. Dr. James Asa Shield, psychiatrist to the Virginia State Penitentiary at Richmond, reports that among 749 white prisoners examined there in 1935 only 21 showed a mental age of 14 years or over, and that among 1,043 colored prisoners there were but two.
3 The Psychology of Prison Language, *Journal of Abnormal and Social Psychology*, Oct.-Dec., 1935, pp. 359–65.
4 Table Talk, *San Quentin Bulletin*, Jan., 1931, p. 11.

674   *The American Language: Supplement II*

This vocabulary has its local variations, but most of it seems to be in general use in American prisons, for the same malefactors move from one to another. A large part of it is identical with the table talk of soldiers and sailors. Milk is *chalk;* macaroni, *dago;* eggs, *cacklers, cackleberries* or *shells,* or, if fried, *red eyes;* potatoes, *spuds;*[1] onions, *stinkers* or *tear-gas;* butter, *grease;* catsup, *red-lead;* soup, *water;* bread, *duffer* or *punk;* sugar, *sand* or *dirt;* roast beef, *shoe-sole, leather* or *young horse;* veal, lamb or mutton, *goat-meat;* coffee, *gargle, suds* or *black soup;* sausage, *beagle, dog* or *balloon;* tea, *dishwater;* sauerkraut, *shrubbery* or *hay;* a meat loaf, *mystery* or *rubber-heels;* biscuits, *cat-heads* or *humpers;* bread and gravy, *poultice;* tapioca, *fish-eyes* or *cats'-eyes,* and a sandwich, *duki* (from *duke,* the hand). Meat as a whole is *pig* and food in general is *swag, garbage, scoff, chow, chuck* or *peelings.* A waiter is a *soup-jockey.* The prison functionaries all have derisive names. The head warden is *the big noise, the ball of fire,* or *the Man;* the guards are *shields, screws, hooligans, roaches, hacks, slave-drivers* or *herders;* the chaplain is a *frocker, goody, psalmer, buck* (if a Catholic priest), *Bibleback* or *the Church;* the doctor is a *croaker, cutemup, sawbones,*[2] *pill-punk, iodine, salts* or *pills;* the barber is a *scraper, chin-polisher* or *butcher.*

A new prisoner is a *fish;* a letter smuggled out of prison is a *kite;* a crime is a *trick* or *caper;* a cell, when not a *bird-cage,* is a *drum;* a drug addict is a *junker, junkie, hype, whang, hophead* or *snowbird.* A prisoner who goes crazy is said to be *on his top, conky, footch, guzzly, beered, loco, blogo, buggy, woody* or *meshuga.* To die is *to go down* or *to slam off.* To escape is *to gut, to mouse, to have the measles, to take* (or *cop*) *a mope, to hang it, to be on the bush, to lam the joint, to go over the wall, to get a bush bond* (or *parole*) or *to crush out.* To finish a sentence is *to get up.* A sentence is a *trick, knock, rap, hitch, bit, stretch* or *jolt.* If short it is *sleeping time,* if for one year it is a *boffo,* it for two a *deuce,* if for five a *five-specker* or *V,* if for twenty a *double sawbuck,* if for life the *book,* the *ice-box* or *all.* The prison is the *big house,* the *college* or the *joint.* A pardon or commutation is a *lifeboat.* An arrest is a

[1] Traced to 1860 by the NED, and said by Partridge to be "the inevitable nickname of any male Murphy." *Murphy* for a potato has been traced to *c.* 1810.

[2] *Sawbones* is in The Pickwick Papers, 1837.

fall, a man is a *gee*, a bed is a *kip*, and the prison morgue is the *greenhouse*. Many euphemisms are in use. At Sing Sing, for example, the death-house is *Box Z*, the section for insane convicts is *Box A*, and the place where dead inmates are buried is *Box 25*. Not a few of the terms reported smell of the lamp, and certainly did not emanate from the common run of prisoners, *e.g.*, *last mile* for the march to the gallows or electric chair, *Cupid's itch* for venereal disease, *pussy bandit* for a rapist, *gospel-fowl* for chicken, *sleigh-bells* for silver, and *toad-hides* for paper money.[1]

Between the world of professional criminals and that of honest folk there is a half-world of part-time, in-and-out malefactors, and to it belongs the army of hoboes, beggars, prostitutes, drug addicts, and so on. Most juvenile delinquents are part of it and remain so, for not many of them can ever hope to be promoted from neighborhood gangs to touring mobs. Indeed, the average bad boy of today, alarming his parents and feeding the fires of editorial writers, is very apt to end tomorrow, not in prison, but upon a clerk's stool in some petty government office, and the girl who abandons her virginity at fifteen is far more likely to celebrate her twentieth birthday on her honeymoon than in the gutter. To the layman all the species of the genus *hobo* look pretty much alike, but there are actually sharp divisions between one and another, though all are

---

[1] I am indebted here to Messrs. Clinton A. Sanders, Joseph W. Blackwell, Jr., Samuel Meyer and the editors of the *San Quentin News*. I have also made use of My San Quentin Years, by James B. Holohan, published serially in the Los Angeles *Times*, in 1936; Prison Slang, by Clinton T. Duffy; San Quentin, n. d.; Can Cant, by J. Louis Kuethe, Baltimore *Evening Sun*, Dec. 9, 1932 (republished as Prison Parlance, *American Mercury*, Feb., 1934, pp. 25–28); English Behind the Walls, by William H. Hine, *Better Speech*, Dec., 1939, pp. 19–20 (sent to me by Mr. Fred Hamann); Convicts' Jargon, by George Milburn, *American Speech*, Aug., 1931, pp. 436–42; Prison Phraseology, by Bruce Airey; Montgomery (Ala.), 1943; A Prison Dictionary (Expurgated), by Hi Simons, *American Speech*, Oct., 1933, pp. 22–23; Underworld and Prison Slang, by Noel Ersine; Upland (Ind.), 1935; Prison Lingo, by Herbert Yenne, *American Speech*, March, 1927, pp. 280–82; More Crook Words, by Paul Robert Beath, *American Speech*, Dec., 1930, pp. 131–34; Hipped to the Tip, by Jack Schuyler, *Current History*, Nov. 7, 1940, pp. 21–22; An Analysis of Prison Jargon, by V. Erle Leichty, *Papers of the Michigan Academy of Sciences, Arts & Letters*, Vol. XXX, 1945, pp. 589–600, and the glossaries in Almanac For New Yorkers, 1939, p. 125; Farewell, Mr. Gangster, by Herbert Corey; New York, 1936; The Professional Thief, edited by Edwin H. Sutherland; Chicago, 1937, and Crime as a Business, by J. C. R. MacDonald; Palo Alto (Calif.), 1939.

alike enemies of bourgeois cage-life. In the same *jungles* near a railroad-yard there may be camped at the same time migratory workers wandering from job to job, *yeggs* fleeing the police, genuine *tramps* who go no further than minor thieving but never work at all, and a miscellaneous rabble of temporary wanderers. The average intelligence of these public nuisances is probably even lower than that of habitual criminals. At the top are the congenital vagabonds, sometimes smart and amusing fellows, who choose to eschew what passes for civilization among us; at the bottom are the incurable drunkards, the drug addicts, the chronic out-of-works and beggars, the fugitives from unendurable jobs or wives, the runaway boys and girls, and the swarms of psychopaths. Some of these persons conduct themselves in a reasonably orderly manner according to codes of their own devising, but the great majority of them are incurably anti-social and teeter precariously upon the verge of crime. Most of the females are either harlots or ex-harlots, and many of the males are homosexuals. At the bottom of the pile are the poor wretches, mainly aging, who find road life increasingly insupportable, and so gravitate dismally toward the big cities, to become beggars and *mission-stiffs*.

It will be recalled that the first investigation of underworld speech in the Fifteenth and Sixteenth Centuries had to do with the talk of such vagrants rather than with the cant of more daring criminals. That speech still excites the interest of the curious, and there is a large literature upon it.[1] In part it is made up of borrowings from criminal cant, in part of loans from the argot of railroad men, and in part of what seem to be original inventions. Many of its terms

---

[1] Many titles are listed in Burke's bibliography. For what follows I have resorted mainly to Hobo Cant, by F. H. Sidney, *Dialect Notes*, Vol. V, Part II, 1919, pp. 41-42; Hobo Lingo, by Nicholas Klein, *American Speech*, Sept. 1926, pp. 650-53; The Argot of the Vagabond, by Charlie Samolar, the same, June, 1927, pp. 385-92; More Hobo Lingo, by Howard F. Barker, the same, Sept., 1927, p. 506; The Vocabulary of Bums, by Vernon W. Saul, alias K. C. Slim, the same, June, 1929, pp. 337-46; Junglese, by Robert T. Oliver, the same, June, 1932, p. 41; Bowery Terms, by H. E. Baronian. *Hobo News*, various dates from 1941 onward; A Dictionary of American Tramp and Underworld Slang, by Godfrey Irwin; London, 1931; Boy and Girl Tramps of America, by Thomas Minehan; New York, 1934; The Hobo, by Nels Anderson; Chicago, 1923; various articles by John Chapman in the New York *Daily News*, 1937-38; Sister of the Road, by Ben L. Reitman; New York, 1937, and the well-known books about tramps by Josiah Flynt (Willard).

are familiar to most Americans, *e.g.*, *jungles* (usually plural), the camp of vagabonds outside a city, sometimes occupied for years; *blind*, the front of a baggage-car, directly behind the engine-tender; *flop*, a place to sleep (*flop-house*, a cheap lodging-house); *mulligan*, a stew made in the jungles of any food the assembled hoboes can beg, borrow or steal; *slave-market*, an employment agency; *main stem* or *drag*, the main street of a town; *crummy*, lousy;[1] *to mooch*, to beg;[2] *hand-out*, food begged at a house-door;[3] *to panhandle*, *to ride the rods*;[4] *hoosegow*, a jail;[5] *bughouse*, crazy;[6] *barrel-house*, a low saloon;[7] *to pound the ties*, and *to rustle a meal*.[8]

Among the more esoteric terms recorded in the literature are *to go gooseberrying*, to rob clothes lines (*gooseberries*); *filling-station*, a small town (once a *tank-town* or *whistle-stop*); *bindle*, the hobo's roll of clothes and bedding (if he carries one he is a *bindle-stiff*); *scissors-bill*, a law-abiding citizen;[9] *rattler*, a freight-car; *red-ball*, a fast freight; *stash*, a hiding-place;[10] *clown*, a rustic policeman; *gay-cat*, a newcomer to the road; *jungle-buzzard*, one who partakes of a meal in a jungle without contributing anything to it;[11] *skid-road*, a city street frequented by hoboes; *tourist* or *snow-fly*, a tramp who goes South in Winter to escape the cold weather; *lump* or *poke-out*, a hand-out (if unwrapped it is a *bald-lump*); *locust* or *sap*, a policeman's stick; *to be fanned*, to be awakened by having it

1 Apparently of English origin.
2 An ancient word of varied meaning. It once meant to play truant, then to peddle things obtained free (*e.g.*, blackberries or wild salads), then to slink along, and finally to beg.
3 Now extended in common usage to mean anything obtained free, *e.g.*, a release by a press-agent. Partridge calls it American, and says that it reached England *c.* 1920.
4 *i.e.*, the steel framework under a freight-car.
5 Cf. AL4, p. 221, n. 1. It seems probable that the spread of *hoosegow* from the Mexican border was effected by hoboes.
6 Samolar, before cited, says that this "was coined by Boston Mary, a notorious female hobo."
7 Traced to 1883 by the DAE and marked an Americanism.
8 In the general sense of to acquire something by putting forth effort, to collect, to get together, to forage around for *to rustle* is traced by the DAE to *c.* 1846. *To rustle cattle*, *i.e.*, to steal them, is not found before 1893.
9 Applied derisively by members of the I. W. W. (*wobblies*) to migratory workers who refused to join their one-big-union.
10 Possibly from *cache*.
11 Samolar, before cited, says that the *buzzard* is "the lowest thing in Vagabondia" — next to the *mission-stiff*, who lives by getting converted at city missions. Says H. F. Kane in A Brief Manual of Beggary, *New Republic*, July 15, 1936: "Beggars who indulge in such hypocrisy and those who habitually frequent the Salvation Army headquarters and various missions represent the lowest and most unethical type of our profession."

applied to the soles of one's feet; *gandy-dancer*, a section hand; *hairpin*, a housewife; *pie-card*, a union card used as a credential in begging; *shark*, an employment agent; *man-catcher*, an employer seeking workers; *stew-bum*, a drunkard; *sit-down*, a meal in a house; *hump*, a mountain; *tin cow*, canned milk; *Peoria*, soup;[1] *drag*, a train; *reefer*, a refrigerator-car; *shack*, a brakeman; *to put it down*, to get off a train, and *to carry the banner*, to walk the streets all night, lacking money for lodging.

The *bums* who congregate in cities and live by panhandling have special names to designate men whose appeals to charity are helped by various disabilities, real or imaginary. A blind man is *Blinky*, a man who holds out that he is deaf and dumb is *D. & D.* (if he claims to be only deaf he is *Deafy*; if only dumb, *Dummy*), a one-legged or legless man is *Peggy*, a one-armed or armless man is *Wingy* or *Army*, a paralytic is *Crippy*, an epileptic is *Fritz*, a man with tremors is *Shaky*, and one pretending to be insane is *Nuts*. Those who exhibit sores, usually made with acid, are *blisters*; those who throw their bones out of joint are *throwouts* or *tossouts*, those who cough dismally are *ghosts*, and those who squat in front of churches or other public buildings and pretend to be helpless are *floppers*.[2] Cripples in general are *crips*. Those who repair umbrellas at street-corners are *mush-fakers* (an umbrella is a *mush*).[3] Those who make and sell objects of wire, *e.g.*, coat-hangers, are *qually-workers*. Those who gaze longingly into restaurants or bake-shops while they gnaw at prop bread-crusts are *nibblers*. Those who dig into garbage-cans are *divers*. Those who pretend to have fainted from hunger are *flickers*. Those with hard-luck stories are *weepers*. Those who practise minor con games are *dingoes*.[4] Those who pick up cigar and cigarette butts are *snipe-hunters*. Homosexuals are common among hoboes, and have a vocabulary of their own. They are called *wolves* or *jockers* and the boys accompanying them are *guntzels, gazoonies, punks, lambs* or *prushuns*.[5] There are generally recognized hobo nicknames for most towns and many railroads. Chicago is *the Village*, Cincinnati is *Death Valley*, Richmond, Va.,

1 Said to be not from the town name, but from *purée*.
2 I take all these names of specialists from Sister of the Road, by Ben L. Reitman, before cited, pp. 300–301.
3 From *mushroom*. Partridge traces it to 1821 in England.
4 I am indebted here to The Beggars are Coming, by Meyer Berger, *New Yorker*, March 11, 1939.
5 See The Language of Homosexuality, by G. Legman, in Sex Variants, by P. W. Henry; New York, 1941, Vol. II, pp. 1149–79.

is *Grantsville*, Pittsburg is *Cinders* or *the Burg*, Spokane, Wash., is *the Spokes*, Walla Walla, Wash., is *the Wallows*, Kalamazoo, Mich., is *the Zoo*, Columbus, O., is *Louse Town*, Little Rock, Ark., is *the Rock*, Joliet, Ill., is *Jolly*, Salt Lake City is *the Lake*, Toledo is *T. O.*, Butte, Mont., is *Brass*, Kansas City is *K. C.*, Cleveland is *Yap Town*, Minneapolis is *Minnie*, Washington is *the Cap*, Terre Haute, Ind., is *the Hut*, and New York is simply *the City*.[1]

Webster 1934 says that the origin of *hobo* is unknown. The DAE says that the suggestion that it comes from " Hello Beau " or " Ho, beau," an alleged greeting of railroad brakemen to tramps and of tramps to one another, "perhaps deserves special attention," but goes no further. Many other etymologies have been proposed. Jack London undertook, without evidence or plausibility, to derive the word from *oboe;* others have suggested that it comes from " Homeward bound," a slogan of soldiers returning from the Civil War; from *Hoboken;* from *homus bonum*, a good fellow; from *hoe-boy*, a California farm-hand of Gold Rush days; from " Ho, bo " or " Ho, bub," a greeting to boys; from " Ho, boy," the cry of mailmen along the Oregon Short Line in the 80s; and from a Japanese word meaning everywhere. All these sound improbable to me. The DAE's first example of the word comes from one of the magazine articles of Josiah Flynt, and is dated 1891. It came into wide use soon afterward.[2] *Tramp* has been traced in England to 1664, but it was not in general use in the United States until the 1880s. *Bum*, which is usually assumed to be derived from the German *bummler*, of the same meaning, first came into use in San Francisco, in the form of *bummer*, *c.* 1855. Applied to predatory soldiers, it was widely popular during the Civil War, but was not shortened to *bum* until *c.* 1870.[3]

Also hanging about the outskirts of the professional criminals are the drug addicts, the prostitutes, and the disorderly children (not a few of them with well-to-do and even rich parents) who

---

1 I take these from Underworld Place-Names, by D. W. Maurer, *American Speech*, Oct., 1940, pp. 340–42, and More Underworld Place-Names, by the same, the same, Feb., 1942, pp. 75–76. Some of the nicknames of railroads are listed in AL4, p. 582.

2 Charles J. Lovell, who has found examples earlier than the DAE's first, suggests that the word may be from the Chinese or some Indian language. He says that it apparently originated in the Seattle-Tacoma area.

3 See AL4, p. 156 and Supplement I, pp. 314–15.

train for entrance into one or another of the three groups. There is nothing inherently criminal about taking drugs, and in many cases it is not even anti-social, but the laws against it have made those who do so partners of the racketeers who supply them, just as Prohibition made even the most moderate boozer a partner of Al Capone. Moreover, small-time criminals themselves often become addicts, and all drug-sellers are criminals, so the relation between crime and addiction is close. The language of the vice and trade has been reported by David W. Maurer,[1] James A. Donovan, Jr.,[2] Victor Folke Nelson,[3] Milton Mezzrow[4] and Meyer Berger:[5] it varies according to the drug used, but has many general terms, some of them borrowed from the vocabulary of criminals. Maurer says that "it changes rapidly, for as soon as a word is generally known outside the fraternity it dies and another is coined to take its place." At the time of writing a wholesaler is a *big man*, a retailer is a *pedlar* or *connection* (not infrequently he is also an *ice-tong doctor*, i.e., an abortionist), a beginning addict is a *joy-popper* or *student*, a finished addict is a *gowster* or *junker*, and is said to have a *monkey on his back*, non-addicts are *square Johns* or *do-right people*, an addict well supplied is *on the mojo* and is said to be *in high*, a standard dose is a *ration, check, deck, bindle, block, card, cube, cap* or *piece*, a half size is a *bird's eye*, to adulterate is *to shave* and an adulterated piece is a *short piece*, a dose injected hypodermically is a *shot, pop, O, bang, jolt, fix-up* or *geezer*, a needle is a *spike, gun, joint, nail, luer,* or *artillery*, and a Federal narcotics agent is *whiskers, gazer, uncle,* or a *headache-man*. Opium is *tar, mud, black stuff, gum* or *hop*, morphine is *white stuff, Racehorse Charlie, sugar, white nurse* or *sweet stuff*, cocaine is *snow, happy dust, C, Heaven dust* or *coke*,[6] and marihuana is *muggles, Mary Warner, mezz, In-*

[1] "Junker Lingo," By-Product of Underworld Argot, *American Speech*, April, 1933, pp. 27–28; The Argot of the Underworld Narcotic Addict, the same, April, 1936, pp. 116–27, and Oct., 1938, pp. 179–92; Narcotic Argot, the same, Oct., 1936, p. 222; Speech of the Narcotic Underworld, *American Mercury*, Feb., 1946, pp. 225–29, and Marijuana Addicts and Their Lingo, *American Mercury*, pp. 571–75.

[2] Jargon of Marihuana Addicts, *American Speech*, Oct., 1940, pp. 336–37.

[3] Addenda to "Junker Lingo," *American Speech*, Oct., 1933, pp. 33–34.

[4] Really the Blues; New York, 1946.

[5] Tea For a Viper, *New Yorker*, March 12, 1938, pp. 47–50.

[6] See Supplement I, p. 346, for *coke* as an abbreviation of *Coca-Cola*.

dian hay, loco weed, Mary Jane, mooter, love weed, bambalacha, mohasky, fu, mu, moocah, grass, tea or *blue sage*.[1]

Opium smoking, says Maurer, is going out, largely because the drug is bulky and smoking it calls for prepared quarters and a somewhat elaborate apparatus. Many of the terms used by smokers are of Chinese origin, *e.g.*, *yen*, the craving; *yen-pok* or *fun* (pronounced *foon*), the prepared pill; *yen-shee-kwoi*, an unsophisticated smoker; *toy*, the box in which opium is kept; *yen-shee* or *gee-yen*, unburned gum; *suey-pow*, a sponge for cleaning the pipe, *yen-shee-gow*, a scraper for the same purpose, and *hop* with its derivative, *hophead*. In English the pipe is a *stem, saxophone, gong, gonger, dream-stick, joy-stick* or *bamboo*. An addict smoking is said to be *hitting* (or *beating*) *the gong, kicking the gonger, kicking the gong around*, or *laying the hip*, the preparation of the opium is called *cooking* (or *rolling*) *a pill*, an addict is a *cookie*, and one who cooks it for others is a *chef*. A marihuana smoker is a *viper, tea-man* or *reefing-man*, a cigarette is a *reefer*,[2] *stick, killer, goof-but, giggle-smoke, gyve* or *twist*, smoking is *viping* or *sending*, a place devoted to *sending* is a *pad* and a peddler is a *pusher*. " A smoker is *high* when contentment creeps over him "[3] and *down* on the morning after. The stump of a cigarette is a *roach*, whiskey is *shake-up*, and the juke-box or phonograph usually present in a *pad* is a *piccolo*. In the days when cocaine was a popular tipple a devotee was a *cokie, snowbird snifter* or *Charlie Coke*, to inhale the drug, often called *Bernice*, was *to go on a sleighride* or *to go coasting*, and a mixture of cocaine and morphine was a *whizz-bang* or *speed-ball*. The vo-

1 I take some of these from The Weed, *Time*, July 19, 1943, pp. 54–56. See also Marihuana Intoxication, by Walter Bromberg, *American Journal of Psychiatry*, Sept., 1934. I am indebted here to Dr. Roger S. Cohen, of Washington.

2 Mr. Hugh Morrison calls my attention to the fact that *reefer* is probably derived from the Mexican Spanish *grifa* or *grifo*, which is defined in Francisco J. Santamaria's Diccionario General de Americanismos; City of Mexico, 1942, as meaning "la persona intoxicada de drogas como la marihuana, la morfina o la cocaina." It was brought to the United States, along with marihuana itself, by Mexicans, who have a tendency, says Mr. Morrison, "to elide the *g* at the beginning of a word." The result was *reefa*, whence *reefer*, though Maurer says that among American addicts *greefo* survives as the name of the dried drug, which is also *muggles, bo-bo bush* or *potiguaya*. The cigarette is always a *reefer*. Webster 1934 and the DAE prefer the spelling *marijuana*, but Santamaria gives *marihuana*.

3 Berger, before cited, p. 47.

cabulary of addicts differs somewhat from place to place. Maurer records that in Chicago (1938) they called themselves *ads, junk-hogs, jabbers, knockers* and *smeckers*, terms apparently not in use elsewhere, and Sanders tells me that prisoners in the Virginia State Prison (1942) had a long list of local names for various mild narcotics and sedatives, *e.g., cement,* codeine; *ping pong,* pantopon; *yellow jacket,* nembutal; *green hornet,* sodium pentobarbital, and *blue devil,* sodium amytal. Most of these were suggested by the colors of the capsules. Elsewhere a sodium pentobarbital capsule is a *goof-pill*.[1]

Maurer says that prostitutes are so stupid and so little group-conscious that they have never developed "the technical vocabulary which characterizes all other criminal groups."[2] Nevertheless, there are trade terms that prevail widely among them, and some are of considerable antiquity, *e.g., landlady* or *madame,* the keeper of a brothel; *boarder,* an inmate; *hustler,* a street-walker; *friend,* a pimp; *hooker,* an old prostitute; *dark meat,* a colored prostitute; *stable,* a group of women under control of one padrone; *cathouse, crib* or *sporting-house,* a brothel; *call-house,* one with no internes, which sends for girls on demand; *to sit for company,* to be on the staff of a brothel; *to be busy,* to be engaged professionally, and *professor,* a house musician.[3] A *creep-joint* or *panel-house* is one in which patrons are robbed, a *roller* or *mush-worker* is a girl who robs them, and a *lush-worker* is one who specializes in drunks, but these last terms belong to the general vocabulary of criminals and are not peculiar to prostitutes. During World War II many patriotic young girls, some of them in their early teens, devoted themselves to entertaining soldiers and sailors on leave. They were usually called *V-girls.* Women who frequent taverns or night-clubs, getting a percentage on the drinks they induce male patrons to buy, are *taxi-drinkers, mixers, percentage-girls* or *sitters.*[4] *Crib,* a very low form of brothel; *cat-wagon,* a conveyance used by touring prosti-

---

[1] Pharmacist Sentenced for Sale of Pentobarbital, *Journal of the American Medical Association,* June 17, 1944.
[2] Prostitutes and Criminals Argots, *American Journal of Sociology,* Jan., 1939, p. 546.
[3] Berrey and Van den Bark list many other terms, but most of them seem to be nonce-words or localisms.
[4] Peter Tamony says in the San Francisco *News-Letter and Wasp,* Feb. 24, 1939, that in that city they are called *B-girls,* and derives the term from *to buzz* or *to put the bee on,* both meaning to wheedle money.

American Slang 683

tutes, and *gun-boat*, a boat used for the same purpose,[1] seem to be obsolete, or nearly so.

The line separating the criminal argots from ordinary slang is hard to draw, and in certain areas the two are mixed. Consider, for example, the language of showfolks. At the top it is highly respectable, and some of it is of considerable antiquity, but on the level of traveling carnivals and low city theatres it coalesces with that of hoboes, Gipsies and thieves. Similarly, the transient slang of jitterbugs and other incandescent youngsters is connected through that of jazz musicians with that of drug-addicts. All showfolks who work under canvas say they are *on the show*, not *in* it, just as pickpockets say they are *on the cannon* and yeggs that they are *on the heavy*, and there are many circus and carnival terms that are identical with criminal terms, *e.g.*, *grift*, an illicit or half-illicit means of getting money; *benny*, an overcoat; *shill*, one hired to entice customers; *cheaters*, spectacles; *mouthpiece*, a lawyer; *to lam*, to depart hastily; *hoosier*, a yokel; *home-guard*, those who do not travel; *leather*, a pocketbook; *moniker*, a person's name or nickname; *office*, a signal, and the various names for money, ranging from *ace* for a $1 bill to *grand* for $1,000.[2] This lingo has been studied by David W. Maurer,[3] George Milburn,[4] Percy W. White,[5] E. P. Conkle,[6] A. J. Liebling,[7] Marcus H. Boulware,[8] Joe Laurie, Jr.,[9] and Charles Wolverton.[10] It is divided into halves, the first of which is that of showfolks proper, who are inclined to be an austere and even somewhat prissy lot, and the second that of their hangers-on, some of whom, as we have just seen, are hardly to be

---

1 The Alexandria (Mo.) *Commercial*, June 22, 1876, reported the hanging of Bill Lee for the murder of Jessie McCarty, one of the crew of a Mississippi *gun-boat*. I am indebted for this to Mr. Franklin J. Meine, editor of Nelson's Encyclopedia.
2 I take most of these from The Language of the Lots, in Hey, Rube, by Bert J. Chipman; Hollywood (Calif.), 1933, pp. 193-97.
3 Carnival Cant; a Glossary of Circus and Carnival Slang, *American Speech*, June, 1931, pp. 327-37.
4 Circus Words, *American Mercury*, Nov., 1931, pp. 351-54.
5 A Circus List, *American Speech*, Feb., 1926, pp. 282-283; More About the Language of the Lot, the same, June, 1928, pp. 413-15.
6 Carnival Slang, *American Speech*, Feb., 1928, pp. 253-54.
7 Masters of the Midway, *New Yorker*, Aug. 12, 1939, pp. 21-25.
8 Circus Slang, Pittsburgh *Courier*, March 20 and 27, 1943.
9 Lefty's Notebook, *Variety*, April 7, 1943.
10 Mysteries of the Carnival Language, *American Mercury*, June, 1936, pp. 227-31.

distinguished from malefactors. But each moiety knows and uses the argot of the other.

That of the showfolks proper is picturesque and often amusing. "Few occupations," says Maurer, "have so colorful a technical vocabulary." A clown is a *paleface*, a *whiteface* or *Joey*, a tattooed man is a *picture-gallery*, a bareback rider is a *rosinback*, a contortionist is a *frog*, *bender* or *Limber Jim*, a freak or snake-charmer is a *geek*, and all performers are *kinkers*. The owner of the show is the *governor* or *gaffer*, the head electrician is *shanty*,[1] a musician is a *windjammer*, a palmist is a *mitt-reader*, a phrenologist is a *bump-reader*, the stake-drivers are the *hammer gang*, those who load and unload the show are *razorbacks*, elephant handlers are *bull men* or *bull hookers*, the barker outside a sideshow is the *spieler*, his talk is the *opening* or *ballyhoo*,[2] a bouncer is a *pretty boy*, a newcomer to the show is a *first-of-May* or *Johnny-come-lately*, and the august master of ceremonies is the *equestrian director*.[3]

Any elephant, male or female, is a *bull*, a zebra is a *convict*, a hippopotamus is a *hip*, a leopard is a *spot* and a tiger is a *stripe*, but any feline is a *cat*. All tents save the *cook-house* and the *clown-alley* are *tops*, and all concessions are *joints* — the *juice-joint* (refreshment-stand), *mug-joint* (photograph-gallery), *grab-joint* (eating-stand), *mitt-joint* (fortune-teller's tent), *sinker-joint* (doughnut-stand), *grease-joint* (hamburger-stand), and so on. All animal cages are *dens*, the show ground is the *lot*, a side-show is an *annex* or *kid-show*, the programme is the *Bible*, the dressing tent is the *pad-room*, the clowns' quarters are *clown-alley*, the latrine is a

---

[1] Apparently from *chandelier*.
[2] The origin of this term still puzzles etymologists. For some of their guesses see AL4, p. 188. In *American Speech*, Oct., 1945, pp. 184–86, Atcheson L. Hench suggested that it might come from a sea term meaning a small West Indian craft of odd rig, apparently a loan from the Carib through the Spanish. But the connection between this *ballyhoo* and the circus *ballyhoo* remains to be established. For the following I am indebted to Mr. Edw. J. Kavanagh, of New York: "In the 40s and 50s many of the traveling tent-shows were conducted by roving Irishmen who spoke both Gaelic and English. In those days the barker had two duties: to talk up the show and to pass the hat. The Gaelic word for *collect* is *bailinghadh*, pronounced *ballyoo* (dissyllable) by Munster speakers and *bállyoo* by Connacht speakers. At intervals in the show would be heard the cry, *Bailinghadh anois* (Collection now)." Other notes on *ballyhoo* are in *American Speech*, Feb., 1936, pp. 101 and 102.
[3] "*Ringmaster*," says Milburn, "is unknown to circus parlance. The stilted phraseology of the press-agent has influenced circus speech, and high-sounding words are often used in preference to simple ones."

donniker, the space behind the big top is the *backyard*, the cheap goods sold by concessionaires are *slum*, the powder used to make lemonade is *flookum*, the diner or club-car on the train is the *privilege-car*, a Ferris wheel is a *hoister*, a merry-go-round is a *jenny*, the last performance of the season is the *blow-off*, the trip to Winter quarters is the *home-run*, the South is *down yonder*, and the show itself is the *opery*. The traveling showmen have borrowed many terms from the stage, e.g., *props, stand, paper* (posters), *dark* (closed), *B. O.* (box office), and *at liberty* (out of work), and others, as I have noted, from the argot of criminals. An outsider is a *clem* or *gilly*, and Milburn says that the old cry of " Hey-rube!," raised when local rowdies attacked a show, is now supplanted by " Clem! "[1]

The larger traveling shows are followed by all sorts of minor enterprisers — operators of gambling devices, sellers of quack medicines, street peddlers, and so on. Some of these are tolerated and others simply exercise their inalienable right to flock along. The street peddlers, who call themselves *pitchmen*, frequently undertake independent tours, and not a few of them have covered the whole country. Their trade journal is the *Billboard* (Cincinnati), which also caters to all other outdoor showmen, and every week they contribute to it what they call *pipes, i.e.*, news reports from the field, describing business conditions and telling of the movements of pitchmen. There are *high* pitchmen and *low*, the former addressing their customers from automobiles or platforms, and the latter operating from the ground level, with their goods displayed on or in a suitcase (*keister*) set upon a tripod (*tripe*). The contents of the *keister* are the *flash*, the audience is the *tip*, to sell is *to turn*, listeners who fade away without buying are *mooches* and are said *to blow*, those who buy are *monkeys, chumps* or *naturals*, when business is bad it is *larry*, to hand out merchandise is *to duke*, and confederates, if they are used, are *boosters, lumpers, sticks* or *shills*. Money is *gelt, take, kale, scratch* or *geedus*. *To cut up pipes* or *jackpots* is to gossip or boast. An indoor stand is a *jam-pitch*.

[1] The English showmen have an entirely different vocabulary. Specimens of it are given in Circus Slang, by Pegasus, *World's Fair* (London), April 3, 1937, and What is an *Auguste?*, London *Observer*, Dec. 15, 1935. The technical vocabulary of tumblers is given in School for Tumblers, *New Yorker*, Feb. 26, 1938, pp. 16-17. That of the roller-skating rinks is in They're Taking the Kinks Out of Rinks, by Pete Martin, *Saturday Evening Post*, May 13, 1944, p. 89.

The various specialists have their own names. One who sells fruit- or vegetable-squeezers is a *juice-worker*, one who takes subscriptions (usually for farm papers) is a *paper man, leaf worker, name-gatherer* or *sheet worker*, one who sells medicines (now usually vitamins) is a *med worker*, and one who deals in horoscopes is a *scape worker*. Plated ware is *floozum*, metal polish is *flookum*, knives are *shivs*, cement is *gummy*, spot-removers or other cleaners are *rads* (from *eradicator*), watches are *blocks*, billfolds are *pokes*, fountain-pens are *ink-sticks*, spectacles are *googs*, a ring is a *hook*, corn cures are *corn punk*, handkerchiefs are *wipes*, and flower bulbs are *horn nuts*. Household articles in general are *gadgets*, and any sort of electrical device is a *coil*. To disperse an audience is *to slough the tip*. To break sales resistance is *to turn the tip*.[1] One of the gifts of pitchmen to the general vocabulary seems to be *phony* or *phoney*, the origin of which still engages lexicographers.[2]

[1] I am indebted here to Mr. William J. Sachs (Bill Baker), who conducts the Pipes for Pitchmen department in the *Billboard*. Many pitchmen's terms are given in Something for Nothing, by John J. Flynn, *Collier's*, Oct. 8, 1932, pp. 15–48; The *Billboard*: Miscellaneous Entertainment, by Alva Johnston, *New Yorker*, Sept. 12, 1936, pp. 31–36; Alagazam, by N. T. Oliver (Nevada Ned), as told to Wesley Winans Stout, *Saturday Evening Post*, Oct. 19, 1929, pp. 26–80; About Carnivals and Pitchmen, by Irving Baltimore, *Editor*, Dec. 2, 1916, p. 518; Pitchmen, by Maurice Zolotow, *Saturday Evening Post*, Sept. 25, 1943, pp. 12–13 and 37–39; Pitchmen Find Business Terrible, *Life*, July 31, 1939, p. 24; Step Closer, Gents, by William D. O'Brien, New York *World-Telegram*, July 6, 1936, and Pitchman's Cant, by Ruth Mulvey, *American Speech*, April, 1942, pp. 89–93. The last is not without errors. The English pitchmen, who call themselves *grafters*, have a quite different vocabulary. Many of its terms are in The Grafters' Corner, by Semi-Detached (Arthur Pearson), *World's Fair*, Jan. 17, 1942, and some are reprinted in the *Billboard*, June 26, 1943, pp. 59–60.

[2] In The Origin of Phoney, *American Speech*, April, 1937, pp. 108–110, Peter Tamony offers strong evidence that it came originally from *fawney*, traced in England to 1781, but the dictionaries continue to mark it "origin uncertain." *Fawney* seems to be derived from Gaelic *fáinne*, a ring. In Grose's Classical Dictionary of the Vulgar Tongue, third ed., 1796, *fawney rig* (not *ring*) is defined as: "A common fraud, thus practised: A fellow drops a brass ring, double gilt, which he picks up before the party meant to be cheated, and to whom he disposes of it for less than its supposed, and ten times more than its real value." Partridge says that the use of *fawney* or *phoney* in the general sense of fraudulent originated in the United States, and was naturalized in England c. 1920. In The American Tramp, *Contemporary Review*, Aug., 1891, p. 253, Josiah Flynt listed *fawney man* as a seller of bogus jewelry. I am indebted here to Mr. Edgar Gahan, of Westmount, Quebec. For other

American Slang

The fakers who hire stores and stage auction sales of phoney jewelry, silverware and other such gimcrackery constitute a variety of pitchmen, somewhat below the salt. Their sales are known in the trade as *grind* auctions. Their business, of course, calls for much more capital than the ordinary pitchman can command, but otherwise they follow his methods pretty closely, especially those he uses in a *jam-pitch*. A study of their argot, by Fred Witman, was published in *American Speech* in 1928.[1] It includes many of the usual pitchmen's terms, and also the following:

> Cold turkey. A price at which merchandise will be sold to the first bidder who names it, without any effort to induce a higher bid.
> Drop, *v*. To sell.
> Freeze, *v*. To alarm the customers by some transparent fraud or other blunder.
> Line. Double the cost.
> Lift, *v*. To recognize imaginary bids, and so stimulate further bidding.
> Mahula, *v*. To go broke.[2]
> Minch. An undesirable spectator.[3]
> Mischcowain, *v*. To monkey around.[4]
> Mitsia. A flashy but defective diamond.[5]
> O. G. (Old girl). A woman who frequents sales without buying.
> Peter Funk. A decoy bidder on articles that fail to bring the prices hoped for.[6]
> Yinceth, *v*. To trim a sucker.[7]
> Zagger. A cheap watch movement in a showy case.

The stage in its various forms shares with the newspapers and the radio the burden of disseminating neologisms in the Republic,

---

proposed etymologies see AL4, p. 187. Also, see Supplement I, p. 511, n. 1; *Phoney*, London *Times Literary Supplement*, Jan. 6 and 20, 1940, pp. 7 and 31, and Origin of *Phoney*, London *Observer*, April 7, 1940.

1 Jewelry Auction Jargon, June, pp. 375–76.
2 The late Dr. William Rosenau of Baltimore, a distinguished Hebrew scholar, told me that *mahula* should be spelled *mechuleh*. It is derived from the Hebrew verb *kala*, signifying to finish and is commonly used for to go bankrupt.
3 Probably a corruption of the German *mensch*.
4 According to Dr. Rosenau *mischcowain* (in which the second *c* should be *k*) is derived from the Hebrew verb *schokaw*, to lie down.

The noun formed from it is *mischkov*, a bed. "Consequently," said Dr. Rosenau, "*mischkowain* in its dual plural form with the -*aim* ending has reference to two persons lying down together and indulging in cohabitation."

5 The correct form is *metziah*. It signifies a find or bargain, and is from the Hebrew verb *motzoh*, a find.
6 Dr. Louise Pound showed in *Peter Funk*, *American Speech*, Feb., 1929, pp. 183–86, that this curious term was in use in New York so early as 1834. It was also used by Walt Whitman in the New Orleans *Crescent*, March 13, 1848.
7 Also, *to yentz*. Witman says: "It also has another meaning, but because of postal regulations I shall omit it." See Supplement I, p. 435.

and its chief organ, *Variety*, has probably set afloat more of them than any other single agency.[1] But in addition to their services in this cultural field stagefolks also use many peculiar terms of their own. Some of them go back to the days of Shakespeare, but most, of course, are more recent, and there is a constant birth of new ones. The first effort that I am aware of to compile an American glossary was made by the highly respectable but stage-struck Dr. Brander Matthews in 1917.[2] In the following list [3] I have omitted terms whose meaning is known to everyone, *e.g., star, box-office, ingénue, one-night stand, angel, hand, S. R. O., properties, understudy, tryout* and *free-list*.[4]

Ad lib, *v.* To insert lines not in the script.

Apron. That part of the stage between the curtain and the footlights.

Backing. Scenery hung behind doors, windows and other openings in the set.

Back-stage. Behind the scenes.[5]

---

[1] See Supplement I, pp. 337-38.

[2] In an article in the *Billboard*, Dec. 22, pp. 8 and 9. It was reprinted as The Vocabulary of the Show Business in his Principles of Playmaking; New York, 1919, pp. 251-64.

[3] In compiling it I have made use of Trouper Talk, by Gretchen Lee, *American Speech*, Oct., 1925, pp. 36 and 37; Stage Terms, by Percy W. White, the same, May, 1926, pp. 436-37; Theatrical Lingo, by Ottille Amend, the same, Oct., 1927, pp. 21-23; Jewels From a Box-Office: The Language of Show Business, by Arnold Moss, the same, Oct., 1936, pp. 219-22; Speech of the Theatre, by W. P. Daggett, *Quarterly Journal of Speech Education*, April, 1923, pp. 154-62; Show Talk and Stage Slang, by Joseph Arnold, *Bookman*, June, 1929, pp. 33-64; A Glossary of Stage Terms and Parlance, in A Handbook For the Amateur Actor, by Van H. Cartmell; New York, 1936, pp. 85-98; A Stageland Dictionary, by Walter J. Kingsley and Loney Haskell, New York *Times*, Oct. 14, 1923, section 8, p. 4; Broadway Glossary, in So You Want To Go Into the Theatre?, by Shepard Traube; Boston, 1936, pp. 243-47; and Theatrical Workers' Slang and Jargon, in Lexicon of Trade Jargon, Vol. III, compiled by the Federal Writers' Project in New York. The argot of the English stage is in A Dictionary of Stage Terms, in Theatre and Stage, edited by Harold Downs; London, 1934, pp. 91-104; English Theatrical Terms and Their American Equivalents, by Henry J. Heck, *American Speech*, Aug., 1930, p. 468, and English Show Slang, *Billboard*, Dec. 18, 1915, p. 193. It is also discussed in *Notes and Queries*, Oct. 24 and Nov. 21, 1942. A bibliography of books and articles on both American and English theatrical argot is in Burke's Literature of Slang, pp. 119 and 120.

[4] *Free-list* is marked an Americanism by the DAE and traced to 1845, but Sir St. Vincent Troubridge, in Notes on DAE, *American Speech*, Dec., 1946, p. 276, gives an English example dated 1806.

[5] In England *to go backstage* is *to go round*. In *American Speech*, Oct., 1942, p. 203, Dwight L. Bolinger shows that *back-stage* has come into general use in the sense of under-cover, not claiming attention.

Bit. A small part.

Blow up, or dry up, or balloon, *v.* To forget one's lines.

Borders. Short curtains or strips of scenery (foliage, etc.) behind the top of the proscenium arch and across the top of the stage; also lights along the sides thereof.

Box set. A setting enclosed on all sides save the one opening to the audience.

Break. The end of a performance.

Business. Any action save spoken dialogue.

Dog. An audience outside New York. To try out a play on the road is *to try it on the dog*.

Doubling. Playing more than one part in the same play.

Dressing. Filling a house with pass-holders likely to applaud.[1]

Drop. A flat, hanging piece of scenery.

Entrance. Any avenue of ingress to the stage, as a door in scenery; also, the actor's use of it.

Fat. Said of a part that gives the performer a good chance to show off his talents.

Featured. Said of an actor whose name appears in the advertising of a play directly below that of the play itself, usually preceded by *with*.

Flies. The region above the stage opening.

Foots. Footlights.[2]

Frohman. The manager of a theatre on the road.[3]

Front of the house. The lobby, box-office and manager's office.[4]

George Spelvin. A name used on play-bills for a minor actor in a walk-on rôle, or to conceal the fact that an actor whose real name is given in one rôle is doubling in another.[5]

Ghost. The company treasurer. The *ghost* is said to *walk* on payday.

Good theatre. Effective on the stage, though maybe deficient in artistic plausibility.

Grip. A stagehand.

Ground-cloth. The stage carpet.[6]

Ham. A bad actor.[7]

[1] The expedient of hiring professional acclaimers has never been in general use on the American stage. Its home is Paris, where the *claque* has been an institution for years. It has produced many terms of its own, *e.g.*, *rieur*, or *rigolard*, one who laughs, *pleureur*, a weeper; *bisseur*, one who cries *bis!* (*i.e.*, encore); *chevaliers du lustre* (knights of the chandelier); *chatouilleur* (tickler), a *claqueur* who devotes himself to one performer. For the Vienna opera *claque* see My Life in the Claque, by Joseph Wechsberg, *New Yorker*, Feb. 19, 1944, pp. 22–25.

[2] Called *floats* in England.

[3] From the name of Charles Frohman (1860–1915), the most celebrated New York manager of the 1900 era. Now obsolete.

[4] In America it is *out front*; in England, *in front*.

[5] See Who is *George Spelvin?*, by Gilbert Swan, *American Mercury*, Nov., 1943. Mr. Swan says that *Spelvin* was invented by Edward Abeles. During one period of three years he appeared in 20,000 performances of 210 different parts.

[6] In England it is the *stage-cloth*.

[7] Possibly from *Hamlet*, a part that all the old-time bad actors either aspired to play or claimed to have played. But the Lexicon of Trade Argot prefers to derive it from the fact that actors formerly used ham-

Heavy. An actor playing serious rôles; the villain of the old-time melodramas.

House. The audience.

House stuff. Equipment which is the property of the theatre rather than of the company.

Legitimate. Any theatrical enterprise devoted to the production of actual plays by living actors, and excluding musical comedy, vaudeville, burlesque, melodrama and the like.

Melodrama. Originally a play with music; now a play marked by scenes of extravagant theatricality.

Mugging. Overdoing facial pantomime.

O. P. (opposite prompt). The side of the stage to the actor's left. Now obsolete.

Open cold, v. To present a play in New York without a tryout elsewhere.

Opry-house. An old, dirty and poorly equipped theatre.

Palmy days. The legendary great days of the stage, often recalled by old actors.

Paper. Free tickets. A *house* is said to be *papered* when it includes many persons admitted on passes.

Plot. The scheme or plan of a performance. The stage hands follow a *scene-plot*, the electricians a *lighting-plot*, and the property-men a *prop-plot*.

Pop. The traditional nickname for the stage doorkeeper.

Prompt side. The side of the stage to the actor's right.[1]

Rep company. A company presenting a répertoire of plays on the road.

Road, or sticks. Any place in the United States save New York.[2]

Script. The typescript of a play.

---

fat instead of cold cream to remove their make-up, and this is supported by a variant form, *ham-fatter*. The term is not listed by Partridge, but it is known in England, and the well-known critic and dramatist, St. John Ervine, used it in the title of an article, *Ham* Acting, in the London *Observer*, Feb. 9, 1936. On July 26, 1938, Stephen Williams, dramatic critic of the London *Evening Standard*, printed in his paper an article (Shakespeare as She is Spoke, p. 7) in which he said: "We hear a great deal about *ham* acting nowadays. As far as I can judge, *ham* acting is the habit of rolling sonorous speeches round the tongue and delivering them with extravagant relish to the gallery. Well, why not? Recent performances of Shakespeare have convinced me that the decay of *ham* acting is a deplorable thing."

Ervine, in the article mentioned, quoted Harcourt Williams as saying, in Four Years of the Old Vic; London, 1936: "I suppose it is an abbreviation of what used to be called *hambone*." In the *Stage* (London), June 1, 1944, Edgar T. Hayes said that *hambone* meant an amateur. *Ham* is also used to designate an amateur radio operator. In this sense it originated in the United States, but Partridge says that it was adopted in England, c. 1936. It is used likewise in the United States to signify any inept and amateurish workman or other person.

[1] Now obsolete. So called because the prompter, now extinct save in stock companies, was stationed there.

[2] In England any place outside London is the *provinces*, and *on the road* is *on tour*.

American Slang

Show business. The stage in all its branches.[1]

Side. A page in the typescript of an actor's speeches, given to him to memorize.

Speech. A unit of an actor's spoken part; it may be one word or a thousand.

Split week. A week on the road divided between two or more towns.

Stand. The engagement of a company, as in *week-stand*.

Straw-hat, hayloft, cowshed or barn. A Summer theatre.[2]

Tank-town. A small town.[3]

Teaser. A short curtain or strip of scenery along the top of the proscenium arch.

Thinking part. A part including no spoken lines.

Tom company. A company presenting "Uncle Tom's Cabin" in the back country, now obsolete.

Top. The price of the most expensive seat in the house, excluding those in the boxes.

Tormenters. Fixed wings or curtains at the sides of the stage, directly behind the proscenium arch.

Trouper. An experienced actor, especially on the road.

Turkey. A failure.

Up-stage. Away from the audience; said of an actor of haughty mien.

Walk on, *v.* To play a part with no lines and little business.

William Winter.[4] A dramatic critic.

Vaudeville, in its heyday, had a rich argot of its own, some of which survives in the general vocabulary of the stage:[5]

Actors' Bible. Originally, the New York *Clipper;* now *Variety.*

Ape. A performer who filches material from others.

Blue. Said of a line or piece of business with obscene overtones.

Brutal brothers. An act in which the performers beat each other up to draw laughs.

[1] The article is usually dropped. Thyra Samter Winslow's *Show Business* (a book) was published in 1926. Some analogues have appeared, *e.g., shipping business* without the article: *Congressional Record*, Dec. 6, 1945, p. 11724, col. 2.

[2] See The *Straw Hat* Theatre, by Joseph Corré, *American Notes & Queries*, July and Aug., 1945, pp. 51–54 and 67–69.

[3] "It consists of nothing but a railroad water-tank." In recent years *filling-station* is substituted.

[4] From the name of the critic of the New York *Tribune* (1836–1917). Now obsolete. In compiling this list I have had the experienced aid of my old colleague, George Jean Nathan. Some of the terms come from England. The NED traces *house* to 1662–63, *business* to 1671, *drop* to 1779, *heavy* to 1826 and *ghost* to 1853, but it marks *grip* U.S. and traces it to 1886.

[5] Many of its terms are listed in Stage Terms, by Percy W. White, *American Speech*, May, 1926, pp. 436–37, and in Vol. III (Theatrical Workers' Slang and Jargon) of the Federal Writers' Project Lexicon of Trade Jargon. The word *vaudeville* was borrowed from the French. The DAE shows that it began to come into use in the United States in the Civil War era. The English prefer *variety*, though it is possible that the latter may be an Americanism. The NED's first example of its use is dated 1886, but the DAE traces it in the United States to 1882, and in the form of *varieties* to 1849.

Dead-pan. A comedian who shows no facial expression.
Deuce spot. The second place on the bill.
Dumb act. One in which there are no spoken words.
Excess-baggage. A wife or other woman traveling with a male performer but not working in the show.
Feeder, or straight man. A performer who serves a comedian by drawing out his jocosities.
Harp. An Irish comedian.
Headliner. A performer whose name appears at the head of the list of acts in the theatre's billing, usually in larger letters than the others.[1]
Heat. A performance.
Hokum, or hoke, or gonk. A time-worn gag, speech, situation or piece of business that is known to wring applause or tears from any audience.
Hoofer, or heel-beater. A dancer.
In one. Said of an act that works before a *drop* hung in the first groove, the nearest to the footlights.[2]
Leaptick. A mattress on which an acrobat lands; also, by metaphor, the pad used to make the belly of a comedian supposed to be fat.
Monologist. A performer offering a monologue, usually without songs or dances.
Neat. Said of a dancing act that avoids buffoonery or acrobatics.
Patter. The lines spoken by a hoofer, acrobat, magician, animal trainer, or other such performer.
Plant. A person in the audience — sometimes the leader of the orchestra — put there to feed a performer.
Pratfall. A fall on the backside.[3]
Production. An act with elaborate scenery and requiring a company of some size.
Professor. The leader of the house orchestra.[4]
Routine. The text or programme of an act.
S. and D. Song and dance.
Single. A performer working alone.
Sister act. Two women working together, usually billed as sisters.
Sitting on their hands. Said of an audience chary with applause.
Slap-stick. An implement used by comedians. It consists of two pieces of wood, in shape like barrel-staves, fastened together at one end, usually with a handle at that end. When it is brought down on the fundament of another performer it makes a loud noise.
Small time. Vaudeville circuits on which performers were required to perform more than three times a day.
Spot. The place of a turn on the bill.[5]
Stop the show, v. To win so much applause that it causes a delay in the performance.

[1] In England a *headliner* is a *top-liner*.
[2] In England *in one* is *in a front cloth*.
[3] Often but erroneously written *prattfall*. The NED traces *prat*, the buttocks, to 1567 and marks it "origin unknown." See Pratt on Prat(t) Falls, by Theodore Pratt, *Variety*, Nov. 29, 1944.
[4] In England he is the *conductor*.
[5] *To play the first spot* is to open the show; in England it is *to play them in*. It is considered undesirable, for the audience is still coming in.

Subway circuit. All the theatres within reach of the New York subways.

Supper-turn. A turn forced to go on at 6 P.M., when the audience in a continuous-performance house is smallest.

Tin-pan alley. The region in New York in which the publishers of popular songs have their offices.[1]

Turn. Any sort of act.

Union. The musicians of the house orchestra; used facetiously.

Vamp. The music played by the orchestra before a performer launches into his song or dance.[2]

Many of these terms, like those given in the preceding vocabulary, are now more or less obsolete, for vaudeville has decayed sadly. At the same time the minstrel show has almost disappeared.[3] Meanwhile, the argot of burlesque, which was once virtually identical with that of vaudeville, has had to be enlarged to take in the vocabulary of strip-tease. The latter was listed by H. M. Alexander in his " Strip Tease " in 1938.[4] From his list, and the help of other authorities,[5] I have put together the following:

Boston version. A show purged of its worst indecencies.[6]

Bump, v. To thrust the hips forward.[7]

Burleycue. Burlesque.

Bust-developer. A performer who croons off-stage while the strip-teaser is at work.

Cacky. Obscene.

Catching the bumps. One of the jobs of the drummer in the orchestra.

Flannel-mouth, or stooge. A *straight man* who acts as *feeder* to the comedian.[8]

1 Its location has varied as the show business has moved uptown. Edward B. Marks says in They All Sang; New York, 1935, p. 74, that the term was invented by Monroe H. Rosenfeld, author of Take Back Your Gold, With All Her Faults I Love Her Still, and other masterpieces of the 80s and 90s.
2 The NED traces *vamp* in this sense to 1882.
3 Some specimens of its argot: *boat*, a train; *burr-head*, a minstrel; *eleven forty-five*, the daily parade of the company; *excess-baggage*, a poor performer; *firstie*, a novice; *high C*, a cornetist; *lumber-buster*, a wooden-shoe dancer; *smut*, burnt cork; *taps*, a drummer; and *wind-jammer*, a trombonist. There is an amusing account of the curious ways of the old-time minstrels in They All Sang, by Edward B. Marks, before cited.
4 New York, pp. 120–23.
5 Especially Mr. Harry Van Hoven.
6 A reference to the fact that Boston has the strictest censorship in the United States.
7 A correspondent writes: " The *bump* is a terrific convulsion in which the lower abdomen, with special emphasis on the *mons pubis*, is shot suddenly forward while the legs and upper torso remain motionless — a sort of double-jointed, free-wheeling hip action. It may be repeated a number of times while a drum beats out the tempo and the artiste clings to a piece of stage drapery."
8 See *feeder* in the Vaudeville wordlist.

Flash. The sudden exposure at the end of an act, presumably of the entire carcass.
  Gadget. A G-string.
  Grind, *v.* To revolve the backside.
  Meat-show. A burlesque show offering strip-teasers.
  Milk, *v.* To wring applause and recalls.
  Painted on the drop. Said of a performer who has no lines to speak.
  Panel. A strip-teaser's diaphanous draperies.
  Parade. The preliminary march across the stage in full costume.
  Quiver, *v.* To rotate or oscillate the breasts.
  Set-up. The performer's figure.
  Shimmy, *v.* To shake the whole body.
  Skull. A comedian's grimace.
  Sleeper-jump. A dressing-room remote from the stage.
  Slinger, or peeler, or shucker, or stripper. A strip-teaser.
  Snake. A sinuous and accomplished teaser.
  Third banana. A comedian who submits to assault by another comedian.
  Trailer. The strip-teaser's exhibitionary strut before beginning to take off her clothes.
  Wham. A strip-tease in which the teaser removes virtually all her clothes.
  Wheel. A circuit of burlesque theatres.
  Yock. A loud laugh.[1]

The recurring efforts to put down strip-teasing have produced, in many cities, rules for its regulation. In New York, in 1941, those rules were as follows:

> Strippers must perform on a darkened stage; all *bumps* must be toward the wings, not frontwise; during *grinds* the hands may stray, but they mustn't touch; the *flash* (the apparent moment of complete nudity) must be at one of the wings, may only last for eight bars of music, and may expose only one breast.[2]

Before the days of the strip-tease the women of burlesque were largely of Brünnhildian build, as indeed were the chorus girls of musical comedy before 1900. They were called *hill-horses* or *beef-trusts*, the last a reference to Billy Watson's famous " Beef Trust " company, the billing of which announced that it offered " two tons of women." When less massive girls began to appear they were called *ponies*. But *hill-horse* disappeared from memory with the old-time horse-cars, and was supplanted by *big horse*.[3] In the 1900 era

[1] My invention of the sober *ecdysiast* to denominate a strip-teaser is described in Supplement I, pp. 584–87. It was denounced as snobbish by Gypsy Rose Lee, the queen of the profession, but made its way in both the United States and England. In the Los Angeles *Daily News*, Sept. 27, 1944, p. 26, it was refined to *ecdysiste*, apparently suggested by *artiste*.
[2] Lid is off Strip-Teasing, by Paul Ross, *PM*, April 1, 1941, p. 23.
[3] The Bigger They Are –, by Lee

there was a distinction between a *chorus-girl* and a *show-girl* or *clothes-horse*. The former simply hoofed and sang in the ensembles; the latter was a more pretentious performer who wore expensive costumes and sometimes had a few lines. In recent years there has appeared the *swing-girl*, who, when shows play seven nights a week, relieves other girls on their nights off.[1] Chorus girls apparently speak the argot of whatever branch of the theatre they happen to adorn, but they also have some terms of their own. In 1943 Earl Wilson, saloon editor of the New York *Evening Post* and a recognized expert on Broadway lexicography, was reporting that those then laboring in the night-clubs were using *to fluff off* to signify getting rid of an unwelcome admirer, *falsies* for the pads which converted them from perfect 32's to perfect 34's,[2] and " Don't give me that *jive* " or " Don't give me that *routine* " as a set reply to honeyed advances.[3] From time to time afterward he added other terms, *e.g.*, *square* or *creep* for a stupid and tiresome person,[4] *body* for any man, *to give him the B.R.U.* (from *brushoff*) for to get rid of him, *to smoke up* for to smarten up, *fractured* for under the influence of alcohol, and *sex appeal* for the aforesaid *falsies*.[5] The ladies of the more decorous ballet, whether Russian [6] or operatic, also have a trade language, made up chiefly of technical terms,[7]

Mortimer, New York *Mirror*, Jan. 12, 1941, magazine section, p. 3. Under date of Jan. 17, 1941, Mr. Mortimer wrote to me: " I have never heard *hill-horse* used during the dozen-odd years I've been on Broadway. I asked Jack Lait about it too, but he doesn't remember it either. [Mr. Lait is editor of the New York *Mirror* and was formerly a theatrical manager. His connection with the theatre began in 1908.] It seems to me that I first heard *big-horses* used seven or eight years ago by Earl Carroll at a rehearsal. He was giving a pep talk to the cast."

1 Lee Mortimer in the New York *Mirror*, Feb. 16, 1947.
2 In the pre-strip-tease age such a pad was called a *heart*.
3 It Happened Last Night, Oct. 6, 1941.
4 Borrowed from the jive vocabulary. Wilson reported in the *Evening Post*, Sept. 28, 1945, that when he appealed to Toots Shor, a Broadway savant, for precise definitions of *square* and *creep* he was told: " A *square* don't know from nothin' and a *creep* is worse'n a jerk."
5 The male ringmaster of a night-club show is always the *master of ceremonies* or *m.c.*, and from the latter has come the verb *to m.c.* In England he is the *compère*, a French word meaning originally a godfather, but extended in slang to mean a crony or the confederate of a quack.
6 Many of the female ballet stars are English, but nearly all use Russian names.
7 It is to be found in The Ballet-Lover's Pocket-Book, by Kay Ambrose; New York, 1945, and The Borzoi Book of Ballet, by Grace Robert; New York, 1946, pp. 351-62.

but so far as I have been able to discover there is no special lingo of opera proper.

There remain the theatre auxiliaries — for example, the box-office crew and the corps of stage-hands. The vocabulary of the former was printed in the New York *Times* in 1935,[1] and that of the latter in *American Speech* in 1928.[2] From the box-office list I take the following:

Annie Oakley, skull or clicker. A pass. See also *ducat*.

Box. The doorkeeper's receptacle for ticket-stubs; also the stubs themselves.

Buy. A ticket agency's purchase of seats.[3]

Count the box, *v*. To count the stubs in the *box*, which see.

Count the rack, *v*. To count the tickets left unsold in the box-office.

Crashing. Getting into a theatre without a ticket.

Dressing a house. Seating an audience in such a manner that it appears to be larger than it is, usually by leaving every other pair of seats vacant.

Ducat. A pass; also, a desirable seat.

Dumps. Tickets returned to the box-office by ticket-agencies.

Gyp. One who charges more than the legal premium on agency tickets.

Hardwood. Tickets for standing-room.

House-seats. A few seats reserved by the management for favored patrons or guests.

Ice. Commissions formerly paid to box-office men.

Murder. A heavy demand for tickets.

Rat, or digger. A sidewalk ticket speculator.

Schlag, or brutal. A very light demand for tickets.[4]

Steerer. One who directs persons turned away from the box-office to a ticket speculator.

Treasurer. A euphemism for ticket-seller.[5]

---

[1] The Strange Vernacular of the Box-Office, Oct. 30. See also The Forty Thieves, by Maurice Zolotow, *Reader's Digest*, Jan., 1944, pp. 91–94.

[2] American Stage-Hand Language, by J. Harris Gable, Oct., pp. 67–70.

[3] The anonymous author of the *Times* article says that there are two kinds of *buys*. One permits a return of 25% of the number brought to the box-office before 7:30 for a night performance and 1:30 P.M. for a matinée; the other is outright, and permits no return of unsold seats.

[4] *Schlag* is Yiddish (and German) for a blow.

[5] The author of the *Times* article says that his informants were Ernest A. MacAuley, treasurer of the Forty-sixth Street Theatre, and Joseph Keith, manager of the Leblang Ticket Agency. "Both Mr. MacAuley and Mr. Keith," he notes, "point out that these expressions are used only in Broadway ticket agencies and box-offices. There are many different idioms used by old-time treasurers, circus, vaudeville and road box-office men and motion picture cashiers that are never heard in the New York legitimate theatres."

American Slang

From Gable's "American Stage-Hand Language," lately cited, and from various articles in *Variety*, come these examples of the argot of stage crews:

Ad curtain. The curtain behind the *asbestos*, so called because it formerly bore advertisements.
Asbestos. The main curtain, usually fireproof.
Booth. The electrician's station.
Carps. The stage carpenter.
Clear. A warning to stage-hands that the curtain is about to go up.
Cover. A property-man who stands in the wings during gunplay on the stage, to discharge a pistol in case that of the actor fails to go off.
Cyclorama, or cyc. A back drop with extensions enclosing the whole stage.
Deck-hand. A stage-hand.
Drop. A hanging piece of scenery.
Flat. A piece of rigid scenery.
Flood. A light illuminating the whole stage.
Fly-floor. A platform midway between the *grid* and the stage floor. To it the *lines* supporting scenery are tied off or *belayed*.
Flyman. A *grip* who handles the ropes supporting scenery.
Grid. A framework high above the stage from which the *lines* supporting the scenery are suspended.
Grip. One who assists the carpenter and *second hand*.
Juice. The electrician.
Line. A rope supporting scenery. Each drop has three — a *short line*, a *center line* and a *long line*.
Operator. An assistant to the electrician.
Pin-rail. A rail on the *fly-floor* to which *lines* are fastened.
Pocket. An electrical outlet.
Practical. Said of scenery or properties that are not merely painted, but really work.
Props. The property-man.
Scene-dock, or organ-loft. The place where scenery belonging to a theatre is stored.
Second hand. The carpenter's chief assistant.
Set. The entire scenery for a scene.
Skate. To slide a *flat* across the stage.
Spot. A small light whose rays are concentrated in one place.
Strike. To dismantle a set.[1]

The argot of the movie-lots shows a good many loans from that of the theatre, but it has also produced some picturesque novelties of its own, chiefly having to do with the technical process of picture making. Most of the following specimens, assembled from

[1] The nautical origin of some of these terms is discussed by S. E. Morison in *American Speech*, Dec., 1928, p. 124.

698 The American Language: Supplement II

various sources,[1] were scrutinized and revised by Miss Anita Loos and the late Edgar Selwyn, to whose friendly aid I am much indebted:

Baby. A small spotlight.[2]
Beard, muff, or feather-merchant. An extra with natural whiskers.
Beef. A laborer.
Best boy. The first assistant to a *gaffer*, which see.
Blupe. An unwanted sound on a sound track.
Boom-jockey. A sound man who follows the action with a microphone.
Bottle. A camera lens.
Breakaway. A chair or other object made of Balsa wood, which falls to pieces when one performer uses it to clout another; also, any simulated glass object made of clear sugar for the same purpose.
Bulber. A photographer.
Bungalow. The metal housing of a sound-proof camera.
Butterfly. A disk of gauze used to diffuse light, or a speck on the camera lens.
Canary. An unidentified noise.
Carbon-monkey. The man who renews the carbons in the lights used on a technicolor set.
Century, or nigger. A cloth shade to shield the camera lens.
Charlie, or walrus. An actor with a mustache.
Civilian. A person not connected with the movies.[3]
Co-ed. A small floodlight carried on the camera.
Cooked. Said of an overdeveloped negative.
Cook's tour. A visit to a movie lot by civilians.
Cow-waddy. A he-man in a Western film.[4]
Cutting-room. The place where movies are edited.
Dolly, *v.* To move up on a shot with the camera.
Double frame, *v.* To slow up the speed of action by printing each *frame* of a film twice.
Dub, *v.* To re-record and combine effects – dialogue, music, etc. – on one film.

1 There is a bibliography of glossaries of motion-picture terms in Burke's Literature of Slang, pp. 121 and 122. Not listed there are Neologisms of the Film Industry, by P. R. Beath, *American Speech*, April, 1933, pp. 73 and 74; Logomachia, by Cecil B. DeMille, *Words*, Oct., 1936, p. 6; Strange Lingo of the Movies, *Popular Mechanics*, May, 1937, pp. 722–26; Glossary of Movie Terms, by James Hogan, North American Newspaper Alliance syndicated article, June 5, 1938; The Playwright in Paradise, by Edmund Wilson, *New Republic*, April 26, 1939;
Movie Talk, by Philip H. Bailey, *Minicam*, June, 1939, pp. 115–18; Hollywood Slang, *Woman's Home Companion*, Aug., 1940, p. 8; Pill? Skull Doily? It's Movie Talk, by Virginia Oakey, Richmond (Va.) *News-Leader*, April 11, 1942, and Filmese, by Louise Pound, *American Mercury*, April, 1943, pp. 155 and 156.
2 *To kill the baby* means to turn the spot out.
3 So used in Screen Notables Shun Night Life, by John Scott, Los Angeles *Times*, Jan. 9, 1938.
4 I take this from *Variety*, which probably invented it.

Extra. A performer in crowd scenes, without lines to speak and usually hired by the day.

Fishpole. An appliance for holding a microphone over the head of a performer.

Frame. Each picture on a film.[1]

Free ride. A meal at the expense of the company.

Gaffer. The head electrician.

Gag-man. One who supplies the working script with comedy.

Galloping. Variable motor speed.[2]

Gimbal tripod. A camera-mount that simulates the motion of a ship.

Gobo. A black screen mounted on a tripod, used for casting shadows.[3]

Grease-room. A make-up room for extras. A make-up man is a *grease-pusher*.

Hays office. The Motion Picture Producers & Distributors of America, Inc., of which Elder Will H. Hays was president, 1922–45. Its chief function is to keep the movies out of trouble, and one of its duties is to censor pictures.[4]

Hollywood. In the movie sense, the whole Los Angeles region. Legally speaking, Hollywood is that part of Los Angeles north of Melrose avenue and west of Vermont avenue.

Independent, or indie. A movie producer not affiliated with one of the big companies; also, the owner of an independent movie-theatre.

Inky. An incandescent light.

Inky-dink. A small *baby*, which see.

In the can. Said of a film that has gone through the cutting and dubbing processes and is ready to be shipped to exhibitors.

Jelly. A gelatine sheet placed in front of a light to diffuse its rays.

Juicer. An electrician. See *gaffer*.

Junior. A spotlight intermediate in size between a *broad* and a *baby*.

Kick. Light reflected from bright objects.

Kill, *v.* To turn off a light.

Klieg eyes. Eye inflammation produced by the glare of lights.[5]

Lens louse. An actor who tries to put himself forward.

Lily. A good *take*, which see.

Location. Any place for making pictures that is not a *lot*, which see.

Loop it. To re-record dialogue in order to improve the reading of a line or to get rid of extraneous voices that were recorded with the original.

Lot. Any permanent place for making pictures.

Lowboy. A low camera base.

Lupe. A tubular light of more than 1500 watts.[6]

Match-box, or pickle. A miniature spotlight.

Matte shot. A film made with a section blocked out, to be filled later on another set.

Mike-boom. An apparatus supporting the microphone.

Mike-monkey. A sound man who manipulates the *mike-boom*.

Milk a scene, *v.* To get everything possible out of it.

---

[1] There are 16 frames to a foot.
[2] A very undesirable fault.
[3] *Gobo* used to be vaudeville argot for a scene played in the dark.
[4] See Supplement I, pp. 641–44.
[5] So called from the name of the Kliegl brothers, inventors of the Klieg arc-light, now obsolete.
[6] From *Lupe* Velez, a female star.

Montage. An effect produced by dissolving into each other a series of short shots with dramatic *crescendo*.

M. O. S. A scene without sound.[1]

Moviola. A machine enabling film editors to see a picture and hear the sound during the cutting process.

Neighborhood-house. A movie-theatre out of the downtown area, usually presenting the second or later runs of pictures.[2]

Orange-peel. A roughened light reflector.

Organ. A portable sound-control apparatus.

Organ-grinder. The operator of an *organ*.

Pan, *v.* To move a camera horizontally.

Pill. A long speech, hard to learn.

Quickie. A movie made in haste, usually by a small company and with little expenditure.

Red-light. Warning over the door of a studio while a scene is being shot.

Retake. A second photographing of a scene after a picture has been completely shot, usually to rectify blunders.

Rifle. A small spotlight throwing a narrow beam.

Roughie. A preliminary sketch made by the art department.

Rushes. Quickly made positives of films shot during the day, for the inspection of directors and other functionaries.

Scoop. A light with a shovel-shaped reflector.

Scrim. A large gauze light-diffuser.

Script-girl. A girl stationed on the set who keeps a detailed record of the shooting of every scene.

Sheepherder, or lung-man. An assistant director in charge of extras.

Shiner. A sun reflector for outdoor work.

Shoot, *v.* To photograph with a movie-camera.

Skip frame, *v.* To hasten the speed of the action by printing only every alternate *frame*.

Skirt. A silk screen fastened over a spotlight to diffuse the light.

Skull doily. A wig.

Soup. The photograph's developer.

Spaghetti. Film.

Speed, or up to speed. Used to indicate that the camera is running film at the standard speed of 90 feet a minute, or 1½ feet a second.

Stand-in. A person of the same height, build and coloring as a principal performer, employed to take the latter's place during the tedious process of focusing the camera and adjusting the lights for a shot.

Standing-board. A device for enabling a performer to rest between scenes without sitting down and thus rumpling his (or her) clothes.

Still. An ordinary photograph of a scene or people in a movie.

Stockade. A protection for the camera when animals are being photographed, or there is other danger of injury to it.

Stunt-man, or -woman. A performer resembling a principal performer,

---

[1] Bradford F. Swan, in Slang-Minting Film Capital Speaks Its Own Language, Providence *Journal*, March 3, 1946, says that this is an abbreviation of *mitoudt sound* in "the heavy dialect of a foreign director."

[2] *Variety* always calls it a *nabe*.

employed to take the latter's place in hazardous scenes, such as wrecks, duels, explosions, and leaps from automobiles and airplanes.

Suck, v. To lift with a block and tackle.

Swing-gang. The night shift of stage hands.

Take. A scene or other unit of a picture.

Titles. The legends used to explain the action of a movie.[1]

Trailer. An advance notice of a new film, with specimen scenes, prepared for theatres in which it has been booked.

Treatment. A first rough draft of a story for a screen play.

Trucking shot. A shot made with the camera moving along with the action.

Western, or horse-opera. A movie dealing with cowboys, Indians, bandits, etc.

Whodunit (Who done it?). A melodramatic movie dealing with mystery and murder.[2]

Yes-man. A sycophantic subordinate.[3]

Zoom. To move a camera up to or away from an object quickly.

Preview, meaning the showing of a picture, before its first public performance, at a special performance for movie critics and other privileged persons, is not a Hollywood invention. The identical verb is traced by the NED to 1607. The noun, however, seems to be an Americanism, for the NED's two examples, one dated 1882 and the other 1899, and both antedating the movies, come from American publications. It has been borrowed by the English, and is now used in senses having nothing to do with motion-pictures, as it is in America. The austere *Literary Supplement* of the London

---

[1] Despite the advent of the talkies they are still sometimes used.

[2] See Supplement I, p. 327, n. 5.

[3] In Origin of Words: *Yes Man*, San Francisco *News Letter & Wasp*, June 30, 1939, p. 10, Peter Tamony says that *yes-man* was invented by T. A. (Tad) Dorgan, the cartoonist, in 1913. It appeared first in a cartoon entitled Giving the First Edition the Once Over, showing the editor and his assistants looking over an edition fresh from the press. The assistants are praising it, and are labelled *yes-men*. "The extension of the term to indicate assistant directors in motion-picture organizations," says Mr. Tamony, "was natural. The early 1920s saw the industry rapidly developing to the stupendous, colossal, flamboyant mystery it now is, and the many who strove for fame and fortune did so with hats in hand." In a short while the late Wilson Mizner was calling Hollywood "the land where nobody noes," and *Variety* nominated one of the assistants of Darryl Zanuck, the producer, for the dignity of *super-yes-man*. Mr. Tamony calls attention to the fact that *yes-men* were known in the Eighteenth Century as *amens*, which appeared in the third edition of Grose's Classical Dictionary of the Vulgar Tongue, 1796. The term is defined thus: "He said *yes* and *amen* to everything; he agreed to everything." For Dorgan see Tad Dorgan is Dead, by W. L. Werner, *American Speech*, Aug., 1929, p. 430. Werner does not list *yes-men* among Dorgan's coinages. Its possible source in the German *jaherr* is noted in Supplement I, p. 431.

Times uses it, for example, as a heading on advance notices of new books.[1] *Release*, in the sense of a new picture just delivered, or about to be delivered, to exhibitors, was apparently borrowed by Hollywood from the jargon of newspaper offices. It arose in the latter when public dignitaries began sending out advance copies of their speeches marked *For release* at such-and-such a time. This legend was presently used by press-agents for a similar purpose, and a document so marked came to be known as a *release*. According to Eric Berger, writing in *Coronet*,[2] *photoplay* was invented by Edgar Strakosch in 1912. The early motion picture producers disliked *movie*, which had begun to displace *biograph, kinetoscope, kinetograph*[3] and *cinematograph*,[4] and in 1912 the Essanay Company offered the princely prize of $25 for something more elegant. The money went to *photoplay*, sent in by Strakosch. The term gained a considerable popularity, and became the name of one of the earliest and most influential magazines for movie fans, edited from 1914 to 1932 by James R. Quirk, but *movie* nevertheless survived.

A term which often puzzles movie fans is *oscar*, the name of a gold statuette awarded each year for various sorts of professional achievement by the Academy of Motion Picture Arts and Sciences, the Hollywood opposite number to the American Academy of Arts and Letters.[5] For the following account of the origin of the word I am indebted to the late Edgar Selwyn:

---

[1] Autumn *Preview*, Sept. 25, 1943, p. 465.

[2] New Models in Words, Nov., 1940, pp. 28 and 29.

[3] Both *kinetoscope* and *kinetograph* were used by Thomas A. Edison to designate his original motion-picture machine of 1893.

[4] *Movie* is not listed in the DAE, but the NED Supplement marks it an Americanism and traces it to 1913. Terry Ramsaye says in Movie Jargon, *American Speech*, April, 1926, p. 357, that it really goes back to 1906–07. *Movie-parlor* came in on its heels, along with *movie-actor, movie-show*, etc. When sound pictures were first heard of they were called *speakies*, but in 1926, when their production was begun on a commercial scale by Warner Brothers, they became *talkies*. The Australians call March of Time reconstructions of history *thinkies*. No short name for colored pictures is in general use.

[5] There are more than twenty annual awards. One goes to the actor adjudged to have given the best performance of the year, another to the actress, a third to the author of the most original screen-play, a fourth to the best photographer, a fifth to the best animated cartoon, and so on. There are also various special awards — for example, one for the most valuable technical improvement of the year, and another (named in honor of the late Irving G. Thalberg) "for the most consistent high quality of production achievement by an individual producer."

Donald Gledhill, secretary of the Academy, and his wife were in Gledhill's office and fell to discussing the impending arrival of a relative called Uncle Oscar. A newspaper man was waiting in an outer office. While this conversation was going on a jeweler arrived with a sample statue. At first glance Gledhill mistook him for the missing relative and said to Mrs. Gledhill, "Here's Oscar now." The newspaper man, thinking he referred to the statue, wrote in his column the next day: "The gold Academy awards are referred to as *oscars* by Academy officials." This was lifted by other newspaper men all over the country, and in a little while the awards were being called *oscars* everywhere.[1]

Many terms associated with the movies are the product of press-agents,[2] *e.g.*, *wampas*, a female aspirant to stardom;[3] *sheik*, a romantic lover;[4] *cobra*, a girl powerfully aphrodisiacal;[5] *vamp*, a more mature woman skilled at conquering and wrecking men;[6] *starlet, sex-appeal*,[7] *it*,[8] *oomph*,[9] *glamor-girl*,[10] *motion-picture*

[1] The term has also come into use outside movie circles, always to designate some symbol of merit. See Among the New Words, by I. Willis Russell, *American Speech*, Dec., 1944, p. 306. *Baltimore & Ohio Magazine*, Nov., 1945, p. 9: Our Annual Report Wins *Oscar* (a bronze trophy offered by the *Financial World*). *Editor & Publisher*, April 5, 1947, p. 7: Promotion *Oscars* Awarded to 6 Newspapers (bronze plaques). There are also derivative *Edgars* and *Gertrudes*, the former, named for Edgar Allan Poe, going to writers and producers of whodunits, and the latter to writers of Pocket Books which sell 1,000,000 copies. See *American Notes & Queries*, July, 1946, p. 53, and *Saturday Review of Literature*, April 26, 1947, p. 24.

[2] *Variety* calls press-agents *flacks*, a World War II term for anti-aircraft fire. It was borrowed from the German *flak*, an abbreviation of *fliegerabwehrkanone*, anti-aircraft cannon. Agents of extraordinary virulence are *blast-artists*. They call themselves *publicists, public relations counsel* or *publicity engineers*. See Supplement I, pp. 578-79.

[3] Suggested by the name of the *Western Associated Motion Picture Advertisers*, made up of advertising and publicity men.

[4] From the title of The *Sheik*, by Edith M. Hull, a sensational novel which made a movie for the late Rudolph Valentino (1895-1926) in 1922. Dwight L. Bolinger reported in The Living Language, *Words*, Oct., 1937, p. 156, that it was moribund by 1931.

[5] New Name is Coined, Los Angeles *Herald*, Jan. 30, 1926: "'That girl surely has appeal—she's a *cobra*.' That's the latest expression one hears around Hollywood." The title of another Valentino picture, with Nita Naldi as the ophidian.

[6] *Cf.* Rudyard Kipling's The *Vampire*, 1897. The abbreviated noun came into general use in England by 1918 and the verb by 1922, but both seem to have been propagated in the United States from Hollywood.

[7] The early history of this term is obscure. The NED Supplement shows that it had reached England by 1927. Howard C. Rice reported in the *Franco-American Review*, 1936, that it had reached France as *le sex-appeal*.

[8] Used by Kipling in Mrs. Bathurst, 1904: "Tisn't beauty, ... or good talk necessarily. It's just *It*. Some women will stay in a man's memory if they once walked down a street." It was spread in the United States by the press agents of the film version of Elinor Glyn's Three Weeks, c. 1922. In 1927 she did a movie called *It*.

[9] A committee organized by press-

cathedral, and the magnificent *super-colossal*. Some of other terms emanating from Hollywood wits have their points, *e.g.*, *to go Hollywood*, meaning, when applied to an actor, to succumb to a suffocating sense of his own importance,[1] and, when applied to a movie writer or other intellectual, to abandon the habits and ideas of civilization and embrace the levantine life of the richer moviefolks; *casting-couch* for the divan in a casting-director's office; *tear-bucket* for an elderly actress playing heart-broken mothers; *finger-wringer*, for a star given to emoting; *baddie* for an actor playing villains; *cliff-hanger*, for a serial melodrama; *sobbie* or *weepie* for a picture running to sadness, and *bump man* for a performer who undertakes dangerous stunts. *Variety* uses *flesh* to designate live players who appear in movie houses.

The queer jargon called *jive*, which had its heyday in the early 1940s, was an amalgam of Negro slang from Harlem and the argots of drug addicts and the pettier sort of criminals, with occasional additions from the Broadway gossip columns and the high-school campus. It seems to have arisen at the start among jazz musicians, many of them Negroes and perhaps more of them addicts,[2] and its chief users were always youthful devotees of the more delirious

---

agents awarded the title of *Oomph Girl* of America to Ann Sheridan, March 16, 1939. See America's *Oomph* Girl, by Noel F. Busch, *Life*, July 24, 1939, p. 64. The term was apparently first used by Walter Winchell, but it was the movie publicists who broadcast it. It aroused a violent discussion when it reached England, a little later. In 1945, when an American manufacturer of footwear tried to register *Oomphies* as a trade-mark for his products, the Registrar of Trade-Marks refused to grant it, apparently on the antagonistic double ground that *oomph* had sexual connotations and was a common adjective, and hence not registerable. On Oct. 16, 1946, sitting in the Chancery Division of the High Court, Mr. Justice Raymond Evershed rejected both contentions and ordered the trade-mark registered. See *Newsweek*, Oct. 28, 1946, p. 44 and Supplement I, pp. 329, 362, 398 and 428.

10 But Eve Brown says in Champagne Cholly; New York, 1947 (reprinted in *Omnibook*, May, 1947, p. 155) that this was invented by Maury Paul, for many years the Cholly Knickerbocker of the Hearst papers.

1 Neologisms, by Dwight L. Bolinger, *American Speech*, Feb., 1941, p. 66.

2 Said Westbrook Pegler in his column of June 24, 1947: "The Musicians' Union in its recent convention adopted a resolution which is significant. . . . The resolution would permit the expulsion of any member who used or carried on traffic in narcotics. . . . Because so many of the members are employed in resorts of the underworld and the twilight world of luxurious and expensive dives run by racketeers, but patronized by more or less respectable clients, they are brought very close to the narcotics trade."

sort of ballroom dancing, *i.e.*, the so-called *jitterbugs*. Earl Conrad says in his foreword to Dan Burley's " Original Handbook of Harlem Jive "[1] that it was " one more contribution of Negro America to the United States " and that it had its rise in " the revolutionary times when it was necessary for the Negro to speak and sing and even think in a kind of code," but this is a romantic exaggeration. It actually arose in the honky-tonks and tingle-tangles of the prejazz era, and many of its current names for musical instruments go back to that era or even beyond, *e.g.*, *bull-fiddle* or *dog-house* for a double-bass; *groan-box* or *box of teeth* for an accordion; *slip-horn*, *slush-pump*, *gas-pipe*, *syringe* or *push-pipe* for a trombone; *thermometer* for an oboe; *iron-horn*, *plumbing*, *squeeze-horn* or *piston* for a trumpet; *pretzel* or *peck-horn* for a French horn; *licorice-stick*, *wop-stick*, *gob-stick*, *blackstick* or *agony-pipe* for a clarinet; *fog-horn*, *fish-horn* or *gobble-pipe* for a saxophone; *box*, *moth-box* or *88* for a piano;[2] *scratch-box* for a violin; *chin-bass* for a viola; *gitter*, *gitbox* or *belly-fiddle* for a guitar; *grunt-iron* for a tuba; *god-box* for an organ; *wood-pile* for a xylophone, and *skin* or *suitcase* for a drum. So with the names for performers, *e.g.*, *skin-tickler*, *skin-beater*, *hide-beater* or *brave boy* for a drummer; *squeaker* for a violinist; *sliver-sucker* for a clarinetist; *whanger*, *plunker-boy* or *plink-plonker* for a guitarist; *monkey-hurdler* for an organist, *gabriel* for a trumpeter; and *brass officer* for a cornetist. Any performer on a wind instrument is a *lip-splitter*.

The jazz band is a variable quantity, and may run from four or five men to what almost amounts to a symphony orchestra. Jazz itself is divided into two halves, the *sweet* kind and the *hot* kind or *jive* or *swing*,[3] of which *boogie-woogie* is a sub-species.[4] All jazz

1 New York, 1944.
2 The standard piano has a compass of 7¼ octaves, or 88 notes.
3 Profiles: Alligator's Idol, *New Yorker*, April 17, 1937, p. 27: " *Swing* is really just another word for *jazz*, but it has come to imply *hot jazz*, as distinguished from the *sweet jazz* developed by Paul Whiteman, with his violins, muted brasses and soft symphonic effects." In Jazz is Where You Find It, *Esquire*, Feb., 1944, Leonard G. Feather said that the standard jazz band at that time consisted of five or six saxophones, four or five trumpets, three or four trombones, piano, guitar, double-bass and drums.
4 *Boogie-woogie* is defined by the New College Standard Dictionary, 1947, as " a type of piano *blues* characterized by a rhythmic ostinato bass with free rhapsodizing in the right hand, composed of numerous short figures in varied rhythms." The use of *blues* here is perhaps inaccurate. *Blues* means a song or instrumental piece of a generally desponding character, like

is based upon a strongly marked rhythm, almost always in four-four time, but the *sweet* variety is otherwise not greatly differentiated from ordinary popular music.[1] A performer who sticks to the printed notes is a *paperman*, and if he ever undertakes conventional music is a *commercial, salon-man, long-underwear* or *long-hair*. An adept at *hot jazz*, which is marked by harmonic freedom and a frequent resort to improvisation, is a *cat*, and if he excels at arousing the libido of the fans (who are also, by courtesy, *cats*) he is said to *send* or *give* or *ride* or to *go to town* or to be *in the groove*, and becomes a *solid sender* or *gate*. The test of his skill is his proficiency at adorning the music with *ad lib.* ornaments called *licks, breaks, riffs, get-offs* or *take-offs*. The wilder they are the better. When swing performers meet to *lick* and *riff* for their own entertainment they are said to hold a *jam-session, clam-bake* or *barrel-house*. Music that is banal or stale is *corny*.[2] *Boogie-woogie* accentuates a monotonous bass, usually of eight notes to the measure.[3] A woman singer is a *canary* or *chirp*. Any wind performer is a *Joe blow*. Tuning up is *licking the chops*. High trumpet notes are *Armstrongs*.[4] Notes are *spots*. Rests are *lay-outs*. To emphasize the rhythm is to *beat it out*. To be out of a job is to be *cooling*. Jazz in Negroid style is *gut-bucket*. To keep good time is to *ride*. The jazz bands have changed much of the conventional Italian terminology of music.

---

that of many Negro spirituals. The *blues* laid the foundations for *jazz*, but they are not necessarily *jazz* themselves.

[1] Its structure is discussed learnedly in So This is Jazz, by Henry Osborne Osgood; New York, 1926, and by the same author in The Anatomy of Jazz, *American Mercury*, April, 1926, pp. 385-95. Its history is recounted in Reflections on the History of Jazz, by S. I. Hayakawa, a lecture delivered before the Arts Club of Chicago, March 17, 1945, and later printed as a pamphlet by the author. See also Is Jazz Music?, by Winthrop Parkhurst, *American Mercury*, Oct., 1943, pp. 403-09.

[2] In Among the New Words, *American Speech*, Feb., 1944, p. 61, Dwight L. Bolinger traces this term to 1938, and connects it with *corn-fed*. In *Corny*, the same, Oct., 1946, Marie Sandoz says that it was in use in Western Nebraska *c.* 1890-1910.

[3] It is discussed learnedly, and with approbation, in the *Étude*, the trade journal of American music-teachers, Dec., 1943, p. 757, and by Nicolas Slonimsky in Jazz, Swing and Boogie Woogie, *Christian Science Monitor*, May 20, 1944. Slonimsky says that it was launched by Meade Lewis and Albert Ammons, Negro pianists, at Carnegie Hall, New York, Dec. 23, 1938.

[4] From Louis *Armstrong*, alias Satchelmouth, alias Satchmo, a famous colored trumpet-player. For his triumphs see Hot Jazz Jargon, by E. J. Nicholas and W. L. Werner, *Vanity Fair*, Nov., 1935, p. 38, and Jazz, by Robert Goffin; New York, 1946.

American Slang

Music played *dolce* is said to be *schmalz* (German for lard), *scherzo* is *medium bounce*, a grace-note is a *rip*, the final chord is a *button*, a drop in pitch on a sustained tone is a *bend*, and a *glissando* is a *smear* or *slurp*.[1]

The vocabulary of the jazz addict is largely identical with that of the jazz performer. He himself is a *hep-cat*, *alligator* or *rug-cutter*. To him those who dislike swing music are *tin-ears*, and are said to be *icky*. A dance is a *rat-race* or *cement-mixer*; anything excellent is *killer-diller*, *murder* or *Dracula*; a girl is a *chick*, *witch*, *drape*, *mouse*, *spook* or *bree*; face powder is *dazzle-dust*; a shot of Cocacola is a *fizz*; a blind date is a *grab-bag*; a hamburger is *ground horse*; a kiss is a *honey-cooler*; money is *moula*; a sandwich is a *slab*; to sit down is to *swoon*; to dance wildly is to *get whacky*; an aggressive girl is a *vulture* or *wolverine*; a fat girl is a *five-by-five*, and a person disliked is a *specimen*, *herkle*, *prune*, *corpse*, *droop*, *fumb*, *gleep*, *cold cut*, *apple* or *sloop*.[2] When he encounters swing

---

[1] For more examples see Presto-Rush, by Arthur Minton, *American Speech*, April, 1940, p. 124-31; What Every Young Musician Should Know, by Meredith Willson; New York, 1938; From the Baltimore *Evening Sun*, by R. P. Harriss, *American Speech*, Oct., 1941, p. 229; The Slang of Jazz, by H. Brook Webb, the same, Oct., 1937, pp. 179-84; A Musician's Word List, by Russel B. Nye, the same, Feb., 1937, pp. 45-48 and Musical Slang Explained, by Gene Krupa, Chicago *Sun*, Feb. 7, 1943, p. 28.

[2] I take most of these from Jabberwocky and Jive, by Nancy Pepper; New York, 1943. Miss Pepper gives some edifying examples of teen-age wit, *e.g.*, "He moved to the city because he heard the country was at war," "He took a bicycle to bed so he wouldn't have to walk in his sleep," and "He cut off his left side so he would be all right." See also It's Swing, by Holman Harvey, *Delineator*, Nov., 1936, pp. 10-11 and 48-49; Débutante's Dictionary, *Vogue*, Nov. 15, 1937, pp. 70 and 144; On the Record, by Carleton Smith, *Esquire*, Nov., 1938, pp. 95 and 179; Jitterbugs are Poison, *Life*, Aug. 8, 1938, p. 56; Manhattan Room, *New Yorker*, Jan. 8, 1938, pp. 34-35; Swing Terms, by S. J. Perelman, *New Yorker*, Sept. 14, 1940, pp. 18-19; Subdebese, *Life*, Jan. 27, 1941, pp. 78-79; Jabberwocky, *Time*, July 26, 1943, p. 56; Teen-Age Slang, New York *Times Magazine*, Dec. 5, 1943; Teen Talk: Slanguage, by Bonnie Gay, Baltimore *Sunday Sun*, Feb. 11, 1945, Sect. A, p. 2; Teen Talk, by Mary Jane Carl, *American Weekly*, July 21, 1946, p. 15; Dan Burley's Original Handbook of Harlem Jive; New York, 1944, pp. 133-50 (Burley conducts a column in jive, Back Door Stuff, in the New York *Amsterdam News*, and has made many contributions to the vocabulary); The New Cab Calloway's Hepster's Dictionary; New York, 1938; new editions, 1939 and 1944 (said by *Variety*, June 22, 1938, to have been written by Ned Williams, a press agent); Hepcats' Jive Dictionary, by Lou Shelly; Derby (Conn.), 1945, and Really the Blues, by Milton "Mezz" Mezzrow and Bernard Wolfe; New York, 1946, pp. 371-80. The last is extremely in-

that really lifts him he says that he has been *sent down to the very bricks*, an experience comparable to suffering demoniacal possession or dying in the electric chair. This slang of the adolescent changes quickly, as is shown by the rapid fading out of *to neck, to pet, to pitch woo, boy-friend* and *red-hot mama*.[1] During the middle 1940s there was a rage for abbreviations, *e.g.*, *natch* (naturally) and *def* (definitely), but the *Circle and Monogram*, the trade journal of the publishers of Webster 1934, was reporting by March, 1947, that they were already " as passé as a yearling egg."[2]

In view of the background of latter-day jive it is not surprising to find that some of its principal terms were originally of indecent significance. *Jazz* itself is one of them. Efforts have been made to derive it from the names of various Negro performers of years ago, *e.g.*, Charles (*Chas*) Alexander or Washington, of Vicksburg, Miss.,[3] a dancing slave named Jasper, alias *Jass* or *Jazz*,[4] and a musician of Chicago named Jasbo (*Jas*) Brown,[5] and certain etymologists have also sought to relate it to a Louisiana-French verb, *jaser*, meaning (varying with the authority) to speed up[6] or to chatter

---

teresting and also authoritative, for Mezzrow has functioned successfully as both jazz musician and marihuana pedlar.

[1] The vocabulary of the 1920s, now nearly all archaic, is to be found in Courtship Slang, by F. Walter Pollock, *American Speech*, Jan., 1927, pp. 202–03. That of the C. C. C. boys of the 1930s is in C. C. C. Speech, by Elwood W. Camp and H. C. Hartman, the same, Feb., 1937, pp. 74–75; C. C. C. Chatter, by Levette J. Davidson, the same, April, 1940, pp. 201–11; C. C. C. Slang, by James W. Danner, the same, April, 1940, pp. 212–13, and an anonymous article in *Life*, Aug., 1933, p. 9. That of youngsters confined in institutions is in Vocabulary and Argot of Delinquent Boys, by Lowell S. Selling, *American Journal of Sociology*, March, 1934, pp. 674–77; The Argot of an Orphans' Home, by L. W. Merryweather, *American Speech*, Aug., 1932, pp. 398–404; and The Growth and Decline of a Children's Slang Vocabulary, by Edmund Kasser, *Journal of Genetic Psychology*, 1945, pp. 129–37. That of streetboys in New York is in Peanuts! The Pickle Dealers, by Julius G. Rothenberg, *American Speech*, Oct., 1941, pp. 187–91.

[2] *Zoot*-suit was especially short-lived. The garment was worn in the East mainly by Negroes and in the West by Mexicans. Its history is set forth in Zoot Lore, *New Yorker*, June 19, 1943. See also American Notes & Queries, July, 1943, p. 54; *Negro Digest*, Aug., 1945, p. 64, and What's in a *Zoot?*, by David Wray, *True Detective*, March, 1943, p. 99.

[3] Words From Names, by Jerome C. Hixson, *Words*, Nov., 1934, p. 10; Where is Jazz Leading America?, by Vincent Lopez, *Étude*, July, 1924.

[4] *Jazzbo, Washed Up*, and *Gravy*, by Walter J. Kingsley, New York *World*, Oct. 25, 1925.

[5] *Jazz* Jargon, by James D. Hart, *American Speech*, April, 1932, p. 245.

[6] *Jazz*, by Peter Tamony, San Francisco *News Letter & Wasp*, March

and make fun,[1] but the plain fact is that *to jazz* has long had the meaning in American folk-speech of to engage in sexual intercourse, and is so defined by many lexicographers, *e.g.*, Godfrey Irwin,[2] Allen Walker Read,[3] Berrey and Van den Bark,[4] Maurice H. Weseen[5] and " Justinian." [6] According to Clay Smith, an old-time traveling performer and song-writer,[7] the transfer of the accompanying noun to the orgiastic music it now denominates occurred in the bawdy honky-tonks of the Western mining-towns, *c.* 1890. " If the truth were known about the origin of the word," he says, " it would never be mentioned in polite society." Tamony says that it was introduced to San Francisco in 1913 by William (Spike) Slattery, sports editor of the *Call*, and propagated by a band-leader named Art Hickman.[8] It reached Chicago by 1915 [9] but was not heard of in New York until a year later.[10] The first New York *jazz-band* appeared in February, 1917,[11] and by August 20 of the same year one was billed at the Holborn Empire in London. Three months later there was one playing at the Casino de Paris.

The decorous DAE does not list *jazz*, but the NED Supplement, while avoiding the original meaning of the term, shows that the musical meaning was well understood in England by 1918, and that *to jazz up* in the sense of to liven or brighten, was in vogue by 1920. The DAE traces *ragtime*, the predecessor of *jazz*, to 1897, but

---

17, 1938, and Hart, just cited. See also *Jazz*, by Robert Goffin, before cited, pp. 62–64.

1 Origin of *Jazz*, *Negro Digest*, April, 1947, p. 53.
2 American Tramp and Underworld Slang; before cited, p. 109.
3 Lexical Evidence From Folk Epigraphy in Western North America; Paris, 1935, p. 62.
4 P. 342.
5 p. 22.
6 America Sexualis; Chicago, 1939.
7 Where is *Jazz* Leading America?, *Étude*, Sept., 1924, p. 595.
8 *Jazz*, by Tamony, before cited. Slattery, according to Tamony, borrowed it from the vocabulary of crap-shooters and used it " as a synonym for ginger and pep," but it was soon used to designate Hickman's music, much to his disgust.
9 I am indebted here to Mr. J. E. Keith, of Ann Arbor, Mich. He says that it was originally applied derisively to the music of a colored band from New Orleans, playing at a night-spot called Lamb's Café, and that it was spread maliciously by union musicians who resented this intrusion. But the Chicago antinomians, knowing the original meaning of " one of the most commonplace of American obscenities," flocked with high expectations to hear the music. Soon there were many imitators.
10 *Variety*, Oct. 27, 1916: " Chicago has added another innovation to its list of discoveries in the so-called *jazz-bands*. The *jazz-band* is composed of three or four instruments and seldom plays regulated music. The College Inn and practically all the other high-class places of entertainment have a *jazz-band* featured."
11 Slonimsky, before cited.

it must be considerably older. The first *blues* were written by W. C. Handy, of Memphis, in 1911. Some of the other terms of *jazz* addicts come from sources almost as blushful as that of *jazz* itself, *e.g., jitterbug, cat, jerk, hot, to blow one's top, I ain't coming,* and *juke*.[1] Dr. Lorenzo D. Turner, the chief American authority on African loan-words in Negro American, says that *juke* is a corruption of a Wolof term, *dzug* or *dzog*, meaning to lead a disorderly life, to misconduct oneself,[2] and that *juke-house*, among the Negroes of the Southeast, means a house of ill repute.[3] *Cat*, according to the NED, has been in use as a synonym for harlot since *c.* 1400. *Boogie-woogie*, according to Zora Neal Hurston, had the original significance, in the South, of secondary syphilis.[4] *Jitterbug*, according to Tamony, is a fan "whose reaction to swing is always physical."[5] The rest scarcely need glosses.[6]

The American underworld is much less given than that of England to the banalities of what is called rhyming slang, *e.g., twist and twirl* for girl; *bowl of chalk* for talk; *bang and biff* for syphilis

---

[1] The obscene significance of many words commonly found in *blues* texts, *e.g., jelly-roll, short'nin-bread* and *easy rider* was noted by Guy B. Johnson in Double Meaning in the Popular Negro Blues, *Journal of Abnormal & Social Psychology*, April–June, 1927, pp. 12–20.

[2] West African Survivals in the Vocabulary of Gullah, a paper read at the Dec., 1938, meeting of the American Dialect Society in New York. See *Dzug, Dzog, Dzuga, Jook, Juke*, by Will McGuire, *Time*, Jan. 29, 1940, p. 8.

[3] In Arnold *vs.* State, 1939, Justice Glenn Terrell, of the Florida Supreme Court, decided that *jukes* were "not retreats which moralists dared to frequent, but rather the arch incubators of vice, immorality and low impulses." I am indebted here to Mr. J. Kenneth Ballinger, of the Tallahassee bar, and to Mr. Arthur T. Young of New York. In Dec., 1945, the grand jury of Tift county, Georgia, brought in a presentment charging that "the roadside houses generally referred to as *jouk-joints* have become a menace to society and the welfare of the people." I am indebted for this to Mr. Lester Hargrett, of Washington.

[4] Story in Harlem Slang, *American Mercury*, July, 1942, p. 84.

[5] *Jitterbug*, San Francisco *News Letter & Wasp*, March 3, 1939. He says that it came into currency "late in 1935." How its meaning was misunderstood in England is told in Supplement I, p. 509.

[6] " The association of marihuana with *hot jazz*," says *Time*, July 19, 1943, p. 56, "is no accident. The drug's power to slow the sense of time gives an improvisor the illusion that he has all the time in the world to conceive his next phrases. . . . Among *hot jazz* players there are few (except the confirmed lushes) who do not occasionally smoke." "Most addicts," adds Maurer in Marihuana Addicts and Their Lingo, *American Mercury*, Nov., 1946, p. 573, "want swing music while they are on a jag. . . . [Certain popular songs] reflect, in a very thinly disguised manner, the close relation of drug-aroused sexual desire to swing music."

(syph); *by the peck* for neck, and *fleas and ants* for pants. Maurer, from whom I take these examples,[1] says that such forms are vastly more prevalent on the Pacific Coast than in the East, but that the common belief that they are introduced there from Australia is erroneous. The Australians use them to some extent, but mainly only as loans from England. "There is a tendency," says Maurer, "to clip one term and allow it to carry the meaning, even though it no longer rhymes, as *twist*, a girl, from *twist* and *twirl*." Not a few such words and phrases were picked up in England by American soldiers during World War II, but they seem unlikely to survive.[2] In 1943 many of them were used in a movie called "Mr. Lucky," but they apparently puzzled and displeased the American fans.[3] They are most used today by the lower varieties of underworld denizens, and seem to be more prevalent in prison than outside, though a few, *e.g.*, *twist*, have some currency and have been adopted by the hep-cats. Campus slang, once a chief source of popular neologisms, has been swamped in recent years by those welling up from the underworld, and the grove of Academe borrows more from the barbarians than it offers them.[4] What passed for collegiate speech formerly had a considerable vogue in the movies, but in 1943

---

1 "Australian" Rhyming Argot in the American Underworld (with Sidney J. Baker), *American Speech*, Oct., 1944, pp. 183-95; Rhyming Underworld Slang, *American Mercury*, Oct., 1946, pp. 473-79.

2 A Dictionary of Rhyming Slang, listing about 500 terms, was published in London in 1941, apparently for the instruction of Americans.

3 Some of those more or less in use in American prisons are in Underworld Slang, by Convict 12627, Jackson, Tenn., 1936. See also English Underworld Slang, *Variety*, April 8, 1931, reprinted in *American Speech*, June, 1931, pp. 391-93; Rhyming Slang, by Alan Tomkins, London *Sunday Dispatch*, Feb. 16, 1941; Adventures in Rhyming Slang, by Alan Dent, *Strand Magazine*, April, 1943, pp. 86-88; and Some Notes on Rhyming Argot, by Sir St. Vincent Troubridge, *American Speech*, Feb., 1946, pp. 45-47.

4 I point, as examples, to *to get in the groove, icky, jailbait* (an adolescent girl, *i.e.*, one whom it would be a penal offense to seduce), *to blow one's top, hep-cat, slick chick, skin-beater* (a drummer) and *pad* (an apartment) in College Slang, by Dorothy M. Schullian, *School & Society*, Sept. 4, 1943, pp. 169-70; and Jive and Slang of Students in Negro Colleges, by Marcus H. Boulware; Hampton (Va.), 1947. In Johns Hopkins Jargon, *American Speech*, June, 1932, pp. 327-38, J. Louis Kuethe reported that "such expressions as *big shot, hot spot, to muscle in, to pay off* and *to scram*" had already "made the journey from the rackets to the classrooms," and in Agricultural College Slang in South Dakota, *American Speech*, Oct., 1936, pp. 279-80, Hugh Sebastian reported several jazz-band terms as prevailing there.

a war correspondent at Hollywood was reporting that it had "suddenly and unaccountably gone into a slump."[1] I should add that he said in the same dispatch that the slang of the jitterbugs was also beginning to lose ground.[2] This last may have been a bit premature, but there is every indication that jive is not long for this life.[3]

In the days of the Federal Writers' Project in New York it planned a "Lexicon of Trade Jargon" that promised to be very useful, but when the project blew up the manuscript was still incomplete, and since then it has reposed, unpublished, in the Library of Congress.[4] One must regret that it was never finished, for the

[1] Hollywood, by Robbin Coons, in various papers of Oct. 16.

[2] Many reports on the campus vocabulary, new and old, are listed by Burke, pp. 130-35. Others are noted in AL4, p. 569. Among yet others that I have encountered are Current College Slang (University of Virginia), by Gilmore Spencer, *Virginia Magazine*, Oct., 1926, pp. 16-17; Keeping Up With Joe Gish (Princeton), *Princeton Alumni Weekly*, May 24, 1929; Handed-Down Campus Expressions, by K. L. Daughrity, *American Speech*, Dec., 1939, pp. 129-30; Current Undergraduate Slang, by H. H. Rightor, *Princeton Alumni Weekly*, May 22, 1931, p. 798; Short Dictionary of Slang, Jargon, Cant (University of Virginia), by John Wyllie, *University of Virginia Alumni News*, Jan., 1936, pp. 80-81; College Slang (University of Denver), *Clarionette*, March 18, 1937; Cadet Slang at the Citadel (Charleston, S.C.), by R. I. McDavid, Jr., *South Atlantic Bulletin*, Dec., 1937, pp. 3-4; A Citadel Glossary, by the same, *American Speech*, Feb., 1939, pp. 23-32; A Dictionary of Exeter Slang, by A. Fisher and Harvey Williams, *Phillips Exeter Bulletin*, April, 1938, pp. 15-20; Slanguage, *Lobo* (University of New Mexico), Oct. 13, 1937; Latest Lingo — Campus, by Joyce Thresher, *Mademoiselle*, Aug., 1943, pp. 62-63; Odd Colloquialisms (University of Nebraska), by M. C. McPhee, *American Speech*, Oct., 1940, pp. 334-35; Missouri University Colloquialisms, by Lelah Allison, the same, Feb., 1941, p. 75; Whitman College Slang, by William White, the same, April, 1943, pp. 153-55; American Schoolboy Slang, by F. V. L., Jr., *American Notes & Queries*, Jan., 1945, pp. 151-52; Campus Slang at Minnesota, by Nancy Calkin and William Randel, *American Speech*, Oct., 1945, pp. 233-34; An Aggie Vocabulary of Slang (Agricultural and Mechanical College of Texas), by Fred Eikel, Jr., the same, Feb., 1946, pp. 29-36; Chapel Hill *Chaff* (University of North Carolina), by Louis Graves, Chapel Hill *Weekly*, April 4, 1937, p. 1. The best recent work on campus slang in England is Public School Slang, by Morris Marples; London, 1940. The German authority is Deutsche Studentensprache, by F. Klug; Strassburg, 1895 For Scandinavia there is Skolpojks ock Studentslang, by R. Berg, *Svenska Låndmalen*, No. 8, 1900.

[3] I am indebted for help here to Messrs. Fred Hamann, Thayer Cummings, William H. Mittler and Tom Bowman.

[4] For a while it seemed to be lost altogether, and not until after a long search did I find it in the Library, and borrow it through the courtesy of Dr. Luther H. Evans, then chief assistant librarian and since 1945 librarian. In this search I was given friendly aid by Mr. and Mrs. Harold Strauss and Messrs. Frederick Clayton, Walter H. Dun-

argots of the trades contain many picturesque terms,[1] and the orthodox dictionaries of slang give them only the most cursory notice. Inasmuch as an adequate account of them would fill a volume twice as large as the present one it will be impossible to do much better here, but we can at least glance at some characteristic specimens. The argot of railroad men may well come first, for it is extraordinarily extensive, has provided the common vocabulary with many familiar phrases, *e.g.*, *to jump the track* and *asleep at the switch*, and in part descends from the much older argots of coaching and the sailing ships.

In its terms for various functionaries and objects it is largely derisory. A locomotive engineer is a *hogger*, *hoghead*, *hog-jockey*, *hog-mauler*,[2] *grunt* or *eagle-eye*; a fireman is an *ash-cat*, *ash-eater*, *blackie*, *diamond-cracker*, *bake-head*, *tallow-pot*, *fire-boy*, *bell-ringer*, *dust-raiser*, *soda-jerker*, *coal-heaver* or *smoke*; a conductor is a *big ox*, *big O*, *skipper*, *brains*, *boss*, *captain*, *drum*, *grabber* (passenger service) or *king* (freight); a brakeman is a *shack*, *hind-hook*, *club-winder* or *ground-hog* (freight) or a *thin-skin*, *baby-lifter* or *dude-wrangler* (passenger); a section-hand is a *donkey*, *gandy-dancer*, *jerry*, *snipe* or *terrier*; the foreman of a section gang is a *king snipe*; a flagman is a *bookkeeper*; a switchman is a *yard goose*; a yardmaster is a *ringmaster*, *dinger* or *bull goose*; a station-master is an *ornament*; a trainmaster is a *master mind*; a master mechanic is a *master maniac*; a train dispatcher is a *detainer* or *delayer*; a car-repairer is a *cherry-picker*, *tonk* or *car-knocker*; an engine-wiper is a *dishwasher*; a round-house machinist is a *chambermaid*, *nut-splitter*, *-buster* or *-cracker*, or *kettle-mender*; a boiler-maker is an *iron skull*; a repairer of air-brakes is an *air-monkey*; a railroad policeman is an *egg*; a clerk is a *paperweight* or *shiny pants*; a Pullman porter is a *bed-bug*; an official is a *brass collar* or *main pin*; a new employee is a *Casey*; one who is unpopular is a

---

can, Henry G. Alsberg, R. I. Garton and Wilmer R. Leech.

1 " The American skilled craftsman," said Ernest A. Dewey in *Labor Today*, Sept., 1941, p. 19, " speaks two languages — his native tongue and the language of his trade. Sometimes humorous, always odd to the uninitiated ear, are the strange terms, titles and phrases he applies to the tools, processes and machinery he uses in his work. Over a period of years these technical and derisive terms have developed into a craft language as distinctive to his trade as the skill in his practised hands."

2 From *hog*, one of the names for a locomotive.

scissorbill or *scissor;* and one who is solicitous for the company's interest is a *stockholder.* A locomotive is a *hog, pig, mill, calliope, smoker, jack* or *pot,* or (if small) a *coffee-pot, kettle, peanut-roaster* or *dinky;* a caboose is a *bouncer, shack, chariot, bedhouse, crib, cage, cracker-box, crumb-box, crummy, louse-cage, dog-house, glory-wagon, go-cart, monkey-wagon, palace, pavilion, shelter-house, buggy, hack, van, parlor, way-car, shanty, hearse, library, saloon, cook-shack, clown-wagon* or *zoo;*[1] a refrigerator-car is a *reefer, reef* or *freezer;* a tank-car is a *can* or *oiler;* a cattle-car is a *cow-cage* or *-crate;* a sleeping-car is a *snoozer;* a locomotive tender is a *tank;* passenger-cars are *cushions,* and a private car is a *drone-cage.*[2] A few miscellaneous examples:

> Asbestos, cobs, slack, real estate, or Pennsylvania. Coal.
> Banjo, or scoop. A fireman's shovel.
> Battleship. A large locomotive or car.
> Beehive. A yard office.
> Bend the iron, or the rust, *v.* To throw a switch.
> Big hook. A wrecking crane.
> Bird-cage, or rubberneck-car. An observation-car.[3]
> Bird-cage, bug torch, or shiner. A lantern.
> Black snake. A train of coal-cars.
> Bootlegger. A train which runs over more than one railroad.
> Bowling-alley. A hand-fired, coal-burning locomotive.
> Brain-plate. A trainman's badge.
> Brownie. A demerit.
> Brownie-box. A superintendent's car.

[1] On the Pennsylvania Railroad a caboose is known officially as a *cabin-car.*

[2] I take most of the above and those following from A Glossary of Railroad Terms, by W. F. Cottrell and H. C. Montgomery, *American Speech,* Oct., 1943, pp. 161-70, but have also borrowed from Lingo of the Rails, by Freeman H. Hubbard, *Railroad Magazine,* April, 1940, pp. 32-55; Railroad Avenue, by the same; New York, 1945; Highball, by Lucius Beebe; New York, 1945; Glossary of Railroad Slang, *Photography,* Jan., 1946, p. 149; The Railroader; by W. F. Cottrell; Palo Alto (Calif.), 1940, pp. 118-39; The Engineer Explains It, by Frank Shippy, *Saturday Evening Post,* April 15, 1939, p. 26; Lingo of the Line, *Tracks,* June, 1945, pp. 28-31; Railroad Stuff, by Stephen J. Lynch, *Writer's Digest,* April, 1942, pp. 30-32; Railroaders Have a Word For It, by Doris McFerran, *American Mercury,* June, 1942, pp. 739-42, and The Rails Have a Word For It, by Lyman Anson and Clifford Funkhouser, *Saturday Evening Post,* June 13, 1942, p. 27. Earlier sources are listed in AL4, p. 583, n. 1, and Burke, p. 110. I am also indebted to Messrs. Paul F. Laning, Phil Hamilton, James F. Rabbitt, Phil Stong, Fred Hamann, J. H. Fountain and Henry B. Brainerd.

[3] A Glossary of Pullman Service Terms, *Pullman News,* Sept., 1922, p. 137.

Bull-pen. The crew room at a terminal.

Bullfighter. An empty car.

Bump, v. To displace another man by right of seniority.

Butterfly. A note thrown or handed from a train.

Candy-butcher or news-butcher. A pedlar selling candy, tobacco, magazines, etc., on a passenger train.[1]

Caterpillar, or sailor, or tin lizard. A streamlined train.

Company jewelry. A trainman's cap, badge and other insignia.

Consist. The make-up and type of cars in a train.[2]

Cornfield meet. A head-on collision.

Crate. A box-car.

Crow's nest, cockloft or penthouse. The cupola of a caboose.

Deadhead. An employee or other passenger riding on a pass; also, an empty passenger car; also, a locomotive being hauled by another.

Deck. The floor of an engine cab; also, the roof of a freight-car.

Die game, v. To stall on a grade.

Dope. Official order; also, a lubricant.[3]

Drag. A slow freight.

Drunkard. A late Saturday night passenger train.

Eye. A signal, *e.g.*, *red-eye* and *green-eye*.

Flip, v. To board a moving train.

Flat wheel. A lame man.

Fog, or putty. Steam.

Garden, or field. A freight-yard.

Gate. A switch.

Get the rocking chair, v. To be retired on pension.

Glory. A string of empty cars.

Gone fishing. Laid off.

Goose, v. To make an emergency stop.

Gut. An air-hose.

Harness. The uniform of a passenger conductor.

Highball. A go-ahead signal; also, a fast freight running on a schedule; as a verb, to speed.[4]

High liner. A fast passenger train.

Hog-law. The federal statute which forbids a train-crew to work for more than 16 consecutive hours.

In the ditch. Wrecked.

1 See *News Butcher, Railroad Magazine*, June, 1940, pp. 97-99. *Butcher* in this sense is traced by the DAE to *c.* 1889, but is undoubtedly older.

2 When *table d'hôte* meals appeared on diners at the beginning of World War I *consist* was borrowed to designate the list of dishes in a given meal.

3 *Dope* appears in virtually all American craft argots as a designation for a liquid of unknown composition.

4 Cottrell and Montgomery, before cited, say that it comes from the name of the first train signals, " which were in the form of painted metal globes hoisted to the cross-arm of a tall pole." To this day the green, or go-ahead signal is the highest. See *Highball*, to Speed, by I. Willis Russell, *American Speech*, Feb., 1944, pp. 33-36.

In the hole. On a sidetrack.

Jerk soup, or jerk a drink, v. To pick up water from a channel between the rails while a train is under way.[1]

Kitchen stove. The firebox of a locomotive.
Ladder. The main track in a yard.
Latch. A locomotive throttle.
Liner. A passenger train.
Main iron, main steel, main stem, or high iron. The main track.
Manifest, red ball, hot shot, or ball of fire. A fast freight.
Mountain pay. Overtime.
Niggerhead. The steam dome atop a locomotive boiler.
Pigpen. A roundhouse.
Ping-pong. Switching duty.
Pike. A railroad.
Possum-belly. The tool-box under a caboose.
Red-cap. A station porter.[2]
Ringtail. A hobo.
Roof-garden, or sacred ox. A helper locomotive.
Sky-rockets. Red-hot cinders from the smoke-stack.
Tea-kettle. An old and decrepit locomotive.
Telltale. Any warning device, but especially the rods which hang over the track on the approach to a bridge, to warn freight-train crews to duck.
Varnish, or plush run. A passenger train.
Whale-belly, or sow-belly. A steel coal-car.
Whiskers, or age. Seniority.
Wildcat. A locomotive pulling no cars.
Wind. Air-brakes.
X. An empty car.
Yard goat. A switching engine.

Pullman porters, cooks and waiters have an argot of their own, e.g., *alarm-clock,* a passenger who snores loudly; *battleship,* an old-fashioned Pullman with sixteen sections and no private rooms; *to buck the bronco,* to sit up all night because no berths are vacant; *eye-drops,* cinders; *to go upstairs,* to carry food from the diner to the day-coaches; *nailer,* a railroad detective; *rubber-tired,* said of a crack express-train; *snake,* a cheap tipper; *tin-can,* a buffet-car;

[1] Origin of *Jerkwater, Engineman's Magazine,* Sept., 1945, pp. 148–49: "In June, 1870, the New York Central made, at Montrose, N. Y., the first installation that permitted locomotives to pick up water on the fly. The term *jerkwater* came into the language to designate localities whose importance consisted almost solely of the water pans between the tracks there." I am indebted here to Miss Esther Johnstone, of Richland, Wash.

[2] Black Metropolis, by St. Clair Drake and Horace Cayton, quoted in *Negro Digest,* Jan., 1946, p. 80: "Tradition has it that on Labor Day, 1890, a Negro porter at the Grand Central Station, New York, tied a bit of red flannel around his black uniform cap so that he could be more easily identified in the crowd. As a consequence he 'cleaned up,' and set a style which became the emblem of America's red-caps."

and *turtle*, a dish-washer.[1] Trolley crews, in the days of their glory, had their jargon, too, *e.g.*, *boat* for a trolley-car, *horse* for a motorman, *poor-box* for a fare-box, *stick* for a trolley-pole and *Sunday* for any day of light traffic,[2] but it is fading out with their art and mystery. So is that of the telegraphers, and for the same reason,[3] though some of it is preserved by radio operators. In the Golden Age of the craft its aristocrats were the newspaper telegraphers, who not only had to be fast and accurate at the Morse Code but also had to master the Phillips Code, which changed almost from day to day.[4] The old-time operators all suffered from *glass arm*, a variety of writers' cramp, but it was cured for the senders when someone invented the *bug*, a semi-automatic key which worked sideways instead of up and down, and for the receivers on the advent of the *mill*, *i.e.*, the typewriter. An unskilled operator was a *lid, ham, bum* or *plug*. To send a message at high speed was to *paste* the receiving operator, who was said to be *burnt up* or to *go under the table*. A wire to a remote place was a *monkey-wire*. At the end of his shift or of the day's or night's work the sender sent *30*.[5] His ordinary symbol of personal greeting to a colleague was *73*.[6] The modern automatic sending machine is an *iron horse*, the

[1] I take these from the Lexicon of Trade Jargon, before cited.
[2] These come from the same Lexicon of Trade Jargon. The trolley-car gave us *to slip one's trolley*.
[3] Said R. E. L. Russell in Twilight Falling On Men of Morse, Baltimore *Sunday Sun*, Aug. 22, 1943: "Little new blood is coming into the trade, for it has long been slowly dying." I am indebted to Mr. Russell, an old newspaper colleague and a famous telegrapher in his day, for help with what follows.
[4] It was launched by Walter P. Phillips, of the Associated Press, in 1876. Every word or phrase in daily newspaper use was abbreviated, *e.g.*, *gb*, Great Britain; *ik*, instantly killed; *td*, Treasury Department; *ac*, and company; *ancm*, announcement; *elcud*, electrocuted; *fapid*, filed a petition in bankruptcy; *hur*, House of Representatives; *pips*, Philippines; *twm*, tomorrow morning, and *scotus*, Supreme Court of the United States. In the 1925 edition of the Phillips Code there were 2500 such abbreviations, and a new one was added whenever a new personality or idea began to appear in the news. Mr. Carl A. Nelson, publisher of the *Telegraph & Telephone Age*, tells me that at the start the operators took down the code words as received, and newspaper editors had to write in their meaning, but that after the typewriter came in operators did the expanding. The code has now been adapted for use with the teletype. See Phillips Code Today, *Telegraph & Telephone Age*, April, 1939.
[5] Its origin is discussed in *American Notes & Queries*, July, 1941, p. 58, and Jan., 1942, p. 156; in the *Editor & Publisher*, May 4, 1940, p. 36, and in the Chicago *Tribune*, Jan. 13, 1940, p. 10, Jan. 15, p. 10, and Jan. 16, p. 10.
[6] 73: Origin of the Symbol, Chicago *Tribune*, May 3, 1941, p. 12. See also Lingo of the Telegraph Operators, by Minnie Swan Mitchell,

receiver is a *printer*, and the girls who paste its tape messages on delivery forms are *paperhangers*. Messenger boys and linemen also have their jargons. To the former a delivery to a distant address is a *breezer* and they themselves are *trotters*, though they seldom go on foot. To the latter a pole is a *stick*, cross arms are *toothpicks*, an insulator is a *bottle*, digging tools are *knives and forks*, climbing spurs are *hooks*, a cant-hook is a *log-wrench* or *mooley-cow*, a safety-belt is a *scared strap*, a transformer is a *pot*, to fall from a pole is to *burn the stick*, and an inexperienced workman is a *grunt*.[1]

Many of these are also used by telephone and power linemen, but both of the latter have some terms of their own. To the telephone men insulation on a wire is *bark*, a pole dipped in creosote is a *black jack* or *black diamond*, a transformer is a *kettle* or *stove*, a service truck is a *loop-wagon*, a safety-belt is a *crupper*, a cross arm is a *slat*, a lineman is a *stump-jumper* or *hiker* or *Joe Hooks*, a foreman is a *gaffer* or *brains*, a power lineman is a *hot monkey*, the company is *Maw Bell*, to get an electric shock is to be *bit* or *burned*, and to be electrocuted is to be *crossed up*. A lineman's helper or other workman who never leaves the ground is a *goofer, gopher*,[2] *groundhog, grunt, click* or *squeak*. The cry of warning when anything drops from a pole is *Headache!*[3] Two terms in use by all electricians, *juice* and *live wire*, long since entered the general vocabulary.

With the movement of communications toward radio and of transport toward gasoline there have appeared some new and pungent argots, *e.g.*, those of the truckmen and taxi-drivers. Not a few terms of the former are borrowed from older crafts, *e.g.*, *bull o' the woods*, a company supervisor, from the lumbermen, and *reefer*, a refrigerator, and *highballing*, running at high speed, from the rail-

---

American Speech, April, 1937, pp. 154-55, and Some Telegraphers' Terms, by Hervey Brackbill, the same, April, 1929, pp. 287-90.

[1] Lineman's English, by Charles P. Loomis, *American Speech*, Sept., 1926, pp. 659-60, and The Lingo of Railroad Linemen, by D. V. Snapp, the same, Feb., 1938, pp. 70-71.

[2] *Go f'r this* or *go f'r that*.

[3] These come from The Vernacular of the Lineman, by Don Wolverton, *Southern Telephone News*, June, 1930, pp. 13-14; Telephone Shop Talk, by Edna L. Waldo, *Writer's Digest*, May, 1927, p. 406-09; Telephone Workers' Jargon, by Jean Dickinson, *American Speech*, April, 1941, p. 156, and Lexicon of Trade Jargon. I am also indebted to Messrs. Edwin R. Austin, Fred Hamann, Edward L. Bernays and J. Earle Miller.

road men. Of the more original words and phrases of the truckmen I offer a few specimens: [1]

> Balloon, or load of wind. A light, bulky cargo.
> Baloney, or doughnut. A tire.[2]
> Bareback, or bob-tail. A tractor without a trailer.
> Barrelling, flying too low, floor-boarding, high-balling, on the bottom, or pouring it on. Running at high speed.
> Boom-wagon. A truck loaded with explosives.
> Boss her, or follow her around, v. To back a trailer into position.
> Box, or tag-along. A trailer.
> Bug juice, or push water. Gasoline.
> Cackle-crate. A poultry truck.
> Candy-wagon. A light truck.
> Cinchers. Brakes.
> Cold. Behind schedule.
> Cop caller. Squeaking brakes.
> Cowboy, Indian, rough-rider, or traffic-whipper. A reckless driver.
> Crash-wagon. An ambulance.
> Dock monkey. A loader.
> Dog. A motor vehicle inspector.
> Emergenson, or anchor. An emergency brake.
> Eskimo. A driver who drives with open windows in Winter.
> Fort, or tin-box. An armored car.
> Gipsy. An independent truckman, usually with but one truck.[3]
> Goose it, v. To feed gasoline in spurts.
> Grounded, v. To have one's license revoked.
> Gunnysacked. Said of a badly used truck.
> Hack-hand, juice jockey, spinner, or tooler. A driver.
> Horse, or mule. A tractor.
> Hot. Ahead of schedule.
> Iron up. v. To put on chains.
> Jesse James. A police magistrate.
> Kidney-buster. A hard-riding truck.
> Line load. A mixed cargo so stowed that its contents may be delivered in a straight line across town.[4]
> Load of post-holes. No cargo.
> Long nose, or rubber heel. A company inspector or spotter.

[1] Most of these come from Truck Drivers Lingo, *Commercial Car Journal*, March, 1938, pp. 18–19. Additions are from the Lexicon of Trade Jargon, and from Taxicab Language, *Christian Science Monitor*, May 27, 1940, p. 14; Truck Drivers Have a Word For It, by Doris McFerran, *American Mercury*, April, 1941, pp. 459–62; Knights of the Line, by James H. Street, New York *World-Telegram*, April 8, 9 and 10, 1937, and Truck Driver Lingo, by Bernard H. Porter, *American Speech*, April, 1942, pp. 102–05. I am also indebted to Mr. Robert J. Icks, of Stevens Point, Wis.

[2] An undersized tire is a *bicycle tire* or *rubber band*.

[3] *American Notes & Queries*, Sept., 1944, p. 85. Also, an out-of-town truck, with no local terminal.

[4] *American Notes & Queries*, Feb., 1945, p. 166.

Men. The police.
Pension run. A short, easy one.
Punctured lung. A leaky radiator.
Scow. A very large truck.
Sleeper, or pajama wagon. A truck with sleeping accommodations, usually over the cab.
Soft coal burner. A Diesel truck.
Soup jockey. A waitress at a roadside stand.[1]
Spook. An insurance or safety inspector.
Sweat-shop. A bullet-proof cab with bad ventilation.
Swinger. A heavy load.
Wobbly hole. Neutral gear.[2]

The lingo of taxi- and bus-drivers differs a bit from city to city, but some of its terms seem to run through the country, e.g.:

Angel. A passenger who takes a cab for the evening, stopping at bars to drink.
Blimp. A worn-out car; a large bus.
Coolie. A driver who works long hours.
Damper. A taximeter.
Donkey. A traffic policeman.
Hack, or rig. A taxicab.
Hod, or scuttle. A Negro passenger.
Hot fare, or stiff. A passenger who fails to tip.
Hungry. Applied to a driver who cadges a tip by pretending to have no change.
Ink. Gasoline.
Jerk. A short trip.
Jockey. A passenger or friend who rides in front with the driver.
Liner. A passenger who asks to be directed to a brothel.
Long-haul, or run. A trip yielding a fare of more than $1.
Neutral, or newt. Silly, brainless.[3]
Tiddly. Smart or superior, as in *tiddly uniform, tiddly sailor*.

[1] Usually addressed as *Jennie* or *Toots*.
[2] The drivers of moving vans use some of these terms, but have many others of their own, e.g., *bagger*, a flight of stairs (*three-bagger*: three flights); *chowder*, small miscellaneous articles; *climber*, a house without an elevator; *doll's house*, a penthouse; *fiddle*, a grand piano; *heel*, the heavier end of a large piece of furniture; *lap*, a round trip from van to apartment; *mountain-climber*, a moving-man; *mouse-trap*, a house or apartment with narrow doors; *sweetheart* or *honey*, an object so large that it must be taken through a window with block and tackle; *Tammany Hall*, a poorly furnished home, and *washboard*, a small piano. I take these from the Lexicon of Trade Jargon; Moving Words, New York *Evening Journal*, Sept. 29, 1936, and Farmer's Market, by Fred Beck, Los Angeles *Times*, Jan. 5, 1946.
[3] I am indebted here to the Lexicon of Trade Jargon and to A Glossary of Taxicab Words and Phrases, by Paul Gould, *New Yorker*, Nov. 3, 1928, p. 94; The Slang of Taxicab Drivers, by Frank J. Wilstach, New York *Times*, Nov. 11, 1928, Sect. 5, p. 21, and The Taxi Talk, by George Milburn, in Folk Say,

American Slang

The lingo of deep-sea sailors (including whalers and fishermen) has produced so large and so accessible a literature [1] that there is no need to deal with it here. Many of its terms have got into the common speech and are familiar to everyone, e.g., *above-board, three sheets in the wind, Davy Jones' locker, on the beach, bilge* (buncombe), *to pipe down, to be taken aback, plain* (originally *plane*) *sailing, ship-shape, half seas over, to give a wide berth to, to run afoul of, to keel over* and *to stand by*.[2] Coastwise, lake and river mariners base their talk upon the lingo of the deep sea, but the pseudonym of Samuel L. Clemens is a sufficient reminder that they also have some terms of their own.[3] The argot of canalboatmen is now almost forgotten, but in its day it showed some picturesque

---

1929, edited by B. A. Botkin. For the last I owe thanks to Mr. L. J. Carrel, of the University of Oklahoma Press. The argot of English taxi-drivers and busmen is listed in Slang, by A. N. Steele, London *Daily Herald*, Aug. 5, 1936, and This is BUSic, London *Evening News*, April 19, 1944. Some specimens: *attic*, a bus deck; *ground floor*, inside; *jockey*, a driver; *the bunk*, the head office; *finger*, an official; *mush*, money; *rabbit*, a passenger; *set*, an accident, and *tub, tank* or *wagon*, a bus.

[1] Nearly all of it in English before 1939 is listed in Burke, pp. 105–08. Works overlooked by Burke or published since include A Glossary of Sea Terms, by Gershom Bradford; New York, 1942; Sea Terms Come Ashore, by George Davis Chase, *Maine Bulletin*, Feb. 20, 1942; Perry Scope's Seagoing Dictionary, by Harley F. Wight; Brooklyn (N.Y.), 1933; Argot of the Sea, by Orlo Misfeldt, *American Speech*, Dec., 1940, pp. 450–51; Sea and Navy Story Writer's Guide, by H. F. Wright; San Diego (Calif.), 1936; Square-Rigger Relics in American Speech, by Nathaniel S. Olds, *Atlantic Monthly*, Sept., 1932, pp. 383–84; Sea Lingo Passing on Modern Liners, New York *Times*, Jan. 31, 1932, Sect. II, p. 8; Seamen's Lingo, by Arthur Richter, New York *Times*, Aug. 29, 1943; On the Lingo of the Sea, Baltimore *Evening Sun* (editorial page), Sept. 1, 1943; Sticktown Nocturne, by H. D. Darrach, Jr., Baltimore *Sun Magazine*, Aug. 12, 1945, p. 1; Nautical Lingo, by H. Phipps Hemming, Newcastle-on-Tyne *Weekly Chronicle*, May 25, 1940; English Sea-terms in Words and Idioms, by Logan Pearsall Smith; London, 1925, pp. 1–27; On the Sun Deck, by Robert Wilder, New York *Sun*, April 10, 1937, p. 24; The Yankee Whaler, by C. W. Ashley; Boston, 1926, pp. 123–46; Charley Noble, Ships, June, 1943, p. 18; Soogie, Soujge, by M. S. Beeler, *American Speech*, April, 1944, pp. 151–52, and Vocabulary for Lakes, Deep Sea and Inland Waters, by Otis Ferguson, the same, April, 1944, pp. 103–111.

[2] Many more are listed in Sea Language Comes Ashore, by Joanna Carver Colcord; New York, 1945.

[3] The calls of the leadsmen on the Mississippi of its palmy days were in feet up to nine feet and in fathoms after that. *Mark twain* was two fathoms, or 12 feet. *Half twain* was two fathoms and a half, or 15 feet. On May 20, 1941 Mr. Albert K. Dawson, of the American Express Company, issued an interview with Captain Tom Greene, of the *Gordon C. Greene*, saying that these calls were then still in use on the Mississippi and its tributaries.

terms, mainly borrowed from the speech of the yokels along the way.[1] The men who load and unload ships are still a large and rambunctious fraternity, and their talk bristles with words and phrases unintelligible to the outsider.[2] A few examples:

Ambulance. A wooden box in which small articles are hoisted.[3]
Big-money boy. A longshoreman handling explosives.
Boilermaker and helper. Whiskey with a beer chaser.
Captain Blood. A harsh boss.
Carrots and peas. Cronies.
Chain-breaker. A strong man.
Chop. Income-tax deducted from wages.
Crumb, or green pea. A man not trustworthy.
Dark cellar. A job on which men are paid less than the union scale.
Draft. A cargo.
Farm. An open space where freight is stacked.
Flame-thrower. A man successful with women.
For the church. Extra work done for nothing.
Glass arm, ten-ton Jack, lamb chop, or poor steel. A weak, lazy or otherwise poor worker.
Golden hours. Overtime.
Hero. A very diligent worker.
Made the parlor. Dead.
Marry the hook, *v.* To live and die a longshoreman.
Mission bell. A drinker of cheap wine.
Pick of the beach. A good worker.
Pie-card job. An office job.
Race-track. The route along which hand-truckmen follow one another.
Reindeer. A hand-truckman who works fast.
Riding. Loading.
Save-all. A safety net hung between ship and pier.
Scavenger. A longshoreman who eats the sailors' leavings aboard ship.
Termite. One who curries favor with the foreman.
Under the hat. Wages under the union scale.
Uphill. The last hour's work.
Warden. The boss.

[1] Erie Canal Colloquial Expressions, by Jason Almus Russell, *American Speech*, Dec., 1930, pp. 97–100; Some Quotations Supplementing the DAE, by Elliott V. K. Dobbie, the same, Dec., 1946, pp. 305–07; Snubbin' Thro' Jersey, by F. Hopkinson Smith and J. B. Millet, *Century Magazine*, Aug., 1887, pp. 483–96.
[2] Its more seemly vocabulary is listed in A Port Dictionary of Technical Terms, published by the American Association of Port Authorities; New Orleans, 1940. See also Port Terminal Operation, by Eugene H. Lederer; New York, 1943. The less austere terms following come from Longshoreman's Lingo, by John Alfred Knoetgen, *Encore*, Sept.–Oct., 1944, pp. 336–38, and the Lexicon of Trade Jargon.
[3] Probably suggested by the fact that it is used to bring injured workers ashore.

To which may be added some terms of the men who build and service ships:[1]

After-birth. The sliding ways which cling to a ship after launching.
Baloney. An electric cable.
Duke. An inspector.
Furniture. Masts and rigging.
Gold room. A warehouse where valuable parts are kept.
Hat. A diver's helmet.
Hole. A drydock.
Jesus slippers. Boots.
Kettle-buster. A boilermaker.
Meat-hook. A wire which ravels out when a steel cable is frayed.
Mill. A marine engine.
Pig. A welding machine.
Rig. A pile-driver.
Shrapnel. Bolts, rivets, etc., that fall upon workmen below.
Snake-rancher. An incompetent workman.
Spider. A painter.
Stick. Any timber more than 6 by 6 inches in size.
Third ear. An informer.
Undertaker bait. A man who takes dangerous risks.
Wheels. Propellers.

The automobile and the airship have both brought in large vocabularies of new terms. Many of those introduced by the former have got into the common speech, *e.g., to park, back-seat driver, road-hog, to step on the gas, garage, detour, filling-station, gas* (for gasoline), *chauffeur, stream-lined, joy-ride, hit-and-run, jaywalker, fender, speed-cop, traffic-light, tourist-camp, safety-zone* and *to thumb a ride*, and the meaning of many more is generally known, *e.g., chassis, limousine, carburetor, tractor, station-wagon, rumble-seat, spark-plug* and *clutch*,[2] but there are others that remain the

[1] I take these mainly from Shipyard Terms of the Northwest, 1944 Style, by Hal Babbitt, *American Speech*, Oct., 1944, pp. 230–32; Navy Yard Talk, by Jack G. Arbolino, the same, Dec., 1942, pp. 279–80, and Lexicon of Trade Jargon.
[2] How long they will last remains to be seen. The bicycle gave us *scorcher, century-run, to back-pedal* and *pedal-pusher* and for years they were known to every schoolboy, but now they are all obsolete, though the bicycle survives. The automobile vocabulary, in fact, has changed considerably since 1900. See The Horseless Carriage, by M. R. Eiselen, *Yale Review*, Autumn, 1936, pp. 134–47, and The Automobile and American English, by Theodore Hornberger, *American Speech*, April, 1930, pp. 271–78. Some of the differences between American and English automobile terms are listed in Supplement I, pp. 457–87. In the Motorists' Companion, by John Prioleau; London, 1936, pp. 457–67, such terms are given in six languages, of which

private property of the men working in automobile plants and of those who sell or repair cars. A few specimens:

Bald-head. A worn tire.
Bare-foot. A car without tires.
Barrel, or hole. An engine cylinder.
Bender, tomato, or puppy. A stolen car.
Canary, or cricket. A squeak in a car.
Chatterbox. A car radio.
Clinchers, or grippers. Brakes.
Firecracker. An engine that misfires.
Ginger-bread. Body trim.
Glimmers. Headlights.
Guess-stick. A slide-rule.
Handshaker. A foreman.
Headhunter. An efficiency man.
Hearse, moose, or steam-roller. A very large car.
Hell's kitchen. A body shop.
Hide. Electric insulation.
Hoop, rubber, or gum. A tire.
Insect. A small defect in a new car.
Juice box. A battery.
Kalsomimer. A body finisher.
Kick the clock, v. To set back a speedometer.
Lid. A hood.
Liquor. An anti-freeze mixture.
Mill. An engine.
Old Man. A portable drill.
Orphan, or off-breed. An obsolete model.
Pot, strainer, or percolator. A carburetor.
Scalding. Welding.
Slushers. Chains.
Snort-pipe. The exhaust.
Tack-spitter. An upholsterer.
Umpire. An inspector.
Wind-bag. An inner tube.
Windmill. A fan.[1]

Jalopy is defined by the New Practical Standard Dictionary, 1946, as "a decrepit automobile or airplane" and marked "origin obscure." Whether it arose among the airmen or the automobile

---

two are English and American. I am indebted here to Mr. Edgar Gahan.

[1] I take these from Slang on Wheels, by Elliott Curtiss, Jr., *Automobile Trade Journal*, Jan. and May, 1937; Kick-Ups and Jack Pads, by G. A. Kahmann, *News & Views* (General Motors), March, 1938, pp. 41 and 45; Lexicon of Trade Jargon; Super-Service Slang, by Nedra Karen Israel, *American Speech*, Dec., 1938, pp. 314–16; Detroit Automobile Slang, by Thelma James, the same, Oct., 1941, p. 240, and How to Buy a Used Car, by Martin H. Bury, revised edition, Philadelphia, 1940.

dealers I do not know, nor am I sure about the spelling, for it has appeared variously as *jalopy, jallopy, jaloppy, joloppy, jollopy, jaloopy, jalupie* and *julappi*. Wentworth says that it was in oral use *c.* 1925, but his first printed example is dated 1934. The Winston Dictionary says that it was used by sports writers in 1924, in the form of *julappi*.[1] Wentworth defines it as " an old (battered) automobile " and notes a derivative, *sub-jalopy*. By 1942 Berrey and Van den Bark had found it in use to designate a racing car and an airplane, and as a verb meaning " to ride in or drive a cheap or small car." It began to attract the attention of amateur lexicographers in 1937 or thereabout, and one of them reported in 1938[2] that it had been employed by used car dealers and taxi drivers " for years." A little before this another reported that he had encountered it in a film starring W. C. Fields, the comedian, " more than seven years ago."[3] In those cradle days it had many rivals, *e.g., can, boiler, crate, knick-knacker, Napoleon, klunk, klunker, goat, goat-nest, stone-crusher, tramp, feed-bag, puddle-jumper, rattletrap, chug-wagon, whoopie, china-closet, slop-can, concrete-mixer, coffee-grinder, dog, hoptoad, heap, knockabout* and *tin*. The etymologies proposed for it are numerous and most of them are highly unpersuasive. I offer the following as horrible examples:

1. " Old broken-down Fords were exported to Mexico, many to *Jalapa*. Hence, in Southern California, any floppy car became a *jalopy*."[4]
2. " In one of Galsworthy's books he refers to an otherwise undescribed horse-drawn carriage as a *shallop*. *Shallop* is derived from the French *challupe*."[5]
3. " *Jaloppy* or *jallape* is of Yiddish-Polish origin and a transliteration of the word *shlappe*, meaning an old horse."[6]
4. " *Jalopy* . . . is simply the first three syllables of the Italian word for dilapidated, namely *dilapidato*, which is pronounced very nearly *jih-lah-pih-DAH-taw*."[7]
5. " Working on the clue that the term is of oriental extraction, we have pin-pointed two possible derivations. One is the Hebrew word *yalleph*, which

[1] Current English Forum, *College English*, April, 1943, p. 439.
[2] Jalopiana, Newark *Sunday Call*, Oct. 23.
[3] Neal O'Hara in the New York *Evening Post*. Reprinted in New Words For Old, Baltimore *Evening Sun* (editorial page), May 17, 1938.
[4] Margaret Ernst, in The Conning Tower, New York *Evening Post*, April 6, 1939.
[5] Eddie Blass in the same. The French word is actually *chaloupe*. It means a form of water craft and has cognates in the Spanish *chalupa*, Italian *scialuppa*, German *schaluppe* and Dutch *sloep*. The NED traces it in English use to *c.* 1578.
[6] Mexetao Sherover in the same.
[7] *Dilapidato*, by Elmer G. Smith, *Time*, July 26, 1937, p. 6.

means a scabby substance, and the other is an Arabian word, *jalab*, meaning a leathern shield, skin or steel [*sic*]."[1]

6. "In Spanish a tortoise is a *galapago*. . . . The word might be used to designate a person or thing having the characteristics of a tortoise, which is noted for its slow motion and the age it attains, some of them living more than 200 years. . . . It is easy to think of natives near the Mexican border referring to old, slow-moving automobiles as *galapagos*, and to understand how *galapago* would become *jaloppy*. . . . Americans have always had trouble with the hard *g*."[2]

7. "The readiest explanation is that *jalopy* is a distorted diminutive form of *gallop*, a term that was frequently used by collegians among the alliterative names painted on their leaping and bucking old open-air taxicabs."[3]

8. "Webster R. Kent, of Memphis, Tenn., suggested in a telegram to *Time*, June 21, 1937, that *jalopy* came either from *gallop*, as mentioned above, or was a euphemistic contraction of *dilapidated*. A more whimsical attempt would relate it to *jollop*, a fowl's dewlap or wattle."[4]

Jitney and *tin-Lizzie* have also engaged the etymologists, but with no more plausible result. The DAE passes over both, but Gilbert Tucker, in his "American English,"[5] traces *jitney* to 1912. On February 4, 1915, the *Nation* defined it as "the Jewish slang term for a nickel," but Webster 1934 suggests that it may come from the French *jeton*, "a counter, token or metal disk," and the New Practical Standard marks it "etymology obscure." It must be older than 1912, but it did not come into general use until *c*. 1915, when it began to be applied to Fords operating as five-cent busses. By 1916 the Legislature of New Jersey and the City Council of Atlantic City were defining *jitney* in this sense: at the start it meant always a five-cent bus, but by 1922 it was applied also to busses charging ten cents.[6] In *American Speech*, in 1933, p. 73, I noted that the term was already obsolescent,[7] but this was presently denied by Miles L. Hanley,[8] W. L. Werner[9] and Harold Wentworth.[10] It is, however, seldom heard today, for high taxes and franchise fees have driven *jitneys* from the streets of most American cities, and the term is but little used for a five-cent piece, though it retains some vitality in the general sense of paltry. *Flivver*, in many situations, is synonymous. It

[1] Recurring Word, Edinburgh *Scotsman*, March 1, 1941.
[2] From an unpublished paper by Sergeant David M. Cleary, of the Field Artillery, 1942.
[3] Jalopiana, before cited.
[4] Jalopiana, before cited.
[5] New York, 1921, p. 271.
[6] *Jitney* and *Jitneur*, by W. L. Werner, *American Speech*, Feb., 1934, p. 74. See also *Jitney*, by H. L. Mencken, the same, Jan., 1927, p. 214.
[7] Feb., p. 73.
[8] Comments, *American Speech*, Oct., 1933, p. 78.
[9] *Jitney* and *Jitneur*, lately cited.
[10] Survival of *Jitney*, *American Speech*, Dec., 1934, pp. 315-16. See also AL4, pp. 86, 93, 189 and 263.

seems to have originated in college slang, and at the start meant a failure. In this sense it was used by Harry Leon Wilson in "Ruggles of Red Gap," 1915. During the same year it was listed by Robert Bolwell as in use on the campus of Western Reserve University[1] and four years later it was reported as high-school slang in the Southwest.[2] It seems to have been applied to a Model T Ford, then the cheapest car on the market, before 1920; later it was also applied to various other inferior contrivances, including destroyers of 750 tons or less. In 1918 Arthur (Bugs) Baer used *flivveritis* in the sense of deterioration or ruin, but apparently without any reference to the Ford.[3] *Lizzie* and its daughter, *tin-Lizzie*, may be derived from *lizard*, which the DAE traces to 1870 as the name of "a sled-like contrivance for hauling logs or other heavy objects."[4] The cowboys of the West also applied it to the metal horn of a saddle.[5] Miss Warnock, lately cited, reported *Lizzie* and *tin-can* as Southwestern campus names for a Ford in 1919. *Tin-Lizzie* followed naturally.

The argot of aviators has been compiled in a workmanlike manner by Fred Hamann.[6] "Aviation," he says, "is less than half a century old, yet no other industry has originated a language as rich in slang, argot, colloquialisms and colorful terms." Many of them are already familiar to everyone, *e.g.*, *to zoom, to bail out, on the beam, to fly blind, air-pocket, blimp, low* (or *high*) *ceiling, to hedge hop, to nose-dive* and *tail-spin*. The airmen, like the railroad men, use many derisory terms in speaking of themselves and their apparatus, *e.g.*, *truck-driver, chauffeur* or *throttle-jockey* for a pilot; *paddlefoot, blisterfoot, ground-gripper* or *dust-eater* for a member of the ground crew; *clerk* or *pencil-pusher* for a navigator; *stooge* or *kid* for a co-pilot; *barrel* or *can* for an engine cylinder; *pants-slapper, blower, wind-mill, butter-paddle, club* or *fan* for a propeller, and *hut, greenhouse* or *pulpit* for a cockpit. Not a few of these terms show *Galgenhumor*, *e.g.*, *meat-wagon* for an ambulance, *first*

---

1 College Words and Phrases, *Dialect Notes*, Vol. IV, Part III, p. 233.
2 Terms of Disparagement in the Dialect of High-School Pupils in California and New Mexico, by Elsie Warnock, *Dialect Notes*, Vol. V, Part II, 1919, pp. 60–73.
3 Vogue Affixes in Present-Day Word-Coinage, by Louise Pound, *Dialect Notes*, Vol. V, Part I, 1918, p. 8.
4 Riding in a *Lizard*, by Mamie Meredith, *American Speech*, Aug., 1931, p. 465.
5 Cowboy Lingo, by Ramon F. Adams; Boston, 1936, pp. 44 and 102.
6 Air Words; Seattle, 1946.

man down for a flyer in trouble whose parachute doesn't open, and *funeral glide* for a landing out of control. Some are also more or less indecent, e.g., *joy-stick* for the pilot's control stick,[1] and *condom* for a wind-cone. The airmen have borrowed heavily from the argot of sailors, e.g., *to trim ship, log-book, tail-wind* and *rigger* (applied to a parachute repairer), and also from that of railroad men, e.g., *hoghead* (the manager of an airport); that of lumbermen, e.g., *haywire;* that of actors, e.g., *barnstormer;* that of automobile-drivers, e.g., *crate, flivver* and *hot* (fast), and that of hoboes, e.g., *hump* (a mountain). The workers in airplane plants use many of these terms also, and their vocabulary is otherwise full of the terms in common use in all metal-working plants, but they also have some that I have not found elsewhere, e.g., *blue ox*, a bombsight; *bones*, the skeleton of an airplane fuselage (body); *Buck Rogers*, a rivet gun; *bug-chaser*, an inspector; *knuckle-buster*, a wrench; *roof-rider*, a crane operator; *sewing-machine*, an automatic riveter or welder; *squawk*, an inspection; *tin-knocker*, a riveter or sheet-metal worker, and *fisterris* and *kajody*, any indefinite object.[2]

Radio is even younger than the airplane, but its impact upon American life has been terrific, and so long ago as 1937 a writer on its vocabulary was calling it the *fifth estate*.[3] That vocabulary is now large, but much of it is of very recent date. The word *radio* itself did not come into general use in the United States until c. 1920,[4] and the English still seem to prefer *wireless*. Until the death of the Hon. Alfred E. Smith on October 4, 1944, there lingered some doubt among American fans as to whether the word should be pronounced *ray-dio* or *rad-dio*, and the learned still disagree about the conjugation of *to broadcast*. The brothers Fowler, in the Concise Oxford Dictionary, give *broadcasted* for the past tense and *broadcast* for the perfect participle; Webster 1934 allows *broadcasted* in the past "in radio senses"; the New Practical Stand-

---

[1] Hamann says that this implement gets its name from its inventor, one Joyce, but Joyce is not identified and the etymology sounds improbable.

[2] There are many lexicons of air argot, but Hamann's, before cited, is the best. The earlier literature is listed by Burke, p. 109. An Encyclopedic Aviation Dictionary, by Charles A. Zweng; Los Angeles, 1944, defines mainly technical terms.

[3] The Fifth Estate Vocabulary, by Julian T. Bentley, *American Speech*, April, 1937, pp. 100-02.

[4] AL4, p. 559.

ard ordains *broadcast* for both past and perfect participle. Many of the terms in use in the studios are loans from the stage, *e.g.*, *to ad lib*, *bit* (a small part), *blue* (indecent), *cast, character, cue, to double, dress rehearsal, flack* (a press-agent), *gag, grip* (a stage carpenter), *lead, emcee, props, show* and *turkey*, and others come from the argot of the movie-lots or the jazz-bands, *e.g.*, *canary, cliff-hanger, continuity, corny, 88, flesh-pedlar* (a talent agent), *groan-box, long-hair, schmalz, script* and *whodunit*.[1] The following, however, seem to be indigenous:

Across the board. A programme that goes on daily at the same time.
Adenoid. A vocalist with a muffled voice.
Arsenic. A boresome programme.
Beard, clinker, fluff, or kick. An error in a performance.
Belcher. A performer who is hoarse.
Belly-punch, buffaroo, or hup-cha-da-bub-cha. A joke which produces hearty laughter.
Bite off, *v*. To cut off a line or number while the show is on the air.
Blast. Over-loud transmission.
Bobble, *v*. To fumble, especially in reading lines.
Burp. An unintended noise.
Chromatics. Emotional acting.
Clambake, or clanaroo. A programme or rehearsal that goes badly.
Clientitis. Trouble with a sponsor.
Cow-hand. One who escorts visitors through a studio.
Crawk. An animal imitator.
Creeper, or mike mugger. A performer who gets too close to the microphone.
Cushion. Music played at the end of a programme to consume time in case it runs ahead of schedule.
Dawn patrol. Performers in early morning broadcasts.
Disk jockey, or pancake-turner. One who changes phonograph records.[2]
Dog. A time-worn song or gag.
Down in the mud, low level, or not enough hop. Singing or speaking too low.
Ear-ache. An actor who over-acts.
Fish-bowl. The client's observation booth in a studio.
Frying. A hissing sound caused by defective equipment.
Gabber, or spieler. A commentator.
Gaffoon. A sound-effects man.
Gelatine. A tenor with a thin voice.
Hash session. A consultation before a broadcast.

[1] Radio Bandmen Speak a Strange Language, by Louis Reid, New York *American*, June 22, 1935; Swing Lingo in Radio Adds Color to Broadcasts, by Martin Codel, Worcester (Mass.) *Telegram*, July 9, 1938.

[2] *American Notes & Queries*, March, 1945, p. 192.

730 *The American Language: Supplement II*

Hook. "That part of the *commercial* which urges you to send in the box-tops."[1]
Lady Macbeth. An emotional actress.
Line. A network.
Log. A record of a broadcast, required by law.
Madame Cadenza. A female vocalist.
Madame La Zonga. A performer who dances nervously at the microphone.
Mama Lucia. A fat contralto.
Mike hog. A performer who tries to monopolize the microphone.
Monkey. A band leader.
Nemo, or remote pickup. A broadcast picked up from outside the studio.
Off the arm. Extemporaneous.
One-lunger, or coffee-pot. A 100-watt station.[2]
On the nose. Running on time.
Out in the alley. Out of range of the microphone.
Pipe, *v*. To send a programme from one place to another by telephone.
Plops. Over-accentuated pronunciations, especially of the letters *b* and *p*.
Plug-ugly. An advertisement interjected into a news announcement or entertainment programme.[3]
Quonking. Side-line chatter which disturbs a performance.
Rover boy. A minor executive of an advertising agency.
Scooper. A singer with slurry enunciation.
Scoutmaster. An advertising agency executive.
Segue. A transition from one musical theme to another.[4]
Sexton. A bass singer.
Signature. The music or other effect which identifies a serial programme.
Sneak in. Music played softly, as a background to dialogue.
Town crier. A singer who sings too loud.
Walla walla. Words uttered by performers in mob scenes.
Weaver. A performer who moves nervously before the microphone.
White meat. An actress.
Woodshed. A hard rehearsal.
Yuck. A soap-opera addict.
Zampa. A florid musical passage.
Zilch. Anyone whose name is not known.[5]

[1] The Fifth Estate Vocabulary, before cited.
[2] *Fortune*, March, 1947, p. 175
[3] In the Interest of Radio, St. Louis *Post-Dispatch* (editorial), April 10, 1945.
[4] Advertisement of Columbia Broadcasting System, Feb. 26, 1944: "Call it *ség-we* or *ség-way*, not *ség-you*."
[5] Most of these come from Radio Alphabet: A Glossary of Radio Terms, edited by Gilbert Seldes, Paul Hollister and a dozen others and published by the Columbia Broadcasting System in 1946. The early authorities are listed in Burke, p. 122. Other works worth consulting are Wireline Webster, issued by the Mutual Broadcasting System, June, 1945; Glossary of Commercial Terms, by J. J. Weed, in *Variety* Radio Directory, 1937-38; New York, 1937, pp. 353-58; Some Radio Terms, by John S. Carlile, *Fortune*, May, 1938, p. 54; Radio Vocabulary, by S. Stephenson Smith, *Quarterly Journal of Speech*, Feb., 1942, pp. 1-7; Radio Jargon, by William White, *Words*, Dec., 1941, pp. 97-101; A Study of the Vocabulary of Radio, by Donald E. Hargis, *Speech Monographs*, XII, 1945, pp. 77-87; Dictionary of Radio Terms; Chicago, 1940; Radio Slanguage, by

The meaning of many radio terms is now familiar to every American, e.g., *web, sponsor, sustaining programme, soap-opera,*[1] *to dial, plug, platter, on the air, commercial, network, canned music* and *static*. Television, usually called *video*, is introducing its own, e.g., *blizzard-head*, a blonde; *flag* or *gobo*, a screen to shade the camera; *ghost*, an unwanted secondary image; *gismo* or *gizmo*, any contrivance which yet lacks a name; *hot light*, a concentrated light; *inky*, an incandescent light; *gilding*, performers' make-up;[2] *womp*, a sudden flare-up of light on the receiving screen;[3] *noise*, spots or a pattern on the picture; *model*, to move gracefully before the camera, as in a fashion-show; *roll it*, the cue to start work, and *stretch*, to stall for time.[4]

Every other trade, profession, sport and hobby has its argot, and it would be impossible to give specimens of all of them. Even such strange folk as aquarium attendants, apple-pickers, dog-breeders, philatelists and social workers talk among themselves in terms unintelligible to the outsider. The best I can do here is to sample those of some scattered groups, taking them in alphabetical order:

Advertising Agents

Art. Anything in the nature of a picture.

Blind ad. An unsigned newspaper or magazine advertisement, usually including a direction to send inquiries in care of the publisher.

Blurb. An encomium of a book on a slipcover, usually signed by someone pretending to literary judgment; now extended to any florid testimonial.[5]

K. W. Strong, *Better English*, March, 1940, pp. 118–19 and Radio Has a Word For It, by Doris McFerran, *American Mercury*, Nov., 1941, pp. 578–81. I am also indebted here to Messrs. Will A. Whitney, J. V. Koehler, Eldridge Peterson, Julian Street, Jr., Joseph Katz and A. K. Dawson. The gestures used in radio studios (speaking, of course, is forbidden) are illustrated in Radio Alphabet, above cited, and described in Lexicon of Trade Jargons, Vol. III.

1 Radio Alphabet, before cited: " [So called] because the early sponsors of these programmes were soap manufacturers."

2 *Video* Make-Up, *Variety*, June 19, 1946, p. 27.

3 *Gobos* and *Gismos*, New York *Times Magazine*, March 3, 1946.

4 These come from Television Talk, issued by the National Broadcasting Company in 1946. See also The Words, *New Yorker*, Dec. 3, 1938, p. 20. The vocabulary of radar is in Radar Nomenclature, *American Speech*, Dec., 1945, pp. 309–10; Radar Language, *Newsweek*, Sept. 10, 1945, p. 92, and Radar, issued by the British Information Services, New York, 1945. That of amateur radio operators, or *hams*, is in Ham Slang, by R. D. Bass, *Words*, Dec., 1938, pp. 138–39, and Jan., 1939, pp. 10–12; and *Ham* Lingo, by Marion Fry, *American Speech*, Oct., 1929, pp. 45–49.

5 See Supplement I, p. 389.

Bookvertising. Advertising by means of books and other printed matter in which the advertiser's product is mentioned only incidentally.[1]

Copy-writer. One who writes the text of an advertisement.

Display-ad. One set wholly or chiefly in large type.

Double-truck. An advertisement covering two facing newspaper pages.

Layout-man. One which lays out an advertisement, indicating the places and themes of the *art*.

Puller. An advertisement that brings in sales.

Reader, or reading-notice. A blurb printed as reading-matter. It is usually thrown in by the publisher in return for a paid advertisement. If it is paid for separately the Postal Act requires that it be marked *Advertisement*.

Space buyer. A functionary who chooses the media in which a given advertisement or series is to be published.

Transitad. An advertisement in a street-car, bus or other public vehicle.[2]

Want-ad. A small advertisement, usually printed under a rubric, e.g., *Help Wanted, Lost and Found*.[3]

Aquarists

Boarder. A fish on exhibition.

Chef. The attendant who cuts up food for the fish.

Goofy. Said of a fish off its feed.

Hybreeding. Hybridizing.

Sleeper. A visitor who comes in, not to see the fish, but to rest.[4]

Apple-pickers [5]

Apple-knocker. A club used to loosen fruit from the boughs; also, a fast apple-picker.

Dope. Any spray used in an orchard.

Drops, or ground stuff. Fallen apples.

Facers. The apples packed at the top of the box.

[1] Coined by Herb Stoeckel, of *Bookbinding & Book Production*, New York.

[2] Coined in 1940 by George E. Frazer, a New York accountant, and now used in the title of National *Transitads*, of which he is president. I am indebted here to Mr. Myron T. Harshaw.

[3] The commonplace quality of these selections from the advertising man's trade argot is compensated for by the lush fancy shown in the terms he invents for his clients, especially those who appeal to female patronage. Many of his names for colors, perfumes and articles of female adornment are borrowed from non-English languages, e.g., *brassière, dirndl, babushka*. See Ici on Parle—, by Marjorie H. Nicholson and Edith Phillips, *American Speech*, Feb., 1926, pp. 257–63; All the Perfumes of America, by Arthur Minton, the same, Oct., 1946, pp. 161–74, and The Language of Fashion, by Mary Brooks Picken; New York, 1939. He is also the progenitor of many euphemisms, e.g., *halitosis, B. O., D. O.* (dog odor), *tissue* (toilet-paper). His latest novelties are frequently noted in *American Speech*.

[4] I take these from Aquarium English, by Ida Mellen, *American Speech*, Aug., 1928, pp. 460–63. Miss Mellen says that the aquarian folk call themselves *aquarists*. In England they used to be *aquarians* and in the United States some of them preferred *aquariist*, with two *i*'s, but *aquarist* now prevails in both countries.

[5] From Lexicon of Trade Jargon, before cited.

Goose walk. An over-abundance of packers applying for work.
Marbles. Extremely small apples.
Skyscraper. A tree which requires an extra long ladder.
Sting. An apple with wormholes.
Push. The boss.
Worm-chaser. An inspector.[1]

Architects [2]

Bird seed. Dotting or hatching on plans.
Calque, *v.* To make a tracing.[3]
Cheater. A reducing glass.
Garbage. Ornamentation.
Nigger, *v.* To fill in details of a design.
Pencil-pusher. A draftsman.
Pig. A brush used to sweep off drawings.
Sky-hooks. Plans showing insufficient structural support.
Slip-sticks. A slide rule.

Bakers [4]

Bottomer. One who places the hulls of pies in plates before baking.
Cracker-breaker. One who knocks off individual crackers from the long strips in which they are baked.
Dumper, shaker, or hot-stuff man. One who removes pies, etc., from pans.
Pan-catcher. One who stacks empty pie pans.
Pie-washer. One who paints pies with a fluid designed to give them a golden-brown color when baked.
Pinner, or sticker. One who impales cookies on the pins of a wire rack preparatory to dipping them in icing.
Pretzel-twister. One who fashions thin strips of dough into the form of pretzels.
Sandwich girl. A girl who spreads filling between the two halves of double-deck crackers or cookies.

Barbers

Acre-and-a-half. A fat-faced man.
Barbed-wire, or squirrel. A tough beard.
Bath. A shampoo.
Box. An angular, craggy-faced man.
Dragger. A non-tipping customer.
Gopher. A man who has not had a haircut in a long time.

---

1 See also Fruit-Drying Phraseology, by Ivy Grant Morton, *Writer's Monthly*, Aug., 1928, pp. 104-05, and Apple-Picking Terms From Wisconsin, by F. G. Cassidy, *American Speech*, Feb., 1943, pp. 74-76.
2 From Lexicon of Trade Jargon.
3 French *calque*, a tracing or imitation.
4 These all come from Dictionary of Occupational Titles, Part I: Definitions of Titles, prepared for the use of "public employment offices and related vocational services" by the Job Analysis and Information Section, Division of Standards and Research, United States Employment Service, Department of Labor; Washington, 1939. This volume of 1287 double-column pages, printed on Bible paper, is one of the masterpieces of New Deal scholarship.

Hob, or hook. A razor.
Jista. A customer who asks for a shave only.[1]
Mop. A lather brush; also, a heavy head of hair.
Panther-water, or squaw-water. Hair tonic.
Scratcher. An electric head-rubbing apparatus.
Steamer. A hot towel.
Tear, v. To cut or nick.
Workhouse. A barber-shop.[2]

Bartenders

Barman. A euphemistic term for bartender.[3]
Cage. A service bar.
Comb. The scraper used to remove suds from a freshly-drawn glass of beer.
Cop's bottle. A bottle of the cheapest whiskey.
Fast house. A bar where most of the trade is in mixed drinks.
Flat. A very small beer.
Fruit salad. An old-fashioned cocktail.
Gas-drinker. A drinker of ginger-ale.
Germ-killer. Benedictine and brandy.
Headache, or auctioneer. A garrulous customer.
Landlord. A steady customer.
Light. An honest glass without a false bottom.
Mickey Finn. A drink containing a quick purgative, given to a drunk to get rid of him.[4]
Pop-skull. An empty whiskey glass.
Sham. A glass with a false bottom.
Shell. A small beer-glass.
Squirt-gun. A seltzer siphon.
Stick. The handle of a beer spigot.[5]
Trance. A customer far gone in liquor.[6]

Baseball-players [7]

Apple, cantaloupe, onion, potato, or tomato. The ball.
Aspirin, or pea. A ball pitched so fast that the batter can barely see it.
Banana stalk. A bat of inferior wood.

1 *Jist a* shave.
2 All these come from Lexicon of Trade Jargon.
3 The most elegant bartenders' organization is the International *Barmen's* Association. But the A. F. of L. union is the *Bartenders'* International League of America, organized in Jan., 1892.
4 The origin of this term has been much debated. See Gem of the Prairie, by Herbert Asbury; New York, 1940, p. 172.
5 *Going behind the stick* or *behind the plank* is going on duty.
6 I am indebted here to Lexicon of Trade Jargon and to Mr. Roy L. McCardell. The names of drinks are discussed in AL4, pp. 148–50, and Supplement I, pp. 252–69.
7 Most of these terms are taken from An Historical Dictionary of Baseball Terminology, by Edward J. Nichols, " a dissertation submitted in partial fulfillment of the requirements for the degree of doctor of philosophy at the Pennsylvania State College," Jan., 1939. This is an admirably accurate, comprehensive and workmanlike study. It has not been published save in abstract, but microfilms and full-sized photographs of the MS. are obtainable from University Microfilms, Ann Arbor, Mich. I have also made some use of Joe McGlone, Provi-

Barker, or yodeler. A coacher.
Bean ball, duster, or Gillette. A ball thrown at a player's head.[1]
Biff, *v.* To bat a ball hard.[2]
Bleachers. The uncovered seats at a ball park.[3]
Blind Tom, guesser, Jesse James, robber, empire, or His Honor. An umpire.
Blue darter, or clothesliner. A low, hard liner.[4]

Bunt. A hit made with an almost motionless bat, causing the ball to fall between home-plate and pitcher's box.[5]

Can o'corn. A fly that is easy to catch.
Charley horse. Muscular soreness in a player's leg.[6]
Chucker, fogger, fooler, or tosser. A pitcher.
Cigar-box, or flea-box. A very small ball-park.
Clinker, boat, or kick. An error.
Collar, or horse-collar. A time at bat without a hit.
County fair, Fancy Dan, or show-boat. A show-off.

dence (R.I.) *Evening Bulletin*, Aug. 2, 1946, p. 30; Down in Front, by Richards Vidmer, New York *Herald Tribune*, June 7, 1941, p. 17; Baseball Guide and Record Book; New York, 1943, pp. 83-92; Gibberish, by C. M. Gibbs, Baltimore *Sun*, Jan. 31, 1935, and the Jargon of Sports-Writers, by Willis Stork; Lincoln (Neb.), 1934. Other papers on the subject are listed in Burke, pp. 115-16. I am indebted for friendly help to Dr. Nichols, Dr. Harold H. Bender, Messrs. Lawrence C. Salter, Fred Hamann, Leo C. Dean, H. Allen Smith, and A. H. Gurney, the late Dr. Logan Clendening, Dr. Victor Johnson, the late Admiral C. S. Butler, Medical Corps, U.S.N., and Messrs. Bill Bryson, Lloyd Lewis and Charles J. Lovell.

1 *Gillette*, of course, was suggested by *close shave*.
2 Traced by Nichols to *Sporting Life*, Oct. 4, 1902. Said to have been coined by William T. Hall, a Chicago sports reporter.
3 Traced by Nichols to 1888.
4 Bewildering are Slang Terms Used in Talk of Baseball Players, by Harold Parrott, Brooklyn *Eagle*, Aug. 9, 1936.
5 Introduced by the Baltimore Orioles and traced by Nichols to 1891. In his introduction to his Dictionary of Baseball Terminology and in Appendix II thereof he shows that of 100 terms for *hit* in vogue in 1938, 74 could be traced to 1918 or before.
6 Traced by Nichols to 1891. Dr. H. H. Bender, chief etymologist of Webster 1934, sent an agent to Bill Clarke, first baseman of the Baltimore Orioles, who said that it came from the name of *Charley* Esper, a left-handed pitcher, who walked like a lame horse. Lawrence C. Salter (private communication, Jan. 14, 1944) sent another agent to Billy Earle, an old-time catcher in the Western League, who said that it was suggested by a horse worked by one *Charley*, ground-keeper at Sioux City. The late Dr. Logan Clendening wrote to me on Nov. 20, 1943: " *Charley horse* is a ruptured muscle. It has exactly the same pathology as string-halt in a horse." In Treatment of *Charley Horse, Journal of the American Medical Association*, Nov. 30, 1946, p. 821, it is described as " injury to a muscle, usually the *quadriceps femoris*." This injury " consists first in a contusion, which results in a *hematoma*. Later the *hematoma* may organize into a *myositis ossificans*, forming soft bone in the muscle." Other etymologies are in *Charley Horse*, by Bill Brandt, *Letters*, Nov. 11, 1935; *American Notes & Queries*, April, 1937, pp. 9-10, and My Thirty Years in Baseball, by John J. McGraw; New York, 1923, p. 52.

Cup of coffee. A brief try-out in the big leagues.
Cushion, hassock, or pillow. A base.
Deer. A fast runner.
Dick Smith, or loner. An unsociable player.[1]
Dipsy-doo. A slow tantalizing curve.[2]
Fan. An enthusiast.[3]
Fireplug. A short, stocky player.[4]
Fireworks. A batting rally.
Fungo. A ball batted in practise; also, the bat used in batting such balls.[5]
Glass arm. A sore throwing or pitching arm.[6]
Grazer, gardener, or pasture-man. An outfielder.
Gun, wing, or soup-bone. A pitcher's arm.
High pockets. A very tall player.
Hind snatcher, or backstop. A catcher.
Hot corner. Third base.
Jockey. A player who bedevils (rides) an opposing player (usually a pitcher) or team.
Jug, jug-handle, hook, mackerel, fish, number two, or snake. A curve.
Lamb, or cousin. A pitcher easy to hit.
Leather player. A good fielder who can't hit.
Lumber, bludgeon, shillelah, or willow. A bat.[7]
Maggot. A club owner.[8]
Manicurist. A ground-keeper.
Muff. To fumble a ball and so miss a play.[9]
Papier mache, or pretty. A player who is easily hurt.
Pay-station. The home plate.

[1] Also used on the race-track. Its etymology is discussed in *Dick Smith*, by Peter Tamony, San Francisco *News-Letter & Wasp*, Sept. 15, 1939, p. 12.
[2] Also spelled *-do, -dew, -dow,* and *dypsido*. "This uncertainty as to spelling," says Nichols, "is typical of terms invented by the players rather than the sports reporters." Traced to 1932. At the start it was sometimes *dinky-doo*.
[3] This is often assumed to be a back-formation from *fanatic*, but William Henry Nugent says in The Sports Section, *American Mercury*, March, 1929, p. 331, that it really comes from *fancy*, which has been in use in England to designate followers of the prize-ring since 1811. The steps, he says, were *fance, fans, fan*. In baseball use the DAE traces it to 1896.
[4] Ducks on the Pond, by Joe Cummiskey, *PM*, April 21, 1943.
[5] The etymology is uncertain. See Expedition Into *Fungoland*, Chicago *Tribune* (editorial page), Oct. 29, 1939, and *Fungo* and *Bingo* Again, by Peter Tamony, *American Speech*, Oct., 1937, pp. 243-44. Traced by the DAE to 1867.
[6] The late Admiral Butler, before mentioned (private communication, Nov. 30, 1943), described *glass arm* as usually *myositis* (inflammation) of the long tendon of the biceps muscle. "Its action," he said, "is three- or four-fold and its relations to synovial sheaths, bursas and joints complicated. Damage of these structures often produces a stiffness and rigidity accompanied by loss of the power to supinate the forearm. . . . The arm feels rigid, and as if likely to break like glass."
[7] Dugout Slang, by Jimmy Powers, New York *Daily News*, Jan. 12, 1937.
[8] Apparently from *magnate*.
[9] Traced by the DAE to 1868.

Peg. A throw.[1]
Pool-table. A smooth infield.
Rhubarb. An altercation on the field.[2]
Rooter. An enthusiastic supporter of a team.[3]
Rubber, or platter. The home plate.
Seventh-inning stretch. The interval after the first half of the seventh inning.[4]
Shotgun, or slingshot. A strong throwing arm.[5]
Shut-out. A game in which one side fails to score.[6]
Southpaw, side-wheeler, cockeye, corkscrew-arm, or twirly-thumb. A left-handed pitcher.[7]
Strawberry. An abrasion caused by sliding for a base.
Teacher, or skipper. A manager.
Texas Leaguer, nubber, blooper, sinker, banjo, bleeder, stinker, pooper, punker, plunker, drooper, humpie, humpback, or squib. A pop fly which nevertheless takes the batter to first base.
Walk. A base on balls.[8]
Wolves. Hostile spectators.
Wood player. A good hitter who can't field.[9]

Beauticians

Bag, or bitch. An elderly fat woman.
Blizzard. A customer who is always in a hurry.

[1] Baseball American, by Ring W. Lardner, in The American Language, second edition; New York, 1921, pp. 392–93, and third edition, 1923, pp. 404–05.
[2] Ball Talk, New York Times Magazine, July 14, 1946. H. Allen Smith, in Rhubarb; New York, 1946: "A colloquialism inserted into the Yankee vernacular by Red Barber, the baseball broadcaster. Mr. Barber in turn picked it up from the prose of Garry Schumacher.... A noisy altercation, a broil, a violent emotional upheaval brought on by an epical dispute — such as whether one grown man had touched another on the body with a ball the size of a smallish orange."
[3] First found by Nichols in the New York Press, July 8, 1890.
[4] Nichols traces it no further back than 1920.
[5] Dugout Slang, by Jimmy Powers, New York Sunday News, Jan. 17, 1937.
[6] Traced by Nichols to 1881.
[7] Southpaw is traced by Nichols to the Chicago Herald, July 24, 1891. Richard J. Finnegan, publisher of the Chicago Times, reports that it was coined by Charles Seymour (d. 1901). He says in a letter to Lloyd Lewis, Nov. 26, 1945: "The pitchers in the old baseball park on the Chicago West Side faced the west, and those who pitched left-handed did so with their *south paws*." Baseball players believe that all left-handed pitchers are more or less balmy, just as musicians believe the same of oboe-players.
[8] Traced by Nichols to 1866.
[9] Nichols, in Appendix I of his Dictionary, lists many terms that baseball has given to the general speech, *e.g.*, *to go to bat for, play-by-play, three strikes and out, hit-and-run, minor league, to pinch hit, something on the ball, on to his curves, on the bench, two strikes on him, grandstand play, double-header, home run, to play ball* and *team-play*. Some interesting history is in Nicknames of Baseball Clubs, by Joseph Curtin Gephart, American Speech, April, 1941, pp. 100–03, and in Baseball and Rounders, by Robert W. Henderson, Bulletin of the New York Public Library, April, 1939, pp. 303–14.

738   *The American Language: Supplement II*

Clinic. A beauty-parlor.[1]
Cocktail. A light facial which freshens the customer for the evening.
Coffee. A mud-pack.
Cosmetology. The care of the skin.[2]
Crepy. Wrinkled.
Daisy. A freckle.
Decision. A woman who has her hair dyed.
Dowager's hump. A deposit of fat at the back of the neck.[3]
Fire-drill. A henna rinse.
Hair-do. A style of dressing the hair.[4]
Hamburger. A "food" cream.
Hand-out. A shampoo.
Harvest. A plucking of the eyebrows.
Hitch-hike. A finger wave.
Joe. A customer who does not tip.
Kitty. Tips.
Meat-grinder. A constant talker.
Pan-handler. A beauty-shop girl.[5]
Perm. A permanent wave.
Pickle. A customer with a forbidding face.
Queen Elizabeth. A haughty customer.
Rainbow. An eye-shadow of a color to harmonize with the complexion.
Retouch, *v*. To dye or bleach hair.
Santa Claus. A customer who appears only at long intervals.
Scratch. An appointment-book.
Screech. A complaining customer.
Skunk bob. Dyed gray hair.[6]
Smear. A bleaching lotion.
Spaniel. A woman who wears her hair in a long bob, suggesting a spaniel's ears.
Sponge. A customer willing to try all the treatments and lotions suggested.
Springtime. An old woman who yearns to be young again, and beautiful.

1 Originally, a *hair-dressing-parlor*. Latterly a *beauty-parlor*, *-shop*, *-shoppe* (*beauté-shoppe*), *-salon*, *-studio* or *-clinic*. In the *William Feather Magazine*, May, 1938, *beauty-marts*, *-bars*, *-chateaus* and *-laboratories* are all reported, and the *Modern Beauty Shop*, 1945, pp. 131, adds *-centers* and *-villas*. See Supplement I, p. 573.
2 This *recherché* term has been recognized in State laws providing for the examination and licensing of practitioners of the science. *Cosmetic*, of Greek origin, is traced in English to 1650, and the adjective *cosmetical* to 1559. *Cosmeticism* appeared in England in 1821. *Cosmetology* is apparently American. It was preceded by *cosmetician* and still has a rival in *beautician*. Both of the latter were suggested by *mortician*. See Supplement I, pp. 567–74.
3 *Modern Beauty Shop*, Dec., 1945, p. 132: "[In dealing with] the *dowager's hump* . . . I place my hands firmly on each shoulder, close to the neck. Using my thumbs only, I move them in a circular massage over the fatty area. Pressure is necessary."
4 Who invented this elegant term I do not know, but it seems to be American and goes back at least to 1936. It has been adopted in England.
5 From *pan*, face.
6 *American Notes & Queries*, June, 1946, p. 40.

Tint, *v.* To dye.
Whiskers. Artificial eyelashes.
White henna. A bleach.[1]

Booksellers [2]

Guck. The gilt stamping on a book.
Interior decorator. A dealer who specializes in sets.
Kangaroo. A shoplifter with capacious pockets.
Looker, or reader. One who haunts bookshops, but never buys.
Plug. A good book that no one wants.
Point. A feature which distinguishes the first issue from other issues of a book.

Brewery Workers [3]

Ausbrenner. A device for burning old pitch off the inner surface of kegs before applying a new coat.[4]
Beer-schiessen. Beer-time for the workers.[5]
Beer-shooter. The man or boy who dispenses beer to the workers at set times.
Bull-work. Heavy labor.
Cooperage. Draft beer containers, whether of wood or metal.
High-kraeusen. A heavy formation of foam on the fermenting beer.[6]
Kaiser's geburtstag, or saltag. Pay day.[7]
Kuehlschift. A cooling tank.[8]
Lauter-tub. A clarifying vat.[9]
Ruh-cellar. A cellar where maturing beer is stored.[10]
Schlaucher. A workman who rinses empty vats with a hose.[11]
Totsäufer. A customer's man.[12]

Bricklayers [13]

Barber, boot, or cobbler.[14] A poor bricklayer.
Belly-whacker. One who lays bricks out of plumb.
Blade. A trowel.

1 I am indebted here to Beauty-Parlor Slang, by E. E. Ericson, *American Speech*, Dec., 1941, p. 311, and to Miss Margaret Dempsey.
2 I am indebted here to News From the Rare Book Sellers, by Jacob Blanck, *Publisher's Weekly*, July 14, 1945, and to Messrs. S. R. Shapiro and H. Allen Smith.
3 Most American brew-workers are Germans, and the rest understand German. This accounts for the number of terms from that language in their argot. I take all these from Lexicon of Trade Jargon.
4 Ger. *ausbrennan*, to burn out.
5 Ger. *schiessen*, to shoot, to burst forth.
6 Ger. *sich kräusen*, to curl.
7 Ger. *geburtstag*, birthday; *salztag*, salt-day.
8 Ger. *kühl*, cool, and *schiff*, a vessel.
9 Ger. *lautern*, to clear or refine.
10 Ger. *ruh*, rest.
11 Ger. *schlauch*, a hose.
12 Sometimes *todsäufer*. A German term meaning dead-drinker. One of a *totsäufer's* chief duties is to weep for the brewery at the funerals of saloonkeepers. See my Happy Days; New York, 1940, p. 44, n. 2.
13 All these come from Lexicon of Trade Jargon. See also Handbook of Brick Masonry Construction, by John A. Mulligan; New York, 1942, pp. 491–508.
14 It is common for workmen to call incompetent fellows by the designations of workers in other trades.

Bull-header. A brick laid on edge.
Fly-blow. One who goes from job to job, borrowing money.
Hog. A difference in the number of courses of bricks in opposite corners to a given height.
Hopping-board. A scaffold.
Monkey. A hod; also, a hodcarrier.
Monkeyshines. Fancy brick work.
Mud. A call for mortar or cement; also, mortar that is too thick.
Slime, or soup. Inferior mortar.
Soldier. Brick laid on its head, as over a window.
Toother. A brick which projects from the end of a wall against which another will be built.

Cannery Workers [1]

Ball-rubber. A worker who seeks to ingratiate himself with the foreman.
Barn-paint. Catsup.
Chef. The man who runs the cooker.
Corn-snitcher. One who cuts bad places out of the ears before they are washed.
Eagle. The owner of a factory.
Eagle Eye. A Federal Pure Food inspector.
Grease-gun. One who oils the machinery.
Gummer. A label machine operator.
Kidney cleaner. Asparagus.
Peeler. One who shucks corn.
Pop-valve. An excitable foreman.
Puffer. A swelled can.
Sewer-trout. Pink salmon.
Snoop. A timekeeper.
Stuffer. A canning-machine operator.
Tail lights. Stuffed olives.

Carpenters [2]

Bone. Hard wood.
Bread and butter. A kit of tools.
Bullstaller. A poor carpenter.
Cellar. A small contractor's shop.
Cheese. Soft wood.
Coffee-grinder. A breast drill.
Floor-logger. A floor-layer.
Freeze, *v.* To glue two pieces of wood together.
George Washington. A hatchet.
Ice cream, or scap. Overtime.
King's eye. A level.
Knocker, or knocking iron. A hammer or hand ax.
Mutt. A water-carrier.
Nail-eater. A lather.
Peg. A nail.

The terms most commonly in use are *shoemaker* and *blacksmith*.

[1] From Lexicon of Trade Jargon.
[2] From Lexicon of Trade Jargon.

Riding the air. Working high up.
Scuffing. Rough planing.
Slicer. A rip saw.
Sword. A saw.[1]
Toothpick. A 12 x 12 inch beam.

Cattlemen [2]

Animal. A bull.[3]
Bite the dust, *v.* To be thrown from a horse; to die.[4]
Bronco, or bronc. An unbroken or half-broken horse.[5]
Bronc-peeler, or buster. A horse-breaker.
Buckaroo, cowhand, cowpoke, puncher, screw, rawhide, or waddie. A cowboy.[6]
Bull-dogger. One who leaps on, wrestles with and throws young steers.
Button. An apprentice cowboy.
Chaps. Leather leggins, hip high.[7]
Chili, or yellow-belly. A Mexican.
Chouse, *v.* To drive cattle roughly.[8]
Coil, string, flingline, whaleline, twine, or gutline. A lasso, or lariat.[9]
Corral. A pen for animals.[10]
Deacon. A young calf.
Dogie. A scrubby calf or other animal.[11]

[1] Language of the Trade, by Ernest A. Dewey, *Labor Today*, Sept., 1941, p. 19.

[2] These come mainly from Western Words, by Ramon F. Adams; Norman (Okla.), 1944, and The Language of the Mosshorn, by Don McCarthy; Billings (Mont.), 1936. Adams points out, p. x, that the cowboy vocabulary is by no means uniform over the cattle country. The popularity of Western fiction has made most Americans familiar with many range terms, but I have included some of them in order to discuss their origin. W. Cabell Greet says in A Standard American Language?, *New Republic*, May 25, 1938, p. 68, that the speech of the cattlemen " derives from the Southern hill type," *i.e.*, that of Appalachia.

[3] Says Mary Dale Buckner, in Ranch Diction of the Texas Panhandle, *American Speech*, Feb., 1933, p. 29: " The cowboy and ranchman would use any amount of circumlocution to avoid calling a spade a spade in the presence of ladies."

[4] This is probably an Americanism, though the DAE does not list it. The NED's first example is from William Cullen Bryant's translation of the Iliad, 1870.

[5] Sp. *bronco*, rough, rude. Traced by the DAE to *c.* 1850.

[6] Cowboy Lingo of the Texas Big Bend, by Haldeen Braddy, *Dialect Notes*, Vol. VI, Part XV, Dec., 1937, p. 620. *Buckaroo* is from the Spanish *vaquero*, of the same meaning. Traced by the DAE to *c.* 1861.

[7] Sp. *chaperejo*.

[8] This term is discussed by Stephens, J., in South Kansas Railway *vs.* Isaacs, 49 *Southwestern Reporter*, p. 691. I am indebted here to Judge Theodore Mack, of Fort Worth, Tex.

[9] *Lasso* is from the Sp. *lazo* and *lariat* from the Sp. *la reata*, both meaning a rope. The former is traced by the DAE to 1833 and the latter to 1835.

[10] From the Spanish. As a noun traced by the DAE to 1839 and as a verb to 1847.

[11] Harold W. Bentley says in A Dictionary of Spanish Terms in English; New York, 1932, p. 87, that it is from the Sp. *adobe*, a mud brick. Another, but improbable etymology, is in *Dogie*, *American Speech*, Oct., 1936, p. 218.

Dude, or tenderfoot. A newcomer unaccustomed to ranch and range life.[1]
Fork, v. To straddle a horse.
Goosehair. A pillow.
Guteater, or bow-and-arrow. An Indian.
Hackamore. A halter made of rope or rawhide.
Hot roll. A cowboy's bedding and other belongings.
Justins. Boots.[2]
Kack. A saddle.
Lamb licker, mutton puncher, or sheep-puncher. A sheepherder.
Leppy. A motherless calf.
Levis. Overalls.[3]
Loco. Crazy.[4]
Maverick. An unbranded stray animal.[5]
Mosshorn. An old steer; also, an old cowboy.
Nester, sod-buster, or soddie. A small farmer or stockman, usually suspected of stealing cattle.[6]
Pants rat, or seam squirrel. A louse.
Phildoodle. An imitation cowboy.
Powders. Orders from the boss.
Presidente. A ranch-owner.
Pull leather, or grab the apple, v. To hold on to the saddle horn with the hands while riding a bucking horse.
Rodeo. A round-up of cattle; also, a show staged by cowboys.[7]
Sidewinder. A rattlesnake.
Sougan. A quilt or comforter.
Squaw side. The right side of a horse.[8]
Stetson, or John B. The cowboy's large hat.[9]

[1] The DAE traces *tenderfoot* to 1875 and *dude* in this sense to 1885. A ranch which entertains visitors is a *dude-ranch*, traced to 1921. There is a *Dude Ranchers'* Association in the Northwest, and it has published a quarterly, the *Dude Rancher*, at Billings, Mont., since 1926.
[2] From Joseph *Justin*, the name of an early maker whose workshop still survives at Fort Worth.
[3] From the name of *Levi* Strauss, who began to make overalls in San Francisco in 1850.
[4] From *loco-weed* (*Astragalus mollissimus* or *Aragallus lamberti*), which causes severe nervous symptoms in cattle eating it.
[5] AL4, p. 189. Traced by the DAE to 1869.
[6] John M. Hendrix, in The Nester, *Cattleman*, March, 1946, p. 84: " A name given to those intrepid souls who broke away from the credit system of East Texas to gain a foothold in the cattle country."
[7] From Sp. *rodear*, to surround, to gather together. Traced by the DAE in the first sense to 1851. The *rodeo* in the second sense has now taken the place of the old-time Wild West show. McCarthy, before cited, says that the word is pronounced *ró-de-o* in Montana and Wyoming, and *ro-dáy-o* elsewhere.
[8] Mr. Bruce Nelson, of Bismarck, N. D., tells me that the Indians used to mount from that side.
[9] Both come from the name of the maker, John Batterson Stetson, of Philadelphia (1830–1906). A. L. Campa says in *Ten-Gallon Hats*, *American Speech*, Oct., 1939, p. 201, that *ten-gallon* does not refer to the cubic capacity of such a hat, but to the braid – Sp. *galón*.

Stinker. A general term of contempt.[1]
Wishbook. A mail-order catalogue.
Wrangling. Rounding up, catching, saddling and riding range horses.[2]

Chautauquans [3]

Bull's eye. A placard bearing a circle with a red, white and blue field, announcing the date and place of a coming chautauqua.
Bureau. The management.
Celebrity, or platform giant. Any speaker notorious enough to bring in a crowd.
Chautauqua salute. Waving a handkerchief.
Crew tent, or pup tent. A small tent at the rear of the main tent, used by the crew as living quarters.
Diplomat, or dip. An advance-agent.
Docott. Ropes and pulleys used to keep the tent taut.[4]
Endorser, grantor, or signer. A guarantor.
Fives. Circuits with five-day programmes.
Hickey. The operation of tightening the tent.
Junk. The chautauqua equipment.
Kitchen. The section of the tent covering the stage and dressing-rooms.
Message. The theme of a lecture.
Morning-hour girl. One who kept the customers' children entertained of a morning.
Sevens. Circuits with seven-day programmes.[5]

[1] Cowboy Lingo Has Enriched Our Language, by Nat McKelvey, *Everybody's Digest*, Aug., 1945, p. 86: "Hollywood stole *stinker* from the cowboy. Originally, he was a newcomer who skinned the buffalo the hunters killed."

[2] The literature of cattlemen's speech before 1939 is listed in Burke, pp. 99–100 and 145–46. Later studies worth consulting are Bronc Peelers, by John L. Sinclair, *New Mexico*, Feb., 1939, pp. 18–20; the glossary in Wyoming: a Guide to Its History, Highways and People; New York, 1941, pp. 459–66; Nebraska Cowboy Talk, by Rudolph Umland, *American Speech*, Feb., 1942, pp. 73–75; Stock Jargon, in Nevada: a Guide to the Silver State; Portland (Ore.), n. d., pp. 75–78; Southwestern Speech, by Haldeen Braddy, *American Speech*, Dec., 1945, p. 306; Lingo of the Cowpoke, in the programme of the National Western Stock Show; Denver, Jan. 13–21, 1945, p. 42, and Waddies' Lingo, by James F. Bender, New York *Times Magazine*, Oct. 20, 1946, p. 35. I am indebted for friendly aid to Messrs. Don Bloch, J. N. Beffel, L. J. Carrel, Don McCarthy, Fred Hamann, Frank Foster and Thomas Caldecott Chubb.

[3] The itinerant chautauqua is now extinct, though the Mother Church, established in 1874 at Chautauqua, N. Y., still exists. Many of the old-time chautauquans have become radio-crooners or public jobholders. I present a few specimens of their argot as relics of a past day, like those of the telegraphers. The itinerant chautauqua flourished from 1904 to 1932. See notes on it by J. R. Schultz in *American Notes & Queries*, Feb., 1942, p. 167, and Dec., 1943, p. 142.

[4] Said by J. R. Schultz, in Chautauqua Talk, *American Speech*, Aug., 1932, p. 408, to have been named after its inventor, *Dr. Ott*, a lecturer.

[5] This comes from the paper by J. R. Schultz, before cited, and

744   *The American Language: Supplement II*

Cigarmakers [1]

Binder. The thin leaf under the *wrapper*, holding the *filler* together.

Blow, *v.* To *case* tobacco by taking water into the mouth and then blowing it out in a fine spray.

Book. A pad of *wrappers*.

Buckeye. A small shop in which cigars made in the back room are retailed in front.[2]

Bunch. *Filler* surrounded by a *binder*.[3]

Casing. Dampening tobacco to make it pliable enough to work.

Cheroot. A cigar, usually of cheap materials, trimmed at both ends.

Cigarmakers' heaven. Philadelphia.

Cuttings. The pieces trimmed from the *tuck* of a cigar, later used as *filler* for a cheaper cigar.

Filler. The tobacco inside the *binder* and *wrapper* of a cigar.

Hand. A group of tobacco leaves, tied at the stem end.

Head. The pointed end of a cigar.

Noodle-twister. A cigarmaker.

Plug. A cigar too tightly made to be smokable.

Skipper. A cigar in which there is a gap between adjoining sections of *wrapper*.

Sprig. A small piece of *filler*.

Stogy. A cigar of cheap materials, loosely made and with a twist at one end.[4]

Tuck. The trimmed end of a cigar.

Wrapper. The thin leaf on the outside of a cigar.[5]

Clergymen [6]

Box (Catholics). A confessional.

Buck, crow, or Galway (Protestants). A Catholic priest.

---

from another by the same, *American Speech*, Oct., 1934, pp. 232-34. Schultz says that a performer working one was said to be *on the sevens*. This recalls *on the —— circus* and *on the heavy*.

1 These come mainly from The Language of the Buckeye, by Norman E. Eliason, *American Speech*, Dec., 1937, pp. 270-74.
2 A Reporter at Large, *New Yorker*, Feb. 15, 1947, p. 59.
3 A cigarmaker is said to *break* a bunch, not to *make* it.
4 Traced by the DAE to 1893, but much older. Named after the *Conestoga*-wagon. See Supplement I, p. 233, and The *Stogie* Comes Into Its Own, by Richard McCardell, *Facts*, Aug., 1945, p. 83.
5 A discussion of the names, mostly Spanish, of cigar shapes and colors would take us too far afield. The former are described, with illustrations, in Tobaccoland, by Carl Avery Werner; New York, 1922, pp. 386-96. Colors run from *claro*, the lightest, through *colorado claro*, *colorado*, *colorado maduro* (the typical tobacco color) and *maduro* to *oscuro*, the darkest. The machine is driving out the old-time cigarmakers. They have a rich folklore, and believe that every member of the craft, at death, is transmogrified into a jackass. Whenever a jackass passed a cigarshop, *c.* 1890, the men stopped work and gave him three cheers, always professing to recognize some departed comrade.
6 So far as I know, there is no report in print upon the argot used by clergymen in their professional bull-sessions. The Catholic Language, by Benjamin Musser, *Eccle-*

Church school, or baby church (Protestant Episcopalians). A Sunday-school.[1]

Episcopate (Colored Methodists). A bishop.[2]

Go-to-Hell collar (Catholics). An ordinary men's collar, sometimes worn by priests on holiday.

Hell-and-damnation fathers (Catholics). Redemptorists.[3]

Kingdom work (Evangelical Protestants). Raising money for church enterprises.

Novitiate (Catholics). A novice.[4]

On the altar (Catholics). Serving at the altar.

Pastorium (Evangelical Protestants). The pastor's house.[5]

Plant (Methodists and Baptists). The church building, including the church itself, the pastorium, and the various meeting-halls, bowling-alleys, refreshment rooms, etc.

Plate (colored Protestants). A collection.

Sawdust trail (Evangelical Protestants). The path of a convert to the mourners' bench.[6]

Southpaw, or left-footer (Catholics). A Protestant.

Stewardship (Evangelical Protestants). The layman's duty to provide whatever money is needed by the clergy.

Turk (Catholics). An Irish-born priest.[7]

Cock-fighters [8]

Billing, or pecking. Teasing cocks before a fight to arouse them to ferocity.

Blinked. Blinded.

---

siastical *Review*, Dec., 1926, pp. 573–83, is an amusing account of the errors made by non-Catholics (and by many Catholics) in using the technical terms of Holy Church. I have borrowed a few terms from it for the brief list below. For the speech of Quakers see the papers listed in AL4, p. 450, n. 1, and p. 589, n. 1. For that of Mormons see the latter note. I have also added a few terms not confined to the clergy, nor even to the saved.

1 *Sunday-school* was coined by Robert Raikes (1735–1811), publisher of the Gloucester (England) *Journal,* who opened the first Sunday-school at Gloucester in 1780.

2 The Episcopacy of Zion Methodist Will be Celebration Highlight, Pittsburgh *Courier,* July 27, 1946: "Bishops Lynwood Westinghouse Kyles, George Clinton Clement were among the outstanding *episcopates* of modern days."

3 Apparently obsolete. See *Converted* *Catholic Magazine,* Oct., 1943, p. 204.

4 *Novitiate* in this sense is denounced by Father Musser, before cited, as an error made by "nine out of ten non-Catholics," but the NED shows that it has been in good usage in England since 1655.

5 AL4, p. 179, n. 3.

6 Billy Sunday: Tabernacles and Sawdust Trails, by T. T. Frankenberg; Columbus (O.), 1917, p. 81: "The phrase originated during Mr. Sunday's first campaign on Puget Sound. The use of sawdust and shavings made a particular appeal to the lumbermen who predominated in that region." See also *American Notes & Queries,* Feb., 1946, p. 168.

7 He is supposed to have an extraordinary facility for getting ecclesiastical preferment.

8 These come from Cocker Cant, Baltimore *Evening Sun,* April 24, 1939, Sect. II, p. 17; English Cock-fighting, *Living Age,* June, 1937,

Buckle, *v.* To fly above the opposing cock.
Cocker. A connoisseur of cock-fighting.
Coupled. Said of a cock whose hip has been dislocated.
Dunghill. A cock which runs from a fight.
Gaff, or heel. A steel spur.
Hang, or to be in. For a cock to jab his spur so far into another that he can't withdraw it.
Kick, *v.* To spur.
Lunged. Gaffed through both lungs.
Main. A series of fights, always odd in number, between the birds of two cockers.
Muffs, or boxing-gloves. Protective pads put over the natural spurs of a cock when in training.
Pitchfork. A very long spur.
Shingle-nail. A short spur.
Shuffle, *v.* To strike with both spurs.
Sick. Nearly dead.[1]

Corset-makers

Bra, breast-shield, or breast-form. A brassière.
Derrière. A backside, usually meaning a massive one.
Drooper, or super-drooper. A pendant bust.
Grapefruit. A medium-sized bust.
Hammock. A large bust.
Teacup. A small bust.[2]

Crap-shooters [3]

Ada from Decatur. A throw of eight.[4]
Big Dick. A ten.[5]
Big Natural. An eleven.[6]
Box-cars. A twelve.
Caroline nine. A nine.[7]
Craps. A three.[8]

---

pp. 350–52; Rooster Fight, by Wayne Gard, *Southwest Review*, Autumn, 1936, pp. 65–70, and High-Flyers, by Peter Tamony, San Francisco *News-Letter & Wasp*, July 28, 1939, p. 9.

1 Cock-fighting has given the general speech many phrases, *e.g.*, *dead game*, *to stand the gaff*, *pitted against* and *to crow over*.
2 Some of these come from Life in a Putty-Knife Factory, by H. Allen Smith; Garden City (N.Y.), 1943, p. 158.
3 This list is based upon one by F. O. Richey, published in the *William Feather Magazine*, Sept., 1943. The variants are from Johns Hopkins Jargon, by J. Louis Kuethe, *American Speech*, June, 1932, p. 331; a note by William Feather in the *William Feather Magazine*, Feb., 1944, and Cries of Crap Shooters, by Clinton Sanders, *American Notes & Queries*, June, 1942, pp. 42–43.
4 Kuethe and Feather: *eighter from Decatur*.
5 Kuethe, Feather and Sanders add *from Boston*, and Sanders offers an etymology.
6 Kuethe omits the *big*.
7 This is from Kuethe. Feather gives *Nina from Carolina*, or *from Argentina*. Richey says that "a nine seems to have no name."
8 Kuethe: *cat-eyes*.

Johnny Hicks. A six.[1]
Little Joe. A four.[2]
Little Natural. A seven.
Phoebe. A five.[3]
Snake-eyes. Two aces.
Viggerish. The cut of the house.[4]

Dairymen [5]

Blue John. Skimmed milk.
Cow salve. Butter.
Eskimo. One who works in a cold-storage room.
Floaters. Oversize rubber shoes worn by dairy workers.
Moo juice. Milk.
Slop. Buttermilk.
Teat-puller. A dairy farmer.

Department-store Salespeople [6]

Bat. A watchful store official.
Blow air, or puff up, v. To rearrange the merchandise displayed on a counter.
Counter-stretcher. An imaginary instrument for lengthening an overcrowded counter.
Dreck. A garment badly made of inferior materials.[7]
Go-giver. An unusually attentive saleswoman.
J. L.,[8] or lemon. A woman who examines many articles but buys nothing.
Mooch. A finicky customer, alert for real bargains.[9]
Pawing. Handling merchandise on display.
Pick-up. The day's receipts of a given counter.
Post-mortem. An article that is out of fashion.
Red circles. Staple goods that must always be in stock.[10]
Schlag.[11] A badly made skirt.

---

1 Kuethe: *Captain Jimmy Hicks of the Horse Marines.*
2 Kuethe adds *from Kokomo.* A writer in *American Notes & Queries,* June, 1941, p. 43, suggests that this may be rhyming slang from *little fo'* (four). This is disputed by D. W. Maurer in the same, Jan., 1945, p. 160. A writer in *American Notes & Queries,* Oct., 1943, p. 112, says that *Little Joe picked the cotton* is "a commonly accepted form."
3 Kuethe makes it *Phoebe the preacher's daughter.*
4 In *Viggerish,* New York *Times Magazine,* Oct. 31, 1943, p. 2, David Shilman suggests that it is an English loan from *vicarage,* suggested by the collection of tithes.
5 From Lexicon of Trade Jargon.
6 These come mainly from Department Store Technical Expressions, by Alice Smart, *American Speech,* Dec., 1938, pp. 312–13 and Consumer Vocabulary, by Mamie Meredith, the same, Feb., 1939, p. 80.
7 Ger. *dreck,* dirt.
8 *i.e.,* just looking.
9 *Mooch* is old English slang for one who idles and hangs about. Partridge says that it may have some relation to the French *mucher,* to hide, or skulk.
10 Miss Smart says that they are circled in red on the order-list.
11 Ger. *schlag,* a blow or shock. Like many other terms in the vocabularies of the Jewish trades, it probably came in through Yiddish.

Wrap-up. A customer easily pleased. Also, an inferior article palmed off on such a customer.

Distillery Workers [1]

Angel teat. A mellowed whiskey of good bouquet.
Beer. The fermented mash, ready for distilling.
Bug juice. Whiskey of low quality.
Bulldozer. An iron used to stamp barrel-heads.
Drop a cook, v. To run mash from a boiler into a fermenting vat.
Goose. A dephlegmater, i.e., a device for purifying spirit coming from a still.
Low wine, or heads. The first product to come off in distilling beer.
Mash. The cooked grain.
Scroll water. Steam curling off the coil of the still.
Set a tub, v. To fill a fermenting vat with yeasted beer.
Slop, or off-falls. The waste remaining after beer is distilled.
Spirit runner. The operator of a still.
Tale-box. A glass-enclosed meter which registers the proof and rate of flow of whiskey coming from a still.
Thief. A metal tube for withdrawing samples from barrels.
Well. A fermenting vat.

Dog-breeders

Butterfly nose. A dog whose nose is speckled with flesh-colored spots.
Button ear. An ear that falls forward, with the point toward the eye.
Daredevil. An Irish terrier.
Diehard. A Scottish terrier.
Flag. The tail of a setter.
French. A dog whose front feet turn slightly outward.
Merle. A mottled blue color in collies and sheep-dogs.
Snipy. A muzzle that is too pointed.
Weedy. Deficient in muscle and bone.[2]

Farmers [3]

Badger, gopher, snake, snake-killer, crackerjack, go-devil, go-dig, or two-row eli. A corn-cultivator that cultivates two or more rows at a time.
Bunch, or dump. A pile of hay.
Bushwhacker. A scythe.
Buster. A plow.
Cluck. A setting hen.
Cob-roller. A small, pudgy pig.

---

[1] These terms come from Stillers' Argot, by Fred Hamann, *American Speech*, Oct., 1946, pp. 193–95; Scotch Whiskey, *Forum*, June, 1946, pp. 135–36 and 180–92, and Lexicon of Trade Jargon.

[2] I take all these from A Dictionary of Dogdom Terms, by Bob Becker, Chicago *Tribune*, Oct. 13, 1939.

[3] The argot of farmers differs so much in different parts of the country that all I can do is to offer a few random specimens, chiefly from the Middle West. They come mainly from Middlewestern Farm English, by Russell T. Prescott, *American Speech*, April, 1937, pp. 102–07; Cornhusking and Other Terms, by Mamie Meredith, the same, Feb., 1938, pp. 19–24, and Lexicon of Trade Jargon.

Crap-shooter. A manure-spreader.
Crow bait, skate, skinflint, or plug. A worn-out horse.
Cut, change, or alter, *v.* To castrate.
Drag. A harrow.
Feathered. Potatoes with part of the skin rubbed off.
Finished. Cattle fat enough for market.
Fired. Corn dried out by drought.
Hatrack, or shell, or canner, or nellie. An old cow.
Hog-lot. An enclosure for hogs.[1]
Juicing. Milking cows.
Lister. A plow used to make a ditch or furrow for planting corn.[2]
Rig. A threshing outfit.
Round-house. A silo.
Spike-pitcher. One who feeds a threshing-machine with bundles of grain.
Springer. A cow about to calve.
Three-titter. A cow that has lost one teat.
Volunteer. Grain which comes up after a field has been cut.[3]

Firemen

Apparatus. The generic name for fire-engine, hook-and-ladder, etc.
Bag. A uniform.
Bagger. Used to designate the numerical order of an alarm, *e.g.*, two-*bagger* (or *deuce*), three-*bagger*, etc.
Big stick. A large ladder.
Blue shirt, or smoke-eater. A fireman.
Bop, probie, or skut. A probationer.
Buff. A fire fan.[4]
Committee work. Cleaning up.
Cork. A short nap.
Dash. A quick opening and shutting of the nozzle to douse a small blaze.
Hit the floor, *v.* To slide down the pole in a firehouse.
Hitting in. The sounding of an alarm in a firehouse.
Kink-chaser. A laggard who says that he was straightening the kinks out

[1] "In the dictionary," says Prescott, "one can find such terms as *piggery* and *pigsty*, which are rarely, if ever, used on American farms, but he will not find *hog-lot* or *hog-house*, which deserve recognition . . . as the terms commonly used." This was published in 1937. Since then the DAE (1940) has listed both terms. It traces *hog-lot* to 1835 and *hog-house* to 1638.
[2] The word is an Americanism, and is traced by the DAE to 1887.
[3] For the argot of workers in the sugar-beet fields of the West see Sugar-Beet Language, by Levette J. Davidson, *American Speech*, Oct., 1930, pp. 10-15; for that of the hopfields, Hopfield Terms From Western New York, by J. R. Shulters, *Dialect Notes*, Vol. V, Part V, 1922, pp. 182-83, and for that of English farmers, Pure English of the Soil, by William A. Craigie, S.P.E. Tract No. LXIV, 1945, pp. 79-107.
[4] Said to be from *buffalo*, and to have been suggested by the fact that the wealthy young men who belonged to the early volunteer fire-companies commonly wore buffalo-skin coats in Winter. See Running Down the Name Fire Buff, New York *Sun*, Nov. 16, 1937, p. 28. Other authorities say that it originated in the fact that many of the early firemen wore *buff* uniforms.

of the line when questioned by his company commander, who has missed his presence in a blazing building.

Looie, or luke. A lieutenant.
Patrolie. A member of a privately-paid fire patrol.
Platform. The fire-alarm dispatcher at headquarters.
Potsy. A fireman's badge.[1]
Ripe, or snotty. Smoky.
Roast. The body of a person burned to death.
Rolling out. Leaving quarters for a fire.
Siamese. A connection for amalgamating two lines of hose.
Spaghetti. Hose.
Squib. A small fire.
Stretch in, v. To lead lines of hose into a building on fire.
Syringe. A water-tower.
Touch-off. An incendiary fire.
Turnouts. Trousers kept beside the bed of a fireman on night duty, designed for quick dressing.[2]
White-coat. An officer above the rank of captain.
Worker. A bad fire.[3]

Fishermen [4]

Balloon. A round inflated rubber bag used to float a net.
Bank, or banks. Any shoal water.
Blink. An undersized mackerel.
Break water, v. To arise from bed.
Bug. A lobster below the legal minimum in weight; on the Gulf coast, any shrimp.
Chance. A job.
Chum, v. To vomit over the side.
Clinkers. The engine-room crew.
Coloring. Tattooing.
Doctor. The crew cook.
Down. North along the coast.
Gurry. The entrails and other wastes of fish.
Hubbly. A rough sea.
Ile-suit. Clothes made waterproof by oiling.

[1] That Word *Potsy*, by A. W. M., New York *Sun*, March 26, 1932: "From the piece of tin can, doubled and redoubled and stamped flat, which is kicked about by the juvenile player of the game *potsy*."
[2] They are wide-bottomed and their ends are left outside rubber boots. The fireman sleeps with a shirt on, and when the man on watch yells "Get out!" the sleeper swings his feet out from under the blankets and steps into the *turnouts*.
[3] I am indebted here to Firemen Invent Their Own Slang, New York *Sun*, March 16, 1932; Fire Department Slanguage, by S. James Lynch, *Writers' Digest*, Sept., 1941, pp. 23–24; Smoke Eaters' Lingo, *New Yorker*, March 31, 1945, p. 41; A Preliminary Glossary of the New York City Firemen, by Leo Blond and Harold J. Jonas, *American Notes & Queries*, April, 1944, pp. 3–8; Where's the Fire?, *Better English*, July–Aug., 1939, p. 39, and Lexicon of Trade Jargon.
[4] These come from Schoonerisms, by David W. Maurer, *American Speech*, June, 1930, pp. 387–95, and Lexicon of Trade Jargon.

Lay. The manner of dividing the catch between the crew and the owner.
Mammy-daddy, *v.* To row with one oar, and then the other.
Monkey. A green hand.
Nippers. Lice.
Outside. At sea.
Redjacks. Waterproof leather boots.
Skunk. An approaching squall.
Soup-barrel. A water-cask.
Stemwinder. One who fishes for sport alone.
Trip. The amount of fish brought to market on one voyage.[1]

Food-dispensers [2]

Acid. Vinegar.
Adam and Eve on a raft. Poached eggs on toast.
Alive (of oysters). Raw.
Arizona. Buttermilk.[3]
Baby, or Sweet Alice. A glass of milk.
Bellywash, or splash. Soup.
Bib. A napkin.
Bird-seed. A cereal.
Blood, hemorrhage, paint, or red lead. Ketchup.
Boiled leaves. Tea.
Bossy in a bowl. Beef stew.
Breath. An onion.
Bullets, Saturday nights, or whistleberries. Baked beans.
Bun pup. A hot dog.
Chocker hole, or submarine. A doughnut.
Chopper. A table knife.
Clean up the kitchen. Hash.

[1] For the argot of crabbers see Crab Talk, by Mamie Meredith, *American Speech*, Aug., 1931, p. 465; for that of sealers, Sealing Nomenclature, by C. G. Porcher, the same, April, 1934, pp. 156–57, and Newfoundland Dialect Items, by George Allan England, *Dialect Notes*, Vol. V, Part VIII, 1925, pp. 322–46, and for that of sports fishermen, Tackle Terminology, by a committee of the National Association of Angling and Casting Clubs; St. Louis, 1945.

[2] The queer lingo used in transmitting orders from table to kitchen was noted by a writer in the Detroit *Free Press* so long ago as Jan. 7, 1852, *e.g., fried bedpost, mashed tambourine* and *roasted stirrups*. In 1876 J. G. Holland, then editor of *Scribner's*, discussed it in his Everyday Topics, p. 386. It was richly developed by the colored waiters who flourished in the 1870s and 80s, but is now pretty well confined to the waitresses and countermen who glorify third-rate eating-houses. The following specimens come from Hash House Lingo, by Jack Smiley; Easton (Pa.), 1941; The Private Language of Eating Joints, Chicago *Tribune*, Nov. 12, 1940, p. 16; A Glossary of Café Terms, by Oran B. Bailey, *American Speech*, Dec., 1943, pp. 307–08; Curb Service, by Theodore Pratt, *New Yorker*, Jan. 8, 1938, pp. 48–49, and the Language of West Coast Culinary Workers, by Robert Shafer, *American Speech*, April, 1946, pp. 86–89. I am also indebted to Mr. Paul McPharlin.

[3] "A waitress," says Shafer, before cited, "thinks any man drinking buttermilk ought to be in Arizona for his health."

Clinker. A biscuit.
Coney Island bloodhound. A frankfurter.
Cow feed. A salad.
Creep. Draft beer.
Curb-hopper, curbie, or car-hop. A waitress serving automobilists at the curb.[1]
Dog-biscuit. A cracker.
Dog-soup, or one on the city. A glass of water.
Echo. Please repeat the order.
Eve. Apple pie.
Fly-cake, or roach-cake. Raisin-cake.
Fly-pie. Huckleberry-pie.
Grass, or leaves. Lettuce.
Gravel-train. A sugar-bowl.
Graveyard stew. Milk-toast.
Hasher. A counterman.
Irish turkey. Corned beef and cabbage.[2]
Looseners. Prunes.
Lumber. A toothpick.
Midnight. A cup of black coffee.
Mike and Ike. Salt and pepper shakers.
Moo. A steak.
Mud, or murk. Coffee.
Pair of drawers. Two cups of coffee.
Raft. A slice of toast.
Salve, or skid-grease. Butter.
Scoop. A spoon.
Sea-dust. Salt.
Shimmy. Gelatine.
Soup. Gravy.
Spear. A fork.
Spla. Whipped cream.
Sport. A liberal tipper.
Stiff, or George Eddie. A patron who does not tip.
White bread. The manager.
Wreath. Cabbage.
Yum-yum. Sugar.[3]

Furniture-workers [4]

Angel-bed. A bedstead without posts.
Ark. A chest.
Barber's chair. An Eighteenth Century corner armchair, with head-rest.
Chiseler. A carver.
Cockroach shop. A small furniture shop.

[1] *Variety*, Sept. 27, 1937, p. 63: "*Curb-hopping* is strictly an American enterprise. It originated during the 1925 Miami land boom, but since then has gained protagonists in practically every city of the United States."
[2] Supplement I, p. 604.
[3] See also Hotel-workers and Soda-jerkers.
[4] From Lexicon of Trade Jargon.

Flatting. Veneering.
Flunky. An apprentice upholsterer.
Horse. A fast, expert carver or upholsterer.
Jabber. A chair-maker.
Lawyer. The lavatory.
Murderer. A poor workman.
Nails. A set of carving tools.
Nova Scotian mahogany. Furniture made of stained pine; a cheap job.
Russian Renaissance. A rush job of carving.
Sausage machine. A machine not equipped with safety devices.
Scratcher. An apprentice carver.
Stuffer. An upholsterer.

Garbage Men [1]

Banjo. A deep shovel.
Big Bubble. A foreman.
Fruit salad. Garbage.
Juggler. The man who hands cans from the sidewalk to men on a garbage truck.
Morgue-wagon. A truck used to haul dead animals.
Mungo. One who retrieves valuable objects from garbage and trash.
Push-a-push. A broom with stiff bristles.
Road-apples. Horse manure.
Shaker-down. The man who empties the cans handed to him by *jugglers*.

Garment Workers [2]

Automobile. A fast operator.
Balmechule. A slow and inferior worker.[3]
Barker. A foreman.
Brooklyn Bridge. A garment difficult to press.
Checkout. A dress that sells well.
Chicky. A garment smart and youthful in design.[4]
Clothing. Men's clothing only.[5]
Coal mine. Shipping or stock room.
Dog. A dress that does not sell well.
Fireman. A presser.
Ford. A copy of an expensive dress selling at a low price.
Honey. The wax used in ironing.
Horses. Boys who push racks of garments through the streets.
Klupper. An incompetent worker.[6]
Mama-house. A firm dealing in dresses for large women.
Pinochle season. The slack season.
Professor. A good cutter.
Schneider. Anyone connected with the garment trade.[7]

---

1 From Lexicon of Trade Jargon. All come from New York City.
2 From Lexicon of Trade Jargon.
3 Yiddish *mechulle*, spoiled, out of order, bankrupt. *Ba'al* is a generic designation for one performing a function, e.g., *ba'al brith*, the father of a boy at a circumcision; *ba'al keria*, one who reads the Torah in a synagogue.
4 French *chic*, stylish.
5 Never used for women's garments
6 Apparently a Yiddish loan.
7 Ger. *schneider*, a tailor.

Schmoosing. Idling around and talking shop.[1]
Shoeshiner. An inefficient presser who puts a shine on the garments pressed.
Shroud. A cheap dress.
Tents. Coats and dresses, size thirty-eight and up.

Glassblowers [2]

Bull gang. Laborers.
Cinder-head. A glassblower.
Cullet, or slocker. Spoiled and refuse glass.
Dog. Scum or melted glass.
Dope. Coloring matter for glass.
Get-up. A day's work.
Glory hole. A small furnace for reheating articles blown.
Heavy. Hot.
Horn-knocker. An inexpert glassblower.
Lehr (pro. *leer*). An annealing oven.
Maggie's room. Place where mixed ingredients are stored.
Necktie, or yink-yank. A wrinkled bottle.
Seeds. Minute bubbles in the glass.
Teaser. A workman who tends the fire and charges the pot.[3]

Glaziers [4]

Board, or plank. Very heavy plate glass.
Butchered. Badly cut by glass.
Chinee, or hot knife. A hard worker.
Flounder foot. A clumsy worker.
Gooey, slime, or smear. Putty.
Jigger. Small truck to carry glass on edge.
Light. Plate or sheet of glass.
Politician, or sky man. A worker who steadies the top of plate glass being moved, the lightest type of work.
Puttyhead. A glazier.
Slaughterhouse. A shop where many accidents occur.

Golfers [5]

Bat. One over par.[6]
Birdie. One under par.[7]

---

1 Yid. *schmus*, talk.
2 Most of these come from Lexicon of Trade Jargon. I am also indebted to The Glass Industry, by William Marks, *Dialect Notes*, Vol. I, Part VII, 1894, pp. 335-36.
3 French *tisard* or *tisart*, the door of a glass furnace.
4 From Lexicon of Trade Jargon.
5 These come mainly from Golf Gab, by Anne Angel, *American Speech*, Sept., 1926, pp. 627-33, and A Caddy's Compendium, by Margaret Erskine Cahill, the same, April, 1937, pp. 155-56.

6 Associated Press dispatch from Jacksonville, Fla., March 15, 1946: "Professional Golfers Association tournament manager Fred Corcoran today coined a long-needed golfing term — *bat*, meaning one over par."
7 Peter Tamony says in *Birdie* and *Eagle*, San Francisco *News-Letter & Wasp*, June 9, 1939, p. 5, that it came in *c.* 1908, at first as *bird*. It is denounced as an Americanism, now in use in England, in Golf, by Bernard Darwin, *Country Life* (London), April 27, 1940. *Bird*, in

Buzzard. Two over par.
Creep. A slow round.
Divot. A piece of turf cut from the course by a stroke.
Dodo. A hole in one.
Double eagle. Three under par.
Eagle. Two under par.[1]
Loop. An eighteen-hole course.
Nineteenth hole. The club bar.
Par. The standard number of strokes for each hole.
Pill, or aspirin. A golf-ball.
Prairie. A badly kept course.
Scotchman. A professional.
Stance. The attitude assumed in hitting the ball.
Stymie. Defined by the New Practical Standard Dictionary as "a condition obtaining when an opponent's ball lies in the line of the player's putt on the green, the balls being more than six inches apart."
Wood-butcher. A poor player.[2]

Hospital Attendants [3]

ABD. An abdominal dressing.
BM. Bowel movement.
BP. A bed-pan.
Cerebral accident. A stroke of apoplexy.
Chase doll, or Mrs. Chase. A dummy used by nurses in training.
Coxey's army. The entourage of interns, nurses and medical students which follows a chief of staff on his round.
Dirty. Used of an operating-room nurse who handles unsterilized articles.
Duck, banjo, or submarine. A urinal.
Float. A relief nurse.
Foundry. A maternity hospital.
GI. Gastro-intestinal.
GU. Genito-urinary.
Gyney. A gynecological patient.
Inkie. An incubator baby.
Kick-off room. A room to which ward patients are taken when dying.
OB. An obstetrical case.
OR. Operating-room.

---

the sense of any person or thing of excellence, is traced by the DAE to 1842.

1 An Americanism. It came in with *birdie*.
2 The full vocabulary of golf would fill pages. Some of its terms, e.g., *stymie*, have got into the general speech. It has also engendered *African golf*, crap-shooting, and *barnyard-golf*, horseshoe-pitching.
3 The argot of nurses, interns and orderlies is mainly borrowed from that of their lords, the doctors, and hence runs to abbreviations, e.g., *GU* and *TB*, and cant terms designed to reassure patients, e.g., *lues*, syphilis, and *new growth*, cancer. The following come mainly from Hospital Talk, by Dorothy Barkley, *American Speech*, April, 1927, pp. 312–14; Hospital Lingo, by Dorothy E. House, the same, Oct., 1938, pp. 227–29, and Lexicon of Trade Jargon. I have also borrowed a few from Berrey and Van den Bark, and am indebted to Dr. Kingsley Roberts, Mrs. Margaret R. George, Miss M. L. Hudson and Mr. John P. Trimmer.

PA. A patient.
Pesthouse. A hospital for infectious diseases.
Pipe. An enema.
Post, or PM. An autopsy.
Premie. A prematurely born baby.
Primip. A mother having her first child.[1]
Probe. A probationer.
Schizy. A patient with mental symptoms.[2]
Scut, or pup. A junior intern.
Stilts. Crutches.
T and A. Tonsils and adenoids.
TB. Tuberculosis.[3]
TPR. Temperature, pulse, respiration.

Hotel Workers [4]

Ace man, or rag. A guest who tips $1.
Admiral. A doorman.
Anvil-, or tombstone-salesman. A guest with a heavy bag.
Aviator, or jockey. An elevator operator.
Beat, flathead, Joe McGee, Joe Baggs, or cold turkey. A guest who fails to tip.
Bird. A towel.
Broom. A lobby-cleaner.
Cave, kennel, box, or stall. A guest-room.
Crock, or jake. A drunken guest.
Drum. A hotel.
Flea-bag. A cheap hotel.
Gun. An elevator.
Oil can. The manager.
Penwiper. A desk clerk.
Quarry. A luxury hotel.
Screw. A room-key.
Scrub. A maid.
Scuttle of clinkers. A pitcher of ice-water.
Simon. A bell-captain.[5]
Wolf. A porter or bellboy who carries too many bags, thus depriving others of tips.
Zoo. The place where the help eat.

House-Painters [6]

Animal. Enamel.
Broom. A large brush used on walls.

[1] From *primipara*. At subsequent deliveries she is a *multip*, from *multipara*, or a *para-two, three*, etc.
[2] From *schizophrenia*.
[3] The patients in tuberculosis sanitoria call taking the cure *chasing*. A hemorrhage from the lungs is *spilling rubies*. See T. B. Talk, by Anders H. Anderson, *American Speech*, Feb., 1935, pp. 77–78. Dr. William B. Bean, of Cincinnati, tells me that tuberculosis is called *jupe* in Southern Ohio and Northern Kentucky.
[4] These come from Hotel Slang, by William Stewart Cornyn, *American Speech*, Oct., 1939, pp. 239–40, and from Lexicon of Trade Jargon.
[5] From *Simon Legree*.
[6] From Lexicon of Trade Jargon.

Catface. A spot missed by a painter.
Grass. Green paint.
Sash tool. A small brush used to paint window sash.
Soup. Paint.
Take the ground, *v.* To be killed in a fall; to fall.

House-Wreckers [1]

Broom clean, *v.* To demolish a building in such a fashion that all the wreckage can be carried away.
Dirt. Everything that falls during a wrecking job — brick, mortar, etc.
Trap. A building dangerous to demolish.

Instalment-House Salesmen [2]

Bekakee, buttons, or spiff. A premium paid to a salesman for selling specified merchandise.[3]
Borax. Inferior goods, especially furniture.[4]
Macher. A boaster.[5]
Number. Double the cost.[6]
Pull, or jerk, *v.* To recover merchandise from the home of a customer who is in default on his payments.
Schlepp, *v.* To move furniture about on the sales floor.[7]
Schmeer, *v.* To flatter a customer.[8]
Schmiss, or schmeiss, *v.* To break off a sale.[9]
Schneid, *v.* To reduce a price.[10]
Schnuck (le). A customer easily persuaded, a sucker.[11]
Schrei, *v.* To talk loudly, to complain.[12]

---

[1] From Lexicon of Trade Jargon.
[2] Most of the terms following come from Furniture Lingo, by Charles Miller, *American Speech*, Dec., 1930, pp. 125–28. Those that are of German origin probably got into English through Yiddish.
[3] Miller, just cited, believes that this word comes from the Hebrew. There is a Hebrew word, *beracha*, meaning a benediction. See Wonder Words, by Benjamin L. Winfield; New York, 1933, p. 20.
[4] E. Jerome Ellison and Frank W. Brock say in Overstuffed Phoneys, *Today*, Jan. 16, 1937, p. 8, that *borax* comes from Ger. *borgen*, to borrow, to buy on credit. "This word," says Winslow Ames (private communication, July 6, 1936), "now denotes through the furniture trade (and also in the architectural magazines) the flimsy, flashy sort of furniture that consists largely of molded ornaments stuck on veneered surfaces." A store selling it is a *borax-house*.
[5] Ger. *machen*, to make, to effect, to perform.
[6] Miller says that this is used by salesmen in the presence of the customer.
[7] Ger. *schleppen*, to move, to drag.
[8] Ger. *schmieren*, to smear, to grease.
[9] Miller thinks it may come, not from Ger. *schmiss*, a blow, but from Ger. *schmitz*, also a blow. It is used, he says, "when it is discovered that a customer cannot make a sufficiently large down-payment, or when a salesman has misquoted a price to his disadvantage and can get rid of it only by discouraging the sale."
[10] Ger. *schneiden*, to cut.
[11] Possibly from Ger. *schnucke*, a small sheep.
[12] Ger. *schreien*, to cry out. The original verb, according to Miller, is also used as a noun, as in "Cut out the *schreien!*"

Showful. Bad; used of business, and also of a person.

Switch, *v.* To divert a customer from a low-priced article to one of higher price, offering a better profit.

T. O. T. Cash.[1]

Turnover, or T. O., *v.* To hand over a customer to another salesman.[2]

Tzorris. Trouble caused by a customer who complains or is in default on his instalment payments.

Verlier. Go away; lose yourself.[3]

Woman's home companion. A house-to-house canvasser.[4]

Laundrymen [5]

Chorus girls. Girls who work the mangles.
Feet. Socks.
Fly. A handkerchief.
Gold-diggers. Those who open the bundles and look for coins in the wash.
Kitchen. A wash-room.
Peanut. A small bundle.
Weasel. A foreman.
Wheels. Washing machines.

Leather Workers [6]

Cellar-rats. Workers who scrape the flesh from hides.
Daubers. Those who oil skins.
Greens. Fresh hides, skins, or pelts.
Japanner. One who applies the enamel to patent leather.
Lumper. One with no specialized skill who helps wherever needed.
Offal. The less valuable parts of hides, usually the head, shoulder and belly.
Sammie. A process in tanning by which skins are placed in damp sawdust to absorb moisture slowly and uniformly, making them soft.
Side. Half a whole hide, cut longitudinally along the backbone, with *offal* attached.
Tripe. Poor quality hides.

Loggers [7]

Barber-chair. A fallen tree which remains attached to the stump.
Brush-cat. A sawmill man's term for a logger.

---

1 Miller calls this "a formation that originated from a decidedly vulgar expression in Jewish. . . . It has become so common that it is used freely, with no consciousness of its vulgar beginning."

2 The object here, says Miller, is to get the aid of the second salesman when the first fears that he is not making headway. The relief man is usually introduced as the sales manager, general manager, or president.

3 Ger. *verlieren*, to lose. "It is employed," says Miller, "when a salesman wants to let another sales-man know that the latter's presence is interfering with a sale."

4 Edward C. Ames says in Note on Suite, *American Speech*, Dec., 1937, p. 315, that the pronunciation *sweet* sounds affected to most customers, and that salesmen wait until a customer uses it before using it themselves. Otherwise it is *soot*. See also Department-Store Salespeople and Shoe Clerks.

5 From Lexicon of Trade Jargon.

6 From Lexicon of Trade Jargon.

7 These come mainly from the glossary in Holy Old Mackinaw, by Stewart H. Holbrook; New York,

Bucker. One who saws felled trees into logs.
Buckskin. A log with the bark peeled off.
Bull-cook. A chore man.
Bull of the woods. A camp boss.
Candy. The opposite of *haywire*.
Cat. A tractor.[1]
Choker. A loop of cable used to noose and hoist a log.
Clam-gun, idiot-stick, or muck-stick. A shovel.
Cock-shop. The camp office and store.
Cork. A shoe- or boot-caulk.[2]
Ding-dong, or gut-hammer. The dinner-bell, usually a steel triangle.
Donkey-doctor. A mechanic who keeps machinery in repair.
Dough-roller, boiler, stewbum, stomach-robber, gut-burglar, sizzler, stew-builder, meat-burner, or mulligan-mixer. A camp cook.
Duff. The litter on a forest floor.
Faller. One who fells trees.
Flathead, sawdust-eater, or humpback. A sawyer.
Flunky. A camp waiter.
Ground lead. The process of dragging logs along the ground.
Haywire. "A term used to denote anything and everything which is either poorly operated or poorly put together."[3]
High-rigger, or -climber. One who cuts the tops from high trees, that they may be used as spars in the handling of logs.
Hook-tender. A straw boss in the timber.
Ink-slinger. A camp clerk.
Ironburner. A blacksmith.
Land-looker, or timber-cruiser. One who surveys new land and maps it out for logging.
Limber. One who cuts the limbs from felled trees.
Macaroni. Sawdust.
Monk. A worker in a lumber-yard.
Push. A foreman.

1938; Logger Talk, by James Stevens, *American Speech*, Dec., 1925, pp. 135–40; Timberland Terminology, by Orlo H. Misfeldt, the same, Oct., 1941, pp. 232–34; Paul Bunyan Talk, by Elrick B. Davis, the same, Dec., 1942, pp. 217–25; Rhymes of a Western Logger, by Robert E. Swanson; Vancouver (B.C.), 1943, pp. 49–56, and Logger-Talk, by Guy Williams; Seattle, 1930. Other authorities are listed in Burke, pp. 101–02. Some early Maine terms are in Joys and Perils of Lumbering, *Harper's Magazine*, Sept., 1851, pp. 517–21. The argot of New Zealand loggers is in *Fiddlers, Ropies* and *Skiddies*, *New Zealand Free Lance*, Aug. 18, 1943, p. 7. I am indebted here to Mr. J. Heenan. I am also indebted to Miss Helen F. Northrup and to Messrs. Stewart H. Holbrook, James Stevens, Washington J. McCormick, Charles E. Brown, Carl B. Costello, Harold H. Sherley, Harold Russell, Fred Hamann, Paul Drus and John B. Martin.

1 From *caterpillar*, but now applied to all tractors.
2 Says a correspondent: "The first logger who heard an Easterner say *caulk* thought he was trying to say *cork*."
3 Timberland Terminology, by M. Misfeldt, before cited, p. 233. See Supplement I, pp. 393–94.

River-driver, river-pig, river-hog, river-rat, or white-water bucko. One who drives logs down a river.
Savage, heathen, timber-beast, or brush-cat. A logger.[1]
Schoolma'am. A forked log.
Show. Any logging operation.
Side-winder. A tree that hits another as it falls.
Skid-road. A path along which logs are dragged to the mill.[2]
Slave-market. An employment agency.
Snoose. Snuff.[3]
Swedish fiddle, briar, or misery-whip. A crosscut saw.
Timber. A cry of warning, signifying that a tree is about to fall.
Tin pants. Waterproofed clothing worn in the woods.
Wanigan, or wangun. A store-house or -room; also, a boat which supplies *river-drivers;* also, debts incurred at the company store.[4]

Machinists [5]

Banana-wagon. A tank on wheels used for refuse.
Barbering. Grinding.
Bitch. A clamp used to hold work on a lathe.
Bunion. A lump on a casting.
Chicago finish. A poor finish.
Funny sheet. A blueprint.
Glue-pot. A belt repairman.

Miners (Coal) [6]

Banjo. A miner's shovel.
Blossom. An outcropping of coal at the surface.
Boll-weevil, hill-billy, or snake-stomper. A new or inexperienced miner.
Bone. Coal full of stone.
Brass nuts. The manager of a mine.
Brattice, or brattish. A wall of wood, canvas or bricks used to cut off parts of the mine where there is gas.

---

1 Williams, before cited, p. 12. Says Davis, before cited, p. 217: "Lumberjacks call themselves *loggers.* To call them *lumbermen* is an invitation to a brawl. To a *logger,* a *lumberman* is a *sawdust-eater* down at the *macaroni-mills.*"

2 Used metaphorically to designate the street of saloons, flophouses, etc., frequented by loggers in town. Harvey C. Muldoon says in *Skid Road,* San Francisco *Chronicle,* Dec. 2, 1946, that the first *skid-road* was in Seattle, and that its vestiges are "more or less defined by the present Yesler way." Other *skid-roads* are Trent avenue in Spokane, Howard street in San Francisco, and West Pender street in Vancouver.

3 From *snooser,* the logger's term for a Scandinavian. The snuff was introduced by Scandinavians, and is very peppery. It is chewed, not snuffed.

4 Abnaki Indian *waniigan,* a trap. Traced by the DAE to 1848.

5 From Lexicon of Trade Jargon.

6 The following terms come from Mining Town Terms, by Joseph and Michael Lopushansky, *American Speech,* June, 1929, pp. 368–74; Lingo — Mine Run, *Writer's Digest,* Nov., 1941, pp. 28–29; Glossary of Current and Common Mining Terms, issued by the Bituminous Coal Institute, revised edition; Washington, 1947, and Lexicon of Trade Jargon. I am indebted here to Miss Virginia Allen, Eric Bender and Fred Hamann.

Breast. The underground chamber where anthracite is mined; in the bituminous mines it is called a room.
Bug-dust. Fine coal particles.
Bug-eye, or -light, or doodle-bug, or lightning-bug. An electric miner's lamp, worn on the cap.
Buggy, or bus. A small truck used underground.
Canary-bird. A device used to detect gas.[1]
Chalk-eye. A miner's helper.
Crawfish, v. To move about on hands and knees.
Dilly. An animal or tractor used for moving coal-cars.
Dirty-neck. A miner.
Fire boss. An inspector charged with detecting gas, insecure roofs, etc.
Flat wheel. A leg or foot injury.
Gaffer. A foreman.
Galloper. An assistant superintendent.
Gob. A place where the coal has been taken out and the earth has fallen in.
Gob-pile orator. A talkative miner.
Hardtail. A horse or mule used in a mine.
Hawbush. A local strike.
Hole. A mine.
Horseback. A bulge of slate into a vein of coal.
Jessie James. A company weigher.
Monster, or rattler. A coal-cutting machine.
Out on the sod. Said of one who has left the mines.
Panther, or niggerhead. A hard rock formation in a vein.
Pennydog. An assistant to the boss.
Pigeon-hole. A small, shallow working.
Pot. A loose fossiliferous formation in the roof of the mine, dangerous to the miner.
Snapper. A brakeman on a motor coal-car.
Soldiers. Posts supporting the mine roof.
Trapper. The doorkeeper of a mine.
Wasp-nest. An accumulation of gas.

Miners (Metal) [2]

Anchor. A pick.
Auto. A wheelbarrow.
Blockhead. A bulwark erected against fire.

[1] Formerly actual canaries were used.
[2] These come from The Lingo of the Mining Camp, by Helen L. Moore, *American Speech*, Nov., 1926, pp. 86–88; Mining Expressions Used in Colorado, by Levette J. Davidson, the same, Dec., 1929, pp. 144–47; Mining Jargon in Nevada: A Guide to the Silver State; Portland (Ore.), n. d., pp. 58–63; The Folklore, Customs and Traditions of the Butte Miner, by Wayland D. Hand, *California Folklore Quarterly*, Jan., 1946, pp. 1–25, and April, 1946, pp. 153–78, and Lexicon of Trade Jargon. The vocabulary of the early California miners is dealt with at length in California Gold-Rush English, by Marian Hamilton, *American Speech*, Aug., 1932, pp. 423–33. They gave the general speech many terms, *e.g.*, *prospector, to pan out, to make a stake, to grubstake, hard-pan, pay-dirt* and *claim-jumper*, and popularized many others that they did not invent, *e.g.*, *gulch, jim-jams, canyon* and *tenderfoot*.

Book-miner. A geologist.
Bootleg. A charge of explosive that explodes but does not break rock.
Cackler. A white-collar employé.
Capon. A miner who evades hard work.
Collar. The mouth of a shaft.
Country rock, or Protestant ore. Waste rock.
Cousin Jack. A Cornish miner.
Gallows-frame. A structure supporting hoisting machinery.
Hacienda. A smelter.
Hardrocker. A miner.
Jack, or steel. A drill.
Mike. A heavy hammer.
Pickey-poke. A soft-rock drill.
Picture-ore. Very high grade ore.
Porcupine, or Dutchman. A drill stuck in the hole.
Sewer-hog. A ditch digger.
Shawn O'Farrell. Whiskey with a beer chaser.
Shifter, gaffer, push, pusher, heeler, or enemy. A shift boss.
Sod-buster, hay-stoper, stubble-jumper, or top-hand. A recruit from the farms.
Spoon. A rod for cleaning out drill holes.
Stone (or rocks) on the chest. Miner's silicosis.
Tar-baby. A man who lubricates hoisting cables.
Wiggle-tail, or widow-maker. An old-fashioned power-drill, making much dust.

Oilfield Workers [1]

Afternoon. The shift from 4 P.M. to midnight.
Barefoot. Said of a hole with no *liner*.
Basket, bulldog spear, fishing tool, or overshot. Devices for recovering *fish* or a section of pipe.
Bean. A small pipe or steel billet inserted in the pipe in a well to restrict the flow of oil.
Belly-buster. A rope stretched across the derrick as a protection to the derrickman.
Biscuit-cutter. A drill bit.
Bleed, *v.* To drain off water at the bottom of an oil-tank.
Blow in, *v.* To begin to flow; said of a well.
Blow-out. An outburst of gas under high pressure.
Boll-weevil. In Texas, a new worker; in California, a Texan or a rotary driller.

[1] The following list is mainly based on Derrick Jargon, by Winifred Sanford and Clyde Jackson, *Southwest Review*, Spring, 1934, pp. 335–45; Language of the California Oil Fields, by Frederick R. Pond, *American Speech*, April, 1932, pp. 261–72; Oklahoma; a Guide to the Sooner State; Norman (Okla.), 1941, pp. 121–22, and Pipe Line Terms, by Leon Hines, *American Speech*, Dec., 1942, p. 280. I am greatly indebted to Mr. Lawrence E. Smith, of the Independent Petroleum Association of America, for revising my first draft and making additions to it, and also to Messrs. T. W. Archer, Fred Hamann, Miles Hart and Alfred M. Landon.

Breathing. The expansion and contraction of gases in an oil-tank as the temperature rises and falls.

Bridge. A collection of debris in a well.

B. S. The sediment in an oil-tank.[1]

Calf-line. The cable used to hoist and handle casing.

Casing. The pipe which lines the well.

Cat plant. A plant in which crude oil is split into lighter fragments by catalysis.[2]

Christmas tree. The group of valves at the top of a well.

Come in, *v.* To begin producing oil.

Core-barrel. A device used to obtain a sample of the sand or rock at the bottom of the hole.

Cut. Impurities in oil.

Daylight. The shift from 8 A.M. to 4 P.M.

Dead. A well that has ceased to flow.

Dead-in-a-hurry. A hauler of nitroglycerin.

Doodlebug. A divining rod.[3]

Dry gas. Natural gas containing no vaporized oil.

Duck's nest. The firebox of a boiler.

Duster. A dry hole.

Farmer, or Sears-Roebuck. A green worker.

Fish, or junk. Anything lost down a well.

Fourble. Four joints of pipe.

Freeze, *v.* To be stuck; said of a drill or pipe.

Go-devil. A device run through a pipe-line to clean out paraffin and other sediment;[4] also, a small charge of nitroglycerin used to detonate the main charge when a well is shot.

Go wild, *v.* To get out of control; said of a well.

Graveyard. The shift from midnight to 8 A.M.

Gusher. A well spouting oil by its own pressure.

Hot-ass. A bench in a locker with a steam-pipe under it.

Joint. A section of pipe, usually 20 feet long.

Liner. The casing which lines the hole in the oil-producing stratum.

Maud. An engine.

Mother Hubbard. A flat-bottomed bit used for drilling in soft soil.

Mouse-trap. A device for securing pipe.

Mud-smeller, or rock-hound. A geologist.

Nipple-chaser, or pusher. A foreman.

One-armed Johnnie. A hand-pump.

Pig-tail. A coil in a refinery pipe, employed to condense vapors.

Roustabout. A laborer on an oil lease, not a member of the rig crew.

Shoot, *v.* To break up the hard stratum at the bottom of a well by exploding nitroglycerin.

---

[1] Robert Shafer says in The Origin of *Basic Sediment, American Speech*, Oct., 1945, p. 238, that *B. S.* originally had its usual vulgar significance, but that *basic sediment* was substituted when oil-men began to grow refined.

[2] See *Cat Cracker* and *Cat Plant*, by M. M. S., *American Speech*, Feb., 1944, p. 46.

[3] See *Doodlebugs*, by Mody C. Boatwright, *Lamp*, Aug., 1946, pp. 10–11.

[4] Almost obsolete. Chemicals now do the work.

Spud in, v. To start drilling.
Stovepipe. Welded or riveted casing.
Sump. A ditch to catch waste oil.
Tank-farm. A group of storage tanks.
Thief-sand. A stratum of sand which absorbs oil from richer strata.
Thrible. Three joints of pipe.
Tour.[1] A work period.
Whiskey-jack. A hydraulic jack.
Wildcat. A well drilled in an area where oil has not been found hitherto.[2]

Packinghouse Workers [3]

Baby doll. An unusually well-finished yearling steer or heifer.
Bath towel. Beef tripe.
Beagles. Sausages.
Bologna, or baloney. A bull of a low grade, fit only for sausage.
Boulevards. The stockyards.
Bowbow. A stunted, aged steer.
Cat. A ram that lacks plumpness.
Cattalo. A steer showing buffalo blood.
Chicken-eater. A thin sow.
Deacon. A calf too young to be slaughtered.
Dog. Any low-grade animal.
Dollie. A choice, light heifer.
Dude. An office worker.
Educated. Said of stock raised at an agricultural college.
Elephant, or hippo. A steer weighing more than 1,500 pounds.
Facer. One who skins the heads of slaughtered cattle.
Grouch. A cattle buyer.
Gut-fatter. One who trims fat from the viscera.
Gut-shanty. The place where sausages are made.
Gutter. One who splits a carcass for the government inspection.
Ham-sniffer. An inspector of hams.
Ham-tree. A rack on which hams are placed.
Header. One who cuts off the heads of slaughtered hogs.
Hooks. The hip-bones of a cow.
Judas. A sheep trained to lead other sheep to the killing-floor.
Knocker. One who stuns the animal with a blow on the head.
Mountain oyster. A sheep testicle.
Mouse. An undersized lamb.
Nanny. An old ewe.
Nelly. An old, thin cow.
Peeler. A skinner.

[1] Pronounced *tower*. Formerly it was twelve hours, but now it is eight. See *afternoon, daylight* and *graveyard*.
[2] The DAE's first example is dated 1903, but *wildcatting*, the verb, is traced to 1883.
[3] From Language of the Livestock Market, by Russell F. Prescott, *American Speech*, Dec., 1935, pp. 269–72; How They Talk in the Stockyards, by A. A. Imberman, Baltimore *Evening Sun* (editorial page), Dec. 15, 1939; Words From South Omaha, by Rudolph Umland, *American Speech*, Oct., 1941, pp. 235–36, and Lexicon of Trade Jargon.

Peewee. A small, stunted pig or lamb.
Scenery-fed. Applied to half-starved sheep or steers.
Slimmer. A remover of fat.
Snatcher. One who removes the viscera from a carcass.
Snooper. A government inspector.
Soo-ey. A whip used in driving cattle.
Stiller. An animal fed on distillery mash.
Sunfish, or tripe. A thin, common animal.
Turp. An inferior animal from the South, supposed to have been fed on turpentine.

Photographers [1]

Acrobat, or distorter. A photographer who specializes in pictures taken at arty angles.

Blow-up. An enlargement.

Box. A camera.

Candid camera. A small hand-camera with a very fast lens, used for making surreptitious shots.[2]

Cheese-cake, or submarine shot. A photograph of a woman showing her legs above the knee.[3]

Cook, v. To develop.

Crop, or guillotine, v. To trim a print.

Dodging. In making prints, to shade parts of the negative in order to keep the shadows from becoming too dark.

Dope. A mixture used to roughen a negative for retouching.

Dynamite. A very rapid developer.

Elbow artist. A newspaper photographer who presses to the front, thus obstructing his fellows.

French it, v. To deceive a *lens-louse* by going through the motions of making an exposure without actually doing so.[4]

---

[1] I am indebted for most of these to Mr. A. Aubrey Bodine, chief of the photographic department of the Baltimore *Sunpapers*, and Mr. Jack Price, photo editor of the *Editor & Publisher*. The rest come from Slanguage of the Amateur Photographer, by Robert Johnston, *American Speech*, Dec., 1940, pp. 357–60, and More Jargon of the Amateur Photographer, by Gene Bradley, the same, Dec., 1941, pp. 316–17.

[2] R. L. Simon says in Miniature Photography; New York, 1937, p. 16, that the term was invented by a San Francisco news photographer in 1925. The first *candid camera* in wide use was the German Leica.

[3] Mr. Jack Price, before cited, says that it was launched *c.* 1912 by James Kane, of the New York *Journal*. He took a photograph of an actress seated on the rail of an incoming steamship, and discovered on developing it that it included more of her person than either he or she had suspected. "That," he exclaimed, "is what I call real *cheese-cake*"—a favorite New York sweet. Other accounts ascribe the coinage of the term to Joe Marsland, *c.* 1925. Discussions of it are in *Time*, Sept. 17, 1934, p. 30; *Broadside*, July, 1943, p. 1; *Saturday Review of Literature*, June 24, 1944, p. 22; and *American Notes & Queries*, Sept., 1945, p. 88; Nov., 1945, p. 123; Jan., 1946, p. 155, and Feb., 1946, p. 172.

[4] The usual plan is to pull the slide but not spring the shutter. Mr. Jack Price, before cited, tells me that this device was invented *c.*

Fuzz-ball. A photograph out of focus.
Glowworm, shutterbug, snapper, clicker, ham, or film-burner. An amateur photographer.
Gun. An apparatus for setting off a flashlight.
Hypo-bender. One in charge of the fixing-bath — hyposulphite of soda.
Lens-louse, or -hog. A publicity-seeker who tries to force himself uninvited into news photographs.
Mugger. A portrait photographer.
Percentage man. A news photographer who makes a large number of exposures, hoping that chance will give him a few good pictures.
Photogenic. Used to describe a good photographic subject.[1]
Pix. An accepted plural for *picture*.[2]
Pop-bottle. A poor lens.
Screwball. A difficult photographic subject.
Shot. An exposure.
Soup. A developer.
Stripper. A photographer specializing in nudes.
Tent. A darkroom.
Thirteen and eight. A warning cry that a *lens-louse* has got into a group about to be photographed.[3]

Plasterers [4]

Airedale, bloodhound, or minute-man. A foreman.
Aviator. A man working on a high ceiling, as in a theatre.
Bottom. The walls.
Butterflies. Lumps in the lime that don't spread out.
Chicken-wire. Light metal lath.
Corker. An easy job, without the delays caused by windows, beams, etc.
Dope. A chemical retarder that prevents plaster from setting immediately.
Hoddy-doddy. An apprentice.
In the boilers. Work underground.
Mudslinger, spreader, or mutt. A plasterer.
Putty. Lime.
Slugger. A hard worker, in a derogatory sense.
Snots. Lumps left on the wall.
Whitewash. A poor plastering job.

Plumbers and Steamfitters [5]

Bicycle Jake, or roller-skater. An overzealous workman.
Cocker. A steamfitter.
Digging for gold fish. Cleaning clogged sewers or toilet bowls.

---

[1] In this sense, apparently an Americanism and a relatively recent invention of Hollywood press-agents. In the early days of photography it was used for *photographic*, and in that sense is traced by the NED to 1839.
  1913 by Wade Mountfort, a New York ship-news photographer much afflicted by bogus French noblemen on incoming ships.
[2] First used, I believe, by *Variety*.
[3] Said to be a repunctuation of Hebrews XIII, 8, thus: " Jesus Christ! The same yesterday, and today, and forever! "
[4] From Lexicon of Trade Jargon.
[5] From Lexicon of Trade Jargon.

Dope, gooey, or gee. The white lead used on pipe-threads to prevent leakage.

Fly swatter. A painter.

Fourteen and a half. The boss is coming.

Good Friday. Pay day.

Hardware. Tools.

Hickey. Any tool.

Jewelry. A tool kit.

Postoffice Workers [1]

Balloon. A large mail-pouch.

Boodle. A valuable letter or package.

Box up, or buck the *case*, v. To sort mail.

Bum. An empty mail-pouch.

Case. A rack of pigeonholes into which mail is assorted according to its destination.

Confetti. Envelopes of less than the usual size.

Czech. An unpopular superior.

Fat stock. Letters too bulky to go through the cancelling machine.

Floating. Loafing on the job.

House. A postoffice.

Humpback. A mail sorter.

Kluck. A used postage stamp on a letter.

Landlord. A high postoffice official.

Nixie. A letter or other piece of mail so badly addressed that it can't be delivered.[2]

Peeling, skinning, or sweeping. Collecting mail from street boxes.

Shedder, or brummie. A stamp fallen from an envelope.

Shoo-fly. A carrier foreman.

Swing-room. A lunch-room or rest-room.

Potters

Clay-belly. A potter.

Doughnut. A woman's stocking worn in the cap as a cushion by men who carry ware on their heads.

Fire-eater. A worker who unloads kilns.[3]

Pugilists [4]

Button. The point of the jaw.

Chiropractor. A wrestler.

---

[1] From Speech in the Post Office, by Paul Bisgaier, *American Speech*, April, 1932, pp. 278–79, and Lexicon of Trade Jargon. I am also indebted to Mr. Hartford Beaumont.

[2] Apparently from the German *nichts*. Traced by the DAE to 1879. See AL4, p. 157, n. 2.

[3] From Lexicon of Trade Jargon. Many other potters' terms are in a poem, From Clay to Roses, by Harry Brokaw, *Congressional Record*, May 2, 1946, p. A2568.

[4] Pugilists as a class are far too stupid to invent an argot of any interest. What passes as such is mainly produced by sports writers. Many of its terms are given in Jargon of Fistiana, by Robert E. Creighton, *American Speech*, Oct., 1933, pp.

Cauliflower, or tin ear. An effusion of blood or serum between the cartilage of the ear and the skin, caused by blows.[1]
Has-been. A played-out pug.[2]
K. O., or kayo. A knockout.[3]
Level, *v.* To fight honestly in a framed bout.[4]
Mouse. A black eye.[5]
Palooka,[6] ham, or tomato. An inferior fighter.
Punch-drunk, slap-happy, slug-nutty, punchy, goofy, or cutting paper-dolls. Feeble-minded as a result of taking too many blows to the head.[7]
Roarer, or breather. One who fights with his mouth open.
Semi-windup. The fight before the last one of the evening.[8]
Solar plexus. A network of nerves behind the stomach and in front of the aorta.[9]
White hope. A white fighter expected to beat a colored champion.[10]

Racetrack Followers [11]

Acey-deucy. A jockey riding with one short stirrup and one long one.
Blind Tom. A track steward.

34–39. I offer a few samples here. A number of pugilistic words and phrases have got into the general speech, e.g., *to hit below the belt, knockout, to throw up the sponge,* and *to take the count.*

[1] Obviously suggested by the resemblance of a *cauliflower-ear* to the vegetable.
[2] Traced by the NED to 1606.
[3] Partridge calls it an Americanism and says that it was first used after 1900. Not in Alfred H. Holt's Phrase Origins, New York, 1936.
[4] Westbrook Pegler's column, March 11, 1947.
[5] Traced by Farmer and Henley to 1857.
[6] Probably borrowed from the racetrack, where it signifies a sorry nag. It may be related to the synonymous *palouser*, which may be derived from the name of the *Palouse* Indians of the Northwest. Holt, before cited, suggests that it may come from the Spanish *peluca,* a term of reproof.
[7] Dr. Harrison S. Martland says in *Punch Drunk, Journal of the American Medical Association,* Oct. 13, 1928, p. 1103, that "the basic lesion is due to traumatic multiple hemorrhages."
[8] Coined by the late Abraham Lincoln Herford. See my Heathen Days; New York, 1943, p. 101.
[9] It was with a blow which shook the *solar plexus* that Robert Fitzsimmons knocked out James J. Corbett at Carson City, Nev., March 17, 1897, but Peter Tamony says in The Advent of *Solar Plexus,* San Francisco *News-Letter & Wasp,* Oct. 27, 1939, p. 18, that the sporting fraternity did not become aware of the term until the effects were explained by Dr. John H. Girdner, of New York, two days later. The old-time English pugilists called the pit of the stomach the *mark.*
[10] Its origin is discussed in *White Hope,* by Steven T. Byington, *American Speech,* April, 1943, pp. 156–68.
[11] These come mainly from English As She is Spoke Where Nags Run, by Hugh Bradley, New York *Evening Post,* May 15, 1936; Race-Track Lingo, by Charles H. Dorsey, Jr., Baltimore *Evening Sun,* April 15, 1940; A Billion Across the Board, *Fortune,* Sept., 1944, pp. 202–14, and Horse English is Very Simple, by Arthur Siegel, Boston *Traveler,* May 26, 1946. I am indebted here to Mr. Bradford F. Swan.

Bug. An apprentice jockey's five-pound weight allowance, lost when he has been riding a year or won a certain number of races.[1]

Dead weight. Lead to bring a jockey's weight up to the amount the horse he rides is required to carry.

Dogs. Temporary fences set up on muddy mornings to prevent horses working out from messing up the track near the inner rail.

Embalmer. A bookmaker who bribes stable boys to dope favorites.

Gumbo. A muddy track.

Gyp. A small owner.[2]

Heavy-headed. Said of a horse which runs with its head low.

High in flesh. Said of a fat horse.

Kentucky position. The fourth place in a race.[3]

Lug in, or lug out, v. To swerve from the course.

Maiden. A horse that has never won a race.

Morning glory. A horse that shows good speed in the morning trials, but does badly in the afternoon.

Night cap. The last race of the day.

Photo finish. A finish so close that only the photograph usually taken can determine the winner.[4]

Ringer. A horse entered under a false name.[5]

Sportsman. One who patronizes racing because he really loves horses.[6]

Stiff. A horse sent out not to win.

Stimulate, v. To dope a horse.[7]

Suicide club. Steeplechase riders.

Tack. A jockey's equipment.[8]

Tap out, v. To bet one's last dollar.

Walk-over. A race in which only one horse starts.

---

1 "When a jockey has such an allowance," says Dorsey, "it is indicated on the programme by an asterisk, hence the *bug*."

2 Dorsey says that the word is apparently derived from *gipsy*, and "has no derogatory significance whatever."

3 "Because," says Bradley, "Kentucky trainers used to tell a client his horse finished fourth when he was way out of the running."

4 The Living Language, by Dwight L. Bolinger, *Words*, May, 1939, p. 74.

5 Defined by Webster 1934 as "one that enters any competition under false representations as to his identity, past performance, or the like; esp., a horse entered fraudulently in a race under a false name to obtain better odds in the betting." The term seems to be an Americanism, for it does not appear in the NED, and Partridge omits it from his Dictionary of Slang and Unconventional English, though he admits the verb *to ring* in the sense of "to manipulate, to change illicitly," and *to ring in* in the sense of "to insert, esp. to substitute, fraudulently." The DAE unaccountably overlooks it, but it is to be found as *ringer-in*, in the sense of an interloper, in *Harper's Magazine*, Feb., 1857, p. 421.

6 "The species," says Bradley, "is about as extinct as a New York starter who knows his business."

7 This elegant euphemism got a large play in the newspapers at the time of the racing scandals in Maryland, 1946.

8 Dorsey says that it is derived from *tackle*.

770   *The American Language: Supplement II*

Wall-eyed. Said of a horse blind in one eye.[1]
Work. Any sort of exercise for a horse, including walking.[2]

Rubber Workers[3]

College. A rubber factory.
Gob. A worker in a rubber factory.
Nerve. Firmness, strength and elasticity in crude or reclaimed rubber.
Plugger. A maker of rubber heels.
Red apple. A non-union man.
Sausage grinder. A tube machine.
Shoddy. Reclaimed rubber.
Wheel. An automobile tire.

Sand-hogs[4]

Bore hole. A tunnel.
Drummy. Loose rock.
Hot cat. Dynamite which fails to explode.
Navvies. Excavators employed on canals, docks, or other maritime projects.
Niggerhead. A dense, hard boulder; also, a cylinder on a power-winch.
Rib. The side of a tunnel under construction.
Slaughterhouse. A job on which there are many accidents.
Smitty. A blacksmith.

Sheepmen[5]

Biddy, or gummer. An old ewe.
Blade-man, or barber. A shearer.
Bum, bummer, orphan, dogie, or leppy. A lamb whose mother has deserted it.
Drag. The rear end of a moving flock.
Drop band. A group of ewes about to lamb.
Gancho. The sheepman's crook.
Granny. A ewe which adopts the lambs of other ewes.
Herder, or jockey. A shepherd.
Marker. A black or spotted sheep.
Nut, *v.* To castrate.

Shoe Clerks[6]

Al, Albert or Andy. A shoe of A width.
Benny. A shoe of B width.
Charley. A shoe of C width.

---

[1] The NED says that this is a misuse of the word. It actually means having an eye "the iris of which is whitish, streaked, parti-colored or different in hue from the other eye, or which has a divergent squint."

[2] Some of these terms have been borrowed from the English, just as racing itself was borrowed. Others have entered into the common speech, sometimes in figurative senses, *e.g., ringer, horse-sense, well-groomed, also ran, to set the pace, tight rein,* and *walk-over.*

[3] From Lexicon of Trade Jargon.

[4] *i.e.,* tunnel excavators.

[5] I take these from The Idiom of the Sheep Range, by Charles Lindsay, *American Speech*, June, 1931, pp. 355–59; Stock Jargon, in Nevada: a Guide to the Silver State; Portland (Ore.), n. d., and Lexicon of Trade Jargon. See also *Cattlemen.*

[6] My authorities here are Lingo of the Shoe Salesman, by David Gel-

Cheaters. Insoles used to palm off over-large shoes.
Chromo. A difficult customer.
Compos, paste, or Mac. The cheapest sort of shoe.
Cowhide, or keg of nails. Men's work-shoes.
Danny, or David, or Dave. A shoe of D width.
Dog. A shoe that is hard to sell.
Early, or Eddie. A shoe of E width.
Float. A customer who walks out while a salesman is getting a shoe to try on.
Forty-four boy. A salesman's helper.
Forward, or up, or front. A customer is entering the store.
Happies. Arches.
Jiffy. A shoe included in a special sale; also, a cork inner sole.
Knock down, or grab, v. To take a customer out of turn.
Lawyer. A friend accompanying a customer, to advise him on his purchase.
M. M. A mismated pair of shoes.
Mrs. McKenzie,[1] or shome.[2] A customer who doesn't buy.
Personal, or P. T. A customer who insists upon being waited on by a favorite salesman.
P. M., spiff, ninety-nine, or skig-last. An unpopular shoe on the sale of which the salesman receives an extra commission, called *push-money*.
Schlach-joint. A store without fixed prices.[3]
Schlock. An overcharge.[4]
Shoe dog. A salesman.
Skig, tinge, P. M. man, or P. M. hound. A salesman eager for *push-money*.
Stock manager. A salesman to whom a turnover is handed.[5]
Thirty-four. Go away.
Thrown out. Said of a customer to whom it was impossible to sell anything.
T. L. A salesman who tries to ingratiate himself with the boss.[6]
Walk. A customer who leaves the store without buying.
Wrap-up. A sale that is easy to make; also, an easily satisfied customer.
Zex. Beware; the boss is watching.[7]

Shoemakers [8]

Bat. A cheap shoe.
Beauty parlor. A dressing and packing room.

---

ler, *American Speech*, Dec., 1924, pp. 283–86, with a vocabulary by J. S. Fox; Shoe-store Terms, by Erik I. Bromberg, the same, April, 1938, p. 150; a United Press dispatch from Lincoln, Neb., July 2, 1936, describing an investigation made by students of Miss Mamie Meredith, instructor in business English at the University of Nebraska, and Lexicon of Trade Jargon.

1 Yiddish *mie ken zie*, I know her.
2 *i.e.*, one who says "Show me this; show me that."
3 Ger. *schlacht*, a battle.
4 Apparently from a Yiddish word meaning a misfortune or curse.
5 "The term is used," says Geller, "to impress the customer with the fact that he is being given more attention for his money."
6 Yiddish *tochus lekker*, arse-kisser.
7 See also *Department-Store Clerks* and *Instalment-House Salesmen*.
8 These come mainly from Lexicon of Trade Jargon.

Bootblacks. Ironers in the finishing and packing departments.
Club sandwich. A high heel in layers of different colors.
Crispin. An old-time shoemaker.[1]
Doughman. A paymaster.
Flat foot. The superintendent.
Tap. A half-sole.
Tripe. Bad leather.

Soda-Jerkers [2]

Bar-mop. A towel.
Belch-water. Seltzer.
Black and white. Chocolate soda or malted milk with vanilla ice-cream; also, coffee with cream.
Black-bottom. A chocolate sundae with chocolate syrup.
Black-cow. Root beer with ice-cream.
Blue bottle. Bromo-Seltzer.
Bottom. Ice-cream added to a drink.
City juice, or moisture. Water.
Coke, or shot. Coca-Cola.
C. O. cocktail, or high-ball. Castor oil in soda.
Eighty-one. A glass of water.
Eye-opener. Castor oil in sarsaparilla.
Hoboken. A mixture of pineapple syrup and chocolate ice-cream.
Hot top, or hot cha. A cup of hot chocolate.
House-boat. A banana split.
Hump. Camel cigarettes.
Java. Coffee.
Oh gee, or red ball. Orangeade.
Scandal soup. Tea.
Spiker. Lemon phosphate.
Sprinkle. Spirits of ammonia.
Straight Kelly. Orange juice.
White-cow. A vanilla milk shake.
White horn. A vanilla ice-cream cone.[3]

---

1 St. *Crispin* is the patron of shoemakers. Both he and his brother, St. Crispinian, practised the craft in Gaul, and both were beheaded at Soissons in 285 or 286. The first trades-union of American shoemakers, formed in 1868, was called the Knights of St. *Crispin*.

2 The *soda-jerker* or *jerk* or *hopper* calls himself a *soda-dispenser* (his trades-union is the Cooks, Countermen, *Soda Dispensers* and Assistants Union) or *fountaineer* (Supplement I, p. 360). His jargon is very much like that of waitresses. (See *Food-Dispensers*.) It includes a number of terms of true cant, designed to prevent strangers understanding what is communicated, and some of them are simple numerals. Thus, *thirteen* or *ninety-eight* signifies that the manager is in sight, and *ninety-five* or *ninety-six* is a warning to the cashier that a customer is getting away without paying his check.

3 On Oct. 8, 1936 the Red Network of the National Broadcasting Company put on an interview with several *soda-jerkers* from Radio City, with Dr. W. W. Beardsley as the interlocutor. The advance notice, dated Oct. 6, said: " The *soda-jerker's* behind-the-counter speech almost amounts to a code, covering any number of subjects in addi-

American Slang 773

Steel Workers [1]

Bogieman. A foreman.
Bone. A hard streak in a piece of steel.
Bug. A large ladle.
Buggy. A traveling crane.
Bull. A large ladle; also, a shop foreman.
Cabbages. Scrap metal pressed into blocks.
Cat's-eye, or wormhole. A gas bubble in crucible steel.
Cheese. A disk-shaped ingot.
Clocks. A timekeeper.
Dickey boy. An efficiency man.
Dynamite. Limestone.[2]
Flush, *v.* To withdraw molten iron from a blast furnace.
Flute. A wave on the surface of a badly rolled sheet.
Healer, or iodine. A first-aid man.
Heat. The contents of one furnace; also, any load of molten steel.
Irish local. A wheelbarrow.[3]
Knobbling. A forging.
Niggerhead. A piece of scrap sticking above the surface of molten steel in a furnace.
Noodles. Material used to stuff cracks in the bottom of a furnace.
Pickle sheets. Sheets from which the scale has been removed by chemicals.
Pulpit. The raised platform from which the mill operations are controlled.
Salamander. The solidified iron on the bottom of a furnace.
Shoe. A plant policeman.
Skull. Iron cooled in a ladle.
Teeming. The act of pouring molten steel.
Umbrella. An ingot that curls when rolled.

Stockbrokers [4]

Airedale. A successful stock salesman.
Bird-dog. An outsider (often innocent) who rounds up customers.
Boiler-room. A telephone-room.
Cats and dogs. Worthless securities.
Cut a melon, *v.* To declare a large extra dividend.
D. K. The opposite of O. K.
Dynamiter. A stock salesman of extraordinary virulence.
Front-money. An *airedale's* expense-account.
Hot stuff. Selling literature.
Irish dividend. An assessment on stock.

---

tion to that of dispensing sodas and sandwiches. In recent years its use has become nation-wide." I am indebted here to Messrs. Theodore R. Goodman and William Feather.

[1] These come from Slang of Steel, *Fortune*, Dec., 1935, p. 44, and Lexicon of Trade Jargon.

[2] From *dolomite*.

[3] See Supplement I, p. 604.

[4] Some of these terms are now virtually obsolete, for the setting up of the Securities and Exchange Commission, on July 6, 1934, greatly crippled constructive salesmanship in Wall Street. Most of them come from Financial Racketeering and How to Stop It, by William Leavitt Stoddard; New York, 1931, pp. 4 and 5. I am also indebted here to Messrs. Dent Smith and Edward L. Bernays.

Lily, or mooch. A customer.
P. O. A Postoffice inspector.
Reefer. A refunding bond.
Reloader. A stock salesman skilled at selling more of the same stock to persons who have already bought shares.
Scenery. Directors elected to give an appearance of respectability to a company.
Tagged. Indicted.[1]

Stonecutters [2]

Banker, or skidway. A structure on which a stone rests while being worked.
Dog. A hook used for lifting stone.
Dutchman. A cemented repair on a finished stone.
Gang. A machine for sawing stone.
Hickey. A small grave marker.
Knot. A dark gray or black patch in granite.
Lumper. A laborer.
Saint Lucia day. Pay-day.
Slant-face. A grave marker with a surface for the inscription at an angle of about 65 degrees.

Structural Iron Workers

Buckeroo. The man who puts his weight against one end of a rivet while the other is being driven.
Button-head. A rivet.
Catcher. The man who catches hot rivets.
Driver. A riveter.[3]
Dutchman. A small derrick, operated by hand.
Flop. A fall not resulting in death.
Framer. A carpenter.
Header. A fall resulting in death.
Hole. The basement of a building under construction; also, the empty space under the workers on high jobs.

[1] Stockbrokers and their clerks have some amusing nicknames for conspicuous stocks, e.g., *Father Divine*, International Telephone & Telegraph; *Nipper*, Northern Pacific; *Monkey*, Montgomery Ward; *Jumpy*, Johns-Manville; *Knockout*, Coca-Cola; *Old Woman*, New York, Ontario & Western; *Betty*, Bethlehem Steel; *Big Steel*, U. S. Steel; *Minnie Mouse*, Marine Midland; *Mop*, Missouri Pacific; *Widow*, West Indies Sugar; *Ukulele*, Union Carbide & Carbon; *Rebecca*, Republic Steel; *Rockies*, Chicago, Rock Island & Pacific; *Sopac*, Southern Pacific; *Whiskey*, Wisconsin Central. I am indebted here to Mr. C. MacCoy, of the New York Exchange and to Traders' Tongue, *Investor's Reader*, Dec. 15, 1943, pp. 4 and 5. Some bond issues have special names, e.g., *Saps*, San Antonio Public Service 4s; *Sows*, South Carolina Power 5s; *Miserys*, Missouri Power & Light 3¾s; *Scarlett O'Haras*, Southern Bell Telephone 3s.

[2] I am indebted here to Mr. Carl Kastrup, of Rockford, Ill. I have added a few quarrymen's terms from Lexicon of Trade Jargon.

[3] A crew consists of a *heater*, who heats the rivets; a *catcher*, a *buckaroo* and a *driver*.

Monday. A sixteen-pound hammer.
Monkey. A member of a raising gang.
Red dot. A hot rivet.[1]

Tanners [2]

Buffing. The operation of taking a light cut from the surface of cattle skins.

Butt. That part of a hide covering the hind-quarters of the animal.

Chamois. If genuine, leather made from the skin of the Alpine chamois. Usually the flesh part of sheepskins, oil-dressed and suede-finished.

Cordovan. Leather made from horse hides, used for shoe uppers.

Crushed. Said of leather in which the natural grain has been artificially accentuated.

Currying. Incorporating oils or greases into leather.

Doeskin. White sheep- and lambskin.

Full grain. The outer surface of a hide from which nothing has been removed save the hair.

Iron. The unit of thickness in sole leather. One iron equals 1/48 inch.

Loading. Materials used to condition leather, *e.g.*, glucose and magnesium chloride.

Ounce. The unit of thickness in upholstery and bag leather. One ounce equals 1/64 inch.

Rawhide. Cattle hide that has been dehaired and limed, and sometimes stuffed with oil or grease, but not tanned.

Russia. Originally a calfskin shoe leather, dressed with birch oil, but now applied to a fancy leather made of either calfskins or cattle hides.

Suede. Leather finished by applying it to an emery-wheel, thus separating the fibres and giving the surface a nap.

Textile-workers [3]

Agafretted. Tangled or snarled work.
Alley. A mill aisle.
Birdseye. Woolen or worsted cloth.
Buggy-rider. A sweeper.
Bull. The factory whistle.
Cut. A length of cloth, usually 60 yards.
Doc. A machinist who repairs looms.
Dungeoneer. A dye-house worker.
Elegazam. Perfect work.
Fly. Fabric particles and dust given off by the looms.
Iron horse. A loom.

[1] I take all these from Lexicon of Trade Jargon.

[2] So far as I know, there is no study in print of the argot of tanners, but the Tanners' Council of America issues a Dictionary of Leather Terminology; third edition, New York, 1941, that lists some of the terminology used in the trade, as opposed to the craft. Says the preface: "Many leathers are known commercially or popularly by names of hides or skins of which they are not actually made.... Names of some skins (like *chamois*) have come to mean a finish as much as a kind of leather. It has even been necessary to insert the word *genuine* before some kinds of leather (like *buckskin*) to distinguish it from its imitators."

[3] From Lexicon of Trade Jargon.

776   *The American Language: Supplement II*

Lint-head. A cotton-mill worker.
Looney. A green worker.
Nurse cloth. Colored goods woven in stripes.
Oatmeal cloth. Cretonne.
Picks. The number of threads to an inch.
Race-horse. A loom geared to high speed.
Scroop. The rustle or crunch of silk.
Squat-head. A company executive.

Tobacco-growers [1]

Bookman, or ticket-maker. A warehouse clerk who records sales.
Bull-gang. Laborers who handle hogsheads.
Duckbill, or spoonbill. A small hand-truck.
Frenchman. A stalk with small, erect leaves, worthless in quality.
Frog-eye. A small speck on a tobacco leaf.
Guinea. Tobacco with *frog-eyes*.[2]
Lug. A leaf low on the stem, of small value.
Pinhooker. One who buys privately, often at bargain prices.[3]
Pole-sweat, or house-burn. Spoiling of tobacco in the process of curing.
Smithfield. "Making a bid by a nod, but calling aloud at the same time a lower price in order to trick other buyers." [4]
Wooden ear. A buyer who raises his own bid.
Yellowhammer. A speculator.

Union Men in General [5]

Beef-squad, or goon-squad. A gang of *goons*.
Brother. Used in addressing or speaking of a fellow union man.
Check-off. Union dues or assessments deducted by the employer and paid to the union.
Featherbedding. Getting pay for work not done.
Goon. Originally, a ruffian hired to intimidate strikers; now, a ruffian menacing workers who refuse to strike.[6]

---

[1] These come from Tobacco Words, by L. R. Dingus, *Publication of the American Dialect Society No. 2*, Nov., 1944, pp. 63–72, and Language of the Tobacco Market, by Robert J. Fitzpatrick, *American Speech*, April, 1940, pp. 132–35. They were all gathered in the Southern tobacco area, where cigar tobacco is seldom if ever grown.

[2] So called, says Fitzpatrick, before cited, "because its freckles resemble those of a *Guinea*-hen."

[3] Mr. Leonard Rapport, of Chapel Hill, N. C., tells me that the term has been traced to the 70s. It may be related to *pin-hook*, a bent pin used as a fish-hook, traced by the DAE to 1840.

[4] I take this definition from Fitzpatrick. He says that "the practise is said to have originated at Smithfield, N. C."

[5] The more seemly terms in use by union men are listed in Labor Terminology, Bulletin No. 25 of the Bureau of Business Research, Harvard University; Cambridge, 1921. I am indebted here to Messrs. James F. Bender, Harry F. Bruning and John S. Grover.

[6] Apparently picked up from Alice the *Goon*, a character in Elzie Crisler Segar's comic strip, Popeye the Sailor. As a verb it is an obsolete form of *to gun*, and is in Chaucer's The House of Fame, III, *c*. 1380. As a noun, defined as "a person with a heavy touch," it was used in The *Goon* and His Style, by Frederick L. Allen, *Harper's Magazine*, Dec., 1921. Mr. Allen tells me

Hooker. "An operative who inveigles union men into acting as spies on their fellows and keeps them *hooked* by threatening to expose them to the union."[1]

Jimmie Higgins. A willing member who does the drudgery of a union.[2]

Kickback, or piece off. A bribe paid by a workman to a foreman or union official for security in his job.

Missionary worker. One who seeks to break down the morale of strikers.

Noble. The commander of a strike-breaking squad.[3]

Picket. A person posted at a struck plant, usually bearing a placard setting forth the strikers' case.

Pork-chopper. A union official who is in the labor movement for what he can get out of it.[4]

Portal-to-portal. From the entrance to the plant or mine back to the same place.[5]

Rollback. A reduction in wages to a former level.

Scab, or fink. One who takes the place of a striker.[6]

Scissor-bill. A non-union worker.

Sit-down, folded arms, crossed arms, or stay-in. A strike in which the strikers remain in the plant but refuse to work.[7]

Struck. Used to designate a plant in which a strike is in progress.[8]

Wildcat, quickie, or outlaw strike. One not authorized by union officials.

Wobbly. A member of the Industrial Workers of the World, or I. W. W.[9]

Yellow-dog contract. A contract whereby workers agree not to join a union.[10]

World War II, though it threw off an enormous number of what, to newspaper lexicographers, appeared to be neologisms, actually produced few that were really new, and not many of them have stuck. Some of the most familiar, *e.g.*, *foxhole, brass hat, M.P.*[11] and *black market*, were legacies from World War I, and others went

---

that it was used in his family before this, and may have been either picked up elsewhere or invented.

1 Associated Press dispatch quoted in *Word Study*, Feb., 1937, p. 4.
2 Miriam Allen deFord, in *American Notes & Queries*, Nov., 1946, p. 127, says that it "was used in the Socialist party at the beginning of the century." Upton Sinclair made it the title of a novel in 1919.
3 *Word Study*, Feb., 1937, p. 4.
4 *Pork-Chopper*, by Miriam Allen deFord, *American Notes & Queries*, Nov., 1946, p. 127.
5 See Among the New Words, by I. Willis Russell, *American Speech*, Dec., 1946, p. 298. His earliest example is from *Time*, Oct. 25, 1943, p. 21.
6 *Scab* is traced to 1806 by the DAE and marked an Americanism.
7 George P. Peter says in *Sit-Down, American Speech*, Feb., 1937, pp. 31-33, that the term was first proposed in 1911, but that it did not come into general use until 1936.
8 *Strike-Struck*, by Hugh Sebastian, *American Speech*, Oct., 1937, p. 235.
9 Organized in Chicago, 1905. An attempt at the etymology of the term is in How *Wobbly* Originated, by Richard W. Hogue, *Nation*, Sept. 5, 1923, p. 242.
10 *Yellow-dog* as a general symbol of worthlessness is an Americanism, traced by the DAE to 1895. It is probably much older.
11 Called a *red-cap* by the English.

back to earlier wars, including the Civil War, e.g., *dog-tag, K.P., a. w. o. l., hike, pup-tent, gook,*[1] *belly-robber, to bust* (to reduce in rank), *commando* (South African War).[2] What differentiated World War II from all others in history, aside from the curious fact that it produced no popular hero and no song, was the enormous number of newspaper correspondents who followed its operations, and the even greater number of press-agents who served its *brass*. Many of these literati were aspirants to the ermine of Walter Winchell, and as a result they adorned the daily history of the war with multitudinous bright inventions, but the actual soldier, like his predecessors of the past, limited his argot to a series of derisive names for the things he had to do and endure, and the ancient stock of profanity and obscenity. All the more observant and intelligent veterans that I have consulted tell me that a few four-letter words were put to excessively heavy service. One of them, beginning with *f*, became an almost universal verb, and with *-ing* added, a universal adjective; another, beginning with *s*, ran a close second to it. The former penetrated to the highest levels, and was the essence of one of the few really good coinages of the war, to wit, *snafu*, meaning, according to Colonel Elbridge Colby, the leading authority on Army speech, "the confusion that comes from sudden changes in orders."[3] Colby says that it is an abbreviation of "Situation normal; all *foozled* up," and other lexicographers have substituted *fouled* for *foozled*, but the word really in mind was something else again.[4] Nor were the two mentioned the only ones of the sort in constant use. The verb in the last clause of I Samuel XXV, 22 also had a heavy play,[5] and so did the ancient Germanic word for backside.[6] Nor were their lesser analogues forgotten.[7]

1 Supplement I, p. 598.
2 The Word *Commando*, by Elliott V. K. Dobbie, *American Speech*, April, 1944, pp. 81–90.
3 Army Talk, second edition; Princeton (N.J.), 1943, p. 230.
4 *Snafu* (pronounced as a word) produced a numerous progeny, e.g., *susfu*, situation unchanged: still *fu; fubar, fu* beyond all recognition; *janfu*, joint Army and Navy *fu*, and *tarfu*, things are really *fu*, but Jeffrey A. Fleece says in Words in *-fu, American Speech*, Feb., 1946, pp. 70–72, that none of them ever "really became part of Army language." Morroe Berger, in Army Language, the same, Dec., 1945, p. 262, adds *G. F. U.*, a soldier who never does anything correctly; *F. O.*, to avoid work, and various others. In *F. O. off* takes the place of the usual *up*.
5 It came originally from the French, and the NED says that it got into English as a euphemism. It is to be found in nearly all the standard writers before the Eighteenth Century.
6 Pronounced *arse* in England, but

The precise provenance of most of the terms that issued from the war is dark and disputed. Where, how and at whose hands *GI* came into use is not known. Colby, before cited, says that in World War I, and perhaps before, the initials stood for *galvanized iron*, as in *GI* [ash]-*can* and *GI bucket*, but that they were transferred early in World War II to *general issue*, as in *GI soap, GI haircut* and *GI food*. All such things were disesteemed by the soldier, mainly because they were purely utilitarian and hence unattractive, so he presently began to transfer the letters, metaphorically, to other things that he didn't admire, *e.g., GI hop* or *struggle*, a dance at an Army post; *GI girl*, a female brought in to dance with him; *GI war*, manoeuvres; *GI sky-pilot*, a chaplain; *GI lemonade*, water, and so on. These terms soon appeared numerously in *Yank*, the soldiers' newspaper, and *GI Joe*, for the soldier himself, and *GI Jane* for his female comrade-in-arms, followed inevitably.[1] But the *Joe* part was

---

ass in this country. It has cognates in all the Germanic languages. It lies defectively hidden in *BAM*, the Navy name for a lady marine, *i.e., broad-assed marine*. During the war a naval officer of rank and fancy suggested that *leatherteat* be substituted, but this stroke of genius was frowned upon by the High Command. The lady marines were known officially as the *Women's Reserve of the Marine Corps*. Their heroic record is given in the *Congressional Record*, Dec. 18, 1945, pp. A6042-43. That of their comrades-in-arms, the *WAVES* of the Navy proper, is in the same, Feb. 11, 1946, p. A685. That of the *SPARS*, who fought with the Coast Guard, is in the same, Jan. 25, 1946, pp. A237-38. *SPARS* was coined by the commander of the outfit, Captain Dorothy G. Stratton. She got it from the Coast Guard motto, *Semper paratus*, always ready.

7 Says Frederick Elkin in The Soldier's Language, *American Journal of Sociology*, March, 1946, pp. 414-22: "Such terms, used by themselves or in combination phrases, are in almost every sentence a soldier says." Elkin adds that "this constant and crude use of obscenity" often shocks recruits, but that "with constant exposure the shock lessens," and "eventually, to a greater or less degree, practically all soldiers adopt it.... Violating the taboos of language gives feelings of courage and freedom,... strength and virility." In the same issue of the same journal, p. 411, Henry Elkin (not the same writer), says: "By pronouncing those 'dirty words,' which he never dared to utter in the presence of Mom or his old-maid schoolteachers, the GI symbolically throws off the shackles of the matriarchy in which he grew up." Testimony to their prevalence in the Army is to be found in many other discussions of soldiers' argot, *e.g.*, Warriors' Slang, by Robert L. Wheeler, Providence (R.I.) *Sunday Journal*, Feb. 4, 1945, Section VI, p. 1, and American Army Speech in the European Theatre by Joseph W. Bishop, Jr., *American Speech*, Dec., 1946, pp. 241-52.

1 Dave Breger claimed in *Time*, Feb. 26, 1945, p. 7, that he was the first to use *GI Joe*, to wit, in *Yank*, June 17, 1942. "I decided on GI," he said, "because of its prevalence

disliked,[1] and soon *GI Joe* became plain *GI*. The latter also had some vogue as an adjective standing alone, as in " Are they very *GI* around here?," always expressing distaste, but it did not last for long. Neither did *GI kraut*, listed in 1945 as in use in the Army of the Occupation to designate a former private in the German Army.[2] Of *kraut* itself Irwin R. Blacker said during the same year: [3]

> *Kraut* and *krauthead* . . . have a somewhat questionable . . . source. They were selected by one of the propaganda branches of the Army to replace the widely accepted *jerry*. The *Stars and Stripes*, early in the Italian campaign, published notification of its intention to use *kraut* because it gave less dignity to the enemy. The word was thereafter popular in print, but was not generally used by the soldiers.[4]

But it was official fiat which substituted the euphemistic *selectee* for the somewhat harsh *draftee* of World War I. The former first appeared in the Selective Training and Service Act of 1940, along with *trainee*. *Trainee* didn't have much prosperity, but *selectee* was in almost universal use until the end of the war. *Evacuee*, which raged among the English, though it was violently denounced by their purists,[5] never made any progress in this country, probably because the only American citizens actually evacuated were the heathen Japanese of the Pacific Coast. Once the war was over *displaced person*, usually abbreviated to *DP*, came into use on both sides of the water.[6] *Stateside*, in the sense of relating to or in the direction of the United States — in other words, *back home* — impinged upon the national consciousness during World War II, but

[1] in Army talk . . . and *Joe* for the alliterative effect."
A writer in the Baltimore *Evening Sun* – *GI* and Other Army Terms, editorial page, March 14, 1945 — reported that it was resented as much as the English *Sammy* had been resented in World War I. Said Wheeler, before cited: "The *GI* doesn't mind being called a *GI* or a *Joe* by other soldiers . . . but there are standard four-letter words for what he thinks about being tagged *GI Joe* by, say, a guy like me." Westbrook Pegler predicted in his column, Jan. 17, 1945, that *GI* would also soon fade, but the *GI Bill of Rights* apparently gave it a new lease of life.

[2] By James F. Bender in Thirty Thousand New Words, New York *Times Magazine*, Dec. 2, p. 22.
[3] Jargon by Command, *Saturday Review of Literature*, Nov. 24, p. 14
[4] The favorite of American headline-writers was the innocuous *nazi*, which almost completely displaced *kraut*, *jerry*, *heinie* and the *hun* of World War I.
[5] War Words in England, by H. L. Mencken, *American Speech*, Feb., 1944, pp. 9 and 10.
[6] Among the New Words, by I. Willis Russell, *American Speech*, April, 1946, p. 140.

a writer in *American Notes & Queries* in 1947[1] said that he had a vague recollection of seeing it in print "fifteen or twenty years ago, used by Americans living temporarily in United States Territories and in the Far East."[2] The introduction of the *pin-up girl* has been claimed by Walter Thornton,[3] but he apparently did not invent the term.[4] *Mae West* for an inflatable life-preserver used by aviators and later for a tank with two turrets, came from the English,[5] as did the German *blitz* and its derivatives, and *blackout*. When *blitz* began to work its way into English use, at the beginning of the war, there were many violent protests from chauvinists,[6] but by 1940 it had been fully accepted, along with *ersatz* and *flak*.[7] Whether or not these terms will survive in the language remains to be seen; probably not. In the United States they are known, but seem to be in infrequent use.

The English invented *blackout* in 1939,[8] but it did not cross the ocean until after Pearl Harbor. *Task-force* had to wait until the resumption of the offensive in the Pacific: it is apparently American, but who coined it I do not know. *V-day*, *VE-day*, *VJ-day* and *V-mail* also appear to be of American origin, though the terms in *-day* may have been suggested by the German *der tag*, one of the

---

1 *Stateside*, Feb., 1947, p. 170.
2 He added that it was used by Walter Karig and Welbourn Kelley in Battle Report, Vol. I; New York, 1944. See also *Stateside*, by Harold A. Welch, *American Notes & Queries*, Sept., 1945, p. 88.
3 *Pin-up Girl*, *American Notes & Queries*, July, 1946, pp. 55–56. He says that "at the outset of World War II" he offered General Powell, then in command at Fort Dix, a collection of 5000 photographs typifying "not the usual glamorous, show-girl type, but the girl back home, wholesome, sweet and vivacious."
4 M. D. C. says in *American Notes & Queries*, Oct., 1945, p. 108, that it was first used in *Yank*, April 30, 1943. "Prior to that date," he adds, "*Yank* had been fumbling for a tag-line with such commonplaces as *dream girl*."
5 Said Fred Backhouse in Pre-War *Mae West*, *Newsweek*, Sept. 4, 1944: "[It] was thought up by an unknown Royal Air Force man before the war and was in common usage when I joined the slang-loving body in 1940. From being slang it moved up into official documents.... The *Mae West* is a bulky canvas and rubber affair, and when worn gives you a bust measurement like that attributed to the actress."
6 War Words in England, before cited, p. 7.
7 On June 19, 1941 the Edinburgh *Evening Dispatch* headed an editorial *Blitz* Comes to Stay, and said: "After all, the word does express something that is not adequately expressed by any English word. And it has doubled its hold by becoming adjective and verb as well as noun." *American Speech*, Feb., 1940, p. 110, shows that it had come into use in the United States in 1939.
8 Global Darkness, *American Notes & Queries*, Oct., 1942, pp. 99–100.

chief proofs of German wickedness in World War I.[1] *Black market*, of course, was a legacy from that war, and was possibly borrowed from the German *schwarzmarkt*, which preceded it. *Lend-lease* was coined by some anonymous Washington onomatologist at the time the thing itself was invented, before Pearl Harbor. The enormous number of abbreviations in use during the war, *e.g.*, *WAC, Pfc, AMGOT*,[2] *SHEAF, ETO* and *Seabee*[3] began to fade the moment hostilities ended, along with the even more numerous abbreviations designating sectors of the home front, but some of them will no doubt be revived when the bugles blow again. The device of calling a military enterprise *Operation* this-or-that shows some sign of enduring.[4] The fate of *to liberate* I do not venture to predict. It signifies to loot and had a large vogue in the Army of Occupation in Germany, *c.* 1946, but the sentence of fifteen years at hard labor imposed upon the master-liberator, Colonel Jack W. Durant, on April 30, 1947, gave it a set-back. It has an American smack, but there is evidence that it was actually borrowed from the English.[5] *Quisling* and its verb, *to quisling* or *to quisle*, also English loans, ran into difficulties on September 8, 1943, when Marshal Pietro *Badoglio* came over to the allies, though his country was still at war, and the English papers began to use *badoglio*, a surrender to the enemy.[6]

Jeep seems to be authentically American, but the history of the

[1] In Among the New Words, *American Speech*, April, 1946, p. 145, I. Willis Russell traces *V-day* to March 16, 1942, *VE-day* to Sept. 18, 1944, and *VJ-day* to the same day. See also Russell's paper in the same, Oct., 1946, pp. 220–222.

[2] *Amgot* (soon shortened to *AMG*) seems to have been an English invention. In *Amgot* (editorial), July 19, 1943, the London *Daily Sketch* described it as "a new word" and said: "It stands for the *Allied Military Government of Occupied Territory*, which is headed by Major-General Lord Rennell."

[3] From *CB*, construction battalion. The New Practical Standard Dictionary says that the *seabees* were "given this name in 1942, soon after they were inaugurated to handle all construction for the Navy in combat zones abroad, such as air bases and landing places."

[4] A writer in *American Notes & Queries*, May, 1946, p. 30, said that it then seemed to be "on the way to becoming a permanent speech figure." He cited its use in *Operation Dixie*, the CIO's name for its attempt to organize Southern labor.

[5] Let's be Honest Again, *Tit-Bits* (London), Dec. 14, 1945: "In the services *scrounging* (or *liberating*, in the current slang) is not generally frowned on."

[6] War Words in England, before cited, p. 6. For the use of *quisling* see *Quisling*, *Life*, May 6, 1940. Major Vidkun *Quisling* was executed Oct. 24, 1945. Said the London *Times*, quoted by *Life:* " *Quis-*

word is almost as obscure as the history of the car itself. The latter was apparently first projected by Captain (later Colonel) R. G. Howie, then in command of the Seventh Tank Company at Fort Snelling, Minn., in 1932. He continued his experiments during the three years following, and in 1936 was given a small grant from Army funds by Major-General Walter C. Short. At the beginning of 1937, assisted by Master Sergeant M. J. Wiley, he began assembling the first car, and during the Autumn of that year it was completed and sent to Fort Sam Houston, Texas, for trials. They brought in favorable reports from the Army bigwigs there assembled, headed by Major-General (later Lieutenant-General) Walter Krueger, and a year later Short sought to keep the invention an American monopoly by applying for a patent on it, in his own name and those of Howie and Wiley.[1] But the *jeep*, so far, was a rather primitive contrivance, and its operator had no seat, but was supposed to lie upon it belly-whopper fashion. In the developments which followed various other persons had some hand, and also different manufacturers, *e.g.*, the Willys-Overland Motors of Toledo, the American Bantam Car Company of Butler, Pa., and the Minneapolis-Moline Power Implement Company. Indeed, there were so many fingers in the pie that after the *jeep* was adopted by the Army and became a vast success, conflicting claims of interest produced a controversy before the Federal Trade Commission,[2] and it dragged on wearily.

The first batch of seventy *jeeps* was produced by the Bantam Car Company in 1940, and delivered to the Army Quartermaster Depot at Holabird, Md., on September 23 of that year.[3] They were given

---

ling . . . has the supreme merit of beginning with a *q*, which (with one august exception) has long seemed to the British mind to be a crooked, uncertain and slightly disreputable letter, suggestive of the questionable, the querulous, the quavering of quaking quagmires and quivering quicksands, of quibbles and quarrels, of queasiness, quackery, qualms and quilp." The "august exception," of course, is to be found in *queen*.

[1] This application was filed on Jan. 23, 1939. The patent, No. 21,195,432, was issued on April 2, 1940.

[2] Docket No. 4959, May 6, 1943. More details are given in Hail to the *Jeep*, by A. Wode Wells; New York, 1946. See also Whose *Jeep?*, *Tide*, Feb. 15, 1944, pp. 21–22.

[3] *PM* reported, March 28, 1944, that the sole survivor of this first batch, affectionately called *Gramps*, was deposited in the Smithsonian Institution a short while before. I take this from *American Notes & Queries*, April, 1944, p. 12.

thorough tests there and at other Army posts, and it was soon resolved to order them in large quantities. It was by then apparent that the United States would soon be in the war, and the fear that the Bantam Company might not be able to produce the new cars fast enough caused the Army to let contracts for them to other companies, including Ford. The fact that the code symbol of Ford on Army cars was GP has led to the surmise that the word *jeep* was born there and then,[1] but there is no evidence for it. Nor is there any evidence that the word came from the same letters in the sense of *general purpose*, for the first *jeeps* were not called, officially, *general purpose cars*, but *half-ton four by four command-reconnaissance cars*.[2] It seems to be much more probable that the name was borrowed from that of a character in E. C. Segar's comic strip, "Popeye the Sailor," which also gave the language *goon*. Eugene the *Jeep* appeared in Segar's drawings on March 16, 1936, and on April 1 of that year the King Features Syndicate, which syndicated his work, took steps to protect both the name and the character. Segar dropped both before his death in 1938, but they had caught the public fancy and survived him.[3] Who first applied *jeep* to the new Army car is not known, but a claim has been made for a Sergeant James T. O'Brien.[4] Inasmuch however, as this baptism is dated 1937, when the car was still in its early experimental stage, the evidence seems to be shaky, but there is evidence that an Oklahoma manufacturer named Erle Palmer Halliburton gave the name to a different car, half truck and half tractor, during the same year.[5]

The fact is that, at that time, *jeep* was in the air, and many other contrivances were so called, *e.g.*, the Link Trainer for aviators. Colby says that it was also applied to a recruit, to ill-fitting hats and coats, and to various other objects.[6] At one time an autogiro was a *jumping jeep*, and the barracks where recruits were quartered was a *jeep-town*. In 1938 Jerome Barry reported that *jeep* was

[1] J. K. Layton in *Life*, Aug. 10, 1942, p. 6.
[2] Colby, before cited, p. 116.
[3] I am indebted here to Mr. Ward Greene, editor and general manager of the King Features Syndicate, and to A Word-Creator, by Jeffrey A. Fleece, *American Speech*, Feb., 1943, pp. 68–69.
[4] Repaired *Jeep* in '37, Moline Mechanics Say, St. Paul *Pioneer Press*, June 6, 1944, and *Jeep*, *American Notes & Queries*, Jan., 1944, p. 155.
[5] *American Notes & Queries*, May, 1944, pp. 26–27.
[6] *Jeep*, by P. Burwell Rogers, *American Notes & Queries*, March, 1944, p. 189.

then in use among soda-jerkers to designate a slow and incompetent colleague,[1] and in 1940 a writer in the Baltimore *Evening Sun* said that it was used among automobile finance men for "one who rides with the adjuster in order to drive back the cars repossessed."[2] The English, during World War II used it for a radio operator and also for a member of the Royal Canadian Naval Volunteer Reserve.[3] In the sense of a bantam car it once had many rivals, *e.g.*, *blitz-buggy*,[4] *baby-buggy*, *bug*, *gnat-tank*, *scout-car*, *leaping Lena*, *puddle-jumper*, *jeepers-creepers*, *midget*, *midgie*, *quad* and plain *bantam-car*. *Peep* was invented to differentiate the half-ton car from a quarter-ton model.[5] *Jeep* quickly passed into most of the European languages. "No Frenchman, Belgian, Dutchman, Luxemburger, Dane, Norwegian or German, and very few Poles or Russians," says Bishop, before cited, "is ignorant of *OK*, *GI* or *jeep*."[6]

The English apparently preferred the *European War* as a designation for the conflict of 1914–18, but in the United States it came to be known as the *World War*, and when another round began in 1939 it naturally became *World War II*. But there were poets who groped for something less prosaic, and one of them was President Franklin D. Roosevelt. So late as the Spring of 1942 he was calling for suggestions, and many flowed in. The Hon. Thomas E. Dewey proposed the *War for Survival*, Mrs. Anne M. Rosenberg *Freedom's War*, Dr. William Lyon Phelps the *War of Liberty*, the Hon. Henry H. Curran the *Necessary War*, and Jack Dempsey the *Fight to Live*. The Hon. Emil Schram, president of the New York Stock Exchange, put his hopes into the *Last World War*, and other less eminent persons contributed the *War to Save Humanity*, the *Fight for Right*, the *War to Save Civilization*, the *War of the Ages*, the *People's War*, the *Survival War*, the *War of World Freedom*, the *War Against Tyrants*, the *Hitler War*, and the *World Order*

---

1 The Jerk, *Saturday Evening Post*, July 16. I take this from *American Speech*, Oct., 1938, p. 235.
2 What Happens When the Finance Adjuster Steps In, editorial page, Oct. 8.
3 Service Slang, by J. L. Hunt and A. G. Pringle; London, 1943, p. 41.
4 *Time*, Sept. 22, p. 20.
5 *Jeep*, by Richard Gordon McClosky, *American Notes & Queries*, Dec., 1943, pp. 136–37.
6 But Maurice Hindus reported in a Moscow dispatch in the New York *Herald Tribune*, March 28, 1944, that the Russians used *Willys*. So did *Tide*, Feb. 15, 1944, p. 22. I am indebted here to Col. R. G. Howie, Col. Francis V. Fitzgerald, Major Eugene C. Merrill, Lieut. W. C. Alcock, and Messrs. Nick M. Carey, F. H. Fenn, W. J. Konicek and M. A. White.

War. There were even cynics who proposed the *Crazy War*, the *War of Illusions*, the *Meddler's War*, the *Roosevelt War*, the *Devil's War*, and *Hell*. How and by whom the votes were counted I do not know, but when the uproar was over it was announced that *World War II* had won by a large plurality, with *War of World Freedom* a bad second, and *War of Freedom* a worse third. Soon after Pearl Harbor, in fact, the Army and Navy had adopted *World War II*, and by the middle of 1942 it was appearing in the *Congressional Record*. By the end of that year it had obliterated all the other proposed names, and prophets were already beginning to talk hopefully of *World War III*.

Ernest K. Lindley and Forrest Davis say in "How War Came"[1] that *United Nations* was coined by President Roosevelt. This was during Winston Churchill's visit to Washington at the end of December, 1941. He was a guest at the White House, and he and Roosevelt discussed the choice of a name for the new alliance. One morning, lying in bed, Roosevelt thought of *United Nations*, and at once sought Churchill, who was in his bath. "How about *United Nations?*" he called through the door. "That," replied Churchill, "should do it." And so it was.

[1] New York, 1942.

LIST OF WORDS AND PHRASES

a, 73, 260, 352, 366, 410, 544
a, article, 92, 93, 94, 139, 143
a, broad, 3, 15, 22, 25 n, 27 n, 28, 32, 69, 73, 79, 81, 110, 131, 136, 151, 170, 181, 185, 186, 187, 210, 214, 215, 224 n, 230, 241, 251, 269, 288, 290, 291, 292, 293, 294, 300, 554
a, final, 90
a, flat, 15, 16 n, 20, 28, 36, 45, 47, 69, 72, 90, 110, 122, 131, 133, 159, 164, 170, 183, 184, 185, 186, 187, 199, 205, 211, 214, 215, 218, 220, 222, 226, 227, 230, 241, 251, 269, 288, 291, 292, 424, 431, 470, 554
a, Norwegian, 454
ä, 293, 431
ä, Swedish, 431
å, 431
aa, 293
AAA, 330
aahaahoo, 164
Aaronic priesthood. 221
aback, 165
Abacuck, 467
Abayomi Karnge, 448
abbé, 318
Abbie, 566; -ann, 494
Abbot, 441
'Abbūd, 441
ABD, 755
abdomen, 25; ábdomen, 48
Abe, 466, 475
Abergavenny, 456
aber nit, 645
Abeshe, 514
abhor, 95

Abie, 466
Abigail, 479, 500
Abindav, 519
abisselfa, 271
abito, 252
ablonogastrigolumpios- ity, 327
Aboideau, 252
aboon, 195
aboose, 84
aborigine, 385
aboudt, 258
about, 73, 227
about to go, 367
above-board, 721
Abozaweramud, 446
abrade, to, 195
Abraham, 467, 516, 517, 518, 519; -s, 416, 420; -son, 430
Abram cove, 661
Abrams, 420; -on, 421
Abrasha, 516
absissas, 319
Abu, 52; -Ahmed, 524; -Jalad, 441; -Rujayli, 441
abwaschen, 254
a-by-itself-a, 271
Abyssinia, 519
ac, 717
accessory, 48
accomplished, 459
accompt, 310
ace, 683
Ace, 501
ace man, 756
ache, 313
acheln, to, 654
aches, 17
Achimelech, 519
acid, 192, 751
Acid, 449
a-come, 219
Acorn, 449

Acosta, 423
acre, 195; -and-a-half, 733
acrobat, 765
across, 174; the board, 729
acrost, 100, 174
acta, 314
acteon, 661
act of oblivion, 211
actor, 246, 333
actors' Bible, 691
actual, 5, 246
ad, 682; -curtain, 697
Adabel, 498
Ada from Decatur, 746
Adam and Eve on a raft, 751
Adámic, 426
Adams, 396, 398, 401, 420, 453, 470
Adam's ale, 661
Adamson, 453
Adam-tiler, 661
Addams, 453
Addamson, 453
áddict, 48
Addielle, 566
Addleston, 421
áddress, 48, 454; addréss. 454
Adelaide, 500
Adenesia, 481
adenoid, 218, 729
adhere, 95
Adina, 519
Aditi, 514
adjective, 333
Adjoil, 501
Adler, 424
ad lib, to, 688, 729
Administration, 322
admiral, 252, 756
adnoid, 218
adobe, 51, 741
Adolf, 465, 516, 519
Adrene, 482

787

List of Words and Phrases

Adrian, 508
Adula, 481
adurt, 253
Advent, 590
adverb, 333
adverbium, 333
advertise, to, 47
ádvertising, 48
advice, 228; ádvice, 49
advise, to, 228
advocate, to, 20
Adyhon, 481
ae, 282, 291, 300
Aeileen, 481
aek, 313
aend, 293
Aerielle, 481
aethecite, 208
aez, 293
afeared, 118, 181
affection, 277
Affie, 494
affordern, 259
AFL, 331
Afong, 443
African golf, 755
aft, 141
after, 74, 187; -birth, 723; -clap, 207; -noon, 205, 762, 764
after while, 152
à Fusil, 413
agafretted, 775
again, 75, 76, 219
against, 100, 202, 203, 219
agali, 266
Agali, 514
Agamemnon, 588
agast, 295
age, 253, 716
-age, 386
agen, 76
agenda, 319
agendums, 320
ager, 89, 181
Aggie, 466
aggravate, to, 338
Aggressor, 587
Aghavni, 523
agin, 113, 153, 226
Agnella, 481, 494
Agnes, 499
a-going, 169
agony-pipe, 705
agreeable, 246; -scoundrel, 646

Agricultural Adjustment Agency, 330
Ague, 449
ah, 22, 70, 82, 125, 159, 184, 185, 192, 203, 215, 216, 225, 230, 251, 288, 293
-ah, 382
Ah, 443
ahdn't, 233
Ah Fu, 443
ahint, 210
ah-ler-herkst, 52
Ahmed, 524
Ahmelda, 481
Ahn-hay-lays, 547
Ah-quah-ching, 561
ah-oo, 227
ahp, 260
ah prays, 264
Ah Sing, 443
Ahuda, 519
Ahuna, 443
Ahwhichaolto, 573
ai, 81, 86, 164, 185, 224
ai, German, 307
aia, 40
aiah, 226
Aiaoua, 545
Aiauway, 546
aidg, 171
aigle noir, 155
aigs, 186
ailded, 358
ailed, 294, 295
Aileen, 481
ain't, 137, 205, 218, 269, 340, 357, 391
ain't done, 393
ain't got none, 372
ain't he has?, 205
ain't I?, 337
ain't never, 392
ain't never done nothin' nohow, 391
ain't nobody, 392
ain't nobody never, 391
ain't nothing, 392, 393
ain't no use, 392
ain't seen nothing yet, 392
ain't you will?, 205
Aiowais, 546
air, 214, 226
-air, 382
aircrahft, 36
airedale, 766, 773

Airlia, 498
air-monkey, 713
Airoy, 501
air-pocket, 727
airsome, 253
-aitches, 17
-aitis, 428
aj, 249
Ajowes, 546
ajskrimsoda, 425
akal, 654
Akana, 443
ake, 313
akerel, 225
akjurejt, 425
akros, 300
Aksarben, 579
Al, 466, 770
Alabama, 552
Alabamy, 544
a la carte, 327
Alamisa, 514
Alamogordo, 564
Alamosa, 555
Alanreed, 541
Alapluma, 481
alarm-clock, 716
alas, 74
Albany, 75
albatross, 232
Albert, 472, 493, 516, 523, 770
Alberta, 493
Alberti, 439
Albert Lea, 562
Alberts, 439
Albrecht, 408
Albright, 408
Alburtis, 493
Alcarla, 481
Alcester, 456
alcove, 47
Alderney, 414
Aldoux, 472
Aldrich, 516
Alease, 481
Aleck, 466
Aleene, 481
Aleese, 481
Alehouse, 588
Aletta, 479
Alette, 521
Alex, 466, 476
Alexander, 398, 517
Alexanderene, 481, 493
Alexandria, 537

List of Words and Phrases

Aldace, 507
Aleyne, 481
Alf, 466
Alfa, 481
alfabet, 296
alfalfa, 151
alfathy, 151
Alfred, 481
Alfredia, 481
Alfretta, 481
Alga, 481
Algeier, 412
Algeline, 480
algerine, to, 208
Algire, 412
alibi, 228
Alice, 481, 499, 510
Alick, 466
Aliece, 481
Aliene, 481
alive, 125, 751
Alkabo, 541
al-Khūri, 441
Alksninis, 428
alky, 671
all, 108, 148, 149, 160, 175, 201, 230, 233, 254, 377, 674
Alla Jo, 481
all both, 215
Allchin, 449
all-day, 204
all dressed up, 337
alle, 202
Allece, 481
Alleen, 481
Allegany, 526
Alleghany, 526
Allegheny, 526, 571
Allen, 396, 398, 420
Allene, 481
Allen George VIII, 501
allerhöchst, 52
allerickstix, 197
alles richtig, 197
alley, 775
Alleyne, 481
Allgeier, 412
Allgeiger, 412
all gone, 254
Allie, 466
Allied Military Government of Occupied Territory, 782
Allie Mae, 488
állies, 48

Allieu, 501
alligator, 707
Alligator, 448, 511; -State, 613
all most, 278, 279
all of a biver, 158
all of a floption, 252
all of a high, 158
all of a slam, 253
all of you, 377
allow, to, 108
all right, 197, 278, 279
allrightest, 388
All Saints, 591
all the farther, 232
Allways, 451
alm, 431
almanac, 96
AlMeda, 481, 494
Almera, 516
Almetana, 480
almond, 96
almost, 278, 279
Almouth, 501
Almroth, 472
Alnwick, 456
Aloha, 481, 516
Alonzo, 503
aloof, 228
Alouise, 494
Alovizo, 514
Aloyd, 481
already, 202, 278, 279
alright, 278, 279, 295, 316
Alsenatha, 481
Alsex, 501
also ran, 770
Altameasse, 481
Altar fire, 593
alter, to, 749
altho, 295, 302, 311
altitudes, 661
Alto, 481
aluminium, 285
aluminum, 85, 284, 285, 316
alumium, 284
alumni, 319
Alvah, 507
Alvarez, 435
Al Verne, 482
Alvin, 516
always, 384
Alys, 481
am, 11, 202

a.m., 324
'am and heggs, 191
Amasca, 482
amas de cabànes, 573
ambar, 151
ambidexter, 661
Ambolena, 497
ambrosia, 215
Ambrosia, 528
ambulance, 722
Amburs, 501
Ameagle, 541
Ameche, 439
ameise, 207
Amel, 501, 506
amen, 701
Amenta, 483
Amer, 501
Amerette, 482
Americana, 318
Ames, 409
AMG, 782
AMGOT, 782
Amici, 439
Amikam, 519
Aminnia, 482
Amleth, 466
Amleto, 466
Amnon, 519
amn't, 357
amœba, 282
a'mond, 96
among, 83
Amor, 508
a'most, 96
amp'itheater, 97
Amsterdam, 537
Amurrica, 24
Amy, 499, 513
am you?, 264
an, article, 92, 93, 94, 139, 202
Ana, 482
anæmia, 282, 286
anæsthetic, 282
Anah, 482
Anajean, 482
Anajoe, 482
an-'all, 247
analog, 295
Analon, 482
analysises, 319
Anamarie, 482
Ananias, 504, 512
ananse, 267
anathemar, 40

List of Words and Phrases

Anchamaunnackkaunack, 530
anchor, 719, 761
Ancient Dominion, 596
ancm, 717
and, 263, 292, 297, 327, 352
'and, 95
and a little of the snapping turtle, 617
Andastoei, 526
Andeech, 426
Anders, 520
Anderson, 396, 398, 400, 401, 430, 433
Anderssen, 433
Andich, 426
Andina, 482
andramarten, 253
Andreas, 519
Andrew, 472
Andrews, 398, 428
Andrice, 482
Andrzejski, 425
Andy, 466, 476, 482, 770
Aner, 482
Anestis, 523
Angel, 488, 521
angel, 652, 688, 720; -bed, 752; -teat, 482
Angelle, 482
Angelo, 521
Angel's food, 596
Anger, 449
Angie, 508
angler, 661, 657
Anglo, 183
Angola, 556
ani, 313
-ania, 584
Aniahwagamut, 552
Aniceta, 482
Anies, 453
Anika, 514
animal, 741, 756
Anita, 521, 522
Anjean, 541
ankura, 267
Anliza, 483
Anmi Ruhamah, 474
Ann, 479, 499, 513
Anna, 520; -belle, 466
Ann Arbor, 561
Annarbor, 539
Annarenia, 480
Anne Arundel, 456
Anneice, 482

Anner, 482, 494
annex, 684; ànnex, 48
annex, to, 25
Annice, 482
Annick, 456
Annie, 510, 521
Anniece, 482
Annie Oakley, 696
Ann McGinty, 582
Ann-rán'l, 456
Annyce, 482
Anonymous, 512
another, 171
another hog off the corn, 233
Anster, 456
Anstruther, 456
answer, 74, 159, 171
ant, 73, 211, 214
an't, 357
Antanaitis, 429
Antanavičius, 429
antelope, 328
Antelope State, 635
antennas, 319
Anthonette, 482
Anthony, 522
antidote, 657
Antietam, 589, 606
antigodlin, 219
anti-goslin, 219
antipasto, 53
Antoinette, 500
Anton, 519, 522
António, 522
anudda, 171
Anvil, 501
anvil salesman, 756
any, 313
any more, 198, 203, 204, 234
anything, 91
Anzac, 331
Anzonetta, 497
Aola, 482
Aorum, 501
ap, prefix, 403
Apache State, 611
Apalachicola, 556
Apalonia, 482
aparador, 243
ape, 253, 691
Ape, 511
aperture, 5
apexes, 320
Apeyard, 568

apiteaser, 53
Apollo, 501, 507
Apollo and St. Peter, 593
Apollos James, 514
apos'le, 96
apothem, 291
apalling, 284
apparatus, 72, 168, 749
appendic, 384
appendicitides, 320
appendicitis, 81, 320
appendix, 384
appendixes, 320
apple, 667, 707, 734; -jack, 181; -knocker, 732; -sauce, 644; -slump, 210; -snits, 254
Apple, 482, 495
apples, 667
aproksimaet, 301
apron, 688
apurn, 99, 185
aquarian, 732
aquariist, 732
aquatic, 62
aquecope, 225
ar, 79, 156, 159, 164, 173, 288
-ar, 382
Ara, 482
arab, to, 162
araber, 162
Arazona, 482
Arbeely, 441
Arben, 501
'Arbīli, 441
arbitrator, 48
arbour, 286
Arbuckle, to, 120
arbus, 151
arcana, 319
Arcelia, 482
Arch, 501
Archambault, 437
Archangel, 512
Archie, 576
Archy, 466
Ardeal, 482
Ardenwald, 542
Ardis, 501, 521
Ardzeooni, 441
are, 218, 292, 356
-are, 382
a'ready, 96
Arene, 482
aren't, 357

List of Words and Phrases 791

are you going to play?, 367
Are You Ready For the Judgment Day?, 509
Argeree, 482
Argigene, 482
Argonaut, 581
Argue, 449
argufy, to, 11, 118
Arind, 482
áristocrat, 49
Arizona, 751; -Dakota, 507
Arjesta, 482
ark, 752
Arkana, 541
Arkansas, 543, 548; -City, 543; -toothpick, 612
arkansaw, to, 120
Árkansaw, 543, 548
Arla, 501
Arlando, 501, 506
Arlenzor, 482
Arlington, 581
Arloine, 482
arm, 246
Armadilla, 482
Armand, 516
Armderdeen, 482
Armemaryetta, 482
Armenfreud, 417
Armilda, 482
Armin, 516
Armista, 482
Armistead, 454
armístice, 49
Armistice, 482
armoir, 154
Armon, 501
armor, 281
Arms, 577
Armstädt, 454
Armstrong, 398, 399, 706
Army, 449, 678
Armyl, 482
arn, 230
Arnez, 482
Arnold, 398, 520
Aronsheim, 422
Aroostook Republican, 595
Arout, 441
Arpád, 524
Arraba, 593
Arrenwintha, 510
Arrow, 501

Arroyo, 574
Arrundel, 456
arse, 778; -kisser, 771
arsenic, 89, 729
arsle, to, 208
Arson, 501
Arsula, 482
art, 731
Arteri, 440
Artery, 440
Artesia, 482
Artesian State, 638
Arthetta, 498
Arthur, 462, 516, 521
Arthur Brisbane, 582
Arthuree, 482
Arthurene, 483
Arthuritus, 482
Artie, 476
artillery, 680
artisan, 47
artist, 246
artiste, 694
artistippus, 661
Artonsia, 482
Arundel, 456
Arupe, 514
Arvesta, 482
Arvia, 498
Arvigne, 482
Arville, 502
-ary, 45
Arylne, 482
Arzonia, 482, 493
Asagumo, 588
Asa Packer, 581
Asaph, 519
asbestos, 697, 714
as big as all outdoors, 144
as big as a whale, 144
Asbjrnsen, 434
Ascension, 590
Aschkenasi, 416
Asco, 540
as crooked as a dog's hind leg, 145
as dumb as a mine mule in low coal, 146
as durable as a hog's snout, 145
Asenath, 482
as fine as frog's hair, 144
as greasy as a muskrat, 145
ashamed, 120
ash-cat, 713

ash-eater, 713
Asher, 417
Ashmead, 472
as hot as a mink, 145
as if, 337
Asigbe, 514
Asing, 443
as jealous as a cat, 145
ask, 45, 171, 187, 205, 214, 230
Askew, 456
Asko, 456
Aslak, 434
asleep at the switch, 713
Asmantas, 428
as mean as a jaybird, 145
asoeshyaeshon, 306
as patient as Job's turkey, 145
Aspenwall, 434
asphalt, 215, 278
asphalte, 278
aspirin, 734, 755
as poor as a race-horse, 145
as poor as Job's turkey, 145
as proud as a dog with two tails, 145
as regards, 337
ass, 73, 778
as safe as a cow in the stockyards, 145
assembly, 99
assenycke, 89
as skittish as a colt, 145
association, 306, 314
as sour as a billy-goat, 145
assume, 205
assure, 192
astern the lighter, 166
asthema, 100
as thick as three in a bed, 146
Asthike, 523
asthmy, 544
Astor, 578
as tough as a biled owl, 145
as tough as a mule, 145
astray, 253
Astri, 520
at, 202, 234, 261
atabrine, 82
at all, 234

List of Words and Phrases

Atatürk, 442
ate, 46, 75, 76, 186
at eleven, 97
Atha, 482
athaletic, 99, 175
Athanasios, 523
Athenai, 540
Athens, 532, 537, 540
Ather, 502
athletics, 385
Athlone, 414
at home, 111
at liberty, 685
Atonement, 590
-atorium, 133
attaboy, 643
attaché, 318
attackt, 357
attackted, 100, 185, 217, 357
Attaresta, 497
Attelia, 482
attic, 100, 721
Attica, 559
attorney-general, 328
Attracta, 466
Atty, 466
au, 199, 224, 228, 260, 288, 291, 410, 423, 424
au, German, 424
Aubert, 438
Aubrigene, 482
Auburn, 482
auctioneer, 734
Aud, 502
Au Dell, 482
Audery, 482
Audie, 482
Audif, 502
Audra, 482
Audrey, 482
auf dem boden, 206
Augier, 437
August, 519
Augusta, 571
Aukštikalnis, 428
Aulana, 482
aunt, 36, 69, 131, 159, 165, 170, 171, 185, 186, 187, 210, 214, 218, 220, 222, 251, 254, 657
Aunt Jane, 528
Aura, 482
Auraria, 554
Aure, 453
Auria, 480

Aurora, 523
aurum, 285
ausbrennan, 739
ausbrenner, 739
Ausby, 502
-auska, 428
auskleiden, 202
ausstecken, 206
Austaphine, 482
Austell, 502
Austin, 398
Australia, 482
Australian and New Zealand Army Corps, 331
Authalene, 482
author, 280, 281
Author, 502
authority, 303
Autice, 482
auto, 761
automata, 319
automobile, 199, 753
Auto State, 629
Autra, 482
Au Train, 561
autsjd, 425
autsch, 51
Avalanche, 595
Ava Marie, 482
Avayd, 482
aviator, 72, 756, 766
-avicius, 428
Aviva, 519
avoid, 192
avoirdupois, 73
Avola, 482
Avram, 519
aw, 40, 57 n, 70, 159, 199, 215, 228, 241, 249, 251, 288, 410, 424
a-wanted, 133
a'-wee, 247
awff, 83
awfn, 96
awful, 172, 203, 390
awfully, 337
Awlster, 456
a.w.o.l., 379, 778
áwol, 379
a-woofin, 220
ax, 286
axed, 154
Axel, 520
axises, 319
ay, 288
Ayanways, 546

Ayavais, 546
ayem, 297
Ayeovai, 546
Ayerst, 456
Aylisse, 481
Aylmer, 471
Ayoouais, 546
Ayooués, 545
'Ayrūt, 441
Ayscough, 456
Aytla, 482
Azadia, 482
Azaleen, 496
Azaña, 316
Azar, 441
azerbert addiz haircut?, 96
azhure, 192
azid, 192
Aziz, 523
az-nu, 296
Aztec State, 611
Azuba, 482
Azuna, 482
azzembly, 99
b, 98, 209, 246, 258, 300, 411
b, Italian, 308
b, Spanish, 307
Baa, 593
baach, 207
baachie, 207
ba'al, 753; -brith, 753; -keria, 753
babe, 646
babes in the wood, 662
Babette, 582
Babtis, 137, 175
babushka, 732
baby, 698, 751; -buggy, 785; -carriage, 249, 250; -church, 745; -doll, 764; -lifter, 713
Baby, 449
Babylon, 537
Baby State, 611
Bacchus, 569
bach, 408
Bach, 52, 408
bachelor, 261
bacilli, 319
bacilluses, 320
back East, 219
back home, 780
backhouse, 232
backing, 688

List of Words and Phrases

Backman, 432
back of the yards, 141
back-pedal, to, 723
back-seat driver, 723
back-stage, 688
back-stand, to, 232
backstop, 736
backyard, 163, 685
bacteria, 319
bacteriums, 320
bad, 389, 390, 645
badder, 387
baddie, 704
badger, 642, 748
Badger, 641; -State, 641, 642
bad job, 657
badlands, 237, 574
badoglio, 782
Baer, 435
Baeumler, 410
Bafata, 514
bag, 121, 737, 749
bagatel, 295
Bagehot, 456
bagger, 720, 749
Baggot, 456
bag o' guts, 181
bags, 649
Bagshot, 456
bahg, 82
bahk, 52
bahr, 171
bahr'l, 171
Baie de Wasal, 561
Bailey, 396, 398, 401, 402
bailif, 294, 295
bailinghadh, 684
Baillie, 402
bail out, to, 727
Baird, 454
baj gasz, 425
bake, 253
Baked-Beans State, 599
bake-head, 713
Baker, 396, 398, 402, 409
Bakken, 434
Balaam, 512
balance, 20
Balassa, 440
balcony, 47
balderdash, 657
Bald Friar, 536
bald-head, 724
bald-lump, 677
Balfour, 454; -Arms, 577

ballas, 307
ballaz, 307
ball of fire, 674, 716
balloon, 674, 719, 750, 767
balloon, to, 689
ball-rubber, 740
Ball's Bluff, 589
ballyhoo, 652, 684
balmechule, 753
baloney, 544, 644, 669, 719, 723, 764
Balpha, 508
BAM, 779
bambalacha, 681
bamboo, 681
bamboozle, to, 643
Bambula, 514
Bament, 438
Bames, 453
bampoolap, 164
ban, 266
banana-stalk, 734
banana-wagon, 760
bandies, to do, 150
band of musk ox, 328
bandore, 160
bang, 680; -and biff, 710; -up, 660; -water, 671
banjo, 160, 714, 737, 753, 755, 760
banjor, 160
bank, 322, 750; -burglar, 668
banker, 774
Bank of the United States, 320
banks, 750
Banner State, 640
bantam-car, 785
Baptist, 175, 386
baptized, 662
baptizz, 386
baq, 446
bar, 137, 580
Baraboo, 528
Baratta, 439
Barbara, 463, 520
barbecue, to, 363
barbed-wire, 733
barber, 252, 739, 770; -chair, 758
Barber, 439
barbering, 760
barber's chair, 752
barbershela, 172
Barbieri, 430

BarBQ, 291
Barbiene, 482
Barclay, 79
bare, 171
Bare Arse, 588
bareback, 719
bare-foot, 724, 762
Barefoot, 449, 451
Barenbaum, 424
Barende-gat, 564
Bareville, 526
Barf, 456
Barfreeston, 456
barge, 73, 179
Barger, 410
Baribault, 528
Baring, 414
bark, 79, 269, 718
barker, 735, 753
Barkersville, 559
bar'l, 120, 188
barlen, to, 654
barley, 79
barman, 734
bar-mop, 772
barn, 79, 222, 691; -paint, 740
Barnegat, 564
Barnes, 398, 405
Barnet, 454
Barnhart, 410
barnstormer, 652, 728
Barnum's, 578
barnyard-golf, 755
baron, 320
Bar-On, 422
barrel, 171, 188, 724, 727; -fever, 662; -house, 677, 706
barrelling, 719
barrens, 574
Barren She, 566
Barrington beggar, 179
barroom, 580
barrow, 151
Barry, 439
Barsa, 441
Barson, 456
Bar State, 611
Bartash, 428
Bartelot, 456
Barth, 159
Bartlett, 456
Bar-Tov, 422
Bartus, 440
Barty, 456

List of Words and Phrases

Barugh, 456
basar, 654
bascal, 201
Bashie, 482
basic sediment, 763
basin, 155
bask, 74
basket, 187, 762
Basket, 536
bas relief, 73
bass, 329
Bassingburne, 468
basura, 243
bat, 241, 644, 747, 754, 771
batatas, 385
batch, 253
Batesville, 562
bath, 73, 74, 131, 214, 218, 733; -towel, 764
Bath, 159
Bathsheba, 482
bath-tub gin, 671
batsman, 324
Batsto, 564
Battenberg, 414
battle, 97; -ax, 133
Battle-born State, 636
Battleground of Freedom, 623
battleship, 714, 716
Battleship X, 588
bauer, 51
Bauer, 409
Bauermeister, 412
baugh, 408
Baugh, 408
Baughman, 408
-baum, 424
baving, 253
baw, 408
bawd, 314
bawg, 82
bawl out, to, 648
bawm, 424
bayas, 307
bayaz, 307
bayou, 151, 574
Bayou State, 631
Bay State, 599
Bay St. Louis, 562
Baysul, 502
bayuk, 574
Bazoo, 595
bdtcd, 92
bdtcdz, 92

be, to, 11, 164, 165, 171, 202, 264, 356, 364
beach, 181
Beaconsfield, 416
beagle, 674, 764
beah, 40, 360
beal, to, 234
bean, 36, 186, 187, 250, 645, 762; -ball, 735
Beanblossom, 449
Be Ann, 483
beany, 150
bear, 127, 329; -hug, 145
Bear, 572
beard, 18, 645, 698, 729
Beard, 454
Bearl, 502, 506
Bearle, 502
Bear State, 611, 613, 627
Beartha, 482
Beaslings, 233
Beastback, 153
beat, 670, 672, 756
beat, to, 672
Beatfred, 482
beat it, to, 672
beat it out, to, 706
Beatrice, 499
beat the gong, to, 681
Beauchamp, 456
Beauclerc, 456
Beaufort, 548
Beaulieu, 456
Beaumont, 438
beauté-shoppe, 738
beautician, 738
beau trap, 662
beauty-bar, 738; -center, 738; -clinic, 738; -laboratory, 738; -mart, 738; -parlor, 738, 771; -salon, 738; -shop, 738; -shoppe, 738; -studio, 738; -villa, 738
beaver, 328
Beaver, 456, 530; -State, 630, 638
Beaworthy, 456
Be Bee, 452
becasse, 155
because, 260
Beck, 398
Becker, 409
bed, 121; -buddy, 217; -bug, 713; -clothes,

246; -fly, 253; -house, 714
bee, 208, 241; -eater, 324
Beecham, 456
Beecher, 473, 503
beef, 698; -squad, 776; -trust, 694
Beef State, 640
beehive, 714
Beehive, 641; -State, 640
been, 186, 187, 250, 394
beer, 748; -schiessen, 739; -shooter, 739
beered, 674
Beetar, 441
Beethoven, 582
beetle-head, 657
Beetrace, 559
Be-faithful, 467
before, 203
Begay, 446
beginning, 284
begone, 646
Begonia, 482
béhave, 49
behaviour, 286
be he (or you) sick?, 356
be I?, 165
Beit Aharon, 422
bekakee, 757
Béla, 524
belch back, to, 195
belcher, 729
belch-water, 772
Belejčak, 427
Belenta, 483
Belfur, 454
Bel Geddes, 452
Bell, 396, 398
Belle Alliance, 588
bellhop, 644
belling, 208
Bellingham, 456
Bellinjam, 456
Belliqueux, 588
bell-ringer, 713
Bells, 562
belly-bacon, 159; -buster, 762; -chete, 664; -fiddle, 705; -punch, 729; -robber, 778; -wash, 751; -wax, 181; -whacker, 739
Belly Cook, 588
belongded, 358
belsh, 657

List of Words and Phrases

Belva, 497
Belvin, 502
Belvoir, 456
Belziabona, 482
Bement, 438
ben, 113, 186
Ben, 475, 524
Ben Ami, 452
bend, 707
bendedz, 425
bender, 684, 724
bend the iron, to, 714
bend the rust, to, 714
Benedetto, 465
Benedict, 465
Benedicto, 465
Benedictus, 465
Benedikt, 465
Benenia, 482
beng, 266
bengree, 653
Ben-Horin, 422
Benito, 465
Benjamin, 518
Benjiman, 502, 506
Benld, 541
Bennet, 471
Bennett, 396, 398, 517
Bennie, 476, 524; -Mae, 482, 493
Ben-Nun, 422
benny, 653, 683
Benny, 770
Benoit, 438
Benson, 435
Bentinck, 456
bent one, 668
Benway, 438
Ben Yaaqov, 422
beracha, 757
Berdella, 482
Berdilia, 480
Berea, 591
berg, 431
-berg, 423, 431
Berg, 432
bergen, to, 654
Bergenbaum, 422
-berger, 425
Berger, 408, 410
Bergh, 432
Berinthia, 497
Berkeley, 79
Berkhampsted, 414
Berkshire, 578
berl, to, 190

Berlin, 502, 542
berlue, 226
Berly, 457
Berlyn, 502
Berna Dean, 482
Bernalillo, 564
Bernard, 454
Bernardine, 482
Bernece, 496
Berneth, 510
Bernhard, 519
Bernhardt, 410
Bernice, 496, 523
Bernie, 476
Bernis, 502
Bernstein, 420, 421, 422
Beronest, 482
berri, 313
berry, 313
Berry, 398; -Jayne, 482
berson, 209
Bert, 476
Bertash, 428
Bertašius, 428
Bertha, 482, 577
Berthella, 482
Berthie, 482, 494
Bertie, 456
Bertok, 440
Beruria, 519
bery, 313
berykejda, 425
Beryl, 502, 506, 518
Besma, 483
Besshunter, 483
Bessie, 483
Bessye, 483
best, 123
best boy, 698
bestest, 387
bestmost, 387
Best Yet, 580
betcha, 298
Beters, 441
Bethany Beach, 556
be that as it may, 368
Bethel, 591
be they?, 165
Bethune, 448
Betress, 483
betrothed, 53
betseleh, 261
Betta, 483
Bette, 483; -Lou, 483
better, 388
better as, 261

betterer, 387
betterest, 387
Bettha, 483
Betti, 483
Bettijune, 483
betting, 98
Betty, 483-499, 518, 523, 774; -Jane, 478; -Jo, 494
Bettye Joe, 483; -Fae, 483
betwattled, 662
between, 209
between him and I, 373
between you and I, 343, 354, 373, 374
between you and we, 374
betzam, 654
Beulah, 518
Beverly, 472, 493, 506
Bewly, 456
Bewsie, 483
Beyer, 410
be yi?, 165
beyond, 220
beyonst, 220
be you?, 356
beytzah, 654
Bezalel, 519
Bezzie, 483
B-girl, 682
Bianco, 439
bib, 751
Bibianna, 483
Bible, 449, 684; -back, 674
biblia, 385
Bicester, 456
bicycle Jake, 766
Bide-a-Wee, 579
biddy, 11, 770
bidon, 155
biece, 209
Bienfaisant, 588
Bienville, 437
biff, to, 735
big, 139, 272
Big Arm, 535
big as a skinned mule and twice as homely, 139
Big Ben, 588
Big Bend State, 639
Big Boss, 511
big bubble, 753
Big Bugaboo, 566
big con, 667, 668, 669
Big Creek, 540
Big Dick, 746; -from Boston, 746

List of Words and Phrases

big doin's, 215
big hook, 714
big horse, 694
big house, 674
big man, 680
big-money boy, 722
big natural, 746
big noise, 674
big O, 713
Bigot, 449
big ox, 713
big shot, 667, 671, 711
Big Soak, 568
big stick, 749
big store, 667
bikus, 260
bild, 311
bile, 171, 214
bilge, 721
Bilious, 449
Bill, 507, 523
Bill Brown's Big Black Hog, 132
Billie, 476
billing, 745
Billy Dee, 502; -Joe, 487
Billye, 483
Billy gun, 269
Biltover, 579
Bimeler, 419
bin, 186, 187, 250
bin-a-go, 247
binder, 744
bindle, 677, 680; -stiff, 677
bineys, 226
bing, 266
bingo, 736
biograph, 702
biorque, 155
bip into, to, 172
bird, 17, 157, 328, 754, 756; -cage, 673, 674, 714; -dog, 773; -sled, 733, 751
Birda, 483
Birdeen, 483
Birdell, 483
Birdella, 483
Birdena, 483
birdie, 652, 754, 755
Birdie, 483
Birdine, 483
Bird in Hand, 536, 579
bird's eye, 680, 775
bird snow, 232
Birge, 453

birk, 195
Birmingham, 46
Birron, 460
Birtha, 482
Birtie, 483
Birvin, 502
bis, 203
Bischof, 409
biscuit-cutter, 762; -shooter, 238
bishop, 221
Bishop, 409, 502
Bishop's Head, 580
bison, 328
bisseur, 689
Bister, 456
Bístricky, 426
bit, 674, 689, 729
bit, to be, 718
Bītār, 441
bitch, 121, 737, 760; -hopper, 165
bite, 228
bite off, to, 729
bite the dust, to, 741
bito, 252
Bitsche, 411
Bitsh, 449
bitter, 98
Bixler, 410
bj, Swedish, 432
Bj, 478
Björk, 432
Bjørnson, 435
Bjurman, 432
Black, 396, 398, 409, 411
black and white, 772
Black Ankle, 534
black-blizzard, 200; -book, 207; -bottom, 772; -coffee, 53; -cow, 772; -diamond, 718; -dishes, 150; -jack, 718; -market, 777, 782; -out, 781; -roller, 200; -smith, 740; -snake, 714; -snaps, 179; -soup, 674; -spot, 217; -stuff, 680
Black Cat, 596
Black Diamond, 581
Black Eye, 445
blackie, 208, 713
Blackie, 594
blackin', 44
Blackman, 423
Black Man, 132

blackstick, 705
Blackthorn Winter, 208
Blackwater State, 635
blade, 739; -man, 770
blaetter, 316
Blaeuwveldt, 406
blage, 160
blague, 160
blah, 647
blanche, 74
Blanche, 499, 523, 572
Blancpied, 438
Blandina, 479
Blanka, 483
blase, 317
blaspheme, 74
blasphemious, 100
Blasphemy, 511
blast, 729; -furnace, 425, 669
Blau-, 424
Blaustein, 424
Blauvelt, 406
Blawfelt, 406
Blawsteen, 424
Blawveldt, 406
bleachers, 735
bleating, 98
Bleba, 483
blech, 647
bleed, to, 762
bleeder, 737
blesfana, 425
bless, to, 171
blickey, 181
blikje, 181
blimp, 720, 727
blind, 677
blind ad, 731
Blind Tom, 735
blink, 750
blinked, 745
blinky, 153
Blinky, 678
blister, 678; -foot, 727
blitz, 781; -buggy, 785; -water, 671
Blitz, 513
Blitzkrieg, 513
blizzard, 737; -head, 731
Blizzard State, 638, 640
bloast, to, 195
bloater, 195
Bloch, 408
block, 680, 686
Block, 408

List of Words and Phrases

blockhead, 95, 761
blogo, 674
Blois, 502
bloo, 85
blood, 84, 751
bloodhound, 766
bloody, 251
Bloom, 409
bloomer, 670
Bloomingdale, 423
Bloomington, 558
blooper, 737
blossom, 760
Blossom, 515
blosz, 425
blough, 209
Blount, 454
blouse, 123
blow, 744
blow, to, 644, 685
blow air, to, 747
blower, 727
blow in, to, 762
Blow-me-Down, 572
blow-off, 685
blow one's top, to, 710, 711
blow-out, 176, 762
blowsabella, 662
blowse, 662
blow-up, 765
blow up, to, 689
blu, 298
blubber cheeks, 662
Bluddy, Pirate, 583
bludgeon, 736
blue, 85, 132, 205, 691, 729; -bottle, 772; -darter, 735; -devil, 682; -liz, 127; -ox, 728; -sage, 681; -shirt, 749; -sky, 149
Blue, 502
Blue Earth, 561
Blue Ball, 536, 580
Blue Beetle, 588
Blue Belly, 536
Blue Eye, 535
bluefish, 329
Blue Grass region, 627; -State, 627
blue hen's chickens, 232, 605
Blue Hen State, 605
Blue John, 747
blue law, 600

Blue Law State, 600
blues, 705, 706, 710
bluff, 573, 574
-blum, 417
Blum, 409
Blumenthal, 423
Blumpy, 438
blunderbuss, 165
Blunt, 454
blupe, 698
blurb, 731
blutwurst, 151
Bly, 456
Blythe, 456
BM, 755
B'nai B'rith, 582
bo, 553
Bo, 483, 502, 506
B.O., 685, 732
boal, 207
boam, 303
boar, 226; -cat, 226
board, 314, 322, 754
boarder, 682, 732
boar's nest, 233
boat, 158, 693, 717, 735
Bob, 476, 513
Bobba, 483
Bobbie, 483
bobble, to, 729
Bobby, 483; -Jean, 483
Bobbye, 483
bobo, 167
bo-bo bush, 681
bob-tail, 719
bob-wire, 138
Bocalvia, 483
bock, 408
Bóclare, 456
body, 695
Body, 451
boees, 188
-boer, 434
Boetcher, 406
boffo, 674
Bogardus, 406
Bogart, 406, 420
Bogdžiūnas, 428
Bogert, 406
boggy, 120
Boghos, 441
Boghossian, 441
bogieman, 773
Bogitzky, 420
Bogoslof, 552
bogus, 20

Boh-ie, 457
Böhn, 413
Boi, 514
boid, 134, 155, 188
-boiger, 425
boil, 87, 17, 214
boiled-leaves, 751; -yarn, 165
boiler, 725, 759; -room, 773
boilermaker and helper, 722
Boise, 544, 588
Boisvert, 438
Bok, 502
bo'le, 181
Boler, 454
Bolitho, 456
boll-weevil, 760, 762
bologna, 764. See also *baloney*
bolt, to, 11
Bolytho, 456
bom, 302
bomb, 137, 230, 302, 303
bombast, 47
Bomgaert, 406
Bonahom, 441
Bonanza State, 635
Boncilla, 483
Bon Coeur, 437
Bond-street, 322
bone, 241, 740, 760, 773; -eater, 198
Bone, 411
bone for, to, 172
bonehead, 645
bones, 643, 728
bong, 266
Bonhomie, 562
Boniface, 439
Bonifazio, 439
bonnarings, 207
Bonnie, 483; -Mae, 483
Bonny Pheasant, 588
boo, 149
boodle, 767
boo-dwahr, 53
Boogaert, 406
boogie-woogie, 705, 706, 710
Boo-ie, 457
book, 214, 674, 744
Book, 385
boo-kay, 53
Booker, 409, 447

bookkeeper, 662, 713
bookman, 776
book-miner, 762
Book of Books, 385
bookvertising, 732
bool, 84
bool-yuh-base, 53
boom, 303, 648; -jockey, 698; -wagon, 719
Boomer's Paradise, 638
Boone, 411, 412
Boonsboro', 589
Boop, 449
boor-b'n, 53
boor-zhwah-zee, 53
boosh, 199
booshel, 199
boost, 648
booster, 670, 685; -box, 670
boot, 228, 739
bootblack, 772
booth, 697
Boothe, 454
Bootjack, 511
bootleg, 762
bootlegger, 714
boo-tuh-nyair, 53
booty, 84
booze, 645, 664
boozefuddle, 158
bop, 749
Bo-peep, 511
borax, 757; -house, 757
Borden, 428
Border-Eagle State, 631
borders, 689
Border State, 629
Boreas, 588
bored, 314
bore hole, 770
bore with too big an auger, to, 146
borgen, 757
bornded, 358
boro, 292
borough, 292
-borough, 402, 534
borrow, to, 82, 216, 237, 292
Bortz, 412
Borz, 412
böse, 431
Boskowitz, 416
boss, 713
bosshart, 654

boss her, to, 719
bossy in a bowl, 751
Boston, 12, 531; -version, 693
bot, 158
Bot Fly, 593
both, 98
bothen, 394
bottle, 698, 718
bottom, 573, 766, 772
bottomer, 733
Bottomley, 456
botty, 208
boucan, 155
Bouchevaldre, 413
boudoir, 53
bought, 362
boughten, 362, 394, 395
bouillabaisse, 53
Boujalad, 441
boulevard, 170, 764
Boulware, 454
bouncer, 669, 714
bounder, to, 181
bound'ry, 96
bounteous, 5
bouquet, 48, 53
bourbon, 53, 628
Bourchier, 457
bourg, 573
bourgade, 573
Bourgeois, 438
bourgeoisie, 53
Bourjaily, 441
-bourne, 534
bouse, 664
bousing ken, 664
bo-ut, 158
boutonnière, 53, 317
Boutross, 441
Bovine, 561
bow, 360
bow-and-arrow, 742
bowbow, 764
Bowcher, 457
Bowen, 403
bower, 51
Bower, 409
Bowermaster, 412
Bowers, 409
Bowie, 457; -knife, 611, 612; -State, 611
Bowlegs, 535
bowler, 3
bowling-alley, 714
bowl of chalk, 710

bowne, 360
Bowry, 456
bowse, to, 664
Bowthe, 454
box, 45, 669, 696, 705, 719, 733, 744, 756, 765; -cars, 746; -office, 652, 688; -set, 689
Box A, 674
boxing-glove, 746
box of teeth, 705
Box 25, 675
box up, to, 767
Box Z, 675
boy, 192, 203, 249; -friend, 708
Boyce, 472
Boyd, 398
Boyer, 410
boys, 188
Bozanna, 483
BP, 755
bra, 52, 746
braces, 250
Bradford, 469, 471
Bradley, 398, 399
Brager, 435
Braggadocia, 535
Bragger, 435
Braham, 416
Brahan, 457
Brahkah, 435
brain-plate, 714
brains, 713, 718
Brainstorm, 594
brake, to, 362
braked, 362
Bram, 516
branch, 573
Brandeis, 424
Brandenburg, 542
brand-new, 11
bran-faced, 662
brang, 167
brashy, 175
brass, 644, 778; -ankle, 215; -collar, 713; -hat, 777; -nuts, 760; -officer, 705; -smith, 324
brassière, 52, 53, 317, 732
brass-yair, 53
brattice, 760
brattish, 760
Brauer, 409
Braun, 409, 422
Braun-, 424

List of Words and Phrases 799

Braunstein, 424
brave boy, 705
Bravo, 561
Brawn, 457
Brawnsteen, 424
Brazell, 483
Braziel, 483
brazier, 620
bread and butter, 740
Bread and Butter State, 630
Bread Basket of the Nation, 630
Bread of Life, 590
breaf, 171
break, 689, 706
break a bunch, to, 744
breakaway, 698
Breakheart Point, 572
break water, to, 750
breast, 761; -form, 746; -pin, 218; -shield, 746
breastner, 252
breath, 171, 751; -harp, 232
breather, 768
breathing, 763
bred, 293
bree, 707
Breeding, 449
breenk, 261
Breeze, 595
breezer, 718
brekker, 649
bre-oon, 43
brer, 265
brerl, to, 190
bres, 171
bresh, 120
Bressler, 411
bretheren, 100
brethern, 120
brethren, 328
Brett, 420
Brewer, 409
Breza, 483
briar, 760
Briarcliffe, 534
Bricabrac, 528
Bricker, 412
Brickyard, 556
Bricquebec, 528
bridge, 763; -smasher, 583
bridle, 228
brief, 172
brigadier, 620

bright, 228, 389
Brightfellow, 449
Brightie, 483
Brilty, 427
Brindle, 535
bring, 209, 261
Bring Home What You Borrowed, 132
brioche, 154
briqué, 155
Bristol, 533
Brlety, 427
broach, 314
broad-assed marine, 779
Broad Axe, 536
broadcast, 729
broadcast, to, 728
broadcasted, 728
Broadmoor, 578
Broadus, 472
Brocas, 469
Brockenbrough, 454
broduck, 209
Broihahn, 410
broke, 362
Broke, 457
Broken Nose, 445
bromine, 81
bronc, 741; -buster, 741; -peeler, 741
bronchi, 320
bronchitides, 320
bronchitis, 81, 320
bronco, 741
bronichal, 100
Bron-ix, 100
Bronstein, 415
bronze, 270
Broo-am, 457
brooch, 314
brook, 168
Brook, 402, 457
Brookenburro, 454
Brooklyn, 588; -Bridge, 753
Brooks, 396, 398, 402, 409
broom, 215, 228, 756
broom clean, to, 757
Brooxie, 483
brosch, 151
broster, 371
brot, 313
brother, 222, 265, 776
brother and sister, 371
brother-in-laws, 328
brothers-in-law, 328

brouge, to, 233
Brougham, 457
broughten, 167
broughtforth, 325
brought on, 132
browcing, 179
Brown, 396, 398, 400, 401, 402, 409, 447
Browne, 402
Brownelle, 502
brownie, 714; -box, 714
Brown Leg, 566
Brownstone State, 600
Bruce, 404
Brücher, 412
Brücker, 412
Bruening, 316
bruh, 265
bruh-uh, 265
brulée, 155
brummie, 767
brunet, 291
Brunetta, 483
brung, 108, 219
Brüning, 316
Brunis, 502
Bruno, 594
brush-cat, 758, 760
brushoff, 695
brutal, 696
brutal brothers, 691
Brutus, 532
Bryan, 410
Bryant, 398
Brytha, 483
bryush, 139
B. S., 763
bub, 108
buba, 266
bubbly-jock, 207
bubeliks, 207
bubli, 207
bubu, 266
bubuwa, 266
Buccleuch, 457
Bucher, 409
Buchwalter, 413
buck, 121, 674, 744
buck, to, 134
buckaroo, 201, 741, 774
bucker, 759
bucket, 108, 129
buckeye, 616, 637, 744; -cabin, 616
Buckeye, 621, 637; -Grocer, 637; -Lake Topics,

800 *List of Words and Phrases*

637; -News, 637; -State, 636, 637
buckle, to, 165, 746
buckra, 247
Buck Rogers, 728
Buckshot, 511
buckshot land, 173
buckskin, 759, 775
Buckskin Joe, 555
buck the bronco, to, 716
buck the case, to, 767
bud, 220
Bud, 502, 506
Buddy, 525
Budeach, 426
budge, 657
budget, 140, 234
Budiac, 426
Buechsler, 410
Buena Park, 528
Buena Vista, 483
buer, 195
buff, 749
Buff, 594
buffalo, 328, 749
Buffalo, 532
buffalo, to, 127
Buffaloe, 449
Buffalo Plains State, 613
buffaroo, 729
buffer, 657
buffing, 775
bug, 159, 248, 249, 668, 717, 750, 769, 773, 785; -chaser, 728; -dust, 217, 761; -eye, 761; -juice, 719, 748; -light, 761; -torch, 714
Bug, 535
Bugeater, 635
Bug-Eating State, 635
Bugg, 451
Bugger, 511
Buggerman, 449
Buggy, 674, 714, 761, 773; -rider, 775
bughouse, 677
Bug Lake, 540
Bugtussle, 535
Buhdeach, 426
Bûhdeeack, 426
buh-er, 192
built like a depot stove, 146
Buklóo, 457

bukra, 266
Bulas, 502
bulber, 698
bull, 84, 110, 121, 226, 644, 652, 684, 773, 775; -cook, 759; -dogger, 741; -driver, 208; -face, 160; -fiddle, 705; -gang, 754, 776; -goose, 713; -header, 740; -hooker, 684; -man, 684; -pen, 715; -work, 739
Bulldog, 587
bulldog spear, 762
bulldozer, 748
bullets, 751
bullfighter, 715
Bullion State, 631, 634
bull of the woods, 759
Bull Run, 589
bull's breakfast, 233
bull's eye, 743
bullstaller, 740
Bulpitt, 449
bum, 230, 303, 457, 678, 679, 717, 767, 770
Bumble Bee, 535
Bumly, 456, 457
bummer, 51, 679, 770
bummler, 679
bummy, 177
bump, 694; -reader, 684
bump, to, 693, 715
bump man, 704
bump off, to, 652
Bun, 502
Bū-Na'ūm, 441
bunch, 744, 748
bungalow, 698
bung-out, 149
bunion, 760
bunk, 721
Bunker, 437; -Hill, 437
bun pup, 751
bunt, 735
bur-b'n, 53
bureau, 83, 743
bureaucracy, 83
bureaucrat, 83
Burg, 679
Burgass, 453
Burge, 453
-burger, 425
Burger, 408
Bürger, 408
-burgh, 539

Burghley, 457
burial-ground, 592
Burk, 432
Burke, 396, 397, 398, 401
Burkeshire Arms, 577
Burl, 506
burlesk, 291, 297
burleycue, 693
Burlin, 502
Burman, 432
burn, 158, 252
Burneace, 496
burned, to be, 718
Burneice, 496
Burnell, 521
Burnett, 578
Burnham, 416
Burnis, 496
Búrniss, 496
Burns, 398, 409
burnsides, 645
Burnt Arm, 572
burn the stick, to, 718
Burnt Pone, 566
burnt up, 717
Burnucc, 496
Burnup, 451
Burnus, 496
burocracy, 294, 295
Burovsky, 427
burp, 729
Burp, 449
burp, to, 644
Burr, 420
Burrell Inn, 542
burr-head, 693
Burroak, 539
burst, to, 175, 355, 356
bursted, 356
Burstein, 420
Burt, 507
Burtha, 482
Burton, 420, 442
Burvine, 502
bury, 197, 313
-bury, 402
Bury, 427
burying-ground, 179
bus, 328, 761
Bus, 511
buses, 327, 328
bush-house, 217
Bushway, 438
bushwhack, to, 150
bushwhacker, 748
busier 'n Hattie's flea, 139

business, 386, 669, 689, 691
busses, 327, 328
bust, to, 143, 175, 185, 355, 356, 778
bust a blood-vessel, to, 355
bust a bronco, to, 355
bust a suspender button, to, 355
bust, to go on a, 355
bust-developer, 693
busted, 165, 356
buster, 355, 748
Buster, 502, 506
Buster Brown, 355
bust-head, 355
bustinest, 355
bust out laughing, to, 355
busy, to be, 682
Busy B., 588
but, 391
Butch, 594
butcher, 228, 674, 715
Butcher, 406
butchered, 754
Butensky, 420
Butler, 396, 398
but one, 391
Butrūs, 441
butt, 215, 775
butte, 237, 573, 574
butter, 97, 195; -bread, 206; -brot, 206; -paddle, 727
butterfly, 698, 715, 766; -nose, 748
Buttermilk, 449
buttery, 111, 185, 207
but that, 391
button, 707, 741, 767; -ear, 748; -head, 774
buttons, 670, 757
butts meat, 215
but what, 337, 391
buy, 696
Buzache, 593
buzz, to, 682
buzzard, 677, 755
Buzzard, 610; -State, 610
Buzzards' Glory, 558
by, 175, 209, 261
By, 449
by a head, 652
Byard, 502, 506
by-blow, 226

by gosh, 425
by his house, 261
Byioba, 483
Byllye, 483
by me, 394
Byrdalyce, 483
Byrdella, 483
Byrl, 506
Byron, 460
Byrtha, 482
Bythella, 483
by the peck, 711
by the time that, 203
Byzantine Botts, 450
c, 281, 284, 285, 291, 292, 294, 296, 300, 303, 304, 432
C, 680
c, French, 572
c, Italian, 52, 308
caa'v, 314
cabaca, 167
cabase, 151
cabbage, 386, 773; -leaves, 161
Cabbage, 449
cabeza, 151
cabin-car, 714
Cabinet, 322
Cabot, 418, 419
cache, 677
cackleberry, 674
cackle-crate, 719
cackler, 674, 762
cacky, 693
Cactus State, 636
Cad, 502
cade, 210
cadet, 230
Cadiz, 533
caecus, 655
caen, 653
Caesar, 466, 513
cafe, 317
caffeine, 87
caffoon, 247
cag, 272
cage, 714, 743
cah, 192
Cahan, 421
cahm, 192
cahn't, 25
Cain, 512
Caintuck, 627
Caitiff, 451
Cajan, 628

Cal, 476
Calais, 44, 49
calamity, 179; -howler, 149
Calara, 483
calcium, 285
Caldeen, 502
Caledonia, 577
Calexico, 540, 541
calf, 74, 171, 199; -line, 763
Calf, 449, 451
Calhoun, 402
calibre, 282
calico, 132
California, 506, 588
Calina, 480
Calis, 50
Calista, 483
Callahumpian, 208
call-house, 682
calliope, 714
callithump, 185
Callowhill, 454
calm, 171, 187, 211, 215, 230
Calneva, 541
Calogeropoulus, 440
Caloyer, 440
calque, to, 733
Calthorp, 469
calv, 385
calvary, 99
calve, 314
Calvert, 411
calves, 385
Calvin, 472, 522; -Victory, 583
Calzona, 541
Cama, 483
Cámbel, 457
Cambridge, 12, 414
Camden and Amboy State, 602
Camel, 457
Camma, 502
Camolia, 483
Camp, 454
cámpaign, 49
Campbell, 398, 400, 405, 435, 453, 457
campement de plusieurs, 573
Camphor, 449
Camp Rest-a-bit, 578
Camyada, 483

can, 4, 69, 73, 249, 367, 653, 714, 725, 727
Canaan, 591
Canada, 573
Canadeo, 439
Canal, 556
Canaliza, 483
canapé, 318
canary, 672, 698, 706, 724, 729; -bird, 761
candelabra, 319
Candelaria, 483
candid camera, 765
candle, 73
Cando, 541
Can Do Ship, 588
candy, 759; -butcher, 715; -wagon, 719
Candy, 451
can I go with?, 169
canned music, 731
canner, 749
cannon, 670; -ball, 581
can o'corn, 735
canoe, 160, 267
cañon, 51, 237, 316. See also canyon
can't, 3, 74, 122, 159, 195
cantaloupe, 734
cante, to, 664
Canton, 584
can't seem, 338
can't see nothing, 246
canyon, 316, 573, 761. See also cañon
cap, 680
Cap, 679
caper, 674
capillary, 48
Capitola, 483
Caplunk, 579
capon, 762
cappi, 653
caps, 153
captain, 713
Captain, 594
Captain Blood, 722
Captain Jimmy Hicks of the Horse Marines, 747
cap the stack, to, 215
capting, 100, 114
caput, 320, 654
car, 73, 86, 89, 230; -hop, 752; -knocker, 713
Cara, 502
Car A, 582

Caral, 483
Carasaljo, 540
Carbena, 483
carbon-monkey, 698
carbox, 215
carburetor, 723
Carcass Creek, 570
card, 88, 227, 680
Cardia, 506
care, 214, 251
Carell, 483
Carew, 454
Carey, 454
carf, 360
cargo, 5
caries, 87
carillon, 50
Carisbrooke, 414
Carl, 483, 520
Carla, 483
Carlee, 483
Carli, 520
Carlina, 483
Carlisle, 404
Carlson, 441
Carlyne, 483
Carmelit, 519
Carmen, 506
Carmencita, 593
Carmichael, 454
Carnegie, 454
Carnell, 483
Carol, 483, 506, 520
Carolie, 483
Caroline, 493
Caroline nine, 746
Caroliny, 544
Carolle, 502, 506
carp, 73
Carpenter, 398, 399, 409, 422, 435
Carpet, 227, 233
carps, 697
Carr, 398, 458
Carrall, 483
carriage, 171, 214
Carrie, 487
Carriell, 483
Carrine, 483, 494
Carrizozo, 565
Carroll, 398, 454, 483
Carroll of Carrollton, 452
Carroll the Barrister, 452
carrots and peas, 722
carry, 86, 251
carry, to, 101, 107, 144

carry on, to, 169
carry the banner, to, 678
carry the mail, to, 669
cars, 248
cart, 214
Carter, 398, 402
Carthage, 532, 537
carton-box, 153
cartoon, 153
Carul, 483
carve, to, 79, 314, 360
Carver, 448
Caryl, 483
Casalegni, 439
Cascade, 483; -Bluff, 583; -Den, 583; -Elf, 583; -Gully, 583; -Moon, 583; -Whirl, 583; -Whisper, 583
case, 657, 767
case, to, 668, 744
Casebeer, 449
Casey, 713
Cash, 502, 506
Cashdollar, 449
cashier, 620
cash 'n carry, 297
Casindania, 483
casing, 763
Caspar, 519
Cassels, 457
Cassidy, 444
Cassilis, 457
cast, 729
cast, to, 360
casted, 360, 362
Castile, 513
casting-couch, 704
Castle, 97
Castor, 583
Castor and Pollux, 588
castor-cat, 208
Castor Oil, 513
cat, 205, 657, 672, 684, 706, 710, 759, 764; -cracker, 763; -eye, 746; -face, 757; -head, 674; -house, 682; -nap, 145; -wagon, 682
catalog, 291, 311; -woman, 176
Catawba, 530
catch, 174; -all, 162
catched, 165
catcher, 774
Catchpoll, 451

catch the bumps, to, 693
caterpillar, 644, 715
Catharan, 483
Catherine, 520
Cathern, 483
catholic, 670
Cat Island, 540
Cato, 513
cat plant, 763
Catrisa, 483
cats, 424
cats and dogs, 773
cats'-eye, 674, 773; -head, 208; -pajamas, 644; -uncle, 217; -water, 208
Cat's Meow, 579
cattalo, 764
cattle-mill, to, 220
cat up, to, 672
cat-up men, 672
caucus, to, 643
caught, 199
cauliflower, 269; -ear, 768
caulk, 314, 759
cavalier, 620
Cavalier State, 597
cave, 756
cavvies, 238
cawf, 83
cawk, 314
cawked, 217
cawnt, 4
Cawtry, 460
Caxambas, 557
cayeute, 639
Cayo Huesco, 557
cayotah, 639
cayote, 639
Cayuga, 565
Cayugy, 565
Cayuse, 641
CB, 782
CCC, 331
C.C.N.Y. Victory, 564
Ceal, 502
Cecil, 457, 469, 506
Cecco, 439
Cecyle, 483
cede, 313
ceiling-buster, 671
celebrity, 743
Celethal, 483
cellar, 740; -rat, 758; -way, 179
Cellow, 502

cement, 48, 682; -mixer, 707
Cementa, 483
cemetery, 592
censor, 280
Centennial State, 613
center, 300, 301, 539
center line, 697
Center Theatre, 286
Centerville, 559, 569, 572
Centipede, 536
Centrahoma, 542
Central Park, 582; -State, 623
centre, 249, 282, 539
Centurlius, 502
century, 698; -run, 723
century of the common man, 121
Ceola, 502
ce-oo, 43
cerebral accident, 755
Cerelia, 498
Cerilla, 483
cert, 669
certain, 79
cert'n'y, 96
cession, 313
Cestaro, 439
c'est moi, 372
ch, 258, 290, 292, 300, 304, 414, 418, 426, 431
ch, German, 52, 151, 307, 408, 414, 426
ch, Italian, 308
cha-cha, 195
Chacsper, 423
chaenj, 300
chafar, 654
Chahmers, 457
Chaim, 519
chain-breaker, 722
chainge, 269
chains, 269
chair, 197
Chair-boor, 34
Chairynne, 483
chaise, 384
chalk, 674; -eye, 761
challupe, 725
Chalmers, 457
chaloupe, 725
chalupa, 725
chambermaid, 713
Chambers, 577
chamois, 775

Champ, 456, 502
Champion, 508
Champwood, 541
Chan, 442, 502, 506
chance, 74, 750
chancellor, 284
chandelier, 684
Chandos, 457
Chang, 443
change, 217
change, to, 231, 749
Chapereau, 423
chaperejo, 741
Chapiro, 423
chapling, 99
Chapman, 398, 399
chaps, 741
character, 38, 729
Charelle, 483
Charentz, 441
chargé d'affaires, 318
Chargoggagaugmanchaugagoggchaubunagungamaugg, 530
chariot, 714
Charity, 468
charivari, 185
Charla, 483
Charlaine, 483
Charlatta, 483
Charlcie, 483
Charleere, 483
Charlena, 483
Charlene, 483
Charles, 462, 465, 483, 510, 513, 523, 531
Charles James, 474
Charles King the Martyr, 590
Charles Little Dog, 444
Charley, 476, 770
Charleye, 483
Charley horse, 735
Charley Noble, 721
Charlie, 483, 523, 524, 698
Charlie Coke, 681
Charline, 483
Charlotte, 521
Charlsie, 483
Charlye, 483
Charlyne, 483
Charlyse, 483
charm, 74
charwoman, 114
Charteris, 457
Charters, 457

Chas, 483
chase, 315
Chase doll, 755
chase the cure, to, 756
Chasey, 425
chassis, 53, 723
Chastain, 502
Chat and Chew, 580
Chateaugué, 437
Chat-N-Nibble, 580
chatouilleur, 689
chatterbox, 724
chattes, 664
chauffeur, 50, 52, 53, 723, 727
Chauncey, 469
Chauncy, 469
chaunk, to, 120
Chautauqua, 560; -salute, 743
chaw, 88, 181
chaw tobacco more than onc't, to, 172
Chayim, 418
cheapen, to, 359
cheater, 683, 733, 771
Checago, 530
check, 680
checkermint, 179
Checko, 439
check-off, 776
checkout, 753
chee, 386
Cheegago, 530
cheep, to, 173
cheer, 137, 197
Cheer, 449
Cheer Up Ship, 588
cheese, 386, 740, 773; -cake, 765
Cheese, 451
cheese it, 644
Cheesewright, 449
chef, 681, 732, 740
Cheggago, 530
Chelsea, 575
Chelsea Court Tower, 577
Chemdah, 519
Chemquasabamticook, 560
Chenang, 565
Chenango, 560, 565
cheque, 282
Chequelin, 437
Cherbourg, 34
cheroot, 744

Cherrie, 434
Cherry, 434
cherry-picker, 713
cherry-picker's nose, 146
Cherubim, 483
Chesnutt, 448
Chestannie, 483
Chester, 439, 471, 472, 517
chestnut, 233
Chet, 475
chevalier du lustre, 689
chew, to, 88, 161
Chiang Kai-shek, 443
chic, 53, 753
Chicago, 5, 132, 216, 530, 548; -finish, 750
Chicahgo, 548
Chicawgo, 530, 548
Chiccago, 530
chick, 53, 707
Chick, 502, 506
Chickahominy, 589
Chickaloon, 552
Chickaugo, 5
Chicken Bone, 564
chicken-eater, 764; -flutter, 165; -wire, 766
Chicken Thief, 536
chicking, 99
chicky, 753
Chief, 581
Chief American Horse, 583
Chief Gall, 583
Chief Iron Tail, 582
chien, 655
Chiesa, 439
Chiggago, 530
chigger, 267
Chikkago, 530
childering, 99
childern, 99, 100, 185
childrens, 386
childs, 240
Chilgren, 431
chili, 741
Chilingirian, 441
Chillicothe, 566
chillun, 200
chimbly, 100, 174
chimley, 164
chimney, 174
china-closet, 725
Chinatown, 563, 582
chin-bass, 705

Chinee, 383, 385, 754
Chineeah, 483
chink, 657
chinners, 645
Chinook State, 641
chin-polisher, 674
chiota, 639
chip out, to, 217
Chirgago, 530
chiropractor, 767
chirp, 706
chisel, to, 644
chiseler, 752
Chiselhurst, 577
chit, 243
Chituni, 441
chiv, 653
chivaree, 185
chix, 233, 297
Chizella, 483
chloride of lime, 269
chlorine, 81
Chlorine, 483
chocker bole, 751
chocolate, 216
Chokamengro, 442
choker, 759
Cholmondelay, 456
choose to run, to, 222
chop, 722
chop-hills, 176
chopper, 751
choppies, 176
Choquette, 437
choral, 72
chore, 169
chorus-girl, 695, 758
chouse, to, 741
chow, 674
Chow, 442
chowder, 252, 720; -head, 165
Cho-Wella, 502
Chris'mas, 96
Christ, 220, 590
Christian, 472; -name, 477
Christianity, 321
Christie, 435
Christine Nancy Luanna Jane Rio Miranda Mary Jane, 512
Christmas, 219, 449; -tree, 763
Christo, 502
Christoria, 483
chromatics, 729

chromo, 771
chronic, 254
Chronos, 440
Chrzanowski, 425
chuck, 219, 674
chucker, 735
Chucklehead, 536
chuffer, 316
chug-wagon, 725
Chulahoma, 562
chum, to, 750
Chumly, 456
chump, 670, 685
Chunky Gal, 566
church, 322
Church, 439, 674
Churchill, 430, 451
Churchman, 408
church-school, 745
churchyard, 592
chymical, 311
chymist, 311
Chyna, 483
ci, 313
Cicely, 499
Cicero, 532
cider, 278
cigar, 86; -box, 735
cigaret, 291
cigarette, 48
cigarmakers' heaven, 744
cigya, 86
Cimarron, 564
cinchers, 719
Cincinnati, 544, 559, 566, 588
Cinderella Hall, 577
cinder-head, 754
Cinders, 679
cinema, 251
cinematograph, 702
CIO, 331
ciote, 639
cipher, 228
ciphering-match, 132
Cirrelda, 483
Cistern Hill, 592
Citamard, 579
City, 539, 559, 679
city juice, 772
Civic Center, 582
civilian, 698
Civilla, 483
ck, 304
cks, 297
clahssic, 314

claime, 259
claim-jumper, 761
Clalie, 483
clam-bake, 706, 729
Clam State, 602
clanaroo, 729
clap, 657
Clapp, 412
claque, 689
claqueur, 689
Clara, 519
Clare, 506
Clarence, 521
Clarendon, 578
ClarEtta, 483, 494
Clarine, 496
Clarion, 595
Clarise, 502
Clarissa, 479, 509
clark, 46, 184, 251
Clark, 398, 406, 471
Clarmond, 502
claro, 744
clasp, 74
class, 187
Clata, 483
clatterwhacking, 232
Claudere, 502, 506
Clauzell, 502
Claverhouse, 457
Clavers, 457
claw, 670; -off, 158
Clay, 471, 507
clay-bank, 173; -belly, 767; -eater, 608; -hiller, 608
Clazene, 483
clean, 184
cleanser, 212
clean up the kitchen, to, 751
clean your plow, to, 138
clear, 697
Clearfield, 569
clear grit, 139
Cleatus, 483
cleaver, 662
clem, 685
Clements, 439
Clemet, 434
Clemetsen, 434
Cleo, 506
Cleodus, 502
Cleopatra, 594
Cleopatria, 484
Clere, 502

clergy, 79
clerk, 46, 79, 251, 727
clessic, 314
Clesta, 484
Cletis, 502
Cletus, 502
Clevanel, 484
Clevern, 502
cleymes, 657
click, 718
clicker, 766
clientitis, 729
Cliff, 475
-cliffe, 534
cliff-hanger, 704, 729
Clifford, 468, 469, 521
Clifford Saber, 523
Clifton, 517
climb-to, 359
climbed, 359
climber, 720
clime, 315
Climena, 484
clinchers, 724
Cline, 409, 411
clinged, 165
clinic, 738
clinker, 729, 735, 750, 752
Clint, 502, 506
Clinton, 469, 522
clipe, 208
clip in to, to, 166
Cloa, 484
clock, 184, 773
Clock, 449
Clodean, 502
Clois, 502
Cloisters, 577
clomb, 359
clombe, 359
Clome, 484
close shave, 735
closet, 210
Cloteel, 494
clothes, 385; -closet, 111; -horse, 695; -line, 735; -press, 111
clothing, 753
Clough, 457
Clover, 583; -Bed, 582; -Colony, 583; -Gem, 583; -Nest, 583; -Plot, 583; -Veldt, 583
CloVera, 484
clown, 677; -alley, 684; -wagon, 714

Cloys, 502
club, 727; -sandwich, 772; -winder, 713
cluck, 748
Cluff, 457
Cluke, 502
clum, 359
clunch, 657
clutch, 723
cly, to, 665
Cly, 484
cly the gerke, to, 664
Cnocknatratin, 593
coach, 255
Coal City, 569
coaleys, 253
coal-heaver, 713
coal-mine, 753
Coal State, 598
coarse ones, 667
coat, 158
cob, 657; -roller, 748
Cobbledick, 449
cobbler, 739
cobra, 703
cobs, 714
Coburn, 421, 457
Cocabelto, 593
Coca Cola, 680
coccuses, 320
cocheter, 155
Cochibo, 552
Cochocton, 566
cockabaloo, 253
cockale, 658
Cockburn, 457
cocker, 746, 766
cockeye, 737
cockloft, 715
cockroach shop, 752
cock-shop, 759
cocktail, 658, 738
coco, 645
C. O. cocktail, 772
cod, 149
coddy, 149
codeine, 87
codster, 208
Cody, 412
Coe, 502
co-ed, 698
Coelho, 436
Coen, 421
Cœur d'Alêne, 539
Cœur-Très-Pur de la Bienheureuse Viêrge

Marie de Plaisance, 571
coff, 313
Coff, 166
coffee, 82, 83, 738; -grinder, 725, 740; -pot, 714
coffin, 110, 216; -nail, 127
Cofflin, 457
Coffman, 410
cof gums, 297
cofi, 515
Coftry, 460
Cogh-, 457
Coghlan, 457
Cohan, 421
Cohen, 396, 397, 398, 400, 401, 419, 420, 421, 422
C. O. high-ball, 772
Cohn, 421
Cohon, 421
Cóhoon, 457
coil, 191, 192, 686, 741
Coiner, 451
Coita, 484, 495
coke, 652, 680, 772
Coke, 408
Cokely, 457
cokie, 681
Coklan, 457
Cola, 508
Colan, 457
Colbath, 461
Colcannon Night, 252
Colclough, 457
cold, 719
cold cocked, to be, 233
cold cut, 707
cold feet, 644
Cold Harbor, 589
cold poke, 670
cold shoulder, 649
cold slaw, 51
cold turkey, 687, 756
Cole, 398, 409, 436
Coleman, 398
Coler, 409
cole slaw, 51
coleus, 384
Colhoff, 444
Colita, 484
Coliver, 420
collar, 735, 762; -day, 662
collection, 277
college, 674, 770
Collins, 398, 409
collote, 639

Colney, 428
colonel, 310, 320
Colonel, 502, 507, 594
color, 159, 281, 301
colorado, 744
Colorado, 555
colorado claro, 744
colorado maduro, 744
coloration, 280, 281
Colo-ray-do, 555
colored, 270
colored man, 211
colorific, 281
coloring, 750
colossuses, 320
colour, 280, 281
Colquhoun, 402, 457
coltish, 658
Columbia, 571
Columbus, 476, 504
comb, 207, 208, 734
combe, 573
Combe, 457
come, 340
come and, 394
comedy, 459
come in, to, 763
come in this house, 220
come-off, 670
Comet, 593
comf'table, 96
coming, 459
Comma, 502, 506
command, 214
commando, 778
commercial, 706, 730, 731
committee work, 749
Commodore, 502, 507
Commodore Vanderbilt, 581
Commoleen, 484
common, 168
communiqué, 318
como esta?, 243
company, 83, 322, 459
company jewelry, 715
Compass, 536
compensate, 4
compère, 50, 695
complaisance, 47
complected, 338
complexion, 277
compos, 771
compromised, 246
Compton, 457
concern, 79

Concklijn, 406
concrete-mixer, 725
condeetion, 234, 235
Condelario, 444
condition, 234
condom, 728
conductor, 692
conduit, 50
Cone, 421
co'ner, 96
Conestoga, 526; -wagon, 528, 744
Coney Island bloodhound, 752
confetti, 767
confided, 359
confidentially, 348
confidently, 348
confiscate, 4, 47
conflab, 100
confrère, 317, 318
Congressional, 581
Congretta, 484
Conighame, 460
Conisborough, 457
conjure, 215
conkerbill, 253
Conkling, 406
conky, 674
Conn, 421
Connace, 484
connection, 277, 669, 680
connexion, 277
Conover, 405, 411
conqueror, 280
Conqueror, 587
conquést, 114
Conrad, 519
consaity, 233
consate, 78
consent job, 668
consist, 715
constable, 83, 215, 459
Constance, 468
Constancia, 521
Constantine, 509
Constipation, 513
constitutiant, 99
constitution, 250
Constitution, 320, 322, 581; -State, 600
Consto, 513
construe, 48
Conte, 439
cóntemplate, 47
conténts, 49

conterary, 99
Contey, 439
continuity, 729
contrary, 232
Contrary Mary, 139
contribution-box, 179
conversation, 277
convict, 684
convoy, to, 25
cony, 658; -catching, 658
Cooglin, 457
cook, to, 765
Cook, 398, 405, 408, 412, 425
cook a pill, to, 681
cook coffee, to, 156, 169
Cooke, 427
cooked, 698
Cookey, 448
cook-house, 684; -room, 132; -shack, 714
cookie, 681
Cook's tour, 698
Coolidge, 427
coolie, 720
cooling, 706
Coom, 457
coon, 211
Coon, 409
cooner, 208
coon's age, 145
coop, 52, 215, 228
Cooper, 228, 398, 402, 406, 457
cooperage, 739
Coosawda, 530
coose, 207
cooshion, 235
cooster, 208
cooter, 267
Cootry, 460
Coots, 457
cop, 653; -caller, 719
cop, to, 653
cop a mope, to, 674
coppa coula, 263
copper, 653
cop's bottle, 734
copying, 252
copy-writer, 732
Coqueisenejigh, 573
Corcoran, 457
cordovan, 775
Cordula, 484
corduroy bridge, 176
Corean, 484

core-barrel, 763
Coreen, 484
Coreine, 484
Corene, 484
Corey, 441
corfen, 360
Corienne, 484
Corilla, 484
Corinn, 484
Corinne, 484
Corinth, 537
Corinthia Marigold Wilkinson Ball Wemyss Alexander Jones Mitchell, 514
Corise, 484
Coritha, 479
cork, 314, 749, 759
corker, 766
Corkran, 457
corkscrew-arm, 737
corn, 3; -barn, 210; -crib, 231; -fed, 706; -house, 210, 231; -punk, 686; -snitcher, 740; -stack, 231
Corn Cob, 592
Corncracker State, 609, 627
Corne, 502
Cornell, 427
corner boy, 253
cornet, 250
cornfield meet, 715
cornfield nigger, 124
Cornhusker, 635
Corn Huskers' State, 635
Cornish Arms, 578
Cornish Queen, 139
cornstarch airs, 166
Corn State, 614
corny, 706, 729
corp, 384
corpse, 384, 707
corpus, 320
Corpus Christi, 544, 591
corral, 51, 741
corral, to, 134
correc', 218
corrector of the press, 284
Correne, 484
Corrine, 484
cortège, 317
Coryl, 496
Coscob, 539

coshtey, to, 155
cosmetic, 738
cosmetical, 738
cosmeticism, 738
cosmetology, 738
Cossett, 438
Costello, 454
costly, 218
Cosy, 484
cot, 158; -betty, 207
cotched, 137
coteau, 237
cotillion, 50, 295
Cotry, 460
cott, 89
cottage cheese, 231
Cottenham, 457
Cottnam, 456
cotton, to, 648
Cotton, 469, 515; -Belt, 610; -Country, 610; -dom, 610; -ia, 610
Cotton Plantation State, 610
Cotton State, 610
Cotton States, 610
cotton to, to, 644
couch, 255
couch a hogshead, to, 664
cou collier, 155
cough, 83, 306, 313
Cough-, 457
Coughlan, 457
Coughlin, 457
Coughtrey, 460
could, 364
coulda, 365
could-a-of, 366
could have, 366
could of, 366
coulee, 574
counselor, 284
Count, 507
counter-stretcher, 747
country, 552; -rock, 762
count the box, to, 696
count the rack, to, 696
county, 542, 570; -fair, 735
coupé, 52, 306
coupled, 746
courber, 278
Courier, 595
court, 89
Court, 577

Courteway, 437
Courthouse, 542
Courtois, 437
cousin, 133, 315, 736
cousin, to, 158
Cousin Jack, 762
co-ut, 158
Coutts, 457
Couwenhoven, 405
Covadonga, 484
cover, 697
Covered Wagon, 588
cow, 86, 122, 291; -boy, 719; -brute, 200; -bug, 232; -cage, 714; -crate, 714; -feed, 752; -flop, 163; -hand, 729, 741; -hide, 771; -juice, 663; -paste, 217; -poke, 741; -puncher, 134; -salve, 747; -shed, 691; -storm, 165; -waddy, 698
Cowan, 421
Cowboy, 595
cowcow, 43
Cow Creek, 540
Coweene, 484
Cowenhoven, 405
Coweta, 484
cowly, 253
Cowper, 402, 457
Cowtry, 460
cowy, 179
Cox, 398
Coxey's army, 755
Coy, 502
Coyne, 421
Coyote State, 638
coyotl, 639
Cozart, 438
Cozella, 484
cozen, to, 314
cozy, 253
CPT, 270
cq, 304
crabat, 247
cracker, 195, 609, 620, 627; -box, 714; -breaker, 733
crackerjack, 748
Crackerland, 609
Cracker State, 609
cracky, 252
craft, 329
cramberry, 164
Crane, 421

crap, 658; -shooter, 658, 749
craps, 658, 746
crashing, 696
crashing chetes, 664
crash-wagon, 719
crass, 73
-crat, 83
crate, 669, 715, 725, 728
crawfish, to, 153, 761
Crawford, 398
crawk, 729
crawss, 83
crazy, 137; -quilt, 593
Crazy Horse, 446
Crazy War, 786
Cream Pitcher of the Nation, 630
creasing-plane, 211
creator, 320
crèche, 317
credie, 669
Credilla, 497
Creed, 520
creek, 79, 80, 170, 186, 574
creep, 695, 752, 755; -joint, 682
creeper, 729
Creighton, 457
Crellon, 502
Crenna, 484
Crenshaw, 454
creole, 628
Creole State, 628
crep, 217, 362
crepe, 317
crepy, 738
Crescent, 322
crew tent, 743
crib, 210, 682, 714
Crichton, 457
crick, 79, 80, 170, 175, 185, 186, 187
cricket, 724
crick in the neck, 80
crickled, 143
crike, 80
Crile, 412
crim. con., 277
criminal connexion, 277
criminal conversation, 277
crimp, to, 120
crip, 678
cripple, to, 121
Crippy, 678

List of Words and Phrases

crisises, 320
crispin, 772
criteria, 318, 320
criterions, 320
crittur, 113
crix, 297
croaker, 674
crock, 756
crocodile tears, 663
Croghan, 457
Cromer, 414
crony, 658
Crook Crab, 132
crook the elbow, to, 663
crop, to, 765
crope, 362
croquignole, 155
cross, 216
crossed arms, 777
crossed up, to be, 718
Cross Keys, 580
crosslegged, 212
crossways, 385
crotch, 179
Crouse, 409
crow, 528, 744; -bait, 749
Crow, 453
Crowan, 457
crowd, 227
Crowell, 453
crow-hop, to, 149, 233
Crowninshield, 454
crow over, to, 746
crow's nest, 715
Crow Wing, 528
cruality, 99
cruel, 390
crum, 295
crumb, 646, 722; -box, 714
crummy, 677, 714
Crunchell, 454
crunnocks, 252
crupper, 718
cruse, 315
crushed, 775
crush out, to, 674
crutch, 179
cryke, 80
Crysick, 449
crystalline, 284
Crystal Star, 448
Cryton, 457
Csokonai, 440
Csongardi, 430
Csüry, 440
cube, 680

Cubéan, 99
Cuckold's Cove, 572
Cudell, 484
Cudjo, 513
cue, 729
cuffer, 253
Cuffy, 513, 515
culchah, 40
cul-de-sac, 50
cullet, 765
cullus, 502
cully, 658
Cumberland, 578
Cumbo, 541
Cumpton, 457
Cuninggame, 460
Cunningham, 398, 470
Cunninghame, 404
cunnyfingered, 232
Cunsbra, 457
cuntery, 99
Cunygam, 460
Cupid, 511
Cupid's itch, 675
cup of coffee, 736
curb, 249, 278, 316; -broker, 278; -hopper, 752; -hopping, 752
curb, to, 278
curbie, 752
curb your dog, 278
cure, 171
Curilee, 502
curl, 191, 192
Curlew, 532
Curl Inn, 579
curly-flower, 269
curmudgeon, 658
currantses, 386
current, 166
curricula, 318
currying, 775
curse, 175
cursetor, 664
cursitor, 664
cush, 653
cushie, 159
cushion, 714, 729, 736
cushti, 653
cuss, 175
Cuss, 451
Custard, 535
Custer, 408, 412
cut, 199, 763, 775
cut, to, 671, 749
cut a melon, to, 773

cutemup, 674
cutie, 646
Cutie, 511
Cutmutton, 451
cut off, to be, 221
cutte, to, 664
cutter, 668
cut paper-dolls, to, 768
cut up Jack and kill Jinny, to, 215
cut up jackpots, to, 685
cut up molly, to, 161
cut up pipes, to, 685
cut the comb of, to, 173
cutting-room, 698
cuttings, 744
cut yourself a piece of cake, 645
Cuyper, 406
Cwnynghame, 460
Cyabell, 122
cyahmly, 86
cyahnt, 86
cyamel, 218
cyandle, 227
cyandor, 227
cyar-, 17, 85, 122, 214, 227
cyc, 697
cyclone, 624; -cellar, 624
Cyclone, 502, 506, 536, 595; -State, 623, 624
cyclorama, 697
cyder, 278
Cylistine, 484
Cylvia, 484, 494
cyo, 171
cyounty, 86
cyow, 86
Cypher, 536
Cyra, 484
Czatkai, 440
Czech, 767
Czyzcwicz, 425
d, 193, 209, 241, 258, 260, 261, 262, 300, 411, 500
d, Norwegian, 435
d, silent, 96, 218, 220
da, 266
d. Ä, 501
daag, 214
Dabaghi, 441
dabimit, 175
Dabney, 484, 493
Dacel, 484
Dachstädter, 412
dad, 111

dada, 266
daddy, 111
Daenliker, 411
daf, 266
Daffodil, 494
dafuwa, 266
dag, 238
Daggett, 532
dago, 674
D'Aguilar, 457
Dágwiller, 457
dahg, 82
dahkey, 211
Dahl, 434
Dahlgren, 432
dahmitory, 230
dahn, 260
Daintree, 457
daisy, 738
Daisybee, 484
Daisy Bell Rise Up and Tell the Glory of Emmanuel, 512
dajije, 266
Dakoming, 540
dal, 431
dalandu, 267
-dale, 534, 563
D'Alesandro, 439
dalfe, 360
Dalgren, 432
Daliah, 519
Daliel, 457
Dallas, 507, 508
dallinger, 654
Dalmac, 577
Dalvin, 502
Dalyell, 457
Dalzell, 457
Dam, 451
dame un dime, 182
damfino, 298
Damfino, 511
damme-boy, 658
damned be him, 372
dampened, 359
damper, 720
damper-pad, 669
Dan, 475, 476, 512
Dana, 484
dance, 36, 69, 122, 131, 159, 187, 214, 218, 227; -hall, 673
dance in the hog-trough, to, 161
dancinest, 387

D. & D., 678
Danelle, 484
danger, 38
danguh, 38
Danial, 484
Daniel, 69, 467, 484, 518, 524
Daniel Conqueror, 448
Daniels, 430
Daniel's Wisdom May I Know Stephen's Faith and Spirit Choose John's Divine Communion Seal Moses Meekness Joshua's Zeal Win the Day and Conquer All, 512
Danine, 484
Danish, 72
da-nite, 296
Danna, 484
Dannine, 484
Danny, 595, 771; -Lou, 484
Dar, 422
DAR, 331
Darbinian, 441
Darby, 79, 454, 455, 456
Dardanella, 484
daredevil, 748
dare I go?, 202
Darel-Gene, 484; -Jean, 484
dare-say, 364
darf, 202
Daring, 587
dark, 79, 685
Dark and Bloody Ground, 627
dark cellar, 722
darkemans, 664
dark horse, 669
Darkies, 449
dark meat, 682
Darlean, 484
Darlene, 484, 498
darling, 374
Darrell-Gene, 484
Darryl, 506
darsn't, 113
darst, 113
dart, 73
Darthilda, 484
Dartmoor, 577
DaRue, 484, 494
Darwin, 465

Daryl, 521
das, 206
dash, 749
dasn't, 169
dast, 169
Dasy, 484, 494
dat, 171
data, 72, 318, 319, 338
daub, 216
dauber, 758
Da'ud, 441
daughter, 199
Daumantas, 429
dauncy, 208, 229
Dauws(e), 406
Dave, 771
Daventry, 457
David, 441, 472, 518, 523, 524, 771
Davies, 402
Davis, 396, 398, 401, 402, 416, 447
Davite, 523
Davy Jones' locker, 721
daw, 314
dawg, 82, 83
Dawnette, 484
dawn patrol, 729
Dāwūd, 441, 523
-day, 781
daylight, 763, 764
Daymono, 502
Dayse, 484
Dayton, 508
dazzle-dust, 707
de, 263, 308, 440
de, Italian, 440
de, Spanish, 436
deacon, 221, 741, 764
dead, 192, 763
dead game, 746
deadhead, 715
dead-in-a-hurry, 763
dead in the shell, 150
dead-man, 176
Dead Man, 535
Dead Mule, 536
dead-pan, 692
dead skin, 670
dead weight, 769
deaf, 80, 81, 174, 211
Deafy, 678
deah, 40
De'An, 484, 494
Deane, 522
DeAnn, 484

List of Words and Phrases 811

dear, 374
dear, to, 359
Death, 449; -Valley, 678
De Bakey, 441
debl, 171
Deborah, 479
debt, 192
debunk, to, 648, 650
début, 317
decádent, 48
decalog, 311
de Casseres, 423
deceased, 358
Decies, 457
decision, 738
deck, 680, 715; -hand, 697
Deck, 511
De Clemente, 439
decollete, 317
décor, 50
décoy, 48
DeDonda, 494
Dee, 502
Dee-áll, 457
DeeAnne, 484
Dee-Dee, 484
Deeds, 409
deef, 80, 81, 120, 174, 185, 186, 187, 211
Deell, 457
deer, 328, 329, 736
Deer, 572
dees, 260
deesh, 235, 260
Déeshees, 457
deestrick, 174, 197
Dee Wayne, 502
def, 80, 81, 211, 708
Defeated, 535
défect, 48
defence, 281, 282, 283, 284, 286
Defender, 446
defense, 279, 281, 283, 285
Defense of the Realm Act, 331
Defiance, 561
deficit, 3, 4
definitely, 295
Degagné, 437
Degonia, 437
DeHarte, 406
Deill, 457
déjeuner, 318
DeJong, 401
DeKina, 484

DeKlerke, 406
DeKype, 406
DeLaine, 502, 506
De la Mare, 457
De La Pasture, 457
Delares, 484
Delargentino, 584
De Lauris, 484
Delavendra, 484
Delavie, 423
delayer, 713
Delbert, 507
Delbrazil, 584
Delbrück, 416
Delcena, 516
Delector, 495
Delette, 484
Delevan, 578
Delft, 99
delicatessen, 51
Delirious, 512
dell, 573, 648
della, Italian, 440
Déllamair, 457
Dellevie, 423
Delmar, 540, 541
Delmarva, 540
Delmarvia, 540
Delor, 507
Deloreans, 584
Delores, 502, 506
De Lores, 484, 494
Deloris, 484
DeLos, 502
DeLoyce, 502
Del Ray, 502, 506
DelRose, 484, 494
Deluft, 99
delve, 360
dé luxe, 49
Delvina, 480
Delymaine, 484
dem, 188, 247
demagog, 295
demand, 214
Demarest, 406
Demetrios, 523
de Meyners, 458
Demis, 484
demi-tasse, 53
Democrat, 595
demonstrate, to, 4
Demosthenes, 523
demuhcrat, 83
den, 171, 684
Dencred, 502

DeNell, 484
Denlinger, 411
denomination, 277
Denva, 493
Denver, 502, 506, 554
Deo, 502, 507
Deoda, 484
dephlegmater, 748
De Pietro, 439
deposite, 311
depot, 211, 318, 337
De Priest, 448
Deputy, 511
Derald, 502
der ältere, 501
Derby, 3, 79
Dereen, 484
der jungere, 501
DeRoin, 502
Deronde, 406
Derounian, 441
Derricksen, 406
derrière, 746
der tag, 781
der wein gehört gekühlt, 202
desate, 78
de Saussure, 438
Deseret, 569
Deseret State, 640
desert, 314; -rat, 138
Desert State, 641
deserve, 79
designer, 669
de Silva, 423
Desire, 593
Des Marest, 406
Desmond, 469
desoive, 155
Des Portes, 438
DesRosiers, 423
dessert, 250, 314
Déssosore, 438
Déssports, 438
det, 266
détail, 48
detainer, 713
detonator, 72
detour, 723; détour, 48
Detta, 484
deuce, 674, 749; -spot, 692
Deucie, 484
Deuteronomy, 512
Devastation, 587
Devereux, 460
device, 285

List of Words and Phrases

devil, 171
Devil, 449
devilinski, 176
Devil's War, 786
devise, to, 285
Devon, 578; Devón, 141
Devora, 519
DeVries, 401
Dévveruh, 460
dew, 84
Dewane, 502
Dewdrop, 484, 495; -Inn, 579
DeWitt, 502
dewnt, 40
Deyell, 457
De Yell, 457
De Young, 401
dey prays, 264
dh, 288, 293, 294, 300, 303
dhan, 300
dhat, 300
dhe, 300
dheez, 300
dhem, 288
dhī, 293
dhīn, 293
dhoe, 301
dhu, 293
di, 308, 440
di, Italian, 440
Diab, 441
diagnose, to, 99
dial, to, 731
Dial, 502
dialect, 228
Dialogue, 449
Dialtha, 484
Diamondback, 596
diamond-cracker, 713
Diamond-Field Jack Davis, 139
Diamond State, 605
Diana, 518
Dianne, 520
diarrhœa, 282
dice, 643
Dice, 537, 561
dices, 386
Dicey Mae, 484
Dick, 476, 523, 746
dickemilch, 208
Dickens, 406
dickey boy, 773
dick-in-a-minute, 232
Dickinson, 406

Dick Smith, 736
Dickson, 406
dicta, 318
did he went?, 246
did it, 346
didn't, 374
didn't none of them, 392
didn't take hardly, 391
did you got, 395
die game, to, 715
diehard, 748
die out, to, 217
Dietrich, 519
Dietz, 409
different than, 337
dig, 272
Di Georgio, 439
dígest, 49
digest, to, 49
digger, 696
digging for gold fish, 766
diklaer, to, 288
Dikran, 523
dilapidated, 726
dilapidato, 725
dilettantes, 319
Dillon, 457
Dillwyn, 457
dilly, 761
diloot, 85
Dimatteo, 440
Dime-a-Mite, 580
Dimitrios, 523
Dimmuck, 457
di'n', 361
Dina, 519
dinah, 668
dindi, 266
din din, 266
Dinette, 497
Dingbat, 449
dingclicker, 158
ding-dong, 759
dinger, 713
dingle-doos, 53
dingo, 678
Dink, 502, 506
Dink Dare, 164
dinky, 714
dinky-doo, 736
dinner's about, 177
di'n't, 361
Diogenes, 582
dip, 670, 743
diplomas, 319
diplomat, 743

diplomata, 319
Dippy, 449
dipsy-dew, 736; -do, 736; -doo, 736; -dow, 736
dip'theria, 97
dip'thong, 97
Dirckssen, 406
dírect, 48
direction, 277
dirndl, 732
dirt, 252, 674, 757
dirty, 755; -camp, 232; -neck, 761
dis, 171
Disa, 484
disahsta, 36
díscharge, 48
disgyíse, 227
dish, 260
dishwasher, 713
dishwater, 674
Dishwater Pond, 540
disk jockey, 729
dismiss, to, 365
displaced person, 780
dísplay, 48
display-ad, 732
Dissonette, 444
distiller, 284
Distler und Derecsenyi zu Dercsen, 440
Distomo, 542
distorter, 765
district, 174, 197
dite, 158
dived, 338
diver, 678
divide, 573
divine, 374
Divorce State, 636
divot, 755
Dixie, 484, 502, 505, 595; -Lou, 484
Dixon, 398, 399
Diyāb, 441
Diyell, 457
dj, 292
d.J., 501
Djagashvilli, 415
djdtcd, 92
djinrichia, 320
Djugashvilli, 415
D.K., 773
dl, 184
do, 266, 294, 363, 542
D.O., 732

List of Words and Phrases

doc, 775
Doc, 502, 506
doch, 203
dock, 248, 249; -monkey, 719
Dockstader, 412
decott, 743
docterin, 99
doctor, 658, 750
Doctor, 516
doctrinal, 47
dodging, 765
Dodis, 484
dodo, 755
Dodo, 514
Do Drive Inn, 580
Doel, 508
doeskin, 775
does you?, 264
does your mother know you're out?, 645
doff, 365
dog, 83, 184, 185, 203, 214, 216, 328, 674, 689, 719, 725, 729, 753, 754, 764, 771, 774; -biscuit, 752; -house, 668, 705, 714; -tag, 778
dog, to, 133
dogie, 238, 741, 770
Dog Pen, 572
dogs, 769
dog-trot house, 232
dogwood, 138; -Winter, 195
doing chores, 114
Doke, 502
Dolaris, 484
dolce, 707
doll, 185, 216
Doll, 451
dollar, 292, 657
dollie, 764
doll's house, 720
dolly, to, 698
Dolly, 480
dolomite, 773
Dolores, 466, 484, 517, 521, 522
Dolph, 476, 507
Dolphin, 536
Dolphus, 502, 506
dolven, 360
don, 365
Don, 476, 524
Donaco, 502

Donald, 521
Donaldine, 524
donate, to, 20
Dondeline, 484
done, 363, 365
done been done, 365
done bought, 365
done burnt up, 365
done did it, 137
done do, 365
done done it, 219, 365
done gone, 365
done got, 365
done it, 142, 346
Don Elda, 484
done married, 365
done show me, 264
Dong, 443
donkey, 163, 713, 720; -doctor, 759
Donna Bee, 484
donner und blitzen, 177
donniker, 685
donor, 280
don't, 123, 260, 337, 342, 348
don't everbody, 393
don't hardly, 392
don't know if, 337
don't nobody, 393
don't you think?, 205
donut, 297, 298
doo, 84
doodlebug, 761, 763
Doodle Bug, 511
do off, 365
do on, 365
door, 184, 214, 230, 314; -shutter, 173
dooty, 84
Doozie, 484
dope, 652, 715, 732, 754, 765, 766, 767
doppich, 202
dor, 314
Dora, 331, 519
Dorabelle, 484
dorado, 613
Dora Lee, 488
Dorathy, 484
Dorcas, 467
Dorchester Gardens, 577
Dorcine, 502
Dorethe, 484
-dorf, 534
do-right people, 680

Doris, 484, 523; -Jean, 484
Dorlye, 484
Dormitory, 230
Doron, 422
Dorotha, 484, 502, 506
Dorothy, 479, 484, 498, 499, 510, 521; -Dot, 525
Dorothye, 484
Dorraine, 484
Dorriss, 484
Dorthea, 484, 523
Dorys, 522
Dose, 449
do she?, 264
do time, to, 673
dotter, 199
double, 668; -cross, 648; -eagle, 755; -header, 737; -sawbuck, 674; -truck, 732
double, to, 729
double frame, to, 698
doubling, 689
Dougall, 404
dough, 310; -beater, 153; -roller, 759
Dougherty, 408
doughman, 772
doughnut, 719, 767
Doughnut, 594
Douglas, 468, 469, 493, 522
Douglass, 448
do-ups, 181
douse, to, 253
dout, to, 238
Dov, 519
dove, 338, 360
Dove, 502, 523
Dover, 566
Dovey, 523
Dovinda, 479
dowager's hump, 738
down, 260, 681, 750
down by the head, 166
down home, 138
down in the mud, 729
down-street, 180
down the Labrador, 253
down the street, 155
down yonder, 685
Doyal, 502
Doyel, 484
Doyle, 502
do you have?, 152

DP, 780
dr., 320
DR, 478
Drabbletail, 226
Drachenblut, 417
drachm, 310
Dracula, 707
draf, 218
draft, 722
draftee, 780
drag, 678, 715, 749, 770
drag-aff, to, 247
dragger, 733
drahmatize, to, 47
drain, 175
Drain, 535
drama, 47
drank, 362
drape, 707
drats, 153
draughtsman, 316
drawed, 165, 362
Dráweda, 457
drawers, 664
Drayton, 588
Drazia, 519
Dreadnaught, 587, 588
dreamed, 226
dream girl, 781
Dream of Allah, 593
dream-stick, 681
Dreamy, 495
dreck, 747
dreen, 120, 154, 175, 185
Dreiser, 424
dremp, 226
dress around, to, 202
dressing, 689
dressing a house, 696
Dressler, 411
dress out, to, 202
dress rehearsal, 729
drew, 362
Drewceller, 494
Drewry, 454
drinked, 165
drinkingest, 388
drinx, 297
driv, 110
drive, to, 233
driver, 774
drive-ur-self, 297
Drogheda, 457
dromedary, 658
drone-cage, 714
droop, 707

drooper, 737, 746
drop, 689, 691, 732; -ball, 253; -band, 770
drop, to, 687
drop a cook, to, 748
drove, 110
drownd, to, 358
drownded, 100, 211, 357
drozzle tail, 158
Druecellar, 484
drug, 361
Druit, 454
Drulla, 484
drum, 674, 713, 756
drummy, 770
drung, 252
Drung, 593
drunk, 362, 645, 646
drunkard, 715
Drusilla, 484
dry-cleansing, 168; -gas, 763; -goods, 248, 249; -hole, 198
dry-land frog, 231
drymop, 168
dry up, to, 689
dt, 258
du, 288, 308
Duane, 465, 502
dub, 262
dub, to, 698
Dub, 502, 506
Dublin, 537
Du Bois, 448
Dubray, 444
ducat, 696
duck, 328, 755; -bill, 776
duck's nest, 763
ducy, 121
dude, 742, 764; -ranch, 742; -wrangler, 713
Dude, 502, 506
dudelsock, 207
Dudelzak, 422
Dudgeon, 449
Dudley, 468, 469
duds, 644, 663
due, 84, 205
duelist, 284
due one a compliment, to be, 172
due to, 337
duff, 759
duffer, 674
Dufresnoy, 572
duivel, 188

duke, 250, 674, **723**
duke, to, 685
duki, 674
dulce, 243
dulcimer, 207
Dullere, 484
Dumaresq, 457
Dumb, 450
dumb act, 692
dumbbell, 646
Dumbell, 449
dumb Isaac, 151
dumbski, 176
Dumérrick, 457
Dummy, 678
dump, 748
dumper, 733
dumps, 696
Duncan, 398, 399
dunch, 252
dungeoneer, 775
dunghill, 746
Dunhuntin, 579
dunk 'n dine, 297
Dunlap, 425
Dunn, 398
Dunrenten, 579
dunt, 260
duódenum, 48
Duphemia, 484
Dupont, 416
Dura, 484
Dürer, 316
DuRonde, 406
Dursteen, 424
Durwood, 521
dust, 84; -eater, 727; -pneumonia, 200; -raiser, 713
Dust, 467
Dust Bowl State, 624
duster, 735, 763
Dustia, 484
Duta, 485
Dutala, 514
Dutchman, 219, 762, 774
duty, 84
DuWayne, 485, 494, 502
Dwain, 502
Dwight, 469, 507
dwy, 252
Dyayell, 457
dyew, 122
Dymoke, 457
Dynama, 485
dynamite, 765

List of Words and Phrases

dynamiter, 773
dypsido, 736
dzadza, 266
dzadzalo, 266
dzagdza, 266
dzambi, 266, 267
Dzhugashville, 415
dziga, 266, 269
Dzimidavičius, 429
Dzio, 425
dzog, 710
dzoga, 266
dzug, 710
e, 18, 71, 72, 73, 79, 158, 185, 260, 291, 292, 300, 306, 402, 409, 410, 500
e, French, 309
eaceworm, 210
'ead, 85
eagle, 740, 754, 755; eye, 713, 740
Eagle, 595; -State, 631
eah, 40
Ealeta, 485
Eames, 453
ear, 214; -ache, 729; -wigger, 667
ear, to, 315
earl, 87
Earl, 507
Earlene, 482
early, 771
Early, 409
Earnberg, 431
Earres, 453
earth, 86
Earthel, 485
Earven, 502
easly, 253
Easlyn, 485
east, 87
Easter, 515
easterly, 253
Eastern Shore Republican, 595
easy, 388
Easy Knee, 528
easy rider, 710
eat, 76
eat crow, to, 648
eating, 260
eatingest, 388
eatmor, 296
eat shop, 580
Eatwell, 580
eaux, 310

Ebaugh, 408
Ebenezer, 591
Eberhart, 411
Ecclesiastes, 512
ecdysiast, 694
ecdysiste, 694
e'cept, 96
echo, 752
Echo, 485, 495
ECITO, 330
eckspres, 310
Economic Intelligence Division of the Enemy Branch of the Office of Economic Warfare Analysis of the Board of Economic Warfare, 330
economics, 72, 250
economy, 282
Ecton, 502
ed, 310, 388
Ed, 475, 476, 478
edads, 177
edah hoe, 557
Edd, 476
Eddene, 485
Eddie, 476, 485, 771
Edel, 417
Edellyn, 521
Edelstein, 421
Edelweiss, 497
Eden, 537
Edenia, 485
Edgar, 518, 703
Edgard, 502, 506
Edgarta, 485
edge, 171, 185
Edgealea, 485
Edice, 485
Edina, 485
Edinburgh, 485, 537
Edith, 519
Edmund, 516
Edna, 521; -Rae, 490
Ednar, 89
Edneau, 485
Edolia, 485
Edonna, 485
Edrin, 485
educated, 764
Eduta, 485
Edward, 462, 472, 485, 510, 516, 518
Edwarda, 485
Edwards, 396, 398, 405

Edwin, 485
Edysol, 502
Edyth, 518
Edythe, 494
ee, 70, 81, 165, 214, 241, 288, 300, 424
Ee-dah-hoo-oo-oo, 557
Eedahoo, 558
eek-, 250
eel, 329
-een, 424
eequal, 288
-eesh, 199
eesue, 199
ee-ther, 32, 77, 78, 186, 187, 214, 230
efekt, 300
effen, 200
ef I had of tuck, 361
ef I taken, 361
egal, 195
Egegik, 552
Egg, 451
egg, 713; -gatherer, 324
Eggleson, 434
eggnog, 159
eggs, 186
Eggs and Bacon, 588
egret caille, 155
Egypt, 615
eh, 70
ei, 291, 410, 424
Eichelberger, 424
EIDEBOEWABEW, 329
Eidel, 485
Eiffel Tower, 582
eigh, 310
Eighteen, 451
Eighter from Decatur, 746
88, 705
eighty-foist, 189
eighty-one, 772
Eigildsen, 434
einmal, 198, 202
Einstein, 424
Eire, 604
Eisenhauer, 409
Eisenhower, 409, 424
Eisner, 424
either, 32, 186, 187, 214, 226, 230
either of these three, 337
ek-, 250, 431
ekal, 164
eksersierz, 306

List of Words and Phrases

-el, 418
Elah, 485
Elaine, 500, 521
Elba, 493
Elbert, 509
elbow, 668; -artist, 765; -grease, 658; -room, 663
Elbow Room, 580
Elcie, 485
elcud, 717
elder, 151, 221
Elderline, 480
Eldo, 502
El Dorado, 613
Eleanor, 499, 518
Eleck, 502
Electamae, 485
elected with, 172
electricity, 72
Eledice, 485
elegazam, 775
Elémer, 524
elephant, 764
Elesten, 502
eleven forty-five, 693
elevingtht, 100
Elgne, 502
Elgretta, 485
Elias, 518
Elicious, 485
Eligh, 502, 506
Elima, 479
Eliot, 469
Elise, 481
Eliza, 513
Elizabeth, 473, 479, 499, 510
elk, 179; -face, 151
Elk Horn, 589
Ella, 463, 485
Ellen, 499, 520
Elleuvinia, 485
Elliott, 396, 398, 399
Ellis, 396, 398, 405
El Louise, 485, 494
Ellsworth, 465
ellum, 100, 175
elm, 175; -peeler, 236
Elmer, 471, 522, 524; -Dee, 502
Elmhurst, 534
Elmonia, 485
El-Mora, 577
Elms, 578
Elnathan, 519
Elodee, 485

Elore, 485
Eloyd, 579
Elpha, 485
El Reno Victory, 584
Elsa, 520
Elseroad, 412
Elsie, 485, 593
Elsroad, 412
Eltham, 414
Eltopia, 567
Eltzroth, 412
eluf, 99
Elura, 485
Elvan, 502
Elvaree, 485
Elvcyd, 502
Elvira, 523
Elvis, 485, 502
Ely, 149
Elza, 502
Elzada, 485
Elzia, 502
em-, 282
Emaelera, 485
Ema Jane, 485
Emalee, 485
Emalou, 485
Emancipation Proclamation, 507
embalmer, 769
Embarras, 528
Embassy, 581
embed, to, 282
embonpoint, 50
embroidery, 215
emcee, 729
Emden, 416
Eme, 485
Emelda, 485
Emer, 485
emergenson, 719
Emeric, 472
em I?, 165
Emi, 485
Emil, 506
Emily, 485, 500
Emitt, 502
Emma, 463, 485, 499, 520
Emmanuel, 518, 590
Emmanuelo, 590
Emmar, 89
Emmet, 472
Emo, 485
Empanel, 282
Empec Court, 577
emperor, 280

empire, 87, 88, 735
Empire, 598; -State, 597, 598; -State Express, 581, 598; -State of the South, 610
Empo, 485
emporia, 319
empt, 253
empty, 253
Empty Basket, 572
Em' Straight-Edge, 139
em they?, 165
em wi?, 165
em yi?, 165
en-, 282
-en, 386
enceinte, 50
enclose, to, 282
Enclyn, 485
encrust, 282
encyclopædia, 282
Endamile, 485
en dat Virginia quintam 597
Endicott, 469
end man, 324
endorse, to, 282
endorsement, 282
endorser, 743
Enel, 502
enema, 320
enemy, 386, 762
energy, 292
engaged, 246
engine, 88
England, 18
English Village, 577
Engracia, 497
enhance, to, 359
Enid, 524
e'nin', 218
enjoy, to, 120, 192
enlarge, to, 211
ennui, 50
enny, 313
Enola, 563
Enolia, 485
enough, 313
enquirer, 282
enquiry, 282
Enrechetto, 485
Enroughty, 454, 455, 456
ensure, to, 282
enthralled, 173
entire, 48
entourage, 50

List of Words and Phrases

entrance, 689
entree, 318
entrench, to, 282
enu, 269
enuf, 300
enuff, 313
enufole, 266
eny, 288, 300
Eola, 485
Eolus, 588
Eötvös, 440
ephedrine, 81
epididymes, 320
epididymides, 320
epididymis, 320
episcopate, 745
Epitaph, 595
épitome, 48, 87
E Pluribus Unum, 508
equal, 164, 195
Equality State, 642
equestrian director, 684
er, 79, 155, 156, 164, 189, 190, 192, 214, 226, 265, 292, 294, 300, 387
Era, 502
eradicator, 686
erbaen, 300
Erdijhelyi, 440
Erdine, 521
Erdis, 508
Erdix, 507
-ere, 382
er hat heimweh, 202
-eria, 133
Eric, 520, 524
Erickson, 398, 430
Erik, 520
Erkert, 459
erl, 190, 191
Erleen, 481
Erliss, 521
Ermyl, 485
Ernadine, 485
Ernest, 518, 523
Ernestine, 485, 520
Ernestyne, 485
Erneze, 485
eroic, 94
Erra, 453
erratums, 320
Errett, 502
Erron, 502
error, 280, 281
errour, 281
ersatz, 781

Ersie, 503
er sollte gesagt haben, 202
erster, 190, 191
Erville, 503
-ery, 133
-es, 436
-es, Portuguese, 436
escheat, 48
Eschscholtzia, 496
Esco, 503
es gibt, 202
eskate, 246
Eskimo, 719, 747
Eson, 503
esophágeal, 48
Espinosa y Pelayo, 436
essen, 307
Essex, 577
-est, 387
establish a raw, to, 252
estate, 246
Esterine, 485
Esther, 521; -Mae, 503
estop, 246
Estra, 503
et, 46, 76, 185, 186, 219
Etalea, 485
Etci, 503
E. T. City, 542
Etelka, 497
(e)ternal, 79
Ethalene, 485
Ethel, 485, 510, 524
Ethelene, 482
Ethelmer, 471
Ether, 513
Ethereal Blue, 594
Ethins, 314
Ethna, 485
Ethol, 485
Ethyl, 485
Ethylyn, 485
etiquet, 295
etiquette, 47
Etna, 485
ETO, 782
Etoyle, 485
Etrulia, 485
etten, 361
étude, 318
eu, 410
Euarda, 485
Eubert, 503
Euclid, 503, 507
Eugen, 519

Eugene, 516
Eugenia, 509
Eulice, 485
eumonia, 253
Eunice, 521
Euphia, 485
Eura, 453
Eurah, 465
Eure, 453
eureka, 613
Eureka State, 613
Euri, 453
Euria, 453
European Central Inland Transportation Organization, 330
European War, 785
Eutanna, 485
Eutaw, 569; -Springs, 569
Eutha, 485
Eutris, 485, 495
Euzelle, 485
evaa, 81
evacuee, 780
Evan, 516
Evannah, 485
Evans, 396, 398
Evarista, 485
Evassa, 485
Eve, 752
Eveline, 485
Evelyene, 485
Evelyn, 500, 505
Evelynne, 485
evening, 144, 173, 218, 253
Evening Star, 582, 592
ever, 81, 172, 237
Everdiena, 485
Everglades News, 595
Everglade State, 613
Evergreen State, 641
Everhart, 411
Ever Mae, 485
Evern, 503
evertite, 296
every, 172
everybody, 369
everyone, 369
everyone-they, 337
everything, 91
E-Vetha, 494
E-Vetta, 485
-evicius, 428
Evilchild, 451
evils, 226
Evitmus, 503

ēvl, 293
evolution, 72
Evon, 485
Evylan, 485
ewa, 240
Ewar, 453
ewe, 658
Ewell, 409
Ewul, 503
-ex, 386
exactly, 218
example, 214
Exaverm, 485
éxcess, 48
excess baggage, 667, 692, 693
excelsior, 597, 598
Excelsior State, 597
exclusive, 99
Executive, 581
exercise, 306
exhaust, 95
exhibit, 95; éxhibit, 48
exhort, 95
Exolda, 485
expectorate, to, 372
expedite, to, 48
expense, 281
expert, 47
explore, to, 139
explosion, 177
explosive, 99
expose, 292
éxpress, 218
express train, 581
exsperimental, 289
Exton, 503
extra, 699
Extra, 511
extraordinary, 7, 18, 39
extra-ordinary, 175
extr'odn'ry, 96
extry, 120
Exum, 497
ex-vice-president, 324
exzerseizah, 259
ey, 78, 288
eye, 269, 292, 300, 715; -brow, 292; -drops, 716; -opener, 772; -winker, 143
Eye, 451
eyeful, 646
eye-ther, 32, 77, 186, 187, 214, 230
Eyre, 453

Eythel, 485
-ez, 436
-ez, Spanish, 436
Ezza, 485
f, 98, 211, 253, 291, 300, 309, 310, 422, 460
f, German, 307
f, Welsh, 460
façade, 317, 318
facer, 732, 764
facies, 87
facultized, 165
Fadjo, 508
Fadwa, 523
Fae, 485
fafa, 266
fah, 40, 192
fahg, 82
Fahrni, 410
Fain, 503
fáinne, 686
Faint-not, 467
fair, 89, 214, 390
Fairview, 572
fairway, 232
fair wind, 166
Fairy, 485, 495; -land, 593
Faith, 468, 479
Falconer, 457
fall, 675
Fall, 159
Fallen Arches, 579
faller, 759
fall guy, 127
falsies, 695
falter, 96
Fama, 487
familyar, 300
famly, 217
fan, 647, 727, 736
fanatic, 736
fance, 736
fancy, 73, 736
Fancy Dan, 735
Fan El, 485
Fanfaron Faaronovich Yomtovson, 415
fani, 560
fanned, to be, 677
Fannie Mae, 488
fans, 736
Fanshaw, 457
fant, 195
fantasia, 47
fantods, 644
fantom, 291, 294

fapid, 717
far, 5, 230
far be it from me, 368
Fareign, 503
Farhat, 523
Farl, 485
farm, 79, 88, 722
farmer, 763
Farmington, 566
far more superior, 388
Farrar, 453
farrier, 620
farther, 79
Fassnakday, 255
fast, 69, 150, 159; -house, 734
Fast Horse, 445, 446
fastly, 121
fastnacht, 208
Fastnacht, 255
Fastrill, 541
fat, 689; -cake, 208; -cat, 166
Fat, 450
fa'ter, 96
father, 22, 71, 101, 241
Father Divine, 774
fathom out, to, 253
fat stock, 767
Fatter, 449
faucet, 101
Faucette, 495
faultive, 211
fause, 195
favor, to, 153
favour, 280, 286
fawg, 82
Fawkner, 457
fawney, 686; -man, 686; -rig, 686
Fay, 506
Faye, 503
Faynola, 485
Fayrene, 485
fayt, 62
Faythe, 485
fear, 171
Fear-not, 467
feather, to, 121
featherbedding, 776
feathered, 749
Featherstonhaugh, 457
feature, 84
featured, 689
feat-yur, 84
February, 175

List of Words and Phrases 819

Feb'uary, 96, 175
Feby, 485, 494
federalist, 320
feed-bag, 725
feeder, 692, 693
feel bad, to, 389
feeld, 288
feel dauncy, to, 200
Feerstonhaw, 457
fees, 261
feesh, 199, 235
Feesonhay, 457
feessure, 199
feet, 758
feetses, 386
Feichter, 414
Feighter, 414
Fein, 417, 424; -stein, 420, 424
feisty, 140
Feivl, 516
-feld, 423
Feleky, 440
Felesta, 485
Felicia, 519
Felix, 519
fell, 573
fella, 174
feller, 90, 253
fellow, 174
Felmet, 503
Fema, 485
Femme, 572
femurs, 320
fen, 573
fence, 658
fender, 723
Feng, 443
Fennick, 457
Fenton, 420, 421
Fenwick, 457
Ferenz, 524
Ferguson, 398, 399, 413
fermentation, 306
Fermetta, 485
fern, 306
Fern, 503
Ferne, 521
Ferndale, 534
Fernós-Isern, 451
Ferra, 485
ferret out, to, 145
ferrididdle, 200
Festonhog, 458
fete, 318
fête, 50, 62, 317

Fétherstonhaw, 567
fettkuchen, 208
fetzen, 654
fetzen, to, 654
Feuerstein, 413
Fever Sheet, 596
few, 84, 226
fey, 207
ff, 460
Ffoulkes, 460
F.F.V., 581
fi, 308
fiancé, 53
fiancée, 50, 318
fibre, 282
fibrillation, 48
fibromas, 320
fi' cents, 96
Fichter, 414
fiddle, 720
fiddle-a-ding, 165
Fido, 594
Fiechter, 414
field, 715
-field, 563
Field, 434
fienal, 288, 289
Fiery Siding, 536
Fiescher, 414
Fietcher, 414
fifteenyearold, 325
fifth, 218; -estate, 728
fifty-fifty, 648
fig, 272
Fight for Right, 785
fightingest, 144, 387
Fight to Live, 785
figure, 84
file, 658
filibuster, 658
filibustier, 658
filler, 744
Filleul, 485
filling-station, 677, 691, 723
fillum, 99, 100
film-burner, 766
Filna, 516
filosofy, 296
filto-kleen, 296
fin, 253
Finace, 503
fínance, 48
financier, 620
find back, to, 237
Findlay, 457

fine, 125; -haired, 120
Fineboy, 448
Finette, 480
finger, 294, 721; -wringer, 704
Fingerville, 568
Finis, 503
finished, 337, 749
fink, 777
Finkelstein, 415, 421; -Arms, 577
Finly, 457
Finn, 421
fipper, 253
fire, 5; -board, 140, 226; -boss, 761; -boy, 713; -cracker, 724; -drill, 738; -eater, 767; -engine, 749; -plug, 736; -ship, 658; -works, 736
fired, 749
fireman, 753
Firenza, 540
Fireworks, 535
first, 379; -class, 248; -rate, 248
firstie, 693
first man down, 727
first-of-May, 684
first reader, 163
Fischer, 422
fish, 261, 269, 662, 674, 736, 763; -bowl, 729; -eyes, 674; -horn, 705
fisher, 313
Fisher, 396, 398
fishes, 328
fishing tool, 762
fishpole, 699
fishuer, 313
Fiske, 461
fissure, 313
fist, to, 253
fisterris, 728
fisticuff, to, 172
fith, 218
fits-u, 296
fit the mitt, to, 667
Fitzgerald, 398
Fitz-Raulf, 469
five-by-five, 707
fives, 743
five-specker, 674
fix, to, 248, 249, 338
fix-up, 680
fizz, 133, 707

List of Words and Phrases

fizzle-dust, 149
Fjeld, 434
flack, 703, 729
Fladen, 434
flag, 731, 748; -collar, 211
flagary, 164
Flag of Our Union, 595
flak, 703, 781
flake, 166
Flake, 503
flame-thrower, 722
Flamingo, 581
flannel-mouth, 693
flared, 166
flash, 685, 694
Flashlight, 596
flat, 573, 697, 734; -foot, 772; -head, 756, 759; -jointer, 666; -out, 220; -toned, 232; -wheel, 715, 761
flatting, 753
Flavel, 503
flavior, 151
flavor, 151
flea-bag, 756; -box, 735
fleas and ants, 711
Flechter, 414
Fledarea, 485, 510
Fleming, 420
flesh, 704; -pedlar, 729
Flesicher, 420
Fletcher, 414
flicker, 678
Flickertail State, 636
fliegerabwehrkanone, 703
flies, 689
Fliesmann, 416
flinch, 217
flingline, 741
flink, 166
Flint, 413, 421
flip, to, 715
flipper, 253
flit, to, 206
flitting, 206
flivver, 726, 728
flivveritis, 727
float, 755, 771
float, to, 208
floater, 747
floating, 767
floats, 689
Floay, 485
Flodeen, 485
Floeeta, 485

flood, 697
flookum, 685, 686
floor, 122; -boarding, 719; -logger, 740
floozum, 686
flop, 677, 774; -house, 677
flopper, 678
Floradawn, 485
Florence, 82, 216, 505, 540; -Towers, 577
Florestine, 485
Florian, 416
Florida, 82; -lime, 269
Floridy, 544
florist, 306
Florns, 503
florrist, 306
Floscella, 485
floss, 654
Flosye, 485
flottant, 155
flounder, 329; -foot, 754
Flouzelle, 495
flow, 246
Flowanna, 485
flowed, 246
Flowerdew, 449
Flower State, 614
flowing, 246
flows, 246
Floyd, 403, 507
fluent, 85
fluff, 729
fluff off, to, 695
Flume, 595
flunkey, 174, 753, 759
flush, 773
flute, 84, 253, 773
fly, 758, 775; -blow, 740; -cake, 752; -floor, 697; -pie, 752; -swatter, 767
fly blind, to, 727
fly-blow, to, 165
Fly-fornication, 467
Flying Angel, 448
Flying Hawk, 446
flying too low, 719
flyman, 697
flyoot, 84
fly the coop, to, 143
F. O., 778
foalded, 358
fochts, 151
foci, 320
focuses, 320
foerth, 288

fœtus, 282
fog, 184, 228, 715; -horn, 705
fogger, 735
foggy, 251
fogy, 663
foi, 308
Foil, 503
foist, 189, 191, 265, 379
Fokes, 460
folded arms, 777
fole, 195
fo le enu, 266
Foljambe, 457
folks, 151
folkses, 386
follow her around, to, 719
Foma, 515
Fomby, 485
Foncilla, 485
Fondanell, 485, 495
Fond du Lac, 561
fone, 296
Fononda, 497
foo, 84
food, 241
Fooks, 460
fool, 195
fooler, 735
Fool Head, 445
Fooljum, 457
foon, 681
footch, 674
foot-mop, 139; -pie, 195
foots, 689
foozled up, 778
for, 204, 234, 352
force, 246
forci, 319
-ford, 534, 563
Ford, 398, 405, 753
for do that, 240
fore, 5
forehead, 95, 186
foreign, 82, 216
Foreigner State, 602
forest, 82, 216
Forest, 436
forever, 300, 316
for-ever, 283
for ever, 282, 283, 286, 300
forevermore, 177
forgetting, 284
fork, 573, 658
fork a horse, to, 138, 742
forkloesher, 301

List of Words and Phrases

formulæ, 319
Forney, 410
fornicator, 47
forrard, 164
Forsha, 485
Forster, 402
fort, 719
Fort Dodge, 583; -Duquesne, 534
for the church, 722
Forthfifth, 449
Fortituda, 480
for to go, 394
fortun, 114
fortune-teller, 658
forty, 668
forty-four boy, 771
forward, 164, 771
fossile, 311
fossnocks, 208
Foster, 396, 398, 402, 406
fotch, to, 248
foto, 291, 295
fotog, 295
fotograf, 296
fotografer, 295
fotographer, 295, 296
fouled up, 778
Foulfish, 451
Foulis, 457
foul-mouthed, 663
Foundation, 322
foundry, 755
fountaineer, 772
four, 222
fourble, 763
four first, 337
Four-Killer, 566
fourscoreandseven, 324
fourteen and a half, 767
Fowls, 457
fox, 328, 329
Fox, 398, 409
foxhole, 777
Foy, 485, 503
Fra, 485
frack-coat, 247
fractured, 695
frag-grant, 175
fragile, 72
Fragoletta, 485
Fraidy, 511
frame, 699, 700
framer, 774
Francelia, 486
Francescone, 439

Francisco, 522
Francopolous, 523
Frank, 439, 462, 497, 522, 523, 524
Frankie Bell, 486
Franklin, 461, 470, 471, 523, 531, 537, 562, 588
Franklin Delano, 470
Franklinina, 486
Franz, 519
frate, 295
fräulein, 53
frawst, 83
Fray, 486
Frechter, 414
Fred, 475, 476
Fred Cut Grass, 444
Freddie Mae, 486
Frederick, 524
Frederique, 503, 506
Freedman, 421
Freedom's War, 785
Free-gifts, 467
Freelin, 486
free-list, 688
Freeman, 398, 595
Free Press, 595
free ride, 699
Free State Brewery, 604; of Maryland, 603
Freestone State, 600
Freewill, 592
freeze, to, 687, 740, 763
Freeze, 515
freezed, 165
freezer, 714
Freeze-ting-haze, 458
freinschaft, 205
Frema, 486
Frena, 498
French, 748
French it, to, 765
Frenchman, 776
French State, 628
frency, 194
frensy, 194
frersh, 198
fresh, 198, 230
fress, to, 255
fressen, 255
Freud, 417
Freude, 417
Freudman, 417
Freund, 409
freundschaft, 205
Freyerstone, 414

Frida, 519
Friday face, 669
Fried, 417
fried bedpost, 751
Frieden, 417
Friedman, 417, 421
friend, 682
Friend, 409
Frietschie, 409
frijole, 51
Fritjof, 520
Fritsche, 409
Fritz, 475, 476, 594, 678
frocker, 674
Froeda, 486
frog, 184, 185, 216, 684; -eye, 776
Frog, 511
frog-eye gravy, 140
Frog in the Middle, 132
Frog Tanks, 553
Frohman, 689
from, 262
From-above, 467
front, 253, 771
front-money, 773
front of the house, 689
front steps, 162
frontyard, 163
froo, 171
Frood, 457
froon, 262
Frost, 435
frostbite, 218
Froude, 457
Frugality, 582
fruit salad, 734, 753
fryer, 210
frying, 729
fu, 681, 778
Fu'ād Sāba, 523
fubar, 778
fubbs, 658
Fuchs, 409
fuehrer, 316
fufu, 266
fuh coat, 192
führer, 316
fukfuk, 266
fula, 266
fulafafa, 266
Fuller, 398, 399
full grain, 775
full house, 652
full stop, 323
fumb, 707

822   *List of Words and Phrases*

fumble-heels, 165
funeral glide, 728
Fung, 443
fungo, 736
funguses, 320
Funny Louis, 560
funny sheet, 760
fur, 89, 253
Furious, 587
furlo, 291
furmentaeshon, 306
furn, 306
Furnace Hill, 592
furniture, 723
furst, 300
Fürst, 408
fuse, 199, 313
fuskit, 236
fuss, to, 663
fustest, 387
fuzz, 668, 670; -ball, 766
g, 57, 92, 98, 99, 114, 260, 291, 300, 411, 425, 431, 438, 460, 500, 726
g, final, 91
g, Swedish, 431
Gaad, 214
Gaarden, 435
gabber, 729
Gables, 577
gabriel, 705
gabrielle, 156
gadget, 686, 694
Gae, 486
gafa, 266
gaff, 746
gaffer, 252, 684, 699, 718, 761, 762
gaffoon, 729
gag, 729; -man, 699
gag, to, 658
Gage, 470
gagen, 76
Gagne, 437
Gahd, 175
gahs, 47
Gail, 506, 520, 522
Gaillard, 438
Gaines, 453
Gainsborough, 421
Gainsburg, 423
galapago, 726
galch, 654
Galeen, 486
galgener, 654
Galilee, 451

Gallagher, 457
Gallaher, 457
gallied, 166
gallop, 726
galloper, 761
galloping, 699
Gallows, 449
gallows-frame, 762
gallus, 108, 153
galón, 742
Galsworthy, 457
Galt, 578
galvanized iron, 779
Galway, 744
galways, 645
Galween, 486
gam, 166
gambol, 315
Game Cock, 582
Gamecock State, 608
Gamelle, 486
Gamoca, 541
gan, 664
Gananoque, 573
gancho, 770
gandy-dancer, 678, 713
gang, 658, 774; -buster, 355
ganglia, 319
gangster, 672
gangway, 165, 212
ganov, 653, 670
GaNun, 452
gaol, 310
gap, 200, 573, 574
Gara, 486
Garabed, 523
garage, 53, 723; garáge, 49
garagee, 253
garbage, 733; -man, 324
Garcia, 435, 555
garçon, 317
garden, 86, 163, 214, 227, 715
gardener, 736
Garden of the West, 614
Gardens, 577
Garden State, 601, 623
garding, 91
Gardner, 398, 425
Gareld, 503, 506
Garfakis, 523
Garfield, 523
gargle, to, 674
Garguerite, 486, 494

Garl, 503, 506
garment, 227
Garnada, 486
Garnet, 472
Garnett, 439
garret, 110
Garrett, 406
garrison, 214
Garrison, 406, 465
Garsha, 555
Garver, 411
garvey, 181
Garvey, 448
gas, 47, 644, 723; -drinker, 734; -mask, 47; -pipe, 705
Gas Hill, 536
gasp, 73
gastritis, 81
gat, 672
gatam, 654
gate, 706, 715
Gates, 409
Gateway to the West, 597, 623
Gatha, 486
Gathergood, 451
Gatling-gun, 672
gatzam, 654
gaunt, 214
Gaunuhnauqueeng, 573
Gauthier, 437
Gawdy, 469
Gawlsworthy, 457
gawn, 83
gay-cat, 677
Gaygun, 457
Gaylene, 486
Gaynelle, 486
Gaytree, 503
gazaroo, 253
Gazelle, 486
gazer, 314, 680
Gazette, 595
gazoonie, 678
gb, 717
Geann, 486
Gearldina, 486
geburtstag, 739
Geddes, 452
gee, 675, 767
Gee, 451
Geechee, 265
geedus, 685
geek, 684
Geeky, 457

List of Words and Phrases 823

geesen, 386
geeses, 386
Gee-Whiz, 511
gee-yen, 681
geezer, 680
gegen, 202, 203
gegin, 76
gehst du mir?, 170
geht es euch allen gut?, 379
geige, 207
geik, 207
Geikie, 457
ge-irl, 18
geisha, 320
gelatine, 729
Gelbfisch, 419, 420
Gelda, 486, 495, 498
Gell, 460
gelt, 658, 685
G-E-M, 579
Gemmalee, 486
Gem of the Mountains, 614
Gem State, 614
gemütlichkeit, 317, 327
Gene, 476, 518
Geneal, 486, 516
General, 594
general-issue, 779; -purpose, 784; -purpose car, 784
Genia, 486
genitive singular, 377
Genius of Liberty, 595
Genóa, 141
Genoese, 385
Gent, 451
Gentervee, 495
gentile, 221
gentleman passenger, 165
gentry morte, 664
genuine, 144, 775
genuinly, 295
genuses, 320
geography, 179
Geoghegan, 403, 457
geografy, 295
geography, 179
Georg, 411
George, 462, 465, 472, 510, 513, 523, 524, 593
George Dewey, 470
George Eddie, 752
Georgeilein, 486
George Spelvin, 689

George Washington, 581, 740
George Washington Thomas Jefferson Andrew Jackson, 512
Georgia May Virginia Dare Martha Annie Louise, 512
Georgian, 577
Geraldine, 484
Gerasimopoulos, 440
Gerber, 411
Germany, 540
germ-killer, 734
Gerold, 503
Geronia, 486
Gerretse, 406
Gerrittsen, 406
Gertrude, 518, 520, 703
Gervaise, 438
Gesnia, 486
Gestapo, 331
get, to, 86, 202
get a bush bond, to, 674
get a feel, to, 180
get a good scald on, to, 177
Getalea, 486
get a parole, to, 674
get awake, to, 202, 254
get-away, 648
get in bad, to, 127
get-off, 706
get one's goat, to, 234
get religion, to, 143
get sick, to, 337
get the rocking chair, to, 715
get together, to, 648
get to go, to, 152, 204
get to windward, to, 165
get-up, 754
get up, to, 674
get whacky, to, 707
Getz, 410
geuil, 189
geyser, 237, 314
Géza, 524
gfar, 654
G. F. U., 778
gh, 310, 408
gh, Italian, 308
Ghaska, 486
Ghost, 451
ghost, 678, 689, 691, 731; -writer, 644

ghotti, 309
ghoughphtheightteeaux, 310
Ghyneth, 486
GI, 755, 779, 780, 785; -Bill of Rights, 780; -bucket, 779; -can, 779; -food, 779; -girl, 779; -haircut, 779; -hop, 779; -Jane, 779; -Joe, 779, 780; -kraut, 780; -lemonade, 779; -sky-pilot, 779; -soap, 779; -struggle, 779; -war, 779
Giacobbe, 439
Gianni Schicchi, 38
gib, 171
gibbet, to, 158
Gibran, 441, 523
Gibson, 398
Gid Inn, 579
Giffersonne, 453
gift, 86
gig, 272
gig back, to, 150
giggle-smoke, 681
Gilbert, 398, 420
gilding, 731
Gilkes, 457
Gilleen, 486
Gillette, 735
gilly, 685
Gilsey, 578
gimbal tripod, 699
gimcrack, 645, 658
ginger blue bird, 177
gingerbread, 663, 724
Gingerich, 410
ginger-leap, 165
Ginsberg, 423
Ginsborg, 420
Ginsborough, 423
Ginsburg, 423
Ginsburgh, 423
Ginsbury, 423
Ginter, 411
Gintner, 411
Ginzberg, 423
Giori, 442
Giovanni, 400
gipsy, 719, 769
Gipsy, 652
Girardeau, 438
girl, 18, 214, 260, 645, 646; -scout, 669
Girl, 449

girl I go with's, 394
girling, 149
girls, 86
Girtha, 486
gismo, 731
git, to, 340
gitbox, 705
gitter, 705
Git-Up-and-Git, 536
give, 171
give a passage, to, 254
give a wide berth to, to, 721
give him goodbye, 205
give him right, 205
give him scissors, to, 172
give him the B. R. U., to, 695
give me a good-bye, 230
given-name, 477
give one the flit-flaps, to, 151
give tittie, to, 121
givey, 121
gizmo, 731
Gizzard, 534
gk, 261
gl, 184
glaans, 300
Gladdis, 486, 494
gladiole, 384
Gladis, 486
gladness, 184
Gladous, 486
glad rags, 234
Gladson, 503
Gladstell, 541
Gladstone, 522, 578
Glad Tidings, 567
Gladyce, 486
Gladys, 486
Glahms, 457
Glamis, 457
Glamora, 486
glamor-girl, 703
glance, 214
Glanda, 486, 495
Glary Ann, 486
Glasgow, 556
glass, 22, 60, 218; -arm, 717, 722, 736
Glassie, 486
glasyers, 664
Glea, 486
glean, 292
gleep, 707

Gleichen, 414
glen, 292, 582
Glen, 582; -Beach, 583; -City, 583; -Hollow, 583; -Rapids, 583; -Rio, 583
Glenace, 503
Glendor, 521
Glenneth, 503
Glenoulia, 486
Glenrico, 528
glick, 205
glide, 360
glim, 658
glimmers, 724
glimpse, 301
glimse, 301
Glineva, 486
Glinner, 486
glissando, 707
Glitha, 495
glo, 298
glod, 360
glode, 360
Gloe, 486
gloo, 85
Glore, 503
Gloria Dei, 590
Gloriola, 486
Glorious Illumination, 448
glory, 715; -hole, 754; -wagon, 714
glose, 314
Gloster, 543
Gloucéster, 543
Glovetta, 486
Glowrene, 486
glows, 314
glow-worm, 766
Glucinda, 486
glück, 205
Glück, 408
glue, 85; -pot, 760
Glue, 449
glut, 173
glutch, to, 253
glutton, 629
glymmer, 664
Glymph, 449
G-man, 671, 672
gn, 310
gnat-tank, 785
gnaw, 360
gnawn, 360
gnew, 360

go, 203, 230
goal, 278
Goat, 511
goat, 328, 658, 725; -meat, 674; -nest, 725
gob, 761, 770
go-back land, 150
go backstage, to, 688
gobbledegook, 53
gobble-pipe, 705
Gobbler's Knob, 568
gobby, 253
go behind the plank, to, 734
go behind the stick, to, 734
gobo, 699, 731
gobos, 731
gob-pile orator, 761
gob-stick, 705
go by the board, to, 165
go by water, to, 181
go-cart, 714
go coasting, to, 681
god, 320; -box, 705
God, 175, 203, 214, 215, 216, 228, 322
go-devil, 748, 763
God from the World, 262
go-dig, 748
go down, to, 674
Godspenny, 451
goelan, 155
goer-by, 226
Goerg, 411
Goering, 316
Goetz, 409, 410
Goforth, 449, 568
gofta, 151
go-giver, 747
go gooseberrying, to, 677
go Hollywood, to, 704
goil, 134, 188, 260
going, 171
goingest, 388
going some, 338
Gola, 265
G'Ola, 486, 494
Golboro, 423
Gold, 417; -berg, 421, 423; -boro, 423; -fish, 419, 420; -hill, 423; -State, 612, 613; -stein, 418, 423, 424, 447;

List of Words and Phrases

-stone, 423; -wyn, 419, 420
gold-digger, 759
golden hours, 722
Golden State Limited, 581
gold room, 723
Goldsborough, 423
Goldston, 423
Golebiewski, 426
Goletha, 486
golluf, 99
Golson, 423
Gomez, 435
Gommerray, 486
Gomorrah, 535
goms, 668
Gondra, 486
gone, 83, 216
gone and done, 394
gone fishing, 715
gone sucker, 615
gong, 187, 681
gonger, 681
gonk, 692
gonna, 365, 367
Gonyer, 437
Gonzalez, 435
goober, 267
Goober, 610; -grabber, 610; -State, 610
Gooch, 454
goochy, 195
Goochey, 437
good, 390, 645
good and, 338, 394
Goodbeer, 431
Good Book, 385
goodby, 324
good-by, 324
good-bye, 324
Good Friday, 767
Goodie Goodie, 580
Goodman, 409
Good Man, 226
good-morning, 248
Goodnight, 535
Good Shepherd, 590
good theatre, 689
goods-train, 250
Good Thunder, 561
goody, 674
gooey, 754, 767
goof, 646; -butt, 681; -pill, 682
goofer, 718

goofy, 732, 768
goog, 686
goo-goo eyes, 644
gook, 778
goom, 120
goon, 646, 776; -squad, 776
go on a sleighride, to, 681
go on the breeze, to, 253
goop, 150
goose, 715, 748; -cap, 208; -egg, 145; -ground, 208; -hair, 742; -heaven, 150; -walk, 733
goose, to, 127, 145, 219, 645
Goose, 511
gooseberries, 677
goose it, to, 719
goot, 217
go over the range, to, 134
go over the wall, to, 674
GOP, 331
gopher, 668, 718, 733, 748
Gopher State, 630
Gor, 427
Gora, 503
Gorčiansky, 427
Gordon, 398, 416, 435, 438, 509, 521
Gordons, 438
Gorfein, 424
Görg, 440
gorilla, 667
Göring, 316
gorming, 158
go round, to, 688
Goschen, 414
Goshen, 570
go slo, 388
go slow, 337, 388, 389
go slowly, 389
go south, to, 150
gospel-fowl, 232, 674
Gospel Swamp, 536
Gossett, 438
gossipest, 388
goster, to, 181
got, 340, 363
Gotha, 503
go through the Temple, to, 222
go to bat for, to, 737
Gotobed, 449, 451
Gotoff, 449

go-to-hell collar, 745
go to oil, to, 253
go to the lake, to, 170
go to town, to, 706
Gott, 536
gotta, 363, 365
gotten, 337, 363, 395
gotten hell, 167
Götterdämmerung, 317
Gottfried, 519
Gouge, 454; -Eye, 535, 536
Goughenheim, 423
Gould, 421
go under the table, to, 717
go upstairs, to, 716
Gourdin, 438
Gourd Neck, 534
Gov, 507
Government, 322
government-man, 672
governor, 111, 218, 280, 459, 684
gove'nor, 186
governour, 280, 281
govrenment, 99
gow, 208
go wild, to, 763
go with, to, 170
gown, 86
gowster, 680
Goy, 503
Gp, 784
grab, to, 771
grab-bag, 707; -gutter, 139; -joint, 684
grabber, 713
grabble, to, 132
grab the apple, to, 742
Grace, 468, 523, 590
Gracella, 494
gracious, 374
grade crossing, 250
Gradena, 486
graet, 288
graf, 298
Graff, 410
graft, 668
grafter, 686
Graham, 398, 405
gra'ma, 97
Gramercy, 575
grampa, 97
Gramps, 783
grand, 683
Grandma, 593

List of Words and Phrases

Grandmother's Fan, 593
grandstand play, 737
Granger, 454
Granite State, 599
granny, 770
grant, 214
Grant, 398, 399, 404, 470
grantor, 743
Grantsville, 679
grapefruit, 746
Grape State, 613
Grapevine, 450
grass, 25, 36, 159, 171, 184, 187, 681, 752, 757
grassee, 179
Grasshopper, 553; -State, 623, 624
Grava-Nell, 486
gravel-train, 752
Graves, 458
grave-stones, 165; -stew, 752; -yard, 592, 763, 764
gravy, 708
Gray, 398, 442
Gray Goose, 596
Gray's Inn-rd., 322
Gray Snow, 545
grazer, 736
grease, 674; -gun, 740; -joint, 684; -room, 699
greasy, 123
great, 76
Great Central State, 636
Great Gut, 540
gredientses, 386
Greece, 540
greefo, 681
Greeg, 427
green, 168, 758; -bag, 658; -beans, 231; -eye, 715
green, to, 262
Green, 396, 398, 402, 409, 461
Greenberg, 421
Greene, 402, 537
greenhead, 663
Greenhorn, 663
green horn, 682
greenhouse, 95, 675, 727
Green Mountain Boy, 599
Green Mountain State, 599
green pea, 722
Greenwich, 5
Greenwood, 438
Gregg, 435, 458

Greguška, 427
Greider, 411
Greig, 435, 458
gren, 431
grenadier, 620
gret, 314
Grevil, 468
Greville, 469
grex, to, 202
grey, 282
grid, 697
grief, 328
Grieg, 435
grieves, 328
grievious, 100
grifa, 681
Griffin, 398
grifo, 681
grift, 668, 683
Grigonis, 428
grimance, 100
grind, to, 694
grind auction, 678
grinders, 659
grindstone, 209
grintstown, 209
grip, 689, 691, 697, 729
grippers, 724
gris gris, 154
grist, 215, 235
Grit, 535
grits, 144, 215
groan-box, 705, 729
Grog, 450
Groom, 228
groove, to be in the, 706, 711
groper, 659
Grosscup, 412
Grosse Pointe, 561
Grosskopf, 412
grouch, 764
ground-cloth, 689; -floor, 721; -gripper, 727; -horse, 707; -lead, 759
grounded, to be, 719
groundhog, 129, 161, 207, 234, 713, 718
groundhog case, 173
Ground Hog's Glory, 536
Ground-Hog State, 631
ground oak, to, 181
grounds, 384
groupe de tentes, 573

grouse, 328, 329
-grove, 563
Grove, 410
Groveline, 486
Grover, 570
Grover Cleveland, 470
groves, 385
growed, 165, 362; -up-pest, 387
grown upest, 226
grub, 11, 644, 663
Gruber, 411
grubstake, to, 761
Grün, 409
grunt, 713, 718; -iron, 705
grunt, to, 219, 255
grunzen, 225
Gruver, 411
Gry, 422
GU, 755
Guam, 588
Guandoln, 486
Guansignougua, 573
guard, 214
Guarinot, 439
Guarito, 486
guba, 266, 267
Gubernator, 449
guck, 739
Guddine, 438
guecha, 320
Guela, 486
Guen, 486
Guengerich, 410
Gueresy, 486
Guertau, 437
gues, 131
guess, to, 248
guesser, 735
guess-stick, 724
gugaw, 659
gugelfranz, 654
gugelfrenzin, 654
Guggenheim, 423
guide, 214
guillotin, 50
guillotin, to, 765
Guilyard, 438
guinea, 776
Guinesberg, 423
gúitar, 49
Guitar, 449
Guizot, 437
gulch, 574, 761

List of Words and Phrases

Gulf State, 614; -States, 614
Gullah, 265
gum, 120, 680, 724
gu-marnín, 248
gumbo, 267, 769
Gumboil, 451
gummas, 320
gummer, 740, 770
gummy, 662, 686
gun, 302, 670, 680, 736, 756, 766; -boat, 683; -moll, 670
gun, to, 776
Gun, 413
Gunderson, 434, 435
Gunnar, 520
gunnysacked, 719
gunpowder, 659
Günther, 411
guntzel, 678
gurry, 750
Gus, 476, 523
Guscas, 425
gush, 235
gusher, 763
Gushing, 450
Gustafsdotter, 431
Gustafson, 430
Gustafsson, 430, 431, 432
gut, 715; -bucket, 706; -burglar, 759; -eater, 742; -fatter, 764; -hammer, 759; -line, 741; -shanty, 764
gut, to, 674
Gutman, 414, 422
Gutmans, 409
guts-ache, 179
gutter, 764
guv'ment, 97
guvner, 218
guy, 652
Guyenn, 503
guyl, 180
Guynzburg, 423
guzzly, 674
Gwendel, 503
Gwendolyn, 518
gwine, 171, 248
Gwladys, 486, 582
gwlgw, 92
gwlts, 92
gwuq, 446
Gwzcarczyszyn, 425

gyarden, 85, 86, 139, 171, 214, 229
gyarlic, 227
gyate, 218
gyide, 227
Gyilil, 486
gyirl, 86, 229
Gyle, 503
gymnasia, 319, gymnasiums, 319
gynæcology, 282
gyney, 755
Gyongyosy, 440
gyp, 232, 696, 769
gyp, to, 652
gyve, 681
gz, 292
h, 251, 300, 418, 426, 427, 432
h, German, 307
h, intrusive, 95, 96, 191
h, silent, 57, 92, 93, 94, 95, 137, 238, 253
h, Spanish, 307
h, Swedish, 432
ha, 308, 370, 422
habben, 366
haben, 366
Habert, 502
Habib, 523
habit, 73, 94
habitual, 94
hacienda, 762
hack, 668, 674, 714; -hand, 719
hackamore, 742
Hackett, 458
hadda, 365, 394
Haddon Hall, 577
hadn't, 233
hæmorrhage, 282
Hagen, 434
Hagiti, 422
Ha Ha, 572
hahly, 212
hai, 308
haid, 171
Haidbura, 427
Hail, 515
Hailstone, 449
hain't, 340
hair, 92; -do, 738
Hair, 449
hair-dressing-parlor, 738

hairpin, 669, 678
Hairston, 447
Hakala, 429
Hal, 475
halb-bruder, 151
Haleene, 482
Haley, 422
half, 90, 131, 171, 199, 230; -brother, 151
half horse and half alligator, 617
half past, 28
half seas over, 659, 721
half-ton four-by-four command-reconnaissance car, 784
half twain, 721
Halili, 422
halitosis, 732
Halkett, 458
hall, 188
Hall, 396, 398, 402, 409, 435, 527
Hallam, 472
Hallijean, 486
hallo the house, 618
Halloween, 486
hallucination, 93
halo, 319
haloes, 319; halones, 319; halos, 319
Halstead street, 141
Halsteinsgaardbakken, 434
halve, 74
Halvor, 520
ham, 689, 690, 717, 731, 766, 768; -meat, 140; -snifter, 764; -tree, 764
-ham, 46
Ham, 451
Hama, 515
Hamblen, 453
hambone, 690
hamburger, 738
-hame, 543
hamfatter, 690
Hamilton, 398, 470, 531
Hamina, 519
Hamlet, 466, 689
Hamleth, 466
Hamlin, 453
hammer gang, 684
hammoc, 295
hammock, 746

Hampton, 447
Ham Shank, 592
Hamtramck, 561
Hancock, 469
hand, 92, 688, 744
Handbag, 511
Händel, 408
handkerchief-head, 270
hand-out, 652, 677, 738
handshaker, 724
handsignment, 252
handsome, 73
handsomebody, 451
handy, 253
hang, 746; -ashore, 253; -by, 226; -out, 133
hang it, to, 674
hangry, 230
Hangtown, 535
Hanina, 519
Hannah, 513
Hannibal, 513
hanno, 308
Hannora, 486, 494
Hanover, 161
Hans, 519
Hansen, 398
Hanson, 398, 434
Hans Walter, 654
happies, 771
happy dust, 680
Haralampopoulas, 440
Harald, 521
Harbaugh, 408
harbor, 285
harbour, 285
Harce, 503
Harcourt, 406
hard, 5, 214; -boiled, 234, 648; -case, 638; -down, 133; -pan, 761
Hard-case State, 638
Hardin, 453
Harding, 427, 453
hardly, 212, 391
hardly hadn't never, 392
hardly nobody, 392
hardrocker, 762
Hardscrabble, 567
hardshelled, 325
hardtail, 761
Hardtimes, 513
hardware, 253, 767
Hardwick Hall, 577
hardwood, 696

hare, 328
harem, 50
Harilaos, 523
Haring, 406
Hark, 449
harken, 294
Harlan, 472, 507
Harlinza, 503
Harman, 409
Harmansen, 406
Harmonia, 592
harness, 715; -cask, 165
Harold, 516, 517, 518, 521, 523
Harolyne, 486
harp, 692
Harper, 398, 399
Harriet, 513
Harrietta, 486, 494
Harris, 396, 398, 401, 402, 409, 416, 429, 430, 440, 447
Harrison, 398, 402, 406, 470
Harrod, 454
Harrus, 429
Harry, 475, 476, 517, 523, 524
Harry Percy of the Union, 608
Harsela, 422
Harshbarger, 410
Hart, 309, 406
Hartford, 79, 458
Hartlein, 410
Hartley, 472
Hartzell, 410
Harutyoun, 523
Harve, 475
harvest, 79, 738
Harvest, 515
Harvesta, 486
Harvey, 471, 517
Harwood, 454
has-been, 768
hase, 307
Hash, 449
hash-brown, 388
hasher, 752
hash session, 729
hasn't, 393
Hassidah, 519
hassoc, 294
hassock, 736
Hastie, 448

hat, 94, 260, 723
-hatchee, 556, 557
Hatchet, 449
Hatchett, 449
hate, to, 121
Hate-evil, 467
Hatetoleaveit, 578
Hathorne, 461
Hathyel, 486
hatrack, 749
Hatrack, 593
Hattie, 480
Haughton, 454
Haughty, 587
haunches, 162
haunt, 230
hausfrau, 51
have, to, 342, 363, 365
have got, 337, 340, 342, 363
haven, 92, 534
haven't, 393
haven't never, 392
Haverhill, 12
have the measles, to, 674
havn't, 302
haw, 314
Hawa, 515
hawbush, 761
haw-haw, 38
Hawkeye, 622, 623
Hawkeye-Record, 623
Hawkeye State, 621
Hawkins, 398, 399
Hawthorne, 454, 461
Hawton, 458
hay, 674; -stoper, 762
Hay, 402
Hayes, 398, 402, 409
Haygait, 460
Haygit, 460
hayloft, 691
Haym, 519
Haynes, 447
Hays office, 699
haywire, 728, 759
hay-wire, to, 177
Haywood-Hayward, 453
H'Doubler, 452
he, 370, 374
heaben, 171
head, 171, 645, 646, 744; -horse, 161
headache, 718, 734; -man, 680

List of Words and Phrases

Headacres, 579
header, 764, 774
headhunter, 724
Headlee, 503
Headlight, 595, 596
headliner, 692
heads, 748
heah, 40
he ain't no good, 167
healer, 773
he-all, 379, 380
healthful, 388
healthy, 388; -respect, 388
he am, 264
heap, 129, 253, 725
hear, 214
heard, 80, 157
hearing chetes, 664
hearken, 79
hearsay, 151
hearse, 714, 724
hearso, 151
heart, 5, 79, 91, 695; -burning, 217
hearth, 79
Hearts and Gizzards, 593
hearty, 79, 98
heat, 362, 692, 773
heated, 362
heater, 774
heath, 573
Heathcote, 458
heathen, 760
heathern, 120
heaven, 171; -dust, 680
heavenly day, 177
Heavenly Rest, 592
heaven's letter, 207
heavy, 690, 691, 754, 769
heavy racket, 668, 669
he be, 356
he been die, 264
heck it, to, 253
hed, 311
hedge, 92, 93; -hog, 95
hedge hop, to, 727
he did, 361
he didn't, 361
hedkworterz, 301
he done, 167, 348, 361
he don't, 370
hee, 225
heebie-jeebies, 644
heel, 720, 746; -beater, 692
heeler, 762

heerd, 80
heesh, 370
hefer, 294, 295
heff, 199
he gone, 264
he (h)aint, 165
heia, 151
Heid, 409
heifer, 295
height, 301
heightht, 100
Heim, 418
-heim, 424, 534
-heimer, 424
-heimr, 434
heinie, 780
Heinie, 594
Heineman, 418
Heinz, 409
Heinze, 138
heir, 93, 94, 95
Heisse, 409
Hele, 486
Helen, 479, 498, 499, 510, 518, 521
Helentzia, 497
Helicon, 583
Hell, 786
hell-and-damnation fathers, 745
Hell Hole Swamp, 568
hello, 237
hello beau, 679
hell's kitchen, 724
Hell's Neck, 536
hell to pay, 567
helluva, 298
Helm, 432
Helma, 520
helmet, 92
help, 122, 200, 360
help Andy, to, 233
helped eat, 364
helpkeeper, 211
helt, 167
hem, 370, 371
he-man, 648
hematoma, 735
hemloc, 295
hemo, 240
hemorrhage, 751
Hemp State, 628
hen, 93; -down, 143; -house, 662
hender, 154

Henderson, 398
Hendrickson, 430
Henerilta, 480
Henrietta, 493
Henrietta Maria, 474
Henriola, 486
Henry, 398, 462, 472, 510, 513, 517, 523, 531
Henry Frederick, 474
he or she, 369, 370
he ought to could, 220
hep-cat, 707, 711
Hepler, 410
he pray, 264
her, 374; -all, 379, 380
Herald, 516, 595
heraldic, 94
Herald of Freedom, 595
he ran, 361
her and you, 394
herb, 86, 92, 94
Herb, 476
Herbert, 517
Herchkeimer, 412
herculean, 94
Hercules, 587
herd, 80
herder, 674, 770
here, 86, 171, 225
-here, 382
hereditary, 94
Here-I-Is, 579
heretical, 94
Herkimer, 412
herkle, 707
Hermann, 409, 519
hermaphrodite, 94
hermetically, 94
Heritage, 577
hern, 368, 369
hero, 722
Herod, 512
heroic, 93, 94
Heroina, 486
Herriman Lake, 540
Herring, 406
Herr Je, 151; -Jesu, 151
herse, 294, 295
Hersh, 517
Hershel, 517
hers'n, 368
Hertasene, 486
Hertford, 458
Hertlin, 410
he run, 361

Herz, 417
Herzl, 417
Herzler, 417
he's, 394
hes, 371
he said, 361
Hesba, 486
he sez, 361
hesh, 370
he shut, 361
het, 260, 362
Hethcot, 458
Heu, 422
he-un, 380
heureka, 613
hevn, 293
hew, to, 313
Hew, 442
Hewgée, 438
hex, 207
hexed, 255
hexen, 255
Hexie, 486
Heygate, 460
Heyman, 418
hey-rube, 685
Heyward, 454, 472
hez, 370
hi, 237, 241, 671
Hialeah, 556
hiatus, 94
Hiburnia, 493
Hiccough, 310
hiccup, 310
Hiccup, 451
Hickerson, 454
Hickey, 232, 743, 767, 774
hickory, 138, 166; -tea, 132
Hickory, 544
Hicks, 398
hickup, 310
hidden, 92
hide, 670, 724; -heater, 705; -out, 671
hiekka, 430
hierling, 306
Hietemäki, 430
Higginson, 454
high, 92, 125, 671, 681; bale, 715; -balling, 719; -bob, 194; -brow, 648, 650; -ceiling, 727; -climber, 759; -iron, 716; -kraeusen, 739; -liner, 715; -pockets,

736; -pitchman, 685; -priest, 221; -rigger, 759; -steppingest, 388; -yallah, 270
High, 410
high C, 693
High Dry, 536
high in flesh, 769
hijack, to, 652, 671
hijacker, 671
High Pine, 446
hight, 301
high-tail, to, 138
High Water, 513
High Wind, 593
hike, 125, 778
hike, to, 648
hiker, 718
Hilah, 479
Hilario, 565
hilarious, 94
Hilata, 443
hilce, 192
hile, 253
Hill, 398, 428, 584
hill-billy, 116, 760; -horse, 694
Hillcrest, 577
hillins, 238
hillock, 73
hills, 192
Hilry, 503, 506
him, 340, 374
him-all, 379, 380
himer, 370
himmel, 654; -sbrief, 207; -steig, 654
himmer, 370
him or her, 370
Himself, 511
hind, 93; -hook, 713; -feet, 162; -legs, 162; -snatcher, 736
Hines, 409
hi-open-bopens, 236
hip, 684
hippo, 764
hir, 371
Hiramette, 486
Hiram Ulysses, 477
Hirata, 443
hireling, 306
hiren, 369
Hirschberger, 410, 417
Hirsh, 517
Hirtzell, 410

his, 370; -all, 380
hiser, 370
his honor, 735
hisn, 369
his or her, 370, 371
his own, 215, 369
hissy, 220
hist, 87, 108, 120, 143, 189, 192, 214
historic, 94
historical, 93, 94
history, 174
histry, 174
hit (it), 96, 120, 173, 192, 200, 220, 735
hit-and-run, 723, 737
hit below the belt, to, 768
hitch, 674; -hike, 738
hitched, 644
hitch-hike, to, 363
Hite, 409
-hithe, 534
Hitler War, 785
hitth, 192
hit the floor, to, 749
hit the gong, to, 681
hit the hay, to, 127
hit the trail, to, 672
hitting in, 749
Hiu, 442
hiumn, 288
hivvely, 205
hiway, 297
hizzer, 370
Hjelm, 432
-hjelm, 434
Hjort, 432
ho, 308
hoar, 314
hob, 734
hobbing-iron, 211
ho beau, 679
hobo, 652, 675, 679
ho bo, 679
Hoboken, 679, 772
ho boy, 679
ho bub, 679
hoc est corpus, 670
Hoch, 408, 410
Hochdeutsch, 207
Hochroth Arms, 577
hocks, 253
hocus-pocus, 670
hod, 720
hodada, 267
hoddy-doddy, 766

List of Words and Phrases

hododo, 267
hoe, 121, 385; -boy, 679
Hoeber, 411
Hoeppler, 410
Hoey, 458
-hof, 433
hofbräu, 51; -haus, 327
Hoffman, 398, 422
hog, 184, 185, 216, 713, 740; -age, 165; -house, 749; -jockey, 713; -law, 715; -lot, 749; -mauler, 713; -pen, 250; -wrestle, 158
hog, to, 150
hog and hominy, 639
Hog and Hominy State, 639
Hog Dutch, 207
Hog Eye, 534
Hogflesh, 451
hogger, 713
hoghead, 713, 728
Hog Island, 536
hog, mud and rocks, 673
hog pig, 208
hog's back son-of-a-bitch, 165
Hog's Diggings, 536
hogses, 386
Hogshead, 449
Hog's Nose, 572
Hogwallow, 564
hoir, 309
hoist, to, 87, 214
hoister, 685
hoke, 692
Hoke, 408
hokum, 692
hokus, 670
hol, 292
hold-fast, 181
holding company, 324; -bond, 324
hole, 92, 149, 723, 724, 761, 774
Holger, 520
Holiday, 536
Holima, 515
Hollenden, 578
Hollene, 503
holler, 89, 100; -horn, 226
hollow, 573
Holloway, 408
Hollweg, 408
Holly Jo, 486

Hollywood, 699
Holme Run, 579
Holmes, 398, 402
Holohan, 461
Holoughan, 461
holp, 200, 226, 360
holpen, 360
Holsti, 429
holsum, 296
holt, 98
holy, 92, 390
Holy, 449
Holy Cross, 591
Holy Fellowship, 590
Holy Ghost, 590
Holy Land, 661
Holy Moses, 512
Holy Paraclete, 590
Holy Rosary, 591
Holy Spirit, 590
holzbock, 209
ho-made, 298
hombre, 243
Home, 458
homebrew, 671
home-guard, 683
homely, 657
home-made cheese, 231
Homer, 466, 507
home-run, 685, 737
hominy, 160, 215
hommie, 208
homœopathy, 282
homo sapien, 384
homus bonum, 679
Hondo, 565
honest, 93, 94, 95
Honest John, 588
honey, 720, 753; -chile, 125; -cooler, 707
honor, 94, 95, 280, 282, 300
honorarium, 95
honorariums, 320
honorary, 280
Honoré, 317
honorific, 280
honour, 280, 281, 282, 306
honourable, 280
hoo, 620
hooch, 641
Hood, 409
hoodoo, 267
hoof, 228
Hoof, 449
hoofer, 692

Hoofer, 411
hook, 573, 686, 730, 734, 736; -tender, 739
hook-and-ladder, 749
hooker, 682, 777
hooks, 718, 764
hooligan, 674
hoop, 228, 314, 670, 724
Hooper, 228
hoosa, 619
hoose, 620
hoosegow, 677
Hoosher, 616
Hoosheroon, 616
Hooshier, 619; -State, 621
hoosier, 618, 619, 670, 683
Hoosier, 615, 616, 617, 620, 621; -Banker, 621; -Business Woman, 621; -Democrat, 621; -dom, 621; -ism, 142, 621; -land, 621; -nest, 616; -State, 615, 620, 621
hoosierize, to, 621
Hooston, 458
Hooton, 458
hoov, 385
Hoover, 411, 412, 583
hooves, 385
hoozer, 620
hop, 652, 680, 681
hope, 94, 226, 234
Hope, 468, 503, 506
Hope-still, 467
hophead, 674, 681
Hop Inn, 579
Hopkins, 398, 399
hopper, 772
hopping-board, 740
hoptoad, 725
Horace, 466, 503
Hore-Belisha, 324
Horicon, 565
horizon, 93
horl, 188
Horlene, 486
horn, 93; -knocker, 754; -nut, 686
horn, to, 175
hornbock, 654
Hornbuckle, 450
Horned Toad, 596
horning, 210
Horres, 486
horrible, 82, 93
horrid, 82, 216

List of Words and Phrases

horror, 280
horrour, 311
hors-d'oeuvre, 50, 53
horse, 89, 93, 94, 717, 719, 753; -collar, 735; -doovers, 53; -laugh, 649; -opera, 701; -sense, 770
horseback, 761
Horse Chops, 572
Horsefoot, 563
Horse Guards, 528
horsehed, to, 149
horseman, 93
horses, 753
Horsetail, 535
Hort, 432
Horton, 454
Hosa, 486
hose, 385
hospital, 92, 94, 322
hoss, 89
Hossegar, 528
host, 92
host, to, 121
hostler, 92, 94
hot, 45, 83, 93, 185, 667, 710, 719, 728; -ass, 763; -cat, 770; -cha, 772; -corner, 736; -fare, 720; -knife, 754; -light, 731; -shot, 716; -spot, 711; -top, 772
Hot Coffee, 534
hotel, 92
Hotham, 458
hother horse, 162
hothouse, 95
hot jazz, 705, 706, 710
hot mamma, 646
hot monkey, 718
Hot'n, 458
Hoton, 458
hot roll, 742
Hotspur, 587
hot stuff, 773
hot-stuff man, 733
Hotun, 458
Hot Water State, 611
Houbre, 413
Houghton, 458
Houlihan, 461
houn, 294
hour, 93, 94, 95. 226
house, 93, 227, 231, 291, 690, 691, 767; -boat, 772; -burn, 776; -moss,

232; -seat, 696; -stuff, 690
House, 577, 578
Houseboat Creek, 540
householder, 93
housekeeper, 212
housen, 181
House of Prayer, 590
Houston, 458
Houver, 413
hoved out, 153
Hover, 411
Hovsep, 523
Hovsepian, 441
how, 227, 255
how ah yuh?, 211
Howard, 398, 448, 454, 468, 469, 517
how are you?, 237
how be yuh?, 211
How Come You, 566
how'd you like to be the ice-man?, 645
howl, 177
Howling Water, 446
how old of a, 394
howsomeber, 247
how's your poor feet?, 645
how that, 220
Howton, 458
Howtun, 458
Hoy, 410, 458
Hoyd, 503
Hoylestown, 572
Hozen, 503
Hrant, 523
Hriar, 523
Hrivnyák, 440
hu, 288
Huachuca, 552
hubba-hubba, 644
hubbly, 750
hübelich, 205
Huber, 411, 413
huckleberry, 149
Huckleberry, 503
Hudak, 427
huddle, 166
Hudson, 398
hudu, to, 267
Hueco, 528
Huerfano, 552
hues, 313
huesco, 557
Huey, 582

huez, 313
huffbrow, 51
Huffton, 458
huge, 93
Huger, 438, 472
huggerum buff, 252
Hugh, 524
Hughes, 398, 442
Hughzetta, 486
Huldah, 479
Hulon, 503
Human, 449, 503, 506
humane, 94
human rifle, 121
humble, 94, 95
humbug, 663
Humbug, 567; -Flat, 535
Hume, 458
humgumption, 253
humility, 94
humor, 94
humorist, 280
humour, 280
hump, 678, 728, 772
humpback, 737, 767
humpers, 674
humpie, 737
hun, 780
hunderd, 99, 100, 175
hundert, 100
hundred, 93, 175
hundret, 209
hungry, 230, 720
hunkle, 217
hunt, 93
Hunt, 398
Hunter, 409
Hunyadi Janos, 440
hup-cha-da-bub-cha, 729
hur, 717
hurricane, 94
hurry, 45
hurting, 98
huse, 313
Hush, 449
husher, 617, 618
hush-money, 644, 663
hussar, 618, 619
hustler, 682
Hustler, 451, 595
hut, 727
Hut, 679
hutchy, 160
Huth, 409
huthering, 204
Huthum, 458

List of Words and Phrases

hutsch, 160
hutschel, 160
hutschli, 160
huzur, 620
huzza, 619
Huzzah, 535
hwen, 288
hwich, 95, 288
Hy, 476
hyæna, 282
hybreeding, 732
Hyde, 427
hydraulic, 94
hyena, 94, 282
Hyena, 588
Hygiene, 486
Hyman, 418
hymaviffa-of-the-bivavva, 175
Hyooston, 458
hype, 674
hypersophic, 346
hyphen, 228
hypo-bender, 766
hypocrisy, 94
hypocrite, 93
hysen, 369
hysterical, 93
Hywana, 486
i, 73, 81, 182, 189, 192, 199, 230, 235, 246, 260, 291, 292, 309, 310, 408, 410, 432
i, long, 72, 125, 137
i, Russian, 308
i, Spanish, 554
I, 230, 297, 352
I ain't coming, 710
I-all, 379
-ian, 441
I are, 171
I ate, 361
Iaways, 546
Ibach, 408
Ibada, 486
Ibar, 497
I be, 165, 181, 218, 356, 357
I been't, 357
I be going, 356
I ben't, 356
Iberville, 437
ibi, to, 267
I bin gone done it, 142
I brang, 361
I bring, 361

i bro, 292
I brung, 361
Ibsen, 582
-ic, 584
I can't seem, 337
ic beo, 356
ice, 125, 696; -box, 674
-ice, 417
Ice, 449, 535
ice cream, 740
ice-cream-soda, 425
iced-cream, 388
Icel, 486
ice-tong doctor, 680
Iceyphenolia, 486
ich, 411, 418, 426
icky, 707, 711
Ida, 520
Idaho, 554, 557, 558, 588
I'd a went, 219
Iddela, 486
Iddog and Menw, 590
idea, 81; ídea, 48
ideaa, 81
idear, 89, 159, 186
idiot, 646
Iditarod, 552
Idoline, 486
I don't think, 643, 645
Idoree, 486
I drag, 361
Idress, 486
Idris, 503
I drug, 361
Iduma, 486
ie, 291, 300, 410
I eat, 361
-ier, 620
iern, 314
I-erst, 456
I et, 361
Ietta, 486
if, 200
iffen, 394
if he be, 368
if he is, 368
if I am, 368
If I hadda been, 368
if I was, 368
If I were, 368
Ifla, 486
if she go, 368
if she goes, 368
ig, 411, 418
I give, 361
I given, 361

Ignatz, 516
I got, 361
I gotten, 361
igneetion, 199
I guv, 361
I gwine do it, 142
I gwine to gone done it, 142
I had tuck, 361
I (h)ain't, 165
I have brought, 361
I have brung, 361
I have did, 354
I have saw, 340, 346, 354, 373
I have took, 361
I have tuck, 361
I hope you good luck, 234
Ihoway, 546
I is, 171, 264
ik, 446, 717
I knowed, 361
I known, 361
Ikola, 429
ikut, 267
Ilana, 519
iland, 292
Ilene, 481
ile-suit, 750
ilet, 156
Ilias, 523
Ill, 449
illahi, 237
ill-gotten, 363
Illipah, 563
ill-shaped, 358
I'll take he, 254
illy, 390
Ilo, 486
Iloath, 503
iltis, 654
im-, 282
Ima Hogg, 450
Imajane, 486
Imari, 524
I might can, 220
I might could, 220
Imilda, 486
I'm is, 226
Immaculate Conception, 591
Imogene, 486, 593
Imojean, 486
implement, 246
impruuvment, 300

Imre, 524
in, 202, 234, 352
in-, 282
-in, 91, 114
in, to be, 746
in a bad row of stumps, 153
inadequacy, 306
in a front cloth, 692
in a swither, 232
in back of, 338
inbred, 48
Incarnation, 590
inch, 232
Inch, 449
incidence, 175
incident, 175
Incomappbeaux, 573
Increase, 467, 468, 562
in creeper, 669
Independence Hall, 583
independent, 699
Indian, 719; -hay, 680
Indiany, 544
indicative present, 377
indice, 385
indices, 319
indie, 699
indorsation, 282
Ineda, 486
Iness, 486
Ine-stine, 424
Inez, 482, 486
infairior, 314
infant, 195
infare, 140
Infernal, 587
inflexion, 277
Inflexible, 587, 588
in forwardness, 211
in front, 689
-ing, 91, 99, 123, 124, 418
Ing, 458
Inge, 458
Ingebertsen, 435
Ingeborg, 520
ingénue, 688
inglorious, 184
inhame, 267
in high, 680
Inice, 486
ink, 720; -slinger, 759; -stick, 686
inkie, 755
inky, 699, 731; -dink, 699
inland, 220

In Memoriam, 594
inn, 579
innernational, 192
inning, 384
innings, 384; to have a good —, 384; to have a long —, 384
Inolia, 486
in one, 692
Inos, 486
Inouye, 443
inquirer, 282
inquiry, 282; ínquiry, 48
ínsane, 49
in search for, 337
insect, 724
insignia, 318
-inskas, 428
instalment, 284
instead, 226
instrument, 246
insuelaeshon, 306
insulation, 306
insurance, 282; ínsurance, 218
intellectual snob, 650
Intercourse, 536
interduce, 99, 175
interésting, 48
interior decorator, 739
intestinal, 47
in the boilers, 766
in the can, 699
in the ditch, 715
in the hole, 716
in the suds, 662
intimate, 277
Intrepid, 587
introduce, to, 175
inveigh, to, 365
inverted commas, 326
Invincible, 587, 588
invite whoever you like, 337
inx, 297
iodine, 81, 82, 674, 773
Iodine, 512; -State, 608
ion, 314
Iovia, 486
Iowa, 545, 548
í-o-wa, 546; -way, 545, 546
Iowegian, 623
Ipswich, 12
ir, 189, 294, 300
Irastus, 507

Irby, 503
Irealia, 486
Irene, 482, 521
Iril, 486
Irish-dividend, 773; -Free State, 604; -local, 773; -Queen, 139; -turkey, 752
Irista, 479
Irita, 496
Irkonen, 420
Irl, 503
Irma, 519, 520
Irmingard, 520
Iron, 230, 314, 775; -horn, 705; -horse, 717, 775; -skull, 713; -Skull, 572
ironburner, 759
Ironfoot, 451
Ironjaw Lake, 540
Ironmonger, 454
Iron Mountain State, 631
iron up, to, 719
Irving, 516
Irwin, 516
is, 218, 352
Isaac, 421, 516, 517, 518
Isabel, 499, 500, 523
Isalona, 486
I sang, 361
Isaphene, 480
I sawed, 354
I see, 354
I seed, 353, 354
I seen, 340, 346, 353, 354, 373
Isenhour, 409
is going to, 367
-ish, 199, 386
is he?, 165
Ishi, 515
ish kabibble, 645
I should worry, 645
Isidor, 516
Isigny, 528
Isma, 486
isolaeted, 300
isolation, 72
Isophene, 497
Isota, 486
is said, 202
Issaquena, 562
Issue, 536
-ist, 386
is to go, 367
istorical, 94

List of Words and Phrases

Istvan, 524
I sung, 361
I swan, 185
it, 206, 220, 352, 703
it ain't me, 346, 347
Italy of America, 611
Itamar, 519
I taken, 360
Itealia, 486
Ithaca, 532
Ithacy, 544
it has, 202
Itiel, 519
-itis, 320
it is him, 372
it is I, 372
it is me, 336, 337, 371, 372, 373, 395
it is not I, 346, 347
is thee?, 382
Ithama, 486
Itmann, 541
it might would, 220
Itrice, 486
it's a bear, 127
Itt, 449
itting, 260
Iturna, 486
I used to could, 220
Ival, 508
Ivan, 442; -Dell, 486
Ivanhoe, 577
I've got, 342
Iverna, 486
Ives, 421, 496
Iville, 486
Ivo, 496, 497
Ivory, 511
Ivy, 503
Ivynnelle, 486
iw, 288
Iwalani, 525
I wan, 361
Iwao Inagaki, 444
I was broke, 361
I Will Arise and Go Unto My Father, 512
I win, 361
I wish, 361
I wisht, 361
I written, 360
Ix, 449
iy, 288
iz, 293
-ize, 285
Izell, 503

Izola, 486
Izydorczyk, 425
izzatso, 298
j, 261, 268, 292
j, Swedish, 432
Jaann, 494
jabber, 682, 753
Jacel, 486
jack, 181, 714
Jack, 475, 476, 513, 518, 594, 762
Jackaline, 486
Jackass Gulch, 535
Jackeson, 453
Jackie Jane, 486
Jacklynn, 486
Jackson, 396, 398, 401, 409, 447, 453, 470, 531
Jack the Dude, 139
Jack White, 165
Jacoba, 486
Jacobs, 439, 441
Jacobson, 430
Jacoby, 454
Jacqueline, 486
Jacques, 523
Jacson, 453
Jaeger, 409
jag, 207
Jahala, 487
jaherr, 701
jail, 249, 278, 316
jailbait, 711
Ja Jaye, 487, 494
jake, 671, 756
Jakson, 453
Jakubauskas, 428
Jakubs, 428
jalab, 726
jalapa, 725
jallape, 725
jallopy, 725
jaloopy, 725
jalopa, 725
jaloppy, 725, 726
jalopy, 725, 726
jalousie, 156
jalupie, 725
Jamanuel, 503, 506
jambalaya, 154
James, 396, 398, 405, 462, 478, 496, 509, 510, 517, 523, 524, 531; -town, 530
Jamie, 475; -Lou, 487
Jamieson, 458

jamoca, 673
jam-pitch, 685, 687
jam-session, 706
Jan, 494, 522
Janann, 487
janders, 100, 211
Jane, 479, 480, 499, 513, 524
Janell, 516
Janet, 518
Janeway, 385
janfu, 778
János, 524
Jansen, 407
Januweys, 385
Japanee, 383
Japanese, 99
jape, to, 234
jargon, 643
Jarmie, 487
Jaroslav, 522
jappaner, 758
järvi, 430
Järvi, 429
Järvinen, 430
Jarvis, 438, 458
Jas, 708
jaser, 708
Jass, 708
Jat, 503
jaundice, 100, 211
Jaundice, 487
jaunt, 214
Java, 772
Jaxon, 453
jay, 668
Jay, 475
Jaybird, 559
Jaydee, 503
jayhawk, 626, 627
Jayhawk, 625, 626; -er, 625
Jayhawker State, 623, 624
Jayjay, 496
Jaymisson, 458
Jayne, 487, 494
Jayrene, 487
jaywalker, 133, 723
jaz, 295
jazz, 705, 706, 708, 709, 710; -band, 709
jazz, to, 709
jazzbo, 708
jazz up, to, 709
Jealous Woman, 594
Jean, 506, 518

Jeanita, 487
Jeannette, 500
jeanses, 386
Jearl, 487
Jed, 475, 476
jedge, 87, 120, 211, 219
jedgy, 120
Jeekel, 458
jeep, 782, 783, 784, 785; -town, 784
jeepers-creepers, 785
Jeeta, 487
Jeffanna, 487
Jefferson, 453, 470, 471, 478, 522, 531, 537; -Territory, 554
Jeffersonian, 577
Jeffie, 476
Jeffreson, 453
Jehovah, 512
Jehuda, 417
Jekyll, 458
Jelačič, 426
Jelássick, 426
Jelessia, 487
jelly, 699; -roll, 710
Jelly, 449
Jemail, 441
Je Nanne, 494
JêNanne, 487
Jenkins, 396, 398, 401, 442
Jennie, 480, 720
jenny, 685
Jennyberry, 487
Jens, 520
Jensen, 398
Jeoneta, 487
jeopardize, to, 20
Jeoraldean, 487
jeppo, to, 200
Jere, 475
Jerell, 503
Jerez, 386
Jericho, 451
jerk, 646, 710, 720, 772
jerk, to, 757
jerk a drink, to, 716
Jerkem Tight, 566
jerker, 176
jerk soup, to, 716
jerkwater, 716
jermak, 441
Jermakian, 441
jern, to, 190
Jerrold, 503
jerry, 713, 780

Jerry, 475, 522
Jerryline, 487
Jerry's Kitchen, 580
Jersey, 253
Jersey Blues State, 601
Jersey lightning, 181
Jersey wagon, 162
Jervey, 429
Jervis, 458
Jess, 476
Jesse James, 719, 735, 761
Jessoise, 487, 510
Jesús, 521
Jesus Christ and Him Crucified, 512
Jesus slippers, 723
jeton, 726
Jewehe, 503
jeweler, 284
jewellery, 284, 286
jewelry, 767
jewlarky, 172
Jew peddler, 176
Jhonestowne, 397
ji, 444
ji, Japanese, 444
jice, 87
jiffy, 771
jig, 272
jigger, 175, 754
Jilks, 457
Jim, 513, 523
jim-jams, 761
Jimmie, 476, 487, 523
Jimmie Higgins, 777
Jimmie Lee, 503, 506
Jimmie Lou, 393
Jimmisson, 458
Jimmy, 524
jimmy-jawed, 172
Jimmy the Harp, 139
jimmy with, to, 149
Jimplecute, 595
jine, 154
Jingo, 511, 513
jinricksha, 320
Jirl, 503
Jírrardo, 438
jiste, 734
jit, 208
jitneur, 726
jitney, 726
Jitney, 535
jitterbug, 705, 710
jive, 695, 704, 705
jkwal, 288

J. L., 747
J'Nette, 487
Jo, 443, 487
Joab, 519
Joan, 463, 499, 518
Joán, 141
Joanita, 487
JoAnn, 487
João, 522
Jocelia, 487
jocker, 678
jockey, 720, 721, 736, 756, 770
jodarter, 172
Jodine, 487
Joe, 425, 475, 476, 487, 513, 521, 738, 779, 780
Joe Baggs, 756
Joe Ben, 477
Joe blow, 706
Joeeda, 487
Joe Goss, 669
Joe Hep, 668
Joe Hooks, 718
Joela, 503, 506
Joe McGee, 756
Joey, 684
joham, 654
Johann, 519
Johannes, 432
Johannessen, 433
Johansson, 431
Johanstoun, 397
Johena, 487
John, 261, 400, 442, 447, 462, 463, 487, 494, 510, 513, 517, 518, 522, 524
Johnah, 487
Johnaline, 487
Johnathon, 503, 506
John B., 742
Johnella, 487
Johnetta, 487
Johngston, 397
John Jacob Astor, 583
John Marie, 487
Johnnesone, 397
Johnnestoun, 404
Johnny Behind the Rock, 139
johnnycake, 160
Johnny-come-lately, 684
Johnny Hicks, 747
Johnnye, 476
johnny-house, 231
Johnny-v, 487

List of Words and Phrases

Johns, 409
John Smith, 398, 400, 401, 444
Johnson, 396, 397, 398, 400, 401, 407, 430, 433, 447
Johnston, 397, 398, 399, 400
John's ton, 397
Johnstoun, 397
John Wilkes, 581
Joi, 487
join, 87, 192
joint, 292, 674, 680, 684, 763
joisie, 253
joist, 87
Joline Joy, 450
jollop, 726
jollopy, 725
Jolly, 679
joloppy, 725
jolt, 674, 680
Joma, 487
Jonaday, 519
Jonah, 487
Jones, 396, 397, 398, 401, 447
Joneses, 398
Jones Point, 539
Joneston, 397
Jong, 406, 443
Jonie, 503
Joniston, 397
Jonnie Lee, 487
Jonson, 397
jook, 710
Jordan, 397, 399, 436
Jordão, 436
Joreath, 487
Jorene, 503
José, 521, 522
Joseph, 441, 462, 475, 510, 522, 523, 524
Joseph Brown of A, 452; of D, 452
Joseph's Coat, 592
Joseph Woodrow, 465
Josh, 476
Joshua, 467
Jotter, 411
jouk-joint, 710
Journal, 595
Jo Verleen, 487
Joveta, 487
jowl, to, 132

Joy-again, 467
joy-popper, 680
Joyrene, 486
JoyRene, 487
joy-ride, 723
joy-stick, 681, 728
Jozelpa, 487
József, 524
Jr., 500, 501
ju, 310
Ju, 593
Juanita, 492, 521
Juanzell, 487
Jubrān, 441
Jucklin, 437
Judah, 417
Judas, 764; -Iscariot, 512
Judean, 521
judge, 87, 211, 219, 261
Judge, 511
Judiciary, 581
Juella, 521
jug, 668, 736; -handle, 736; -heavy, 668; -stiff, 669
juggler, 753
Juhana, 524
juice, 697, 718; -box, 724; -jockey, 719; -joint, 684; -worker, 686
juice, to, 176, 749
juicer, 699
juke, 710
Julaine, 487
julappi, 725
Julia, 493, 523
Julian, 518
Julius, 517
Jumayyil, 441
Jumbo State, 640
Jumpertown, 592
jumping jeep, 784
Jumping Jesus, 149
Jump-off Joe, 567
jump-over, 176
jump the track, to, 713
Jumpy, 774
Jun., 500
June, 486, 503, 521
Juneesia, 487
Jung, 409
jungle, 652; -buzzard, 677
Jungle Cat, 596
jungles, 676, 677
Junian, 503
junior, 699

Junior, 500
junk, 743, 763; -hog, 682; -house, 710
Junk, 449
junker, 674
junkie, 674
juoti, 310
jupe, 198, 756
juper, 198
jupiter, 322
Jupiter, 472, 557
juror, 280
Jusamere Home, 578
Jussi, 524
Just-a-Bite, 580
justice, 285
justins, 742
just now, 253
jute-ball, 673
Juva, 487
Jymme, 487
k, 96, 98, 261, 292, **294**, 296, 300, 303, 304, 310, 408, 411, 414, 418, 431
k, French, 572
k, German, 307
k, Swedish, 431
ka, 237
kabas, 654
Kabo, 437
Kabotchnick, 418
kack, 742
Kadane, 441
kadifter, 208
kadoowy, 175
Kaelber, 411
kafa, 266
Kahn, 421
kai, 240
kaif, 580
kain, 261
Kaintuck, 627
kaiser's geburtstag, 739
Kajakanikamak, 572
kajody, 728
Kakakiwing, 528
Kakekekwaki, 572
kala, 687
Kalamazoo, 561
kale, 685
Kallar, 429
Kallio, 429
Kalliokowski, **429**
Kalman, 516
Kaloola, 487
kalsomimer, **724**

Kamescro, 442
Kamlo, 442
kamook, 237
Kamp Takiteze, 579
Kanada, 296
Kanadian, 296
kanata, 573
Kanawha, 570
Kane, 429
kangaroo, 739
Kangasniemi, 429
Kann, 421
Kanorado, 540
Kansas, 543; -language, 152; -Nebraska, 507
Kansaw, 543
Kanterbury, 304
kantleek, 296
Kantner, 411
Kanzadah, 487
Kanzas, 543
Kanzaw, 543
Kaplan Court, 577
Kar, 440
kara, 266
Karácsonyi, 440
Karamouzis, 440
Karen, 519, 520, 522
Karikanta, 430
Kark, 503
Karl, 520, 523
Karla, 487
Karldene, 487
Karleen, 487
Karlette, 487
Karloff, 427
Karlsen, 406
Karlson, 432
Karlssen, 433
karv, 314
Kashatta, 487
Kassab, 441
Kassanumganumkeag, 560
Kasumi, 588
Kate Douglas Wiggin, 583
Katharine, 479
Katherine, 498, 499, 510
Kathern, 483, 494
Kathleen, 520
Kathryn, 494
Katibah, 441
Katz, 421, 424
katzenjammer, 51
Katzenstein, 420

Kaufmann, 410
Kaunismäki, 429
Kaval, 427
Kavulič, 427
Kaye, 420
kay-hun, 422
Kayns, 458
kayo, 768
Kazan, 503
K. C., 679
Kedjerski, 425
keecorn, 253
keeds, 260
keel over, to, 721
keel up, to, 165
Keely, 458
Keen, 409
keen-kutter, 296
keep your hair on, 645
keerpet, 233
keetchen, 260
Keethly, 458
keff, 199
keg, 272
kegge, 272
keg of nails, 771
Keighley, 458
Keightley, 458
Keileranny, 593
Keim, 418
keint, 122
keister, 685
Kekoalauliionapalihauliu-liokekoolau, 525
Kekroppamont, 446
Keldora, 487
Keleel, 503
Kelin, 416
Kelley, 399, 430
Kellicocam, 593
Kellogg Koiled Kords, 296
Kelly, 399, 401
Kelonymos, 516
kelpie, 196
Kelvoryvybegg, 593
Kemp, 454
ken, 664
Kenesaw Mountain, 507
KenMore, 452
Kennedy, 399, 439, 453
kennel, 756
Kenneth, 517, 521, 522
Kennis, 503
Kenora, 572
Kenova, 540

Kent, 304, 425
Kentuck, 627
Kentucke, 627
Kentucky Home, 582
Kentucky position, 769
Ken-Tuck-You-Inn, 579
kep', 218
kerb, 278
kerbstone, 278; -broker, 278
Kergzo, 437
Kermon, 521
kern, 190
Kerr, 458
Kerry, 487
Kesti, 429
ketch, 174
ketch, to, 120, 159
kettle, 174, 262, 670, 714, 718; -buster, 723; -mender, 713
Keturah, 479, 487
Keturakaitis, 428
Keturakat, 428
Kevrok, 523
Kewpie, 487, 495
Keynes, 458
Keystone, 563; -State, 598
Key West, 557
Khalil, 523
Khatchadouryan, 441
kibosh, 644
kick, 699, 729, 735
kick, to, 746
Kick, 449
kickback, 777
kicker, 648
kick-off room, 755
kick the clock, to, 724
kick the gong, to, 681
kick the gonger, to, 681
kid, 727; -show, 684
kidder, 198
kiddie-klothes, 296
Kidney, 449
kidney-buster, 719
kidney cleaner, 740
kids, 260
Kieffer, 410
Kiel, 542
Kiercereau, 437
Kiergerau, 437
kikanamoso, 561
Kilgren, 431
kill, 573
kill (kiln), **96**

List of Words and Phrases 839

kill, to, 699
Killbridge, 449
killer, 681; -diller, 707
Killer, 451
killjoy, 644
kill the baby, to, 698
Kill van Kull, 564
kiln, 96
Kiln, 562
Kilroy was here, 645
kimona, 673
Kimona, 487
kin, 269
kind, 214, 227, 261
kinda, 394
kinder, 198
kin-éen, 48
kinetograph, 702
kinetoscope, 702
king, 713; -snipe, 713
-king, 443
King, 397, 399, 436, 507
King Bird of the Jayhawkers, 624
kingdom work, 745
King Klean, 580
Kingman, 443
King of Prussia, 536, 579, 580
King of William, 452
Kingsbridge Vanity Court, 577
king's eye, 740
King Solomon, 512
kink-chaser, 749
kinker, 684
kinky, 668
kin-néen, 82
kin'ness, 96
Kinnicum, 460
kiota, 639
kiote, 639
Kiote, 596
kip, 675
Kip, 406
Kipp, 406
Kirby, 458
Kirchman, 408
Kirkby, 458
Kirkcudbright, 458
Kirkkomäki, 430
Kirkóobry, 458
Kiskiminetas, 529
Kisser, 451
kiss her, to, 92
Kissimee, 556

kitchen, 260, 743, 758; -closet, 210; -stone, 716
Kitchener, 542
kitchi, 574
kitching, 91, 100
kite, 674
kitel, 209
Kit-Kat, 596
kittle, 120, 174
kitty, 738
kivi, 430
Kiviniemi, 430
Kiwanis, 487, 495
Kizize, 487
Kjaerret, 434
kl, 184
klaliff, 296
klapot, 151
klauen, 665
klavern, 296
Kla-Williams, 448
kleagle, 296
klearflax, 296
Klein, 409, 411, 416, 424
KleinSmid, 452
KlenDshoj, 452
klenzo, 296
Kleo Murl, 503
Klieg eyes, 699
Klimb Inn, 579
Kline, 411, 424
klonvocation, 296
kloof, 207
kloran, 296
klotsy, 255
klotzig, 255
kluck, 767
kludd, 296
klunk, 725
klunker, 725
klupper, 753
Klypa, 428
knick-knacker, 725
Knight, 399
knives and forks, 718
knob, 573
knobbling, 773
Knoche, 411
knock, 674
knockabout, 725
Knockadawe, 593
knock down, to, 771
knocker, 682, 740, 764
knocking iron, 740
knock off, to, 644
knockout, 768

Knockout, 774
Knollys, 458
knot, 774
knout, 151
know, 230
know from nothing, to, 392
knowledgeable, 254
known, 167
Knox, 411
Knuckle, 595
knuckle-buster, 728
Knut, 520, 521
Knutsen, 433
K. O., 768
Kobe, 542
Koch, 408, 412, 414
kochi, 552
Kodiak Bear, 596
kof, 313
kofta, 151
Kohan, 421
kohen, 422, 424
ko-hén, 422
Kohl, 409
Kohler, 409
koh'n, 422
Koith, 503
kok, 446
Koken, 421
Kohn, 421
Kohon, 421
Kokosh, 237
kold-kist, 296
kolfactor, 150
Kolin, 416
Kolodziejcak, 425
kol-pak, 296
Komal, 503
komically, 296
komusta, 243
Kona, 487
konceived, 296
Koncevičius, 428
Končius, 428
koncocted, 296
Konover, 405
Konstantinos, 523
Konza, 543
Kool Kave, 580
koolsla, 51
Koral, 487
Koran, 503
Koren, 503
Korene, 484
Kormos, 440

840 *List of Words and Phrases*

Kortesmäki, 429
Korzybski, 425
Koscielniak, 426
Kosciuszko, 425
Kosh, 414
kosher, 671
Koskenniemi, 429
Koski, 429
Kosola, 429
Köster, 408
Kothe, 412
Köthe, 412
kougholpn, 310
Kowai, 515
Kowalczyk, 425
koyott, 639
K. P., 778
kping, 266
krachen, 609
krächzen, 202
Kraemer, 409
Kraeutler, 410
krais, 220
kraisiz, 220
kraistiz, 220
Kramer, 409
Krámoris, 426; Kramóris, 426
krasligged, 212
Kraus, 409
kraut, 780; -head, 780
kraze, 296
Kreidler, 410
Kreil, 412
Kreitzer, 410
Kress, 426
Kreuzer, 410
Krieg, 513
krike, 80
kroflite, 296
Krom Elbow, 565
Kromme Ellebog, 565; Zee, 528
kruxingiol, 155
Krzyzanowski, 425
ks, 292, 294
Kuban, 427
Kucharz, 425
Kuchuk, 427
Kudisch, 427
Kuefer, 410
kuehlschift, 739
kühl, 739
Kuhn, 409, 414
Kühn, 424
Kühne, 409

Kuiper, 406
Ku Klux Klan, 296
kulo, 267
kulor, 301
kum-a-part, 296
Kumhavarest, 578
Kum-on-Up, 579
kump, 151
Kunigunde, 520
kunkura, 267
kunu, 267
kurious, 296
Kurt, 519
Kurtz, 409
kuta, 267
Kuta, 515
kutz, 296
kutzit, 296
kuupae, 306
Kuvulič, 427
kvist, 431
kw, 292
kwality, 18
kwik, 298
kwí-nin, 82
kwinine, 82
kwintesens, 301
kyind, 86
kyow, 114
Kyun, 424
l, 63, 262, 284, 300, 308, 309, 500, 556
l, French, 52
l, silent, 96
l, Swedish, 432
la, 440, 470, 494, 542
-la, 418
la, Italian, 440
L. A., 547
LaBelle, 487
La Boheme, 582
labor, 282, 300
laboratory, 36, 47
laborious, 280
labour, 249, 280
laboured, 280
labourer, 280
labouring, 280
Labourite, 280
LaBovith, 423
Labovitz, 423
Lacahabarratu, 593
Lacene, 487
lacunas, 319
ladder, 716
Laddie, 503, 506

Ladelle, 487
LaDellys, 487
ladened, 359
Ladora, 542
La Doris, 494
LaDuska, 487
Lady Bird, 496
Ladye, 487
Lady Haley, 165
lady-killer, 649
Lady Macbeth, 730
Lady of the Lakes, 629
laebor, 301
laf, 311
LaFaun, 510
Lafayette, 450, 470, 531
LaFern, 487
LaFerry, 503, 506
laff, 297
Laff-a-Lot, 579
lage, 664
lagniappe, 149, 154
La Guardia, 439
La-Ha Way, 564
Lahoma, 487
Lah Sahl, 470
lai, 241
Laiche, 413
laid, 362
laig, 120
lain, 362
Lainde, 515
lain down, 167
Laird, 458
La Joie, 438
Lajos, 524
La Junta, 565
Lake, 430, 679
Lake Amos, 530
Lake Erie, 512
Lake George, 565
Lake Pelican, 583
Lake Pontchartrain, 583
Lakeside, 569
Lake State, 629, 630
Lake States, 630
Lala, 487
Lalabelle, 487
LaLahoma, 487, 494
Lalan, 487
lam, 672
lam, to, 672, 683
Laman, 515
La Mar, 516
lamb, 678, 736
lamb chop, 722

Lambert, 406
lamb licker, 742
laméntable, 48
Lamiza, 497
Lamm, 417
Lammaerts, 406
Lamminmäki, 429
Lämmle, 417
LaMoe, 435
Lamont, 444
LaMorte, 487
Lamp, 429
Lamppinen, 429
lam the joint, to, 674
land, 123, 199; -looker, 759; -louper, 149
-land, 434
landa, 267
Landi, 439
Landis, 439
landlady, 682
landlord, 734, 767
lando, 267
Land of Enchantment, 636; of Flowers, 614; of Heart's Desire, 636; of Opportunity, 636; of Red Apples, 638; of Steady Habits, 600, 601; of the Cactus, 636; of the Dakotas, 636; of the Delight Makers, 636; of the Montezumas, 636; of the Mormons, 640; of the Red People, 638; of the Rolling Prairies, 623; of the Saints, 640; of the Sky, 607; of the Wooden Nutmegs, 599
Landrew, 506
landu, 267
Lane, 399
Lang, 409
Lange, 409
Langhorne, 454
Langley, 588
Langon, 454
Lanivine, 487
Lanthanum, 285
Lantz, 409
LaOba, 487
lap, 664, 720; baby, 195
lap, to, 233
LaPhalene, 487

Lapierre, 438
lapish, 254
läppisch, 255
Lapriel, 487
Larada, 487
larceny, 100, 668
Larceny, 487
larceny in his heart, 668
larch, 73
Larch, 437
L'Archeveque, 437
la reata, 741
large, 212, 237
Large Bier, 583
lariat, 741
La Riviere, 437
Lark, 581
Laro, 438
Larocca, 440
La Rocca, 440
Laron, 503
Larraby, 437
larrapin, 220
larrikin, 220
larry, 685
Larry, 476
Lars, 432
Larsen, 433
larsensy, 100, 315
Larson, 399, 430
Larssen, 432
LaSalle, 470, 497
Lasarian, 487
Lascelles, 458
Lashaway, 438
lass, 73
Lássels, 458
lassen, 202
Lassie, 594
lassie loaf, 253
lasso, 741
last, 22, 69, 74, 171, 187, 205
Last Hope, 592
last mile, 675
Last World War, 785
latch, 73, 716; -pin, 153
LaTerulia, 487
lath, 74
Lathal, 503
Latrina, 487
Laudenslager, 412
laufer, 51
Lauffer, 410
laugh, 74, 184, 187, 195, 214, 218

Laughinghouse, 449
Laughter, 499
Lauginia, 487
Launceton, 414
launch, 214
launder, to, 363
laundered, 363
laundried, 363
laundry, 187
Laureau, 438
Laurel, 503, 506
L'Aurelia, 487
Laurentsen, 434
LaUrine, 513
Lausia, 487
Lautenschläger, 412
Lautenschleger, 412
Lautenslager, 412
Lauter, 409
lautern, 739
lauter-tub, 739
lava, 215
Lava, 487
Lavalette, 487
lavandera, 243
LaVassar, 487
La Vaughn, 521, 522
LaVaughne, 487
Laverne, 506, 516, 521
LaVeta, 498
LaVey, 423
LaVieve, 487
Lavisa, 487
lavish, 120
Lavoie, 437
LaVon, 516
law, 89, 238, 668
lawd, 40
Laweelhanna, 528
Laweese, 487
Lawfer, 410
Lawisaquik, 528
lawn, 199, 314
lawns, 385
law of Moses, 89
Lawrence, 409, 421, 434
Laws-an-j'l-uhs, 546
lawyer, 753, 771
lay, 751
lay, to, 261, 362
Lay, 450
Layard, 458
Lay-fat, 450
layout, 706; -man, 732
Layson, 458
lay the hip, to, 681

Layvee, 422
Lazella, 487
Lazette, 488
lazo, 741
lazy-gal, 195; -wife, 195
L'Dean, 488
Lea, 402, 458
lead, 729
LeAda, 488
Leader, 595
lead horse, 162
Leading Wren, 311
Lead State, 613, 631
leaf, 252; -worker, 686
Leafy Ella, 488
leag, 292, 311
Leaky, 593
Leandrew, 503
Leannette, 488
leaped, 362
leapfrog, 163
Leap Frog, 592
leaping Lena, 785
leaptick, 692
Lear, 524
Learlene, 488
learn, 79
learned, 340
Learn-wisdom, 467
Learsi, 579
leastest, 387
leathe, 295, 670, 674, 683; -coat, 160; -player, 736; -teat, 779
L'Eau Froid, 528
leave, to, 202
leave me go, 202
leaven, 202
leaves, 752
Leavy, 422
Lebanon, 556
lebben, 248
Leberstein, 421
Lebita, 488
lebm, 218
Lecher, 413
Lecheux, 413
Lecompton Constitution, 507
Lector, 503
Ledell, 488
Lederman, 422
Lédnicky, 426; Lednícky, 426
Lee, 399, 402, 405, 416,

422, 423, 458, 470, 488, 506, 522
Leeanard, 503
Leeds, 422
leeftenaunt, 85
Leel, 460
Lee Loy, 443
Lee-man, 423
Lee Ona, 488
leer, 754
le'er, 192
leery, 663
Leesburg, 589
Leeshman, 458
Lée-vee, 422
Leeven, 458
Leevy, 422
leftenant, 46, 85, 251
left-footer, 745
Leftwich, 416
leg, 121, 185
Legare, 438
Legene, 516
Legion, 581
legislátive, 114
Legislator, 581
legitimate, 690
Legna, 488
Legnial, 503
Legrée, 438
Lehi, 515, 569
Lehman(n), 423
Le Houx, 437
lehr, 754
Lehrensteinfeld, 416
Lehrer, 416
Leibelsperger, 411
Leibensperger, 411
Leibman Manor, 577
Leibowitz, 421
Leicester, 458
Leichet, 413
Leidy, 421
Leif, 520
-leigh, 534, 577
Leigh, 402
Leilani, 525
Leimoni, 525
-lein, 418
Leipersberger, 411
Leipsic, 556
Leishman, 458
Leiston, 458
LeJeune, 516
Lejitta, 488
Le Kew, 458

Leletia, 488
Lelis, 503
Lem, 504
Lemial, 503
leming, 100
Lemitar, 564
Lemma, 488
lemon, 747
LeMon, 503, 506
Le Moyne, 437
Lemster, 458
Lemuel, 503
Lemul, 503
len, 383
lend, to, 199, 204, 362, 395
lended, 362
lend-lease, 782
lend me look, to, 240
Lendol, 488
length, 92
lengtht, 100
lengthways, 384
lengthy, 20
Lenin, 415
lens, 383; -hog, 766; -louse, 699, 766
Lens, 542
lent, 362
Lent, 451
Lentz, 409
Lenva, 488
Leo, 519
Le Olive, 494
Leominster, 458
Leon, 417, 422, 523
Leona, 488
Leonodine, 488
Leopold, 519
Leota Glee, 488
lep, 362
Lepha, 488
Lephair, 495
Lepoline, 488
lepper, 362
leppy, 742, 770
Le Queux, 458
Leroy, 507
Leroyal, 488
lerrers, 192
Lesbia, 569
Lesc, 413
Lesch, 413
Lesher, 413
Lesley, 503, 506
Leslie, 506, 517

List of Words and Phrases

Lessecq, 413
Lessig, 413
Lessly, 503
Lester, 458
let, to, 202
let-down, 176
Letha, 488
lether, 292, 294, 295
let me tell you-o-ou, 645
l'etoile du Nord, 630
Letress, 488
L'Etta, 488
letten, 167
Lettucia, 488
LeTulle, 488, 491
leuch, 195
Leumiza, 488
Levala, 488
Levanne, 422
Levantia, 480
Levay, 422
Leve, 422
levee, 318
Levee, 422
Leveen, 422
level, to, 768
level crossing, 250
Leven, 422, 458
Levene, 422
Levenson, 422
Leventhal, 420
Lever, 422
Leverett, 469
Levesson-Gower, 456
Levey, 422
Levi, 422
Levie, 422
LeVie, 423
Levien, 422
Levin, 417, 422
Levina, 480
Levine, 422
Levins, 422
Levinsohn, 417, 422
Levinson, 422
levis, 742
Levis, 423
Levison, 422
Levitan, 422
Levitas, 422
Levitski, 422
Levitz, 422
Levon, 523
LeVon, 503
Levonna, 488
Levvy, 422; Lévvy, 422

Levy, 401, 421, 422
Lew, 476, 524
Lewellys, 408
Lewes Delaware, 507
Lewin, 422
Lewis, 397, 399, 401, 409, 416, 422, 442
Lewisohn, 420, 422
Lewison, 422
Lewy, 422
Lewynne, 423
Lexine, 488
Ley, 458
Leyetta, 488
Leyette, 495
Leylan, 423
li, 440
li, Italian, 440
Li, 423, 442
liable to snow, 337
Lian, 441
lib'ary, 96
liberate, to, 782
Liberty, 558, 559
library, 220, 714
liburty, 288
license, 329, 386
lices, 386
licht, 307
lick, 219, 573, 706; dab, 175
lick, to, 706
licking the chops, 706
Lick Log, 566
Lick Skillet, 534
licorice, 100; -stick, 705
lid, 717, 724
Liddane, 488
lie, to, 261
Lie, 423
Liebknecht, 422
lied, 362
Lietsche, 422
lieutenant, 46, 85, 250
life, 125, 228
lifeboat, 674
lift, to, 262, 687
liftenant, 85
Lig, 503
Liggon, 458
light, 734, 754
light a rag, to, 668
Lighthead, 449
lighting-plot, 690
lightmans, 664
lightning-bug, 761

lightwood, 161
Ligretta, 488
like, 228, 337, 338, 394, 395
like a hog to war, 173
like a lead nickel with a hole in it, 146
like for, 394
like I'd been shot at and missed, 146
likerish, 100
like siz, 151
like to froze, 219
lik-kewer, 53
Lile, 460
Lilienthal, 417
Lillard, 503
Lillian, 510
Lillious, 488
Lillywhite, 449
Lilon, 503
lily, 699, 774
-lily, 390
Lim, 458
limb, 372
limber, 759
Limber Jim, 684
lime, 687
limerick, 162
Limerick, 540
Limesprings, 539
limited, 581
Limon, 503
limousine, 723
limp-to-quaddle, to, 165
Linccolne, 453
Lincoln, 453, 470, 531
Lincolna, 488
Lincon, 453
Linda, 520
line, 697, 730
Line, 322
line load, 719
liner, 716, 720, 763
Linger Longer, 579
lingreesa, 167
linguica, 167
lining, 99
link, 239
Link, 476
Linkhern, 453
Linkhorn, 453
links, 384, 385
lint-head, 116, 776
lion, 639
Lion, 587

Lionel, 517
Lion's Den, 639
lions of the West, 639
Liora, 488
lip, 644; -splitter, 705
liqueur, 50, 52
liquor, 724
Lisle, 460
listen, 97
lister, 749
lite, 298
litenant, 85
literati, 319
literatur, 84
little buzzard, 145
Little Cloud, 445; Delaware, 605; Flower, 591; Georgetown, 540; Gold Dollar, 139; Hope, 592; Ida, 614; Joe, 747; Joe from Kokomo, 747; Joe picked the cotton, 747; Rat, 593; Rhody, 601
little fo', 747
little natural, 747
little small, 155
little ways, 337
Litvinov, 415
live hard against, to, 253
Livelsberger, 411
Livelsparger, 411
Lively Experiment, 601
Livenspire, 411
Liver, 449
Livera, 488
liverish, 253
Liverius, 480
Liverpool, 537
livers, 139
livesey, 458
live wire, 718
livier, 252
Livingston, 421
Livzy, 458
Liyān, 441
Liza, 515
lizard, 727
Lizard State, 610, 611
Lizinka, 497
Lizzie, 727
Ljungvist, 432
'll, 367
ll, Spanish, 307
Llewellyn, 508
llo, 308
Lloa, 488

Lloyd, 471, 521
Lloyd George, 403
Lloydine, 488, 493
lo, 292, 440
lo, Italian, 440
loaden, to, 358
loadened, 358
loading, 775
load of post-holes, 719
load of wind, 719
loafer, 51
Loaine, 488
loan, 158; -shark, 648
loan, to, 337, 355, 362, 395
Loarn, 503
Lo Bella, 488
Loberta, 488
loblolly, 193
Local, 536
locate, to, 48, 248, 249
location, 699
Loce Ahng-hayl-ais, 546; Ahng-hell-ess, 547
loch, 307
locker, 262
loco, 674, 742; -weed, 681, 742
Loco, 535
locoed, 127, 219
locust, 677
Locust, 488
Lodell, 503
lodge, 212
Loeb, 417
Loe Mae, 488
Loenial, 503
Loeties, 503
Loew, 417
Lowenstein, 422
Loewenthal, 420
log, 184, 185, 216, 228, 230, 251, 730; -book, 728; -wrench, 718
logger, 760
Logtown, 562
Loid, 504
loidy, 188
Lois, 521; -Rae, 490
loiter, 192
Lok, 442
Lömoe, 435
lon, 199
London, 459, 537
lonely, 390
loner, 736
Lone Star State, 640

Lone Wolf, 445
long, 175, 230; -faced, 217; -hair, 706, 729; -haul, 720; -sparred, 166; -underwear, 706
Long, 399, 409
longger, 300
Long Giland, 192
long holidays, 250
long line, 697
long nose, 719
longshoreman, 324
longsome, 175
Longstreet, 406
Longueuil, 437
Long Visitor, 445
Lonnie, 530
Lonzetta, 488
Lonzo, 503
loobricate, 85
loodicrous, 85
looie, 750
look, to, 205
Look, 442
look-after, 253
looker, 739
Look See, 579
look the berries, to, 140
looney, 776
Looney, 450
loop, 755; -wagon, 718
loop, to, 699
Loophole, 449
loose, to, 358
loosed, 358
loosen, to, 358
loosener, 752
Looson-Gore, 456
loot, 85
lootenant, 85
lop, 254
Lopez, 435
lopsided, 663
Lorama, 488
Loran, 504
LoRayne, 488
Lord, 323
Lord and Lady, 572
lordlily, 390
lordly, 390
Lord's bread-wagon, 218
lore, 89
Loree, 488
Lorenz, 409
lore of Moses, 89
Loretta, 480

List of Words and Phrases

lorn, 314
Lorna Jo, 488
lorry, 250
Lo-ruhmah, 488
Los, 547
Los Ahng-hay-lays, 547
Los Angeles, 545, 546, 547, 548, 553, 554, 571
Los Angeles de Porciuncúla, 547
Los Anggeles, 547; Angguh-lus, 547; Angheles, 547; Anjeles, 547; Anjileez, 547; Anjilus, 547; Anjuhliz, 546
Loss Anjileez, 546
loss, 216
lost, 83
Lost Gap, 562
Los Vigiles, 565
lot, 215, 684, 699
Lotawana, 497
Lotolia, 488
Lotta Joy, 579
Lotus, 504
Lou, 437
Louah, 488
LouCille, 488
loud, 227, 390
lo-ud, 158
loud noise, 646
Loughborough, 458
Louie, 476, 523
Louiezon, 488
Louis, 518
Louise, 487, 499, 500, 510
Louisiana Purchase, 508
Louis Seize, 449
Louis XVI, 449
lounge-lizard, 644, 649
Lounoma, 488
Lououn, 504
louse, 646; -cage, 714
Louse, 567
Lousella, 488
Louse Town, 679
Lousetta, 488
Lousy Level, 535
Louwillie, 488
Louza, 488
Louzella, 488
Louzon, 488
love, 121; -hole, 121; -weed, 681
Loveall, 449
Love Joy, 592

Lovel, 442
Loveladies, 564
Lovelady, 488
lovely, 374
Lo Venia, 494
Loven Kisses, 511
Loventine, 488
Lovewear, 437
Lovie, 480
LoVina, 488
loviner, 387
Loving, 525
Lovis, 504
Lovorn, 488
lowboy, 699
low ceiling, 727
Lowe, 408
Löwe, 408, 417
Lowell, 419, 420
Lowell Island, 540
Low Freight, 528
low level, 729
low pitchman, 685
Lowther, 409
low wine, 748
Loxi, 488
Loy, 488, 504
loyal, 192
Loyal, 542
Loyalhanna, 528
Loyal Lodge No. 296 Knights of Pythias Ponca City Oklahoma, 508
Loyd, 504
Loy Lee, 443
lozenge, 175
lozenger, 100, 175
L. Q. C. Lamar, 583
L'Rue, 488
Lu, 524
LuAlice, 488
Luana, 516
Luanda, 488
Luchow, 414
Luciel, 518
LuCiel, 488
Lucifer, 595
Lucile, 521, 523
Lucille, 518
Lucina, 480
Lucinda, 488
Luck, 511
Luckie, 525
Lucky Dog, 596
Lucy, 513

lud, 158
Luda, 488
Ludor, 579
Ludwig, 409
lueed, 310
Luena, 488
luer, 680
lues, 755
Lufburra, 458
luftenand, 85
lug, 646, 776; -wagon, 165
lug, to, 181
Lugarda, 488
lug in, to, 769
lug out, to, 769
lugubrious, 85
Luimneach, 540
luke, 750
Luke, 442
lukewarm, 85
Lulu, 518, 521, 561
Lum, 476, 504
lumber, 736, 752; -buster, 693; -room, 162
lumber, to, 226
lumberman, 760
Lumber State, 628
lumens, 319
lumina, 319
lump, 677
lumper, 685, 758, 774
lunatic, 85
lund, 254, 431
Lung, 449
lunged, 746
lung-man, 700
lupe, 207, 699
Lural, 504
Luray, 584
LuReign, 504, 506
Lurella, 480
Lurid, 85
lusa, 560
lush, to, 663
Lush, 488
lush-worker, 682
lustig, 207
lusty, 207
Lutellia, 488
lutenand, 85
Luther, 465, 471, 472, 522, 523
Lutine Clipporine Blanchine Annie-Ann, 521
Luttie, 488
Luvader, 495

Luvan, 504
Luvardia, 504
Luvna, 488
Luweoda, 488
Luzelle, 488
Luzertta, 480
-ly, 389, 390
Lyal, 504
Lyall, 504
Lygon, 458
Lyle, 504
Lyligh, 488
Lyman, 503, 506
Lympne, 458
Lynch, 399
Lyncoln, 453
Lyndyll, 488
Lynel, 504
Lynn, 506
Lynovecta, 488
lynx, 239
Lysander, 507
Lyska, 488
Lysle, 504
m, 300, 500
ma, 240
Määrälä, 429
Mabele, 488
Mable, 488, 494
Mac, 403, 404, 452, 504, 771
Macamic, 572
macaroni, 759; -mill, 760
Macaulay, 403
MacDonald, 400, 405
Macedonia, 591
Macena, 488
MacEochain, 403
Mac Eoghain, 421
Mac Gregor, 404, 405
mach, 314
machen, 757
macher, 757
Mack, 403, 429, 476
Mackékrun, 458
mackerel, 736
Mackey, 426, 429
Mackinac, 561
Mackinaw, 5
MacLaughlin, 408
MacLevy, 420
Maclíkuddy, 458
MacSuibhne, 403
mad, 159
Madalyne, 488
madame, 682

Madame, 488
Madame Cadenza, 730
Madame La Zonga, 730
mad-ax, 239
Madeliene, 488
Madelline, 488
Madelyn, 488
made the parlor, 722
Madison, 470, 531
Madison Square, 575
Madline, 488
Madlyne, 488
Madolene, 488
Madora, 488
maduro, 744
Mae, 488
mael, 312
Maela, 488
Ma'ene, 488
maenkaind, 288
Maeola, 488
Mae West, 781
Mafalda, 488
Magalone, 488
mágazine, 48, 114
Magazine, 511
Magdalene Arms, 577
Maggie, 480
Maggie's room, 754
maggot, 736
Maggot, 451
Maggotty Cove, 572
magnate, 736
Magnease, 488
Magnolia State, 630
Magnus, 434
Magnusholmen, 434
Mahan, 458
mahaqua, 529
Mahershalhashbaz, 467
Maheu, 453
Mahleen, 488
mahm, 111
Mahmūd, 523
mahn, 247, 269
Mahn, 458
mahnah-wauk-seepe, 526
Mahon, 458
Mahony, 454
mahsk, 47
mahula, to, 687
maid, 254
maiden, 769
MaIlDeCVoelpfocAP*pd-al*d*tlftnransnfSrpFS*s, 69

mail, 312
Maimai, 488
main, 746; -drag, 677; -iron, 716; -pin, 713; -steel, 716; -stem, 646, 677, 716
mainer, 388
Mainwaring, 458
Mainzeis, 458
Majel, 488
Major, 594
major-general, 208
Majoribanks, 456
makai, 240
Makamik, 572
makara, 267
make a lot of bag, to, 177
make a meal, to, 254
make a stake, to, 761
make fire, to, 253
Makehate, 451
make him scratch where he don't itch, to, 161
Mäkelä, 429
make ménage, to, 156
make off, to, 141
maker, 669
make wonder, to, 253
Maki, 429
mäki, 429, 430
makings, 127
Mäkitalo, 429
Mäkivuori, 429
Makkako-tan-engree, 442
Malaoa, 488
malary, 120
Malcolm, 517
Malcum, 506
male, 226, 312; -cow, 234; hog, 226, 234
Male, 561
Malene, 504
Malixia, 488
mall, 75
Mallard, 532
Mallūk, 441
Malma, 488
Malone, 439, 563
Malooly, 441
malt, 360
Malta Jean, 488
Ma'lūli, 441
Malvern Hill, 507
máma 48
mama-house, 753
Mama Lucia, 730

List of Words and Phrases 847

Mama's Baby, 511
Mamel, 488
M'Amis, 488, 494
mamma, 25, 111
mammæ, 319
mammal, 73
mammas, 319
mammy-daddy, to, 751
man, 269, 443
-man, 324
Man, 674
Manaloa, 489
mañana, 316, 318
Manassas, 489, 589
man-a-waukee, 526
man-catcher, 678
Mandalina, 489
mandate, 73
Mandze, 515
Manhattan, 565
manicurist, 736
Manifee, 489
manifest, 716
Manila, 489, 493
man I'm going to marry, 53
-mann, 423
Mannahatta, 565
mannequin, 73
männerchor, 317
Mannering, 458
Manners, 458
Manning, 439
Mano, 523
Manoel, 522
manonim, 237
Manoog, 523
Manor, 577
manse, 73
Månson, 432
Manti, 569
Manuel, 522
Manvin, 504
man-wau, 526
Maomi, 489, 494
maqua, 529
maracle, 154
marb, to, 238
Marblehead, 588
marbles, 733
Marcalee, 489
Marcantonio, 439
Marcellette, 489, 494
marchez, 238
marchons, 238
Marco Polo, 582

Marcus, 517
Mardela, 540
Mardella, 489
mare, 203
Maréchal, 317
Marenisco, 542
Marette, 498
Margaline, 489
Margaret, 479, 480, 498, 499, 509, 518, 521, 523
Margelina, 480
Margell, 489
margery prater, 664
Margileth, 489, 495
Margorilla, 509
Margot, 520
Marguerite, 518
Marhattianna, 542
Maria, 505, 513, 521
María de los Delores, 521; del Pilar, 521; del Rosario, 521
Mariana, 504
Marianne, 500
Marie, 499
Mariedythe, 489, 494
Mariel, 489
marihuana, 681
Marijo, 489
marijuana, 681
Marilyn, 498
Marine, 489
Marino, 439
Marion, 504, 505, 521
mark, 670, 768
Mark, 472, 517
marker, 770
Markowitz, 420
Marks, 436
mark twain, 721
Mark Twain, 583
Markus, 506
Marlborough, 458
Marlowe, 420, 429
Marlynne, 498
marmalade, 269
Marmette, 489
Marolyn, 521
Marques, 436
married, 646
marronguin, 155
marry, 91
marry the hook, to, 722
Marsala, 439
Marschula, 489
Marseille, 489

Marshall, 399, 439, 442, 444, 470
Marshbanks, 456
marshmeller, 89
Marston, 406
Marsylvia, 489
Martha, 480, 513
Martha Dandridge, 470
Marthamarcella, 489
Martha's Vineyard, 539
Martin, 46, 397, 399, 401, 436, 517, 523
Martines, 436
Martini, 439
Mart'n, 46
Marttinen, 430
Martyl, 489
Mărŭn, 441
Marvee, 489
marvel, 79
marvelous, 284
Marvin, 517
Mary, 91, 442, 463, 479, 489, 499, 509, 510, 513, 521, 591; Ann, 518; Arms, 577; Jane, 523, 681; Jo, 493; John, 442; Warner, 680
Mary Beatrice Love Divine Ceeno Tatrice Belle Caroline, 512
Marye, 489
Maryea, 489
Maryland Free State, 602, 603, 604
Marylynn, 489
Maryneal, 541
Marynell, 489
Maryville, 553
marzipän, 317
mash, 748
mash, to, 269
mashah, 516
mashed tambourine, 751
masher, 644, 645
mash potatoes, 388
mask, 47
Maskew, 459
Mason, 399
mass, 322, 323
Massachóosets, 543
Massachusetts, 543
Massasip, 544
Massátchusetts, 543
masseur, 53
Masten, 406

master maniac, 713
master mind, 713
master of ceremonies, 50, 695
Ma'Su, 489
matairiel, 314
match-box, 699
Matches, 449
Matchihundupemabtunk, 560
Mateel, 489
mateeryaliez, 306
Mater Dolorosa, 466, 517
materialize, 306
Matha, 489
Mathilde, 489
Matilda, 499
Matina, 489
matrixes, 320
matterated, 158
matte shot, 699
Matthew, 453
Matthew Mark Luke John Acts of the Apostles, 512
Mattie, 480
mattock, 239
Matykiewicz, 425
Matzola, 439
Maud, 499, 763
MauDee, 489
Maudella, 489
Maudleigh, 489
Maugham, 458
mauka, 240
maul-drag, to, 155
Maunaloa, 525
Maungau, 515
Maureen, 489
Maurice, 454, 517, 524
Maurus, 524
Maury, 454
Mauva, 489
Mauzell, 489
Mava, 489
Mavance, 489
maverick, 219, 742
Mavontiene, 489
maw, 40, 111
Maw, 451
Maw Bell, 718
Mawlbra, 458
Mawm, 458
Max, 517
may, 195, 202, 367, 446
maybe, 261

Maybelle, 488
Mayble, 488
may can, 133, 364
May-dá-me, 488
Mayer, 415, 458
Mayeu, 453
Mayhem, 449
Mayhew, 453
Mayhoe, 453
Maymire, 489
Mayo, 453, 504
Mayola, 489
mayor, 203
mayorality, 99
Mayowe, 453
Mayozie, 489
Mayry, 489
Mazelle, 489
mazuma, 151
Mazura, 489
Mazzola, 439
M. B., 511
mba, 266
mbakara, 266, 267
mbu, 266
mbubu, 266
m. c., 50, 695
m. c., to, 695
Mc, 403, 583
McCarthy, 399
McCoy, 670, 671
McCreadyville, 583
McCullough, 408
McDonald, 399
McGeoghegan, 403
McGillicuddy, 403, 583
McGonigle, 583
McIlhatton, 403
McKaba, 441
McLaughlin, 453
McNara, 494
McNificent, 298
McNora, 489
McShea, 426
McSweeney, 403
McTwiggan, 583
McZena, 483
me, 248, 340, 373, 374, 375
Me, 511
M'Eachern, 458
Meagher, 458
meese, 638
Mehron, 523
me-all, 379
meals, 173
mean, 350

me and Jim, 374
meant, 359
measle, 383
measles, 219
measure, 185
meat-burner, 759; -drinker, 738; -hook, 723; -pie, 250; show, 694; -wagon, 727
Mecca, 489
mechuleh, 687, 753
Meddler's War, 786
media, 318
Media, 489
mediæval, 282, 286
Medicine Hat, 572
Medina, 414
medium bounce, 707
Medrith, 489
med worker, 686
meeter, 301
meeting-house, 170, 185
meet-up, 165
Mega, 489
Megerditchian, 441
Megnies, 458
mek a jump, to, 247
Melassia, 495
Melbourine, 489, 493
Melcena, 489
Melchett, 416
Melchisedek priesthood, 221
melee, 318
Meleke, 526
Melirn, 504
melk, 230
Melleoke, 526
Mellona, 497
melodrama, 690
Melone, 439
melt, 360
Melvin, 517
Melwakee, 526
Melwarik, 526
memo, 730
memoranda, 319
Memory Grove, 592
Memphis, 559
men, 720
Menahem, 519
menance, 100
Mencken, 595
Mendel, 519
Mendong Gomba, 538
Mengiz, 458

Mengues, 458
meninges, 319
Meniol, 489
Mennel, 458
Mennes, 458
mens, 386
men's, 325
menses, 386
Men-tung-Ssu, 538
menu, 53
Menyas, 458
Menyies, 458
menyou, 53
Menzas, 458
Menzheis, 458
Menzies, 458
Menziz, 458
meracle, 154
Mercidean, 489
mercy, 79
Mercy, 468
Merd-, 495
Merdelle, 489, 495
Merdena, 495
Merdine, 489, 495
Merdis, 495
Merhize, 489, 510
merle, 748
Merle, 496, 504, 506
Merma, 489
Meroah, 489
Merrick, 453, 458
merry, 91
Merry Lou, 489
merry-me-got, 253
mes, 516
mesa, 51, 573
mesh, 313
meshuga, 671, 674
mesot, 209
message, 743
Messiah, 590
messu, 516
mestizo, 243
Mészöly, 440
Meta, 520
metallurgy, 284
Metarie, 489
Meteor, 595
meter, 301
method, 209
Methodis', 218
Methodist meeting-house, 322
métier, 318
Metlakatla, 552

metziah, 687
Mevasher-Tov, 519
Mew, 331
meyer, 207
Meyer, 399, 401, 410, 519
Meyers, 410
Meynell, 458
Meyrick, 458
mezz, 680
M'Gillycuddy, 458
Mia, 489
Miami, 544, 566
micen, 386
Michael, 463, 524
michagami, 561
Michel, 409
Michelson, 430
Michigan, 561
mich wundert, 203
Mickey, 489, 594; Finn, 734
Micki, 489
microphonitis, 36
Micsza, 426
Micuda, 427
midget, 785
midgie, 785
midnight, 752
Midnight Bell, 593; Sun, 596
midoudt sound, 700
midsummermadness, 325
Midwinter, 449
mie ken zie, 771
mien, 315
Mierzejewski, 426
miet, 288
might, 261
might-a-of, 366
might can, 364
might could, 133, 364
might have, 366
might he will come, 261
might of, 366
might ought to go, 133
might would, 364
mighty, 172
Mighty G., 588
mighty near, 390
Mihály, 524
Mike, 475, 523, 762
Mike and Ike, 752
mike-boom, 699; -hog, 730; -monkey, 699; -mugger, 729
Miki, 489

mikinak, 561
Mikolajezyk, 425
Milada, 489
Milca, 489
Milderd, 494
Mildred, 521
Mildren, 489
Milford Haven, 414
milioke, 526
milk, 230, 269; -gap, 699
milk, to, 694
milk a scene, to, 699
Milk Wagon, 588
mill, 269, 714, 717, 723, 724
Millais, 458
Millar-Millard, 453
Millay, 458
Mille Lacs, 561
miller, to, 121
Millerstown, 530
Millickie, 526
Millinee, 489
Milliner's Arms, 572
Miller, 396, 397, 398, 399, 401, 409, 422, 439
Millie Mike, 442
Mills, 399
Milltown, 553
Mill Wheel, 593
Milma, 480
Milo, 522
miloaki, 526
Miloma, 541
Milon, 507
Miloslav, 522
Milta, 489
Milton, 517, 522, 523
Milton H. Smith, 582
Miltonic, 98
Milwackey, 526
Milwacky, 526
Milwarick, 526
Milwaukee, 526, 529, 588
Milwaukie, 526
minch, 687
mind, 230
mine, 261
minet, 155
Mingies, 458
Mingiss, 458
Minian, 489
miniature, 7
minister's face, 226
Ministry of Economic Warfare, 331
minne, 574

List of Words and Phrases

Minnesoti, 171
Minnewa, 489
Minnich, 411
minnie, 155, 156
Minnie, 679; -Mouse, 774
minon, 156
minor league, 737
Minuleta, 379
minute-man, 766
Minx, 449
Miriam, 518, 519
miring-branch, 217
Mirror Lake, 540
Mirta, 489
Mirth, 496
mis, 131
Mis, 452
Misak, 523
misbobble, 177
Mis-Campbell, 452
miscellany, 47
mischcowain, to, 687
mischievious, 100
mischievous, 48
mischkov, 687
mischkowain, 687
misch-masch, 151
miselaenyus, 301
Misery, 588, 774
misery-whip, 760
Misha, 517
Mishilimackanac, 5
misiz, 131, 221
Mis-Kelly, 452
Miss, 53, 428
misseded, 359
Misses, 53
Misses Smith, 328
missionary worker, 777
mission-bell, 722; -stiff, 676, 677
Mississippi, 544, 588
Missouri, 544, 588; -Compromise, 508
Miss Smiths, 328
misted, 359
Mister, 53, 511
misty-moisty, 232
Mitchell, 399, 405, 409, 442
mitgehen, 254
mitsia, 687
Mitsugi, 444
Mitsuji, 444
mitt-joint, 684; -reader, 684

Mitzie, 696
MiXail, 442
mixer, 682
mix-max, 151
miz, 131, 221
miziz, 131, 221
mizriz, 221
Mizzoura, 544, 545
Mizzoury, 544
M. M., 771
-m'n, 324
m'nisose, 544
Moark, 541
mob, 667, 671
mobilize, 72
Mocolee, 489
Modaine, 489
model, to, 731
moder, 258
moderatest, 388
modern, 40
Modjeski, 425
Modrel, 504
modren, 99, 100
Modrzejewski, 425
Moe, 562
Mohammed, 572
mohasky, 681
Mohawk, 529
Mohelia, 489
Mohonri, 515
Mohr, 402
moider, to, 253
moineau, 155
Moïse, 517
moisture, 772
Molasse, 582
molasses, 219, 329, 386
Mokownquando, 446
Mole, 458
Molinari, 439
Molitoris, 427
moll, 667; -buzzer, 670
Molly, 594
Molly b'Damn, 139
molten, 360
Molvene, 489
molybdenum, 285
Molyneaux, 458
mom, 111
Moma, 489
mommy, 111
Momo, 515
Momulu Massaquoi, 448
mona, 269
Mona Lisa, 577

Monar, 504
Monday, 459, 775
Monday Morning, 594
Moneta, 439
money, 645
Moneysunk, 579
Mongeon, 432
moniker, 683
Monima, 489
monk, 759
Monk, 504, 506
monkey, 685, 730, 740, 751, 775; -hurdler, 705; -shines, 740; -wagon, 714; -wire, 717
Monkey, 774
Monkeydo, 511
monkey on his back, 680
Monkey State, 639
Monne Fay, 521
monologist, 692
Monroe, 531
Monsieur, 53
Monson, 432
monster, 761
monstrous, 172
Monsūr, 523
montage, 700
Montague, 416
Montana City, 554
Monte, 523
Monteze, 489
Montgomery, 458
Montgomery Ward, 446, 459
Monumental City, 604
Monument State, 604, 641
Monzell, 504
moo, 752
moocah, 681
mooch, to, 127, 677, 685, 747, 774
mood, 294
moo-errn, 18
moo juice, 747
mooley-cow, 718
Moonean, 495
moor, 168, 253, 573
-moor, 577
Moore, 396, 397, 399, 401, 402, 413
moose, 328, 724
Moose, 504, 506, 572
Mooseasuck, 531
Moose Factory, 572
Moosejaw, 572

List of Words and Phrases   851

Moosetocmaguntic, 560
moosic, 84
Moosonoe, 572
moot, 84
mooter, 681
mop, 262, 734
Mop, 774
mor, 292
Mór, 524
Mora, 564
moral, 216
Moran, 426, 441, 454
Morani, 569
Moray, 458
Mord, 504
more, 214, 230, 387; beautifuller, 387; better, 387; betterer, 387; fresher, 387; gladder, 387; greater, 387; hotter, 387; larger, 387; nor, 269; outer, 388; resteder, 387; righter, 387; stronger, 387; surer, 387; taller, 387; than, 269
-more, 534
More, 402
moreder, 387
More-fruit, 467
Moreira, 436
Morene, 495
morer, 387
More-trial, 467
Moretti, 439
Morey, 436
Morgan, 399
Morgenthau, 424, 435
Morgenthaw, 424
morgue-wagon, 753
Moris, 427
Moritz, 517
Mormon State, 640
morning, 254; -glory, 769; -slippers, 237
Morning, 515
morning-hour girl, 743
Morocco, 537
Moroni, 515
Morphine, 513
Morris, 399, 405, 416, 436, 517
Morrison, 399, 403
morsch, 151
mortician, 738
Mortimer, 517

Morton, 416, 430, 517
Morveen, 489
M. O. S., 700
Mosco, 504
Moscovitz, 422
Moscow, 537, 540
Moses, 416, 467, 516, 517
Moses Bull Bear, 444
Moses Moke, 525
Mosetta, 489
Mosiellee, 489
Moskva, 540
Moslyn, 489
Mosolete, 497
Mosquito State, 601
Mossaback, 449
mosshorn, 742
Mossy Lee, 489
most, 152, 387; anybody, 337; best, 387; bitterest, 387; hardest, 387; nearest, 387
mostest, 387
mostly, 218
most unkindest cut of all, 387
Motare, 489
mothback, 233
moth-box, 705
mother, 111, 459
Mother Hicks, 572; Hubbard, 763; of Presidents, 597, 637; of Rivers, 599; of Southwestern Statesmen, 639; of States, 597; of Statesmen, 597
motion-picture cathedral, 703
Motubizanto, 593
motzoh, 687
Mouakad, 441
moula, 707
mould, 286, 316
Moule, 458
Moultrie, 472
mountain, 328; -climber, 720; -oyster, 764; -pay, 716
mountainious, 99, 100
Mount Alta, 528; Calvary, 590; Comfort, 592; Cuba, 556; Vernon, 581; Washington, 563, 564
Mountbatten, 414, 587

mounting, 137
mourn, 18
mouse, 328, 673, 707. 764, 768; -trap, 720, 763
mouse, to, 674
mouthpiece, 683
movie, 702; -actor, 702; -cathedral, 644; -parlor, 702; -show, 702
movies, 251
moviola, 700
Moyer, 410
Moyett, 489
Moynian, 459
Moynihan, 459
M. P., 777
Mr., 220, 222; Bates, 667; Fakus, 669
Mrs., 131, 221, 222, 428; Chase, 755; John Smith, 473; Jones Smith, 472; McKenzie, 771
Mt. Joy, 536
mu, 681
Mu'aqqad, 441
mucher, 747
muckered, 253
muckle-dun, 143
mud, 680, 740, 752; -guard, 250; -hen, 107; -slinger, 766; -smeller, 763
Mudcat State, 630
Mud-waddler State, 631
Mueller, 397
Muench, 411
muff, 736, 746
mugg, to, 669
mugger, 766
mugging, 669, 690
muggles, 680, 681
muggs, 135
Muggsie, 594
mug-joint, 684
muhnch-ou-z'n, 52
Muir, 402
mukka, 207
mukkus, 207
mukluk, 239
mule, 719; -foot, 236
Muller, 397, 408, 414
Müller, 397, 408, 409
mulligan, 677; -mixer, 750
Mullinewks, 458
mullock, 217
multip, 756

multipara, 756
mum, 111, 663
mumma, 110
mummy, 110
mumps, 219
Mumu, 515
Münchhausen, 52
München, 540
Munger, 454
Mungo, 513, 753
Munian, 459
Munich, 540
municipial, 99
Munson, 432, 434
Muntgummery, 458
Muqabba'ah, 441
Murdena, 489
murder, 696, 707
murder, to, 253
murderer, 753
Murel, 504
Murfreesboro', 589
Muriel, 463, 504
murk, 752
Murley, 521
Murphy, 399, 401, 403, 674
Murray, 91, 399, 454, 517; Hill, 575
Murry, 458, 518
Murt, 504
Murta, 459
Murtagh, 459
Murva, 489
muscle in, to, 671, 672, 711
Muscle Shoals, 569
Muscogee, 556
muse, 313
múseum, 48
mush, 151, 678, 721; -faker, 678; -worker, 682
mush, to, 238
mush and molasses, 132
mushmillion, 137
mushroom, 678
music-box, 176
musick, 311
muskellunge, 329
muskie, 329
muskrat, 170, 328
Muskrattown, 540
musky, 329
Mussel, 569
mústache, 48

mustang, 237
muster-bread, 158
mutt, 645, 740, 766
mutter, 307
mutton corn, 215
muttonhead, 645
mutton puncher, 742
Muzelta, 489
my, 125, 230, 261, 375
Myda, 489
Myers, 399
Myerscough, 459
Myldredth, 516
myll a ken, to, 664
Myllymäki, 429
mynt, 664
myositis, 736
myositis ossificans, 735
Myricille, 489
Myrick, 453
myrrh, 310
my son, 254
mystery, 674
Mystia, 489
n, 92, 99, 151, 193, 228, 262, 300, 368, 500
n, silent, 96
'n, 297
na, 267
nab, 664
nabe, 297, 700
nabor, 291
Nacirema, 579
Nachman, 519
nachtigall, 207
Nadda, 489
NaDine, 489
Nadinola, 489
Naevene, 489
Naftali, 417
Naftzinger, 411
Nafziger, 411
nail, 680; -eater, 740; -sick, 165
nailer, 716
Naio, 489
Naith, 504
naïve, 318
Najala, 489
Najīb, 523
naked, 175
Nıked Place, 566
Nalwottoge, 556
name-gatherer, 686
Nammūrah, 441

Namora, 441
nanan, 155
Nancy, 513
nanny, 764
Nanotuck, 556
nanse, 267
Naomi, 489, 519
Naparia, 489
Napoleon, 593, 725
nap'tha, 97
Narasona, 498
narrow, 151; -gutted, 165
nary, 181
Narylyn, 489
nary none, 392
Nary Red, 536
Nasi, 422
Nasrine, 489
Nassamasschaick, 530
Nassau, 472
nasty-faced chowder-head, 180
Nat, 475, 476
Natalie, 517, 518
natch, 708
Natchez, 562
Natchovtasmuck, 530
Nathan, 518
Nathaniel, 467, 518
nation, 310
native, 328; -horse, 328
natschelnik, 151
natueral, 300
natur, 114
natural, 685; -looking, 153
nature, 84, 320
Natusio, 588
nat-yur, 84
naught, 283
naughtin, 114
Naumkeag, 531
Nausch, 416
Nauvelene, 489
Nauwot, 556
Navelle, 489
Navel of the Nation, 623
nav gajikanes, 442
navvy, 770
Nawwatick, 556
Nawwatuck, 556
nay, nay, Pauline, 645
Nazarene, 489
Nazary, 454
Nazi, 331, 780
ndo, 266

List of Words and Phrases

neah, 40
near, 390
neat, 315, 692
neb, to, 204
Nebraska, 563
Nebrasky, 544
nebulæ, 319
nebulas, 319
Necessary, 450
Necessary War, 785
neck, 573
neck, to, 708
Neck City, 536
neck her, to, 92
neckid, 120
necktie, 754
Ned, 476
nee, 318
need, to, 202
Needa, 489
needle, to, 652, 671
Needy, 567
nee-ther, 78, 214
Negro, 171, 211, 322
Nehemiah, 467
Neidich, 411
Neidig, 411
neighborhood, 297; -house, 700
neighbour, 286
neither, 186, 214
neither-are, 337, 338
neither don't, 393
neitshr, 288
neked, 175
Neketia, 489
Neldagae, 489
nellie, 749
Nellie, 480
nellify, to, 194
Nello, 504
Nelly, 764
Nelma, 489
Nels, 476
Nelson, 397, 399, 401, 476, 521
Nenzil, 504
nephew, 211
Nephi, 515, 569
Nequiltpaalis, 573
n er g, 292
Nerton, 504
nerts, 643
Nerva, 489
nerve, 770
Nerve, 511

nervous, 164
nesieri, 288
nester, 742
nestes, 139, 200, 386
nesteses, 139
nests, 200
net, 283, 316
nett, 283
network, 731
Neukirch, 408
Neumann, 409
neuralgia, 175
Neuralgia, 512
neuraliga, 99, 175
neuritis, 81
neu-tone, 297
neutral, 720
Neuzze, 416
Nevada, 504, 506, 588
Neval, 489
never done nothin', 391
new, 84, 205
New, 531, 532
New Amsterdam, 532
Newana, 489
Newark, 566
Newbedford, 539
Newengland, 539
New England of the West, 630
new ground, 226
new growth, 755
Newhampshire, 539
Newkirk, 408
New London, 553, 572
Newman, 399, 409
Newnes, 459
Newnz, 459
New Philadelphia, 566
New Purchase greenie, 618
news, 84, 313; -butcher, 715
News, 595
Newsholme, 402
Newsom, 402
newspack, to, 232
New Spain, 601, 602
newspaper man, 324
New Sweden, 605
newt, 720
Newt, 475
Newton, 433, 522, 531
New Virginia, 571
New York, 539, 565, 588
next, 123

ng, 182, 185, 192, 228, 261, 290, 294, 411
ng, German, 307
ngandu, 267
Ngola, 265
nguba, 266, 267, 610
Ni, 404
Nias, 504
nibbler, 678
nibby, 232
Nibthaska, 563
nice, 241
nicerer, 388
Nichols, 397
Nicholsdaughter, 431
Nicht, 450
nicht nichts, 394
nichts, 767
nick, 155
Nicolson, 431
Nicoma, 489
Nieca, 489
Niedermann, 422
Niel, 317
niemals nicht keine, 394
Niemi, 429
Nieminen, 429
nifty, 644
niggah, 211
nigger, 698, 733; -baby, 163; -head, 716, 761, 770, 773
Nigger Hill, 536
nighdt, 258
night, 125, 254; -cap, 769
Night Glow, 582; Walker, 44
Niinimäki, 429
Nils, 476, 520, 521
Nilson, 432
nimshy, 158
Nina, 519
Nina from Argentina, 746; from Carolina, 746
Ninaview, 528
nineteenth-hole, 652, 755
ninety-eight, 722; -five, 772; -nine, 771; -six, 772
Ninnie, 521
nip, to, 177
Nip and Tuck, 534
nippent, 252
Nipper, 774
nippers, 751
nipple-chaser, 763
Nira, 513

854   List of Words and Phrases

Nishan, 523
nisht zu wissen fin gornisht, 392
Nissie, 489
Nissley, 410
nite, 291, 295
Nitsua, 579
Nitul, 517
Nix, 489
nixie, 767
nk, 192
nna, 267
no, 204, 260, 394; -account, 143
Noah, 468
Noba, 490
Nobie, 496
noble, 777
Noble, 507, 508
nobody, 391
nobody ain't never, 393
nobody don't, 393
nobody hadn't ought to, 393
noch, 203
nochtogal, 207
Nodaway, 579
Noffsker, 411
Nogales, 552
nohow, 391, 392
noise, 192, 668, 731
Noles, 458
Nolia, 490
Nolwotogg, 556
nomen, 333
Nomus, 507
none are, 337
nonessential, 325
no nothing, 392
Nonotuck, 556
nood, 84
noodle, 773; -twister, 744
Noodle, 534
noodleje, 181
nook, 228
Nookie, 490
nooz, 84
no puedo ver nada, 246
norate, to, 226
Nordamyrth, 490
nor do not, 393
Norena, 521
Norfolk, 5
Norissa, 490
Norkaitis, 428
Norkat, 428

Norman, 518, 521
Normangee, 541
Normarie, 490
nor-not, 393
nor nothing, 393
Norreys, 459
Norris, 459
Norsworthy, 454
north, 88
Northallerton, 414
North Amherst, 566
Northampton, 96
Northbrook, 414
North Star State, 630
Norvain, 490
Norvetta, 498
Norwotock, 556
Nose Dive, 594
nose-dive, to, 727
no-see-um, 239
nosegent, 664
Nosodak, 540
not, 251, 393, 394
not be no, 394
notch, 573, 574
not enough hop, 729
Noter Dayme, 54
nothing, 91, 171
nothin' nohow, 392
nothin' scarcely, 391
No Time, 568
Notluf Farm, 579
not-neither, 393
not never, 392
not never no more nohow, 392
Notre Dame, 54; de l'Assumption de MacNider, 571; de Lourdes de Montjoli, 571
Notrr Damme, 54
nought, 282, 283
noun, 333
Nousiatinen, 430
Nova Scotian mahogany, 753
novelet, 302
Novert, 504
novitiate, 745
Novsepian, 441
now, 260
Noyce, 504
NRA, 513
ns, 269
nu, 84, 298
nubber, 737

nucleus, 292
nuclus, 292
nude, 84
nue, 300
Nuel, 504
Nuessli, 410
nuez, 313
nuffin, 171
nuf sed, 298
nuklene, 296
nullify, to, 194
number, 757
Number Nine, 536
number two, 736
nuna, 267
nunny-bag, 252
nunu, 267
Nürnberg, 317
nurse cloth, 776
nursement, 121
nuse, 313
nut, 645, 648; -buster, 713; -cracker, 713; -splitter, 713
nut, to, 770
Nutmeg State, 599
nuts, 648
Nuts, 678
nuts over, to be, 127
nyam, to, 267
nyamnyam, to, 267
nye-ther, 78
nyew, 122
nyewz, 84
nygle, to, 664
Nyitray, 440
Nykänen, 429
Nylan, 504
Nylotis, 490
nymphæums, 320
Nynn, 490
nyoung, 269
nyow, 114
Nypenn, 541
Nye Sverige, 605
nyu, 84
o, 45, 71, 73, 82, 114, 158, 184, 185, 186, 199, 203, 226, 228, 230, 236, 241, 258, 260, 288 291, 292, 310, 367, 410, 431, 443, 459, 521, 546
O, 404, 680
ö, German, 50, 189, 431
ø, Norwegian, 434
o, Spanish, 554

List of Words and Phrases

ö, Swedish, 431
O', 403
Oadeous, 504
Oarly, 504
Oatmeal, 450
oatmeal cloth, 776
Oaxim, 490
OB, 755
Oba, 504
Obanon, 490
Obear, 438
Obelisk, 536
obertenne, 208
Oberzine, 490
Obey, 451
Obie, 504
O'Brien, 399, 403
Oblong, 534
oboe, 679
obscurantist, 25
obsequies, 385
Oby, 504
Ocala, 556
O Cathain, 421
Occum, 504
Oceail, 504
Ocean Towers, 577
Oceaphus, 504
O Ceochain, 421
Ochsenschwanz, 417
Ocie, 504
Ocllo, 497
Ocoee, 556
O Comhdain, 421
O Comhghain, 421
O'Connor, 399, 403
octopodes, 319
octopi, 319
od, 504, 506
Odas, 504
Ode, 504
O'Dell, 406
odeona, 237
Oder, 504
Odessa, 556
Odis, 504
Odix, 504
Odle, 406
O'Donnell, 403
O'Donovan, 403
odorous, 280
odour, 280; -less, 280
O'Dwaine, 490
Odyle, 490
Odys, 504
odzo, 267

oe, 282, 410, 434
O. E. A., 163
œcology, 282
œconomy, 282
œcumenical, 282
œdema, 282
Oehler, 408
Oehm, 409
Oehrle, 409
œsophagus, 282
of, 234, 262, 352, 365, 366
ofay, 270
of easy virtue, 663
off, 83, 241, 254, 778
offa, 394
offal, 758
off-breed, 724
offeecial, 199
offen, 394
offence, 281, 282, 284
offend, to, 211
offense, 281, 285
offer, 216
off-falls, 748
office, 216, 683
Office of Solid Fuels Coordinator for War, 330
office with, to, 220
off of, 337
off the arm, 730
of'n, 96
often, 96
O. G., 687
ogalallah, 490
Ogeal, 490
O Giorgi de Tisasko, 442
Ogpu, 331
Ogrodowski, 425
Oguerracatam, 593
oh, 70
O'Henry, 504
O-he-ó, 543
oh gee, 772
oh girlie, 177
Ohio, 543
Ohler, 408
Ohlson, 432
Ohmart, 504
Ohowo, 543
Ohta, 444
oh yeah, 97, 645
oh, you son-of-a-bitch, 646
oi, 87, 155, 157, 164, 188–

93, 203, 214, 241, 255, 292, 410
Oid, 504
oil, 87, 190, 191, 192, 214, 241, 253; -can, 756
oiler, 714
oilily, 390
Oil State, 598
oj, 249
Ojo Caliente, 565
O. K., 648, 650, 773, 785
Okai, 448
Okaloosa, 560
Okasaki, 443
Okay, 535
Okazaki, 443
Okemah, 490
Okey, 504
Okie, 637
Okla, 490, 493
okoboji, 582
Oktibbeha, 562
okus, 670
ol, 310
Ol, 504
ola, 267
Olaf, 520
Olamae, 488
Olander, 504
Ol-aw-baw-ma, 552
old, 203
Old Bay State, 599; Bullion, 635; Colony, 599; Crow, 446; Dirigo, 629; Dominion, 596; Glory, 542; Granny Hobble-Gobble, 132; Hawk-eye, 622; Ironsides, 588; Line State, 602, 604; Miss, 488; Mo, 588; Nick, 588; North State, 607; Town, 166; Town Turkey, 166; Webfoot, 638; Woman, 774
older, 388
oldern than me, 337
old-fashion, 388
old man, 724
Ole, 432
Oleah, 504
Olene, 482
Ole Olesen, 432
Oler, 408
Olesen, 432, 433
Olessen, 432
Olgalene, 482, 490, 494

Olinzea, 490
Olive, 524
Oliver, 439
Olivieri, 439
Ollie, 476
Ollus, 504
Ollywood, 96
olo, 310
O'Loughlin, 403, 432
Olson, 399, 432
Olva, 504
-om, 402
Omadell, 490
Omae, 504
Omaha, 563
omaloor, 253
O-mán-ha, 563
Omar, 508
Omarchadha, 403
omelette, 269
Omelia, 490, 494
omnibus, 327
O Muircheartaigh, 403
on, 187, 202, 203, 216, 226, 234, 251, 352, 370
ona, 267
on account of, 337
Onan, 512
on a pig's back, 253
once, 100, 198, 202, 394; -over, 652
onct, 120
one, 269, 370
One, 450
one-armed Johnnie, 763
one at a clatter, 150
One Eye, 536
one-he, 338, 395
Oneida, 529
O'Neill, 403
one-lunger, 730
Onema, 490, 495
one-night stand, 688
one-one, 269
one on the city, 752
onery, 97
ones, 100
onfinancial, 155
Ong's Hat, 564
on his, 92
on his top, 674
Oníghons, 460
onion, 734
Onions, 460
-onis, 428
Onis, 504

on last week, 226
onliest, 387
only, 337, 338, 394
Only, 450, 535
Ono, 444
Onoh, 444
onor, 300, 306
onour, 95
on pump, 177
o'n'ry, 97, 161
Ontario, 565
on the air, 731
on the altar, 745
on the attick, 206
on the beach, 721
on the beam, 727
on the bench, 737
on the bottom, 719
on the bush, to be, 674
on the cannon, 683
on the circus, 744
on the drop edge of yonder, 217
on the heavy, 683, 744
on the I. C., 669
on the lam, 667, 672
on the mojo, 680
on the nose, 730
on the road, 690
on the sevens, 744
on the show, 683
on to his curves, 737
on tour, 690
Onus, 504, 506
on yesterday, 226
Onza, 490
oo, 70, 84, 215, 241, 292, 294, 309
Oolooah, 490
oomph, 644, 703, 704
Oomph Girl of America, 704
oomphies, 704
oonah, 269
Oong, 443
-oosh, 199
Oota, 490
Ootram, 459
O. P., 690
Opaloma, 490
open cold, to, 690
opening, 684
open the door, Richard, 645
operation, 782
Operation Dixie, 782

operator, 697
opery, 544, 685
Opferkuchen, 408
oph, 310
Ophni, 504
opium, 292
opry-house, 690
opum, 292
or, 327
OR, 755
-or, 279, 280, 281
Ora, 506
Orabelle, 490
Orah, 519
Oral, 504
Oran, 504
orange, 82, 216; -peel, 700
Orange, 506; Free State, 604; River Colony, 604; State, 614
orator, 216, 280
oratour, 280
Oravell, 504
Orban, 504
Orbra, 504
Orcellia, 509
Orderway, 461
ordinry, 32
Ordis, 490
Ordway, 461
Oregon, 567
Orel, 504
or else, 672
Oren, 422, 508
Orene, 490, 494
orfan, 292
organ, 700; -grinder, 700; -loft, 697
Organ, 450
O'Rhaitia, 490
Oriel, 504
Original Bugg, 451
Orilla, 490
Oris, 504
Orlen, 504
Ormal, 504
Orman, 504
Ormie, 506
ornament, 713
Ornberg, 431
Örnberg, 431
ornery, 97, 161
Orpha, 504
orphan, 724, 770
orphanest, 388
Orray, 504

Orr-Lyda, 490
Orsamus, 504
Orsavilla, 490
orthoggerafey, 310
Ortice, 490
Orv, 504, 506
Orville, 521
-ory, 45
os, 320
osaginang, 561
oscar, 702
Oscar, 669
Oscaretta, 490, 493
oscuro, 744
Osey, 504
OSFCW, 331
O'Shea, 437
Oshie, 494
Osia, 437
Osie, 504, 506
Osman, 504
O-So-Kozy, 579
O sole mio, 505
Osro, 507
Osett-cum-Gawthorpe, 324
Ostella, 490
Ostenia, 490
ostler, 92
OSuileabhain, 403
O'Sullivan, 403
otel, 92
otha, 171
Othal, 504
Othema, 490
other, 171
Othul, 504
Otis, 470
O'Toole, 403
Otshingumbo, 267
Otta, 490
Ottilie, 482
Ottis, 504
Otto, 519
ottomobile, 199
O Tuathail, 403
Otwa, 504
ou, 227, 292, 294, 310
Ouaricon, 567
oubain, 87
ouch, 51
ough, 310
oughta, 219
oughtn' to never, 392
ought to could, 364
Ouida, 492

ounce, 775
oup, 258
-our, 280, 281, 316
ouren, 369
Our Father, 590
ourfathers, 325
Ouriconsint, 567
Our Lady's Bubbies, 572
ourn, 368, 369
Our Saviour, 590
'ouse, 95
out, 120, 227, 230
outen, 390
outen, to, 202
out front, 163, 689
Outhouse, 450
out in the alley, 730
outlandishest, 388
outlaw strike, 777
out on the sod, 761
outplay, to, 365
Outram, 459
outside, 425, 751
outsider, 221, 222, 234
Ouzinkie, 552
ov, 300
Ova, 490, 495
Oval, 504
oven, 662
over-den, 208
overhalls, 96
overshot, 762
overtake, to, 365
over the left, 644
Overy, 504
-ovice, 417
Ovid, 504, 507
-ovitch, 417
ow, 86, 294
Owaelah, 490
owanga, 267
Owego, 565
Owens, 397, 399
owl, 328
Owl, 596
own, 369
ox, 231
Ox, 535
oxens, 137, 386
Oxford, 537, 562, 578; Knolls, 577
oxter, 253
Oyonna, 490, 510
o you kid, 645
oyster, 190, 192
Oyster, 449; -State, 604

Oxx, 449, 459
Ozark State, 631
Ozell, 490
Ozmay, 504
Ozro, 504, 507
p, 98, 258, 300, 411, 500
pa, 111
PA, 756
Pabodie, 438
Pabody, 438
pachshu, 151
pack guts to a bear, to, 173
packwater, 139
pact, 306
pad, 681, 711; -room, 684
pad, to, 217
paddlefoot, 727
pædagogy, 282
pædiatrics, 282
pænology, 282
Pagé, 437
Paglia, 439
pah, 563
Pahk, 444
Pahoja, 545
Pahotcha, 545
Pahranagat, 563
Pahroc, 563
Pahrump, 563
pahs, 101
Pahucka, 545
Pah Ute, 563
pail, 110, 129, 185; -feed, 238
painted on the drop, 694
Paint Pot, 536
pair of drawers, 752
Paiut, 563
Päivärinta, 429
pajama wagon, 720
pakt, 306
pal, 653
palace, 714
palate, 73
Palatka, 556
paleface, 270, 684
Palia, 439
Palinchas, 545
Pallis, 504
pallor, 280
palm, 71, 79, 171, 215
Palmer, 399, 578
palmetto, 608; -banner, 608; -cockade, 608; -flag, 608; -speech, 608

Palmetto State, 605, 608
palmy days, 690
Palmyra, 537
palooka, 768
pa'lor, 96
palouse, 768
Palouse, 233
palouser, 233, 768
pamphlet, 73
pan, 738; -catcher, 733
pan, to, 700
Panayiotis, 523
Pancake, 450, 536
pancake-turner, 729
panegyrist, 25
panel, 694; -house, 682
Panhandle, 640
panhandle, to, 640, 677
panhandler, 640, 652, 738
Panhandle State, 640, 641
pannam, 664
Panola, 560
Panorama Special, 580
pan out, to, 761
pant, 74, 383
panther, 761; -water, 734
Pantomina, 415
pantry, 73, 111
pants, 73, 384; -rat, 742; -slapper, 727
pap, 111
papa, 111, 171; pápa, 48
paper, 669, 685, 690; -bag, 207; -man, 686, 706; -mill, 324; -poke, 207; -pusher, 669; -sack, 207
paperhanger, 669, 718
paper-mill employee, 324
paperweight, 713
papier mâché, 736
papiette, 155, 156
papillote, 156
Papini, 439
Pappadimitracoupoulos, 440
Pappapolychronopoulos, 440
Pappas, 440
pappy, 111, 171
par, 163, 755
Para, 504
parade, 694
Paradine, 490
Paradise, 536
paraffin, 73
Paragould, 540

paragraf, 296
paramount, 47
pararie, 220
parasol, 73
para-three, 756
paratoed, 215
paratroop, 384
para-two, 756
pare, 297
parenthesis, 320
Parhaniemi, 429
pariah, 73
parin, 155
Paris, 537
Parishhawampitts, 552
park, 261
park, to, 723
Park, 444
Parker, 399, 402, 405, 469, 578
Park-lane, 322
park 'n dine, 297
parks, 385
Parkside Arms, 577
parler, 654
parlor, 163, 714
Parnethia, 479
parrot, 73
pars, 333
parse, to, 333
parson, 79
Parsonage, 450
part, 88, 269
partake of fresh air, to, 177
part earthquake and a little steamboat, 617
Parthenais, 437
Partney, 437
Partrick, 454
Parzola, 490
Pasadena, 554
Pascagoula, 562
Pasco, 504
pasej, 300
Pashia, 437
pass, 74, 75, 101, 122, 131, 184, 199, 230; -word, 151
passapool, 163
Pass aux Huitres, 528
passenger, 73
passer, 669
pass in one's chips, to, 134
passionate, 253

passive, 73
pass the time of day, to, 143
past, 25, 74, 199, 214
paste, 771
paste, to, 717
pastor, 22
pastorium, 745
pasture-man, 736
Pat, 475
Patapsico, 100
pâté, 318
pater, 111
path, 25, 45, 73, 74, 184, 187, 218, 227
pathetiker, 388
pa'ticular, 186
patio, 51
patootie, 133
patriarch, 221
Patrick, 454, 472
patrico, 664
pat'ridge, 98, 218
Patriola, 490
Patriot, 581
patrolie, 750
patter, 692
Patterson, 399
Patti Jo, 490
pau, 240
Paul, 441, 465, 517, 521
Paulala, 490
Paul Revere, 581
Pauncefote, 459
Pava, 490
pavement, 251
pavilion, 714
paw, 111
pawed, 249
pawing, 747
Pawn, 542
pawnded, 358
paw-pawer, 121
Pay and Save, 580
Paybodie, 438
Paybody, 438
pay-dirt, 761
Payment, 537
Payne, 399
pay off, to, 711
pay-station, 736
pea, 385, 734
Peabody, 438
peach, 644
Peachy, 411
peanut, 758; -roaster, 714

Pearce, 214
Pea Ridge, 589
Pearl, 524; City, 559; Harbor, 513
pearl-diver, 133
Pearline, 490
pease, 385
Pechel, 469
pechly poorly, 164
peckerwood, 270
peck-horn, 705
pecking, 745
Pecsal, 469
Peculiar, 534
ped, 258
pedagog, 311
pedagogy, 282
pedal-pusher, 723
pediatrics, 282
pedler, 680
peel, 260
peeler, 694, 740, 764
peeling, 674, 767
peep, 785
Peeps, 459
peery, 662
Peetry, 459
peewee, 765
pe'formance, 96
peg, 737, 740
Peggy, 678
Peg-Leg Annie, 139
Peirce, 214
pek, 446
Pelican State, 628
peluca, 768
Pelzer, 411
pemmican, 237
penadie, 237
penalize, 72
Pencilla, 490
pencil-pusher, 727, 733
pencil-trimmer, 200
Pendleton Hill, 530
pénicillin, 48
Peninsula State, 613
penman, 669
Pen-Mar, 541
Pennsylvania, 714; of the West, 631
Penn Yan, 540
pennydog, 761
pennydog, to, 151
Pennypacker, 406
Penobscot, 526
penology, 282

Pensacola, 556
pension run, 720
Pentacost, 449
Pentapang, 528
penthouse, 715
penwiper, 756
peon, 51
peonage, 51
People's War, 785
Peoria, 678
pe-pippa, 161
Pepper, 411
Peppiss, 459
Peppiz, 459
Pepys, 459
per, 320
pércent, 49
percentage-girl, 682; -man, 766
perch, 329
percolator, 724
Percy, 469
Percy Bysshe, 463
perdreaux, 155
perdure, to, 220
Pereida, 436
Perenna, 480
Père Noël, 317
perfect, 49, 164
perféct, to, 49
Pericles, 514
Perkins, 399
Perlmutter, 422
perm, 738
Permelia, 490
Permission, 450
Perreira, 436
Perry, 399, 429, 436, 531; Clees, 514
pers, 214
Pershin, 411
Pershing, 410, 412, 542
persimmon-beer, 159
personal, 771
Persotia, 490
perspiration, 175, 218
per year, 320
Pesach, 519
Peshach Pessi, 415
peso, 658
pess, 199
pest, 199
pesthouse, 756
pet, to, 708
pete, 668
Pete, 475, 523

Peter, 463, 513, 523; Funk, 687; Rock, 592
Péterka, 426
Peterson, 399, 401, 430, 433
Peterssen, 433
Pete's Hamburger Place 580
Petit, 416
Petoskey, 561
Petrie, 459
petrol, 230
Pettersson, 432
Petticoat, 450
Petula, 490
Petulengro, 442
petwene, 209
peuil, 189
pf, 411
Pfaelzer, 411
Pfaffenberger, 411
pfannhase, 160, 208, 232
Pfc, 782
Pfeffer, 411
Pfeffernüsse, 317
Pfirsching, 410, 411
ph, 97
ph, French, 309
Phadalee, 490
phænomenon, 282
Phalla, 490, 495
Phaye, 490, 494
pheasant, 329
phenomena, 318
phenomenon, 282
Pheotine, 490
Phil, 476
Philadelphia, 559
Philadelphy, 544
Philadulphia, 24
phildoodle, 742
Philelle, 490, 493
Philena, 480
Philippa, 493, 499
Phillie Joe, 498
Phillips, 397, 399, 416, 428
Philoxemus K. Hunks, 473
Phin, 504
Phoebe, 485, 494, 747; the preacher's daughter, 747
Phoebus, 516
phoney, See *phony*
phony, 648, 686, 687

Phony War, 648
photo finish, 769
photogenic, 766
photographic, 766
photoplay, 702
Phra, 490
phreight, 295
phth, 310
phthink, to, 310
phthisic, 310
phtholognyrrh, 310
Phygenia, 490
Phylistice, 490
Phyllis, 463
Phynis, 503
physick, 311
Piano, 450
piazza, 211
Pibaudière, 438
PICAO, 330
picayune, 154
Picayune, 562
Piccadilly, 578
piccolo, 681
pickaninny, 160
pickerel, 329
Pickering, 468
picket, 777
Picketwire, 564
Pick Eyes, 572
pickey-poke, 762
pickle, 738; -sheets, 773
Pickle, 450, 592
pick of the beach, 722
pick putter-and-ache man, 262
picks, 314, 776
pick-up, 747
picnic grounds, 385
Pictorial Review, 512
picture, 100; -gallery, 237, 684; -ore, 762
picturegallery, 325
piddy, 97
pie-card, 678
pie-card job, 722
piece, 169, 226, 671, 680
piece of calico, 649
piece-of-eight, 658
piece off, 777
piece of wood, 180
Pierce, 214, 461
Pie Town, 564
pieu, 155
pie-washer, 733
pig, 272, 674, 714, 723;

733; -pen, 250, 716; -sty, 350, 749; -tail, 763
pigeon-hole, 761
Pigeon Snow, 208
piggery, 749
piggle, to, 238
pigheaded, 145, 663
Pigs Eye, 561; Landing, 561
Piira, 429
pike, 329, 716
Pike, 634
Pike countyan, 634
piker, 647
Pike's Peak or bust, 355
Pilar, 522
Pile O' Bones, 572
Pilipauskas, 428
Pilipavičius, 428
pill, 315, 698, 700, 755; -punk, 674
Pill, 511
pillgarlick, 164
pillow, 736
pills, 674
Pimple, 450
Pinch Gut, 566
pinch hit, to, 737
Pinckney, 447, 472
pineapple, 667
Pine State, 609
pine-tree, 204
Pine Tree Limited, 581; State, 628
Ping, 511
ping pong, 682, 716
pinhead, 645
pinhooker, 776
pink, 270
Pink, 451, 504
pinken, to, 359
Pinkie's Tin Shack, 580
pinkletink, 166
pin-money, 663
pinner, 733,
pino, 201
pinochle season, 753
pin-rail, 697
pin-up girl, 781
pinxter, 181
Pioneer, 582
pio, 646
pipe, 685, 756
pipe, to, 730
pipe down, to, 721
pips, 717

Pirillä, 430
pisen, 87, 174
piston, 705
pitcher, 100
pitchfork, 746
Pitchfork, 451
pitchman, 685
pitch woo, to, 708
pit-coal indigo, 599
pitiyanqui, 244
pitoskig, 561
Pitt, 534
pitted against, 746
Pittsbourne, 534; -burgh, 534, 539; -cliffe, 534; -dale, 534; -dorf, 534; -field, 534; -hame, 534; -heim, 534; -hithe, 535; -side, 534; -leigh, 534; -more, 534; -stade, 534; -stead, 534; -stein, 534; -steppe, 534; -thorpe, 534
Pittsburg Landing, 589
pity, 97
Piute, 563
pix, 766
pixilated, 167
pizen-neat, 158
Pizzi, 439
plaak, 62
place, 315, 580
pladder, 657
plahnt, 36
plaice, 315
plain, 389
Plain Dealer, 595
plain sailing, 721
Plaintiff, 450
plank, 754
plant, 692, 745
plant, to, 644
Plantation State, 601
plaque, 62
Plaquemine, 560
plätchern, 654
plate, 745
platform, 750; -giant, 743
platinum, 285
Plato, 562
Platon Pantolonovich Lokshentopov, 415
platschen, to, 654
platter, 731, 737
play ball, to, 737
play-by-play, 737

List of Words and Phrases

Playground of the Nation, 630
playgrounds, 385
play jig, to, 252
play possum, to, 270, 648
play the C, to, 668
play the first spot, to, 692
play them in, to, 692
Plaza, 576, 577, 578
pleach, 263
plead, 195
pleaded, 362
Pleas, 504
Pleasant, 504; -Dreams, 592; -Grove, 490; -Hill, 559
Pleasantina, 490
pleased, 195
pleasuh, 38
pleasure, 38, 98; -grounds, 385
pled, 362
Ples, 504
pleureur, 689
Plez, 504
plink-plonker, 705
plodnik, 151
plops, 730
plot, 690
plotting, 98
plough, 286
Plover, 532
plow, 209
plug, 717, 731, 739, 744, 749; -ugly, 730
plugger, 770
plumbing, 705
plunker, 737; boy, 705
Plunkett-Ernle-Erle-Drax, 324
Plush, 535
plush run, 716
Plymouth Rock, 531
p.m., 324
PM, 756
P.M., 771
P.M.-hound, 771; -man, 771
pn, 310
pneumonia, 253, 310
P. O., 774
poached, 220
poarched egg, 220
po' buckras, 215
Pocahontas, 581
pocket, 697

pocketbook, 110
pod, 158, 249
podzo, 267
Po-ell, 454
pœnology, 282
Poffenberger, 411
point, 739
Point Loma, 528
Pó-is, 459
poison, 87, 174, 192
Poison, 536
Poitevin, 438
pok, 261
poke, 161, 200, 204, 207, 219, 229, 670, 686; -out, 677
Poke, 505
Polack, 75, 427
Polak, 427
Polar Star State, 629
pol. econ., 649
pole-sweat, 776
pólice, 48, 218
Polish piano, 141
politician, 754
Poll Infamous, 588
Polly's Jim, 514
Polo, 490
polpisy, 166
Poltny, 459
Polygraph, 596
polypuses, 320
Pomalee, 490
Pompey, 532
pompion, 160
ponch, 260
Ponce de Leon, 581
pond, 187, 574
ponhaws, 208
pon hosh, 232
ponhoss, 160, 208
Ponjola, 594
Ponsonby, 459
Pontefract, 459
Ponto, 594
pony, 694
pooch-jawed, 161
Poodletown, 536
pool-table, 737
poon, 248
pooper, 737
poor, 122; -box, 717
poor craft, 166
Poorgrass, 451
Poor Man's Protection, 593

poor steel, 722
poosh, 199, 235
poot, 121
Pootuppag, 528
pop, 680, 690; -bottle, 766; -skull, 734; -valve, 740
Pope, 588
popper, 24
porciúncula, 547
porcupine, 762
pork-chopper, 777
poroskint, 296
-port, 534, 563
portage, 252
portal-to-portal, 777
Porter, 399
Portia, 593
portière, 317
Portishead, 459
Portlandville, 559
portly, 120
Porto Rico, 246
portry, 100
Ports, 412
Port Tobacco, 528
Portugee, 383, 385
Port Wine, 536
Portz, 412
poseetion, 234
position, 234
possible, 223
possum, 160; -belly, 716
Possum, 511
Possum Kingdom, 568
post, 756; -mortem, 747
Post, 595
postage-stamp, 76
postes, 200, 386
Postlethwaite, 454
postoffice, 163
posts, 200
pot, 269, 714, 718, 724, 761
potados, 385
potassium, 285
potater, 120
potato, 385, 734; -hill, 260; -thump, 158
potatoes, 386
potatus, 385
potheaded, 208
potiguay, 681
potlatch, 641
pot-pie, 250
Potsdam, 542
potsy, 750
Potts, 532

862   List of Words and Phrases

Pottsylvania, 532
Potwin, 438
Poughkeepsie, 564, 565
Poulos, 440
poultice, 674
pound, 209, 662
pound hair, to, 233
pound the ties, to, 677
pount, 209
pour it on, to, 719
Poverty Flat, 570; Hill, 536
powders, 742
powder-wagon, 669
Powell, 399, 403, 454, 493
power, 86
Powerful, 587
power of, 137
Pownsfoot, 459
pow-wow, 160
Powys, 459
Pozzet, 459
pphoughtluipsh, 309
practic, 285
practical, 697
practice, 285
practique, 285
practise, 285
practise, to, 285
practize, 285
practize, to, 285
Praestegaard, 434
prairie, 220, 573, 755
Prairie Dog, 595; State, 614, 615
Praise-God, 467
praline, 154
pram, 249
prat, 664, 692
pratfall, 692
Pratt, 427
pray, to, 264
praya, 40
Preacher, 511
précise, 318
predigen, 654
premie, 756
Prescott, 434
present, 246
Preserved, 468
President, 322, 581
presidente, 742
President's War Relief Control Board, 330
Presindia, 516
prespiration, 99, 175, 218

Press, 595
Pressler, 411
Preston, 507
pretence, 281
pretty, 133, 215, 736; -boy, 684
Pretyman, 459
pretzel, 705; -twister, 733
Preus, 409
preview, 701
price, 228
Price, 399, 403, 409
Prichard, 403
pricker, 179
priest, 221
pright, 258
primip, 756
primipara, 756
prim up, to, 162
primp up, to, 162
Prince, 508, 594; -George's, 325, 539; of Wales, 588
príncess, 48
Princess Mary, 48; Royal, 588
pring, 209
Pringle, 472
Prins, 406
printer, 718
Priscilla, 479
Prittyman, 459
privilege-car, 685
pro, 649
probably, 175
probe, 756
probie, 749
pro'bition, 97
prob'ly, 96, 175
Prodestant, 209
production, 692
proelonggaeshon, 301
professor, 682, 692, 753
prog, 252
program, 286, 302, 311, 316
progress, to, 20
Prohibition, 513
projick, to, 172
prolog, 311
prompt side, 690
pronomen, 333
proof, 228
proofreader, 284
propaganda, 319
properties, 688

prop-plot, 690
props, 685, 697, 729
prospecti, 319
prospector, 761
Prosser, 426
protectu, 297
protein, 87
prótest, 49
protést, to, 49
protestant episcopal church, 322
protozoa, 320
proud, 253
prove, 294
proven, 337
provided, 337
Providence, 531
providing, 337
provinces, 690
Provisional International Civil Aviation Organization, 330
prowness, 100
Pruchniewski, 426
Prucia, 490
Prudence, 479
prug, 180
prun, 297
Prune Barge, 588
prune, 707; -heddler, 176
Prunice, 490
prushun, 678
prygge, to, 665
Przybysz, 522
ps, 310
psalm, 215, 230, 269, 294, 310
psalmer, 674
psa'm, 269
Psceschaggo, 530
pshaw, 310
psozzyrrzz, 310
P. T., 771
public, 304; -enemy, 672
publicist, 703
publicity, engineer, 703
publick, 304
public relations counsel, 703
public school, 41
publicte, 304
publik, 304
publike, 304
publique, 304
publyke, 304
puck, 252

List of Words and Phrases

puckerin', 253
Puckhunkonnuck, 530
puddin', 44
pudding, 214
Pudding, 512
puddle-jumper, 725, 785
Pueblo de Nuestra Señora la Reina de Los Angeles de Porciuncúla, El, 547
Puerto Rico, 246
puffer, 740
puff-up, 254
puff up, to, 747
Pugh, 403
pug-nose, 663
Puhakka, 430
puke, to, 634
Puke, 536, 641; State, 631, 634
Puker, 626
Pulis, 505
Pulitzer, 421
pull, 214
pull, to, 757
puller, 732
pull leather, to, 742
pulpit, 727, 773
Pulteney, 459
Pumfret, 459
pump, to, 659
pumpernickel, 51
Pumphrey, 403
pumpion, 160
pumpkin, 160
Pumpkinville, 568
punch, to, 127, 260
puncher, 741
punch-drunk, 768
punchy, 768
puncture lung, 720
punk, 674, 678
punker, 737
Punsunby, 459
pup, 756; -tent, 743, 778
puplicke, 304
puppy, 724
Puppytown, 536
Purcell, 454
pure, 292
purée, 678
purfektly, 300
Puritan State, 599
Purity, 593
Purl, 521
purp, 133

Purple, 450
purse, 110
Purse, 461
pursy, 96
Purum, 442
push, 733, 759, 762; -money, 771; -pipe, 705; -water, 719
push-a-push, 753
pusher, 669, 681, 762, 763
puss, to, 175
pussybandit, 675
pussyfoot, 145
pussy-gut, 96
pu'sy, 96
put, to, 197, 214
put a bad mouth on, to, 215
put it down, to, 678
put on the spot, to, 644
putrid, 649
put right into it, to, 180
putter, 262
put the bee on, to, 682
put the heat on, to, 672
put-together, 133
putty, 715, 766; -head, 754
PWRCB, 330
py, 209, 258
pyjamas, 282
Pyola, 490
Pyöriasaari, 429
pyx, 314
q, 288, 291, 500, 783
Qay, 490, 494
Qa'zān, 441
qu, 292
quad, 785
quagmire, 73
quail, 328, 329
Quaintillia, 490
quaker, 322
Quaker City, 598; State, 598
quality, 18, 73
qually-worker, 678
quándary, 48
quanity, 175
Quannah, 505
quantity, 175
quarrel, 195, 216
quarry, 756
Quashie, 513
qua'ter, 96
queen, 260

Queena, 490
Queen Anne's, 325, 539
Queen Elizabeth, 738
Queen Esther, 512
Queenie, 594
Queen State, 604
Quejette, 490
Quenshhague, 530
Quenshukeny, 529
questionary, 320
questionnaire, 320
quick, 298, 337
quickie, 700, 777
quick-shyn, 297
Quida, 490
quien, 655
Quiercero, 437
quieten, to, 358
Quiet Love, 448
quill, 295
quill-wheel, 149
quin, 260
Quineshakony, 530
quinine, 48, 81, 82
Quinn, 421
Quinneshockeny, 530
quint, 166
Quinta, 496
quintuplet, 73
quisle, to, 782
quisling, 782
quisling, to, 782
quite, 172
quiver, to, 694
Quohquinapassakessamanagnog, 529
quonking, 730
quotation marks, 326
quotes, 326
Quo Vadis, 512
quuf, 165
quyerkyn, 665
qwéye-nine, 48
r, 45, 88, 90, 91, 98, 101, 121, 131, 133, 134, 135, 159, 192, 193, 197, 205, 218, 221, 225, 261, 263, 292, 300, 303, 414, 500, 556, 563
r, German, 307
r, intrusive, 238
r, medial, 96, 171
r, silent, 15, 27, 32, 38, 40, 164, 171, 186, 192, 214, 223, 228, 230, 255, 261, 265

864   List of Words and Phrases

r, sounded, 15, 16, 20, 24, 36, 183, 184. 185, 186, 222, 226, 251
rabais-shop, 155
Rabbi, 511
rabbit, 329, 721
Rabbit Hash, 535
rabies, 87
Raccoon, 535
race-horse, 776
Racehorse Charlie, 680
race-track, 722
Racheal, 490
Rachel, 518
Rachelle, 490
rack, 253
racket, 286, 644, 648, 667
racketeer, 648, 672
racquet, 286
rad, 307, 686
Rada, 505
raddio, 77, 728
radio, 72, 728
Radio, 512, 513
radish, 171, 261, 386
Rae, 490
raft, 74, 752
rag, 670, 756
Ragine, 490
Ragna, 520
Rags, 594
ragtime, 709
Ragtown, 536
Rahn, 410
Rah-tone, 555
raillery, 18
railroad station, 211
Rain, 449
rainbow, 738
raise in pay, 250
raisin, 77
Raleigh, 75, 459
rale McKay, 671
ralize, 40
rallery, 18
Rally, 459
rally-kaboo, 149
Ralph, 463, 523
ram, 110
Ram, 450
Ramarion, 490
Rames, 453
rampike, 252
rampole, 252
Ramsay, 404
Randa, 515

Randolph, 471; of Roanoke, 542
rang, 263, 361
ranpike, 252
ransation, 220
Raola, 490
rap, 674
rapids, 573
rapture, 84
rapt-yur, 84
raquette, 286
rare, to, 214
Rascal, 512
rash-un, 77
rassle, 79, 174
Rastus, 515
rat, 328, 646, 696; -race, 707
Rat, 512, 535
Rathbon, 459
Rathbone, 459
rather, 251
rathskeller, 51
ration, 77, 680
Raton Pass, 555
Ra-toon, 555
Rat Portage, 572
ratskiller, 51
Ratskin, 450
rattler, 677, 761
Rattlesnake Shake, 593
rattletrap, 725
rattling, 172
Rat-Trap, 536
Rauch, 408
Rautenbusch, 411
Ravenscliffe, 534; -leigh, 534; -stein, 534; -wood, 534
Ravola, 490
raw, 253
Rawautoaqwaywoaky, 446
rawhide, 741, 775
Rawhide State, 640
Rawly, 459
rawr egg, 192
Ray, 475, 490, 506, 523
Raychel, 490
raydio, 77
raynbo, 298
ray-shu, 77
Razor, 535
razorback, 684
-rd., 322
re, 542

-re, 286, 316
reach, 314
reader, 732, 738
read for the minister, to, 169
Reading, 416
reading-notice, 732
real, 172, 389, 390
real down, 172
real estate, 714
reality, 99
really, 389
real McCoy, 670, 671
real McKaye, 671
rear, to, 214
Reasta, 490
rébate, 48
Rebecca, 518, 774
rébound, 48
recede, 313
receipt, 100
récess, 48
recipe, 100
Reckawack, 528
recompense, 281
reconcile, 48
Reconciliation, 590
Record, 595
Recorder, 595
recovering, 459
red, 89; -ball, 677, **716**, 772; -cap, 716, 777; -eye, 669, 715; -lead, 674; -light, 700; -nose, 153
Red, 594
red apple, 770
Red Bird, 581
Red Bone, 592
Red Cedar, 446
red circles, 747
Red Dog, 535
red dot, 775
rede, 315
Redeemer, 590
red eyes, 674
red-hot mama, 708
redjacks, 751
Red Lion, 536, 579
Red Lion-square, 322
ReDonda, 490
Red Owl, 445
Reed, 399
reef, 714
reefa, 681
reefer, 678, 681, 714, 774

List of Words and Phrases

reefing-man, 681
Ree-o-Grand, 555
Reese, 459
reesede, 313
reesin, 77
reflection, 277
Refolla, 490
refuse, 292
Regeneration, 590
regenwurm, 655
Regina, 520, 572
regyarder, 86
rehaul, to, 173
Rehoboth, 556
reich, 52
Reichardt, 409
reindeer, 722
reinge, 269
Reinette, 490
reins, 269
Reis, 436
Reizenstein, 421
Reklaw, 540
release, 702
reliable, 20
reloader, 774
Reluctant Dragon, 588
remainter, 209
remote pickup, 730
Remus, 592
Renascence, 302
Renaud, 437
rench, 120, 169
rended, 362
reng, 260
Rennert, 578
Reno, 437, 438
rense, 169
rent, 158
Reo, 505
repeat, 98
rep company, 690
Rephord, 505
Representative, 581
réprieve, 49
Republic, 595
Republican, 595
réquest, 49
rerled, 190
resate, 78
résearch, 49
reseed, 313
résign, 49
resort, 170
respectable, 348
respective, 348

réstarong, 50
restaurant, 50
résumé, 318
rétail, to, 49
retain, 98
retake, 700
retch, 314
Retel, 505
retouch, to, 738
rettesh, 261
return ticket, 250
Reuss, 409
réveille, 49
revelation, 221
Revelstoke, 414
Revola, 490
revu, 292
Rex, 542, 595
Reynolds, 399
Rheufina, 490
rheum, 315
Rhey, 490, 494
rhino, 659
Rhodeisland, 539
Rhondda, 459
Rhone, 410
rhūbarb, 737
Rhumelle, 490
Rhygene, 490
Rhys, 459
rib, 770; -sticker, 138
ribbon, 261
Riccardi, 439
Rice, 399, 421
Ricebird, 608
Rice State, 608
Richard, 415, 463, 467, 523
Richards, 399, 409, 439, 444
Richardson, 399
Richmond, 531
RiDant, 452
ride, 89, 125
ride, to, 706
ride the air, to, 741
ride the rods, to, 677
Ridgely of Hampton, 452
Ridge Runner, 588
riding, 722
rieur, 689
riff, 706
riff, to, 706
rifle, 228, 700
rifraf, 295
rig, 720, 723, 749

rigger, 728
right, 309, 338
righting, 310
right smart, 143
rigolard, 689
rike, 52
rile, to, 87, 185
Riley, 399
rime, 291, 294
rind, 175
rine, 175
ring, to, 361, 769
ring down the curtain on, to, 652
ringer, 769, 770
ringer-in, 769
ring in, to, 769
ringmaster, 713
ringtail, 716
rink, 232
rinse, 99, 169
Rio de las Animas Perdidas en Purgatorio, El, 564
Rio Grande, 555
rip, 707
ripe, 750
rip-roaring, 617
Rip Van Winkle State, 607
rised, 362
rise in pay, 250
rise of, 226
Rising Sun, 536, 580
risqué, 318
rite, 309
Rite Spot, 580
Rittenhouse, 413
Rittershausen, 413
Rittinghuysen, 413
Ritz, 578
Riverdale, 569
river-driver, 760; -hog, 760; -jack, 232; -pig, 760; -rat, 760
rivet, 98
Rivven, 459
riz, 154
rjspekt, 288
roach, 674, 681; -cake, 752
Roach, 436
road, 158, 322, 690; -apple, 753; -bog, 145; 723
roadways, 385

List of Words and Phrases

roarer, 768
roast, 750
Roast, 450
roast beef, 218
roasted stirrups, 751
roasting-ear, 160
rob, 185
robber, 735
Robert, 462, 463, 510, 518, 520, 521
Robert E. Lee, 581
Roberts, 397, 399
Robertson, 399, 400
Robeson, 448
Robinson, 397, 399, 421, 447, 595
robm, 97
Rob Peter and Pay Paul, 593
Rocha, 436
Rocille, 490
Rock, 679
Rockaway, 528
Rockefeller, 412
rock-hound, 763
Rockies, 774
Rockne, 427
Rock-ribbed State, 599, 628
rocks on the chest, 762
Rocksylvania, 559
Rocky Mountain Rocket, 581
ro-dáy-o, 742
rode, 89
rodear, 742
rodeo, 742
rodéo, 51
Rodgers, 425
Rodintha, 480
Rodriguez, 435, 436
Roentgen, 582
Rofey, 505
roger, 665
Roger, 467, 518
Rogers, 397, 399, 405, 436
Roggenbrot, 207
Roggenfelder, 412
roil, 87
rokenbrod, 207
Roland, 505
role, 318
Rolen, 505
Rolin, 505
Rolla, 505, 508
roll a pill, to, 681

rollback, 777
roller, 682; -skater, 766
Rolleston, 459
Rollin, 505
rolling out, 750
roll it, to, 731
rollitsh, 181
Rollo, 505
Rolston, 459
Roma, 496
Roma Jean, 488
Romalice, 490
Roman, 505
rómance, 48
Romany, 665
Rome, 18, 537
Rome bouse, 665
Romeo, 514
römer, 659
Romero, 444; -ville, 528
Romey O., 514
Romney, 459
Romulus, 532
Ronal, 505
Ronald, 505
Rondell, 516
Ronell, 505
Röntgen, 50
Rontha, 459
roof, 328; -garden, 716; -rider, 728
roofes, 328
roofs, 328
roodge, 230
rook, 228
rooleje, 181
room, 215, 228
Room, 18
Roosevelt, 407
Roosevelt War, 786
rooster, 228, 248, 249
root, 85, 228
rooter, 737
Rootham, 460
rootle, to, 165
rooves, 328
roovis, 328
Rope's End, 579
Rosario, 522
Rose, 399, 430, 490, 519, 523, 524
Rosebush, 423
Rosecrans, 412
Rosedale, 562
Rose Grove, 559
Rosehill, 423

Rosel, 498
Rosellini, 439
Rosenberg, 421, 423
Rosenfelder, 422
Rosenkrantz, 412
Rose of Sharon, 592, 593
Roseola, 490
Rosia, 490
Rosiena, 490
Rosie Pete, 422
Rosile, 490
rosinback, 684
Ross, 399, 421, 435
Rössel, 409
Rossignol, 438
RossKam, 452
Rossmore, 577
Rossoff Terrace, 577
Rosynook, 578
rotatory, 47
Rothstein, 421
Rothwell, 459
Rotsly, 460
rotten, 251
rotten, to, 359
rotwelsch, 654
ro-ud, 158
Roudebush, 411
roue, 318
rouge, 51, 230
rough, 310; -rider, 719
roughie, 700
Rouleau, 437
Roumaine, 490, 507
round-house, 749
round-up, 134
rousin' oil, 132
roustabout, 763
route, 85
routine, 85, 692, 695
Rover, 594
rover boy, 730
Rowdy, 505, 506
Rowe, 423
Rowell, 459
rowt, 85
Roxaner, 490, 494
Roxie, 523
Roxly, 460
Royal, 502, 505, 507; Blue, 581; Palm, 581
Royalene, 490
Royce, 409
Rozetta, 490
Rubba, 438
rubber, 724, 737; -check,

List of Words and Phrases

669; -heel, 674, 719; tired, 716
rubberneck, 644, 647, 649; -car, 714
rub out, to, 671
Ruburdia, 490
Ruby, 506
ruckus, 153
rud, 158
-rud, 434, 435
Rue, 505
Ruffen, 459
rug-cutter, 707
Rugh, 408
R U going 2 the Cside, 291
ruh, 739; -cellar, 739
rulah, 40
rule, 212
Rulo, 437
rum, 51
Rumba Jo, 490
rumble-seat, 723
rummer, 659
Rumny, 459
Rump, 451
run, 573, 720
run, to, 269
run a blind calf over, to, 173
run afoul of, to, 721
rung, 361
runnin'er, 226
Runt, 475
Runtgen, 50
rursh, 198
rush, 198
Rushdooni, 441
rushes, 700
Rushville, 584
Ruskin, 421
Russel, 438
Russell, 399
Russia, 775
Russian Renaissance, 753
Russo, 439
rustle, to, 677
rustle a meal, to, 677
rustle cattle, to, 677
Rustler, 595
Rustler-Herald, 596
Ruth, 499, 510, 521, 524
Ruthven, 459
Rutledge, 447, 472
rutschen, 205
rutschi, 205

Ruusu, 430
Ruy, 490
Ryan, 399
Rye-o-Grand, 555
Rylda, 490
s, 44, 46, 50, 62, 98, 100, 192, 193, 248, 262, 269, 281, 284, 285, 292, 294, 300, 364, 368, 402, 408, 409, 414, 424, 432, 433, 439
-s, 368, 384, 385, 386
s, German, 307
s, long, 321
s, silent, 97
Saari, 429
Saba, 497
sabe, 171
Sabra, 490
Sacheverell, 459
Sachs, 424
sack, 161
sacks, 297
SaCoolidge, 452
Sacred Heart Gin, 592
Sacred Heart of Jesus, 591
sacred ox, 716
saddle, 73; -horse, 208
saddle, to, 253
saddy, 206
Sadelle, 490
Sadye, 494
-saetr, 434
safen, to, 359
safety-zone, 723
Safronia, 490
sag, 232
sag dank, 206
sägebock, 209
Sage-brush State, 636
sage-hen it, to, 138
Sage-hen State, 636
Sage State, 636
Saginaw, 561
Sahara, 570
sahtsch, 260
sai, 382
Saidee, 490
Saidhe, 490
sailor, 715
saint, 222
Saint Cross, 590
Saint Esprit, 590
Saint-Henri des Tanneries, 571

Saint-Jean-Baptiste de l'Ile Verte, 571
Saint Lucia day, 744
Saint Patrick, 513
Saint's Rest, 592
sala, 243
salamander, 659, 773; -stone, 659
Salathia, 490
Salem, 531
Sal Hepatica, 512
Saliba, 441
Salim, 523
Saline, 491
Salinskas, 428
sallet, 229
Sally Ben, 491
Salom, 523
Salomica, 505
Salomon, 665
salon-man, 706
saloon, 714
saloot, 85
salt, 74
Salt Lake City, 588; State, 640
salts, 674
salute, 85
salvage corps, 100
salve, 199, 752
Salwyn, 517
salztag, 739
sam, 446
Sam, 475, 476, 478, 513, 514, 515, 523
Sambo, 513
Sam Buck, 514
Sam Buck Jeemes Ribber Highoo, 514
same like, 269
Sammie, 758
Sammy, 476, 780
samourai, 320
Samuel, 467, 475, 510, 516
Samuel Morse, 583
samurai, 320
San Antone, 547
San Antonio, 545, 547
Sanchez, 435
sand, 673, 674; -hiller, 608; -lapper, 608
Sandas, 509
S. and D., 692
Sanders, 399
Sandhill, 430
Sandhill pavement, 177

868   *List of Words and Phrases*

Sand Hill State, 611
Sand-lapper State, 608
Sands, 459
Sandtown, 556
sandwich, 663; -girl, 733; -shop, 580
Sandy, 594
Sandy Hook, 564
Sandys, 459
Sanford, 516
sang, 359, 361
Sanger, 408
Sänger, 408
San Ildefonso, 565
sanitaria, 319
San José, 539
San Juanito, 556
sank, 361
Sank, 505
Sanko, 515
sanky-poke, 195
San Luis, 555
Sans Souci, 537
Santa Claus, 534, 738
Santa Fé, 539, 564
Santone, 547
Santonyo, 547
Saorstat Eireann, 604; Maryland, 604
sap, 644
Saphrona, 491
sapphire, 310
Saps, 774
Sapsed, 459
Sarah, 421, 513, 516, 519
Sarben, 563
sarcomas, 319
Sardis, 507, 542
sarmin, 248
Sarou Khan, 441
Sasheverel, 459
sash tool, 757
Saspamco, 541
sa'sparilla, 96
sass, 108
sassy, 120, 175
sat, 362
Satan, 320, 472
Satana, 593
Satchel, 512
Satchelmouth, 706
Satchmo, 706
Satis, 505
sattelgaul, 208
Saturday night, 751
Saturdays, 205

saturn, 322
Satyra, 491
satz, 160
sauce, 314
saucy, 175
Sauer, 409
sauerkraut, 51
sauerteig, 151
säufer, 205
Sault Sainte Marie, 561
sausage, 386; -grinder, 770; -machine, 753
Sausage, 512
Sauvolle, 437
savage, 667, 760; -corpse, 100
save, 171, 254
save-all, 722
Save-a-Nickle, 580
Save-U-More, 580
savey, 149
Savile, 454
Savior, 280
Saviour, 280, 323
saw, 314, 346; -buck, 208
sawani, 557
sawbones, 674
sawdust, 673; -eater, 760; -trail, 745
saw gourds, to, 153
Sawkulich, 452
sawr, 192
saw wood, to, 648
sax, 297
Sax, 424
saxophone, 281
Saydhe, 490
saying, 121
Saylor, 409
scab, 777
Scaccia, 439
scalding, 724
scallion, 250
scandal-proof, 659
scandal soup, 772
scap, 740
scapegallows, 662
scape worker, 686
scarcely, 391
scared strap, 718
scarlet, 214
Scarlett O'Hara, 774
scavenger, 722
scene-dock, 697
scene-plot, 690
scenery, 774

scenery-fed, 765
scenic, 72
sceptic, 286
Sceva, 505
sch, 51, 250, 408, 414
sch, German, 307
Schack, 414
Schalom, 417
schaluppe, 725
Schapierer, 423
Schapira, 423
Schapiro, 423
Scharf, 409
Scharlott, 491, 494
schedule, 36, 46, 250, 313
scheme, 253
Schenkakko, 530
Schermerhorn, 405
scherzo, 707
schiessen, 739
schiff, 739
schiltren, 258
schimmel, 255
Schimmelpfenning, 432
schizophrenia, 756
schizy, 756
Schjøth, 434
schlach, 696; -joint, 771
schlacht, 771
Schlacht, 408
Schlachter, 409
schlag, 747
schlauch, 739
schlaucher, 739
schleckerig, 151
Schleicher, 414
Schlens, 414
schlepp, to, 757
schleppen, 757
Schlesinger, 421
Schloch, 414
schlock, 771
schlürfen, 151
Schmal, 409
schmalz, 707, 729
schmeer, to, 757
schmeiss, to, 757
Schmetterling, 421
Schmidt, 399, 409, 410
schmieren, 757
schmierkäse, 51, 320
schmiss, 757
schmiss, to, 757
schmitz, 757
Schmoch, 415
schmoosing, 754

Schnaebeli, 411
schneid, to, 757
schneiden, 757
schneider, 753
Schneider, 409, 414
Schneittacher, 421
schnitte, 254
schnitz, 160, 230
schnucke, 757
schnuck(le), 757
Schoach, 415
Schoch, 414
Schoenberg, 418
Schön, 409, 424
Schöndufter, 417
Schooch, 415
Schoock, 414
Schooh, 414
schoolma'am, 760
schrei, 655
schrei, to, 757
Schreiber, 409
schreien, 757
schreiling, 655
Schreiner, 414
Schroeder, 435
Schuerkaigo, 530
Schultz, 399, 426
Schumacher, 409
Schurz, 415
schussel, 206
schussle, 205
Schuyler, 189, 405, 448, 469
schwartenmagen, 151
Schwartz, 401
Schwarz, 409, 411
Schwarzmann, 423
schwarzmarkt, 782
schweizer, 51
schyool, 229
scialuppa, 725
Sciortino, 439
Scioto, 566
scissor, 714; -bill, 714, 777
scissors, 385; -bill, 677
Scochoch, 415
scoff, 674
scoffle, to, 121
Scone, 459
Scoon, 459
scoop, 700, 714, 752
scoop, to, 195
scooper, 730
scoots, 194
scorcher, 723

score, 98
scotchman, 755
Scott, 399, 435, 439, 470
scotus, 717
Scout, 595
scout-car, 785
scoutmaster, 730
scow, 720
scram, to, 671, 711
scrammed, 254
scraper, 674
Scrap Island, 166
scratch, 685, 738; -box, 705
scratch, to, 652
scratcher, 669, 734, 753
screech, 738
screw, 674, 741, 756
screw, to, 659
screwball, 766
screwbore, 180
scrim, 700
scrip, 669
script, 690, 729; -girl, 700
scriptchaa, 81
scripture, 81
scroll water, 748
scroop, 776
Scroop, 459
Scrope, 459
scrounge, to, 782
scrub, 756
scudge, 253
scuffing, 741
scut, 756
scuttle, 720
scuttle of clinkers, 756
scythe, 96
sdreet, 98
se, 370, 382
sea, 292, 328; -crab, 662; -dust, 752
Sea, 584
Seaboard, 536; Air Line, 322; Airline Railway, 509
Seaholm, 432
sealed, 222
sealing, 222
seam squirrel, 742
seance, 318
search, 79
Searchlight, 595
Sears-Roebuck, 763
seb, 446
secetary, 175

secretary, 3, 4, 5, 36, 175, 211
secretry, 4, 32, 96
Secundo, 450
Sebastopol, 163, 164
sebm, 97
2nd, 501
II, 501
Second Bull Run, 589
second hand, 697
Second Manassas, 589
second reader, 131
sects, 131
Sedber, 459
Sedburgh, 459
see, 292
Seebee, 782
seed, 313, 754
Seegar, 439
segue, 730
ség-way, 730
ség-we, 730
ség-you, 730
Sellrite, 580
Seely-Brown, 451
seemed, 238
Seemer, 459
see monkeys, to, 194
seen, 346
Seena, 491
see them, 269
seez, 260
sehen, 353
seight, 309
Seiler, 409
sei peso, 246
seiz pesos, 246
selectee, 780
self, 122
Selig, 417
Seliger, 417
Seligman, 417
Selma, 520, 523
Selmer, 521
Seloo, 459
Selous, 459
Selpha, 521
Selwyn, 517
Seminole State, 614
Semion, 505
semi-windup, 768
semper paratus, 779
sempt, 238
sen, 433
-sen, 399
Senator, 581

Senator Few Clothes, 139
Senator Henry Cabot Lodge, 583
send, 667
send, to, 706
sending, 681
senkah, 269
señor, 318
sent, 171
sent down to the very bricks, 708
senter, 301
Senus, 505
separeishn, 288
sepia, 270
seppä, 430
Seppänen, 430
sequelæ, 320
Serene, 491
seres, 386
sergeant, 79
Sergeant, 511
serie, 385
series, 385
Serigny, 437
Seroco, 541
serpent, 79, 164
Serra, 439
serums, 320
Serutan, 579
serv, 199
servant, 79
serve, 164
service, 79, 285
seshon, 313
Sessel, 457
session, 313
Sestee, 505
set, 171, 362, 697, 721
set a tub, to, 748
set the pace, to, 770
set-up, 694
Seven-by-Nine, 536
sevens, 743
seventh-inning stretch, 737
seventy, 221
several, 120, 233
severial, 233
sew, to, 312
Sewell, 459
Sewer, 450
sewer-hog, 762
sewer-trout, 740
sewing-machine, 728
Sewlliea, 491

sex, 131, 386
Sex, 450
sex appeal, 695, 703
sexton, 730
Seymore, 506
Seymour, 539, 459, 469, 516
sez you, 645
's Gravenhage, 540
sh, 46, 98, 131, 182, 192, 193, 261, 269, 290, 300, 309, 310, 414
sh, German, 424
shack, 678, 713, 714
shacket, 210
Shackway, 437
shad, 253, 329
Shain, 424
Shakakko, 530
shake down, to, 652
Shakelady, 451
shaker, 733; -down, 753
Shakespeare, 423, 453
shake-up, 681
shaklin, 181
Shaky, 678
Shalins, 428
shall, 261, 336, 366, 367
shallop, 725
shallot, 250
shall you play?, 367
sham, 734
Shambo, 437
Shampoo, 437
shamus, 668, 669, 670
Shandos, 457
shandrámadan, 247
Shane, 409, 424
Shangreau, 444
shanty, 684, 714
Shapera, 423
Shapereau, 423
Shapero, 423
Shapiro, 423
shark, 659, 678
Shark, 587
Sharmeen, 491
Sharon, 591
sharooshed, 253
Sharp, 409
Sharpsburg, 589, 606
shart, 247
shassis, 53
Shato, 553
shave, to, 680
Shaw, 399

Shawmut, 531
Shawn O'Farrel, 762
shay, 384
she, 348, 588; -all, 379, 380; -brick, 662
SHEAF, 782
Sheba, 593
Shecago, 530
shedder, 767
shedyul, 313
shee, 50
sheep, 328; -herder, 700; -puncher, 742
sheeps, 386
sheet, 246; -worker, 686
Shelby, 493
Shelby Lee, 491
shell, 734, 749
shellacked, 644
Shelley, 453
shells, 674
Shell State, 614
Shelta, 491
shelter-house, 714
Shelvia, 491
shem, 314
Shem, 519
she may can, 220
Sheperd, 425
she pray, 264
Shercaggo, 530
Shergold, 577
Sheridan, 470
sherif, 295
Sherley, 453
Sherman, 470
sherris, 386
sherrivarrie, 185
sherry, 386
Sherwood, 418, 419, 425; Hall, 577
shes'n, 368
shet, 88, 113, 175, 362
shet 'at doh, 89
she-un, 380
shew, to, 302
shield, 674
Shifrah, 519
shifter, 762
Shikkago, 530
shill, 683, 685
shillelah, 197, 736
Shiloh, 589, 591
shilshite, 209
Shimidzu, 443
Shimizu, 443

List of Words and Phrases

shimmel, 255
shimmy, 752
shimmy, to, 694
Shimmy, 593
Shinbone, 536
shiner, 700, 714
shingle-nail, 746
shinkafa, 266
shiny pants, 713
Shippe, 477
shipping business, 691
ship-shape, 165, 721
shipy, 748
ShirLee, 491, 494
Shirley, 493, 506, 516, 518
Shirt Tail, 535
shite-poke, 176
shiv, 653
shivel, 179
shlappe, 725
sho, 297
shobiz, 297
shocard, 297
Shock, 414
shoddy, 770
shoe, 773; -dog, 771; -hombre, 243; -maker, 740; -sole, 674; -string, 163; -round, 194; -shiner, 754
Shoemaker, 409
shofar, 316
shoffer, 316
sho-f'r, 52
Shoholm, 432
shome, 771
shon, 202
Shongaloo, 560
shoo-fly, 767
shoo fly, don't bother me, 645
shool, to, 166
shoot, 121
shoot, to, 700, 763
shoot crap, to, 658
shoot her, to, 92
shootinest, 387
shoot the chutes, to, 652
shop-lift, 659
shoppe, 580
Shoppee, 451
shopping, 111
Short, 409
short-con worker, 667
Shortino, 439

short line, 697
short'nin-bread, 710
short piece, 680
Shortsleeve, 450
Shoshana, 519
shot, 680, 766, 772
shotgun, 737; -house, 140
should, 202, 394
Shoulder Blade, 446
should of, 167
should of went, 167
shovel, 179
Shovel, 450
shover, 669
show, 297, 729, 760; -boat, 735; -girl, 695
show, to, 361
show business, 691
showed, 361
showfer, 53
showf'r, 53
showful, 758
showfur, 53
Show Me State, 631, 634
shown, 361
shrank, 361
shrapnel, 723
Shrewsbury, 459
shrine, 591
shrink, to, 361
shrivel, 179
Shriver, 409
Shrobsb'ry, 459
shroud, 754
shrubbery, 674
shrunk, 361
shucker, 694
shud, 288
shuffle, to, 746
Shultz, 553
shum, 269
shumac, 175
shure, 313
shut, 88, 175; -out, 737
shutterbug, 766
shuur, 313
si, 292, 382
Si, 475
Siamese, 750
Sibeth, 491
Sibyl, 499
sich, 188
sich kräusen, 739
sick, 746
sick'em, 215
sickener, 208

Sickman, 450
sic semper tyrannis, 597
Sid, 475
side, 691, 738; -draft, 151; -walk, 249, 251; -ways, 385; -wheeler, 737; -winder, 742, 760
-side, 534, 563
siden, to, 238
Sidney, 438, 468, 469, 472, 493, 506, 516
Sidra, 498
sie, 378
Sie, 448
Sieglinde, 520
sierra, 51, 573
Sierra Valley News, 595
siesta, 51
siffer, 205
sige, 269
sight-draft, 151
sight of the eye, 233
signature, 730
signer, 743
Signora, 53
Sigrid, 520
sik dollar, 246
Sikoch, 415
silk, 138
Sillanpää, 429
silscheit, 209
Silva, 436
Silva de Dias, 436
Silverland, 636
Silver Meteor, 581
Silver State, 613, 636
silver thaw, 252
sim, 370
Simcha, 417
Simko, 440
Simmons, 399, 459
Simon, 518, 756; Legree, 756
Simoon, 593
sipi, 574
Simpson, 399, 477
Simung, 515
Sin, 488
Sina, 491, 515
Sinay, 422
Sinclair, 439, 454, 459
sinct, 100
Sin-deny, 467
sinecure, 72
sing, to, 359, 361, 672
Sing, 459, 491

872   *List of Words and Phrases*

singer, 261, 294
singingest, 226
singink, 192
single, 692
Sin-jun, 454
sink, 99
sink, to, 361
sinker, 737; -joint, 684
Sinner, 450
Sinsinati, 293
Sinskey, 418, 419
Sinus, 450
Sion, 505
Sioux State, 636
Siranui, 588
Sireen, 491
Siro, 505
Sir Walter Raleigh, 513
sis, 370
Sissil, 457
sister, 222
sister act, 692
sisteren, 328
sistren, 328
sit, 241
sit-down, 678, 777
sit for company, to, 682
sit in the butter-tub, to, 166
sit 'n eat, 297
sitter, 682
sitting on their hands, 692
Sivola, 491
sivvy beans, 215
siwash, 237, 641
six, 260
Six, 450
six dollars, 246
six nations, 320
size, 269
sizzler, 759
sj, Swedish, 432
Sjöholm, 432
Sjöstrand, 432
Skalička, 440
skate, 246, 749
skate, to, 697
skedyul, 313
skee, 50
skeehaw, 175
skeerce, 120
ski, 50
-ski, 176, 426
skiddoo, 643, 644
skid-grease, 752

skid-road, 677, 760
skidway, 774
skift, 149
skig, 771; -last, 771
skimmelton, 185
skin, 269, 705; -away, 149; -beater, 705, 711; -flint, 659, 749; -tickler, 705
skinning, 767
-skiold, 434
skip frame, to, 700
skipper, 713, 737, 744
skirt, 644, 700
skit, 149
skite, 175
Skokie Club, 582
skookum, 237, 641
skrivel, 179
skulch, 158
skull, 694, 773; -doily, 698, 700
skull-drag, to, 155
skunk, 329, 751
skunk bob, 738
Skunk Grove, 559
Skunktown, 350
skut, 749
sky, 214, 227; -hooks, 733; -juice, 673; -man, 754; -parlor, 663; -rocket, 716
-sky, 422
skyscraper, 733
slab, 707
slack, 714
slack-jaw, 173
slacks, 297
Slaght, 408
Slaithwaite, 459
slam off, to, 674
slang, 643
slant-face, 774
slap-happy, 768
slap-stick, 692
Slare, 506
slat, 718
slate, 665
slates, 665
Slaughter, 409, 556
slaughterhouse, 754, 770
slave-driver, 674; -market, 677, 760
slax, 297
sleek, 11
sleep, 260
Sleep, 451

sleeper, 720, 732; -jump, 694
sleep in, to, 204
sleeping time, 673, 674
Sleepy Eye, 534, 561
sleigh-bells, 675
Sleyman, 441
slicer, 740
slick, 11
slick chick, 711
slide, to, 348
slime, 740, 754
slimmer, 765
slinger, 694
slingshot, 737
slinky, 253
slip, 260; -horn, 705; -sticks, 733
slip one's trolley, to, 717
slipova, 296
slit, to, 360
sliver-sucker, 705
slob, 252
slobber-chops, 165
slocker, 754
sloep, 725
Slo-it, 459
sloomiky, 149
sloop, 707
slop, 747, 748; -can, 725
slough the tip, to, 686
slouinglie, 99
slow, 337, 338
slowcome, 153
slud, 348
slug, to, 169
slugger, 766
slug-nutty, 768
slum, 673, 685
slunk, to, 252
slurp, 707
slurp, to, 151
slush-bucket, 662; -bump, 705
slushers, 724
smack, 253
small, 237
Small, 309
Smallbones, 451
small time, 692
smart-money, 659
smartski, 176
smatchy, 253
smear, 662, 707, 738, 754
smearcase, 51, 149, 201, 202, 231, 320

List of Words and Phrases

smecker, 682
smelling chete, 665
smelt, 329
Smelt, 451
Smialkowski, 426
smicket, 226
Smid, 406
Smith, 396, 397, 398, 399, 400, 401, 402, 405, 409, 410, 421, 425, 430, 436, 441, 442, 447
Smithfield, 776
smithur, 400
Smithville, 553
smitty, 770
smoke, 713; -eater, 749
smoker, 714
smoke up, to, 695
smooth, 171; -bore, 236
smoothen, to, 359
smoove, 171
smorgasbord, 317
smothersome, 153
smut, 693
smutter, 158
smutty, 659
Smy, 451
Smyrna, 556
Smyth, 402
Smythe, 402
Snabel, 411
Snabely, 411
snafu, 778
snag, 121
snag-gag, to, 181
snake, 197, 694, 716, 736, 748; -eyes, 747; -fence, 145; -killer, 748; -rancher, 723; -stomper, 760
snake's hips, 643
Snak-Shak, 580
Snap-Apple Night, 252
snapper, 761, 766
snatch, to, 667
snatched up, 162
snatcher, 765
Snavely, 411
snaz, 253
Snead, 409
sneak in, 730
sneaksby, 662
sneck, 197
Snedeker, 421
Snediker, 421
sneege, 269
sneeze, 269

snew, 181
Sniedt, 409
snip, 662
snipe, 713; -hunter, 678
snits, 160, 233
snoop, 740
snoop, to, 179
snooper, 765
snoopy, 161
snoose, 760
snooser, 760
snoot, 87, 175
snoozer, 714
Snort Creek, 559
snort-pipe, 724
snot, 766
snot, to, 121
snots, 167
snotty, 750
snouge, 149
snout, 87, 175
snow, 680; -fly, 677
snow, to, 181
Snowball, 450
snowbird, 674; -snifter, 681
snudge, 659
snug, 158
Snussle Inn, 579
Snyder, 399, 409
so, 267
soap-boxer, 648
soap-opera, 731
soar, 314
sobbie, 704
Sochs, 415
Social Circle, 534
Society Hill, 592
sock, to, 659
socks, 237, 297
Socorro, 564
so crooked he could hide behind a corkscrew, 146
soda-dispenser, 772; -jerker, 713, 772
Sodawasser, 450
sod-buster, 742, 762
soddened, 359
soddie, 742
soddy, 177
sodium, 285
Sodom, 535, 570
sody, 544
soe, to, 312
Sofa, 450

soft, 83, 123, 389, 670
soft coal burner, 720
softmouth, to, 195
soft-soap, 649
sofy, 171
-sohn, 417, 422
Sohn, 501
soive, to, 190
Sol, 475
solar plexus, 768
soldier, 620, 740, 761
Solen, 505
solicitor, 280
Solid Muldoon, 595
solid sender, 706
Solis Cohen, 418
sollybuster, 161
Solomao, 505
Solomon, 477, 505, 517, 518
Solon, 505, 507
Solveig, 520
some, 337
somebody else's, 395
some place else, 394
Somerset, 472
something, 91
something on the ball, 737
somewhere, 174
somewheres, 100, 174, 394
So Mote It Be, 593
son, 323, 450
-son, 399, 402, 417, 433
Son, 501, 505
Sonia, 488
Sonntag, 412
Sonny, 525
son-of-a-bitch, 219; -of-a-gun, 219
son of Lloyd, 403
Sonora, 491, 493
sont, 171
soo-ey, 765
soogan, 174
soogie, 721
soon, 228
sooner, 637, 638
Sooner, 512
sooner dog, 638
Sooner State, 637
Soonkookian, 441
soot, 758
Sopac, 774
Sophia, 493
sore, 314; -back, 194

sorehead, 644
sorry, 251
sorta, 366, 394
sorted, 98
so so, 267
sot, 171, 362
so that, 205
Sotheby, 459
sotnik, 151
Souadabscook, 529
sougan, 742
soujge, 721
soul-driver, 659
soup, 292, 668, 671, 700, 740, 752, 757, 766; -barrel, 751; -bone, 736; -jockey, 674, 720
Soup, 450
souper, 670
source, 314
sourdough, 138, 238
Sour Owl, 596
South Dakota, 588; Mountain, 589; Wind, 581
Southey, 459
southpaw, 745
southpay, 737
sove, 254
sovereign, 301
soviet, 72
sovran, 301
sow, to, 312
sow-belly, 716
Sowers, 409
so worse, 394
Sows, 774
sox, 297, 298
spa, 168
space buyer, 732
spack, 181
spaghetti, 700, 750
Spahn, 410
Spangler, 410
spaniel, 738
Spanish Rose, 139; State, 636
spark-plug, 723
sparrick, 180
SPARS, 779
Sparta, 532, 537
sparteine, 87
spasm, 219
Speaker, 505, 507, 581
speakies, 702
spear, 752

Special, 440
Speciale, 440
specie, 383
specify, to, 215
specimen, 707
speck, 181
spectacle, 385
speech, 260, 691
speed, 315, 700; -ball, 681; -cop, 723
spell, to, 252
Spellaci, 439
spelling-bee, 304; -class, 304; -match, 304; -school, 304
Spencer, 399, 468, 469
Spencer-Churchill, 451
Spengler, 410
sperl, to, 190
Speziale, 440
spider, 185, 723
Spider's Den, 592
Spider Web, 592
spielen sie morgen?, 367
spieler, 684, 729
Spielmann, 409
spiff, 767, 771
spigot, 101, 204
spike, 680; -pitcher, 749
spiker, 772
spill rubies, to, 756
Spilman, 409
Spinach, 450
spinner, 719
Spirit of Democracy, 595
spirit runner, 748
spirochetes, 320
spit, 262; -blower, 163
spitch, 260
spla, 752
splash, 751
spleeny, 158
spliced, 663
splint-shin, 236
split-fig, 659
split week, 691
Spohn, 410
spoir, 309
Spokes, 679
sponge, 98, 738; -cake, 237
sponsor, 731
spook, 228, 707, 720
spool-pig, 149
spoon, 228, 248, 762
spoonbill, 776

spoonfuls, 328
spoonsful, 328
sport, 752
sporting-house, 682
sportsman, 769
spose, to, 174
spot, 269, 684, 692, 697, 706
Spot, 594; Cash, 594
spouty, 173
sprag, 233
sprang, 361
spread, 208, 669; -water, 151
spreader, 766
sprig, 744
spring, to, 361
springer, 749
springtime, 738
sprinkle, 772
spritz, 20, 202
spritzen, 202
Spritzwasser, 450
sprung, 361
spucken, 635
spud-digger, 138; -glommer, 138; -row, 138
spud in, to, 764
Spud Peeler, 588
spuds, 674
spun out, 253
Spuyten Duyvil, 189
squalid, 215
squam, 574
square, 204, 390, 695; -shooter, 648
square John, 680
square the yards, to, 166
squat-drop, 132; -head, 776
squatter, 624; -law, 624; -sovereignty, 624
Squatter State, 623
squaw, 160; -man, 243; -side, 742; -water, 734
squawk, 728
squeak, 718
squeaker, 705
squeal, to, 644
squeechy, 175
squeeze-horn, 705
squib, 737, 750
squin, 210
squirrel, 329, 733; -turner, 121
squirt-gun, 734

List of Words and Phrases 875

sqwqw, 92
Sr., 501
sred, 131
Srilda, 491
srink, 131
S. R. O., 688
ss, 545
SS. Cyricus and Julieta, 590
SS. Gluvias and Budoke, 590
-st., 322
stable, 682
-stad, 435
-stade, 534
-stadir, 434
staff, 74
stage, 253; -cloth, 689
stag-party, 647
Stahl, 409
stake, 221
stake president, 221
St. Albans, 578
Stalin, 415
stalk, 314
stall, 670, 756
stallded, 359
stalled, 151
stalted, 151
stamp, 208
stamp, to, 75
stamps, 659, 665
stance, 755
stand, 685, 691
stand, to, 269
stand by, to, 721
Stand-fast, 467
Stand-for-them, 446
stand-in, 700
standing-board, 700
Standing Elk, 446
stand in the paper, to, 169
stand-table, 200
stand the gaff, to, 746
Stanhope, 459
Stanley, 468, 469, 516
Stannup, 459
St. Ansgarius, 590
star, 652, 688
Star, 696
Star-Gazette, 595
starigan, 252
Star in a Mist, 592
staripen, 653
starlet, 703

start-naked, 124
stash, 677
state, 246, 322
State of Camden and Amboy, 602; of Rhode Island and Providence Plantations, 601; of Spain, 602
stateside, 780
States Rights, 508
static, 731
station, 337; -wagon, 723
statistic, 384
status, 72
Stauffer, 410
Stavros, 523
stawk, 314
stawmerre, 258
stayed, 261
stayed to home, 234
stay-in, 777
stay up, to, 179
St. Charles City, 554
St. Clair, 439, 459, 491
St. Clergy, 450
St. Cwfig, 591
St. Cyffelach, 590
St. Delta, 590
St. Denis, 438, 439
-stead, 534
steal, to, 269
steamer, 734
steam-heat, 260
steam-roller, 724
Stee-fen, 99
steel, 762
Steel, 409
Steel State, 598
-steen, 424
steepy, 118
steer, 171, 231
steerer, 696
Stefan, 519
Stefanovitch, 442
steig, 654
-stein, 422, 424, 534
Stein, 409, 424
Steinbeck, 424
Steinberg, 422
Steinmetz, 415
steishn, 288
Stella, 523
stem, 681
stemwinder, 751
sten, 431
Stenola, 491

Stepaside, 572
Stephen, 99, 402, 518, 524
Stephens, 399, 430
step on the gas, to, 723
steppe, 151
-steppe, 534
Steps to the Altar, 593
Sterilize, 512
Sterling, 507
stern, 79
stern foremost, 165
Stetson, 742
Steve, 523
Stevens, 399, 402, 421
Stevenson, 406, 442
stew, 120, 671; -builder, 759; -bum, 678, 759
stewardship, 745
Stewart, 399, 400, 404, 405, 421
St. Francis, 325
St. Gaffo, 590
stick, 269, 669, 681, 685, 717, 718, 723, 734
stick, to, 206
stick 'em up high, Jack, 671
sticker, 669, 733
sticks, 690
stick-up, 671
stiff, 669, 720, 752, 769
stiffs, 668
stigmata, 320
still, 148, 203, 206, 700
stiller, 765
Stilletto, 596
stilts, 756
stimbitt, 260
stimulate, to, 769
stimuli, 319
-stine, 424
Stine, 409
sting, 670, 733
sting, to, 668
stingaree, 166
stinker, 646, 737, 743
stinkers, 674
stir, 653
St. James, 590
St. James's-place, 325; -street, 322
St. John, 454, 590
St. John in the Wilderness, 590
St. John's, 539
St. Jones, 572

Stkachango, 530
Stktschagko, 530
St. Llanwddog, 590
St. Luke, 590
St. Mark, 590
St. Mary, 590
St. Mary Magdalene, 590
St. Mary-of-the-Woods, 325
St. Mary's, 325, 539
St. Mary the Blessed Virgin, 591
St. Mary the Virgin, 590
St. Maur, 439, 459
stockade, 700
Stockfarm, 592
stockholder, 714
stock manager, 771
stockyards, 384, 385
stogy, 744
Stoke-on-Trent, 324
stole, 254
Stolen, 450
stomach-robber, 759
stomp, to, 76
stomping, 76
stone, 158; -crusher, 725
Stone, 399, 409, 425, 430, 438
Stoneleigh, 534
stone on the chest, 762
stone pony, 133
Stone River, 589
Stonewall, 470
stood, 261
stood in bed, 261
stooge, 647, 727
stool, 158
stoop, 211
stop, 45, 246, 251
stop over, to, 648
stopper, 233
stop the show, to, 692
store, 248, 249; -church, 591
storey, 282, 283
stork, 314
Storm, 515
story, 283, 316
sto-un, 158
Stourton, 459
stove, 718
stovepipe, 764
Stover, 410
stow, to, 254
stow you, 665

St. Paul, 561, 590
St. Peter, 590
St. Peter Port, 590
Strabogie, 459
Strabolgi, 459
Strachan, 459
Strachatinstry, 449
Strachey, 459
straddle-bug, 179
Strahn, 459
straight Kelly, 772
straight man, 692, 693
strainer, 724
strand, 431
strange, 206
strangle-goose, 662
strata, 72, 318
Stratford Arms, 578; -House, 578
Strawton, 459
Stratton, 459
stratums, 320
Straus, 423
Strauss, 423
strawberry, 673, 737
strawdiny, 39
straw-hat, 691
Strawn, 459
Straws, 423, 424, 536
Straytchy, 459
stream-lined, 723
streel, 253
street, 98, 322; -car, 250, 251
strength, 92, 175, 246
strengths, 92
strengtht, 100
strenth, 175
stretch, 674
stretch, to, 659, 731
stretch in, to, 750
strickened, 359
strictly, 218
strife, 328
strike, to, 697
string, 741; -beans, 231
stripe, 684
stripper, 694, 766
strives, 328
stommell, 665
stromp, 179
strong, 180; -arm, 648
Strongface, 448
struck, 777
struwwel, 202
struwwely, 202

St. Tyclecho, 590
stubble-jumper, 762
stuboy, to, 179
Stub-Toe State, 635
studdle, to, 166
student, 680
Studis Fat, 450
stuffer, 740, 753
stump, to, 643
Stump, 411
Stumpf, 411
stump-jumper, 718
stun, 158
stunde, 647
stunt, 647; -man, 700
Sturgeon, 505
St. Ursula and the Eleven Thousand Virgins 590
Sturton, 459
Stuyvesant, 405, 406
St. Wrthwl, 590
stymie, to, 652, 755
St. Ynghednoddle, 590
Suad, 519
Suango, 515
sub-japoly, 725
Sublimity, 567
submarine, 751, 755; -shot, 765
Submarine, 513
subway circuit, 693
súccess, 49
succor, 281
such, 188, 260
Such, 450
such an one, 94
such a one, 94
suck, to, 701
sucker, 615; -word, 668
Sucker, 614, 641; -State 614
Sucksmith, 451
suds, 384, 662, 674
Suduta, 515
Sue, 506
suede, 775
Sŭekevičius, 428
suey-pow, 681
Suffrage State, 642
sugar, 680; -daddy, 649
Sugar, 505, 512
Sugar Loaf, 564
Sugar State, 628
Sugarwater, 450
suicide club, 769

suitcase, 705
suite, 758
Suitsme, 579
Suits Us, 580
Sukevicius, 428
Sula, 480
Sulaymān, 441
sulfur, 291
Sullivan, 399, 401
sumac, 175
summers, 212
Summer-side, 208
Summer Sigh, 593
Summer vacation, 250
summus, 212
sump, 764
Sumpad, 523
Sun, 595
Sunbeam, 512
sunbrite, 296
Sunburst, 582
Sunday, 412, 717; -school, 745
Sunday Night Supper, 509
Sunflower, 562, 592; -State, 623, 624
sunfish, 765
sung, 359, 361
Suni, 515
sunk, 361
Sunny Piazzi, 450
Sun Queen, 581
Sunset City, 553; State, 611, 638
Sunshine, 450; State, 636
sup, 292
super, 670; -colossal, 704; -drooper, 746
super and slang, 670
Super-Chief, 581
Superview, 577
super-yes-man, 701
supper-turn, 693
suppose, to, 174
súpreme, 218
su'prise, 96
sure, 313, 337, 388, 389, 390
surface-coal, 219
Surgailis, 428
Surrey, 578
survae, 306
survey, 306
Survival War, 785
Susannah, 479

susfu, 774
suspenders, 250
Susquehanna, 526
Susquehanny, 544
Sussex, 578
sustaining programme, 731
Susanah, 491
susy, 121
Sutheby, 459
Suthy, 459
Sutzanna, 579
Suvada, 491
Suwanee, 556
Sva, 491
Swaffer, 459
swag, 674
swallick, 180
swamp, 215, 216, 574; -root, 194
swamped, 668
Swamp State, 608
swan, 215, 216
Swan, 491
Swanson, 433
swarp, 153
Swartz, 411
Swayback Maru, 588
sweat, to, 360
sweat-shop, 720
Swedish fiddle, 760
sweeping, 767
sweet, 250, 269, 374, 389
Sweet Alice, 751
sweet alyssum, 269
sweetheart, 720
Sweetheart, 525
Sweet Home, 592
sweet jazz, 705, 706
sweetpotato, 325
sweet religion, 269
sweets, 64, 462
sweet stuff, 680
swelled, 110
Swellhead, 536
Swenssen, 433
Swill, 450
swing, 705; -gang, 701; -girl, 695; -room, 767
swinger, 720
swinkeltree, 209
switch, to, 758
Switzerland of America, 540, 599, 602, 613, 629, 641

swivit, 193
Swoffer, 459
swoggle, to, 121
swole, 110
swollen, 151
swoon, to, 707
swoonded, 358
sword, 741
swullen, 151
sxw, 93
Sycamore, 450
Sylvan, 516
Sylvia, 421, 436, 516, 519
Symons, 459
sympathetic, 246
Symphorosa, 497
syndicate, 667
syndrome, 87
Synge, 459
Synn, 505
synthesises, 320
Syooel, 459
Syracuse, 532
Syreath, 491
syringe, 705, 750
Syrjäniemi, 429
syth, 96
Syveta, 491
sz, German, 307
Szczepanski, 425
Szécskay, 440
Szigligeti, 440
Szybczýnski, 425
Szymkiewicz, 425
t, 44, 53, 97, 100, 131, 192, 193, 209, 218, 241, 258, 262, 292, 300, 411, 500
t, Russian, 408
t, silent, 96
t, voiced, 97, 98
ta, 267
taalsman, 406
Taavetti, 524
Tabitha, 467
table, 97
Tachera, 436
tack, 769; -spitter, 724
tackle, 769
tacks, 297
tactic, 383
Taelman, 406
tag-along, 719
tagged, 774
tahm, 192
Tahwahnah, 491

tailer, 176
Taillefer, 455
tail-light, 740; -spin, 727; -wind, 728
tailor, 280
tain't no place for nobody, 393
take, 241, 685, 701
take a mope, to, 674
take a puke, to, 634
take for a ride, to, 652, 671
take goodby, to, 151
take his commission, to, 236
taken, 110, 133, 220
taken aback, to be, 721
takened, 221, 360
taken off, 167
take-off, 706
take the count, to, 768
take the ground, to, 757
Tal, 505
Talapoosa, 530
tale, 292; -box, 748
tal e, 292
Taliaferro, 447, 454, 455
Taiicia, 491
talk, 203
talkies, 702
talk short, to, 195
talk underground, to, 165
Tallahassee, 556
Tallifer, 455
Tallman, 406
tallow-pot, 713
Tallulah, 496
Taloah, 491
Talvio, 429
Tammany Hall, 720
Tamora, 491
Tamošitis, 428
Tampa, 556
T and A, 756
Tandy, 505
tangle-foot, 649
tank, 219, 714, 721; -farm, 764; -town, 677, 691
Tank, 450
tantalum, 285
tantoaster, 180
tao, 243
tap, 101, 772
tap out, to, 769
täppisch, 202

taps, 693
tar, 73, 269, 680; -baby, 762
Tar-boiler, 606
tard, 230
tarfu, 778
Tarheel, 194, 606, 607; Banker, 607
tarif, 295
tarnation, 172
Taro Sazuki, 444; Tanaka, 444
tarrible, 171
tarrier, 171
Tarryall, 555
tart, 73
Tart, 450
Tasceil, 491
task-force, 781
tassel, 169
Tastee, 580
tasteful, 388
Taste Rite, 580
tasty, 388
taterdemaelyon, 306
Tatro, 437
tatterdemalion, 306
taught, 314, 340
taut, 314
Tavor, 422
tax, 297
taxi-drinker, 682
Taylor, 397, 399, 401, 409, 416, 442, 507
T. B., 536, 755, 756
tch, 261
tchahtch, 261
Tchoupitoulas, 560
td, 717
te, 208
tea, 292, 681; -cup, 746; -kettle, 716; -man, 681
teacher, 221, 737
Teacher's College, 325
Teakettle, 588
team-play, 737
tear, 214, 734; -bucket, 704; -gas, 674
teared, 165
teaser, 691, 754
teat, 171; -puller, 747
TeAta, 491
Teats, 450
Teck, 414
Tecumseh, 507
tee, 292

Tee, 505
Teebo, 437
teem, to, 238, 315
teeming, 773
teer, 301
Teigmouth, 459
Teixeira, 436
teksiz, 218
Telefer, 455
telegraf, 295
Teletha, 491
tell it to Sweeney, 645
telltale, 716
Temperance, 479
temptāshn, 293
Temure, 406
tenderfoot, 742, 761
Ten Eyck, 405
Ten Eyre, 406
ten-gallon hat, 742
Tennessee, 588
Tennga, 541
Tennyson, 406
tent, 766
ten-ton Jack, 722
tents, 754
Tenya, 491
Tera, 505
Terbert, 505, 506
Teretha, 491
Terhune, 430
Terhunen, 430
Terjesen, 435
terled, 190
term, 79
termatter, 75
termayter, 75
termite, 722
Terrace, 577
Terrapin State, 602, 604, 605
Terrence, 518
terrible, 171
Terrible, 587
terrier, 171, 713
territory, 5
territóry, 114
terror, 38
terrour, 311
Terry, 476, 594
Tesa, 491
Tesnus, 541
testatrixes, 320
Tetaw, 437
tete-a-tete, 327
tetnit, 179

List of Words and Phrases

Tetreault, 437
Texana, 491
Texarilla, 491
Texarkana, 540
Texas, 218, 491; -leaguer, 737
Texhoma, 540
Texola, 491
Teyna, 491
tfip, 192
th, 92, 98, 171, 192, 205, 209, 218, 241, 246, 248, 253, 258, 260, 288, 290, 291, 292, 293, 294, 300, 303, 424, 435, 456, 458, 459
th, German, 424
th, Norwegian, 435
th, silent, 96
-th, 328
Thad, 475
Thaddies, 505
Thadine, 498
Thaine, 505
-thal, 422, 423
thaler, 657
Thallis, 491
thar, 87
-thar, 382
Tharyn, 491
that, 205, 206, 303, 352, 369, 375, 382
that-a-way, 169
that's for sure, 236
that-there, 382, 383
that-there-way, 169
that-un, 380
thaut, 306
Thava, 491
the, 38, 73, 97, 263, 288, 352, 382
theater, 291, 301
theatre, 48, 282, 286
Théâtre Français, 317
Thebes, 537
thee, 382
thee is, 382
The Hague, 540
their, 301
theirn, 368, 369
theirselves, 366
their wife, 394
Thelbert, 505
Thella, 491
Thelma, 510
The-Lord-is-near, 467

them, 188, 218, 340, 348, 375
the malaria, 394
them-all, 380
the man that, 375
Themious, 505
the'mometer, 96
them-there, 382
them-uns, 380
then, 337
Theobold, 459, 472
Theodora, 493
Theodore Roosevelt, 470
Theophilus, 505
Theople, 505
Theoplies, 505
Theorda, 505
Theos, 521
Theral, 491
there, 87, 241, 261, 382
the reason was because, 337
there you be, 356
Therica, 491
thermometer, 705
these, 218, 375
these-here, 382, 383
these kind, 337
thesen, 369
thesises, 320
Theumissen, 406
they, 218, 369
they-all, 380
they all known, 167
they-alls, 380
they be, 165, 356
they beat, 361
they beaten, 361
they be good, 356
they bet, 361
they (h)aint, 165
they is, 264, 377
they'm, 165
they taken, 361
they takened, 361
they tooken, 361
they tuck, 361
Theyva, 491
Thibeau, 437
thicken, to, 359
thick-joint, 160
thick-milk, 208
Thiebaud, 437
thief, 748; -sand, 764
thimble, 670
think for, to, 180

thinkies, 702
thinking part, 691
thinnen, to, 359
thinnening, 359
thin-skin, 713
thir, 301
third, 99
3rd, 501
III, 501
third banana, 694
third degree, 652
third ear, 723
third-termite, 644
thirteen, 772
thirteen and eight, 766
30, 616
thirty-four, 661
this, 260, 382
this-a-way, 169
this-'ere, 382
this-here, 382, 383, 394
this-hyar, 382
thish-yer, 382, 383
this h-yere, 383
thisn, 369
thiss, 288
this-un, 380
this-yer, 382
this-yere, 382
tho, 291, 295, 301, 302, 311
Thoas, 505
thoid, 87, 107, 189, 190, 191
thoidy-thoid, 188
Thomas, 397, 399, 401, 428, 447, 462, 463, 510, 517, 521, 523
Thompson, 397, 399, 400, 401
thon, 370, 371
thon's, 370, 371
Thor, 508
thoro, 291, 311
thorofare, 311
thoroly, 311
thorough, 45
-thorpe, 534
Thorstad, 435
Thorvald, 520
those, 340, 375
thosen, 369
those-there, 382
thot, 313
thou, 381, 382
thou be, 356
thought, 203, 241, 306

List of Words and Phrases

thout, 171
Thrantham, 505
thrash, 79
three-bagger, 720, 749
three-card monte man, 667
three-ring, 652
Three Rivers, 572
three sheets in the wind, 721
three strikes and out, 737
three-titter, 749
thresh, 171
thrid, 99
thro, 302
Throniall, 505
throttle-jockey, 727
through, 171, 310, 337
Through-Much-Tribulation-We-Enter-Into-the-Kingdom-of-Heaven, 468
throw away, 269
throwed, 362
thrown out, 771
throwout, 678
throw up the sponge, to, 768
thru, 291, 295, 301, 311
thruout, 311
thruu, 301
Thuda, 491
thuh, 38
thumb, 171, 294
thumb a ride, to, 723
thunder, 171; -hole, 220; -pump, 176
Thunder, 587
thurd, 300
Thurolene, 491
thusly, 390
Thusnelda, 497
thuyty-thuyd, 189
-thwaite, 402
ti, 308
Ti, 542
Tia Juana, 528
Tibbald, 459
tick, 269, 644
ticket-maker, 776
tickey, 181
tickle, 254
Tickle, 450
tickled pink, to be, 649
tiddly, 720; -sailor, 720; -uniform, 720

tidy, 254, 663
t'ief, to, 269
tier, 184, 301
Tiercero, 437
Tierra Amarilla, 565
tie-up, 158
tiffin, 243
Tiger, 588
Tigertown, 568
tight, 390; -wad, 648
tight rein, 770
Tijuana, 528
Tikvah, 519
Tilbury Court, 577
till, 151, 203, 239
tillacume, 237
tilt, 252
Tim, 594
timber, 760; -beast, 760; -cruiser, 759
time, 125
Times, 595; -Herald, 595
Timothy, 518
Timpahute, 563
tin, 249, 725; -box, 719; -can, 716, 727; -cow, 678; -ear, 707, 768; -knocker, 728; -lizard, 715; -lizzie, 127, 726, 727; -pants, 760
tin-a-fix, 155
Tin Cup, 555
tinge, 771
Tinja, 552
tinker-tonker, 149
Tinmuth, 459
tin-pan alley, 693
tint, to, 739
Tiog, 565
Tioga, 565
tip, 685
tipe, 311
tip over, to, 236
Tippecanoe, 558
tippetybounce, 210
tire, 249, 286, 316
tired, 230
Tiresaver, 581
Tirrit, 459
tisard, 754
tisart, 754
tissue, 732
tit, to, 151
titles, 701
tivis, to, 166
tiwana, 528

Tiwauni, 515
Tjarda van Starenburgh Stockouwer, 407
T. L., 771
TNT, 593
to, 141, 239, 292, 301, 312, 352, 364, 365
T. O., 679
T. O., to, 758
Toad, 449
toad-hides, 675
toat, to, 193, 194
Tobacco State, 628
toboggan, 252
toby, 669
Toby, 475
tochos, 151; -lecker, 771
today, 97, 324
to-day, 286, 324
Toe Nail, 592
tog, 670
togeman, 665
togogo, 267
to home, 111
toil, 87, 214
toime, 248
tokens, 208
toko, 267
tole, 96
Tolee, 491
Tolliver, 454, 455
Tom, 397, 475, 513, 523, 524
Tomahawk, 595
tomahto, 75
Tomaline, 491
Toman, 427
tomato, 75, 724, 736, 768
tomatoeses, 386
tomatto, 75
tomayto, 72, 215
tomb, 668
Tombstone, 553
tombstone salesman, 756
Tom-cat, 226
Tom Collins, 386
Tom company, 691
Tomi, 491
Tomme, 491
Tommie, 491, 496; Ann, 491; Mae, 518
Tommye, 491
Tommy-gun, 671
tomorrow, 324
to-morrow, 324
Tom-thumb, 659

List of Words and Phrases

Tonbridge, 459
tongue, 313
tonguey, 118
tonic, 168
tonk, 713
Tonkajo, 491
Tonopah, 563
tonsillitis, 81
tony, 648
Tony, 522
too, 203, 269, 292, 301, 312
toob, 84
to of done, 366
took, 110
took after, 237
tookis, 151
tool, 246, 670
tooler, 719
Toosh, 459
tooth, 203
toother, 740
toothpick, 718, 741
Toothpick State, 611
Toots, 720
Toovone, 491
top, 684, 691; -hand, 762; -hole, 648, 649; -liner, 692
Topaz, 537
Topock, 552
toppingly, 649
tore-downdest, 387
Torial, 512
Torl, 505
tormenters, 691
Törnwall, 432
torpedo, 667, 671
Torrey, 570
tort, 314
tortilla, 51
Tortolia, 552
tory, 320
Tosa, 491
tosser, 735
tossle, 169
tossout, 678
tossted, 358
T. O. T., 758
tot, to, 267
tota, to, 267
Totah, 441
total loss, 646
Total Wreck, 553
tote, to, 144, 194, 200, 267
Totoventz, 441
totsäufer, 739

Totus, 491
touch, to, 663
Touche, 459
touch-off, 750
tough cud, 179
toun, 397
toune, 397
tour, 764
tourer, 195
tourist, 386, 677; -camp, 723
tout, to, 652
Tout, 451
towards, 203
tower, 764
Towers, 577
to what, 394
-town, 539, 563
town crier, 730
Townzella, 491
towre, to, 665
Towser, 594
Towson, 576
Toxie, 505, 506
toy, 192, 670, 681
Toycen, 435
TPR, 756
tractor, 723
Tracy, 517
trading, 111
traffic-light, 723; -whipper, 719
trafic, 295
trailer, 694, 701
Traina, 491
trainee, 780
training-school, 132
trait, 314
traler, 297
tram, 250, 251
Trames, 453
tramp, 676, 679, 725
Trampleasure, 451
trance, 734
transitad, 732
trap, 757
trapee, 383
trapper, 761
traps, 662
trassel, 171
traumas, 319, 320
traveler, 284, 669
Traveler's Rest, 592
traveller, 282, 284
Travette, 491
Travois, 505

tray, 314
treaded, 362
tread water, to, 362
treasurer, 696
Treasure State, 613, 635
treated, 238
treatment, 701
Trechsler, 408
Tree Planters State, 635
Trematon, 414
tremendious, 99, 217
tremor, 280
Tres Piedras, 565
Tressler, 411
trestle, 171
tret, 238
Trevania, 491
Trevelyan, 459
Trevilian, 459
Tribby, 468
trible, 764
Tribulation, 592
tríbunal, 48
Tribune, 595
trick, 674
triddler, 217
Trigger, 512
trigger-man, 644, 667, 671
trim, to, 659
trim ship, to, 728
Trinity, 590
trink, 233
triolet, 25
trip, 192, 751
tripe, 685, 758, 772
Triumph, 562
trod, 362
trodding, 362
Trois-Rivières, 572
Troostenburg de Bruyn, 407
Trotsky, 415
trotter, 718
Trouble, 512
trouper, 691
trout, 329
Trout, 572
trouts of the Rocky Mountain, 328
t'row, 192
Troxler, 408
Troy, 532, 537
truck-driver, 727
trucking shot, 701
True, 505, 506

Truman, 471
trunx, 297
trust-buster, 355
truwy, 269
try, 125
try and, 337, 338, 394
tryninge, 665
try on the dog, to, 689
tryout, 688
Tryphena, 491, 495
ts, 261
Tsankawi, 582
Tschakko, 530
Tschechener, 206
T'Serclaes, 452
tsh, 292
tshassis, 53
tshinguhmbuh, 267
Tsino, 442
Tsipora, 519
Tsur, 442
tte, 310
tu, 308
tub, 199, 721
Tubal, 508
Tubbs, 532
Tubbsville, 532
tube, 84, 205
tuck, 744
Tucker, 399
tuckout, 165
tucks, 198
Tudor, 577; Manor, 577
tullegram, 24
Tulsa, 544
Tulsey, 544
Tulsy, 544
tun, 397
tunnel, 185
tung, 292, 313
Tuomikoski, 429
Turin, 537
Turk, 659, 745
turkey, 138, 691, 729
Turkey, 562
Turkey Tracks, 592
turkler, 166
túrkwoyze, 62
Turlington, 454
turn, 252, 693
turn, to, 685
turned over, 253
Turner, 397, 399, 405, 406
turnip, 670
Turnipseed, 450

turnouts, 750
turnover, to, 758
turn the tip, 686
Turnton, 454
Turnwall, 432
turp, 765
turpentine, 218; -whiskey, 608
Turpentine State, 606
turpmtine, 218
turquoise, 62
turrón, 317
turtle, 717
Turtleskin, 592
Tuscaloosa, 530
Tuskegee Victory, 584
tut, 205
tuta, to, 267
tüte, 205
tutor, 280
tutor, to, 121
tuu, 301
TVA, 331
Twe, 448
twell, 151
twelve, 122
Twentieth Century Limited, 581
twenty, 97
Twerp, 593
twict, 100
Twilight, 592
twill, 151
twine, 741
twinly, 252
twirly-thumb, 737
twirp, 646
twist, 681, 711
twist and twirl, 710, 711
twist-bud, 160
twister, 127
Twitty, 491
twm, 717
two, 292, 301, 312
two-bagger, 749
Two Bellies, 446
Two-Bits, 512
two doctor, 225
two-row eli, 748
two strikes on him, 737
Twyla, 498
Twylah, 491
txw, 92
tyb of the buttery, 665
Tydfyl, 491
Tye, 505

Tyi, 491
Tyler, 470
tympani, 318
tyown, 86
type, 125
typhoid, 228
Typhosa, 479
tyre, 286, 301
Tyrwhitt, 459
Tyson, 435
tyune, 122
tzorris, 759
Tztchago, 530
u, 45, 51, 73, 83, 84, 114, 186, 192, 199, 205, 214, 235, 241, 281, 291, 292, 294, 297, 300, 435, 459
u, French, 50
u, German, 51, 414
u, Norwegian, 434
U, 297
Uarda, 491
U Are Here, 297
u-bet-u, 297
Ubre, 413
udder, 151
u-do-it, 297
u-dryvit, 297
ue, 310, 397, 410
Uel, 505
Uffie Grunt, 450
Ughtynton, 451
Ugly, 449
uh, 215, 265, 288
Uhl, 409
Uhlan, 505
uh-oo, 227
uhreeb'n, 261
uhrgucker, 151
ui, 189, 191
Ujváry, 440
uka, 240
U Kan Kum Inn, 578
Ukdene, 491
ukudu, 267
Ukulele, 774
ula, 267
Ulala, 491
Ulelia, 480
Ulestine, 495
Ulianov, 415
Uliey, 505
Ullainee, 491, 496
ultraaustere, 325
Ulys, 506
Ulysses, 466, 477, 513;

List of Words and Phrases

Hiram, 478; Simpson, 477, 478
Ulyssia, 491, 493
Um-Ahmed, 524
Umatilla, 582
umble, 94
umbrella, 773
umkleiden, 202
umpire, 87, 88, 724
Umsted, 454
-un, 380
Una Lee, 488
-unas, 428
unbend, to, 359
uncle, 254, 663, 680
Uncle, 165; Sam, 478; Tom, 270
Uncle Sam's Pocket Handkerchief, 605
Uncle Tom's, 579
uncommon, 172
underlain, 362
underminded, 359
undermine, to, 365
under secretary, 324
under-secretaryship, 324
underskirt, 237
understudy, 652, 688
undertaker, 723
under the hat, 722
Une, 505
uneeda, 297
unelse, 198
Uneveigh, 491
unfeed, to, 195
-ung, 418
Unified State Political Department, 331
union, 86, 322, 693
United Nations, 786
United Nations Relief and Rehabilitation Administration, 330
United Staids, 209
United States of America, 505
university, 322
University, 576
unless, 198
unloose, to, 358, 359
unloosed, 358
unloosen, to, 358, 359
unmrella-'tick, 248
Unnionz, 460
Unous, 578
unplezant, 300

UNRRA, 330
-uns, 381
until, 156
u-otto-buy, 297
up, 241, 260, 362, 771, 778
Upalco, 569
upheader, 181
uphill, 722
up in the Chandalar, 552
Upjohn, 403
upon, 73
Upperco, 408
Upson Downs, 579
up-stage, 691
upstuck, 207
up to speed, 700
u-put-it-on, 297
ur, 189, 292, 294, 300
Ura, 505
Urakeze, 588
Urath, 491
Urban, 427
urbane, 300
Urcell, 491
Ure, 453
Ureatha, 491
Uren, 452
Uretha, 495
Uri, 519
Urian, 507
Urlda, 491
urmin, 300
Urquhart, 459
Ursula, 482
urth, 293
Urxula, 505, 506
us, 371
U S, 505
USA, 330
U. S. A., 330
us-all, 380
use, to, 269, 364
used to, 363, 364, 365
used to come, 364
used to could, 394
used to didn't, 364
used to was, 364
u-serve, 297
use-to-be, 364
-ush, 199
us'n's, 394
Usona, 505
usquebaugh, 207
usted, 378
us-uns, 380
Ut, 450

Utah, 569
Utahna, 491, 493
utensil, 48
Utica, 532
Uticy, 544
Utis, 505
uu, 292, 300
Uue, 453
Uva, 491
uw, 288
v, 98, 137, 181, 191, 218, 241, 246, 253, 258, 260, 291, 300, 411, 422, 432
V, 668, 674
v, German, 307
v, silent, 96
v, Spanish, 307
v, Swedish, 432
Vabalaitė, 428
Vabalas, 428
Vablienė, 428
vacation, 251
Václav, 472
Vacquensbac, 413
Vadna, 491
Vae, 491
vagabond, 664
vagarant, 99
vagrant, 72
vahst, 36
vahyoo, 314
Valanciunas, 428
Valančiunas, 428
Valeita, 491
Valentine State, 613
Valentino, 439
Valerica, 491
valet, 44, 53
VaLeta, 491
Valfred, 491
Valla, 491
vallas, 307
vallaz, 307
Valoise, 491
Valora, 487
valorous, 280
valour, 280
Valourd, 505
val-u, 84
value, 84
Valuzki, 425
vamp, 693, 703
vamp it, to, 253
van, 263, 407, 714
Van, 406, 407
Vancouver, 583

Vandenberg, 407
Vanderbilt, 407, 578
Vandergrift, 407
Vanderveer, 407
Vander Veer, 407
Vandervelde, 407
Vandetta, 491
Vandeveer, 407
Vandeventer, 407
Van Deventer, 407
Van de Venter, 407
Vandiver, 407
Van Dyke, 401
Vangele, 491
vanillar, 24, 89, 186
Vanis, 505
Van Kouwenhoven, 405, 411
Vann, 448
Vannelda, 496
Vannice, 407
Vannuys, 407
Van Nuys, 407
Van Roosevelt, 407
van Tets van Goudriaan, 407
vaporous, 280
vaquero, 741
Varbel, 491
Vardrene, 491
Vared, 422
Varice, 491
variete, 317
variété, 317
varieties, 691
variety, 691
Varington, 460
varmint, 100
Varnas, 428
Varney, 468
varnish, 716
Vart, 523
VaRue, 491
vas, 258, 320
Vaseline, 491, 513
vasha, 263
Vasilos, 523
vassal, 73
Vassar College, 582
Vassar-Smith, 421
Vasso, 505
Vater, 501
vaudeville, 53, 317, 691
Vaudie, 505
Vaughn, 506, 523
Vaughncille, 491

Vaux, 459
Vavelle, 491
vayas, 307
vayaz, 307
Vaye, 491
vayse, 215
V-day, 781, 782
Veal, 450
VE-day, 781, 782
Vedder, 508
veesion, 199
vega, 574
Vekol, 552
Vella, 491
Velma, 506
Velondia, 491
Velva Jo, 491
Velvalee, 497
Velvet-Ass Rose, 139
velyiew, 314
Vema, 491
Venazulia, 491, 493
vendue, 207
Veneriece, 491
Venie, 492
Venton, 509
Venus, 322, 451, 569
Venus Arms, 577
Veon, 505
Ver, 492
verb, 333
Verbilee, 505
verbum, 333
Verdavelle, 492
Verdine, 489
Verdmont, 570
verdrübt, 205
verdure, 314
Ve Ree, 492
verger, 314
veribest, 296
Verily, 512
Verl, 505
Verle, 505
verlier, 758
verlieren, 758
Verma, 492
Vermilla, 492
Vermont, 570
Vernace, 505
Vernal, 505
Vernet, 505
Verney, 469
Vernola, 492
Vernon, 517
Veronica, 519

Veroqua, 492
verse, 190
versenken, to, 655
Vershire, 541
vertebræ, 320
very, 172, 205, 269
very good, 172
Veskel, 505
Vesle, 434
Vesnelle, 492
Veston, 505
Vesuvius, 587
Vetelia, 492
V-Etta, 492, 518
vex, to, 338
Veyo, 542, 569
V-girl, 682
vhen, 258
vi, 308
Viadell, 492
vicarage, 747
vice-president, 324; of the United States, 320
victor, 280
Victory, 584, 587, 588
Victrola, 512
vid, 263
video, 731
Vienna, 540
-view, 563
viggerish, 747
Vigner, 413
vigor, 280
vigorous, 280
vigour, 280
vigourless, 280
Viig, 435
vil du gaa med?, 170
Vilentia, 492
Villa-de-Luxe, 578
village, 192, 573
Village, 678
Villa Real de Santa Fé de San Francisco de Assisi, La, 564
-ville, 534, 539, 573
Villers, 459
Villiers, 459
villitch, 192
vin, 253
-vin, 434
Vin, 505
Vincennes, 448
Vincent, 472
Vinch, 460
Vinciguerra, 439

List of Words and Phrases

Vinegar, 450
Vinnierenn, 492
vinyard, 291
Viola, 556
Violet, 566
víolin, 218
Violintta, 492
Viora, 492
viper, 228, 681
viping, 681
VirDen, 452
Virgil, 466, 507
virgin, 121
Virginia, 466
Virgin Mary, 512
Virgle, 505, 506
Virjama, 492
Virma, 579
Viropa, 541
virtue, 79
Virtus, 505
visa, 318
vis-à-vis, 318
visé, 318
visit, 260
visitor, 280
VisKocil, 452
Visscher, 406
Vital, 505, 506
Vitalis, 519
Vitoline, 492
Viviaette, 492
Vivian, 506
V-J, 505
VJ-day, 781, 782
Vlčansky, 427
Vlchansky, 427
Vlene, 492
V-mail, 781
voad-veal, 53
vodu, 267
vodu da, 267
vodudoho, 267
vodusi, 267
vodvil, 297
voi, 308
voice, 192
Voionmaa, 429
Vokes, 459
Volney, 507
voloominous, 85
voltmeter, 73
vol-um, 84
volume, 84
volunteer, 749
Volunteer State, 639

Vomera, 492, 495
vomick, 120
von, 262, 407, 505
Vonda, 492
Vondilee, 492
von Donop, 414
von Frandke, 413
Vonnez, 492
Vonzo, 503
voodoo, 267
Vookes, 460
vootsie, 208
vortexes, 319, 320
vortices, 319
Vosmaer, 406
Voulkes, 460
vous tous, 376
Vox, 459
Vox Populi, 595
Voy, 492
Voyd, 505, 506
Vrench, 460
vrow, 207
vudu, 267
vuduna, 267
Vulkánskee, 427
Vulon, 505
vulture, 707
Vuolijoki, 429
vur, 253
Vura, 492
Vurl, 505
vurry, 24
vus, 260
vy, 422
Vyrillia, 492
Vyskocil, 452
w, 137, 164, 191, 246, 258, 260, 263, 291, 300, 432
w, Swedish, 432
W. A. A. C., 330
Waaf, 331
Wäänänen, 429
Wa-a-wa, 579
Wabash, 558
Wac, 330
WAC, 330, 782
W. A. C., 330
wach werden, 202, 254
Wacile, 492
Waco, 528
Waddell, 454
waddie, 741
Wade, 523
wadgetty, 166
Waffle, 450

Wagensbach, 413
Wages, 535
waggon, 282
Wagner, 399, 415
wagon, 282, 316, 721
Wahl, 435
Wah-Leah, 492
Wahlelu, 492
Wahneta, 492
wahz, 159
waikiki, 240
Wain, 429
Wäinömöinen, 429
wainscoat-plow, 211
Wait, 454
waiting, 98
wait on, to, 239
Waive, 492
wake, 362
waked, 362
Waldburgia, 520
Waldegrave, 459
Walderich, 471
Waldo, 471, 507
walk, 74, 737, 771; -over, 769, 770
Walker, 397, 399
walkin, 114
Walking Coyote, 446
Walkingstick, 450
walk to, to, 691
Wall, 421, 536
Wallace, 399, 425
Wallammassekaman, 446
walla walla, 730
Wallawalla, 539
walled-eye, 770
Wallows, 679
Wall Street, 582
Walnut City, 559
walrus, 698
Walsena, 492
Walsh, 399
Walt, 475
walten, 471
Walter, 421, 463, 472, 510
Waltherene, 482
Wames, 453
wampas, 703
wampus, 197
wamus, 207
Wanahda, 492
Wanamaker, 409
Wanda Verline, 492
wanderlust, 51
Wanerta, 492

Waneta, 492, 516
Wanetta, 492
Wang, 562
wanga, 267
wangun, 760
wanigan, 760
waniigan, 760
Wanita, 492
Wanna Noit, 298
Wannemacher, 409
Wanneta, 492
Wanoka, 492
want, 234, 394; -ad, 732
want in, to, 204
want off, to, 207
want out, to, 204, 234
want to get off, to, 207
want to go, to, 97
Wanza, 492
Wanzenknicker, 417
war, 230
War Against Tyrants, 785; for Survival, 785; of Freedom, 786; of Illusions, 786; of Liberty, 785; of the Ages, 785; of World Freedom, 785, 786; to Save Civilization, 785; to Save Humanity, 785
warant, 295
Ward, 399, 405
warden, 722
Warfel, 408
Warner, 409
Warren, 399, 470, 471
Warrenetta, 492
warrior, 280
warsh, 174
War Shipping Administration, 330
Warwick, 459
was, 159, 219, 260
Wascott, 540
was für, 155, 160, 203, 254
wash, 174, 215, 216, 360
Wash, 450, 476
washboard, 720
washdub, 262
washed up, 708
washen, 360
was he with?, 169
Washington, 399, 405, 447, 453, 469, 470, 471, 472, 476, 531, 537, 556
Washington pie, 163

wash-off, 121
Washtub, 593
wasp, 216; -nest, 761
Wasserman, 422, 423
wassermucker, 151
Wasserzweig, 421
waste, 153
Wat, 475
watch, 251
Watch-Your-Step Church of God, 591
water, 97, 215, 216, 674; -sobbed, 173
Waterloo, 588
Waterman, 423
Waterproof, 534
Wathena, 492
Watkins, 399
Wauchope, 459
Waukop, 459
Wauhilla, 492
waumus, 148, 149
Waunita, 492
waur, 288
Wave, 505
WAVES, 779
waw, 40
Wawlgrave, 459
Wawrzynski, 425
way, 253; -car, 714
Way Down Upon the Swanee River, 509
Wayne, 507, 522
ways, 384, 385
Waywayanda, 579
Wazell, 505
WCTU, 331
weal, 203
wealberow, 209
weald, 573
we-all, 379, 380
we-alls, 379, 380
Wealthena, 479
we am, 171
weapon, 246
wear, 203
we are getting company, 202
wear-u-well, 297
weasel, 758
weather, to, 121
weaver, 730
Weaver, 399, 400, 409
web, 731
Webb, 399
we be, 165, 356

Weber, 399, 409
we be ready, 356
Webfeet, 638
Webfoot, 638
Webfoots, 638
Web-foot State, 638
We-Blu-Inn, 579
Webster, 530
wed, 165, 238
Wedlock, 449
weed, to, 165
Weeda, 492
weeded, 238
weedy, 748
Weego, 565
weehaw, 151
Week, 248, 435
Weems, 459
Weepah, 563
weeper, 678
weepie, 704
weesh, 234
weesit, 260
we (h)aint, 165
we hat, 267
Weinberg, 418
Weinburg, 424
Weinstein, 421, 422, 424
Weiss, 409
Welch, 399
Welcomyn, 579
we lived to Milwaukee, 141
well, 748
well-groomed, 770
Wells, 399
Welo, 492
welt, 220
Weltha, 492
we'm, 165
Wemyss, 459
Wen, 443
Wendoweeat, 578
We'nesday, 96
Weona Place, 579
we prays, 264
wer, 300
werden sie morgen spielen?, 367
Werner, 409
Wertly, 460
Wescott, 460
Wesley, 465, 472, 519, 524
Wesleyan Victory, 584
wes'n, 368
west, 557

List of Words and Phrases

West, 399, 559
West by God Virginia, 641
Westcot, 460
Western, 701
Westernism, 126, 142
Western Virginia, 571
Westinghouse, 412
Westkan, 541
Weston-super-Mare, 324; -under-Lizard, 324
West Point, 562
West Virginia, 570
Weta, 492
Wettin, 414
we-uns, 172, 380, 381
we uns gone done it, 142
we uns gwine to gone done it, 142
wh, 203, 209
Whale, 450
whale-belly, 716
whaleline, 741
Whalley, 460
wham, 694
Wham, 450, 534
whang, 674
whanger, 705
wharrel, 195
Wharton, 468
what, 261, 314
what-all, 169
What Cheer, 535
what for, 148, 155, 160, 203, 254
Whawly, 460
Wheat State, 630
wheel, 203, 694, 770
Wheeler, 399, 425
wheels, 667, 723, 758
whee-up, 158
Wheirmelda, 495
whelp, 220
when, 95
where, 95, 203
where are we at?, 394
where he went?, 246
where you at?, 264
Whestone, 505
whet, 162; -stone, 162
whetter, 162
which, 95, 203, 394
whiddle, to, 659
whiff, 177
Whiff, 594

whig, 320
while, 230
whiles, 180
while-u-wait, 297
whip cream, 388
Whirlwind, 594
whisker, 716
Whisker, 449
whiskers, 667, 680, 739
whiskey, 277, 278; -jack, 764
Whiskey, 567, 774
Whiskeytown, 567
whisky, 277, 316
Whist, 451
whistleberries, 751
whistle-pig, 161, 234
whistler, 669; -stop, 677
Whitam, 460
-white, 402
White, 397, 399, 401, 439, 441
White Bird, 446
white bread, 752
white-cap, 176
White Cloud, 592
white-coat, 750
white-cow, 772
White Elephant, 596
whiteface, 684
White Falcon, 596
Whitefield, 460
white henna, 739
white hope, 768
white horn, 772
White Horse, 536
white lie, 663
white meat, 730
White Mountain, 564; State, 599
white-nose, 253
white nurse, 680
white stuff, 680
whitewash, 766
white-water bucko, 760
Whitfield, 460
Whitie, 594
whittlety-whit, 153
whizz-bang, 681
who, 336, 342, 374, 375, 394
WHO, 330
who-all, 169, 379
who are you looking for?, 337
who did he marry?, 374

who do you love?, 348
whodunit, 297, 701, 729
whom, 336, 342, 348, 374, 375
whoop, 314
whoopee, 644
whoopie, 725
whoosher, 617
whore, 314
whose, 375
whosen, 369
who's yere?, 618
whot, 300
why, 230
Whynot, 563
Whytham, 460
Wichner, 413
wic-i-up, 149
wid, 188, 192
Widow, 774
Widower's Choice, 592
widow-maker, 762
wife, 646
wig, 272
wiggle-tail, 762
Wightwick, 460
Wilbarine, 498
Wilbraham, 460
Wilbram, 460
wilcox, to, 166
wild, 328
Wilda, 492
wildcat, 716, 764, 777
wildcatting, 764
Wildfire, 587
Wild Irishman, 583
Wildis, 516
wild pig, 328
wile, 315
wilful, 291
Wilhelm, 519
Wiljamaa, 430
Wilkes-Barre, 539
will, 261, 336, 366, 367
Will, 475, 476, 477
Will-A, 478
Willard, 518, 578
Will-B, 478
will can, to, 204
Willcke, 412
Willedra, 492
Willena, 492
Willene, 482
Willetta, 492
Willia, 492
William, 462, 463, 492,

509, 510, 513, 518, 521, 523, 524
Williamina, 492
Williams, 396, 398, 399, 429, 444, 447
Williamsburg, 531
Williamson, 399, 401
William Winter, 691
Willie, 512, 524; Mae, 492
Willie ⅜, 508
Willieva, 492
Willis, 399
Willith, 492
Williweze, 492
Willkie, 412
Willola, 492
willow, 736
Willow, 492
will you play?, 367
Willys, 785
Wilson, 396, 397, 399, 400, 401, 430, 461, 470
Wilsonia, 492
Wilvarine, 492
wimen, 313
wimmen, 313
Wimmie, 492
Winar, 425
wind, 716; -bag, 724
Wind, 515
winder, 90
Winder, 460
Windi, 492
windjammer, 684, 693
windmill, 724, 727
window-light, 237
Windsor, 414, 577; Castle, 577
winegar, 181
wine needs cooled, the, 202
wing, 528, 736
Wingy, 678
Winiarecki, 425
Winiwini, 515
Wink, 535
Winnaretta, 492
Winnell, 492
Winnepesaukee, 529
Winnipesaukee, 529
Winola, 492
Winston, 421
Wint, 508
Winthrop, 469
Winwar, 439

wipe, 686
Wipers, 528
wir bekommen besuch, 202
wire, 670; -road, 132
wireless, 728
Wirt, 412
Wisconsin, 567
Wisconsin Illinois, 507
Wise, 409
wise-crack, 609; -cracker, 609
wish, 230, 234, 359; -book, 138, 743
wished, 359
wish I was, to, 337, 338
wisht, to, 394
Wiso, 579
Wister, 412
Wistinghausen, 412
wit, 188, 209
witch, 203, 707
with, 188, 234, 254
without, 171, 394
withouten, 390
Wittick, 460
wittles, 181
wo, 291
wobbly, 677, 777; -hole, 720
Wohlgemuth, 421
Wohlgeruch, 417
woife, 248
woik, 192
woikus of de woild, 192
woild, 192
woith, 260
woken, 362
woken up, 362
wolf, 646, 678, 756
Wolf, 588
Wolseley, 460
wolverine, 629, 630, 707
Wolverine, 630; -State, 629, 631
wolves, 737
woman, 246
woman alive, 177
womanishest, 388
woman's, 325
woman's home companion, 758
women, 310, 313
womens, 386
Women's Auxiliary Air Force Service, 331

Women's Reserve of the Marine Corps, 779
Women's Royal Naval Service, 331
womp, 731
Wona, 492
wonder, to, 203
Wonder Home, 592
Wonder State, 611
Wonder State Herald, 611
Wong, 442, 443
won't, 342
won't never, 392
wood, 385; -buck, 208; -butcher, 755; -fish, 200; -pile, 705; -player, 737; -shed, 730
-wood, 534
Wood, 399, 409, 436
wooden ear, 776
Wooden Nutmeg State 599
Woodhouse, 439
Woodmere, 534
woodpecker, 659
Woodrow, 465, 470
Woodrow Joseph, 465
woods, 385
Woods, 399
Wood Violet, 582
woody, 674
woollen, 286
wooly breeches, 200
Woolzly, 460
Wooster, 5, 543
wop-stick, 705
Worcester, 5, 543, 566
work, 770
worker, 750
workhouse, 734
working man, 324
workman, 324
works, 385, 668
World Health Organization, 300
World Order War, 785
World War, 785
World War II, 785, 786
World War III, 786
worm-chaser, 733
wormhole, 773
worn outest, 226
Worrick, 459
worry, 45
worser, 387

worsest, 387
Worster, 5
worth, 260
Wörth, 412
Wortley, 460
Worton, 468
wot, 314
would, 364
woulda, 365, 366
would have, 366
wouldn't be for knowing, 133
wouldn't that jar you?, 645
would of, 366
wow, 646
wrack, 315
wrangle, to, 201
wrangling, 743
wrapper, 744
wrap-up, 748, 771
Wras, 505
wreath, 328, 752
Wreatha, 492
Wren, 331
wrestle, 174
wright, 309
Wright, 399
wring-jaw, 159
Wriothesley, 460
write, to, 309
writing, 98
Wroberta, 492, 494
wrong, 294, 389
wrote, 348
Wrotham, 460
Wrottesley, 460
WSA, 330
wug, 175
wuk, 248
wunnenberg, 655
wunst, 100
Wuorijäri, 429
Würfel, 408
wush, 230, 360
Wüster, 412
Wyatt, 454
Wyena, 492
Wylvia Jayne, 492
Wymola, 492
Wyneese, 492
Wynelle, 492
Wyvine, 492
x, 291, 292, 293, 294, 297, 408, 458
x, German, 307

X, 716
Xanthe, 498
Xeres, 386
Xie Mae, 492
Xina, 492
Xmay, 492
x pose, 292
Xylia, 498
y, 408, 436, 544
y, glide, 84, 86, 122, 243, 164, 171, 173, 205, 214, 218, 227, 230, 250, 291, 292, 300
y, Spanish, 307, 436
Yaaqov, 519
Yabel, 492
yacht, 294
yahyin, 654
Yakaze, 588
Yakov Vladimirovich Voronin, 415
Yale, 505
y'all, 264, 378
yalleph, 725
yaller, 89, 120, 137
Yallow, 451
yam, 160, 267
-yan, 441
yan, to, 267
yander, 120
Yankee, 132, 610, 621; -jumper, 162; -State, 636
Yankee Land of the South, 610
yap, 670
yap, to, 252
Yap Town, 679
Yaqūb, 441
yaram, 665
yarb, 86, 129
yard, 157, 163, 269; -goat, 716; -goose, 713
Yardena, 519
Yarmouth, 12
yarry, 252
Yartin, 440
yat, 446
yawd, 157
Yawl, 460
Yayts, 460
Yazzi, 446
ye, 375
ye all, 376
Yearick, 411
yearl, 87

yearth, 86
yeast, 87
Yeast, 449
Yeats, 460
yegg, 676
Yehiel, 519
Yehuda, 519
Yélahchich, 426
yella, 263
yeller, 89
yellow, 644, 668; -belly, 741; -jacket, 682
Yellow Boy, 445
yellow-dog contract, 777
yellowhammer, 776
Yellow-hammer State, 610, 611
Yellow Leaf, 592
Yellow Man, 446
Yellow Medicine, 561
yelper, 236
yen, 681; -pok, 681; -shee, 681; -shee-gow, 681; -shee-kwoi, 681
Yenkel Voroner, 415
yeno, 269
yent, 269
yentz, to, 671, 687
yenu, 269
yeppit, 165
Yerdith, 498
yere, 86
Yeredor, 422
yern, 292, 294, 295
yes, 97, 204, 645; -man, 647, 701
yeste'dy, 96
yesterday, 188
yes, we have no bananas, 645
yet, 203
Yetza, 492
yew, 310
yeye, 269
Yick, 505
Yididya, 519
Yigoel, 519
yinceth, to, 687
yink-yank, 754
yinnah, 215
yip, 158
yistidy, 96
y'll all, 379
YMCA, 331
yo, 308
yock, 694

yodeler, 735
Yoder, 411
Yoel, 519
yoking, 669
yolk, 179
Yonah, 519
Yondah, 492
yonder, 101
Yong, 444
yoonah, 269
Yopp, 450
York, 531
you, 215, 269, 292, 352, 373, 375, 377
you-all, 92, 101, 123, 125, 144, 169, 172, 173, 200, 231, 234, 247, 264, 375
you-alls, 378
you-all's, 380
you and I, 373
you and your folks, 377
you are all, 375
you be, 165, 356
Youghal, 460
you (h)aint, 165
you is, 171, 264
You Know Me Al, 579
you'll, 378
you'm, 165
voung, 269
Young, 399, 409, 444
young horse, 674
Young Man Afraid of His Horse, 445
Young Man Whose Very Horses are Feared, 445
Youngquist, 432
your, 18, 122, 352
You-reen, 513
youren, 369
yourn, 368, 369
yours comradely, 390
yourself, 260
yours friendly, 390
yous, 380
you-uns, 375, 380, 381
you-unses, 381
Ypres, 528
Ypsilanti, 561
yrr, 310
yuck, 730
yuck, to, 226
Yuer, 453
yuh prays, 264

yum-yum, 752
yur, 18
yuself, 260
Yuvon, 505
Yvette, 497
Yvonne, 485, 497, 582
z, 98, 193, 250, 262, 300, 310, 435, 458, 545
z, Italian, 308
z, Spanish, 435
Zach, 476
Zadean, 492
Zadeikis, 428
Zadoc Kahn, 424
Zadonna, 492
zagger, 687
Zala, 492
Zale, 505
zampa, 730
Zane, 570
Zannis, 492
Zanola, 492
Zanzibar, 583
Zaphenathpaneah, 467
Zay, 505
Zazelle, 492
Zdenka, 492
Zdzislaw, 522
ze, 269
zed, 250
Zedore, 505
zee, 250
Zee, 505
Zeema, 492
Zeev, 519
Zefferine, 492
Zehringer, 413
Zelda, 519
Zella, 498
Zellmer, 508
Zelmer, 505
Zelo, 522
zel rond, 155
Zelvateen, 492
Zémanovic, 426
Zemma, 492
Zenana, 492
Zeno, 508
Zenoda, 492
Zepheretta, 480
Zephro, 505
Zephyr, 581
Zercher, 410
Zeriah, 479

Zerietha, 492
Zerinque, 413
Zerrilla, 480
Zerrubabel, 467
Zessie, 492
zex, 771
Zeylus, 505
zh, 98, 193, 292, 300
Zheekako, 530
Ziba, 492
Zicaro, 439
zickus, 655
Zigzag, 535
zilch, 730
Zilliacas, 429
Zilwaukee, 561
Zimmerman, 409, 412
Zina, 479, 516
zinc, 99
Zine, 505
Zino, 537, 591
Ziona, 492, 519
Zippa, 492
Zle, 493
Zmuday, 425
Zmudzinski, 425
Zoan, 493
Zoda, 493
Zoheth, 505
Zola, 493; Mae, 496
Zonza, 493
zoo, 714, 756
Zoo, 679
zoom, 701, 727
Zota, 505
Zoualda, 493
Zoya, 491, 493
Ztschaggo, 530
Zucca, 439
Zudeen, 493
Zuericher, 410
Zula, 566; Bell, 493
Zuma, 493
Zur-Ayre, 422
Zurr, 505
zwicken, 655
zwicker, 655
Zwilla, 493
Zylphia, 493
Zymole, 493
zz, 310, 545
Zzelle, 493

INDEX

It would burden this Index unduly, and serve no useful purpose, to enter all the references to *American Speech*, *Dialect Notes*, the New English Dictionary and the Dictionary of American English. The entries are therefore confined to those which go beyond the mere citing of these indispensable authorities.

Abbatt, William, 158 n
Abbreviations, 329–31
Abeles, Edward, 689 n
Abercrombie, Lascelles, 37
Abramson, Samuel H., 421, 423
Académie Française, 309
Academy of Motion Picture Arts & Sciences, 702, 703
Academy of Sciences, Arts and Letters of Albuquerque, 128 n
Accent, 21, 25, 60, 114, 250
Accents, 316–18
Acland, F. A., 316 n
Actors' speech, 6, 7, 17, 26, 27 n, 33, 35, 42, 728, 729
Acts of the Fourth International Congress of Linguists, 15 n, 89 n, 115 n
Adam and Eve, 5
Adamic, Louis, 425, 426
Adams, Charles F., 258
Adams, Clifford R., 520 n
Adams, Franklin O., 535 n
Adams, Franklin P., 374
Adams, Harold E., 257 n
Adams, Joey, 420
Adams, John, 334, 470, 474 n
Adams, John Quincy, 20, 474

Adams, Ramon F., 727 n, 741 n
Adams, W. P., 166 n
Addison, Joseph, 302
Ade, George, 145, 645, 646, 672 n
Adjectives, 387, 388
Adverbs, 388–90
Advertising argot, 731, 732
African languages, loans from, 247, 265 n, 266, 267, 514, 515, 610, 710
Agate, James, 649 n
Ager, Cecilia, 297 n
Agnew, Joyce G., 470 n
Agnus, Felix, 579 n
Agronsky, G., 519 n
Ahrend, Evelyn, 251 n
Aiken, Janet R., 77 n, 303 n, 341
Airey, Bruce, 675 n
Alabama, given-names in, 482, 484, 488, 490, 491, 492 n, 496; nicknames of, 610, 611; place-names in, 542, 551, 552 n; speech of, 13, 105, 107, 115, 116, 129–31, 154 n, 357, 359 n, 387, 390
Alabama Anthropological Society, 551
Alaska, place-names in, 542, 552; speech of, 238, 239
Albany Institute, 47 n, 406 n

Albany Microscope, 599 n
Alciatore, Roy L., 53
Alcock, W. C., 785 n
Alden, Raymond McD., 327 n
Aldington, Richard, 40
Aleichem, Sholom, 415
Alexander, Charles, 708
Alexander, Donald M., 297
Alexander, Henry, 46 n, 99, 112, 115 n, 190, 191, 255, 354, 360 n, 373
Alexander, H. M., 693
Alexander, P., 327 n
Alexandria (Mo.) *Commercial*, 683 n
Alford, Henry, 389
Aliens' Restriction Act, 419 n
Allen, Bernard M., 363 n
Allen, Frederick L., 776 n, 777 n
Allen, F. Sturges, 137
Allen, Harold B., 170, 596 n
Allen, Virginia, 760 n
Allen, W. H., 202, 205, 206
Allentown (Pa.) *Morning Call*, 210 n, 410 n
Allgemeiner Verein für Vereinfachte Rechtshreibung, 307
Allison, Drew, 291
Allison, Lelah, 712 n
Allison, Vernon C., 121 n
Alsberg, Henry G., 713 n

i

Alsopp, Fred. W., 553
Alta Californian, 374 n
Alumni Bulletin (University of Virginia), 376
Ambrose, Kay, 695 n
Amend, Ottilie, 389, 688 n
American Academy of Arts and Letters, 33
American Academy of Language and Belles Lettres, 20
American Anthropological Association, 332 n
American Anthropologist, 446 n
American Antiquarian Society, 11
American Bantam Car Company, 783, 784
American Bookman, 371 n
American Council of Learned Societies, 67 n, 112, 156, 162, 216 n, 332 n, 398, 405 n
American Dialect Society, 105, 106, 108, 109 n, 111 n, 118 n, 124 n, 183 n, 188, 200 n, 255, 268 n, 574, 710 n
American Folk-Lore Society, 254 n
American-German Review, 412 n, 529 n, 579 n
American Guide Series, 131, 156 n, 174 n, 182, 193 n, 200, 216, 221 n, 238, 611 n, 743, 761 n, 762 n, 770 n
American Historical Review, 462 n
American Journal of Education, 273 n
American Journal of Philology, 213 n, 284
American Journal of Psychiatry, 681 n
American Journal of Sociology, 682 n, 708 n, 779 n
American Library Association, 551 n
American Magazine, 115 n

American Medical Association, 282 n, 285
American Mercury, 111 n, 117 n, 192 n, 193 n, 248 n, 260 n, 263 n, 264 n, 270 n, 379 n, 383 n, 388 n, 419 n, 427 n, 511 n, 581, 670 n, 671 n, 675 n, 680 n, 683 n, 689 n, 698 n, 706 n, 710 n, 711 n, 714 n, 717 n, 731 n, 736 n
American Museum, 321
American Notes & Queries, 91 n, 115 n, 239, 262 n, 323 n, 326 n, 362 n, 522 n, 541 n, 542 n, 630, 635, 645 n, 691 n, 703 n, 708 n, 712 n, 717 n, 719 n, 729 n, 735 n, 738 n, 743 n, 745 n, 746 n, 747 n, 750 n, 765 n, 777 n, 781, 782 n, 783 n, 784 n, 785 n
American Philological Association, 335, 549 n
American Philosophical Society, 162 n, 263
American Rifleman, 569 n
American Scholar, 343 n, 391 n
American Slavic and East European Review, 426
American Society of Newspaper Editors, 383
American Speech, 18 n, 27 n, 29, 32, 34, 45 n, 49 n, 54 n, 60 n, 61, 63 n, 67, 68 n, 74, 97 n, 98 n, 100, 106, 109 n, 138, 164, 168, 184, 193 n, 196 n, 203 n, 228, 233, 234, 236, 270 n, 290, 296 n, 297, 325 n, 337 n, 358, 362 n, 371, 372, 378, 379, 389, 429, 542 n, 551 n, 554, 567 n, 574 n, 607 n, 650, 696, 726, 728 n, 781 n
American Speech Reprints & Monographs,

67 n, 118 n, 217 n, 332 n, 570 n
American Standard. See General American
American Weekly, 707 n
American Youth for Democracy, 359 n
Americana, 462 n
Ames, Edward C., 758 n
Ames, Winslow, 592 n, 757 n
Ames, Winthrop, 498 n
Amherst (N.H.) Evening Record, 539 n
Amigos, 436 n
Ammons, Albert, 706 n
Amsterdam News, 447 n, 707 n
Anderson, Anders H., 756 n
Anderson, Charles B., 482 n
Anderson, Nels, 676 n
Anderson, V. A., 29
Andrews, Charlton, 48 n
Angel, Anne, 754 n
Anglia, 77 n, 268 n
Anglic, 289, 303
Anglic: an Edukaeshonal Revue, 303 n
Anglic Illustrated, 303 n
Anglo-French, loans from, 95 n
Anglomania, 14, 15 n, 17, 20, 21–24, 26, 33, 45, 187, 463 n, 577, 578
Anglo Sacsun, 293 n
Angoff, Charles, 581
Animals, names of, 328, 329 n
Annals of Iowa, 147 n, 559 n
Anson, Adrian C., 508
Anson, Lyman, 714 n
Answers, 650
Antigua, speech of, 247
Anti-Semitism, 32 n
Apartment-house names, 576, 577
Apollonius Dyscolus, 335
Apostrophe, use of, 325
Appalachia, given-names in, 118, 483, 487, 492 n, 501 n, 502 n, 503 n, 504 n, 505 n; place-names in, 118; people

of, 116, 117, 126; speech of, 16, 79, 103, 104, 115–19, 120, 128, 131, 136, 137, 139, 144, 146 n, 153, 157, 160, 161, 170, 171, 172, 173, 196, 200, 204, 207, 208, 213, 216, 218, 219, 220, 224, 226, 228, 233, 234, 239, 357, 358, 380, 387, 390, 741 n
Appalachia, 564 n
Apple-pickers' argot, 732, 733
Aquarists' argot, 732
Arabic given-names, 523; surnames, 441
Arbolino, Jack G., 723 n
Arcadian Magazine, 172 n
Archer, Stanley C., 155
Archer, T. W., 762 n
Archer, William, 299 n, 301 n
Archibald, Mildred E., 334 n, 389
Archimedes, 613 n
Architects' argot, 733
Archives of Speech, 71 n
Arensberg, Charles C., 425 n, 439 n, 440 n
Arizona, nicknames of, 611, 638; place-names in, 535, 552, 553; speech of, 127, 131, 132, 140, 221
Arkansas, given-names in, 485, 487, 489, 500, 510, 511 n; nicknames of, 611, 612, 627, 630; place-names in, 528, 542, 543, 553
Arki-Yavensonne, 479
Arliss, George, 33
Armagh, Archbishop of, 320 n
Armenian given-names, 523; surnames, 441
Armfield, Blanche Britt, 513 n
Armour, J. S., 49 n
Armstrong, George H., 572
Armstrong, Louis, 706 n
Arnall, Ellis, 125
Arnold, Joseph, 688 n
Arnold, Matthew, 302 n

Aronsky, Gershon, 422 n
Arrow Points, 551
"Arthur the Rat," 67, 130, 199
Arts Club of Chicago, 706 n
Arvedson, George, 461 n
Asbury, Francis, 619 n
Asbury, Herbert, 671 n, 734 n
Ashley, C. W., 721 n
Asquith, Cynthia, 37
Associated Press, 348 n, 374 n, 398 n, 444 n, 470 n, 477, 513 n, 717 n, 754 n, 777 n
Association of Shorthand Reporters, 55 n
Association Phonétique Internationale, 61, 62
Aston, J. W., 528 n
Aswell, James A., 543 n
Atherton, H. E., 196 n
Atkinson, Arthur R., 295 n
Atlanta, speech of, 121
Atlanta Journal, 119 n, 330, 609
Atlantic Monthly, 6 n, 119 n, 164 n, 180, 228 n, 444, 445, 462 n, 535 n, 546 n, 553 n, 615, 721 n
Atlantic Monthly Style-Book, 94
Attmore, William, 193
Auctioneers' argot, 687
Aurand, A. Monroe, Jr., 206 n
Austen, Jane, 339, 374
Austin, Edwin R., 718 n
Austin, Ethel, 481 n, 484 n
Austin, Mary, 573 n
Australia, speech of, 58, 256 n, 711
Author & Journalist, 108 n, 360 n
Authors & Printers Dictionary, 278, 282, 283, 323, 324 n
Automobile terms, 723–27
Automobile thieves' argot, 668, 669
Automobile Trade Journal, 727 n

Avery, Myron H., 568 n
Avery, S. P., 296 n
Axley, Lowry, 234, 378, 379
Ayearst, Morley, 250 n, 251, 316 n
Ayres, Harry Morgan, 66, 67, 248 n
Ayres, Leonard P., 352
Azrael, Louis, 576 n

Babbitt, E. H., 135, 188, 189, 351
Babbitt, Hal, 723 n
Babel, Tower of, 5 n
Backhouse, Fred, 781 n
Bacon, Charles R., 602
Bacon, Francis, 21 n
Badlian, Richard, 441 n, 523 n
Badoglio, Pietro, 782 n
Baeyer, Adolf, 599 n
Bailey, Mrs. L. B., 507 n
Bailey, Nathan, 661 n
Bailey, Oran B., 751 n
Bailey, Philip H., 698 n
Baker, Alfred, 299 n
Baker, Benjamin M., Jr., 48 n
Baker, F. Sherman, 46 n
Baker, Marcus, 552
Baker, Sidney J., 256 n, 651, 711 n
Bakers' argot, 733
Baldwin, Worth B., 512 n
Balfour, Arthur J., 39
Ball, Alice M., 318 n, 324, 325 n
Ball, Carleton R., 319 n
Ballinger, J. Kenneth, 710 n
Baltimore, speech of, 97 n, 99 n, 128, 129 n, 162, 163, 204, 362 n, 662 n
Baltimore, Irving, 686 n
Baltimore American, 579
Baltimore & Ohio Magazine, 703 n
Baltimore *Catholic Review*, 465 n
Baltimore *Commercial*, 599 n, 600 n
Baltimore *Evening Sun*, 44 n, 67 n, 162 n, 248 n, 256 n, 295 n, 317, 322,

327, 362 n, 398 n, 414 n, 486 n, 491 n, 524 n, 534 n, 580 n, 603, 604, 669 n, 675 n, 707 n, 721 n, 725 n, 745 n, 764 n, 768 n, 780 n, 785
Baltimore *News-Post*, 509 n, 576 n
Baltimore *Sun*, 256 n, 286 n, 298 n, 317, 322, 327, 348 n, 384, 411 n, 412 n, 413 n, 420 n, 421 n, 423 n, 426 n, 450 n, 561 n, 646 n, 649, 707 n, 717 n, 721 n, 735 n, 765 n
Bamboo English, 241
Bancker, Gerard, 532
Banker, Pierre A., 449 n
Bankhead, Tallulah, 496
Banks, Ruth, 270 n
Baptist Record, 393
Barbadoes, speech of, 248 n
Barber, Red, 737 n
Barber, T. R., 299
Barbers' argot, 733, 734
Barclay, Alexander, 609, 655, 656
Bardsley, Charles W., 406 n, 438 n, 451, 453 n, 454 n, 466 n, 467, 468 n, 469 n
Barge, William D., 558
Barker, Ernest A., 318 n
Barker, Howard F., 184 n, 399 n, 401 n, 402, 408, 416 n, 446, 447, 448, 450 n, 456 n, 461, 462 n, 676 n
Barker, Lewellys F., 508 n
Barkley, Dorothy, 755 n
Barkley, William, 303, 304
Barnes, Walter, 338, 343 n
Barnes, Will C., 551, 552, 553
Barnett, A. G., 248 n
Barnum, P. T., 659 n
Baronian, H. E., 676 n
Barr, Lockwood, 479 n
Barrère, Albert, 258
Barrett, L. L., 86 n, 423 n
Barrie, J. M., 463 n

Barrows, Sarah T., 77 n
Barrs, James T., 124, 543 n
Barry, Jerome B., 242 n, 784, 785
Barry, Phillips, 297 n
Bartenders' argot, 734
Bartenders' International League, 734 n
Bartle, Kemp P., 565
Bartlett, John R., 12 n, 103, 126, 154, 188, 209, 271 n, 355, 376, 381, 607, 611, 617, 618, 627, 628
Bartlett's Familiar Quotations, 379 n
Barzun, Jacques, 210 n, 325
Baseball argot, 734–37
Basler, George E., 195 n
Bass, R. D., 731 n
Bates, Ralph O., 250 n
Battenberg, Prince Louis of, 587
Battles, names of, 588, 589
Baugh, A. C., 29
Baum, Paull F., 162 n
Baumann, Elda O., 32 n, 408 n, 409, 410
Bayer, Henry G., 529
Bayonne (N.J.) *News*, 56 n
B. E., 656, 657, 659, 661, 662, 663 n, 664, 665
Beadle, J. H., 142, 601
Bean, R. Bennett, 229 n
Bean, William B., 198 n, 756 n
Beardsley, W. W., 772 n
Beath, P. R., 675 n, 698 n
Beatty, Willard W., 446 n
Beauchamp, William H., 565
Beaumont, Hartford, 88 n, 243 n, 438 n, 767 n
Beauticians' argot, 737, 738
Beche le Mar, 240, 264
Bechman, Frank E., 594 n
Beck, Fred, 720 n
Becker, Bob, 748 n
Beckwith, Martha W., 248 n

Beebe, Lucius, 714 n
Beeler, M. S., 721 n
Beerbower, G. M., 357 n
Beffel, J. N., 743 n
Beggars' argot, 656
Bel Geddes, Norman, 452 n
Bell, Alexander Melville, 59, 296 n
Bell, Charles N., 573
Bell, Margaret V., 381 n
Bell, Thomas, 427
Belloc, Hilaire, 54, 55, 69, 83, 97
Bell's Life in London, 660 n
Bell System Technical Journal, 352 n
Benardete, Dolores, 260, 264 n
Bender, Eric, 760 n
Bender, Harold H., 735 n
Bender, James F., 35, 36, 45 n, 47 n, 75, 78 n, 81, 82, 85, 96 n, 99 n, 193 n, 424 n, 743 n, 776 n, 780 n
Benedict XV, 464
Benitez, Carlos C., 244 n
Bennett, J. A. W., 256 n
Bennett, John, 266 n, 267, 268 n, 269 n
Bennett, Mr. Justice, 299, 300
Bent, Silas, 363 n
Bentham, Jeremy, 304 n
Bentley, Harold W., 528 n, 529 n, 551, 741 n
Bentley, Julian T., 728 n
Benton, Thomas Hart, 635
Benton Harbor (Mich.), speech of, 129 n
Bentz, Dorothy, 248 n
Beowulf, 573 n
Berg, Carl A., 291, 294 n
Berg, R., 712 n
Berger, Eric, 702 n
Berger, Meyer, 678 n, 680, 681 n
Berger, Morroe, 778 n
Bermuda, speech of, 248 n, 473 n
Bernays, Edward L., 718 n, 773 n
Berns, Mayme, 347 n

Bernstein, Herbert B., 379
Berrey, Lester V., 176, 356, 646, 650, 651, 657, 682 n, 709, 725, 755 n
Berry, Erik, 108 n
Better English, 731 n, 750 n
Better Speech, 675 n
Better-Speech Week, 343
Beverage Retailer Weekly, 386
Bevier, Thyra J., 368
Bey, Constance, 124 n, 174 n
Bibb, J. C., Jr., 481 n
Bible, 5 n, 21 n, 92, 93, 262, 272, 277, 299 n, 304 n, 322, 323 n, 351, 356, 376, 417, 466, 467, 468, 512 n, 514 n, 516 n, 591 n, 615 n, 766 n, 778
Bierce, Ambrose, 653 n
Billboard, 33, 114 n, 423, 452 n, 685, 686 n, 688 n
Binyon, Claude, 394
Biological Survey, 538
Bird, Robert M., 643 n
Birss, John H., 565 n, 610 n
Bisgaier, Paul, 767 n
Bishop, Joseph W., Jr., 779 n, 785
Bissell, Clifford H., 94 n
Bituminous Coal Institute, 760 n
Black, George F., 397 n, 404, 435 n, 439, 457 n, 458 n, 460 n
Black, John W., 70, 72 n
Blacker, Irwin R., 780
Blackstone, William, 304 n
Blackwell, Joseph W., Jr., 675 n
Blaisdell, Thomas C., 379 n
Blanchard, George W., 159 n
Blanck, Jacob, 739 n
Blandford, F. G., 44, 45, 46, 48 n, 248
Blanton, Thomas L., 392
Blass, Eddie, 725 n

Bloch, Bernard, 15, 16, 88, 89, 111, 112, 115 n, 212 n
Bloch, Don, 40 n, 481 n, 580, 743 n
Bloch's Book Bulletin, 518 n
Blond, Leo, 750 n
Bloom, Margaret, 142 n
Bloomfield, Leonard, 66 n, 70, 90, 98 n, 141, 309 n, 346 n
Blue Laws, 600
Board on Geographic Names, 537, 538–40
Board on Geographical Names, 325, 529, 542, 546, 547, 550
Boardman, James, 6 n
Boas, Franz, 544 n
Boatwright, Mody C., 763 n
Bodine, A. Aubrey, 765 n
Boise *Idaho Statesman*, 557 n, 558 n
Bolinger, Dwight L., 374 n, 688 n, 703 n, 704 n, 706 n, 769 n
Bolitho, Hector, 456 n
Boll, Ernest, 326 n
Bonaparte, Joseph, 602
Bonaparte, Louis Lucien, 61
Bond, C. A., 593
Bond, George, 77 n
Bond, Richard P., 145, 296 n
Boock, Darwin F., 377
Bookbinding & Book Production, 732 n
Bookman, 168 n, 227 n, 303 n, 688 n
Booksellers' argot, 739
Boone, Daniel, 152, 412, 413
Booth, Edwin, 26 n
Booth, Ernest, 670 n, 672 n
Booth, John Wilkes, 597
Bootleggers' argot, 667, 670, 671
Borden Company, 593 n
Boston, speech of, 4, 14, 15, 17, 27 n, 30 n, 31, 32, 69, 74 n, 88, 102 n, 111, 121, 134, 157, 167,

168, 178, 180, 183, 210, 227, 314; surnames in, 401
Boston *Courier*, 113
Boston *Globe*, 45 n, 167 n, 168 n
Boston *Herald*, 34 n, 44 n, 75, 463 n, 531 n, 647 n, 648 n
Boston *Journal*, 557
Boston Mary, 677 n
Boston *Post*, 115 n
Boston Public Library, 293 n
Boston *Transcript*, 158 n
Boston *Traveler*, 75 n, 535 n, 768 n
Boswell, James, 76, 80 n, 304, 387
Botkin, B. A., 119 n, 721 n
Bottomley, Horatio, 457 n
Boucher, Jonathan, 9, 159, 160
Boulder (Colo.) *Daily Camera*, 449 n
Boulware, Marcus H., 683, 711 n
Bowcock, James M., 122 n, 217 n, 490 n
Bowditch, N. I., 449
Bowen, B. L., 184, 185
Bowie, James, 612
Bowie, Lucy Leigh, 160 n
Bowie, Oden, 612 n
Bowie, Rezin P., 612
Bowles, J. D., 448 n
Bowman, Isaiah, 162 n
Bowman, Tom, 712 n
Bowman, William D., 462 n
Box-office argot, 696
Boyd, Julian P., 321 n
Boyd, Stephen G., 567
Boykin, Mrs. Ocllo G., 497
Bozarth, Theodore W., 322 n
Bracher, Frederick, 567 n
Brackbill, Hervey, 718 n
Brackenridge, H. H., 263
Braddy, Haldeen, 741 n, 743 n
Bradford, Roark, 106
Bradford, Gershom, 721 n

Index

Bradley, A. C., 38 n
Bradley, Gene, 765 n
Bradley, Hugh, 768 n, 769 n
Bradley, J. Franklin, 310 n, 368
Bradley, Omar N., 398
Bradley, William R., 87 n
Bragg, Braxton, 589
Brainerd, Henry B., 714 n
Brandenburg, George C., 353 n
Brandt, Bill, 735 n
Branner, John C., 553 n
Brannon, Peter A., 551
Branson, C. C., 449 n
Brant, Sebastien, 655, 656
Brazil, given-names in, 522 n
Breger, Dave, 779 n, 780 n
Brehm, Walter E., 330
Brennan, Francis, 466 n
Brewer, David J., 287 n
Brewery workers' argot, 739
Brewster, Paul G., 145
Bricker, John W., 412
Bricklayers' argot, 739, 740
Bridgeport (Conn.) *Post*, 620 n
Bridger, Clyde A., 558 n
Bridges, Robert, 36, 37, 38, 39, 71, 314, 315, 319
Brierley, G. H., 451 n
Briggs, John Ely, 623 n
Bristed, Charles Astor, 114
British Academy, 37
British Admiralty, 537
British Broadcasting Corporation, 36–39, 43, 50, 62, 543, 546
British Foreign Office, 282
British Museum, 256 n
Broadcasting, 35 n
Broadside, 765 n
Broadway Journal, 610
Brock, Frank W., 757 n
Brodeur, Arthur G., 107 n

Brodie, Fawn M., 516 n
Brodinsky, B. P., 579 n
Brody, Alter, 260, 262
Brogan, D. W., 649
Brokaw, Harry, 767 n
Bromberg, Erik I., 771 n
Bromberg, Walter, 681 n
Bronstein, Arthur J., 46 n, 70
Brooklyn, speech of, 87, 107, 155, 181, 188–93, 265; surnames in, 401 n
Brooklyn *Eagle*, 421, 735 n
Brooks, Cleanth, Jr., 13, 14, 124, 129, 130, 137, 138 n, 264 n
Brooks, Van Wyck, 480
Brother Jonathan, 600, 601, 604, 605, 607, 608, 609, 613, 628, 629, 634, 636, 639
Browder, Earl, 415 n
Brown, Aaron V., 639
Brown, Bertram H., 264 n, 379 n
Brown, Calvin S., Jr., 117, 216 n
Brown, Carlton, 668
Brown, Charles Brockden, 474
Brown, Charles E., 759 n
Brown, Donald M., 210 n
Brown, E. P., 561 n
Brown, Eve, 704 n
Brown, Gould, 344 n, 387 n
Brown, H. Glenn, 161 n
Brown, Irving, 442 n
Brown, Jasbo, 708
Brown, John, 447, 623
Brown, John Taylor, 301 n
Brown, Rollo W., 143
Brown, Thomas J., 573
Browne, Oscar, 55 n, 70, 87
Browne, P. A., 371 n, 387 n
Browne, Thomas, 281
Bruce, J. Douglas, 217
Bruner, Helen, 237, 238
Bruning, Harry F., 776 n
Brunson, Alfred, 571
Bryan, G. S., 537 n
Bryan, W. J., 635

Bryant, Bessie B. M., 612 n
Bryant, Margaret M., 341 n
Bryant, William Cullen, 188, 293 n, 741 n
Bryn Mawr College, 23
Bryson, Artemisia B., 220, 569 n
Bryson, Bill, 735 n
Buck, Carl D., 141
Buckingham, J. S., 480 n
Buckle, Henry T., 388 n
Buckner, Mary Dale, 741 n
Buffalo *Evening News*, 402
Bühler, G., 499 n
Bühnenaussprache, 17
Bulgarian, spelling of, 308
Bulkeley, Benjamin R., 647 n
Bullard, Robert E., 291
Bulletin of the Institut Général Psychologique, 70 n
Bulletin of the Linguistic Society, 112 n
Bulletin of the New York Public Library, 453 n, 651 n, 737 n
Bulletin of the University of South Carolina, 266 n, 341 n
Bulletin of the Virginia State Library, 570
Bulletin of the Washington Geological Survey, 570 n
Bullitt, William C., 474
Bungalow names, 578, 579
Burdette, Robert J., 623
Burgess, Cool, 645 n
Burgess, Gelett, 499
Burglars' argot, 668
Burke, Edmund, 383 n, 393
Burke, James P., 670 n
Burke, W. J., 174, 256 n, 650, 651 n, 655, 656, 665, 676 n, 688 n, 698 n, 712 n, 714 n, 721 n, 728 n, 730 n, 735 n, 743 n, 759 n

Burkitt, Robert, 446 n
Burlesque-show argot, 693–95
Burley, Dan, 705, 707 n
Burlington (Iowa) *Hawkeye & Patriot*, 622, 623
Burnell, A. C., 256 n
Burnham, Josephine M., 151, 152, 394 n
Burns, Robert, 485 n, 632 n, 661
Burpee, Lawrence, 573 n
Burt, Frank H., 564
Burt, Struthers, 352
Burwell, M. A., 176, 177
Bury, Martin H., 724 n
Busch, Noel F., 704 n
Bus-drivers' argot, 720
Business Week, 129 n
Butcher, Jesse S., 33 n
Butler, C. S., 735 n, 736 n
Butler, Edward H. (Son), 501
Butler, Nicholas Murray, 66
Butler, Samuel, 87
Butterfield, Roger, 508 n
Buxbaum, Katherine, 147, 501 n, 503 n, 504 n
Byington, Steven T., 94 n, 193 n, 325 n, 359 n, 394 n, 768 n
Byrnes, James F., 77
Byron, Lord, 338, 339, 389 n, 390, 460
B.Z. am Mittag, 412 n

Cabell, James Branch, 473
Cabot, George, 418 n
Cabot, John, 418
Caboto, Giovanni, 418 n
Caffee, N. M., 124
Cahill, Margaret E., 754 n
Cain, James M., 32
Cairns, Huntington, 411
Cajans, speech of, 131
Caldwell, N. W., 558
California, given-names in, 482, 484, 485, 486, 487, 489, 490, 492, 496, 502 n; nicknames of, 611, 612, 613; place-names in, 528, 529, 533,
542 n, 553, 554; speech of, 107, 133, 134, 140, 182, 208, 221, 357, 761 n
California Folklore Quarterly, 174 n, 761 n
Calkin, Nancy, 712 n
Callan, Charles J., 465 n
Calloway, Cab, 707 n
Cambridge History of English Literature, 321 n
Camden, William, 448, 468, 469, 471 n, 474, 493
Camp, Elwood C., 708 n
Campbell, Alfred S., 564 n
Campbell, Frank, 645 n
Campbell, George, 334 n
Campbell, Killis, 265 n
Campbell, Marilyn, 551 n
Campbell, Oscar J., 343 n
Campora, Vincenzo, 439 n
Canada, given-names in, 496; place-names in, 571–73; speech of, 127, 158, 248–51; spelling in, 286, 316
Canadian Geographic Board, 571, 572
Canadian Geographical Journal, 572
Canadian Geographical Society, 286 n
Canadian Historical Association, 286 n
Canadian Jewish Chronicle, 421 n
Canadian Journal, 248 n
Canalboatmen's speech, 207
Canal-boat names, 583
Canby, Henry S., 371 n
Cannell, Margaret, 445 n
Cannery workers' argot, 740
Cannon, Hughie, 644 n
Cannon, Pat, 75
Canon Law, 463, 464, 472
Cantril, Hadley, 448 n
Cape Cod, given-names on, 474, 482 n, 489 n; speech of, 132, 164, 210
Capitalization, 320–23

Capone, Al, 667 n, 671 n, 680
Carey, Nick N., 785 n
Cargill, Oscar, 49 n
Carl, Mary Jane, 707 n
Carl, Pitt F., Jr., 575, 576
Carlile, John S., 730 n
Carlisle Indian School, 444
Carlisle (England) *Journal*, 649 n
Carlson, John Roy, 441
Carlton, Lilyn E., 340 n
Carlton, Theodore, 340 n
Carlton-Britton, P. W. P., 419
Carlyle, Thomas, 283
Carnegie, Andrew, 290, 305, 311
Carpenter, Charles, 117 n, 119 n
Carpenters' argot, 740, 741
Carr, Joseph W., 121 n, 132, 157, 158, 178, 179, 360, 461 n, 500 n
Carr, William, 578 n
Carrel, L. J., 721 n, 743 n
Carrick, Earl of, 472
Carrière, J.-M., vi, 20 n, 436, 437, 479 n, 530 n, 531 n, 534 n, 536 n, 600 n, 609 n, 613 n, 630 n, 631 n
Carroll, Earl, 695 n
Carruth, W. H., 148, 149, 559
Carter, C. W., Jr., 352 n
Carter, Robert, 223
Carter, W. L., 500 n
Cartmell, Van H., 688 n
Cartwright, George, 254
Case, Francis, 318 n
Case & Comment, 506 n
Cash, W. J., 124 n
Cassidy, Frederic G., 141, 235, 236, 571, 733 n
Cassidy, Marshall, 594 n
Catholic given-names, 464, 465, 466, 472
Catlett, L. C., 380
Cattell, Owen, 496
Cattleman, 742 n
Cattlemen's speech, 51 n, 126, 127, 136, 174, 177,

201, 216, 219, 233, 238, 741, 742, 743
Cavanagh, Dermot, 192 n
Caxton, William, 655
Cayton, Horace, 716 n
C.C.C. boys' argot, 708 n
Cecil, David, 37
Census Bureau, 538
Central-Western speech. See *Middle Western speech*
Century Dictionary, 64, 275, 349
Century Magazine, 27 n, 119 n, 326, 380, 381, 415 n, 453 n, 480 n, 567 n, 588, 722 n
Cermak, Anton J., 373
Cerri, Nicola, Jr., 239 n
Chadwick, Henry, 384
Chaldee language, 5
Chamberlain, A. F., 249
Chambers, Gilbert, 361 n
Channing, William E., 474
Chapel Hill (N.C.) *Weekly*, 712 n
Chapin, Florence A., 128 n
Chapin, R. F., 291
Chapman, John, 676 n
Chapman, Maristan, 119 n
Chapman, R. W., 42
Charles I, 474
Charles II, 404, 596, 597
Charleston, speech of, 122 n, 213, 214, 225, 268 n
Charlotte (N.C.) *News*, 124 n
Charlotte *Observer*, 485 n
Charlottesville, Va., speech of, 14
Charteris, Leslie, 322 n
Charters, W. W., 340
Chase, George D., 135, 157, 158, 164, 165, 721 n
Chattanooga *Times*, 217 n
Chaucer, Geoffrey, 47, 80, 113, 206, 280, 359, 391, 643, 776 n
Chautauquans' argot, 743
Chemical Abstracts, 285 n
Cherry, Donald L., 541 n
Chesapeake Bay country, speech of, 161, 162, 229

Cheshire, Giff, 360 n
Chesterfield, Lord, 76, 277
Chesterton, G. K., 473
Chicago, speech of, 70, 141, 682; surnames in, 400, 401
Chicago *Herald*, 737 n
Chicago *Herald-Examiner*, 371 n
Chicago *Sun*, 707 n
Chicago *Times*, 737 n
Chicago *Tribune*, 259, 294, 295, 317, 322, 462 n, 511 n, 512 n, 530 n, 640, 669 n, 717 n, 736 n, 748 n, 751 n
Chicanot, E. L., 252 n
Chidsey, Donald B., 135 n
Child, F. J., 106
Chinese given-names, 524; surnames, 442, 443
Chinese language, loans from, 666, 681
Chinook jargon, loans from, 133, 200, 237, 641
Chipman, Bert J., 683 n
Chrisman, Lewis H., 462 n, 579
Christian Science Monitor, 58 n, 78 n, 239, 256 n, 286, 706 n, 719 n
Chronicles of Oklahoma, 566 n
Chubb, Thomas Caldecot, 511 n, 743 n
Church, Hayden, 302
Churches, names of, 589–91
Churchill, Winston, 44, 45, 77, 373, 451 n, 786
Cicognani, Amleto G., 466
Cincinnati *Republican*, 619
Circle & Monogram, 708
Circus argot, 684, 685
Civil War, 14, 17, 22, 126, 188, 258, 274, 322, 375, 381, 480, 515, 534, 589, 595, 597, 604 n, 608, 610, 611, 623, 636, 679, 691 n, 778
Clader, Will-A, 478 n
Clagett, A. Henry, 48 n

Clancy, Daniel Francis, 462
Clarendon, Earl of, 280
Clarionette, 712 n
Clark, Andrew C., 291, 293 n
Clark, Champ, 456 n, 632, 634
Clark, I. E., 332
Clark, John Drury, 552
Clark, Thomas Campbell, 477 n
Clark, Thomas D., 359
Clark, Victor S., 243
Clark, Walter, 606
Clarke, Bill, 735 n
Clarke, Hewson, 659 n
Classical Journal, 319 n
Clay, Henry, 355
Clayton, Frederick, 712 n
Cleary, David M., 726 n
Cleator, P. E., vi, 297 n, 370 n
Cleaves, Mrs. B. J., 163 n
Clemens, Samuel L., 94, 129 n, 173, 265 n, 287, 363, 374, 383, 390, 549 n, 634, 721
Clement, F., 271 n
Clements, Nancy, 121 n
Clendening, Logan, 735 n
Clergymen's argot, 744, 745
Cleveland, Grover, 470, 473, 634 n
Click, 356 n
Clifford, James L., 90 n
Climate, effects on speech, 4
Clinton, George, 532
Clough, Wilson O., 238 n, 571
Coale, W. B., 239, 240
Coal-miners' argot, 760, 761
Coast and Geodetic Survey, 537, 538 n
Coates, Robert M., 193 n
Cobb, Collier, 195
Cobb, Irvin S., 193 n
Cocheu, Lincoln C., 405 n
Cock-fighters' argot, 745, 746
Cockney speech, 4, 7, 34, 40, 43, 92, 94, 191, 253, 255 n

Index

Cockrum, Helen, 511 n
Codel, Martin, 729 n
Cody, Buffalo Bill, 412
Coffy, Mrs. R. C., 511 n
Coffman, George R., 162 n
Cohen, H. B., 44 n
Cohen, Moïse K., 517 n
Cohen, Roger S., 681 n
Cohen, Solomon Solis, 422 n
Coke, Thomas, 619 n
Colburn, Warren, 335
Colby, Elbridge, 778, 779, 784
Colby, Frank O., 36, 41 n, 45 n, 46 n
Colcord, Joanna C., 721 n
Cole, C. C., 557, 558
Coleman-Norton, P. R., 456 n
Coleridge, Hartley, 472
Coleridge, S. T., 280, 301 n, 338, 387, 499
Collections of the State Historical Society of Wisconsin, 561 n
College English, 49 n, 298 n, 341 n, 367 n, 725 n
College Entrance Examination Board, 371
College-paper names, 596
College slang, 711, 712
College Standard Dictionary, 370, 705 n
Colleges, names of, 596 n
Collier, Jeremy, 467 n
Collier's, 686 n
Collins, F. Howard, 94
Collitz, Hermann, 561 n
Colman, Norman J., 634
Colorado, given-names in, 481, 488, 494 n; nicknames of, 599, 613, 636; place-names in, 535, 554, 555; speech of, 127, 134
Colorado Magazine, 555
Colorado Writers' Project, 555
Columbia Broadcasting System, 33, 34, 730 n
Columbia University, 28 n, 66, 67
Columbus, 439 n

Columbus (Neb.) *Daily Telegram*, 177
Combs, Josiah, 32, 33, 117, 118 n, 124, 138 n, 153 n, 291, 447 n, 547 n, 565 n
Comfort, 488
Comfort, Anne W., 382 n
Comic strips, 348
Commentary, 421 n, 516 n
Commercial Car Journal, 719 n
Commission on Trends in Education, 26 n
Common Sense, 374 n
Commonweal, 374 n, 672 n
Communists, 32 n, 415 n
Conch dialect, 137
Concise Oxford Dictionary, 275, 280 n, 282, 283, 728
Concordia (Kansas) *Blade-Empire*, 625
Condit, Mrs. D. J., 511 n
Congressional Record, 99 n, 100 n, 226 n, 289, 318, 325 n, 330, 383 n, 390 n, 392 n, 440 n, 444 n, 477 n, 479 n, 504 n, 518, 635 n, 691 n, 767 n, 779, 786
Con-men's argot, 667, 668
Conkle, E. P., 176, 683
Connecticut, given-names in, 479, 507; nicknames of, 599, 600, 601; place-names in, 555, 556; speech of, 129, 134, 135, 210
Conrad, Earl, 265 n, 705
Contemporary Review, 256 n, 686 n
Converse, Charles C., 369, 370
Converse, Sherman, 275
Converted Catholic, 448 n, 745 n
Cook, Frederick A., 412
Cooke, Jerry, 427 n
Coolidge, Calvin, 222, 474
Coolidge, Lowell W., 566 n
Coons, Robin, 712

Cooper, C., 73
Cooper, J. Fenimore, 20, 78, 103 n, 257, 474, 622
Copland, Robert, 655, 656
Corbett, James J., 768 n
Corcoran, Fred, 754 n
Cordon, Guy, 245 n
Corey, Herbert, 675 n
Cornell, Lillian, 427
Cornhill Magazine, 480
Cornyn, William S., 756 n
Coronet, 702
Corré, Joseph, 691 n
Correct English, 46 n
Corset-makers' argot, 746
Costello, Carl B., 322 n, 759 n
Cottenham, Earl of, 459 n
Cottrell, W. F., 714 n, 715 n
Couch, Darius N., 415 n
Couch, W. T., 14 n, 86 n, 104 n, 108 n, 190 n, 212 n, 264 n, 266 n
Council of State Governments, 328
Counterfeiters' argot, 669
Country Gentleman, 593 n
Country Life, 754 n
Courtney, T. J., 669 n
Covenant Quarterly, 430 n
Covered Wagon, 488 n
Cowan, J. Milton, 478
Cowper, William, 338, 393, 457 n
Cows, names of, 593
Cox, James M., 637
Craig, G. Dundas, 671 n
Craigie, William, 284, 311, 312, 313, 315, 316, 328, 362 n, 373, 374, 749 n
Crandall, John S., 210
Crap-shooters' argot, 746, 747
Craver, B. N., 87 n
Crawford, Nelson Antrim, 152
Creighton, Robert E., 767 n
Cresswell, Nicholas, 9
Crile, George W., 412

Criminals' cant, 652-75
Cripps, Stafford, 383 n
Criswell, E. H., 200
Croessmann, H. K., 36 n, 671 n
Cromley, Ray, 444 n
Cross, Ephraim, 67 n
Cross, Tom Pete, 477 n
Crow, C. L., 220
Crowell Company, Thomas Y., 109 n
Crowningshield, Gerald, 184, 185
Crucian Creole, 247
Cruikshank, George, 660 n
Crumb, D. S., 173, 365
Cruttendon, Daniel, 334 n
Culkin, William E., 562 n
Cummings, Homer S., 672 n
Cummings, Thayer, 712 n
Cummiskey, Joe, 736 n
Curme, George O., 199 n, 342 n, 343 n, 344, 363, 369
Curren, Henry H., 785
Current History, 675 n
Current Religious Thought, 591 n
Currie, Anne, 46 n
Currie, C. W. Y., 598 n
Curtenius, Peter T., 532
Curtiss, Elliott, Jr., 724 n
Curzon, Marquess, 279
Custer, George A., 412
Czech given-names, 472; spelling of, 309 n; surnames, 427
Czechoslovak Student Life, 427 n

Daggett, Windsor P., 33, 144 n, 688 n
Dahlgren, John A., 432 n
Dairymen's argot, 747
Dale, E. E., 127 n
Dale, Francis, 438 n
Dale, George N., 329 n
Dallas *Morning News*, 569 n
Daly, Augustin, 33
Dancy, W. E., 569 n
Danish language. See Dano-Norwegian language

Danner, James W., 708 n
Dano-Norwegian language, loans from, 12, 168, 170
Dante Alighieri, 23 n
Danton, Annina P., 53 n
Darlington, James H., 361 n
Darrach, H. D., Jr., 721 n
Dart, Henry P., 562 n
Darwin, Bernard, 754 n
Date-lines, 323
Daughrity, K. L., 712 n
Davenport-Ffoulkes, Trevor, 460 n
Davidson, Levette J., 127 n, 554, 555, 708 n, 749 n, 761 n
Davies, Constance, 79 n
Davis, Arthur K., Jr., 224, 230
Davis, Burke, 486 n
Davis, Edwin B., 189, 291, 293
Davis, Elmer, 77
Davis, Elrick B., 759 n
Davis, Forrest, 786
Davis, Jeff, 476 n
Davis, John W., 621
Davy, Humphry, 284
Dawson, Albert K., 721 n, 731 n
Dawson, Edward, 557 n
Dayton (O.) *Journal*, 27 n
Dean, Dizzy, 348 n
Dean, Leo C., 638, 735 n
Dean, Richmond, 582
Dearden, Elizabeth J., 161, 162, 195, 196, 207 n, 224, 225
DeBaun, Everett, 406 n, 653 n, 670 n, 671 n
De Boer, John J., 343 n
de Camp, L. Sprague, 53 n, 63 n, 202, 205, 552, 565
De Casseres, Benjamin, 518 n
Decennial Publications of the University of Chicago, 141 n
de Crespigy, Claude, 46 n
Defoe, Daniel, 304 n, 339

deFord, Miriam Allen, 541 n, 777 n
Deiler, J. Hanno, 155 n, 413
Dekker, Thomas, 656, 665
Delattre, Pierre, 308 n
Delaware, nicknames of, 605; place-names in, 531 n, 556; speech of, 104, 122 n, 136, 162, 201 n, 204, 207, 378; surnames in, 401
Delcamp, E. W., 392 n
Delineator, 707 n
Dellquest, Augustus Wilfrid, 462 n
Delmarva, 136, 161, 224 n
Delta Kappa Epsilon Quarterly, 331 n
DeMille, Cecil B., 698 n
Dempsey, Jack, 785
Dempsey, Margaret, 739 n
Denham, Edward, 167 n
Denham, John, 302 n
Denison, E. W., 480 n
Dennis, Leah A., 124 n, 130, 389 n
Dent, Alan, 711 n
Denver, James W., 554
Denver *Tribune*, 134
Department-store argot, 747, 748
Dery, Charles F., 239, 432 n
de Saussure, Ferdinand, 54 n
de Sélincourt, Basil, 280 n
Des Moines *Tribune*, 492 n
de St. Cosmé, John Baisson, 526
Detroit *Free Press*, 629, 751 n
DeVane, William C., 26 n
Devils' names, 593
DeVinne, Theodore L., 326
Dewey, Ernest A., 713 n, 741 n
Dewey, George, 470
Dewey, Godfrey, 287 n
Dewey, Melvil, 287 n
Dewey, Thomas E., 45 n, 129 n, 355, 785

DeWitt, Marguerite E., 27 n, 28 n
DeWitt, Simon, 532
Dexter, F. B., 555
Dialect Notes, 100 n, 106, 111 n, 117, 119 n, 132, 133, 137, 139, 143, 150, 151, 153, 154, 157, 159 n, 164, 174, 175, 179, 180, 194, 197, 252, 377, 565 n, 647 n, 727 n
Dialects, American, 101, 257-70; English, 102, 105; Italian, 102 n
Dickens, Charles, 283, 339, 355, 674 n
Dickerson, Edwin T., 440 n
Dickinson, Jean, 718 n
Dictionary of American English, 52 n, 79, 97 n, 106, 108, 113 n, 126 n, 134 n, 135 n, 142 n, 145, 148 n, 159, 160 n, 169, 179, 181 n, 194, 237 n, 238, 249 n, 284, 321, 355, 357, 358, 365, 366, 369, 381, 384, 477 n, 515, 528 n, 543, 563, 574, 578 n, 581 n, 593 n, 596, 597, 598, 599, 600, 601, 604, 605, 606, 607, 608, 609, 610, 613, 615, 616 n, 617 n, 624, 627, 628, 629, 630, 635, 637, 638, 639, 647 n, 658 n, 672 n, 677 n, 679, 681 n, 688 n, 691 n, 709, 714 n, 736 n, 741 n, 742 n, 749 n, 760 n, 764 n, 767 n, 776 n, 777 n
Dictionary of National Biography, 499
Dictionary of Occupational Titles, 733 n
Diekhoff, John C., 54 n
Dillinger, John, 670 n, 672 n
Dilworth, Thomas, 271, 272, 273
Dingus, L. R., 199 n, 124 n, 224, 226, 392 n, 776 n
Diphthongs, 87, 228, 230, 231, 241, 249 n, 258, 291, 300

Distillery workers' argot, 748
Divine, Father, 448 n
Dixon, Campbell, 40
Dixon, Jeremiah, 604 n
Dobbie, Elliott V. K., 722 n, 778 n
Dobie, J. Frank, 569
Dockstader, Lew, 412
Dods, A. Wilson, 512 n
Doe, Jane, 418 n, 517 n
Dog-breeders' argot, 748
Dog News, 595 n
Dog World, 594 n
Dogs' names, 594, 595; vocabulary of, 351 n
Domesday Book, 463 n
Donaldson, William, 217
Donehoo, George P., 567
Donovan, James A., Jr., 680
Donut Institute, 298
Doone, Jice, 256 n
Dorgan, T. A., 701 n
Dorsey, Charles H., Jr., 768 n, 769 n
Dorson, R. M., 115 n
Doty, Ed, 624 n
Doty, Iva, 291
Double negative, 340 n, 346, 353, 390-94
Douglas (Ga.) *Enterprise*, 124 n
Douglas-Lithgow, R. A., 561 n
Dow, C. W., 83 n
Downs, Harold, 688 n
Draemel, Milo S., 567 n
Drake, C. M., 553
Drake, Joseph Rodman, 532 n
Drake, St. Clair, 716 n
Dreiser, Theodore, 348
Dresser, Paul, 348
Drew, Frank, 556 n
Driscoll, Charles B., 624 n
Driscoll, David, 193 n
Drug addicts' argot, 680-82
Drus, Paul, 759 n
Dryden, John, 304 n, 339
Dude Rancher, 742
Dude Ranchers' Association, 742
Dudek, J. B., vi, 427, 481 n, 522

Dudley, Fred A., 153
Duff, Peter, 283 n
Duffin, Ruth, 39
Duffy, Clinton T., 675 n
Dunaway, Wayland F., 116 n
Duncan, John M., 20 n
Duncan, Walter H., 712 n, 713 n
Dundee (Scotland) *Telegraph and Post*, 645 n
Dunglison, Robley, 223, 365
Dunlap, A. R., 96 n, 395, 564 n
Dunlap, Fayette, 438 n
Dunn, Jacob Piatt, 558 n, 616, 618, 619, 620
Durant, Jack W., 782
Durling, E. V., 463 n, 509 n
Dust Bowl, speech of, 200
Dutch Guiana, speech of, 248 n
Dutch language, loans from, 51, 144, 148 n, 181, 188, 189, 193, 206, 207, 529, 564, 572, 574; surnames from, 405, 406, 407
Duwamish language, 92 n
Dyche, Thomas, 47 n
Dykema, Karl W., 65

Eager, W. M., 256 n
Eames, Frank, 572, 573
Eames, Wilberforce, 453
Earle, Billy, 735 n
Earle, John, 360, 453
East Anglia, speech of, 10, 12, 79
Eastern Public Speaking Conference, 27 n, 65
Eastern Shore of Maryland, speech of, 122 n, 128, 136, 161, 162; of Virginia, 122 n, 136, 228, 229, 231, 232
Eastman, Charles A., 445
Ebner, Hieronymous W., 653 n
Ecclesiastical argot, 744, 745
Ecclesiastical Review, 744 n, 745 n

Eckstorm, Fannie H., 167 n, 526 n, 560
Eclectic Magazine, 307 n, 348 n, 468 n, 480 n
Eddis, William, 8, 160 n
Edelson, Jack, 393 n
Eden, Garden of, 5
Edgell, Henry W., 210 n
Edgerton, William B., 125 n
Edinburgh *Evening Dispatch*, 12 n, 647 n, 781 n
Edinburgh *Evening News*, 85 n
Edinburgh *Scotsman*, 648 n, 726 n
Edison, Thomas A., 702 n
Editor, 128 n, 686 n
Editor & Publisher, 316, 317, 318, 322, 323, 327, 329 n, 330, 360 n, 383 n, 478 n, 609 n, 703 n, 717 n, 765 n
Edson, H. A., 216 n, 386 n
Educational Method, 347 n, 353 n
Educational Research Bulletin, 337 n
Educator-Journal, 340 n
Edwards, Bryan, 160 n
Edwards, Davenport, 140 n
Edwards, Eleanor T. D., 622 n
Edwards, J. G., 622, 623
Egan, Pierce, 660, 661
Eggleston, Edward, 106, 142
Egypt (Illinois), 139, 140
Ehrensperger, Edward C., 568, 570
Eich, Louis M., 115 n
Eighteenth Century English, 6, 7, 14, 19, 47, 183, 272 n, 361 n, 393, 467
Eikel, Fred, Jr., 712 n
Einarsson, Stefan, 400 n
Eiselen, M. R., 723 n
Eisenhower, Dwight D., 409 n
Ekwall, Eilert, 19 n, 84 n, 568 n

Elementary School Journal, 351 n
Eliason, Norman E., 72 n, 270 n, 744 n
Elizabeth of England, 358, 620, 656
Elizabethan English, 117, 118
Elkin, Frederick, 779 n
Elkin, Henry, 277 n, 779 n
Ellet, Marion, 625
Ellis, Alexander J., 61, 74 n, 105, 257 n, 299 n, 305, 310, 372
Ellis, Anthony L., 401 n
Ellis, Brobury Pearce, 36 n
Ellis, Havelock, 371, 372
Ellis, William, 362 n
Ellison, E. Jerome, 757 n
Ellison, Louise B., 511 n, 512 n
Ellsworth, Ephraim Elmer, 471 n
Elmer, Ebenezer, 471
Elmer, Jonathan, 471
Elmore, Frank H., 551
Elocutionists, 26, 27 n
Elyot, Thomas, 58 n
Emberson, Frances G., 173 n
Emeneau, M. B., 254, 255
Emerson, Oliver F., 183, 184, 185, 565 n
Emerson, R. W., 95 n, 387, 507
Emerson Quarterly, 114 n
Emery, Alice S., 381 n
Emmet, Robert, 472 n
Emsley, Bert, 64 n, 68
Encore, 262 n, 386 n, 665 n, 722 n
Encyclopaedia Britannica, 102 n, 282
Encyclopedia Americana, 4 n, 545 n, 546 n, 622, 630
Engineman's Magazine, 716 n
England, dialects of, 7, 8, 10–13, 19; given-names in, 464 n, 505 n; place-names in, 574 n; speech of, 3, 4, 6, 92, 93, 94, 98 n, 357; surnames in, 400, 402

England, George Allen, 114 n, 158 n, 179, 253, 254, 751 n
Englische Studien, 124 n
English Association, 37
English Dialect Society, 11 n, 105
English Journal, 24 n, 48 n, 310 n, 336 n, 343 n, 345 n, 347 n, 353 n, 368 n, 370 n, 387 n
English Lunch Club of Harvard, 124 n
English Place Names Society, 574 n
English Received Pronunciation. See *Southern English Standard*
English Studies, 7 n, 58 n, 296 n
Enos, J. B., 462 n
Enroughty, Lemuel N., 456 n
Entsler, Beverly, 511 n
Epler, Blanch N., 195 n
Ericson, Eston E., 76 n, 187 n, 612 n, 739 n
Erie Canal, 597
Ernst, C. W., 168 n
Ernst, Margaret, 725 n
Ersine, Noel, 675 n
Erskine, John, 55 n
Ervine, St. John, 39, 46 n, 690 n
Eskimo language, 332; loans from, 238
Espenshade, A. Howry, 526 n, 536 n, 567
Esper, Charley, 735 n
Espinosa, Aurelio M., 183
Esquire, 53 n, 645 n, 705 n, 707 n
Essanay Company, 702
Essays and Studies by Members of the English Association, 38 n
Étude, 318, 706 n, 708 n, 709 n
Euphemisms, 215, 226, 231, 233, 234, 236, 592, 741 n, 749 n
Eure, Thad, 453
Evans, Charles, 271 n
Evans, Luther H., 712 n
Evans, Mary S., 256

Index

Evans, Medford, 125
Everett, Edward, 7 n, 20
Evershed, Raymond, 704 n
Every Saturday, 359 n, 473 n
Everybody's Digest, 743 n
Ewell, Richard S., 497
Ewen, C. L'Estrange, 403 n, 418 n, 419 n, 438 n, 456 n
Ewing, Thomas, 507 n
Exeter, Marquess of, 457 n
E. Z. Speling, 292

Faber, A. D., 270 n
Facts, 744 n
Fairmont (W.Va.) Times, 235
Falk, Adalbert, 307
Fallersleben, Hoffman von, 653 n
Farmer, John S., 142, 355 n, 595, 627, 656, 768
Farmers' speech, 216, 748, 749
Faröese, spelling of, 312
Farquhar, Francis P., 554 n
Farr, T. J., 119 n, 217
Farrar, William M., 637
Farris, Tennessee, 569 n
Fassett, Frederick G., Jr., 488 n
Faught, Ray C., 159 n
Faulkner, William, 106
Faust, Albert B., 412, 413
Fawcett, Edgar, 15 n
Faxon, Philip, 256 n
Faxon, Winthrop, 596 n
Fay, Frank J., 463 n
Feather, Leonard G., 705 n
Feather, William, 345 n, 646, 773 n
Featherstonhaugh, Duane, 457 n
Fecher, Charles E., 162 n
Federal Bureau of Investigation, 668, 672 n
Federal Trade Commission, 782
Federal Writer's Project,

138, 178, 193 n, 555, 560 n, 561, 563 n, 564, 566 n, 568, 569, 571 n, 622, 623 n, 636 n, 639 n, 688 n, 691 n, 712
Feipel, Louis N., 93, 528 n, 533 n
Fenn, F. H., 785 n
Fenning, Daniel, 272
Ferguson, D. W., 204 n
Ferguson, Otis, 721 n
Ferguson, William, 618
Fernós-Isern, A., 451 n
Fessenden, Thomas G., 358, 368
Fiechter, F. C., Jr., 414
Field, Eugene, 126 n, 623 n
Field, Frank, 481 n
Fielding, Henry, 339
Fields, Lew, 259 n
Fields, W. C., 725
Fielstra, G. E., vi
Filson, John, 152 n
Financial World, 703 n
Fink, P. M., 568, 569
Finley, John, 616, 617, 621
Finley, States Rights Gist, 508 n
Finnegan, Richard J., 737 n
Finnish language, 430; given-names, 524; spelling, 309 n; surnames, 429, 430
Firemen's argot, 749, 750
Fischer, Walther, 378 n
Fishbein, Morris, 499
Fisher, B. H. P., 463 n
Fisher, H. A., 712 n
Fisher, Vardis, 138 n
Fishermen's argot, 750, 751
Fiske, John, 10, 461
Fithian, Philip V., 223
Fitzgerald, Francis V., 785 n
Fitzpatrick, Lillian Linder, 562, 563
Fitzpatrick, Robert J., 776 n
Fitzpatrick, T. J., 558, 559
Fitzsimmons, Robert, 768 n

Flanagan, John T., 221 n, 535 n
Flandrau, Charles E., 630
Flaten, Nils, 169, 170, 520, 521
Fleece, Jeffrey A., 778 n, 784 n
Flesch, H., 416, 417 n
Flint, Timothy, 599 n
Flom, George T., 435 n
Flood, Noacian, 5
Florida, given-names in, 481, 482, 484, 488, 490, 511 n; nicknames of, 613; place-names in, 556, 557; speech of, 136, 137, 357, 386, 390
Florida Historical Society Quarterly, 556 n
Flowers, Paul, 501
Flynn, John J., 686 n
Flynt, Josiah, 620, 621, 676 n, 679, 686 n
Fogg, Wendell R., 100 n, 158 n
Foley, Michael, 56 n
Fonetik Crthografi, 288, 291
Food-dispensers' argot, 751, 752
Football elevens, nicknames of, 596 n, 635 n
Forbes-Robertson, Johnston, 36
Forbidden words, 121, 144, 145
Forby, Robert, 74 n, 105, 361 n
Ford Motor Company, 784
Forest, Jon R., 293 n
Forest Service, 533
Forgers' argot, 669
Forrest, Nathan Bedford, 387
Förster, Max, 527 n
Fort Smith (Ark.) Times-Record, 125
Fortune, 730 n, 768 n, 773 n
Forum, 370 n, 371 n, 670 n, 748 n
Foster, Frank, 743 n
Foulk, Ruby Oliver, 290
Fountain, J. H., 714 n

Fountain Inn (N.C.), *Tribune*, 450 n
Fowle, William B., 339
Fowler, H. W., 52 n, 83, 84, 280, 281, 282, 325 n, 327, 368, 728
Fowler, William C., 21, 365
Fox, J. S., 771 n
Fox-Davies, A. C., 419 n
France, given-names in, 464 n, 505 n; speech of, 90 n
France, Robert, 258 n
Francis, Frances, 237, 238
Franco-American Review, 703 n
Frank, Glenn, 45 n
Frank, Waldo, 93
Frankau, Pamela, 281 n
Frankenberg, T. T., 412 n, 745 n
Franklin, Benjamin, 20, 107 n, 209, 271, 302 n, 321, 470
Fransson, G., 462 n
Franzén, Carl G. F., 347
Fraser, John Foster, 40
Frazer, George E., 732 n
Freeman, 191 n
Freeman, Douglas S., 497 n
Freeman, Edward A., 383 n
French, N. R., 352 n
French and Indian War, 534 n
French-Canadians, speech of, 145
French dictionaries, 349; pronunciation, 90; speech, 90 n; spelling, 308, 309; surnames, 436–39; vocabulary, 349
French language, loans from, 49 n, 51, 77, 95 n, 127, 144, 151, 154, 155, 156, 160, 167, 172, 206, 207, 213, 238, 249, 252 n, 277, 278, 286 n, 384, 529, 562, 566, 571, 572, 573, 574, 654, 655, 666, 691 n, 695 n, 708, 725, 726, 753 n, 754 n, 778 n
French Review, 347 n, 349 n

Freud, Sigmund, 516 n
Frey, J. William, 148 n, 332 n
Freyre, Gilberto, 522 n
Fries, Charles C., 333 n, 341, 342, 359, 361 n, 367
Frohman, Charles, 689 n
Frontier, speech of, 127 n
Frontier & Midland, 174 n
Frontier Times, 480 n, 521 n, 612 n
Fruit, John P., 153
Fry, Marion, 731 n
Fucilla, Joseph G., 439
Fuld, Ernest, 319 n
Fuller, M. Cordelia, 135
Fulmore, Z. T., 569
Fulton, Deoch, 462 n
Funk, Charles E., 303, 462 n
Funk, Isaac K., 287 n, 303 n
Funk, Wilfred J., 351 n
Funkhouser, Clifford, 714 n
Furniture workers' argot, 753
Fwnetik Orthqgrafi, 287, 288

Gable, J. Harris, 696 n, 697
Gadsden (Ala.) *Times*, 125
Gaelic language, loans from, 206, 684 n, 686 n; spelling of, 312
Gaffney, Wilbur, 385
Gahan, Edgar, 686 n, 724 n
Gaines, Helen F., 505 n
Gaines, Helen Sue, 221 n
Galaxy, 22 n, 320 n, 400
Galsworthy, John, 725
Gannett, Henry, 549, 554, 555, 556, 562, 564
Ganong, W. F., 572
Garbage men's argot, 753
Gard, Wayne, 746 n
Gardiner, Alan H., 462 n
Gardner, Mrs. J. P., 481 n
Gardner, Marjorie, 481 n, 485
Garfield, James A., 636
Garland, Hamlin, 478 n

Garment workers' argot, 753, 754
Garrett, R. M., 127 n
Garrison, W. L., 448
Garton, R. I., 713 n
Gaskell, Elizabeth C., 358
Gates, Floy Perkinson, 200
Gatewood, Dr., 478 n
Gaulden, J. Andrew. 511 n, 512 n
Gause, John T., 291, 292
Gay, Bonnie, 707 n
Gazzam, Joseph P., 633
Gehman, Sara, 209
Geikie, A. S., 248
Geller, David, 770 n, 771 n
General American, 15, 30, 31, 32, 33, 34, 35, 58 n, 90, 95, 103, 110, 125, 131, 135, 153, 157, 175, 178, 181, 183, 184, 186, 187, 196, 197, 199, 200, 218, 221, 222, 250
General Education Board, 156
General Land Offices, 538
General Southern American, 4, 12, 16, 28, 31, 32, 91, 98, 104, 122, 129, 171, 187, 218
Genung, B. M., 293 n
Geoghegan, Richard H., 530 n
Geographic Board, 526, 527, 528 n, 529, 530 n, 538–40, 549 n, 568
Geographical Board. See Board on Geographical Names
Geographical Review, 563 n
Geological Survey, 533, 537, 549 n, 552
George II, 321
George V, 414
George, Margaret R., 755 n
Georgia, given-names in, 483, 486, 490, 492 n, 508, 511 n, 514, 515; nicknames of, 609, 610, 627; place-names in, 534, 542 n; speech of, 13, 14 n, 104, 116, 119 n, 121, 124 n, 130, 137, 138,

Index

357, 359 n, 381, 386, 387, 390, 543 n
Georgia Historical Review, 268
Georgia Teachers College, 476
Georgia's Health, 511 n
Gephart, Joseph C., 737 n
Gerard, John, 386
Gerlach, F. M., 351
Gerling, C. J., 48 n
German American Annals, 155 n, 202 n, 413 n
German Coast of Louisiana, 155, 413
German dialect, 258, 259; dictionaries, 349; given-names, 349; place-names, 574; pronunciation, 90; spelling, 307; surnames, 397, 399, 407–15; vocabulary, 349
German language, loans from, 51, 75, 76, 108, 140, 142, 144, 149, 150, 151, 155, 156, 160, 168, 170, 172, 175, 177, 181, 195, 197, 201–10, 213, 229, 230, 232, 254, 255, 257, 320, 376, 529, 653, 654, 655, 666, 701 n, 703 n, 739 n, 747 n, 753 n, 757 n, 758 n, 767 n, 771 n, 781, 782
Gerould, Gordon Hall, 23 n
Gettysburg Address, 288
Gibbs, C. M., 735 n
Giblens, V. E., 146 n
Gibran, Kahlil, 441 n
Giessner Beiträge zur Erforschung der Sprache und Kultur Englands und Nordamerikas, 114 n
Gilbert, W. H., 235
Gilder, Richard Watson, 287 n
Giles, Almira M., 30
Gilfillan, Joseph A., 562
Gillette, J. M., 340 n, 350
Gingrich, F. W., 202 n, 210 n
Gipsy language, loans from, 206 n, 207, 653, 665 n; surnames, 443

Girdner, John H., 768 n
Giric, 405
Girl, Christian, 449 n
Gist, States Rights, 508
Gist, William H., 508
Given-names, 462–525; Appalachian, 188; Arabic, 523; Armenian, 523; boys', 500–09; Chinese, 524; Finnish, 523–524; German, 519, 520; girls', 479–500; Greek, 523; Gullah, 514, 515; Hawaiian, 525; Hungarian, 523, 524; initials as, 477–79; Japanese, 524, 525; Jewish, 516–19; middle-names as, 472–74; Mormon, 515, 516; Negro, 507–15; nicknames as, 475–77; Norwegian, 520, 521; Portuguese, 522; Puritan, 466–68; Scandinavian, 520, 521; Slav, 522; slaves', 513, 514; Spanish, 521, 522; surnames as, 468–73; synthetic, 479–98; Syrian, 523
Gladstone, J. H., 306
Gladstone, W. E., 472 n, 578
Glasgow *News*, 116 n
Glass, Montague, 259, 262
Glassblowers' argot, 754
Glaziers' argot, 754
Gledhill, Donald, 703
Glottal stop, 181, 182, 192, 193 n
Glover, Joseph G., 128
Glyn, Elinor, 703 n
Godey's Lady's Book, 86 n
Godkin, E. L., 620
Godley, Margaret W., 557
Goff, John, 614 n
Goffin, R. C., 256 n, 706 n, 709 n
Golding, Arthur, 113
Goldsmith, Oliver, 388 n
Goldwyn, Samuel, 419
Golfers' argot, 754, 755
Gonzalez, Ambrose E., 269 n, 270 n

Good Housekeeping, 256 n
Goodman, Theodore R., 773 n
Goodner, Marguerite C., 580
Goodrich, Chauncey A., 275
Goral, B. E., 425 n
Gordon, Adam, 8
Gordon, J. W., 570 n
Gordon, Lucilla, 256 n
Gould, Charles N., 566
Gould, George M., 282 n
Gould, Paul, 720 n
Government Printing Office, 246, 276, 285, 317, 318 n, 323, 326, 327, 329, 528
Gower, John, 281, 390
Graduate Magazine of the University of Kansas, 625 n
Graham, L. V., 627 n
Graham, William A., 606, 607
Graham's Magazine, 258
Grammarians, 333–35, 339, 340, 342, 343, 354, 367, 369, 395
Grand Rapids, surnames in, 401
Grand Rapids (Mich.) *Press*, 128 n
Grandgent, C. H., 69 n, 73, 77 n, 88, 91 n, 106
Grant, Jesse, 477 n
Grant, U. S., 448, 461, 470, 477, 589, 636
Granville-Barker, H. G., 39
Graves, Louis, 712 n
Gray, Giles W., 88 n
Gray, Thomas, 348 n
Gray, W. S., 351 n
Gray, Zane, 570
Gray of Fallodon, Lord, 39
Great Lakes region, speech of, 104, 140
Greek dictionaries, 349; given-names, 523; surnames, 440; vocabulary, 349
Green, B. W., 223, 225, 226, 227, 230, 454

Green, Theodore F., 290
Greenberg, Doris, 373 n
Greene, Robert, 656
Greene, Tom, 721 n
Greene, Ward, 784 n
Greenough, C. N., 179
Greet, W. Cabell, 14, 29, 32, 34, 35, 36, 44 n, 63 n, 66, 68, 86, 104, 108 n, 115, 122 n, 124, 126, 129 n, 136, 158, 159, 161, 190, 212, 224, 225, 230, 264 n, 266 n, 741 n
Gregg, Darrell L., 196 n
Gregory, William, 310
Greig, J. Y. T., 40, 647
Grieg, Edvard H., 435
Griffin, William J., 72 n, 148 n, 170
Grill, Erma V., 176
Grose, Francis, 11, 105, 588 n, 643, 648 n, 651, 659, 660, 661, 662, 663, 664, 665, 686 n, 701 n
Gross, Milt, 259, 262, 304
Grosscup, Peter S., 412
Grove, W. Alan, 343 n
Grover, John S., 776 n
Grumbine, Lee L., 210 n
Grymes, Charles, 454 n
Gubbins, Nathaniel, 40
Gudde, Edwin G., 551, 553
Guggenheim family, 518
Guinea dialect, 136; people, 235
Guinea Neck, speech of, 224, 225, 229
Guiterman, Arthur, 583
Gullah dialect, 101, 264, 265–69; given-names, 514, 515
Gunsky, Frederic R., 390 n
Gunter, Gordon, 221 n
Gunther, John, 443
Gurney, A. H., 735 n
Gustafson, Ralph, 289
Gwatkin, Miss, 650
Gyles, John, 629

Hackett, Roger C., 386 n
Hadley, Herbert S., 633
Hadley, L. Nixon, 181, 564 n
Hadley, Will-B, 478 n
Hairston, Samuel, 447
Halbert, H. S., 551, 562 n
Hale, Edward E., 532, 573 n, 574 n
Haliburton, Thomas C., 112 n, 114, 599
Hall, A. Rives, 252
Hall, Basil, 80
Hall, Carrie A., 592
Hall, Fitzedward, 23
Hall, Grover C., 265, 470 n
Hall, James, 535
Hall, Joseph Sargent, 118, 119
Hall, Leonard C., 585 n
Hall, Louise, 194 n
Hall, Robert A., Jr., 346, 349
Hall, William T., 735 n
Halleck, Fitz-Greene, 532 n
Halliburton, E. P., 784
Halliwell-Phillipps, J. O., 11 n, 357 n
Halsema, James, 243 n
Hamann, Fred, vi, 483 n, 487 n, 492 n, 501 n, 503 n, 645 n, 671 n, 675 n, 712 n, 714 n, 718 n, 727, 728, 735 n, 743 n, 748 n, 759 n, 760 n, 762 n
Hamburger Tageblatt, 529 n
Hamilton, Alexander, 32, 43, 83, 90, 91
Hamilton, Ben, Jr., 285 n, 448 n
Hamilton, J. G. deRoulhac, 117 n
Hamilton, Marian, 535 n, 761 n
Hamilton, Phil, 714 n
Hamilton, W. S., 364
Hamilton (N.Y.) *Democratic Reflector*, 565 n
Hamman, Louis, 48 n
Hammett, S. A., 599 n
Hammond, Otis G., 564
Hancock, John, 469
Hand, Learned, 419
Hand, Wayland D., 174 n, 761 n
Handy, W. C., 710

Haney, John L., 48 n
Hanley, Miles L., 6 n, 29, 63 n, 77 n, 108 n, 111, 211, 421 n, 726
Hanley, O. W., 143
Hanna, Margaret M., 318 n
Hanna, Phil Townsend, 554 n
Hanover (Pa.) *Sun*, 411 n
Hansen, Marcus L., 11 n, 112, 405
Happy Hours, 473 n
Harap, Henry, 340 n
Hardin, Achsah, 671 n
Harding, W. G., 471, 637
Hardy, Thomas, 339
Hargan, James, 673
Hargis, Donald E., 730 n
Hargrett, Lester, 481 n, 710 n
Harlan, James, 472 n
Harman, Thomas, 663, 664, 665
Harper, Francis, 138 n
Harper, G. McL., 414 n
Harper's Magazine, 100, 114, 126 n, 159 n, 258 n, 309 n, 356 n, 467 n, 475, 583 n, 615, 624 n, 628, 759 n, 769 n, 776 n
Harrington, John P., 308 n
Harris, Henry L., 243 n
Harris, Jesse W., 140
Harris, Joel Chandler, 106, 262 n, 265, 270 n, 376, 377
Harris, Rachel S., 115 n
Harris, William T., 287 n, 296 n
Harrison, Benjamin, 547, 636, 637
Harrison, Mrs. Burton, 15 n
Harrison, E. J., 359 n
Harrison, James A., 268, 269, 270
Harrison, William, 663, 664
Harrison, W. H., 470, 474
Harrison Anti-Narcotic Act, 671 n
Harriss, R. P., 707 n

Harshaw, Myron T., 732 n
Hart, James D., 708 n, 709 n
Hart, J. M., 197
Hart, John, 57 n
Hart, Miles, 762 n
Harte, Bret, 653 n
Hartford Courant, 32, 72 n, 76 n, 90
Hartman, H. C., 708 n
Harvard University, 28 n
Harvey, Bartle T., 127
Harvey, Holman, 707 n
Haskell, Loney, 688 n
Hastings, James, 464 n
Haugen, Einar, 98 n, 433 n, 435 n
Hausen, T. Josephine, 200, 201
Havens, Barrington S., 383 n, 437 n
Hawaii, given-names in, 522, 524, 525; speech of, 239–41; surnames in, 436, 443, 444
Hawaii Educational Review, 239 n
Hawaiian language, loans from, 240
Hawthorne, Nathaniel, 461
Hay, John, 453 n
Hayakawa, S. I., 706 n
Hayden, J. F., 291, 293 n
Hayden, Marie Gladys, 174
Hayes, Edgar T., 690 n
Hayes, Francis C., 124 n, 194 n
Hayes, James J., 291, 292, 293
Hayes, Patrick Cardinal, 465
Hayes, Rutherford B., 636
Hayford, James, 341 n
Hays, Will H., 699
Haywood, Big Bill, 633
Head, Richard, 665
Healy, Ned R., 476 n
Hearn, Lafcadio, 444 n
Hebrew language, loans from, 653, 654, 687 n, 725, 757 n
Heck, Henry J., 541 n, 688 n

Heckewelder, John G. E., 567 n
Heenan, J., 759 n
Heffner, R.-M. S., 57 n, 72, 198
Hegner, Robert W., 629
Heil, Johann Alfred, 114 n
Heindel, R. H., 58 n
Heintze, Albert, 411 n, 417 n
Heltman, H. J., 29 n
Hemming, H. Phipps, 721 n
Hempl, George, 65 n, 91 n, 96
Hench, Atcheson L., 124, 154 n, 162 n, 210 n, 224, 232, 382, 570 n, 601 n, 684 n
Henderson, Leon, 77
Henderson, Robert W., 737 n
Hendrix, Joseph M., 742 n
Henley, W. E., 460 n, 768 n
Hennepin, Louis, 526
Henrici, Frederick W., 47 n
Henrietta Maria, 474
Henry, P. W., 678 n
Henry, Thomas R., 596
Hepburn, James C., 443 n
Herbert, George, 467 n
Herford, A. L., 768 n
Herkimer, Nicholas, 412
Herman, Lewis, 15 n, 240, 241, 261
Herman, Marguerite S., 15 n, 240, 241, 261
Herrick, D-Cady, 478
Herriford, Merle, 270 n
Herring, Lila M., 592
Herriott, Frank I., 147
Herskovits, Melville J., 446 n
Heumann, Johann, 653 n
Heydrick, B. A., 202, 206
Hibbard, Addison, 270 n
Hibbitt, George W., 211, 413 n
Hickey, William, 330 n, 459 n

Hickman, Art, 709
Hicks, Joseph L., 136 n
Hicks, Wilson, 256 n
Hiero II of Syracuse, 613 n
Higginson, T. W., 11, 287 n
Hijackers' argot, 668, 669
Hill, A. A., 49 n, 89, 162 n, 224 n, 230, 553
Hill, D. H., 589
Hill, J. F., 516 n
Hill, Robert T., 543 n
Hillhouse, J. T., 94 n
Hills, E. C., 351 n, 628 n
Hilton, James, 281 n
Hindus, Maurice, 785 n
Hindustani language, loans from, 666
Hine, William H., 675 n
Hines, Leon, 762 n
Hispania, 308 n
Historical Collections of Ohio, 637 n
Hitler, Adolf, 255, 518
Hixson, Jerome C., 462, 472 n, 531 n, 708 n
Hoar, George F., 11
Hoben, Lindsey, 331
Hobhouse, Leonard T., 388 n
Hobo News, 676 n
Hobos' argot, 675–79
Hochberger, Simon, 508 n
Hodder, George, 460 n
Hoffman, Charles Fenno, 614, 621, 630, 641
Hoffman, George E., 141
Hoffman, William S., 481 n
Hogan, Charles H., 220, 547
Hogan, James, 698 n
Hogrefe, Pearl, 156 n
Hogue, Richard W., 777 n
Holbrook, Stewart H., 549, 758 n, 759 n
Holiday, 195 n, 564 n
Holinshed, Raphael, 663
Holland, J. G., 751 n
Holland, Lady, 497 n
Holley, Marietta, 187 n
Hollingsworth, Leta S., 353 n

Hollister, Howard K., 191, 192
Hollister, Paul, 730 n
Holloway, William, 11
Hollywood, speech of, 27 n, 42, 100, 281 n, 297, 697–704, 712, 729, 743 n, 766 n
Holmes, Urban T., 351 n, 509
Holohan, James B., 675 n
Holt, Alfred H., 456 n, 458 n, 496 n, 548, 563 n, 768 n
Holt, Henry, 287, 305
Holzinger, John J., 262
Hooker, Thomas, 600
Hoops, Johannes, 174 n, 423 n, 453 n
Hoosier, Harry, 619 n
Hoosier Farmer, 621 n; *Legionnaire*, 621 n; *Motorist*, 621 n; *Sentinel*, 621 n
Hoover, Herbert, 45 n, 411, 412
Hoppin, Mrs. R. H., 168, 198 n
Hopwood, David, 256 n
Hornberger, Theodore, 723 n
Horne, Herman H., 511 n
Horses' names, 593, 594
Horsford, Eben N., 561 n
Horton, Robert W., 583 n
Hospital argot, 755, 756
Hotel names, 578
Hotel workers' argot, 756
Hotten, John Camden, 653, 654
Hough, H. B., 167 n
Houghton, Alanson B., 458 n
Houkon, Magda, 521 n
House, Dorothy E., 755 n
Houseman, Percy A., 285 n
House-painters' argot, 756, 757
House-wreckers' argot, 757
Housman, Laurence, 374
Howard, Henry, 493
Howard, O. O., 448
Howard, Rollin, 645 n
Howe, Hezekiah, 275

Howell, George Rogers, 406 n
Howells, George R., 47 n, 85
Howells, W. D., 169, 358 n, 374
Howie, R. G., 783, 785 n
Howson, Roger, 402 n
Hoyt, Vernon L., 177
Hubbard, Freeman H., 714 n
Hubbell, A. F., 191, 192
Hudson, Arthur P., 511 n, 512 n, 513 n
Hudson, M. L., 755 n
Hudson Valley, speech of, 14, 45, 69, 181, 184, 187
Hughes, Arthur H., 556
Hughes, Dorothy J., 541
Hughes, Herbert L., 156 n
Hulbert, James H., 284
Hull, Cordell, 125
Hull, Edith M., 703 n
Hull, John A. T., 631, 632
Hultzén, Lee S., 63 n, 112
Human Biology, 383 n
Hume, David, 20 n
Humphreys, David, 113, 354, 368, 648 n
Hungarian given-names, 524; surnames, 440
Hunsicker, Isaac, 209 n
Hunt, Duane G., 465 n
Hunt, J. L., 785 n
Hunt, Leigh, 400 n
Hunt, Leland O., 356
Hunt, Rockwell D., 624 n
Hunter, Estelle B., 78
Hunter, George Burton, 298, 299, 305
Hunter, J. Marvin, 480 n, 521 n
Hunter College, 28 n
Hurd, Seth T., 335 n
Hurston, Zora Neale, 270 n, 710
Hutt, James N., 537 n
Hussey, Roland B., 166
Huxley, Aldous, 472
Hyacinth, Socrates, 218 n, 381, 534 n, 640 n
Hyde, A. B., 619 n
Hyde, J. J., 492 n
Hydrographic Office, 537

Hygeia, 499 n
Hynes, Gregory, 370
Hyphen, use of, 324, 325
Hyphenated surnames, 448, 451

Icelandic language, 7 n, 400 n; surnames, 431 n
Ickes, Harold L., 77, 538, 658
Icks, Robert J., 719 n
Idaho, nicknames of, 614; place-names in, 544; speech of, 138, 221, 232 n
Illinois, given-names in, 483, 485, 490, 491, 492 n, 496, 501 n, 504 n; nicknames of, 614, 615, 623; people of, 143; place-names in, 534, 535, 541, 558; speech of, 104, 107, 115, 116, 123, 139–41, 359 n, 378
Illinois Patriot, 622 n
Imberman, A. A., 764 n
Immigration, early, 8, 9, 102; interstate, 9, 10, 235
Independent, 268 n
India, speech of, 256 n
Indian Bureau, 445
Indian languages, 332; loans from, 134, 138, 144, 172, 225, 237, 238, 526, 527–30, 552, 553, 554, 555, 556, 557, 559, 560, 561 n, 562, 563, 565, 566, 567 n, 571, 572, 573 n, 574 n, 619, 638, 760 n
Indian place-names, 225; surnames, 444–46
Indiana, given-names in, 476 n, 483, 485, 488, 492 n; nicknames of, 615–21; place-names in, 528, 534, 558; people of, 143; speech of, 104, 107, 115, 123, 141, 142–47, 204 n, 359 n, 387
Indiana Democrat, 615, 619
Indiana Historical Society Publications, 616 n
Indiana History Bulletin, 143

Index

Indiana History Conference, 142
Indiana Magazine of History, 558 n, 616 n
Indiana University, 332 n
Indiana University Bulletin, 112 n
Indianapolis *Journal,* 616, 617, 621 n
Indianapolis *Sentinel,* 616 n
Indianapolis *Star,* 146 n
Indianapolis *Times,* 392 n
Ingleman, Anna A., 120 n
Ingraham, Edward D., 449
Initials as given-names, 477, 478, 479
Inn names, 579, 580
Instalment-house argot, 757, 758
Interior Department, 538
International Barmen's Association, 734 n
International Correspondence Schools, 66
International Journal of American Linguistics, 92 n, 332 n
International phonetic alphabet, 61–66, 199, 255, 290
Intonation, 54–56, 102, 204
Investor's Reader, 774 n
Iowa, given-names in, 472, 482, 486, 487, 492 n, 503 n, 504 n; nicknames of, 621–23; people of, 147, 148; place-names in, 535, 542, 558, 559; speech of, 104, 107, 147, 148, 155, 357
Iowa, State University of, 28 n
Ireland, speech of, 7, 91 n, 197, 213 n, 248, 257, 365; surnames in, 402
Irish Free State, 403
Irving, Washington, 20, 470, 531 n, 533, 549, 607, 617 n, 649 n
Irwin, Godfrey, 665, 672 n, 676 n, 709
Isles of Shoals, speech of, 180

Israel, Nedra Karen, 724 n
Italian dictionaries, 349; given-names, 466; loans from, 52, 140, 725; spelling, 308; surnames, 439, 440; vocabulary, 349
Ithaca (N.Y.), speech of, 183, 184
Ives, George B., 94 n

Jaberg, Karl, 112 n
Jackson, Andrew, 355, 639
Jackson, Clyde, 762 n
Jackson (Miss.) *News,* 513 n, 592 n
Jackson Whites, 180, 181
Jacobs, Arthur D., 383 n
Jahveh, 5
Jamaica, speech of, 248 n
James I, 474
James, A. Lloyd, 37, 38, 41, 42, 43, 50, 54 n, 57, 58, 63, 68, 74, 81, 83, 89, 101 n, 104 n, 456 n, 460, 543 n, 546 n, 548 n
James, Henry, 23, 24, 90
James, Henry J., 164, 165, 166
James, Ollie M., 476 n
James, Thelma, 724 n
James, William, 287 n
James Sprunt Historical Publications, 194 n
Jamestown (N.Y.) *Post Journal,* 77 n
Jamieson, John, 146 n, 485 n
Jamieson, T. H., 656 n
Japanese given-names, 524, 525; surnames, 443, 444
Jazz jargon, 704–10
Jefferson, Thomas, 333, 413 n, 414 n, 455, 470
Jenks, William L., 561 n
Jensen, Paul, 138
Jespersen, Otto, 61 n, 87 n, 342, 372, 381, 387
Jewish dialect, 100, 259–62; given-names, 516–19; surnames, 415–25
Jewish Forum, 415 n
Jewish leaders, 32 n

Jive jargon, 704–10
Jockey Club, 594
Johansen, David M., 435 n
John o'London's Weekly, 76 n, 95 n, 255 n, 278 n, 358 n
Johns Hopkins Alumni Magazine, 561 n
Johns Hopkins University, 162, 335
Johnson, Alexander, 437 n
Johnson, Alice M., 242
Johnson, Andrew, 447, 639
Johnson, C. W. L., 328 n
Johnson, E. Gustav, 430, 431, 432
Johnson, Falk, 111 n
Johnson, Gerald W., 602 n
Johnson, Guy B., 268, 269 n, 710 n
Johnson, H. P., 124
Johnson, Hugh S., 66
Johnson, Jed, 476 n
Johnson, Robert A., 362 n
Johnson, Roger A., 191, 192, 356
Johnson, Samuel, 6 n, 76, 81, 107 n, 280, 281, 301, 304 n, 338
Johnson, Spud, 182
Johnson, Victor, 735 n
Johnston, Alva, 686 n
Johnston, Joseph E., 507 n
Johnston, Robert, 765 n
Johnstone, Esther, 716 n
Jonas, Harold J., 750 n
Jones, Brooke, 366
Jones, Charles C., Jr., 270 n
Jones, Daniel, 28 n, 30, 37, 41, 42, 55 n, 61 n, 62, 65 n, 70, 72 n, 76, 81, 85, 92, 96 n, 101 n, 299, 301 n, 310 n
Jones, Gomer Ll., 40
Jones, Hugh, 7, 8
Jones, John, 100
Jones, John Paul, 474 n
Jones, Joseph, 96 n, 579
Jones, Joseph S., 113 n
Jones Metabolism Equipment Company, 298
Jonson, Ben, 281
Joos, Martin, 249 n

Jordan, Philip D., 623 n
Journal of Abnormal & Social Psychology, 673 n, 710 n
Journal of American Folk-Lore, 254 n, 528 n
Journal of American Insurance, 668 n
Journal of Education, 462 n, 561 n
Journal of Educational Psychology, 353 n
Journal of Educational Research, 347 n
Journal of English & Germanic Philology, 11 n, 46 n, 69 n, 77 n, 209 n, 265 n
Journal of Genetic Psychology, 340 n, 708 n
Journal of Infectious Diseases, 455
Journal of Negro Education, 265 n
Journal of Negro History, 510 n
Journal of the Acoustical Society of America, 72 n
Journal of the American Medical Association, 48 n, 256 n, 285 n, 298 n, 320, 369 n, 379 n, 392 n, 416, 423 n, 452 n, 682 n, 735 n, 768 n
Journal of the Illinois State Historical Society, 140 n, 558 n
Journal of the Washington Academy of Sciences, 235 n
Joyce, P. W., 257 n
Joyce, William, 193
Jud, Jakob, 112
Judd, Henry P., 241 n
Judy, William L., 594
Juiliter, Mrs. Pieter, 99 n
Justin, Joseph, 742 n

Kadison, Alexander, vi, 83 n, 96 n, 318 n, 361 n, 366 n, 421 n, 425 n, 449 n, 461 n, 501 n, 508 n, 535 n, 672 n
Kahmann, G. A., 724 n
Kahn, E. J., Jr., 296 n

Kahn, Morton C., 248 n
Kane, Elisha K., 270 n
Kane, H. F., 677 n
Kane, James, 765 n
Kansas, given-names in, 491; nicknames of, 601, 623–27; place-names in, 541, 559; speech of, 108, 120 n, 129, 148–52, 204 n, 359 n, 378, 390
Kansas City Star, 152 n, 627
Kansas City Times, 632, 633
Kansas Humanistic Studies, 265 n
Kansas University Quarterly, 148, 149 n
Kapmarski, J. A., 237 n
Karig, Walter, 781 n
Karloff, Boris, 427 n
Kasser, Edmund, 708 n
Kastrup, Carl, 592 n, 774 n
Katibah, H. I., 441 n, 524 n
Katz, Joseph, 731 n
Kavanagh, Edw. J., 684 n
Kayfetz, B. G., 422 n
Kean, Mrs. Charles, 74 n
Keating, L. Clark, 97, 352 n, 522 n, 531 n
Keats, G. A., 463 n
Keats, John, 463 n
Keen, Ed L, 478
Keene, Francis B., 560 n
Keenleyside, H. L., 572
Keith, J. E., 709 n
Keith, Joseph, 696 n
Keith, Walling, 125
Kekule von Stradonitz, Stephan, 412 n, 413 n
Keller, Ben D., 235 n
Kelley, Blaine A., 210 n
Kelley, Welbourn, 781 n
Kellogg, Allen B., 146 n
Kellogg, Walter Guest, 339 n
Kelly, George A., 583 n
Kelly, Machine-Gun, 672 n
Kelly, Myra, 262
Kemal, Mustapha, 308, 442 n
Kennedy, Arthur G., 12 n, 100 n, 105 n, 114 n, 115 n, 255 n, 271 n,

291 n, 293 n, 303 n, 311, 325 n, 352 n, 461 n
Kennedy, J. S., 374
Kennedy, Lou, 190, 193 n
Kenny, Hamill, 234, 541, 551, 570
Kenrick, William, 87, 96 n
Kent, Frank R., 602 n
Kent, Webster R., 726
Kentucky, given-names in, 471, 491; nicknames of, 627, 628; place-names in, 533, 559; speech of, 80, 115, 119 n, 123, 141 n, 152, 153, 194 n, 204 n, 229, 270 n, 359 n, 378, 380, 390, 756 n; surnames in, 401
Kenyon, John S., 15, 18 n, 25, 28, 30, 31, 46 n, 49, 61 n, 62, 63, 64, 68 n, 76, 77 n, 78 n, 82, 84, 85, 89, 90, 97, 98, 103, 190, 197, 390, 544, 547
Kephart, Horace, 117 n, 119 n, 392 n, 568, 569
Key, Francis Scott, 447 n, 474
Kibbe, Pauline R., 221 n
Kidd, Bj, 478
Killheffer, Marine, 113, 114
Kimmerle, Marjorie M., 433 n, 434
King, Charles, 477
King, Durward, 489 n, 491 n, 512 n
King, Edith Morgan, 579
King, Lincoln, 370
King Features Syndicate, 784
King James Bible. See *Bible.*
Kingman, Dong, 443 n
Kingsley, Charles, 283 n
Kingsley, Walter J., 688 n, 708 n
Kinnicutt, Lincoln N., 561 n
Kipling, Rudyard, 384, 390, 472, 703 n
Kiplinger, W. M., 388 n
Kirchner, G., 672 n
Kirk, K. E., 591 n

Index

Kirkman, Samuel, 354
Kirkpatrick, E. A., 350
Kit-Kat, 376 n
Klaeber, Fr., 170 n
Klein, Nicholas, 676 n
Kliegl brothers, 699 n
Kline, Priscilla C., 366 n
Klipple, Carmelita, 220
Kloss, Heinz, 241 n
Klug, F., 712 n
Knebel, John, 653
Kneen, J. J., 451 n
Knickerbocker Magazine, 126 n, 531, 533 n, 549, 608, 629
Knights of St. Crispin, 772 n
Knoetgen, John A., 722 n
Knopf, A. A., 286
Knott, Thomas A., 15, 27 n, 30, 31, 32 n, 49, 63, 64, 65, 68 n, 76, 78 n, 82, 84, 85, 103, 190, 344, 547
Knox, John, 466 n
Kober, Arthur, 259
Koch, Frederick H., 414
Koehler, J. V., 731 n
Koehler, Olga Hazel, 554
Koenig, Walter, Jr., 352 n
Kökeritz, Helge, 44 n, 47, 77 n
Kolehmainen, John I., 429, 430
Konicek, W. J., 785 n
Kouwenhoven, Wolphert Gerretse, 405 n
Kramer's Nieuw Engelsch Woordenboek, 148 n
Kramoris, Ivan J., 426, 427, 522
Krapp, George Philip, 14, 15, 25, 28, 46 n, 55 n, 56 n, 63, 66, 73 n, 77 n, 78 n, 84, 85, 86, 108 n, 113, 140, 257 n, 258 n, 263, 264, 265, 282, 293 n, 366, 367, 368, 379, 453 n, 532 n
Krenek, Ernest, 533 n
Kretsinger, Rose G., 592
Kroeber, A. L., 349, 554
Krumpelmann, John T., 204 n, 220, 234
Krupa, Gene, 707 n

Kruse, Ed. C., 306 n, 310 n
Kuethe, J. Louis, 162, 560, 644 n, 675 n, 711 n, 746 n, 747 n
Kuhns, L. Oscar, 409 n
Kuntz, Paul G., 165 n
Kurath, Hans, 13, 16, 29, 46 n, 67, 102 n, 104, 111, 112, 115 n, 134, 135, 156, 157, 161, 196, 199, 201 n, 202, 208, 209, 210, 222 n, 228, 231, 348 n

Laase, Leroy T., 71
Labor Today, 713 n, 741 n
Labrador, speech of, 254
Ladies' Repository, 293 n, 413 n
Lafayette, Marquis de, 470
Laird, Charlton, 5 n
Lait, Jack, 695 n
Lamb, Charles, 301 n
Lambert, Mrs. Breckenridge, 497 n
Lambert, Marcus B., 148 n, 201
Lamp, 763 n
Lancaster (Pa.) *Gazette*, 609
Lancet, 48 n
Landes, Henry, 570
Landis, Kenesaw Mountain, 507
Landon, Alfred M., 357, 624, 762 n
Landor, Walter Savage, 95
Langland, William, 281
Language, 64 n, 66 n, 70 n, 72 n, 90, 104 n, 105 n, 119 n, 141 n, 201 n, 236, 249 n, 255 n, 357 n, 390 n, 557 n
Language Monographs, 199
Laning, Paul F., 714 n
Lardner, Ring W., 90, 333, 361, 366, 737
Larsen, Thorleif, 25, 48 n, 52, 85
Larson, Cedric, 595
Larson, M. Burneice, 496
Latham, Robert G., 334
Latimer, Hugh, 87 n
Latin language diction-

aries, 349; loans from, 77, 95 n, 654, 655, 670 n; vocabulary, 349
Laubach, Frank C., 291
Laubscher, G. G., 224, 226
Laughlin, Hugh C., 124 n, 194 n
Laundrymen's argot, 758
Laurie, Joe, Jr., 683 n
Law, Andrew Bonar, 472 n
Lawler, Frank, 296 n
Lawrence, D. H., 204 n
Lawrence (Mass.) *Telegram*, 359 n
Layton, J. K., 784 n
Leacock, Stephen, 371, 649 n
Learned, Henry D., 49 n
Leathers, Mrs. John A., 512 n, 513 n
Leather workers' argot, 758
Ledbetter, W. M., 632, 633
Lederer, Eugene H., 722 n
Lee, Francis B., 180, 181
Lee, Francis Lightfoot, 474
Lee, Gretchen, 688 n
Lee, Gypsy Rose, 694 n
Lee, Ivy, 503 n
Lee, Joshua Bryan, 476 n
Lee, Richard Henry, 474
Lee, Robert E., 470, 589
Lee, Rose Hum, 524 n
Lee, Thomas J., 273 n
Leech, Wilmer R., 713 n
Leechman, Douglas, 388 n
Legler, Henry E., 571
Legman, G., 678 n
Lehman, Benjamin H., 127 n, 133, 139 n, 232, 233
Lehmanowsky, John J., 618 n
Leichty, V. Erle, 675 n
Leibensperger, Elmer I., 411 n
Leland, Charles G., 258, 442 n, 653 n
LeMoyne, Charles, 437 n
Lenin, Nikolai, 415 n
Leonard, Sterling A., 336,

337, 338, 343 n, 345, 346, 367, 371
Leong Gor Lum, 442 n
Lessing, Bruno, 262
Leterz Political & Theological, 293 n
Levels of speech, 345, 347, 353
Levene, Moses, 519
Lew, Donaldine, 524 n
Lewis, Lloyd, 478 n, 507 n, 735 n, 737 n
Lewis, Meade, 706 n
Lewis, Sinclair, 170, 451 n, 645 n, 646 n
Lewis, Wyndham, 40
Lexicon of Trade Jargon, 688 n, 689 n, 691 n, 712, 717 n, 718 n, 719 n, 720 n, 722 n, 723 n, 724 n, 731 n, 732 n, 733 n, 734 n, 739 n, 740 n, 747 n, 748 n, 750 n, 752 n, 753 n, 754 n, 755 n, 756 n, 757 n, 758 n, 760 n, 761 n, 764 n, 766 n, 767 n, 770 n, 771 n, 773 n, 774 n, 775 n
Liberian Patriot, 448 n
Liberian surnames, 448 n
Liberty, 374
Librarian of Congress, 383, 712 n
Library of Congress, 712
Liebling, A. J., 683
Life, 256 n, 318, 348 n, 427 n, 476 n, 488 n, 492 n, 535 n, 634 n, 668 n, 686 n, 704 n, 707 n, 708 n, 782 n, 784 n
Life in London, 660 n
Lightall, W. D., 248 n
Lighthouse Board, 537, 538 n
Ligon, Richard 160 n
Lincoln, Abraham, 117 n, 322 n, 415 n, 448, 453, 470, 472 n, 582
Lincoln's Gettysburg Address, 118 n
Lindbergh, Charles A., 498
Lindley, Ernest K., 786
Lindsay, Charles, 770 n

Lindsay, Dorothy N., 221, 222
Linemens' argot, 717
Linford, Dee, 571
Linguaphone Institute, 67
Linguistic Atlas of Italy and Southern Switzerland, 112
Linguistic Atlas of New England, 28, 82, 88, 133, 157, 164, 178, 222 n, 356, 372, 374, 393
Linguistic Atlas of the Middle Atlantic States, 162
Linguistic Atlas of the United States and Canada, 13, 109, 110, 112, 115 n, 136 n, 140, 146, 156, 195, 199, 211, 212, 231, 236, 255
Linguistic Society of America, 67 n, 124 n, 156, 196 n, 203 n, 212 n, 236 n, 332 n, 336, 341 n, 428 n, 476 n, 478
Lintheads, 481
Literary Digest, 34, 303 n, 351 n
Lithuania, 428 n, 429 n; surnames of, 427, 428, 429
Litscher, Daniel, 401 n
Litvinoff, M. M., 415
Lively, Morris U., 535 n, 544 n
Livengood, William W., 274 n
Liverpool Daily Post, 297 n, 320 n
Liverpool Echo, 46 n, 370 n, 451 n
Living Age, 745 n
Livingood, Louis J., 210 n
Livingston, C. H., 257 n
Livingston, Robert R., 413 n
Lloyd, Charles A., 368, 369 n
Lloyd, Elwood, 553 n
Lloyd, John Uri, 270 n
Lloyd, R. J., 88
Loan-words, treatment of, 49–53, 316–20
Lobo, 712 n

Locke, John, 286 n, 334 n, 388 n
Lockwood, Belva, 497
Lodge, Henry Cabot, 418 n
Loggers' argot, 758–60
Lohrfinck, Rosalind C., vi
Lomax, Elsie, 378
Lomoe, Wallace, 435 n
Lomonosov, M. V., 308
London, Jack, 679
London County Council, 287
London *Daily Express,* 303, 304 n, 330 n, 459 n, 649 n
London *Daily Herald,* 45 n, 278 n, 721 n
London *Daily Mail,* 39
London *Daily Sketch,* 281 n, 782 n
London *Daily Telegraph,* 283 n, 578 n, 592 n, 650
London *Daily Telegraph & Morning Post,* 40 n, 358 n
London *Evening News,* 721 n
London *Evening Standard,* 39 n, 46 n, 690 n
London *Mercury,* 318
London *Morning Post,* 103 n, 248 n, 256 n, 283 n, 451, 650
London *News Chronicle,* 44 n, 456 n, 648 n
London *News-Review,* 256 n
London *Observer,* 39 n, 256 n, 278, 279, 283 n, 315, 359 n, 362 n, 366, 382 n, 477 n, 685 n, 687 n, 690 n
London *Spectator,* 649 n
London *Star,* 645 n
London *Sunday Dispatch,* 711 n
London *Sunday Express,* 40 n, 299 n
London *Sunday Times,* 460 n
London *Times,* 39, 283, 284, 296, 300 n, 302, 306 n, 314 n, 318, 320 n,

322, 323 n, 386, 421 n, 649, 650, 782 n
London *Times Literary Supplement*, 276, 304 n, 306 n, 314 n, 331 n, 368 n, 391 n, 463 n, 467 n, 660 n, 687 n, 701 n
Long, Charles M., 560
Long, E. Hudson, 377 n
Long, Stephen H., 543 n
Longfellow, H. W., 360 n, 390, 597
Long Island, place-names of, 528; speech of, 357
Longshoreman's argot, 722
Longstreet, A. B., 271 n
Longworth, Tom, 477 n
Loomis, Charles P., 718 n
Loos, Anita, 333 n, 698
Lopes, Albert R., 436 n
Lopez, Vincent, 708 n
Lopushansky, Joseph, 760 n
Lopushansky, Michael, 760 n
Los Angeles *Daily News*, 694 n
Los Angeles *Examiner*, 374
Los Angeles *Herald*, 703 n
Los Angeles *Times*, 546, 675 n, 698 n, 720 n
Lotz, Benjamin, 210 n
Louisiana, given-names in, 486, 489, 492 n, 503 n, 510, 511 n, 513 n, 517 n; nicknames of, 628; place-names in, 529, 534, 559, 560; speech of, 105, 120 n, 123 n, 131, 154–59; surnames in, 413
Louisiana Historical Quarterly, 560 n, 562 n
Louisiana State University Studies, 13 n, 124 n, 129 n, 551 n
Lounsbury, Thomas R., 49 n, 95, 287 n, 311, 372
Lovell, Charles J., vi, 167, 286 n, 293 n, 321, 322, 436 n, 480 n, 539 n, 543 n, 565 n, 613 n,
628, 631, 636 n, 638, 679 n, 735 n
Lowden, Mrs. Frank O., 582
Lowell, J. R., 78 n, 106, 113, 114 n, 142, 653 n
Lower, Mark Antony, 451 n
Lowman, Guy S., Jr., 111, 161, 195, 196, 208, 212, 224, 231, 232
Lucas, Mrs. George, 516 n
Lumbermen's argot, 158, 174, 207, 233, 234, 297, 728, 758–60
Lunch-room names, 580
Lund, Lenora, 512 n
Luther, Martin, 653
Lydenberg, H. M., 462 n
Lydgate, John, 281
Lyell, Charles, 7 n
Lyman, Dean B., 234
Lyman, Rollo L., 335
Lynch, S. James, 750 n
Lynch, Stephen J., 714 n
Lynd, Robert, 648 n

Macaulay, Rose, 37
MacAuley, Ernest A., 696 n
MacCarthy, Peter A. D., 41, 62
MacCoy, C., 774 n
MacDonald, J. C. R., 675 n
MacDonald, J. Ramsay, 472 n
Machinists' argot, 760
Mack, Theodore, 221 n, 741 n
Mackenzie, Compton, 366 n
Mackintosh, W. L. S., 168
MacLaurin, Lois M., 321 n
MacLeish, Archibald, 244 n
Macnamara, H. C., 44
Macphail, Andrew, 251
Macy, William F., 166
Mademoiselle, 712 n
Madison, James, 470, 624
Madison Quarterly, 122 n
Magazine names, 596

Magazine of History, 532 n, 564 n
Magazine of New England History, 565 n
Mahaffy, John P., 371
Mahn, C. A. F., 5 n
Maine, given-names in, 488; nicknames of, 509, 628, 629; place-names in, 560; speech of, 15, 107, 111, 129, 157–59, 175 n, 198, 208, 229, 759 n
Maine Bulletin, 721 n
Malone, Kemp, 59, 77, 105 n, 129 n, 162, 203 n, 284
Malory, Thomas, 387
Malungeon people, 235 n
Mammen, Edward W., 30, 64
Man, A. P., Jr., 131, 224, 226
Manchester (England) *Evening News*, 25 n
Manchester *Guardian*, 50 n, 647 n, 649, 650
Manchester *Guardian Weekly*, 248 n
Manila *Graphic*, 242
Manitoba, place-names in, 572
Manly, J. M., 106
Manly, William Lewis, 624 n
Manning, William, 99 n
Manu-smriti, 400
March, F. A., 296 n
Marckwardt, Albert H., 97 n, 112, 140, 141, 143, 146, 168, 170, 199, 338, 339
Maritime Commission, 583, 584
Marks, Edward B., 693 n
Marks, Percy, 133
Marks, William, 181, 754 n
Markwell, Dawes, 210 n
Marlowe, Julia, 33
Marples, Morris, 712 n
Marr, Charles, 532 n
Marryat, Frederick, 339, 438, 531
Marsh, George P., 21, 22, 334, 360

Marshall, Elihu F., 273 n
Marshall, Martha A., 553
Marshall, Vance, 256 n
Marshall (Mo.) *Democrat-News*, 500 n
Marsland, Joe, 765 n
Martha's Vineyard, speech of, 164, 166, 168, 210
Martin, John B., 759 n
Martin, J. Victor, 44, 45, 46, 48 n, 248
Martin, Lawrence, 563
Martin, Maria Ewing, 566
Martin, Pete, 685 n
Martin, Stanley, 555
Martland, Harrison S., 768 n
Marx, Karl T., 579 n, 580 n
Marye, William B., 561 n
Maryland, given-names in, 482, 485, 486, 491, 515; nicknames of, 602–05; place-names in, 528, 536, 539, 540, 560, 580; speech of, 8, 87, 100, 101, 104, 115, 122 n, 128, 155, 159–63, 169, 201 n, 204 n, 207 n, 224 n, 225, 231, 359 n; surnames in, 408, 411, 412, 447 n
Maryland Declaration of Rights, 603
Maryland Historical Magazine, 257 n, 460 n, 561 n
Mason, Charles, 604 n
Mason, C. P., 437 n
Mason, George, 367
Mason and Dixon Line, 604
Massachusetts, given-names in, 522; nicknames of, 599; place-names in, 530 n, 540, 561; speech of, 157, 165–68, 210, 387; surnames in, 436, 449
Massengill, Fred I., 541, 569
Massingale, Sam C., 100 n
Master Detective, 485 n
Mather, Cotton, 357, 386
Mathews, M. M., 64 n, 79 n, 128 n, 137 n, 140, 159 n, 223, 385
Matson, Charlotte, 481 n
Matthes, Gerard H., 569 n
Matthews, Albert, 108 n, 140, 625 n
Matthews, Brander, 17 n, 51, 287 n, 688
Matthews, W., 209 n
Matthews, William, 115 n, 255 n, 651
Matthias, Virginia P., 153
Matthison, Edith Wynne, 33
Maurer, David W., 666, 667, 668, 669, 670 n, 672, 673, 679 n, 680, 681, 682, 683, 684, 710 n, 711, 747 n, 750 n
Maverick, Maury, 53, 547
Mawer, Allen, 574 n
Maxfield, Ezra K., 158, 159, 202, 204, 205, 382
May, Ida, 608
Mayan language, 349
McArthur, Lewis A., 550, 567, 570
McAtee, W. L., 108 n, 143, 144, 160 n, 328, 536 n
McCardell, Richard, 744 n
McCardell, Roy L., 734 n
McCarthy, Don, 741 n, 742 n, 743
McCarthy, Justin, 672 n
McClellan, George B., 589
McClosky, R. G., 785 n
McCormick, Katharine L., 564 n
McCormick, S. D., 168 n, 227 n
McCormick, Washington J., 759 n
McCosh, James, 373 n
McCoy, Kid, 670 n
McCracken, George, 210 n, 457 n
McCraw, William C., 640
McCutchan, J. Wilson, 224
McCutcheon, R. J., 327 n
McDavid, Raven I., Jr., vi, 78 n, 109 n, 110 n, 112, 119 n, 121 n, 124, 146 n, 147 n, 188 n, 212, 214, 215, 216, 357 n, 361 n, 472 n, 491 n, 508 n, 568 n, 712 n
McDermott, John F., 437
McDevitt, William, 291
McDowell, Tremaine, 263, 265 n
McFerran, Doris, 714 n, 717 n, 731 n
McGee, W J, 478
McGlone, Joe, 734 n
McGowan, Samuel, 323 n
McGraw, John J., 735 n
McGroarty, William Buckner, 455 n
McGuire, Will, 710 n
McHugh, John A., 465 n
McIntyre, L. Julian, 290
McJimsey, George D., 570, 574 n
McKee, John D., 182 n
McKeehan, Alice E., 347 n
McKelvey, Gerald G., 210 n
McKelvey, Nat, 743 n
McKinley, William, 636
McKnight, George H., 17 n, 102 n, 372, 374, 462 n
McLay, W. S. W., 250 n
McLean, Margaret P., 30
McMillan, California C., 506 n
McMillan, James B., 124, 129, 130, 131, 370 n
McNamee, Graham, 36 n
McNary, Laura K., 554
McPharlin, Paul, 751 n
McPhee, M. C., 712 n
McPherson, Douglas, 322 n
McQuesten, Gertrude, 114 n
McRae, Annie, 556
McWhorter, A. W., 533 n, 568
Mead, Tom C., 488 n
Mead, William E., 135
Meade, Janet H. C., 290
Meany, Edmond S., 570
Mechem, Kirke, 624, 625, 626, 627
Medbury, Stutley, 366 n

Index

Medill, Joseph, 295 n
Meech, Sanford B., 333 n
Meek, C. S., 340
Meek, Mrs. G. A., 436 n, 482 n, 486 n, 487 n, 480 n, 492 n
Meine, Franklin J., 683 n
Mellen, Ida M., 578, 579, 728 n
Meloney, W. B., 224 n
Melton, M. E., 340 n
Melville, Herman, 387
Mencken, H. L., 117 n, 164 n, 168 n, 287 n, 316 n, 317 n, 371 n, 379 n, 462 n, 472 n, 475 n, 489 n, 497 n, 506 n, 602 n, 726, 739 n, 768 n, 780 n, 781 n, 782 n
Menner, Robert J., 6 n, 101 n, 191, 192, 204 n, 259, 260, 262, 325 n, 346, 354 n, 362 n, 373, 375
Meredith, George, 339, 374
Meredith, Mamie, 176, 318 n, 328 n, 528 n, 645, 727 n, 747 n, 748 n, 751 n, 771 n
Merriam, George and Charles, 275, 276
Merrill, Eugene C., 785 n
Merryweather, L. W., 708 n
Messenger boys' argot, 718
Mexican War, 639
Meyer, Samuel, 675 n
Meyers, James Cowden, 450, 481 n
Mezzrow, Milton, 680, 707 n, 708 n
Miami (Fla.) *Daily News*, 607 n
Michener, Earl C., 330
Michigan, given-names in, 488, 496, 505 n; nicknames of, 629, 630; place-names in, 536, 537, 540, 542, 561; speech of, 104, 107, 141, 168, 204 n; surnames in, 401, 406
Michigan Historical Magazine, 561 n

Middle English, 70, 202 n, 225 n, 382 n
Middle-names, 470, 471; as surnames, 472–74
Middle West, speech of, 56 n, 90, 91 n, 100 n, 104, 359 n, 384
Middleton, Jimmie Bugg, 487 n
Milburn, George, 675 n, 683, 684 n, 685, 720 n
Milford Haven, Marquess of, 587 n
Millar, H. Johnstone, 306 n
Miller, Charles, 757 n, 758 n
Miller, Frank, 627
Miller, J. Earle, 718 n
Millet, J. B., 722 n
Millgate, 25 n
Milton, John, 301, 328, 338, 351, 388 n
Milwaukee *Journal*, 236, 237, 331
Milwaukee *Sentinel*, 308 n
Minehan, Thomas, 676 n
Miner, Virginia Scott, 558 n
Miners' speech, 138, 216, 238, 760–62
Minicam, 698 n
Minneapolis *Journal*, 322 n, 359 n
Minneapolis-Moline Power Implement Company, 783
Minnesota, given-names in, 488, 491; nicknames of, 601, 630; place-names in, 528, 534, 540, 561, 562; speech of, 97, 104, 168–70, 196, 249; surnames in, 401, 402, 409
Minnesota Geographic Board, 562 n
Minnesota Geological and Natural History Survey, 562 n
Minnesota Historical Society, 562 n
Minstrel-show argot, 693 n
Minton, Arthur, 576, 577, 707 n, 732 n

Misfeldt, Orlo, 721 n, 759 n
Mississippi, given-names in, 490, 491, 505 n, 513 n; nicknames of, 630, 631; place-names in, 534, 562; speech of, 105, 115, 121, 154 n, 157, 170–72, 265 n, 354 n, 387
Missouri, given-names in, 487, 489, 500; nicknames of, 611, 631–35; place-names in, 534, 535, 542 n, 550, 574; speech of, 104, 107, 116, 123, 172, 173, 200, 359 n; surnames in, 437
Missouri Alumnus, 172 n
Missouri Historical Review, 174 n, 544 n, 550
Mitchell, A. G., 256 n
Mitchell, James, 166 n
Mitchell, Minnie Swann, 717 n
Mitchell, W. Fraser, 467 n
Mitteilungen der Akademie zur Wissenschaftlichen Erforsehung, 413
Mittler, William H., 712 n
Mizner, Wilson, 701 n
Mobile trade language, 560
Modern Beauty Shop, 738 n
Modern Language Association, 26, 61, 66, 212 n, 232, 335, 336, 341 n, 408 n, 428 n, 550 n, 551
Modern Language Journal, 67 n, 294 n
Modern Language Notes, 49 n, 94 n, 105 n, 117 n, 129 n, 216 n, 223 n
Modern Language Quarterly, 311 n
Modern Language Review, 252 n
Modern Philology, 13 n, 102 n, 477 n
Modjeska, Helen, 425 n
Moffatt, Donald, 511 n
Moffett, H. Y., 345, 346

Index

Monatshefte für deutsche Unterricht, 201 n
Monkhouse, Allen, 647
Monroe, B. S., 184
Monroney, A. S. Mike, 290 n
Montana, nicknames of, 613, 635; place-names in, 525; speech of, 174, 204 n, 249, 761 n
Montgomery, H. C., 714 n, 715 n
Montgomery, James, 625 n
Monthly Magazine & American Review, 321 n
Monthly South Dakotan, 638
Montreal, speech of, 249, 250, 254 n
Montreal *Gazette*, 100 n
Montserrat, speech of, 248 n
Moon, G. Washington, 23
Moor, Edward, 11 n
Moore, E. S., 256 n
Moore, Helen L., 761 n
Moore, Matilda E. B., 612 n
Moore, Pal, 413
Moore, Raymond C., 625
Moore, W. F., 572
Morehouse, Harry Gwynn, 388 n
Morehouse, Mrs. Robert L., 490 n
Moreno, Henry M., 554 n
Morgantown (W.Va.) *Post*, 362 n
Morison, S. E., 158 n, 697 n
Morley, Christopher, 285
Mormon, Book of, 569 n, 640, 641
Mormons, given-names of, 515, 516; speech of, 221, 222, 745 n
Morris, William, 338
Morrison, Estelle R., 378, 379
Morrison, Hugh, 75 n, 102 n, 192 n, 193 n, 307, 308, 349 n, 505 n, 521 n, 588 n, 681 n

Morrow, Robert C., 323 n
Morse, Jedidiah, 273
Morse Code, 717
Mortimer, Lee, 695 n
Morton, Ivy Grant, 733 n
Morton, James F., 370
Morton, John, 430 n
Moses, 516
Moses, Elbert R., 60 n
Mosier, Mrs. Charles I., 481 n
Moss, Arnold, 688 n
Motor Land, 554 n
Mott, Frank Luther, 147
Mott, Gertrude, 553
Mott, Lewis F., 253
Mountfort, Wade, 766
Movie argot, 697–704, 729
Movies, influence of, 33
Moving-van drivers' argot, 720 n
Moyer, Paul, 309
Moyers, Clyde, 410 n
Mudd, S. W., 633
Muldoon, Harvey C., 760
Mulgrave, Dorothy L., 30, 31
Mullen, Kate, 127 n
Müller, Max, 348, 349
Mulligan, John A., 739 n
Mulvey, Ruth, 686 n
Mumford, Lewis, 93
Munroe, Helen L., 248 n, 250 n
Murdoch, John, 543 n
Murray, Amelia M., 530 n, 609 n, 613, 614, 619, 628, 631 n
Murray, Gilbert, 301 n
Murray, James A. H., 344, 345
Murray, Lindley, 335 n, 367
Musicians' argot, 704–10
Musser, Benjamin, 744 n, 745 n
Mussey, Barrows, 189 n
Mutual Broadcasting System, 730 n
Mynders, Alfred, 217
Myrdal, Gunnar, 270

Nahuatl language, 349
Naldi, Nita, 703 n

Namm och Bygd, 574 n
Nanticoke people, 235 n
Nantucket, speech of, 164, 166, 168, 210
Nares, Robert, 87 n, 88 n, 96 n
Narragansett Bay speech-area, 210, 211
Nason, Elias, 461 n
Nathan, George Jean, 691 n
Nation, 55 n, 77 n, 270 n, 298 n, 467 n, 624 n, 625 n, 726, 777 n
National Association of Angling and Casting Clubs, 751 n
National Association of College Women, 487 n
National Association of Teachers of Speech, 27 n
National Broadcasting Company, 35, 731 n, 772 n
National Council of Teachers of English, 24, 337, 341 n, 343
National Education Association, 311, 370
National Education Association Journal, 294 n
National Geographic Magazine, 195 n
Nation's Business, 538 n
Natoma (Kansas) *Independent*, 151 n
Naval vessels, names of, 584–88
Neal, John, 601
Nebraska, given-names in, 484, 485, 491; nicknames of, 635; place-names in, 562, 563; speech of, 174–78, 196, 270 n, 357, 385, 387, 706 n
Negro Digest, 383 n, 511 n, 515 n, 708 n, 709 n, 716 n
Negroes, given-names of, 509–15; leaders of, 32 n; speech of, 8, 14, 32, 86, 101, 107, 130, 131, 160, 171, 172, 209, 227, 247,

Index

248, 263–70, 358, 379;
surnames of, 402, 446,
447, 448
Neill, Robert T., 612 n
Neitzel, Stuart, 216 n
Nelson, Bruce, 446 n,
742 n
Nelson, Carl A., 717 n
Nelson, John H., 265 n
Nelson, L. E., 353 n
Nelson, Victor F., 680
Nelson, William, 446
Neuren Sprache, Die,
88 n
Neutral vowel, 71, 73, 81,
90, 226, 269
Nevada, given-names in,
488; nicknames of, 613,
636; place-names in,
563; speech of, 178,
761 n, 770 n
Nevada State Historical
Society, 563
Neville, Marcus, 515 n
Newark (N.J.) *News*,
535 n
Newark *Sunday Call*,
725 n
New Bedford *Standard-Times*, 167 n
New Brunswick, speech
of, 110, 252
Newcastle-on-Tyne
Weekly Chronicle,
721 n
New Deal, 329, 330, 603,
733 n
Newell, R. H. (Orpheus
C. Kerr), 560 n
New England, given-names in, 467, 468, 471;
place-names in, 12;
speech of, 11, 12, 16, 17,
22, 86, 88, 90, 103 n, 104,
110, 112–14, 128, 157,
169, 170, 185, 187, 198,
207, 210, 211, 249, 356,
357, 372, 387; surnames
in, 402
New England Magazine,
168 n
New England Primer,
272, 273
New England Quarterly,
115 n, 366 n, 469 n,
555 n

New English Dictionary,
65 n, 76, 80, 85 n, 160 n,
211, 238 n, 272 n, 277,
278, 279 n, 280 n, 282,
283, 286, 296 n, 302 n,
314, 328, 344, 349, 353,
355, 356, 358, 363 n, 366,
369, 374, 382 n, 383, 384,
385, 388 n, 393 n, 400 n,
477 n, 573 n, 578 n,
592 n, 597, 613 n, 657 n,
663 n, 664 n, 670 n,
672 n, 691 n, 692 n,
701 n, 710, 725 n, 741 n,
745 n, 766 n, 770 n,
778 n
Newfoundland, place-names of, 572 n, 574;
speech of, 249, 252, 253,
254, 357, 358, 387
Newfoundland Nomenclature Board, 571
New Hampshire, given-names in, 507; nicknames of, 599; place-names in, 529, 530, 540,
563, 564; speech of, 15,
157, 159, 178–80, 257;
surnames in, 461 n
New International Encyclopedia, 545 n, 622,
631, 635
New Jersey, given-names
in, 505 n; nicknames of,
599, 601, 602, 623; place-names in, 536, 542, 573;
speech of, 104, 180–82,
201 n, 204, 388; surnames in, 401
New Jersey Public Library Commission,
564 n
Newlin, Claude M., 202,
205, 223
New London (Conn.)
Day, 450 n
Newman, Benjamin, 70 n
Newman, Robert G.,
450 n
New Masses, 244 n
New Mexico, nicknames
of, 636, 638; place-names in, 529 n, 564,
565; speech of, 127, 136,
182, 183, 221
New Mexico, 743 n

*New Mexico Historical
Review*, 128 n
New Orleans, speech of,
121, 127; surnames in,
401
New Orleans *Crescent*,
687 n
New Orleans *Picayune*,
166, 492 n
New Practical Standard
Dictionary, 64 n, 279 n,
546, 547, 724, 726, 728,
755, 782 n
New Republic, 32 n,
104 n, 115 n, 122 n,
126 n, 193 n, 325 n,
677 n, 698 n, 741 n
News & Views, 724 n
Newspaperman, 256 n
Newspaper names, 595,
596
Newsweek, 245 n, 357,
522 n, 704 n, 731 n,
781 n
Newton, Emmett, 632
Newton, F. H. J., 96 n
Newton, Simon, 462, 463,
471 n
New York, given-names
in, 482, 483, 488, 492 n,
502 n; place-names in,
528, 529, 565, 574; nicknames of, 597, 598;
speech of, 4, 14, 16, 22,
27 n, 30 n, 31, 32, 103 n,
104, 108, 135, 155, 170,
183–93, 203, 204 n, 357,
390, 392 n
New York *American*,
729 n
New York Board of Geographic Names, 565 n
New York City, surnames in, 400, 401
New York *Daily News*,
295, 594, 676 n, 736 n
New York *Evening Journal*, 720 n
New York *Evening Post*,
293 n, 532 n, 695 n,
725 n, 768 n
New York *Evening Star*,
619
New York *Herald Tribune*, 42 n, 43 n, 76 n,
317, 318, 328 n, 349 n,

xxviii *Index*

405 n, 420 n, 421 n, 471, 478 n, 496, 672 n, 735 n, 785 n
New York *Journal,* 765 n
New York *Journal-American,* 463 n
New York *Mirror,* 530 n, 533, 534 n, 536 n, 695 n
New York *Press,* 737 n
New York Public Library, vi, 462 n
New York Singing Teachers' Association, 28 n
New York *Staats-Zeitung,* 414 n
New York State Department of Education, 29
New York State Museum, 565 n
New York *Sun,* 329 n, 400 n, 401 n, 452, 557 n, 626, 721 n, 749 n, 750 n
New York *Sunday News,* 737 n
New York *Times,* 47 n, 48 n, 56 n, 67 n, 83 n, 129 n, 192 n, 193 n, 212 n, 303, 310 n, 322 n, 326 n, 351 n, 361 n, 373, 376, 379 n, 420 n, 421 n, 423 n, 425 n, 438 n, 473, 505 n, 532 n, 535 n, 569 n, 647 n, 648 n, 650 n, 671 n, 688 n, 696, 720 n, 721 n
New York *Times Magazine,* 36 n, 45 n, 168 n, 192 n, 193 n, 256 n, 373 n, 470 n, 496 n, 649 n, 707 n, 731 n, 737 n, 743 n, 747 n, 780 n
New York *Times Saturday Review of Books,* 376 n
New York *Tribune,* 691 n
New York *World,* 129 n, 708 n
New York *World-Telegram,* 316 n, 366 n, 686 n, 719 n
New Yorker, 181 n, 256 n, 259 n, 262, 287 n, 295 n, 296 n, 298, 323 n, 348 n, 392 n, 400 n, 427 n,

452 n, 453 n, 454 n, 457 n, 488 n, 523, 533 n, 577 n, 579 n, 583 n, 588 n, 644 n, 647 n, 678 n, 680 n, 685 n, 686 n, 705 n, 707 n, 708 n, 720 n, 731 n, 744 n, 750 n, 751 n
New Zealand, speech of, 256 n, 759 n
New Zealand Free Lance, 759 n
New Zealand Free Press, 256 n
Nice, Margaret M., 350, 351 n
Nicholas, E. J., 706 n
Nicholas, Madaline, 246 n
Nichols, Edward J., 734 n, 735 n, 736 n, 737 n
Nicklin, John B. C., 455 n
Nicklin, T., 41, 49 n, 70, 95 n
Nicknames, personal, 475-77; of States, 596-642
Nicolay, J. G., 453 n
Nicols, John B., 507 n
Nicolson, Marjorie H., 732
Niles' Register, 598, 605
Nineteenth Century and After, 46 n, 304 n
Nixon, Phyllis J., 110 n, 224, 231
Nixon, Rachel Ann, 491 n
Nixon, William J., 291, 292
Noah, Mordecai M., 619
Nock, Albert Jay, 262 n
Nock, S. A., 389
Norris, P. W., 237
North, Lord, 534 n
North American Newspaper Alliance, 596 n, 698 n
North American Review, 77 n, 181 n, 268 n, 339 n
North Carolina, given-names in, 483, 489, 490, 491, 510, 511 n, 512 n, 513 n; nicknames of, 605-07; place-names in, 542, 544, 565, 566; speech of, 115, 119,

122 n, 124 n, 154 n, 162, 193-96, 207 n, 224 n, 225, 229, 359 n, 378, 379 n, 380, 386
North Country, speech of, 11, 12, 13, 38
North Dakota, nicknames of, 636; place-names in, 541, 542 n, 566; speech of, 196
North Dakota Geographic Board, 566 n
North Dakota Historical Quarterly, 566 n
North Georgia Review, 138 n
Northern American. See *General American*
Northrup, Helen F., 759 n
Northwest, speech of, 127 n
Northwest Quarterly, 558 n
Northwestern Pioneer & St. Joseph's Intelligencer, 616, 620
Northwestern University Studies in the Humanities, 351 n
Norton, Arthur A., 267
Norton, Charles L., 640 n
Norton, Theodore E., 321 n
Norwegian given-names, 520; surnames, 432-35
Norwegian language. See *Dano-Norwegian language*
Norwegian-American Studies & Records, 433 n
Notes & Queries, 688 n
Nouns, 383-86
Nova Scotia, place-names in, 573 n; speech of, 252, 254
Noyes, Gertrude E., 665
Nugent, William H., 736 n
Nye, Bill, 623 n
Nye, Russel B., 707 n
Nykerk, John B., 146 n

Oakes, John, 256 n
Oakey, Virginia, 698 n

O'Banion, Dion, 671 n
O'Brien, James T., 784
O'Brien, William D., 686 n
Och, J. T., 529 n
O'Connor, Harvey, 518 n
Odum, Howard W., 162 n
Ogilvie, Mardel, 29
O'Hara, Joseph M., 466 n
O'Hara, Neal, 535 n, 725 n
Ohio, given-names in, 535; nicknames of, 636, 637; place-names in, 566; speech of, 16, 25 n, 104, 123, 141, 169, 196–99, 204 n, 234, 357, 381, 756 n; surnames in, 401, 411
Ohio Almanac, 321
Oilfield argot, 762–64
Okakura, Y., 303 n
Okies, 481
Oklahoma, given-names in, 481, 482, 483, 484, 485, 486, 487, 488, 489, 490, 491, 492 n, 493 n, 494, 495 n, 496, 498, 502 n, 503 n, 504 n, 505 n, 506, 507, 508, 510, 511 n, 513 n; nicknames of, 637, 638; place-names in, 553, 542, 544; speech of, 123, 199, 200, 366, 390
Oklahoma City Oklahoman, 361 n, 450 n, 476 n, 483 n, 484 n, 485 n, 486 n, 487 n, 489 n, 490 n, 491 n, 492 n, 493 n, 496 n, 502 n, 503 n, 504 n, 505 n, 508 n, 511 n, 513 n
Oklahoma City Times, 481 n, 482 n, 483 n, 484 n, 485 n, 487 n, 488 n, 489 n, 490 n, 497, 498, 502 n, 503 n
Old English, 21, 202 n, 255 n, 349, 359; its vocabulary, 349
Olds, Nathaniel S., 721 n
Oliphant, Samuel Grant, 400 n

Oliver, Mrs. James D., 170 n
Oliver, N. T., 686 n
Oliver, Robert T., 676 n
Olmsted, Frederick Law, 610
Omnibook, 704 n
Ondis, Lewis A., 198
Ong, Walter J., 327 n
O'Neill, Eugene, 57 n
O'Neill, J. M., 29
Onions, C. T., 39, 328 n
Ontario, speech of, 141 n, 204 n, 249
Opportunity, 137
Orbeck, Anders, 10, 11, 112, 453
Oredownik Jezykowy, 425 n
Oregon, nicknames of, 630, 638; place-names in, 535, 542, 550, 551, 567; speech of, 104, 107, 200, 201, 208, 232 n
Oregon *Argus*, 615
Oregon Geographical Board, 550 n
Oregon Historical Quarterly, 551 n
Oregon Historical Society, 550 n
Ormin, 301, 302 n
O'Rourke, L. J., 340, 341
Ortega, Joaquin, 182 n
Ortleb, Ruth, 60
Osborn, E. B., 358 n
Osgood, Henry O., 706 n
O'Sullivan, Ivo, 496 n
Oswald, Victor A., Jr., 98
Otis, David, 415 n
Ottawa *Journal*, 45 n, 99 n, 250 n
Oursler, Mary C., 450
Outing, 384
Overland Monthly, 128 n, 375 n, 381 n, 534 n, 606, 640 n
Owen, Marie B., 611
Owen, Robert L., 289, 290
Owens, Bess Alice, 119 n
Owens, Hamilton, 602, 603
Oxford Book of Light Verse, 348 n

Oxford English. See *Southern English Standard*.
Oxford University Press, 283
Ozarks, given-names in, 482, 485; people of, 105, 116, 119, 120, 126; speech of, 105, 116, 119, 120, 129, 132, 156, 159, 173, 200, 332, 357, 358, 361 n, 362 n, 366, 378, 379, 380, 385, 387, 391. See also *Appalachia*.

Pacific Coast, speech of, 104
Packinghouse argot, 764, 765
Padín, José, 244, 245
Page, Thomas Nelson, 377
Page, Walter Hines, 24 n
Paget, Richard, 70, 98, 356
Paine, Gustavus Franklin, 482 n, 489 n
Paine, Gustavus Swift, 453 n, 474, 563
Paine, Henry G., 287 n
Paine, Robert Treat, 474
Painters' argot, 756, 757
Palacio, El, 564 n
Palestine, Jewish names in, 519
Palestine Gazette, 422 n, 519
Palestine Post, 422 n, 519 n
Palimpsest, 622 n, 623 n
Palmer, A. Smythe, 385
Palmer, Harold E., 44, 45, 46, 48 n, 74 n, 75, 79, 95 n, 248, 342
Palmer, Harold S., 240, 434 n
Palmer, P. E., 571
Palmer, Robert B., 256 n
Palsgrave, Jean, 6 n
Paltsits, Victor H., 532 n
Papers of the Michigan Academy of Science, Arts and Letters, 141 n, 675 n
Parade, 524 n

Pardue, Leonard G., 508 n
Park, Wilmer R., 220, 364 n
Parker, Dorothy, 595
Parkhurst, Winthrop, 706 n
Parler, Mary Celestia, 212 n, 215
Parmenter, C. E., 71 n, 76
Parmenter, Mary, 482 n
Parrant, Pierre, 561 n
Parrots, vocabulary of, 351 n
Parrott, Harold, 735 n
Parry, W. H., 197, 198
Parsons, Usher, 549, 567
Parton, James, 400 n
Parton, Nat, 476 n
Parton, Sara P. Willis (Fanny Fern), 400
Partridge, Eric, 220 n, 256 n, 329 n, 355 n, 384, 463 n, 638, 647 n, 648 n, 650, 651, 660, 661, 662, 665 n, 666 n, 671 n, 672 n, 673 n, 677 n, 678 n, 690 n, 747 n, 768 n
Passy, Paul, 61
Patrick, George Z., 329 n
Patterson, George, 254 n
Pattison, Mark, 383 n
Paul, Maury, 704 n
Paulding, James K., 617 n
Pauly, Karl B., 412 n
Payne, L. W., Jr., 13 n, 130, 222 n, 264 n
Pearce, J. W., 154, 155
Pearce, Thomas W., 128 n, 564
Pearson, Arthur, 686 n
Peavey, Harris Booge, 513 n
Peck, Epaphroditus, 437 n
Peckham, John, 464 n
Pedersen, Holger, 61 n
Pedlar's French, 663
Pegge, Samuel, 11
Pegler, Westbrook, 441 n, 704 n, 768 n, 780
Pei, Mario A., 308 n
Penang *Gazette*, 96 n
Pendleton, Paul E., 119 n
Penn, William, 411 n
Pennsylvania, given-names in, 471, 512 n; nicknames of, 598; place-names in, 528, 529, 536, 580; speech of, 16, 103 n, 104, 107, 108, 115, 120 n, 129, 136, 147, 155, 156, 169, 201-10, 230, 239, 354, 381, 387; surnames in, 401, 410, 411, 412, 413, 449
Pennsylvania Geographic Board, 567 n
Pennsylvania-German language, 201, 205 n, 206, 207, 208, 213, 230, 233, 234, 408; loans from, 128, 148, 156, 201-10; surnames, 410, 411
Penzl, Herbert, 77 n, 112, 115 n
Pepper, Nancy, 707 n
Pepys, Samuel, 107 n, 373
Perelman, S. J., 707 n
Perkins, Anne E., 158 n, 198
Perkins, Frances, 66
Perkins, Henry A., 72 n, 73 n
Perkins, T. W., 379
Perley, Harriet, 487 n
Perrin, P. G., 114 n, 358 n
Perth Amboy *Evening News*, 564 n
Pestalozzi, J. H., 335 n
Peter, George P., 777 n
Peters, Samuel A., 570 n, 600
Peterson, Eldridge, 731 n
Petit Journal (Montreal), 572 n
Phelps, William Lyon, 785
Philadelphia, speech of, 8, 203, 204; surnames in, 401, 409 n
Philadelphia *Bulletin*, 322 n
Philippines, speech of, 88 n, 241-43
Phillips, Edith, 732 n
Phillips, Walter P., 717 n
Phillips, Mrs. Wendell B., 164
Phillips Code, 717
Phillips Exeter Bulletin, 712 n

Philological Quarterly, 147 n
Phonemes, 54
Phonetische Studien, 213 n
Phonograph, 66-68
Phonotype Journal, 299 n, 310
Photographers' argot, 765, 766
Photography, 714 n
Picken, Mary B., 732 n
Pickering, John, 17, 78, 126, 223, 353, 356, 357, 362 n
Pickett, George E., 497
Picking, H. F., 537
Pickpockets' argot, 670
Pidgin English, 240, 258 n, 261 n, 264
Piedmont, speech of, 16, 161, 196, 204, 214, 215, 232
Pierce, Franklin, 461, 471
Pierce, Robert M., 65 n
Pierce, Shanghai, 212 n
Pierce Egan's Life in London, 660 n
Pike county dialect, 126
Pike, Kenneth L., 57 n, 68 n
Pike, Robert E., 437 n, 438 n
Pilgrim Fathers, 6 n
Pilkington, Richard, 296 n
Pilot, William, 252 n
Pineys, 180
Pipe Rolls, 403
Pipes, Nellie B., 550 n
Pitch pattern. See *Intonation*
Pitchmen's argot, 685, 686
Pitman, Benn, 299 n, 310 n
Pitman, Isaac, 70, 299, 310
Pitman, Isaac James, 299, 300
Pitt, William, 534 n
Pittsburgh *Courier*, 683 n, 745 n
Pittsfield (Mass.) *Berkshire Evening Eagle*, 450 n, 452 n
Pius X, 464 n
Place-names, 525-75; Appalachian, 118

Plasterers' argot, 766
Platt, William, 382 n
Pleasures of Publishing, 323 n, 348 n
Plumbers' argot, 766, 767
Plurals, false, 219, 269, 318, 319, 320, 383-86
PM, 695 n, 736 n, 783 n
Poe, Edgar Allan, 265 n, 610, 703 n
Polish language, spelling of, 309 n; surnames, 425, 426, 427
Polk, James K., 474, 639
Pollard, Mary O., 216 n
Pollock, F. Walter, 708 n
Pollock, Thomas C., 26 n
Pollok, Thomas P., 554 n
Ponce de León, 614
Pond, Frederick R., 762 n
Pooley, Robert C., 6 n, 337, 347, 353, 389
Pope, Alexander, 387
Pope, J. S., 330
Popular Mechanics, 698 n
Popular Science Monthly, 350 n
Popular songs, 348
Population Bulletin, 245 n
Porcher, C. G., 751 n
Porter, Bernard H., 719 n
Port Folio, 362 n
Portland *Oregon Journal*, 551 n
Portuguese language, loans from, 167, 240; given-names, 522; surnames, 436
Posidonius, 335
Post, Emily, 53
Postoffice argot, 533, 537, 767
Potter, George R., 115 n
Potters' argot, 767
Potts, F. G., vi, 75, 90 n, 91, 99 n, 210 n, 384 n, 438 n, 574 n
Pound, Louise, vi, 16, 24, 29, 46 n, 48 n, 52 n, 78 n, 82, 96 n, 97 n, 100 n, 105, 174, 175, 176, 257 n, 296, 297, 314 n, 318, 359 n, 363 n, 371, 384, 387 n, 388 n, 394 n, 402 n, 562, 647 n, 687 n, 698 n, 727 n

Powell, W. A., 605
Power, Anabel, 513 n, 592 n
Power, H. Darcy, 303 n
Powers, Jimmy, 736 n
Prairie Schooner, 325 n
Pratt, Theodore, 692 n, 751 n
Prenner, Manuel, 506, 513 n
Prescott, Russell T., 748 n, 749 n, 764 n
Prettyman, William, 202, 206
Price, Jack, 765 n
Price, Lawrence M., 313 n
Price, Malvern Hill, 507 n
Priest, George N., 655
Priestley, Joseph, 371
Primer, Sylvester, 213, 214, 223, 229, 230, 233 n
Prince, J. Dyneley, 189 n, 565 n
Prince Edward Island, place-names in, 572
Princeton Alumni News, 491 n
Princeton Alumni Weekly, 373 n, 712 n
Pringle, A. G., 785 n
Printers' Ink, 36 n, 348 n, 377 n
Prioleau, John, 723 n
Prior, Matthew, 303
Priscian, 335
Prison slang, 672-75
Proceedings of the American Antiquarian Society, 11, 12 n, 555 n
Proceedings of the American Philological Association, 210 n
Proceedings of the Bostonian Society, 168 n
Proceedings of the British Academy, 327 n
Proceedings of the Modern Language Association, 216 n
Proceedings of the Nantucket Historical Association, 166 n
Proceedings of the New

Jersey Historical Society, 564
Proceedings of the New York Historical Society, 565 n
Proceedings of the Second International Congress of Phonetic Sciences, 46 n, 224 n
Prohibition, 602, 629, 648 n, 667, 668
Pronouns, 242, 246, 254, 269, 368-83
Propeller, 491 n
Prosser, William S., 291
Prostitutes' argot, 682, 683
Providence (R.I.) *Evening Bulletin*, 735
Providence *Journal*, 46 n, 108 n, 212 n, 322, 483 n, 484 n, 489 n, 491 n, 536, 614, 617, 618, 700 n, 779 n
Providentissima Mater Ecclesia, 464 n
Publications of the American Dialect Society, 109 n, 118 n, 124 n, 130 n, 154 n, 174 n, 194 n, 224 n, 266 n, 776 n
Publications of the East Tennessee Historical Society, 568 n
Publications of the Mississippi Historical Society, 562 n
Publications of the Modern Language Association, 6 n, 23 n, 49 n, 54 n, 60, 77 n, 89 n, 117 n, 118, 223 n, 233 n, 248 n, 257 n, 271 n, 313 n, 327 n, 333 n, 336 n, 343 n, 494 n, 565 n, 566 n
Publications of the Ohio Archeological & Historical Society, 566 n
Public Health Service, 609
Publishers' Weekly, 739 n
Puckett, N. N., 446, 509, 510, 513, 514

Puerto Rican Teachers' Association, 245
Puerto Rico, given-names in, 522 n; speech of, 243-46
Puerto Rico Libre, 245 n
Pugh, Delia H. Biddle, 18 n, 460 n, 497 n
Pugilists' argot, 736 n, 767, 768
Pullen, Jr., T. G., 413 n
Pullman, George M., 582
Pullman-car names, 582, 583
Pullman News, 714 n
Pullman porters' argot, 716, 717
Punch, 86
Punctuation, 325, 326
Puritan given-names, 466-68
Pusey, William A., 80
Putnam's Monthly, 453, 473 n, 501
Pyles, Thomas, 49 n
Pylon, 448 n

Quaife, M. M., 630
Quakers, speech of, 382, 745 n
Quarterly Journal of Speech, 27 n, 29, 30 n, 31 n, 46 n, 60 n, 65 n, 68 n, 70, 71 n, 72 n, 76 n, 88 n, 115 n, 224 n, 249 n, 256 n, 268 n, 730 n
Quarterly Journal of Speech Education, 18 n, 27 n, 688 n
Quarterly Journal of the New York State Historical Association, 532 n
Quarterly Review, 284, 285
Quebec, place-names in, 572; speech of, 108, 249
Quebec Geographic Board, 571, 572
Queen, Johnny, 644
Queen's Quarterly, 99 n, 373 n
Query, 40 n
Quilt names, 592
Quincy, Josiah, 474 n
Quinn, Robert H., 450 n

Quirk, James R., 702
Quisling, Vidkun, 782 n, 783 n
Quotation marks, 326
Quynn, Allen George, 501 n

Rabbitt, James F., 714 n
Racing argot, 736 n, 768-70
Rackham Foundation, 141
Radio argot, 728-31; pronunciation, 33-39, 62, 250
Radio Times, 50 n
Radio Weekly, 34 n
Rafferty, Keen, 182 n
Raikes, Robert, 745 n
Railroad argot, 138, 713-17, 728
Railroad Magazine, 714 n, 715 n
Raleigh, Walter, 494
Raleigh (N.C.) *News-Observer*, 511 n
Ramsay, David, 9
Ramsay, Robert L., 173 n, 349, 350, 390, 550, 562, 568, 574
Ramsaye, Terry, 702 n
Randel, William, 170, 365, 567, 712 n
Randolph, John, 221 n
Randolph, Vance, 106, 119, 120, 121, 132, 173, 332, 361 n, 362 n, 366, 378, 379, 380, 385, 388, 391, 592, 593 n, 671 n
Rankin, K. L., 53 n, 393 n
Ransom, C. F., 148 n
Ransom, Jay Ellis, 92 n
Ransom, John E., 119 n
Rapport, Leonard, 776 n
Ratcliffe, S. K., 37
Raubicheck, Letitia, 29 n, 30, 31
Raven-Hart, R., 74
Ray, J. B., 621
Rayburn, Sam, 475
Rea, Mrs. Vernon A., 536 n
Read, Allen Walker, 7, 10, 11, 20 n, 58, 101 n, 115 n, 140, 144, 159 n, 166 n, 172, 174 n, 209 n, 256, 271 n, 296 n, 346 n, 533 n, 543 n, 544, 545, 546 n, 548, 550, 558, 559, 574, 709
Read, William A., 46 n, 69 n, 124, 545 n, 551, 552 n, 556, 557, 559, 628 n
Reader's Digest, 459 n, 496 n, 696 n
Reardon, Daniel L., 563 n
Rebolledo, Antonio, 182 n
Received Pronunciation. See *Standard Southern English*
Received Standard English. See *Standard Southern English*
Red Book, 374 n
Red River Valley, speech of, 155, 156
Reece, Byron H., 119 n
Reed, Carroll, 208
Reed, H. B., 151 n
Rees, Byron J., 166
Reese, George H., 98 n
Reflex, 418 n, 517 n
Reform, 307
Reid, Loren, 29
Reid, Louis, 729 n
Reid, Thomas R., Jr., 137
Reinecke, Aiko Tokimasa, 239
Reinecke, John E., 239, 436 n, 442 n, 443, 444, 522 n, 524, 525
Reitman, Ben L., 676 n, 678 n
Renault, Raoul, 553 n
Rennicks, James F., 476 n
Rennicks, Mrs. James F., 487 n
Reno, Conrad, 438
Reno, Jesse Lee, 438 n
Reno, Jesse Wilford, 438 n
Reno, Victor T., 438 n, 670 n
Restoration, 321
Reuter, E. G., 547
Revolution, American, 6 n, 8, 16, 19, 101, 183, 256, 263 n, 304 n, 321, 335 n, 367, 469, 471, 539 n, 627; Loyalists in, 157

Reynaud, Paul, 648 n
Reynold, Horace, 375
Reynolds, Helen Wilkinson, 564 n, 565 n
Rhame, John M., 270 n
Rhode Island, given-names in, 483, 484, 489, 491; nicknames of, 601; place-names in, 549, 567, 568; speech of, 210-12
Rhode Island Geographic Board, 568
Rhyming slang, 666 n, 710, 711
Rice, Elmer, 421 n
Rice, Howard C., 703 n
Rice, Moyle Q., 90
Rice, Thomas D., 257
Rice, Wallace, 363 n, 371, 389
Rice, William O., 139, 143
Richards, I. A., 37, 58
Richardson, Albert D., 615 n
Richardson, B. T., 256 n
Richardson, Lewis C., 245, 246
Richardson, Samuel, 393
Richey, F. O., 746 n
Richey, Frank, 392 n
Richie, Eleanor L., 555
Richmond, Edson, 146
Richmond, Va., speech of, 14, 121
Richmond *News-Leader*, 456 n, 698 n
Richmond *Times-Dispatch*, 122 n, 217 n, 224 n
Richter, Arthur, 721 n
Richter, Conrad, 210 n
Rickenbacker, Eddie, 77
RiDant, Hugh, 452 n
Riedel, E., 154
Rigby, Elizabeth, 481 n
Rightor, H. H., 712 n
Rigney, Agnes, 29 n
Riley, James Whitcomb, 106, 145, 619, 621
Ripley, R. L., 402 n, 506, 512 n
Ripman, Walter, 299 n, 301 n
Ritchie, Albert C., 603

Rittenhouse, William, 413
Roback, A. A., 190 n, 421 n, 516 n, 517
Robb, Arthur, 330 n, 331 n
Robbins, T. H., Jr., 511 n
Robert, Grace, 695 n
Roberts, Ernest B., 290
Roberts, Kingsley, 755 n
Robertson, David A., 210 n, 573 n
Robertson, Mrs. John W., 481 n
Robertson, Stuart, 343 n
Robinson, Erdis, 508 n
Robinson, M. P., 570 n
Robinson, Ted, 456 n
Roche, Edward P., 556
Rochester, E. P., 450, 476, 481 n
Rochester *Times-Union*, 41 n
Rockefeller, John D., 474 n, 503 n
Rockefeller Foundation, 42
Rockwell, Kenneth, 482 n
Rodman, Lida Tunstall, 194 n
Rogers, J. A., 619 n
Rogers, P. Burwell, 784 n
Rogers, Samuel, 47
Rogers, Will, 100 n, 361, 370, 386, 393 n, 477 n
Rollins, Hyder E., 219, 481 n
Roman personal names, 475
Romanic Review, 370 n, 529 n
Romany. See *Gipsy language*
Rome (N.Y.) *Sentinel*, 317 n
Roosevelt, Eleanor, 66, 369
Roosevelt, Franklin D., 45, 66, 77, 244, 373, 470, 471, 603, 785, 786
Roosevelt, Theodore, 242, 305, 355, 470, 538
Rosecrans, W. S., 412, 589
Rosenau, William, 687 n
Rosenberg, Anne M., 785
Rosenblum, Marcus, 518 n

Rosenfeld, Monroe H., 693 n
Rosenthal, Alice, 595 n
Rosenthal, Harold, 256 n
Rosenwald Fund, 216 n
Rositzke, Harry A., 72 n
Ross, Charles G., 477 n
Ross, James, 243 n
Ross, Leonard Q., 259
Ross, Nancy Wilson, 138
Ross, Paul, 694 n
RossKam, Charles K., 452 n
Rosten, Leo Calvin, 259
Rotarian, 291, 525 n
Rothenberg, Julius G., 392 n, 646 n, 708 n
Routh, James, 154, 155, 156 n
Roy, Pierre-Georges, 572, 573
Royal Academy of Dramatic Art, 37
Royal Air Force, 781 n
Royal Canadian Naval Reserve, 785
Royal Society of Canada, 286 n
Royal Society of Literature, 37
Royall, Ann, 129 n, 223, 375
Rubber workers' argot, 770
Runyon, Damon, 333 n
Rupp, I. Daniel, 520 n
Ruppenthal, J. C., 150, 151
Ruskin, John, 338
Russell, Bertram, 39
Russell, Harold, 759 n
Russell, I. Willis, 130, 703 n, 715 n, 777 n, 780 n, 782
Russell, Jason A., 179, 184, 185, 461 n, 722 n
Russell, R. E. L., 717 n
Russell, Thomas, 461 n
Russell, William, 290, 291
Russian language, loans from, 151 n, 329; spelling of, 308; surnames, 427, 428
Ryan, John A., 383 n

Ryman, Mrs. James N., 507 n

Saba, speech of, 248
Saber, Clifford, 523
Sachs, William J., 686 n
Sage, Evan T., 532
Sailors' argot, 721, 728
Salem (Ore.) *Capital Press*, 638
Salisbury, Marquess of, 457 n
Salisbury (Md.) *Times*, 363 n
Salmagundi, 649 n
Salter, J. L., 412 n
Salter, Lawrence C., 735 n
Saltonstall, Leverett, 75
Salvation Army, 298, 677 n
Samolar, Charles, 676 n, 677 n
Sampson, George, 314
Samuel, Maurice, 415 n
San Antonio (Tex.) *Light*, 476 n, 569 n
Sanchez, Nellie Van de Grift, 528 n, 547 n, 553, 554 n
Sanders, Clinton A., 675 n, 682, 746 n
Sandhogs' argot, 770
Sandilands, John, 252 n
Sandoz, Marie, 706 n
Sandson, William, 431 n
Sanford, Winifred, 762 n
San Francisco, speech of, 102 n; surnames in, 401
San Francisco *Call*, 709
San Francisco *Chronicle*, 760 n
San Francisco *Examiner*, 316 n
San Francisco *News*, 482 n
San Francisco *News Letter & Wasp*, 672 n, 682 n, 701 n, 708 n, 710 n, 736 n, 746 n, 754 n, 768 n
San Juan (Puerto Rico) *El Imparcial*, 245
San Juan *El Mundo*, 245
San Juan *World Journal*, 245

San Quentin Bulletin, 673 n
San Quentin News, 675 n
Santamaria, Francisco J., 681 n
Saroyan, William, 441, 523 n
Sartoris, Jane D., 96 n, 381, 383 n
Saturday Evening Post, 259, 283, 508 n, 669 n, 685 n, 686 n, 714 n, 785 n
Saturday Review of Literature, 36 n, 94 n, 245 n, 286 n, 302 n, 305 n, 317, 318, 319 n, 348 n, 352, 363 n, 366 n, 371 n, 373 n, 375 n, 383 n, 500 n, 558 n, 560 n, 596 n, 703 n, 765 n, 780 n
Saul, Vernon W., 676 n
Savage, Howard J., 236
Saxe, Joseph, 255 n
Saxo Grammaticus, 466 n
Sayce, A. H., 371
Sayler, J. Abner, 419
Scandinavian Studies & Notes, 435 n
Scarborough, Katherine, 450 n
Schack, William, 25 n
Schele de Vere, M., 12, 222 n, 381 n, 438, 599, 601, 609, 611, 613, 614, 618, 623, 627, 628, 629, 630, 637, 638, 641, 642
Scheuermeier, Paul, 112
Scheyer, David, 645 n
Schlauch, Margaret, 382
Schlesinger, Arthur M., 469, 470
Schmidt-Wartenberg, H., 171
Schmitt, Mrs. Fred., 481 n
Schnabel, D. C., 377 n
Schnirring, Mrs. F. W., 481 n
Schoch, Alfred D., 92, 414, 557 n
School & Society, 353 n, 711 n
Schoolcraft, Henry R., 549, 565
Schoolma'am, her labors,

17, 18, 23, 182, 239, 333, 334, 343, 345, 346, 347, 354, 360, 361, 363, 367, 388, 389, 544, 625, 626
School Review, 16 n, 25 n, 46 n, 314 n
Schram, Emil, 785
Schramm, Wilbur L., 59, 60
Schreiber, Heinrich, 653 n, 654
Schullian, Dorothy M., 711 n
Schultz, J. R., 743 n, 744 n
Schumacher, Garry, 737 n
Schuricht, Herman, 408 n
Schuyler, Jack, 675 n
Schweizer Journal, 520 n
Science, 87 n, 308 n, 543 n
Science & Society, 343 n
Scientific Monthly, 349 n
Scopes trial, 639
Scotch-Irish, speech of, 13, 16, 116, 117, 204, 206, 207, 213
Scotland, speech of, 7, 12, 13, 90, 91 n, 257; surnames in, 400, 402, 404, 458 n
Scott, DR, 478
Scott, Fred Newton, 24, 370
Scott, John, 698 n
Scott, Lewis A., 532
Scott, Walter, 354
Scott, Winfield, 470
Scotticisms, 114, 118
Scottish Educational Journal, 12 n
Scottish schoolmasters, 16
Scottish surnames, 435
Scranton, Pa., speech of, 205
Scranton Times, 452 n
Scribner's Magazine, 134 n, 257 n, 751 n
Scripture, E. W., 59
Scully, Frank, 317
Scypes, George S., 381 n
Sealock, Richard B., 551, 558
Seaman, H. W., 40, 73, 74 n, 79, 282 n, 286 n, 362 n
Seaman, John, 168 n

Seashore, C. E., 59, 432 n
Sebastian, Hugh, 711 n, 777 n
Securities and Exchange Commission, 773 n
Seegers, J. C., 215
Seely, Pauline A., 551, 558
Seely-Brown, Horace, 451 n
Segar, Elzie C., 776, 784
Seidleman, Morton, 270 n
Seifert, Lester, 208
Selbysville (Del.) *Delmarva News*, 541 n
Seldes, Gilbert, 730 n
Selling, Lowell S., 708 n
Selwyn, Edgar, 698, 702, 703
Senior, Nassau W., 472
Senn, Alfred, 426, 428 n, 520 n
Sephardic Jews, names of, 518
Seymour, Charles, 737 n
Seymour, N. P., 197
Shadwell, Thomas, 373 n
Shafer, Henry B., 505 n
Shafer, Robert, 547, 554, 751 n, 763 n
Shaftesbury, Earl of, 302, 313 n, 357
Shakespeare, William, 21 n, 23 n, 50, 76, 78 n, 206, 257 n, 281, 285, 351, 356, 359, 372, 376, 387, 389 n, 423 n, 453, 466, 609, 634, 648 n, 657 n, 663 n, 688, 690 n
Shands, H. A., 170–72, 265 n, 354 n, 544 n
Shankle, George Erlie, 329, 598, 599, 600, 602, 605, 606 n, 607, 610, 611, 613, 614, 623, 628, 629, 630, 631, 635, 636, 638
Shapiro, S. R., 739 n
Shapleigh, Mrs. F. E., 158 n, 184, 185
Shaw, George Bernard, 37, 39, 41, 296 n, 302, 303, 304, 315, 362 n
Shaw, O., 525 n
Shaw, Roger, 672 n
Shaw, Thomas S., 115 n

Shearin, Hubert G., 119 n, 153
Sheba, S., 525 n
Sheepmen's argot, 770
Shekener language, loans from. See *Gipsy language, loans from*
Sheldon, Esther Keck, 6 n, 64 n, 102 n, 106, 388 n
Shelley, P. B., 463 n
Shelly, Lou, 707 n
Shenandoah Valley, speech of, 14, 122 n, 224 n, 225, 228 n, 229, 232
Shepard, John P., 501 n
Shepard, Odell, 135 n, 530 n, 556
Shepherd, William G., 668 n
Sheridan, Ann, 704 n
Sheridan, Philip H., 470
Sheridan, Thomas, 6, 17, 96 n
Sherley, Harold H., 759 n
Sherman, W. T., 448, 470, 507
Sherover, Mexetao, 725 n
Sherwin, Reider T., 529 n
Sherwood, Adiel, 137, 354, 365, 368, 375, 557
Shewmake, Edwin F., 223, 226, 227, 228, 376 n
Shield, James Asa, 673 n
Shilman, David, 747
Shipbuilders' argot, 723
Ship names, 583–88
Shippy, Frank, 714 n
Ships, 721 n
Shoe clerks' argot, 770, 771
Shoemaker, Henry W., 206, 207, 208, 567
Shoemakers' argot, 771, 772
Shoplifters' argot, 670
Shor, Toots, 695 n
Short, Walter C., 783
Shoup, Thomas B., 511 n
Shovel, Cloudsley, 450 n
Shulters, J. R., 749 n
Sidney, F. H., 676 n
Siegel, Arthur, 768 n
Siegle, John W., 163 n

Sierra Club Bulletin, 554 n
Siler, Hayden, 384 n, 502 n, 504 n
Simmerman, Charles, 181
Simms, W. G., 608
Simon, R. L., 765 n
Simons, Hi, 675 n
Simonson, Harry, 555 n
Simpler Spelling Association, 287 n
Simplified Spelling, 287–316
Simplified Spelling Board, 287, 293, 294, 298, 299, 301, 303 n, 305, 311, 313 n
Simplified Spelling Society, 282, 287, 299, 300, 303, 306, 312 n, 313 n, 314
Simpl Orderli Speling, 289
Simpson, Claude M., Jr., 211, 446 n
Simpson, J. H., 499 n
Sims, William Rice, 171
Sinclair, John L., 743 n
Sinclair, Upton, 777 n
Singulars, false, 173, 233, 318, 319, 320, 383–86
Sisam, Kenneth, 325 n
Sizer, Miriam, 450 n, 502 n
Skeat, W. W., 13 n, 105, 109 n, 301 n
Skeel, Emily E. F., 5 n, 274
Skelton, Reginald, 324 n, 326 n
Skillman, W. J., 180 n
Skinner, Ray E., 68
Slattery, William, 709
Slav given-names, 522
Slaves, names of, 513, 514
Slonimsky, Nicolas, 706 n, 709 n
Slovak Review, 526 n, 522 n
Slovak surnames, 426, 427
Slovene surnames, 426
Smalley, E. V., 567 n
Smallfry, Simeon, 223 n
Smart, Alice, 747 n
Smiley, Jack, 751 n
Smith, Adam, 334 n

Smith, Alfred E., 77, 379, 598, 670 n, 671 n, 728
Smith, Arthur G., 291
Smith, Arthur H., 443 n
Smith, C. Alphonso, 194 n, 224, 376, 377
Smith, Carleton, 707 n
Smith, C. E., 235
Smith, Clay, 709
Smith, Dent, 773 n
Smith, Edgar W., 97 n, 470 n
Smith, Edward F., 465 n
Smith, Eldon E., 367 n
Smith, Elisabeth F., 239 n
Smith, Elmer G., 725 n
Smith, Elsdon C., 498 n, 500
Smith, Esther, 481 n
Smith, F. Hopkinson, 722 n
Smith, Grace Partridge, 139, 558 n
Smith, H. Allen, 735 n, 737 n, 739 n, 746 n
Smith, Herbert W., 164, 165
Smith, Jere, 617
Smith, John, 79, 286 n, 407
Smith, Joseph, 516
Smith, J. S., 448 n
Smith, Lawrence E., 762 n
Smith, Logan Pearsall, 36, 51 n, 321 n, 371 n, 721
Smith, Madorah E., 239, 240
Smith, Maurice G., 446 n
Smith, Nicholas, 400 n
Smith, Ralph, 609
Smith, Rebecca W., 217
Smith, Reed, 266 n, 268, 269 n, 343
Smith, Saba, 497
Smith, Seba, 112 n, 304
Smith, Sebastian, 115 n
Smith, S. Stephenson, 730 n
Smith, Sydney, 497
Smith, William C., 239, 241 n
Smith, W. R., 579
Smith College, 28 n, 42
Smithsonian Institution, 537, 538 n, 783 n
Snapp, D. V., 718 n

Snyder, Joseph F., 31
Snyder, M. Robert, 551
Social Forces, 78 n, 121 n, 147 n, 188 n
Social Security Board, 396, 401, 461
Society for Pure English, 36, 318
Society for Pure English Tracts, 36 n, 39 n, 42 n, 46 n, 51 n, 70 n, 71 n, 84 n, 99 n, 103 n, 104 n, 256 n, 312 n, 314 n, 318 n, 319 n, 325 n, 328 n, 356 n, 362 n, 371 n, 373 n, 749 n
Society for the History of the Germans in Maryland, 408 n
Society for the Prevention of Cruelty to Southern Accents, 125
Soda-jerkers' argot, 772, 785
Soldiers' papers, names of, 596
Sölmund, Olaf, 414 n
Sonkin, Robert, 190 n, 260
Souders, D. A., 440 n
South, speech of. See General Southern American
South Africa, speech of, 256 n
South African War, 778
South Atlantic Bulletin, 712 n
South Atlantic Quarterly, 266 n
South Carolina, given-names in, 472, 484, 491, 503 n, 510, 514, 515; nicknames of, 608, 609; place-names in, 568; speech of, 105, 123, 204 n, 212–16, 229, 369 n, 381, 384, 387, 390
South Dakota, nicknames of, 638, 639; place-names in, 568; speech of, 216
Southern Commercial Congress, 607 n
Southern English Standard, 16, 24, 25, 30, 32

Southern Folklore Quarterly, 511 n, 512 n, 513 n
Southern Literary Messenger, 223 n, 377 n
Southern Telephone News, 718 n
Southey, Robert, 60, 61, 302, 303, 338, 531 n, 593
Southwest Courier (Oklahoma City), 486 n, 487 n
Southwest Review, 221 n, 569 n, 746 n, 762 n
Southwestern Reporter, 741 n
Spackman, W. M., 449 n
Spadino, E. J., 30, 31
Spaeth, Sigmund, 348
Spanish language, loans from, 51, 133, 137, 144, 151, 182, 183, 201, 221 n, 243, 246, 529, 541 n, 552, 553, 554, 555, 557, 566, 572, 574, 666, 677 n, 681 n, 726, 741 n, 742 n, 744 n, 768 n; dictionaries, 125; given-names, 521, 522; New Mexican, 127, 134, 182, 183; Puerto Rican, 243, 244; spelling, 307, 308; surnames, 435; vocabulary, 349
Sparks, Chauncey, 125
Special Service Digest, 386 n
Spectator, 302 n
Speech levels, 34 n, 50, 198
Speech Monographs, 32 n, 83 n, 730 n
Spelling, 305 n, 306 n, 307 n
Spelling-bee, 304
Spelling-pronunciation, 4, 7, 85, 90, 91
Spelling Reform Association, 295 n, 305, 306, 309 n
Spence, Lewis, 12
Spencer, Gilmore, 712 n
Spenser, Edmund, 494
Spiller, Robert E., 26 n
Spofford, A. R., 296 n
Sporting Life, 660 n, 735 n

Index

Spradley, Isabel, 121 n, 592, 593 n
Springer, John, 240 n
Stage, 690 n
Stage-hands' argot, 697
Stalin, Joseph, 415 n
Stambolsky, Alexander, 308
Standard Dictionary, 64, 65 n, 275, 276 n, 303 n, 349, 371
Standard Southern English, 26, 27, 28, 33–45, 58 n, 96, 183 n, 249, 250
Staniford, Daniel, 353
Stanley, Oma, 217, 218, 219, 270 n, 332, 357, 365, 379, 392 n
Stark, James, 404 n
Starnes, Val. W., 381
Stars and Stripes, 283, 780
State Government, 328
State Department Style Manual, 318 n, 323, 324, 326
St. Crispen, 772 n
St. Crispinian, 772 n
Steadman, H. M., 118 n
Steadman, J. M., Jr., 18 n, 194, 372, 374
Steamfitters' argot, 766, 767
Stearns, Mrs. Albert T., 437 n
Stedman, Adelaide, 58 n
Steele, A. N., 721 n
Steele, Richard, 374, 393, 644
Steel-workers' argot, 773
Stein, Kurt M., 259
Steinbach, Reuben, 343 n
Steinbeck, John, 319 n
Steinitz, Wolfgang, 307 n
Stene, Aasta, 56
Stephens, Ferris J, 478
Sterling (Kansas) *Bulletin*, 492 n
Stern, Max, 397 n
Sterne, Laurence, 277
Stetson, John B., 742 n
Stevens, James, 759 n
Stevens, Walter B., 632
Stevens, W. O., 167 n
Stevenson, Robert Louis, 460 n

Stewart, George R., 525, 526, 530, 534 n, 541 n, 542 n, 567, 574 n, 575
Stewart, William C., 51 n, 547 n
St. Croix, speech of, 247
St. Gaudens, Paul, 179, 180, 438 n, 450 n, 480 n, 484 n, 488 n, 490 n, 504 n, 507
St. Giles's Greek, 663
Still, Elmer G., 291
Still, James A., 487 n, 501 n, 568
Stimpson, George, 515 n
St. John, Francis R., 482 n, 491 n
St. Kitts, speech of, 247
St. Louis *Post-Dispatch*, 48 n, 544 n, 632 n, 633, 730 n
St. Louis *Republican*, 134 n
St. Louis, speech of, 129 n
St. Martin, speech of, 248
Stockbrokers' argot, 773, 774
Stoddard, Albert H., 268, 269
Stoddard, Richard Henry, 460 n
Stoddard, W. L., 773 n
Stoeckel, Herb, 732 n
Stokes, William N., Jr., 221 n
Stone, Walter C., 35 n
Stonecutters' argot, 774
Stong, Phil, 317, 714 n
Stork, Willis, 735 n
Stout, Wesley W., 686 n
Stoven, Elizabeth M., 221 n
Stowe, Harriet Beecher, 265 n, 283, 473
St. Paul *Pioneer Press*, 784 n
Strakosch, Edgar, 702
Strand Magazine, 711 n
Stratton, Charles S., 659 n
Stratton, Dorothy G., 779 n
Strauss, Harold, 712 n
Strauss, Johann, 501
Strauss, Levi, 742 n
Street, James H., 719 n
Street, Julian, Jr., 731 n

Street, Thomas E., 507 n
Stress, 4, 47–49, 54, 72
Strip-teasers' argot, 693, 694
Strong, K. W., 731 n
Strong, William D., 254
Struble, George G., 242 n
Structural iron workers' argot, 774, 775
Strunsky, Simeon, 303, 473
Studies in Linguistics, 109 n, 110 n, 124 n, 141 n, 156, 167 n, 212 n, 666 n
Studies in Philology, 59 n, 187 n, 665 n
Sturtevant, E. H., 66 n, 102 n, 111, 112, 189 n, 334 n, 342, 544
Subjunctives, 368
Sullivan, W. G., 366 n
Sunday, Billy, 412, 745 n
Supplement to Language, 84 n, 112 n
Surnames, 396–461; as given-names, 468–73
Survey Graphic, 524 n
Sutherland, Edwin H., 675 n
Svenska Låndmalen, 712 n
Swadesh, Morris, 70 n, 141
Swaen, A. E. H., 573
Swaffer, Hannen, 45 n
Swan, Bradford F., 108, 601 n, 700 n, 768 n
Swan, Gilbert, 689 n
Swanson, Robert E., 759 n
Swanson, Roy W., 430, 529 n, 562
Swanton, John R., 557 n
Swartwout, R. E., 322 n
Swedish language, loans from, 168, 317; place-names, 574 n; surnames, 430
Swedish-American Historical Bulletin, 529 n, 562 n
Sweet, Henry, 61, 62, 67, 199
Sweet, J. H., 168 n
Swift, Jonathan, 301, 339, 357
Swinburne, A. C., 653 n

Swinburne, Louis, 134
Swinton, John R., 551 n
Swope, Mrs. Isaac G., 159 n
Sydney (Australia) *Bulletin*, 458 n
Sydnor, F. W., 455, 456
Syfert, V. A., 558 n
Sylvester, A. H., 533 n
Symonds, P. M., 353 n
Syracuse *Post-Standard*, 36 n
Syrians, given-names of, 523
Systematized Spelling, 287, 288

Taft, William H., 636
Tagalog language, loans from, 243
Talbert, E. W., 558 n
Taliaferro, name and family, 455
Tall Talk, 617 n
Tamony, Peter, 645 n, 672 n, 682 n, 686 n, 701 n, 708 n, 709, 710, 736 n, 746 n, 754 n, 768 n
Tan Eyck, Conrad, 629
Tannehill, W. M., 621
Tanners' argot, 775
Tanners' Council of America, 775 n
Tannous, Afif I., 524 n
Taos (N. Mex.) *Valley News*, 182
Tanner, Myrtle L., 221 n
Tappan, Benjamin, 447 n
Tarlau, Jacob, 424 n
Taschenbuch für Geschichte und Alterthum in Süd-Deutschland, 653, 654 n
Tatler, 644
Taxi-drivers' argot, 720
Taylor, Bert L., 259
Taylor, Henry J., 366 n
Taylor, Jay L. B., 121 n, 173 n
Taylor, Myron C., 472, 473, 474
Taylor, Rupert, 132
Taylor, Zachary, 597
Teachers College, Columbia, 5, 362 n

Teen-age slang, 707, 708
Telegraph & Telephone Age, 717 n
Telegraphers' argot, 717, 718
Telephone-exchange names, 575, 576
Television argot, 731
Temple, William, 80
Temple, William (American), 193 n
Tennessee, given-names in, 487, 488, 502 n, 503 n, 504 n; nicknames of, 639; place-names in, 534, 535, 568, 569; speech of, 115, 117, 119, 123, 136, 140 n, 216, 217, 229, 357, 359 n, 378, 384, 386
Tennyson, Alfred, 301 n, 338
Tennyson, Hallam, 472
Terhune, Albert Payson, 181 n, 430 n
Terrell, Glenn, 710 n
Texas, given-names in, 482, 485, 486, 487, 490, 491, 493, 502 n, 507 n, 510, 511 n, 513 n; nicknames of, 610, 640; place-names in, 528, 534, 535, 541, 542 n, 544, 569, 570; speech of, 104, 105, 108, 120 n, 123, 126, 136, 154 n, 217-21, 357, 364 n, 365, 379, 392 n
Texas Christian University, 476
Textile-workers' argot, 775, 776
Text-quote, 326
Thackeray, W. M., 338, 339, 354, 389 n
Thalberg, Irving G., 702 n
Thaw, Harry K., 23 n
Thaxter, Celia, 180, 435 n
Thayer, Alexander W., 407
This Week, 256 n, 512 n
Thomas, Charles K., 18, 27, 28, 29, 30, 31, 45 n, 63 n, 64, 82, 184, 185, 186, 187, 190 n, 260, 262
Thomas, Russell, 387

Thompson, B. F., 565 n
Thompson, Denman, 113 n
Thompson, Dorothy, 66
Thompson, George W., 89 n, 264 n
Thompson, John W., 450 n
Thompson, Lawrence S., 522 n
Thompson, Thomas P., 5 n
Thorndike Century Senior Dictionary, 546
Thorndike, E. L., 390
Thornton, R. H., 150 n, 224, 284, 354, 362 n, 600 n, 608, 614, 615, 617, 621, 639
Thornton, Walter, 781
Thornton, Willis, 593
Thousand Islands, place-names in, 572
Thresher, Joyce, 712 n
Thurston, W. C., 362 n
Tibbals, Kate W., 382 n
Tibet, place-names of, 538 n
Ticknor, George, 20
Tide, 783 n, 785 n
Tidewater, speech of, 13, 14, 74, 75, 104, 122, 123, 124, 128, 136, 212, 228
Tidwell, J. N., 265 n
Tiffin, Joseph, 60
Tifft, 478 n
Tilden, William, Jr., 473
Tilly, William, 26, 30
Timbre, 57, 58
Time, 286 n, 373 n, 681 n, 707 n, 710 n, 725 n, 726, 765 n, 777 n, 779 n, 785 n
Tit-Bits, 782
Tobacco-growers' argot, 776
Today, 757 n
Toepel, Dooley, 98 n
Tolar, S. B., 511 n
Toledo *Blade*, 392 n
Tomkins, Alan, 711 n
Toms, William L., 146 n
Tooke, John Horne, 339
Tooker, William W., 565
Topham, Mrs. Wellman, 481 n

Index

Topographical terms, 570, 573, 574
Toro Nazario, J. M., 246 n
Toronto *Saturday Night*, 251 n, 499 n
Toronto *Week*, 248 n
Torreya, 108 n
Torrio, Johnny, 671 n
Townsend, Charles W., 46 n
Townsend, Edward W., 188
Townsfolk, 485 n
Town Topics, 14 n
Toynbee, Arnold J., 116 n, 126 n
Tracks, 714 n
Trager, George L., 15, 77 n, 167, 370 n, 555
Train names, 581
Trampleasure, Jane G., 451 n
Tramps' argot. See *Hobos'*
Transactions of the Alabama Historical Society, 552 n
Transactions of the Albany Institute, 15 n, 47 n, 85 n
Transactions of the Modern Language Association, 213 n
Transactions of the Royal Society of Canada, 572 n
Transactions of the Wisconsin Academy of Sciences, Arts and Letters, 571 n
Traube, Shepard, 688 n
Travelers, English, 101
Treadway, Allen T., 75
Tressider, Argus, 122 n, 224, 228, 229, 230
Treviño, S. N., 60 n, 71 n, 76
Trimmer, John P., 755 n
Trinidad, speech of, 248 n
Trolley crews' argot, 717
Trollope, T. A., 95 n, 649 n
Trotsky, L. D., 415
Troubridge, St. Vincent, 688 n, 711 n

Troy (N.T.) *Sentinel*, 145
Truckmens' argot, 718–20
True Detective Mysteries, 488 n, 667 n, 670 n, 708 n
Trueblood, Thomas C., 249 n, 256 n
Truesdell, Leon E., 10 n
Truman, Harry S., 173, 244, 477, 478, 648 n
Trumbull, James H., 530 n, 549, 555
Trumbull, John, 189 n
Tucker, Gilbert M., 15 n, 726
Tucker, Kathryn, 490 n
Tucker, N. B., 265
Tucker, R. Whitney, 201 n, 202, 203, 204
Tugwell, Rexford G., 244
Turkish, spelling of, 308
Turner, Leslie, 221 n
Turner, Lorenzo D., 266, 267, 268, 446, 514, 515, 710
Turney, Douglas, 182
Tuskegee Institute, 510
Tweedie, W. M., 252
Tydings, Millard E., 603
Tyler, John, 470
Tyler, Royal, 112
Tyler's Quarterly Historical & Genealogical Magazine, 455 n
Tyng, Ed, 329 n
Tyson, F. H., 283 n, 314 n, 362 n, 592 n

Ukrainian surnames, 427
Umland, Rudolph, 743 n, 764 n
Uncle Remus's Magazine, 376
Union men's argot, 776, 777
Unitarianism, 468
United Nations Weekly Bulletin, 330 n
United Press, 418, 440 n, 442 n, 446 n, 478, 507 n, 771 n
United States Naval Institute Proceedings, 537 n, 588 n
University Magazine, 195 n
University Microfilms, 734 n
University of Arizona Bulletin, 551 n
University of California Publications in Anthropology and Ethnology, 554 n
University of California Publications in English, 574 n
University of Colorado Studies, 433 n
University of Missouri Studies, 173 n, 390 n, 550 n
University of Nebraska Studies in Language, Literature and Criticism, 562 n
University of Texas Studies in English, 265 n
University of Virginia Alumni News, 712 n
University of Virginia Studies, 124 n
Unwin, William, 393 n
Upham, Warren, 562
Upshaw, William D., 602
U. S. Geographic Board. See *Geographic Board*
Utah, nicknames of, 640, 641; place-names in, 542, 569, 570; speech of, 221, 222

Vachell, Horace A., 649
Valentine, John, 596
Valentino, Rudolph, 703 n
Vanbrugh, John, 373 n
Vance, Zebulon B., 607
Van den Bark, Melvin, 176, 177, 356, 625 n, 646, 650, 651, 657, 682 n, 709, 725, 755 n
Vanderbilt, Cornelius, 497
Vandiver, Willard D., 631, 632, 633
Van Doren, Irita, 496

Van Hoven, Harry, 693 n
Vanity Fair, 57 n, 706 n
Van Langehove, G. Ch., 255 n
van Patten, Nathan, 109 n, 265 n
Variety, 39 n, 121 n, 295, 297, 317, 319 n, 394 n, 420 n, 427 n, 485 n, 683 n, 688, 692 n, 697, 698 n, 700 n, 701 n, 703 n, 704, 707 n, 709 n, 711 n, 730 n, 731 n, 752 n, 766 n
Varro, 335
Vasché, Joseph B., 297 n, 553, 554
Vassar College, 28 n
Vaudeville, argot of, 691–93, 699 n
Velez, Lupe, 699 n
Venable, John, 564 n
Vera, Eugenio, 245 n, 246 n
Verbs, 353–68
Vermeule, C. C., 564 n
Vermont, given-names in, 483; nicknames of, 599; place-names in, 570; speech of, 222
Verney letters, 366
Ver Nooy, Amy, 565 n
Verwyst, Chrysostom, 561 n, 571
Vidmer, Richards, 735 n
Viking, Valdemar, 317 n, 394 n
Villard, Oswald Garrison, 383 n
Villaronga, Mariano, 245 n
Vincennes (Ind.) *Sun*, 620
Virchow, Rudolf, 307
VirDen, Ray, 452 n
Virgin Islands, speech of, 247, 248
Virginia, given-names in, 471, 484, 488; nicknames of, 596, 597; place-names in, 531, 540, 542, 570, 574 n; speech of, 84, 86, 115, 120 n, 124 n, 136, 162, 194, 201 n, 207 n, 223–32, 358, 359 n, 381, 387,
392 n; surnames in, 408, 454, 455, 456
Virginia Literary Museum, 222 n, 223, 365
Virginia Magazine, 712 n
Virginia Piedmont, speech of, 105, 123, 225, 226, 228
Virginia Quarterly Review, 119 n
Virginia Tidewater, speech of, 13, 74, 104, 123, 124, 128, 195, 214, 224, 225, 227, 380
VisKocil, Helen, 452 n
Vizetelly, Frank H., 17 n, 33, 34, 36, 57 n, 73 n, 76, 82, 90, 349 n, 368, 545, 546
Vocabulary, 348–52
Vogue, 707 n
von KleinSmid, Rufus B., 452 n
von Puttkamer, R. V., 307
Vowel Shift, 70
Vowles, Guy R., 379

Wagner, Richard, 415 n
Wainwright, Charles W., 48 n
Walbran, John T., 572
Walcott, Fred G., 338, 339
Waldo, Edna L., 718 n
Wales, speech of, 7, 257; surnames, 400, 402
Walker, Francis C., 25, 48 n, 52, 85
Walker, John, 6, 17, 47 n, 70, 85, 88 n, 96 n, 284
Walker, Robert G., 159 n
Walker, Stanley, 295 n, 511 n
Walker, William, 658 n
Wall, Arnold, 256 n, 651
Wallace, E. R., 366 n
Wallace, Henry A., 121 n
Wallace, K. R., 29
Wall Street Journal, 444
Walsh, Chad, 74 n, 224, 230, 231
Walshe, Maurice, 278 n
Walter, Bruno, 421 n
Walter, Dorothy C., 519 n
Ward, Artemus, 354, 653 n
Ward, Ida C., 74 n, 96 n, 101 n
Ward, Mary L., 362 n
Ward, Paul W., 649 n
Ward, William, 367
Wardlaw, Patterson, 341 n
Warfel, Harry R., 103 n, 272 n, 273, 274, 275, 339 n, 468 n
Warner, Charles Dudley, 390, 549 n
Warner, James H., 132
Warnick, Florence, 160, 161
Warnock, Elsie, 727 n
War of 1812, 101, 126, 142, 152, 257, 534, 627, 648
Warrack, Alexander, 118
Warren, Joseph, 470
War with Mexico, 142
Washington, Booker T., 405, 447 n
Washington, Charles, 708
Washington, George, 405, 447, 564 n, 597
Washington, Laurence, 453
Washington *Daily News*, 359 n
Washington Historical Quarterly, 570 n
Washington *Post*, 40 n, 371
Washington (city), speech of, 129 n
Washington (State), nicknames of, 641; place-names in, 570; speech of, 232, 233, 249
Wasson, R. G., 519 n
Waterman, T. T., 239 n
Watson, Billy, 694
Watson, Foston, 467 n
Watts, Isaac, 87 n, 369 n
Weathers, Nelda A., 146 n
Webb, H. Brook, 707 n
Webb, Mary W., 481 n
Weber, Joseph, 259 n
Webster, Clarence M., 115 n
Webster, Noah, 6, 7, 17,

21, 90, 126, 129 n, 134, 185, 194, 277, 283, 302 n, 304 n, 310, 311, 321, 334, 389, 468
Webster's American Dictionary, 5 n, 80, 81, 84, 185, 274, 275, 281, 284, 285, 318, 349
Webster's Compendious Dictionary, 274, 284, 318, 349
Webster's Dissertations on the English Language, 17, 77, 78, 79, 81, 84, 85, 86, 94, 103, 112, 223, 333, 384
Webster's Grammatical Institute, 274 n, 371
Webster's New International Dictionary, 48 n, 53 n, 64, 65, 66, 76, 85, 148 n, 275, 276, 279 n, 285, 286, 319, 325 n, 327, 349, 371, 379, 547, 622, 679, 681 n, 708, 726, 728, 735 n
Webster's Philosophical and Practical Grammar, 339, 391
Webster's Spelling-book, 4, 5, 17, 271–74, 276, 304 n, 471 n, 479
Wechsberg, Joseph, 689 n
Wecli Fonetic Advocat, 293 n
Weed, J. J., 730 n
Weed, J Spencer, 478
Weekley, Ernest, 48, 368 n, 451 n, 462 n, 464 n, 471 n, 499, 657 n, 670 n
Weekly News Bulletin of the American Civil Liberties Union, 245 n
Weeks, Abigail E., 119 n, 153
Weeks, R. L., 173
Weimarisches Jahrbuch für deutsche Sprache, Literatur und Kunst, 653 n
Weinstock, Herbert, 408 n
Weiss, George, Jr., 189 n
Weiss, Hymie, 671 n
Welch, Francis X., 129 n

Welch, Harold A., 781 n
Wellard, James Howard, 40, 46 n
Weller, George, 181 n
Wellman, Paul I., 632, 633, 634
Wells, A. Wode, 782 n
Wells, Guy H., 557
Wells, Harry L., 547 n
Wells, H. Bartlett, 479 n
Wells, H. G., 301 n, 305
Welsh language, loans from, 204
Wemyss, Earl of, 457 n
Wentworth, Harold, vi, 29, 49 n, 100, 106–09, 120 n, 129, 135 n, 137, 140, 146 n, 148, 150, 154 n, 161, 164 n, 169, 173, 179, 193 n, 194, 202 n, 204, 231, 232, 234, 357, 358, 359 n, 360 n, 362 n, 363, 364, 365, 375, 379, 380, 381, 382, 386, 387, 388, 389, 390, 544 n, 725, 726
Wentworth, John B., 159 n
Werner, Carl A., 744 n
Werner, W. L., 701 n, 706 n, 726
Weseen, Maurice H., 650, 709
Wesley, John, 280, 388 n
Wesort people, 235 n
West, immigration to, 90; speech of, 18 n, 90, 126, 127 n, 142, 152, 257
West, Robert, 29
West, V. Royce, 672 n
Western American. See *General American*
Western Associated Motion Picture Advertisers, 703 n
Western Observer, 622 n
Westinghouse, George, 412
Westminster Gazette, 279 n
Westminster Review, 5 n
West Virginia, nicknames of, 599, 640, 641; place-names in, 541, 570; speech of, 104, 115, 118 n, 119 n, 155, 169,

201 n, 204, 231, 233–35, 359 n, 390
Wharton, Don, 513 n
Whatcoat, Richard, 619 n
Wheatley, Katherine E., 123 n
Wheeler, Robert L., 779 n
Whiskey Rebellion, 205
White, Mrs. Arthur W., 498
White, E. B., 159 n
White, Henry A., 184, 185
White, M. A., 785 n
White, Percy W., 683, 688 n, 691 n
White, Richard Grant, 22, 26, 78, 335, 453 n
White, Stanford, 23 n
White, Stewart Edward, 132
White, Whitman, 712 n
White, William, 730 n
White, William Allen, 318, 473
White, William W., 40 n
Whitehall, Harold, 83, 84, 112, 146, 147
Whitehead, Charles E., 533 n
Whitehead, Henry S., 247
Whiteman, Paul, 705 n
Whiting, B. J., 115 n
Whitman, Walt, 20, 296, 553, 595, 610, 687 n
Whitmer, R. P., 362 n
Whitmore, W. H., 561 n
Whitney, Alvin G., 565 n
Whitney, Annie W., 268 n
Whitney, Frederick L., 340 n
Whitney, J. D., 573 n, 574 n
Whitney, Will A., 731 n
Whitney, William D., 23 n, 74, 334, 371
Whittaker, James, 467 n
Whittier, J. G., 414
Who's Who in America, 508, 535 n
Why-Not-Me? Club, 372 n
Whyte, John, 367
Wickard, Claude, 77

Wiener, Alexander S., 383 n
Wiener, Earl, 517
Wiener, Frederick B., 508 n
Wiener, Leo, 179
Wiener, Samuel G., 517 n
Wigan, Alfred, 74 n
Wight, Harley F., 721 n
Wilde, Oscar, 339
Wilder, Robert, 721 n
Wiley, M. J., 783
Wilhelm II, 307
Wilke, Walter H., 31
Wilkinson, Lupton A., 268
Wilkinson, Paul, 149 n
Willard, Josiah Flynt. See *Flynt*
Willard, Rudolph, 315 n
William & Mary Quarterly, 159 n, 455 n
William Feather Magazine, 345 n, 392 n, 463 n, 646 n, 738 n, 746 n
Williams, Cratis D., 124 n, 154 n, 194 n
Williams, Edna R., 315 n
Williams, Guy, 759 n, 760 n
Williams, Harcourt, 690 n
Williams, Harvey, 712 n
Williams, Henry T., 536
Williams, Ned, 707 n
Williams, Stephen, 690 n
Williamson, A. B., 30
Williamson, A. W., 562
William the Conqueror, 455
Willis, N. P., 474
Willkie, Wendell L., 412
Willys-Overland Motors, 783
Wilmington (Del.) *Delmarvia Review*, 541 n
Wilson Bulletin, 108 n
Wilson, Charles M., 119 n
Wilson, Earl, 695
Wilson, Edmund, 698 n
Wilson, George P., 30, 64, 69, 108, 109 n, 110 n, 124, 194 n, 196, 224
Wilson, G. M., 340
Wilson, Henry, 461
Wilson, Howard M., 481 n

Wilson, Meredith, 707 n
Wilson, Woodrow, 351, 369, 370 n, 419 n, 473, 597
Wilson Company, H. W., 598 n
Wilstach, Frank J., 720 n
Wilt, Napier, 122 n
Winchell, Walter, 330 n, 671 n, 704, 778
Winder, W. H., 460 n
Windsor, Duke of, 44, 472
Winfield, Benjamin L., 757 n
Wingfield, Fred S. C., 287, 288, 289
Winnipeg *Free Press*, 250 n
Winship, A. E., 561 n
Winslow, Thyra Samter, 691 n
Winston Dictionary, 725
Winter, William, 691
Winterich, J. T., 383 n
Winwar, Frances, 439 n
Wirt, William, 412
Wisconsin, nicknames of, 641, 642; place-names in, 528, 571; speech of, 104, 141 n, 170, 235-37, 733 n; surnames in, 408, 433 n
Wise, C. M., 46 n, 121, 123, 156, 157, 268
Wister, Owen, 412
Witherspoon, John, 19, 78, 158, 353, 357, 358, 382, 648 n
Withington, Robert, 79 n
Withycombe, E. G., 463 n
Witman, Fred, 687
Witzell, Edward F., 479 n
Wolfe, Bernard, 707 n
Wolfe, Julia W., 115 n
Wolsley, Garnet, 472
Wolverton, Charles, 683 n
Wolverton, Don, 718 n
Woman's Home Companion, 698 n
Wood, Aaron, 618
Wood, J. S., 645 n
Woodard, C. M., 194 n

Woodberry, Charles J., 95 n
Woods, H. Curtis, Jr., 673 n
Woods, Ralph L., 670 n
Woodson, Carter G., 447
Woodward, C. M., 224, 232
Woofter, Carter, 233, 234 n
Woolf, H. B., 362 n
Woolf, James D., 348 n
Wooster, David, 566 n
Worcester, Joseph E., 69, 275
Worcester (Mass.) *Telegram*, 729 n
Word, 307 n
Worde, Wynken de, 655
Words, 53 n, 97, 325 n, 374 n, 462 n, 472 n, 489 n, 531 n, 566 n, 596 n, 698 n, 703 n, 708 n, 730 n, 731 n, 769 n
Word Study, 46 n, 192 n, 350 n, 533 n, 568 n, 575 n, 777 n
Wordsworth, William, 281, 414
Workman, William D., Jr., 155 n, 240 n, 369 n
Works Progress Administration, 552
World Almanac, 32 n, 400 n, 462 n, 601, 610, 611, 613, 614, 621, 628, 629, 631, 635, 636, 641
World Language Foundation, 290
World's Fair, 685 n, 686 n
World War I, 36 n, 259, 298, 331, 414 n, 461, 477 n, 542 n, 594, 777, 779, 780
World War II, 34, 56, 66, 141, 193, 255, 283, 323, 329, 331, 479, 481, 542, 583, 585, 586, 594, 596, 648 n, 650, 668, 669, 671 n, 682, 703 n, 711, 715 n, 777-86
Woulfe, Patrick, 403 n, 404 n, 421 n, 439, 452 n
Wray, David, 708 n
Wrenick, Bernard C., 301

Index

Wright, Aldis, 105
Wright, Almroth, 472
Wright, H. H., 555
Wright, H. F., 721 n
Wright, Joseph, 11 n, 105, 109 n, 11 n, 139 n, 354, 356, 357, 360 n, 368, 375, 381, 382, 386, 387, 388
Wright, Muriel H., 566 n
Wright, Thomas, 11 n, 357 n
Wrigley, Sarah, 616 n
Writer, 270 n
Writer's Digest, 668 n, 714 n, 718 n, 750 n, 760 n
Writer's Monthly, 114 n, 179, 310 n, 733 n
Wulbern, Helen P., 419, 421 n
Wyatt, Isabel, 382 n
Wyclif, John, 281
Wyld, H. C. K., 6 n, 27 n, 37, 42, 43, 44, 48 n, 62, 73, 79, 84, 86 n, 89, 96 n, 99, 100, 107, 302 n, 366 n, 373, 387
Wyllie, John, 712 n
Wyoming, nicknames of, 636, 642; place-names in, 571; speech of, 221, 237, 238
Wythe, George, 455

Yale Review, 723 n
Yank, 779, 781 n
Yankee, 115 n
Yankee dialect, 112–14, 257; drawl, 112
Yenne, Herbert, 675 n
Yerkes, D. Lorraine, 450 450 n, 481 n, 496 n
Yezierska, Anzia, 262
Yiddish language, 419 n; loans from, 151, 190, 260, 392 n, 646, 666, 670, 671, 696 n, 725, 726, 747 n, 753 n, 754 n, 757 n, 758 n, 771 n
Yidgin English, 262
Yoder, Donald H., 410, 411
Yonge, William, 76
Young, Arthur T., 710 n
Young, Brigham, 641
Young, Edward, 303
Young, Ella Flagg, 370
Young, J. H., 523 n

Youth's Companion, 310 n
Yoxall, Harry W., 57 n
Yukon (Okla.) *Sun*, 491 n
Yule, Emma S., 242
Yule, G. Udny, 353 n
Yule, Henry, 256 n

Zachrisson, R. E., 289, 303
Zanuck, Darryl, 701 n
Zeitschrift für Ortsnamenforschung, 574 n
Zerler, Mary, 29 n
Zeta Beta Tau Quarterly, 517 n
Ziadeh, Farhat, 441 n, 524 n
Ziff, William B., 422 n, 519 n
Zimmer, Norbert, 529 n
Zimmerman, H. E., 162 n
Zimmerman, Jane Dorsey, 30, 31, 66 n, 67
Zolotow, Maurice, 686 n, 696 n
Zwart, Elizabeth Clarkson, 492 n
Zweng, Charles A., 728 n